A GUIDE TO TWENTIETH CENTURY LITERATURE IN ENGLISH

A GUIDE TO

EDITED BY
HARRY BLAMIRES

METHUEN
LONDON & NEW YORK

TWENTIETH

AUSTRALIA · CANADA
THE CARIBBEAN
THE GAMBIA · GHANA

CENTURY

INDIA · IRELAND
KENYA · NEW ZEALAND
NIGERIA · PAKISTAN

LITERATURE

SOUTHERN AFRICA
SRI LANKA · UGANDA
UNITED KINGDOM

IN ENGLISH

Phillips Memorial
Library
Providence College

First published in 1983 by
Methuen & Co. Ltd
11 New Fetter Lane, London EC4P 4EE

Published in the USA by
Methuen & Co.
in association with Methuen, Inc.
733 Third Avenue, New York, NY
10017

© 1983 Harry Blamires, Peter
Quartermaine, Arthur Ravenscroft

Printed in Great Britain

*British Library Cataloguing in
Publication Data*
A Guide to twentieth-century literature
in English.
1. English literature—20th century—
Dictionaries
I. Blamires, Harry
820'.9'09321   PR471

ISBN 0-416-56180-2
ISBN 0-416-36450 0 (pbk.)

*Library of Congress Cataloguing in
Publication Data*

Main entry under title:
A Guide to twentieth-century literature
in English.
1. English literature—20th
century—History and criticism.   2.
English literature—Commonwealth of
Nations authors—History and
criticism.   3. Authors, English—20th
century—Biography.   4. Authors,
Commonwealth of Nations—20th
century—Biography.
I. Blamires, Harry
PR471.G78 1983
820'.9'0091   83-13181

ISBN 0-416-56180-2
ISBN 0-416-36450-0 (pbk.)

CONTENTS

THE GUIDE p 1

CONTRIBUTORS

Harry Blamires: Ireland and the United Kingdom
Peter Quartermaine: Australia, Canada, New Zealand
Arthur Ravenscroft: The Caribbean, The Gambia, Ghana,
India, Kenya, Nigeria, Pakistan, Southern Africa, Sri Lanka, Uganda

LIST OF AUTHORS
BY COUNTRY

Australia

Astley, Thea
Beaver, Bruce
Boyd, Martin
Brennan, Christopher
Buckley, Vincent
Buzo, Alexander
Campbell, David
Carey, Peter
Dawe, Bruce
Dobson, Rosemary
Dransfield, Michael
Fitzgerald, R. D.
Furphy, Joseph
Hall, Rodney
Herbert, Xavier
Hibberd, Jack
Hope, A. D.
Keneally, Thomas
Lawson, Henry
Lindsay, Jack
Lindsay, Norman
McAuley, James
McCrae, Hugh
Malouf, David

Australia contd

Mathers, Peter
Moorhouse, Frank
Murray, Les
Neilson, John Shaw
Oakley, Barry
Palmer, Vance
Porter, Hal
Porter, Peter
Richardson, Henry Handel
Shapcott, Thomas
Slessor, Kenneth
Stead, Christina
Stow, Randolph
Wallace-Crabbe, Chris
Webb, Francis
White, Patrick
Wilding, Michael
Williamson, David
Wright, Judith

Canada

Atwood, Margaret
Birney, Earle

Canada contd

Callaghan, Morley
Cohen, Leonard
Davies, Robertson
Dudek, Louis
Grove, F. P.
Hine, Daryl
Klein, A. M.
Layton, Irving
Leacock, Stephen
Levine, Norman
Livesay, Dorothy
MacLennan, Hugh
Mitchell, W. O.
Moore, Brian
Munro, Alice
Ondaatje, Michael
Pratt, E. J.
Reaney, James
Richler, Mordecai
Ross, Sinclair
Scott, F. R.
Skelton, Robin
Smith, A. J. M.
Weibe, Rudy

The Caribbean

Barbados
Brathwaite, Edward Kamau
Clarke, Austin Chesterfield
Lamming, George

Dominica
Rhys, Jean

Guyana
Harris, Wilson
Mittelholzer, Edgar
Nicole, Christopher

Jamaica
Hearne, John
McKay, Claude
Mais, Roger
Patterson, Orlando
Reid, Vic S.
Salkey, Andrew

St Lucia
St Omer, Garth
Walcott, Derek

Trinidad
Anthony, Michael
de Boissière, Ralph
James, C. L. R.
Khan, Ismith
Naipaul, Shiva
Naipaul, V. S.
Selvon, Samuel

The Gambia

Peters, Lenrie

Ghana

Aidoo, Ama Ata
Armah, Ayi Kwei
Awoonor, Kofi
Sutherland, Efua Theodora

India

Anand, Mulk Raj
Bhattacharya, Bhabani
Chaudhuri, Nirad C.
Das, Kamala
Desai, Anita
Desani, G. V.
Ezekiel, Nissim

India contd
Jhabvala, Ruth Prawer
Lal, P.
Malgonkar, Manohar
Markandaya, Kamala
Mehrotra, Arvind Krishna
Mehta, Ved
Moraes, Dom
Nahal, Chaman
Nandy, Pritish
Narayan, R. K.
Parthasarathy, R.
Ramanujan, A. K.
Rao, Raja
Sahgal, Nyantara
Singh, Kushwant

Ireland

Beckett, Samuel
Behan, Brendan
Bowen, Elizabeth
Broderick, John
Buchanan, George
Clarke, Austin
Colum, Padraic
Devlin, Denis
Dunsany, Lord
Ervine, St John
Friel, Brian
Gogarty, Oliver St John
Gregory, Lady Augusta
Hanley, James
Harris, Frank
Heaney, Seamus
Hewitt, John
Iremonger, Valentin
Johnston, Denis
Johnston, Jennifer
Joyce, James
Kavanagh, Patrick
Kennelly, Brendan
Kinsella, Thomas
Lavin, Mary
Ledwidge, Francis
Leonard, Hugh
Longley, Michael
MacDonagh, Donagh
McGahern, John
Mahon, Derek
Martyn, Edward
Montague, John
Moore, George
Muldoon, Paul
Murphy, Richard
O'Brien, Edna

Ireland contd
O'Brien, Flann
O'Brien, Kate
O'Casey, Sean
O'Connor, Frank
O'Donovan, Gerald
O'Faolain, Sean
O'Flaherty, Liam
Plunkett, James
Robinson, Lennox
Rodgers, W.R.
Russell, George W. (AE)
Shaw, G. B.
Somerville, E. O.
  and Ross, Martin
Stephens, James
Synge, John M.
Tressell, Robert
Trevor, William
Yeats, W. B.

Kenya

Ngugi wa Thiong'o

New Zealand

Adcock, Fleur
Baxter, James K.
Brasch, Charles
Curnow, Allen
Davin, Dan
Doyle, Mike
Duggan, Maurice
Fairburn, A. R. D.
Frame, Janet
Glover, Denis
Hyde, Robin
Ihimaera, Witi
Johnson, Louis
Joseph, M. K.
Mander, Jane
Mansfield, Katherine
Mason, R. A. K.
Mulgan, John
Sargeson, Frank
Satchell, William
Shadbolt, Maurice
Smithyman, Kendrick
Stewart, Douglas
Tuwhare, Hone
Wendt, Albert (from Samoa, often
  grouped under the 'NZ'
  umbrella in bibliographies)

Nigeria

Achebe, Chinua
Aluko, T. M.
Amadi, Elechi
Clark, John Pepper
Ekwensi, Cyprian
Okara, Gabriel I. G.
Okigbo, Christopher
Soyinka, Wole
Tutuola, Amos

Pakistan

Ali, Ahmed
Ghose, Zulfikar

Southern Africa

Abrahams, Peter
Bosman, Herman Charles
Brutus, Dennis
Butler, Frederick Guy
Campbell, Roy
Cloete, Stuart
Fugard, Athol
Gordimer, Nadine
Head, Bessie
Jacobson, Dan
La Guma, Alex
Millin, Sarah Gertrude
Mphahlele, Es'kia
Mtshali, Oswald Mbuyiseni
Nortje, Arthur
Paton, Alan Stewart
Plaatje, Solomon Tshekisho
Reitz, Deneys
Rive, Richard
Schreiner, Olive
Serote, Mongane Wally
Smith, Pauline Janet
van der Post, Laurens

Sri Lanka

Wijenaike, Punyakante

Uganda

Okot p'Bitek

United Kingdom

Abercrombie, Lascelles
Abse, Dannie
Adams, Richard

United Kingdom contd

Aldington, Richard
Amis, Kingsley
Arden, John
Arnim, Countess von
Auden, W. H.
Ayckbourn, Alan
Bainbridge, Beryl
Ballard, J. G.
Baring, Maurice
Barker, George
Barker, H. Granville
Barrie, J. M.
Bates, H. E.
Bawden, Nina
Bedford, Sybille
Beer, Patricia
Beerbohm, Max
Belloc, Hilaire
Bennett, Alan
Bennett, Arnold
Benson, E. F.
Bentley, Phyllis
Berry, Francis
Betjeman, John
Binyon, Laurence
Blackburn, Thomas
Blackwood, Algernon
Blake, George
Blunden, Edmund
Bolt, Robert
Bond, Edward
Bottomley, Gordon
Bottrall, Ronald
Bradbury, Malcolm
Bragg, Melvyn
Braine, John
Bridges, Robert
Bridie, James
Brighouse, Harold
Brittain, Vera
Brooke, Jocelyn
Brooke, Rupert
Brophy, Brigid
Brown, George Mackay
Brownjohn, Alan
Bruce, George
Buchan, John
Bunting, Basil
Burgess, Anthony
Byatt, A. S.
Cameron, Norman
Cary, Joyce
Causley, Charles
Cecil, David
Chaplin, Sid

United Kingdom contd

Chesterton, G. K.
Childers, Erskine
Christie, Agatha
Church, Richard
Clemo, Jack
Common, Jack
Compton-Burnett, Ivy
Connolly, Cyril
Connor, Tony
Conquest, Robert
Conrad, Joseph
Cooper, William
Coppard, A. E.
Cornford, Frances
Coward, Noel
Craig, Gordon
Cronin, A. J.
Davie, Donald
Davies, Rhys
Davies, W. H.
Day Lewis, C.
De la Mare, Walter
Delaney, Shelagh
Dennis, Nigel
Doughty, C. M.
Douglas, Keith
Douglas, Norman
Doyle, Arthur Conan
Drabble, Margaret
Drinkwater, John
Duggan, Alfred
Du Maurier, Daphne
Duncan, Ronald
Dunn, Douglas
Durrell, Lawrence
Eliot, T. S.
Empson, William
Enright, D. J.
Evans, Caradoc
Ewart, Gavin
Farrell, J. G.
Fenton, James
Firbank, Ronald
Fisher, Roy
Flecker, James Elroy
Fleming, Ian
Flint, F. S.
Ford, Ford Madox
Forster, E. M.
Fowles, John
Fraser, G. S.
Fry, Christopher
Fuller, Roy
Galsworthy, John
Garioch, Robert

United Kingdom contd

Garnett, David
Gascoyne, David
Gerhardi(e), William
Gibbon, Lewis Grassic
Gibbons, Stella
Gibson, Wilfrid W.
Gittings, Robert
Godden, Rumer
Golding, William
Gosse, Edmund
Graham, W. S.
Grahame, Kenneth
Graves, Robert
Green, Henry
Greene, Graham
Greenwood, Walter
Grenfell, Julian
Griffiths, Trevor
Grigson, Geoffrey
Gunn, Neil
Gunn, Thom
Gurney, Ivor
Hall, Radclyffe
Hampton, Christopher
Hardy, Thomas
Hare, David
Harrison, Tony
Hartley, L. P.
Heath-Stubbs, John
Heppenstall, Rayner
Herbert, A. P.
Hill, Geoffrey
Hill, Susan
Hilton, James
Hobsbaum, Philip
Hodgson, Ralph
Holbrook, David
Holtby, Winifred
Houghton, Stanley
Housman, A. E.
Hudson, W. H.
Hughes, Richard
Hughes, Ted
Hulme, T. E.
Humphreys, Emyr
Huxley, Aldous
Isherwood, Christopher
Jacob, Violet
James, Henry
James, M. R.
Jameson, Storm
Jennings, Elizabeth
Johnson, B. S.
Johnson, P. Hansford
Jones, David

United Kingdom contd

Jones, Glyn
Jones, Gwyn
Jones, T. H.
Kavan, Anna
Kennedy, Margaret
Keyes, Sidney
Kipling, Rudyard
Kirkup, James
Koestler, Arthur
Larkin, Philip
Lawrence, D. H.
Lawrence, T. E.
Leavis, F. R.
Lehmann, John
Lehmann, Rosamond
Lessing, Doris
Lewis, Alun
Lewis, C. S.
Lewis, Percy Wyndham
Lindsay, Maurice
Linklater, Eric
Livings, Henry
Logue, Christopher
Lowry, Malcolm
Lucie-Smith, Edward
Macaulay, Rose
MacBeth, George
MacCaig, Norman
MacCarthy, Desmond
MacDiarmid, Hugh
Machen, Arthur
MacInnes, Colin
McKenna, Stephen
Mackenzie, Compton
Mackintosh, Elizabeth
MacNeice, Louis
Manning, Olivia
Marsh, Edward
Masefield, John
Mason, A. E. W.
Maugham, W. Somerset
Mercer, David
Mew, Charlotte
Middleton, Stanley
Milne, A. A.
Mitchell, Adrian
Mitchison, Naomi
Mitford, Nancy
Monro, Harold
Montague, C. E.
Morgan, Edwin
Mortimer, John
Mortimer, Penelope
Mottram, R. H.
Muir, Edwin

United Kingdom contd

Munro, Neil
Murdoch, Iris
Murry, J. Middleton
Myers, L. H.
Nesbit, E.
Newbolt, Henry
Newby, P. H.
Nichols, Peter
Nicholson, Norman
Nicolson, Harold
Noyes, Alfred
Orton, Joe
Orwell, George
Osborne, John
Owen, Wilfred
Patten, Brian
Paulin, Tom
Peake, Mervyn
Pinter, Harold
Pitter, Ruth
Plomer, William
Potter, Beatrix
Powell, Anthony
Powys, J. C.
Powys, Llewelyn
Powys, T. F.
Prescott, H. F. M.
Priestley, J. B.
Prince, F. T.
Pritchett, V. S.
Pym, Barbara
Quiller-Couch, A.
Raine, Craig
Raine, Kathleen
Ransome, Arthur
Rattigan, Terence
Raymond, Ernest
Read, Herbert
Read, Piers Paul
Reed, Henry
Reeves, James
Renault, Mary
Richards, Frank
Richardson, Dorothy
Rickword, Edgell
Ridler, Anne
Roberts, Michael
Rolfe, Frederick W.
Rosenberg, Isaac
Sackville-West, V.
Saintsbury, George
Saki
Sansom, William
Sassoon, Siegfried
Sayers, Dorothy L.

United Kingdom contd

Scannell, Vernon
Scott, Alexander
Scott, Paul
Scott, Tom
Scovell, E. J.
Scupham, Peter
Shaffer, Peter
Sherriff, R. C.
Silkin, Jon
Sillitoe, Alan
Simpson, N. F.
Sisson, C. H.
Sitwell, Edith
Sitwell, Osbert
Sitwell, Sacheverell
Smith, Iain Crichton
Smith, Stevie
Smith, S. Goodsir
Snow, C. P.
Sorley, Charles H.
Soutar, William
Spark, Muriel
Spencer, Bernard
Spender, Stephen
Spring, Howard
Squire, J. C.
Stallworthy, Jon

United Kingdom contd

Stewart, J. I. M.
Stoppard, Tom
Storey, David
Strachey, Lytton
Strong, L. A. G.
Swinnerton, Frank
Symons, Arthur
Taylor, Elizabeth
Thomas, D. M.
Thomas, Dylan
Thomas, Edward
Thomas, R. S.
Thompson, Flora
Thwaite, Anthony
Tolkien, J. R. R.
Tomlinson, Charles
Tonks, Rosemary
Toynbee, Philip
Travers, Ben
Tuohy, Frank
Upward, Edward
Waddell, Helen
Wain, John
Waley, Arthur
Wallace, Edgar
Walpole, Hugh

United Kingdom contd

Warner, Rex
Warner, Sylvia Townsend
Waterhouse, Keith
Watkins, Vernon
Watson, William
Waugh, Evelyn
Webb, Mary
Welch, Denton
Weldon, Fay
Wells, H. G.
Wesker, Arnold
West, Rebecca
White, T. H.
Whiting, John
Williams, Charles
Williams, Emlyn
Williamson, Henry
Wilson, A. N.
Wilson, Angus
Wilson, Colin
Wingfield, Sheila
Wodehouse, P. G.
Woolf, Virginia
Wright, David
Wyndham, John
Young, Andrew

Note: writers who left their homeland to work largely in another English-speaking country are not necessarily listed under the country of their birth.

PREFACE AND ACKNOWLEDGEMENTS

This work is designed to provide the student and the general reader with a compact and readable guide to the important literature of our century in English (outside the United States). It contains over 500 entries on individual writers, alphabetically arranged, and space is proportionately distributed between Africa, Australia, Canada, The Caribbean, India, Ireland, New Zealand, Pakistan, Sri Lanka and the United Kingdom. The aim has been to make the Guide at once a handy reference book for academic purposes and a companionable source of pleasure and illumination for all who love literature. In compiling the work, the contributors have striven to achieve a qualitative authority by weighting the Guide in favour of the established figures of the age and other significant writers whom students and informed general readers would wish to know about. Thus substantial articles are provided on those major novelists, poets and dramatists whose reputation has already gained them a place in academic studies, and on others whose work seems to the contributors to be deserving of equivalent attention. Shorter entries extend the coverage over a broad cross-section of interesting lesser writers chosen on the basis of literary quality and of evident impact on the reading public.

Articles supply biographical details helpful for placing writers in their context and interesting personal information that can shed light on their work, but the Guide gives priority throughout to the character and quality of the work itself, exemplifying what is representative and significant in the output of the writers concerned. The contributors have eschewed the kind of comprehensiveness which issues in directory-style lists of publications and capsulated curricula vitae. Rather we have tried to cater for the reader who would wish to have salient examples of an author's work described with sufficient attention to detail to give an idea of its character and importance. And since the purpose throughout is thus to give the reader an impression of what each author's work is like, judicious selectivity has been essential. In the case of minor authors, whose entries are necessarily brief, the tendency has often been to focus on one or two works which can best illustrate the author's particular talent and convey something of its characteristic flavour. While the space allotted to major authors makes less stringent demands upon selectivity and indeed allows of sketching a writer's total achievement in outline, the same principle has been applied of also fastening in some detail on particular works crucial to his development as a writer and representative of his central artistic attainment.

The desire to give a view of literature from the inside has determined the method of presentation. Ensuring that a major writer's career and achievement as a whole are summed up and that works of crucial significance are at the same time usefully described presents the problem that it does not always make for readability to interrupt the general survey of a writer's output with thoughtful commentary upon an outstanding work or with structural clarification of a large-scale opus. Entries on particular books have therefore been appended to the articles on certain major writers. These sub-entries give concise descriptions of individual works that have gained special recognition through their significance in the cultural or social history of the period. Where a book mentioned in an article is to be the subject of a sub-entry, its title is marked by an asterisk. This is a matter of presentation, not of relative grading. While the inclusion of a sub-entry on a book is certainly an indication of its quality and importance, the lack of a sub-entry carries no converse implication. With the majority of writers it has been found that sufficiently substantial accounts even of very important books could be readably accommodated within the general survey without upsetting the balance. In this as in other respects rigid adjustment of the entries to a single pattern has been avoided. Writers differ enormously in the range and variety of their output: they also differ widely in the extent to which they involve themselves in matters of public interest relevant to their creative work: and finally they differ in the degree to which exploration of their personal lives can shed light on their work. For all these reasons it has been accepted that a too standardized general format for all articles would act as a straitjacket. The shape of the entries is flexibly adjusted to the character of the career and output of the writers concerned.

The contributors have not played down their own critical opinions, believing that articles devoid of such judgements must necessarily be lifeless. The views of known critics and fellow-writers are cited where it seems desirable to balance pros with cons in literary evaluation. Indeed the Guide makes its bow to literary critics by the use it thus makes of them in commentary. With a very few exceptions, it does not include entries on critics unless they are also themselves creative writers.

In compiling a survey which attempts to sum up the individual achievements that make up twentieth-century English literature over so wide an area of the English-speaking world, the contributors have inevitably undergone much heart-searching about whom to include and whom to exclude, especially in the case of newer writers. Where a limited amount of space is available the distinction between those writers who just get in and those who just fail to get in cannot be a very meaningful one: but we believe that the net has been thrown widely enough for the Guide as a whole to form a balanced conspectus of the literary scene from 1900 to the present day.

The editor and publisher would like to thank the following for their kind permission to reproduce copyright material: The Cresset Press (now part of the Hutchinson Publishing Group Limited) for Frances Cornford's 'Youth' in Poems and 'The Revelation' in Mountains and Molehills in Collected Poems; The Dolmen Press Limited for 5 lines from Austin Clarke's 'Return from England' in Ancient Lights; W. S. Graham and Faber & Faber Limited for 8 lines from 'Since All My Steps Taken' in The White Threshold.

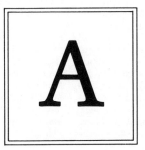

A

ABERCROMBIE, LASCELLES (1881–1938). Poet and critic, born in Cheshire. He became a university teacher at Leeds, then at Oxford. He was one of the poets represented in the first volume of *Georgian Poetry* (1912) and then co-operated with Wilfrid Gibson (q.v.), John Drinkwater (q.v.) and Rupert Brooke (q.v.) in a short-lived quarterly, *New Numbers*, which he founded in 1914 and published from his Gloucestershire cottage. Its final issue (1915) included Brooke's celebrated war sonnets. Abercrombie was also involved with Gordon Bottomley (q.v.) and others in the movement to revive verse drama. His verse plays include *The Sale of Saint Thomas* (1911) and *End of the World*, which appeared along with Bottomley's play *King Lear's Wife* in the second volume of *Georgian Poetry* (1915). Abercrombie cultivated Georgian dignity and self-conscious beauty of phrase. Edward Thomas (q.v.) found his 'Mary and the Bramble', which Yeats (q.v.) later included in his *Oxford Book of Modern Verse* (1936), 'rather loose and eloquent, with nice feeling', but such was his contemporary reputation that he was given a collected edition in the *Oxford Poets* in his own lifetime in 1930. Later critical taste has reacted against his cloudiness and turgidity.   [HB]

ABRAHAMS, PETER (1919–). Journalist and novelist, born in the slums of Vrededorp, Johannesburg, South Africa. Some limited schooling and the discovery of Lamb's *Tales*, Palgrave's *Golden Treasury* and Keats's poetry kindled literary ambitions even in the face of poverty and racial discrimination. By the mid-1940s he had become the first black South African novelist since Plaatje (q.v.). In 1939 he took ship as a stoker and after two years at sea settled in London, employed by the *Daily Worker* until his first book, *Dark Testament* (1942), was published. These short stories convey the painful longings for personal or artistic fulfilment of sensitive, isolated characters, usually destitute and subject to racial prejudice or political oppression. As the autobiography *Tell Freedom* (1954) suggests, Abrahams's understanding of desolate loneliness springs from his own formative experiences and is at the heart of all his fiction, whether about prostitutes, murderers, artists or political leaders. It is his greatest strength as a novelist, even though it leads often to romantic sentimentality when the isolated character finds release in communion with another.

The urgent need for communication across personal, racial and political barriers gives considerable power to his first three novels, *Song of the City* (1945), *Mine Boy* (1946), *The Path of Thunder* (1948). *Mine Boy*, about life in the black urban slums and on the gold mines, won Abrahams some critical acclaim; the most sanguine of his South African books, it shares with *Cry, the Beloved Country* (Paton, q.v.) an optimistic, postwar vision of racial harmony based on individual change of heart rather than political process. Yet Abrahams's and Paton's authentic, realistic descriptions of Johannesburg's black ghettos did much to focus international attention upon South Africa's political iniquities.

So did *Tell Freedom* and his account of a visit to South Africa in 1952, *Return to Goli* (1953), which first appeared as articles in the *Observer*, for which Abrahams wrote regularly between 1952 and 1964. In 1957 he moved to Jamaica and was editor of the *West Indian Economist* and controller of radio news until he resigned in 1964.

Abrahams's experience of human isolation and of racial impediments to humane understanding has enabled him to achieve in his later novels an acute analysis of political situations. It shows first in his historical novel *Wild Conquest* (1950), about the triangular relationship of Barolong, Boers and Matabele (partly inspired by Plaatje's *Mhudi*). *A Wreath for Udomo* (1956) is prophetic in its imaginative positing of problems that the leaders of former colonies would have to wrestle with.

This Island Now (1966), though set in the Caribbean, draws much from his African experience. Like *A Wreath for Udomo*, it looks into the future and presents a political leader who sacrifices personal peace of mind to his passionate determination, this time, to slash a way for his black people through neo-colonialist economic bonds that still deny them their full humanity. As President Josiah curbs local capitalism, foreign economic power, then the freedom of the press, even the independence of the judiciary, he sees each step as a ruthlessly unhappy but necessarily chosen means of carrying through 'the great work of his life, the liberating of the land and its people'. Each act leaves him more lonely than before, especially when he has to use force against his own people for their eventual good and 200 are killed in riots. For a moment he has doubts, but they pass: 'If this way is wrong then there is no way out for the people of the so-called under-developed world'. Josiah is very sympathetically presented but the views of his opponents are also eloquently put, especially Judge Wright's plea for the rule of law. Yet Abrahams does suggest that in the Third World, with its prodigious problems of poverty and the other long-term effects of colonialism, western notions of individual human rights may be irrelevant luxuries. Despite characteristic, though fewer, lapses into triteness and sensationalism, *This Island Now* is an important novel of ideas, with tragic dimensions.   [AR]

ABSE, DANNIE (1923–). Poet and dramatist, born in Cardiff, South Glamorgan, Wales, educated there and at King's College, London. He served in the RAF and is a doctor by profession. His family background is Jewish. His volumes of poetry include *After Every Green Thing* (1949), *Tenants of the House* (1957), *Poems, Golders Green* (1962), *Selected Poems* (1970), *Funland* (1973) and *Collected Poems* (1977). The poetic voice is companionably conversational, engagingly close to the reader's ear. The concerns are those of the unpretentiously sceptical mind reflecting on the stuff of daily life – a return to the hometown, a remembered schoolmaster, a night at an Auschwitz film, the death of his father, a record of Caruso:

> Loved not for themselves those tenors who sing
> arias from 'Aida' on horned, tinny
> gramophones – but because they take a man back
> to a half forgotten thing.
>
>   ('Sunday Evening')

In *Way Out in the Centre* (1981), whose title distances the writer from passionate extremisms ('Yet here I am in England way out in the centre'), there are poems about the predicament of reconciling the poet's human sensibilities and the doctor's professional responsibilities.

Abse's plays include *House of Cowards* (prod 1960); *Fire in Heaven* (prod 1948), a verse play dealing with a pacifist's dilemma, later revised in prose as *In the Cage* (see *Three Quester Plays*, 1967); and *Pythagoras* (1976). He has also written novels, including *Ash on a Young Man's Sleeve* (1954) about growing up in Cardiff. His autobiography, *A Poet in the Family* (1974), contains interesting reminiscences of literary London in the 1940s and 1950s. Abse was Visiting Writer in Residence at Princeton University, New Jersey, from 1973 to 1974. [HB]

ACHEBE, CHINUA (1930–). Novelist, born at Ogidi in Eastern Nigeria. His mother tongue was Igbo, but he learned some English at home, as his father, Isaiah Okafor Achebe, was a teacher in the Church Missionary Society's village school. Achebe attended this school and in 1944 he went to Government College, Umuahia, for his secondary education. In 1953 he was one of the first graduates of the then University College of Ibadan in Nigeria. The next year he began a career in broadcasting that culminated in his appointment in 1961 as Director of External Broadcasting in Lagos. He resigned after the massacres of Igbos in Northern Nigeria in 1966, and went back to the Eastern Region. When it declared its independence as Biafra in 1967 and the Civil War began, he worked for the Biafran authorities, travelling more than once to western Europe and the United States to gain help for the Biafran cause. After the end of the Civil War in 1970, he was Research Fellow in African Studies at the University of Nigeria, Nsukka, until in 1972 he took up a university teaching appointment in the United States. He returned to Nigeria in 1977. In 1974 he was awarded an honorary doctorate by the University of Southampton and the next year by the University of Stirling. His published works consist of four novels (*Things Fall Apart*, 1958; *No Longer at Ease*, 1960; *Arrow of God*, 1964; *A Man of the People*, 1966); a short novel for children (*Chike and the River*, 1966); two collections of short stories (*The Sacrificial Egg and Other Stories*, 1962, and *Girls at War*, 1972); a volume of poetry (*Beware Soul Brother*, 1971; in the USA *Christmas in Biafra and Other Poems*, 1972); and a collection of essays (*Morning Yet on Creation Day*, 1975).

For inventiveness in language and novelistic technique, for profound insight into tragic human experience, for satirical sophistication, Achebe must still be regarded as the anglophone African novelist of most considerable stature. His first novel, *Things Fall Apart*, opened new possibilities for the African novel in English, and has deservedly become a classic in less than twenty years. It tells the tragic story of the rise and fall of the strong, self-made man Okonkwo against the background of the gradual, and equally tragic, disintegration of his people's culture, during the time of the first Igbo contact with white missionaries and colonial officials in Eastern Nigeria. Although both hero and society are presented with great sympathy, the one is shown to have suppressed all his natural affections in order to gain his fellows' respect, while the other is seen to be too rigid in its culture to be able to counteract the allurements that Christianity holds for its less fortunate and socially unaccommodated members. Achebe has himself acknowledged that his aim was to persuade his fellow Africans (and the outside world also) that the pre-colonial African past had a highly developed culture that was orderly and humane. Much of the authenticity of his re-creation of this culture derives from the oral tradition he imbibed in his own family as a child, but he does not sentimentalize the African past. He presents its weaknesses as well as its strengths with great vividness and integrity. The most marked linguistic characteristic is his use of Igbo proverbs literally translated into English, a device that makes for surface authenticity but is also a means of demonstrating, through the characters' speech, how Igbo society is simultaneously strengthened and seriously limited by its traditional wisdom inherited through gnomic folk sayings. The story is not simply a lament for the past but an analysis in fiction of a process of historical change.

Although *Arrow of God* provides an even richer evocation of traditional culture than *Things Fall Apart*, it is more than a similar novel on a larger scale. The organic daily life of the Umuaro clan is drawn in great detail, but the detail is necessary for realizing fully the part played by the priest Ezeulu in that society, for Ezeulu is the most complex and ambitious piece of characterization Achebe has yet attempted. The tragedy evolves from the conflict within him between the demands of his semi-divine office as priest of the clan's protecting deity and Ezeulu's very human desire for personal power. The theme of the novel is a man's use of the power he already wields, his desire to extend it and the effects of his misuse of it upon himself and his people. Again Achebe uses Igbo proverbs, but with further refinements, as a means of conveying a sense of the twilit area between a man's terrestrial existence and his function as a semi-spirit mediating with the deity on his people's behalf. It is here that Ezeulu stumbles tragically. Both priest and people are handled with extraordinary sympathy and human understanding, but Achebe succeeds in achieving a remarkable artistic detachment, with the final, wry paragraph of the novel calling in question the people's over-simple interpretation of Ezeulu's downfall.

In *No Longer at Ease* the cohesiveness of pre-colonial Igbo culture has become a hollow mockery, just as the chief character Obi's youthful, British-university-inspired idealism is seen to be without foundation before the harsh realities of corruption in modern Lagos. What is satirically laid bare, without overt authorial comment, is the chaotic, rootless bewilderment of modern West African city life, again fully reflected in the characters' speech, as they switch from Igbo, to pidgin or to English, according to their relationships with other people. The general crisis of culture is particularized, and humanized, in Obi's career, with Achebe's satire sympathetically underlining the absence of any larger mode for personal integrity to work within.

A Man of the People is a bitter satirical farce. Achebe attacks the sort of political corruption and thuggery that characterized Nigeria between Independence and the military coups of 1966. He does so not by conventional means, but by using the narrator Odili as an anti-hero

who lucidly analyses the evils around him, while taking a very active part in them himself. The only clue to Odili's real fictional function is the false, pseudo-sophisticated speech that Achebe places in his mouth. Perhaps Achebe's greatest strength as a novelist is the steady refinement of his control over his characters' speech as a means of conveying rather than stating insights and moral valuations.

Achebe's poems in *Beware Soul Brother* show how the physical horrors and spiritual obscenities of the Civil War darkened the world of his imagination frighteningly, but he displays his characteristic honesty by facing the horrors head-on in the poems, sustained by a very real faith in his people and their future, provided they can be true to themselves and draw strength from their past.

Most of the essays in *Morning Yet on Creation Day* form an impressive contribution to the continuing debate about the nature of African literature in the English language. The profound awareness of the great shadow that colonialist Europe has left upon African thought and feeling, and the high seriousness, expressed wittily and in vivid, vigorous language, make the best of these essays wise and enlightening. [AR]

ADAMS, RICHARD (1920-). Novelist, born in Berkshire. He was for twenty years a civil servant until the immense success of his children's book *Watership Down* (1972) enabled him to turn full-time writer. It is a full-length tale of the adventures of a company of rabbits whose search for new quarters brings experience of various societies in bondage, and who learn the hard way the value of freedom and initiative. The locale is a topographically exact area of West Berkshire; geographical and natural detail is painstakingly researched. The fantastic saga *Shardik* (1974) is intended for adults. It focuses on the long-prophesied reincarnation of the mighty bear Shardik, an agency of divine power built in the mould of C.S. Lewis's (q.v.) Aslan, but a shade beastlier in that he kills men with a cuff, devours the carcasses of sheep and befouls the ground. Round the moral question whether his authority is to be harnessed to lead his people to victory or accepted in wholly disinterested submission a busy epic narrative unfolds that culminates for Shardik in the suffering, humiliation and sacrifice ordained for God's chosen vessel. In *The Plague Dogs* (1977) Adams turns back from an imaginary to an actual locale, the Lake District, for the adventures of two dogs who escape the savage human brutalities of ARSE (Animal Research, Scientific and Experimental) to roam the countryside. They are rumoured to be carrying plague. The human hunt and the publicity it arouses are an opportunity for heavy ridicule of media men and other authorial aversions. *The Girl in a Swing* (1980) puts the *Tannhäuser* myth in a contemporary context; and the hero runs a china shop in Newbury. [HB]

ADCOCK, FLEUR (1934-). Poet, born at Papakura, near Auckland, New Zealand, and educated in England in 1939-47 and at Victoria University of Wellington, New Zealand. After university teaching and library work in New Zealand in 1959-62 she settled in England in 1963 and now works as a librarian in London. Her first collection, *The Eye of the Hurricane* (1964), displayed an accomplished command of a variety of lyrical forms. Sensitivity and taut control were balanced in exploring dimensions of the everyday as mother and lover. Her classical training shows in a poem such as 'Note on Propertius I.5' but it is a strongly individual and personal voice that is most evident in her work. Of the twenty-six poems in *Tigers* (1967) half were reprinted from the previous book, but with the new works the collection represented an extension as well as a consolidation of her range. In poems such as 'For a Five-Year-Old' and 'The Water Below' her ability to render the subtleties of human emotion with complex precision while still retaining firm control over the verse itself is impressive. *High Tide in the Garden* (1971) enhanced her achievement and contained three fine poems expressing her feelings as an expatriate New Zealander which stand as perceptive and honest records of the expatriate experience. *The Scenic Route* (1974) made extensive use of an Irish setting, and was well received. Poems in *The Inner Harbour* (1979) reflected a visit to her home country. [PQ]

AIDOO, (Christina) AMA ATA (1942–). Poet, short-story writer and dramatist, born and educated in Ghana, graduating in 1964. While still a studen she won a Mbari literary prize and started writing her very sensitive first play, *The Dilemma of a Ghost* (1965), about the personal pains of a young Ghanaian and his Harlem-born wife on returning from America and trying to discover themselves and integrate their rural Ghanaian and American expectations of marriage. Despite weaknesses, it is a work of inventive stagecraft; C. Pieterse calls it a 'distinguished socio-domestic morality'. In addition to researching into indigenous drama in Ghana, she has travelled extensively in America, Europe and East Africa. Since about 1965 her poems, short stories and critical reviews have appeared in most African literary periodicals. Her second play, *Anowa* (1969), is her own version of an old Ghanaian legend which she first heard from her mother as a song. Her collection of short stories, *No Sweetness Here* (1970), reveals a confident, dramatic use of dialogue, an elegiac mood in her handling of African values and opportunities betrayed and a subtle but incisive satirical gift. Her stories illustrate her admiration of oral African techniques of narration. Her first novel, *Our Sister Killjoy* (1976), lacks the assurance of her shorter fiction.   [AR]

ALDINGTON, RICHARD (1892–1962). Novelist and poet, born in Portsmouth, Hampshire, the son of a solicitor, and educated at Dover College and (for one year) at London University. He came to light as a poet of the Imagist school that cultivated exactness of vocabulary, liberation from established rhythms, and sharp particularity of image. His first volume, *Images* (1915), was followed by *Images of War* (1919) and *Images of Desire* (1919). 'The triumph of technical skill is that it should be unobtrusive', he wrote in his introduction to the *Complete Poems* (1948). Aldington's technical skill is evident; he achieves the economy, the freedom of phrasing and the clarity of image that he valued:

A church spire
Holds up a little brass cock

To peak at the blue wheat fields.
('London: May 1915')

but his total poetic output lacks weight. Aldington married Hilda Doolittle, the American poet, in 1913, but the marriage was dissolved in 1937. His second wife was Netta McCulloch. The First World War swept Aldington into the army and to the Western Front in 1916 and left him nervously broken and shell-shocked in 1918. As man and as writer he was permanently damaged by the war. Ten years after it ended he wrote his war novel, *Death of a Hero* (1929), 'a memorial in its ineffective way to a generation which hoped much, strove honestly, and suffered deeply' (Dedicatory Letter). It is a scathingly vituperative outburst against the folly of war and the imbecility of men, 'a vendetta of the dead against the living'. The book opens with the death in battle of Captain George Winterbourne. The bitter authorial voice – ostensibly that of a narrating friend – unfolds the story of George's life. He is the lifelong victim of stupidity – parental, educational, social, moral, political. Accepted 'goodness' emerges as hypocrisy, religion as bogus, tradition as humbug. But the sledge-hammer irony is too crude, the venom too diversely distributed. Fury unleashed at the humbug of the older generation, at middle-class smuggery and philistinism, at conventional morality and religion, creates the illusion that the bloody holocaust was somehow the product of sexual inhibition and prudery – 'the supreme and tragic climax of Victorian cant'. What Aldington does succeed in conveying most powerfully is the way the harrowing experience of the front-line soldier cuts him off from meaningful communication with civilians at home, so that the soldier on leave finds himself 'gesticulating across an abyss'. In general Aldington shrieks so hysterically that the book's very existence seems to constitute a poignant expression of human promise cut off and artistic poise knocked sideways. Later novels include *The Colonel's Daughter* (1931), *All Men Are Enemies* (1933) and *Very Heaven* (1937). Aldington wrote a biography of D.H. Lawrence (q.v.), *Portrait of a Genius, But . . .* (1950), and assaulted the idealized 'Lawrence of Arabia' myth in *Lawrence of Arabia; A Biographical Enquiry* (1955). His autobiography, *Life for Life's Sake* (New York, 1940; London, 1968), contains interesting portraits of many literary contemporaries, including Pound and Eliot (q.v.), Yeats (q.v.) and Ford (q.v.), D.H. Lawrence and Norman Douglas (q.v.), Ian S. MacNiven and Harry T. Moore have edited *Literary Lifelines* (1981), letters exchanged between Aldington and his younger admirer, Lawrence Durrell (q.v.), both of them expatriates, between 1957 and 1962.
[HB]

ALI, AHMED (1912–). Diplomat, Urdu writer, critic, novelist in English, born in Delhi, India, and educated at Aligarh and Lucknow. A founder of the Progressive Writers' Movement, which greatly influenced Urdu culture in the 1930s, he lectured at Allahabad University. After working for the BBC in India, he joined the Pakistani diplomatic service in 1950, retiring prematurely in 1960. Author of some volumes of Urdu short stories, he has translated Indonesian and Urdu poetry into English, written an unusually sensitive article on Raja Rao (q.v.)

and produced two novels in English. *Twilight in Delhi* (1940), warmly praised by E.M. Forster (q.v.), is a recording, and elegiac celebration, of the fast-fading Muslim culture of Old Delhi early in the twentieth century. The private concerns of Muslim families are presented against a rich background of life within the old city walls later demolished by the British. L. Brander emphasizes 'Muslim exuberance' (e.g. in the pigeon-flying, kite-flying and marriage scenes) set against a general mood of 'Muslim acceptance of fate' and regards the novel as 'the most remarkable description of oriental customs and ceremony in English'. *Ocean of Night* (1964) contrasts past Muslim splendours with 1930s sordidness in Lucknow.   [AR]

ALUKO, T.M. (Timothy Mafalarurso) (1918–). Civil servant, administrator and novelist, born in Ilesha, Nigeria. On entering Lagos Technical College he hoped to study literature but it wasn't on offer that year so he chose engineering. In 1950 he obtained a London BSc in civil engineering, then worked as an engineer until he became senior lecturer in engineering in Lagos University in 1966. In 1971 he was appointed Commissioner for Finance in the Mid-West State government. His novel *One Man, One Wife* (1959), which satirizes Yoruba Christians and polygamists, was the first Nigerian novel in English to be published in Nigeria. With six novels behind him Aluko has, however, won little critical attention, most of it hostile, like B. Lindfors's dismissive comment: 'It is hard to take such a light-hearted comedian seriously'. Aluko's comedy is cerebral not emotive, and he applies it to the stresses between modern and traditional life which most African writers treat tragically. With considerable linguistic sophistication he often implants in authorial narration the clichés and superficial attitudes he mocks, which unwary readers can mistake for his own. His delight in the droll is vital and celebratory rather than malicious or superficial. In *One Man, One Matchet* (1964) he satirizes a demagogue, in *Kinsman and Foreman* (1966) the improper demands made on a civil servant's influence by his relations. *Chief the Honourable Minister* (1970) unconvincingly attempts serious satire of national politics, but Aluko regains some of his poise in *His Worshipped Majesty* (1972), about the transition from chiefly rule to modern administration. *Wrong Ones in the Dock* (1982) is an indignant and solemn fictional exposé of the workings of the Nigerian legal system.   [AR]

AMADI, ELECHI (1934–). Of the Ikwere tribe, Amadi is a soldier, administrator and novelist. Born in Aluu, near Port Harcourt, Nigeria, he graduated from Ibadan University in mathematics and physics. He later became a land surveyor, then a Federal Army officer. In 1965 he turned to teaching. During the Civil War (1967–70), he was imprisoned by the Biafran government, escaping at the fall of Port Harcourt to rejoin the Federal forces. After the war he worked for the Rivers State government and became its Commissioner for Information. He has written two accomplished novels, *The Concubine* (1966) and *The Great Ponds* (1969), an account of his wartime experiences, *Sunset in Biafra* (1973), and, less successfully, two plays in one volume, *Peppersoup and The Road to Ibadan* (Ibadan, 1977).

Both novels are set in a pre-colonial village environment, not unlike the Igbo setting of *Things Fall Apart* (Achebe, q.v.). Against the vivid realization of such a culture, Amadi creates in *The Concubine* a subtle interplay of tensions between individual aspirations and the custom-sanctified influences of tribal communality. In *The Great Ponds* the near-idyllic culture is brought to catastrophe by forest warfare quite as devastating for the villagers as the First World War was for Europeans. Amadi's particular strengths lie in his delicate handling of relationships between individuals and his completely convincing presentation of the villagers' belief in the presence of their gods, with the supernatural world as real and immediate as the mundane. Men are not lessened but magnified by their acceptance of the gods, even when suffering and near-intolerable sacrifice are ordained.   [AR]

AMIS, KINGSLEY (1922–). Novelist and poet, born in London, educated at the City of London School and at Oxford University. He was Lecturer in English at University College, Swansea, from 1949 to 1961, then held a fellowship at Peterhouse, Cambridge, for two years before turning full-time writer. His best-selling novel, *Lucky Jim* (1953), presents a resentful young university lecturer, Jim Dixon, up against all-round phoniness, academic, cultural and social; and journalists gave him archetypal status as the Angry Young Man of fiction. In *That Uncertain Feeling* (1955) Jim is metamorphosed into John Lewis, humble librarian pursued by a wealthy councillor's wife. Slapstick high jinks with cars and fights and dressing-up are laid on by Amis's non-stop laugh-production line, and the prose simmers with verbal flippancies. *I Want It Now* (1968) starts as a scathing satire on the self-inflated media man, but twists itself into a dubious parable of salvation through sex ('I've had to give up trying to be a dedicated, full-time shit'). Amis's comic inventiveness and his eye for current shoddinesses and shams continued to entertain his public through the 1970s with novels whose ironic perspectives and verbal vitality give them a certain cachet. He has also displayed his versatility by trying his hand at a James-Bond-style spy story, *Colonel Sun* (1968); a period detective novel, *The Riverside Villas Murder* (1973); pictures of an imaginary Catholic England, *The Alteration* (1976); and a future Russianized one, *Russian Hide-and-Seek* (1980). But a streak of immaturity emerges in *Jake's Thing* (1978), whose sustained farce about genitals and sex therapy becomes strenuously unfunny.

As a poet (*A Frame of Mind*, 1953; *A Case of Samples*, 1957), Amis first worked in the mode of Larkin, projecting the no-nonsense posture with individual downrightness:

> Should poets bicycle-pump the human heart
> Or squash it flat?
>
> ('A Bookshop Idyll')

It has been argued that Amis is a better poet than novelist. When *Collected Poems 1944–1979* (1979) was published, Anthony Powell (q.v.) praised highly his gift for bringing off in his poetry 'something exceedingly difficult in all the arts – the appearance of being very ordinary, while not being ordinary at all'.

Amis is an authority on science fiction. See his *New*

Maps of Hell: A Survey of Science Fiction (New York, 1960; London, 1961) and the anthology he has edited, *The Golden Age of Science Fiction* (1981).   [HB]

ANAND, MULK RAJ (1905–). Art critic, editor, short-story writer, novelist, born in Peshawar, India, son of an Indian Army subedar. After graduating from Punjab University (1924) he was at University College, London in 1926–9 and Cambridge from 1929 to 1930. Between 1930 and 1945 he divided his time between literary London and Gandhi's pre-independence India, then, settling in Bombay, began his long editorship of *Marg*, a quarterly journal of the arts. He married the actress Kathleen van Gelder (1939, divorced 1948) and the dancer Shirin Vajifdar (1950). He has published over forty books, including some fifteen novels and seven volumes of short stories, is a Sahitya Akademi Award Winner and has been translated into about forty languages. After publishing books on Persian painting, Indian curries, Indian poetry, Hindu art, an essay on heroism and a volume of short stories between 1930 and 1934, he brought out his first two novels, on which his reputation rests firmly, *Untouchable* (1935) and *Coolie* (1936). Despite vastly different outlooks and techniques, Anand with *Untouchable*, R.K. Narayan (q.v.) with *Swami and Friends* (1935) and Raja Rao (q.v.) with *Kanthapura* (1938) established the Indian novel in English as a viable form. Indian literary circles have, ever since, heatedly debated its propriety, even its authenticity, but the now venerable three have gone on for over forty years, writing in English (not their mother-tongue) to convey experience that is distinctively Indian. Whatever cultural theories are thus exemplified, violated or refuted, their writings took the novel in English into new, hazardous, but also exhilarating linguistic and stylistic waters in the 1930s. They have been followed by many other Indian authors and, since the early 1950s, by African writers like Achebe (q.v.), Soyinka (q.v.) and Tutuola (q.v.).

Compared with Narayan and Rao, Anand has been undeservedly underestimated both in India and abroad, usually on the grounds that his political purposes are too transparent in much of his work; for instance, W. Walsh writes that his 'semi-marxist categories, his furious . . . indignation, and his habit of undue explicitness . . . make him a writer whose work has to be severely sieved'. What his writings do reveal is a polished, cultivated, cosmopolitan mind, very sceptical of religion and transcendental metaphysics, but with a vital, passionate faith in ordinary human potential. Like Dickens, he is angered by the corrosive effects upon the human spirit of poverty and oppression of any kind, and, again like Dickens, is able to draw upon vivid memories of childhood, to depict the elemental realities of life that press upon the masses of the abject poor in India. No other Indian writer in English has so whole-heartedly demystified and deglamorized Indian life, whether of beggars, graduates or princes. What sustains Anand's fiction is his assertion of the preciousness of life in the face of all that would overwhelm it; however inimical nature or mankind or both, most of his major characters attain a real dignity, even if it is very fragile, which opens their concerns movingly to readers of different backgrounds and cultures. That anger, reproach, accusation of society,

have gone into Anand's rendering of the social conditions in his novels cannot, and need not, be denied. In most of his books these emotions are mediated in genuinely literary ways, often through earthy, 'simple' characters parodying the speech of the pompous and arrogant; for instance, the NCO Kirpu's mocking of military orders-of-the-day and Sepoy Lalu's parody of the Bishop of Chetpur's militant sermon to uncomprehending Hindu, Sikh and Muslim troops in Flanders (both in *Across the Black Waters*, 1940).

S. Cowasjee rightly declares that Anand's chief strength lies in his being a political novelist. Indeed his 'political' emotions more often than not vitalize rather than vitiate his writing. What merit might lie in the maudlin novella *Lament on the Death of a Master of Arts* (1967) derives from the fudged attempt to attribute the character's real and symbolic deaths to poverty, cruelty and outmoded social conventions. In *The Woman and the Cow* (1960; reissued as *Gauri*, 1976), the long-suffering Gauri's final, resolute desertion of a once tender but now brutalized husband makes of the novel not simply a story about marriage in a drought-stricken village, but also an Indian parable of contrasted responses to conditions that could extinguish life itself.

Untouchable is still the most admired of Anand's novels, with critics enthusiastically praising its unity of construction (it deals with the events of a single day). As an Untouchable street-sweeper, Bakhu, who has cleaned latrines since he was 6, is doomed to a despised, unchangeable, hereditary occupation. He seems to accept it stoically, like his father who believes unquestioningly that it is the piety of higher-caste Hindus 'which prevents them from touching us'. But Bakhu is more spirited; when the 'piety' of others makes him the victim of three particularly humiliating incidents, anger and rebelliousness surge through him. His secret fantasizing after literacy and sahib-hood cannot sustain him, but the novel ends with the subdued consolation he gathers from hearing Gandhi preach against untouchability and over-hearing a conversation about a casteless Indian society, when latrines will have been mechanically cleansed. Though the reader becomes very involved in Bakhu's experiences, Anand succeeds throughout in portraying him as illiterate and shamefully confined mentally and spiritually by his environment. The criticisms of society that the novel evokes arise less from Bakhu's limited consciousness than from the hypocrisy, arrogance and spite enacted in word and deed by the 'respectable' characters whose paths he crosses.

Like Bakhu, and for similar, sound reasons, Munoo in *Coolie* is a representative figure, not a fully individualized character; his travels from a Kangra hill-village to Sham Nagar, Daulatpur, Bombay and Simla, in various exacting menial jobs which lead to his death from tuberculosis, symbolize the movement of millions of Indians from village innocence to urban experience. This wider-ranging, episodic design allows Anand a panoramic treatment of social problems, with a great variety of types of people revealing their virtues or vices in their reactions to a simple, warm-hearted, often destitute youth.

Similar social changes and their effects upon a young man stirred into aspirations beyond his immediate, claustrophobic environment are more fully analysed in the trilogy consisting of *The Village* (1939), in which the peasant-boy Lalu chafes under age-old conventions. *Across the Black Waters* (1940), about Lalu's disenchantment with European values in the trenches of Flanders, and *The Sword and the Sickle* (1942), with Lalu back in India resisting new prejudices based not on religion but on money. *The Big Heart* (1945) shows individual hereditary coppersmiths at the mercy of capitalist factory owners, with trade unionism precariously emerging from the conflict. Cowasjee has somewhat exaggeratedly claimed that *Private Life of an Indian Prince* (1953) 'is a Dostoevskian novel on the grand scale', but the book does demonstrate how Anand's non-categorical mind penetrates the nature of mental anguish in a subject who would seem well outside the author's sympathies. Largeness of heart is indeed what makes Anand an attractive novelist, though his technical skills should not be overlooked, nor the authority and sureness with which he brings to light the trampled lives of the dispossessed in the Third World. G. Parry has observed that Anand's 'authorial voice has the command, flexibility, and poise of a master of English', whereas the 'stylized English' he 'imposes on his low characters works because it acknowledges the distance that necessarily exists between the subject and the reader'.   [AR]

ANTHONY, MICHAEL (1932–). Novelist, born in Mayaro, Trinidad. He lived in England in 1954–68, in Brazil in 1968–70 and then returned to Trinidad to work as a journalist. His first three novels are remarkable for the freshness, deceptive simplicity and authenticity with which the perceptions of youthful characters are caught. *The Games Are Coming* (1963) interweaves differing motives and tensions in three characters' excitement over the outcome of a cycling championship race. Anthony's finest achievement is his creation in *The Year in San Fernando* (1965) of the 12-year-old country boy, Francis, learning new experiences and gaining insight into adult behaviour during a year spent as servant and schoolboy in the town of San Fernando. P. Edwards and K. Ramchand argue that 'an area of experience has been sounded' but 'there is no attempt . . . to suggest that the boy has now "reached maturity" '. The novel engages us vividly in 'a peculiarly open state of consciousness', without Francis making moral judgements on the sometimes sordid adult goings-on. *Green Days by the River* (1967) focuses upon an older but more perplexed lad savouring contradictory loves before a shotgun marriage. *Streets of Conflict* (1976) is set in Brazil during the student riots of 1968 and implies a choice between love and life or revolution and death, but theme and method are not as finely integrated as in the earlier novels.   [AR]

ARDEN, JOHN (1930–). Dramatist, born in Barnsley, South Yorkshire, educated at Sedbergh School, King's College, Cambridge, and Edinburgh College of Art. He first practised in architecture. He married the actress Margaretta D'Arcy in 1957 and she has collaborated with him in the composition of plays. Arden's first London production was *The Waters of Babylon* (prod 1957), a complex, busy play about a Polish exile, Krank, who leads · a double life as day-time architect and night-time keeper

of a disorderly house, and gets involved in political bombing and an attempted Premium Bond swindle. *Serjeant Musgrave's Dance* (prod 1959, pubd 1960) won Arden his reputation. An epic drama in the Brechtian tradition, it has a scatter of songs, fitful didactic reflection, a big cast and the panoramic sequences of the chronicle form. Labelled 'An Un-historical Parable', it is set vaguely in the years between 1860 and 1880. Serjeant Musgrave and three privates arrive at a mining town in winter in the middle of a strike. They are deserters from a colonial war, and they have brought the body of their dead comrade to his home town in a box. Musgrave, it eventually emerges, intends to gather the populace together for a recruiting meeting, to tell the truth about the battlefield, to display the victim's skeleton, to charge the citizens with the guilt of implicit involvement, and to turn the guns on them in righteous retribution. The dragoons arrive to arrest the deserters just in time. Arden stands back from moral judgement and explores the inherent duplicities of idealism in action. Episode by episode Arden often makes an impact through the theatrical distinctiveness and variety of theme and setting, but he tends to sacrifice dramatic thrust and concentration to proliferation of multiple motifs.

The Workhouse Donkey (prod 1963, pubd 1964), subtitled 'A Vulgar Melo-drama', achieves unity of theme in its satire of small-time municipal corruption affecting local government, local politics and the police, but the element of farcical burlesque seems to embody a nihilistic ambivalence that is resolved only in belly-laughs. The downfall of Charlie Butterthwaite, Napoleon of local government, is effected in a morass of gerrymandering, and the virtuous new police chief who tries to clean things up seems to belong to another play with a moral spine. Arden moved to sixteenth-century Scotland and adopted a synthetic Scots idiom for *Armstrong's Last Goodnight* (prod 1964, pubd 1965). Called 'An Exercise in Diplomacy', it is a study of James V's attempts to bring a marauding Border chieftain to heel through the intermediary diplomacy of Sir David Lindsay. Its composition was sparked off by Arden's perception of a correspondence between Conor Cruise O'Brien's efforts in the Congo (recorded in his book *Katanga and Back*) and the events of the old Scottish ballad of 'Johnny Armstrong'. As a chronicle play, it recaptures the feel of a half-barbaric, half-civilized age and its problems, and thus carries conviction, but that human impress upon action which gives intensity to drama is inadequately articulated. Arden's *Left-Handed Liberty* (prod and pubd 1965), a play about the Magna Carta, was written to commission from the City of London for the 750th anniversary of the signing of the charter. *The Hero Rises Up* (prod 1968, pubd 1969) takes Nelson off his column with a vengeance, and *The Island of the Mighty* (prod 1972, pubd 1973) gives an ironic picture of King Arthur as a lame, hobbling monarch. *The Ballygombeen Bequest* (prod 1972) is about absentee landlordism in Ireland.

Arden, a rebel against the established theatre and against the literary tyranny of the fixed dramatic text, has spoken of his ideal of a thirteen-hour play, an audience coming and going and a theatre with the 'characteristics of a fairground or amusement park' (Preface to *The Workhouse Donkey*). He characterized himself and his dilemma in the radio play *The Bagman* (prod 1970). Versatile in style, he has used verse and prose, and has tried his hand at epic, problem play, melodrama, fable, farce and several forms of theatrical experimentation. See his critical book, *To Present the Pretence: Essays on the Theatre and Its Public* (1978). *Silence Among the Weapons* (1982), set in the Roman Republic in the first century BC, is his first novel.   [HB]

ARMAH, AYI KWEI (1939–). Novelist, born in Takoradi, Ghana, and educated at Achimota School. He graduated in social studies from Harvard University, Boston, Massachusetts, and in fine arts from Columbia University, New York. After working as a television scriptwriter and school-teacher in Ghana, translator in Algeria, journalist in France and literature lecturer in the United States, he settled in Tanzania in 1970.

His first novel, entitled *The Beautyful Ones Are Not Yet Born* (1968) from a motto on a Ghanaian bus, won him immediate critical acclaim. The everyman-like hero's isolated life of private integrity is set against a society whose ingrained corruption is registered through intensive use of imagery of disease, excrement, rot. Achebe (q.v.) calls it 'a sick book' which 'imposes so much foreign metaphor on the sickness of Ghana that it ceases to be true'. *Fragments* (1970) also bitterly exposes false social values; the hero's alienation from his community leads to his committal to an asylum, but it is the demented society which is alienated from itself by its frenzied whoring after the gods of western affluence.

In *Why Are We So Blest?* (1972) R. Fraser sees the influence of Afro-American rejection of racial co-operation in America in the early 1960s and of 'the occasional fire-and-brimstone' qualities of James Baldwin. The novel ranges widely over white–black relationships in America and Africa. Ingeniously constructed to accommodate large themes of racial confrontation, its two major African characters are again élitist failures, with the chief white character a near-allegorical figuring of the universal white destruction of black ways and values.

The title of *Two Thousand Seasons* (1973) refers to an ancient prophecy of the length of time Africans would suffer foreign conquest and spiritual rape. The narrator, a griot during the slave-trade, gives a rhythmical, threnodic account of his people's history: sufferings under Muslim conquest, epic trek to freedom, forsaking the true way, betrayal by selfish rulers into the hands of European slavers. Reiterating throughout that 'the way, our way' is of reciprocity among individuals, and creation only of what is truly needful, he punctuates the pitiful history with exhortations to return to the austere, unselfish, caring, and therefore fulfilling, ways of the past. 'White' becomes an epithet for the arid, the destructive, the hideous in African experience. The influence of Frantz Fanon is evident. Armah's novels are fired by an intense moral sense, yet Achebe's dissatisfaction, mentioned above, may well point to a pervading nihilism in Armah's outlook. His concrete rendering of moral dereliction is always more eloquent than the attempts, strongest in *Two Thousand Seasons*, to indicate alternatives. *The Healers* (1978), dealing with the destruction of the Ashanti empire in the nineteenth century, as much

through its own disunity as from British military prowess, asserts the need for African solidarity and unity in the twentieth century. No novelist is bound to draw political blueprints, but Armah engages deliberately with political themes – with more spiritual fervour than political analysis.   [AR]

ARNIM, MARY ANNETTE VON (née Beauchamp; pen-name 'Elizabeth') (1866–1941). Novelist, born in Sydney, Australia, a cousin of Katherine Mansfield. In 1891 she married Count August von Arnim whom she met on a tour of Italy. Her life with him and their three children on his Pomeranian estate provided the material for her amusing domestic sketches, *Elizabeth and Her German Garden* (1898), where her husband figures under such denominations as 'the Man of Wrath'. In numerous succeeding novels (which include *The Adventures of Elizabeth in Rugen*, 1904; *The Pastor's Wife*, 1914; and *The Enchanted April*, 1923) she developed her distinctive vein of humorous irony. A felicitous turn of phrase, a sparkling wit and an easy control of narrative movement mark her best work. After her husband's death in 1910, 'Elizabeth' had an affair with H.G. Wells (q.v.), but in 1916 she became the third wife of Frank Russell (Earl Russell), Bertrand Russell's brother, from whom she was separated three years later. The experience provoked her celebrated novel *Vera* (1921), in which a trusting young girl, Lucy Entwistle, emotionally afflicted by her father's death, is pounced upon by a middle-aged widower of uncontainable selfishness, vanity and possessiveness. His first wife (Vera) has died in a tragic accident. Much of the book is high comedy until it becomes too late to save Lucy from Everard Wemyss's clutches. The tone then turns sour and Wemyss proceeds to devour his wife's happiness and smother her spirit. It becomes plain that Vera was driven to suicide. See also Arnim's autobiography, *All the Dogs of My Life* (1936).   [HB]

ASTLEY, THEA (1925–). Novelist, born in Brisbane, Queensland, Australia. After graduating from the University of Queensland in 1947 she taught at schools in Queensland in 1944–8 and in New South Wales in 1948–67. She has taught English at Macquarie University, Sydney, since 1968. *Girl with a Monkey* (1958) proved her talent for original and convincing satirical comment on provincial middle-class prejudices, the potentially destructive aspects of which are seen in *A Descant for Gossips* (1960). *The Well-Dressed Explorer* (1962) focused on a selfish but misunderstood character whose life and death evoke a wry blend of wonder and horror. In its combination of complex characterization, wit and breadth of approach this novel represented an advance over earlier work. *The Slow Natives* (1965) had affinities with *A Descant* but showed greater confidence and possessed more credibility in character studies and situation. The convincing exploration of the lives of ordinary people continued in *A Boatload of Home Folk* (1968) in which an impending hurricane symbolizes that challenge against which human pettiness is measured in her books. The dominating power of a single personality is again the focus of *The Acolyte* (1972), this time a blind musician. *A Kindness Cup* (1974) underlined her undeniable strength as a charter of the constant tensions – and possible explosive violence – arising from the juxtaposition of spiritual or moral values and everyday affairs. *Hunting the Wild Pineapple and Other Related Stories* (1979) further demonstrated her talent as a writer, though the complex format raised problems.   [PQ]

ATWOOD, MARGARET (1939–). Poet, novelist and critic, born in Ottawa, Ontario, Canada. She graduated from the University of Toronto in 1961 before going on to further study at Radcliffe College and Harvard University, Cambridge, Massachusetts. In 1964–8 she was a university teacher in Canada but the publication in 1969 of her novel *The Edible Woman* and the poetry collection *The Animals in That Country* confirmed her as a major new talent (she had received two prestigious Canadian poetry prizes in 1967). Her writings since have amply demonstrated her talents as a passionate and intelligent feminine observer of Canadian life. A constant focus in her work is the potentially destructive nature of human relationships (whose claustrophobic dimension provides the 'animal' and 'cannibalistic' volume titles), a theme which is already apparent in her second poetry collection *The Circle Game* (1964). A commitment to Canada which is as tenaciously held as it is intellectually impressive informs much of her poetry and criticism. An example of this in poetry is *The Journals of Susanna Moodie* (1970) which re-created the experiences of the pioneer Canadian settler and author, while the novel *Surfacing* (1972) brought together mental and physical landscape in a brilliant probing of self-realization which extends issues of identity and fulfilment opened up by her earlier novel. The exploration of related themes over several works is a feature of her creative method, and the poems in *Procedures for Underground* (1970) both maintain the concerns of earlier volumes and complement *Surfacing* in their disturbing, sometimes witty, fingering of the delicate strands of human passion and identity. *Survival: A Thematic Guide to Canadian Literature* (1972) gave compass for her mythopoeic involvement in Canadian writing and is exemplary in its masterly blend of thought-provoking critical propositions and determinedly practical and unpretentious notes for individual further reading. Begun, in her own words, as 'a short, easy-to-use guide to Canadian literature', *Survival* emerged as 'a cross between a personal statement . . . and a political manifesto'. It is easily the most readable and stimulating guide available, bringing to the realm of criticism the informed concern of the creative writer. The book is both challenging reading in itself and also a valuable, committed introduction to a tradition of which Margaret Atwood herself is very aware of forming an important living part. The poetry collection *You are Happy* (1974) further enhanced her reputation and was followed by a well-chosen *Selected Poems* (1976). The novel *Lady Oracle* (1976) was an exploration of the boundaries of sanity through the life of a young woman menaced by her secret obsessions. Further stories (*Dancing Girls*, 1977) and poems (*Two-Headed Poems and Others*, 1978) were followed by *Life Before Man* (1979), a bleak novel which probed the elemental forces governing human relationships in the 'modern' world.   [PQ]

AUDEN, W.H. (Wystan Hugh) (1907–73). Poet, born at York. His father was a doctor with scholarly interests in archaeology, the classics, and Icelandic sagas. His mother was the daughter of a parish priest and herself a devout Anglo-Catholic. Auden was only a year old when the family moved to Birmingham where his father became Schools Medical Officer. The Midlands industrial landscape and the Pennine moorlands (visited on holidays) stamped permanent memories on his imagination. After five years at a preparatory school in Surrey, where Christopher Isherwood (q.v.) was a fellow pupil, he was sent to Gresham's School, Holt, where his first published poem ('Dawn') appeared anonymously in the school magazine, *The Gresham*, in 1922. From 1925 to 1928 Auden was at Christ Church, Oxford. He had won an exhibition in natural science, but he changed subjects twice, finally settling down to English and studying under Nevill Coghill. Coghill told later how Auden replied at their first interview to the stock question about what he intended to do in life. 'I am going to be a poet.' 'In that case', Coghill said, 'you should find it very useful to have read English.' 'You don't understand', Auden said. 'I'm going to be a great poet.'

Much has been written by Auden's contemporaries at Oxford about the powerful impact he made. Rex Warner (q.v.) spoke of his 'amazing intellectual ebullience', voracious appetite for facts and ideas, and brilliantly voluble conversation. John Betjeman (q.v.) confessed that while he himself was the old-type undergraduate, 'trivial, baroque . . . a diner with a great admiration for the landowning classes', their houses and parks, he found Auden 'already aware of slum conditions in Birmingham and mining towns and docks', and many have testified to the commanding oracular status which Auden assumed without any self-consciousness or pretence. Among others whose university careers overlapped with his at Oxford were Stephen Spender (q.v.) (whom he knew intimately), and Cecil Day Lewis (q.v.) and Louis MacNeice (q.v.) (whom he actually met only much later). Christopher Isherwood and Edward Upward (q.v.) sometimes visited him from Cambridge. These writers later became naturally associated in the public mind for their critical judgements on contemporary capitalist society, for their experiments in bringing urgent social and political issues into literature, and indeed for generally bursting open all the so-called 'Georgian' inhibitions over what it was appropriate for poetry to be about and in what idioms it was appropriate for poets to speak.

After leaving Oxford in 1928, Auden spent a year in Berlin learning German and then held school-teaching posts. A visit to Iceland with Louis MacNeice in 1936 led to their collaboration in *Letters from Iceland* (1937), which includes Auden's 'Letter to Lord Byron', a lively pastiche of *Don Juan* in *ottava rima*. He paid a visit to Spain in sympathy with the republican cause in 1937, and to China with Christopher Isherwood in 1938. He collaborated with Isherwood in three verse plays of which the most effective (though none has worn well) was *The Ascent of F6* (1937), which allegorizes the challenge of the contemporary crisis in the tragedy of a heroic expedition to scale a supposedly haunted mountain. The climbers are overwhelmed in an avalanche. In 1939 Auden and

Isherwood both decided to settle permanently in the USA. (Auden became a US citizen in 1946.) Thereafter he spent periods teaching at various universities and colleges in the US and lived otherwise much of the time in New York. In 1956, however, he returned to England, having been elected Professor of Poetry at Oxford for a period of five years, and in 1958 he acquired a farmhouse in Kirchstetten, Lower Austria, as a summer home.

By the time the early collections of verse (*Poems*, 1928, 1930 and 1934) and *Look, Stranger* (1936) (US *On This Island*) were published, Auden was celebrated as the leading figure in the new movement, the 'poets of the Thirties'. From the first his strengths included an astonishing technical control of metre and form, and a disconcertingly versatile mastery of tone and idiom. At one moment the orchestration is opulently grand,

> O love, the interest itself in thoughtless Heaven,
> Make simpler daily the beating of man's heart;

at the next moment it is lyrically chaste,

> Now the leaves are falling fast,
> Nurse's flowers will not last;

Auden can plunge into dramatic monologue with a touching emotional thrust,

> To settle in this village of the heart,
> My darling, can you bear it?

Above all he is master of the casual, conversational approach,

> A shilling life will give you all the facts . . .

But the strident, revolutionary clamour, familiar in Day Lewis, is not often heard in Auden. *Spain* (1937), however, whose royalties were devoted to medical aid for Spain, has that immediacy and urgency which in so many contexts make Auden's work irresistible:

> Yesterday the installation of dynamos and turbines,
> The construction of railways in the colonial desert;
> Yesterday the classic lecture
> On the origin of Mankind. But today the struggle.

A crucial development occurred when Auden was converted to Christianity and returned to the Anglican Church in 1940. 'It has taken Hitler to show us that liberalism is not self-supporting', he said, and recorded how, on the personal side, Charles Williams (q.v.) unknowingly exercised a remarkable influence on him. 'I met an Anglican layman, and for the first time in my life felt myself in the presence of personal sanctity.' Soon Kierkegaard became favourite reading. A significant literary product of Auden's new thinking was *New Year Letter* (1940), a ramblingly reflective poem in octosyllabic couplets, stimulated by the outbreak of war. It is a piquant blend of philosophical and moral musing with concrete personal recollection. It was published in the US as *The Double Man*, which in fact was Auden's own title, glossed in an epigraph from Montaigne: 'We are, I know not how, double in ourselves, so that what we believe we disbelieve, and cannot rid ourselves of what we condemn.'

The concept of the double man has been found useful in characterizing Auden himself, a devotee of order in art, a defender of traditional orthodoxy in his thought, and a writer who worked with punctuality and discipline at his craft, yet who seems to have been incorrigibly eccentric and disorderly in many aspects of personal and domestic life. Consciousness of dichotomy threads its way through *New Year Letter*. Positive moments of experience are remembered when 'art had set in order sense / And feeling and intelligence'. 'Great masters who have shown mankind / An order it has yet to find' deserve all the greater honour –

> If, weaker than some other men,
> You had the courage that survives
> Soiled, shabby, egotistic lives.

And, at the conclusion of 'The Sea and the Mirror', a long verse commentary in dramatic form on Shakespeare's *The Tempest*, Caliban delivers a personal epilogue to the audience, and explains the impossibility of leaving our 'shambling, slovenly, makeshift world' to dwell permanently in the world the Muse inhabits, 'that world of freedom without anxiety, sincerity without loss of vigour, feeling that loosens rather than ties the tongue'. Art temporarily restores harmony and relationship for beings for whom 'the real Word is the only raison d'être'.

But the distinctive thing about Auden is that philosophical, moral or theological generalization always carries a massive freight of living imagery. He does not leave abstractions unqualified, unillustrated. The line between the middle class and the workers becomes 'the railroad above which houses stand in their own grounds, each equipped with a garage and a beautiful woman, sometimes with several, and below which huddled shacks provide a squeezing shelter for collarless herds who eat blancmange and have never said anything witty'. Similarly the nostalgic sentimentality behind so many a human cry for escape becomes: 'Carry me back, Master, to the cathedral town where the canons run through the watermeadows with butterfly nets and the old women keep sweetshops in the cobbled streets . . . carry me back to the days before my wife had put on weight, back to the years when beer was cheap and the rivers froze in winter.' The influence of Joyce is evident.

'The Sea and the Mirror' was published alongside *For the Time Being: A Christmas Oratorio* (1945), a dramatic sequence in nine sections: 'Advent', 'The Annunciation', 'The Temptation of St Joseph', 'The Summons', 'The Vision of the Shepherds', 'At the Manger', 'The Meditation of Simeon', 'The Massacre of the Innocents', 'The Flight into Egypt'. After a series of movements in verse, the penultimate section, a prose apologia by Herod, is a satirical rehearsal of contemporary secularist themes. The influence of the Eliot of *Murder in the Cathedral* and *Four Quartets* is evident at many points.

The Age of Anxiety (1947) completes a quartet of long poems which evidenced a period of unflagging industry and inspiration. Labelled 'A Baroque Eclogue' and dedicated to John Betjeman, it is prefixed by three lines of the 'lacrimosa dies illa' from the *Dies Irae*, foreseeing the misery of coming judgement on mortal man. It presents four lonely, displaced characters, Quant, an Irish-American shipping clerk and a widower, Malin, a Medical Intelligence Officer in the Canadian Air Force currently on leave, Rosetta, a well-to-do buyer for a department store ('Why were the men one liked not the sort who proposed marriage and the men who proposed marriage not the sort one liked?'), and Emble, a young man who enlisted in the Navy while in his sophomore year at a Mid-Western university, an anxious fellow whose attractiveness readily grants him 'a succession of sexual triumphs' that aggravate rather than alleviate his unease. These four come together in a New York bar on All Souls' Eve. External dialogue is interwoven with private thought and dream, and a narrative voice sustains a detached commentary. The sheer brilliance and variety of much of the verse, the infinitely resourceful imaginative reconstructions of individual memory, dream and longing, and the uncanny verbal ingenuity in matching mood with image entrance the reader moment by moment; but overall cohesion of design and clarity of narrative projection are lacking.

If there has been a tendency to neglect Auden's longer poems, it is understandable in that his output of shorter poems was prolific and they bring all his qualities into play. But the longer poems prove that what he does well he can do in great profusion and at great length, and they add much to our awareness of his ultimate seriousness, his profundity and his consistency.

Auden declared that 'biographies of writers . . . are always superfluous and usually in bad taste'. Knowledge of the raw material of a writer's personal experience, he insisted, is not going to help explain 'the peculiar flavour of the verbal dishes he invites the public to taste: his private life is, or should be, of no interest to anybody except himself, his family, and his friends' (A Certain World, A Commonplace Book, 1970). The notion of the poet dishing up courses appetizing to the reader's palate accords with his refusal to assume a vatic authority or to claim influence on public events. But it is difficult to ignore all aspects of Auden's private life. In 1935 he married Erika Mann, a German émigré, at a Registry Office in order to provide her with a British passport. ('He had never set eyes on her before the wedding', her brother tells us. 'His telegram agreeing to the marriage consisted of a single-word: DELIGHTED.') Auden's homosexuality involved him with various partners and more especially in a protracted relationship with the writer Chester Kallman, with whom he collaborated in various libretti including those for Stravinsky's The Rake's Progress (1951) and Hans Werner Henze's Elegy for Young Lovers (1961) and The Bassarids (1966). Drama and opera were a lifelong interest. He also supplied the libretti for Paul Bunyan (prod 1941) and The Duchess of Malfi (prod 1946), both by Benjamin Britten, a younger product of Gresham's School, Holt, who shared lodgings with him in New York in 1940.

T.S. Eliot observed 'but a poem is not poetry − / That is life', and Auden liked to quote Valéry's words − 'a poem is never finished but only abandoned'. He shared Eliot's sense of the poet's total production as a single work only completed at death. He insisted that poetry is 'a game of knowledge'. He presented himself neither as hag-ridden romantic nor as authoritative legislator but as a happily occupied craftsman.

> After all, it's rather a privilege
> amid the affluent traffic

to serve this unpopular art which cannot be turned
> into background noise for study
> or hung as a status trophy by rising executives.

So he wrote in 'The Cave of Making' (from About the House, 1966), a memorial poem to Louis MacNeice. And he sums up his own personal ambition with the same air of detachment.

> I should like to become, if possible,
> a minor atlantic Goethe,
> with his passion for weather and stones but
> without his silliness
> re the Cross.

Auden's powerful personal appeal is due in part to the contrast between his unassuming way of shrugging off claims to grandeur and his actual achievement. For he brought to bear a unique insight, perhaps not into individual hearts and minds, but into the moods and longings, the fads and fashions, the worries and apprehensions prevalent in the decades through which he lived. He did this, not so much as seer or satirist, but as verbal wizard with a hundred different voices at his disposal. There are poems of rare charisma like the tender 'Lullaby' ('Lay your sleeping head, my love, / Human on my faithless arm') or the moving lament for lost love, 'If I could tell you' ('Time will say nothing but I told you so'), a villanelle apparently addressed to Chester Kallman. Alongside these are the irresistibly subtle musings of, say, 'Musée des Beaux Arts' or the infectiously personal freshness of 'Many Happy Returns' or 'On the Circuit'. Add to these the catchy balladry of 'Miss Gee' and the rollicking metrics of 'Night Mail', and plainly the variety and memorability evidence a poetic range, in both technique and substance, probably unmatched in our century.

Collected Longer Poems (1966) and Collected Shorter Poems 1927-1957 (1966) have been superseded by Collected Poems (1976), edited by Edward Mendelson, who has also written a critical study, Early Auden (1981). Among Auden's prose works, see especially the collection of critical essays, The Dyer's Hand (London, 1963; New York, 1962). W.H. Auden, a Tribute (1974), edited by Stephen Spender, contains memories by many who knew Auden personally. See also Humphrey Carpenter, W.H. Auden, a Biography (1981). [HB]

AWOONOR, KOFI (formerly George Awoonor-Williams) (1935-). Poet, born at Wheta, Ghana. He attended the universities of Ghana, London and New York, Stony Brook, and worked in the Institute of African Studies, Legon, in 1960-4, and for the Ghana Film Corporation in 1964-7. After researching and teaching in the United States, he was imprisoned without charges on returning to Ghana in 1975.

His verse collections, Rediscovery and Other Poems (1964), Night of My Blood (1971), Ride Me, Memory (1973), make him the anglophone African poet who has most committedly turned to vernacular oral traditions for poetic inspiration, though using English. 'My God of Songs Was Ill', about finding new inspiration, expresses his faith in the old culture: 'My god burst into songs, new strong songs / That I am still singing with him'. He has described how he uses devices from traditional African culture:

'Traditional oral poetry of the Ewes, with its emphasis on lyricism, the chant, repetition of lines, symbolism, and imagery transfused into English through the secondary influence of Pound, Dylan Thomas'. The rhythmic effects he can achieve are illustrated in 'The Sea Eats the Land at Home', about natural destruction in a coastal village:

> Goats and fowls were struggling in the water,
> The angry water of the cruel sea;
> The lap-lapping of the dark water at the shore,
> And above the sobs and the deep and low moans,
> Was the eternal hum of the living sea.

In his poetry no less than on the public platform and in his book *The Breast of the Earth: A Survey of the History, Culture and Literature of Africa South of the Sahara* (1975) he eloquently pleads the existence of a rich African culture before the white colonialists arrived; his poetry attempts to bridge the gap between pre-colonial and post-independence African culture. He has particularly responded to the African sense of community: 'the communion we forged / the feast of oneness whose ritual we partook of' ('Rediscovery'). He has also written poetry in Ewe; the clarity and lyricism of his English verse owe much to Ewe poetic tradition and characterize him sharply among anglophone African poets. He is always more aware of a communal type of audience than, say, Okara (q.v.), another poet much influenced by vernacular practices.

With G. Adali-Mortty, Awoonor edited the anthology *Poems from Ghana* (1970). Achebe (q.v.) thinks highly of his very ambitious novel, *This Earth, My Brother . . .* (1972), an intensely emotive treatment of a character and a people adrift without enduring values.   [AR]

AYCKBOURN, ALAN (1939–). Dramatist, born in London and brought up mainly in Sussex. He has worked in the theatre since leaving school and by 1976 had five plays running simultaneously in London. He is director of productions at the Theatre in the Round at Scarborough. His success is not that of a politically committed propagandist or a sensation-monger but of a craftsman who believes in the well-made play, has a Pinterian ear for living conversation, and is a master of pure humour, psychological and situational. His numerous successful productions include *Standing Room Only* (prod 1962),

Relatively Speaking (prod 1967) and *Time and Time Again* (prod 1971). *How the Other Half Loves* (prod 1969) brings two living rooms together on stage ('smart period reproduction' and 'more modern, trendy and badly looked after') to juxtapose the marital lives of boss Frank Foster and employee Bob Phillips. Bob is having an affair with Frank's wife Fiona and, under suspicion, the two guilty ones quote the same couple, the Featherstones, as their alibi to cover an evening they spent together. The high point of the play is the fusion on stage of two separate dinner parties, the Fosters' and the Phillips', at which the innocent Featherstones are guests. Ayckbourn's ingenuity in contriving this disaster-fraught conversational ensemble guarantees its comic impact.

Ayckbourn's most celebrated achievement to date has been the comic trilogy *The Norman Conquests* (prod 1974), consisting of *Table Manners, Living Together* and *Round and Round the Garden*. Norman is an amusing study in steam-rollering self-assertiveness. Exuding tyrannical good-humour, disastrous candour and cheap witticisms, he infuriates, dominates and captivates. The six characters of the trilogy form a family group and Ayckbourn's manipulative legerdemain with domestic cross-currents and family fireworks has a riotous, deadly accuracy. The three plays dovetail contemporaneously. Each has four scenes. Events cover a single weekend. Thus the second and third plays gradually fill in the gaps of their predecessors with between-the-scenes and behind-the-scenes developments. The work loses momentum in the third play, but by this time Ayckbourn has rung the changes on Norman's sexual conquests with side-splitting thoroughness. *Just Between Ourselves* (1978) teeters on the edge of graver matters in tracing the mental deterioration of a wife whose well-meaning husband and insufferably protective mother-in-law drive her into a catatonic trance. *Taking Steps* (pubd 1980), a cunningly structured domestic romp, is appropriately dedicated to Ben Travers (q.v.), the ingenious deviser of Whitehall farces in the 1920s. In *Way Upstream* (prod 1982) Ayckbourn goes to the lengths of demanding from the stage-engineers a full-sized cabin cruiser (flat-bottomed) afloat in water. This suggests a ship of state aboard which the human comedy acquires allegorical overtones. See also Ian Watson, *Conversations with Ayckbourn* (1981).   [HB]

B

BAINBRIDGE, BERYL (Margaret) (1934–). Novelist, born in Liverpool and educated at art schools. She has worked as an actress in repertory theatres and as a clerk in a publisher's office. She has also worked as a cellar woman in a bottle factory, and this experience gave her the setting for her highly successful fifth novel, *The Bottle Factory Outing* (1974). It is a tale of two English girls, Freda and Brenda, who work at a London wine-bottling factory run and largely staffed by Italians. Freda, large, outgoing, domineering, centres on the owner's nephew romantic dreams as comically exaggerated as those of Joyce's Gerty Macdowell in *Ulysses*; and she tries to bring some of these dreams to fruition by arranging a Sunday outing for the factory employees. Brenda, her flat-mate, a slight, withdrawn, unprepossessing girl, is nevertheless as incapable of saying 'No' to male advances as Freda is of getting the chance to say 'Yes'. Freda's pursuit of her dreams is a headlong dash to her doom. For the outing proves a fiasco, then a tragedy. The novel has thrust and point in exploring the relationship between dream and reality. Beryl Bainbridge manages plots of escalating comedy and grotesqueness with consummate skill. She is brilliant at scattering humour over seemingly gruesome terrain.

Sweet William (1975) centres on Ann Walton, a Londoner working with the BBC. She is suddenly swept off her feet by a rising playwright who turns out to have a divorced wife, a family, a present wife, and a ready talent for bedding down with all and sundry. Pregnant, reduced

to the status of a kept woman ('I've been taken over, requisitioned'), Ann cannot break the spell woven by a totally selfish and dishonest predator whose brash confidence and fluent manipulation of the vocabulary of emancipation takes her rational and moral sense captive. ('He was bigger than she in every way. She was petty and cynical.') The irony is sharp, the humour irresistible. *A Week-end with Claude*, Beryl Bainbridge's first novel (1967), has now been radically rewritten (1981). It explores again the emotional and nervous cost of sexual permissiveness. An old assortment of friends descend for a weekend on Claude, a middle-aged antique dealer, and the presiding genius of the story. Claude, self-appointed mentor of the young, exudes claptrap about the need to choose life, to be self-creative,· and not to give in, while behaviour consonant with his code turns the place into a virtual mad-house. But neither in clarity of presentation nor in sureness of tone does the book fully match up to the best of the novels.

Among other novels *Harriet Said* (1972) and *The Dressmaker* (1973) are horror stories with a difference. *Young Adolf* (1978) develops the fancy that in 1912 Hitler fled to Liverpool to avoid conscription. *Winter Garden* (1980) follows English visitors on an 'artists' ' excursion to Russia.

Critics have attempted to pinpoint the qualities of Beryl Bainbridge's style by detecting the influence of Pinter, Stevie Smith and Muriel Spark. Her brilliance lies in the matter-of-fact blandness with which irony and humour are planted in situations of emotional stress or of macabre horror. Her forte is the tragedy and comedy of human self-delusion. The collisions and discrepancies between dream and reality have always provided literature with sombre tragedy and high comedy, but not very often, as in Beryl Bainbridge's case, with both at the same time and sometimes in the same breath. [HB]

BALLARD, J.G. (James Graham) (1930-). Novelist and short-story writer, born in Shanghai, China, and educated at King's College, Cambridge. He pioneered a brand of science fiction in which nature turns on technological man and reverses his progress catastrophically. Geophysical upheavals transform the earth's climate and submerge our temperate regions in flood and vegetation in *The Drowned World* (1963). A cancerous proliferating crystallization vitrifies forest, creature and city in *The Crystal World* (1966). Technical and social structures collapse in the 1000-unit residential manhive of *High Rise* (1975). Predatory birds and tropical vegetation suddenly invade suburban life in Shepperton in *The Unlimited Dream Company* (1979). The reversions and upheavals are technically ingenious but strike no deep human note. [HB]

BARING, MAURICE (1874-1945). Novelist and man of letters, born in London, the younger son of Lord Revelstoke. He grew up in the grand social world of country houses and town houses (see his autobiography, *The Puppet Show of Memory*, 1922), was educated at Eton and Cambridge and read widely in many languages. As a personality he created a legend for his spontaneous levities, verbal and practical (he once casually threw out of a train window an expensive new coat he found too big to pack into his suitcase). He held posts in the diplomatic service, was a newspaper correspondent in Russia and the Balkans and served in the RFC in the First World War. He never married. As a Catholic convert, Baring became associated in the public mind with Chesterton (q.v.) and Belloc (q.v.). He was a highly productive and accomplished writer in several fields. His plays include *The Grey Stocking* (prod 1908), about unhappy marriage; *The Green Elephant* (prod 1911), a farce; *A Double Game* (prod 1912), about the 1907 revolutionary movement in Russia; and *His Majesty's Embassy* (1923), a story of a heart-breaking love affair, which Shaw (q.v.) praised highly. Baring's novels re-create the high social life of the time with painstaking fidelity and unnecessary documentary fullness. Familiar figures recur from book to book so that 'sometimes it seems to us that he wrote only one novel, and that all his separate ones are like great chapters' (Paul Hogan, ed., *Maurice Baring Restored*, 1970). Characters naturally discuss ideas, art, literature and music, giving intellectual substance to the fictional world. The theme of passion at loggerheads with honour or duty, the fruit of early blunders, mischances or misunderstandings, is a prevailing one. *Cat's Cradle* (1925), perhaps the best, tells the story of a woman, Blanche, married unwillingly to a Roman nobleman, who then falls deeply in love with a younger man, Bernard, but does not betray her husband. Long after, widowed, she faces the agony of having her own young ward's hand sought by

Bernard. *C* (1924) is a story of the anguished love of Caryl Bramsley for the shallow and sensual Leila, captivating sexual exploiter and consumer. Other novels are *Daphne Adeane* (1926), *The Coat Without Seam* (1929) and *Robert Peckham* (1930). Baring is also noted for his somewhat precious, if high-spirited, exercises in literary spoofery. Characteristic are *Lost Diaries* (1913), imaginary snippets from journals by such figures as William the Conqueror and Mark Antony, and *Dead Letters* (1910), imaginary communications involving such jeux d'esprit as an interview with Nero and a letter from Lady Macbeth to Lady Macduff, inviting her to Forres. ('P.S. Don't forget to bring Jeamie. It will do Macbeth good to see a child in the house.') See also his letters to Lady Juliet Duff, written from France between 1915 and 1918, which Michael Russell has edited under the title, *Dear Animated Bust* (1982). [HB]

BARKER, GEORGE (1913-). Poet, born in Loughton, Essex. The family moved to Chelsea, London, shortly after his birth, and he was educated at Marlborough Road School, Chelsea, and at Regent Street Polytechnic. At the time of the poet's birth, Barker's father was a police-constable ('I had been cast a little low / In the social register', *True Confessions*). His mother was from an Irish peasant family in Drogheda, and what he owed to her powerful personality can be gauged from the sonnet 'To My Mother':

> She is a procession no one can follow after
> But be like a little dog following a brass band.

Leaving school at the age of 14, Barker had various jobs, including work on wallpaper design and in a garage. A fencing accident in 1932, in which he blinded his brother in the right eye, left its legacy of guilt. ('Therefore I render to my hell hand's Abel / The no less agonized blood my hand has bled', he writes in the Dedication to *Calamiterror*.) Barker got to know Middleton Murry (q.v.), David Gascoyne (q.v.) and Michael Roberts (q.v.) (see 'Elegy on the Death of Michael Roberts') and his *Thirty Preliminary Poems* was published in 1933. The publication of *Poems* in 1935 by Faber and Faber marked the beginning of an influential acquaintance with T.S. Eliot (q.v.), to whom he later addressed one of the 'Personal Sonnets' supplementary to *Eros in Dogma* (1944) as well as 'Verses for the 60th Birthday of T.S. Eliot' and 'Elegiacs for T.S. Eliot' (*Dreams of a Summer Night*, 1966):

> I believe him to have been a spy of the gods
> Disguising himself as publisher, policeman,
> Verger and bank clerk, in order the better
> To report on the state of the unreal city.

Barker married Jessica Woodward in 1935 and at first lived as a writer in a Dorset cottage under patronage from Faber and from the Royal Society of Literature. In 1939 he became Professor of English Literature at the Imperial Tohoku University in Sendai, Japan (the 'Pacific Sonnets' record his exile), but he moved to the USA in 1940, and thereafter he has lived fitfully in the USA, England, Italy and Spain (where he was made an honorary bullfighter in 1951). His first marriage broke down in 1940, but Barker is the proud father of several children, and he married Elspeth Langlands in 1964. He has held visiting professorships and fellowships at New York, York and Wisconsin.

Barker's output includes novels and plays. His early poetry has a clamant wordiness. The grand style, the romantic stance and the lack of social concern put him out of key with the fashionable Pylon poets of the 1930s. He was readily classed with Dylan Thomas (q.v.) and with David Gascoyne as a master of personal histrionics from whom a torrent of images flowed as from a verbal volcano, but there were signs too of that response to the discipline of objectivity which later gave quality to his best work. Thus, in *Calamiterror* (1937), from presentation of violence inherent in human birth itself there is traced the poet's own development from subjectivity. Here, and in succeeding volumes, *Lament and Triumph* (1940), *Eros in Dogma* (1944) and *News of the World* (1950), there are lapses into rhythmic anarchy and metaphorical incoherence. This is the price Barker pays for an intense internal scrutiny of the self, a self sored by probing, jarred by the recurrent collision of flesh with spirit, and quivering with febrile animosity against accepted recipes for reconciliation. Barker boasts and worries about copulation: he cannot shake off the guilt of sexuality implicit in the defiance of the spirit that its restless animal demand seems to involve. A man's and his bride's nightmares after consummation are sharply counterpointed with the theme of crucifixion in 'The Bridal Nightmare I and II' (*News of the World*). The rub and thrust of physical sex send an electric current through many a poem, a current whose positive is joyous affirmation and whose negative is angry repugnance. In this respect the climax of Barker's work is *The True Confessions of George Barker* (1950; enlarged version, 1955) which, because of its indecencies, Faber preferred not to include in the *Collected Poems 1930–1955*. Barker always enjoyed the Byronic privilege of exhibiting his raw nerve-ends to the world, and here he assumes a jaunty Byronic thoroughness of self-exposure that stops short of no inference, personal or universal, however devastating. Barker is a poet who rarely astonishes by individual lines of unforgettable inevitability, but the sheer energy of this poem makes an impact. And the vitriolic assault on the Scots in 'Scottish Bards and an English Reviewer' (*The View from a Blind I*, 1962) has a Skeltonic raciness. Barker's best work (such as 'To My Son', 'Resolution of Dependence' and personal tributes already cited), in which rhetoric is judiciously tempered by terseness and lucidity, is perhaps his least characteristic. In this respect the evident influence of the later Yeats proved a healthy one. Indeed, in the short lyrics of *Villa Stellar* (1978) Barker found a way of domesticating the old gusto by pickling unpremeditatedness in small containers. Moods of self-analysis, of disillusionment, and of hope lost are captured with agonizing thoroughness; but there are lights as well as shadows. Barker's images still leap into the reader's field of vision and grab his attention.

> I mean those allegorical
> instances that vault like acrobats into the ring of
> our lives.   [HB]

BARKER, HARLEY GRANVILLE   (1877–1946). Dramatist and stage director, born in Kensington, London, the son of an estate agent and an actress who trained him for the stage from the age of 13. He played Marchbanks in Shaw's *Candida* in 1900 and his own comedy, *The Marrying of Ann Leete*, was produced in 1902. From 1904 to 1907, with John E. Vedrenne, he directed historic productions of Shaw (q.v.), Galsworthy (q.v.), Yeats (q.v.), Ibsen and others at the Court Theatre. His continuing sponsorship of Shaw (he played many Shavian parts himself) was influential and his later Shakespearean productions were memorable. His interpretative bent was towards psychological realism in close dependence upon the text, and his series of *Prefaces to Shakespeare* (issued in five volumes, 1927, 1930, 1937, 1945, 1947) brought this interest into line with his immense practical knowledge of stagecraft. His 'problem' play, *The Voysey Inheritance*, was first produced at the Court Theatre in 1905. Edward Voysey's inheritance from his father is an ostensibly flourishing solicitors' business, but it is sustained by misappropriation of clients' funds. Edward, already distressed by being let into the secret, faces a sharpened moral conflict when his father suddenly dies. Shall he come clean immediately to the ruin of many trusting clients, or shall he go on cheating long enough to safeguard the position of poorer clients, leaving only the wealthy ones to lose out? The dilemma is simplified into a choice between priggery and humanity. *Waste* was produced in 1907 by the Stage Society, the group formed in 1899 to perform plays of quality with limited commercial prospects. It is the tragedy of Henry Trebell, rising politician on the brink of a great progressive achievement in disestablishing the Church of England and devoting its resources to secular educational purposes. He is, however, in his sister's words, a man with 'power over men and women and contempt for them'. A passing light-hearted affair with a married woman results in her pregnancy and death after an abortion, his loss of a promised seat in the cabinet, and his suicide. The topicality of the political issues dates it, but Barker's plays are good to read if only because some of his best writing is in the stage directions. *The Madras House* (prod 1910), perhaps his most Shavian play, portrays the development of a family millinery business in terms of the demands of the New Woman and the coming commercial exploitation of mass-fashion.   [HB]

BARRIE, J.M. (Sir James Matthew) (1860–1937). Dramatist and novelist, born in Kirriemuir, Angus, Tayside, Scotland, the ninth of ten children of Presbyterian parents, David Barrie and his wife, Margaret Ogilvy. David Barrie was a handloom weaver, industrious and ambitious for his children. Margaret Ogilvy was a frail but strong-willed woman, dominant in her household, and her son David was the apple of her eye. When the boy died at the age of 13 in a skating accident, she was permanently scarred. In particular James became a substitute for the irreplaceable David, the recipient of his mother's demanding affection and of her reminiscences of girlhood and youth. Her spirit hovers over his work, and she was a woman for whom the mother–son relationship was a matter of love and wonder, whereas the wife–husband relationship was a matter of duty, and sexual experience a regrettable part of it. Emotional currents produced by her disturbing maternal possessiveness emerge later in an idealized memoir, *Margaret Ogilvy* (1895), a vehicle of evident autobiographical pathos.

Barrie was educated at Glasgow Academy, Forfar Academy, Dumfries Academy and Edinburgh University. He early developed a taste for books and set his heart on a literary career. After taking his MA he turned to writing, first in Edinburgh, then in Nottingham as a journalist on the *Nottingham Journal*. After a brief spell of freelancing from home, he moved to London in 1885. His first novel, *Better Dead*, was published in 1887 at his own expense. It was followed in 1888 by *Auld Licht Idylls*, a collection of pieces he had already published in the *St James's Gazette*. They were sketches of Scottish life centred on the puritanical sect, the Auld Lichts, to which the Ogilvy family belonged. Barrie's Kirriemuir experiences also supplied the material for *A Window in Thrums* (1889). Thrums is Kirriemuir. Sly humour about its inhabitants and recognizable caricatures of relatives aroused some dislike in Scotland. It was this kind of work, in which the externals of Scottish personality are transmuted into facile and profitable entertainment, that earned Barrie the reputation of having founded the Kailyard School. But he was now well established commercially and the novel *The Little Minister* (1891), an unlikely story of a Scottish minister who falls in love with a gipsy, crowned his early successes.

However, it is as a dramatist that Barrie will keep a place in literary history. A stage version of *The Little Minister* was put on in 1897. *Quality Street* (prod 1902) ran for 459 performances. Set at the time of the Napoleonic Wars, it is a study of two sisters of whom the younger, Phoebe, has a protracted and interrupted romance with a doctor who turns captain and goes off to fight. The life of middle-class maidenhood, with its heroisms of frustration and its brave bursts of playfulness, hangs expectantly in abeyance while an implausible hero moves through the long years to a clear indication of what he is about. *The Admirable Crichton* (also prod 1902) was another success. It makes its point neatly, reversing the relative status of lord and butler when they are marooned on a desert island and natural ability is all that counts. The dialogue is lively, the humour pervasive, and the ironies implicit in the upending of accepted standards are smoothly engineered. The paradoxes have a Shavian aspect, but there is neither Shaw's wordiness nor his acidity.

Peter Pan was performed in 1904 but published only in 1928, with a revealing dedication 'To the Five', the sons of Sylvia Llewelyn Davies, whose children's world Barrie had entered long ago, had filled with fantasy and fun, and had now transmuted into a heady cocktail of whimsy and sentimentality, magic and humour. Subtitled 'The Boy who would not grow up', the play opens at the children's bedtime in the London home of the Darlings. Wendy and her younger brothers, John and Michael, are put to bed. Peter Pan flies in with the fairy Tinker Bell and carries them off to the Neverland of perpetual childhood where childish dreams, feminine and masculine, of peaceful home-making and heroic battle with wicked pirates, are realized in a riot of dramatic fantasy. Captain Hook, villainous pirate chief, is a fearsome creature whose false arm, with a hook at the end, is his most damaging weapon. The crocodile that ate the lost arm pursues him still with whetted appetite, but involuntarily gives audible warning of his approach, having swallowed an alarm clock. There is genuine sympathy with the child mind: there is sentimentalization of childhood and parenthood too. 'Oh for an hour of Herod!' Anthony Hope is said to have exclaimed after the first performance of the play; but it became and remained the perennial Christmas alternative to pantomime.

If *Peter Pan* is Barrie's most popular play, *What Every Woman Knows* (prod 1908) is probably his sturdiest. Altogether robuster in feeling, it presents a Scottish family, the Wylies, whose menfolk have been successful in business and seek to do their best for daughter Maggie. Father and brother finance a poor but clever and ambitious young man's education provided that he will marry Maggie, should she wish, at the end of it all. The bargain is made and fulfilled. John Shand, the beneficiary, becomes a successful MP, but career and happiness are threatened by passion of a different brand for Lady Sybil Lazenby. In the upshot Maggie wins. She is a clear-headed Scottish Candida who knows all about men. The play has humour, polish and dramatic economy.

Barrie's growing appetite for sentimental fantasy is evident in *Dear Brutus* (prod 1917), a somewhat moralistic parable of people who regret the might-have-been life their mistakes have denied them. Entry into the magic wood on Midsummer Eve teaches them that 'the fault, dear Brutus, lies not in our stars'. It lies in themselves. Their lives go just as widely awry in the might-have-been situations magic has made real for them. *Mary Rose* (prod 1920) is a dramatic version of a highland legend like the story James Hogg told in his narrative poem, *Kilmeny*. There is a Hebridean island on which a girl disappears in childhood for twenty days, then again as a wife and mother for twenty years. After a ghost-like return to meet her grown son, the island finally calls her home. Barrie's last play, *The Boy David* (prod 1936), was a failure.

There is much that is ambiguous in the personal story of Barrie's relationships with dearly idolized women, yet its mysteries are pertinent to his idiosyncratic output. Margaret Ogilvy moulded him. He married Mary Ansell, an actress, in 1894, but they were divorced in 1909, Mary having fallen in love with Gilbert Cannan, the playwright. Back in 1897 Barrie had begun his lifelong intrusion into the family of Sylvia Llewelyn Davies to whom he was deeply devoted and whose five sons he generously and fondly made himself responsible for after their father's – and later their mother's – death. It is clear that Barrie was impotent and his marriage unconsummated. The fourth and last loved woman in his life was Cynthia Asquith who became his secretary and the major beneficiary under his will, and who wrote *Portrait of Barrie* (1954).

Barrie was made Rector of St Andrews University in 1919 and Chancellor of Edinburgh University in 1930. He accepted a baronetcy in 1913 and was invested with the OM in 1922. Viola Meynell edited *Letters of J.M. Barrie* (1942). See also Barrie's autobiographical book, *The*

Greenwood Hat (1930), and Janet Dunbar, *J.M. Barrie, the Man Behind the Image* (1970).   [HB]

BATES, H.E. (Herbert Ernest) (1905–74). Born in Northamptonshire and educated at Kettering Grammar School. He published some thirty novels and a similar number of volumes of short stories. A Squadron Leader in the RAF in the Second World War, he temporarily used the pseudonym 'Flying Officer X'. The very successful novel, *The Purple Plain* (1947), is a story of the Burma campaign in 1945 and *Fair Stood the Wind For France* (1944) of adventure in occupied France. In each case a crashed airman heroically escapes and a native girl supplies sexual solace. Pre-packaged melodramatics, stiff upper lips and such like are served up as though from the Fiction Department of the wartime Ministry of Information. *The Darling Buds of May* (1958) is one of a contrasting group of novels presenting the Larkins, a rumbustiously unconventional family living hilariously. That is to say there is a mother who is very fat and a father who keeps saying 'Perfick' and everybody eats too much. Many readers have found it uproarious. Critics prefer the short stories, and especially those which picture country life. Alan Cattell edited *Selected Stories* (1975). There are four volumes of autobiography, beginning with *The Vanished World* (1969) and ending with *The World in Ripeness* (1972).   [HB]

BAWDEN, NINA (1925–). Novelist, born in London and educated at Somerville College, Oxford. She married H.W. Bawden in 1946 and Austen Kark in 1954. She has three children. Her first novel, *Who Calls the Tune* (1953), was published in the USA as *Eyes of Green*. *Tortoise by Candlelight* (1963) excellently exemplifies her power to get inside the child mind and explore ramifications of fantasy and fact stimulated by the impingement of half-understood adult conflict and frustration. The heroine of *A Woman of My Age* (1967), Elizabeth Jourdelay, encounters the marital strains of middle life, brought to crisis during a holiday in Morocco, with a finely measured blend of ironic self-knowledge and feminine self-ignorance. In *The Birds of the Trees* (1971) Bawden makes a compassionate study of a teenager from a good family who takes to drugs and becomes totally withdrawn. The effect on a younger sister and brother of the parents' necessary concentration of sympathy upon their problem child is sensitively analysed. In *Familiar Passions* (1979) Bridie's husband leaves her after thirteen years. She is jolted back into the past in search of her mother – for she was an adopted child – and ironic surprises are neatly distributed.

Nina Bawden has a highly proficient narrative technique, an engaging sense of humour and refreshing psychological wisdom. Her fictional world is confined to suburban family life into which the poor seem to intrude as outsiders, but the weight of a healthy moral sturdiness is felt through the interplay of acute inner self-criticism on the part of husband or wife in conflict. Bawden's polish and ease give the impression of a writer whose natural talent takes all tears out of authorship. She can be relied upon not to be cheap – and not to strain after a masterpiece.   [HB]

BAXTER, JAMES K. (Keir) (1926–72). Poet, born in Dunedin, New Zealand, and educated at Quaker schools in New Zealand and England. He returned home aged 13 after over three years away 'quite out of touch with my childhood companions and uncertain whether I was an Englishman or not'. He has described his early verse-making as a form of therapy for the isolation he felt at this time, and in 'A Family Photograph. 1939' ('a rather Robert Lowellish poem') he evoked a recurrent theme: 'the Calvinist ethos which underlies our determinedly secular culture like the bones of a dinosaur buried in a suburban garden plot'. A pervasive sadness characterized much of his early lyric poetry ('a sense of grief has attached itself to my early life, like a tapeworm') but *Beyond the Palisade* (1944) and *Blow, Wind of Fruitfulness* (1948), which established him as the leading New Zealand poet of his generation, also demonstrated his powerful use of landscape, and seascape, in exploring spiritual conflict and the sense of loss – 'what happens is either meaningless to me, or else it is mythology'. *The Fallen House* (1953), though technically assured, often lapsed into rhetorical gesture but *The Iron Breadboard* (1957) revealed a formidable talent for parodying his fellow poets in New Zealand. A drink problem had long been part of his unconventional way of life, but in 1957 he went teetotal and also became a Catholic. *In Fires of No Return* (1958), a selection, reflects this religious involvement while maintaining the development of the personal dramatic lyric. A five-month UNESCO grant to study school publications in India produced some of the best poems in *Howrah Bridge* (1961), and these works achieved a new spareness of expression with which to probe 'the threefold aspect of the modern world – monotony, atrocity, anarchy'. *Pig Island Letters* (1966) was an important collection in establishing flexibility with sureness of form and voice; in the best poems an unrivalled sharpness of observation fixes a finely understated exploration of personal public worlds. It is the sure tuning of laconic comment and daring pathos which gives these poems their richly human dimension, though sometimes the tone can be forced or the references too limited to enable the free structure to stand. The critical work *Aspects of Poetry in New Zealand* (1967) gives valuable insights into not only his own work but also that of his contemporaries in New Zealand, as does the essay 'Notes on the Education of a New Zealand Poet' in *The Man on the Horse* (1967), while his poetic stature was reaffirmed with the selection *The Rock Woman* (1969). This volume, his first published overseas ('perhaps a milestone. I trust it is not also a tombstone'), was a selection from his entire work made to define his achievement. The underlying theme is 'the private hell' which 'a writer just cannot avoid' exploring and understanding; the religious poems focus this suffering in a particular way. His work still shows an ear for 'the unheard sounds of which poems are translations' – a striking gift when he uses it well, but sometimes dangerously seductive in his more 'public' poems. From this period he was increasingly engaged in community work; in 1959 he helped to found a Narcotics Anonymous Group in Auckland, and from 1970 he lived alone in a Maori commune at Jerusalem on the Wanganui river. *Jerusalem Sonnets* (1970) is a loose sequence of thirty-nine poems and *Jerusalem Daybook* (1971) a collection of prose and verse reflecting his new existence. Two volumes of plays were also published in 1971: *The Sore-Footed Man/The Temptations of Oedipus* and *The Devil and Mr Mulcahy/The Band Rotunda.* He was correcting the proofs of *Autumn Testament* (1972) at the time of his death. Always an unconventional figure, he had abandoned his studies at Otago University ('Aphrodite, Bacchus and the Holy Spirit were my tutors') in 1944 and later worked for his degree extramurally at the University of Victoria. Poet, postman, labourer and staunch friend of the Maori, 'Heemi' was a gifted poet who welcomed the public role of the bard even if, like his fellow poet Allen Curnow (q.v.) – who once called him 'an oracle without a cave' – he preferred to move from 'questions which present themselves as public and answerable, towards the questions which are always private and unanswerable'. As he put it himself 'The poem is / A plank laid over the lion's den'. He borrowed boldly from the poets he loved – especially W.B. Yeats (q.v.) and Robert Lowell – but always to make something his own. Another fellow poet, Mike (Charles) Doyle (q.v.), published the fine study *James K. Baxter* in 1976; *The Bone Chanter: Unpublished Poems 1945–1972* appeared the same year and added to Baxter's already impressive output. *James K. Baxter as Critic* was edited by F. McKay in 1978 and *Collected Poems* by J.E. Weir in 1979. [PQ]

BEAVER, BRUCE (1928–). Poet, born in Sydney, New South Wales, Australia. He was educated at schools there until 1943: 'I hated school; I would day-dream in class'. A variety of jobs and periods of recurrent ill-health followed. In 1958 he went to New Zealand, returning in 1962. His first book, *Under the Bridge,* was published in 1961 – 'from then on I didn't look back as a poet'. He received an invalid's pension in 1967, but between bouts in hospital continued to write: *Seawall and Shoreline* appeared in 1964 and *Open at Random,* his favourite book, in 1967. *Letters to Live Poets* (1969) marked a change in tone and established a new depth and range, extending a form already used in his second collection. One influence was *Pig Island Letters,* published three years earlier by the New Zealand poet James K. Baxter (q.v.). Many of Beaver's poems reflect his immediate environment of the Sydney shoreline suburb of Manly, at best attaining an impressively honest expression of everyday, personal experience. Past and present, local and universal, are held in a complex poetic tension. In *Lauds and Plaints, Poems 1968–1972* (1974) – 'the most important book I've written' – a sense of mortality featured increasingly in a work which was, like *Letters,* a *livre composé. Odes and Days* (1975) is a poem sequence, and the range of Beaver's poetic voice is further illustrated in *Death's Directives* (1978) and *As It Was . . .* (1979). The publication of *Selected Poems* in 1979 made possible a proper appreciation of his achievement. [PQ]

BECKETT, SAMUEL (1906–). Novelist and dramatist. He was born at Foxrock, Dublin, Ireland, of a well-to-do Protestant family, and the day was both Friday the 13th (April) and Good Friday. He was educated at Portora Royal School, Oscar Wilde's old school, at Enniskillen. He went to Trinity College, Dublin, in 1923 and took a first-class BA degree in French and Italian in 1927. Among his early interests were chess, cricket and golf as well as cycling; he toured France on two wheels in the summer of 1926. In 1928, after teaching for two terms at Campbell College, Belfast, he went as exchange Lecteur at the École Normale Supérieure to Paris, where he first met James Joyce (q.v.). From 1930 to 1932, he was back in Dublin as Assistant Lecturer in French at Trinity College and he took his MA degree in 1931. Twenty-eight years later (1959) the University of Dublin was to make him an honorary D Litt. He was awarded the Nobel Prize for Literature in 1969.

Beckett's involvement with Joyce in Paris was a crucial influence. In 1929 he edited essays on *Finnegans Wake* (*Our Exagmination . . .*) by close Joycean disciples who were already enthusiastic for the 'Work in Progress' ten years before its publication. Another crucial formative influence is indicated in Beckett's short critical study, *Proust* (1931), a fine exercise in aphoristic penetration. Beckett, like Eliot (q.v.), responded to the associative abundance of the Joycean and Proustian worlds by devising a recipe for literary economy – in Beckett's case an economy of substance which gradually strips his imaginative world of the personal and civilizational accoutrements of life except in so far as they impinge selectively upon his characters as algebraic symbols of abstract place, function or possession. The bicycle, for instance, in *Molloy* becomes a mechanical extension of man's physical inefficiencies. The Proust study also points the way to Beckett's coming Cartesian obsession with the antithesis between the outer world and the inner world. It is from the former that the Proustian involuntary memory enables us to 'escape into the spacious annexe of mental alienation, in sleep or the rare dispensation of waking madness'. Likewise Beckett's hero, Murphy (*Murphy**), not having a mind built 'on the correct cash-register lines for doing sums with the petty cash of current facts', seeks the sanctuary of mental alienation. Tragic, yet absurd, aspects of the individual's imprisonment in a degenerating body become dominant Beckettian concerns.

The first of Beckett's creative works was the poem *Whoroscope* (1930), and the first prose fiction was the volume of short stories *More Pricks than Kicks* (1934), in which Belacqua Shuah (Belacqua personifies indolence in Dante's *Purgatorio*) is defeated in his ambition for immobility by the conspiracy of circumstance and more especially of designing women. Four years after this self-conscious experiment in picaresque came the first novel, *Murphy* (1938), of which 1500 copies were printed. Half of them were still unsold by 1942. Stylistically the book is at once a comic burlesque of exhausted fictional techniques of plotting, character, presentation, narrative and dialogue, and an attempt to revivify the novel form by frankly implausible subjection of human and psychological interest to the shock display of verbal jugglery.

Beckett settled in Paris in 1937. The death of his father in that same year had left him with a small annuity which was to be his main means of support until theatrical success came his way in the 1950s. He was active in the French Resistance during the war and narrowly escaped betrayal to the Gestapo. He was later awarded the Croix de Guerre and the Médaille de la Résistance. It is notable that Beckett, who had proved temperamentally unfit to hold down a teaching post at Trinity College, Dublin, and had undergone psychoanalytical treatment in London for a grave neurotic condition with severe and debilitating physical symptons, was capable of rising so effectively to practical emergencies. He fled from the Gestapo into the unoccupied zone with his future wife, Suzanne Deschevaux-Dusmenil, and worked as an agricultural labourer in the village of Roussillon. Here he suffered a serious breakdown. Lacking access to psychiatric treatment, he found his relief in committing his confusion to paper. This was the genesis of his last strictly English novel, *Watt*. His biographer, Deirdre Bair (*Samuel Beckett*, 1978), describes its composition as 'his daily therapy'. 'Beckett wrote *Watt* in a desperate attempt to stave off complete mental breakdown and filled the book with dialogues and scenes from his own life.' The book remained in manuscript until it was published in Paris in 1953 (New York, 1959; London, 1963). Watt's pilgrimage ends, like Murphy's, in a lunatic asylum, where his fellow inmate, Sam, learns his story and is able to recount it with the rollicking imbecile logic that properly appertains to it as a registration of man's failure to contact and belong. The household to which Watt is earlier assigned as servant is a Kafkaesque establishment run under the elusive Mr Knott with mad fastidiousness over trivialities in a riot of disproportion. Watt's inner life of restless cerebration in pursuit of an unattainable thought-out relationship between appearance and reality is recorded in scintillatingly precise yet enigmatic prose. Watt's transition from Mr Knott's employment to his fenced enclosure adjoining Sam's comes as no shock.

After the war a rich phase of creative activity followed during the period of what Beckett has called 'the siege in the room' when, back in Paris between 1946 and 1950, he wrote his trilogy of French novels later translated as *Molloy*, *Malone Dies* and *The Unnamable*. Beckett made his own English version of these novels. Pilgrimage and counter-pilgrimage, which were merged in *Murphy*, are disentangled in *Molloy* (Paris, 1951; New York, 1955; London, 1959), with Molloy journeying back to his mother and struggling against physical disabilities, in part 1. In part 2 the agent Moran carries out mysterious orders to find Molloy. Relics of fictional verisimilitude and plausibility intrude only comically amid the shifting insubstantialities of act and setting. *Malone Dies* (Paris, 1950; New York, 1956; London, 1958) presents a cripple on his deathbed, addressing himself to a consideration of his possessions and his condition. 'I am working with impotence, ignorance', Beckett averred, and indeed the extremes are tested in *The Unnamable* where the paralysed unnamed sits in a container. Identities are merged and objectivity disappears in a farrago of expressionist fantasy. In these books Beckett had hit upon the first-person monologue as his fictional form. The speaking voice accosts the reader, stripped of external circumstance, of direct temporal, spatial or narrative placement. Seeing himself as 'doomed to spend the rest of my days digging up the detritus of my life and vomiting it out over and over again', Beckett yet accepted the positive aspect of being able to make the dark side of his personality work for him.

*Waiting for Godot** (1955, first London production) turned the tide of Beckett's fortunes with a tremendous success, and he followed it up with a series of plays in which his studies in deprivation and immobility are transferred from the page to the stage. Beckett's style had always been rich in sharp counter-shafts that shatter the equilibrium of an atmosphere, an idiom or a posture, in ironic mockery. Brought to the theatre, this gift, and his superb sense of the pathos of clowning, made an immediate impact. Beckett's verbal skill is vast. He can capsulate into successive phrases the essence of those multifarious currencies that sustain our social and professional postures, serious or comic, courteous or rude. Pastiche is distilled into a working dialogue compounded of all currencies and giving recognition to none. As an instrument of acrid nihilism or hearty tomfoolery, it is apt and effectual. In making it serve both ends at once, Beckett turns the tables on his public and himself. After *Waiting for Godot*, *Happy Days** (prod London 1962) perhaps reveals the blend of nullity and humour at its mellowest. *Endgame* (prod 1958) is more sombre, less fresh in spirit. Hamm, the protagonist, is confined to his armchair, while his parents, Nagg and Nell, pop up and down in their dustbins. *Krapp's Last Tape* (prod 1958) brings present and future grotesquely together as Krapp, an alcoholic old man, listens to one of the many tapes on which he has recorded a running commentary on his life. *Embers* (broadcast 1959), *All That Fall* (broadcast 1957), two radio plays and the one-act *Play* (prod 1963), in which the heads of three characters stick up from the necks of urns, are all experimental pieces.

During the 1970s Beckett wrote a handful of short plays and sketches which continue to register human mystification and incapacity before the pathos of life and the ineffectiveness of attempts to connect or comprehend. *Breath* (prod 1970), indeed, consists of a single cry beginning as vagitus and ending as death-rattle. *Not I* (prod 1973) expands this chill commentary on man's seventy-year span into a rambling monologue from an illuminated Mouth to which an Auditor listens and responds only by raising and lowering the arms in helpless compassion. In *That Time* (prod 1976) Listener's aged face is visible and his breath is audible as his own voices, A, B and C, flow around him in recollection. In *Footfalls* (prod 1976) dialogue between May, in her forties, and the Voice of her Mother of 89 is tormentingly supplemented by May's pacing to and fro along a narrow strip of stage:

> Will you never have done? (*Pause.*) Will you never have done . . . revolving it all?

Not I, *That Time* and *Footfalls* are among the pieces collected together in *Ends and Odds* (1977).

Murphy was the first of Beckett's novels and the only one to approximate in any degree to the conventions of the form. The approximation is ironic. Murphy, a Dubliner living in London, seeks to escape the 'current' facts of the big world (that 'colossal fiasco') for the isolated life of the mind, and he discovers by working in a lunatic asylum 'that self-immersed indifference to the contingencies of the contingent world which he had chosen for himself as the only felicity'. While enjoying a self-induced trance in his rocking chair he is burned to death by his gas-fire.

Murphy's quest for peace is balanced by a quest for Murphy on the part of Irish acquaintances whose tangled relationships give them various motives for seeking him out. These characters, Neary, Wylie, Celia Counihan, and their man Cooper, are all grotesque caricatures, but Celia Kelly, a prostitute who loves Murphy sufficiently to try to help him at the cost of her career, is realized with some tenderness in spite of Beckett's claim, 'All the puppets in this book whinge sooner or later, except Murphy, who is not a puppet'. Idioms exploited in the book touch every level of utterance from mock-metaphysics and grand literary allusiveness to music-hall gags and tap-room crudity. Beckett's handling of the pursuit of Murphy, Murphy's ingenious devices for living without effort and eating without cost, and absurd caricatures such as Miss Carridge the landlady, issue in raw farce, but the book is saved from comic nullity by the curious touch of seriousness with which the quest for sanity in insanity is invested.

Waiting for Godot, a 'tragi-comedy in two acts', was written in French as *En Attendant Godot* and later translated into English by the author. Two tramp-like figures, clad in the relics of respectability and equipped with the fragmentary remnants of cliché-thinking and verbal consequentiality, are waiting inexplicably for someone (Godot) who never comes. Their unlikely names, Vladimir and Estragon, shed no light on human identities and they are bereft of definable locale, property, place, connection or function in society. Vladimir and Estragon are visited by Pozzo, a person of apparent substance, who drives Lucky, slave and carrier, before him, roped like an animal and controlled by a whip. (Marlowe's *Tamburlaine*, in which conquered kings are harnessed, bitted, reined and whipped, seems to be an influence.) The bluster of Pozzo, showy, empty and tyrannical, and the crazy rhetorical mish-mash poured out by Lucky, seem to represent the most that human civilization is likely to provide in the way of answer to those who wait, and the total effect might be one of searching pathos were it not that Beckett turns his patient victims into double-act clowns who mess about with hats and boots and tumble in horse-play. The anguish of human rootlessness and meaninglessness consorts with crude pantomime, and there is no anchor for dignity.

Happy Days, a play in two acts, has only two characters: Winnie, a woman of about fifty, and Willie, a man of about sixty. The dialogue is largely Winnie's. She is embedded up to above her waist in a mound against an expanse of scorched grass and the audience can only presuppose the passing of an atomic holocaust. Willie, however, can at least crawl on his hands and knees. The extraordinary force of the play resides in the flow throughout of a chattering monologue by Winnie that exploits the habitual idioms of cheerful and sentimental if rather vapid suburban life in a situation of frustration so total as to render them grotesquely out of key. Nostalgically reminiscing about her past, examining her face or her teeth in a mirror, rehearsing the clichés of conventional morality, or fiddling with the handbag, parasol and other few fragments of civilization left to her, Winnie sustains a patter by which Beckett subjects the currencies of our thinking and posing to a piercing scrutiny. Within the context of near immobility and surrounding sterility the noises we spend our time making are shown up for what they are.   [HB]

BEDFORD, SYBILLE (1911–). Novelist, born in Charlottenburg, Germany. She married Walter Bedford in 1935. Outside fiction she has written up some famous trials of the age in journalistic or book form: the John Bodkins Adams trial, the Auschwitz trial, and, in *The Faces of Justice* (1961), the trial of six Algerians for murder. She completed her full-scale biography of Aldous Huxley (q.v.) in two volumes in 1974. Her novel *A Legacy* (1957) is a study of two German families, while *A Favourite of the Gods* (1963) and its sequel, *A Compass Error* (1968), together trace the careers of Anna Howland, an American born in the 1870s, her daughter Constanza, born in 1893, and granddaughter Flavia, our contemporary. Anna marries an Italian prince and leaves him, outraged by his infidelities. Constanza is as promiscuous and generous as her mother was strait-laced and unforgiving ('everything that happened to her mother went to shape what happened to herself', Flavia observes). The clash of values is not just a matter of psychological and temperamental contrast but of changing mores, of conflicting national and cultural characteristics and traditions. Bedford has a gift for crisp dialogue ostensibly quivering with oblique scoring-points, and the communication by quick-fire witticism can be entertaining. But the elaborate personal and sexual manoeuvres in the cause of duty or happiness sometimes seem to lack human centre and the sprinkled references to events and personalities of the day do not fill out a significant sociohistorical canvas.   [HB]

BEER, PATRICIA (1924–). Poet, born in Exmouth, Devon, and educated there and at Exeter University. She married J.D. Parsons, an architect, and she has lectured in English at the University of Padua and at Goldsmiths' College, London. *Loss of the Magyar* (1959) was followed by *The Survivors* (1963), *Just Like the Resurrection* (1967), *The Estuary* (1971) and *Driving West* (1975). *Selected Poems* (1979) adds a few 'New Poems' to pieces from these volumes. Patricia Beer's autobiography, *Mrs Beer's House* (1968), is informative about her upbringing among the apocalyptic Plymouth Brethren: it sheds lights on an intensely economic output in which the dread of commitment or conviction is allied with technical exactitude in imagery and craftsmanship. Like Yeats (q.v.), Beer sucks the reader into the heart of compulsive inner argument and self-scrutiny. Dilemmas remain unresolved. A half-facetious, yet curiously astringent off-handedness seems to push ultimate seriousness to arm's length. Ironic deflation of religious attitudes in 'The Baptism' (at the expense of total immersion by the Brethren) and 'A Visit to Little Gidding' (at T.S. Eliot's expense) is immaculately executed and yet leaves a sour taste. Death is a recurrent theme. In 'Called Home', which ruefully recalls how the Brethren spoke of death, the poet pins her hope on atheistic fellowship in a way which seems to strip negation of its last dimension:

Believers cannot help. I must have some
Ally who will keep non-company
With me in a non-life.   [HB]

BEERBOHM, MAX (full name Sir Henry Maximilian) (1872–1956). Caricaturist, essayist and novelist. His family were prosperous merchants from Memel on the Baltic. Julius Beerbohm, Max's father and himself a youngest son, settled in England in about 1830, traded as a corn-merchant, and married an English-woman, Constantia Draper. When she died he married her sister Eliza (English law necessitated a journey to Switzerland for the purpose). Sir Herbert Beerbohm Tree, the famous actor-manager who dominated the stage of his day, was a son of the first marriage and Max the youngest child of the second. He was educated at Charterhouse and went up to Oxford in 1890. There he quickly developed his flair for caricature, wit and parody. The Oxford of Pater and the cult of aestheticism provided an appropriate backcloth for his cultivation of a dandified pose – elegant, leisurely and urbane – and his display of flippant irony and outrageous paradox. The concern for style became a dominant element in his artistic make-up, and self-dramatization proved a source of subtle humour in his essays. Soon Beerbohm's acquaintances included Will Rothenstein the artist, who encouraged him as a caricaturist, and Oscar Wilde, whose paradoxical epigrams certainly influenced his own. ('The gods have bestowed on Max the gift of perpetual old age', Wilde averred.) In London Rothenstein introduced Beerbohm to the 'decadents', Aubrey Beardsley, Arthur Symons (q.v.) and Lionel Johnson. His friendship with Beardsley resulted in Beerbohm's becoming a contributor to the *Yellow Book*. This quarterly made its first appearance in April 1894. Beerbohm's contribution was 'A Defence of Cosmetics', a frivolous essay ironically rapturous about the power of artifice to improve on nature. It suffered the sensational critical disapproval that the allegedly scandalous journal provoked. ('As far as anyone in literature can be lynched, I was', Beerbohm used to say later.)

Beerbohm settled down in London to the life of writer and caricaturist, contributing to journals, mixing much with the Wilde group (without sharing their homosexual interests). He visited America in 1895 but was back in London for the Wilde trial, which put an end to the circle he had known so well. He lived a busy and observant social life; he published *Caricatures of Twentyfive Gentlemen* in 1896, and in the same year collected some of his essays in *The Works of Max Beerbohm* (the essay on cosmetics appears as 'The Pervasion of Rouge'). The essays abound in exquisite trifling and elegant stylistic mannerisms in which good taste is fastidiously preserved by pervasive irony. 'It is very gratifying to be recognized in one's lifetime', he said of the *Works*, and in the closing essay, 'Diminuendo', the autobiographical self-scrutiny is charmingly posed: 'Already I feel myself to be outmoded. I belong to the Beardsley period'.

The Happy Hypocrite (1897) tells the story of Lord George Hell, a Regency rake ('They say he was rather like Caligula, with a dash of Sir John Falstaff') who falls in love with Jenny Mere. She 'can never be the wife of any man whose face is not saintly' and she rejects him. Lord George has a saintly mask fitted. Thus he wins Jenny and, ashamed now of his old name, signs himself 'George Heaven' on the marriage register. The mask is torn off by a vengeful former mistress, but Jenny finds George's own face even dearer than the mask now. The preoccupation with masks is symptomatic both of Beerbohm and of his age. The moral is clear. 'If you live up to a good mask . . . perhaps it will become first nature to you', Beerbohm explained many years later.

In 1898 Beerbohm was asked to succeed Shaw (q.v.) as dramatic critic for the *Saturday Review*. Shaw himself had suggested Beerbohm to Frank Harris (q.v.), the editor. Shaw signed himself out in May to let in 'the incomparable Max', who then held the post for twelve years. Meantime further volumes of essays came out in 1899 (*More*) and 1909 (*Yet Again*). Beerbohm's literary connections grew. He introduced himself to Chesterton (q.v.) by letter: the two very different writers met and got on famously. He knew George Moore (q.v.) and has left us amusing impressions of him. He knew and liked Belloc (q.v.) and Galsworthy (q.v.). Shaw he admired more coolly; Yeats (q.v.) he disliked. Meredith he thought 'the greatest author alive and possibly the greatest English author since Shakespeare' (David Cecil, *Max, A Biography*, 1964). It was after a memorial service for Meredith in Westminster Abbey in 1909 that a girl approached Beerbohm and asked for his autograph, respectfully calling him 'Mr Barrie'. Unabashed by the disturbing misidentification, he took her book and wrote: 'Aye lassie, it's a sad day the noo. J.M.B.'

In 1910 Beerbohm married Florence Kahn, an American actress, and in the following year retired to settled domesticity in Rapallo. There he lived until his death, apart from the years of the Second World War which he spent back in England. *Zuleika Dobson* (1911) achieved considerable reputation for its sustained and mannered irony. In this comically fantastic tale Zuleika, adorable granddaughter of the Warden of Judas College, comes to Oxford and infatuates undergraduates to mass suicide for love. Later works are *Even Now* (1920), which includes a memorable record of a visit to Swinburne ('No. 2. The Pines'), and *Seven Men* (1919). The latter contains fine imaginary studies of literary and social figures. Beerbohm is projected as narrator and partaker, and the subtle blend of humour, parody, satire and fantasy is irresistible. 'Enoch Soames', the first study, features a 'decadent' poet who sells himself to the Devil for a (disappointing) preview of his posthumous literary reputation. ' "Savanarola" Brown' introduces us to a would-be dramatist whose unfinished blank-verse tragedy, 'Savanarola', is surely the most hilarious parody of Elizabethan drama ever written.

Beerbohm was acclaimed as a broadcaster for his nostalgic reminiscences. He was knighted in 1939.　　[HB]

BEHAN, BRENDAN (1923–64). Dramatist, born in Dublin, Ireland. His father, Stephen Behan, was a house-painter, but one who knew his way about books and would read Dickens, Zola and Shaw to his family in the evenings. His mother, Kathleen, would sing from her great repertoire of songs and ballads. Kathleen's mother-in-law by her first marriage (she was a young widow when she became Mrs Behan) was given three years at Birmingham Assizes in 1939 when found in IRA company with gelignite in her corsage; she was 77 at the time. Behan himself became an IRA courier at the age of 15. He left for England on a bombing expedition, was followed by the police, arrested in Liverpool with dynamite in his possession, and after remand at Walton Gaol was tried at the Assizes in February 1940. His youth saved him from penal servitude. He was sent for three years to the Borstal institution at Hollesley Bay, Sussex, and fell into the care of the enlightened and humane Governor, C.A. Joyce. This story is told (with graphic licence appropriate to autobiographical fiction) in *Borstal Boy* (1958). His friendship with English fellow delinquents and experience of 'decency' on the part of authority was crucial. 'After Borstal he found it impossible to hate Englishmen any more' (Ulick O'Connor, *Brendan Behan*, 1970). Freed and deported in December 1941, he soon reassumed the role of flamboyant revolutionary, shot a policeman after the Dublin Easter parade in April 1942, and found himself in Mountjoy Gaol with a fourteen-year sentence at the age of 19. It was here that he began to write. He contributed an article on his Borstal experiences to *The Bell* in April 1942 and wrote his first play, *The Landlady*. It was to have been produced by the convicts had not rehearsals provoked a riot among political prisoners.

Behan was transferred in 1943 to the internment camp in the Curragh. Here there were more opportunities for study, and he perfected his Gaelic. He was released under a general amnesty just after Christmas 1946, and launched himself into bohemian circles in postwar Dublin where alcoholism and bisexual promiscuity were in vogue as well as revolutionary politics, sparkling talk and roaring balladry. Behan's exhibitionist tendencies nurtured an extravagant self-projection, first as self-made slum rebel, then as hectoring inebriate trampling on conventions of social politeness and respectability. There was another side too: a genuine interest in unspoilt folk-culture took him on visits to Gaelic-speaking Kerry, and he wrote many Gaelic poems in the late 1940s. By 1951 he had started work on *Borstal Boy*, a book which he described as 'a novel', thereby removing any possible criticism of its factual reliability. He supported himself by regular articles for the *Irish Press* and by writing and performing in ballad programmes for the Irish radio. But positive achievement was steadily undermined by drinking habits that were especially dangerous because of a mild diabetic condition. Behan's marriage in 1955 to Beatrice French-Salkeld provided him with support and understanding which at first sustained him through many months of fruitful work, but which his fatal addiction was ultimately to subject to intolerable strain.

The Quare Fellow, a play based on experience in gaol, was put on at a little Dublin theatre (the Pike Theatre) on 4 December 1955 and was an immediate success. The action takes place in Mountjoy Gaol, Dublin, during the twenty-four hours leading up to the execution of an unnamed murderer, the 'quare fellow', and explores the prison community's reaction to the event. The victim himself does not appear, but talk continually centres on him while preparations are made for the hanging and the burial and the last night in the death-cell. The play is not strong in structure; it lacks dramatic thrust and climax; but dialogue sparkles with wry surface comedy, while a pervasive moral urgency underlies the cunning juxtaposition of day-to-day prison banter and routine with on-the-spot recollections of what really happens at hangings which are gruesome and horrific. The whole macabre

paraphernalia of the hangman's tools and trade are on show. A deeper gravity emerges through the character of Warder Regan, a devout and humane Catholic who can see through the cant of legalized brutality. 'You forget the times the fellow gets caught and has to be kicked off the edge of the trap hole. You never heard of the warders down below swinging on his legs the better to break his neck, or jumping on his back when the drop was too short.'

After the Dublin success of *The Quare Fellow* it was presented in May 1956 by the Theatre Workshop at the Theatre Royal, Stratford, London, and fell into place alongside Osborne's *Look Back in Anger* (q.v.) as part of the new blast of social realism hitting the theatre. It was soon after transferred to the West End and made the author's name as a vibrant recorder of Irish personality and Irish fluency, grave and gay, in the tradition of O'Casey (q.v.) and Synge (q.v.). The sensational success of the play in England and America gave Behan an international audience, promoted via popular press and television, for his escalating public act as roistering Irish gasbag and ribald iconoclast. Arrests for drunken disorderliness occurred on both sides of the Atlantic.

In 1957 Behan wrote *An Giall*, the Gaelic play later to be translated and adapted as *The Hostage*. The scene is a Dublin brothel where a kidnapped English Tommy is held hostage by the IRA in an attempt to save one of their men who is due to be hanged in Belfast. The Tommy, a Cockney, falls in love with Teresa the 'skivvy', a simple country girl, but he is accidentally killed when police raid the house at the end. The racy Irish humour, the macabre ironies of the situation and the final bloodshed form a moving background to a sincere meeting between two innocent young people who have so much in common that national differences seem absurd. When the English version was made (*The Hostage*) for the Theatre Workshop in 1958, additional characters were fitted in and the tone of the play altered to accommodate current theatrical fashion. The cheapening of the work irritated lovers of the Gaelic original who saw a 'blown-up hotchpotch' substituted for a 'small masterpiece' (Ulick O'Connor, op. cit.). But audiences loved it, and *Borstal Boy* (1958) provided Behan with a simultaneous spectacular success in another medium. Nevertheless his career as a writer, increasingly overwhelmed by the alcoholism that killed him, was virtually at an end. *Brendan Behan's Island* (1962) was dictated, but two impressive early short stories ('A Woman of No Standing' and 'The Confirmation Suit') as well as a less successful radio play (*The Big House*) were sandwiched into it between chapters of taped chatter about Ireland. *Richard's Cork Leg*, a play left unfinished at his death, descends overmuch to stale music-hall jokes. *Confessions of an Irish Rebel* (1964), another taped work, is neither reliable nor inspired.   [HB]

BELLOC, HILAIRE (1870–1953). Novelist, historian, essayist, poet and miscellaneous prose writer, born at La Celle St Cloud near Paris of mixed ancestry. His grandfather, Hilaire Belloc, a painter, had married Louise Swanton from Ballydehob, County Cork, who translated Moore's *Irish Melodies* into French and wrote a life of Byron. His father, Louis Belloc, married Bessie

Parkes, a great granddaughter of Joseph Priestley, the scientist. She knew George Eliot, Thackeray, Trollope, Mrs Browning and Mrs Gaskell, whom she accompanied to Yorkshire when she was working on the Brontë biography. The Bellocs came to London soon after Hilaire's birth and thereby escaped the siege of Paris that followed the fall of the Empire. Louis died when Hilaire was but two and Mrs Belloc moved to Sussex (Slindon, near Arundel) in 1877. In 1880 Hilaire was sent to school at the Oratory, Edgbaston, for the family was staunchly Catholic, but holidays were often spent in France. Young Belloc voluntarily did service with the French Army and did not go up to Oxford (Balliol) until 1893. He distinguished himself at the Union, became President in 1894, took a first in History in 1895, but failed to get an All Souls' Fellowship. The rejection remained a lifetime's disappointment. In 1896 he went to America to marry Elodie Hogan whom, on first meeting in London five years before, he had determined to make his wife, but who had since seemed to be inaccessible because of her apparent vocation to the religious life.

The married pair settled in Oxford, Belloc giving University Extension lectures and coaching. His *Verses and Sonnets* was published in 1896 and *The Bad Child's Book of Beasts* made a hit the same year. *More Beasts (for Worse Children)* followed in 1897. *Danton*, Belloc's first of many historical biographies, was published in 1899. The Bellocs moved to London in 1901, and in the following year Hilaire was naturalized as a British citizen. He was hard at work on his second historical study, *Robespierre* (1901), in 1900 when he undertook the famous walk from Toul (his old garrison town) to Rome, the plan being to write down whatever occurred to him – about landscape, people and general subjects, its fruit being *The Path to Rome* (1902). The Alps and a blizzard defeated his attempt to cover the ground in a straight line, but the feat was one of considerable endurance. Belloc lived on bread and ham, slept rough, and packed his record of it all with interest and vitality, the personal stamp nowhere more evident than in the intermittent exchanges between *auctor* and interrupting *lector* ('Pray are we to have any more of that fine writing?').

Belloc published his fictional political satire, *Emmanuel Burden*, in 1904. He had met Chesterton (q.v.) in 1900 and the literary relationship which Shaw (q.v.) dubbed 'Chesterbelloc' was born. Chesterton himself illustrated several of Belloc's satirical novels; but the 'establishment' figures and fashions which their mockery pilloried now have a dated topicality. (*But Soft, we are Observed*, 1928, is a later instance of the genre.) Belloc's comic irreverence survives more palatably, more durably, in the satiric verse. *Cautionary Tales* was added in 1907, *More Peers* in 1911, and *New Cautionary Tales* in 1930. The ironic projection of the truly Horrible Child was a healthy antidote to virtuous domestic sentimentality. The aristocracy were always a favourite target. Young John Vavasour de Quentin Jones 'was very fond of throwing stones' and as a result was disinherited in favour of Miss Charming, 'who now resides in Portman Square/And is accepted everywhere' (*New Cautionary Tales*). There is an eighteenth-century flavour about Belloc's most aphoristic couplets and a Swiftian ring about the octosyllabics in such poems as 'Lord Lundy'.

His Lordship is a dismal failure in parliament –

> Thus, if a member rose to say
> (As members do from day to day)
> 'Arising out of that reply . . .'
> Lord Lundy would begin to cry.

He suffers the final indignity of banishment to the governorship of New South Wales. Belloc's more serious verse is accomplished rhetoric, rhythmically alive.

Belloc was elected Liberal MP for Salford in 1906, but retired from the House in 1910, 'relieved to be quit of the dirtiest company it has ever been my misfortune to keep'. The disillusionment is articulated in *The Party System* (1911), written in collaboration with Cecil Chesterton. Belloc had a radical disgust of what he saw as manipulation of parliamentary democracy by the wealthy and the powerful, but this was allied with a dread of economic totalitarianism (see *The Servile State*, 1912) that made him the advocate of Distributism – the wide diffusion of small ownership – for which the medieval guild system was a precedent.

Belloc bought the house King's Land, in Sussex, in 1906 and this was where he lived for the rest of his life. *Marie Antoinette*, his then biggest biographical study, came out in 1909 and, as at all times of his life, volumes of miscellaneous essays (often collected from regular journalism) periodically made their appearance (*The Hills and the Sea*, 1906; *On Nothing*, 1908; *On Everything*, 1908; *On Anything*, 1910; *On Something*, 1910, and so on). These short but shapely exercises cover a wide range of varied interests. Some are casual and chatty, others more gravely contemplative. There are memories of travel, accounts of odd experiences, ironical squibs, and forceful judgements on contemporary attitudes; and one meets Belloc's personality at its most relaxed and forthcoming. The clarity of style is often notable, the mannered rhetoric well sustained. Of course, here as elsewhere, the high style, whether direct or ironic, can be taxingly self-conscious, the jocularity overbearing, the forthrightness too strident, the take-it-or-leave-it tone too rigid.

As a historian (he wrote a four-volume *History of England*, 1925–32) Belloc did not try to mute his prejudices in the interests of objectivity and he had too much imagination to be willing to limit himself to the scientifically ascertainable. He sought to bring the past back to life by a pictorial concreteness of scene and an emotional revivification of character. This did not make him a historian's historian. But his weekly articles on the military situation throughout the First World War in *Land and Water* made his name known everywhere, at home and at the front.

Belloc was a man of restless energy, a torrential personality who made a legend of his attachment to the Catholic faith and the wine-bottle ('Strong brother in God and last companion, Wine'). His hectoring affirmations ('The Church is Europe; and Europe is the Church', *Europe and the Faith*, 1920) limit the audience for his Catholic apologetic, but he was a controversialist to be reckoned with. His public oratory could be captivating, his private talk riotously engaging. 'When you get talking, Hilary,' Max Beerbohm said to him, 'you are like a great Bellocking ram, or like a Roman river full of baskets and dead cats'. Freelance writing and lecturing, necessitated by lack of a fixed income, eventually drained him of his resources, but he had published well over a hundred books when this became apparent.   [HB]

BENNETT, ALAN (1934–). Dramatist, born in Leeds, West Yorkshire, educated there and at Exeter College, Oxford. He contributed monologues and sketches to the revue *Beyond the Fringe*, produced in Edinburgh in 1960. *Forty Years On* (prod 1968) uses the device of annual performances by boys at a school to stage successive skits that blend satire with nostalgia. *Getting On* (prod 1971) has a powerful portrait of a middle-aged Labour MP whose energies and idealism have been philosophized by drab experience into depersonalized rhetoric. His virulent verbalism gives ample scope for Bennett's notable linguistic virtuosity. *Habeas Corpus* (prod 1973), a cheap sex farce enlivened by slapstick with falsies, scarcely bears comparison with it, and even less with *The Old Country* (prod 1977) in which there is cunning presentation of a Philby-type exile in Moscow receiving a visit by relations from home. The nostalgic element, the faintly sinister overtones and the inner dialectic of the central dilemma are all discreetly managed, as it gradually emerges that an exchange of spies has been arranged. Bennett's prose has vitality and punch: neatly structured, it is the product of a literary mind yet never becomes merely 'literary'. In *Enjoy* (1980) he goes back to his home area to present a family in the last back-to-back house in Leeds. Their natural conversation is counter-pointed with the jargon which social investigators bring to bear on their lot and with the clichés of the media which mythologize them. The blend of authentic Yorkshire dialogue and humour with the idioms of contemporary pseudo-thought has a Joycean richness.   [HB]

BENNETT, ARNOLD (1867–1931). Novelist, born above a down-at-heel draper's shop at Shelton, Hanley, Staffordshire, the eldest of nine children, six of whom survived. His father, Enoch, bettered himself with a grim determination that cost the family much privation. He articled himself to a solicitor at the age of 29, studied at night and became a solicitor himself five years later, when Arnold was nine. The family was Wesleyan Methodist and the combination of puritanical prejudice with the domineering temperament of the father was formidable. A vivid impression of a complex father–son relationship can be gained from *Clayhanger* (1910), in which autobiography is deeply ingrained. Bennett's father was to be struck down in 1900 by what was called softening of the brain and was perhaps general paralysis of the insane. Stages of similar degeneration (Enoch was only 57) are pictured with harrowing detail in the account of Darius Clayhanger's end. When Bennett reached a comparable age, his own eccentricities may have strengthened a notion that he would end like his father. He mentioned such a premonition to Dorothy Cheston Bennett, and she recalled it when Bennett deliberately drank tap water in Paris and so brought on the typhoid that killed him.

Bennett left Newcastle under Lyme Middle School at the age of 16 to go reluctantly into his father's office, but he failed his law examination and made up his mind to break away. He mastered shorthand, went up to London in 1888 to a clerkship with a firm of solicitors, and soon found himself with friendships in which he could share his interest in books and music, and through which he made contact with writers. Chesterton (q.v.) observed of the eager aspirant from the Midlands that he looked like someone who had come up for the Cup and forgotten to go back. In 1893 he became assistant editor of *Woman* and three years later editor. As 'Marjorie' he ran a gossip column and answered readers' letters, thereby learning much about the female mind. He also wrote reviews and short stories, and laid the foundations of a lifelong career in journalism that culminated in the weekly articles which boosted the sales of the *Evening Standard* in the 1920s and for which he was paid £300 a month (see *The Evening Standard Years, Books and Persons*, ed. A. Mylett, 1974). In this last decade of his life he was making and breaking reputations, having achieved the status of a national literary grand panjandrum. Bennett's character contained dichotomies. The money-making journalist, yacht-owner and purveyor of potboilers was sometimes at war with the serious artist; but there is little disagreement about the cluster of novels that stands out from a massive output to place him among great writers. His eighty-odd titles include volumes of autobiography (*The Truth About an Author*, 1903); criticism (*The Author's Craft*, 1914); and pocket philosophy. His *Journals* were edited by N. Flower and published in three volumes after his death (1932–3); and three volumes of *Letters*, edited by J. Hepburn, have been added to these (1966–70). Bennett made many attempts to turn successful playwright, most of them vain, though *Milestones* (1912), written in collaboration with Edward Knoblock, made money.

Bennett's first novel, *A Man from the North* (1898), was written under inspiration from George Moore's (q.v.) Potteries novel, *A Mummer's Wife*; his second, *The Grand Babylon Hotel* (1902), is a light-hearted mystery tale which opens with an American millionaire's lightning purchase of a hotel, whose waiter has refused his daughter's request for steak and beer. The deal is completed in time for the meal to be served. The organization of sumptuous hotels fascinated Bennett and he made it the subject of his last novel, *Imperial Palace* (1930.)

Bennett's true quality first emerged in *Anna of the Five Towns* (1902). Set in Bursley, one of the Five Towns, it brings the life of the Potteries into the English novel with an assurance of registration which in scope and detail has compelling artistic power. Anna Tellwright's relationship with her wealthy but miserly father is subtly articulated. 'He belonged to the great and powerful class of house-tyrants, the backbone of the British nation', and Anna, a well-meaning young woman whose genuineness and integrity stop short of heroism, confronts domestic and spiritual constraints steadily, ultimately giving stability and loyalty precedence over an onrush of unexpected passion in settling for a mate.

In 1903 Bennett went to Paris and France became his main home for the next nine years. Here, on the rebound from a seven-week infatuation with Eleanor Green, who refused to marry him (she was 18, and twenty years his junior), he married Marguerite Soulié in 1907. Soon after, living in a rented house near Fontainebleau, he started work on his masterpiece, *The Old Wives' Tale** (1908), an epic study of two women from one of the Five Towns in the Potteries. It was slow to catch on at first, but Bennett himself knew its worth. 'This day is the most important of my life', he told his wife on the day of publication. 'I shall never be able to do better.'

Bennett has been called a 'connoisseur of the normal': he knows how real people live and what they have to cope with; he has a genius for hitting on trivialities of event or temperament that cease in fact to be trivial and become the burning stuff of family embarrassment, tension or strife. No writer better keeps the reader aware of how important to daily human well-being are meals, health, money and warmth. The age-long struggle of the English against cold and draughts, rheumatism, influenza and indigestion is among his specialities.

Clayhanger traces the childhood and young manhood of Edwin Clayhanger (born 1856), son of a self-made Potteries printer, Darius Clayhanger. It is one of our great studies of growing up under repressive paternal authority. Bennett invests the plain, ordinary young man here with the interestingness he gave to the very ordinary Anna Tellwright. The dogged resilience of illusionless Midlanders in the face of life's frustrations runs like a low-voltage current through Bennett's Potteries novels. The historical canvas of *Clayhanger* has depth without intrusiveness. Bennett cunningly leaves a big question mark over the strange behaviour of Hilda Lessways, who mysteriously diverges from Edwin into an impossible marriage, and he inserts a footnote forecasting the publication of another novel dealing with Hilda's previous history. Neither *Hilda Lessways* (1911), which complements *Clayhanger* from the woman's point of view, nor the third novel, *These Twain* (1916), a record of subsequent warfare in marriage, matches *Clayhanger* in all-round convincingness.

However, Bennett struck gold again in *Riceyman Steps* (1923) and *Lord Raingo** (1926). *Riceyman Steps* is the story of Henry Earlforward, a Clerkenwell second-hand bookseller, who in middle life marries a widow, Violet Arb. His ingrained miserliness makes domesticity impossible, while his ingrained gentleness makes rebellion unthinkable. Sustained by a golden-hearted, self-sacrificing servant, Elsie, the two drift meaninglessly to death from prolonged under-nourishment. The ironic intensity of the tragedy is uncanny. Doom closes in on a woman who has 'at hand all the materials for tranquil happiness' stultified by the absurd 'volition of her loving husband'.

Bennett was not an easy man to live with. Obsessional rigidities were strangely compounded in him with warm-hearted generosity. His marriage broke down in separation. In 1922, at the age of 55, he formed a permanent attachment with a young woman in her twenties, Dorothy Cheston, who adopted his surname and bore him a daughter, Virginia, in 1926. Marguerite Bennett wrote two books about her husband, *Arnold Bennett* (1925) and *My Arnold Bennett* (1931).

The Old Wives' Tale chronicles the lives of two sisters, Constance and Sophia Baines, daughters of a draper in Bursley. An incident in a Paris café in 1903 was the genesis of the story. Bennett saw a fat, ageing woman, fussy and repulsive, the butt of the restaurant. He was struck by the pathos of the fact that once she must have been a charming young girl, and he determined to write a book about 'the development of a young girl into a stout old lady'. He got to grips with the long-pondered scheme in 1907 and completed the book in one of his most fruitful bursts of creative energy. The book is at once a melancholy lament on the human damage wrought by time and a packed registration of what the stolid will and unbeaten spirit of Midland women can achieve in the face of it. The central characters are convincing at every stage from girlhood (they are in their teens in the 1860s) to old age. Constance, the elder sister, is sober, earnest, conscientious, obediently responsive to the family need for her to go into the drapery business. Sophia is inclined to be giddy, impulsive, romantic and has irrepressible ambitions to break out. Their father is a bed-ridden paralytic and the moral pressure to equate virtue with pleasing him is suffocating. Constance predictably marries Samuel Povey, the archetype of unimaginative thrift and conscientiousness, while Sophia is lured into the grip of Gerald Scales, a showy and worthless commercial traveller who inherits a fortune, whisks her off to Paris, ruins himself by fatuous extravagance and abandons her. Sophia makes her own indomitable way in foreign isolation, living through the Siege of Paris and the Commune. Book I covers the lives of the girls up to Sophia's disappearance from Bursley, books II and III the careers of Constance and Sophia respectively, and book IV brings the two sisters together in Bursley for their old age. It must be accepted that the Paris scenes lack some of the winning naturalness with which Potteries life is transcribed, but in structure, in range and particularity of characterization, in panoramic fullness of event and portraiture, in the sheer inventiveness by which an epoch is re-created, and in overall thematic continuity of vision, the achievement is a triumphant one.

Lord Raingo was the fruit of Bennett's brief sally into official life. At the instigation of his friend, Lord Beaverbrook, he was put in charge of the wartime Ministry of Information in May 1918 and worked hard as an administrator to the end of the war, when he refused the reward of a knighthood. By contrast his hero, Sam Raingo, a self-made millionaire, makes a peerage a condition of taking charge of propaganda as Minister of Records towards the end of the war. Raingo has a heart condition and for the last third of the book he is on his death-bed. There is a moving contrast between Raingo's strained yet not unkindly relationship with his classy, self-absorbed wife, Adele – an absent-minded woman lukewarm in wifely emotions – and his tender love for Delphine – his plebeian mistress, a generous-hearted girl, grateful but worried by an obligation to a man at the front. Raingo, who revels in power and notoriety and is given to introspection, is at once realist and romantic, alternately suspicious and impressionable in response to the wizardry of the Prime Minister and the warmth of Delphine. The main force of the book lies in the account of ministerial infighting and inter-departmental intrigue involving the war cabinet, the service chiefs, and top civil servants. The stark, implicit contrast between the war game in London and the mistily remote business of blood and mud at the front has cool ironic power. Andy Clyth, the Prime Minister, is a brilliantly executed portrait of Lloyd George, and his secretary, Rosie Packer, of Lloyd George's mistress,

Frances Stevenson. Winston Churchill is portrayed as the aggressive Tom Hogarth, Minister of Munitions. [HB]

BENSON, E.F. (Edward Frederick) (1867–1940). Novelist, born at Wellington College, Somerset, son of its headmaster, E.W. Benson, later Archbishop of Canterbury, and educated at Marlborough College and at Cambridge. *Dodo* (1893) launched a successful series of light society novels. A later series, the 'Lucia' novels of the 1920s and 1930s (recently reprinted), turns the comic mockery on small-town middle-class life. Lucia is a lovably snobbish and dynamic socialite with a naughty itch to tease, and there are high jinks with false teeth and bicycles, for instance, in *Trouble for Lucia* (1939). But it is all too strenuously bright. Benson's current reputation rests rather on the autobiographical *As We Were: A Victorian Peep Show* (1930), a delightfully polished evocation of the Victorian age, its manners and personalities, and a mine of gossipy anecdote amusingly recounted. It was followed by *As We Are* (1932). [HB]

BENTLEY, PHYLLIS (1894–1977). Novelist, born in Halifax, West Yorkshire, and educated at Cheltenham Ladies College, Gloucestershire. She found her material chiefly in her native West Riding. Early novels included *Environment* (1922), *The Spinner of the Years* (1928) and *Carr* (1929), but it was *Inheritance* (1932) that became her most celebrated work. Its human material draws on her own family past. The history of the Oldroyd family of local mill-owners symbolically sums up the textile industry's rise and decline from Luddite riots to the 1926 slump. Phyllis Bentley was fascinated by the ambitious dynamism of the mill-owners and the civilizing radicalism that put a brake on it. *A Modern Tragedy* (1934) again focuses on the inter-war depression. Bentley kept returning to the Oldroyd family, whose saga is concluded in *A Man of his Time* (1966). Her style, however, is flaccid and her work lacks imaginative intensity. See her autobiography *O Dreams, O Destinations* (1962). [HB]

BERRY, FRANCIS (1915–). Poet, born in Malaya, educated in England. After war service, he graduated at London University. Since then he has held university posts at Sheffield and London, where he is now Professor of English at Holloway College. *The Galloping Centaur: Poems 1933–1951* (1952) selects from earlier volumes which include the two long narrative poems *The Iron Christ* (1938) and *Fall of a Tower* (1943). Berry's style manifests something of Hopkins's vigour and splendour in moulding language to the poetic demand foot by foot and line by line. The pulsing energy and tumbling fluency are the product of disciplined skill. An angular consonantal percussiveness coexists rhythmically with compulsive forward movement. The theme of *The Iron Christ* is summed up in the epigraph: 'In 1902, Chile and Argentina were going to war. But, as the result of a sermon, a Christ is made from the guns on the frontier fortresses, and erected on the highest point of the Andes, between the two countries. War is averted.' The description of the manufacture and transportation of the statue is turbulent with action and packed with vivid imagery:

Cold cracks the nerves, as higher still
The Iron Christ climbs, reaching desert plateau
Glinting blue in steel regard of stars.
At twenty thousand feet, the terminus,
Train presses buffers in, expiring in
A hiss of steam that comes down damp.

Fall of a Tower tells how, out of devotion to the sun, a fanatic blows up a cathedral tower that casts oppressive shadow all around it. Later collections of verse include *Morant Bay* (1961), whose title poem deals with a nineteenth-century negro uprising in Jamaica, and *Ghosts of Greenland* (1966). Berry's critical book *Poet's Grammar* (1974) analyses the use of particular grammatical forms in poetry. [HB]

BETJEMAN, JOHN (Sir) (1906–). Poet and writer on architecture, born in London. His father intended him to succeed to the control of the family business, but young Betjeman preferred poetry. The story of the consequent tension and of much else in the poet's early life is told in the autobiographical poem, *Summoned by Bells** (1960). T.S. Eliot was among the boy's teachers at his Highgate preparatory school. After Marlborough, where he suffered much, came Oxford, where he enjoyed himself too much, failed Divinity Moderations, and was sent down. It was a great disappointment:

I'd seen myself a don,
Reading old poets in the library,
Attending chapel in an MA gown
And sipping vintage port by candlelight.
(*Summoned by Bells*)

Betjeman taught briefly at a private school and then got a job on the staff of *The Architectural Review*. His first prose book, *Ghastly Good Taste* (1933), presents the 'depressing story of the rise and fall of English Architecture'. In the introduction he wrote for a new edition in 1970 Betjeman has something to say about his rebellion against his own class. He 'felt obliged to be in sympathy with the strikers' in the 1926 General Strike. 'I was, in fact, a parlour pink, and bored by politics. I was also Anglo-Catholic, and thought I had found the solution of life in the teaching of Conrad Noel, the Red Vicar of Thaxted.' Betjeman's passion for architecture is a deep human concern whose values far transcend those of mere aesthetics. The numerous works of topographical and architectural interest which he wrote or edited (many of them illustrated) are the work of an ebullient and exuberant commentator and critic with strong likes and dislikes, and one who has an enormous repertoire of intimate and detailed reference to churches, stations and buildings of all kinds scattered throughout the country. For Victorian architecture he has a special affection. The books include *Vintage London* (1942) and *First and Last Loves* (1952), a collection of essays. The breadth of his range can be seen in *A Pictorial History of English Architecture* (1970), while the sharp eye for Victorian grandeur and Victorian finesse focuses in *London's Historic Railway Stations* (1972) on dramatic glimpses of St Pancras, Liverpool Street and the rest.

Betjeman has lived by writing and, since the war, by turning himself into a distinguished performer on the television screen. His poetic output began with *Mount Zion* (1931). When *Collected Poems* (1958) came out, with an introduction by the Earl of Birkenhead, sales reached figures unknown for poetry (over a hundred thousand, it is said) since the days of Scott and Byron. Betjeman's fluency in high-spirited if unadventurous versification is often irresistible. If it leads him to write sometimes at a very modest level of poetic intensity, there is never a hint of pretentiousness. The idiom never masquerades in false dignities and the poet knows exactly what he is doing. 'These verses do not pretend to be poetry. They were written for speaking on the wireless', he writes in introducing *Poems in the Porch* (1954). Betjeman is aware, not without justifiable combativeness, of what stern Leavisite evaluation can do to a muse as undemandingly genuine as his:

> Even today,
> When all the way from Cambridge comes a wind
> To blow the lamps out every time they're lit,
> I know that I must light mine up again.
> *(Summoned by Bells)*

Sometimes Betjeman writes satire with a sting, as when he pillories the businessman with 'plump white fingers made to curl / Round some anaemic city girl' in 'The City' or mocks the complacent, insensitive don in 'The Wykehamist':

> It's something to become a bore,
> And more than that, at twenty-four.

But more often what Betjeman loves and what he pokes fun at are one and the same, notably the Church of England, whose buildings, practices and internal rivalries he knows inside out. Above all, known and loved places are deftly evoked in his poetry – small towns, London suburbs, and familiar southern beauty spots. Particular places serve as settings for reflective, nostalgic or ironic studies of the changing human scene. It is the study of a building and its site – 'St Saviour's, Aberdeen Park, Highbury, London N' – into which is compressed a moving record of the poet's parentage, background and religious dedication.

The serious Betjeman, touched by fear and by anticipation of death in 'The Cottage Hospital' or by the intrusion of distress on steady middle-class life in 'Oxford: Sudden Illness at the Bus-stop', has extensive sympathies. His wry sensitivities reach out with rare acuteness to the mood of a night-club proprietress as she opens up her premises in the morning in 'Sun and Fun'. But poems with a stronger vein of humour have done most for Betjeman's wide popularity. 'The Licorice Fields at Pontefract' is a nice reply to 'Down by the Salley Gardens'. It introduces the Betjemanian Amazonian who leaves her lover 'winded, wilting, weak', and who figures so athletically in 'The Olympic Girl':

> Oh! would I were her racket press'd
> With hard excitement to her breast
> And swished into the sunlit air
> Arm-high above her tousled hair.

Betjeman was knighted in 1969, and his appointment as Poet Laureate in 1972 was generally welcomed. His subsequent volume, *A Nip in the Air* (1974), showed no falling-off. John Guest has selected *The Best of Betjeman* (1978), a Penguin book.

Summoned by Bells is an autobiographical poem in nine 'chapters'. It gives an 'account of some moments in the sheltered life of a middle-class youth'. Blank verse is the medium chosen as being 'best suited to brevity and rapid changes of mood and subject'. At a few points stanzaic lyrics are interposed. In Chapter I ('Before MCMXIV') the extremes of joy and pain in infancy are represented by the 'safe old bear', Archibald, and the hateful nurse, Maud, who 'smelt of soap'. Chapter II ('The Dawn of Guilt') presents Betjeman's father, a wealthy manufacturer whose earnest ambition for his son to succeed him in the works ('the fourth generation') is to end in hopeless disappointment and in alienation as the poet pursues his chosen vocation. Chapter III takes us through schooldays at Highgate and the boy-bard's efforts to interest his American master, Mr Eliot, in *The Best of Betjeman*, his first verses. Later chapters treat of holidays in Cornwall, attendance at a prep school at Oxford, life in Chelsea, and the torments of the public school regimen at Marlborough:

> Doom! Shivering doom! Inexorable bells
> To early school, to chapel, school again:
> Compulsory constipation, hurried meals . . .
> The dread of beatings! Dread of being late!
> And, greatest dread of all, the dread of games.

As Betjeman moves through adolescence, tension between father and son reaches a climax. The last chapter (IX) takes us to Oxford in the 1920s – wining, dining, house-parties, everything but work. Betjeman is sent down and gets cold comfort from his tutor, C.S. Lewis (q.v.): 'You'd have only got a Third'. The poem is shot through with evidence of Betjeman's nostalgic affection for places and buildings.   [HB]

BHATTACHARYA, BHABANI (1906–). Novelist, born in Bhagalpur, India. He studied at the universities of Patna and London. In 1935 he married Salila Mukerji. He has worked as a journalist and for the Indian Ministry of Education, has visited many foreign countries and taught in the University of Hawaii.

The Bengal famine of 1942–3 stirred him into writing *So Many Hungers!* (1947), a brutally realistic novel about three million people having to die 'to make thirty new millionaires'. He writes vigorously about Indian social problems, with compassion for the downtrodden. In *Music for Mohini* (1952) the heroine successfully fuses modern attitudes with traditional attitudes in an arranged marriage. *A Goddess Named Gold* (1960) ingeniously uses a legend-like framework to present communal solidarity as effective counter to business greed. *Shadow from Ladakh* (1966 – Sahitya Akademi Award, 1967) surveys Indian society impressively, but the central love relationship is heavily symbolic. *A Dream in Hawaii* (1978) is about a professor turned holy man, who is caught up in 'supermarket' religion but succeeds in retaining his integrity. Bhattacharya is at his best as social satirist, his most satisfying novel being *He Who Rides a Tiger* (1954), where narrative and satirization of caste and wealth are skilfully integrated. He has also published non-fiction, translations of Tagore and a short-story collection, *Steel Hawk* (1968).   [AR]

BINYON, LAURENCE (1869–1943). Poet, and an authority on oriental art. He became Keeper of Oriental Prints and Drawings at the British Museum. He wrote poetry throughout his life, and *Collected Poems* was published in two volumes in 1931 and reissued in 1943. Binyon has been more praised for the integrity of his diction than read for any immediacy of impact. Yeats chose 'Tristram's End' for the *Oxford Book of Modern Verse* to represent an output that has consistent mellifluous dignity but is often tapestried and remote. In the celebrated 'For the Fallen' the high academic craftsmanship was brought to bear on the subject of the war dead with a sureness of touch that caught a national mood:

> They shall not grow old, as we that are left grow
>   old:
> Age shall not weary them, nor the years condemn.
> At the going down of the sun and in the morning
> We will remember them.

Similarly a posthumous poem, 'The Burning of the Leaves', caught the spirit of national reaction to the bombing raids of the Second World War:

> Now is the time for stripping the spirit bare,
> Time for the burning of days ended and done

Binyon published a highly regarded translation of Dante's *Divine Comedy* in terza rima: *The Inferno* (1933); *The Purgatorio* (1938); *The Paradiso* (1943).   [HB]

BIRNEY, EARLE (1904–). Poet and playwright, born in Calgary, Alberta, Canada, and educated at the University of Toronto and the University of California, Berkeley. After a distinguished academic career in Canada as both teacher and creative writer he became a freelance writer and lecturer in 1968. A prolific and urbanely witty writer, his experience of the depression in the 1920s and 1930s made a lasting impression; he was a Marxist for many years and a strong interest in history and the immediate social fabric still characterize his work. *Now Is Time* (1945) reflected his wartime experiences, as did the accomplished picaresque novel *Turvey* (1949). An imaginative radio play, *The Destruction of Vancouver* (broadcast 1952), was included in the poetry collection *Trial of a City* published that year. The semi-autobiographical novel *Down the Long Table* (1955) explored leftist activities in Toronto and Vancouver during the Depression. An inventive interest in word pattern and rhythm characterize the formal aspect of his poetry; in his own words 'free form tending towards the "concrete" and mixed media'. In the Preface to *Selected Poems 1940–1966* (1966) he described his poems as 'signals out of the loneliness into which all of us are born'. Later collections such as *Rag and Bone Shop* (1971), *Bear on the Delhi Road* and *What's So Big about Green* (both 1973) reaffirmed the variety of his tatent, amply documented in the two-volume *Collected Poems* (1974). He has edited collections of Canadian poetry, and (with Margorie Lowry) has also edited *Lunar Caustic* (1963) by Malcolm Lowry (q.v.), whom he knew, and Lowry's *Selected Poems* (1962). *The Creative Writer* (1966) is literary essays. The

Rugging and the Moving Times: Poems New and Uncollected was published in 1976 and *The Ghost in the Wheels: Selected Poems 1970–1976* in the following year.   [PQ]

BLACKBURN, THOMAS (1916–77). Poet, born in Hensingham, Cumberland, the son of the vicar. He was educated at Bromsgrove School and Cambridge but was sent down. His autobiography *A Clip of Steel* (1969) tells a remarkable tale of paternal oppression and acute nervous tensions in boyhood. (Father supplied the 'clip' – to render nocturnal erections painful and forestall involuntary emissions.) Blackburn's eventual recourse to alcohol had devastating effects, but the demons were exorcized. He took a degree at Durham University and taught English at St Marylebone Grammer School and the College of St Mark and St John, Chelsea. His volumes of poetry include *The Outer Darkness* (1951), *The Holy Stone* (1954), *In the Fire* (1956), *The Next World* (1958), *A Smell of Burning* (1961), *A Breathing Space* (1964), *The Devil's Kitchen* (1975) (for children) and *Selected Poems* (1976). Yeats (q.v.) was the dominant influence on Blackburn, whose poetry explores the emotional complexities of the inner and the domestic worlds by carrying on a compulsively rational tussle with the irrational. Analytical self-probing is directed towards generalization: poetry is therapy for the self and philosophy for others.

> It takes a third way between sanctity
> And madness, this artistic way, and
> Proclaims what its makers lack – the serenity
> Of a good life.

> ('The Makers')

'San Lorenzo' (*A Breathing Space*) examines very acutely 'the duplicity / Of being human' as evidenced in marrying the widow of a loved husband killed by cancer, and assimilating her past. Blackburn's range of tone and substance may be gathered from comparing the profoundly moving prayer of 'Hospital for Defectives' with the cheerfully dry ironies of the poem on lecturing in English Literature, 'Teaching Wordsworth'. Blackburn's novel, *The Feast of the Wolf* (1971), traces the disintegration of an English professor who fails to exorcize the demons of alcohol and violence, and climbs to his death on a Welsh mountain.   [HB]

BLACKWOOD, ALGERNON (1869–1951). Short-story writer and novelist, born in Kent, the son of Sir Arthur Blackwood, Secretary to the Post Office. He was educated at a Moravian school in Germany, at Wellington and at Edinburgh University. His autobiography, *Episodes Before Thirty* (1923), gives a lively account of his wandering life and numerous occupations in Canada and the USA before his return to England, where his first collection of stories, *The Empty House* (1906), proved so successful that he made writing his career. Subsequent collections include *John Silence* (1908), *Pan's Garden* (1912), *The Dance of Death* (1927) and *Tales of the Uncanny and the Supernatural* (1949). Blackwood's exploitation of the supernatural was based on a serious interest in the possibility of paranormal extensions of consciousness. In the novel *The Human Chord* (1910) his hero is taken to a remote house in Wales where a clergyman is investigating the latent power of sound on the theory that 'the properties of things are merely the "muffled utterances of the sounds that made them''. The thing itself is its name.' His ultimate experiment is to try to name the ineffable Name, and there is inherent risk of releasing diabolical instead of divine energies. Thus Blackwood anticipates the 'spiritual thriller' of Charles Williams (q.v.), but his rhetoric is less disciplined even than Williams's and the theological basis less articulate. A later novel, *A Prisoner in Fairyland* (1913), was dramatized as *The Starlight Express* (1914) for which Elgar wrote incidental music. Blackwood's literary career ended with an Indian summer as a story-teller on television.   [HB]

BLAKE, GEORGE (1893–1961). Scottish novelist, born in Greenock, Strathclyde, Scotland, and educated at Greenock Academy. While serving in the First World War he was wounded at Gallipoli; in the Second World War he served in the Ministry of Information. He worked professionally in journalism and publishing. Keenly opposed to false literary romanticization of Scotland, Blake wrote numerous novels about industrial Glasgow and Clydeside. *The Shipbuilders* (1935) provides an impressive documentation of the effect of the inter-war slump on Clydeside shipyards at the commercial and at the personal level. The story opens with the ceremonial launching of a ship by the firm of Pagans whose boss privately knows that 'there was not a single order on the books'. Built around the lives of Leslie Pagan, young shipyard boss, and Danny Shields, journeyman riveter, who were side-by-side as officer and batman through the war and now inhabit their separate worlds, the book is authentic about the way of life of both rich and poor, and conditions in the depressed areas are vividly brought home. Among later novels are the successful series *The Westering Sun* (1946), *The Five Arches* (1947) and *The Voyage Home* (1952). *The Piper's Tune* (1950) chronicles the interwoven lives of two Clydeside families, those of Rab Rollo, wealthy yacht-owner, wanton and wilful, and Wee Moray Marr, an ambitious boat-builder, from the early 1930s to 1946. Though again packed with documentary interest, the novel diffuses narrative content too widely and sags under its own weight. Blake's non-fiction works include *The Heart of Scotland* (1934) and *Down to the Sea* (1937) as well as the critical study *Barrie and the Kailyard School* (1951).   [HB]

BLUNDEN, EDMUND (1896–1974). Poet and prose writer, born in London of parents who were both schoolteachers. They moved to Yalding, Kent, where Edmund was brought up, attending the local grammar school until he won a scholarship to Christ's Hospital, Horsham. This 'Bluecoats school' was where Charles Lamb, Coleridge and Leigh Hunt had been educated, and Blunden was to interest himself in all three of them (see *Leigh Hunt: A Biography*, 1930; *Charles Lamb and his Contemporaries*, 1933). He also wrote a history of the school (*Christ's Hospital: A Retrospect*, 1923) and contributed a dramatic piece in verse and prose, *A Dede of Pittie*, to the school's quatercentenary celebrations in 1953. He won a classics scholarship at Queen's College, Oxford, in 1914, but did not take it up till after the war. While still at school he had

arranged the publication of his first book of verse, *Poems* (1914), with a Horsham bookseller.

Blunden joined the Royal Sussex Regiment in 1914. His service in France betweeen 1916 and 1918 included action on the Somme front and in the Ypres salient. The third battle of Ypres, as it began on 31 July 1917, is vividly described at the climax of Blunden's most distinctive prose work, *Undertones of War* * (1928) ('I had to thrust aside my *Cambridge Magazine* with Siegfried Sassoon's splendid war on the war in it; sent my valise to the dump; and fell in'). The book contains poems too, and 'Third Ypres' depicts the first day of the same offensive in blank verse with concentrated dramatic power:

> Runner, stand by a second. Your message. – He's
>   gone,
> Falls on a knee, and his right hand uplifted
> Claws his last message from his ghostly enemy,
> Turns stone-like. Well I liked him, that young
>   runner,
> But there's no time for that.

After the war Blunden went to Oxford, but war experience had left him unfit for settling down to student life there and he moved to London in 1920 as assistant editor of *The Athenaeum* (under Middleton Murry (q.v.)), to which he continued to contribute when it was shortly taken over by *The Nation*. Early postwar volumes of poems included *The Waggoner and Other Poems* (1920) and *The Shepherd and Other Poems of Peace and War* (1922). In 1924, prompted in the first place by Ralph Hodgson (q.v.), Blunden went out to Japan to become Professor of English Literature at the Tokyo Imperial University. The appointment proved remarkably successful in both academic and human terms, as can be gathered from the verse tribute, 'The Author's Last Words to His Students', with which Blunden marked his departure from Japan in 1927. He returned to England and to Kent, with the manuscript of *Undertones of War* in his baggage, and in 1931 became a Fellow of Merton College, Oxford, where he taught in the English school. The book, *We'll Shift our Ground, or Two on a Tour; Almost a Novel* (1933) – also almost an autobiography – was written in collaboration with Sylva Norman, the Shelley scholar, whom Blunden married in 1933. Blunden's own critical biographies include an important study, *Shelley* (1946), as well as his volume, *Thomas Hardy* (1941), in the 'English Men of Letters' series. He left Oxford for London again in 1943 to work on the staff of the *Times Literary Supplement*. He married Claire Margaret Poynting in 1945, and in 1947 returned to Japan as cultural Liaison Officer to the British Mission in Tokyo. The Japanese honoured him by election to membership of the Japanese Academy in 1950. From 1953 to 1964 he was Professor of English Literature at Hong Kong University. He was elected to the Professorship of Poetry at Oxford in 1967 in succession to Robert Graves (q.v.), but ill-health compelled him to resign the post in 1968.

Blunden's enthusiastic work on John Clare, whose poems he edited in 1920, is characteristic of his own poetic affinities with writers who have observantly and affectionately recaptured in verse the detail of the countryside. Memorable early poems like 'The Barn' and 'The Pike' have a tough verbal delicacy like the disciplined delicacy of the strong-fingered concert-pianist. Exercises in fastidious pastoralism, like 'Almswomen' and 'Forefathers', have a sturdiness of fibre that enables sentiment to ring clear and true. In later lyrics Blunden is sometimes something of a sage moralist, deriving tokens of our universal nature and destiny from particular personal whim or observation (as in the title poem of *After the Bombing*, 1949, or 'Young Fieldmouse' from *New Poems* included in the 1957 collection, *Poems of Many Years*):

> We try our makeshifts, one by one they pass;
> It tries; but in the end, in the long green grass,
> The infant body stiffens, and the frame
> Of the universe, to us, dies a little with the same.
>   ('Young Fieldmouse')

There persisted throughout Blunden's poetic career intermittent uneasy reminders of war's shadow – an eye for symbolic incongruity and disparate juxtaposition opened wide by the early encounter with massive and unnatural violence; but on the other hand 'The Sum of All', *Poems 1930–1940*, voices a mood in which a rehabilitated self has confidently come to terms with life. Unobtrusive strength inhabits a refined technique in Blunden's best work. One might apply to him what he wrote in a chapter on Gilbert White in *Nature in Literature* (1929): 'It is not necessary to make a noise in order to win immortality'. Robyn Marsack has edited *Selected Poems* (1982).

Undertones of War is one of the most telling personal records we have of the First World War. Blunden took part in action near Neuve Chapelle in what was a diversion from the Somme offensive further south on 30 June 1916, was himself moved into the Somme area for the offensive of 3 September, and was up north again in the Ypres salient before the end of 1916: he was still there for the battle of 31 July 1917. His book (which includes some poems) differs from other personal reminiscences, such as those by Sassoon (q.v.) and Graves, in that the war is not seen in the context of interrupted peace. It opens when, at Shoreham in 1916, Blunden hears that he has been ordered to France, and it closes in early 1918 as he is sent back to England for six months in a home training centre. Episodes of home leave are passed over in silence: personal links with home are not mentioned. Blunden fastens on the war scene with a sombre intensity of focus, yet with an extraordinary detachment ironically indicative of enormities that passion, heroics or grandiloquence could never match. Sometimes the gap between headquarters map work and front-line butchery is devastatingly evident through the deadpan narrative coolness. The work is an elaborate mosaic of experiences, impressions and reflections shattering in their unadorned immediacy. Understatement and surface flippancy seem to function often as the only idiom that deeply bruised human sensitivities dare trust themselves to.   [HB]

BOLT, ROBERT (1924–). Dramatist, born in Manchester, educated at Manchester Grammar School and Manchester University. He was a schoolmaster at Millfield School, Somerset, from 1952 to 1958. *Flowering Cherry* (prod 1957), a comedy with a Chekhovian base, was a commercial success and freed Bolt for writing. *A*

Man for All Seasons (prod 1960), another great commercial success, is a historical play about Sir Thomas More with a 'story rather than a plot' (Author's Preface), whose style is a 'bastardized version' of the Brechtian. It has neither the literary dimensions of analytical insight nor the dramatic cohesion of a developing human pilgrimage. *Vivat! Vivat Regina!* (prod 1970), another exercise in transposed history, has alternate episodes figuring Mary Queen of Scots and Elizabeth I of England. There is cunning stagecraft, but it cannot animate the literary clichés.   [HB]

BOND, EDWARD (1934–). Dramatist, born in North London of working-class parents and educated there. His first play, *The Pope's Wedding*, was staged in 1962. Written in East Anglian dialect, it shows Scopey, a good-hearted farm-worker, gradually infected by the obsessions of an aged, half-witted village recluse whom his young wife looks after by inherited obligation. There is strong, terse dialogue here, and even more so in *Saved* (prod 1965), in which young layabouts amuse themselves by rubbing a baby's face in its own excrement, throwing lighted matches into its pram and stoning it to death. In this kind of human context Len, another well-meaning hero, tries to get in touch and be helpful. Bond's social indignation is evident; he has a sense of humour; but his shock tactics scream at the gods. *Early Morning* (prod 1968), a grotesque, phantasmagoric work, includes a lesbian relationship between Queen Victoria and Florence Nightingale and an assassination plot by Disraeli and Prince Albert. *Lear* (prod 1971) is an extravagantly horrific parable on corruption by power; while *Bingo* (prod 1973) illustrates personal corruption by showing a retired Shakespeare making money out of a dubious land transaction, telling his daughter Judith how he hates her, and refusing to take an interest in his dying wife. *The Fool* (prod 1975) makes of the mad nineteenth-century East Anglian poet, John Clare, a pretext for another excursion into sensational violence. *The Woman* (prod 1978) fastens on the Trojan War and the fate of Hecuba for a bitty sequence of episodes embodying a clumsy sermon about war and peace. Bond divides the critics. There are those who complain that he has nothing but common liberal clichés to communicate, and those who discern a Brechtian dimension in his theatrical embodiment of dissatisfaction with society.   [HB]

BOSMAN, HERMAN CHARLES (1905–51). Journalist and short-story writer, born at Kuils River near Cape Town, South Africa. Of Afrikaner birth, he received an English education in Johannesburg which awakened an interest in English literature and American frontier humour. After teaching in a frontier-like environment near Groot Marico, Western Transvaal, he served a four-and-a-half years' sentence from 1926 for shooting his stepbrother dead in the heat of a quarrel. He became a journalist, spent nine years in Europe and worked again at journalism in South Africa until his death.

As 'Herman Malan' he published two volumes of romantic verse in the 1930s, then a novel, *Jacaranda in the Night* (1947), but his steadily growing literary reputation rests on his short stories, *Mafeking Road* (1947), and various posthumous collections of short fiction, *Unto Dust*

(1963), *Jurie Steyn's Post Office* (1971), *A Bekkersdal Marathon* (1971), and essays and sketches in *A Cask of Jerepigo* (1957). *Cold Stone Jug* (1949) is a painful, though laughter-filled, account of a sensitive man's prison experience. The *Mafeking Road* and *Unto Dust* stories about rural Afrikaners form a comic counterpart to the tragic writings of Pauline Smith (q.v.); Bosman uses a narrator, Oom Schalk Lourens, whose wry, laconic pose of emotional detachment allows for great variety of tone, from light-hearted shrewdness of observation ('Splendours from Ramoutsa'), through low-key irony which tilts at many South African shibboleths ('Marico Scandal'), to satire ('Veld Maiden') and unsentimental pathos ('The Rooinek'). *Willemsdorp* (1977) is a posthumous novel. *Collected Works* (2 vols) appeared in 1981.   [AR]

BOTTOMLEY, GORDON (1874–1948). Poet and dramatist, born in Yorkshire, the son of a businessman, and educated at Keighley Grammar School. He was afflicted by tubercular haemorrhages which dogged him from 1892 for the rest of his life, disabling him from employment and compelling him to live quietly in the country, where he made literature his life-interest. Strongly influenced by Rossetti, he became a poet and verse-dramatist romantically unconcerned with the immediate contemporary world but convinced that 'art is a distillation of life and nature – not a recording or a commenting, and only incidentally an interpretation'. *King Lear's Wife* (prod 1915), a dramatic prelude to Shakespeare's play, revolves around the death of Lear's wife, Hygd, while *Gruach* (1921, prod 1923), a prelude to *Macbeth*, shows Macbeth carrying off Morag, the restless and rebellious future Lady Macbeth, on the eve of her wedding to a less sensational partner. Bottomley's plays are close to Yeats's (q.v.) in spirit and in style. His mother was a Gordon, and increasing interest in the Celtic movements and in the Japanese Nō plays turned him into a kind of Scots Yeats, tackling historical and legendary material in *The Women from the Voe*, *The White Widow*, *Fire at Callart* and *Deirdre*. These he called his 'plays for the Theatre Unborn' as opposed to his earlier 'plays for the Theatre Outworn' (*King Lear's Wife* etc). See *Gordon Bottomley, Poems and Plays*, ed. C.C. Abbott (1953).   [HB]

BOTTRALL, RONALD (1906–). Poet, born in Cornwall, educated at Redruth County School and Pembroke College, Cambridge. He has held academic posts in Finland, Singapore and Florence, and been British Council representative in Sweden, Italy, Brazil, Greece and Japan. His early poetry, *The Loosening and Other Poems* (1931) and *Festivals of Fire* (1934), won immediate critical acclaim from F.R. Leavis (q.v.) and others. A disciple of Pound, he emulated his master's cosmopolitan sophistication and his work is often metaphorically dense and obliquely allusive. Indeed it often seems too exuberantly overcharged with clamant talk to yield digestible fruit, yet Edith Sitwell (q.v.), introducing Bottrall's *Selected Poems* (1946), noted how his poems 'draw wealth from depth: they have a sheer ripple of thew and muscle'; and Charles Tomlinson (q.v.), introducing Bottrall's *Collected Poems* (1961), found a vein of 'moral resistance' running through the seemingly negative evocations of our spiritual wastelands of muddle, waste

and unfulfilment. *Poems 1955–1973* (1974) includes 'Talking to the Ceiling', a sustained and engaging poem about Bottrall's Cornish childhood. *Reflections on the Nile* (1980) includes reflective and descriptive pieces of welcome lucidity and precision.   [HB]

BOWEN, ELIZABETH (1899–1973). Novelist, born in Dublin, Ireland. Her father came of a Welsh family that had been granted an Irish estate by Oliver Cromwell. The author inherited Bowen's Court near Kildorrery, County Cork, on her father's death in 1928. Her history of the home, *Bowen's Court* (1942), contains formative childhood memories. When she was 7 her father suffered a mental illness and her mother brought her to England. She was educated at Downe House School, Kent. In 1923 she married Alan Charles Cameron and settled at Headington, Oxford, but returned to Ireland for some years after her husband's death in 1952. She was awarded a D Litt by Trinity College, Dublin, in 1948 and by Oxford University in 1956.

In *Notes on Writing a Novel* (1945) Elizabeth Bowen defined the purpose of a novel as the 'non-poetic statement of a poetic truth' whose essence is 'that no statement of it can be final'. In fact Bowen brings a sharp poetic sensibility to bear on her study of close human relationships and the loneliness that subsists within them. Her method effectively combines the meticulousness of Henry James with the clarity of Jane Austen. Her subtle sense of the social comedy, especially of the emotional and psychological complexities below the surface of humdrum family and social interchange, has penetration, irony and often humour. She focuses generally on a girl or woman whose emotional antennae are hyper-sensitive and whose personal hunger for love or security keeps her teetering on the edge of unhappiness. Bowen's is a feminine world into which so-called 'social issues' scarcely intrude, but detached authorial reflection often adds philosophic dimension ('Habit is not mere subjugation, it is a tender tie: when one remembers habit it seems to have been happiness', *The Death of the Heart*). The first novel, *The Hotel* (1927), pictures a scene of postwar triviality into which a vulnerable but intelligent young woman, Sydney Warren, is thrust. In *The Last September* (1929) Lois Farquar, a 19-year-old English orphan, is at an Irish country house in 1920 for the Troubles. In *To the North* (1932) Emmeline Summers commits herself ingenuously to a perverse poseur, Markie Linkwater.

In the two great central books of the author's career, *The House in Paris* (1936) and *The Death of the Heart* (1938), the vulnerability of the young is exposed with painful thoroughness as the sins of the fathers are visited upon the children. *The House in Paris* portrays the child Leopold, an unlooked-for offspring, locked within himself in lonely isolation. In *The Death of the Heart*, Portia Quayne is the unwanted fruit of a ridiculous liaison that destroyed the settled married life of her father and sent him on pointless travels with an incongruous partner. Orphaned and bequeathed at 16 to a stepbrother and his wife, Portia finds herself in a lovelessly insensitive household and falls in love with a worthless poseur, Eddie, who can no more answer her emotional needs than can her shallow relatives. The very depth and persistence of her unanswerable idealistic demands make her alienation and isolation inevitable. She is inwardly damaged in a tragi-comic sequence of rejections. The study brings to full maturity Bowen's uncanny gift for registering the maturing experience of sensitive women and in particular for tracing the transmutation of girlish innocence and idealism into wounded understanding. There are descriptive passages in the book, such as the opening scene in Regent's Park in winter, that tingle with atmosphere. Technical narrative adroitness and acute psychological perception guarantee memorability.

The Heat of the Day (1949) is set in wartime London and brilliantly recaptures the feel of it. The personal story is counterpointed tellingly against the unfolding national drama. Stella Rodway, a widow in her late thirties, is visited by an agent, Harrison, himself in love with her, who knows that her lover, Robert Kelway, is selling his country. Though the two men are somewhat unconvincing and the dénouement rather stagey, Stella's dilemma is searchingly probed. The prose has at times both intellectual intensity and metaphorical vigour. Bowen has a sharp eye for incidents that crystallize the intricacies of tangled relationships or states of mind. The later novels, A World of Love (1955), The Little Girls (1964) and Eva Trout (1969), show a movement away from naturalism to a more poetic sense of characters as universal human symbols.

As a short-story writer Bowen concentrated on rendering 'the significance of the small event'. The Collected Stories of Elizabeth Bowen (1981) contains over seventy stories. It has an introduction by Angus Wilson who notes 'her determination that life seen will only survive on the page when it has met the strictest demands from form and elegance'. Reviewing the collection, William Trevor (q.v.) observed that Elizabeth Bowen was inspired by the unfamiliar, that many of her stories echo with mystery and are charged with the connection between past and present. Her point of view as an artist took colour from her feeling that 'the Anglo-Irish were really only at home in mid-crossing between Holyhead and Dun Laoghaire'. There are some autobiographical chapters in the posthumous Pictures and Conversations (1975).   [HB]

BOYD, MARTIN (1893–1972). Novelist, born in Lucerne, Switzerland, during one of his parents' tours of Europe. The quest for a true spiritual home is a recurrent theme in his writing. Both his parents came from old and distinguished colonial families of Victoria, Australia, who had settled before the population boom which followed the gold rushes of the 1850s. After an idyllic childhood, and education at Trinity Grammar School, Melbourne, he failed his entrance examination to Melbourne University and entered a theological college. This he soon abandoned and took up the study of architecture. At the outbreak of the First World War he enlisted in England and later transferred to the Royal Flying Corps. He felt out of place in Melbourne after the war and in 1921 returned to England to try his hand at writing. In 1948 he returned to his grandfather's house at Berwick, Victoria, but fell ill during a trip to England in 1951 and never returned. From 1957 he lived in Rome. His first three novels were published under the name of Martin Mills and with the third of these, The Montforts (1928), he

found his true vein with a chronicle history of his mother's à Beckett family. In tracing the changes brought about in an English family by migration to Australia, Boyd also explores the urban social scene in Melbourne at a time when the outback, rural tradition still predominated in Australian fiction. The Picnic (1936) anticipates his later 'Langton' novels in drawing upon family history; the autobiography A Single Flame (1939) describes his restlessness during the 1930s and his abhorrence of fascism. Lucinda Brayford (1946) marked a return to family chronicle with one-third of the book set in England and the remainder in Australia. The Cardboard Crown (1952) concentrates more upon a particular episode of family history which is nevertheless related to those upon which successive novels focus. The book deals with the generation of Boyd's grandparents and Outbreak of Love (1957) extends this treatment into his own parents' times. A Difficult Young Man (1955) explores his own generation and When Blackbirds Sing (1962) forms the second part of this story. The move to Rome was mirrored in Much Else in Italy (1958), 'A Subjective Travel Book', while Day of My Delight (1965) was 'An Anglo-Australian Memoir' of largely autobiographical pieces. Although strongly rooted in personal and family experience Boyd's fiction displays masterly handling of time and perspective in its exploration of the intricate relations between personal fate and family inheritance. He himself wrote that 'the greatness of a novel depends on its content of humanity'; largely neglected during his lifetime as an expatriate from both Australia and England, recent recognition of his achievement suggests that time may prove his opinion – and the value of his writings.   [PQ]

BRADBURY, MALCOLM (1932–). Novelist, born in Sheffield, South Yorkshire, and educated at the universities of Leicester, London and Manchester. After holding a university teaching post in English at Birmingham from 1961, he became Professor of American Studies at the University of East Anglia in 1970. Eating People Is Wrong (1959) portrays life at a redbrick university in the Midlands, in particular the antics of Professor Stuart Treece, head of the English Department, bachelor, ineffective idealist and liberal humanist at odds with all tendencies towards academic utilitarianism ('our function is to talk about what is good when the rest of the world is talking about what is profitable'); but serious treatment of this liberal dilemma is swamped in farce, palatably salted by wit. Stepping Westward (1965) follows an angry young Nottingham writer to a mediocre American university as writer-in-residence, but the satire is now weakened by sheer inflation and over-documentation; and The History Man (1975) suffers from the same excesses. In Rates of Exchange (1983) an English academic goes lecturing in East Europe in the new decade of Thatcherite Sado-Monetarism.   [HB]

BRAGG, MELVYN (1939–). Novelist, born and brought up at Wigton, Cumberland, and educated at the local grammar school and at Wadham College, Oxford. He has worked as a producer for BBC television and has become widely known as a television personality. 'As a novelist, he has re-created the life of twentieth-century Cumberland with outstanding success', Norman

Nicholson, a fellow Cumbrian, has written (*Times Literary Supplement*, 20. 8. 76). *For Want of a Nail* (1965) is an emotionally powerful study of growing up in the Wigton area. The book is rich, indeed poetic, in texture: from infancy Tom Graham's fantasy world of day-dreaming impinges on the real world, and as he grows older, might-have-been sequences are interleaved with the have-beens. Victim of a weak father, a wayward mother, a deceptive 'uncle' and other less-than-adequate pastors and mentors, Tom, a sensitive boy, is surrounded by vividly real people. In tracing his adolescent confrontation with religion and with the onset of sex, Bragg manages for the most part to skate nimbly round the clichés of the rebellion pattern. Intra-family relationships are analysed with insight and acumen. In *The Second Inheritance* (1966) there is a uniquely complex pattern of family interaction under the dominion of a dour and ambitious Cumbrian, Nelson Foster, self-made farmer whose work is his exclusive obsession. The family circle, its tensions, its backchat, its quarrels and its humour come alive. Nelson's son, John, cannot escape the devoted parental tyranny, but the world of middle-class culture and of sexual exaltation impinges on his earthy environment through the neighbouring family of Colonel Langley. Here as elsewhere it is often exciting to see what Bragg can make words do in serving his descriptive and analytical purposes. *Without a City Wall* (1968) has a Cumbrian heroine; *The Nerve* (1971), a study in nervous breakdown, has a London setting; but in *Josh Lawton* (1972) Bragg reverts to Cumbria for a swift village tragedy caused by a young wife's adultery. *The Hired Man* (1969), the story of a Cumbrian farm-labourer, John Tallentire, covering the period from 1898 to the early 1920s, became the first novel of a trilogy about four generations of the Tallentire family. *A Place in England* (1970) and *Kingdom Come* (1980) continue the chronicle, which eventually fans out from the base in Cumbria to London and America, as younger generations get involved in the world of literature, television and pop music.

In *Speak for England* (1976) Bragg recorded the reminiscences of some sixty men and women who have lived and worked in his native Wigton. A fascinating picture of the social history of our century is unfolded by a well-chosen cross-section of the inhabitants.   [HB]

BRAINE, JOHN (1922–). Novelist, born in Bradford, West Yorkshire, and educated at St Bede's Grammar School, Bradford. After false starts at various jobs and a period of war service in the navy, he worked in the public library at Bingley and made himself a qualified librarian. He later held county library posts with Northumberland and the West Riding until the enormous success of his first novel, *Room at the Top* (1957), enabled him to turn full-time writer. He married Helen Patricia Wood in 1955 and has four children. He now lives in Surrey. *Room at the Top* was quickly associated with Kingsley Amis's (q.v.) *Lucky Jim* (1954) and John Osborne's (q.v.) *Look Back in Anger* (1956) as a key book of what was called the 'Angry Young Man' movement. Joe Lampton, its hero, is an ambitious northerner, hyper-sensitive to the way the middle and upper classes have cornered the material good things of life and deny such young men as he the

social footing, poise and gloss necessary to success. Orphaned by a German bomb in the war, he establishes himself in suburbia as a local authority clerk in the Treasurer's department. There he is seized with ambition to rise to the top. Amateur theatricals give him contacts that cross the social barriers. Irritated and stimulated by his unacceptability to the social establishment, he finds Susan Brown, a wealthy businessman's daughter, not only loving and lovable, but also personally and socially covetable. On the other hand an older, more experienced married woman, Alice Aisgill, involves him in a torridly passionate liaison where commitment is sexually rapturous and personally total. When the testing time comes, Joe chooses Susan and success, while Alice is abandoned and commits suicide. Joe's capacity for devastating self-judgement adds force and subtlety to the portrayal. In the sequel, *Life at the Top* (1962), Joe learns by experience the superficiality and aridity of life at the top, and the backlash of the torrid love affair which he sacrificed in his climb still troubles him in family life. Braine's strength lies in his skill at analysing the potent currents of self-interest that sweep over the individual's attempts to live in genuine emotional self-involvement as a human and sexual being, and often corrupt his proper respect for the personalities of others.

Among later novels are *The Jealous God* (1965), *The Crying Game* (1968), *Stay with Me till Morning* (1970; in USA as *The View from Tower Hill*) and *Waiting for Sheila* (1976). There is a revealing analysis of a novelist's tendency to exploit all experience in the interest of his literary career in *The Queen of a Distant Country* (1972) – a novel that should be read alongside Braine's subsequent textbook of literary craftsmanship, *Writing a Novel* (1974), an enlightening indication of how thoroughly he has worked at his craft. The narrator of the novel, Tom Metfield, himself a novelist, looks back over personal experiences that became fictional fodder. His gradual, piecemeal acquisition of material for his 'first novel' plainly sheds light on the genesis of *Room at the Top*. The ironic reduplication involved in this trick of writing in the first person qua writer surveying his own life as means to his own fiction has a Kierkegaardian flavour. The moral investigation of exploitation – of self, others, sex, experience of all kinds – is basic to Braine, who misses profundity perhaps only through lack of overall psychomachic clarity and consistency. He is a writer to his finger tips, with a lively mind, a gift for acute observation and deadly deflation. *One and Last Love* (1981) portrays a smugly successful middle-aged writer with an acute appetite for feminine adulation, literary and sexual. [HB]

BRASCH, CHARLES (1909–73). Poet and editor of *Landfall**, born in Dunedin, New Zealand, and educated at Oxford University. After travel to Europe, Africa and the United States, and two visits to New Zealand, he finally returned there after the Second World War. Together with Denis Glover (q.v.) he founded the periodical *Landfall* in 1947 as a forum for cultural debate: 'To relate: that is one of the chief social – and spiritual – functions of the arts'. The journal's historical importance might be compared with that of the earlier *Bulletin* (q.v.) in Australia. He retired as editor in 1966. His early poetry collections *The Land and its People*

(1939) and *Home Ground* (1943) were concerned with a mythopoeic approach to New Zealand which at its best produced a fine poem such as 'The Islands (ii)' but also led to much over-solemn verse. *Disputed Ground* (1948) was in similar vein, but *The Estate* (1957) and *Ambulando* (1964) struck a quiet elegiac note, the latter volume revealing more personal dimensions at times.

Landfall, 'A New Zealand Quarterly', was founded by Brasch in 1947. His first editorial, for March 1947, announced the journal's chief concern to be 'with the arts of which literature is one' and against all expectation it went on to set new standards not only for the level of contributions and quality of production but also for efficiency and sheer survival. Under . Brasch's editorship (1947–66) it provided a forum for discussion and an opening for numerous New Zealand writers. In 1951 it received its first grant from the State Literary Fund. In the third number Brasch described it as having been 'planned in the light, though not in the image, of three English literary journals' – the *Adelphi*, the *Criterion* and the *Dublin Review*. The title of the journal was taken from the bicentennial poem 'Landfall in Unknown Seas' by the New Zealand poet, Allen Curnow (q.v.). A useful selection of published material, including editorials, was collected in *Landfall Country* (1962) edited by Brasch. [PQ]

BRATHWAITE, EDWARD KAMAU (formerly L. Edward) (1930–). Poet, critic, historian, born in Bridgetown, Barbados, and educated at Harrison College (Barbados), Pembroke College, Cambridge, in 1950–4, and the University of Sussex (D Phil, 1968). In 1960 he married Doris Monica Welcombe. After serving as an education officer in Ghana from 1955 to 1962 he was appointed to the University of the West Indies, St Lucia, and became Senior Lecturer in History at Mona, Jamaica, in 1972. A founder-member of the Caribbean Artists Movement, London, in 1966, he has co-edited the West Indian journal *Savacou* since 1970. He has won various awards, including a Guggenheim Fellowship (1972).

Brathwaite's poems were published in Caribbean literary periodicals before his first volume, *Rights of Passage*, appeared in 1967. It was followed by *Masks* (1968) and *Islands* (1969), the three being reprinted together as *The Arrivants: A New World Trilogy* (1973). A slim volume, *Days and Nights*, came out in 1975 and a longer work, *Mother Poem*, in 1977. In addition to plays for school use in Ghana, Brathwaite has published numerous critical articles, historical monographs and *The Development of Creole Society in Jamaica* (1971).

His professional training as a historian has interacted fruitfully with his gifts as a poet in the *Arrivants* trilogy, which, in a structure of separate poems that constitute 'movements', not unlike those in *Four Quartets* by T.S. Eliot (q.v.), explores the history, culture and present-day situation of Caribbean man, victim of slavery and colonialism. If the method has been broadly suggested by *Four Quartets*, with even odd phrases and cadences derived from Eliot, the work is nevertheless highly original and Brathwaite a technically very accomplished poet with a rich imagination.

Rights of Passage is divided into four parts, *Masks* into

six, *Islands* into five: each part consists of from three to seven separate poems of varying length, related to one another (and to other poems throughout the trilogy) thematically or by deliberate verbal reiterations or inversions. Not only does the structure thus resemble a complex musical composition, but the verse form in individual poems captures the rhythms of such Caribbean and plantation forms as work songs, blues and calypso, in a conscious effort to naturalize popular verbal art within a modern 'literary' poem. The dominant theme of *Rights of Passage* is rootlessness and enforced migration, especially of the African diaspora caused by slavery. Out of his despair over this rootlessness, the poet feels his way through the rhythms of song and dance that slavery in the western hemisphere built upon native African musical expression, and so gathers into the movement of his verse fragments of an African cultural heritage that give new insights into Caribbean man's identity. He laments not only the fate of slaves on the middle passage but also the sufferings of today's black dispossessed, 'path-less, harbour-less', from Cape Town to 'Chicago, Smethwick and Tiger Bay'. Different personae dramatize the roles that dispossession has forced upon slaves and their descendants: the communal voice of the leaderless black masses ('New World A-Comin' '); the subservient Uncle Toms who nevertheless 'dare to remember' the Golden Stool of Ashanti ('Tom'); the black man who acts out the white stereotype of the Negro:

> a fuck-
> in' negro,
> man, hole
> in my head,
> brains in
> my belly

> ('Folkways')

Such are the means Brathwaite uses to assemble an intricate kaleidoscopic impression of bitter black experience in the New World – a counterpointing of hopelessness and high spirits, of mockery, irony, satire.

Masks explores the culture of the slaves' ancestors in its modern living forms in Africa, especially in the Ashanti region of Ghana. It is the poet's pilgrimage to find his people's cultural origins and psychological genealogy, in the history of black empires, in the ways of life of savannah and forest, of river and sea coast, in the fashioning of ceremonial drums, in celebrations of the agricultural year, in appeals to the gods for guidance, in commemorations of disasters and meditation upon the transcendence of disaster, in invocation to the Divine Drummer to 'knock' the representative persona awake and into true independence. *Masks* is a religious poem put to cultural, political and psychotherapeutic purposes on behalf of a whole people; African ritual is used both to search for the genuine identity of the deracinated blacks and to affirm their essential vitality. *Masks* repeatedly, in G. Rohlehr's words, 'returns to the dance, symbol of transcendence'. This exploration is not the nostalgic African dream of some earlier West Indian writers, but a realistic appraisal of racial energies expressed in differing yet similar sensuous modes on both sides of the Atlantic.

Islands attempts a new stock-taking of Caribbean man,

continuing the religious mood and imagery of *Masks* by probing the possible ways in which God, the remote fisherman, may be trying to gather his fish, the common people of the black diaspora: old bridges of song (spirituals, blues, work songs) collapse in the mechanized cities, but the primeval rhythm isn't totally expunged; the Ananse tales are thin remnants of a plenteous African mythology; a blind fisherman (clearly a poet-figure) hears the song of the 'keeper of the tribe' and hopes light will come before her song ends. It is an ambivalent world of past catastrophe, present uncertainty, future possibility – separation from ancient founts of life is imaged in sea overwhelming firm land, in (at a cricket match) the lack of sound men 'to hole up de side'. Yet the dumb gods speak kinetically through the *pocomania* dancer possessed, and they 'still have their places' in nature upon the islands ('they speak to us with the voices of crickets / with the shatter of leaves'). The alternating currents of suffering remembered and sustenance received are skilfully figured in 'Caliban', where the limbo dance enacts both the claustrophobia of 'tween-decks on a slave ship, and support from the gods raising the dancer upright again from under the limbo stick. An important constituent of the islanders' experience is mounting rage at all the outward signs of neo-colonial 'development' and materialism. This rage accompanies the poet's welcoming of sensuous receptivity, of dreams, of the Word of love no less than the angry words needed 'to refashion futures / like a healer's hand'. Violence, it is hinted, is probably necessary before the people can possess themselves fully and legitimately. Part IV, 'Possession', recapitulates the islands' history, not in lamentation and anger as in *Rights of Passage*, but as a process of coral growth stimulated but not destroyed by irritants and pain. Uncle Tom is no longer seen as a figure of nullity only but merges with the image of a magnificent tiger, caged but still containing its natural powers. In the final part, 'Beginning', the West Indian carnival, the *vodoun* ceremony, dancing and drumming become sources of potential growth: 'now waking / making / making / with their / rhythms some- / thing torn / and new'.

These brief comments on so complex a poetic work as Brathwaite's trilogy necessarily over-simplify, but one does wonder whether the ending isn't too facile, the grounds for regeneration and restitution too flimsy. Brathwaite's achievement lies in the width and coherence of his poetic imagination realized through mastery over a wide range of disparate metrical forms and, in K. Ramchand's words, 'an ease of entry at all points of a linguistic scale . . . from . . . sedate Standard English . . . to . . . dialect'. Nevertheless, that very ease sometimes finds irresistible the temptation of punning for mere gamesomeness, the kind of weakness which may explain why Ramchand dismisses the later work *Mother Poem*, the first long poem in a new trilogy, as 'self-satisfied and gimmicky', though M. McWatt finds it 'a powerful and rhythmic evocation . . . of the poet's motherland'.   [AR]

BRENNAN, CHRISTOPHER (1870–1932). Poet, born in Sydney, New South Wales, Australia, of Irish immigrant parents. After a Jesuit schooling he read classics and philosophy at Sydney University. In 1892 he obtained a two-year travelling scholarship to Berlin where he studied classics and acquired a profound understanding of ancient and modern literatures. He fell in love with the daughter of his landlady, and she joined Brennan in Sydney in 1897 after he had found employment there in the public library. In March 1897 Brennan published *XVIII Poems* (eight copies only) and in July *XXI Poems*, subtitled 'Towards the Source', a collection which revealed the extent of his reading in romantic and symbolist literature of the nineteenth century. *The Prose of Christopher Brennan* (1962) contains contemporary critical writings which illuminate his aims in poetry, including his interest in the *livre composé*, which he defined as 'the sublimation of a whole imaginative life and experience into a subtly ordered series of poems, where each piece has, of course, its individual value, yet cannot be interpreted save in its relation to the whole'. In 1908 he took over responsibility for French lectures at Sydney University and his own *livre composé*, *Poems*, was published in 1914; it was reprinted in 1972. This volume included seventeen poems from the 1897 collection within a single five-movement structure, linked by their exploration of man's yearning for a lost Eden – a hopeless quest which yields the recognition that even the mere search can lend meaning to life in this post-lapsarian world. Man seeks paradise in the fabric of civilization and empire and in sexual union, but failure leads him to Lilith, the Lady of Night. A passage from *The Symbolist Movement in Literature* (1899) by Arthur Symons (q.v.) which Brennan marked in his own copy expressed the nature of the poem sequence: 'All love is . . . a desire of the infinite in humanity, and, as humanity has its limits, it can but return sadly upon itself when that limit is reached'. Man's search is doomed to failure, and the final sequence, entitled 'The Wanderer', expresses the attempt to find fulfilment within the flux of time. The Epilogue to the volume, entitled '1908', is unusual in its local and autobiographical references.

Brennan was appointed to an associate professorship in German and Comparative Literature at Sydney University in 1920, but he had a drink problem and in 1922 he left home to live with a woman he referred to as 'Vie'; her accidental death three years later was a cruel blow. In June 1925 his wife's separation proceedings came to court, and amid growing scandal he was dismissed from his university post. He died in 1932, having turned again to the Catholic Church in the last month of his life. His work can only be fully understood within the context of nineteenth-century European poetry and philosophy, although the images of personal isolation and of physical and spiritual desolation in 'The Wanderer' suggest comparison with Australian writers such as Henry Lawson (q.v.) and Patrick White (q.v.). He had become an agnostic in 1890 and *Poems* is in one sense a record of the spiritual restlessness which characterized his life – 'the fate of the soul intoxicated with perfection'. It is on the 1914 sequence that his reputation rests; the two volumes

of war poetry, *XV Poems: The Burden of Tyre* (1953) and
A Chant of Doom (1918), do not enhance it.   [PQ]

BRIDGES, ROBERT (1844–1930). Poet and critic, born
at Walmer on the Kent coast into a well-to-do middle-class
family. He was educated at Eton and at Corpus Christi
College, Oxford, where he read Greats. He lived his life to
a predetermined plan, first to practise medicine, then to
settle down as a poet. After training at St Bartholomew's
and service as physician at other London hospitals, he
moved to the country in 1881 and married Monica
Waterhouse, an architect's daughter, in 1884. From 1881
to 1907 he lived at Yattenden, Berkshire, and from 1907
to his death at Boar's Hill near Oxford. Long years of
comfortable, genteel independence as poet and man of
letters gave something of their character to his poetic
output. A conscious craftsman, he devoted himself to the
manufacture of poems as things of beauty, artefacts
whose technical impeccability should match up to a high
notion of the quasi-sacramental status of the beautiful in
man's thirst for God. His disciplined mastery of prosody,
his fastidious metrical sensitivity, and his dexterity in
fashioning the felicitous phrase gave to the best work in
his three series of *Poems* (1873, 1879 and 1880) and his
Shorter Poems (1890) the kind of easily assimilable
distinction which anthologists exploit most happily.
Choice, mannered verses like 'A Passer-By' ('Whither, O
splendid ship'), 'I love all beauteous things' and 'Spring
goeth all in white' were thus to become widely known; and
so were more perceptively observant descriptive pieces
such as 'London Snow' and 'November'. Bridges, as a
nineteenth-century poet, thus gave studied artistry and
novelty of cadence to the lyric of his day, but, for all his
skill as a practitioner, there is in him too often a straining
after borrowed dignity and an excessive reliance upon
ready-made 'poetic' vocabulary and overworn devices.
Lines are sprinkled with *ye* and *thee, cometh* and *goeth,
o'er* and *'neath* and *'mong, 'tis* and *'twere, noughtsoever,
agaze, meseem'd* and the like.

Bridges became Poet Laureate in 1913. His last work
was a long philosophical poem, *Testament of Beauty*
(1929), for which he used an unrhymed Alexandrine
whose metrical basis is syllabic rather than accentual.
The four books of the poem ('Introduction', 'Selfhood',
'Breed' and 'Ethick') argue with much exemplification the
testimony of Beauty that God is love; but the argument is
embalmed in an idiom so precious, bookish and contrived
that the effect is that of a verbal museum. 'He being then a
housecarl in Loyola's menie', says the poet of his former
young companion in study, Gerard Manley Hopkins. It is
ironic that the friendship and correspondence between
the two poets and Bridges's editing of Hopkins's poems
for posthumous publication now give Bridges a surer
place in literary history than his own poetic output.   [HB]

BRIDIE, JAMES (pseudonym of Dr O.H. Mavor)
(1888–1951). Scottish dramatist, the son of a well-to-do
engineer and born into a cultured home in Glasgow,
Strathclyde, Scotland. (See his autobiography, *One Way
of Living*, 1939, issued under his own name.) He was
educated at Glasgow Academy and Glasgow University,
qualified as a doctor in 1913 and served in the RAMC
during the war. In his subsequent medical career he rose

to be Professor of Medicine in the Anderson College of
Glasgow. He married Rona Bremmer in 1923 and had two
sons. He was 40 years old by the time his first play, *The
Sunlight Sonata*, was produced in Glasgow in 1928, and
thereafter he wrote over thirty plays as well as numerous
adaptations, revised versions, and scripts for radio and
film. Of these the most celebrated are the biblical plays
on the one hand and certain 'plays of ideas' with a
Scottish setting on the other. *Tobias and the Angel*, the
first of the biblical plays (first produced at the Festival
Theatre, Cambridge, in 1930), is a 'plain-sailing dramatic
transcription of the charming old tale told in the Book of
Tobit in the Apocrypha' (Author's Note). Tobit's son
Tobias is sent from Nineveh to Rages to try to rescue the
family from poverty by collecting an old debt from a
wealthy merchant, Gabael. The porter, Azarias, who
accompanies him, is the angel Raphael in disguise. He
strengthens Tobias in his adventures en route and
enables him to marry Sara, daughter of Raguel of
Ecbatana, whose previous seven husbands have been
strangled on their wedding nights by the demon
Asmodeus. The naturalness of Bridie's dialogue, the
homeliness of the characterization, the spontaneous
gaiety of tone, and the sprinkling of piquant modernities
on a narrative frank in its supernaturalisms, give a sturdy
directness and a winning unaffectedness to a
presentation that has built-in narrative richness and
charm. The recipe was repeated (if without quite the
same degree of freshness and flair) in *Jonah and the
Whale* (prod 1932), which contains an entertaining little
scene in the Belly of the Whale ('Would you mind very,
very much if I shipped four gallons?' asks the thirsty
whale considerately of its tenant. 'Can you swim?'), and
Susannah and the Elders (prod 1937) where, among the
liberties taken with the apocryphal original, the Elders
are transformed into Assyrians – 'modern, cultivated,
respected and respectable old civil servants of the class
easily recognized as gentlemen' (Preface).

'A Play is a Story told by Actors,' Bridie avers revealingly in the same Preface, and indeed his weakness is that
the driving impetus is often narrative rather than
dramatic. There is again a ready-made interest in the
material of his first big London success, *The Anatomist*
(prod 1930), a dramatic rendering of the nefarious doings
of Burke and Hare, murderers and corpse-suppliers to the
nineteenth-century Edinburgh anatomist Dr Knox, a man
'so theatrical in his life and habit that it is possible to
transfer him almost bodily to the stage' (Author's Note).
But the play has diverse dramatic interests. A love story
involving Knox's assistant is spatchcocked on to the main
theme which itself fails to attain full cohesion in either the
airing of moral problems or the definition of Knox's role.
In *A Sleeping Clergyman* (prod 1933) weakness of structure is evident again. A chronicle play covering seventy
years, it explores the theme of heredity in an animated
genealogical history of an eminent bacteriologist, Sir
Charles Cameron, at once genius and eccentric. Two
preliminary generations of illegitimacy, of mingled
caddishness and brilliance, are unfolded in a series of
scattered 'shots'. The flavour of different periods is aptly
caught, but the sequences have anecdotal interest rather
than dramatic thrust. It is as though a novel had been
clumsily adapted for the stage.

Mr Bolfry (prod 1943) is a more tightly structured play. Two young soldiers, as well as a young niece, are wartime guests at the West Highland manse of a strict Wee Free minister, the Reverend McCrimmon. The young people, oppressed by the pious atmosphere, try their hand at midnight conjuration, and the Devil appears in the form of Mr Bolfry, to take on the company in argument. The company's wishful assumption next morning, that they have had a communal nightmare, is shot to pieces when the umbrella left behind by the visitant walks out of the room. The culminating impact of the work relies rather on the shock of the walking umbrella than on any meaningful working-out of the human and theological issues raised initially in the collision of attitudes between McCrimmon and his guests; but the entertainment value of the play is high. There is dramatic vitality again in the gradual unmasking of a villainous murderer in *Dr Angelus* (prod 1947), though tension flags through over-protraction of the dénouement, and the young doctor hero (Johnson) has to be made naïvely trustful to the point of stupidity not to see through his wicked senior (Angelus) sooner.

Bridie was instrumental in founding the Glasgow Citizens Theatre in 1942, and one of its purposes was to encourage modern Scottish playwrights. Eric Linklater described him as 'a man of no great physical attraction, but his appearance in maturity acquired a ponderous, craggy, and magnificent benignity' (*Dict. of Nat. Biog., Twentieth Century, 1951-1960*, pp. 722-4). [HB]

BRIGHOUSE, HAROLD (1882-1958). Lancashire dramatist. He belonged to the group, 'the Manchester School', who wrote north-country drama for the Gaiety Theatre, Manchester, when Miss A.E. Horniman ran it from 1907 to 1921. Brighouse's most celebrated play, *Hobson's Choice* (1916), set in the 1880s in Salford, shows a strong-willed elder sister doggedly taking on a blustering, drunken father, shoemaker and retailer, who has bullied his three daughters and his workmen, and effectively taming the tyrant. William Tydeman has argued in the 'Dramatists' volume of *Great Writers of the English Language* (ed. J. Vinson, 1979) that Brighouse's continuing reputation as a one-play dramatist fails to do justice to the varied range of his achievement, and he pleads the claims, not only of his sensitive one-acters, but also of full-length plays such as *The Odd Man Out* (1912), *Garside's Career* (1914) and *Zack* (1916). [HB]

BRITTAIN, VERA (1896-1970). Novelist, born in Newcastle under Lyme, Staffordshire, and educated at St Monica's School, Kingswood, and Somerville College, Oxford. Her novels, which include *The Dark Tide* (1923) and *Not Without Honour* (1924), are not distinguished, but her autobiographical books have a continuing fascination. *Testament of Youth* (1933) in particular gives a memorable account of her experience as a Red Cross nurse in the First World War, experience from which she emerged as a convinced pacifist. Its sequel, *Testament of Experience* (1957), covers the subsequent years up to 1950, years of writing, lecturing and campaigning in progressive causes. It records her marriage in 1925 to Professor G.E. Catlin, the political philosopher, and the birth of her daughter, the politician Shirley Williams.

Testament of Friendship (1940) is a tribute to her friend, the novelist Winifred Holtby (q.v.). [HB]

BRODERICK, JOHN (1927-). Novelist, born in Athlone, Ireland. He wrote a series of novels critically observant of provincial life in the Irish Midlands, including *The Waking of Willie Ryan* (1965) and *An Apology for Roses* (1973). The focus tends to be on unlovable characters such as Tony O'Reilly, the prosperous, go-getting, overbearing builder of *The Pride of Summer* (1976). His wife, Olive, takes refuge from him in the home of a couple of old dears who happen to be Protestants, and O'Reilly has recourse to the local dirty-tricks department to prise her out. Broderick thus contrives a framework for examining a cross-section of small-town life. On the strength of this he has been likened to Balzac. But the authorial designing hand is too patently and heavily applied, condemnation is distributed with schoolmasterly obtrusiveness, and the reader's sympathies are but fitfully engaged. [HB]

BROOKE, JOCELYN (1908-66). Novelist, born at Sandgate, Kent, the son of a Folkestone wine merchant. He was educated at Bedales (after running away from King's School, Canterbury, twice in a fortnight) and at Worcester College, Oxford. He failed to settle happily in the family business, joined up in the RAMC in 1939, re-enlisted after the war, then bought himself out when he began to publish. His most celebrated work is the trilogy of semi-fictionalized autobiography, *The Military Orchid* (1948), *A Mine of Serpents* (1949) and *The Goose Cathedral* (1950), now reissued together as *The Orchid Trilogy* (1981). Brooke was from childhood a keen and knowledgeable botanist. The lifelong search for the prized *orchis militaris* is never fulfilled, though closely related and quite rare forms of the orchid turn up from time to time. This theme, together with one based on a parallel enthusiasm for fireworks, gives a kind of overall shape to recollections and musings that are not presented chronologically but in thematic counterpoint across the years. Brooke's father had a country cottage at Bishopstoke in the Elham valley. This region, a focus of rich memories of childhood happiness, and the contrasting home on the coast were balanced for Brooke like Proust's two ways. The trilogy exercises a sustained but rather wayward charm. It recaptures not only the magic of childhood but the ironic comedy of the child's view of his elders in deft imaginative strokes. The recollections of army life and the picture of Oxford in the 1920s, where Brooke and his contemporaries ape the artificialities of manners inspired by Firbank, Wilde and Huxley, are entertaining if less remarkable. Brooke repeatedly homes in on childhood:

> How could one identify that core of reality among the *personae* of my own fabrication? Only by evoking my childhood could I achieve any conviction of my own reality.

Brooke's output included poetry (*The Elements of Death*, 1952), technical books on botany, and another five novels. Of these Anthony Powell (q.v.) has described the heavily autobiographical *The Dog at Clambercrown* (1955) as 'perhaps Brooke's best book', but *The Image of* the *Drawn Sword* (1950), though also autobiographical, is more decisively 'a novel'. It is reminiscent of Rex Warner's (q.v.) Kafkaesque novel, *The Aerodrome*. Reynard Langrish, living in a country cottage with his widowed mother, is called upon by a regular officer, Roy Archer. Reynard is immensely attracted to Roy, who puts pressure on him to join army recruits training locally. The pressure is at first friendly (and unmistakably homosexual). The invitation offers escape from the drab, routine life of a bank clerk, and the conflict between quotidian 'commonsense' and the rash project of 'enlistment' acquires overtones of a spiritual struggle to achieve the daring of surrender. But fantasy encroaches escalatingly on reality. The vague emergency that the new forces are training to counter and the mysterious tyrannical powers apparently at their disposal give an increasingly sinister and bizarre flavour to a tale which, unfortunately, ends in pure melodrama. Brooke's work suffers from limitations in the study of character and from consequent deficiency in human interest.   [HB]

BROOKE, RUPERT (1887–1915). Poet, born at Rugby, Warwickshire. His father was a schoolmaster there, later a housemaster, and the boy was eventually éducated in his own father's 'house'. He went up to King's College, Cambridge, in 1906, read for the Classical Tripos and then, in 1909, turned to study English literature. He won a scholarship with an essay, *John Webster and the Elizabethan Drama*, which was later published (1916), and King's College elected him to a fellowship in 1913. Brooke travelled a good deal, staying in Switzerland, Germany, the South Sea Islands and North America. When war came he joined the Artists' Rifles and then was given a commission in the Royal Naval Division. In October 1914 his brigade was briefly active in the Antwerp Expedition to aid the relief of the Belgians. Then, in February 1915, his division embarked for the Dardanelles and, after an attack of dysentery, he died in a hospital ship. He was buried at Skyros. He had published a volume, *Poems*, in 1911 and *1914 and Other Poems* (1915) came out soon after his death. This volume included the dramatic war sonnets which helped so much to turn Brooke into a legend. The legend was manufactured immediately. Discerning contemporaries were aware that they were in at its making and that it would last. Brooke's extraordinary personal attractiveness was basic to it. He embodied youthful freshness and the image of poethood. Meeting Brooke, Siegfried Sassoon (q.v.) spoke of an 'assured perception that I was in the presence of one on whom had been conferred all the invisible attributes of a poet. To this his radiant good looks seemed subsidiary.' Henry James (q.v.), whose last literary work was a Preface for Brooke's *Letters from America* (1916), spoke of Brooke's death as 'a stupid and hideous disfigurement of life and outrage to beauty'.

The continuation of the legend has been guaranteed by devoted biographical work (Edward Marsh's (q.v.) *Memoir* prefaced to the *Collected Poems* of 1918 was the first such sketch), some of it so thorough that we are told how Brooke's prehensile toes enabled him to strike a match with his feet, and we are invited to consider the possibility that he contributed to a Boxing Day burlesque the line, 'I sometimes think you love me for my cardigan

vest alone' (see Christopher Hassall, *Rupert Brooke*, 1964). The legend is the richer for the fact that Brooke appears to have been one of the most photographed young men of his generation. Disentangling the man from the myth, we find an engaging, restless, zestful personality who fell inconveniently in love with Noel Olivier when she was a Bedales schoolgirl of 15, with Katherine Cox at the point when she was involved with Henry Lamb the artist, and with Cathleen Nesbitt, the actress, just when Ka Cox had begun to need him. There was also Taatamata of Mataia in Tahiti, who survives bare-breasted in a photograph. Nevertheless Brooke's last message to Ka, received after his death, began: 'Dear child, I suppose you're about the best I can do in the way of a widow. . . . My dear, my dear, you did me wrong: but I have done you very great wrong. Every day I see it greater.'

Brooke belonged to a group of lively young people who were somewhat self-consciously kicking over the Victorian traces. He did what they did and did it rather passionately. They roamed abroad and gathered in parties at home; they rambled and camped in the country; they produced plays (Brooke himself helped to found the Marlowe Society at Cambridge and acted in *Dr Faustus*); and above all they talked. Nor was the talk all aesthetic and academic – though Brooke's group impinged through Lytton Strachey (q.v.) and Virginia Stephen (Woolf (q.v.)) on what was later to become the 'Bloomsbury group'. Under the influence of H.G. Wells (q.v.), Hugh Dalton and William Morris's *News from Nowhere* Brooke espoused the socialist cause and joined the Fabians. Indeed he succeeded Dalton as President of the Cambridge Fabian Society and in 1910 he joined in planning a caravan tour to speak on Poor Law Reform at open-air village meetings. He was self-reflective but never precious. The impression his appearance could make on men like David Garnett (q.v.) ('His complexion, his skin, his eyes and hair were perfect') and Edward Thomas (q.v.) ('No one that knew him could easily separate him from his poetry') was something to be joked about by his closest friends. 'So you were frank and boyish?' Frances Cornford (q.v.) asked when he had just met Henry James. 'Oh yes, of course I did the fresh boyish stunt, and it was a great success', he replied.

Brooke is not a war poet in the sense that Siegfried Sassoon and Wilfred Owen (q.v.) are war poets. He did not survive to have experiences of fighting to record. The symbolic poignancy of his poetry – as of his life – is that the war intrudes to put an abrupt termination to riches that belong to peace. Brooke was a careful poetic craftsman from the start, using the languid cadences and lush poeticisms of the 1890s to neat effect in 'Day that I have lived', and probing his imaginative resources with new promise in the sonnet, 'Seaside':

> In the deep heart of me
> The sullen waters swell towards the moon,
> And all my tides set seaward.

Brooke was himself a moving spirit behind the first volume of *Georgian Poetry* which Edward Marsh edited in 1912, and 'The Old Vicarage, Grantchester', by which he was represented, is a lively outburst from Germany of nostalgia for England and home in octosyllabics whose judiciously heartfelt phrases preserve their freshness:

Here tulips bloom as they are told;
Unkempt about those hedges blows
An English unofficial rose.

Brooke's study of Elizabethan literature and especially of Metaphysical poetry gave substance and incisiveness to his most mature work. Flecker hailed him as 'our Donne Redivivus' and others noted the influence of Marvell. There is a jaunty cavalier humour in 'The One before the Last' (girls, not drinks), a harsh protest against sentimental idealization of the central personae in 'Menelaus and Helen', and a realistic verbal regurgitation of seasickness in 'A Channel Passage'. The five war sonnets, which did most for the legend, followed hard on the heels of 'The Great Lover', a paean of praise for the things of peace - plates and cups, wood-smoke and crusts, and 'the rough male kiss / Of blankets'. The poem is rich with Brooke's perceptive sensuousness. 'Peace', the first sonnet ('Now God be thanked Who has matched us with His hour'), caught the public mood grandly, and the apt touch was sustained through the others ('These laid the world away; poured out years to be / Of work and joy') to reach its climax in 'The Soldier' ('If I should die, think only this of me'). Death turned the last into one of the best-known poems in our literature.

Brooke's will named Wilfrid Gibson (q.v.), Lascelles Abercrombie (q.v.) and Walter de la Mare (q.v.) as his heirs; and the royalties from his works were thereby ploughed back into English poetry. G. Keynes edited The Poetical Works (1946) and The Letters of Rupert Brooke (1968), and Christopher Hassall, Brooke's biographer, edited The Prose (1956). See also Timothy Rogers, Rupert Brooke, a Reappraisal and Selection (1971). [HB]

BROPHY, BRIGID (1929-). Novelist, born in London, and educated at St Paul's Girls School and St Hugh's College, Oxford. In 1954 she married Michael Levey who is Director of the National Gallery. She is a vegetarian and a campaigner for animals' rights. Her first novel, Hackenfeller's Ape (1953), is a fable about a biologist's personal involvement with two rare apes whose mating he is anxious to observe, and it skates lightly on the edge of humour and satire. The Finishing Touch (1963) is an exercise in Firbankian pastiche that delicately sketches the naughtinesses of two lesbian co-headmistresses and their pupils at a girls' boarding ('finishing') school in France. Brophy's other novels include Flesh (1963), In Transit (1969) and Winter Palace (1978). The last named, dedicated to Michael Foot, experiments in imposing symbolic dimensions on the tale of a Ruritanian court, bringing Kafka to the aid of Anthony Hope. Brophy tried to revitalize Shavian-style drama with The Burglar (1967), she has written books on Mozart and Aubrey Beardsley, and in Prancing Novelist (1972) has produced 'a defence of fiction in the form of a critical biography in praise of Ronald Firbank'. [HB]

BROWN, GEORGE MACKAY (1921-). Poet, novelist and short-story writer born in Stromness, Orkney, Scotland, the son of a tailor who was also postman. He was educated at Stromness Academy and at Newbattle Abbey, Lothian, where Edwin Muir was principal. He took his MA at Edinburgh University in 1960 and returned

to Orkney to write. He became a Roman Catholic in 1961. Published volumes of verse include The Storm (1954), Loaves and Fishes (1959), The Year of the Whale (1965), Fishermen with Ploughs (1971) and Selected Poems (1977). The poetry is deeply concerned with the Orkney people and their way of life. The intensity of the local and individual portraiture is achieved by a fearless perceptive accuracy that never cartoonifies or diminishes its object, for the pervasive sense of a continuing community at war with the elements and at grips with their own flesh gives individual studies a universal and, at times, heroic stature. Moreover the present is threaded through with the primitive and mythic past, and religious symbolism enriches the comprehensiveness. Brown's guide to Orkney, An Orkney Tapestry (1969), provides an illuminating commentary on his work.

Brown's volumes of short stories include A Calendar of Love (1967), A Time to Keep (1969), The Sun's Net (1976) and Andrina (1982). They have the same interests as the poetry. Full of insight and humanity, they ransack the past for tales of fishing and piracy, crime and mystery, and fix the present in accounts of momentous changes in the lives of simple, ordinary folk. Of the novels Greenvoe (1972) is a variegated human tapestry of life on the island of Hellya. Woven of the present and the past, incorporating passages of legend, ritual, poetic recollection and inner dialogue, it is vigorously alive, intensely compassionate and often acutely funny. The coming of 'Black Star', a secret defence project, which dossiers the islanders, bulldozes their homes and pollutes their sea, is a horrifying picture of organized devastation that finally seals the island off from the world. Magnus (1973) reconstructs the lives of Orcadians in the twelfth century, when Magnus Erlendson became Earl of Orkney. The King of Norway insisted on double rule by a shared earldom there. Conflict ended in Magnus's murder. [HB]

BROWNJOHN, ALAN (1931-). Poet, born in London, educated there and at Oxford. He lectures in English at Battersea College of Education, London, and has been a Labour Party candidate for Parliament. Published volumes of verse include The Railings (1961), The Lions' Mouths (1967) and Warrior's Career (1972). He has written a novel for children, To Clear the River, under the pseudonym 'John Berrington'. Brownjohn reflects on life's complexities with a steady exactness, concerning himself, he says, 'with love, politics, culture, time'. His later volume, A Song of the Good Life (1975), contains 'The Ship of Death', a notably quiet but penetrating allegorization of man's end: a series of not over-venomous satirical vignettes of contemporary types (like the drop-out of 'Going Up') and, in the extended drama, 'A Love Song', a moral satire of easy adultery. More recently still, A Night in the Gazebo (1980) for the most part continues to take stock ironically and uneasily of a drably disintegrating human scene. [HB]

BRUCE, GEORGE (1909-). Scottish poet, born in Fraserburgh, Grampian, Scotland, and educated at Fraserburgh Academy and Aberdeen University. After thirteen years as a schoolmaster in Dundee he began to work for the BBC in 1946 as producer, first in Aberdeen, and later in Edinburgh and London. He has since been

Fellow in Creative Writing at Glasgow University. His first published verse was *Sea Talk* (1944). *The Collected Poems of George Bruce* (1971) garnered his output to date. Bruce is intimately concerned with the lives of the fishing folk in the rugged environment of north-east Scotland (see 'Sea Talk', 'Death Mask of a Fisherman' etc.) and his style has an austere, sinewy restraint appropriate to the harsh background and the demand it makes on human patience and stubbornness. The fisherman's lot is symptomatic of a mortal condition which Bruce examines with a tellingly dry compassion. The portrait of his father, head of a herring-curing firm, 'A Man of Inconsequent Build', and the celebrated poem on the East Port, St Andrews, 'A Gateway to the Sea', finely illustrate how Bruce's concentration on the personal and the local achieves a philosophic dimension. [HB]

BRUTUS, DENNIS (1924–). Poet and anti-apartheid activist, born of South African parents in Harare, Zimbabwe (Salisbury, Rhodesia). He studied at Fort Hare University College and the University of the Witwatersrand, before teaching in South African schools for fourteen years. Banned by the South African government in 1961 from taking part in political activities, he was arrested in 1963. When he escaped to Mozambique, the Portuguese authorities returned him to South Africa and he was shot in the back when attempting another escape in Johannesburg. He served an eighteen-months' hard-labour sentence on Robben Island, the gaol for black political prisoners. In 1966 he left South Africa with his wife and children on a one-way 'exit permit', first settling in London, where as President of the South African Non-racial Olympic Committee he worked tirelessly and travelled extensively to mobilize international opinion against apartheid. More than any other individual he was responsible for the exclusion of South Africa and Rhodesia from the Olympic Games. In 1970 he moved to the United States and became a Professor of English at Northwestern University, Evanston, Illinois. In 1973 he visited China as an official guest.

In 1962 Brutus was awarded the Mbari (Nigerian) prize for poetry; in 1963, while he was in prison, Mbari published his first collection of poems, *Sirens, Knuckles, Boots*. The title poem records the accompaniment to black living in South Africa, the strident sounds of a violent social system: 'the siren in the night / the thunder at the door / the shriek of nerves in pain'. Sometimes he conveys the general conditions of apartheid experience through precise accounts of particular deprivations and his reactions to them, more often through the conceit of a troubadour celebrating his passionate love of his country as a woman whose body and spirit he tries to make himself one with, despite the violation they both suffer. The emotions range from indignation, through bitterness and rage, to a desperate hopefulness and unwilling vindictiveness, occasionally to disillusion. J.P. Clark (q.v.) claims that 'Brutus cuts a tough figure of great bravura' and that much of the verse in this first volume is 're-modelled rhetoric'. Though grounds for these gibes can be found in some poems, by no means all the energy of movement and inventiveness of language is attributable to poetic histrionics, while to reduce the working of his

rhetoric to the stale whiff of mimeography is to overlook the poet's use of the troubadour idea as a largely convincing means of giving order and direction to his emotions. When Brutus fails, the effect is of an honest manoeuvre gone gauche; the sensibility is warm, delicate, generous, passionate. If the attitude is sometimes too posed, as in 'Miles of my arid earth' and 'Under me', the underlying conceit makes the collection pleasingly cohesive. And not all the poems have public themes; some of the most moving use the same erotic mode in dealing with the relationship between himself and his wife, and underline in the description of sexual release the sustaining role she plays, even when he feels most destitute in spirit. Thus the erotic imagery enables him to bring private and political emotions into meaningful relationship, and to convey also the latent violence that a gentle nature can be provoked into. Though Brutus often catches 'glimpses of a glinting spear' of retribution for the future, his real nature comes across as tender and compassionate, especially in 'Nightsong: City' and 'It is your flesh that I remember best'.

In 1968 Brutus's second volume of verse appeared, *Letters to Martha and Other Poems from a South African Prison*. The 'Letters to Martha' and 'Postscripts' poems in this collection are painful revelations of prison experience and of the violable interior life of a sensitive man in captivity. Intended to help a friend understand what her newly arrested husband will be subjected to, these poems, though so personal a confession, constitute also a public tribute to all the wretched, those defeated by the experience no less than those who miraculously retain integrity: one man gives up smoking so that he can't be bribed into sodomy, another finds refuge 'in fainting fits and asthmas / and finally fled into insanity'. Violence from the warders and among the prisoners themselves, lack of music, realization that the voices in the prisoner's heart shouting 'Destroy! Destroy!' express the impatience of the incarcerated whom only political change can release, joy in the movement of clouds and birds barely glimpsed through a cell window, enduring the 'cement-grey' environment but also the 'horrors / that people the labyrinth of self' – what distinguishes this poetry is the pared austerity of the language. It is clear that in coming to terms with prison Brutus found the richer, more metaphoric language of his earlier verse inadequate and developed instead a poetry of direct, plain statement, which would read like prose but for his firm control over the rhythm; the measured tone of conversational understatement detonates the appalling truth that a poem enunciates, not during the actual reading but in the silence that follows, when the reader has grasped the full implications of the seemingly commonplace words as borne by the movement of the verse.

Not surprisingly, Robben Island stimulated the most powerful poetry Brutus has written and has coloured all his subsequent writing about many other landscapes, in his poems of exile in two booklets, *Poems from Algiers* (1970) and *Thoughts Abroad* (1970), and in *A Simple Lust* (1973), which contains all the verse of the preceding books as well as poems previously uncollected. *Stubborn Hope* (1979) is a further collection that draws upon all of Brutus's writing career. Despite the enlarged sympathies learned on Robben Island, the later work inevitably suffers by comparison with *Letters to Martha*, even though one understands readily the exile's nostalgia and his pain at having to count himself one of 'the D.P.-type / who is our age's mendicant and jew'. There is sometimes a self-indulgent slackness of expression, and yet an important element in Brutus's poetry is his perception of urges towards uninhibited sensuality working simultaneously with a religious desire for self-discipline. *Strains* (1981) is a further collection.   [AR]

BUCHAN, JOHN (1st Baron Tweedsmuir) (1875–1940). Novelist and historical biographer, born in Perth, Tayside, Scotland, the son of a Free Kirk minister, and educated at Hutcheson's Grammar School, Glasgow, Glasgow University and Brasenose College, Oxford. In 1900 he moved to London, where he began to study law, but in 1901 he accepted the invitation of Lord Milner, High Commissioner for South Africa, to return with him as private secretary and assist in the task of rebuilding the administration after the Boer War. Back in England in 1903, he returned to the Bar. In leisure time he became a keen mountaineer, fisherman and walker. In 1906 he married Susan Grosvenor (whose grandmother was a niece of the great Duke of Wellington). He now abandoned law and went into partnership with Thomas Arnold, the Edinburgh publisher, and in 1911 he entered the political field as Conservative candidate for Peebles and Selkirk. When the First World War broke out Buchan was too ill for combatant service (in a babyhood accident a wheel had gone over his skull) and he served first as correspondent for *The Times* on the Western Front, then as an intelligence officer and finally as Director of Information. He had started the publication of a popular history of war in monthly volumes in the autumn of 1914. He was eventually near enough to the centre of things to be occasionally summoned to the War Cabinet.

After the war his conservative notions of civilized values and personal rectitude put him at loggerheads with intellectual and literary fashion, but he was already an established writer. He had contributed to the *Yellow Book* in the 1890s and published several prewar novels including *Prester John* (1910), an African adventure story for boys involving a missionary who claims to be the reincarnated spirit of Prester John, fifteenth-century Abyssinian king, and destined to lead an African rising. Buchan's war experiences, his travel, his knowledge of governing circles and his grasp upon world affairs give something rather more than ephemeral escapist interest to his successful series of adventure stories that began with *The Thirty-Nine Steps* (1915). The hero of this story (which later made a very successful film), Richard Hannay, reappears in its successors, *Greenmantle* (1916), *Mr Standfast* (1919) and *The Three Hostages* (1924). The two middle volumes, dealing with wartime espionage, compass a vivid view of the stretched-out battle-lines, overt and underground, military and psychological, of Europe in conflict. The four novels were gathered together as *The Four Adventures of Richard Hannay* in 1930. Buchan's war is not the war of Sassoon (q.v.), Graves (q.v.) or Owen (q.v.). It is an organized,

directed business whose individual events contribute to a vast pattern. The world map is spread out in the writer's mind. Europe at war is a vast playground for adventurous Outward-Boundery, the conflict at once a grave game and a perilous examination-system for worthwhile career-making. In his autobiography, *Memory Hold-the-Door* (1940), Buchan conceded that his work in intelligence revealed 'at close quarters the intricate mechanism which directed the war at home. . . . Slowly I began to see the War as a gigantic cosmic drama, embracing every quarter of the globe and the whole orbit of man's life . . . it had an apocalyptic splendour of design.' The stories have unflagging narrative thrust and inventiveness but indulge extravagant implausibilities. Buchan used Hannay also in *The Courts of the Morning* (1929) and *The Island of Sheep* (1936). Another hero, Dickson McCunn, a retired grocer with his 'ragamuffin boys from the Gorbals', made his first appearance in *Huntingtower* (1922), and Sir Edward Leithen, a lawyer, figures as protagonist in four novels, including *John Macnab* (1925).

In addition to some twenty-six novels, Buchan published a number of historical biographies, including *Montrose* (1928), *Sir Walter Scott* (1932), *Oliver Cromwell* (1934) and *Augustus* (1937), four books he described as 'a confession of faith' enabling him to define his own creed and thereby clear his mind. Buchan became a Companion of Honour in 1932, Lord High Commissioner to the Assembly of the Church of Scotland from 1933 to 1934, and was raised to the peerage as Lord Tweedsmuir in 1935 on his appointment as Governor-General of Canada.

Resurgent critical appreciation of Buchan has been provoked by the publication of *The Best Short Stories of John Buchan* (1980), edited by David Daniell, who notes Buchan's interest 'in the small moment at the point of balance of very large events'. Buchan's posthumous last novel, *Sick Heart River* (1941), has also been reissued (1981). Its autobiographical content gives it a special poignancy. Leithen, terminally ill but determined 'to die standing, to go out in his boots', undertakes his last adventure in rescuing an obsessed genius from the freezing far north of Canada. Buchan's son, William Buchan, has written *John Buchan, A Memoir* (1982).   [HB]

BUCHANAN, GEORGE (1904–). Novelist and literary journalist from County Antrim, Northern Ireland. He attempted to escape the bonds of fictional naturalism and give his novels the qualities of poetry – economic, reflective, non-dramatic. *Rose Forbes* (part 1, 1937; parts 1 and 2, 1950) is a distilled picaresque study of a supposedly simple Irish girl who nevertheless thinks and writes like a novelist while learning the way of sexual emancipation. The technique adopted, with its episodic bittiness and brevity, detracts from overall fluency. *A Place to Live* (1952) is a study of a hotel manager who rejects the world of public abstractions for that of domestic privacies, but it scarcely comes alive. *Green Seacoast* (1959) and *Morning Papers* (1965) are autobiographical. Buchanan has also published volumes of poetry, including *Bodily Responses* (1958) and *Possible Being* (1980). The verse is often engagingly ruminative in substance but prosaic in idiom and tone.   [HB]

BUCKLEY, VINCENT (1925–). Poet, born in Victoria, Australia. After a Jesuit schooling he studied at Melbourne and Cambridge Universities. He returned to Australia after war service and worked as a public servant before joining the English Department at Melbourne University, where he is now a professor. At first he published poetry, *The World's Flesh* (1954), but the two volumes of essays that followed, *Essays in Poetry, Mainly Australian* (1957) and *Poetry and Morality* (1959), established the powerful religious and aesthetic commitment which is characteristic of his work. The former also demonstrated his international stance in criticism, although he has always stressed the need for Australia to recognize the special importance of its own literature. *Masters in Israel* (1961) and *Arcady and Other Places* (1966) strengthened his reputation as a poet, while *Poetry and the Sacred* (1968) set out his fundamental beliefs in discussion of a wide range of literature. 'The Golden Builders' (1972) – reprinted in *Golden Builders and Other Poems* (1976) – underlined his deep sense of place in its moving attribution of spiritual significance to personal memories intricately embedded in the historical and human fabric of Melbourne. The range and flexibility of this work represented a widening of his poetic scope; his article 'Imagination's Home', pulished in *Quadrant* (Sydney) in March 1979, is illuminating on influences and intentions. Later collections of poetry include *The Pattern* and *Late Winter Child* (both 1979).   [PQ]

BULLETIN, THE (1880–). A weekly Sydney journal which played an important role in fostering Australian self-awareness in the period up to and beyond Federation in 1901. Under the editorship of J.F. Archibald, who founded it with John Haynes, the journal encouraged 'short stories, or ballads, especially on bush, mining, sporting, social, or dramatic themes', though Archibald's literary advice to contributors – 'Boil it down' – often encouraged a tendency towards melodrama. Writing in 1907 of Sydney twenty-seven years before he claimed: 'What was most Australian in spirit had been lost by the secessions first of Victoria and then of Queensland'. *The Bulletin* was to stand for 'more humanity in the laws, more freedom in the Parliaments, more healthy independence in the press'. In spite of certain lapses (for example its opposition to coloured immigration) the journal did represent an important radical vehicle for national expression; Archibald's aim was a popular journal written largely by its readers and for a time he came near to realizing this. The work of Henry Lawson (q.v.) and Joseph Furphy (q.v.) was first published by the journal and these two writers gave fine expression to many of the central preoccupations of *The Bulletin*. As Vance Palmer (q.v.) expressed it in his influential critical work *The Legend of the Nineties* (1954): 'In the shearing-sheds, in small country settlements, at camp-fires along countless tracks, existed a scattered audience and an army of potential contributors, and as *The Bulletin*'s national outlook widened it began to draw them into its civilization, at first unconsciously, and then with deliberate intent'. Reference to the '*Bulletin* school' of writers and the legend of which they form part (the facts allow of other interpretations) is still necessary to understand the positions taken up on occasions by contemporary writers and

critics; a good example of this continuing debate is *Melbourne or The Bush* (1974) by Chris Wallace-Crabbe (q.v.). A.G. Stephens (1865–1933) worked for *The Bulletin* from 1894 until 1906 and contributed articles for the influential 'red page' inside the cover. In 1899 he described Henry Lawson as 'splendidly parochial. That increases his claim upon his country, but decreases his claim upon literature.' In the Introduction to *The Bulletin Story Book* (1901, reprinted 1973) he commented: 'in this book it has not been attempted to choose examples of work characteristically Australian. The literary work which is Australian in spirit, as well as in scene or incident, is only beginning to be written.' These were – and in some ways still are – important issues, and *The Bulletin*'s fame is assured by the popular expression it gave to such topics during a crucial period of Australia's history.   [PQ]

BUNTING, BASIL (1900–). Poet, born in Scotswood on Tyne, Northumberland. He was imprisoned as a conscientious objector in the First World War. He has been editor, music critic and diplomat, has lived in Italy, the USA and Iran, has held university posts abroad and has been President of the Poetry Society. A disciple of Pound, he published a volume of poems in Milan in 1930 but made his great impact in England in the 1960s with *Briggflatts* (1966), an autobiographical poem, and *Collected Poems* (1968). Hugh MacDiarmid (q.v.) has compared him with Hopkins as a case of delayed recognition, seeing his poems as the most important since T.S. Eliot's *Waste Land* (q.v.). Others have lamented his contrived literary allusiveness and parade of erudition. 'I have set down words as a musician pricks his score, not to be read in silence, but to trace in the air a pattern of sound', Bunting himself claims (Preface to *Collected Poems*), but this is scarcely the full recipe for writing such as:

> By the dategroves of Babylon
> there we sat down and sulked
> while they were seeking to hire us
> to a repugnant trade.
>
> ('The Spoils')

or for:

> White marble stained like a urinal
> cleft in Apuan Alps,
> always trickling, apt to the saw.
>
> ('Briggflatts')

Bunting's work has an inner animation and an outer crispness of statement that is too fast-moving to be always easy to digest. He has encouraged neither exegesis ('There is no excuse for literary criticism', he avers) nor biographical commentary ('My autobiography is *Briggflatts* – there's nothing else worth speaking about'), but his allusive density rewards scrutiny. See the later *Collected Poems* (1978).   [HB]

BURGESS, ANTHONY (1917–). Novelist, born in Manchester. His full name is John Anthony Burgess Wilson. He had a Catholic upbringing and was educated at the Xaverian College, Manchester, and at Manchester University. His career has included army service, colonial service in Malaya and schoolmastering. His first novel, *A Vision of Battlements*, was written in 1949 but not published until 1965. Its hero (or anti-hero) is a failed composer and the novel is structured mock-heroically on the framework of Virgil's *Aeneid*. The novels known as the 'Malayan Trilogy' (*Time for a Tiger*, 1956; *The Enemy in the Blanket*, 1958; *Beds in the East*, 1959) were Burgess's first publications. They deal with the racial and social situation in postwar Malaya. A suspected brain-tumour brought Burgess home from Malaya in 1959. Believing that he had only twelve months to live, he wrote five novels in the year to help provide for his 'widow', and used pseudonyms for two of them in order to conceal his over-productivity. One of the five, *The Wanting Seed* (1962), is set in the future and pessimistically projects the working-out of a cyclic view of history in terms of the Pelaphase-Interphase-Gusphase cycle. The Pelagian phase of sentimental liberal humanism is followed by a transitional reaction of disillusioned brutality, and in turn by an orthodox Augustinian phase that recognizes original sin.

A Clockwork Orange (1962) is another anti-utopian exercise. It underlines Burgess's position as a renegade Catholic who has found no refuge in liberal humanism and remains deeply sceptical about the relevance of social idealism to a creature so depraved as man. The scene is England in an undated future. The lingo of teenage delinquents, 'nadsat', with its Slav roots, indicates an assimilation of Soviet influence. Alex and his gang steal, torture, rape and kill, while the respectable middle classes hide behind closed doors. When the police finally catch up with Alex he is rescued from gaol by a well-meaning, sentimental government scheme for Reclamation Treatment. It builds up in Alex an association between violence and sickness that turns him into a creature without moral choice, a 'clockwork orange'. But the marginal effects of the conditioning are such that music, sex and art are also associated with sickness. Burgess's targets are both the humanitarians and the conditioners, liberalism and totalitarianism. The book might have had more coherence had he settled for the one or the other. Its ancestry is clear. It is bred of *Brighton Rock* out of *1984*; but Evelyn Waugh of *Decline and Fall* gets in the saddle from time to time. For Burgess's work is highly derivative – from Joyce (q.v.), Huxley (q.v.), Waugh (q.v.), Beckett (q.v.) and others – and the imitativeness often has a curiously ingenuous obviousness.

Burgess is at his most entertaining when his sense of humour takes over. *Inside Mr Enderby* (1963) presents F.X. Enderby, a middle-aged poet who has withdrawn from the wicked world and is most at home when composing poetry on the lavatory. What gives the novel validity is the sheer farce of his role as the honest ingenuous comic who puts his foot in it and is trapped into matrimony by a glamorous journalist. Enderby's falsely presumed insanity and attempted suicide are Waugh-like slapstick. The Joycean mannerisms and the verbal resourcefulness supply apt imagery for comic day-dreaming. The story of Enderby was continued in *Enderby Outside* (1968) and *The Clockwork Testament or Enderby's End* (1976). Burgess's attempt in *Tremor of Intent* (1966) to invest a stock spy story (ingenious and versatile as such) with symbolic overtones conducive to allegoric reading in theological terms was not successful.

He left England to live on the Mediterranean in 1968. He interested himself in an obscene and blasphemous Roman dialect poet, Belli, some of whose sonnets he translated in *Abba Abba* (1977), a short novel built around a possible meeting between Belli and Keats.

Burgess is indefatigably prolific and inventive, but pays the price of hasty over-productivity. Deficiencies in artistry are evident both in the faltering structure of his novels and in half-thought-out philosophical schemas. The epic novel *Earthly Powers* (1980) is narrated by a writer born in 1890 and now in his eighties, who claims familiarity or contact with various great figures of his age. Though somewhat coarse-grained in verbal and imaginative texture, the work has immense verve and energy. *The End of the World News* (1982) weaves narrative strands (on the pattern of watching three television channels at once) in a projection of the end of history. [HB]

BUTLER, FREDERICK GUY (1918–). Poet, drama-tist, critic, born in Cradock, South Africa. He studied at Rhodes University and Oxford. After war service abroad, he lectured in Johannesburg in 1948–50 and was Professor of English at Rhodes University in 1950–78. Dedicated to the English-language cultural heritage in South Africa, he edited the *Oxford Book of South African Verse* (1959) and books on the 1820 (British) Settlers, but has also declared: 'English, as the chosen language of millions of Blacks, has a great and exciting future in Africa'.

His best poetry belongs to *Stranger to Europe* (1952; enlarged 1960) and *On First Seeing Florence* (1968); stimulated by his war experience, it expresses a restrained but very real love of life and anguish at its destruction – see 'Bomb Casualty', 'December 1944' and 'Air Raid Before Dawn'. His return from Europe, the fount of his settler culture, sharpened awareness of his African environment; much of the verse in *South of the Zambezi* (1966) ingeniously seeks to domicile English rhythms and European cultural references within the South African landscape, through a humane, unsentimentally compas-sionate sensibility. *Selected Poems* appeared in 1975. His plays include *The Dam* (prod 1953), *The Dove Returns* (prod 1956), *Take Root or Die* (prod 1966; pubd 1970). *Karoo Morning* (1977) is the highly attractive, well-written first volume of an autobiography. [AR]

BUZO, ALEXANDER (1944–). Dramatist, born in Sydney, New South Wales, Australia. After graduating from the University of New South Wales in 1965 he worked at various jobs, an experience he draws upon in his writing. The success of *Norm and Ahmed* (1967) was a turning-point in the success of modern vernacular drama in Australia. A brief work depicting a chance street-corner encounter between a 'typical' Australian and a student from 'the South-East Asian sub-continent', it depended upon a faultless ear for local speech-rhythms in its probing of the uncertainties and prejudice underlying the Australian suburban dream. Later plays approach the mannered in their close exposure of the urban, commercial and sexual rituals with which individuals seek to conceal their inner loneliness and isolation. *The Front Room Boys* and *Rooted* (both 1969) ruthlessly depicted the microcosm of office life and civil service power structure, while *The Roy Murphy Show* (1970) was a farce centred on a television sports commentator. *Tom* (1972) was again set in the glittering but brittle world of business executives; *Coralie Lansdowne Says No* (1974) followed the painful accommodation of ideals and illusions to reality in the personal conflicts surrounding Coralie's need to face the facts – her age among them. *Macquarie* (1971) was a historical play set in the early eighteenth century. Buzo himself describes *The Front Room Boys* as 'a gag-style comedy which . . . also attempts to explore the baffling relationship between the rulers of our society and the world' and it is this note which marks his best work. Recent works include *Martello Towers* (1976) and *Makasar Reef* (1979), and Buzo's approach to theatre can be gauged by his rejoinder to critical reviews of the former: 'the theatre is a practical place where what works in rehearsal and in performance with an audience can be deemed to have worked full stop'.

[PQ]

BYATT, A. S. (Antonia Susan) (1936–). Novelist, born in Sheffield, South Yorkshire. A Cambridge graduate and sister of the novelist Margaret Drabble (q.v.), she attempted in her second novel, *The Game* (1967), to portray a relationship between two sensitive sisters upon whom conflicting religious, ideological, and personal influences have played unsettlingly. Quakerism, Anglo-Catholicism and fanatical do-goodery compete with the mores of the media. But what begins as a novel with moral and philosophical dimensions – and interesting exploration of the relationship between real and fictive worlds – seems to lose its bearings in the morass of cliché values it earlier examined objectively. *The Virgin in the Garden* (1978) centres various personal stories on a Yorkshire schoolmaster's production of his own verse drama in Coronation Year, 1953. Heavily literary in tone, the book is overladen in substance and perhaps casts a shadow on Byatt's conviction that 'the unwritten novel is an enormous bag into which everything can be put' (*The Times*, 28.10.78).

[HB]

C

CALLAGHAN, MORLEY (1903–). Novelist, born in Toronto, Ontario, Canada. He went to Toronto University and the Osgoode Hall Law School. He has lived in Toronto nearly all his life and this human and urban setting, together with firm Christian beliefs, characterizes his most successful work. After law school Callaghan worked as a reporter on the Toronto *Daily Star* where he met Ernest Hemingway, who encouraged him to write. His first novel, *Strange Fugitive*, was published in 1928 and a collection of short stories, *A Native Argosy*, in the following year. In *That Summer in Paris* (1963) – which remains a good biographical and stylistic introduction to his work – Callaghan tells of his time in Paris during 1928 where he again met Hemingway, and also James Joyce (q.v.) and Scott Fitzgerald. Callaghan's first novel, like the two that followed it, *It's Never Over* (1930) and *A Broken Journey* (1932), was set in the contemporary world of deprivation and corruption and was indebted to Hemingway in its laconic style. His attitude to life underwent a major religious change during 1933 and this had a direct effect upon his writing; he abandoned the stress upon physical action, violence and seeming futility which had characterized his early work and espoused a position of Christian humanism in his work. *Such is My Beloved* (1934) centres upon the dilemma of a priest whose official position (but not his spirit of belief) is destroyed by the offence he gives to the establishment of church and state in trying to help two prostitutes. In *They Shall Inherit the Earth* (1935) the apparently contradic-

tory similarity of the saint to the sinner is again emphasized, as it is in *More Joy in Heaven* (1937), the story of a paroled convict who becomes disillusioned and dies fighting for his former comrades. Callaghan brings out the elements of true charity and self-sacrifice in the convict Kip Caley, even though in the judgement of both church and state he remains nothing better than a sinner and a criminal. With their neat plots and selective characterization, his early works are essentially social fables of moral predicament. Opinion divides on whether these straightforward but attractive works or later books, in which he has adopted a more overtly symbolic and structured manner of writing, represent his best work. *The Loved and the Lost* (1951) illustrates Callaghan's fine ability to use the city (Toronto) as both setting and symbol in attempting to work out the Christian ethic in the modern world of racial tension. *The Many Colored Coat* (1960) set up a complex series of parallels with the biblical story of Joseph in its exposure of the false values of contemporary life. The less successful *A Passion in Rome* (1961) took as its literal and symbolic setting the choice and installation of a new pope after the death of Pius XII. *A Fine and Private Place* (1975) returned to a Toronto setting in its moving exploration of the fascination exercised by an ageing writer upon a graduate student who feels compelled to attempt a critical assessment of him. Callaghan is also an accomplished short-story writer, showing a striking ability to create within small compass a vision of the truly universal within the apparently mundane. In addition to the early collection he has published *Now That April's Here* (1936) and the two-volume *Morley Callaghan's Stories* (1959). The novel *Close to the Sun Again* was published in 1977.   [PQ]

CAMERON, NORMAN (1905–53). British poet, born in India, educated at Fettes College and at Oxford. After a spell as an education officer in Nigeria, he worked in advertising, and during the war was engaged in propaganda warfare. He became a Roman Catholic in 1950. Verse published in *The Winter House* (1935) and *Work in Hand* (1942) was gathered in the posthumous *Collected Poems 1905–1953* (1957) and introduced by Robert Graves (q.v.). Cameron's poetry has no recourse to modernist experiment in form, but derives precision and authority from his vigilant exactitude in the choice of words and from his epigrammatic dexterity. It can be argued, writes John Press, in *A Map of Modern English Verse* (1969), that 'the course of true poetry in our century descends from Thomas Hardy through Edward Thomas, W.H. Davies, Norman Cameron, and Alun Lewis, to finish in Graves himself; and that modernism, as Philip Larkin has observed, "is fun no more . . ." ' (not Press's own view).
                                                                         [HB]

CAMPBELL, DAVID (1915–79). Poet, born in New South Wales and educated in Sydney and at Cambridge University. After war service he took up farming and lived on a station near Canberra, in the pastoral landscape which features so often in his work. *Speak with the Sun* (1949) and *The Miracle of Mullion Hill* (1956) showed his craftsmanlike care with language in their strong sense of the different, but not opposing, influences of immediate landscape and literary tradition. Poems such as 'Harry Pearce' and 'The Stockman' interpreted contemporary Australian life and land within a mythopoeic outlook similar to that of Judith Wright (q.v.). *Poems* (1962) included the fine sequence 'Cocky's Calendar' in which the basic rhythms of Australian country life were interpreted with blended simplicity and sophistication. *Selected Poems, 1942–1968* (1968) included a new section, 'Talking to Strangers', and an enlarged edition was published in 1973 which reprinted selections from work in *The Branch of Dodona* (1970). Also in 1970 he edited an anthology, *Modern Australian Poetry*. Although pastoral images give life to so much of his work he is careful to distinguish between ends and means – 'I do not think of myself as a pastoral poet: a poet thinks with the images nearest to hand'. *Starting from Central Station* (1973) charted a personal journey through time and space; *Moscow Trefoil* (1975) was a joint translation from the Russian with Rosemary Dobson (q.v.). Later verse included *Deaths and Pretty Cousins* (1975) and *Words with a Black Orpington* (1978). *Flame and Shadow: Selected Short Stories* appeared in 1976 and the poetry collection *Man in the Honeysuckle* in 1979.   [PQ]

CAMPBELL, ROY (Ignatius Roy Dunnachie) (1902–57). Poet, born in Durban, South Africa, into a family who owned sugar estates in Natal. The father, Dr S.G. Campbell, watched over his children's education, urging equally their physical and intellectual development. The upbringing was individualist and patrician, and the sons enjoyed a large freedom on the Natal estates and on visits to their uncle in Rhodesia.

In 1919 Campbell went to Oxford for a year's private study, which introduced him to the work of T.S. Eliot (q.v.) (one of whose earliest admirers he became) and of the modern French poets. After a footloose period in Paris and the South of France, he returned to England in 1921, and, to his family's consternation, married at the age of 19. For him and his wife, Mary, there followed two lean years in a Welsh village. Here he wrote *The Flaming Terrapin* (1924), which detonated upon the Georgian literary scene with pyrotechnic brilliancy. In some 1400 lines, it celebrates all that is vital in nature and man, through the myth-like symbol of a gigantic terrapin which hauls Noah's Ark into a newly cleansed world, with Noah and his sons as phoenix-like renewals of degenerate mankind. Within the formal restraints, mostly of rhymed couplets, the verse moves with great flexibility and muscularity, a cascade of images of fire, light, electric current, of natural objects magnified and imbued with volcanic potential.

Most reviewers hailed Campbell's youthful, vigorous individuality that gusted across Georgian idiom and versification as that of a new poetic pioneer, though some dismissed it as flamboyance. It was the voice of an outsider that had learned its heroical accents in a province of empire. In a 1931 essay Alan Paton (q.v.) wrote: 'We are subjected to a succession of shocks, shaken out of our composure'. And this is probably the view of Campbell's work that still prevails fifty years later, owing largely to his scornful attack on literary England in *The Georgiad* (1931) and his final estrangement of intellectual England through his championing of Franco in the Spanish Civil War. But for these two 'non-poetic' causes, his reputation as a poet might be higher today, for much of the poetry of his later years is neither satirical nor arrogant, and often achieves a rare delicacy of line and sentiment. Whether the poetic meteor acclaimed in the 1920s could ever have become a seminal influence upon later English poetry is doubtful, but literary London indeed called in its bond after allegiance to Franco followed upon *The Georgiad*. 'In every herd there is some restive steer' is Campbell's image for the poet's relationship with society, and his worship of the individualist was a simplistic, overpowering emotion which made him scornful of little men who made up the herd, and distrustful of ideologies that favoured the masses. By the mid-1930s, he and Mary were living in Spain as Roman Catholic converts and to them Franco was defending the Christian Spain of ancient, colourful, individualist values against the dingy masses. It was a myopic but innocent romanticism rather than any vicious intellectual fascism, and the Campbell who fought on the same side as the Nazi and fascist contingents in Spain served the anti-Nazi cause in 1939–45.

After *The Flaming Terrapin* appeared, Campbell returned to South Africa. In 1926, with Plomer (q.v.) and van der Post (q.v.), he started *Voorslag* ('Whiplash'), intended to be 'a monthly magazine of South African life and art'. Its forthright questioning of established racial and cultural attitudes raised so much antagonism that financial backing was threatened; in the third number

Campbell announced his resignation as editor and soon left for England. *The Wayzgoose* (1928) was his pungent reply to the South Africa that had made the *Voorslag* endeavour impossible – a 'garden colony', 'Where pumpkins to professors are promoted / And turnips into Parliament are voted'; the satire was aimed at recognizable personalities, but through them at sterile provincialism and intellectual atrophy. After three years in England he lashed out at another kind of provincialism – that of the metropolis. *The Georgiad* flays the emasculated poetic of the Georgians and the soft-centred intellectuality of Bloomsbury; its satirical venom was intended to avenge what he felt as personal treacheries suffered at the hands of some of the literary figures he attacks. The move soon after to Provence, and later Spain, was to a physical and cultural climate he found altogether more warm and congenial.

Adamastor had appeared in 1930, the work of a maturing poet who can now control the flood of images of fiery energy, and value experiences of calm no less than of tireless movement, as in the closing lines of 'Mass at Dawn', describing return from a night's fishing: 'But when with food and drink, at morning-light, / The children met me at the water-side, / Never was wine so red or bread so white'. The volume includes Campbell's best-known shorter poems, from the deft satirical epigrams like 'On Some South African Novelists' to the calmer, though self-conscious, 'Rounding the Cape', 'The Serf' and 'The Zulu Girl', in which a surface quietude is undercut by ominous hints of the accountability to which white South Africa will eventually be called. In 'Tristan da Cunha' the island images poetic aloofness but also a new, painful, sense of a South African's exile in Europe's 'wintry space', though in 'Horses on the Camargue' he finds in an unspoiled space of southern Europe 'Spirits of power and beauty and delight' that compensate for those he celebrates in 'The Zebras'.

Campbell's gratified feeling of affinity with south-western Europe marks most of the poems in *Flowering Reeds* (1933) and *Mithraic Emblems* (1936). There is contemplative detachment from past clangours of spirit, while the characteristic Campbell energy is now channelled into the honing of a sparser, more economical versification. 'The Flame', for instance, and 'The Flower' are oblique love poems of peace and silence, at a remove from passion, of a calm but deep contentment, marred by some diffuseness of imagery, but striving for the moment when 'There dawns a presence such as only / Of perfect silence can be born' ('The Secret Muse'). That Campbell is remembered chiefly as the poet who 'swaggers in the clashing spurs of rhyme' (*The Wayzgoose*) is partly due to his autobiographical *Light on a Dark Horse* (1951) but also indicates an unwarranted neglect of his post-*Georgiad* poetry. One must except here *Flowering Rifle* (1939), in which the Franco-apologist displaces the poet in virtual self-parody of his early satirical style. Among the uncertain treatments of Second World War themes and some political axe-grinding, *Talking Bronco* (1946) does contain one of his most distinguished poems, 'Luis de Camões', his tribute to a poet who 'Wrestled his hardships into forms of beauty'. Campbell's own debts in craftsmanship to Spanish and French poets are amply repaid in translations of *Poems of St John of the Cross*

(1951) and Baudelaire's *Les Fleurs du Mal* (1952).

Campbell spent his last years in Portugal, where he was killed in a motor accident.   [AR]

CAREY, PETER (1943–). Short-story writer, born at Bacchus Marsh, near Melbourne, Victoria, Australia. After failing to complete a science course at Monash University he went into advertising, first in Melbourne and then in Sydney: 'I was a child of Menzies and General Motors and thought that advertising might be interesting'. His interest in fiction was aroused by the work of fellow Australian writers Morris Lurie and Barry Oakley (q.v.) and he also cites William Faulkner as an important early influence: 'structurally, probably the thing that influenced me most was *As I Lay Dying*'. At first Carey's own stories were published in magazines in Australia, but in 1974 he published *The Fat Man in History*, a collection which established him as a major new talent in contemporary Australian fiction. The book sold well and went into paperback; Carey now writes full time and lives in Sydney. He describes his writing as springing from an interest in 'extending reality, pushing behavioural patterns to their logical limits'; in another vein he wryly observes that 'there are no easy answers, for someone . . . who at nineteen years of age went into advertising with fuck-all education, no reading, no nothing'. The difficulty – and enjoyment – that his works offer lies in their startling blend of closely observed day-to-day life and subtly distorted 'reality'. We quickly recognize elements from our own experience but find ourselves drawn into a world we hardly dare to confront. Stories such as 'Crabs' and 'American Dreams' demonstrate his ability to render modern hopes and fears with both wit and compassion. His second collection, *War Crimes* (1979), confirmed his talent and his standing; the title story is a powerful 'acting out' of elemental ambition in an industrial setting which is indeed a story for our time. A selection from both Australian collections was published in Britain in 1980 under the title *The Fat Man in History*.   [PQ]

CARY, JOYCE (1888–1957). Novelist, born in Londonderry, Northern Ireland. His father, Arthur Cary, had married Charlotte Joyce, uniting county landowning stock, long rooted in the Inishowen peninsula, County Donegal (though deriving originally from Devonshire), with the Derry business family that provided the novelist with his Christian name. The Carys were one of those Anglo-Irish families who had been impoverished by failing to oppress their debt-ridden tenants. The family moved to London and Joyce's upbringing centred there, with periodic visits to relations back in Northern Ireland. Joyce's mother died when he was 9 and his father's subsequent marriage to a cousin soon ended in a second bereavement which deeply shocked Joyce, by then at school at Clifton. His first ambition was to be an artist and, after he left Clifton, his father supported him as an art student in Paris. From Paris he moved to Edinburgh under the influence of Charles Mackie, the Scottish painter, who saw the dangers for him in the undisciplined café-life of French Bohemia. Cary himself gradually realized his lack of adequate artistic talent and then set his heart firmly on becoming a writer. (He published a volume of *Verses* in Edinburgh in 1908.) In order to procure a safety net under literary aspirations he went up to Trinity College, Oxford, in 1909 to read law. A notable friendship with Middleton Murry (q.v.) began, and Cary introduced him to bohemian Paris. (It was not to be long before Cary had to watch Murry rise meteorically in the London literary world while he was himself unknown. When the two met in 1954 after a gap of forty years their positions had reversed.) The fiasco of his law finals (he got a fourth) and the total unresponsiveness of Gertrude Ogilvie with whom he had fallen in love drove Cary out of England in 1912. He went off to the Balkans to fight for Montenegro against the Turks. His experiences in the Balkan War are recorded in *Memoir of the Bobotes*, published posthumously in 1964 with Cary's own illustrations. Cary was back in England in 1913 and, after casting about for a career, was accepted for the Colonial Service as an assistant district officer in Nigeria. As such, his civilian status became military when the First World War began. He fought in the Cameroons, was wounded, and came home in 1916 at last to marry Gertrude ('Trudy') Ogilvie. Small private incomes on either side provided a basic stand-by, but, though he was already working unceasingly with his pen, lack of alternative career prospects pinned the young husband in Nigeria until 1920, when ill-health made retirement more necessary and acceptance of some short stories by *The Saturday Evening Post* opened up new possibilities. For the rest of their days, the Carys lived in Parks Road, Oxford, bringing up four sons. For many years they suffered intermittent periods of financial strain during Cary's long haul to establish himself as a selling writer. The tide finally turned in the 1940s and success came. Sadly, Trudy was stricken with cancer and died in 1949. Cary himself was struck down in 1955 by disseminated neuritis, a disease which kills by increasing paralysis of the whole body.

Family misfortunes of the Carys and Joyce's own personal frustrations as man and writer help to explain his persisting concern with injustice. The demand of some of his major characters for a justice denied them in the world as it is has religious rather than social implications. Divine Providence seems to be worryingly under question, and Cary aligns himself neither with optimistic progressivism nor with angry disillusionment. His books do not play down human corruptibility, but human fortitude and cheerfulness shine. Cary is not a philosophical novelist, though the rhetoric of William Blake gives a drift to his preoccupation with ideals soured in action, with efforts nullified by the ways of the world, and with aspirations dissipated through being misunderstood, fantasized or baulked by counter-aspirations. Cary's major characters function without lucid cerebral direction. They live on their nerves, carried, sometimes frenziedly, on a tide of non-rational, self-generated activity.

It was not until 1932 that Cary's first novel, *Aissa Saved*, got into print. Together with *The African Witch* (1936) and *Mister Johnson* (1939) it forms a group of African novels in which Cary brings native peoples up against a white civilization and culture by which they are lured into enthusiastic self-identification with what they do not understand. Idealistic white administrators and missionaries are bewildered by wildly erroneous assimilation of their mores and message. Aissa's experience of conversion culminates in the ritual slaughter of her own baby while she sings in grotesque rapture: 'All de tings I lak de mos / I sacrifice dem to His blood'. Mister Johnson's hilarious and pathetically half-educated dreams of grandeur, stimulated by entry into the white man's ways through mission school and an administrative clerkship, also culminate in murder. In *Charley is my Darling* (1940) the culture-gap is transported to wartime England, where evacuation brings London slum children to Devon, and Charley Brown, isolated in mockery by his shaven head (he is lousy), and frustrated of worthwhile imaginative outlet, becomes a gang-leader in housebreaking raids.

Cary published a novel of a different kind in *A House of Children* (1941). Its setting is Donegal and it is frankly autobiographical, disguising the names of places and people known to him in his boyhood visits to Northern Ireland. The use of the first-person narrator for the first time launches Cary on what was to be his most successful mode of fictional presentation. The influence of James Joyce's (q.v.) *A Portrait of the Artist as a Young Man* is evident in the shaping of the work round a series of epiphanies rather than in a structured plot. But Cary comes most magnificently into his own in the first trilogy, *Herself Surprised** (1941), *To Be a Pilgrim* (1942) and *The Horse's Mouth* (1944), where he invests himself successively with the contrasting personae of three parties to a triangle, two of them men at opposite extremes of outlook and temperament, the other a woman of captivating feminine full-bloodedness. The assumption of individual roles so diverse in highly authentic autobiographic self-presentation is an outstanding feat of verbal impersonation. And Cary achieved a comparable, perhaps more complex and disciplined, display of mimetic virtuosity in his second trilogy, *Prisoner of Grace* (1952), *Except the Lord* (1953) and *Not Honour More* (1955). Again the situation is triangular and the woman has first word. Nina tells the story of Chester Nimmo, her husband (*Prisoner of Grace*), then Nimmo, now at the end of his life, recounts his early days (*Except the Lord*), and Jim Latter, Nina's cousin and lover, writes his confession in the death-cell (*Not Honour More*), for he has murdered Nina in jealousy. Nimmo is the inspired prophetic reformer and wielder of political power whose self-mesmerization and adjustment of cause to expedience stop just short of hypocrisy. Latter is the extreme representative of law and order whose claims for supposed duty shade off into paranoid brutishness. The public background here, as elsewhere in Cary, gives one a rich awareness of the twentieth-century scene, for Cary's overall objective sense of historic change counterbalances the exuberant self-identification with vivaciously eccentric personalities. Some critics have charged that Cary's fluency betrays him; that structure is sacrificed to a tumbling sequence of bitty episodes and that dramatic thrust is dissipated in a cascade of ill-differentiated events; but the overpowering prodigality of Cary's vision and technique is undeniable. See also the *Selected Essays*, ed. A.G. Bishop (1976), and Malcom Foster, *Joyce Cary: A Biography* (1969).

Herself Surprised, To Be a Pilgrim and **The Horse's Mouth** form a trilogy designed 'to show three characters, not only in themselves, but as seen by each other'. They are Sara Monday, Thomas Loftus Wilcher and Gulley Jimson, and they narrate their stories in that order. Sara, a cook, has married into her employer's family and then, as a widow, become first the mistress of Jimson, then housekeeper and mistress of Wilcher. She is essential Woman, moral in intention but constitutionally susceptible to man in search of mother and mistress. Her racy self-portrayal, shot through with moral overtones, has called out comparison with Defoe's Moll Flanders. She is woman the preserver and destroyer. Wilcher recalls her 'gaiety, her obstinate resolve that others should enjoy what she found good: warmth, food, affection, soft beds, a domestic sensuality about which her religion was like the iron bars nailed to a child's tuck box'; and to Jimson she becomes 'the old female nature' who 'attempted to button up the prophetic spirit, Gulley Jimson, in her placket-hole, got a bonk on the conk, and was reduced to her proper status, as spiritual fodder. But what fodder.' Sara sees herself 'the victim of mysterious events and her own soft heart' while to Wilcher she is 'the devoted unselfish servant and mistress' and to Jimson she is 'cunning, vain, lecherous, self-deceiving, a man-catcher' who at all costs, even at the cost of a man's soul, will make her nest in the world.

Tom Wilcher (*To Be a Pilgrim*) narrates as a crochety old man on the verge of senility, knowing that he is passé and out of touch. He has been a prudent, cautious man, safe about financial practicalities and therefore a complete foil to Jimson. His brothers and sister long ago committed themselves in decisive action, but he has withdrawn too much into himself. The alternate representation of his 'present' in the 1930s and of his past, by recall of the previous generation, makes for moving emotional parallels and a revealing glimpse of the changing decades in modern England. Sara has been imprisoned for stealing from him – to support Gulley. He would like to marry her on her release, but he is now in the care of his niece after incidents of indecent exposure.

For Gulley Jimson (*The Horse's Mouth*) Wilcher is 'five feet of shiny broadcloth and three inches of collar ... Genus, Boorjwar; species, Blackcoatius Begoggledus Ferocissimouse. All eaten up with lawfulness and rage; ready to bite himself for being so respectable'. The style is the man. Jimson, Wilcher's opposite, is a man of faith and decision, committed in certitude to the personal vocation to paint. He is Cary's greatest comic study, hilariously personifying the anarchic romantic artist who flouts all convention and respectability, scorns the cultural establishment, and battens cunningly on others in total disregard of moral obligation. Yet he is lovably single-minded and irrepressibly on the side of life. The compelling vivacity of the man survives even the descent to cartooneries of slapstick and farce to which Cary's headlong zest impels him. [HB]

CAUSLEY, CHARLES (1917–). Poet, born in Launceston, Cornwall, educated there and at Peterborough Training College. He returned to teach in Cornwall after the war. His service as a rating in the Royal Navy from 1940 to 1946 inspired poetry representative of the ordinary seaman and left a continuing mark on the imagery of later peacetime verse.

The first published volume was *Farewell, Aggie Weston* (1951). The work of successive volumes was garnered in *Collected Poems, 1951–1975* (1975). Causley excels at the ballad and at stanzaic poems in regular swinging metres that smack of Kipling (q.v.), Chesterton (q.v.), Housman (q.v.) and even Betjeman (q.v.). A romantic vein softens harsh reality in poems about warships and naval men, but it does not dilute their colourful spiritedness.

> Oh mother my mouth is full of stars
> As cartridges in the tray,
> My blood is a twin-branched scarlet tree
> And it runs all away.
> ('Song of the Dying Gunner A.A.l')

The winning accessibility and freshness of Causley's work is the product of refined workmanship. He has published numerous books of stories and verse for children. [HB]

CECIL, DAVID (Lord) (1902–). Biographer and critic, youngest son of the 4th Marquess of Salisbury, educated at Eton and Oxford. He was Goldsmith's Professor of English Literature at Oxford from 1948 to 1970. His biographical study of the poet William Cowper, *The Stricken Deer* (1929), was a contemporary success. Later studies included *Sir Walter Scott* (1933), *Jane Austen* (1935), *Hardy the Novelist* (1943) and *Max* – on Sir Max Beerbohm (q.v.) – (1964). [HB]

CHAPLIN, SID (1916–). Novelist, born in Shildon, County Durham. He worked as a miner from 1931 to 1950. The Durham region and the mining community provided the material for his first book, a collection of short stories, *The Leaping Lad* (1946), and likewise for his novels, *My Fate Cries Out* (1949), which goes back to the eighteenth century, *The Thin Seam* (1950) and *The Big Room* (1960). In *Sam in the Morning* (1965), however, Chaplin moves to London to place his Durham-bred hero, Sam Rowlands, in the monolithic headquarters of a giant company, where the question of rising to the top or dropping out with an idealistic dream-girl is at issue. Sam has the gift of the gab and a cheerful effrontery that cannot fail. His successor, Harry John Brown, in *The Mines of Alabaster* (1971), who also disseminates capsulated pseudo-profundities that keep the girls agog, is lured to Tuscany from a broken acting career and a breaking marriage by two regulation dream-girls. Chaplin's characters often converse in quick-fire repartee, exchanging oblique, ironic epigrams vaguely resonant with more than meets the ear. His descriptive canvas is a packed one, his narrative presentation busy, his style poetically alive. Basic moral concerns are involved in his characters' choices and philosophical attitudes are in the air – made serious by an awareness of death and of the necessary stability of marriage. [HB]

CHAUDHURI, NIRAD C. (1897–). Prose writer, born in Kishorganj, Bengal, India. He was educated in the University of Calcutta, but his energetic independent, encyclopedic mind owes much to his enlightened parents. His failure to achieve the academic career for which he seemed equipped led to decades of poverty, until, in his mid-50s, *The Autobiography of an Unknown Indian* (1951)

established him as a man of letters. *The Autobiography* is, paradoxically, both egotistical and, through its stringent confrontation of self, objective and exploratory. Chaudhuri revels in the discomfort of interpreting India as if he were an alien, by means of a vivid, honest, engaging account of the growth of his own personality. The achievement, as W. Walsh states, 'rests . . . on an inward life and coherence'. *A Passage to England* (1960) is a distinctive traveller's tale of the surprising extent to which actual experience confirmed the England of his reading and imagination. *The Continent of Circe* (1965) analyses and tries to account for the miseries and shames of contemporary Indian life – with courage and (what Indian controversy over the book often ignores) with pain. *Clive of India* (1975) and *Scholar Extraordinary* (1975), a biography of F.M. Muller, extend Chaudhuri's role as an interpreter of the convoluted Indian-British relationship.
[AR]

CHESTERTON, G.K. (Gilbert Keith) (1874–1936). Journalist, essayist, thinker, novelist, biographer, poet and critic. The son of an estate agent, he was born in London, educated at St Paul's and later at the Slade School of Art. At St Paul's began his long friendship with E.C. Bentley, the inventor of the clerihew. While at the Slade, he attended the English course at University College, where he found W.P. Ker's lectures a lively stimulus. By 1901, when he married Frances Blogg, he was a well-known journalist, writing regularly for the *Daily News*, *Speaker* and *Bookman*. From 1905 he wrote in the *Illustrated London News*, keeping up a weekly column until his death. Chesterton's political and social enthusiasms were anti-imperialistic (he was pro-Boer) and anti-establishment: he shared the view his friend Hilaire Belloc (q.v.) and his brother Cecil Chesterton voiced in their book *The Party System* – 'that there were not two real parties ruling alternately, but one real group "the Front Benches", ruling all the time' (*Autobiography*, 1969). He was a liberal defender of the small unit against giant uniformities; his anti-capitalism took the form of Distributism – a belief in small ownership and distribution of the nation's property, especially its land, among its people: he regretted the Fabian attack on property itself. ('It is the negation of property that the Duke of Sutherland should have all the farms in one estate; just as it would be the negation of marriage if he had all our wives in one harem', *What's Wrong with the World*, 1910). The *Eye Witness*, a periodical run by Belloc and Cecil Chesterton, was responsible for forcing the Marconi scandal on the public and, in Chesterton's view, first made the people aware of the corruptibility of English politicians. (The scandal blew up in 1912 over the premature sale of shares in a planned project to establish a government network of radio stations. Ministers were alleged to have been among the purchasers.) He took over the editorship of *New Witness* (*Eye Witness*'s successor) when Cecil joined the army in 1916, and ran it until 1923. It was succeeded in turn by *G.K.'s Weekly* (1925) which ran until Chesterton's death. How far the massive, lifelong journalistic output frustrated or damaged Chesterton's more creative work is a question, but his determination was to influence current thinking. ('I have never taken my books

seriously; but I take my opinions quite seriously', *Autobiography*.)

In finding his way from fashionable agnosticism to Christianity, Chesterton was helped by Frances, a firm Anglo-Catholic: his friends Belloc and Maurice Baring (q.v.) played their part in his eventual movement from the Church of England to the Church of Rome in 1922. The Catholic synthesis, in its full institutional and dogmatic rigour, proved a congenial framework for the life and thought of a man who was early disturbed by 'vague and visionary revolt against the prosaic flatness of a nineteenth-century city and civilization', who pursued coherence and rationality through related aspects of social, intellectual and spiritual life, and who was above all aware of the paradox embedded in the truth and reality confronting him as man and writer at every level of experience. ('There is always something fanciful about the conjunction of the world that the poet sees and the place he lives in', op. cit.) Chesterton attacked popular literary prophets of the day (Shaw (q.v.), Wells (q.v.) and Kipling (q.v.) among them) for their errors in *Heretics* (1905), was challenged to lay his own philosophical cards on the table, and published *Orthodoxy* in 1908. Belloc spoke of Chesterton's 'unique, his capital genius for illustration by parallel, by example'. This gift, and Chesterton's aphoristic brilliance, make his Christian apologetic both startling and illuminating; and the scintillating parallels and paradoxes of *Orthodoxy* are married in the maturer study, *The Everlasting Man* (1925), to broader and more systematic scholarship.

Chesterton's literary life was entangled with that of eminent contemporaries. There was plenty of controversy, but it generally coexisted with warm friendship. He cherished Belloc (who later wrote *On the Place of G.K. Chesterton in English Letters*, 1940), Baring and Ronald Knox. He won the admiration of Max Beerbohm (q.v.). He admired, and disagreed with, Yeats (q.v.) and Wells. Verbal duels with Shaw, in print and on platform, were a national entertainment. The flavour of it lingers for us in Chesterton's *George Bernard Shaw* (1909). This is one of those literary biographies in which he managed to compensate for lack of what pedants call scholarship by inspired shafts of divination and boisterous conviviality in exposition. He was happy to put on paper a general knowledge unchecked and uncorroborated, yet *Robert Browning* (1903), which Beerbohm urged him to write ('A man should write on Browning while he is young'), is a delight, though Chesterton cheerfully conceded that it was a projection of his own views 'in which the name of Browning was introduced from time to time' (op. cit). The exaggeration is endearing; for there are great insights into Browning's mind and his work. ('He was a kind of cosmic detective who walked into the foulest of thieves' kitchens and accused men publicly of virtue.') *Charles Dickens* (1906) has enjoyed comparable popularity in spite of its inaccuracies. In *The Victorian Age in Literature* (1913) Chesterton is on ground where his knowledge is relevant and his view of the period penetrating. In *Chaucer* (1932) the thinness of the literary scholarship is apparent. The motives the book serves are better served in the theological biographies, *St Francis of Assisi* (1923) and *St Thomas Aquinas* (1933), the latter a lucid and probing study that the most expert scholarship acclaimed with astonishment.

Chesterton's serious poetry (he was a good parodist) includes 'Lepanto', an exercise in blazing rhetoric ('The other day in the trenches we shouted your "Lepanto",' John Buchan (q.v.) wrote to him in 1915), and *The Ballad of the White Horse* (1911), a sustained narrative which describes King Alfred's vision of the Virgin Mary –

> I tell you naught for your comfort,
>   Yea, naught for your desire,
> Save that the sky grows darker yet
>   And the sea rises higher.

– the King's subsequent rallying of the Wessex men, his penetration of the Danish camp as a minstrel, his burning of the cakes and his defeat of the Danes at Edington.

The first of Chesterton's fantastic novels was *The Napoleon of Notting Hill* (1904). The idea for it flashed upon him as he wandered one day about the streets of North Kensington. It became a reality when he found himself broke, for he outlined it to his publishers and sucessfully demanded £20 to get on with it. Auberon Quin, King of England (chosen by lot), is modelled on Max Beerbohm. Seeking fun, he grants the London boroughs the dignity of armed city guards. Adam Wayne of Notting Hill is his counterpart – in seriousness and enthusiasm – and goes to war in protection of a threatened little street. Notting Hill is destroyed by the other boroughs. *The Man Who Was Thursday* (1908) is perhaps the best of Chesterton's fantasies, exploiting to fine purpose his fondness for leading the reader up the garden path. The hero is entangled in the machinations of an anarchistic revolutionary plot and given the name of Thursday – for each of the sinister group is called after a day of the week. Stage by stage, amid extraordinary adventures, it is revealed that each of the group, except the terrifying leader, Sunday, is in fact a detective spying on the proceedings. In *The Ball and the Cross* (1909) a young Catholic Highlander, who takes insults to the Virgin Mary gravely, and an atheist, who takes his atheism seriously, vainly try to fight it out, but wherever they go the representatives of modern civilization interrupt and prevent them: they finish up in an asylum. *Manalive* (1912), vintage Chesterton in its meaningful topsy-turvydoms, and *The Flying Inn* (1914) belong to the same genre.

Of all Chesterton's works the short stories of criminal detection, the *Father Brown Stories*, have proved the most popular. They appeared in a series of volumes, *The Innocence of Father Brown* (1911), *The Wisdom of Father Brown* (1914), *The Incredulity of Father Brown* (1926), *The Secret of Father Brown* (1927) and *The Scandal of Father Brown* (1935). Father Brown, the innocent-seeming Roman Catholic priest and solver of teasingly odd criminal problems, was modelled on Fr J. O'Connor (see J. O'Connor, *Father Brown on Chesterton*, 1937) whom Chesterton first met in 1904 and who received him into the Catholic Church in 1922. Chesterton tells in his *Autobiography* how he first met Fr O'Connor at Keighley in Yorkshire. As the two men walked together over the moors to Ilkley, O'Connor shocked Chesterton by recounting an instance of perverted practices that had come his way. Later Chesterton heard two Cambridge under-graduates speak of the priest as a man shut off from reality by ignorance of the evil in the world. The irony inspired Chesterton with the notion of 'a priest with a knowledge of evil deeper than that of the criminal he is converting' and the first story, 'The Blue Cross', was conceived. The ingenuous-seeming priest with his 'shapeless little figure, which seemed to find its own hat and umbrella as unmanageable as a mass of luggage' ('The Absence of Mr Glass', *The Wisdom of Father Brown*), is a physically battered version of Fr O'Connor; but his quick observation and profound understanding of human nature enable him to turn the tables on the hasty judgements of the man in the street and on the expertise of the professional in interpreting events of apparently baffling complexity. Penetration into twisted states of mind and eccentric practices is his forte. Judicious words of wisdom bubble up richly from the well of moral theology at which the priest's pastoral and detective interests alike are nourished. See also M. Ward, *Gilbert Keith Chesterton* (1944). W.H. Auden (q.v.) edited *Chesterton: A Selection from his Non-Fictional Prose* (1970). [HB]

CHILDERS, ERSKINE (1870–1922). Born in London, educated at Haileybury and Cambridge. He served in the British forces in the Boer War and was a major in the air force in the First World War. His extraordinary novel, *The Riddle of the Sands* (1903), is a solemn warning about the menace to England of German war preparations correctly projected as likely to come to a head in some ten years' time. It is at once a yachting story, packed with technical interest for the initiated, and a tale of espionage carried out on the German coast, where long-term plans for future invasion of England are already under rehearsal. Childers, whose mother was Irish, espoused the Irish republican cause, joined the anti-treaty forces and was executed by the Free State forces in 1922. Frank O'Connor (q.v.) gives a first-hand picture of Childers at this stage in *The Only Child*. See also Andrew Boyle, *The Riddle of Erskine Childers* (1977). [HB]

CHRISTIE, AGATHA (née Miller) (1890–1976). Detective novelist, born in Torquay, Devon, of a wealthy American father. She married Archibald Christie in 1914 and, after divorce, the archaeologist Max Mallowan in 1932. Mystery still surrounds an odd episode in 1926 when she disappeared from her Surrey home to turn up ten days later in Harrogate, apparently suffering from amnesia. Christie has been claimed to be the most widely read British author in the world. From the publication of *The Mysterious Affair at Styles* (1920) she steadily produced detective novels notable for ingenuity of plotting. Her skill in planting clues, trailing red herrings and turning the tables on the reader at the end proved captivating. Her Belgian detective, Hercule Poirot, neatly matches up to an Englishman's story-book notion of a foreigner (he appears in over forty books) and Miss Jane Marple, the old lady who knows her English villagers inside out, is a useful counterpoise. No distinction of style is claimed for Agatha Christie, but her staple presentation, largely dialogue, is eminently readable. Some of her stories have been adapted for the stage. Her play, *The Mousetrap* (prod 1952), has now run continuously in

London for over thirty years. The author also wrote straight novels under the name 'Mary Westmacott'. Personally, she had the breeding and charm of the English upper middle class; that she had wit too is evidenced by her appreciative comment on the advantage of having an archaeologist for a husband: 'The older you get, the more interesting he finds you'. *An Autobiography* (1977) has been published posthumously. [HB]

CHURCH, RICHARD (1893–1972). Novelist, journalist and poet, born in London, the son of a post office sorter and a school-teacher. His mother came of the Midland yeoman family which had felt itself disgraced by the behaviour of cousin Marian Evans – George Eliot – in living with another woman's husband. Church, for a quarter of a century a civil servant by profession, published a dozen novels, twenty volumes of verse, and some thirty other works, mostly collections of essays. The trilogy of novels (*The Porch*, 1937; *The Stronghold*, 1939; and *The Room Within*, 1940) was intended, on the basis of his own experience, to portray 'amongst the individual drama, the workings of the British Civil Service, showing how it is based on the Stoic philosophy' (*Over the Bridge*). The novels read interestingly alongside the three-volume autobiography (*Over the Bridge*, 1955; *The Golden Sovereign*, 1957; and *The Voyage Home*, 1964) but the novels have dated and the autobiographies are richly alive. The evocation of childhood in *Over the Bridge* is refreshingly sensitive and spirited, recapturing 'the first five joyous years of my life spent so peacefully among the labyrinthine streets covering the Battersea marsh'. Church is penetrating and generous in his portraiture of lovable parents, entrancing foils to each other in temperament and motivation, struggling cheerfully and zestfully on their modest income. *The Porch*, by contrast, though illuminating in its account of a young man's start in the Civil Service as a minor clerk in the Food and Drugs Analysis Department at the Custom House, is cloyingly sentimental in tone and substance. *The Stronghold* carries the story forward into the First World War to show the effect of the war on social patterns and personal careers. Church's last novel, *Little Miss Moffatt* (1969), more contemporary in flavour, relies too much on caricature in its study of Malcolm Moffatt, celibate Anglican priest and dogmatic elder brother of an easy-going architect with a charming wife and daughter. Malcolm's dangerously passionate concern for the spiritual welfare of his secularly brought-up niece leads him into strange aberration. As an essayist, Church muses equably on a variety of topics – nature, travel, literature, domestic life and so on – in elegantly palatable prose. His poetry is not distinguished (see *Collected Poems*, 1948). It is the autobiographical volumes that deserve the critical praise accorded them and that seem likely to survive. [HB]

CLARK, JOHN PEPPER (1936–). Dramatist, poet, critic, born at Kiagbodo in the Niger delta, Nigeria, and educated at Ughelli and University College, Ibadan. After graduating in 1960, he worked as a journalist for two years. In 1962–3 he was a Parvin Fellow at Princeton University, New Jersey, then wrote a vitriolic book, *America, Their America* (1964). His first volume of verse

was *Poems* (1962). Some of its poems reappeared in *A Reed in the Tide* (1965) together with new pieces; a further collection, *Casualties: Poems 1966/68*, was published in 1970. *A Decade of Tongues* (1981) is a selection from these three volumes. Clark's first play, *Song of a Goat*, appeared in 1961 and again, with two others, *The Masquerade* and *The Raft*, in *Three Plays* (1964). On returning from Princeton, Clark did research into Ijaw mythology, which inspired his adaptation as a play in English (*Ozidi*, 1966) of the traditional Ijaw epic drama performed in seven days to dance, music and mime; he also made a film of it, *The Ozidi of Atazi*, and has translated the entire epic as *The Ozidi Saga* (1975). In 1966 Clark became lecturer, and later Professor, of English in the University of Lagos. In 1970 he published a lively, forthright collection of his critical writings, *The Example of Shakespeare: Critical Essays in African Literature*, including the now celebrated 'The Legacy of Caliban', which uses the Caliban metaphor to discuss searchingly the black writers' use of English.

The four verse plays constitute Clark's most important work so far, revealing a preoccupation with Ijaw tribal settings in the Niger delta and characters who courageously and tragically assert their individuality against hereditary curse or inimical fate; for instance, in *Song of a Goat*, Zifa's personal love of his wife Ebiere makes him reject the traditional way of dealing with his own impotence – giving her to his younger brother and offering the sacrifice of a goat to obviate the gods' normal disapproval of incest. Ebiere's seduction of her brother-in-law, without the stipulated cleansing rites, leads to the deaths of all three, but also to the birth of Tufa, whose inherited guilt plays itself out tragically in *The Masquerade*. Clark's use of verse drama for themes of fated humanity led critics to regard him as an imitator of Greek tragedy, but the similarities depend rather on general correspondences between ancient Greek and traditional Ijaw culture. K.D. Lipenga has, however, demonstrated the fructifying influence of Lorca on at least one scene in *The Masquerade*. Some commentators have disparaged the 'awkwardness' of Clark's dramatic verse, but G.W. Hill refers to the language of the dialogue as 'raw-edged with awkward juxtapositions' but 'at times, beautifully achieved'. Clark has also been accused of lack of practical experience of the theatre but his first three plays have been successfully staged in various countries. *Ozidi* presents considerable production problems but there is great power in the presentation of the central character's tragedy: 'Like a river at a whirlpool I am come to / A spinning stop'. [AR]

CLARKE, AUSTIN (1896–1974). Poet and dramatist, born in Dublin, Ireland. His father was an official of the Dublin Waste Water Department. Clarke spoke of an eccentric great-grandfather, a skinner, who wore wigs of different colour during the week and wrote satirical ballads for local ballad-singers. He was educated at Belvedere College, Joyce's old school, and at University College, Dublin, where he took his MA and became Lecturer in English from 1917 to 1921. He married Nora Walker and had three children. He spent some years in England, reviewing for major literary journals, and went back to settle finally in Ireland in 1937 – but only to return to England in his dreams:

> When I had brought my wife
> And children, wave over wave,
> From exile, could I have known
> That I would sleep in England
> Still, lie awake at home?
>
> ('Return from England')

Memories of childhood in Ireland and of the London years are feelingly recaptured in the autobiographical reminiscences, *Twice Around the Black Church* (1962), where Clarke quotes with approval Ibsen's definition of poetry:

> Poetry – 'tis a Court
> Of Judgment on the soul.

Clarke first published narrative poems on mythological Irish heroes, *The Vengeance of Fionn* (1917), about the love of Diarmuid and Grainne, and *The Sword of the West* (1921), about Concobar and Cuchullin. For all the surging vigour of these works, they represent a romantic phase from which he escaped in *Night and Morning* (1938), where terse outbursts like 'The Choice' (a surgeon's decision to sacrifice baby, not mother, in childbirth) focus on immediate Irish realities and are taut with commitment. But Clarke then interrupted his 'straight' poetic output, involving himself for some seventeen years in the work of preserving verse drama after its decline at the Abbey Theatre. He founded the Irish Lyric Theatre Group. His own plays include *Sister Eucharia* (prod 1941) and *The Viscount of Blarney* (prod 1944).

When Clarke returned to poetry, the later volumes marked an extraordinary recrudescence of inventiveness and inspiration. They include *Ancient Lights* (1955), *Flight to Africa* (1963), *Old-fashioned Pilgrimage* (1967) and *The Echo at Coole* (1968), and they reveal the full maturing of an astonishingly crisp and forceful utterance on the part of a poet who is absorbed in himself and his country, and ruthless in frank exposure of both. His is a rebellious nature in conflict with itself and its ideological environment; but humour sauces his acerbities. The characteristic emotional violence, whether of inner analysis or external comment, is disciplined by an assonantal technique derivative from Gaelic poetry.

> Teresa had heard the Lutherans
>   Howling on red-hot spit
> And grill, men who had searched for truth
>   Alone in Holy Writ.
> So Martha, fearful of flame lashing
>   Those heretics, each instant,
> Never dealt in the haberdashery
>   Shop owned by two Protestants.

This packed and sturdy poem, 'Martha Blake at Fifty-One', from the fine collection, *Flight to Africa*, registers the facts of Martha's physical collapse and death with searing penetration and compassion. The full intensity of Clarke's personal self-exploration can be gauged from the uniquely powerful record of his experience in a mental hospital in *Mnemosyne Lay in Dust* (1966), which takes us into the company of strange fellow inmates and into the padded cell ('Fists hushed on a wall of inward-outness'). So late a poem as *Tiresias* (1971), a narrative

about the relative copulatory delights of women and men, throbs with sexual energy. Clarke is among the most profoundly original of twentieth-century poets yet his work is rooted in Gaelic tradition. He also wrote three novels that were banned in his homeland. His *Collected Poems* (1974) was published shortly after his death. Clarke was a founder member of the Irish Academy of Letters in 1932 and became President in the year 1952–3. Dublin University gave him an honorary Litt D in 1966, and the Orator applauded his mastery 'in a world of the imagination which spans the gap between old Irish and modern English writing'.   [HB]

CLARKE, AUSTIN CHESTERFIELD   (1934–). Novelist, born in Barbados. He went to school in Barbados and to university in Toronto, Ontario, Canada, where he now lives. He also holds periodic visiting lectureships at United States universities. North American black consciousness has influenced his first five novels. *The Survivors of the Crossing* (1964) and *Among Thistles and Thorns* (1965), both set in Barbados, are respectively about an abortive political revolt against white plantocracy and its self-despising black hangers-on, and an adolescent's abortive cultural revolt, both protagonists being inspired indirectly by the Harlem Renaissance of the 1920s. Like Selvon (q.v.), Clarke deals in his Toronto novels, *The Meeting Point* (1972), *A Storm of Fortune* (1973) and *The Bigger Light* (1975), with black characters' attempts to discover their true selves in an indifferent, even inimical white society. L.W. Brown summarizes Clarke's themes as 'black awareness, national identity, the hateful ambiguities of the West, and the heroic potential of the black peasant', perspicaciously observing that he extends the North American dimension of West Indian literature initiated by Claude McKay (q.v.). Clarke's strengths are complex, meticulous characterization and vigorous dialogue. *The Prime Minister* appeared in 1978, while *Growing up Stupid under the Union Jack* (1980), which was awarded the *Casa de las Americas* fiction prize, finely balances nostalgic celebration of a Barbadian childhood with satirization of its imperial milieu. *When He was Free and Young and He Used to Wear Silks* (1971) consists of impressively crafted stories.   [AR]

CLEMO, JACK (1916–). Poet and novelist, born in St Austell, Cornwall. He attended Trethosa Village School, but can claim to be largely self-educated. His autobiography, *Confession of a Rebel* (1949), traces the development of a social misfit reared on the edge of poverty in an area where the china-clay industry has encroached on farming and defaced the landscape. Isolated by temperament, he has suffered partial, then total and permanent, deafness. From childhood he has also known periods of intermittent blindness and eventually, in 1955, he lost his sight too. He had told how he derived literary inspiration from friendship with young girls, but the central driving force has been a deeply religious sense of Christianity as 'a redemptive invasion of nature by divine grace', a view elaborated in his theological book, *The Invading Gospel* (1958). In his novel *Wilding Graft* (1948) Clemo is concerned to show 'the freedom of God . . . to create a point of contact at any level of the human personality –

not only in the so-called higher levels of idealism and spirituality, but in the undisciplined instinct, a direct grafting into the lifeblood of passion instead of into the cool bony structure of reason' (*Confession of a Rebel*). Thus Garth Joslin, in the novel, receives his grafting through the girl he eventually marries. Browning and T.F. Powys (q.v.) are among Clemo's mentors, but he sometimes writes of sex like a converted D.H. Lawrence (q.v.). The tension between nature and divine grace runs like a high-voltage current through his poetry (*The Clay Verge*, 1951; *The Map of Clay*, 1961; *Cactus on Carmel*, 1967; *The Echoing Tip*, 1971; *Broad Autumn*, 1975). The paradoxical entanglement of spiritual reality with the violent and the harsh is voiced in imagery of vividness and power. In 'The Excavator' the grim machine shields the poet on a stormy Sunday night like a new rock of ages, water dripping on to him from its bar like a baptism.

> The bars now hinged o'erhead and drooping form
> A Cross that lacks the symmetry
> Of those in churches, but is more
> Like His Whose stooping tore
> The vitals from our world's foul secrecy.

Clemo has been awarded a Civil List pension. He married Ruth Grace Peaty in 1968. *The Marriage of a Rebel* (1980) tells the story of his search for a partner, a search by a man convinced that God had destined him for marriage while the Devil had tried to render him unmarriageable.

[HB]

CLOETE, STUART (1897-). Novelist and short-story writer, born in Paris, educated in England. At 17 he joined the army, serving throughout the First World War and until 1925. He then took up farming in South Africa.

Cloete has published some fifteen novels, eight volumes of stories and some works of non-fiction, including *A Victorian Son* (1971) and *The Gambler* (1973), autobiographies. Most of his fiction is set in southern Africa and is best characterized in his own words: 'a novel should provide an escape from the present and transport the reader into other situations, where he can . . . lose himself and forget his worries'. Yet the series of 'Boer' novels, beginning with *Turning Wheels* (1937), his first book, which was banned in South Africa, and ending with *Rags of Glory* (1963), deals realistically with the history of the Afrikaner people up to Britain's defeat of the two republics in 1902, through presenting individuals caught up in, and often confused by, historical events. Consequently he conveys vividly the origins of South Africa's political problems. H. Maes-Jelinek remarks that his writings suggest 'not justice but blind fate rules the world, and the best human beings can do is to fulfil themselves according to their nature'.

The Curve and the Tusk (1953) is a novel about elephant-hunting and elephant behaviour and *The Abductors* (1970) about the white-slave traffic.   [AR]

COHEN, LEONARD (1934-). Poet, novelist, songwriter and singer, born in Montreal, Quebec, Canada, and educated at McGill University, Montreal, and Columbia University, New York. He began his career as a poet with *Let Us Compare Mythologies* (1956) and *The*

Spice Box of Earth (1961), both unremarkable volumes in a predominantly traditional-romantic strain. A preoccupation with human relationships, often from an initially Jewish viewpoint, informed the more experimental volume *Flowers for Hitler* (1964) and also characterized many of the songs which brought him international fame in the mid-1960s. *The Favourite Game* (1963), like its successor *Beautiful Losers* (1966), displayed impressive dexterity in its handling of language and situation. Its story of the Jewish boy from Montreal who becomes a poet and folk singer invites an autobiographical reading and perhaps because of this the book lacks adequate structure and characterization. In *Beautiful Losers* style is dominant; there is no attempt at 'realism' in the black humour of character and situation with which Cohen seeks to depict the spiritual, and sexual, depths of contemporary society. Prose approaches the 'poetic' in an experimental tour de force, at times both disturbing and amusing but ultimately somewhat over-wrought. The poetry collection *Parasites of Heaven* (1966) was followed by *Selected Poems, 1956–1968* (1968) and *The Energy of Slaves* (1972), in which Cohen widened his poetic approach with mixed success. *Death of a Lady's Man* (1978) was a rather over-ambitious book whose format included differing drafts and other material offering shifting prespectives on the 'text'. A useful approach to his very varied work is provided by the essays in *Leonard Cohen: The Artist and His Critics*, edited by M. Gnarowski (1976).   [PQ]

COLUM, PADRAIC (1881-1972). Poet, dramatist and novelist, born at Longford, County Leinster, Ireland, where his father was in charge of the workhouse. He started working life as a Dublin railway clerk, but was soon involved with Yeats (q.v.), AE (George Russell, (q.v.), Douglas Hyde and others in the foundation of the National Theatre. His early play, *Broken Soil*, was put on by the Irish National Theatre Society in 1903. *The Land* (prod 1905) followed, and Colum was regarded as a new 'peasant' dramatist of the same breed as Synge (q.v.). As a poet Colum was among the protégés cherished by AE who included him in his collection, *New Songs* (1904). 'Colum will be our principal literary figure in ten years', Russell averred, somewhat to the chagrin of the young James Joyce (q.v.). Colum's early collection of verse, *Wild Earth* (1907), contains some of his best work. Colum was also an associate of James Stephens (q.v.), with whom he founded the *Irish Review* in 1916, and of Joyce himself. He married Mary Maguire, also a writer, and the two later collaborated in the volume of reminiscences, *Our Friend, James Joyce* (1959). Colum's output includes over a dozen plays and some twenty volumes of stories for children, but it is as a poet that he is chiefly remembered. *Collected Poems* (1953) shows the consistency and the fine simplicity of his lyrical gift. Accepted stanza forms are managed with fluency and directness: musically and idiomatically they have the genuine flavour of folk-song and ballad. One of the most touching pieces, 'She Moved Through the Fair', set to music, has attained immense popularity:

> My young love said to me, 'My brothers won't mind,

And my parents won't slight you for your lack of
kind.'
Then she stepped away from me, and this she did
say,
'It will not be long, love, till our wedding day.'

Colum went to America in 1914 and settled there,
becoming a lecturer at Columbia University. He published
A Treasury of Irish Folklore in 1955. The late novel, *The
Flying Swans* (1957), is a detailed record of the life of
Ulick O'Rehill, whose father Robert has been too
romantic, unpractical and wilful to foster his Irish estate
and regain (by profitable marriage) the long-lost lands of
his aristocratic forebears. Robert lifts a herdsman's
daughter to his side as bride, then forsakes her. Ulick's
upbringing is documented with the fullness and verisimilitude
of autobiography. Benedict Kiely has prefaced a
reissue of Colum's *The Poet's Circuits, Collected Poems of
Ireland* (originally 1960), marking the centenary of the
poet's birth. [HB]

COMMON, JACK (1903–68). Novelist, born in Newcastle
upon Tyne, Tyne and Wear, the son of a railwayman,
educated at the local elementary school and at a
commercial college. He moved to London in the late
1920s, helped Middleton Murry (q.v.) with his *Adelphi*,
worked on film scripts and as a reviewer, and published a
collection of socio-political essays, *The Freedom of the
Street* (1938), which George Orwell (q.v.) called 'the
authentic voice of the ordinary man', but he never gained
by literary recognition an escape from the need to work at
menial jobs. He is now remembered for his two strongly
autobiographical novels, *Kiddar's Luck* (1951) and *The
Ampersand* (1954), which were reissued in one volume in
1975. The first re-creates his childhood and early adolescence
in Newcastle with an astonishing fullness of recall
that makes it an important social document. Against the
background of the shabby streets, the troubled home with
its overworked father and drunken mother, the pubs, the
pawnshops, the market and the school, human portraits
stand out in Dickensian vitality and Dickensian oddity.
The sequel takes the hero through commercial college to
his first job in a solicitor's office, from which he is sacked
for theft. The depth of the cultural chasm between
classes as sensed by an intelligent victim of the divide is
wryly, rather than rancorously, conveyed. But the victim
muffs his own opportunities by laziness and dishonesty
and emerges as a self-centred and unlikeable young man.
Failure to simplify the emotional appeal and to focus the
reader's sympathy decisively perhaps accounts for the
neglect of books which are rich in evocative detail. [HB]

COMPTON-BURNETT, IVY (Dame) (1884–1969).
Novelist, born at Pinner, Middlesex, the daughter of a
London doctor who had five children by his first wife and
seven by the second. The author was the eldest child of
the second marriage and was 16 when her father died. By
this time the family home was at Hove, Sussex. The
widowed mother, a domineering neurotic, survived for
another ten years and then the author herself succeeded
to a role of harsh domination which her four younger
sisters found so intolerable that they fled to London in
1915, though Compton-Burnett had recourse to the family

solicitor in her attempt to restrain them. (Two of the girls
later committed suicide.) Meanwhile both brothers had
died, the first of pneumonia, the second on the Somme –
shortly after administering a heavy blow to his devoted
sister by getting married. The intensity of the family grip
prior to the break-up of the Hove household remained an
obsession throughout the author's career as a novelist. It
is too soon after her death for a full and objective disentangling
of the personal psychological history underlying
this obsession.

Ivy Compton-Burnett had been educated at Addiscombe
College for the Daughters of Gentlemen, at Hove,
and had proceeded to Royal Holloway College in the
University of London, where she took her degree in
classics in 1906 and gained second-class honours. Her
familiarity with Greek tragedy has been cited as relevant
to the concentrated sequences of unfolding disaster
which infuse her novels with ironic fatalism. Her early
rejection of Christianity is relevant to her pessimistic
refusal, as a novelist, to allow of effectively redemptive
agencies operative on human development, and to her
adoption of an ethical stance which assumes that crime
can pay in terms of personal fulfilment as well as in terms
of material gain. In 1919 Compton-Burnett began to share
her London flat with Margaret Jourdain, an expert on
antique furniture, and the companionship lasted until
Miss Jourdain's death in 1951.

Ivy Compton-Burnett's first novel, *Dolores* (1911), a
sentimental study in feminine self-sacrifice, with roots in
George Eliot's *Middlemarch*, was one which she later
preferred to forget, and her fiction career began
seriously fourteen years later with the publication of
Pastors and Masters (1925). The setting is a private
school and the plot centres on the pretentious headmaster's
plan to publish a stolen manuscript as his own.
The father of two of the boys, Mr Bentley, prefigures
what is to come in later novels as a study in parental bullying:
he is adept at twisting every statement by his children
against them. Thereafter, in *Brothers and Sisters* (1929),
Men and Wives (1931), *More Women than Men* (1933) and
A House and its Head (1935), the pattern of the canon is
firmly established. In the country houses of smaller
landed gentry, against a negligible visual background and
in an environment from which the appurtenances of
cultural, professional or even sporting life are rigidly
excluded, members of tightly knit families conduct
dialogues that fasten on details of personal bearing and
personal relationship with a ravenous appetite for
scoring off each other, sometimes good-humouredly, often
maliciously. The warfare of conversation is carried on in
choice diction, deliberate in tone, shapely in phrasing.
There is an almost liturgical power to mesmerize in the
unceasing flow of well-placed words in stylized idiom of
which even cooks and kitchenmaids are capable. One
seems to be listening to the voice of an embittered Lady
Bracknell or a Jane Austen who has acquired a diabolical
tail, so frequently are surface politenesses resonant with
ulterior overtones and so widely diffused is the talent for
sustained conversational brinkmanship on the edge of
overt acrimony. The gift for scathing repartee that knocks
a gushing or pretentious utterance stone dead is also
widespread. It is the only defence against tyrants like
Duncan Edgeworth (*A House and its Head*) whose

unfailing agility at putting other people in the wrong in the name of specious dutifulness is the torment of two daughters and of his heir, a nephew. Widowed in his late sixties, he unexpectedly marries a young wife, but the resultant new heir turns out to have been fathered by the nephew. Murder of the child is engineered by the younger daughter, Sibyl (she has married her cousin), and she throws suspicion on her father and stepmother. Neither just retribution nor fit change of heart overtakes either the father who is unlivable with or the infanticidal daughter. Thus the exercise of power and the greed for money thread black strands of evil through family lives. Children are rendered miserable by exacting demands for premature responsiveness to adult hunger for flattery or servitude. Compton-Burnett dissects men and women who devour the happiness of others – by domination or by the blackmail of advertised suffering and 'sacrifice' – with the thoroughness of Meredith, whom she resembles also in the orchestration of witty backchat.

After *A House and its Head* followed *Daughters and Sons* (1937), *A Family and a Fortune* (1939), *Parents and Children* (1941), *Elders and Betters* (1944) and *Manservant and Maidservant** (1947). Between Edgar Gaveston and his brother Dudley (*A Family and a Fortune*) there exists an inescapable bond (sometimes it is between parent and child) which so often in these novels has a primacy that stultifies normal marriage relations in advance. Another character, Aunt Matty, is a full-scale study of predatory self-dramatization. Her lameness provides the moral leverage for extracting incessant homage. Here as elsewhere well-meaning, unselfish people tend to be beaten into ineffectiveness or to die sadly neglected, and the moral tone is consequently enigmatic. Nevertheless there are always detached or sarcastic characters to highlight the silliness of emotional charlatans and torpedo their self-indulgent histrionics. In *Elders and Betters* there flourishes a female fiend, Anna Donne, adopting the guise of a blunderingly frank plain-speaker. She cunningly diverts an invalid's bequest to herself, though it is intended for her Aunt Jessica's family who have long looked after the invalid (Aunt Sukey). She then subtly drives Aunt Jessica to suicide, when concealment of her crime seems to be at risk. Anna thus successively exploits Aunt Sukey's weakness – an incessant demand for sympathy – and Aunt Jessica's weakness – a tendency to excessive self-abnegation and self-blame. The action drifts to a 'happy ending', when Anna deceives her cousin Terence (Jessica's son) into marriage. The picture of the servants' lot is sharpened by Anna's treatment of them as beings who have no call on human sympathy or interest. Downstairs life is more fully represented in *Manservant and Maidservant*, which may be regarded as a peak and a turning-point. The later novels tend to be repetitive. They include *The Present and the Past* (1953), *A Father and His Fate* (1957) and *A God and His Gifts* (1963). Compton-Burnett's attachment to contrived 'plots' and to uniform stylized diction has invoked criticism, but her dialogue is a sensitive instrument of character revelation and her wit has a unique, inimitable mordancy.

Manservant and Maidservant was issued in the USA under the title *Bullivant and the Lambs*. Horace Lamb is a domestic tyrant in his mid-fifties and he specializes in miserly economies on food and warmth. His brutal treatment of his five children, whose ages range from 7 to 13, has made him a figure of detestation to them and has alienated his wife, Charlotte. 'Horace had married her for her money, hoping to serve his impoverished estate, and she had married for love, hoping to fulfil herself. The love had gone and the money remained, so that the advantage lay with Horace.' Horace's dependent cousin, Mortimer, a good-hearted fellow, fond of the suffering children and now in love with Charlotte, is about to take them all away when the attachment is revealed to Horace and so stuns him that he ostentatiously reforms, becoming a model father. Mortimer and Charlotte can no longer in good conscience contemplate breaking up the family. The past, however, remains in the children's minds and they dread its possible recurrence. Hence the two boys, Jasper and Marcus, on impulse fail to warn their father when he is setting out on a walk that will probably take him over an unsafe bridge to his death. In fact it does not, but a young footman tries to get rid of Horace by the same means later. In each case Horace is provided with opportunities for parading himself unbearably in roles of injured innocence, ill-paid generosity and persecuted virtue. In culmination he becomes ill and, near to death, enacts the final inflated gestures of mercy and magnanimity. But he recovers, and the novel ends where it began. The life of the servants' hall, involving the butler Bullivant (Wodehouse's Jeeves transfigured), is fully recorded and adds an ironic chorus to the bogus heroics upstairs.   [HB]

CONNOLLY, CYRIL (1903–74). Critic, born in Coventry, West Midlands, educated at Eton and Balliol College, Oxford. He founded the literary magazine *Horizon* in 1939 and remained its editor until it ceased publication in 1950. He was an influential reviewer and literary essayist. His one novel, *The Rock Pool* (1936), studies the disintegration of Edgar Naylor in a Riviera resort. Half stockbroker and half 'self-appointed biographer of Samuel Rogers', Naylor is 'neither very intelligent nor especially likeable'. Scathing satire on the English cultural scene from which Naylor has escaped is swallowed up in the picture of savage selfishness and corruption among those who batten on him and destroy him at Trou-sur-Mer. The book has a rare aphoristic brilliance. Connolly's *The Unquiet Grave* (1944), first published under the pseudonym 'Palinurus', is a collection of pensées, culled and original, gathered into pattern around the mythical figure of Virgil's Palinurus, the Trojan pilot who fell overboard and was drowned. *The Evening Colonnade* (1973) is a collection of essays. *A Romantic Friendship* (1975), edited by Noel Blakiston, is a collection of Connolly's letters to Blakiston, mostly dating from the 1920s. Connolly was a widely read, much travelled writer whose literary personality seemed much larger to those who knew him than his creative output can account for.   [HB]

CONNOR, TONY (1930–). Poet, born in Manchester. He left school at 14 and worked in the textile industry until 1960. After teaching at Bolton Technical College, he went to the USA and there he became Professor of English at Wesleyan University, Middletown, Connecticut, in 1971. Generally labelled a 'domestic' poet, he has used accepted verse forms simply and economically to achieve strength and directness in handling homely personal themes. *With Love Somehow* (1962) was followed by *Lodgers* (1965). In the latter there are portraits of his father ('My Father's Walking-Stick') – 'Swindler, con-man, and embezzler . . . I was five / when he disappeared with a Royal Warrant / out for his arrest' – and his mother ('My Mother's Husband'), and some self-analysis in the light of this lineage ('A Death by the Seaside'), as well as lively studies of earthy Lancashire characters. *Twelve Secret Poems* (1965) develops a more indirect idiom: images tumble out in surrealistic sequences; and this mode of presentation is pressed further in *Memoirs of Uncle Harry* (1974): 'Uncle Harry, my mother's favourite brother, was incarcerated in the local mental hospital long before I was born. He died there when I was twelve years old, without my ever having met him, yet he brooded over my growing-up' (Foreword).

Connor has also written several plays. [HB]

CONQUEST, ROBERT (1917–). Born in Worcestershire, educated at Winchester College and Oxford. Himself a poet (*Poems*, 1955; *Arias from a Love Opera*, 1969; *Forays*, 1979), he edited the influential anthology *New Lines* (1956) and thus gave recognizable shape to what came to be called the 'Movement'. Conquest distinguished the current poetic trends from those of the 1930s and 1940s, laying stress on traditional qualities of proportion, neatness and lucidity, decrying irrational addiction to metaphor and the sacrifice of intellectual backbone to highly charged sensuous or emotional intent. 'Poetry is written by and for the whole man, intellect, emotions, senses and all.' Elizabeth Jennings (q.v.), Philip Larkin (q.v.), Kingsley Amis (q.v.), Donald Davie (q.v.) and John Wain (q.v.) were among the poets represented. See also *New Lines II* (1963), a second collection 'broader in scope'. Conquest's publications include novels, one of them, *The Egyptologists* (London, 1965; New York, 1966), written in collaboration with Kingsley Amis, and several political studies of the Soviet Union. [HB]

CONRAD, JOSEPH (1857–1924). Novelist, naturalized English subject, born in Poland at Berdichev within Russian-controlled Podolia. His full name was Josef Teodor Konrad Nalecz Korzenowski. His father, Apollo, and his mother, Evelina, were both members of landowning families, but Apollo, who was himself a writer and the translator of Shakespeare and Hugo, took a leading part in nationalist agitation against Russian domination and was arrested in 1861. He and his wife were exiled and their son accompanied them. Conrad's mother died of tuberculosis in 1865 when he was 7, and his father, thereafter increasingly depressed and morbid, died similarly in Cracow in 1869. Conrad was the terrified companion of his father's last melancholy months. 'I don't know what might have become of me if I had not been a reading boy', he recalled later in *Notes on Life and Letters* (1921). Apollo was given a patriot's funeral, young Joseph walking at the head of an enormous procession.

Uncle Thaddeus, Eva's brother, took responsibility for the orphan, who startled everyone at the age of 14 by announcing his determination to go to sea. He won his way against opposition and was sent off to Marseilles in 1874 to join the French merchant navy. The fact that he was liable to Russian conscription for up to twenty-five years, and in the ranks, made it important for him to attain some other citizenship before returning home. He was briefly an apprentice on the *Mont Blanc* but managed to overspend his adequate allowance in Marseilles's bohemia and had to make the first of many appeals for more money to an increasingly exasperated but magnanimous uncle.

In 1876 he sailed to the West Indies as a steward on the *Sainte-Antoine* and soon after was mixed up in smuggling arms into Spain. The mysterious episode is important for the connection it has with Conrad's later novel, *The Arrow of Gold* (1919), in which Doña Rita, a beautiful Basque peasant girl who has been transformed into a sophisticated lady and for a time the mistress of Don Carlos, the Spanish Pretender, becomes the centre of Carlist intrigue. Monsieur George is involved in gunrunning for the cause, falls in love with Rita and fights a duel for her. Conrad, and later his widow, spoke of the novel's factual and autobiographical basis – Conrad had a scar on his left breast that was attributed to the duel. After Spain, however, money drove him to the gaming tables at Monte Carlo, where he lost what he had (it was borrowed) and then shot himself, narrowly missing his heart. The scar might more accurately be assumed to represent this less glamorous episode.

Recovered, Conrad decided to join the English Merchant Marine, though he knew no English. He served first on the *Mavis*, a steamer carrying coal in a voyage to Constantinople, and next on the *Skimmer of the Sea*, a coaster. 'The North Sea was my finishing school of seamanship', he wrote. 'My teachers had been the sailors of the Norfolk shore; coast men with steady eyes, mighty limbs and gentle voice.' Then he sailed to Australia in *The Duke of Sutherland* and in 1880 passed his examination as second mate. The same year he embarked for Australia again, this time as an officer in the *Loch Etive*, a wool-clipper. He was later to give a picture both of its captain and of a rescue operation on the ship's return voyage in *The Mirror of the Sea* (1906).

Conrad's next ship was the *Palestine*, a worn-out vessel with a cargo of coal for Bangkok, which sprang a leak in the Channel in a storm and had to put into Falmouth for repairs. It eventually sailed in September 1882 and was approaching Java head when the cargo caught fire and the crew took to the boats. This is the basis of the story *Youth* (1902) where the *Palestine* has become the *Judea* and where Conrad vividly recalls the first impact of the East upon him. Soon after he was second mate on the *Riversdale* on a voyage to Madras. His return voyage on the *Narcissus* furnished material for *The Nigger of the 'Narcissus'** (1897). Conrad passed his first mate's examination in 1884 and two years later he gained his Master's Certificate. It was during a voyage to the Far East as first mate on the *Highland Forest* in 1887 that a flying spar damaged his back so that he had to spend some time in hospital in Singapore. After treatment he served on a local steam trading ship owned by an Arab, the *Vidar*, whose voyages through the Malay Archipelago supplied him with material used later in the Malayan novels, *Almayer's Folly**, *An Outcast of the Islands** and *The Rescue**. William Charles Olmeijer, a trader encountered at Tandjong Redeb on the Berouw river in Borneo, became Almayer. Captain William Lingard, owner of a schooner and discoverer of the shipping channel in the Berouw river, became Conrad's Tom Lingard, patron of Almayer and hero of The Rescue. In 1888 Conrad accepted command of the Otago, his first captaincy, which left its mark on The Shadow Line (1917), and which he resigned in 1889, keeping up his practice of changing jobs with startling frequency. It was during this year, in London, that he began to write Almayer's Folly, the manuscript of which accompanied him at sea for many years.

After a visit to Poland and his uncle Thaddeus in 1890, Conrad fulfilled a strange childhood ambition to visit the Congo. It was a depressing and debilitating experience that left him permanently damaged in health (a victim of recurrent malarial gout). Its literary fruit was 'Heart of Darkness' (1902), a study in human failure. The figure of Kurtz, agent at a remote trading post, is dramatically built up in many anticipatory references before he is actually encountered and turns out to be 'hollow at the core', a victim of the power to corrupt that the wilderness exerts by calling up in the human heart the darkness at its own heart. Conrad's last substantial voyages were made as first mate of the Torrens, the clipper on which he met John Galsworthy (q.v.) as a passenger.

In 1894 Fisher Unwin accepted Almayer's Folly for publication on the recommendation of Edward Garnett (who later edited Letters from Joseph Conrad 1895-1924, 1928), and An Outcast of the Islands followed in 1896, to be favourably reviewed by H.G. Wells (q.v.). Conrad married Jessie George in the same year. The couple had two sons. Novels came out in swift succession: The Nigger of the 'Narcissus' (1897), Lord Jim* (1900), Youth (1902) (the volume containing 'Heart of Darkness') and Typhoon (1903). Meanwhile the Conrads lived first in Essex, then in Kent. Literary acquaintances accumulated and included Ford Madox Ford (q.v.) with whom Conrad collaborated in two novels, The Inheritors (1901) and Romance (1903), and who left lively recollections of Conrad in Joseph Conrad: A Personal Reminiscence (1924) and Return to Yesterday (1931). Conrad's output reached its artistic climax in Nostromo* (1904), but financial success came only with Chance (1914), which was serialized in the New York Herald before publication. Its complex plot exploits Conradian formulas with an eye on the popular market. ('It's the sort of stuff that may have a chance with the public', Conrad said.)

As a writer Conrad is naturally associated with the sea, but his interest is essentially in human beings. The sea, or the jungle, or the stress of social danger, supplies the challenge and perils that test a man's worth. 'The temporal world rests on a few very simple ideas, notably . . . on the idea of Fidelity', Conrad wrote in his autobiography, Some Reminiscences (1912) (later reissued as A Personal Record). Men are proved as Captain MacWhirr is proved in Typhoon when he rides the storm in the Nan-Shan and deals courageously with 200 fighting Chinese coolies and the danger of mutiny. Others, like Kurtz, Almayer and Willems (the 'Outcast') are tried and succumb. Conrad refines the pattern of stress and counter-stress by developing conflicting loyalties (as in The Rescue) or other mitigating complexities, like those in

Tsarist Russia pictured in Under Western Eyes (1911), where Razumov runs into difficulties when trying to aid a fugitive fellow student and revolutionary assassin, and betrays him to the police. Conrad's earlier work undoubtedly suffers from being over-written. He does not always keep his footing above the abyss of sentimentality into which a novelist can easily slither down the slopes of over-simplified ethics and idealized love. In some works ironic thrust is strengthened and moral stance disinfected by the use of the narrator, Marlow, whose attitude supplies a non-authorial point of judgement – or an enigmatic refusal to judge. The prevailing flavour of Conrad's work remains pessimistic. Men are 'the victims of nature' and the tragedy is that 'they are conscious of it'. There is no felt religious dimension to temper the melancholy.

Conrad was fully recognized in his last years. He refused a knighthood some months before his death.

Almayer's Folly was Conrad's first novel. Kaspar Almayer, son of expatriate Dutch settlers in Buitenzorg in Java, left home to work in the Macassar warehouses of Hudig and Co. He won the patronage of Tom Lingard, 'King of the Sea', who promised him his fortune in exchange for marrying his adopted half-caste daughter. The couple are established in a new trading station at Sambir on the Patai river on the east coast of Borneo, Almayer nursing visions of future wealth from the discovery of gold in the interior. The story opens twenty years later. Almayer is a failure inhabiting a scene of decay. He has just spent everything on building a new house for the use of the new English settlers expected through the development of the British Borneo Co., but in fact the development does not materialize and the area is left in Dutch control. Visiting Dutch seamen label the house 'Almayer's Folly'. Almayer exists in a dubious relationship with Lakamba, Rajah of Sambir, and with Syed Abdulla, chief of the local Arab trading post. Illicit gunpowder-trading arouses the suspicion of the Dutch authorities, and Dain Maroola, a rajah's son from Bali, has to flee when his gun-laden brig explodes, killing Dutch sailors. What finally breaks Almayer is that his loved daughter Nina, whom he sent away to Singapore for a 'white' upbringing, now goes off with Dain. Almayer had long dreamed devotedly of taking her away with him to Europe and prosperity. He sets fire to the home they have shared together, retreats to the 'Folly', succumbs to opium and dies.

An Outcast of the Islands deals with the river settlement of Almayer's Folly, Sambir. Conrad's interest had been aroused by a 'mistrusted, worn-out European' reputed to have brought the Arabs into the river. He conceived Peter Willems, a Dutch boy picked up by Captain Lingard and established as a confidential clerk with Hudig and Co. in Macassar. He is settled in a home in return for marrying a half-caste woman who is in fact Hudig's illegitimate daughter. He embezzles money, is dismissed, re-rescued by Lingard and sent up to Almayer's trading station at Sambir, where he is so enslaved in love for Aissa, whom he meets there, that he is able to be used by Lakamba and Babatchi in their design to weaken the white man's influence. Willems betrays the secret of the river entry on which Lingard's (and therefore Almayer's) trading prosperity depends. Thus the Arabs take over.

Lingard's confrontation with the man who has betrayed him is a climax in the career of the vain, self-deceiving, prevaricating creature that Willems essentially is. Ultimately Aissa herself kills Willems when he is desperately trying once more to escape ignominiously from his own past. The date is about five years after Almayer's settlement in Sambir and therefore some fifteen years before the final collapse of Almayer's career recorded in *Almayer's Folly*. The bringing together of two men adopted by Lingard and each deceived by his own delusions of future grandeur is infused with sombre tension. For all the wordiness, there is an interesting exploration of basic human loneliness in the mutually uncomprehending relationship of passion between Willems and Aissa, who are isolated in the prisons of their respective racial, civilizational and sexual identities.

The Rescue belongs with the early Malayan novels described above in that its chief character is Tom Lingard, but the manuscript was laid aside in 1898 and taken up for completion twenty years later. The scene is off the Shore of Refuge. Lingard is pledged to the support of Rajah Hassim and his sister Immada who have been ousted from their country. Hassim saved Lingard's life and Lingard has devoted himself energetically to the cause of restoring him. It is the eve of the climax. A new and different obligation arises to confound Lingard's motives and feelings. A yacht is stranded where its wealthy white owners will inevitably bring peril upon themselves and upon his complex dealings with warring Malay factions. At this crucial juncture Lingard finds himself falling in love with Edith Travers, wife of the yacht-owner, and, as a result of the distracting claims of the new rescue operation, becomes unwittingly involved in what is effectively a betrayal of the local cause and people he has long cherished. Edith Travers, a spirited woman, manages her tedious husband, her soothing long-time admirer, d'Alacaer, and her new Byronic Man of Fate with enough percipience and subtlety to keep the over-protracted, over-elaborated tensions of heart and conscience above the level of melodrama.

The Nigger of the 'Narcissus' was based on a voyage Conrad made from Bombay to Dunkirk in 1884 as second mate of the *Narcissus*. 'Most of the personages I have portrayed actually belonged to the crew of the real *Narcissus*', Conrad said. The book was 'an effort to present a group of men held together by a common loyalty and a common perplexity in a struggle not with human enemies'. The tale is a fine exercise in suspense. James Wait, a massive negro in the *Narcissus* crew, falls ill, takes to his bunk, and seems to be dying. His condition undermines the morale of the crew, overshadowing their lives and holding them in a 'weird servitude'. But Captain Allistoun, old Singleton and Donkin are immune to the blackmail of suffering. Uncertainty about Jimmy's real condition and whether he is shamming thus erodes the crew's solidarity – even to the point of near-mutiny – as surely as the challenge of storm strengthens it. Conrad appended a preface to the tale in which he defined the character of artistic communication as primarily an appeal to the senses. 'My task . . . is by the power of the written word to make you hear, to make you feel – it is,

before all, to make you see.'

Lord Jim is perhaps the best known of Conrad's novels. In Singapore Conrad heard the story of Augustus Podmore Williams, son of a Cornish rector, who had been mate on the *Jeddah* in 1880 when its officers abandoned it, damaged in a storm, apparently leaving its passengers, a thousand Muslim pilgrims, to. drown. The *Jeddah* did not in fact sink but was towed into port. In the novel the ship is the *Patna*. The captain and the engineers lower a boat and shout out to Jim (a 'simple and sensitive character') to jump. He does so unthinkingly in the rush of the moment, though fundamentally he is not one of them and would despise thus to save his own skin. Afterwards he alone does not run away but faces the Court of Inquiry which deprives him of his certificate. Conrad gives his impulsive act the dimensions of a 'fall' linking him with reprobates, and the insidious inner and outer consequences of the disgrace haunt his attempts at rehabilitation, attempts that Marlow, the narrator, himself initiates. Eventually he becomes trading manager in a remote tropical community at Patusan, where he rises fully to the opportunity for personal redemption, saves an ill-treated girl from her stepfather, makes her his 'wife', and brings peace and prosperity to the community by skill, integrity and courage that win universal trust and affection. He is respectfully known as 'Lord Jim'. But piratical white blackguards intrude, and Jim pledges himself as guarantee to the natives in the attempt to get rid of them peaceably. They betray him, and this time Jim deliberately makes the choice that atones for the past, surrendering himself and forfeiting his life.

Nostromo was 'the most anxiously meditated of the longer novels', Conrad said, representing 'a subtle change' in the nature of his inspiration. In it he created a South American republic, Costaguana, comprehensively pictured in terms of geography, society, industry, transport, institutions and political history. Costaguana has had a series of unstable governments, and the latest President, the Dictator Don Vincente Ribiera, has to flee a revolutionary outbreak. The government has had the support of Charles Gould, English owner of the San Tomé silver mine, who has struggled to run the mine profitably and humanely under the terms of a government 'concession' granted in exchange for royalties. Nostromo, an Italian, trusted alike by aristocrats and workers for his courage and incorruptibility, is put in charge of a consignment of silver that must be conveyed out of the country before rebels can lay hands on it. The lighter carrying the silver is damaged in a collision and run aground on a small island where Nostromo buries the silver. Lighter and cargo are presumed sunk. Nostromo decides to keep the secret and enriches himself by furtive night visits to the island.

'Nostromo has never been intended for the hero', Conrad wrote in a letter. 'Silver is the pivot of the moral and material events affecting the lives of everybody in the tale.' Silver is a demonic influence, political and personal, rotting the governing system, the domestic virtues of Gould and the integrity of Nostromo. Conrad spoke of his ambition 'to render the spirit of an epoch in the history of South America'. Certainly he succeeded in portraying a humanly rich and vital drama of entangled public and private idealism and cynicism, service and self-interest, whose ultimate pessimistic implication seems to be that moral virtue, peace and fruitful achievement can never defeat the crushing inhumanity of materialistic expediency.　　　　　　　　　　　　　　　　　[HB]

COOPER, WILLIAM (pseudonym of Harry Summerfield Hoff) (1910-). Novelist, born in Crewe, Cheshire, educated there and at Christ's College, Cambridge. He was a schoolmaster in Leicester from 1933 to 1940. After war service in the RAF he joined the Civil Service in 1945 and rose to be Personnel Consultant to the UK Atomic Energy Authority in 1958. He married Joyce Barbara Harris in 1950 and had two daughters. He published four novels under his own name in the 1930s and 1940s before making his mark as William Cooper with *Scenes from Provincial Life* in 1950. Threat of libel action caused the suppression of its sequel, *Scenes from Metropolitan Life*, but *Scenes from Married Life* (1961) partners the first volume, which has been credited with ushering in the anti-hero of the 1950s in the person of Joe Lunn, the narrator. Lunn, provincial schoolmaster in what is obviously Leicester, is the innocent at large, bungling his way through absurd crises with the girl he likes to sleep with and doesn't want to marry. He doesn't fit into the conventions of school-teaching, still less of matrimony. Social mores are comically downgraded and the self ironically debunked in flat, deadpan narrative. The total effect of playing down all gravities and profundities in the interests of immediate personal satisfaction is amorally comic rather than cynical. Cooper's lucid economic idiom is the product of disciplined artistry. In the second book Lunn, now 39, is ingenuously caught up in the Civil Service machinery and paradoxically turning the tables on his past by choosing a wife and finding marriage blissful. There is delightful humour in this ironic upshot, but it is a pity that we are asked to believe Lunn capable of writing the kind of novels he inhabits. Of the intervening publications *The Struggles of Albert Woods* (1952) takes us into the world of science and technology, *Disquiet and Peace* (1956) into Edwardian high society and *Young People* (1958) to a redbrick university in the 1930s. *You're Not Alone* (1976) is the diary of a doctor much involved in giving sexual advice. Cooper's range is narrow: the focus allows piquant comic counterpoint between life's banalities and individual caprice; but the serious substance of life – in terms of felt human need – scarcely intrudes. *Scenes from Metropolitan Life* was eventually published in 1982.　　　　　　　　　　　　　　　　　[HB]

COPPARD, A.E. (Alfred Edgar) (1878-1957). Short-story writer. He tells us (in his effervescent autobiography *It's Me O Lord*, 1957) how he was born at Folkestone, Kent, 'the son of George the tailor and Emily Alma the housemaid' and by the age of 10 was slaving for a London tailor whose sempstresses turned out men's trousers at one-and-ninepence a pair. What it was like can be gathered from Coppard's short story. 'The Presser', from the collection *Silver Circus* (1927). Coppard was 40 years old before he threw up his job as commercial clerk to write full-time. The numerous collections of short stories include *Adam & Eve & Pinch Me* (1921), *Clorinda Walks in Heaven* (1922), *The Black Dog* (1923) and *The Field of Mustard* (1926). Coppard's 'chief idols were the Thomas Hardy of *Life's Little Ironies* and Henry James of the short stories'. 'Dealing with a complication or an episode, true or untrue, in which he perceives some significance or interest, the writer has to find the character or characters most likely to bring it to a successful issue.' Thus he defined the method of the short-story writer (op. cit.). Coppard was a fine craftsman with sensitivities attuned to handling delicate fable-like fantasy with allegorical overtones ('Marching to Zion'), the purely extraordinary or paranormal that leaves the reader guessing (title story of *Adam & Eve & Pinch Me*), or movingly realistic instances of direct human love, courage or loss ('Weep Not My Wanton' or 'The Black Dog'). Many a story centres on a sudden moment of revelation, an uprush of emotion or imagination transfiguring the ordinary and impinging on the extraordinary. The exquisite workmanship fashions little masterpieces of compression and economy from material that lesser writers would have expanded. 'The Black Dog' is a novel in miniature. Doris Lessing (q.v.) has chosen and introduced *Selected Stories* (1972). Coppard's work as a poet is not now regarded as significant (*Collected Poems*, 1928).　　　　　　　　　　　　　　　　　[HB]

CORNFORD, FRANCES (1886-1960). Poet, born at Cambridge, Cambridgeshire, where her father, Sir Francis Darwin, the son of Charles Darwin, lectured in botany. She married a university teacher, F.M. Cornford, a classicist. Their son Rupert John (1915-36), a young writer and a Marxist, was killed while fighting in the Spanish Civil War. Frances Cornford's first publication, *Poems* (1910), contained a celebrated verse epigram about Rupert Brooke whose friend she was:

A young Apollo, golden-haired
　Stands dreaming on the verge of strife,
Magnificently unprepared
　For the long littleness of life.

The volume also contained a triolet that fascinated anthologists, 'To a Fat Lady Seen from the Train:

O why do you walk through the fields in gloves,
　Missing so much and so much?
O fat white woman whom nobody loves . . .

The fruit of subsequent volumes (*Spring Morning*, 1915; *Autumn Midnight*, 1923; *Different Days*, 1928; *Mountains and Molehills*, 1934; and *Travelling Home*, 1948) was gathered in *Collected Poems* (1954). They give evidence of a fastidious craftsmanship, a reflective vein of totally unpretentious directness, and an epigrammatic gift that continued to capsulate moments of wonder, perception or illumination in neat stanzas, like 'The Revelation':

In my dark mind you kicked a stone away.
There in the light a full-grown Purpose lay;
And half in terror, half in glad surprise
I saw his unknown coils and sleeping eyes.
　　　　　　　　　(from *Mountains and Molehills*, 1934)
　　　　　　　　　　　　　　　　　[HB]

COWARD, NOEL (Sir) (1899–1973). Dramatist, born in Teddington, Middlesex. He performed as a child actor in *Peter Pan* in 1911, and in the 1920s established himself as a uniquely talented man of the theatre, acting, writing, composing and directing. He typified in his plays and in his public self-projection the flippant sophistication of an amoral, hedonistic postwar society. *The Vortex* (prod 1924) portrays Florence Lancaster, a shallow middle-aged woman trying to be indefinitely young, while *Hay Fever* (prod 1925) centres on Judith Bliss, retired actress whose histrionic family join with her in off-the-cuff recapitulations of scenes from her successes that hilariously bewilder their guests. Coward has an acute ear for the vapid chatter of bright young things and fading older things, for feminine cattiness and bitchiness, for inconsequential party-time conversational ensembles. His plays are neatly constructed and the dash of theatrical wizardry is winning. In *Private Lives* (prod 1930) a divorced couple, simultaneously remarried, find themselves in adjacent hotel suites on their honeymoon. In *Blithe Spirit* (prod 1941) Charles Condomine dabbles in spiritualism and so finds his deceased first wife intruding upon his second marriage. After the accidental death of the second wife he has two rival preternatural visitants to deal with. 'Let's be superficial and pity the poor Philosophers', says Elyot in *Private Lives* and Coward confesses in his Preface to *Play Parade, volume 5* to a gnawing suspicion that he was 'nothing but a jester, a foolish, superficial, capering lightweight with neither depth nor real human understanding'. It must be accepted that whatever he touches in his farces he taps for its laughs with the single-mindedness of the comic script writer, and that the simmering flippancies, in the absence of moral anchorage or emotional insight, bypass opportunities for true satire and deep irony. Coward's more serious (and less effective) works include the patriotic epic spectacular *Cavalcade* (prod 1931). He wrote two autobiographical volumes, *Present Indicative* (1937) and *Future Indefinite* (1954). See also, G. Payne and S. Morley, eds, *The Noel Coward Diaries* (1982). [HB]

CRAIG, GORDON (1872–1966). Actor, artist and stage designer, son of the architect Edward Godwin and the actress Ellen Terry. He became widely known throughout Europe, where most of his life was lived after 1904. Craig established himself as apostle of new non-naturalistic techniques in décor, staging and lighting, and in *The Art of the Theatre* (1905) and *On The Art of the Theatre* (1911) argued for theatre as product of the all-embracing artistic vision of the stage director ('The Art of the Theatre is the same in one respect as any other art. It is the work of one man'). Craig ran a magazine *The Mask* from 1908 and again after the war until 1929. He wrote *The Theatre Advancing* (1921), *Henry Irving* (1930) and *Ellen Terry and Her Secret Self* (1931), and Max Beerbohm (q.v.) called him 'one of the three or four best living writers of English'. In his *Index to the Story of My Days* (1957), a collection of autobiographical jottings, and in his son's biography (Edward Craig, *Gordon Craig*, 1968) he emerges as a toweringly temperamental, exacting and wanton genius. [HB]

CRONIN, A.J. (Archibald Joseph) (1896–1981). Novelist, born in Dumbartonshire, Scotland. He lost his father in childhood but struggled to take a medical degree at Glasgow University. General practice in Scotland and South Wales afforded rich experience but inadequate remuneration. His autobiography, *Adventures in Two Worlds* (1952), describes the first night of his honeymoon, spent down a mine shaft amputating the leg of a trapped miner. A successful novel, *Hatters Castle* (1931), initiated a second career as a best-selling popular novelist, noted for *The Stars Look Down* (1935) and *The Citadel* (1937). The latter traces the struggle of an idealistic and altruistic young doctor in the pre-Health Service days. Sentimental and predictable Cronin may be, but his critical record of the inter-war private-enterprise medical jungle is sharp and notable. [HB]

CURNOW, ALLEN (1911–). Poet. born in Timaru, New Zealand, and educated at the University of Canterbury and at Auckland University. He joined the Christchurch paper *The Press* and from 1935 to 1948 worked there as, variously, reporter, sub-editor and drama critic. In 1949 he joined the news and sub-editorial staff of the *News Chronicle* in London and in 1950 went to the United States. The following year he was appointed Lecturer in English at Auckland University; he retired as Professor in 1977. As a student at Auckland he was associated with the radical quarterly *Phoenix* (1932–3), and his early collection *Enemies* (1937) – one result of his association with Denis Glover (q.v.) – reflected his interest at that time in poetry of satiric comment, social and political. *Not in Narrow Seas* (1939) foreshadowed later poetry and criticism in tracing the enmeshed personal and national destinies of New Zealand life; the structure of a poetic sequence with prose commentary proved ideal for the exploration of 'The Unhistoric Story' of New Zealand history. Curnow's mythopoeic approach found further powerful expression in his editorship of *A Book of New Zealand Verse, 1923–1945* (1945) in which his own selection was supported by a substantial introduction. Arguing as it did for the need 'to cut our losses; to provide some ground upon which the worth of our verse can be estimated', the anthology was widely influential. Its significance was maintained by a revised edition (1951) and the book established him as a controversial critic as well as a major poet in his own right. His Introduction saw the New Zealand poet trying 'to keep faith with the tradition in the language while his imagination must seek forms as immediate in experience as the island soil under his feet'. Such stress upon the local and the particular (always central in his own writing) was balanced by insistence that 'local reference ought never to decide our estimate of a poet's worth'. Five collections of poetry from *Island and Time* (1941) through to the fine *At Dead Low Water* (1949) revealed an increasingly complex probing of time and history, often from an intensely personal starting point, as in the title poem of *At Dead Low Water. Poems 1947–1957* (1957) was followed by his editing of *The Penguin Book of New Zealand Verse* (1960) which, like the earlier anthology, contained a long critical introduction. His persuasive contention that the best New Zealand poetry reflects an 'island theme' is supported by those poems (his own amongst them) included in the selection, but his thesis did not find universal acceptance. Curnow described his book as 'the record of an adventure, or series of adventures, in search of reality. . . . There is an island story here, which is the human and historical context of the poetic vision'. The stress upon the 'vital discovery of self in country and country in self', and the importance given to New Zealand's colonial past and continuing isolation, were criticized as personal obsessions by some other poets. James K. Baxter (q.v.) – included in the Penguin book – wrote of Curnow's 'deeply held personal fiction of the spiritual isolation of New Zealand' and deplored his 'negative preoccupation with Colonialism' (*Aspects of Poetry in New Zealand*, 1967). Later experts may disagree with Curnow's views, but they will have to visit the site. *A Small Room with Large Windows* (1962), a volume of selected poems, brought together the best of his work to date, while his continuing talent for humour and satire was demonstrated by *Whim*

Wham Land (1967). Recent poetry in *Trees, Effigies and Moving Objects* (1972) and *An Abominable Temper* (1973) reaffirmed his poetic involvement in defining the delicate yet vital relationship between the particular (whether human personality or chance sensation) and the undifferentiated context of time and place within which each must find its significance – in one sense a transposition to the personal dimension of his 'island thesis' with regard to New Zealand, adrift upon the seas of history. *Collected Poems, 1933–1973* (1974) illustrated the extent and range of his poetic achievement, bringing together a variety of poems from twelve published collections. A selection of his plays is available in *Four Plays* (1972). He remains an impressive poet and a critic who has formulated and propounded issues of crucial importance for all New Zealanders. *An Incorrigible Music* (1979) explored some violent aspects of man's physical and spiritual world, including the murder of Aldo Moro in Italy. [PQ]

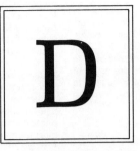

DAS, KAMALA (1934–). Poet, writer of stories in Malayalam and English, born in Malabar, India, to a Malayalam poetess of the Nayar matriarchal community. After a few years' schooling in Calcutta, where her father worked, she was married to K. Madhava Das (1949) and had three sons. The frequent erotic themes in her poetry are probably a form of psychological compensation for the lack of affection in her childhood home. She published nine volumes of Malayalam fiction (1953–72). Her first book of English poetry, *Summer in Calcutta* (1965), gives the now classic riposte to the common complaint that Indians writing in English cannot be 'truly' Indian: 'The language I speak / Becomes mine, its distortions, its queer-nesses / All mine, mine alone ... but it is honest'. A. Jussawalla judges her poetry too 'confessional', N. Ezekiel (q.v.) praises its 'urgency' and regrets its 'improvised air', but D. Kohli convincingly argues that her 'intimacy' with the Indian landscape provides a 'synthesis ... of the changing reality of love ... and the ... unchanging contours' of that landscape. Despite occasional metrical slackness, *Summer in Calcutta* achieves uncommon frankness, vigour, intensity. *The Descendants* (1967) is more uneven; *The Old Playhouse* (1973) is a selection; the autobiography *My Story* (1976) is patently therapeutic; the stories in *A Doll for the Child Prostitute* (1977) unfortunately do not add lustre to her literary achievement. [AR]

DAVIE, DONALD (1922–). Poet, born in Barnsley, South Yorkshire, educated at the grammar school there and at St Catherine's College, Cambridge. After war service in the Royal Navy, he held university posts at Cambridge and Dublin, at Essex (Professor of English), at Stanford University, California, and (since 1978) at Vanderbilt University, Nashville, Tennessee. Davie, who has written critical books on Ezra Pound and Thomas Hardy (q.v.), and whom John Press described as 'perhaps the finest critic of his generation', early pleaded for a return to clarity and traditional form in his critical book, *Purity of Diction in English Verse* (1952) ('there is no necessary connection between the poetic vocation ... and ... exhibitionism, egoism, and licence'). His first volume of verse, *Poems* (1954), was followed by *Brides of Reason* (1955) and *A Winter Talent* (1957), and in 1972 he gathered his output to date in *Collected Poems 1950–1970*.

Here Davie emerges as a poet of studied artistry, highly disciplined in thought and manner, who can annotate moments of experience or moods of reflection with a captivating precision – as in the justly praised 'Remembering the Thirties' or 'Obiter Dicta'. It may be argued that content is too neatly packaged; that jingles polish gravities down to seeming trivialities, smooth worry down to mere wit. Davie was aware of this problem:

> The practice of an art
> is to convert all terms
> into the terms of art.

By the end of the third stanza
death is a smell no longer;
it is a problem of style.

('July 1964')

'I am not a poet by nature, only by inclination', he has conceded; but he has more than once replied convincingly in verse to the critical charge of alleged emotional thinness. In *Six Epistles to Eva Hesse* (1970), determined to show what traditional English verse forms can encompass, he experimented with sustained argument in running four-foot couplets that have a gossipy, Swiftian verve and punch:

No, Madam, Pound's a splendid poet
But a sucker, and we know it.

Among later collections *The Shires* (1974) is a poetic tour of the English counties and *In the Stopping Train* (1976) has a concluding poem that takes us back to Davie's native Barnsley. In *Three for Water Music* (1981) Davie is indebted to Eliot's *Four Quartets* in both substance and style. It is a sequence of meditations ('The Fountain of Cyanë', 'Wild Boar Clough' and 'The Fountain of Arethusa') stimulated by recalls of specific localities and moving, like Eliot's, between a studied and a more conversational idiom. Davie's central concern, however, is the poetic imagination and the relation between contrivance and inspiration. He sees his own 'precarious Springs' of creativity conserved beyond the 'misted panes / Of mystifying memory' in the silence of a 'conservatory'.

Davie is a writer of intellectual stature. It is clear that his early description of himself as a 'pasticheur of late Augustan styles' underestimated the importance of what he was about in accepting poetry as a discipline, examining his own progress with scrupulous integrity and recognizing the poet's moral responsibility. He has never become pretentious. *Trying to Explain* (1980), a collection of essays and articles, includes a revealing autobiographical piece called 'A West Riding Boyhood' – 'If my universe is verbal, so be it – I am happy in my glittering envelope.' *These the Companions* (1982) is a volume of autobiographical recollections. Davie edited *The New Oxford Book of Christian Verse* (1981). [HB]

DAVIES, RHYS (1903–78). Novelist and short-story writer, born at Porth, Glamorgan, Wales, and educated at the county school there. His autobiography, *Print of a Hare's Foot* (1969), contains a lively picture of his Welsh upbringing. Author of over thirty volumes, Davies focuses on Welsh backgrounds and Welsh people with the compelling intensity of Caradoc Evans (q.v.) but without his sourness and with greater versatility. His narrative presentation is both technically proficient and highly economic. His first novel, *The Withered Root* (1927), is a story of a religious revival in Welsh coal valley. Among later novels *The Painted King* (1954) is a full-length study of the career of Guy Aspen, a successful actor-composer in the mould of Ivor Novello, whose real life is eroded into the play world, while *The Perishable Quality* (1957), a study of a Welsh girl turned high-class London whore, contains in Iolo Hancock a roistering poet in the mould of

Dylan Thomas (q.v.). In *Nobody Answered the Bell* (1971) Rose involves her lesbian partner Kenny in concealing the murder of her dead father's mistress, and the two live in increasingly lunatic isolation from the normal world. Davies's economy in range and presentation give him particular effectiveness as a short-story writer. Early stories, printed in magazines, earned him the approval of D.H. Lawrence (q.v.), whom he visited in France in his last days, and critics proclaimed him a Welsh Chekhov. *Collected Stories* (1955), which followed fifteen volumes in this genre, is rich in studies of lively, if sometimes stagey, Welsh quirkiness. See the almshouse ladies who refuse to use the newly installed WC in 'The Contraption' or the donkey that refuses to pass the pub door without its morning pint of beer in 'Alice's Pint'. *The Best of Rhys Davies* (1979) is Davies's own selection of twelve stories, mostly with Welsh backgrounds, exploring what Davies calls 'the lapses into disorderliness of mind and the hidden impulses which provide the best prompting for the tiny, concentrated explosion short stories should contain'. [HB]

DAVIES, ROBERTSON (1913–). Novelist and playwright, born at Thamesville, Ontario, Canada, and educated at Upper Canada College, Queen's University, Kingston, Ontario, and Balliol College, Oxford. Experience as a professional actor, drama teacher and literary editor was followed in 1960 by his appointment as Professor of English at Massey College, University of Toronto. He became Master of the college in 1962. Davies is the author of over fifteen plays, five novels and some dozen publications in the realm of theatre. Much of his writing is witty and urbane comment on what he sees as the provincial shortcomings of Canadian culture. This approach is clear in Davies's early journalism, collected as *The Diary of Samuel Marchbanks* (1947) and *The Table Talk of Samuel Marchbanks* (1949); *Samuel Marchbanks' Alamanack* was published in 1967. The trilogy of novels set in Salterton (recognizable as Kingston) extends issues raised in these journalistic pieces: *Tempest Tossed* (1951), *Leaves of Malice* (1954) and *A Mixture of Frailties* (1958) all adroitly blend melodrama and romance to satiric purpose. A later trilogy, *Fifth Business* (1970), *The Manticore* (1972) and *World of Wonders* (1975), explored alienation and pretension at a deeper level and established Davies as a serious novelist. In his early plays he concentrated on social issues related to the 'Marchbanks' writings, and these works are collected in *Eros at Breakfast* (1949). Later plays are gathered in *Hunting Stuart* (1972) and tend towards a deeper and more abstract, Jungian probing of human values. The contribution Davies has made to Canadian culture goes beyond any listing of publications; he is, for example, a former Governor of the Stratford Shakespeare Festival (on which he wrote three books in collaboration with Tyrone Guthrie). His writings are but one facet of a widely cultured observer of the Canadian scene whose witty comments on Canadian mores over three decades have become progressively more serious. *One Half of Robertson Davies* (1978) carries the subtitle, 'Provocative Pronouncements on a Wide Range of Topics'. [PQ]

DAVIES, W.H. (William Henry) (1871–1940). Poet, born in Newport, Gwent, Wales, and brought up by his grandparents. His father, a publican, had died in Davies's infancy and his mother remarried. Davies was a cousin of Sir Henry Irving. When his grandmother died she left him a very modest income (ten shillings a week) and he went off to America to live as a tramp. It was his habit to shelter from cold winters in prison and to make periodic trips to England on cattle boats. When train-jumping in Canada he slipped and had his foot severed. In the station waiting room, immediately afterwards, waiting for the doctor to arrive, he lit his pipe and smoked. Back in England, with a wooden leg, he slept in doss-houses and wrote poems. Having printed some at his own expense and failed to sell them, he dispatched copies to various people, including Bernard Shaw (q.v.). Shaw was impressed by the poems. 'His work was not in the least strenuous or modern: there was in it no sign that he had ever read anything later than Cowper or Crabbe. . . . There was indeed no sign of his ever having read anything otherwise than as a child reads. The result was a freedom from literary vulgarity which was like a draught of water in a desert.' Shaw's encouragement and recommendation helped to launch Davies in the literary world. He was eventually given a Civil List pension; he married Helen Payne in 1923 and settled in rural Gloucestershire. Once established as a poet, he wrote too much. His poems were gathered together (636 of them) as *Collected Poems* in 1942 and (749 of them) as *Complete Poems* (ed. Daniel George) in 1963. The characteristic note of unaffected sincerity is admirably evident in the celebrated 'Leisure':

What is this life if, full of care,
We have no time to stand and stare.

Davies uses standard lyrical forms for clear observation of country things and direct reflection on the homelier matters and moods of life. Admirers have compared him to Clare. 'There was inevitability in his slightest verses; unique observation in his tiniest reflections of the natural world', said Dylan Thomas (q.v.) (*Quite Early in the Morning*, 1954). 'Truly Great' lists his modest needs for happiness – garden without and books within, a convenient legacy and a gentle wife. Davies is best discovered through his revealing *Autobiography of a Super-Tramp* (1908) for which Shaw wrote the Preface quoted above. [HB]

DAVIN, DAN (1913–). Novelist, born at Invercargill, New Zealand, and educated at the Marist Brothers' School there; later at Otago and Oxford universities. After war service he joined Oxford University Press and compiled the *Introduction to English Literature* (1947) with John Mulgan (q.v.). His writing reflects strongly his New Zealand background and many characters in his books grapple with feelings of isolation, a dimension of New Zealand national consciousness which is compounded by nostalgia for the strength of service comradeship. *Cliffs of Fall* (1945) was set, like so many of his works, in the Southland of Davin's own youth and depicted a conflict of freedom and repression which recalls the work of Frank Sargeson (q.v.). *The Gorse Blooms Pale* (1947), his only collection of short stories, provided a vivid picture of Southland life though here, as

elsewhere in his writings, the loving attention to detail serves a wider aim of personal understanding and fulfilment. The extent to which biographical material is always used for artistic ends was evident in *For the Rest of Our Lives*, published the same year; a fictional account of a New Zealand division in North Africa, it sought to draw personal experience into a wider questioning of human values and moral uncertainty. *Roads from Home* (1949) was the most successful of his books based on personal background. *Crete*, published in 1953, was an official war history, and in the same year he also edited *New Zealand Short Stories* and *Katherine Mansfield's Short Stories*. *The Sullen Bell* (1956) was set among New Zealand exiles in London but *Brides of Price* (1972) marked a fresh approach to new material. A collection of stories entitled *Breathing Spaces* was published in 1975. [PQ]

DAWE, BRUCE (1930–). Poet, born at Geelong, Victoria, Australia, and educated at Northcote High School and at Melbourne and Queensland universities. After holding a variety of jobs and making numerous attempts with poetry and prose, he published *No Fixed Address* (1962) in which poems such as 'Public Library, Melbourne' and 'Happiness is the Art of Being Broken' showed his ability to express the wonder of the mundane in writing of ordinary people. *A Need of Similar Name* was published in 1965. The balance between humour and tragedy is fine in his work: he shows its dependence upon situation or viewpoint, as in the vernacular poem 'The Not-So-Good Earth' in his next collection *An Eye for a Tooth* (1968). In *Beyond the Subdivisions* (1969) he further demonstrates his skill at employing free verse to capture the overlooked or deliberately disregarded aspects of ordinary Australian suburban existence; in 'Homecoming' the return of bodies from Vietnam raises this commitment to 'the lost people in our midst for whom no one speaks, and who cannot speak for themselves' to the heroic level. Rightly acclaimed as an important voice in Australian poetry in his concern for 'homo suburbiensis', he sees his own work as showing 'the strain of being a "bridge" poet, between an anti-intellectual populace and the anti-popular (or non popular) academic world'. In his honesty, humour and modesty he stands as a self-made man, shying away from academic disputes – 'they have aesthetic theories . . . I'm comparatively confused' – but charting the inner fears of city-dwellers, 'the personal landscape of loneliness and isolation'. *Condolences of the Season* (1971) was selected poems, while in 1978 appeared *Sometimes Gladness: Collected Poems 1954–1978*. [PQ]

DAY LEWIS, CECIL (1904–72). Poet and novelist, born in Ballintubber, County Laoighis, Ireland, the son of a Church of Ireland clergyman. His mother could trace her descent from Oliver Goldsmith's uncle. She died when he was only 4 and his autobiography (*The Buried Day*, 1960) makes much of the personal effect of this early deprivation and the consequent emotional pressures upon him from a possessive widowed father. The personal record invites comparison in this respect with Louis MacNeice's (q.v.) *The Strings are False*. The Lewises came to England (the father to a London living) and Cecil was educated at Sherborne (the Sherborne pictured in Alec Waugh's *The Loom of Youth*) and at Wadham College, Oxford. Meanwhile his father moved to a twenty-year incumbency at Edwinstowe in Sherwood Forest, where the incursion of the mining industry upon the old farming community and upon the fading aristocracy of the 'Dukeries' made a lasting impression on Cecil ('it was at Edwinstowe that my social conscience was born' – *The Buried Day*). In his last year at Oxford Day Lewis got to know Auden (q.v.) (he was already familiar with Rex Warner) (q.v.) with whom, along with Spender (q.v.) and MacNeice, he was to be firmly linked in the public mind. He had already published his first volume of verse, *Beechen Vigil* (1925), and contributed to *Oxford Poetry* (1925). He seems to have lost interest in Greats and took only a fourth-class degree; whereupon he went to join L.A.G. Strong on the staff at Summerfields, a prep school. After a spell in Scotland, he moved to Cheltenham College, but his extreme left-wing politics made things difficult for him and the promising prospects opened up by entry into the detective novel field with *A Question of Proof* in 1935 (he used the pseudonym 'Nicholas Blake') enabled him to forsake schoolmastering for full-time writing and also to join the Communist Party. He dropped the connection later ('the errors of judgement, the naiveté, the muddleheadedness are obvious enough today', *The Buried Day*), served with the Home Guard in Devon during the war, and in 1968, after Masefield's (q.v.) death, attained the ultimate respectability of the Poet Laureateship.

Day Lewis first attracted public attention with *Transitional Poem* (1929). From the start he had 'a metrical strictness and an intellectual sternness which were impressive and refreshing'. So wrote Spender in *World Within World*, noting that Day Lewis's talent was more traditional than Auden's; indeed that Day Lewis was a writer 'steeped in the work of ... the Georgians', though to some extent correcting the 'blurred quality' of the Georgians by his use of contemporary imagery. MacNeice had made a similar point in *Modern Poetry* (1938) – 'Day Lewis, whose theme is the modern industrial world, its economics and its politics, takes his images especially from such things as pylons, power-houses, spies, frontiers, aeroplanes, steam-engines'. *From Feathers to Iron* (1931), a sequence celebrating the conception and birth of the first child of his first marriage, is exhilarating in rhythm and image, strenuous yet fluent in articulation, and is carried on the current of Day Lewis's zest for 'the interplay of private and public meaning' (*The Buried Day*). Indeed it may be questioned whether he was ever again to convey so vividly a sense of work spontaneously thrown off and at a high creative temperature:

> Come out in the sun, for a man is born today!
> Early this morning whistle in the cutting told
> Train was arriving, hours overdue, delayed
> By snow-drifts, engine-trouble, Act of God, who
>   cares now?
> For here alights the distinguished passenger.
> Take a whole holiday in honour of this.

Yet in *Magnetic Mountain* (1933), a violently revolutionary product of the Marxist phase, there is often vigour without concentration, vehemence without thrust:

> When you're in the cart and you've got a weak
>   heart,
> When you're up the pole and you can't find your
>   soul ...

At its crudest the vehemence has a heavy-handed, poster-like stridency, and we are shouted at from a poetic soap-box:

> Hands off! The dykes are down.
> This is no time for play.
> Hammer is poised and sickle
> Sharpened. I cannot stay.

In succeeding volumes, *A Time to Dance* (1935) and *Overtures to Death* (1938), for all the technical expertise, there is a pervasive deficiency of imaginative intensity. Day Lewis can put the ballad form to work with polemical effectiveness (see 'Johnny Head-in-Air') and can voice tellingly the late 1930s' sense of impending horror (see 'Bombers'); but there are times when bold concrete metaphor seems to masquerade as meaning, and times when the futilities of the age are registered with a too grating, too wilfully devastating ridicule (see 'Newsreel'). In *Word Over All* (1943) Day Lewis moves, more at ease, within standard patterns of response to the war – its fears, toils, pains and comradeships. Here the utterance is rarely hollow, though it is sometimes rather cerebrally clever than charged with emotion. At least the political placards have been taken down and the scaffolding of official literary disillusionment dismantled.

Day Lewis made verse translations of Virgil's *Georgics* (1940), *Aeneid* (1952) and *Eclogues* (1963), using Virgil 'as a text rather than a springboard'. Each version 'is line-for-line and aims at a precise explication of the original' (the poet's Foreword to the edition of 1966, which brought the three works together). He has written novels under his own name as well as the numerous murder mysteries (by 'Nicholas Blake') featuring the detective Nigel Strangeways who has been said to resemble his creator. Day Lewis's critical work includes *The Poetic Image* (1947) and *The Lyric Impulse* (1965), two sets of lectures delivered at Cambridge and Harvard respectively. Ian Parsons has chosen and introduced *Poems of C. Day Lewis 1925–1972* (1977). Sean Day-Lewis, the poet's son, has written a biography, *C. Day-Lewis, An English Literary Life* (1980). [HB]

DE BOISSIÈRE, RALPH (1907–). Novelist, born in Trinidad into a long-established French-Creole family. Like Mais (q.v.) in Jamaica, de Boissière reached manhood during the time of the inter-war anti-colonial movement, in which he joined energetically. He claims that victimization by the Trinidadian authorities brought him to destitution, and he emigrated to Australia (1948), where he has since worked as salesman, car-factory worker and clerk.

His first two novels, set in Trinidad, contribute an authentic, unequivocally left-wing voice to the early phase of modern West Indian literature, but (probably because they were published in Australia) have been neglected in the Caribbean and Europe. *Crown Jewel* (1952; London, 1981), a social-protest novel, contrasts

Trinidad's natural beauty and violent history, white economic exploitation and black poverty in the 1930s; its jostling dramatis personae use a wide range of proletarian dialect. Themes of racial and economic struggle (against British and American imperialism in the 1940s) recur in *Rum and Coca Cola* (1956). *No Saddles for Kangaroos* (1964), which F.M. Birbalsingh regards as de Boissière's most accomplished book, is about trades union activists in an Australian car factory embattled against owners and corrupt police.   [AR]

DE LA MARE, WALTER (1873–1956). Poet, storyteller and essayist, born at Charlton, Kent, the sixth child of a Bank of England official of Huguenot ancestry. He was educated at St Paul's Cathedral Choir School, where he edited the *Chorister's Journal*, and he worked in the offices of the Anglo-American Oil Company for nearly twenty years. He began to write in journals like *The Sketch* and *The Pall Mall Gazette*: for these pieces and for his first volume of poems, *Songs of Childhood* (1902), he used the pseudonym 'Walter Ramal' (reversing part of his surname), but he identified himself on the title-page of his first novel, *Henry Brocken* (1904), 'his travels and adventures in the rich, strange, scarce-imaginable regions of romance', a book which included several poems. Henry's journeys take him out of reality and he encounters fictional characters like Jane Eyre, Bottom the Weaver and Lemuel Gulliver. From the start De la Mare's work was self-consciously literary both in the author's concern for stylistic finesse and in his claim upon a reading reader. In 1908 he was already sufficiently recognized to be awarded a Civil List pension and he turned to full-time writing, living thereafter quietly in the country. He had married Constance Elfrida Ingpen in 1899 (she died in 1943) and there were four children, of whom Richard, the eldest boy, was to become Chairman of Faber & Faber, his father's publisher. De la Mare was reticent about details of personal history and cultivated authorial privacy, but ubiquitous passages in prose and verse point to the seminal influence of a sensitive impressionable childhood. In the last long poem, *Winged Chariot* (1951), a meditative sequence of reflections on the enigma of time ('The subtlest of confusions known to Man'), De la Mare recalls childhood misery when he was out to tea and his mother failed to turn up at the expected time to take him home.

> So, in a flash, my heaped-up years I span
> To fill *this* Now, as, with uplifted pen,
> I match that child with this scarce-changed old
>   man.

It was *The Listeners and Other Poems* (1912) that fully established De la Mare's public reputation as a poet, and *Peacock Pie* (1913), ostensibly a volume for children, gave to a now growing public such poems as the touching 'Nicholas Eye' (he is a donkey) and the whimsical 'Miss T':

> It's a very odd thing -
>   As odd as can be -
> That whatever Miss T. eats
>   Turns into Miss T.

De la Mare practised the art of short-story writing for more than half a century, fashioning his pieces with disciplined selectivity and painstaking craftsmanship. Here, as in the poetry, the finish and precision of his artistry and the steady consistency of his imaginative power guarantee respect. If, here or there, an excursion into fantasy or absurdity is too laboured or protracted, as perhaps in 'The Orgy' (from *On the Edge*, 1930), where a frustrated young man impulsively piles up a debt of £200,000 for his uncle and guardian in a riotous spree at a London store, more often the distinctiveness of the situation explored and the fine complexities of its emotional implications convey a sense of rare psychological acumen. One might cite 'At First Sight' from the same collection, where a well-to-do young man, Cecil, has an affliction that prevents him from raising his eyes. Equipped with an eye-shade, he lives in a world of carpets and pavements, feet and ankles, skirts and trousers, and nevertheless manages to fall in love with a shop-assistant. Here the impact, comic and pathetic, derives from the ironic interplay of social and psychological cross-currents. In 'Missing' (from *The Connoisseur*, 1926) it derives from the unintentional unveiling of murder by a defensive, conscience-burdened man who buttonholes a stranger in a café. In 'The Almond Tree' and in 'Miss Duveen' (from *The Riddle*, 1923) we share the child's view - in the first case of a parental rift and in the second case of being befriended by a woman neighbour who has to be put away for lunacy. That De La Mare can resist sentimentalizing the child is finely evident in 'In the Forest' (from *The Wind Blows Over*, 1936), where crude unconscious childish selfishness is self-revealed in a boy's account of family tragedy. The powerful novel, *Memoirs of a Midget* (1921), the autobiographical record of a woman so diminutive that she is regarded as a freak, was reissued in 1982.

An awareness of oddity, a grasping after crucial questions that are floating above the words, a feeling that one has been deposited on an original bridgehead in unreality – these are the reader's responses to De la Mare. In poetry the lyrical gift is so unfaltering, the verbal artistry so delicate, that it won the admiration of fellow poets, Eliot and Auden included. The volumes of verse were numerous and many prose works had poems interspersed (such as *Ding Dong Bell*, 1924, and *The Three Royal Monkeys*, a story for children). Throughout, the dream world is constantly granted precedence over reality. 'It is the inward life that matters', De la Mare told Russell Brain (*Tea with De la Mare*, 1957). And 'why must a poem have a meaning?' he asked. Indeed, as Charles Williams (q.v.) early observed, 'De la Mare's poetry seems, at first reading, to communicate nothing but itself' (*Poetry at Present*, 1930), and in *Winged Chariot* occurs:

> 'What *is* this Poetry,' self whispered self,
> 'But the endeavour, faithfully and well
> As speech in language man-devisèd can,
> To enshrine therein the inexpressible?'

Many a lyric is concerned with events and experiences that seem to clamour for interpretation, but at the heart of things lies what is not understandable, not known.

> Oh, no man knows
> Through what wild centuries
> Roves back the rose.

>   ('All that's Past')

The poet's mode of expression is like the character of Martha who used to 'tell us her stories / In the hazel glen'.

> Her voice and her narrow chin,
> Her grave small lovely head,
> Seemed half the meaning
> Of the words she said.

('Martha')

Thus the reader is often left with what is not cleared up, not finished ('He said no more that sailor man', 'The Englishman'), and one of De la Mare's most celebrated poems, 'The Listeners', conjures up an atmosphere of uncanny, unfathomable mystery. Impenetrable eeriness is rendered palpable in images of spellbinding suggestiveness. Tremulous awareness is evoked of meaning undisclosed but momentous, of happenings and beings hidden but inapprehensibly strange. The vein is worked on a larger scale in the late long poem in decasyllabic quatrains, *The Traveller* (1945), where the horseman's mythic quest ('Was he man or ghost?') over an astonishingly surrealistic landscape, representing the eye of the earth, links him with life's courageous venturers as the child of genius who 'explores pure fantasy's unbounded realm'. The work seems to bring to a climax a lifetime's fitful teetering on the edge of being delivered from the inhibitions of terrestrial coherence and material rationality.

But the known and notable achievement of De la Mare remains the succession of lyrics in which varied established stanza forms are filled with new life by virtue of inner metrical subtleties and matching novelties of natural perception or symbolic divination. Many were assembled in the *Collected Poems* he arranged himself in 1942 and in the *Collected Rhymes and Verses* that followed in 1944. All are now available in *The Complete Poems of Walter de la Mare* (1969). Well read in earlier poetry, De la Mare has admittedly a ready-made reservoir of phrase and image that, once tapped, can flow with too much facility, and the writer who does as much in verse as he did for the adult or juvenile 'childhood' market will generally risk triteness and insipidity. Nevertheless the output as a whole has integrity, and its 'core' has uniqueness. [HB]

DELANEY, SHELAGH (1939–). Dramatist, born in Salford, Lancashire. She brought a winning touch of Lancashire down-to-earthness to her study of a working-class girl, Jo, in *A Taste of Honey* (prod 1958, pubd 1959). Alternately harried and neglected by her mother Helen, Jo has an affair with a black man while Helen honeymoons with a brash car salesman. The northern practice of mutual rudeness between intimates is neatly exploited at varying levels of irony and literalness, and the dialogue lives. The more panoramic picture of working-class life in *The Lion in Love* (prod 1960, pubd 1961) lacks the freshness and spontaneity of its predecessor. *Sweetly Sings the Donkey* (1964) is an autobiography. [HB]

DENNIS, NIGEL (1912–). Novelist and dramatist, born in Surrey but educated in Southern Rhodesia and in Germany. He has held important critical and editorial posts in journalism, working for *Time* magazine, *Encounter* and *The Sunday Telegraph*. He is an experimental novelist with scintillating techniques at his finger tips. His first novel was *Boys and Girls Come Out to Play* (in USA as *Sea Change*) (1949), but it was *Cards of Identity* (1955) that fully revealed the literary equipment of the virtuoso. It is concerned with an 'Identity Club' that meets at an English country house for its summer conference, and with 'the modern method of assuming that people are not real at all, only self-painted, and of proceeding to make them real by giving them new selves based on the best available theories of human nature'. Case-histories presented at the conference explore the multiple identities involved in the assumption of public office for ceremonial purposes, in ambiguous sexuality, in secret service work, in sudden conversion from Marxist to Christian commitment and in acting. The satire is devastatingly shrewd and funny. Lavish technical resources – Joycean hyperbole and parody – are harnessed to show up the common element of false self-projection in human roles that Dennis dislikes. The work presupposes a sophisticated readership alert to cultural fashion and current intellectual vagaries, and the presentation is extravagantly expansive. More intense and controlled is the brief fable-like study of wartime captivity, *A House in Order* (1966), which reduces its vision of human effort, hope and limitedness to a microcosmic Beckettian symbolism, taut and exact, never artificial, always humanly convincing. Dennis's plays include *The Making of Moo*, a satire on Christianity (partnered with a dramatic version of *Cards of Identity* in *Two Plays and A Preface*, 1958), and *August for the People* (1962), a satire on the press and its public. [HB]

DESAI, ANITA (1937–). Novelist, born in Mussoorie, India. She went to school and university in Delhi, married Ashvin Desai (1958) and has four children. Her early novels, *Cry, the Peacock* (1963) and *Voices in the City* (1965), examine the spiritual yearnings of unusually sensitive characters from affluent, orthodox Hindu backgrounds, who under the stresses of modern conditions, in seeking forms of fulfilment not consonant with their upbringing, destroy themselves in insanity, dissipation, suicide or despair. In closely textured prose, Anita Desai seizes on the details of outward reality as images of the landscapes of interior being; similarly, her central concern with individuality is projected through vivid realization of social conditions. *Bye-Bye, Blackbird* (1971) is about two Indians defining, through their experiences of England, their relationships with India's rich past and seemingly maze-like present. Shayamala Narayan prefers it to the earlier novels, and praises *Where Shall We Go This Summer?* (1975) for the sympathetic rendering of a wife's painful but uncatastrophic revolt against everyday dreariness. *Fire on the Mountain* (1977), which won a Sahitya Akademi Award and the Winifred Holtby Prize, explores the desolations of a family group of individually lonely women. Anita Desai's use of the language is admirably conscious, confident, sophisticated. *Clear Light of Day* (1980) is an accomplished novel, which delicately traces an embittered woman's childhood and youth, as she comes to understand her own human inadequacies in her relationships with others. [AR]

DESANI, G.V. (Govindas Vishnoodas) (1909–). Indian writer, born in Nairobi, Kenya. A journalist from 1935 to 1945, he lectured for the British Ministry of Information during the Second World War and broadcast for the BBC. After the war he spent fifteen years of meditation in Indian, Burmese and Japanese monasteries. He contributed a weekly column for the *Illustrated Weekly of India* from 1960 to 1968, and became a Professor of Philosophy in the University of Texas, Austin, in 1969.

Desani's one celebrated book, *All About H. Hatterr* (1948; revised edition, 1970), is a highly original work of philosophic sportiveness and verbal exuberance; with babu-like loquacity, Hatterr narrates his attempts to practise spiritual instruction received in turn from seven Indian sages. A torrent of absurd, idiosyncratic, rhetorical, colloquial English, it draws upon many registers of language usage, showing easy, un-priscian familiarity with the languages, cultures and topography of Europe and Asia. Imperial British and native Indian shibboleths are vigorously but good-humouredly ridiculed. On seeking to practise in real life each of the sages' transcendental instructions, the naïve Hatterr is roughly, fantastically discomfited, but bounces back with inextinguishable vitality. Only when he disregards the last sage's dictum does he prosper. It is a superb affirmation of life.   [AR]

DEVLIN, DENIS (1908–59). Poet, born in Greenock, Strathclyde, Scotland, of Irish parents who returned to Dublin when he was about 12. He was first intended for the priesthood. He studied at University College, Dublin, at Munich University and at the Sorbonne, Paris, then lectured in the English Department at University College, Dublin, before entering the Irish diplomatic service in 1935. He rose through various consular posts to be Ambassador to Italy. His *First Poems* (1930) and *Lough Derg and Other Poems* (1946) have been gathered and supplemented in *Collected Poems* (1964) with an Introduction by his literary executor, Brian Coffey. Devlin said, 'the poetic works of x must be the revelation of a single person to the world' and 'The poet justifies the works of man to God'. Coffey discerns his 'catholic conscience . . . schooled in the great book of European learning'. Devlin is not a light-weight poet: he 'sought mastery' and attained it. The telling range of his concerns is evident from 'The Tomb of Michael Collins', 'The Colours of Love' (written to his wife Caren) and 'The Heavenly Foreigner'. He has deliberation and a passionate dignity.

> It was being in the making of heaven, intoned in the terrestrial
> Rehearsal of the faithful, being with her.
>   ('The Heavenly Foreigner')
>   [HB]

DOBSON, ROSEMARY (1920–). Poet, born in Sydney, New South Wales, Australia. After graduating from university there she studied and taught art before working with publishers in London. She married in 1951, and after her return to Australia lived in Sydney and, more recently, in Canberra. Her deep interest in painting is evident in her first volume, *In a Convex Mirror* (1944), and is extended in her second book, *The Ship of Ice* (1948). In the Introduction to a 1963 selection she ably rebutted the criticism that her poetry reflected 'not life, but someone else's imitation of life', arguing that 'every artist should have complete freedom of choice' in selecting those ideas which have 'enlarged the poet's experience or stirred his imagination'. Her own response to paintings as artefacts frequently informs her work to advantage, contributing to its characteristic finely wrought stasis of time and emotion. *Cock Crow* (1965) demonstrates a skill in the creative handling of classical myth and *Selected Poems* (1973) provides a good introduction to her work. *Australian Voices* (1975) was her judicious selection of 'poetry and prose of the 1970s' and *Moscow Trefoil* (1975) a volume of translations from the Russian made in collaboration with David Campbell (q.v.). Later collections of poetry are *Greek Coins* (1977) and *Over the Frontier* (1978).   [PQ]

DOUGHTY, C.M. (Charles Montague) (1843–1926). Travel writer and poet, born in Suffolk, the son of a clergyman, and educated at Cambridge University. His wide travels included an exploration of Arabia that bore fruit in the publication of *Travels in Arabia Deserta* (1888). It is his poetry that belongs to the twentieth century. A few enthusiasts have made high claims for the 30,000-line epic, *The Dawn in Britain* (six volumes, 1906), in which various mythologies jostle, and whose blank verse reeks of artifice and often sacrifices flow in the measuring out of utterance, word by word:

> He would he a lavrock were, that, all day, might
> He, o'er her, singing flit, from toft to croft.

Later poems are *Adam Cast Forth: A Sacred Drama* (1908), *The Cliffs* (1909), *The Clouds* (1912) and *Mansoul, or The Riddle of the World* (1920). The stylistic vagaries of the last-named may be gauged from the poet's climactic vision of Mansoul's Dream City:

> Of all this, gone there-up, I took account;
> Dedale, emailed, deviseful, gem-dight work.
>   [HB]

DOUGLAS, KEITH (1920–44). Poet, born in Tunbridge Wells, Kent. He was educated at Christ's Hospital, and went to Merton College, Oxford, to read English in 1938. Edmund Blunden (q.v.) was his tutor and wrote the Introduction to the *Collected Poems* (1966). Douglas served in North Africa in the tank corps from 1941 to 1943 and was killed in the invasion of Normandy in June 1944. In October 1942, frustrated with his inactivity at base, he drove off to the Alamein battlefield in disobedience of orders. His book *Alamein to Zem Zem* (1946) is a vivid record of the campaign up to the time when he was wounded at Zem Zem and hospitalized in Palestine. 'I never lost the certainty that the experience of battle was something I must have', he wrote. And 'War was his ideal subject', Ted Hughes (q.v.) has observed (Introduction to *Selected Poems*, 1964), noting how the pressure of death, premonition of which obsessed him, brought meaning and urgency to his work. His style, after some early decorativeness, became astonishingly pure. 'His triumph lies in the way he renews the simplicity of ordinary talk' (Ted Hughes, op. cit.). 'Certainly you will never see the long metrical similes and galleries of images again', Douglas himself wrote of his work in August 1943. Actually there is evidence that Douglas had begun to find his own voice early on (see 'On Leaving School', for instance, written in 1937). But the impact of his war poetry, with its ruthless ironic contrasts (see 'Cairo Jag') and laconic understatement (see 'Simplify me when I'm Dead') is devastating. In 'How to Kill' the gunner defines his 'sorcery' in focusing the sight on 'the soldier who is going to die' and blowing to dust the smiles and movement that 'his mother knows'. In 'Vergissmeinicht' (Forget me not) an enemy corpse is found with a picture of his girl, 'Steffi', and her message on it ('Vergissmeinicht').

> But she would weep to see today
> how on his skin the swart flies move;
> the dust upon the paper eye
> and the burst stomach like a cave.

There is no overt moral questioning about war and no sense of ideological purpose; rather the reality of war is recorded with a dispassionateness peculiarly corrosive of the reader's comfort.

Desmond Graham has written *Keith Douglas 1920–1944, A Biography* (1974) and has edited the *Complete Poems* (1978). [HB]

DOUGLAS, NORMAN (1868–1952). Novelist and travel writer, born in Falkenhorst, Austria, of Scottish parentage, and educated mostly in Germany. His early interests were scientific. He served in the Foreign Office in St Petersburg until financial independence enabled him to go to Italy and then to settle at Capri. He married Elsa Fitzgibbon in 1898 and he collaborated with her in the volume *Unprofessional Tales by 'Normyx'* (1901), but he was divorced in 1903. Apart from the war years, which brought him back to England from 1941 to 1946, he spent most of the rest of his life resident in Italy or France. He became the most celebrated travel writer of his time. *Siren Land* (1911), about Italy, and *Fountains in the Sand* (1912), about Tunisia, were followed by *Old Calabria* (1915), which is generally considered his finest book. A 'full-bodied book' Douglas himself declared it (*Late Harvest*, 1946) and indeed we encounter in it a mind bubbling with enthusiasms and pouring out descriptive vignettes, gossipy anecdotes, historical facts, detail of flora and fauna and charming discursive reflections on people and things. It is the writing of a man at ease with life, an unashamed connoisseur of pleasure, and able, with lightly worn erudition, to indulge fascinating digressions about the lore of herbs, the Flying Monk of Copertino or Milton's indebtedness in *Paradise Lost* to the *Adamo Caduto* of Serafino della Salandra.

The same talents, brought to bear in fiction, produced *South Wind* (1917), a novel that has been constantly reprinted since. Thomas Love Peacock has been cited as an influence on this corpus of conversations between human individualists and eccentrics in a Mediterranean island called Nepenthe (an idealized Capri). Douglas rejected the charge that it is plotless in his book *Alone*

(1921). 'How to make murder palatable to a bishop: that is the plot.' In fact, the 'conversion' of Mr Heard, a colonial Anglican bishop, by the various pagan advocates of humanistic hedonism is but a slender thread in the work and not its most effective. Indeed the theme reminds us of the world of reality that Douglas evades. '*South Wind* was the result of my craving to escape from the wearisome actualities of life', he said, and justly, in *Late Harvest*. Peacock's novels were short. *South Wind* is long. The abrupt changes of topic which gave vitality to the travel books militate here against narrative consequentiality. The characters are not established as credible. Instead of authentic personalities, a host of witty disembodied voices is about our ears, leading us by degrees to 'a clear-cut, all consuming sense – of the screamingly funny insignificance of everything'. The reader is asked to sustain too patiently the notion that life filled with minor and major briberies and corruptions is a joke and, for all the book's packaged delights section by section, its superciliousness ultimately freezes the reader's smile. Noting the same 'lack of the story-teller's art', Richard Aldington declares two other novels, *They Went* (1920) and *In the Beginning* (1928), to be 'failures' (*Pinorman*, 1954). Douglas is pictured as James Argyle in D.H. Lawrence's (q.v.) *Aaron's Rod*. [HB]

DOYLE, ARTHUR CONAN (Sir) (1859–1930). Novelist and detective-story writer, creator of Sherlock Holmes, born in Edinburgh, Scotland, of Irish stock. He studied medicine and practised for a time as a doctor. He turned to writing to supplement his income. His training in clinical diagnosis stood him in good stead when he decided to capitalize on the taste for mystery and problem-solving in the sphere of criminal investigation. Wilkie Collins was no doubt an influence, but Doyle's achievement was to hit upon a formula for exercising the reader's brain not too strenuously, locating the deductive procedures in the mind of a fascinating personality and reproducing the atmosphere of a Victorian environment eminently susceptible to nostalgic idealization. Herein lies the continuing appeal that has institutionalized the Sherlock Holmes cult in clubs and quasi-scholarly research. Holmes has a nice blend of intellectual acuteness and human idiosyncrasy, of awe-inspiring charisma and sympathetic accessibility. His unerring capacity for sorting things out is backed by the fact that all the resources of national communications and official know-how seem to be naturally at his disposal in putting the world right. Such authority and power confer mythic status. Doyle's masterstroke was to equip the great man (and through him the reader) with a friend, Dr Watson, who is not at all quick on the uptake. Holmes's career began in *A Study in Scarlet* (1887) and continued in *The Sign of Four* (1890). From 1891 he made regular appearances in the *Strand Magazine*. Collected stories were published as *The Adventures of Sherlock Homes* (1892), *Memoirs of Sherlock Holmes* (1894) and *The Return of Sherlock Holmes* (1905). The full-length Holmes novel, *The Hound of the Baskervilles*, was published in book form in 1902. Somewhat perversely, Doyle came to regard his historical novels, set in the fourteenth century,

The White Company (1891) and *Sir Nigel* (1906), as his best work, and lamented the public preference for Sherlock Holmes. In later life he became a Spiritualist.

[HB]

DOYLE, MIKE (pseudonym of Charles Doyle) (1928–). Poet, born in Birmingham, England. He was educated at Victoria University College, University of New Zealand, and at Auckland University, having gone to New Zealand in 1951 while serving in the Royal Navy. For a time he taught at Auckland University but is now Associate Professor of English at the University of Victoria, British Columbia, Canada. In New Zealand he edited *Numbers*, together with James K. Baxter (q.v.) and Louis Johnson (q.v.). The three poets represented an approach to New Zealand poetry which denied the stress placed upon a regional 'island story' by Allen Curnow (q.v.) and instead held that 'the truly national literature is not regional, but universal'. In his own writing this 'anational and non-regional' perspective leads to a wealth of allusions to personal friends and to the mainstream of western thought. After his first collection, *A Splinter of Glass* (1956), he joined with Baxter, Johnson and Kendrick Smithyman (q.v.) in publishing *The Night Shift*, 'Poems on Aspects of Love', the following year. *Distances* (1963) showed his distinctive voice to good effect and *Messages for Herod* (1965) at times achieved a wry and spare immediacy in some respects comparable to Baxter's. Also in 1965 he edited *Recent Poetry in New Zealand*, an anthology which complemented the 1960 Penguin selection of Curnow. *Earth Meditations: 2* (1968), *Earth Meditations* (1971) and *Earthshot* (1972) explored fundamental human issues in a wide range of verse forms and voices. *Stonedancer* (1976) was an impressive and in many ways more even book which included many previously published poems. In 1970 he published a critical study of the New Zealand poet R.A.K. Mason (q.v.) and in 1976 *James K. Baxter*, a fine study of a fellow New Zealand poet.

[PQ]

DRABBLE, MARGARET (1939–). Novelist, born in Sheffield, South Yorkshire, educated at Mount School, York, and Newnham College, Cambridge. In her first novel, *A Summer Bird-Cage* (1963), she effectively reproduced the twittering inanities of an immature feminine type masquerading as liberated Oxbridge. Breathless, headlong, first-person narrative – chiefly a matter of parties, dress, drink, gossip and sex – plunges the reader into a morass of flippancies and vapidities as Sarah, allegedly brainy, recounts the marriage story of her sister Louisa, who is plainly silly. In *The Millstone* (1965) the clever academic, now called Rosamund Stacey, becomes pregnant, is subjected to NHS ante-natal clinic, maternity hospital and baby-feeding, and thereby learns a thing or two about life that Oxbridge neglected but that ordinary folk know all about. These novels sometimes read like the propaganda of an ironic male chauvinist out to illustrate the irremediable silliness of women. Indeed *The Realms of Gold* (1975) is a full-scale study of brainy archaeologist, Frances Wingate, who keeps her lover's discarded dentures inside her bra for emotional comfort. *The Middle*

Ground (1980) centres on Kate Armstrong, a popular columnist whose researches for a television documentary, 'Women at the Crossroads', spark off a personal self-exploration.

[HB]

DRANSFIELD, MICHAEL (1948–73). Poet, born in Sydney, New South Wales, Australia, and educated at the grammar school there. His early death from heroin addiction has led to undue emphasis upon those poems which deal, with disturbing honesty, with his illness, whereas his first collection, *Streets of the Long Voyage* (1970) – 'for my friends and for Australia' – already showed that complex human response to family, friends and country which was to characterize his best work. Acutely aware of both the beauty and the tenuousness of mortal happiness – a perception which his addiction sharpened to tragic proportions – his poetry brings both lyricism and precise observation to bear upon everyday experience. Poems such as 'Outback', 'Bum's Rush' and 'Last Post' reveal a rare fluency in handling rich human themes without sentimentality, and against them the 'drug poems', such as 'Still Life with Hypodermic', 'Overdose' and 'Fix', acquire their true and tragic significance. *The Inspector of Tides* (1972) confirmed his position as an outstanding Australian poet of the 1970s. *Drug Poems*, published the same year, reprinted some works from earlier collections in a volume which testified to his courage in facing and translating the joys and horrors of addiction. *Memoirs of a Velvet Urinal* was published in the United States, also in 1972. The 1978 volume, *Voyage into Solitude*, was edited by Rodney Hall (q.v.).

[PQ]

DRINKWATER, JOHN (1882–1937). Poet and dramatist, born in Essex. He gave an account of his family background in *Inheritance* (1931), an autobiographical volume with a sequel, *Discovery* (1932). His father had abandoned schoolmastering for the stage and Drinkwater linked himself with an amateur group, the Pilgrim Players, who turned professional as the Birmingham Repertory Company in 1913 ('for some years I was actor, producer, manager and odd-job man', *Inheritance*, Preface). Drinkwater contributed to the first volume of *Georgian Poetry* (1912), but his poetry is insipid and undistinctive. There is some energy in the rhythmic rhetoric of his verse playlet, *Cophetua* (1911), but succeeding verse dramas (see *Rebellion*, 1914) abound in pretentious diction and dressed-up commonplaces. Drinkwater turned to prose for history plays concerned with the human problem of leadership. Of these *Abraham Lincoln* (1918) had most success. Episodic sketches of key moments in Lincoln's career are linked by grandiloquent verse commentary from didactic chroniclers. The other 'leadership' plays are *Oliver Cromwell* (1921) and *Robert E. Lee* (1923). (See *Collected Plays*, 2 vols, 1925.) The comedy *Bird in the Hand* (1927) plays neatly and amusingly, if tritely and datedly, with the stubborn class-consciousness and inverted pride of a country landlord whose daughter falls in love with the local squire's son.

[HB]

DUDEK, LOUIS (1908–). Poet, born in Montreal, Quebec, Canada, and educated at McGill University there and Columbia University, New York. He taught in New York from 1946 until 1951, when he joined the English Department at McGill. In the 1940s he was one of a group of progressive 'proletarian' poets, including Irving Layton (q.v.) and Raymond Souster, with whom he jointly published *Cerberus* in 1952. His first book, *East of the City* (1946), was followed by two volumes in 1952, *The Searching Image* and *Twenty-Four Poems*. The best work in these collections is simple and poignant, uniting imagistic brevity with a lyrical delight in existence. The mechano-urban civilization of today is criticized or redeemed by a fleeting perception or random image. *Europe* (1955) employed a discursive form which accommodated meditative and aesthetic philosophy, personal narration and the occasional development of character and context; *En México* (1958) and *Atlantis* (1967) were also in this vein. As a personal document the series has considerable interest and its sustained poetic and intellectual note is unique in Canadian poetry, but the loose narrative lapses at times into tedium. *Atlantis*, in particular, is marred by awkward poetic 'reflections'; *Europe* remains the more successful work. In *Laughing Stalks* (1958) Dudek expressed his feelings in more humorous vein in a volume which included adroit parodies of Canadian poets and gibes at critics. One aspect of his promotion of contemporary poetry was his editorship of the magazine *Delta* (1957–66). *Collected Poetry* (1971) established his achievement for a new generation and was followed by *Epigrams* (1975). *Selected Essays and Criticism* (1978) was edited by M. Gnarowski; *Technology and Culture* (1979) collected six essays written between 1969 and 1975.   [PQ]

DUGGAN, ALFRED (1903–64). Novelist, born in Buenos Aires, Argentina. His father was of Irish descent, but his mother, when widowed, became Lord Curzon's second wife in 1917, and Duggan was educated at Eton and Oxford. He travelled in the Middle East in pursuit of material for the British Museum. His career as a writer of historical novels began in 1950 with the publication of *Knight With Armour*, and successive titles included *The Little Emperors* (1951), *Conscience of the King* (1951), *The Lady for Ransom* (1953) and *Leopards and Lilies* (1954). Duggan was compared with Robert Graves (q.v.) as one of the great historical novelists of the century. He was a scrupulous historian. 'The theme of this book is that Cerdric Elesing, founder of Wessex, was really a Roman of Britain, bearing the Celtic name of Coroticus', he writes in *Conscience of the King*. Coroticus narrates his own story in old age, dating clearly the successive events of his career from 451 to 531 and revealing himself a cunning and unscrupulous adventurer guilty of fratricide ('I was lucky enough to be born without the silly handicap of natural affection'). The coming of the Saxons is comprehensively depicted by accurate use of available evidence, invention taking over only where evidence is lacking. Yet 'everything I have written could be defended by historical argument', Duggan said of the book. This method is applied to some of the less accessible periods of history. *The Lady for Ransom* traces the career of an

orphaned Norman, Roger, in the service of Roussel de Balliol whose exploits took him to Romania in 1069. We are present at the defeat of the Byzantine Emperor, Romanus Diogenes, by the Turks at Manzikert and observe his subsequent downfall. Roger narrates his story in December 1096 when he is 44 years old and has retired to a monastery and when Alexius Comnenus has ascended the throne. Roger's adventures immediately precede events depicted in Sir Walter Scott's *Count Robert of Paris*. Duggan's forte is fidelity to historical detail and the novels, fascinating as historical narrative, are best read with an atlas at one's elbow.   [HB]

DUGGAN, MAURICE (1922–74). Short-story writer, born in Auckland, New Zealand, and educated at university there. He lived in London and travelled in southern Europe in 1949–53, and, after holding various jobs in New Zealand upon his return, worked in advertising from 1961. His first collection, *Immanuel's Land* (1956), painted a disturbing and at times bitter picture of experience and *Summer in the Gravel Pit* (1965), which reprinted three stories from the earlier book, further illustrated his control of a series of independent but interrelated stories which in form as well as content mirror the fragmentary and deceptive nature of experience. Many of the stories invite a linked reading by their sequential narrative and overlap of characters but in general Duggan's very form of writing seems to defy novelistic reading and to assert the impenetrable misunderstandings that go to form human relationships. A disillusioned view of human nature is offset to some extent by his compassionate interest in the poor unfortunates who, like the 'burnt ones' in the stories by Patrick White (q.v.), so often people his world. The lengthy story 'Along the Ridout Road that Summer', from *Summer in the Gravel Pit*, points the way to the extended fiction form first used in *O'Leary's Orchard and Other Stories* (1970), in which the same character, now aged, reappears; 'Riley's Handbook' is a long monologue in which again the reader's own assumptions are implicitly questioned by the ambiguousness of the writing itself.   [PQ]

DU MAURIER, DAPHNE (Dame) (1907–). Novelist, born in London and educated in Paris, the daughter of the actor Sir Gerald du Maurier and granddaughter of George du Maurier, author of *Trilby*. She is now Lady Browning, widow of the late Lieutenant-General Sir Frederick Browning. Her spate of best-selling novels reached full flow with *Jamaica Inn* (1936), a Cornish smuggling tale, and *Rebecca* (1938), story of an unsophisticated young girl swept into marriage with a wealthy widower and overpowered by the grip of her beautiful predecessor, Rebecca, on her new home and its inhabitants. Proficient presentation and a sweeping narrative line cannot conceal the melodramatic implausibilities and the excessive reliance upon overworked fictional traditions. Daphne du Maurier has more recently turned to material from family history (*Mary Anne*, 1954; *The Glass Blowers*, 1963). Non-fiction works include *Gerald* (1934), a portrait of her father, *The Du Mauriers* (1937) and the autobiographical book *Growing Pains* (1977), subtitled *The Shaping of a Writer*.   [HB]

DUNCAN, RONALD (1914–82). Dramatist and poet, born in Rhodesia. His father's name was 'Dunkelsbuhler': of German birth, he had been brought up in England and married an English girl. She came back to England to bring up their two children and her husband died in Rhodesia in 1918. In his richly informative autobiography, *All Men Are Islands* (1964), Duncan tells how his education at a boarding school 'on the east coast of Yorkshire' prepared him for life's future miseries by surpassing them all in advance. After reading English at Cambridge, he was driven by social idealism to take a job for a time in a Yorkshire coal-mine. He joined the Peace Pledge Union, he got to know Benjamin Britten, Ezra Pound, Eliot, even Stravinsky, and visited Gandhi at his ashram near Wardha. He married Rose Marie Hansom in 1941. Duncan started his own community farm in Devon but the enterprise did not last. He broke through to the public with his verse play, *This Way to the Tomb* (1946), which was performed at the Mercury Theatre, London. The revival of verse drama there made it seem 'that we had the theatre of "realism" on the run. But the victory was brief. Within a few years naturalism became the fashion again. The only change was that the convention of Shaftesbury Avenue duchesses fiddling with flower vases was replaced by Jimmy Porters picking their noses in public' (Introduction to *Collected Plays*, 1971). A masque and anti-masque, with music by Britten, *This Way to the Tomb* presents the fourteenth-century St Antony, who gives up a wealthy and powerful abbacy to become the hermit of Zante and the martyr to his own austerities. The present-day anti-masque revisits the scene with television crew to discredit the legend of the saint's miraculous anniversary revisitations. The influence of Eliot is marked in the handling of the martyrdom (cf. *Murder in the Cathedral*) and sometimes in verbal and rhythmic echo. Duncan felt that, like Eliot, he moved nearer 'to finding a solution to the problem of language in the contemporary situation' (op. cit.) in a later play, *The Catalyst* (1958), but *St Spiv* (produced as *Nothing up My Sleeve*, 1950) is a remarkable exercise in picturing cockney life in London and on the Epsom racecourse with the kind of verve and vividness achieved by Ben Jonson in *Bartholomew Fair*. *The Seven Deadly Virtues* (prod 1968), in which scenes from life are interleaved with diabolic and angelic commentary, is an ingenious exercise in moral diagnosis. Duncan's poetry includes *The Solitudes* (1960), a sequence of surgically analytical love poems, and *Man* (Part 1, 1970; Part 2 and 3, 1972; Parts 4 and 5, 1974), an exercise in sustained speculation. Duncan has also published three volumes of short stories. The title story and 'Mandala' in *A Kettle of Fish* (1969) blend the urbane and the bizarre disturbingly, but the tales in *The Uninvited Guest* (1981) are sometimes naïve in substance and slipshod in style. Duncan has added two further volumes of autobiography – *How to Make Enemies* (1968) and *Obsessed* (1977), the latter concerning his love affair with the actress, Virginia Maskell.   [HB]

DUNN, DOUGLAS (1942–). Poet, born in Inchinnan, Strathclyde, Scotland, and educated at the Scottish School of Librarianship and at Hull University. He worked as a librarian in Scotland, Ohio and at Hull University before turning freelance writer in 1971. His first volume of poems, *Terry Street* (London, 1969; New York, 1973), was succeeded by *The Happier Life* (1972), *Love or Nothing* (1974) and *Barbarians* (1978). The first of these contained neatly delineated but flatly dispassionate vignettes of the city scene. Dunn's tendency is to dismiss the shallowness of human lives with a derogatory shrug. He has pushed the deflationary devices of such poets as Philip Larkin (q.v.) to a new extreme. In 'Remembering Lunch' (*St Kilda's Parliament*), for instance, disillusionment and self-deprecation become all-pervasive: protest and passion evaporate in a lassitude of spirit so nugatory that utterance itself seems otiose and the very words mock themselves.

> We are far gone in our own decay. I admit it
>   freely,
> Longing no more for even the wherewithal of
>   decent sufficiency
> Or whatever hypothetical brilliance makes it
>   possible.

Dunn's earlier technique sometimes falters, but there is clever Cavalier pastiche, of both mood and form, in 'On Her Picture Left With Him' (*New Poems 1977–78*, edited Gavin Ewart). And in *St Kilda's Parliament* (1981) Dunn moves on a new level of imaginative and verbal assurance in drawing on the living 'mythology' of Scottish life on Clydeside. In range of mood and fineness of touch the volume justifies the poet's own claim: 'I like to see these poems as delegates from my own imagination, gathered to sit in its own house'.   [HB]

DUNSANY, LORD (Edward John Moreton Drax Plunkett) (1878–1957). Irish dramatist and short-story writer, born in London and educated at Eton and Sandhurst. He served in the Boer War and the First World War. He combined the life of a literary man and a sporting aristocrat. He wrote several volumes of short stories beginning with *Time and the Gods* (1906). In these and in some of the plays he invented a synthetic mythology with pseudo-classical and oriental nomenclature. The short dramas, *The Gods of the Mountain* (1911), *King Argimenes and the Unknown Warrior* (1911) and *The Golden Doom* (1912), are simple moral fables, stylized in rhetoric and action, to which a menacing sense of supernatural destiny adds potency. In *The Glittering Gate*, put on at the Abbey Theatre, Dublin, in 1909, two dead ex-burglars meet before the gate of heaven. When one of them successfully attacks the lock with the tools of his trade, it swings open to reveal nothing at all. (See *Five Plays*, 1914.) *The Travel Tales of Mr Joseph Jorkens* (1931) and *Jorkens Borrows Another Whiskey* (1954) were the first and last of five books of tall stories narrated at the Billiards Club by Joseph Jorkens, generally at the price of a drink. Dunsany also wrote *Fifty Poems* (1929) and the autobiographical *Patches of Sunlight* (1938).   [HB]

DURRELL, LAWRENCE (1912–). Poet and novelist, born in Julunder, India, of British parents. He was educated at the College of St Joseph, Darjeeling and then, when his family came back to settle in Bournemouth, at St Edmund's School, Canterbury. The family moved out to Corfu in 1935 and Durrell's life since has included spells in Greece, Rhodes, Argentina and Yugoslavia as well as in Egypt. The list of jobs he has held includes night-club porter and motor racer; but official service claimed him during the war when he served in the British Information Offices in Cairo and Alexandria. After the war he worked briefly for the British Council, did periods of service as an embassy press attaché and came eventually to rest as an English teacher in Cyprus, whence the troubles dislodged him in 1956. The success of the novel *Justine* (1957) gave him financial freedom as a writer and he settled in the south of France. Durrell has been three times married. There were two children by his first wife, Nancy. He met his second wife, Eve, in Egypt, and his third wife, Claude, in Cyprus. The three island books reflect three phases of his wanderings, *Prospero's Cell* (1945) being a 'Guide to the Landscape and Manners' of Corfu, *Reflections on a Marine Venus* (1953) a corresponding book on Rhodes, and *Bitter Lemons* (1957) 'a somewhat impressionistic study of the moods and atmospheres of Cyprus during the troubled years 1953-6' (Preface).

Durrell made his first literary reputation as a poet. Some small early volumes were published in the 1930s but Durrell has said, 'I date my poetic appearance from the publication of *A Private Country* in 1943' (Preface to *Collected Poems*, 1960). Later volumes include *Cities, Plains and People* (1946), *The Tree of Idleness* (1955) and *Vega & Other Poems* (1973). James A. Brigham edited the *Collected Poems 1931–1974* (1980). Landscapes – especially those of the eastern Mediterranean – are recreated with sensuous evocativeness and with sensitivity to the golden classical past, and there are many lyrics that, like a commentary, take the reader back to the scenes of the novels and the travel books; but perhaps Durrell's most effective poetic gift is the intrusive analysis that acts as countercheck upon vague or nostalgic recollection of persons or places:

> I saw the street-lamp unpick Theodora
> Like an old sweater, unwrinkle eyes and mouth,
> Unbandaging her youth to let me see
> The wounds I had not understood before.
>   ('A Portrait of Theodora')

Durrell's wit vitalizes a resourceful vocabulary and a polished versification, enabling him to combine humour and seriousness with rare thrust:

> The baby emperor
> reigning on tuffet, throne or pot
> in his minority knows hardly what
> he is or is not –

Thus begins 'Clouds of Glory', and the Wordsworthian basis is meaningfully exploited. Durrell often thrives on derivation. His accomplishment as a pure comic poet can be gauged from the 'Ballad of the Good Lord Nelson' or the 'Ballad of the Oedipus Complex'. His verse dramas have not elicited critical acclaim, though *Sappho* (1950), the first, was put on at the Edinburgh Festival in 1961, and all three of his plays have been performed abroad. In *An Irish Faustus* (1963), called 'A Morality in Nine Scenes', Faustus saves Queen Katherine of Galway from a curse by himself encountering hell. At the end he takes an advisory job in a pardoner's factory that produces bogus relics and indulgences.

Durrell's first two novels, *Pied Piper of Lovers* (1935) and *Panic Spring* (1937), were not distinctive, but *The Black Book*, his third, was a savage and comic outburst against the smug conventionalities of English life or – as he called it – 'the English death'. Durrell cast inhibitions aside in what he later called 'a two-fisted attack in literature by an angry young man of the thirties' and there was no possibility of publication in England for a work so frank in its vocabulary and in its record of sexual activities. Durrell has since admitted his attachment to the book 'because in the writing of it I first heard the sound of my own voice' and indeed the vigour of the prose, the surrealistic presentation of inner life and outer event and the passages of concentrated imagery that are carried on a verbal tide generally too full account for the attention a Paris edition elicited from a small public in 1938. The association of English middle-class respectability and the English climate with personal and civilizational moribundity, and the corresponding association of freedom and vitality with the sunny Mediterranean, is imaginatively useful; but the trouble is that Durrell's recommended alternatives to the stabilities he despises seem to be chiefly eastern scenery and promiscuity. Increasingly in the novels the brothel becomes a symbol of emancipation. Thus *The Black Book* anticipates the mature fiction in the values it derides as well as in the reduplicative technique involved in interweaving the memoirs of Lawrence Lucifer, the narrator, with those of the 'dead' writer, Death Gregory.

*The Alexandria Quartet** brought Durrell's experience of Egypt and the diplomatic service to bear upon a story in which secret gun-running provides an undercurrent to (and an excuse for) heady erotic entanglements and headier sexual permutations. The four volumes skilfully package espionage and coition for the middlebrow in luxurious prose. The sensuous verbal denseness does justice to the physical feel of the Alexandrian world, and set pieces stamp out landscapes, vignettes and moods like precious jewels. The subsequent double-decker, *Aut Tunc Aut Nunquam*, consisting of *Tunc* (1968) and *Nunquam* (1970), does not represent any advance on this achievement. The notion of a 'firm' with a worldwide network of power and influence, which can take over the lives of those it employs, is impressively utilized at the start. The opportunities the firm offers scientists and inventors like the hero, Felix Charlock, provide an excellent basis for examining the character of freedom, and particularly the relative significance of ineffective personal independence and of controlling institutional 'benevolence'. But this interesting theme is submerged under the outpourings of garrulous caricatures and a welter of indigestible material from the bawdy to the horrific. The extravaganza concludes with the manufacture of a female robot. *Monsieur, or the Prince of Darkness* (1974) explores a love triangle which turns out, in *Livia, or Buried Alive* (1978), to be a fictionalized version of what has happened to another trio. The two novels, together with *Constance* (1982), form part of a planned quincunx, a further exercise in shifting angles of vision and multiplying interpretations.

The Alexandria Quartet is a tetralogy of novels: *Justine* (1957), *Balthazar* (1958), *Mountolive* (1958) and *Clea* (1960). All are set largely in Alexandria, the first three in the years before the Second World War and the fourth during the war. Durrell calls parts 2 and 3 'siblings' of part 1 (only *Clea* is a 'sequel') for they 'overlap, interweave, in a purely spatial relation. Time is stayed.' The method is neither Proustian nor Joycean in that the novels illustrate Bergsonian 'Duration' and 'Space-Time'. 'The central topic of the book is an investigation of modern love' (Preface to *Balthazar*). Darley, a school-teacher, the narrator of *Justine*, has Durrell's own initials. He moves in parts 1 and 2 through two of the three liaisons which occupy him over the series – with Melissa, a night-club dancer, Justine, the Jewish wife of Nessim, a wealthy Coptic businessman, and Clea, an artist with whom he finds peace in part 4. Darley's convincing and fervent record of personal experience in *Justine* turns out to be in important respects an erroneous and inadequate reading of events, attitudes and motives, when he turns in *Balthazar* to enrich his own version of things (already in manuscript) from the interlinear corrections made by Balthazar, a doctor, and from other new sources of information. Justine's previous lover, Arnauti, wrote a book about her, and another significant character, Pursewarden, is a writer (as well as a diplomat). Durrell is therefore able to interweave ever-multiplying re-interpretations from the mouths and pens of his characters. *Mountolive* furthers the process of continuous re-correction. It emerges that Nessim and Justine are deeply involved in smuggling arms to Palestine, while Darley and Pursewarden are secret agents: so there is ample basis for deception and multiple motivation. Moreover Mountolive, now British Ambassador, was in Alexandria years earlier as a junior embassy official and had a love affair with Leila Hosnani, Nessim's mother.

Technically speaking, the multi-dimensional effect in the presentation of character and event is something of a tour de force; but the 'investigation of modern love' turns out to be a shuffling and re-allocation of sexual partners tedious in its permutational predictabilities and laced with prescribed variants, pederastic, lesbian and incestuous. In terms of background and atmosphere Alexandria is reproduced with variety and richness – its streets, cafés, brothels, carnivals, funerals and other teeming activities. In terms of basic artistic function the city is really the fantasy world where sexual inhibitions can be dispensed with. An undercurrent of reflection points to 'the mutability of all truth'. In total mutability one comes 'face to face with the meaning of love and time'. But the shallowness of relationships explored ill befits the attempts of participants to make experience a breeding ground for aphoristic profundities.   [HB]

E

EKWENSI, CYPRIAN (1921–). Novelist, of Igbo origin but born in Minna, Northern Nigeria, educated in Ibadan, Achimoto (Ghana), Lagos and London. After teaching and working as a pharmacist from 1947 to 1956, he worked in Nigerian broadcasting from 1956 to 1961. Resigning as Nigerian Director of Information in 1966, he headed Biafran External Publicity throughout the Civil War, 1967–70. Later he became Managing Director of a newspaper group.

Despite elements of popular romance, thriller narrative, mild sexual titillation and deliberate moralizing – often transmitted in clichéd language – his novels are important because he describes social conditions with sharp realism, capturing the general mood of ordinary Nigerians at the mercy of rapid social change. An ability to register the pulses of popular feeling probably springs from the origins of his career, with *When Love Whispers* (1947) and similar works produced on the small printing presses of the Onitsha market in Eastern Nigeria. *People of the City* (1954) was the first anglophone African novel to deal with the unhappiness, rootlessness, yet excitement of young rural people first experiencing urbanization. *Jagua Nana* (1961) is an acute characterization of a Lagos prostitute trying desperately to win respectable security before her charms wear out. *Beautiful Feathers* (1963) satirizes African politicians and top civil servants. *Iska* (1966) reveals Ekwensi's serious social purposes in his treatment of the massacres of Igbos in Northern Nigeria, while his role as vivid chronicler of change is confirmed by *Survive the Peace* (1976), set in war-stricken Eastern Nigeria as the Civil War ends.   [AR]

ELIOT, T.S. (Thomas Stearns) (1888–1965). Poet, dramatist and critic, born in St Louis, Missouri, USA. His father, Henry Ware Eliot, was a prosperous businessman of firm Unitarian convictions. There were four elder daughters and one other son; then the poet was born after a nine-year gap. He had a hernia in childhood that limited him in playing games and later kept him out of active service in the First World War. The family had a holiday home at East Gloucester on the Massachusetts coast, where Eliot learned to sail, a hobby he cultivated when he progressed from Milton Academy to Harvard in 1906. The Mississippi at St Louis and the sea off Cape Ann near Gloucester were to thread themselves for a lifetime through Eliot's imagery. And the fact that his ancestor, Andrew Eliot, had emigrated to New England from East Coker, Somerset, in the seventeenth century became the basis of a symbolic theme of return to be worked out in his poetry and lived out in his life. A member of the American puritan aristocracy, Eliot was assumed to be destined for a distinguished academic career. He spent a year at the Sorbonne from 1910 to 1911 and returned for another three years at Harvard to study for a Ph D (with a thesis on F.H. Bradley's Theory of Knowledge). In 1914 he went to Merton College, Oxford, having been awarded the Sheldon Fellowship, staying briefly in Paris and Marburg, as well as London, on the way. (Personal memories of Bavaria on the eve of the First World War are juxtaposed with imagery of the public calamity in the first section of The Waste Land*.) In London Eliot quickly made the acquaintance of his compatriot, Ezra Pound, and through him of Wyndham Lewis (q.v.), Ford Madox Ford (q.v.) and other writers. Pound's influence on Eliot has perhaps been exaggerated ('Mr Eliot was lifted out of his lunar alley-ways and fin-de-siècle nocturnes, into a massive region of verbal creation in contact with that astonishing didactic intelligence, that is all', said Wyndham Lewis in Blasting and Bombardiering); but Eliot acknowledged its importance.

In 1915 Eliot married Vivienne Haigh-Wood at a registry office without informing his family at home in advance. On a visit to Massachusetts shortly afterwards he faced his parents with the apparent abandonment of academic ambition for obscurity in London. 'Father and son parted bitterly' (Robert Sencourt, T.S. Eliot, A Memoir, 1971), and the sadness of it was to reverberate years later in the rift between 'Henry' and 'Thomas' in Murder in the Cathedral*. Eliot earned his living first by schoolmastering (he taught English to the young John Betjeman at Highgate School) and then, more congenially, by working for Lloyds Bank. Here he rose to a well-paid position in the foreign branch before he left the bank's service in 1925. Meanwhile his literary connections had accumulated, partly through his introduction to Lady Ottoline Morrell's circle at Garsington. Richard Aldington (q.v.), Virginia Woolf (q.v.), Sacheverell Sitwell (q.v.) and Middleton Murry (q.v.) figure among numerous contacts. The relationship with James Joyce (q.v.) began somewhat inauspiciously in Paris when Eliot was the bearer of a parcel from Ezra Pound to Joyce that in fact contained an old pair of shoes. Eliot edited Lady Rothermere's The Criterion from its first issue in 1922 and continued to do so when it was taken over by Faber and Gwyer (later Faber and Faber), the publishing firm of which Eliot became a director for the rest of his life.

Eliot's rapid rise to a position of unique dominance in English letters, first as poetic revolutionary, then as literary mandarin on the Johnsonian scale, began with the publication of Prufrock and Other Observations (1917), Poems (1919) and The Waste Land (1922). Poems 1909–25 (1925) gathered together the vital early output that redirected the development of English poetry by breaking away from standardized Georgian poeticism and seeking in the cadences and idioms of contemporary life a current of vitality and tension equivalent to its moods and its mores. The juxtaposition, in imagery and rhythm, of rich fragments from the literary past with the living colloquial accents of the present provided both heady verbal ensembles and an apt medium for registering the condition of a disintegrating society. Techniques of seventeenth-century metaphysical poets, Donne especially, were revivified to give intellectual spine to imagery and rescue it from 'poetic' predictability. The novel stylistic concentration provoked bewilderment and hostility, partly because it involved playing down surface narrative and logic, often to the point of extinction, and forcing the reader to derive his own intellectual inferences and emotional bearings from the assembled imagery and impressions.

Eliot's conversion to the Church of England was a turning-point. He was baptized in 1927 and in the same year he became a naturalized British citizen. He forthwith proclaimed himself a classicist in literature, a royalist in politics and an Anglo-Catholic in religion. 'Journey of the Magi' (1927) is seminally charged with the paradox of birth through death which baptism itself represents and which the kingdoms of the world 'should be glad of'. Ash Wednesday (1930) is a poem of penitence, purgation and self-surrender; but for all its emphasis on the drag of sense and the pull of the past, its tensions are disciplined within phrases of the liturgy that stir up a ground swell of faith and hope. Eliot's spiritual pilgrimage is clearly documented, but the exact character of the domestic turmoil he endured will be publicly understood only when time has permitted a full account of how Vivienne's instability developed into insanity. The burden of coping with her became too much, and when Eliot went to America to deliver the Charles Eliot Norton poetry lectures (see The Use of Poetry and the Use of Criticism, 1933) in the session 1932–3, he arranged for a legal separation and never returned to her.

Eliot's work on the religious pageant, The Rock, staged at Sadler's Wells in June 1934, led to the commissioning of Murder in the Cathedral. It was written at the request of George Bell, Bishop of Chichester, for performance in the cathedral at the Canterbury Festival, 1935. It was shortly afterwards produced in London at the Mercury Theatre and its success initiated a revival of poetic drama. Eliot made of the martyrdom of St Thomas à Becket a stylized yet deeply interior study of the conflict between worldly and spiritual demands upon man in all ages. But 'I shall not preach to you again', Thomas says in his last sermon in Murder in the Cathedral and in Eliot's succeeding plays religious implications are conveyed only in overtones and half-pressed ambiguities, while verse moves acceleratingly towards the undoctored rhythms of conversation, and surface obviousness of substance becomes ever more suspiciously obvious. The Family Reunion (1939) has curious interest in its almost claustrophobic worrying at questions of guilt and expiation relevant to Eliot's own personal dilemma as husband and son. The threatening estrangement between Edward and his wife Lavinia in The Cocktail Party (1949) is averted by the guidance and wisdom of the unidentified stranger (Sir Henry Harcourt-Reilly): the implication is that disjointed human relationships can be put right with divine assistance at a certain price. The Confidential Clerk (1953) is superficially a farce of labyrinthine mysteries over the identities of illegitimate offspring and the obligations of their parents, but a parable emerges, with psychological and spiritual implications, on the themes of human vocation, the need for self-knowledge, openness and commitment of the will.

The work that set the crown on Eliot's lifetime of poetic endeavour was Four Quartets* which began with the publication of the first 'quartet', Burnt Norton, in 1936 and was gradually completed by the addition of East Coker (1940), The Dry Salvages (1941) and Little Gidding (1942). The whole makes a compressed epic, distilling the experience and study of a lifetime, with an anchorage in places crucial to Eliot in his personal development as man and poet. Eliot now had a unique capacity for blending personal and professional, historical and racial, cosmic and religious layers of significance in images and symbols at once dense and lucid, and the mastery of connotational multiplicity was attuned to a sacramental and incarnational reading of man's role in life. The work has the quality of a *Paradiso*, as *The Waste Land* had those of an *Inferno* and *Ash Wednesday* those of a *Purgatorio*. (See Harry Blamires, *Word Unheard, A Guide through Eliot's Four Quartets*, 1969.)

Vivienne Eliot died in 1947 after fourteen years of separation and Eliot felt the shock deeply at a time when public honours were crowding upon him. He was awarded the Nobel Prize in 1948 and received the OM in the same year. His literary standing in America and Europe was no less eminent than at home, but he suffered increasingly from emphysema and his last years might have been sad ones had he not married his secretary, Valerie Fletcher, in 1957. The union was an immensely happy one, and the happiness is reflected both in the dedication to *The Elder Statesman* (1959) and in the play itself. Eliot's sense of fun was a sustaining characteristic throughout his life. It made him the friend and admirer of Groucho Marx. It glints in the lines of *Old Possum's Book of Practical Cats* (1940) and often between the lines of more overtly serious works. He liked to break 'the law of gravity'; but he lived out his 'return' seriously enough, and his ashes were taken after cremation, as he instructed, to St Michael's Church in the ancestral village of East Coker.

The Waste Land, a poem of some 400 lines (the first draft was drastically reduced with Pound's help), uses techniques of connotational multiplicity and of literary allusiveness that enable a vast range of meaning to be compressed into economic lines and cryptic images. The work has achieved a monumental status as the most intense poetic confrontation with postwar European disintegration that the 1920s and 1930s produced. There is neither clear narrative line nor logical consecutiveness. The angle of vision shifts from shot to shot as in a film. Tiresias, the blind two-sexed prophet, reveals himself in part III as the spectator before whom the fluid sequences take their shape. 'What Tiresias *sees*, in fact, is the substance of the poem', Eliot avers in his Notes. The five sections of the poem are I 'The Burial of the Dead', II 'A Game of Chess', III 'The Fire Sermon', IV 'Death by Water' and V 'What the Thunder Said'. A route of a kind can be found through them by following Eliot's own advice to consult Jessie Weston's book on the Grail legend, *From Ritual to Romance*, and Frazer's *The Golden Bough*, but Eliot's actual presentation discourages linear reading, even on the symbolical and anthropological level. Indeed, overtones carry a connotational polyphony which has its purely personal line relative to the poet's private life, its more social concern with postwar London, its themes of conversion and self-sacrifice, purgation and salvation, and its flashbacks to wartime slaughter and destruction, as well as to momentous landmarks of actual or literary history. Fragmentariness is of the essence of what is a study of a fragmented civilization. Nevertheless the work achieves its own artistic order and thrust in the skilful juxtaposition of images and references that call out their own responses. The cataclysm of nightmare destruction accompanies the image of the mysterious third party on the road to Emmaus; the neurosis of a

bored, sophisticated woman of leisure is cheek-by-jowl with cockney pub chatter of abortions and Sunday dinner; a seduced London typist takes her place alongside the human flotsam of Spenser's 'Sweet Thames' on which Elizabeth and Leicester once flirted together; the crowd of war dead flows over London Bridge and the motors bring their customers to Mrs Porter's brothel. Ultimately, though the dry rock cannot be stricken to bring forth water and the cock of betrayal crows aloud,

> The awful daring of a moment's surrender
> Which an age of prudence cannot retract

is at least called for; and the peace which acceptance of the challenge would bring – the peace which passeth understanding – is proclaimed in Sanskrit: 'Shantih shantih shantih'.

Murder in the Cathedral, a verse play about the murder of Thomas à Becket, has two parts that are separated by an Interlude (the Archbishop's sermon on Christmas Day 1170). The scene moves between the Archbishop's Hall and the cathedral at Canterbury, and the date moves from 2 December to 29 December 1170, the day of Becket's murder. Highly stylized in form, the play shows the influence of Greek tragedy, *Samson Agonistes*, and the medieval Moralities. Thomas's spiritual pilgrimage is the dominating interest, and his martyrdom at the hands of Henry II's knights is made symptomatic of every man's vocation to costly self-surrender to the divine will. The struggle between church and state reflects the conflict between the spiritual and the temporal that dogs human experience in all ages. The pattern of movement through trial and suffering to sanctity is paralleled with the pattern of Christ's atonement and resurrection, with the seasonal pattern of movement through the death of winter to the birth of spring, and even with the sexual pattern of human procreation whereby woman 'dies' in love to man in order to give birth. Eliot is enabled to load his action with these dimensions of meaning by skilful use of a female Chorus whose words involve them and their audience in the protagonist's destiny as part-sharers and would-be rejectors of its cost. The action is largely interior in that the Tempters whose dialogue with Thomas supplies the tension are personifications of his inner impulses.

Four Quartets, a poem in four sections, *Burnt Norton, East Coker, The Dry Salvages* and *Little Gidding*, is a series of meditations on the nature of temporal experience and in particular how it can be humanly transcended. There are given moments of revelatory joy in which the stillness of eternity is realized, and there is a discipline of prayerful self-abnegation that leads to comparable mystical transcendence of earth's inadequacies. Eliot analyses 'the point of intersection of the timeless / With time' in its personal and philosophic aspects. The union of the two 'spheres of existence', eternal and finite, is actualized archetypally in the life of Christ. The same union is actualized in every individual revelatory moment, in every life of Christian discipline, and indeed institutionally in the sacramental life of the church. 'Incarnation' is the appropriate defining term:

> Here the impossible union
> Of spheres of existence is actual,

Here the past and the future
Are conquered, and reconciled.

The emphasis upon timeless moments as scattered events whose clustering will provide the pattern and meaning of life asserts a reading of human experience in direct contradiction to linear temporal thinking in terms of evolution and forward progress. Grasping at the future – morally, intellectually, spiritually – is futile, and to this extent our civilization stands under judgement. The poet works out this principle in the structure of the poem itself. There is no progressive linear argument over all. Rather there is a series of concrete experiences whose gathered significance makes a pattern. The concrete experiences are at once private to the poet and analogously available to his readers, for the poet takes the reader inside the experiences and not only shares his reflections but compels a mutual exchange with the reader himself. 'My words echo thus / In your mind'. *Burnt Norton* takes us to a house and garden near Chipping Campden where a sudden shaft of sunlight floods a dry pool with illumination. From this revelatory moment the meditative sequences ripple out one by one, touching the poet's own personal and professional problems, the significance of works of art, the condition of our civilization, the larger human predicament and deeper religious implications. These themes recur in succeeding sections. *East Coker* takes us first to the Somerset village from which Eliot's ancestors set off for the New World in the seventeenth century, *The Dry Salvages* to East Gloucester on the coast of Massachusetts where Eliot went yachting in his young manhood, and *Little Gidding* to the village in Huntingdonshire where Nicholas Ferrar established an Anglican community in 1625.

As the poet eschews linear progress, and patterns his work like his thought around the garnering and 'recovery' of key moments, so he adopts a musical structure for the work, not only in the sense that successive passages have rhythmic and tonal variety such as rich orchestration produces, and that crucial words and phrases are repeated and developed like the 'figures' and motifs of symphonic movements, but also in the sense that words are enriched by overtones resonant with 'harmonics' in the form of additional connotations. Eliot's use of echo, for aural cross-reference within the poem and outside it, enables him to garner meanings with extraordinary subtlety, sometimes so as to hint at paradox as well as at harmonious correspondence. The style thus achieved is in perfect consonance with a reading of life that finds meaningful 'echoes' all about us.   [HB]

EMPSON, WILLIAM (1906–). Yorkshire-born poet and critic, educated at Winchester College and Cambridge, where he read mathematics. He has held university chairs in English Literature at Tokyo, Peking and Sheffield (1953–71). *Seven Types of Ambiguity* (1930), his critical investigation into double meanings in poetic diction, was a highly influential book. His anti-Christian study of *Paradise Lost, Milton's God* (1961), put the cat among the critical pigeons. Much of Empson's poetry (*Poems*, 1935; *The Gathering Storm*, 1940; *Collected Poems*, 1949, revised 1961) pushes verbal ambiguity and concentration beyond the point of maximum demand

upon the reader, who has to be helped with explanatory notes. Empson's indebtedness to Donne is evident: he shares Donne's delight in argument and in the use of scientific metaphor; he tussles with words, teasing the maximum meaning out of the minimum utterance. For the most part the riddling complexity is not that of a worried, angst-ridden being, but of a detached, tough, sceptical mind. The terse idiom, the nonchalant verbal shrug, the polish achieved in testing forms like terza rima and the use of ironic refrains made Empson a fashionable model for the 'Movement' poets of the 1950s. Though Empson can hold the sustained attention only of those readers who relish poetry as an intellectual obstacle race, one remains aware of a direct, unabashed persona behind the tangled text.   [HB]

ENRIGHT, D.J. (Dennis Joseph) (1920–). Poet and novelist, born at Leamington Spa, Warwickshire, and educated at Leamington College and Downing College, Cambridge, where he read English. He has had an itinerant academic life, holding university posts in Egypt, Birmingham, Japan, Germany, Bangkok, Singapore and Leeds. An instinct for putting his foot in it when abroad has more than once landed him temporarily in trouble with the authorities. His volumes of poetry include *The Laughing Hyena* (1953), *Bread rather than Blossoms* (1956), *Addictions* (1962), *Unlawful Assemblies* (1968), *Selected Poems* (1969), *Daughters of Earth* (1972), *The Terrible Shears* (1973) and *Sad Ires* (1976). Enright's is a distinctive minor talent exercised by a humane intelligence that makes verse jottings on what life throws up here and there about the world to stimulate wry, rueful or deprecatory reflection. It may be the super-efficient German disposal services ('No Offence'), the over-dragooned Chinese ('Small Hotel'), or the smooth foreign diplomat encountered at a party ('Meeting the Minister for Culture'). A down-to-earth stance and an easy conversational contemporaneousness in immediate response to the immediate are characteristics. Sometimes the outcome is prosiness and banality. At other times deep anger smoulders under dismissive surface detachment and ostensibly negative interest in hardship or suffering. (See 'Black Country Women' from *The Laughing Hyena* or 'The Short Life of Kazuo Yamamoto' from *Bread rather than Blossoms*.) Downgrading of the bogus and the shoddy is effected by ironic juxtaposition of idioms:

> He speaks to the maidenforms of Jerusalem
> Blessed are the paps which never gave suck
>   ('The Stations of King's Cross', *Sad Ires*)

Enright complained in *Memoirs of a Mendicant Professor* (1969) of 'a consistent and blank lack of interest in my subject-matter', but William Walsh's *D.J. Enright, Poet of Humanism* (1974) is a generous full-length study that deals also with Enright's novels, set in the Middle and Far East – *Academic Year* (1955) (which gives an autobiographical picture of English teachers in an Egyptian university), *Heaven Knows Where* (1957), *Insufficient Poppy* (1960) and *Figures of Speech* (1965). In editing *The Oxford Book of Contemporary Verse 1945–80* (1980), Enright's preference for 'the poetry of civility, passion and order' over the extremes of the 'violent' and the 'namby-pamby' has produced an overload of humour, wit and satire. Too often the reader wilts under the limp hand of fashionable over-postured unpretentiousness. *Collected Poems* (1981) assembles all his own work that he wishes to retain.   [HB]

ERVINE, ST JOHN (1883–1971). Dramatist, born in Belfast, Northern Ireland. (He added the 'St' to his original name, John Greer Ervine.) He was for a time manager of the Abbey Theatre, Dublin. Early works included novels, a biographical study, *Sir Edward Carson and the Ulster Movement* (1915), and naturalistic problem plays of Ulster life written for the Abbey. In *Mixed Marriage* (prod 1911) marriages made across the Catholic–Protestant divide arouse sectarian bigotry with disastrous consequences. Sectarian tension erupts in *The Orangeman* (1914), while in *John Ferguson* (1915) a God-fearing Ulster Protestant endures domestic grief and afflictions of appalling severity and yet remains steadfast in faith. Ervine has been credited with doing for divided Belfast in these early plays what O'Casey (q.v.) was later to do for divided Dublin.

Ervine was not an easy man to deal with. After a row with the Abbey actors he left the theatre, went to serve in the First World War, and was wounded. In the inter-war years he had successes on the London stage in the field of domestic problem plays. In *The First Mrs Fraser* (1929) James Fraser finds himself unloved and betrayed by his young second wife, Elsie, and still heavily dependent on his former wife, Janet, who never wanted their divorce. The two women are brought to confrontation and the grown-up children of the first marriage contribute to the tangle. Sharper and less obvious in its ramifications is the issue in *Robert's Wife* (1938) where Robert Carson's fine work in the church as vicar and likely Dean seems to be put at risk by his doctor-wife's management of a clinic that handles birth-control and by his pacifist son's propaganda directed subversively at the military. Real dilemmas of principle and expediency are intelligently explored. Ervine returned to Ulster settings in *Boyd's Shop* (1936) and *Friends and Relations* (1947). He wrote three books on the theatre, including *The Theatre in My Time* (1933). He also wrote biographies of Parnell, General Booth and Oscar Wilde, as well as the full-scale eulogistic opus, *Bernard Shaw, His Life, Work, and Friends* (1956). He was among the original members of the Irish Academy of Letters formed at Yeats's (q.v.) instigation and under Shaw's (q.v.) presidency in 1932.   [HB]

EVANS, CARADOC (1878–1945). Novelist and short-story writer from Rhydlewis, Dyfed, Wales. He was for twelve years a draper's assistant, but studied at the Working Men's College in London and then worked in journalism. Inspired with the idea of writing up remembered tales of Welsh country characters on the lines of Barrie's (q.v.) *Auld Licht Idylls*, he produced a collection of short stories, *My People* (1915). Though his widow, the writer 'Oliver Sandys', has told us in *Caradoc Evans* (1946) how Caradoc 'loved the capel and at heart was a thorough-going Methodist', the hypocrisy of the Welsh capel was his central target, and from the first he aroused hostility in Wales for the brutish habits, the squalid savageries and the accompanying religious hypocrisy he attributed to the Welsh peasantry. What is sheer

fantasy and what is factually based in his more ghastly portrayals is a matter of dispute. In his first story, 'A Father in Sion', Sadrach of Danyrefail keeps his mentally failing wife and mother of their eight children barred and padlocked in a stable loft and takes her out for a weekly airing with a cow's halter over her shoulders. In 'Be this her Memorial' a miserably poor woman scrapes together the price of a Bible for presentation to a departing minister by sickening to death on a diet of roasted rats. Two other volumes of stories followed, *Capel Sion* (1916) and *My Neighbours* (1919), and Evans became notorious for his virulence and bitterness.

His three-act comedy, *Taffy* (1924), was put on at the Royalty Theatre, London, in 1923. Set in a Cardiganshire village, its action revolves around the selection of a new minister for Capel Sion by the local 'Big Heads' (Deacons), and the hypocrisy and ulterior self-seeking involved is ruthlessly exposed. The heroine Marged is a forceful study of a woman with a mind and will of her own who finally induces the new young preacher to renounce the pulpit for the land and do a man's job. The blend of earthiness and lilting rhetoric anticipates Dylan Thomas's *Under Milk Wood* (q.v.). In Evans's novel, *Nothing to Pay* (1930), social documentation of the life of a draper's assistant in Wales and London is harsher and more telling than in Wells's *Kipps* (q.v.) ('We Welsh are ideal shop assistants because we are meek and mild hypocrites and born liars'). The central theme is of lifelong miserliness on the part of Amos Morgan, whose death from consumption, the final irony, contains at least one consolation: ' "It's o-rait," said Sara. "There's nothing to pay for death." Amos thanked God for the first time in his life.' Later novels are *Wasps* (1933) and *Morgan Bible* (1943).

Evans's style reproduces the idiom and word-order of Welsh in an English with a distinctly biblical force, rhythm and picturesqueness. An a stylist he was meticulously economic. He 'says as much in half a dozen lines as any man since Swift', Gwyn Jones (q.v.) observed in *The Welsh Review* at the time of Evans's death. Technically he achieves his subtlest effects by what he leaves unsaid, and he claimed to have learned this art from listening to Marie Lloyd. But he gained the hostility he asked for. The Welsh character is under judgement for greed, dishonesty, fantasy-building ('The Welsh are actors; they are make-believers') and the cloaking of self-interest under hypocritical religiosity ('The Welsh are not shackled with constancy: they are holy and evil at the same time'). Evans has been compared, understandably, with T.F Powys (q.v.) for his sardonic humour, his sinewy prose and his grim record of earthy sexuality and savagery.   [HB]

EWART, GAVIN (1916–). Poet, born in London, educated at Wellington and Cambridge. He was for many years an advertising copywriter. In *Poems and Songs* (1939) and in postwar collections like *Londoners* (1964) and *Pleasures of the Flesh* (1966) he worked a vein of irreverent mockery with such ready verbal and metrical ingenuity that he successfully bridged the gap between comic light verse and 'poetry'. Versatile in structural experimentation and a master of pastiche, Ewart has continued to mock the absurdity of the humanly trivial and the humanly solemn with indiscriminate off-handedness. If *The Collected Ewart 1933–1980* (1980) illustrates that the adolescent bravado which contributed 'Phallus in Wonderland' to Geoffrey Grigson's (q.v.) *New Verse* in 1933, when its author was only 17, has never been outgrown, it is sprinkled with wit, glittering with polish and highly entertaining whenever the jokes come off. Witness the updating of Sir Thomas Wyatt's famous complaint that he was forsaken of his former mistresses – 'They flee from me that sometime did me seek / With naked foot stalking within my chamber':

> At this moment in time
> the chicks that went for me
> in a big way
> are opting out;
> as of now, it's an all-change situation.

Ewart edited the *Penguin Book of Light Verse* (1980). [HB]

EZEKIEL, NISSIM (1924–). Poet, born in Bombay, India. He graduated as an MA from Bombay University in 1947. He spent three years in London and in 1952 married Daisy Jacob by whom he has three children. Since 1961 he has taught English and American literature at Bombay University, and held visiting fellowships in Leeds (1964) and Chicago (1967). He has also edited literary magazines and collections of essays and been an art critic.

Ezekiel is a major Indian poet in English, who, although using traditional western verse forms, reacted against the prolixities and spiritualizings of poets like Aurobindo Ghose (1872–1950). He regards himself as 'modernist but not avant-garde' and claims 'never to have written an obscure poem'. In his earlier verse especially, feeling is precipitated within a humane, rational, reflective medium to produce a poetry of scepticisms about the validity of moral categories, the reality of human experiences, the poet's own individual worth. The more clearly he perceives his own moral need – the basic simplicities of living, 'And patiently to build a life with these' (title

poem of *A Time to Change*, 1952) – the more he wryly discovers failure of achievement, as in the sense of what remains incomplete beyond sex:

> Remote from the exploring act
> I knew that both were undefined,
> Who lived in day-dreams not in fact:
> Reflections of the cheated mind.
>
> (*Sixty Poems*, 1963)

Poems in *The Third* (1958) and *The Unfinished Man* (1960) refine Ezekiel's finely worked but tentative, unegotistical self-analysis by which the crooked courses of actual experience are followed from aspiration to disillusioned but not despairing destinations. 'Enterprise' (*The Unfinished Man*) begins 'It started as a pilgrimage' and ends:

> The trip had darkened every face,
> Our deeds were neither great nor rare.
> Home is where we have to gather grace.

Two of Ezekiel's finest poems occur in *The Exact Name* (1965): 'Night of the Scorpion' lovingly satirizes the alarmed use of traditional remedies, worse than the actual scorpion's sting, culminating in the victim's own ambivalent coda: 'Thank God the scorpion picked on me / and spared my children'. In 'Poet, Lover, Birdwatcher' images from birdwatching delicately fuse the potential gains sought in poem-making and love-making 'By poets lost in crooked, restless flight'.

The most recent poems in *Hymns in Darkness* (1976) still record disappointment with life but in language that does not resist abstract philosophizing, thus lending point to D. Kohli's comment (1974) that Ezekiel has failed 'to accept or discover or create a framework of values'.

'Five Latter-Day Psalms' (1978), in the Bombay periodical *Debonair*, is both an acknowledgement and an assessment of his religious background.   [AR]

FAIRBURN, A.R.D. (Arthur Rex Dugard) (1904–57). Poet, born in Auckland, New Zealand, and educated at the grammar school there, where he began a lifelong friendship with R.A.K. Mason (q.v.). He spent six years working as an insurance clerk before leaving Auckland for a five-month stay on Norfolk Island in 1926. Upon his return he worked at various jobs and in late 1930 left for London, where, faced with what he saw as the surrounding decadence, early hopes gave way to disillusion. He travelled around England during 1931, married and returned to New Zealand in 1932 where he was on relief work during the Depression until 1934. He later worked as an editor, a radio scriptwriter and a university teacher of literature and art. Together with R.A.K. Mason he was responsible for that first awakening of the New Zealand sensibility in the 1930s, criticizing the prevailing cultural dependence upon Britain and propounding a confidence in immediate, local perceptions which was later to find expression in the poetry and criticism of Allen Curnow (q.v.). Fairburn's first collection, *He Shall Not Rise* (1930), was published in England and contained much lyric material only republished in *Collected Poems* (1966). Indeed, the concluding title poem suggested burial of a poetic 'self' and the later collections, *Strange Rendezvous* and *Three Poems* (both 1952), show a greatly increased range and control. The latter book includes the important long satiric poem 'Dominion' (completed in 1936 and first published in 1938) in which his experiences of the New Zealand Depression serve to focus his dislike of British colonialism and nationalistic sentiment blends with lyric celebration of local scenery. Although lacking overall unity, the poem remains a tour de force which expresses both the disillusionment of the time and also the hope for renewel – which in literature his own writings partly helped to bring about. A vigorous personality in many fields and a romantic humanist with tendencies to social commentary in his published works, Fairburn played an important role in the literary and political activities of the Auckland 'Phoenix' group, but although he wrote in *We New Zealanders* (1944) 'This is my country, and I am very glad to belong to it – in spite of everything', the book also contained frank comment on the shortcomings of the society.   [PQ]

FARRELL, J.G. (James Gordon) (1935–79). Novelist, born in Liverpool, Merseyside, educated at Rossall School and Oxford. A dabbler in the bizarre and the grotesque (*The Lung*, 1965; *A Girl in the Head*, 1969), he gave some solidity to his fourth novel, *Troubles* (1970), by portraying a group of eccentrics in a decaying Irish hotel, the Majestic, against the background of increasing terrorism and counter-terrorism in the years 1919 to 1921. The Majestic and its inhabitants owe something to Mervyn Peake (q.v.), but the hotel's 'imperceptible slide towards ruin' (cats infest the Imperial Bar and trees sprout through the floor of the Palm Court) acquires symbolic value over against the intermittent foreign and home press-cuttings about currently collapsing social orders.

Nostalgia for lost Anglo-Irish grandeurs and the increasing sense of being marooned on alien territory add ironic dimensions to the preoccupations of the human cranks. If sureness of artistic purpose seemed to be lacking in this very funny book and if impetus and direction tended to get lost in overloaded narrative, Farrell's overall intention became clear when it was succeeded by two other novels studying events in British imperial history – *The Siege of Krishnapur* (1973), dealing with a group of Europeans caught up in the Indian Mutiny, and *The Singapore Grip* (1978), dealing with events leading up to the Fall of Singapore in the Second World War. Both books are notable for the meticulously researched emphasis on the current of daily life that flows on under the shadow of historic calamities. Farrell, who spent part of his boyhood in Ireland (his mother was Irish), was living alone in a farmhouse in West Cork when he died. In *The Hill Station* (1981) John Spurling has edited an unfinished novel that Farrell was working on when he died, his diary of a tour of India in 1971, and some personal appreciations of Farrell. [HB]

FENTON, JAMES (1949–). Poet, born in Lincoln, and educated at Repton and Oxford, where he won the Newdigate Prize in 1968. He has worked in literary journalism for the *New Statesman* and *The Sunday Times*. His collection *The Memory of War: Poems 1968–1982* (1982) is one of the most distinctive recent offerings from younger poets. Fenton is a highly accomplished poetic technician. He manages to combine a fullness of concrete detail with a teasing ambiguity over the attitude of the narrating voice. Thus a scene will be realized with the maximum clarity while any simplistic assimilation of its significance is defied. This approach is refined tellingly in 'A Staffordshire Murderer' and in 'A German Requiem'. The latter, looking back on the devastation of a city by bombing in the Second World War, shows Fenton's incisive yet inconclusive brooding at its most powerful:

But come. Grief must have its term? Guilt too,
then.
And it seems there is no limit to the resourcefulness of recollection.

At several points in this highly charged poem there are echoes of the cadences and idioms of Eliot's *Four Quartets* which are uncannily emphatic without seeming parasitical. [HB]

FIRBANK, (Arthur Annesley) RONALD (1886–1926). Novelist, born in London. His grandfather, Joseph, at first a Durham miner, then a worker on railway construction, rose to great wealth as a contractor. Ronald's father, Sir Thomas, an MP, married the daughter of an Irish vicar. Ronald was not strong physically. Sensitive and nervous, he left Uppingham School after six months and was educated by private tutor and later at Trinity Hall, Cambridge. Among his friends were Robert Ross, Rupert Brooke (q.v.) and Wilde's son, Vyvyan Holland, as well as Lord Alfred Douglas. He was received into the Roman Catholic Church: its ritual, its religious orders and its fashionable laity always fascinated him as a writer. The aestheticism of the 1890s, the world of the Café Royal,

and fin-de-siècle writers, French and English, left their mark upon his life and work. He loved Italy and travelled a great deal. His father's death, in 1910, shocked by bringing to light an unexpected depletion in the family fortune. Ronald shrank from its implications. 'He wore exquisite clothes, massed rare flowers in his rooms, ate little but delicately, drank quantities of champagne, and mocked at those who had the low taste to drink ale and stout', wrote I.K. Fletcher in *Ronald Firbank* (1930), a volume to which Lord Berners, Augustus John and Osbert Sitwell (q.v.) contributed reminiscences of Firbank. He was unfit for war service and by the time the 1920s arrived he had acquired a legendary status by his bohemian eccentricities. He died in Rome.

Firbank's first story, *Odette d'Autrevernes*, was published in 1905, but it gave little promise. His reputation rests chiefly on *Vainglory* (1915), *Inclinations* (1916), *Caprice* (1917) and *Valmouth* (1919). Huysmans and Maeterlinck have been cited as influences on these works; the English literary lineage surely includes Peacock, Meredith and Wilde. The plots are nebulous; the brilliant dialogue is often impressionistically bereft of signposts to indicate the speaker, his posture or his manner, so that his identity has to be dug out from the contextual composition, while his tone of voice and his mood have to be gleaned from the shaping of the utterance itself. Firbank achieved great skill in planting and articulating dialogue so that the needed inferences can be deduced by the attentive reader – but not everyone would want to be bothered, for many a page reads like the text of a play with the names of the speaking characters excised from the left-hand margin. Firbank's interests, like his technique, limit his readership. Society ladies and their hangers-on preoccupy him; ecclesiastics, black people and lesbians haunt his pages.

Vainglory contains something of a self-portait in the writer, Claud Harvester. ('He has such a strange, peculiar style. His work calls to mind a frieze with figures of varying heights trotting all the same way.') Through a symphony of multifariously orchestrated conversation trickles the story of Mrs Shamefoot's campaign to immortalize herself in some cathedral by a commemorative stained-glass window. The humour is rich in witty aphorism and light irony, though there are times when the compulsive verbal scintillation drives itself into self-parody. *Caprice* is mellower, more charming, less clamantly garrulous. Miss Sinquier, stage-struck daughter of the cathedral close, runs away to London and launches herself in *Romeo and Juliet* only to die by getting caught in a mousetrap when she is dancing on the empty stage on the morning after the first night. *Valmouth* pictures an English resort healthy enough, with the aid of Mrs Yajnavalka, a black masseuse, to sustain a colony of centenarians. The marriage of Mrs Yajnavalka's niece to Mrs Thoroughfare's son is the climax. The milieu is an ecclesiastically conscious Catholic society. A more serious human interest threatens to intrude into this tale, but generally a pervasive air of mock reality conditions the unique genre that Firbank contrived. Anthony Powell wrote a Preface to *The Complete Ronald Firbank* (1961). Mervyn Horder has edited *Ronald Firbank, Memoirs and Critiques* (1977), which includes personal reminiscences by Osbert Sitwell, Augustus John, Wyndham Lewis (q.v.)

and others and reveals appropriately that Firbank wrote his novels fragment by fragment on blue postcards. [HB]

FISHER, ROY (1930-). Poet, born in Birmingham, West Midlands, educated in schools there and at Birmingham University. He has had an academic career in higher education and joined the American Studies Department at Keele University in 1971. He came under the influence of the poets of the American Black Mountain group. His provocatively modernist experimentation put him out of key with English trends in the 'Movement' era. *City* (1961, enlarged 1962) is a collage of the postwar and prewar Birmingham scene in verse and prose in which sometimes - as in the childhood memories of bereavement in a bombing raid that are captured in the poem 'The Entertainment of War' - there is powerful directness and compression. 'The imaginary comes to me with as much force as the real, the remembered with as much force as the immediate', Fisher writes, and *The Ship's Orchestra* (1966) is a prose poem projecting the inner life of a bandsman on a cruise with a surrealist vividness and discontinuity. The imaginative density makes for a taxingly congested text, as it does in the volume *The Cut Pages* (1971).

The collection, *Poems 1955-1980* (1980), gathers Fisher's work to date. If the abrupt transitions tend to make passages of his work less than readily accessible, the economy, force and sheer imaginative ingenuity give it a peculiar compulsiveness. Fisher would justify a poem's existence by the possibility that 'somebody may have his perceptions rearranged by having read it' and has embraced Carlos Williams's slogan, 'No ideas but in things'. [HB]

FITZGERALD, R.D. (Robert David) (1902-). Poet, born in Sydney, New South Wales, Australia. He abandoned his science studies at university there and later spent five years in Fiji as a surveyor before transferring to the Commonwealth Department of the Interior. *Moonlight Acre* (1938) included the fine poem 'Essay on Memory', a foreshadowing of later work in which he explores personal and national history within a flexible monologue. 'Heemskerck Shoals', first published in *The Bulletin* (q.v.) in 1944, purports to be the musings of the seventeenth-century Dutch navigator Abel Tasman after the near wrecking of his ships off Fiji. It is a fine achievement within the Australian tradition of 'voyager poems' and was reprinted in a 1960 anthology of that title edited by Douglas Stewart (q.v.). *Between Two Tides* (1952) drew upon his knowledge of Fiji; he commented that he felt it time poets 'got round to narrative again' and that he was 'tired of being referred to as a "philosophical poet" ', though his true story of a ship's boy raised in Tonga and drowned in London years later also focuses the poet's meditations on eternity and human transience. *The Wind at My Door* (1959) reflected upon the flogging of Irish convicts at Castle Hill, New South Wales, in 1804; it gave his enduring interest in the complex interrelation between past and present a deeply personal dimension since his earliest ancestor in Australia was a government-employed doctor who arrived in 1798 - 'I see him in that jailhouse yard'. One Maurice Fitzgerald was among the convicts flogged, and the poet proudly seeks to claim 'his irons as heraldry' in a work which successfully blends historical re-creation and personal statement. Often considered his finest poem, it was reprinted in *Southmost Twelve* (1962). The following year he published a discerning theoretical-critical study, *The Elements of Poetry*, in which he commented: 'I consider poetry has a function as a way of insight and of appreciating values in life and environment. It is not just written to be itself'. In 1970 he edited for publication the letters of his fellow poet Hugh McCrae (q.v.), and in 1976 himself published *Of Places and Poetry*. [PQ]

FLECKER, JAMES ELROY (1884-1915). Poet and dramatist, born in Lewisham, London. Disappointing himself and his family with a third in Greats at Oxford, he worked briefly as a schoolmaster, then went to study oriental languages at Cambridge so that he could enter the Foreign Service. His diplomatic career in Constantinople, Smyrna and Beirut was interrupted, then terminated by the consumption which killed him. Flecker had poetic standards that were not readily satisfied by current taste: he disliked the 'sham manliness', 'sham religiosity' and 'sham roughness' of Masefield's narrative poems; and he achieved some imaginative vitality in his best work, for all its Georgian decorativeness. There are notable poems evoking the atmosphere of the East. The imagery and rhythms of *The Golden Journey to Samarkand* (1913) and especially of the celebrated 'Gates of Damascus' have a hypnotic seductiveness. Flecker gained a considerable posthumous reputation for his five-act play *Hassan* published and produced in 1922. Hassan, a confectioner of Baghdad, is accidentally trapped with the Caliph in the hands of revolutionary Beggars. Saving the Caliph, he is richly rewarded, but soon learns how capricious is the favour of princes. Flecker mixes with this the tragic theme of how Rafi, King of the Beggars, suffers for his attempt to avenge the Caliph's appropriation of his beloved Pervaneh among the women of his harem. The dialogue is mannered ('Am I not a desert waiting for the rain?' asks the seductive Yasmin) and the verse choruses are spicily oriental. See Flecker's *Collected Prose* (1920) and *Collected Poems* (revised 1946). [HB]

FLEMING, IAN (1908-65). Novelist, born in London, educated at Eton and Sandhurst. He served in naval intelligence in the Second World War, and later established himself as a best-selling novelist with espionage and secret service stories centring on the British agent James Bond, handsome super-hero through whom Fleming projected dream fulfilment in acts of daring and all-round mastery. 'He is Fleming's dream of a self that might have been' (John Pearson, *The Life of Ian Fleming*, 1966). The books, highly spiced with violence and sex, turned James Bond into a cult, and their sales topped forty million before Fleming died. The series began with *Casino Royale* (1952) and includes *Diamonds are Forever* (1956), *Thunderball* (1961) and *On Her Majesty's Secret Service* (1963). [HB]

FLINT, F.S. (Frank Stewart) (1885–1960). Poet and translator, born in London. He left school at 13 but by diligent study worked his way into the Civil Service and rose to become Chief of the Overseas Section (Statistics Division) of the Ministry of Labour. His literary importance derives from his connection with T.E. Hulme (q.v.) and Ezra Pound and more particularly from his role in the Imagist movement of which some claimed him to be the founder, though he himself attributed the honour to Pound. (Quarrels between the participants helped to confuse the issue.) Certainly Flint's first-hand knowledge of the French symbolist poets was important in the genesis of the movement, which sought to disinfect poetry of traditional concerns and ornament, to fasten on momentary phases of experience, and to communicate them with verbal exactness and rhythmic freshness in images that capsulate each intellectual and emotional complex. The American poets Amy Lowell and Hilda Doolittle, as well as Richard Aldington (q.v.), were involved in the movement.

Flint contributed to Pound's anthology *Des Imagistes* (1914) and to the subsequent collection *Some Imagist Poets* (1915). His own volumes of verse, apart from the early *In the Net of Stars* (1909), were *Cadences* (1915) and *Otherworld: Cadences* (1920), which contain pieces characteristic of his method.

> On black bare trees a stale cream moon
> Hangs dead, and sours the unborn buds.
>
> ('Eau-Forte')
>
> [HB]

FORD, FORD MADOX (1873–1939). Novelist, poet and critic, born in Surrey. His name, before he changed it after the First World War, was Ford Hermann Hueffer. His father was Dr Francis Hueffer, a music critic. His maternal grandfather was Ford Madox Brown, the painter. Of Brown's two daughters one, Lucy, married Dante Gabriel Rossetti's brother, William Michael, himself a biographer and art critic, and the other, Catherine, married Dr Hueffer. Ford was to write on both Brown and Rossetti (*Ford Madox Brown - His Life and Work*, 1896; *D.G. Rossetti, A Critical Essay*, 1902). Nurtured in the pre-Raphaelite 'hot-house' (his own word) and educated at an advanced co-educational school, Ford then began perversely to fancy a career in the army or the Civil Service, and his grandfather did not approve – Ford's business was to be a genius. His prolific writing career began with the publication of a fairy story, *The Brown Owl*, when he was only 18. Ford had his rebellion nevertheless: he affected aristocratic idiosyncrasies in speech and bearing, and he would reconstruct his own educational past to the requisite public-school pattern in conversation. He became a Roman Catholic in 1892, and he married a former schoolfellow, Elsie Martindale, in 1894. Henry James (q.v.) used the young writer as a model for the character of Merton Densher in *The Wings of the Dove* ('he looked vague without looking weak – idle without looking empty').

Ford's reputation as an amiable fibber and patronizing poseur cannot be separated from his flair for penetrating the hearts of his characters and investing himself with their authentic identity. The total self-investment is uncannily telling. But this imaginative self-involvement is only half the secret of Ford's brilliance as a novelist. After coming into contact with Joseph Conrad (q.v.) in 1897, he became a keen and alert craftsman. The two writers collaborated in *The Inheritors* (1901) and *Romance* (1903). Together they hammered out innovatory doctrines of the 'new Form' needed by the English novel; for its past glories were too much the accidental fruits of genius and its system of patterning around successive dramatic situations was now exhausted. They turned to French practitioners (Stendhal, Flaubert and Maupassant) and to Henry James (q.v.) for guidance. Essentially they sought an escape from direct narration, authorial instruction, and sequential orderliness that is false to the character of human experience. They developed devices that would enable the reader to forget the writer, to forget that he was reading and to be submerged in a carefully contrived verisimilitude. The verisimilitude was subtly doctored to produce a pervasive suspense of cumulative intensity, and accordingly techniques were refined for conveying information crucial to the plot by oblique means. Thus hints would be dropped, important items of fact would be casually slipped in, and a character's parenthetic or offhand observation might ring a resounding bell for the attentive reader. A remark that was in its context apparently little more than a throwaway could be highly significant when put aside some other point held in the mind from another chapter. A fresh terminology enshrined the new precepts: there was much talk of the 'time-shift', of the *progression d'effet*, and even of the 'unearned increment' – an expression used for the electric force that could be sparked off by weighted cross-reference and by juxtaposing superficially innocuous actions or statements. Ford was indeed a great literary theoretician and crusader. He started *The English Review* and edited it memorably from 1908 to 1909. Contributors ranged from celebrities such as Hardy (q.v.) and James to newcomers like Pound and Wyndham Lewis (q.v.). He published critical studies, *Henry James* in 1913 and *Joseph Conrad* in 1924. There are portraits of contemporary writers in *Mightier than the Sword* (1938) and Ford's critical work culminated in the sweeping historical study, *The March of Literature from Confucius to Modern Times* (1939).

Theorizing about the novel bore fruit in the Tudor trilogy about Katharine Howard. Ford dedicated the first book, *The Fifth Queen* (1905), to Conrad. The second, *Privy Seal*, followed in 1907, and the third, *The Fifth Queen Crowned*, in 1908. Katharine's career at court and the intrigues that culminate in her execution are traced within a richly realized sixteenth-century world. The detailed visual clarity of the reconstruction is remarkable, the inner energy of the dramatis personae compelling. The trilogy is a fit precursor of the works by which Ford's claim to rare greatness is justified, *The Good Soldier** (1915), a tour de force that brings massive artistic expertise to bear upon a story of tragic passion, complex in its ambiguities and disturbing in its impact; and *Parade's End**, a sequence whose four books, *Some Do Not* (1924), *No More Parades* (1925), *A Man Could Stand Up* (1926) and *Last Post* (1928), traces the career of

Christopher Tietjens, a Yorkshire gentleman, 'the last Tory', through shattering front-line experience in the First World War. Like Dowell, the hero of *The Good Soldier*, Tietjens is the victim of a ruthless, ravenous wife. Ford modelled him on Arthur Marwood who had helped to finance *The English Review* and who died in the war. Of the later novels Ford himself thought especially highly of *The Rash Act* (1933), a novel of the Depression, which has been reissued (1982).

Ford himself chose active service in the war though he was 40 when it began, and experience in the trenches involved gassing and shell-shock. After the war he lived much in France and America. His marriage had broken down well before the war, and his association with Violet Hunt provoked a damaging scandal when Elsie Hueffer brought an action against her for describing herself as Ford's wife. Violet's own reminiscences (*The Flurried Years*, 1926) give a lively picture of Ford 'refusing to be confronted with any of the problems that beset an author unfortunately doubled with a man'. Among her successors were Stella Bowen, who wrote a study of Ford, *Drawn from Life* (1940), and Janice Biala, the painter with whom he spent his last years. ('O Father Ford, you've a masterful way with you, / Maid, wife and widow are wild to make hay with you', began James Joyce's parody of 'Father O'Flynn'.) There are four scattered volumes of often fascinating, if unreliable, memoirs: *Ancient Lights* (1911), *Thus to Revisit* (1921), *Return to Yesterday* (1931) and *It was the Nightingale* (1934). 'This book . . . is full of inaccuracies as to facts, but its accuracy as to impressions is absolute', Ford wrote of the first. R.M. Ludwig edited the *Letters* (1965).

The Good Soldier brought to full fruition Ford's studied methodology for revitalizing the novel. John Dowell, an American, is the protagonist: his admired and loved friend, Captain Edward Ashburnham, is the good soldier – and an English gentleman whose charitable and emotional commitments prove too costly for himself and for his wife, Leonora. Dowell's adulterous wife, Florence, supposedly suffering from 'a heart' and thus concealing her infidelities, has an affair with Edward and, when her past comes to light, commits suicide. So too, ultimately, does Edward himself: whereupon Nancy Rufford, the young girl he has finally grown to love undemandingly, goes mad. Dowell is left with the demented Nancy at the end. Leonora alone escapes the doomed circle in remarriage. 'The Saddest Story', Ford first called the book, but the wartime publisher could not accept that and the present title was suggested in irony that misfired, Ford tells us. The presentation of events in elaborately disturbed chronological sequence and by a recorder (Dowell) too deeply and immediately involved to be reliable produces a rich mine for interpretative speculation. The 'intricate tangle of references and cross-references' astounded Ford himself when he looked back on the book twelve years after publication. He was delighted to hear it called 'the finest French novel in the English language'. It is fine indeed; but neurotically oppressive and remorseless.

Parade's End, a tetralogy of novels, gives a vivid portrayal of the effect of the First World War on English society. There is some chronological overlap in the first three volumes. *Some Do Not*, the longest and probably the best, covers events at home from 1912 to the hero's return from leave to the Western Front in 1916. *No More Parades* and *A Man Could Stand Up* fill out events to date, cover the war in France, and take the story up to the Armistice. Christopher Tietjens, a lumbering, heavily built fellow, is the younger son of a wealthy Yorkshire family. Their home at Groby is modelled on that of the Marwoods at Busby in North Yorkshire. Christopher, a mathematician in government service, has a brilliant brain, immense generosity of spirit and proud Yorkshire stubbornness in not pursuing self-interest or even self-defence against calumny ('His private ambition had always been for saintliness'). Essentially he is a man whose integrity and altruism invite malice, whose sheer goodness makes others uncomfortable, and whose reticence fuels the resentful urge to damage him. In his civilian career (sacrificed because 'he won't fake statistics to dish the French with') others pick his brains and climb to the top on his disinterested intellectual originality. In his military career he is martyred for his heroic persistence in preferring the interests of his men to the demands of administrative red tape. In his personal life he is ruined by unjust denigration. His wife, Sylvia, a beautiful but arrogant and utterly dishonest woman, is a complex study in evil, notably in malignancy and possessiveness. Her hatred reaches him even in France through the iniquitous intrigues of the High Command, yet she knows what wickedness she is involved in ('How was it possible that the most honourable man she knew should be so overwhelmed by foul and baseless rumours?'). Tietjens's chivalry and high-mindedness enable her to keep him in play in spite of known deception and adultery and the existence of a 'son' whose paternity is in doubt. His decency likewise ('some do not') keeps him from making love to Valentine Wannop, a congenial, scholarly, idealistic girl, until they are united at the Armistice. The suspense implicit in this delay gives tension to the first three volumes. The range of characterization is immense; the war scenes are devastatingly cool and unforced; the technique of presentation interleaves the inner life with the hectic outer activity, mingling the biggest military and political issues with the acutest personal concerns. The overall pattern of the work catches a momentous civilizational change in sharp human terms. Ford himself came to regret the fourth novel, *Last Post*, a postwar epilogue that supplies a sentimental happy ending. He eventually wished it to be forgotten and the Tietjens saga to stand as a trilogy. [HB]

FORSTER, E.M. (Edward Morgan) (1879–1970). Novelist, born in London. He reported entrancingly on his ancestry in his biography, *Marianne Thornton* (1956), a study of his great-aunt whose life spanned ninety years. The Reverend Charles Forster (the writer's grandfather), an Irishman, chaplain to the Bishop of Limerick, married Marianne's sister Laura. He was a scholarly clergyman who produced ten books and ten children. Eddie, the fourth, became an architect, married Lily Whichelo, and died of consumption four years later (1880) when his son, Morgan, was a baby. Aunt Marianne left Morgan £8000 when she died in 1887 and thereby enabled him to study classics and history at King's College, Cambridge (he had intensely disliked his experience of the English public school as a day boy at Tonbridge), and to travel. His books began to sell as the value of the bequest diminished. At Cambridge a great influence on Forster was Goldsworthy Lowes Dickinson, exponent of 'the Greek spirit', whose biography he wrote in 1934, and with whom he travelled to India in 1912. Forster had already stayed in Italy and Greece and in 1922 he was back in India as Secretary to the Maharajah of Dewas, an experience of which he later gave an account in *The Hill of Devi*, 1953. The Mediterranean background and the Indian background together provided fictional material that was crucial to Forster's aim of showing up the inadequacy of respectable English middle-class values.

In *Where Angels Fear to Tread* (1905) the Herritons of Sawston represent those values; Mrs Herriton dominating and narrow-minded, her daughter Harriett self-righteous and intensely dislikeable, and her son Philip priggish and sentimentally self-protective. They are trying to refine away the vulgarity of Lilia, Mrs Herriton's silly widowed daughter-in-law. She is dispatched to Italy with a friend and marries Gino, a feckless, impetuous, uninhibited Italian without class or culture. After her death in childbirth, ambassadorial attempts by the Herritons to rescue the baby for an English upbringing (fools rush in) are in some respects hilariously comic but have sour implications and even some tragic consequences. Scathing portrayal of certain English characteristics already show Forster moving into strenuous hedonistic didacticism ('dull', 'petty' and 'respectable' are terms of maximum opprobrium), but the verve of the book, the vivacity of the style and the deftly economic control are impressive.

The Longest Journey (1907) is, for Lionel Trilling (*E.M. Forster*, 1944), 'perhaps the most brilliant, the most dramatic and the most passionate of his works', but Forster himself admitted that 'most readers' dismissed it 'as a failure', and indeed deficiencies of structure are evident. Rickie Elliot fails to realize the youthful vision of his Cambridge days and loses the inner life in marriage to a woman he has subjectively endowed with a reality she does not possess. He is one of 'those poor slaves' of Shelley's 'Epipsychidion':

Who travel to their home among the dead
By the broad highway of the world, and so
With one chained friend, perhaps a jealous foe,
The dreariest and longest journey go.

By contrast Rickie's half-brother, Stephen Wonham, is ignorant, crude and immoral but belongs with Gino on the side of 'life'. Yet so provocative is the Forsterian ethic that Frank Swinnerton could describe Stephen as 'an incalculable and savage bore for whom the author has a mystical veneration' and one who 'never succeeds in being for the reader anything but a tiresome oaf who would be better dead' (*The Georgian Literary Scene*).

Much tidier in design and more refreshing in tone is *A Room with a View* (1908). It is in part a diverting comedy of manners in which Lucy Honeychurch, after much heart-searching, finally opts for 'life' in the shape of George Emerson, a railway clerk who kisses on impulse, instead of for unnaturalness in the shape of Cecil Vyse, moneyed and superior, who makes a speech before kissing even his fiancée. Thus Lucy is saved, and her future will at least be spent in a room with a view. The symbolic scheme is reinforced by much pillorying of narrow, fenced, middle-class respectabilities, and much eulogizing of the living freedom exercised by those whose radical reading-list includes Byron, Housman (q.v.), Butler and Gibbon. There is much too about not despising our bodies (in their better moments young men bathe frolicsomely in a country pond and their boisterous horse-play causes the 'world of motor-cars and Rural Deans' to recede healthily), much about the 'holiness of direct desire' and the necessity to 'act the truth'. The Forsterian message is pressed home more gravely in *Howards End* (1910) where the collision is between the Wilcox family (Howards End, symbol of England, is their family home), who are solidly efficient but narrow in their sensitivities, and the half-German Schlegel sisters who are interested in culture and sensitive to human needs. The Wilcoxes' world is that of commerce, imperialism and philistinism, while the Schlegels are socialists and go to symphony concerts. Forster's motto is 'Only connect', and the need for cross-fertilization is evident. The design of the book is a subtle fabric of event and symbol, showing the price paid when the well-meaning impulses of blinkered personalities go awry.

Forster's work as a novelist was consummated in *A Passage to India** (1924) which explores the obstacles in the way of sympathetic communication between the English and the natives in British India, and in which personal dilemmas are painstakingly articulated. Forster's characters have reality, though they are generally enmeshed in moralistic dichotomies designed to illustrate that English middle-class respectability, public school education and immersion in conventionality unfit one for the finer commerce of human contact. The Forsterian ethic is based on respect for 'passion and truth' (the two are scarcely distinguishable) and for 'personal relations'. At times it derives its force from caricature and is sauced with parenthetical gibes at Christianity. Forster's later work includes two collections of essays and articles, the fruit of successful journalism and broadcasting, *Abinger Harvest* (1936) and *Two Cheers for Democracy* (1951). His critical work, *Aspects of the Novel* (1927), represents the Clark Lectures delivered at Cambridge. It includes some misjudgements: Scott is declared 'trivial' and Henry James is disparaged; Joyce's *Ulysses* does not 'come off' for its aim is to 'degrade all things'. Forster spent his last years in residence at King's College, Cambridge, as an honorary Fellow.

A Passage to India is set in pre-1914 British India. It portrays the gulf between the Anglo-Indian administration and the natives and the sometimes comic, sometimes tragic, failures to achieve real friendship across the divide. Forster shows both the bad and the good (but especially the bad) in British attitudes, and likewise both the good and the bad (but the bad with some indulgence) in Indian attitudes. K. Natwar-Singh could thus write in 1969 that Forster 'to some extent, provided the corrective' to the view of India popularized by Kipling, and that the book 'remains the outstanding example of an Englishman's honest effort to understand and interpret this country and its complex people' (O. Stallybrass, ed., *Aspects of E.M. Forster*, 1969). Forster's humane and liberal formula is neatly articulated in the plot. Mrs Moore, a woman of unaffected kindness, brings Adela Quested to India to marry her son (by her first marriage), Ronny Heaslop, City Magistrate at Chandrapore. The local British bureaucracy lives the insulated life of an occupation force in office and club, but Cyril Fielding, principal of the local college (and 'a disruptive force'), tries to make genuine personal contact with the Indians. So do Mrs Moore and Adela Quested, who are taken on a visit to the Marabar Caves by Fielding's valued friend, Dr Aziz. Adela accuses Aziz of assault in the darkness of the cave, but at his trial she retracts, suddenly aware that she suffered a hallucination. Though Fielding remains throughout convinced of Aziz's innocence, the complex suspicions and misunderstandings bred of the racial gulf and of the official discrepancies in national status leave the two friends finally separated for all their mutual affection. [HB]

FOWLES, JOHN (1926-). Novelist, born in Leigh-on-Sea, Essex, and educated at Bedford School and Oxford. His novels are remarkable for range of substance and for recurrent emotional intensity, as well as eventually for sheer size. *The Collector* (1958), however, is a concentrated, tragic study of a psychopath who cunningly traps and imprisons the girl he loves. It is presented through the captor's record and the doomed captive's diary. ('What she never understood was that with me it was having. Having was enough. Nothing needed doing.') In *The Magus* (1966) Nicholas Urfe takes a job as schoolmaster on a Greek island where the 'magus', Maurice Conchis, with lavish expenditure of ingenuity and cash, manipulates a massive machinery of fake paranormality that entraps Nicholas and keeps the reader guessing. There is inventiveness in the proliferation of sensational plots and mysteries, but narrative presentation is conventional. The extravagant orgy of implausibilities would seem to require either a genuine flavour of the preternatural or evident parodic irony, and neither is achieved. *The French Lieutenant's Woman* (1969) is the study of a love triangle of the 1860s, set largely in Lyme Regis. Fowles manages to reflect archetypally, through his hero's relationships with a woman of the age and a woman of the next age, the movements of mind and heart that sustained, and those that gradually undermined, Victorian mores and social ethos. He achieves an authentic evocation of the Victorian moral climate and effective use of Victorian idiom while at the same time conducting with the reader, and over the characters' heads, an authorial dialogue about changes in society. Alternative last chapters, melodramatically 'happy' and un-Victorianly inconclusive, are provided. An allusive density of scientific and historical observation gives body to a somewhat simplistic 'progressive' message. Later novels are *Daniel Martin* (1977), a rewritten version of *The Magus* (1977) and *Mantissa* (1982). [HB]

FRAME, JANET (1924-). Novelist, born in Dunedin, New Zealand, and educated at Otago University and at Dunedin Teachers Training College. She taught for a time and later worked as a private nurse-companion in Dunedin; the short stories published as *The Lagoon* (1951, revised 1961) were written during this period. After suffering a nervous breakdown she spent several years in a mental hospital, an experience reflected with disturbing directness in *Faces in the Water* (1961) and relevant to the insistent questioning of 'reality' with which all her writings are concerned. She left New Zealand in 1956 – London is now her home – and her first novel, *Owls Do Cry* (1957), was a vivid depiction of the Withers family and the small New Zealand coastal town of 'Waimaru'. Janet Frame's characters are compelled to probe the uncertain dimensions which underlie mundane reality, and through what would 'normally' be called madness often gain awareness of worlds previously suppressed by social conventions, established religion or political formality. Her constant concern at both a human and an artistic level is with the obstacles to fulfilling communication with others: 'One is alone, one must decide alone'. This leads in her writing to the occasional deliberate distortion of language to reflect the revelations: 'In my family words were revered as instruments of magic'. *The Edge of the Alphabet* (1962) pursues this theme: 'One day we who live at the edge of the alphabet will find our speech. Meanwhile our lives are hollow'. The title of *Scented Gardens for the Blind* (1962) points to a similar concern with the 'grotesque, purposeless' lives of those 'beyond the range of human language'. *The Adaptable Man* (1965) is an unnerving exploration of modern values in a deceptively peaceful English setting. The bizarre consequences for society of a man wrongly declared officially dead after a car accident are traced with disquieting humour in *The Rainbirds* (1968) while *Intensive Care* (1970) extends the apocalyptic aspects of earlier novels in asserting the ultimate ability of the human personality to survive the computer-planning of modern technology. The individual as writer is central in *Daughter Buffalo* (1972), an extended meditation on mortality which takes as its setting the meeting between an elderly New Zealand author and a young American doctor in New York; here as elsewhere Frame's tendency to intrude as omniscient author and commentator sometimes detracts from the impact of the work as fiction, but she is nevertheless an original and profound explorer of countries of the mind. *The Pocket Mirror* (1967) is poetry. *Living in the Maniototo* (1979) employed a subtly shifting location in its disturbing exploration of contemporary values. The narrator comments at one point on her New Zealand town where streets are named after battles but individuals' names are lacking: 'it is literature and our imagination which tells us about those who fought'. It is a remark which could apply to much of Frame's best writing. [PQ]

FRASER, G.S. (George Sutherland) (1915-1981). Poet and critic, born in Glasgow, Strathclyde, Scotland, and educated at Glasgow Academy, Aberdeen Grammar School and Aberdeen University. His first career, as a literary journalist, was interrupted by war service from 1939 to 1945. It was succeeded, from 1959, by an academic career at the University of Leicester, where he became Reader in Modern English Literature. His early poetry – *The Fatal Landscape* (1943) – associated him with the somewhat ephemeral 'New Apocalypse' movement of the 1940s which reacted against politico-social concern with a new vein of romantic personalism. *Home Town Elegy* (1944) includes 'Christmas Home Letter' in which Fraser's wartime recall of Aberdeen life ('the little, lovely taste of youth we had') transfigures the commonplace with an unobtrusively controlled directness and simplicity. Fraser, and his fellow Scot Norman MacCaig (q.v.), were two of the 'Apocalyptic' group who proved to have staying power as literary figures; but Fraser's importance is primarily that of an indefatigable editor and critic whose reviews and publications did much to encourage new poets and to further sympathetic understanding of twentieth-century poetry. See *The Modern Writer and His World* (London, 1953; New York, 1955), *Vision and Rhetoric* (London, 1959; New York, 1960) and *Essays on Modern English Poets* (1977).

The posthumous *Poems of G.S. Fraser* (1981), edited by Ian Fletcher and John Lucas, includes some previously uncollected poems on poets and poetry which display Fraser's rare blend of penetration and readability (see 'Flash Harry' on George Barker (q.v.) and 'Two Letters from, and a Conversation with, a Poet'). Fraser has always excelled in this vein. His early poem, 'For Yeats', was notably discerning:

> you
> Seemed a man greater than your loyalties,
> But your mind saw it; and you made
> A pattern of the history of our time.

[HB]

FRIEL, BRIAN (1929–). Irish dramatist, born in Omagh, County Tyrone, Northern Ireland. He forsook schoolmastering for full-time writing in 1960. He began publishing short stories in 1962 and *A Saucer of Larks* (1969) selects from his two earlier volumes of stories. As a dramatist he scored a notable success at the Dublin Theatre Festival in 1964 with *Philadelphia, Here I come!* (1965), which analyses the psychological complexities behind a young Irishman's decision to emigrate to the United States. On the eve of departure Gareth O'Donnell is presented in dual personae, public and private, whose contrasting attitudes ransack the occasion for its comic, sentimental and ironic potential. In the succeeding plays, *The Loves of Cass McGuire* (prod 1967) and *Lovers* (prod 1967), the failure of experience to match up to the human demand for love and happiness is handled with wistful pathos. *The Freedom of the City* (prod 1973) is probably the best play to have come out of the current Irish Troubles. It is set in Londonderry in 1970. Troops use CS gas in dispersing marchers at a civil rights demonstration and two young men and a mother flee for shelter accidentally into the mayor's parlour in the town hall. The rumour spreads that the trio are forty armed rebels, and they are shot when they emerge to surrender. Friel counterpoints the half-comic dilemma of the trio with voices from a post-mortem tribunal of inquiry and from a broadcast of a requiem mass in their honour. The total effect is powerfully ironic.

Living Quarters, produced at the Abbey Theatre, Dublin, in 1977, is an altogether more sombre, even claustrophobic tragedy of a heroic, middle-aged Irish commandant and his young second wife. *Translations* (prod 1980) goes back to Donegal in 1833, when the Royal Engineers, working on the Ordnance Survey of Ireland, are anglicizing place-names with some local help. The theme of betrayal is movingly articulated. 'Brian Friel has now produced a more significant body of work than any other playwright in Ireland', Seamus Heaney (q.v.) has observed in a review of the play in the *Times Literary Supplement* (24.10.80). [HB]

FRY, CHRISTOPHER (1907–). Dramatist, born at Bristol, Avon. His father had given up a building business to devote himself to the poor and sick as a Church of England lay worker. Worried and overworked, he died in 1910. Fry's mother was also a devout Anglican, though she came of a Quaker family. Parental influence, and in particular the arduous self-sacrifice of the father, left its mark on Fry's thinking. He was educated at Bedford Modern School and then, after a short spell as a schoolteacher, turned to repertory. Financial need drove him back briefly for a second spell of teaching before he finally threw in his lot with the theatre. From 1934 to 1936 he was director for the Tunbridge Wells Repertory Players. Here he produced and acted in the first English performance of Shaw's *Village Wooing* in May 1934. Fry first drew attention to himself with a religious festival play, *The Boy with a Cart* (prod 1937, pubd 1939), a fresh and simple presentation, in loosely linked episodes, of the legendary life of St Cuthman of Cornwall. Cuthman has lost his father and meets the challenge of family ruin by making a cart, harnessing himself and pulling his mother about the country in search of a place in which to settle and build a church. A stylized chorus and frank use of the miraculous give a folky flavour to the work.

War service interrupted Fry's career as a dramatist and in particular his work on the tragedy *The Firstborn* (1946), which was produced at the Edinburgh Festival in 1948. *The Firstborn* deals with the vocation to serve and free his people that drives Moses into tragic action against the family of the Pharaoh who has brought him up and would still wish to cherish him. The costly personal struggle, set against the lurid background of the plagues, is presented with sombre intensity. Fry's decision to put titular emphasis on the Pharaoh's son, Rameses (who is slain in the last plague with all the other firstborn sons), is symptomatic of his thinking. 'Rameses is the innocence, humanity, vigour and worth which stand on the enemy side, not altering the justice or necessity of Moses's cause, but linking the ways of men and the ways of God with a deep and urgent question mark' (Foreword to Second Edition). By the time *The Firstborn* was acted Fry had already made his name in the field of comedy with *A Phoenix Too Frequent*. The renaissance of poetic drama consequent upon the prewar success of Eliot's *Murder in the Cathedral* bore fruit after the war in a series of new productions at the Mercury Theatre, London, where *A Phoenix Too Frequent* was presented in 1946. It is a short play whose scene is an underground tomb near Ephesus at night. ('The story was got from Jeremy Taylor who had it from Petronius.') Dynamene, a beautiful young widow, is determined to follow her lost husband ('Virilius') faithfully into death by starving herself in his tomb, and her servant, Doto, is with her. A young soldier on guard duty (Tegeus-Chromis) intrudes and in his living virility, for all his deep respect for Dynamene's noble idealism, the power of life prevails over the impulse to useless self-immolation. The theme recurs persistently in Fry's work.

So too does his love of paradox, his humour, his metaphorical abundance and his concern with questions basic to the human predicament ('the desire to find / A reason for living').

The success of *A Phoenix Too Frequent* was followed in 1948 by the triumph of *The Lady's Not For Burning*, a play with a medieval setting in which this time a male hero, Thomas Mendip, is intent on death by execution (for supposed murder) until moved by the distress of a lady, Jennet Jourdemayne, victim of a local witch-hunt and condemned to be burnt. The reciprocal personal impacts transform both. The first cast included John Gielgud, Richard Burton, Pamela Brown and Claire Bloom. Fry's verbal decorativeness is at its richest, his metaphorical inventiveness at its most dazzling, his tone at its gayest. He regarded the play as his first 'Comedy of the Seasons' and imbued it with the bouncing vitality of spring. *Thor, with Angels* (1948), a religious play in graver vein, set in 'a Jutish farmstead, AD 596' and performed first at the Canterbury Festival, appeared in the same year, and it was two years later that the second 'Comedy of the Seasons', *Venus Observed**, was put on by Laurence Olivier at the St James's Theatre, London. For his autumnal play Fry presents a middle-aged duke whose spring-like sexual interests threaten an Indian summer. *A Sleep of Prisoners* (1951) belongs among Fry's explicitly religious plays. Its characters, in their dreams, are identified with biblical figures whose experiences have significant parallels with their own. The consequent movement towards self-knowledge works out a pattern much used by Fry. Continuing the sequence of 'seasonal' plays, *The Dark is Light Enough* (1954) embodies the ripe tranquillity of age in Countess Rosmarin Ostenburg, whose incorruptible compassion cannot be monopolized by either side when her Austrian home is overrun by Hungarian revolutionaries in the winter of 1948–9. The mature dramatic craftsmanship with which Fry makes his psychological exploration of conflicting personal loyalties and ideals gives status to this work. Fry remained resolutely a writer whose gift was to celebrate life with gaiety and wonder, and who preferred even the whimsical humours of bathos and paradox to prevalent monochromatic naturalism and theatrical slumming. Thus it was that by the time he wrote his study of Henry II and Becket, *Curtmantle* (1961), the fashionable denigration of poetic drama had contrived to put the verse dramatist culturally in the dock. It was not until 1970 that the sequence of 'seasonal' plays was rounded off with *A Yard of Sun*, a summer comedy set in Siena in July 1946, which shows the three sons of Angelino Bruno, one an ex-partisan, another an ex-blackshirt and the third an ex-war profiteer, coming together again at their old home.

Fry has translated and adapted French plays, notably Anouilh's *L'Invitation au Château* as *Ring round the Moon* and Giraudoux's *La Guerre de Troie n'aura pas lieu* as *Tiger at the Gates*. His lively autobiographical study, *Can You Find Me, A Family History*, was published in 1978.

Venus Observed. The Duke of Altair is a middle-aged widower interested in astronomy. He is determined to put an end to a lifetime's philandering by marrying one of his past mistresses. The aid of his son Edgar is commandeered for selecting the new 'mother'. Three contestants arrive at Stellmere Park, the Duke's mansion:

they are the Venus, Juno and Minerva of the competition. The surprise arrival of Perpetua diverts the Duke's aspirations and for the first time puts son in rivalry with father. The play has a coherent symbolic fabric. If the Duke is seeking rest and stability from desires endlessly teased but unsatisfied by the teeming world of beautiful women, so all men are in search of the eternal that Perpetua represents. The searching of the heavens through a phallic telescope is linked with the Duke's more personal probings, for his observatory is furnished with a bed and serves a double purpose. From his lofty hide-out the Duke and Perpetua are rescued just in time after flaming feminine jealousy has set fire to it. Like all the others in the action, the two fully discover themselves through crisis and testing.   [HB]

FUGARD, ATHOL (1932–). Actor, director and playwright, born in Middelburg, Cape Province, South Africa. He grew up in Port Elizabeth and studied at Cape Town University from 1950 to 1953. After six months hitch-hiking through Africa and two years as a seaman in the Far East, he married the Cape Town actress Sheila Meiring, in 1957. While clerk in a Native Commissioner's Court in Johannesburg (1958) he 'began to understand how my country functioned', and became involved in non-professional theatre in the black ghetto townships; the two activities inspired *No-good Friday* (prod 1958) and *Nongogo* (prod 1959). (Both were published in 1977.) They are plays about individuals trying to rise humanely above their sordid surroundings, recognizing their own short-comings and countering despair with martyrdom in *No-good Friday*, with stoicism in *Nongogo*. After a year in British theatre in 1960, Fugard chose double theatrical isolation by working with amateur actors in South Africa's black townships, under the most primitive physical conditions and increasingly hampered by apartheid legislation. From 1963 he was with Serpent Players, an amateur group in the Port Elizabeth township of New Brighton, whose members included factory workers and domestic servants. Most of Fugard's very inventive and passionately humane theatre work has been accomplished under improvised circumstances; he had had much practical experience of 'poor theatre' when New York friends sent him Grotowski's *Towards a Poor Theatre* during the period 1967–71, when the South African government withheld his passport. After Grotowski, the most stimulating influences on his thinking have been Brecht, Camus, McLuhan, Lowell and R.D. Laing. Since 1972 he has been able to work periodically in Britain and America.

In *The Blood Knot* (prod 1961, pubd 1963), two coloured brothers, one able 'to pass for white', the other of Negro appearance, find dangerous relief from racial tensions that affect their blood relationship through a role-playing game that stops within the periphery of violence; while not symbolic, it dramatizes powerfully the claustrophobia and unremitting tension of South African race relations. *Hello and Goodbye* (prod 1965, pubd 1966) and *People Are Living There* (prod 1969, pubd 1970) show lower-middle-class whites desperately seeking their identity, trying to affirm life amidst drabness and futility. Both illustrate Fugard's technical resourcefulness in making powerful and compassionate drama with sparse settings, semi-articulate characters and small casts (there are only two performers in *Hello and Goodbye*, though the persuasive illusion is created here – and elsewhere – of the off-stage presence of another character).

Boesman and Lena (prod 1969, pubd 1973) is the most intense and tragic of Fugard's plays. A coloured man and woman, destitute and dispossessed upon mudflats at night, are presented as the discarded rubbish of South African society, with a virtually silent old African on the point of death providing a pair of eyes from which Lena draws fragile confirmation of her individuality. It is a brilliant exposition of a couple's habituated intimacy: Boesman beats Lena to deny his own nullity, she taunts him to deny hers, while they remain inextricably Boesman-and-Lena. Stagecraft of this quality has made Fugard an important dramatist of the English-speaking world.

From Fugard's work with Serpent Players developed *Sizwe Bansi Is Dead* (prod 1972, pubd 1974), a bitingly satirical indictment of South Africa's pass laws, and *The Island* (prod 1973, pubd 1974), about black political prisoners, both plays created scene by scene in rehearsal by Fugard 'directing' the actors John Kani and Winston Ntshona and recording their contributions to what became the scripts. Kani and Ntshona shared the New York Tony best-actor award (1975) for their performances in these plays.

Fugard has since written *Statements after an Arrest under the Immorality Act* (prod 1974, pubd 1974), about South African miscegenation laws, and *Dimetos* (prod 1975, pubd 1977), with a non-South-African setting and a new psychological dimension but characteristic in its sensitive treatment of isolation and guilt. *A Lesson from Aloes* (1981) finds a rugged human capacity for faith and tenacity of purpose in the very midst of the defeat and self-betrayal that are the inevitable accompaniment of apartheid in South Africa. His plays are staged and televised in Europe and America. He has also made films, *Mille Miglia*, *Boesman and Lena* and *The Guest* (script pubd 1977), in the latter playing with great sympathy the drug-addicted Afrikaans poet and naturalist, Eugène Marais (1871–1936). He plays Smuts in Attenborough's film *Gandhi*. He has written a novel, *Tsotsi* (1980). [AR]

FULLER, ROY (1912–). Poet, born in Failsworth, Lancashire. He was educated at private schools and began his professional career as a solicitor in 1933. From 1941 to 1946 he served in the Royal Navy. Since the war he has been solicitor to the Woolwich Equitable Building Society, of which he became a Director in 1969. He has also been Vice-President of the Building Societies Association and a Governor of the BBC. Fuller married Kathleen Smith in 1936 and their son John Fuller (born 1937) is himself a poet. Fuller published his first volume, *Poems*, in 1939. He shared the fashionable concerns of the literary 1930s and learned a good deal, as a poet, from Auden (q.v.), whose exact prosiness and metrical facility he assimilated, and with whose sense of impending cataclysm he was infected.

> There are bounds
> To feeling in this suburb, but nothing can save me

> Tonight from the scenic railway journey over
> Europe to locate my future grave . . .
> ('To My Brother')

In fact the war gave him the opportunity to find his particular voice as a poet in registering the facts of life in the services. In *The Middle of a War* (1942) and *A Lost Season* (1944) he observes events with a dry clarity in a tone that shrugs off prophetic pretension and grandiloquent gesture. Fuller cultivated a sardonic precision in recording the impact of the war and, later, of the postwar scene. His *Collected Poems* came out in 1962 and one can see the earnestness and integrity with which Fuller has worked at his craft through a lifetime. Yet the question of how far talent alone can take a poet in the absence of decisive commitment is aired in 'Dialogue of the Poet and His Talent'. Fuller has wit, ingenuity and straightforwardness of contact but his work conveys no sense of having been forged under pressure. It does not quiver with the stress of necessity to speak. There is neither compulsiveness nor emotional intensity. The wry self-consciousness evident early on in his work ('My photograph already looks historic') later becomes clinically analytical in 'The Final Period' and coolly ironic in 'At a Warwickshire Mansion':

> I have been acting
> The poet's role for quite as long as I
> Can, at a stretch, without it being exacting.

This extreme detachment (see also 'To Posterity'), while frank and exact, is yet curiously remote. Later still, in *Buff* (1965), the poet's voice gives way to those of imagined characters. Subsequent volumes include *Off Course* (1969) and *An Old War* (1974).

The range of Fuller's poetic comment and of his technique have won recognition. He was Professor of Poetry at Oxford from 1968 to 1973. Yet a sense of failure seems to haunt him; and indeed there are limits to the fruitfulness of manufacturing poetry out of pervasive dissatisfaction, reticence and professed unwillingness to grapple. The characteristic self-deprecatory detachment renders his first autobiographical book, *Souvenirs* (1980), strangely impersonal and evasive. He characterizes himself as an 'elderly buffer' in the collection of verse *The Reign of Sparrows* (1980). And a second autobiographical volume, *Vamp Till Ready* (1982), covering the years from Fuller's adolescence to the 1940s, fastens on prewar and war-time moods and attitudes with an emphasis on the seeming 'preliminariness' of human experience. (The popular song quoted in the title ran 'My life is only a vamp till ready. I've played the long introduction through'.)

The Individual and His Art (1982) (ed. V.J. Lee) selects from the whole poetic output, an output in which Alan Brownjohn (q.v.) finds 'a continuous, highly individual commentary on the malaise of the time' (*Times Literary Supplement*, 17.9.82). [HB]

FURPHY, JOSEPH (1843–1912). Novelist, born in Victoria, Australia, of Irish parents. After a scant education he worked for a time at farm jobs and on the goldfields. He married in 1866 and set up as a farmer, but later worked for seven years driving a bullock team in the Riverina area of New South Wales and in Northern Victoria. Ruined by drought in 1884, he moved with his family to Shepparton, Victoria, where he worked in his brother's iron foundry for the next twenty years, writing in the evenings. From 1889 he contributed short pieces to *The Bulletin* (q.v.) – one of many writers whose works found their way into print in this way – but *Such is Life* (1903) was the only work published during his lifetime. He wrote some poems and stories in later life, but when the family moved to Western Australia in 1905 the creative period was over. A bushman and self-made man, Furphy nevertheless inherited from his family a love of books, and his familiarity with Shakespeare and the Bible is apparent from both the style and the calculated digressions of *Such is Life*. This work was first published by *The Bulletin*, though a larger version had been in manuscript since at least 1897. Sections removed on the editor's advice were later published in revised form as *Rigby's Romance* (1946) and *The Buln-Buln and the Brolga* (1948); the former was also published in serial form in 1905–6. *Such is Life: Being certain extracts from the Diary of Tom Collins* has been recognized as a complex and carefully constructed work in which 'Tom Collins' is something more than simply a persona, yet certainly not identifiable with the author. Furphy sought to capture the truth of bush life by claiming to record it in random fashion, and it is the discursive Collins who, as Furphy expressed it in a letter of 1899, 'obviously unfolds the patchwork web of life'; but the reader is expected to catch connections and disparities of which Collins himself remains unaware. The book is richly human and amusing, though Furphy's homespun philosophy and learning overburdens the tenuous structure. Only just over a thousand copies were sold in Furphy's lifetime, and he died almost unnoticed. The preface to the 1917 reprint of the work, however, stressed its special value for Australians, and his own description of the book – 'temper, democratic; bias, offensively Australian' – appealed to many on both artistic and political grounds. His real achievement lay in the originality of his subject-matter and form, both of which were a deliberate challenge to works such as the ever-popular *Geoffry Hamlyn* (1859) by Henry Kingsley, and in his unsentimental depiction of the Australian bush and its people. [PQ]

G

GALSWORTHY, JOHN (1867–1933). Dramatist and novelist, born in Surrey into a wealthy family which provided the pattern for the Forsyte dynasty of his most famous work. His own father supplied the model for old Jolyon Forsyte, the most genial and lovable of the bunch. Galsworthy was educated at Harrow and New College, Oxford. He was called to the Bar in 1890. A celebrated meeting with Conrad (q.v.) occurred in 1893 when Galsworthy was one of the passengers on Conrad's last voyage as first mate of the *Torrens*. Galsworthy and he spent evening watches together and Conrad asked him to his cabin on the last evening. They were to become friends as writers later.

Galsworthy's work as a playwright led to his being grouped with Barrie (q.v.), Shaw (q.v.) and Granville Barker (q.v.) as representing a renaissance of British drama. Shaw and Barker accepted his play *The Silver Box* for performance at the Court Theatre in 1906. It reveals Galsworthy's compulsive interest in social problems and the moral issues they bring to light. A drunken young gent and an unemployed labourer are both involved in what are technically 'thefts', but only the latter carries the can. *Strife* (prod 1909) gives a disturbing picture of the bitterness engendered by a strike at a Welsh tin-plate works. Galsworthy registers the moods and attitudes of conflicting employers and workers with a scrupulous impartiality, laying stress on the stubbornness of the two protagonists, each in his own way a man of principle and fortitude. That suffering bears more heavily on the starving men and their families is tragically brought home: yet the emphasis on aspects of underlying humanity and vulnerability common to opponents across the barriers of social class is strong. The play was 'received with acclamation', as Galsworthy noted, and Conrad applauded its 'intellectual honesty' (H.V. Marrot, *The Life and Letters of John Galsworthy*, 1935). In *Justice* (prod 1910) the machinery of justice ruins a clerk who is trying to rehabilitate himself after a prison sentence. In *The Skin Game* (prod 1920) the struggle is between Hillcrist, the aristocrat, and his neighbour, the newly rich manufacturer, Hornblower, who threatens to ruin the locality with a factory. These plays, together with *The Eldest Son* (prod 1912), *Loyalties* (prod 1922) and *Escape* (prod 1926), are consistently neat in construction, economic and often telling in dialogue. Galsworthy probes the social conscience disquietingly in his plays, betraying genuine compassion, sensitivity to suffering, notable sympathy for the underdog, and sometimes an uncomfortable awareness of how precarious the equilibrium of the social fabric is.

Galsworthy's early novels had been published by him under the name 'John Sinjohn'. He attributed to Ada, his wife, the impulse for him to embark on a career as a writer as well as the inspiration for sustaining it. The remarkable marriage – recently more fully investigated by Catherine Dupré (*John Galsworthy*, 1976) – cannot be ignored in any penetrating estimate of his human interests as a novelist. Ada was the wife of his cousin

Arthur when she and John fell in love. It is clear that Ada quickly regretted her marriage in 1891 to Major Arthur Galsworthy, and John was soon made aware of the misery of her position. The pair became lovers in 1895 but the relationship remained a concealed one for nine long years. The need to keep up appearances in a family of Forsytean closeness and respectability was a motive for concealment; a genuine desire not to hurt the feelings of John's much loved father was another; the importance of not being cut out of his will was no doubt a third. When the old man died, in December 1904, the pair immediately allowed their relationship to establish evidence for divorce, and they married in 1905. Major Arthur's attitude to a relationship which he later professed to have been unaware of for several years (he was away in South Africa in the Boer War) is one of many ambiguities that indicate how tense and strained were the lives of the lovers, how fraught with potential guilt and rebellion. Later ostracism compounded the psychological complexities. It is not surprising that when Galsworthy produced his first novel of distinctive power (*The Man of Property*, 1906) it bore the stamp of an experience that was to be deeply embedded in much of his fiction thereafter. The protest against respectable servitude to a failed marriage was linked in Galsworthy's own experience to his dissatisfaction with the bourgeois code of acquisitive ownership. The critique of possessiveness in money and marriage, launched in *The Man of Property*, runs through the subsequent parts of the trilogy that Galsworthy later called *The Forsyte Saga**. Soames Forsyte, embodiment of the Forsytean money ethic, dominates this trilogy, and the post-marital life of his daughter Fleur is central to the second trilogy, *A Modern Comedy* (*The White Monkey*, 1924; *The Silver Spoon*, 1926; and *Swan Song*, 1928). The 'Forsyte Chronicles' (the term covers the nine novels) were further expanded in the third trilogy, *End of the Chapter*, 1935 (*Maid in Waiting, Flowering Wilderness* and *Over the River*), the product of Galsworthy's last years.

The Forsyte Saga was an immense contemporary success. Galsworthy spoke of it as 'embalming the upper-middle class' and was perhaps aware of the relish for good living that he had uncomfortably juxtaposed with irony at the expense of the good livers. His own dilemma, personal and social, seems to have turned his fiction into a lifelong apologia. There is further evidence of the way he used his own experience (see *The Dark Flower*, 1913) in the actress Margaret Morris's book, *My Galsworthy Story* (1967), recounting how, at 22, she impinged too passionately on Galsworthy's middle-aged domesticity. Galsworthy died full of honours, having received several honorary degrees as well as the Order of Merit (1929) and the Nobel Prize for Literature (1932).

The Forsyte Saga, a trilogy, grew by stages out of *The Man of Property* (1906). It presents an upper-middle-class family in the Victorian heyday. The Forsyte tribe, vast and graspable only with the aid of a diagrammatized family tree, exemplify conservative tenacity and backbone in a world of possessiveness. Their mental climate of ownership is disturbed by the figure of Irene, whose beauty cannot be owned nor her personality possessed. Soames Forsyte (the 'Man of Property') marries her, but loses her to a lover who is tragically killed. Galsworthy returned to the story with a brief interlude, 'Indian Summer of a Forsyte', published in *Five Tales* (1918), then continued the series with *In Chancery* (1920), a full novel, 'Awakening', another brief sketch (also 1920), and finally *To Let* (1921). The trilogy, with its interludes, he then called *The Forsyte Saga*. *The Man of Property* opens in the year 1886 and the last novel, *To Let*, in 1920. Galsworthy pursues his central theme of possession or non-possession by balancing against Soames (the dyed-in-the-wool Forsytean) his more attractive cousin Jolyon, who is sufficiently ill adjusted to the Forsytean mould to marry indiscreetly and to paint water colours. It is eventually in Jolyon's devoted, unselfish keeping that the beautiful Irene finds happiness. But Soames's relentless possessiveness towards his lost wife is never laid to rest, and the bitterness of the family feud between Jolyon and Soames bears down brutally in the next generation on the love of Jon (son of Jolyon and Irene) and Fleur, Soames's daughter by his second wife, Annette.

Gilbert Murray praised Galsworthy the novelist as *Scriptor Eroticus* and indeed an intensity of erotic sensibility pervades the book, though Irene, who is encountered by the reader only through the minds of other characters, is little more than a mysterious symbol. But Galsworthy tried to pin down some broader social issues: it is not only beauty that impinges on the bourgeois Victorian world; there is the intrusion of war (the Boer War), the encroachment of divorce, of democracy, even of the petrol engine. At his best Galsworthy has clarity and indeed some subtlety in dramatic presentation; but too often dialogue seems to convey that the speakers (even man and wife) have lived incommunicado since their last appearance before the reader, and that they have stored up their cryptic interchanges for official delivery in his presence. Nor can Galsworthy be exculpated from the charge of relying on cliché sentiment in relation to old age, children and dogs, not to mention relationships between fathers and sons or daughters. There is also too much automatic nostalgia; too much slickly engineered sentiment about the passage of time. Yet Conrad praised the work, *To Let* especially – 'it escapes from the particular into the universal by the sheer force of its inner life'.

[HB]

GARIOCH, ROBERT (1909–81). Poet, born in Edinburgh, Lothian, Scotland, educated there at the high school and the university. He saw war service, was a schoolmaster, and in 1971–3 was Writer-in-Residence at Edinburgh University. The most readily enjoyable of the recent poets to have used Lallans in the tradition of Fergusson and Burns, Garioch captures amusing aspects of Scottish life and character with a nutty raciness and vigour. *The Masque of Edinburgh* (1954) is a lively dramatic fantasy on his native city. But Garioch is much more than a heady entertainer. His adoption of the canny pose and the 'daftness' of the man in the street gives a fierce ironical punch to his onslaughts on public pomposity and hypocrisy. The Edinburgh Festival is his target in 'Embro to the Ploy'.

The tartan tred wad gar ye lauch;
nae problem is owre teuch.

Your surname needna end in -och;
they'll cleik ye up the cleuch.
A puckle dollar bills will aye
preive Hiram Teufelsdröckh
a septary of Clan McKay.

James Campbell, reviewing a new paperback edition of
Garioch's *Collected Poems* (1977) in the *Times Literary
Supplement* (8.8.80), notes that 'his Scots enacts a consciousness which has sunk so far from sight as to have
reached the degradation of a protected species'. Certainly there is deep reverence for the Scottish literary
tradition, as well as superb craftsmanship, in Garioch's
resuscitation of its old forms and idioms. By fusing the
current vernacular with classical Scots he makes his
language a resonant instrument for both ripe humour and
raw satire. See *Complete Poetical Works* (1983).   [HB]

GARNETT, DAVID (1892–1981). Novelist, born in
Brighton, East Sussex, into a distinguished literary
family. His father, Edward Garnett, was a highly influential publishers' reader and literary adviser, and his
mother, Constance Garnett, translated numerous
Russian classics into English. He studied botany at the
Imperial College of Science and Technology and served
briefly in France with the Friends War Victims Relief
Mission in 1915. Later in the war he worked on the land
as a conscientious objector, then turned to book-selling,
publishing, journalism and writing. His three autobiographical volumes, *The Golden Echo* (1954), *Flowers of
the Forest* (1956) and *The Familar Faces* (1962), cover
respectively childhood and youth up to 1914, the First
World War years, and the 1920s and 1930s. These are
light, gossipy records of one whose lot and delight it was
to be familiar with the 'big' names of the Bloomsbury
group. Garnett made his own name as a writer with *Lady
Into Fox* (1922), the tale of how Mr Tebrick's wife, Silvia,
is suddenly changed into a fox and gradually accom-
modates her manners and habits to the new condition.
The story is told in a demure, mannered prose which gives
it the flavour of a fable. Garnett spoke of it as the
'reductio ad absurdum of the problem of fidelity in love'
and indeed the sharper ironies ('However you may be
changed, my love is not', says Mr Tebrick to the vixen)
mock both 'a true conjugal fidelity that it would be hard to
find matched in the world' and the conventional pieties
that sustain it. (Mr T. christens his wife's cubs, declaring
himself their godfather.)

In *A Man in the Zoo* (1924) John Cromartie, after a
lovers' tiff, successfully offers himself to the zoo so that
its collection can be completed with a caged specimen of
homo sapiens. ('Visitors are requested not to irritate the
Man by personal remarks.') In *The Sailor's Return* (1925)
a seaman tries to settle in an English village with his black
wife. Other early books are *Go She Must* (1927) and *No
Love* (1929). Garnett's later fiction output of the 1950s
and 1960s (*Aspects of Love*, 1956; *A Net for Venus*, 1959;
Ulterior Motives, 1966) takes up modish sex recipes in a
frivolously hedonistic vein. Garnett's work as an editor
includes *The Selected Letters of T.E. Lawrence* (1952) and
Carrington: Letters and Extracts from Her Diaries (1970).
                                                          [HB]

GASCOYNE, DAVID (1916–). Poet, born in Harrow,
Middlesex. He was educated at Salisbury Cathedral
Choir School and at Regent Street Polytechnic. He
published his first poems, *Roman Balcony* (1932), when he
was 16, and his sole novel, *Opening Day*, a year later.
Poetic affiliation became evident in his book, *A Short
Survey of Surrealism* (1935), and in his second volume of
poetry, *Man's Life is This Meat* (1936). Surrealistic
imagery, garish in its extravagance, is used to depict a
disjointed personal and social world:

> An arrow with lips of cheese was caught by a
>   floating hair . . .
> And a wild growth of lascivious pamphlets became
>   a beehive
>
>   ('The Rites of Hysteria')

Gascoyne lived in France from 1937 to the outbreak of
war. *Poems 1937–1942* came out in 1943, and the Paris
pictured in 'Noctambules', which is subtitled 'Hommage
à Djuna Barnes', has its affinities with the Paris of
Djuna Barnes's *Nightwood*. Lurid imagery of desolation,
anguish and violence is insistent and ominous in its
impact:

> And in a Left-bank café where
> At about half-past four
> Exiles are wont to bare
> Their souls, a son-and-heir
> Of riches and neurosis casts
> His frail befuddled blonde
> Brutally to the floor
> And with despairing fists
> Tries to blot out the gaze
> Of her wet senseless eyes –.

The poem ends with the note of dereliction at the 'hour of
Night's ending', when a timeless 'vigil of despair' is maintained on the edge of the abyss of war. Thus readiness to
dredge up imagery from the depths of dream and neurosis
meets in the 1943 volume with a sharp awareness of
world catastrophe ('Who can not by now hear / The
hollow and annihilating roar / Of final disillusion?',
'Zero', September 1939). Surrealistic excesses begin to
be purged. 'A Wartime Dawn', for instance, is a powerfully disciplined exercise in 'incommunicable desolation'.
And we hear a more nonchalant tone of voice, characteristic of the later Gascoyne, in 'Farewell Chorus', which
rings down the curtain on the 1930s in measured
resignation:

> And so the long black pullman is at last departing,
>   now,
> After those undermining years of angry waiting
>   and cold tea.

We hear it again in the moving 'Elegy' to a friend who,
apparently overwhelmed by the war, committed suicide
in Dublin in 1941.

Gascoyne increasingly brings Christian symbols to
bear on the contemporary world. His Christ in 'Ecce
Homo' is one who is crucified before centurions in 'riding
boots, black shirts and badges and peaked caps'. He wept
over Jerusalem and now weeps over the bombed cities of
Europe. The religious cry is addressed to a 'Christ of
Revolution and Poetry' whose cross is the 'tree of human

pain'. Gascoyne's main later volumes are *A Vagrant and Other Poems* (1950) and *Night Thoughts* (1956), a long dramatic work written for radio production in 1955. It is in three parts: 1, 'The Nightwatchers'; 2, 'Megalometropolitan Carnival'; 3, 'Encounter with Silence'. The nightmare parody of city decadence and sterility in part 2 is impressively countered by the solitary rural quietude of part 3; but over the work as a whole poetic energy tends to be dissipated in repetition. See *Collected Poems* (1965, reprinted 1970 and reissued 1978), edited by Robin Skelton. See also Gascoyne's *Paris Journal 1937–1939* (1978) which sheds light on the early years and on the devastating anxieties and blockages that have plagued him and limited his productivity. *Journal 1936–1937* (1980), a more recently discovered document, begins in September 1936 and covers the previous nine months in a candid attempt 'to make a record of what I am'.   [HB]

GERHARDI(E), WILLIAM (1895–1977). Novelist, born in St Petersburg, Russia, of British parents. His grandfather had come from Manchester and set up a cotton spinning mill in St Petersburg. His father built a vast mansion overlooking the Neva, but the revolution reduced him to poverty. The story of Gerhardi's Russian upbringing is told with great verve and zest in his autobiography, *Memoirs of a Polyglot* (1931), which covers too his five years in the British Army, his early days as a writer and his initiation into the London literary world of the 1920s. Gerhardi was sent with the British Military Mission to Siberia during the abortive allied intervention in Russia of 1918 to 1920. His first novel, *Futility* (1922), paints a scathingly amusing picture of the 'comic opera attempts to wipe out the Russian revolution'. An Englishman of Russian upbringing falls in love with Nina, one of the three bewitching daughters of Nikolai Vasilievich whose career out-Chekhovs Chekhov. Nikolai's Siberia goldmines are always just about to begin to pay. On the strength of the elusive wealth a multitude of hangers-on clog and dog him with their dependency. He finally goes east on the trans-Siberian railway to try to sort out business problems produced by the revolution, and their pursuit of him is riotously comic. The second novel, *The Polyglots* (1925), returns to the allied intervention in Russia and has personal autobiographical interest. Gerhardi was taken up by Lord Beaverbrook who tried vainly to turn *The Polyglots* into a best-seller.

Jazz and Jasper (1928), a novel of the 1920s, culminates in the atomic disintegration of the earth with a handful of refugees in a hotel on a mountain top as the last survivors. Arnold Bennett (q.v.), who spoke of the book's 'wild and brilliant originality', is amiably caricatured as Vernon Sprott, 'a writer of talent but a merchant of genius', and Lord Beaverbrook as Lord Ottercove. *Jazz and Jasper* was retitled *My Sinful Earth* in 1947 and again as *Doom* (Gerhardi's chosen title which the publishers disliked) in 1971. Gerhardi's most ambitious novel is *Of Mortal Love* (1936), which treats 'of the succeeding stages of transformation of love erotic into love imaginative; of love entrancing into love unselfish; of love tender into love transfigured' (notes to Collected Edition of 1948). Gerhardi saw it as a 'simple love story'. Its hero,

composer Walter Smith, is entranced by Dinah Fry who turns to him in dissatisfaction with her husband Jim. Divorce proceedings produce an ironic volte-face and when finally divorced Dinah finds herself as desperately dependent on Jim as she was earlier on Walter. Finally she dies of diphtheria. Walter's successive deprivations change the character, not the force, of his love. D.H. Lawrence (q.v) praised Gerhardi's humour, and it is the humour that turns *Of Mortal Love* into something distinctive. Gerhardi is clever at simplifying the intricacies of human response in amusing, concrete terms. Vanity and self-deception, in distinguishable male and female modes, are explored with an irony which is all the more endearing because the characters remain innocently lovable. Thus Gerhardi's peculiar blend of pathos and comedy is unique and the neglect of Gerhardi during the 1950s and 1960s is hard to understand. He eventually added an 'e' to his surname, which should be pronounced 'Jerhardy'. He spent his last decades as a semi-recluse. *God's Fifth Column, a Biography of the Age 1890–1940*, published posthumously in 1981, has entertaining sections on Tolstoy, Tchaikovsky, Proust and other notables, but the philosophical reflections scarcely add up to a cogent thesis.   [HB]

GHOSE, ZULFIKAR (1935–). Poet and novelist, born in Sialkot, India (now Pakistan). His family emigrated to London in 1952 and he graduated from Keele University in 1959. First journalist, then schoolmaster, he was appointed to the English Department, the University of Texas, Austin, in 1969.

Ghose's muted verse is direct and conversational; its sharp observation suggests poise, but without disguising the poet's unresolved crisis of identity. *The Loss of India* (1964) laments his pre-Partition, boyhood India, while he looks within himself for origins 'as / an exiled monarch rules a map for a kingdom' ('To My Ancestors'). 'Born of this continent', he writes of India ('This Landscape, These People'), 'I was a stranger', but in the final line 'stranger' deliberately undermines the stated acceptance of England as home. *Jets of Orange* (1967) reveals a 'huge sense of loss' but displays a 'tourist sensibility' (D. Kohli). *The Violent West* (1972) steels this sensibility into satirization of western ways – love: 'we make spring-mattressed love with its / Kleenex anti-climax'; environmentalism: 'bringing cosmetics to geography'.

Ghose has published *Confessions of a Native-Alien* (autobiography, 1965) and the novels: *The Contradictions* (1966), *The Murder of Aziz Khan* (1967), *The Incredible Brazilian* (in three parts, 1972, 1975, 1979).   [AR]

GIBBON, LEWIS GRASSIC (pseudonym of James Leslie Mitchell) (1901–35). Novelist, born at Hillhead of Seggat, Auchterless, Grampian, Scotland, and brought up from the age of 8 in a farmcroft at Drumlithie. After working in local journalism he served from 1918 as a clerk, first in the army (which took him to the Middle East), then in the RAF. He turned full-time writer in 1928, wrote sixteen books in seven years, and died at the age of 34, leaving a wife, a daughter and a son.

His publications include biography and archaeology as

well as short stories and novels. Most were issued under his own name, including the historical novel, *Spartacus* (1933), about the revolt of the Italian slaves under the Thracian gladiator in 73 BC. The pseudonym was used for his major achievement, *A Scots Quair*, a trilogy of novels first gathered into one volume in 1946 and comprising *Sunset Song* (1932), *Cloud Howe* (1933) and *Grey Granite* (1934). The setting is Gibbon's native countryside, the Mearns. The peasant society is figured with extra-ordinary vitality and realism, and the style adopted – lilting, rhythmic, rich in 'the speak' of the region – does for Scotland what Synge did for Ireland. A curiously pervasive use of the second person pronoun in plumbing the thoughts and feelings of the characters adds intimacy and immediacy. We follow the story of Chris Guthrie, a crofter's daughter, from childhood to old age through three marriages, feeling the impact of the First World War and the infiltration of the country society by political radicalism. *Sunset Song* is impressive for its sheer flow and its moving personal story, though Gibbon's rhetoric wrings the last ounce of emotion from such events as the execution of Chris's first husband, Ewan Tavendale, as a deserter from the Western Front. In the later volumes the narrative core is weaker. Characters enter trailing family connections that proliferate in floods of gossip and anecdote; yet their portrayal remains lively and vivid. Gibbon's feeling for the Scottish earth and the Scottish people, their local history, their toils and drudgeries, their humour and their vigour, is as unforgettable as anything in our 'regional' literature. The transmutation of local speech idiom and cadence into an instrument of genuinely poetic flexibility is a distinctive achievement. *A Scots Hairst* (1967), edited by Ian S. Munro, contains short stories, essays, juvenilia and fragments from an unfinished manuscript. The reissue in 1981 of Mitchell's early novel, *The Thirteenth Disciple* (1931), makes available an autobiographical study of an Aberdeen tenant-farmer's son and young journalist who goes to Central America to explore the culture of the Maya (the subject of Mitchell's *The Conquest of the Maya*, 1934).

[HB]

GIBBONS, STELLA (1902–). Novelist, born in London and educated at the North London Collegiate School and University College, London. She scored a well-deserved success with her first book, *Cold Comfort Farm* (1932), a hilarious parody of fashionable pseudo-primitive rural fiction, burlesquing such writers as Mary Webb (q.v.), D.H. Lawrence (q.v), T.F. Powys (q.v.) and their rash of imitators. A brisk heroine, Flora Poste, on a visit to the Starkadder family at Cold Comfort Farm, deals summarily with rooted obsessions and taboos, finally packing off reclusive Aunt Ada Doom (who saw some-thing nasty in the woodshed) to Paris on an aeroplane. Subsequent publications include novels (*Westwood; or, The Gentle Powers*, 1946; *Here Be Dragons*, 1956; *The Snow Woman*, 1969), short stories (*Christmas at Cold Comfort Farm*, 1940; *Conference at Cold Comfort Farm*, 1949) and *Collected Poems* (1951).

[HB]

GIBSON, WILFRID WILSON (1878–1962). Poet, born at Hexham, Northumberland. He was privately edu-cated and devoted his life to poetry. He was in at the plan-ning of *Georgian Poetry* by Edward Marsh (q.v.), and was himself one of the young poets represented in the first volume, *1911–1912*. He also collaborated with Rupert Brooke (q.v.) and others in the quarterly anthology *New Numbers* which came to an end with its fourth issue when the First World War broke out in 1914. *Collected Poems 1905–1925* (1925) garnered what Gibson wished to reprint from numerous earlier volumes, including *Daily Bread* (1910), *Battle* (1916) and *Neighbours* (1920). Later volumes include *The Outpost* (1944) and *Within Four Walls* (1950). Frank Swinnerton (q.v.) (*The Georgian Literary Scene*, 1935) speaks of Gibson's 'sober natural-ism' as a 'poet devoted to simple narrative, telling quiet stories without number, always with feeling and reti-cence'. Inevitably the level of intensity is too low and the control of words too slack over much of Gibson's prolific output, but there is an engaging transparency and direct-ness in his best work. The built-in melodrama of 'Snow', for instance, should be contrasted with the effective nar-rative impact of 'Flannan Isle' or 'The Money'. The latter tells how £4.17s. 5d is found tied round the neck of a poor woman whose death from starvation it could have fore-stalled. But it was the money saved years ago by her husband-to-be for their furniture and discovered on his corpse after a pit accident. She has died rather than spend it. Similarly, in the shorter human studies the senti-mentality of, say, 'Martha Caffrey' should be contrasted with the ironic crispness of 'Henry Turnbull', who gets 'two greasy pennies' change when buying his pint, which are used later in the day in laying him out –

> and so he lies
> With tuppence change till Doomsday on his eyes.

Situations bereft of stock narrative trappings serve Gibson best. In 'Breakfast' soldiers are eating supine because shells are bursting over them when one of them wagers 'a rasher to a loaf of bread' that, given the right full-backs, Hull United would beat Halifax.

> Ginger raised his head
> And cursed, and took the bet, and dropped back
> dead.

'Ragtime' recapitulates one of Sassoon's (q.v.) themes in pointing the contrast between the swaggering actress in khaki and false moustache with her 'squeaky notes' and 'lascivious patter' and the 'dank trenches where men crouch and shiver'.

[HB]

GITTINGS, ROBERT (1911–). Poet, born in Ports-mouth, Hampshire, and educated at Oxford. He worked as producer and scriptwriter for the BBC from 1940 to 1963. His published verse includes *Famous Meeting* (1953) in which Gittings revives the Browningesque dramatic monologue for Wellington reflecting on a casual meeting with Nelson just before Trafalgar (title poem); for Livingstone mentally addressing Stanley ('The Explorers'); and for Boswell musing on his friendship with Johnson ('London Journal'). The monologue form recurs, this time in a series of lyrics, in 'By the Lake' (from

Matters of Love and Death, 1938), a sequence based on Frieda and D.H. Lawrence (q.v.) at Lake Garda. Gittings is a competent poetic craftsman. (See *Collected Poems*, 1976.) *Out of This Wood: A Country Sequence of Five Plays* (1955) is a series of one-act sketches of poets (including Herrick, Cowper and Emily Brontë) and is not exciting. Gittings, however, has distinguished himself as a literary biographer in *Young Hardy* (1975) and *The Old Hardy* (1978).   [HB]

GLOVER, DENIS (1912–80). Poet, born in Dunedin, New Zealand, and educated at Auckland Grammar School and Canterbury University College, where he later taught English (1936–8 and 1946–8). In 1936 he founded the Caxton Press which established a lasting New Zealand tradition of fine printing, particularly for poetry, and, together with the journal *Landfall* (ed. Charles Brasch, q.v.), which is still printed by the Caxton Press, provided an invaluable arena for literary talent. In the 1930s he gained a formidable reputation as a satirist, and *The Arraignment of Paris* (1937), aimed at a group of local women poets, demonstrates how well deserved this was. *The Wind and the Sand* (1945) opens with 'The Road Builders', and several other poems illustrate what was to be a continuing belief in the intrinsic worth of human endeavour. This approach informs his verse commentary for a film, *The Coaster*, first printed in *Landfall* in 1949 and later included in the collection *Sings Harry* (1951). The 'Harry' persona proved a successful device for commenting indirectly upon life in a series of humanly appealing poems which nevertheless ultimately lead away from society and towards nature as a source of values. In his next collection, *Arawata Bill* (1952), this tendency is developed through the half-realistic, half-mythic title character, a lone gold prospector (based on an actual person, William O'Leary) whose adventures 'are meant to personify . . . all the unknown prospectors who essayed rough and wicked country that is not yet fully explored'. Bill assumes the status of a folk-hero, his calculatedly understated and laconic poems about physical hardships suffered in the search for true gold suggesting spiritual trials undergone on behalf of all those New Zealanders who ask:

> What unknown affinity
> Lies between mountain and sea
> In country crumpled like an unmade bed . . . ?

Necessarily limited in scope, the poems are still a powerful evocation of the 'man alone' theme which features prominently in mythopoeic interpretations of New Zealand writing. 'Arawata Bill' is the eternal romantic:

> R.I.P. where no gold lies
> But in your own questing soul
> Rich in faith and wild surmise.

A similar admiration for this bent of character fills a fine poem on 'Dirty Mick' Stimson, a well-known local boatman:

> High in those hills your name is forgotten.
> But the legend lives in the yachts
> Ghosting to anchorage mud.

Enter Without Knocking (1964) was a volume of selected poems (an enlarged edition was published in 1972); *Diary*

to a Woman (1971), a volume of love poems, gave his work a new and unexpected dimension. Later poetry collections have included *Dancing to My Tune* and *Wellington Harbour* (both 1974) and *Come High Water* (1977). *Hot Water Sailor* (1962) is autobiographical.   [PQ]

GODDEN, RUMER (1907–). Novelist, born in Sussex, and brought up partly in India. She married her second husband, J.H. Dixon, in 1949 and has two children. She lives in Henry James's (q.v.) former home, Lamb House at Rye, by permission of the National Trust. Among her early Indian novels *Black Narcissus* (1939) is about an Anglican sisterhood and *Breakfast with the Nikolides* (1942) is a study of girlhood troubled by an insensitive, domineering mother whose horribleness to daughter and husband lacks authenticity. *Fugue in Time* (1945) (in USA as *Take Three Tenses*) attempts to convey the personality of a London house ('The house, it seems, is more important than the characters', it begins), a family home, over several generations. *The River* (1946) is a short but telling and tragic story of two girls growing up in a large house by a river in Bengal. *In This House of Brede* (1969), a massive study of an enclosed Benedictine nunnery, shows Godden's craftsmanship at its peak, but vitality, thrust and intensity are sacrificed to the accumulation of pedestrian detail. *The Peacock Spring* (1975) returns to India and New Delhi, whither two girls are whisked by their father from their English boarding school. Rumer Godden is a Roman Catholic convert. She has a copious output as a writer of children's books. She collaborated with Jon Godden in the autobiographical *Two under the Indian Sun* (1966).   [HB]

GOGARTY, OLIVER ST JOHN (1878–1957). Irish poet and raconteur, born in Dublin, Ireland, educated at Stonyhurst, Trinity College, Dublin, Oxford and Vienna. He became a distinguished surgeon. His limericks went the rounds orally and early established him as a notorious wit.

> There was a young man from St Johns
> Who wanted to Roger the swans.
> 'Oh no,' said the porter,
> 'Oblige with my daughter,
> But the birds are reserved for the dons.'

A characteristic jape was Gogarty's verse 'tribute' paid to Irish regiments returning to Dublin from the Boer War in 1900 and solemnly printed in the snobbish *Irish Society*. Initial letters of each line, read acrostically, ran, 'The whores will be busy'. Gogarty supported Sinn Fein, was devoted to Michael Collins and became a member of the first Free State Senate in 1922. Ironically this made him a target of the anti-treaty rebels and in 1923 he was seized by terrorists and escaped being shot only by feigning bowel trouble, diving into the Liffey and swimming to safety. A strong swimmer, he had already rescued men from drowning more than once. His courage, his skill as a surgeon, his wit, his knowledge of literature and his conversational brilliance made him not only a dominant Dublin personality familiar with men like Yeats and Moore, but also, in due course, a lion of London society and a successful writer and lecturer in the USA.

As a student he briefly shared accommodation with

James Joyce (q.v.) in the Martello Tower, but the friendship could not survive Joyce's caricature of him as Buck Mulligan in *Ulysses*. Gogarty tried his hand at drama. *A Serious Thing*, produced at the Abbey Theatre in 1919, ostensibly a play about the Roman occupation of the Holy Land, is a satire on British rule in Ireland. His poetry (see *Collected Poems*, 1952) is highly accomplished but it is now generally accepted that Yeats (q.v.) vastly overrated him in including seventeen of his poems in the *Oxford Book of Modern Verse*. His book of memoirs, *As I was going down Sackville Street* (1936), is a lively, spontaneous hotchpotch in which he 'never allows himself to be manacled by the tyranny of relevance' (Ulrick O'Connor, *Oliver St John Gogarty*, 1964). *Tumbling in the Hay* (1939) is of the same genre.   [HB]

GOLDING, WILLIAM (Gerald) (1911–). Novelist, born in Cornwall. He spent most of his childhood and boyhood at Marlborough where his family occupied a house on the green. Golding's father, Alec Golding, was a master at Marlborough Grammar School. 'Incarnate omniscience', Golding called him. 'I have never met anybody who could do so much, was interested in so much, and who knew so much.' But he eventually rejected his father's Wellsian rationalism as 'too neat and slick'. Two fragments of autobiography covering the early years ('Billy the Kid' and 'The Ladder and the Tree') were included in *The Hot Gates*, a collection of occasional pieces published in 1965. Golding was educated at 'a dame school', at the grammar school, and then at Brasenose College, Oxford, where he changed from science to English after two years and took his BA in 1935. He 'wasted the next four years' as writer, actor and producer for small theatrical companies, but in 1939 he was appointed English master at Bishop Wordsworth's School, Salisbury, and in the same year he married Ann Brookfield by whom he has one son and one daughter. After service in the Royal Navy from 1940 to 1945 he took up his post again at Bishop Wordsworth's School until literary success enabled him to become a full-time writer in 1961. ('To go on being a schoolmaster so that I should have time to write novels was a tactic I employed in the struggle of life.') He was Visiting Professor at Hollins College, Virginia, USA, from 1961 to 1962.

In a lecture called 'Fable' (included in *The Hot Gates*) which Golding delivered first in California in 1962 and repeated at various American universities, he revealed how the war transformed him into a moralist. 'Before the second world war I believed in the perfectibility of social man; that a correct structure of society would produce goodwill; and that therefore you could remove all social ills by a reorganization of society.' After the war he realized 'that man was sick – not exceptional man, but average man'. Accepting now that 'man is a fallen being . . . gripped by original sin' he embarked on his first and most celebrated novel, *Lord of the Flies** (1954), and his subsequent work has revolved around the theological truism that man's 'nature is sinful and his state perilous'. Anticipating odium, he proclaims himself frankly a 'fabulist' and a 'moralist'. In *Lord of the Flies* he reverses the conventional tale of boys marooned on an island and putting up a good show. 'I decided to take the literary convention of boys on an island, only make them real boys instead of paper cutouts with no life in them: and try to show how the shape of the society they evolved would be conditioned by their diseased, their·fallen nature.' In fact they regress to savagery. They 'try to construct a civilization on the island; but it breaks down in blood and terror because the boys are suffering from the terrible disease of being human'.

The inevitable exclusion of the adult world (not to mention the female sex) from *Lord of the Flies* proved helpful to a writer whose strength lies neither in intellectually active dialogue nor in subtle analysis of sophisticated persons and their relationships. Golding's strength lies rather in the metaphorical resources and imaginative power brought into play for detailed amplification of moral tensions and elaboration of physical background. These gifts were tested again to the maximum in *The Inheritors* (1955), Golding's second novel, where the trappings of civilization and the mentality of rational maturity are once more stripped away, this time to present a Neanderthal family living in harmony in the closing days of their era. They are defeated and supplanted by more 'advanced' and therefore supposedly 'superior' representatives of homo sapiens, but the inheritors, our progenitors, take over with demonic savagery. Golding's ingenuity in representing the utterance and thought patterns of prehistoric man makes the book a tour de force, and incidentally it brings to fruition an interest in archaeological digging nourished in Golding's Wessex boyhood and delightfully recorded in the essay 'Digging for Pictures' (*The Hot Gates*).

Pincher Martin* (1956) is concerned with the fate of a lost soul, allegorized in the figure of Christopher Martin who clings to the imaginary 'rock' of self-centredness and rejects God. If Martin is a mock-up Prometheus, Sammy Mountjoy, the artist-hero of *Free Fall* (1960), Golding's next study in human disintegration, is ironically matched with Dante in pursuit of a Beatrice he destroys. In this case Golding juggles with chronology in presentation (so that, for instance, seminal events of Sammy's childhood are late revealed) but the tale is told in Sammy's own words as he seeks in middle life to track down his fall from grace. The girl he seduced and forsook in young manhood, Beatrice Ifor ('She was simple and loving and generous and humble'), is insane at the end, paying the price not only of Sammy's deficiency in 'vital morality' ('the forge in which all change, all value, all life is beaten into good or bad shape'), but also of the defective education that moulded him. *The Spire* (1965) brings this group of studies in dynamic human wilfulness to a climax with the story of Jocelin, dean of a cathedral, whose obsessive determination to erect a spire against all laws of architectural soundness partakes somewhat of saintly unworldliness and all-conquering faith, but much more of selfish readiness to ride roughshod over all personal and religious interests that conflict with his private passion. The medieval setting makes the recourse to imagery of angel and devil in conflict for Jocelin's soul appropriate and effective. The derivation of events from the extraordinary history of the spire at Salisbury cathedral adds authenticity. The symbolism and the careful analysis of Jocelin's spiritual condition are rooted in a living Christian tradition, and the moral over-simplifications of *Free Fall* are avoided.

The Pyramid (1967), with its picture of boyhood in pre-war England, has a more personal flavour. *Darkness Visible* (1979), a study of evil, traces the career of Matty, a child mutilated in the London blitz and suffering permanent psychological damage, and that of Sophy, a child deserted by her mother, and an amoral psychopath. Frank Tuohy (q.v.) notes 'the menacing system of correspondences and meanings which underpins the book' and commends it for 'an intensity of vision without parallel in contemporary writing'. *Rites of Passage* (1980) again breaks new ground. Set on board ship bound for Australia in Napoleonic days (the title refers to the ceremony of crossing the Line), it counterpoints the experience of two passengers, a young man of means, Edmund Talbot, en route for a post under a governor, and a poor parson, Robert Colley, both of whom keep journals. Social, moral and sexual parallels and contrasts undergird a work of neat historical reconstruction.

It may be argued that Golding carves out his moral and structural patterns too mechanically, that he tends to protract the central, developmental section of his plots tediously, delaying the predictable dénouement by undue prolongation of anticipatory suspense, and that he looks at women from the outside only. But he is an artist who experiments boldly with substance and style, sets himself formidable tasks, and never forfeits the thoughtful reader's respect.

Lord of the Flies is a fable based on Ballantyne's *The Coral Island*. Golding inverts Ballantyne's pattern, in which three English boys, Ralph, Jack and Peterkin, are wrecked on an island in the South Seas and survive by their pluck and resourcefulness. Golding's parallel trio, Ralph, Jack and Piggy (aged about 13), are surrounded by a crowd of largely younger boys: they have all been ejected from a shot-down aeroplane on to a tropical island in a future world war. At first the older boys attempt to organize social life and plan sensibly for possible rescue under the leadership of Ralph. Assemblies are held, a code of rules is agreed, and the decision is made to keep a fire continuously burning so that its smoke can mark their presence. But such intentions – the remnants of civilized order and adult wisdom – are eroded in a regress to savagery that is initiated by Jack. A Christ-figure, the younger boy Simon, is killed sacrificially in the excitement of a mock pig-hunt; Piggy, short-sighted but brainy, is more intentionally dispatched in the struggle for power; and Ralph, the ousted leader and representative of reason, is himself being hunted to death by all the others by the time rescue arrives. 'By the end he has come to understand the fallen nature of man', Golding has explained (*The Hot Gates*). The use of symbols strengthens the artistic coherence of what is a forceful statement about boyhood and about human nature.

Pincher Martin, issued in New York as *The Two Deaths of Christopher Martin*, is a study of moral damnation. As the book opens, Christopher Martin (Lieutenant RNVR) is rolling in mid-Atlantic, having been blown off the bridge of his destroyer in a wartime torpedo attack. Eventually he clings to a rock, climbs on to it and, to all appearances, makes a long, heroic, superhuman effort at survival there against appalling physical difficulties. In his own mind he becomes Ajax and Prometheus in one. But it is revealed at the end that the whole effort at self-rescue was a vision compressed into the drowning man's last moments. The accompanying mental flashbacks over a lifetime of evident greed and selfishness that earned him his nickname 'Pincher' provide an unnerving ironic commentary. The imagined 'heroisms' on the rock reflect the habit of self-glorification in a man who has climbed in life 'over the bodies of used and defeated people', who could dramatize any situation in his own favour, and who was in fact arranging his rival's death at the moment when the torpedo struck. The struggle for survival is an assertion of independent identity in the face of God, and the climax makes concrete Martin's rejection of God ('I spit on your compassion! . . . I shit on your heaven!'). 'Just to be Pincher is Purgatory', Golding has himself explained; 'to be Pincher for eternity is hell.'   [HB]

GORDIMER, NADINE (1923–). Novelist and short-story writer, born in Springs, near Johannesburg, South Africa. In 1949 she married G. Gavron, and in 1954 Reinhold Cassirer. Although a frequent visitor abroad, she has chosen to live and work in South Africa, despite her hatred of apartheid. Her fiction has chronicled, very substantially, the damaging effects of oppressive racial laws upon the human potential of white South Africans, while making very clear the brutal burdens that black people bear. Her first volume of short stories, *Face to Face* (Johannesburg, 1949), appeared the year after the Afrikaner Nationalist government assumed power, and each succeeding book has reflected the hardening grip of racist legislation upon every aspect of South African life. Each has also taken the pulse of white liberal, and more radical, sentiment, and, as Ursula Edmands has pointed out, the mood has changed from muted hope for the future in her first novel, *The Lying Days* (1953), to the near-despair of *The Late Bourgeois World* (1966); and, one might add, the poised resolutions, appropriate to time and situation, in *The Conservationist* (1974) and *Burger's Daughter* (1979).

A Guest of Honour (1971), the only novel so far that she has not set in South Africa, is the fulcrum of her writing career. The events take place in a newly independent black African state, and concern an Englishman's breaking out of his lifelong liberalism and learning how to know reality and himself afresh; it can also be read as a speculative raid into the area of possible options for white South Africans when black majority rule comes about. The apparently senseless death of the central character, James Bray, has led some commentators to interpret the theme of the novel as the futility of action, thus overlooking the importance of Bray's liberating decisions and actions, both political and private. Not only does Bray discard ideals which he has always tried to live with integrity, but he has the courage and vitality to do so after middle age and in response to a new understanding of the realities of a neo-colonialist situation. Moreover, he is seen to do so with the same inner integrity that has always informed his actions – no mere bending to a tide but the result of feeling and intelligence working together. When Nadine Gordimer returns to a South African setting in *The Conservationist*, it is a new beginning in her fiction.

While her novels and many of her short stories report

sensitively and with chilling accuracy upon South African economic, social and political divisions and tensions, they are seldom overtly political. She has said that her interest in politics has arisen from her concern for individuals and for personal relationships. But because racial politics in South Africa affect every individual and every personal relationship, her major preoccupation has inevitably drawn her to the larger implications, and these she has faced honestly, clinically, logically, satirically, but above all compassionately. In her early work (the stories in *The Soft Voice of the Serpent*, 1953, and the novel *The Lying Days*) this very interest in the interior lives of her characters was chiefly responsible for over-attention to detail, a use sometimes of simile and metaphor for their own sakes, creating distraction in the stories, showing fleshy substitute for solid bone structure in the novel. In the stories of *Six Feet of the Country* (1956) and of *Friday's Footprint* (1960) this weakness, though rarer, still occurs. But she begins to overcome it in her second and third novels, *A World of Strangers* (1958) and *Occasion for Loving* (1963), through a more subtle use of the tensions between individual and society as a sustained structural framework. *A World of Strangers* is largely analytical, but without being comprehensive, because the central character, working temporarily in South Africa, returns to England, when he finds it impossible to keep a foot in both black and white South Africa and remain uninvolved. *Occasion for Loving* deals with a white liberal, Jessie Stilwell, whose personal inclinations are all for withdrawal into herself, of escape even from the demands of her eldest child's love. Against her will, she becomes involved, in a protective role, in the love affair between a white woman and a black man. It is Gordimer's first large-scale attempt to integrate personal dilemmas with a panoramic view of South Africa's social problems; despite some unnecessarily discursive passages, the novel is a valid fictive statement on the insidiousness of racism, which prevents whites, however hard they try, from treating a black man 'like any other man', for the simple reason that the black 'isn't a man, won't be, can't be, until he's free'.

The last fuzz of superfluous detail disappears in *The Late Bourgeois World* (1967), the most economical of the novels. In the form of Liz van der Sandt's interior monologue on the day she learns of her former husband Max's suicide, it reviews their life together and their attempts to make common cause with African political movements. Max had rejected his family's wealth and attitudes, Liz the world of her father's shoddy little small-town shop, yet these backgrounds rise up and destroy their marriage: Max's upbringing has dulled him to others' true needs and ultimately robbed him of his self-respect, while Liz's has made her expect from him an impossible embodiment of 'Truth and Beauty'. Yet Max loses everything 'in his attempts to love', and however much Liz may speak in the accents of despair, the novel ends with her contemplating a fringe renewal of political activity and perhaps a sexual relationship across the colour-line which might even be called love, based simply on what each has and can give to the other.

The writing of *A Guest of Honour* had a technically liberating effect on Nadine Gordimer that is revealed by even the most cursory reading of *The Conversationist* and *Burger's Daughter*. There is a breaking away from traditional novelistic procedures, an exhilarating taking of risks that have been skilfully gauged and carried through with, in the best sense, a fine professionalism: the abrupt shifts in time sequence, the sudden changes from first-person monologue to third-person narration and back, the leap-frogging of actual and imagined conversations, the modulations from realism to a tentative, suggestive symbolism. These devices come into play to set up, beyond the narrative level, an intricate structure of meaning which becomes a devastating (though in *The Conservationist* entirely implicit, in *Burger's Daughter* subtle and complex) analysis and commentary upon white South Africa, yet Gordimer does not abandon the accustomed use of detailed observation to give actuality. This new technical versatility makes great demands on the reader too; some reviewers of *The Conservationist* failed to see that the incident involving Mehring and a young woman near the end doesn't describe his death but is a confused amalgam of reality, revulsion, fantasy and sheer panic existing only in Mehring's mind. In the final two pages we learn that this hysteria has driven him to flee the country. *The Conservationist* explores the inner life of an outwardly healthy, confident, successful capitalist, able only to use other people or look for his reflection in them, but incapable of any reciprocal relationship. What leads to his moral collapse is the obsession he develops with the body of a black victim of murder which the police have perfunctorily buried where they found it on Mehring's hobby farm or, as he would have it, private conservation area. Nadine Gordimer's return to South African themes is accompanied by a new historical sense, which ironically expresses itself in the final, solemn planting by black farm-labourers of the unknown black man's remains in the white landowner's soil, an oblique symbolism of both dispossession and re-possession. So unobtrusive is this symbolism, however, that the partly decomposed corpse washed up by flood water perhaps also figures Mehring's unwitting discovery of his own unsightly, real self.

Against a background of events from Treason Trials to post-Soweto-1976, *Burger's Daughter* focuses on the opposite end of the political spectrum. Rosa Burger is the .daughter of courageous, noble-minded Marxists of Afrikaner origin who both die in South African prisons. That she has been entirely moulded by their attitudes and assumptions and has an identity only as her father's daughter is the particular burden she is shown to free herself from. It is a stumbling, painful, wandering process she undergoes from the first shock of realizing on her father's death that relief and sorrow were the same thing for her, and the narrative techniques tax the reader's concentration severely, but legitimately, in order to follow Rosa's need to remove the laminated layers of her parents' influences and arrive at her own, experienced grasp of being a person in her own right and adjusting the precarious balance between that and a truly committed sense of social responsibility. It involves rejecting emotionally, at great nervous and mental cost, the entire ambience of her growing up, and finding her way afresh into her own kind of social commitment. Though she reflects: 'I don't know the ideology: / It's about suffering. / How to end suffering. / And it ends in suffering', her final position, like her parents', leads her too into a South African prison.

Though not as compelling a novel as its predecessor, *July's People* (1981) marks a further development in Gordimer's determination to press harder upon her readers' imaginations. In the enormous uncertainties that follow upon some future civil upheaval, a 'decent' white liberal couple and their black servant July gradually find not only that their psychological roles are becoming reversed but that all the comfortable assumptions on which their former lives and relationships had been based were in fact falsified by the apartheid political, social and economic system. The image-laden language of intense, because unfamiliar, experience reveals pain, bewilderment, fear, as the three major characters learn new disconcerting truths about themselves and their past lives. If there seems to be no political or even personal certainty, that is because the readers are being asked, whatever their convictions, to confront the unthinkable, for the sake of a wiser apprehension of their present condition.

It is Nadine Gordimer's aseptic understanding of the corrosive effects of a system which cripples humanity that gives her writing its strength and originality. Moreover, she knows herself to be, though protesting, a part of that system and each of her novels has been also an attempt to record its blight upon herself. Warmth and feeling are very deliberately controlled, but the impact of her writings would be impossible without them. More readily discernible in the short stories, from *The Soft Voice of the Serpent* right through to *Not for Publication* (1965), *Livingstone's Companions* (1972) and *A Soldier's Embrace* (1980), unromantic warmth and feeling are at the heart of her work; they are responsible for her ability to touch our sense of the tragic pity of human life arrested, distorted or destroyed by an infamous political dispensation.

In 1961 she won the W.H. Smith Award, in 1969 the Thomas Pringle Award, in 1972 the James Tait Black Memorial Prize and in 1975 the Booker Prize. [AR]

GOSSE, EDMUND (Sir) (1849–1928). Critic, born in London. He became librarian to the House of Lords in 1904, exercised enormous influence in the world of letters and published numerous critical and biographical works, including books on Browning, Donne, Jeremy Taylor, Coventry Patmore, Sir Thomas Browne and Swinburne. But his most popular book is *Father and Son* (1907), a record of his remarkable upbringing. Gosse's father, Philip Gosse, a distinguished zoologist, was a member of the Plymouth Brethren, an exclusive sect which imposed inflexible prohibitions on secular interests. Philip Gosse's *Omphalos* (1857) had defended the cosmogony of Genesis and the doctrine of the 'fixity of species'. *Father and Son* traces the tragic dilemma of the son in fashioning his inner life for himself in the face of the strange puritanical tyranny. [HB]

GRAHAM, W. S. (William Sydney) (1918–). Poet, born on Clydeside, Scotland, educated at Greenock High School and Newbattle Abbey College for adult education. He has lived mostly in Cornwall since 1943. He is plainly a gifted virtuoso with words and equally plainly has not come to rest with a verbal method that can guarantee lucid communicability. His early volumes, *Cage Without Grievance* (1942), *The Seven Journeys* (1943) and *The White Threshold* (1949), are cluttered with indigestible imagery in the manner of Dylan Thomas, though the austere voice of a persona struggling towards self-realization begins to be heard in *The White Threshold*.

> Since all my steps taken
> Are audience of my last
> With hobnail on Ben Narnain
> Or mind on the word's crest
> I'll walk the kyleside shingle
> With scarcely a hark back
> To the step dying from my heel
> Or the creak of the rucksack.

The Nightfishing (1955), a long poem in seven sections, centring on a night fishing for herring, has a surer lyrical and rhythmic appeal than most of the work in previous volumes. There is a strong autobiographical thread running through the poem. Over against the shifting background of the 'forming and breaking sea', the poet pursues his search for self-definition and self-recognition.

> Within all the dead of
> All my life I hear
> My name spoken out
> On the break of the surf.

Malcolm Mooney's Land (1970), a poem in five sections, covering five days during which Malcolm is frozen up, refines a sparse and cultivatedly awkward mode of utterance that is aptly suited to Graham's continuing and unassuming confrontation with the mystery of words and the mystery of things. Yet this volume and the subsequent *Implements in their Places* (1977) provoke the question how far Graham's self-conscious obsession with poetry about poetry hinders him in awaking a felt response even to his own isolation. See also *Collected Poems* (1979). [HB]

GRAHAME, KENNETH (1859–1932). Children's writer, born in Edinburgh, Lothian, Scotland. He lost his mother when he was 5 and was brought up in England by his grandmother. He rose from being a clerk in the Bank of England to the position of secretary. His early books, *Golden Age* (1895) and *Dream Days* (1898), overturn the nineteenth-century child cult and show children coolly summing up the inhibiting adult world of 'Olympians'. The books establish the stereoscopic technique in which 'the child's-eye view is given fresh depth and solidity by the adult commentator' (Peter Green, *Kenneth Grahame*, 1959). Grahame's celebrated tale *The Wind in the Willows* (1908) grew from bedtime stories told to his son Alastair, who was to die tragically in 1920 by what was perhaps self-inflicted decapitation on a railway line. Its setting is an idealized river bank where the Good Life is lived by a harmonious community of Rat, Mole, Badger, Otter and the like, who neither marry nor work but tramp around, eat meals and mess about with boats. The black sheep is Toad, a conceited, thriftless, irresponsible fellow corrupted by modern gadgets. In the capture of Toad Hall by the Wildwooders (stoats, ferrets, weasels etc.) and the subsequent ousting of the invaders a parable of social conflict is implicit. Many of Toad's adventures parody those of Ulysses. [HB]

GRAVES, ROBERT (1895–). Poet, born in London, the son of Alfred Percival Graves, a well-known Irish poet whose father had been Bishop of Limerick. A.P. Graves was the author of 'Father O'Flynn' and many other songs fitted to Irish folk tunes and published by Charles Villiers Stanford. Graves justly lamented that whereas songs to Moore's words had become known as Moore's, his own name was lost from his work. A.P. Graves was left a widower and 'my mother married my father largely, it seems, to help him out with his five motherless children', Robert wrote. The second wife, Robert's mother, was German, her family that of von Ranke, the historian. The 'von' on Robert's birth certificate ('Robert von Ranke Graves') was to be an embarrassment to him in prewar schooldays. A.P.'s own mother was Scottish; the English strain in Robert was therefore hard to find. He was educated at prep schools and at Charterhouse. His entry to Oxford was delayed for five years by the First World War, which scarred him for life. Memory of those who died about him, guilt at his own survival, nightmare symbolism and delirious imagery linger for a lifetime in his poetry from the encounter with front-line terror and bestiality.

Superficially Graves exorcized the demon in his autobiography, *Goodbye to All That* (1929). It traces his childhood, makes much of his misery as a sensitive boy among philistines at Charterhouse, but is very largely concerned with the war. Graves enlisted in the Royal Welch Fusiliers in August 1914 and was soon out in France in the Béthune area. He had had five months in the trenches when he met Siegfried Sassoon (q.v.) on the same front in November 1915, and the important friendship began in a sharing of poetic interests. After a period at base Graves rejoined his battalion at the front in March 1916 and he was gravely wounded in the Somme offensive in July. Indeed his death was officially reported and *The Times* printed an obituary. The latter part of the autobiography tells of his first marriage to Nancy Nicholson and early attempts to make good in the postwar literary world. It is the cool vividness with which action at the front is presented that makes the book an important document. The edgy Gravesian personality gives it tartness. Graves's father (A.P. Graves) thought it necessary to set the record straight in the last chapter of his own reminiscences, *To Return to All That* (1931): 'Robert Graves' – 'In writing of him I must point out that there is much in his autobiography that I do not accept as accurate'. Looking back on the book twenty-eight years later, Graves himself noted its climactic significance as marking the point when, Byronically, he shook the dust of England from his feet and went to settle in Majorca with Laura Riding, the poet. 'It was my bitter leave-taking of England where I had recently broken a good many conventions; quarrelled with, or been disowned by, most of my friends; been grilled by the police on a suspicion of attempted murder; and ceased to care what anyone thought of me' (Prologue to 1957 edition).

For the rest of his life Graves lived by writing. Poetry was his main concern and he was enabled to make it so by

the success of his historical novels, notably *I, Claudius* and *Claudius the God* (1934), a lively reconstruction of events in first-century imperial Rome through the mouth of Claudius, who was Emperor from AD 41 to AD 54. Graves traces the story of intrigue at the top through the reigns of Claudius's predecessors, Augustus, Tiberius and Caligula, and, in the second novel, deals with events in Claudius's own reign, including his military campaign in Britain. Dialogue is updated in idiom. Characterization is generalized and psychological investigation does not go deep, but the books are alive with busy, gossipy narrative of public and private affairs, and spiced with the debaucheries of Augustus's daughter, Julia, and Claudius's notorious wife, Messalina. A shadow of fatality is thrown over the action by the divine curse on the destroyers of Carthage voiced by the Sibyl at Cumae in the opening chapter. Among other historical novels *Count Belisarius* (1938) takes us to the Byzantine age of the Emperor Justinian, and *Sergeant Lamb of the Ninth* (1940) with its sequel, *Proceed, Sergeant Lamb* (1941), to the eighteenth century and the American War of Independence. *Wife to Mr Milton* (1943) tells Marie Powell's story in her own words. Of Graves's non-fictional prose, which includes biography (*Lawrence and the Arabs*, 1927) and criticism, the most significant work is his mythographical study, *The White Goddess* (1948). He called it a 'historical grammar of poetic myth', but it is indeed the credo of a twentieth-century poet, shut off from bardic status, who resolves his private uncertainties by rehabilitating the Muse. Loss of the matriarchal ideal, with which she is identified, is equated with the rise of arid intellectualism and the decline of poetry. The book is packed with lore and fascinating in argument. *Greek Myths* (1955), originally published in two volumes, is a product of the same scholarship.

Graves's poetic output began with *Over the Brazier* (1916) and in the next few years the annual volumes issued included *The Pier-Glass* (1921) and *Whipperginny* (1923). Graves's later practice was intermittently to publish *Collected Poems*, fastidiously removing verses which no longer satisfied him and revising those he included. Such are the collected editions of 1948, 1959 and 1965. To these he added *Poems 1965–1968* (1968), *Poems 1968–1970* (1970), *Poems 1970–1972* (1972), *Collected Poems 1975* (1975), marking his 80th birthday, and *New Collected Poems* (1977). 'I write poems for poets. . . . For people in general I write prose. . . . To write poems for other than poets is wasteful', he wrote in the Foreword to *Poems 1938–1945* (1945). It was in character to speak as a man unconcerned to win sympathy, and he passed devastating judgements on many contemporary poets in *The Crowning Privilege* (1955). As a poet Graves belongs to no group. Using traditional verse forms, he voices the tensions of the inner life, sometimes wryly, sometimes heart-rendingly, with a metaphorical notation that makes him something of a twentieth-century metaphysical:

> Is there no life, nothing but the thin shadow
> And blank foreboding, never a wainscot rat
> Rasping a crust?

('The Pier-Glass')

The public scene does not intrude, but private knowledge

of incongruities and inconsequentialities is effectively universalized:

Time and Space
Do but amuse us with their rough-house turn,
Their hard head-on collision in the tunnel.

('Midway')

Graves's sharp sense of the physical world is one anchorage and his recurring exploration of love is another. 'Poetry is the profession of private truth, supported by craftsmanship in the use of words', he maintained (*Poetic Craft and Principle*, 1967), and steadily constructed a lifelong poetic self-study from aggregative lyric fragmentation. Quality of technique and integrity of statement are sustained at a level which the 'minor' poet cannot usually match; yet there is an unaccountable dearth of the compulsive memorability that gives decisive status to a handful of poems by many a lesser practitioner. Graves was Professor of Poetry at Oxford from 1961 to 1966. See also his *On Poetry: Collected Talks and Essays* (1969) and Paul O'Prey, ed., *In Broken Images: Selected Letters of Robert Graves, 1914–1946* (1982). [HB]

GREEN, HENRY (pseudonym of Henry Vincent Yorke) (1905–73). Novelist. He spent his early childhood in Gloucestershire at the family home, Forthampton Court, within sight of Tewkesbury Abbey. He was educated at a private school in Kent and at Eton ('It was a humane concentration camp'). The First World War intruded upon a life of hunting and pheasant-shooting when Forthampton Court became a convalescent home for officers resting en route again for the front and death. There was therefore early experience of an odd human environment touched by the 'imminence of death'. At Oxford Green read English. He also completed his first novel, *Blindness* (1929). It is the inner story of John Haye, who has to reconcile himself to a life of blindness as a result of an accident at the age of 17. It has been noted that Green's university education left little mark on his work. Certainly he has nothing to say overtly on the religious, philosophical, aesthetic or political level. 'There is not in his work a single 'thinking' character who can come to terms with life through his intellect as well as through blood, bones, and nerves', writes F.R. Karl (*A Reader's Guide to the Contemporary English Novel*, 1961). But the experienced contrasts of social extremes in ways of living and thinking sank deep. From Oxford he went to work in his father's factory at Birmingham, living in lodgings, doing a forty-eight-hour week, moving in turn through the stores, the pattern department, the iron-foundry, the brass-foundry and coppersmithery. He found time also to support Aston Villa, attend the cinema, drink, and write nightly and at weekends. Work became a personal passion: work (or its absence) became a crucial theme in his novels.

Living (1929) is a study of men at work at a Birmingham factory: its polarities are masters and men on the one hand, youth and age on the other. The owning family directs the firm largely from London, though young Dupret, the heir, occasionally steps out of his cocooned existence to intrude disastrously into the alien world of human action and real 'living'. Mr Craigan, an ageing moulder, a skilled, old-fashioned craftsman and a bachelor, is firm in affection, in prejudice and in authority in the home. His family is an acquired one – widower Joe Gates, a substitute son, and young Lily Gates, a loved substitute granddaughter for whose future happiness, as wife to trustworthy Jim Dale, he schemes with pathetic ineffectiveness, since she falls in love with the showier but spineless Bert Jones. The frustrated elopement (the couple get as far as Liverpool) mingles pathos and high comedy piquantly. In this book Green's terse, laconic style has sometimes an awkwardness that is absent from later books. There is a forced air of strain about the sub-Joycean indirection in thought-infused narrative.

Green married the Hon. Mary Adelaide Biddulph in 1929. His career thereafter seems improbably 'conservative' for a novelist whose poetic qualities matured rapidly and whose awareness of modern civilization was a deeply disturbed one. He became Managing Director of H. Pontifex & Co., manufacturing engineers for the food trade, and was for a time chairman of the British Chemical Plant Manufacturers' Association. With the approach of the Second World War he realized that a birthdate that had saved him from the previous war made him ripe for its successor; he wrote an 'interim autobiography', *Pack My Bag, A Self-Portrait* (1940), out of anxiety 'to put down what comes to mind before one is killed, and surely it would be asking much to pretend one had a chance to live'. It is a hasty, perhaps premature record of 'how one changed from boy to man'.

Green has extraordinary versatility in coverage of the social scene and in tone of presentation. *Party Going* (1939), the product of eight years' work, takes us to Victoria Station, London, on an evening when dense fog has brought the railways to a halt. A party of young society people, bound for France on the boat train at the expense of their wealthy and therefore much cultivated young host, Max Adey, gather for a frustrating wait spent largely in the station hotel. From here they can overlook the seething mass of delayed commuters below who are prevented by steel doors from seeking refreshment and rest inside the hotel. The potential threat this mass represents to the class to which the blasé, self-indulgent, leisured young people belong is faintly hinted at. The book is essentially a social comedy at the expense of aimless competitive sex-play and group-chatter. Age, illness and loneliness are uncomfortably present in eccentric Miss Fellowes, an aunt of one of the girls, who tenderly picks up a dead pigeon, washes it in the ladies' lavatory and ties it up in a brown paper parcel. However, the shell of youthful selfishness is not cracked by such human need, which, like the crowds on the station, offers a threat to routine composure. When Julia Wray sees Miss Fellowes's exhaustion 'she heard the authentic threatening knock of doom she listened for so much when things were not going right'. Most of the numerous young people are in fact immensely dislikeable. The complex pattern of their individual self-adjustments in a web of selfish cross-purposes and subtle misjudgements is skilfully controlled in an ever-moving arabesque reminiscent of Ronald Firbank. Green's next novel, *Caught* (1943), was the product of his war duties in the Auxiliary Fire Service. Its central figure, Richard Roe, is himself an auxiliary fireman and is damaged by a bomb. *Loving* (1945) takes us to an Irish castle in wartime; it is the servants below stairs whose occupation is 'loving' – as it was the workers in *Living* who did the 'living'. The dominant figure is the self-important butler, Raunce.

Back (1946) has been described as 'probably the finest English novel about the return to civilian life of a war-veteran' (Edward Stokes, *The Novels of Henry Green*, 1959). Charley Summers comes home with an artificial leg and torn nerves. He is obsessed with the memory of his prewar mistress, Rose, who has died while he was abroad. It is revealed that Rose has an illegitimate half-sister, Nancy Whitmore. She resembles Rose so closely that Charley believes she is Rose herself, trying to escape her own past. The book makes a penetrating study of self-discovery, as Charley gradually comes face to face with the real Nancy, herself a young war-widow, and a woman of great warmth, straightforwardness and feminine protectiveness. Imagery of the 'rose' is symbolically exploited as appropriately as imagery of birds was in *Party Going*. *Back* has been called a modern *Romance of the Rose*. *Concluding** (1948) is perhaps the culminating achievement of Green's psychological penetration and his structural virtuosity. The two later novels, *Nothing* (1950) and *Doting* (1952), issued from Green's eventual decision that dialogue alone must be the dominant mode of communication between novelist and reader. The unrevealing realism of the dialogue and the elimination of commentary is debilitating in effect.

Concluding, a novel, takes us to an undated future and a state institution somewhere in England for training girls as civil servants. The institution is run by two spinsters, Miss Edge and Miss Baker, and occupies a fine estate and a former stately home in the country. There is no Orwellian agony or stridency in the cool picture of human nature withered by subjection to endless official rules and regulations, commissions and meetings, enquiries and reports. ('Everyone was frozen in the high summer of the State.') Repressed girls intrigue, conspire and plot, and two mysteriously disappear overnight, making the authorities terrified of outside investigation. A prevailing denial of sexuality symbolizes the dead hand of organized sterility. On the estate lives ageing Mr Rock, famous scientist, whose long-forgotten great discovery entitles him to continued tenancy of a cottage from which Misses Edge and Baker are desperate to evict him. A man rooted in the earth (a 'rock'), keeper of a pig, a goose and a cat, and bearing about him the authority of independent thought and enquiry, he symbolizes the lost individual culture now submerged under statism and bureaucracy. His 35-year-old daughter Elizabeth is uninhibitedly in love with the school economics tutor. At a time of anniversary celebration and also of crisis (caused by the missing pupils) what Miss Edge calls 'odious deviations from what is usual' are subterraneously at war with the brave new world. Green's remarkable capacity for manipulating interrelated motives and counter-motives, explicit and implicit, in telling situation and dialogue, produces brilliantly amusing conversational sparring.   [HB]

GREENE, (Henry) GRAHAM (1904–). Novelist and dramatist, born at Berkhamsted, Hertfordshire. His father, C.H. Greene, was headmaster of Berkhamsted School where Greene was educated. His childhood was not a happy one, but *The Lost Childhood and Other Essays*

(1951) records how Marjorie Bowen's novel *The Viper of Milan* determined his vocation to write when he was 14 years old ('Imitation after imitation of Miss Bowen's magnificent novel went into exercise books'). It also records how, after running away from school, he was sent to a psychoanalyst in order to be 'correctly orientated', and was thereby 'wrung dry . . . fixed in my boredom'. Greene read history at Balliol College, Oxford, and in 1925 produced a volume of verse, *Babbling April*. After Oxford he worked for a time as a journalist in Nottingham and it was here in 1926 that he was received into the Roman Catholic Church ('I had not been converted to a religious faith. I had been convinced in the probability of its creed', *Journey Without Maps*, 1936). He married Vivien Dayrell-Browning in 1927, having now joined the staff of *The Times*, and after the publication of his first novel, *The Man Within* in 1929, he turned to full-time writing. This book and its two successors had failed commercially and he was almost penniless when the success of *The Stamboul Train* (1932) turned the tide of his fortunes. It was the first of a series of books that he called 'entertainments' out of a desire to distinguish them from the more thoughtful 'novels'. *A Gun For Sale* (1936), *The Confidential Agent* (1939), *The Third Man* (1950) and *Our Man in Havana* (1958) come into this category of melodramatic thrillers. The last two provided scenarios of notable films.

It's a Battlefield (1934) was a more thoughtful work and it won praise from Ezra Pound and Ford Madox Ford (q.v.). An ironical picture of England in the mid-inter-war period of Ramsay MacDonald, trunk murders, communist meetings and upper-class sensitivity to the Red scare is sketched in bold strokes. At issue is the fate of Jim Drover, a London bus driver, a harmless man but a communist, who is condemned to death for killing a policeman. He did so impulsively in protecting his wife from a truncheon blow during a demonstration. A variety of worthy and worthless motives, political and personal, involve people at various levels in concern for the man's reprieve, and the situation enables Greene to explore the ramifications of injustice and its human cost with ironic power. The characters of Caroline Bury (modelled on Lady Ottoline Morrell) and more especially of Mr Surrogate (modelled on Middleton Murry (q.v.)) give some passages of the book a Huxleyan flavour. The next novel, *England Made Me* (1935), is one for which Greene has expressed a special affection. 'The subject – apart from the economic background of the thirties and that sense of capitalism staggering from crisis to crisis – was simple and unpolitical, a brother and sister in the confusion of incestuous love' (Author's Introduction to 1970 edition). The confusion concerns the twins, Kate and Anthony Farrant, 'continually on the edge of self-discovery', which they ward off self-protectively. They end by evading themselves and enter into superficial relationships with others.

*Brighton Rock** (1938) was the first of Greene's novels to make explicit his deep interest in the distinction between the Catholic ethic, rooted in the idea of grace and of dependence on the church's sacraments, and humanistic notions of right and wrong that lack spiritual dimension and supernatural orientation. So anxious is Greene to break down secular evaluations of human behaviour that he henceforward investigates the intrusion of divine love into lives far from heroic in the familiar sense and indeed infected with corruption. In *The Lost Childhood* he wrote, 'With the death of James the religious sense was lost to the English novel, and with the religious sense went the sense of the importance of the human act. It was as if the world of fiction had lost a dimension.' Greene has striven to restore that dimension. He lays bare the anguish and weakness of broken men and women on the edge of despair, but he restores to human experience the status of the contingent. The heart breaks under the eye of God: it is not just happiness but salvation that is at issue. Greene seeks signs of God's love and mercy where the sinful human heart is moved, even perversely, by selfless and compassionate impulses and he does not stop short of acts of 'love' that are sinful – for instance, adultery or altruistic suicide. In this way he arrives at a more refined implicit distinction than that between pagan and Catholic ethic; it is a distinction between formulated Catholic morality and the unknowable ways of God's mercy.

Journey Without Maps (1936) is a travel book, the fruit of a visit to Liberia which took Greene on foot into French Guinea. Later he visited Mexico (1938) in order to investigate and report on religious persecution there, and he wrote *The Lawless Roads* (1939) as a result, a travel book of special interest because it includes the story that is the basis of *The Power and the Glory** (1940), Greene's finest novel to that date, in which his formidable powers reach maturity. There is forceful economy in style, dramatic impact in presentation, artistic cunning in structure, and overbearing pressure of tension and atmosphere. Add to this the focusing of moral and spiritual universality upon a human dilemma of current civilizational moment, and Greene's outstanding pre-eminence as a writer is evident.

The same powers are at work in *The Heart of the Matter** (1948), a story set in West Africa where Greene had worked for the Foreign Office in 1941–3. This is the novel which best of all indicates the danger that Greene's doctrine of sanctified sin may topple over into moral anarchy. These two works represent Greene at his peak. The plot of *The End of the Affair* (1951) revolves around an adulterous affair between Bendix, a novelist, and Sarah, the wife of a civil servant. Seeing her lover knocked to the ground in a wartime air raid, Sarah bargains with God in sudden desperate prayer ('I'll give him up for ever, only let him be alive') and thereafter deserts her lover for God. *A Burnt-Out Case* (1961) is set at a leper hospital run by a Catholic community in the Belgian Congo. Querry, a world-renowned architect, has come to the end of the road in his work and in his relationships as a lover of women. He is burnt out, his natural manhood mutilated by success as the natives are mutilated by leprosy. He finds contentment in working at the hospital and atonement in being killed for an 'adultery' he has not committed.

Greene's plays, written when he 'needed a rest from novels', include *The Living Room* (1953), *The Potting Shed* (1958) and *The Complaisant Lover* (1959). His books for children include *The Little Fire Engine* (1950) and *The Little Steam Roller* (1953). There is an autobiography, *A Sort of Life* (1971). 'And if I were to choose an epitaph for all the novels I have written', the autobiography tells us, 'it would be from (Browning's) *Bishop Blougram's Apology*:

> Our interest's on the dangerous edge of things.
> The honest thief, the tender murderer,
> The superstitious atheist, demi-rep
> That loves and saves her soul in new French books –
> We watch while these in equilibrium keep
> The giddy line midway.

It also tells us how early failure taught him the crucial difference between discrimination in words and 'love of one's own words – that is a form of self-love which leads the young writer to the excesses of Charles Morgan and Lawrence Durrell'. The interest in 'innocent wickedness' and the passion for economy have persisted. *The Human Factor* (1978), a novel started in 1967 but put aside for ten years when Kim Philby published his memoirs, studies a Foreign Office double-agent who gets away to Moscow just in time and who has been seduced by decency and gratitude into treachery. And *Dr Fischer of Geneva* (1980), a little masterpiece of compression, tells of a Swiss multimillionaire and widower who revenges the failure of his marriage on the world's poor by giving parties at which expensive presents can be won by taking part in dangerously humiliating games. A second autobiographical volume, *Ways of Escape* (1980), brings Greene's personal story up to date.

Brighton Rock deals with gang warfare and protectionist rackets in Brighton. Charles Hale, a newspaper reporter, is murdered by a gang that is avenging the loss of its former leader and is now led by Pinkie, a ruthless, depraved boy of 17 for whom nothing has any savour unless he is doing someone down in taking it. A worthy but irreligious woman, Ida Arnold, big-breasted and big-hearted, interests herself stubbornly in getting justice done because she believes in 'fair play'. She represents the norm of healthy pagan decency. Pinkie marries Rose, a waitress, to prevent her from witnessing against him. The two are Roman Catholics, aware that their marriage at a registry office is no true union and that they are living in sin. For Pinkie 'the infliction of pain' is 'the finest of all sensations'; one murder leads to another; and his climactic depravity is a cunning attempt to murder Rose herself, who loves him deeply and loyally, by a fake suicide pact. Pinkie is a complex study: the psychological profile of delinquency is made up of a squalid home background that has identified sex with loveless routine, and a snubbed and stunted personality, socially and mentally 'trapped', that is hungry to prove itself in domination. At the same time the most sordid acts are negatively measured against ingrained Catholic presuppositions that give a spiritual dimension to the work.

The Power and the Glory has its setting in southern Mexico during the 1930s. Under the administration of President Calles in the 1920s there had been a bitter struggle between the state and the Roman Catholic Church and open persecution of the clergy. Greene visited Mexico in 1938 at a time when only some of the states had softened their official attitude. The novel is an account of a 'whisky priest' on the run, for whom escape into the next state would mean safety, but who is finally cornered and executed. The unnamed priest is counter-balanced by an unnamed lieutenant, representative of the persecuting state. Greene involves the two, hunter and hunted, in an elaborately designed end-game. The priest is a complex study in human weakness: he has a daughter, is given to the bottle, and has been vain and self-indulgent in enjoyment of priestly authority and petty influence; yet he can draw on reserves of strength. The strength lies in a fundamental capacity for self-knowledge, humility, compassion and trust in God. When the test comes, he puts priestly obedience (the call to absolve a dying man) before personal safety, and recrosses the state border to face certain arrest and death. Greene has managed to present an inner flowering of Christlike love and self-sacrifice which is free of the familiar trappings of heroism and respectability. Towards the end the priest is capable of a selfless prayer for his bastard daughter: 'O God, help her. Damn me, I deserve it, but let her live for ever.'

The Heart of the Matter is perhaps the author's finest study in the characteristic interwoven themes of love and despair, salvation and damnation. The setting is a West African port during the Second World War. Major Henry Scobie is Deputy Commissioner of Police and has been denied the promotion due to him. He is a Roman Catholic, an incorruptible officer and a man of compassion unable to see those he loves suffering. Solicitude for his wife, Louise, who does not fit in and is desperate for a passage to South Africa, leads him into unwise acceptance of a loan from a Syrian storekeeper, Yusef, who is involved in diamond smuggling. The act gradually enmeshes Scobie in corruption. When his wife has gone, he befriends a young widow, Helen Rolt, rescued from a torpedoed vessel. His compassionate concern involves him in a tender companionship and in adultery. When his wife returns he finds himself knotted in a web of falsehood through trying to shield her from knowledge that he believes would hurt her. His sympathy prevents him from breaking with either woman; yet he cannot be absolved in the confessional without promising amendment. Keeping the hurtful truth from Louise means taking communion in a state of sin. 'I offer up my damnation to you. Take it. Use it for them.' He carefully prepares suicide, considerately making it appear like death from a heart attack. He has chosen hell in order to remove the burden of himself from Helen, Louise and God alike. After it all comes out, the priest is not so sure that it is as simple as that. 'I think . . . he really loved God.' [HB]

GREENWOOD, WALTER (1903–74). Novelist, born in Salford, Lancashire. He left school at 13, having already worked part-time at delivering milk and news-papers and in a pawnbroker's shop. Later he worked as clerk, as stable groom for a cotton millionaire, as ware-houseman and as signwriter. He experienced unemploy-ment himself and *Love on the Dole* (1933), his first novel, is an authentic account of the personal realities of the 1930s' slump in the industrial north. Greenwood brings out the humiliations and tyrannies of poverty, the sheer damage it does to personal relations, how it disfigures and ages men and women, nullifies hope, rots the spirit and ultimately erodes moral integrity. Family life under the 'Means Test' is pictured with devastating accuracy,

and there is powerful pathos in the portraits of frustrated young lovers. The success of the book initiated a produc-tive career for Greenwood as a writer of novels, of which *His Worship the Mayor* (1934), a scathing picture of local corruption, is perhaps the next most effective. [HB]

GREGORY, LADY AUGUSTA (1852–1932). Drama-tist, born in County Galway, Ireland, into a Protestant family (Persse) of the Anglo-Irish landed gentry, and educated at home. At the age of 28 she married Sir William Gregory of Coole Park, 63 years old and a retired colonial governor. In widowhood, from 1892, she learned Irish, took up Irish folklore, translated ancient sagas and threw herself, with Yeats (q.v.) and Edward Martyn (q.v.), into founding the Irish National Theatre. The generosity of an Englishwoman, Miss A.E. Horniman, enabled them to convert the old Mechanics' Institute in Abbey Street, Dublin, into the Abbey Theatre, of which she, Yeats and Synge (q.v.) were the first directors. On the opening night, 27 December 1904, there were performances of Yeats's *On Baile's Strand* and Lady Gregory's one-act comedy, *Spreading the News*, an amusing little piece in which deafness, coincidence and peasant imaginativeness together manufacture from nothing a rumour of adultery and murder that sweeps through a country fair. Playlets such as this neatly display Irish antics in folky idiom ('Kiltartanese'). In *The Workhouse Ward* (prod 1908) two old paupers survive by virtue of hearty mutual hostility – perhaps a symbol of Ireland, Lady Gregory suggested: 'it is better to be quarrelling than lonesome'. One of her most popular one-acters has always been *The Rising of the Moon* (prod 1906) in which police are keeping watch at a seaport for an escaped political prisoner. There is a £100 reward for his capture; but when he does appear, the sergeant is alone and he is gradually cajoled into forfeiting the reward and helping the man to get away by sea. Lady Gregory was capable of profundity when she touched the nerve of Ireland's public and private grief. *The Gaol Gate* (prod 1906) is a miniature masterpiece, distilling ironic diversities of that grief into a brief interview between the mother and wife of a captured moonlighter and the gaol gatekeeper.

Of Lady Gregory's more ambitious historical efforts *The White Cockade* (prod 1905) goes back to James II hiding in a barrel after the Battle of the Boyne, and *Devorgilla* (prod 1907) to the one-time Queen of Breffny at Mellifont Abbey forty years after her adultery with Macmurrough of Leinster which led to the first English invasion of Ireland. The three-act play, *Grania* (see *Irish Folk-History Plays*, 1912), presents an Irish legendary love triangle similar to that of Synge's *Deirdre* in dialogue too stately to live. The short play was undoubtedly Lady Gregory's medium. 'The Abbey Theatre would have come to naught but for Lady Gregory's talent for rolling up little anecdotes into one-act plays', said George Moore (q.v.) (*Vale*). Lady Gregory was gracious hostess at Coole to many writers, including Shaw (q.v.) and O'Casey (q.v.). Yeats especially found peace and refreshment at Coole, which was his annual summer sanctuary. 'It was her sym-pathy and help that gave the poet to Ireland', O'Casey said. Thus the great paid their tribute to Coole, and now Lady Gregory's granddaughter Anne (the subject of Yeats's verses 'For Anne Gregory') has given us the child's angle on the great at Coole as she and her sister saw them. In *Me and Nu: Childhood at Coole* (1970) we see the little girls trying to discover whether Mr Yeats really does keep his pyjama trousers on under his day clothes, and responding with indignation when Shaw breaks Lady Gregory's wartime butter-or-jam-but-not-both regulation by buttering his slice, craftily turning it upside down on his plate, and then asking for the jam. See also Elizabeth Coxhead, ed., *Lady Gregory: Selected Plays* (1960), and Lady Gregory, *Our Irish Theatre* (1913).   [HB]

GRENFELL, JULIAN (1888–1915). Poet, son and heir of Lord Desborough. He joined the regular army after education at Eton and Oxford and died of wounds in France in May 1915. His poem 'Into Battle' was published on his death in *The Times*. This inspired poem made him a legendary embodiment of romantic gallantry. It speaks nobly of the fighting man's calling, his zest and his readiness in the face of destiny.   [HB]

GRIFFITHS, TREVOR (1935–). Playwright from Manchester, a former teacher and a committed Marxist. He was concerned in *Occupations* (prod 1970) with the dialectic of revolution and went back to a 1920 Fiat strike in Italy for his material. *Sam Sam* (prod 1972) looks at the effect of our capitalist-orientated educational system on the working class. In *The Party* (prod 1973, pubd 1974) a young radical-turned-prosperous-television-producer holds a night gathering at his home to listen to a fervent Trotskyist veteran. The time is May 1968 and background television shots of the Left Bank student riots in Paris provide an ironic commentary on an analysis of the relationship between Marxist rhetoric and action. *Comedians* (prod 1975) makes its point through a group of amateur stand-up comics who are training for professionaldom. Under audition, it is the chaps who pepper their turns with racist and sexist jokes who get the approval of the adjudicator. The theatrical establishment has no time for humour that might disturb social complacency. Griffiths's protests are as aridly conventionalized as his targets, but his theatrical ingenuity is considerable. [HB]

GRIGSON, GEOFFREY (1905–). Born and brought up in Cornwall. An Oxford graduate, he was a literary journalist during the inter-war years and in 1933 founded the magazine *New Verse*, which aggressively backed the Auden (q.v.) group and flayed the Sitwells (q.v.) ('The fun and slaughter now make me, if I recall them, rather sick', *The Crest on the Silver*). Himself an accomplished and entertaining minor poet (*Collected Poems*, 1963), Grigson became an indefatigable editor (over thirty titles) and his prose output (over forty titles) includes numerous critical and topographical books. His autobiography, *The Crest on the Silver* (1950), contains both an entrancing evocation of a Cornish childhood and some vivid vignettes of the London inter-war literary scene. The *Concise Encyclopaedia of Modern World Literature*, which Grigson edited (1963, revised 1970), is a readable and lively, if sometimes edgy and unbalanced survey. Grigson has continued to publish occasional volumes of verse like *The Fiesta* (1978) and *History of Him* (1980). The latter, if it contains outbursts of anger directed at the moralist, the bogus poet and the 'verse-reviewing squirt', also contains

poems of fresh but teasingly ambivalent celebration of the natural world, in which the visual effects are often sharp, yet unforced. *Twists of the Way* (1981) too has some barbed pieces, including studies of a dry-as-dust don and of a desiccated academic poet, 'Thin-White Recites Thin White Poems He Has Written':

> the poems
> He recites are so pleased with themselves,
> They are clapping themselves.

The Private Art: A Poetry Notebook (1982) is a commonplace-book. *Blessings, Kicks and Curses* (1982) is a collection of critical essays and reviews. *Collected Poems 1963–1980* (1982) complements the earlier collection (1963). Characteristics of Grigson's verse are his energy, his acerbity, and what Peter Scupham (q.v.) has called his 'singular conversational lyricism'.   [HB]

GROVE, F.P. (1879–1948). Canadian novelist and short-story writer, born Felix Paul Greve at Radomno on the Polish-Russian border. Recent researches suggest that his own account of his early life in the 'autobiography' *In Search of Myself* (1946) is romantic fiction. In 1881 his family moved to Hamburg and in 1898 Grove entered Bonn University. From 1902 he worked as a freelance writer and translator but emigrated to Canada about 1910 and in 1913 became (as F.P. Grove) a school-teacher there. The following year he married Tena Wiens (his second marriage) and began the hard struggle to become a successful writer, often depending upon his wife's earnings as a teacher. He was naturalized in 1921. His heavily realistic – and at times melodramatic – collections, *Over Prairie Trails* (1922) and *The Turn of the Year* (1923), were set in northern Manitoba where he and his wife had taught in 1917–18. *Settlers of the Marsh* (1925), the brooding and violent story of a young Swedish immigrant's emotional and psychic tensions, was banned for a time in Canada but *A Search for America* (1927), subtitled 'The Odyssey of an Immigrant', wove together romance and aspects of the accepted innocent immigrant myth and achieved considerable commercial success. In spite of ventures in publishing and farming Grove never attained the success he wished for. His fascination with evolutionary deterministic theories reached its clearest literary expression in the strangely allegorical novel *The Master of the Mill* (1938). *Consider Her Ways* (1947) is an absorbing Swiftian allegory of the ant world, based on the 'ant book' which he kept from 1933 on. Although Grove's autobiographical fictions have somewhat diminished his status as the well-born yet pioneering writer he claimed (and clearly longed) to be, he remains of importance for his use, albeit in a crude and repetitive manner, of the basic rural patterns of Canadian life for the exploration of spiritual values in the 1920s and 1930s.   [PQ]

GUNN, NEIL (1891–1973). Novelist, born in Latheron, Caithness, Scotland, son of a crofter-fisherman, educated locally and in Galloway. He became a civil servant and extended his knowledge of his native Scotland as an exciseman. In 1937 he resigned the service and settled in the Highlands to write. His first novel, *The Grey Coast* (1927), is set on the coast of the Moray Firth where crofters wrest a meagre living from the land and young fishermen, finding the days of the sailing-boat numbered, lose heart and emigrate to Canada. The human cost is studied in the story of orphaned Maggie Sutherland, niece of a miserly sailor-turned-crofter, whose heart is under desperate economic siege by a well-to-do crofter she cannot like. The book is intense at the personal level and searching in its social implications, but a happy ending is engineered.

Morning Tide (1931), technically a maturer book, takes us to a Caithness fishing village where a boy, Hugh, is involved in a spirited assertion of his personality within the remote community. In succeeding novels such as *Highland River* (1937), *Young Art and Old Hector* (1942) and *The Green Isle and the Great Deep* (1944) Gunn continues to give the infectious intensity of man's universal human pilgrimage to his studies of the lives of crofter-fishermen and the struggles of the young. *The Silver Darlings* (1941), set in the early nineteenth century, is a spacious and moving drama of crofters who have been evicted from the glens to make way for sheep. Settled along the north-east coast, they build up the new herring fishing industry, and their struggle against sea and plague has epic grandeur. The young hero's name, Finn, itself endows him with archetypal status. Gunn's characters are fervently alive, and his implicit protest against forces of dehumanization is counterbalanced by a strain of Celtic symbolism, for his mind is that of a poet. In later novels, such as *The Well at the World's End* (1951), there is a movement away from earthiness to mystical romanticism. Non-fiction works include *Whisky and Scotland: A Practical and Spiritual Survey* (1935) and *The Atom of Delight* (1956), an autobiography. [HB]

GUNN, THOM (1929–). Poet, born at Gravesend, Kent, educated at University College School, London, and – after National Service in the army from 1948 to 1950 – at Trinity College, Cambridge. He held a fellowship at Stanford University, California, for a time, and he taught English at Berkeley in the University of California from 1958 to 1966. He has settled in America. His published volumes include *Fighting Terms* (1954), *The Sense of Movement* (1957), *My Sad Captains* (1961), *Touch* (1967), *Moly* (1971) and *Jack Straw's Castle* (1976). *Poems 1950-1966* (1969) was his own selection. Gunn has described himself as one of the 'National Service generation', sharing some of its characteristics, 'i.e. lack of concern with religion, lack of class, a rather undirected impatience'. He came to the fore as one of the so-called 'Movement' poets represented by Robert Conquest's (q.v.) anthology, *New Lines* (1955). 'Movement' poetry is generally marked by neutrality of stance, abjuration of romantic flight, and intelligent incisiveness. But Gunn's early work earned him the label, 'Sartrean existentialist': it seemed to recommend energetic risk, choice and movement by which the individual can assert himself in an objectively 'valueless world'. Like the boys on motor-cycles in 'On the Move', men must 'dare a future from the taken route'.

> At worst, one is in motion; and at best,
> Reaching no absolute, in which to rest,
> One is always nearer by not keeping still.

Likewise in 'Claus von Stauffenberg' the Germans who devised the abortive 1944 bomb plot against Hitler 'chose the unknown, and the bounded terror, / As a corrective'. The admiration for toughness involves tension between meaning and the necessary devices of poetry; but Gunn's work also includes the calm personal self-scrutiny of 'Thoughts on Unpacking' and the moving reflections on Shelley's drowning in 'Lerici'.

The initial 'undirected impatience' achieves a sadly comprehensive articulation in 'Misanthropos' (from *Touch*). This sequence of poems presents the apparently sole survivor of an atomic war in Beckettian desolation. He runs fearfully into other survivors with whom communication has to be renewed and the cycle of human destiny begun again. In *The Passages of Joy* (1982) Gunn has completed his progress from well-fashioned stanzas to free verse and from identifying with the leather-jacketed motor-cycling brigade to frolicking 'hedonistically with acid-heads and newly liberated gays', as Ian Hamilton puts it, much of it 'done with the dizzy relish of one who has believed that he would never get to write about such things' (*Times Literary Supplement*, 23.7.82). See also *The Occasions of Poetry, Essays in Criticism and Autobiography* (1982). [HB]

GURNEY, IVOR (1890–1937). Poet and composer, born in Gloucester, the son of a tailor. He was educated at King's School, Gloucester, as a cathedral choirboy, and was a pupil of Sir Herbert Brewer, the cathedral organist, alongside one David Davies (who perhaps recalled his precocious fellow pupil subconsciously when he adopted the name 'Ivor Novello'). Gurney won a scholarship to the Royal College of Music. Sir Charles Stanford, whose pupils included Vaughan Williams and many other future composers of distinction, called Gurney potentially 'the biggest of them all'. But he was too erratic to be readily teachable. Gurney early began to set poems to music and five volumes of his songs have been published posthumously. He joined the army in 1915 and was in the forward area in France early in 1916. He was wounded in the arm in the Battle of the Somme in April 1917. Back at the front in time for the Passchendaele battle, he was gassed in August and sent back to 'Blighty'. In October 1918 he was discharged after a breakdown as a victim of 'shell-shock'. Though he returned to the Royal College in 1919 for a time, increasing mental instability took him back to Gloucester, where he worked variously as cinema pianist, labourer and clerk. By 1922 he was calling at the local police station every morning asking for a revolver so that he could shoot himself. He was certified, and spent the rest of his life in asylums, where some of his best poetry was written.

Gurney's first volume of verse, *Severn and Somme* (1917), sold well enough to go into a second edition. His second volume, *War's Embers*, came out in 1919. His third collection, called *Rewards of Wonder*, was turned down by the publishers. Edmund Blunden (q.v.) edited *Poems of Ivor Gurney* (1954) and prefixed a Memoir, but more manuscripts have come to light since that date, and P.J. Kavanagh has now edited *Collected Poems of Ivor Gurney* (1982) with a substantial Introduction and with Appendices.

As a poet Gurney never cultivated Georgian quietness

or mellifluousness. Traces of the influence of Housman (q.v.), Clare, Hopkins and, above all, Edward Thomas (q.v.) have been found in what Edmund Blunden called his 'search for the shrewdly different in phrasing and in metring'. He brought an unsparing personal intensity to bear upon what confronted him and wrestled with word and form to respond to it. Both in the poems celebrating Gloucestershire and in those portraying life at the front there is at once an emphasis on the particular and a totally unaffected way of transfiguring the scene in the light of a rarely intensified perception. P.J. Kavanagh has noted in Gurney's lyric poetry the absence (for the most part) of love poetry and of the intricacies of human relations. 'He is concerned with personal epiphanies, the sense of enlargement suddenly granted, say, by the silhouettes of certain trees in certain lights.' Edmund Blunden claimed that Gurney's war poems 'express part of the Western Front secret of fifty years ago with distinctive, intimate, and imaginative quickness'. The word 'secret' is telling. For the battlefield presents strange epiphanies. In 'First Time In' the captain leads his men for the first time from the billet up to the front. Forward progress through the battle-scarred landscape is detailed unsparingly till the area is reached where 'men are maimed and shot through', where 'iron and lead rain', where 'the stuff of tales is woven'. They enter a dug-out to join the 'heroes of the story', and:

> Never were quieter folk in tea party history,
> Never in 'Cranford', Trollope, even. And, as it
>   were, home
> Closed round us. They told us lore, how and when
>   did come
> Minnewerfers and grenades from over there east;
> The pleasant and unpleasant habits of the beast
> That crafted and tore Europe.

Knowledge of the poet's condition naturally renders some of the poems of protest and of suicidal despair intolerably painful. It also lifts them above the reach of criticism. Yet in confinement Gurney's mind continued to recapture the Gloucestershire days and the strange comradeship of the Western Front with an urgency that twists word and syntax to its will without ever forfeiting immediacy or naturalness. See also Gurney's *War Letters*, edited by R.K.R. Thornton (1982). [HB]

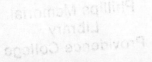

H

HALL, RADCLYFFE (1886–1943). Novelist, born in Bournemouth, Dorset. She began first to publish as a poet and then, more successfully, turned to fiction. After *The Forge* (1924) and *Adam's Breed* (1926) came the *The Well of Loneliness* (1928), the story of a woman, Stephen Gordon (so called because her parents had wanted a boy), whose lesbian nature, in spite of one fulfilling relationship, is a lifelong torment ('God's cruel: He let us get flawed in the making'), alienating her from her mother and turning her into an outsider. Deeply autobiographical in substance, the book is grossly over-written and steams with sentimentality, but it voiced a deeply felt demand for sympathy and understanding for the plight of sexual inverts. It caused a storm of protest and was banned. Radclyffe Hall's claim for open recognition of lesbian relationships, expressed aggressively in her behaviour as well as in her writing, made her a notorious figure on the inter-war literary scene. She had a thirty-year-long companionship with Una Lady Troubridge, an artist.   [HB]

HALL, RODNEY (1935–). Poet and novelist, born in England. He emigrated to Australia as a child and was educated at Brisbane Boys College. For ten years from 1957 he was a scriptwriter and actor with the Australian Broadcasting Corporation radio in Brisbane, and also film critic in 1966–7. Since 1967 he has been poetry editor of *The Australian* and now lives south of Sydney. He has published over ten books in all, including two novels, all of them marked by a restless questioning of accepted attitudes and an imaginative exploitation of varied technique. Early poetry included *Penniless till Doomsday* (1961) and *Forty Beads on a Hangman's Rope* (1963). *The Autobiography of a Gorgon* and *The Law of Karma* (both 1968) demonstrated an exacting use of language and an ability to draw upon historical and cross-cultural sources, the latter volume tracing the original soul as it 'degenerates from one stage of dehumanization to another, through eleven life cycles'. His first novel, *The Ship on the Coin*, 'a fable of the bourgeoisie', was published in 1973. Through dexterous handling of an allegorical story set in classical times but in contemporary terms, it sought to show that 'disastrous things and ridiculous things can happen' when the norms of power and profit go unquestioned. *A Place Among the People* (1975) was set in Brisbane of the 1950s and explored more fully personal and existential questions. *Selected Poems* (1975) also included an important section of new poems, 'The Owner of My Face'. Later poetry includes *Black Bagatelles* (1978).   [PQ]

HAMPTON, CHRISTOPHER (1946–). Dramatist, born in the Azores, educated at Lancing College, Sussex, and at Oxford, where his first play *When Did You Last See My Mother?* was produced (1966) while he was still an undergraduate. *The Philanthropist* (prod London, 1970; New York, 1971), a comedy, studies a bachelor don whose philological interests provide insulation and escape from human involvement. He proves too self-indulgently undemanding to throw off his emotional isolation. The verbal facility sharpens at times into wit as characters voice the anti-progressivism of post-protest disillusionment. Accounts of wholesale genocide of Brazilian Indians, and in particular a sensational case of slaughter in the early 1960s when the gathering of a tribe for an annual feast was made a convenient opportunity for a bloody bombing attack, stirred Hampton to research recent Brazilian political history for *Savages* (prod 1973). The play is an illuminating document with a solid protest content abut USA-supported dictatorship and the urban guerrilla movement; but the episodic construction – half-chronicle, half-collage – gives it minimal theatrical cohesion, and thrust derives from extra-theatrical commentary. *Treats* (1976), a slighter play, concerns a girl's oscillation between a considerate, easy-going lover and a more self-centred and violent one. [HB]

HANLEY, JAMES (1901–). Novelist and short-story writer, born in Dublin, Ireland. He went to sea in 1914 and served for ten years as a merchant seaman. He began to write in 1929, read widely, taking a special interest in Strindberg, and published *Drift*, his first novel, in 1930. Since then a steady output of novels and short stories numbers nearly forty titles, besides plays for theatre and television, critical works (*J.C. Powys*, 1969; *Herman Melville*, 1971) and an autobiography, *Broken Water* (1937). *Boy* (1932) is a turbulent, compassionate and tragic study of a 13-year-old Liverpool boy, Arthur Fearon. He escapes to sea as a stowaway and exchanges parental bludgeoning and slave labour in the docks as a boy-scavenger for the vice and cruelty of sea-mates, one of whom saddles him with an Alexandrian girl prostitute and with syphilis. This tense and gloomy book was followed by the first volume of what was to become a massive five-novel cycle – *The Furys* (1935), *The Secret Journey* (1936), *Our Time is Gone* (1940), *Winter Song* (1950) and *An End and a Beginning* (1958). The saga centres on Dennis Fury, a seaman, his wife Fanny, a towering study in womanhood, almost mythical in scope, and their son Peter, who has done fifteen years for murder by the time the last novel opens. Hanley, whom a reviewer has called 'an isolated giant of English literature', elicited high claims for his stature as a major novelist from writers as diverse as E.M. Forster (q.v.), Henry Green (q.v.), Herbert Read (q.v.), J.C. Powys (q.v.), W.H. Auden (q.v.) and C.P. Snow (q.v.). Certainly his most mature work, exemplified by *The Closed Harbour* (1952), is Conradian in intensity and profundity. It is a powerful study, taut and searching, in the disintegration and head-long plunge to insanity of a 50-year-old French captain of the merchant marine, Eugene Marius. Marius has lost his ticket and lies under a cloud because he (and only one other) survived the sinking of the ship he captained and in which his own nephew went down. In fact he killed his nephew by a blow struck in anger. Technically a fine seaman, personally he is broken in spirit, tormented by conscience, haunted by fabricated terrors. The strain is intensified by his mother's unyieldingly harsh judgement and the tacit condemnation of his sister's distress (the nephew was her son). Hanley's greatness can scarcely be in dispute. As recently as 1973, in *A Woman in the Sky*, he focused with characteristic intensity on the personal

tragedy of an old woman torn by bureaucracy from a happily shared terrace house and deposited alone in a high-rise block of flats. His latest novel, *A Kingdom* (1978), centres on the funeral of a Welsh village blacksmith, which brings his two daughters together at the old home for a touching rediscovery of the past. *The House in the Valley*, originally published in 1951 under the pseudonym 'Patrick Shone', has been reissued in the author's name as *Against the Stream* (1982). It is the story of a boy abandoned by his mother and bereft of his father during the Second World War, and his subsequent experience at the hands of maternal and paternal grandparents. [HB]

HARDY, THOMAS (1840–1928). Poet and novelist, born in a cottage at Higher Bockhampton, near Dorchester, Dorset.

> Our house stood quite alone . . . Snakes and efts
> Swarmed in the summer days, and nightly bats
> Would fly about our bedrooms,

he was to write in his earliest known poem, 'Domicilium'. Hardy's father was a stonemason and he played the fiddle. His mother had hopes of getting Thomas a place at Christ's Hospital, London, but in fact he was educated at the British School, Dorchester. At 16 he was apprenticed to John Hicks, a local ecclesiastical architect. Hardy studied assiduously and later spoke of these early Dorchester days as a time that saw 'the professional life, the scholar's life, and the rustic life, combined in the twenty-four hours of one day'. In 1862 Hardy moved to London to work as a Gothic draughtsman on church design and restoration in the office of Arthur Blomfield and he published a light satirical sketch, 'How I Built Myself a House', in *Chambers's Journal* for 18 March 1865. At this time Hardy studied modern languages at King's College, took an interest in contemporary literature, and was captured by the 'advanced' thought of John Stuart Mill, Darwin and Herbert Spencer. In 1867 he left London and went back to help John Hicks in Dorchester. A year later the manuscript of his first novel, *The Poor Man and the Lady* (unpublished), was on offer and in 1869 Meredith, as reader for Chapman and Hall, called Hardy for interview, not to accept the book, but to offer good advice. The years 1871 to 1895 saw the publication of the Wessex novels, which soon enabled Hardy to turn professional writer, to marry and eventually to settle in Dorchester at Max Gate, the house he had designed.

Jude the Obscure (1895), the last of the novels, aroused bitter controversy and hostility through its representation of the crushing of the human spirit by established social, religious and moral codes. Thereafter Hardy turned to the publication of poetry (he had long practised its composition). 'Perhaps I can express more fully in verse ideas and emotions which run counter to the inert crystallized opinion', he noted. Thus, while Hardy is a nineteenth-century novelist, whose fiction falls outside the scope of this *Guide*, he is a twentieth-century poet both by chronology and in spirit. The published volumes are: *Wessex Poems* (1898), *Poems of the Past and the Present* (1902), *Time's Laughingstocks* (1909), *Satires of Circumstance* (1914), *Moments of Vision* (1917), *Late Lyrics and Earlier* (1922), *Human Shows, Far Fantasies*

(1925) and *Winter Words* (1928). Hardy is twentieth-century in spirit in that the effects he seeks and the idiom he cultivates have little in common with the fastidious graces of Victorianism and Pre-Raphaelitism. His readiness, in pursuit of directness and authenticity, to run the risk of seeming prosaic or unpolished separates him from the Victorians. Nevertheless the architecture of his poems (there are nearly a thousand of them) is consciously 'Gothic' in the way it subsumes irregularity of metrical detail under a master plan of shape and stress. The consequent interplay of spontaneity with stanzaic design gives sturdiness and tension to a most individual utterance.

Hardy often versifies incidents and encounters in human relationships and shifts in personal attitude that sum up the oddity or contrariness of things. Life's ironies of coincidence and change call out the pessimist in him. The grey vein at its bitterest represents God ('By the Earth's Corpse') surveying the now cold globe after all the wrongs endured upon it and recovering the mood in which he overwhelmed it in the days of Noah:

> That I made Earth, and life, and man
> It still repenteth me.

The same vein runs through powerful poems of personal observation like 'The Darkling Thrush', characteristic in the sharp concreteness of the descriptive writing:

> The tangled bine-stems scored the sky
> Like strings of broken lyres -

and characteristic too in that the sudden burst of joyful song which lights up the winter landscape seems so little justified by what is evident on the terrestrial scene that the poet must assume the bird to have some reason for hope not disclosed to him. Hardy's directness of expression sometimes seems like a hard-won directness, but the sense of strain, awkward at times, makes for an awareness of thoughts and words grappled with and brought to book:

> We kissed at the barrier; and passing through
> She left me, and moment by moment got
> Smaller and smaller, until to my view
> She was but a spot.
> ('On the Departure Platform')

It was in 1870 that Hardy went for Hicks, the architect, on a professional visit to St Juliot, Cornwall, met the vicar's sister-in-law, Emma Gifford, and fell in love. (The first meeting is celebrated in 'When I set out for Lyonesse' and 'She opened the door'. See also Carl J. Weber, ed., *Dearest Emmie: Thomas Hardy's Letters to his First Wife*, 1963.) The couple were married in 1874 against the opposition of the socially superior Giffords. (Emma's father called Hardy a 'base churl'.) The story of the marriage relationship is one of deterioration, complicated by Emma's tendency to mental unbalance and by Hardy's growing fondness for London society, feminine especially. The warm friendship between Hardy and Florence Henniker, the writer, did not help. (See E. Hardy and F.B. Pinion, eds., *One Rare Fair Woman: Thomas Hardy's Letters to Florence Henniker 1893-1922*, 1972.) Nor later did the appearance in the Hardy household, in a secretarial capacity, of youthful Florence Dugdale, the

future second Mrs Hardy. Emma's death in 1912 thus put an end to a relationship whose early happiness had been darkened by division and bitterness. The shock of bereavement was deepened by perusal of autobiographical papers Emma left behind. Hardy destroyed the evidence of bitterness but preserved his wife's autobiographical sketch, now published as *Some Recollections* (1961). Hardy's remorseful reaction to the loss was deep and lasting, and his tangled feelings became vocal in some of his finest poems. (See Carl J. Weber, ed., *Hardy's Love Poems*, 1963.) Many of them combine a devastating honesty towards himself with poignant recollections of Emma's earlier days (like the famous 'Beeny Cliff'), or rueful memories of his later neglect of her and alienation from her (like 'Had You Wept', 'The Division', 'The Going' and 'Your Last Drive'). Speaking of some of these remarkable poems (the twenty-one 'Poems of 1912-13' in *Satires of Circumstance*) to A.C. Benson at Cambridge, Hardy said he had written some poems about his wife and was wondering about publication. He described them as 'very intimate . . . but the verses came . . . one looked back through the years and saw some pictures; a loss like that makes one's old brain vocal'. Indeed the poems give the reader an acute and intimate encounter with his sorrow and voice an astonishing resurgence of love:

> Woman much missed, how you call to me, call to
> me,
> Saying that now you are not as you were
> When you had changed from the one who was all
> to me,
> But as at first when our day was fair.
> ('The Voice')

The last major work, *The Dynasts**, published in three parts (1904, 1906 and 1908), a work totally different in scope and pretension, was a vast poetic enterprise for a man to undertake in his sixties, but Hardy's inspiration remained fruitful into his eighties.

The second Mrs Hardy (F.E. Hardy) published *The Early Life of Thomas Hardy* (1928) and *The Later Years of Thomas Hardy* (1930) from autobiographical material dictated by her husband. They have been issued in one volume as *The Life of Thomas Hardy* (1962). Harold Orel edited Hardy's *Personal Writings* (1966) and R.H. Taylor *The Personal Notebooks* (1978). R.L. Purdy and M. Millgate are now editing *The Collected Letters of Thomas Hardy*. Vols 1 (1978) and 2 (1980) cover the years to 1901. See also Robert Gittings, *Young Thomas Hardy* (1974) and *The Older Hardy* (1978).

The Dynasts, an epic-drama in three parts of the war with Napoleon, contains nineteen acts and 130 scenes, and the action covers the years 1805 to 1815, from the Napoleonic threat to invade Britain to the Battle of Waterloo. As early as 1875 Hardy was making notes on a possible 'Iliad of Europe from 1789 to 1815'. As he tells in his Preface to *The Dynasts*, his local knowledge of Weymouth (George III's summer watering-place during the Napoleonic War) and the southern coastal district that had been under threat of invasion combined with his interest in his kinsman Sir Thomas Hardy (in whose arms Nelson died) to fix his mind on the 'vast international tragedy' whose fringes he had touched in *The Trumpet Major*. Hardy imposes on the presentation of earthly history 'contrivances of the fancy' in the shape of phantasmal Intelligences (Spirit of the Pities, Spirits Sinister and Ironic, Chorus of the Pities, Chorus of the Years etc.) whose interspersed commentaries on human action provide a choric counterpoint of sombre necessitarian pessimism.

The vast cast, human and supernatural, runs into hundreds, but the work 'is intended simply for mental performance' and indeed the stage directions sweep over battlefields, cities, mountain ranges, countries and continents. The six acts of Part I include the Battle of Trafalgar and the Battle of Austerlitz and end with the death of Pitt. Part II sweeps from Jena and Tilsit to Wellington's Peninsular campaign and Sir John Moore's death at Coruna. Meanwhile one watches the developing rift between Napoleon and Josephine occasioned by Napoleon's desire for an heir. There are scenes at 'The Field of Wagram', 'The Field of Talavera', 'The Tuileries', 'Petersburg, The Palace of the Empress-Mother' and 'The Lines of Torres Vedras' interspersed with scenes in Brighton and London. The Archduchess Maria Louisa of Austria accepts Napoleon's offer of marriage in Act V and, as Empress, gives birth to his son in Act VI. The seven acts of Part III follow Napoleon to Moscow and back on his disastrous Russian campaign, deal with the exile to Elba, and bring the whole work to its culmination at Waterloo.

The human dialogue of the important characters is largely in blank verse, but Hardy resorts to prose for scenes involving peasants and common soldiers. The blank verse is often stilted and awkward in its strenuous seeking after dignity.

> Nought that we can scheme
> Will help us like their own stark sightlessness!

Napoleon avers. For the over-world scenes Hardy experiments with metrical and stanzaic variety, but often not felicitously. The reader is tempted to echo the Spirit of the Pities:

> This tale of Will
> And Life's impulsion by Incognizance
> I cannot take.

The dominant philosophical motif of the work (as well as its scenic character) may be glimpsed from the direction that closes the Battle of Austerlitz, when the scene suddenly 'becomes anatomized and the living masses of humanity transparent. The controlling Immanent Will appears therein, as a brain-like network of currents and ejections, twitching, interpenetrating, entangling, and thrusting hither and thither the human forms'.   [HB]

HARE, DAVID (1947-). Dramatist, born in St Leonard's-on-Sea, Sussex, and educated at Lancing College and at Cambridge. He began writing at a time when conventions of avant-garde theatre lured playwrights to indiscriminate parody and ridicule in the hope of being credited by reviewers with the dubious dignity of 'making a statement' about 'postwar society'. He believes that his plays should be puzzling, but the mixture of satirical realism, farce and fantasy smacks of disorientation. Thus Slag (prod 1970, pub 1971) has been said to make a comment about educational institutions. In

fact the all-female cast – Ann the headmistress, Elise her sexy assistant and Joanna the rebellious women's-libber – when they are not discussing coition, genitals and orgasms, are engaged in farcical knockabout. But at least Elise has the wit to observe: 'This is not the way women speak together, it's not the way they live. It doesn't ring true.' Later plays include The Great Exhibition (1972), about an MP who exposes himself on Clapham Common, Knuckle (prod 1974), a thriller that attacks the profit motive, Fanshen (prod 1975), a Brechtian documentary about the Chinese revolution, and A Map of the World (prod 1983), which fastens on a UNESCO conference on poverty to investigate world problems. Hare, gifted and cunning in the use of words, would seem to have the makings of a powerful dramatist if he could shake off stereotyped theatrical postures left over from the radicalism of the 1960s.   [HB]

HARRIS, FRANK (1856–1931). Journalist, born in Galway, Ireland, the son of a naval officer of Welsh birth. Sent to the Ruabon Grammar School in Wales, he ran away to America at the age of 15. A wild career included cattle-rustling, boot-blacking, hotel work, presence at the Battle of Plevna and study at Lawrence University, Heidelberg and Göttingen. Back in England in the 1880s he effected a meteoric rise in journalism and successively edited the Evening News, the Fortnightly, the Saturday Review and, later, various lesser journals. Wells (q.v.), Shaw (q.v.), Beerbohm (q.v.), Hardy (q.v.) and Kipling (q.v.) were among his contributors to the Saturday Review. To Wells he was the 'superlative example of the outside adventurer' (Vincent Brome, Frank Harris, 1959). Adept at getting himself sacked, he indulged in sharp practice financially, in orgies sexually, and certainly descended to crude blackmail. Yet his personal dynamism, panache and editorial flair gave him significance in the careers of several great writers. His melodramatic short stories (The Elder Conklin & Other Stories, 1894) won scarcely deserved critical acclaim from writers like Patmore and Meredith. His play, Mr and Mrs Daventry (1900), with a plot borrowed from Wilde, made money. His book, The Man Shakespeare (1909), is extravagant biographical criticism. His biography, Oscar Wilde: His Life and Confessions (1918), impressed the judicious. (Wilde's memory will have to stand or fall by it', Shaw said, op. cit.) His vast five-volume autobiography, My Life and Loves (1923-7), is a packed compendium of gossip, reflection and self-revelation whose reliability is questionable throughout. It won notoriety for its portraiture of the contemporary great and famous, and for its brash accounts of sexual gymnastics by a connoisseur of female genitalia.   [HB]

HARRIS, WILSON (1921-). Novelist, born in New Amsterdam, British Guiana (now Guyana). He went to school in Georgetown, Guyana, and began work as a government surveyor in the 1940s, becoming Senior Surveyor for the Government of British Guiana from 1955 to 1958. During this period two collections of his poems were published in Guyana, The Well and The Land (1952) and Eternity to Season (1954; reprinted London, 1978), both of which touch on themes that were to receive much fuller treatment in his novels. In 1958 Harris emigrated to

London, where he has lived ever since, apart from numerous visits, often as a writer-in-residence, to the United States, Canada, the Caribbean, Australia and various European countries.

Since 1960 Harris has published some of the most remarkable novels in English to have appeared since the end of the Second World War. The first four, known as the 'Guiana Quartet', are: Palace of the Peacock* (1960), The Far Journey of Oudin (1961), The Whole Armour (1962), The Secret Ladder (1963). They are set in the forests and on the rivers of the Guyanese interior, and are much concerned with themes relating to the racial and cultural constituents of life in Guyana, though always with a much wider significance for many contemporary human problems throughout the world. Harris's writings are highly original, unusually imaginative, intense attempts to break down and through the barriers within which individuals and communities isolate themselves from their fellows. By means of an extraordinary expansion of the artistic frontiers of the novel genre, Harris tries to bring to life, and to nurture, dimensions of the human imagination that have long lain dormant, in order to create a free, flexible, exploratory sensibility capable of sustaining individuality within communality and of converting communal exclusivenesses (which otherwise detonate distrust and hostility) into the more insightful, more supple imaginative creativity that humanity needs for survival in our times. In his own words, at a conference in Denmark in 1971: 'We need to re-think our biases if our concern is with the creation of the future as a capacity to sustain contrasting elements and talents in community'. Stasis he sees as a danger to the creative imagination, fluidity as the opportunity by which the imagination and the practical faculty can reach out to save mankind from cultural straitjacketings that can destroy not only man's imaginative life but his very existence too.

Each of his novels is a new attempt to embody this kind of vision, each continues where its predecessor stopped, though not as conventional sequels, since each takes off from, but also subsumes, what the others have achieved – yet each is an independent work in its own right. Since the first four novels, Harris has published: Heartland (1964), The Eye of the Scarecrow (1965), The Waiting Room (1967), Tumatumari (1968), Ascent to Omai (1970), Black Marsden (1972), Companions of the Day and Night (1974), Da Silva da Silva's Cultivated Wilderness and Genesis of the Clowns (in one volume, 1977), The Tree of the Sun (1978), and The Angel at the Gate (1982). Two volumes of stories have also assaulted the bounds of the imagination through adaptations and expansions of the fragmentary survivals of Carib and Arawak myths: The Sleepers of Roraima (1970) and The Age of the Rainmakers (1971). Explorations (1981), a selection of Harris's talks and lectures, augments in a non-fictional mode the reader's apprehension of Harris's concepts of history and art, and fiction in particular.

The nature of Wilson Harris's extraordinary imagination and of the colossal tasks he has set it, the urgency of his concern for the human condition in this century, and the complexity of his vision have impelled him to create an entirely new kind of fiction. Although his themes, settings and characters are rooted in the realities of human life and experience, the novels themselves cannot be described as 'realistic' in manner or form. The central character in Palace of the Peacock, for instance, is at times a fictional characterization of a man of our own times, at times a historical sixteenth-century person, at times the alter ego of the narrator, at times a projection of aspects of all the other characters in the novel, and, indeed, all of these things simultaneously. An added convolution derives from his name, John Donne. In the same novel, Harris's desire to destroy the fixity of implacable, inflexible and, therefore, dangerous modes of thought and feeling leads him to describe rock strata in the imagery of river currents, and currents of water in the imagery of geological strata – not merely to provide somersaults for agile minds but to induce new ways of thinking and experiencing. The reader who relies solely upon his rational faculty is soon lost in a Wilson Harris novel, unless he submits to the pull of its powerful undertow: he must throw away his old fictional maps, and with the unpredictable help he is given by the novelist must find a new route for himself that depends not on fixed landmarks but on the changing, shifting and challenging new relationships among them.

Harris is neither a 'popular' nor 'élitist' artist. Although he is not readily accessible to all readers, is in fact 'difficult' for most, the importance of what he has been attempting has begun to receive ever-increasing recognition. It is no accident that during the 1976–7 season he worked among the people of Salisbury at the St Edmund's Arts Centre as holder of the Southern Arts Writing Fellowship, a sign alike of the growing esteem in which he is held in Britain, and of his own willingness to keep in touch with people in living communities. Reviewing Companions of the Day and Night in The Financial Times (London) in 1975, M. Seymour-Smith wrote: 'It seems to me to be outstanding in the fiction of the past 25 years: Asturias obtained the Nobel Prize for writing just such strange works, and this was a just award. Harris is in such a class.'

Not only is Wilson Harris's art as a novelist original, revolutionary and excitingly exploratory, but its end is directly concerned with confronting many of the cultural and social problems that face modern man and his continued existence as a sentient and feeling creature. His writing forms an incalculable contribution to the literature of the Third World and to the growth and quality of the human creative imagination. Many readers do find Harris a 'difficult' writer, and there are two helpful books on him: Michael Gilkes, Wilson Harris and the Caribbean Novel (1975), and Hena Maes-Jelinek, Wilson Harris (Boston, 1982).

Palace of the Peacock remains the most appropriate of Harris's books for an entry into his complex, fluid imagination, even though it presents the reader with problems of understanding (though not necessarily of apprehension). Some of the characters recur in later novels, and in theme, technique and intention the subsequent books constitute an organic development from it. Though, like its successors, it is grounded, sometimes with great particularity of detail, upon reality, its aim is to undermine the accepted notions of literary realism. A modern journey up a Guyanese river re-enacts and re-interprets a historical one and both come together as a single spiritual quest. At the heart of the 'story' lies a commentary upon the Third World's experience of colonialism and of all the historical 'accidents' of history flowing from it, yet the novel offers itself as a demolition of categorical thinking (historical and otherwise), an attempt to recover for the human imagination a prerational mobility that has never wholly disappeared. Thus plot, setting, characterization shift kaleidoscopically under the reader's eye in an ever-questing movement of exploration. So much that is non-rational (but not irrational) can be puzzling, but it is exhilarating and enriching to cast one's preconceptions overboard and allow the work to sweep one into new insights.　　　[AR]

HARRISON, TONY (1937–). Poet, born in Leeds, and educated at Leeds Grammar School and at Leeds University. He has had university posts in Nigeria and Prague as well as at Newcastle. His translations for the stage include *The Misanthrope* (1973) and the libretto for Smetana's *The Bartered Bride* (1978). He now works for the Metropolitan Opera in New York. *The Loiners* (1970) (Loiners are citizens of Leeds), his first collection of verse, marked him as a poet capable of considerable metaphysical subtlety and also of earthy directness.'Thomas Campey and the Copernican System' is a richly textured portrait of a Leeds character who sells old books and clothes from a hand-cart. 'Allotments' gives blunt impressions of early days in wartime Leeds:

> The graveyards of Leeds 2
> Were hardly love-nests but they had to do –
> Through clammy mackintosh and winter vest
> And rumpled jumper for a touch of breast.

By contrast 'The Nuptial Torches' pictures the wedding night of Philip II of Spain, lit by the blazing bodies of heretics. It ends with a resonant instance of Harrison's power over words:

> *Come, Isabella, God is satisfied.*

Continuous (1982) includes a group of 'sonnets' (of sixteen lines on the model of Meredith's *Modern Love*) which constitute part of a work in progress started earlier in *The School of Eloquence* (1978). Harrison's most unforgettable poems here are those on his own family life. Direct and heartfelt, they reflect his attachment to his working-class background and lay bare the tangled emotions consequent upon being uprooted from it by his education. 'You weren't brought up to write such mucky books', his mother said of *The Loiners*. And 'Book Ends' tells how she used to mock the way he and his father sat in silence. '*You're like book-ends, the pair of you.*' Now, after her death:

> Back in our silences and sullen looks,
> for all the Scotch we drink, what's still between's
> not the thirty or so years, but books, books, books.

In this collection, indeed, there are poems like 'Long Distance I' and 'II' which catch aspects of his father's bereavement in vivid images and in an unfalteringly natural voice; and they have the searing yet controlled intensity of great peotry.　　　[HB]

HARTLEY, L.P. (Leslie Poles) (1895–1972). Novelist, born in Whittlesey, near Peterborough, Cambridgeshire. The family home was Fletton Tower. Hartley's father, a man of culture who called his son Leslie after Sir Leslie Stephen, was a solicitor by profession, but the family had an income from brick-making, as does the novelist-hero of Hartley's late novels, *The Brickfield* and *The Betrayal*. Hartley, who was to write subtly and deeply of the brother–sister relationship, had two sisters. He was educated at Harrow and he served in the Norfolk Regiment during the last two years of the First World War. Then he went to Balliol College, Oxford, to enjoy the social and academic pursuits of the soldiers-turned-students whom he later pictured so delightfully in *The Sixth Heaven*. Thereafter Hartley made writing his career, though for many years his output consisted mainly of reviews to be found in weekend journals like *Spectator* and *Time and Tide* and in Sunday newspapers. An early volume of short stories, *Night Fears and Other Stories*, appeared in 1924, and the following year saw the publication of Hartley's first novel, *Simonetta Perkins*, a light-hearted book that is reminiscent of Henry James both in its basic theme and in its cosmopolitan atmosphere. Lavinia Johnstone (Simonetta's real name), a respectable American girl from Boston, is visiting Venice with her mother and is temporarily infatuated by a handsome gondolier, Emilio. The gondolier presents a romantic contrast to the young American whom Lavinia's mother wishes her to marry.

It was not until 1944, when Hartley was nearing 50, that his substantial output as a novelist really began with the publication of *The Shrimp and the Anemone*. This study of childhood centres on a nervous little boy, Eustace, who is afflicted with what Hartley later called 'sisteritis' (*My Sisters' Keeper*, 1970). It is the first volume of the trilogy *Eustace and Hilda**, a work notable both for moving psychological analysis and for brilliant evocation of upper-middle-class life. Hartley's gift for delicate nuance, fastidious exactitude and velvet-gloved irony operates effectively on the inner life and on the social scene. Upper-class life in an Edwardian country house is re-created with enticing finesse in *The Go-Between* (1953). Leo Colston looks back fifty years on some hot summer days of 1900 when he was a boy of 13 and a guest of a rich school-friend's family, the Maudsleys, at Brandham Hall, Norfolk. Marian Maudsley, his friend's elder sister and a beautiful young woman he adores, is destined to marry Viscount Trimington, another object of the boy's idealistic hero-worship; but she is in love with a most ineligible local farmer, Ted Burgess. Young Leo is used as a messenger boy between the lovers for secret assignations, and is thereby gradually introduced to the facts of life. The culminating spectacle of the two lovers copulating on the ground administers a psychological shock that gives Leo a breakdown and causes a social furore that drives Burgess to suicide. The boy's response to adult whim, pretence or self-revelation is analysed with pathos and humour. The manner in which his innocence is abused raises the kind of moral issue which Hartley likes to entertain. The framing of the story in retrospect, between the middle-aged hero's browsing in his diary and final revisitation of the scene, recalls the structure of *Wuthering Heights*. (Emily Brontë was one of Hartley's favourite authors.) Harold Pinter worked on the script when the story was filmed. This book and the trilogy are Hartley's best-known works. In between them he published *The Boat* (1950), a comment on civilian life during the Second World War. The setting is a country village and the hero is a middle-aged writer frustrated in his symbolically individualistic desire to boat on the river, and living at loggerheads with the villagers.

Hartley averred that the novelist must create a world which the reader can live in, a world which 'must exist independently of the author's testimony, but not of his sensibility, not of his feeling for it, which must be as strong as, if not stronger than, the feeling he has for his own life. And to be that it must, in some degree, be an extension of his own life' (*The Novelist's Responsibility*, 1967). He confessed himself 'a moralist' (The novelist . . . must believe that *something matters*'), he was acutely conscious of the fading values of contemporary civilization, the advance of collectivism, and the devaluation of the individual. Thus *Facial Justice* (1960) has affinities with *Brave New World* and *1984* as in part a prophetic satire on a soulless future society that has abolished social injustice and irons out inequalities of individual intelligence or beauty. In pursuit of facial justice surgery appeases envy by 'beta-fying' girls with beautiful alpha-plus faces; but the heroine falls in love with an angel and discovers spiritual renewal. Two of the later novels, *The Brickfield* (1964) and *The Betrayal* (1966), form a single work of considerable power. In the former Richard Mardick, ageing bachelor novelist, opens his long-burdened heart to a young friend, Denys, to whom he is blindly devoted. The story he tells is of an idyllic and secret youthful first love for Lucy Soames which culminated in tragedy. Lucy apparently drowned herself under the false impression that she was pregnant. The idyll of Richard and Lucy has overtones of Meredith's *The Ordeal of Richard Feveral*. The burden of shame Richard carries into old age is rather the product of hyper-sensitivity and of lifelong concealment than of real guilt, but it enables Denys, in *The Betrayal*, to subject him to prolonged mental harrassment and blackmail. The mounting parasitical intrusion into Richard's heart and home culminates in a devastating persecution where everything conspires to present the victim as the villain. Ironic escalation of this paradox salts the final tragedy with Kafkaesque farcicality. As in all his best work Hartley brings careful symbolism and highly civilized verbal craftsmanship into play by focusing upon a sensitive soul whose intensified dilemmas have a universal relevance.

Eustace and Hilda is a trilogy of novels issued separately as *The Shrimp and the Anemone* (1944), *The Sixth Heaven* (1946) and *Eustace and Hilda* (1947). Eustace and Hilda, brother and sister, are the children of Alfred Charrington, a middle-class widower whose home at Anchorstone, a Norfolk seaside resort, is run by his late wife's sister. Hilda, four years older than Eustace, is a masterful, strong-willed child whose urge to dominate her brother has been given free play through Eustace's need of a substitute 'mother'. He is a nervous child with a weak heart. The first book opens with the symbolic

swallowing of a shrimp by an anemone, and the trilogy explores the developing relationship between brother and sister through childhood and into adulthood in terms of the inordinate emotional demand Hilda makes on Eustace, the complex network of real and imaginery obligations woven between them by her dominance and by his submissive ambition for her, and the havoc wrought on other potential relationships by the unbreakable childhood bonds of mutual dependence. In the first book Hilda's moral and emotional authority impels Eustace, unwillingly, to make himself pleasant to an old invalid, who thereupon cultivates him and then promptly dies, leaving him her fortune and delivering him into further permanent indebtedness to his sister.

The Sixth Heaven opens in Oxford in 1919. Eustace is now 23 and an undergraduate. While his younger sister, Barbara, a healthy specimen of uncomplicated normality, marries happily in integrated disregard of social ambition, Eustace's social predilections and personal needs involve him in relationships with the Anchorstone aristocracy. Hilda has sublimated her masterfulness in founding and running a clinic, thus making a name for herself. ('The clinic was an extension of Eustace.') Eustace is side-tracked into dancing attendance on a substitute Hilda, Lady Nelly Staveley, a society woman of Meridithean stamp. She takes him to Venice where much of the action of the third book, *Eustace and Hilda*, is placed. Hilda's excessive demandingness frightens off the Staveley heir who has been deeply attracted to her and whom Eustace would have her marry. The shock of rejection causes paralysis. Eustace, blackmailed by her suffering, comes home to tend her and propel her about in a bath chair. A shock he devises restores her; but he is worn out and dies himself. In presentation the devices of interior monologue and articulated day-dream (apprehensive or self-fulfilling) are employed sometimes with a Joycean blend of hyperbole, pathos and hilarity. Movement between reality and mental day-dream is neatly controlled.   [HB]

HEAD, BESSIE (1937–). Novelist, born in Pieter-maritzburg, South Africa. She worked as a teacher and a journalist until she went into exile in Botswana in the mid-1960s. She married Harold Head in 1961 and has one son. All three of her strange, ambiguous novels are set in Botswana. As narratives they seem to be about the inturned private problems of each of the central characters, but their power and originality lie in Bessie Head's creating in each a structure of political meaning discernible shadow-like below the surface story. Their themes are closely related and mutually illuminating, with emphasis upon the voluntary curbing of lusts which, if allowed full rein, bring disaster upon individual lives and radiate outwards destructively through communities. Individuals withdrawing into a cell of privacy do so in order to recuperate and then return to communal tasks with new vigour; hence the frequency of images of 'control' and 'imprisonment'.

In *When Rain Clouds Gather* (1968) a black South African political activist escapes into Botswana to find peace and reconstruct his own identity. Makhaya eventually joins with other characters, all markedly individualist, trying to re-make their lives in a physically inhospitable locale, where under the technical guidance of an English agricultural expert, himself a spiritual exile, they labour stoically to create a new self-sufficient rural economy for themselves and the villagers, despite the opposition of a self-indulgent chief and a self-seeking 'new' politician. Through the surface detail of mundane agricultural activities, the novelist projects an intense imaging of harsh, physical, co-operative creativity – no rural paradise but a tough, hugely demanding yet ultimately fulfilling enterprise. What the novel affirms is beneficent private austerity, the dissolving of selfish reserves in individual hearts, reverence for the lives of ordinary people. In the political kingdom of independent Africa the implications are clear.

Structurally, *Maru* (1971) is more adventurous and brings the private and political dimensions splendidly into correlation. Maru, a paramount chief-elect, and his close friend, Moleka, become bitter enemies for the love of a racially outcast, half-Bushman or Masarwa woman, Margaret. The end, related in the first few pages of the novel, shows Maru and Margaret married and living in distant, bleak country, after Maru's renouncing of political power. Though he manipulates others' lives to win Margaret, Maru knows that he, and not Moleka, has the strength to endure his people's contempt for having married an 'untouchable'. His abdication is not an evasion of responsibility, for his marriage also becomes a symbolic political act on behalf of the Masarwa people, even of all the outcast of mankind.

*A Question of Power** (1974) is the most ambitious and most disturbing of the novels. The central character's descent into mental illness enables the novelist to range over the worst obscenities of both the private imagination and many cultural polities and show them to be conjoined. One could describe the novels as religious and political, suggesting an ideal which demands that iron personal integrity should accompany all political action. In 1977 Bessie Head published a volume of short stories, *The Collector of Treasures. Serowe: Village of the Rain Wind* (1981) is a re-creation, partly from written sources, but mainly from almost 100 oral informants, of the history of the Bamangwato capital (in Botswana) and of the remarkable line of chiefs, beginning with Khama the Great, who ruled there from 1875 to 1959.

A Question of Power is one of a number of novels by African writers that in the 1970s provided disturbing critiques of various African political dispensations; the others are Soyinka's (q.v.) *Season of Anomy*, Armah's (q.v.) *Two Thousand Seasons*, Gordimer's (q.v.) *The Conservationist* and Ngugi's (q.v.) *Petals of Blood*. Elizabeth, the chief character in *A Question of Power*, is presented as descending into the ultimate form of alienation and exile, mental illness, and the process is recorded with a frightening vividness that might suggest it is autobiographical, but nowhere in this novel has Bessie Head slipped into confusing the identities of novelist and character. Elizabeth is a coloured South African in Botswana, working with other exiles in a remote village, helping the Batswana make the semi-desert fertile in a vegetable-growing co-operative. Ironically, while she is toiling her way on the land into acceptance by the Batswana, whenever she goes home at night she is over-

whelmed by hallucinations from her own sub-consciousness which take vivid cinematic shape before her. Two male figures, Sello and Dan, dominate her nightly terrors. Sello, a God of both Goodness and Viciousness, is nevertheless a projection of love as 'mutual feeding', while Dan is adept at 'the mechanics of power'. The illness provides its own cure when Elizabeth becomes conscious of her acceptance in the new community. Through the mental illness, the novelist establishes a necessary connection between lust for power over scapegoat-people and the lust for personal sexual licence: personal morality is firmly associated with political justice.   [AR]

HEANEY, SEAMUS (1939–). Poet, born in County Derry, Northern Ireland, brought up on a farm and educated at Queen's University, Belfast, where he later became Lecturer in English. He moved into the Irish Republic in 1972 and, after a period as a freelance writer, became Head of the English Department at Carysford College of Education, Dublin. *Eleven Poems* (1965) was followed by *Death of a Naturalist* (1966), poems whose scenes and people positively reek of Ireland. Heaney moulds phrases that are both precise and warmly evocative. Symbolic overtones enrich such direct and intimate pieces as the frequently quoted 'Digging', about the substitution of the poet's 'squat pen' for the father's and grandfather's spade ('a big coarse-grained navvy of a poem', he later called it), and 'Follower', about following father behind the horse-plough as a child:

> But today
> It is my father who keeps stumbling
> Behind me, and will not go away.

'Docker' is a forceful study of an Ulster Protestant dock labourer rich in its implications. In subsequent volumes Heaney continued to fashion terse phrases, heavy with meaning, charged with feeling, as in 'Elegy for a Still-born Child' from *Door into the Dark* (1969). 'The Peninsula' and 'Bogland', from the same collection, Heaney himself has said, 'by an act of attention, turn a landscape into an image and that image, in turn, has implications beyond the poem'.

> Every layer they strip
> Seems camped on before.
> The bogland might be Atlantic seepage,
> The wet centre is bottomless.

After *Wintering Out* (1972) came *North* (1975) which won the 1976 W.H. Smith Literary Award. 'His is the most striking talent to come out of Ireland since that of the late Patrick Kavanagh', Stephen Spender (q.v.) wrote in a review of it (*Sunday Telegraph*, 24.8.75). The style remains crystal-clear, the words are wiry with argument. In writing of urgent matters like the 'Troubles' (see 'Whatever You Say Say Nothing') Heaney has learned from the advice proffered him by Michael Laverty and versified in 'Fosterage': 'Don't have the veins bulging in your biro'. But the poetic vocation is no less demanding:

> It said, 'Lie down
> in the word-hoard, burrow
> the coil and gleam
> of your furrowed brain . . .'

In *Field Work* (1979) Heaney has pursued his self-excavation with a Yeatsian intensity and a testing connotative resonance to establish himself among the three or four most powerful speaking voices in contemporary poetry. Light has been shed on his work as a poet by his *Preoccupations, Selected Prose 1968–1978* (1980) which contains autobiographical sketches of childhood and youth as well as revealing critical essays:

I suppose the feminine element for me involves the matter of Ireland, and the masculine strain is drawn from the involvement with the English language. I began as a poet when my roots were crossed with my reading.

[HB]

HEARNE, JOHN (1926–). Jamaican novelist, born in Montreal, Quebec, Canada. He served in the RAF (1943–6) and graduated from the University of Edinburgh in 1949. A school-teacher in London and Jamaica from 1950 to 1959, he taught in the university at Kingston, Jamaica, from 1962 to 1967 and has been Director of the Creative Arts Centre there since 1968. Hearne has published six novels: *Voices under the Window* (1955), *Stranger at the Gate* (1956), *The Faces of Love* (1957; *The Eye of the Storm*, USA, 1958), *Autumn Equinox* (1959), *Land of the Living* (1961), *The Sure Salvation* (1981). He has also written plays and co-operated with John Morris (pseudonym of Morris Cargill) on two thrillers.

Hearne's fluent narratives of manly action prompted by generous impulses, which often bring disastrous consequences, exhibit a richly sensuous responsiveness to Caribbean landscape. Although political concepts form a background (communism in *Stranger at the Gate*), he concentrates on individuality, especially its development in relationships among professional or intellectual lovers. W. Cartey remarks that Hearne's 'superlatives of sensory reactions' can clutter his style but 'lend a . . . grand dimension to his work'. His finest novel, *Land of the Living*, achieves genuine tragedy within a vividly realized, rather than analysed, framework of politico-racial issues.

[AR]

HEATH-STUBBS, JOHN (1918–). Poet, born in London. He read English at Queen's College, Oxford, and has since been a schoolmaster and a lecturer at the College of St Mark and St John, London. He has also held visiting professorships in Egypt and the USA and was Gregory Fellow in Poetry at Leeds University from 1952 to 1955. *Selected Poems* (1965) garnered work from eight previous volumes, including *Wounded Thammuz* (1942), *The Divided Ways* (1947), *The Swarming of the Bees* (1950), *A Charm Against the Toothache* (1954) and *The Triumph of the Muse* (1958). Heath-Stubbs concedes modification in his later work of his early 'Neo-Romantic style of the 1940s'. In fact he is an extremely versatile craftsman, with a vast range of subject-matter and a mind enriched with erudition. His humour may be academic: it is none the less lively (see 'Use of Personal Pronouns: A Lesson in English Grammar'). The memorial poem to Sidney Keyes, 'The Divided Ways', and the religious poem, 'The Hill', represent his grander, graver manner. There are poems about Plato and Dionysius the

Areopagite, about Titus and Tiberius, about Tchaikovsky and Mozart, about the Parthenon and a pub at Notting Hill Gate. There is a hilariously wry self-portrait 'Epitaph' and a sturdy manifesto of poetic principle, 'Ars Poetica':

The words come to you from the commercial
districts:
From the shop-bench, and from working in the
fields;
But contrary to much of the practice of the age
There is something to be said for politely
requesting them
To wipe the mud off their boots
Before they tread on your carpet
(Supposing you own one).

The output as a whole is that of a well-stocked mind and a highly cultivated poetic sensitivity. Some of the writing in *The Watchman's Flute* (1978) shows how much Heath-Stubbs has learned from Auden (q.v.) about the mastery of metrically transfigured conversational prose. *Naming the Beasts* (1982) proves him again to be one of those poets whose store of wisdom and wit, as well as his verbal and imaginative resourcefulness, makes continuing productivity, even after a lifetime, richly worthwhile. [HB]

HEPPENSTALL, RAYNER (1911–81). Novelist, born in Huddersfield, West Yorkshire. He had a career as producer for the BBC. His early novel, *The Blaze of Noon* (1939), was a rather pretentious exercise in acclamation of Lawrentian values. Later novels, *The Connecting Door* (1962) and *The Woodshed* (1962), mark him as a fastidious recorder of impressions and recollections. The latter shows Harold Atha, a writer, revisiting his West Riding home area for his father's funeral and casting his mind back to earlier days. Portraiture and anecdote are vivid and piquant, but the whole lacks shape and thrust. *Two Moons* (1977) is an interesting experiment in juxtaposing private and publicized disasters respectively narrated on the left and right hand pages in parallel. [HB]

HERBERT, A.P. (Sir Alan Patrick) (1890–1971). Humorist in prose and verse, born in Surrey and educated at Winchester College and Oxford. He began to contribute to *Punch* in 1920, and in 1924 was made a member of the staff. He was Independent MP for Oxford University from 1935 until university seats were abolished in 1950. He took a special interest in the reform of the divorce law (see his novel, *Holy Deadlock*, 1934) and in the cause of authors' rights. His novel, *The Water Gipsies* (1930), is a light-hearted story of watermen and bargees, but the more satirical shafts here and in the high-spirited legal series, *Misleading Cases in the Common Law* (1927; 1930; 1933), are acute and purposeful. Herbert's output in both prose and verse was enormous and he drew enthusiastic praise from such writers as Barrie (q.v.), Wells (q.v.), Belloc (q.v.), Kipling (q.v.) and Bennett (q.v.). His technical fluency at light versification was a steady stand-by (see *A Book of Ballads; Being the Collected Light Verse of APH*, 1931; revised 1948). In prose his hilarious caricature of the social follies of the day made the regular epistolary outpourings of Topsy, the zestful Modern Woman, a great *Punch* attraction (see *The Topsy Omnibus*, 1949). Herbert also wrote for the stage and provided scripts for successful musical shows. See the autobiography, *A.P.H. His Life and Times* (1970).   [HB]

HERBERT, XAVIER (1901–). Novelist, born at Port Hedland, Western Australia. The family moved to Fremantle when he was about 12 and he received his early education there. In 1923 he moved to Melbourne where he worked for a time in pharmacy and as a medical student but three years later he struck out on a search for experience which took him to Sydney, Darwin, the Solomons and Fiji. In 1930 he sailed to England, hoping to make a living as a writer, and by the end of 1932 had written *Capricornia*, supported meantime by the woman he was later to marry. The book was not published until 1938, five years after this return to Australia, but was at once acclaimed as an outstanding and highly individual novel of epic scope. The work drew upon Herbert's experience of the wild Northern Territory and at one level is a scathing account of the destruction of the indigenous culture by the white man during a period from the 1880s to the 1930s; yet he himself has described the vast canvas as only 'background to a story of which the deep motive was the father–son relationship'. The power of the work undoubtedly derives from the strong sense of place and from the sheer creative force which informs the book, in which tragedy is both balanced and compounded by Herbert's wry humour. *Soldier's Women* (1961) again achieved part of its effect through inclusiveness, but here his sense of form and of control is surer. The novel is a moving exploration of the extremes of passion under wartime conditions. In 1963 he published *Disturbing Element*, an autobiographical work which provides an intriguing introduction to the man, though the practice of altering the names of places and people renders it of mixed autobiographical value. The publication in 1975 of *Poor Fellow My Country* brought Herbert renewed attention. Over 900,000 words in length, the book extends the interests and methods of *Capricornia* in its literal and spiritual charting of the writer's land. The period covered is from 1936 until 1942, with an epilogue which takes in Australia some thirty years later. Herbert's indignation and pessimism are clear, but so are the shortcomings of his method, with too much reliance placed upon the rather wooden hero Jeremy Delacy. Yet in spite of this, and of certain overbearing attitudes on the part of the author, in its sheer inventiveness, commitment and bulk the book is an important and unique vision of Australia's recent past from a point of view rooted in the present.   [PQ]

HEWITT, JOHN (1907–). Poet, born in Belfast, Northern Ireland. He retired in 1972 from a career in art gallery work, spent first in Belfast, then (from 1957) in Coventry. His *Collected Poems 1932–1967* (1968) is a delightful cluster of finely moulded verses, traditional in form, which includes nature lyrics deriving from his lifelong love of the Glens of Antrim. Always conscious of himself as 'an Irishman of Planter stock' –

> This is my home country. Later on
> perhaps I'll find this nation is my own
>   ('Conacre')

– Hewitt has written of the Irish question with quiet passion:

> This is our fate: eight hundred years' disaster,
> crazily tangled as the Book of Kells;
> the dream's distortion and the land's division,
> the midnight raiders and the prison cells.
>   ('An Irishman in Coventry')

In 'The Colony' he has drawn an implicit parallel between the situation in a remote Roman domain at the time of imperial decline and that of Ulster. Particularly distinctive and entertaining are Hewitt's wryly amusing poems of anecdotal portraiture drawn from Belfast family history ('My Grandmother's Garter', 'Eager Journey', 'A Victorian Steps Out', 'Betrayal' and 'No Second Troy'). In the later collection, *The Rain Dance* (1978), the Ulster voice remains sober, exact and modest:

> With what I made I have been satisfied
> as country joiner with a country cart.

Rites in Spring (1980) is a collection of autobiographical sonnets containing vivid memories of Belfast childhood and the Troubles. See also Alan Warner, ed., *The Selected John Hewitt* (1982).   [HB]

HIBBERD, JACK (1940–). Dramatist, born at Warracknabeal, Victoria, Australia, and educated at the Marist Brothers' College in Bendigo, where he grew up. He graduated in medicine from the University of Melbourne in 1964 and practised in the city until 1973. In 1970 he returned from a year in England to join the Australian Performing Group in Melbourne as writer and director and now writes for the theatre full-time. His first play, *White with Wire Wheels* (1970), deals corrosively with the obsessions of three young executives; its world view invites comparison with *The Front Room Boys* by Alex Buzo (q.v.). *Dimboola* (1974) broke very different ground while again reflecting his interest in local sub-culture and speech patterns; in the form of a country wedding breakfast, this ribald work involved extended audience participation (even in the breakfast) and became a great popular success. *A Stretch of the Imagination* (1973) was an extended monologue by one Monk O'Neil, 'a bizarre individual only too keen to declare and extemporize on his idiosyncrasies and obsessions in a comico-serious fashion'. Monk's rambling recollections of his past as death approaches create a powerful sense of human fragility and worth against a background of Australian landscape and legend. Hibberd's work is distinguished over all by an interest in 'imaginative structures' rather than 'naturalistic plays' ('psychological explanation . . . bores me to death') and unflinching dedication to the cause of truly popular theatre – 'a theatre for the populace that deals with legendary figures and events, perennial and idiosyncratic rituals, mythically implanted in the nation's consciousness'. *Three Popular Plays* (1976) well illustrates this approach.   [PQ]

HILL, GEOFFREY (1932–). Poet, born in Bromsgrove, Worcestershire, educated at Bromsgrove County High School and Keble College, Oxford, now Lecturer in English at Cambridge University. He has published judiciously. *For the Unfallen: Poems 1952–1958* (1959) contained poems that are strenuously disciplined in form and charged with meaning for readers who are prepared to dig out subtleties and brood on them. Painful uncertainties in the face of love and death, faith and suffering, are tortured into verse of matching exactingness. The celebrated poem 'Genesis' is a miracle of compression. It is in the first place an account of the six days of physical creation, catching the heave and shock and thrust of bursting natural life in imagery of rare power:

And where the streams were salt and full
The tough pig-headed salmon strove,
Curbing the ebb and the tide's pull,
To reach the steady hills above.

But it is also a record of the birth of cruelty and terror, the making of comforting myth and fantasy, and finally acceptance of inescapable suffering:

By blood we live, the hot, the cold,
To ravage and redeem the world:
There is no bloodless myth will hold.

Readily quotable early poems such as this – and 'God's Little Mountain' or 'The Bidden Guest' – give but a foretaste of the poet's later density. *King Log* (1968), more public in its interests – as the epigraph from Bacon indicates ('From moral virtue let us pass on to matter of power and commandment') – contains in 'Funeral Music' a sequence of ten sonnets on bloodshed in the Wars of the Roses, in which Hill attempts 'a florid grim music broken by grunts and shrieks'. A notable short poem puts Ovid in the Third Reich to observe that 'Innocence is no earthly weapon', and 'September Song', commemorating a 10-year-old concentration camp victim, cuts painfully near the bone. 'Annunciations', meditations on love, is taxingly tangled in its imagery, but yields a lot to patient exegesis. *Mercian Hymns* (1971), a sequence of prose poems centring on King Offa, which recalls the work of David Jones in its merging of past and present, is superficially more approachable:

King of the perennial holly-groves, the riven sandstone: overlord of the M5: architect of the history rampart and ditch, the citadel of Tamworth . . .

In *Tenebrae* (1978) Hill returns to the stricter forms of the earlier collections. It includes two sonnet sequences.

Critical opinion is now prepared to call Hill 'the outstanding poet of his generation'. Along with poets such as Basil Bunting (q.v.) and Roy Fisher (q.v.), he has appealed to a taste left unsatisfied by the narrowness and obviousness of the more readily assimilable post-'Movement' verse. Nevertheless, his scholarliness, his wide-ranging allusiveness, and his reliance on historical and literary figures for the seeds of composition limit his potential readership. Thus *The Mystery of the Charity of Charles Péguy* (1983), a long poem in sturdy pentameters and quatrains, builds its reflections around the aspirations and fate of Péguy, the patriotic French poet, ardent Catholic and socialist whose massive poetical works included *Le Mystère de la Charité de Jeanne d'Arc*, and who founded and edited the polemical topical review *Cahiers de la Quinzaine*. Péguy volunteered for service in 1914, refused a commission, and was killed in the battle of the Marne. [HB]

HILL, SUSAN (1942–). Novelist, born in Scarborough, North Yorkshire, and educated at King's College, London. She has carved out a distinctive place for herself in focusing insight and compassion on the tensions of daily living and relating. She presents her characters through snatches of terse dialogue that has an incantatory formal directness peculiarly effective in conveying stress and revealing the heart. *Gentleman and Ladies* (1968) studies the old. Ladies of Haverstock have their enclosed lives prised open by the arrival of a middle-aged bachelor. *A Change for the Better* (1969), set in a Scarborough-like resort, has balancing portraits of two women victims of domestic tyranny – Deirdre Fount, whose mother, Mrs Oddicott, is overbearingly possessive, interfering, all-consuming; and Flora Carpenter, whose husband, Major Bertram Carpenter, is disintegrating into senile tetchiness. The death of the two tyrants brings a change for the better. *I'm the King of the Castle* (1970) concentrates on the way a motherless boy torments a fatherless boy and drives him to suicide, and the unrelieved blackness and intensity are purchased at some cost in plausibility. *In the Springtime of the Year* (1974) is an intimately felt fictional record of a young wife coming to terms with the sudden death of her husband. Susan Hill concedes that she was 'heavily influenced' by William Trevor (q.v.) in her early career. In the collection of short stories *A Bit of Singing and Dancing* (1973) she exercises the same compulsion upon her readers as in the novels. [HB]

HILTON, JAMES (1900–54). Novelist and journalist from Lancashire. He made a hit with *Lost Horizon* (1933), a novel which takes us to Shangri La, a hidden Tibetan-style land where men live unageingly in tranquillity and contentment. His second great success, *Goodbye, Mr Chips* (1934), is a sentimental life-story of a master at a public school. Master and school epitomize their kind rosily. [HB]

HINE, DARYL (1936–). Poet, born in Barnaby, British Columbia, Canada. He graduated from McGill University, Montreal, Quebec, in 1958 before going on to further studies at the University of Chicago, Illinois. He left Canada in 1959 to live in Europe, mainly France, and returned to the University of Chicago in 1967 as Assistant Professor of English. He edited the magazine *Poetry* from 1968. *The Carnal and the Crane* (1957) illustrated his wide-ranging and at times calculatedly bizarre style and *The Devil's Picture Book* (1960) enlarged an already impressive command of poetic form. In this book, as in *The Wooden Horse* (1965) and *Minutes* (1968), his classical scholarship is applied to contemporary situations in poems which exploit the ironic juxtaposition of myth and mundane reality. *The Prince of Darkness and Co.* (1961) attempted a similar approach in the novel form, centring on literary eccentricity, but the book fails to bring alive the complex literary demands of the structure. *Polish Subtitles* (1962), 'Impressions from a Journey', was less ambitious, but successful as a perceptive and provoking travel book. In *The Homeric Hymns* (1972) his imaginative translations of what were originally oral works evidence an ideal fusion of his poetic and classical impulses. [PQ]

HOBSBAUM, PHILIP (1932–). Poet, born in London, educated at Belle Vue Grammar School, Bradford, and at Downing College, Cambridge, where the influence of F.R. Leavis (q.v.) was superimposed on his working-class radicalism. With Edward Lucie-Smith (q.v.) Hobsbaum founded the so-called 'Group' of the 1950s, bringing discussion-group techniques of candid mutual criticism to bear upon new work shared in poetry workshops. He and Lucie-Smith edited *A Group Anthology* in 1963. Hobsbaum became Lecturer in English at Queen's University, Belfast, in 1962 and moved to Glasgow University in 1966. His own poetry deflates the poet's persona: there is a characteristic transition from teaching 'a modest Irish miss' in a Donne seminar to seducing her on the floor in 'A Lesson in Love':

> Which is the truer? I, speaking of Donne,
> Calling the act a means and not an end,
> Or at your sweet pudenda, sleeking you down . . .

Undoctored experience is recorded with just such workaday deliberateness. Volumes of verse include *The Place's Fault* (1964), *In Retreat* (1966), *Coming Out Fighting* (1969) and *Women and Animals* (1972). See also his *Tradition and Experiment in English Poetry* (1978).
[HB]

HODGSON, RALPH (1871–1962). Poet, born at Darlington, County Durham. He was always secretive about his personal life, but L.A.G. Strong left a portrait of him as a man of personal charm yet having a streak of ferocity, fond of children, a connoisseur of boxing, a fancier of bull-terriers and an evader of fashionable literary cliques (*Green Memory*, 1961). He went to Japan in 1924 and taught English literature at the Imperial University, Sendai. In later days he was resident in the USA. He published three volumes of poetry: *The Lost Blackbird and Other Lines* (1907), *Poems* (1917) and *The Skylark and Other Poems* (1958); then *Collected Poems* (1961). The 1917 volume contained poems which anthologists have made known as widely as any written this century, notably 'Time, you old Gipsy Man', 'Stupidity Street', 'The Bells of Heaven', which neatly voices indignation against the treatment of circus animals, pit ponies and hunted hares, and 'The Bull', which surveys in compassionate retrospect the days of youth and leadership now departed from a deposed and dying bull. Hodgson's two dominant themes are celebration of beauty and innocence – especially as represented by birds – and a sense of the damage done by man to the natural world and its birds and beasts. 'The Song of Honour' is a sturdy paean of praise, a *benedicite* with something of the energy of Christopher Smart's 'Song to David'. 'Eve' is a strange, fairy-tale account of the Fall in jaunty rhythm. Hodgson's distinctive rhymes and rhythms are crucial to his gift for clinching experiences of intense delight with irresistible memorability, and for entering feelingly into the world of animal kind.
[HB]

HOLBROOK, DAVID (1923–). Poet, born in Norwich, Norfolk, educated at the City of Norwich School and at Downing College, Cambridge. He is married and has four children. He was a tank officer during the Second World War and took part in the invasion of Normandy, landing on D-Day 1944 and being wounded shortly afterwards.

There are vivid battle scenes in his novel about the landing, *Flesh Wounds* (1966). Holbrook's volumes of verse include *Imaginings* (1961), *Against Cruel Frost* (1963), *Object Relations* (1967) and *Old World, New World* (1969). *Selected Poems 1961–1978* (1980) makes a pleasingly observant and homely collection, for Holbrook's verse fastens on moments of day-to-day experience from which some meaningful moral insight, some extension of human sympathy, or some sense of the transcendent can be derived. Graceful verses, alive with magnanimity of spirit, record how he accompanies his wife in purchasing a maternity gown, watches his infant son trundling across the lawn on his tricycle, alarmingly traps his daughter's fingers in a door, or builds a bonfire on a frosty day when Benjamin Britten has died. Holbrook's rootedness in personal domesticities and country life is in tune with his one-man campaign for the dignity and depth inherent in the homely simplicities of life and under threat from the new media-induced barbarism of trendiness, permissiveness and mental servitude. The campaign began in the field of education in influential books like *English for Maturity* (1961), *English for the Rejected* (1964) and *Children's Writing* (1967), which encourage creativity and exploration in children, and was then forcefully directed at the intellectual agencies of moral and cultural decomposition in such books as *Sex and Dehumanization in Art, Thought, and Life in Our Time* (1972) and *The Pseudo-Revolution* (1972).
[HB]

HOLTBY, WINIFRED (1898–1935). Novelist, born at Rudston, East Yorkshire, and educated at Scarborough and Somerville College, Oxford. From 1916 to 1917 she did a year's nursing in a London nursing home where the actor Sir Herbert Beerbohm Tree died suddenly in her arms, and in 1918 she interrupted her Oxford studies to serve in the Women's Army Auxiliary Corps. An enthusiast for progressive social causes, Holtby put much of her literary energies into journalism and was for many years a director of *Time and Tide*. She published her first novel, *Anderby Wold*, which contains an interesting portrait of her father, in 1923. Subsequent novels include *The Land of Green Ginger* (1927), *Poor Caroline* (1931) and *Mandoa, Mandoa!* (1932), the last a satire on British imperalism and the product of a visit to South Africa. Scarlet fever in girlhood left Holtby a victim of Bright's Disease and she was dead by the time her most significant novel, *South Riding* (1936), came out. Influenced by her mother's experience as a county alderman, she set herself to portray life in south-east Yorkshire in such a way as to reflect the impact of local government administration on the human scene. It may be argued that in human substance the lack of sustained imaginative intensity leaves the book as dense with banalities as a realistic radio serial, yet the documentary fullness in investigating many areas of life (farming, a school, a lunatic asylum, a community living in shacks, local government intrigue etc.) has its value and the author's sensitivity to the sufferings and frustrations of her fellow creatures is acute. A Spanish proverb used as epigraph seems to sum up her philosophy: ' "Take what you want", said God. "Take it – and pay for it." ' In *Testament of Friendship* (1940) by her friend Vera Brittain (q.v.), Winifred Holtby emerges as a warm-hearted, outgoing personality, though she was seized by periodic misgivings that her work was 'anaemic and poor to the tenth degree'.   [HB]

HOPE, A.D. (Alec Derwent) (1907-). Poet and critic, born at Cooma, New South Wales, Australia, and educated at Sydney University. He won a travelling scholarship to Oxford, and upon his return to Australia after the war lectured in state schools, at the Sydney Teachers Training College and at Melbourne University. He also worked as a vocational psychologist and did broadcasting work before being appointed Professor of English at Canberra University College (now the Australian National University) in 1951. Hope has always championed classical and international standards in the arts, and this has often led him into conflict with Australian writers and critics. His widely anthologized poem 'Australia', first published in the 1944 edition of *Australian Poetry*, expressed his dissatisfaction with postwar Australia, 'Where second-hand Europeans pullulate / Timidly on the edge of alien shores'. The poem closes, though, with an almost mystical turning to Australia as 'The Arabian desert of the human mind' which may yet offer 'some spirit which escapes / The learned doubt, the chatter of cultured apes / Which is called civilization over there'. Such ambivalence has often characterized Australian writing, and Hope's powerful restatement of it, although expressing his personal reaction to a particular period, has acquired an almost classic status.

In 1943 and 1944 Hope was joint author of two issues of a Sydney magazine entitled simply *Number One* and *Number Two* (after *Number Three* of 1948 the magazine ceased publication). It was in these pages that Hope made his first appearance as a critical and pungent observer of society, and his poems were included in H.M. Green's *Modern Australian Poetry* (1946). The Sydney magazine had satirized avant-garde trends such as the Adelaide magazine *Angry Penguins* and, along with the poets James McAuley (q.v.) and Harold Stewart, Hope was seen by some as representing a negative critical attitude – attempting a classical revival against romanticism. Yet both Hope and McAuley gave a vital intellectual lead during the coming decades and their careers foreshadowed the growing 'academic' status of poetry in Australia during the 1950s, when influential poets were increasingly associated with universities. Although his impact on the poetic scene had been immediate, it was not until 1955 that Hope published his first collection of verse, *The Wandering Islands*. A second collection, *Poems* (1960), made clear the positive beliefs underlying Hope's unease in a world which was so lacking by heroic standards. One central belief is that the decay of a rich variety of poetic forms is a sign of the decay of civilization itself, and in *Poems* Hope employs various poetic forms while maintaining a constant concern with the role of the poet in modern times. His inaugural lecture given at Canberra in 1952 broached this topic and Hope returned to it again in his 1956 article 'The Discursive Mode: Reflections on the Ecology of Poetry', which was reprinted in *The Cave and the Spring* (1965). This collection of essays on poetry also included 'Literature versus the Universities', in which Hope voiced the fear that academic research would soon begin 'on the still

unwritten works of living authors'; dislike of what he terms 'the great academic machine' is another aspect of his profound distrust of many of the values which modern man has established in literature as in life.

Much of Hope's best writing has probed the sexual frustrations and fears of modern life and at times his poems offended against accepted standards. Hope has never sought notoriety, although in arguing his case he has exploited to the full his talent as a satirist and in his technical virtuosity, as in his attitudes, has at times invited comparison with Pope or Swift. It would be mistaken, though, to consider him an 'intellectual' poet in any narrow sense for he has always stressed the mysterious nature of the sexual and other forces which motivate man. The title poem of *The Wandering Islands* expresses the essential solitariness of the human condition which brings with it the need for contact, however random or hurtful:

> An instant of fury, a bursting mountain of spray,
> They rush together, their promontories lock,
> An instant the castaway hails the castaway,
> But the sounds perish in that earthquake shock.

Collected Poems (1966, enlarged edition 1972) included Book V of *Dunciad Minor*, a contemporary version of Alexander Pope's *Dunciad* (1728) in which Hope not only castigates other writers and critics but also defines his own artistic and critical positions. The poem dates from 1950, but it was not until 1965 that an outline and lengthy extracts appeared in the Sydney journal *Southerly*, the complete poem being eventually published in 1970.

Introducing *Selected Poems*, published in 1963 in the 'Australian Poets' series, Hope characterized the 'chief . . . heresy of our time' as that 'which holds that by excluding those things which poetry has in common with prose . . . one can arrive at the pure essence of poetry'. This belief he connects 'with that irritable personalism which is partly a heritage of the Romantics, the view that poetry is primarily self-expression'. In contrast to this view of poetry as expressing the personality of the poet Hope states 'on the contrary, . . . poetry is principally concerned to "express" its subject and in doing so to create an emotion which is the feeling of the poem and not the feeling of the poet. In this I am at one with T.S. Eliot, a poet whose poetry I cannot bring myself to like at all'. In its blend of scholarship and iconoclasm, bitterness and humour, sacred and profane, Hope's writing demands from the reader the same constant reassessment which it reveals on the part of its author. *Native Companions* (1974) is a valuable collection of 'Essays and Comments on Australian Literature' over the thirty years until 1966 and provides a good introduction to his critical opinions. His most recent book of poetry is *A Late Picking: Poems 1965–1974* (1975). *The New Cratylus* (1979) was an uneven critical book at times too conservative and testy to do justice to the best of his own poetic work.

[PQ]

HOUGHTON, STANLEY (1881–1913). North-country dramatist, born in Cheshire. He became a critic and reviewer on the *Manchester Guardian*, and wrote *The Dear Departed* (prod 1908), *The Younger Generation* (1910) and *Hindle Wakes* (1912) for Miss Horniman's repertory company at the Gaiety Theatre, Manchester.

Hindle Wakes (1912) was justifiably a great success. The basic problem is of relationship between friends from boyhood when one has risen to be a mill-owner and the other remains a weaver in his employment. Their respective son and daughter superimpose a moral problem on the social one when they stay at a Llandudno hotel together without any honourable intentions. The action is in touch with reality and the idiom is alive. [HB]

HOUSMAN, A.E. (Alfred Edward) (1859–1936). Poet and classical scholar, born at Fockbury near Bromsgrove in Worcestershire. His father was a solicitor. Alfred Edward was the eldest of seven children and helped to bring up the rest. His mother, a devout Anglican, died on his 12th birthday and the event contributed to the undermining of his faith and happiness; but his father married his cousin Lucy two years later and the relationship between the boy and his stepmother was trusting and affectionate. At Bromsgrove School Housman won prizes in poetry contests and got into print in *The Bromsgrove Messenger* in 1874. He won an open scholarship to St John's College, Oxford, in 1877. There he helped to found and edit an undergraduate magazine called *Ye Rounde Table* and contributed witty verse parodies to it, but he pursued his classical studies in such lofty disregard of the Greats syllabus that, for all his developing scholarship, he was ill equipped for the examinations and failed his finals in 1881. He had to return to Oxford a year later to gain a pass degree. For nine years he worked as a civil servant in the Patent Office. During these years he studied with astonishingly strenuous and single-minded self-discipline, publishing a series of papers in learned journals on such writers as Horace, Propertius, Ovid, Aeschylus, Euripides and Sophocles. So effective was this endeavour to wipe out the Oxford disgrace that in 1892 he was able to summon seventeen top scholars to support him in applying for the vacant Chair of Latin at University College, London. He was appointed to the post and held it until 1911 when he became Professor of Latin at Trinity College, Cambridge. As a don, Housman gave himself to arduous and painstaking editing, concentrating especially on the unlikely and undistinguished Latin poet, Manilius. Housman's equipment as a textual critic excelled that of any contemporary in the field, yet it was devoted for a lifetime chiefly to the production of five volumes establishing the text of Manilius's *Astronomicon* (1903–30). His austere dedication to narrow specialization where few could judge him is underlined in the preface he wrote for the last volume of Manilius ('the reader whose good opinion I desire and have done my utmost to secure is the next Bentley or Scaliger who may chance to occupy himself with Manilius').

Housman was a man of enigmatic character. He declined honorary degrees, the Order of Merit and the Laureateship (on the death of Bridges). His frigid reserve and unsociable remoteness were notorious and they cannot be explained as simply concomitants of laborious scholarship. His temperament, often withdrawn and defensive, was that of a deeply wounded and frustrated personality. Whilst at Oxford he had become passionately attached to a tall, handsome young man, Moses Jackson, with whom he shared rooms. The thwarted infatuation, with the aberrant personal destiny it conferred, seems to have become a matter of lifelong embitterment. The pathos reaches us now through such verses as 'Epithalamium' (which refers to Moses's marriage),

Friend and comrade yield you o'er
To her that hardly loves you more,

(*Last Poems*)

through the posthumously published outcries, 'Shake hands, we shall never be friends, all's over' and 'Because I liked you better / Than suits a man to say', and through the poem provoked by Oscar Wilde's downfall, 'Oh who is that young sinner with the handcuffs on his wrists?'

Housman's poetic output consists of *A Shropshire Lad* (1896), *Last Poems* (1922) and the posthumous *More Poems* (1936). (See *Complete Poems*, 1956.) Housman was never a Shropshire lad, but the Shropshire hills fringed the setting of his Midlands childhood. The Shropshire of the poems is a contrived pastoral region to which names like 'Shrewsbury', 'Clun', 'Bredon', 'Wenlock Edge' and 'Wrekin' give some local flavour, while words like 'rick', 'fold', 'barn' and 'stack' testify to rural pursuits. The setting is idealized, but scarcely Arcadian in that its young inhabitants are burdened by life's frustrations and contrarieties. Time and happiness fly away: the young and the beautiful die; the army claims its victims and the gallows has its share. Housman's simple verse forms (often quatrains) are meticulously fashioned with a classical precision; contrast and paradox are finely balanced; yet the emotional directness of dialogue, exhortation and lament touches sensitive nerves in the reader. The splendid poses do not destroy spontaneity.

Into my heart an air that kills
From yon far country blows:
What are those blue remembered hills,
What spires, what farms are those?

(*A Shropshire Lad*, XL)

Unforgettable phrases and haunting cadences are charged with nostalgia and melancholy over loves and beauties dreamed of and lost. 'Poetry indeed seems to me more physical than intellectual', Housman said in his lecture, *The Name and Nature of Poetry* (1933). 'And I think that to transfuse emotion – not to transmit thought but to set up in the reader's sense a vibration corresponding to what was felt by the writer – is the peculiar function of poetry.' See also *Selected Prose*, ed. John Carter (1961), and *The Letters of A.E. Housman*, ed. Henry Maas (1971). In *A.E. Housman: The Scholar-Poet* (1979) R.P. Graves has uncovered what remained to be uncovered in the story of the enigmatic personality who paid male prostitutes in Paris and whose gauche social bearing Max Beerbohm (q.v.) compared to that of an 'absconding cashier'. [HB]

HUDSON, W.H. (William Henry) (1841–1922). Novelist and naturalist, born at Quilmes in Argentina of Anglo-American stock. His fascinating autobiography, *Far Away and Long ago* (1918), vividly recalls a carefree boyhood spent roaming on the pampas: it is rich in quirky human portraiture and evocative description. Typhus, followed by rheumatic fever, left Hudson weakened for life at the age of 16. He came to England and settled permanently in 1875. He married a singer who ran a boarding house in Bayswater and struggled to make his way as a writer. Hudson, who became naturalized, was awarded a British Civil List pension which literary success eventually enabled him to resign. Much of his output is that of the pure naturalist, but *The Purple Land* (1885) and *Green Mansions* (1904) are novels with South American settings, and the latter, 'a romance of the tropical forest', achieved some celebrity for its portrait of the narrator's tragic beloved, Rima, half-woman, half-bird-goddess ('All the separate and fragmentary beauty and melody and graceful motion found scattered throughout nature were Rima's gifts'), whom Epstein was to sculpt for the Hudson Memorial in Hyde Park. Among later books *A Shepherd's Life* (1910) gathers its country lore around the figure of an old Wiltshire shepherd. 'Hudson writes as the grass grows', said Joseph Conrad (q.v.), one of many who praised his refreshing naturalness as a stylist, a naturalness more evident to subsequent generations in the unforgettable autobiography than in the fiction.　　[HB]

HUGHES, RICHARD (1900–76). Novelist, born in Weybridge, Surrey, of Welsh stock, educated at Charterhouse and Oxford. He lived much of his life in Wales. He first tried his hand as poet (*Gipsy Night*, 1933) and playwright (*The Sisters' Tragedy*, 1922), but made his name with the immensely successful first novel, *A High Wind in Jamaica* (1929), an extraordinarily compelling work, *sui generis*, about a family of young children who are captured unintentionally by pirates while on their way from their Jamaican home to school in England. Facets of the child mind – the tangle of the innocent with the almost demonic, the ingenuous with the calculating, the severely practical with the fantastic – are vividly explored; and the collision with the grown-up world involves real blood and pain as well as farce and irony. The compact, restless, sinewy prose style makes the book a tour de force. The sea story, *In Hazard* (1938), is another: it challenges Conrad's *Typhoon* in portraying the crew of a steamer caught in a hurricane. Apart from some children's books Hughes's subsequent efforts were concentrated on a planned trilogy, *The Human Predicament*, designed 'as a long historical novel culminating in the Second World War', of which two volumes came out in Hughes's lifetime, *The Fox in the Attic* (1961), set in the year 1923 at the time of Hitler's Munich *Putsch*, and *The Wooden Shepherdess* (1972), which takes events up to the Night of the Long Knives in 1934. The work is panoramic in its coverage. It darts between England, Germany, America and even Morocco, shedding light on crucial political, social and ideological developments through the cunningly interknit relationships of both rich and poor families, and providing a richly diversified conspectus of the inter-war world. The posthumously published short stories, *In the Lap of Atlas, Stories of Morocco* (1979), derive from Hughes's residence in Tangier where he acquired a house in the 1930s.　　[HB]

HUGHES, TED (1930–). Poet, born in Mytholmroyd, West Yorkshire, in the mixed West Riding environment of town and moorland. The family moved to Mexborough, a mining town, when he was 7. There he went to the grammar school, thence for two years into the RAF, and on to Pembroke College, Cambridge, with an English Exhibition – though he soon dropped English for anthropology and archaeology. After Cambridge Hughes earned his living as a gardener, a night-watchman and a reader for Pinewood Film Studios. He married the American poet Sylvia Plath in 1956 and went to America to teach and write, returning to England in 1960. His marriage ended in separation in 1962, and he married Carol Orchard in 1970. Hughes's poetry was received with great acclaim for its freshness in rejecting the cold-blooded, cultivated urbanities of 'Movement' verse made fashionable by Philip Larkin (q.v.) and others. His volumes of verse include *The Hawk in the Rain* (1957), *Lupercal* (1960), *Wodwo* (1967), *Crow* (1970), *Crow Wakes* (1971), *Eat Crow* (1972), *Cave Birds* (1975), *Gaudete* (1977) and *Moortown* (1979). From the start Hughes's style had a craggy belligerence, a clamant explosiveness. His recurring concern with the animal world is not that of the objective nature poet: he enters into the animal's being in order to savour the brutal directness of act and purpose by which natural survival is guaranteed (see 'Hawk Roosting'). The untamed, primitive energies of the natural world, its single-minded decisiveness, provide a parable for men.

> No indolent procrastinations and no yawning
> 　stares,
> No sighs or head-scratchings. Nothing but
> 　bounce and stab
> And a ravening second.
>
> 　　　　　　　　　　　　　　　　('Thrushes')

This Lawrentian theme tends to surface at the human level in what appears to be admiration for sheer physical persistence (see 'The Retired Colonel') and even of mindless violence. The Crow poems involve universalized annotation of man's world and its absurdity, sometimes in a ferociously mocking vein.

> When God said: 'You win, Crow,'
> He made the Redeemer.
>
> When God went off in despair
> Crow stropped his beak and started in on the two
> 　thieves.
>
> 　　　　　　　　　('Crow's Song of Himself' from *Crow*)

The black comedy is at least a relief from humourlessness. The figure of Crow himself, a product of Hughes's anthropological studies, derives from the Raven, the trickster hero of North American mythology, but Hughes has insisted that his 'main concern was to produce something with the minimum cultural accretions of the museum sort'. Hughes's determination not to 'make a trophy' of known religious/mythological background is matched by an apparent refusal to concern himself overmuch with the artifices of his craft. His exuberant imagery, pressed into runic antiphon or poured into vatic declamation, can degenerate into sheer welter. The long narrative poem, *Gaudete*, in which an Anglican priest is abducted by spirits into another world while spirits substitute a duplicate of him at home, tells a melodramatic story of possession. The demon-priest seduces half the women in the village with a promise of a new incarnate saviour. His visitation comes to a climax with murder in the church basement which is full of naked, drugged wives, rapt in ritualistic hocus-pocus. In reviewing the title sequence from *Moortown*, Peter Scupham (q.v.) has spoken of Hughes's 'rape of the intellect. This is due to the total lack of aesthetic distancing, the rejection of checks and balances, the even-handed intensity which equates all experiences'. Anthony Thwaite (q.v.), reviewing Hughes's *Selected Poems 1957–1981* (1982), writes, 'His is a copious talent which seems to change direction, soar, lose height, lose itself, recover, and then inexplicably repeat its own worst faults again and again' (*Times Literary Supplement*, 25.6.82).

Hughes has written radio plays and has also written a good deal for children both in verse (*Meet my Folks*, 1961; *Season Songs*, 1976) and prose (*How the Whale Became*, 1963). [HB]

HULME, T.E. (Thomas Ernest) (1883–1917). Critic and philosopher, born in Staffordshire and educated there and at Cambridge University. He was associated with Ezra Pound, F.S. Flint (q.v.) and others in the Imagist movement and himself wrote a handful of short poems, but his central interest was in philosophy and aesthetic theory. An anti-romantic, he lamented the decay of classical discipline, precision and objectivity, and the cult of emotional self-indulgence, naïve humanism and trust in progress. 'Like Plato and Socrates, he drew the intellectual youth of his time around him', the sculptor Jacob Epstein said of him. He was killed on the Western Front. Herbert Read (q.v.) collected and edited his essays in *Speculations* (1924). [HB]

HUMPHREYS, EMYR (1919–). Novelist, born in Prestatyn, Clwyd, Wales, educated at the University Colleges at Aberystwyth and Bangor. After six years as a schoolmaster, he joined the BBC as producer in 1955, and was Lecturer in Drama at the University College of North Wales, Bangor, from 1965 to 1972. University and school backgrounds are utilized in *A Change of Heart* (1951) and *Hear and Forgive* (1952) respectively, the former set in Wales, the latter in London. Both books tussle with practical problems of moral behaviour, *Hear and Forgive* the more tidily and convincingly. The narrator, a rising young novelist and scripture teacher, David Flint, is driven to search his conscience over his desertion of a dull wife and his liaison with a wealthy woman who offers leisure and freedom for authorship. Humphreys makes a serious analysis of the moral and spiritual condition of a Christian caught up in the corruptions of the educational rat race and the easy codes of current sexual permissiveness, facing the human cost of adultery with unfashionable honesty. Other novels include *A Man's Estate* (1955) and *National Winner* (1971). Humphreys's technique is conventional and his portraiture generally unremarkable, but the underlying earnestness is sometimes perceptively diagnostic of our moral condition. *The Anchor Tree* (1980) is an especially thoughtful novel in which a Welsh historian visits a small township in Pennsylvania. Dimen-

sions are enriched by appropriate historical flashbacks to the Second World War and to the Welsh pioneers who settled in the same area in the eighteenth century. [HB]

HUXLEY, ALDOUS (1894–1963). Novelist and miscellaneous prose writer, born at Godalming, Surrey, the third son of Leonard and Julia Huxley. His grandfather was the great Victorian biologist, Thomas Henry Huxley. His mother, née Arnold, was Matthew Arnold's niece. He was educated at Eton and at Balliol College, Oxford, where he took a degree in English in 1915. Huxley suffered eighteen months of near-total blindness after an attack of *keratitis punctata* at the age of 16, and it unfitted him for war service. During the war he became a known figure among Lady Ottoline Morell's guests at Garsington Manor, near Oxford, where pacifists like Bertrand Russell and Clive Bell were encountered among a wide circle of intellectuals, including the Sitwells (q.v.), D.H. Lawrence (q.v.) and sometimes serving soldiers like Robert Graves (q.v.). Here Huxley met Maria Nys, a Belgian refugee, who became his wife in 1919. Huxley published four volumes of poetry between 1916 and 1920. He was for a time a teacher at Eton – an ineffective one, he claimed – but he began to establish himself in the literary world when in 1919 he joined the editorial staff of *The Athenaeum* under Middleton Murry (q.v.) (T.S. Eliot (q.v.) had been offered the post and had asked too high a salary), and in 1920 became drama critic for the *Westminster Gazette*. The successful publication of *Limbo* (1920), a volume of short stories, and *Crome Yellow* (1921), his first novel, rapidly brought him fame and financial security.

Thenceforward Huxley had a career as a successful writer. He lived in southern France during the early 1930s, travelled a good deal, became increasingly concerned over the European drift towards war and joined the Peace Pledge Union. He propagated his anti-war thesis that means determine ends in the politico-philosophical treatise, *Ends and Means* (1937), which he called a 'cookery book of reform'. In 1937 the Huxleys went to the USA and settled in southern California for the rest of their lives. Huxley's struggle against grave deterioration of eyesight led him to the unorthodox Bates method ('Perfect Sight Without Glasses') of ophthalmological treatment, and with such success that he recommended its techniques in *The Art of Seeing* (1943). His first wife died of cancer in 1955, and in 1956 he married Laura Archera who was later to write revealingly of his last years in *This Timeless Moment* (1968). After a struggle against cancer, which affected his tongue in 1961, he died in 1963.

Huxley's literary progress thrust two successive and contrasting popular images upon him. He was first the dazzling and irreverent young man of letters of a new, liberated age, and he was last the philosophical sage withdrawn from a shoddy civilization into mystical transcendence of its follies. The great early novels which swept Huxley into pre-eminence as the young students' idol of the late 1920s and 1930s were *Crome Yellow, Antic Hay* (1923), *Those Barren Leaves* (1925) and the crowning triumph, *Point Counter Point* (1928). In each of these novels, so markedly different from the work of dominant older writers of the time, members of artistic and intellectual coteries of the day figure as participants in an unfailingly dazzling display of conversational virtuosity. Plot and action matter less. Huxley created characters with an intellectual life, capable of quoting at length from highbrow books they have read – not necessarily even in their own tongue – and the recipe made a heady diet for young people who, better educated than their parents, wanted the fact to be evident in their taste. In *Crome Yellow* and *Those Barren Leaves* he used the device used by Thomas Love Peacock, and to comparable satiric effect, in gathering his characters together at a house party. The fantastic portraiture of *Crome Yellow* had its appeal enhanced by readily identified (if sometimes disputed) caricatures of known contemporaries of the Garsington world. Priscilla Wimbush was seen as drawn from Lady Ottoline Morrell and Mr Scogan from Bertrand Russell. (It is Mr Scogan who prophesies the scientific utopia later to be realized in *Brave New World*.) An element of broader farce intrudes into *Antic Hay* in the person of Theodore Gumbril who markets Patent Small-Clothes with built-in pneumatic seats, the ingenious fruit of boyhood discomforts on the cold hard pews in the school chapel. An appropriate symbol of the social scene pictured is the absurd circular dance of half-animalized beings implied in the title ('My men like satyrs grazing on the lawn / Shall with their goat-feet dance the antic hay': Marlowe, *Edward II*). *Those Barren Leaves* takes us to Mrs Aldwinkle's palatial home at Vezza on the Italian Riviera. *Point Counter Point** takes place in London. In terms of artistic structure and psychological insight, Huxley was now at his peak. He built for himself a niche as satirist, scathing and witty in denunciation of human vice and folly. Yet he managed to assume therein the pose of the Byronic roué experienced in what he castigates and illumined by its glamour. The wit is always the saving feature. When it falters, the running analysis of sexual liaisons, in terms of competing and varying demand and denial, tends to turn the emotional scenario into a fictional chartist's commentary on an erotic stock-market.

For Huxley the novelist *Brave New World** (1932) was the turning-point. This is a hair-raisingly prophetic picture of social and psychological engineering come-of-age in a fantastic future world state where technology has ironed out instability, obliterated independent thought and made passion obsolete. It has a serious enquiry into the character of freedom at its core, as the epigraph from the Russian philosopher Berdyaev implies. In succeeding novels, *Eyeless in Gaza* (1936) (in which there was recognizable use of family history that brought a reproof from his stepmother), *After Many a Summer* (1939) and *Time Must Have a Stop* (1945), fiction is increasingly a vehicle for intellectual speculation and for advocacy of ideological positions. The character of time is a crucial interest. The pursuit of mystical experience gathers momentum. It led Huxley into active experimentation with drugs as a means of escape to paranormal states of perceptiveness. *The Doors of Perception* (1954) and its sequel, *Heaven and Hell* (1956), gave cultural status to the taking of psychedelic trips. The piquancy savoured by the reading palate in the earlier Huxley's deliciously packaged denigration of current moral corruption and decadence proved to be symptomatic of a

larger dichotomy in the Huxleyan make-up. For the fastidious polymath and seeker after mystical illumination had a persisting streak of obsessive Swiftian disgust with human anatomical facts. Ideal and reality were never reconciled.

Huxley's vast output included volumes of essays (*On the Margin*, 1923; *Proper Studies*, 1927), short stories (*Mortal Coils*, 1922; *Brief Candles*, 1930), and plays (*The Gioconda Smile*, 1948), as well as historical biography (*Grey Eminence*, 1941; *The Devils of Loudon*, 1952). His last novel, *Island* (1962), he called 'a kind of reverse *Brave New World*', but there are those who find his utopia only a refined version of his anti-utopia, for it relies on genetic control, drug-dependence and replacment of the family by Mutual Adoption. In summing up Huxley it is relevant to note what Philip Quarles, the novelist in *Point Counter Point*, writes about 'the novel of ideas' and the way it restricts characterization to that small percentage of people who have ideas to express. 'Hence the real, the congenital novelists don't write such books. But then I never pretended to be a congenital novelist.' Quarles's comments on the novel also underline Huxley's drive towards encyclopedic multiplicity ('One sentence, and I am already involved in history, art, and all the sciences') and his technical experimentation in 'the musicalization of fiction' by contrapuntal interweaving of distinct yet related themes ('A novelist modulates by reduplicating situations and characters').

Sybille Bedford (q.v.), the novelist, has written a two-volume biography, *Aldous Huxley* (1974), and Grover Smith edited the *Letters* (1969). See also Julian Huxley, ed., *Aldous Huxley, 1894–1963, A Memorial Volume* (1965).

Point Counter Point gives a comprehensive satirical picture of postwar London society by cunning simultaneous presentation of a series of couples entangled in various marital or non-marital relationships and cross-relationships. The pursuit of happiness by a generation given over to self-indulgence and obsessive self-analysis is a unifying satiric theme, and many contemporary types are deftly capsulated in epigrammatic definition. There is a ferment of phrase-making, flippancy and cynicism. Formal Proustian sequences of extended psychological analysis are interlaced with brittle conversational fireworks that recall Firbank. The aged artist John Bidlake is said to be based on Augustus John, the fascist leader Everard Whebley on Oswald Mosley and the editor Denis Burlap on Middleton Murry (q.v.). Burlap is a fascinatingly comic study in self-intoxicated pseudo-spiritualized pretentiousness masquerading as childlike simplicity. Mark Rampion, a frank portrayal of D.H. Lawrence, is finely conceived, and his outbursts are so sympathetically enunciated that parody is submerged in authenticity. Stabilizing polarities are provided by Rampion's polemic in favour of instinct and human wholeness, and the converse arid cerebralism of Philip Quarles, a novelist whose views and talents reflect Huxley's own. ('He could manage the complications as well as anyone. But when it came to the simplicities, he lacked the talent – that talent which is of the heart, no less than the head, of the feelings, the sympathies, the intuitions, no less than of the analytical understanding.')

Brave New World is an anti-utopian fantasy of the

future. The year is 632 AF (After Ford). Totalitarian scientific control governs all human life, physical and mental, from the incubation of babies in bottles to the assignment of each (pre-conditioned) being to its appropriate (pre-determined) function in society. Mentally active Alpha pluses are in control at the top and contentedly mindless Epsilons do the drudgeries at the bottom. 'Community, Identity, Stability' is the motto. Hypnopaedia (education during sleep) engineers economically convenient human needs and socially appropriate human likes and dislikes. The universally distributed drug soma keeps uncomfortable thought, emotional stress or possible suffering at bay. ('Christianity without tears – that's what *soma* is,' says Mustapha Mond, Resident World Controller for Western Europe.) Stability and efficiency have made all heroism, nobility, romance, and effort against odds redundant. 'Everyone belongs to everyone else' and the old exclusivenesses of family, monogamy, privacy and creative individual thought are outlawed. Sexual promiscuity is morally obligatory. Hygiene is the supreme value. 'Mother' is an obscene word. 'Our Ford' is recalled with awe and the characters respectfully make the sign of the T (commemorating the first T-model) on their stomachs. Bernard Marx, an Alpha plus psychologist, brings back a 'Savage' from a holiday visit to the Mexican Reservation where descendants of the pre-civilized past live in their old way. John, the 'Savage', loves his mother and is familiar with Shakespeare: he wants the brave new world to match up to ideals that include poetry and passionate attachments. The reality drives him to suicide.

[HB]

HYDE, ROBIN (pseudonym of Iris Williamson) (1906–39). Novelist, born in Cape Town, South Africa, shortly before her parents sailed to settle in Wellington, New Zealand, where she was educated, like Katherine Mansfield (q.v.), at Wellington Girls' College. After early work as a journalist she left for England via the east in 1938 and died in England the following year. *Persephone in Winter* (1937) was the fullest of her early collections and showed her genuine perceptions still clouded by traces of an adolescent style. The two novels, *Passport to Hell* (1936) and its less successful sequel *Nor the Years Condemn* (1938), are brilliant pictures of New Zealand life in the early decades of this century and, together with the early stories of Frank Sargeson (q.v.) and a work such as *Man Alone* by John Mulgan (q.v.), provide a valuable understanding of social conditions and human tensions. *Check to Your King* (1936) used a semi-historical approach similar to that of the previous works in charting the spiritual as well as factual history of Baron de Thierry, a nineteenth-century utopian settler in New Zealand. Her best novel is *The Godwits Fly* (1938), an intricate and moving study of a colonial upbringing and sensibility through the fortunes of the Hannay family who settle in Wellington just as her own parents had done; in 1936 she wrote 'it's just dawned on me that I'm a New Zealander'. *Dragon Rampant* (1939), written in six weeks, was a fine travel book on China, where she had spent six months. The posthumous publication of *Houses by the Sea* in 1952 (with a very useful introduction) made available some fine poetry written during the period 1935–9 and also reprinted the best of her early verse.

[PQ]

I

IHIMAERA, WITI (1944–). Maori novelist and short-story writer, born at Gisborne, New Zealand, where he attended high school before spending three years at the University of Auckland learning to write – 'and consequently failing my exams'. He obtained his BA at Victoria University, Wellington, in 1971. His collection of stories, *Pounamu, Pounamu* (1972), has been reprinted several times – 'it's given Maori kids an idea of what it's like to be a Maori, the emotional experience'. *Tangi* (1973) was the first novel by a Maori, which he wanted 'to celebrate Maori culture at its greatest, and also at its death if we don't watch out'; it is his own favourite, which he describes as having been written 'for the critics, and for myself'. The novel *Whanau* (1974) also depicted 'a rural Maori culture in a process of change' but *The New Net Goes Fishing* (1977) was the first of a trilogy which will explore Maoris in an urban setting. Together with Hone Tuwhare (q.v.) Ihimaera has defined a strong Maori voice in New Zealand literature, but he is rightly wary of being type-cast as a 'Maori writer'; 'the development of Maori literature', he stresses, 'is to the benefit of Maori and pakeha [non-Maori] alike'. His work in the New Zealand Ministry of Foreign Affairs can only enrich this generous outlook on his own cultural loyalties, an outlook which has, at its best, produced writing which defies any easy categorization in its imaginative fusion of the living Maori heritage and the pakeha world. [PQ]

IREMONGER, VALENTIN (1918–). Poet, born and educated in Dublin, Ireland. He was involved with the Abbey Theatre and the Gate Theatre until he went into the Irish Foreign Service in 1946, eventually to hold ambassadorial posts in Sweden, India and Luxembourg. His verse play, *Wrap Up My Green Jacket*, broadcast by the BBC in 1947, is the tragedy of Robert Emmet, revolutionary of the 1803 rising against the British. Iremonger's poetic output has been sparse but distinctive. *Horan's Field and Other Reservations* (1972) contains what he has written since 1950 along with what he would wish to retain from the earlier volume, *Reservations* (1950). The poetic voice is incisive, the attitude often worried, bewildered, sad. In such a mood he recollects childhood war games as precursors of life's struggle:

> The depredation of orchards was the intuitive
>   beginning
> Of the later scramble for food.
>
> ('Backward Look')

Iremonger has a melancholy awareness of the collision between private and public worlds and an even more desolating sense of the individual's interior dividedness:

> In the room, between the lamplight and the door's
>   shadow,
> My fear stands, monstrous as a naked man . . .
>
> ('Alone by Night')

'This Houre Her Vigill' brilliantly defines childish bewilderment at an untimely death. 'Horan's Field' casts nostalgically back to the seedy Sandymount environment of childhood and the companions of play, regretting their passing with inconsolable sense of loss.   [HB]

ISHERWOOD, CHRISTOPHER (Christopher William Bradshaw) (1904–). Novelist, born in Cheshire, and educated at St Edmund's School, Hindhead, Surrey, where in his last year he made friends with W.H. Auden (q.v.), his junior by two-and-a-half years, and then at Repton, where a fellow pupil was Edward Upward (q.v.). He went up to Corpus Christi College, Cambridge, in 1923 where he and Upward entered the arena of current literary controversy in what he later challed 'a state of raging cerebral excitement'. Together they wrote stories picturing fantasy worlds where all the conventional taboos of society could be overthrown. (See Isherwood's *Lions and Shadows: An Education in the Twenties*, 1948.) Isherwood did no academic work in his second year, treated the examination questions flippantly, and was asked to withdraw from Cambridge or to face expulsion. He spent some years in London, then taught English in Berlin from 1930 to 1933. His friendship with Auden developed and the two of them collaborated in three verse plays, *The Dog Beneath the Skin* (1935), *The Ascent of F6* (1936) and *On the Frontier* (1939), visited China together in 1938, and finally both decided to settle in the USA in 1939. Isherwood chose California, became friendly with Aldous Huxley (q.v.) and Gerald Heard, and took up Vedanta philosophy. (See his *An Approach to Vedanta*, 1963, and *Essentials of Vedanta*, 1969.) He worked as a Hollywood screen-writer and, in 1946, became an American citizen.

Isherwood's first novel, *All the Conspirators* (1928), is a novel of rebellion, the battle of son against mother, the continuing war of the young against the conventions of family, employment and routine, upheld by the older generation. ('My generation – right or wrong' was the cry of author and hero alike, as Isherwood later observed.) A meeting with a shell-shocked war veteran sparked off the idea for his next novel, *The Memorial: Portrait of a Family* (1932). 'It was to be about war: not the War itself, but the effect of the idea of "War" on my generation', he explained in *Lions and Shadows*, and later, in a letter, 'I libelled the whole of our family pretty severely in *The Memorial*'. Isherwood's method of turning autobiography into fiction proved more fruitful, however, when he turned to his Berlin days in *Mr Norris Changes Trains* (1935) and *Goodbye to Berlin* (1939). The latter included as an episode the short story *Sally Bowles* (1937), and this was later turned into the play *I am a Camera*, by John van Druten, and into the musical *Cabaret*. The Berlin books were gathered together as *The Berlin Stories* (1946). Mr Norris, encountered en route to Berlin by the narrator,

William Bradshaw (Isherwood's two generally unused names), introduces him to communist circles but is in fact a spy in the camp. The mystery of his machinations provides narrative spine for a lively series of impressions of the Berlin scene on the eve of the Nazi take-over. (The character of Norris, a fascinating study, was based on Gerald Hamilton, then working in the Berlin office of *The Times*, who later wrote a memoir, *Mr Norris and I*, for which Isherwood supplied a prologue.) Sally Bowles, again based on a real person, Jean Ross, is a promiscuous cabaret actress. In *Goodbye to Berlin* 'William Bradshaw' becomes 'Christopher Isherwood' ('a convenient ventriloquist's dummy, nothing more', the preface notes). The book's sections, Isherwood adds, are 'the only existing fragments of what was originally planned as a huge episodic novel of pre-Hitler Berlin' to be called *The Lost*. In 'A Berlin Diary (Autumn 1930)', the first fragment, we read, 'I am a camera with its shutter open, quite passive, recording, not thinking' and *The Berlin Stories* together give a vivid record of the last days of the Weimar Republic, the political tensions, the decadence, the brutality and the misery which Isherwood witnessed at first hand.

In 1933 an Austrian film director, Berthold Viertel, working in Gaumont-British London studios suddenly decided to employ Isherwood as a script-writer on the strength of *The Memorial*. (Margaret Kennedy (q.v.) had just walked out on him in order to work on the film of her *Escape Me Never*.) The experience provided the material for Isherwood's first novel from his USA home, *Prater Violet* (1946). Slight in substance, tenuous in human interest, it is a series of impressions rather than a structured novel. It manifests clearly that inability to escape the autobiographical mode which limited the rest of Isherwood's output. Fascination with the self – unless the particular self is boundlessly fascinating – restricts a writer's appeal to a circle of devotees. In his subsequent career Isherwood has never been able to throw off the role of up-and-coming rebel who lets off steam on paper somewhat indiscriminately. This is evident in later novels such as *Down There on a Visit* (1962) and *A Meeting by the River* (1967), as well as in the autobiographical studies, *Kathleen and Frank* (1971) ('Kathleen' and 'Frank' are his parents) and *Christopher and His Kind* (1976). Of the last he wrote to Spender:

> The absolutely basic themes in my book are being queer and being political and being a pacifist Quaker and being a movie writer and being a Vedantist.

'The dominant theme is the effect that his homosexuality had on every aspect of his life', Brian Finney writes in *Christopher Isherwood: A Critical Biography* (1979), to which the present writer is indebted.   [HB]

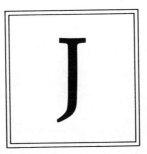

JACOB, VIOLET (née Erskine) (1863–1946). Poet, born in Montrose, Scotland. She married Major Arthur Jacob and spent some time in India. She wrote two novels and several volumes of verse, mostly Scottish dialect. The representative collection, *The Scottish Poems* (1944), contains neat, fluent lyrics, racy and spirited, that voice homely moral sentiments and a touching love for Scottish scenes and ways, and do so with freshness and humour:

> Guidman, ye sit aside the lum
> Sookin' yer pipe, yer doag at heel,
> And gin the Lord should strike ye dumb
> Wha'd be the waur, ye soor auld deil?
> And wha wad ken the dandy lad
> That, at the preachin', socht ma ee,
> When twa pond ten was a' we had
> And ye was cried in kirk wi' me.

('The Guidwife Speaks')

[HB]

JACOBSON, DAN (1929–). Novelist and short-story writer, born in Johannesburg, South Africa, educated in Kimberley and the University of the Witwatersrand. After working as teacher, journalist and businessman, and on an Israeli kibbutz, he settled in Britain in 1958. In 1954 he married Margaret Pye.

The Trap (1955) and the more substantial *A Dance in the Sun* (1956) are set in bleak, isolated localities in the Northern Cape and deal with the powerful, submerged tensions that snap in situations of intimate proximity but mutual incomprehension between whites and their black labourers. Jacobson observes human behaviour judiciously, as his characters perform their lives in a landscape of both grandeur and aridity; both books contain a latent symbolism of the South African political dispensation. Almost all his novels centre around questions of power, either of an individual over his own fate and others' lives or of its exercise within authoritarian political systems – sometimes both simultaneously. This preoccupation is discernible even in his least sombre novel, *The Price of Diamonds* (1957), which treats tenderly the personal relationship between two Jewish business partners. Despite the satirization of a meagre physical setting and provincial attitudes, there is great warmth in the near-tragic pathos with which the two partners come to understand each other, and Jacobson renders Jewish domestic scenes and speech with mischievous affection.

His irritation with the shibboleths of his Jewish and South African upbringing is confidently contained in the panoramic sweep of *The Beginners* (1966), which followed his attempt at a novel of inter-racial love, *Evidence of Love* (1960). *The Beginners* established him as a novelist of fine craftsmanship – competent, dexterous, analytical. It presents the third generation of a Jewish immigrant family, caught in a mesh of ambivalent allegiances, to South Africa, Europe, Israel. There is indulgence in the central character, Joel Glickman's, frequent crises of identity, but the book remains a remarkably comprehensive chronicle of the post-1945 white South African way of life, and it does move outward into the larger concerns of the post-Nazi, nuclear era.

With *The Rape of Tamar* (1970) Jacobson embarks upon his first real technical innovations. The result is an unusual modern novel, about self-seeking ambition and the use of power, that re-tells the rape of King David's daughter Tamar by her brother Amnon. The cynical narrator, who also acts as prompt in the tragedy, is David's clever, time-serving nephew, Yonadab; he reveals his own lack of moral centre by the tone with which he comments on the same lack in others. Yonadab often addresses the modern reader as a fellow cognoscente of human nature and of fiction. Jacobson makes no attempt to explain 'realistically' how such a narration can be made and Yonadab even invites us to dismiss it all as fantasy. Nevertheless, the device succeeds in giving a mordant view of the sordid motives that scheme around any centre of power. It is as much an expansion of 2 Sam. 13, as an analysis of personal jealousies and intrigue in the corridors of power.

Indirect narration and characters even more self-centred than Joel Glickman and Yonadab mark Jacobson's next two novels. *The Wonder-Worker* (1973) is a chillingly clever study of an extreme form of alienation – schizophrenia. Timothy Fogel believes that his mediocre life will be transformed by a divine revelation that will grant him a sort of psychic philosopher's stone; he 'achieves' it through silencing the young woman he has been obsessed with since childhood. Though still absorbed in character analysis, *The Confessions of Joseph Baisz* (1977) moves out again into wider political themes in the 'ramshackle dictatorship' of the Republic of Sarmeda, modelled geographically and politically partly on South Africa, partly on western accounts of communist states. With these two novels Jacobson proclaims himself a sophisticated humanist, at the expense of the abundant warmth of his pre-1973 fiction.

An accomplished short-story writer, Jacobson has published some seven volumes, of which *Beggar my Neighbour* (1964) is probably the finest. He won the Rhys Memorial Prize (1959) and the Maugham Award (1964).

[AR]

JAMES, C.L.R. (Cyril Lionel Robert) (1901–). Historian and political theorist, born and educated in Trinidad. Always a champion of black people against colonialist methods and attitudes, his books *A History of Negro Revolt* (1938) and *The Black Jacobins* (1938) helped nurture black political awareness in the 1940s and 1950s. He grew up, in his own words, steeped in 'the literature, philosophy and ideas of Western civilization' and 'educated by Marxism'. He and Alfred Mendes published the journal *Trinidad* (1929–30) and belonged to the group who wrote for *The Beacon* edited by Albert Gomes (1931–3). They tried to shock middle-class West Indians into regarding blacks as human beings, and their fiction introduced social realism into West Indian writing. With few opportunities for black authors in Trinidad, James emigrated to London in 1932. His *Minty Alley* (1936) was one of the first West Indian novels to treat black proletarian life seriously and convincingly. While registering the gulf of misunderstanding between middle class and proletariat, it is no mere political tract but a vivid celebration of human resilience under economic and social limitations. This influential Third World spokesman engagingly reveals his personality in *Beyond a Boundary* (1963).

[AR]

JAMES, HENRY (1843–1916). Novelist and short-story writer, born in New York City. His father, Henry James, was a theologian of the Swedenborgian school. He brought up his sons in accordance with experimental anti-indoctrinational principles that demanded purposefully unsystematic variety in schooling, immersion in intelligent conversation and travel abroad. Both sides of the family were of Northern Irish extraction. James's brother William became a distinguished pragmatist philosopher and psychologist, a Harvard professor and author of *The Varieties of Religious Experience*. The James family had homes in Albany and Boston. They lived for periods in France, Germany, Switzerland and England. After a brief start at Harvard Law School in 1869, Henry withdrew to devote himself to writing, and he set out for Europe. On this occasion he at first found London cheerless (he had stayed there with his family for some months at the age of 12) and he suffered from homesickness, but he managed to meet William Morris and Ruskin. He was soon in Italy, consciously saturating himself in its culture and atmosphere. James visited Paris in 1875 and came into contact with Flaubert and Maupassant as well as with Turgenev. Like Turgenev, James was to make psychological motives and confluences the ground bass of his fictional structures. Personally he preferred Maupassant to Flaubert, though his New England sensibilities took a jolt when Maupassant received him one day in the company of a masked but otherwise naked lady. France meant much to him. But in December 1876 he came to London, this time to settle. He became a notable diner-out, was accepted by the great (*Daisy Miller* made him something of a lion) and delighted in the opportunity to immerse himself in high society. 'I think a position in society is a legitimate object of ambition', he said, and he wanted 'to be taken seriously' by the English. (His *English Hours*, a collection of evocative essays on his adopted country, published in 1905, was reissued in 1981 with an Introduction by Leon Edel.)

The contrast between Europe and America became for James a dominant interest and source of inspiration. The dichotomy was a complex one. Europe's rich culture contrasted with America's newness, rawness and brashness. On the other hand America's freshness, 'innocence' and enthusiasm contrasted with Europe's decadence, sophistication and depravity. T.S. Eliot (q.v.) described James as 'difficult for English readers because he is an American ... difficult for Americans because he is a European' and perhaps not 'possible for other readers at all'. James was 'possessed by the vision of an ideal society' yet aware, without bitterness, of the 'disparity between possibility and fact'. In the creation of his special world of thought and feeling, his integrity and the exacting nature of his perception provoked his astonishing punctiliousness with words.

James's output divides naturally into three periods and they have been facetiously differentiated as James the first, James the second and the Old Pretender. *Roderick Hudson* (1876) shows a young American artist corrupted abroad. Roderick is a promising young sculptor brought from Massachusetts to Rome to nurture his talent. He fails to profit from the opportunity and comes to a tragic end. *Daisy Miller* (1879) displays a guileless American girl, eager and ingenuous, made the victim of European misunderstanding and censure. The pattern thus established achieved its finest form in *Portrait of a Lady* (1881). Isabel Archer has been brought up in Albany and her expatriate aunt, Mrs Touchett, invites her to her English home. Doomed by consumption, her cousin Ralph finely conceals his love for her by wit and banter. At Ralph's urging her uncle, old Mr Touchett, makes Isabel an heiress. Bright, idealistic, eager for experience and self-perfection, she refuses both her American suitor, Caspar Goodwood, and the highly eligible English aristo-crat, Lord Warburton. Then, in Italy, she falls prey to an unscrupulous expatriate American connoisseur, Osmond. He marries Isabel for her money, and is abetted by the sinister Madam Merle, who turns out to be the mother of Osmond's daughter, Pansy. After a tense crisis, Isabel determines to forfeit happiness and remain faithful.

Two shorter novels of this first period that have remarkable vitality are *The Europeans* (1878) and *Washington Square* (1881). The former brings to Boston two Europeans of American ancestry, Felix Young and his sister Eugenia, now Baroness Münster of Silberstadt-Schreckenstein. At the home of their uncle Mr Wentworth, a sober good-hearted New Englander, they and their three cousins, Clifford, Charlotte and Gertrude (together with close friends among their neighbours), become involved in a choreography of emotional cross-currents fastidiously directed by James and lit with sunny humour. Dialogue and authorial comment are alike full of flavour and freshness, and indeed recall Jane Austen. *Washington Square* (itself compared by Graham Greene with the work of Jane Austen) has an altogether graver tone. Catherine Sloper, due to inherit her father's wealth (he is a fashionable New York doctor), becomes the prey of a self-seeking suitor, Morris Townshend. He breaks her heart and she suffers lifelong spinsterhood. The theme is close to that of *Portrait of a Lady* and foreshadows *The Wings of the Dove*. The claustrophobic pressures exerted on Catherine by her angry father, silly aunt and designing suitor oddly recall the tensions of Richardson's *Clarissa Harlowe*.

James was more concerned with specifically English themes in his middle period, the period of *The Tragic Muse* (1890), *What Maisie Knew* (1897), *The Spoils of Poynton* (1897) and *The Awkward Age* (1899). In *The Awkward Age* he pictures a vital London circle of friends who gather round Mrs Brookenham diverting themselves with scintillating conversation in which there is ceaseless half-flippant dissection of each other. The serious theme is that Nanda Brookenham, virtually adopted by ageing Mr Longdon (who once hopelessly loved her grand-mother), is sought by Mitchy whom she does not love and is reluctantly unwanted by Vanderbank whom she adores; this in spite of Longdon's plan to settle a fortune on her to facilitate marriage to Vanderbank. James makes a devastating study of brittle worldliness, dominated by

the fascinating, malicious Mrs Brookenham, who has Vanderbank too much in her grip. The contrasting fortunes of Nanda and her cousin Aggie, who are handled according to opposite codes (over-early and over-delayed initiation into adulthood) at the 'awkward age', present a serious critique of English social practice. The book is written largely in dialogue. (James was eager for success on the stage, but his *Guy Domville* (1895) was booed at the St James's Theatre and later plays failed to make the impact he desired.)

James's last period makes him a major twentieth-century novelist. The old American/European dichotomy returns in works of impeccable artistry and distinct poetic power, *The Wings of the Dove** (1902), *The Ambas-sadors** (1903) and *The Golden Bowl** (1904). James had now attained subtle mastery in the art of registering failures or near-failures of human adjustment at the social and cultural level and at the level of personal relationships where clarification and mutual under-standing can easily be impeded by inadequate aware-ness. The passage of mood into mood, the confusion of motive with motive, the ambiguities inherent in the inter-play of conflicting impulses prolonged and unresolved – such evanescent complexities James strove to pinpoint with exactitude, and developed, for both dialogue and commentary, an exquisite fastidiousness of phrasing, inimitable at its finest, but inviting parody when precision evaporates in prolixity.

In 1897 James had obtained the lease of Lamb House at Rye and he moved in for the following summer. Ford Madox Ford (q.v.), who had a bungalow at Winchelsea, has left a lively picture of James at Rye in *Return to Yesterday* (1932). Conrad (q.v.) visited Ford and thus met James, the two men respecting each other as writers rather than liking each other as persons. Kipling (q.v.) too was a near and familiar neighbour. Friendship with Wells (q.v.) turned sour when, in the novel *Boon*, Wells ridiculed James's wordiness with the image of a hippo-potamus trying to pick up a pea. When war came and America remained neutral, James applied for naturaliza-tion, becoming a British subject in July 1915. He was awarded the OM in the following December, only a few weeks before his death. Leon Edel, who wrote the five-volume biography, *The Life of Henry James* (1953–72), is editing the *Letters*: vol. 1 (1974), vol. 2 (1980). See also Henry James, *The Art of the Novel* (1935) (Collected Prefaces to the Collected Edition) edited by R.P. Blackmur.

The Wings of the Dove is patterned on the familiar Jamesian basis of inter-relationship between the pursuit of wealth and the passion of love. Mrs Lowden of Lancaster Gate takes over her niece, Kate Croy, on condi-tion that she breaks off all connection with her father, a waster. Installed at Lancaster Gate, with prospects of inheriting from her aunt if she keeps in with her, Kate wishes to marry Merton Densher, a journalist without means whom her aunt dislikes. When Milly Theale, an American heiress, comes on the scene and reveals to Kate that she will soon die of a fatal illness, Kate abets Densher in making love to Milly so that he can marry her, inherit her money, then marry Kate as a widower. Milly is responsive and loves him; but the sordid trick is eventually revealed to her. She calls Densher to her for a last interview before turning her face to the wall and dying. Densher has been left a lot of money but cannot now bring himself to take it. He wants to marry Kate without it, and she refuses. The moral and emotional subtleties inherent in the deterioration of Kate and Densher, and in the ambiguous bond that finally binds the trusting, deceived and generous Milly to her deceiver, even after death, are finely registered in James's probing prolixities. But the sadness of the tale is somewhat oppressive, the character of Kate depressingly unpleasant.

The Ambassadors is based on a theme that gives ample scope for James's quiet irony and exploration of nuance. Mrs Newsome, a wealthy and respectable American widow, has dispatched her somewhat ingenuous ambassador and intended future husband, Strether, to recall her son, Chad, reputed to be involved in Paris with an undesirable woman. The family business requires his presence at home in Woollett, Massachusetts. Strether is editor of a journal and no philistine, but the delicacy of the mission and of his unsuspicious nature makes it possible for him to have the wool pulled over his eyes. The 'beautiful' character of the relationship between Chad and the gracious Countess de Vionnet shakes him free of the values that belong to Woollett. Sarah Pocock, Mrs Newsome's daughter, is dispatched to check up on spy and spied-on, and proves an ambassadress of tougher allegiance, for whom Strether is now a lost man. There is humour as the fragile charm veiling the illicit liaison is tentatively probed and sometimes quick-wittedly protected. James's presentation is what he called the 'scenic method', the characters themselves (Strether notably) being in direct communication with the reader and obviating the need for authorial intervention.

The Golden Bowl is perhaps James's finest novel. An impoverished Italian prince, Amerigo, marries Maggie Verver, daughter of a wealthy American widower and art collector. Maggie adores her husband and her father. But Amerigo has already had an affair with Maggie's dear friend, Charlotte Stant, which only terminated because of lack of the means on either side to make marriage possible. Soon Charlotte marries Maggie's father. The two former lovers have no intention of renewing their relationship and spoiling two marriages, but there is constant familiar contact and James weaves an intricate pattern of delicate emotional and situational complications. Maggie has a baby and, as Charlotte and Amerigo are thrown together, so the young mother and her father are paired at home. The old relationship of Amerigo and Charlotte is renewed, and eventually Maggie's eyes are opened to the fact. But Maggie's unselfishness and quiet endurance enable the situation to be redeemed, breakdown forestalled and the relationships of the two married couples restored. James's later style is always in danger of engulfing under a weight of words the fine minutiae which they are assembled to illuminate: nevertheless the ultrasensitive fabric of inference and suggestion here sustains a subtle sense of passion and torment just below the surface as the story of the quartet unfolds. The cracked golden bowl, symbol of the defective love affair, is smashed on the floor at the climax.   [HB]

JAMES, M.R. (Montague Rhodes) (1862–1936). Fellow of King's College, Cambridge, and later Provost of Eton, a biblical scholar and palaeontologist. He wrote a series of ghost stories, starting with *Ghost Stories of an Antiquary* (1904, and second volume, 1911), which were gathered in *Collected Ghost Stories* (1931). There is knowledgeable use of antiquities – cathedrals, country mansions, witchcraft etc. – which have a genuine general historicity. Verisimilitude is strengthened by detailed pseudo-scholarship referring to legends, manuscripts, places and sources. James relies for atmosphere on a sense of evil lingering from past crime and ancient devilry, and there is no attempt to disinfect the creepiness by explaining mysteries away.   [HB]

JAMESON, STORM (1891–). Novelist, born and brought up at Whitby, North Yorkshire, daughter of a sea-captain. She gained a scholarship to Leeds University and then proceeded to King's College, London. She married Guy Chapman in 1924. She has published some fifty books, over forty of them novels, and specialized in family chronicles like the Whitby shipbuilding trilogy, *The Triumph of Time* (1932) (*The Lovely Ship*, 1927; *The Voyage Home*, 1930; *A Richer Dust*, 1931), whose heroine's lifetime runs from 1841 to the 1920s. Of later, maturer novels *Cousin Honoré* (1941), set in Alsace, covers the inter-war period. *The Green Man* (1952) studies a land-owning family from 1930 through fifteen years of social disintegration, and *A Cup of Tea for Mr Thorgill* (1957) portrays a brilliant young Oxford don who recants his communist sympathies. The two-volume autobiography *Journey from the North* (1969–70) is a sprawlingly zestful record, frank in personal confession, informative in picturing literary life. Naomi Mitchison (q.v.) commends the early novel *Company Parade* (1934), now reissued (1982), as an accurate 'factual picture of England after the First World War'.   [HB]

JENNINGS, ELIZABETH (1926–). Poet, born in Boston, Lincolnshire. Her father was a doctor and his death elicited a characteristically searching poem about their relationship:

> There was love now I see of a strange kind.
> We could move about in each other's mind.
> ('For My Dead Father')

Again she directed attention to the relationship in a poem addressed to Veronica Wedgwood, 'To One Who Read My Rejected Autobiography' ('this childish tale of love and grief'). The author was educated at Oxford High School and St Anne's College, Oxford. She worked for some time in the Oxford City Library and later as a publisher's reader, before becoming a freelance poet in 1961. In a book she wrote for children, *Let's Have Some Poetry* (1960), she described the early development of her interest in poetry. Chesterton's 'Lepanto' first opened her eyes as a schoolgirl, showing her 'an entrance into a world that I knew to be *mine*'. In starting to write her own poetry she delighted from the first in the formalities of rhyme and scansion, and was encouraged in 'literary sincerity' by a wise uncle who praised the genuine directness of a simple little poem about a dead bird above her more pretentious efforts:

I held it in my hand
With its little hanging head;
It was soft and light and whole,
But it was dead.

Jennings's first little book, *Poems* (1953), which gained
her an Arts Council Prize, was followed by *A Way of Looking* (1955). These, and the subsequent volumes – *A Sense
of the World* (1957), *Song for a Birth or a Death* (1959),
Recoveries (1961) and *The Mind Has Mountains* (1966) –
were all represented in the *Collected Poems* of 1967. The
collection showed a rare lyrical gift operative over the
years with a candour that makes personal experience
and reflection vulnerably accessible. Jennings is a Roman
Catholic. She regards poetry as at once a matter of
discipline and 'possession', and she can sustain limpid
clarity and naturalness of idiom within conventional
metrical design, marrying sensibility to artistry. The
ordering and clarifying function of poetry is crucial to
her. ('One does not know what one thinks until one sees
what one writes.') The power of poetry – and its paradox
(for it can give delight even in the registration of deep
grief) – lies in 'the sense of order and purpose' it imparts,
where 'nothing seems wasted or pointless'. There is
unobtrusive firmness of metrical pattern in poems of
sympathetic observation such as 'Old Woman' and 'Old
Man' (*A Sense of the World*), yet there is no hint of pretentiousness or contrivance. The sincerity is authentic as
the daylight. An engagingly open self-analysis in poems
such as 'To a Friend With a Religious Vocation' and 'At a
Mass' (*Song from a Birth or a Death*) foreshadows the
later, graver self-exposure in stress and sickness.
Jennings's predominant note is a strange, tingling
quietness. One may cite 'For a Child Born Dead' (*A Way of
Looking*) which was written in quick response to her
sister's loss:

But there is nothing now to mar
Your clear refusal of our world.
Not in our memories can we mould
You or distort your character.

Much in the subsequent volumes, *The Animals' Arrival*
(1967) and *Lucidities* (1969), is of a piece with her best
work in directness and simplicity. Looking back, in the
poem 'In Retrospect and Hope', she confesses that she
likes best her poem 'Fountain', one of many records in
verse of her visits to Italy. It 'gave form, music, and
sensuousness to what was originally an intellectual
problem – the problem of the meaning of power' (*Let's
Have Some Poetry*). The sequence of hospital poems in
Recoveries (1961) had a lucidity and compassion that
were recaptured in the later records of nervous breakdown and of life in a mental hospital. (See *The Mind Has
Mountains* and *The Animals' Arrival*.) There is uncanny
coolness in observation and steady precision in self-
exploration. *Moments of Grace* (1979) scarcely matches
up in quality to the best of her earlier work (which is well
represented in *Selected Poems*, 1979), but there are
poems in *Celebrations and Elegies* (1982) which recapture
the old lyrical warmth and simplicity.   [HB]

JHABVALA, RUTH PRAWER (1927–). Novelist,
born in Cologne, Germany, of Polish parents, and educated at Hendon and London University from 1945 to
1951. She married C.S.H. Jhabvala in 1951 and settled in
India; they have three children.

Her novels deal with tensions, personality clashes and
middle-class urban attitudes within the traditional Indian
joint-family, as in *To Whom She Will* (1956; her first
novel), *The Nature of Passion* (1957) and, more penetratingly and ironically, *The Householder* (1960); or with
Europeans in India trying to understand both country and
people, as in *Esmond in India* (1958) and *Heat and Dust*
(1975); or with both, as in *A Backward Place* (1965) and *A
New Dominion* (1973; as *The Travelers*, USA). The
cumulative effect is of constriction, though *A New
Dominion* attempts a wider view and, consequently, an
impressionistic structure that bemused reviewers. S.C.
Harrex describes her as 'exposing . . . sentimentality,
snobbery, vanity, pretentiousness, and hypocrisy', but B.
Rajan writes less enthusiastically of 'the ironies of cross-
talk and its interplay', especially in *Get Ready for Battle*
(1962). She herself has said her work 'is only one
individual European's attempt to compound the puzzling
process of living in [India]'. She has published four
volumes of stories and written film-scripts.   [AR]

JOHNSON, B.S. (Bryan Stanley) (1933–73). Novelist
and poet, born in London and educated at London University. His novels attracted more attention than his poetry
(*Poems*, 1964; *Poems Two*, 1972) because of his bold if
ineffective attempt to take over largely unoccupied post-
Joycean terrain. *Travelling People* (1963) eschews tradi-
tionalism for variegated stylistic presentation through
screen scenario, letters, journal, newspaper reporting
etc. *House Mother Normal* (1971) is a series of interior
monologues by inmates of a geriatric home who are
classified as NERs (no effective relatives). *Christie
Malry's Own Double Entry* (1973) expands the image of
credit-and-debit accounting to track the escalating
career of a psychopath through pointless violence to
mass-murder by cyanide. Johnson's heavy reliance on
devices and ideas from Beckett and Joyce is too little
supported by verbal precision and imaginative insight for
his work to be other than rather emptily derivative; but
there is human substance in *House Mother Normal*, and
the hero of *Christie Malry's Own Double Entry*, in converse with the author, justly queries: 'Your work has been
a continuous dialogue with form?'   [HB]

JOHNSON, LOUIS (1924–). Poet, born in Wellington,
New Zealand, and educated at the Teachers' Training
College there. His youth was spent in the farming areas of
the North Island, but in 1944 he returned to Wellington
where he worked in teaching, broadcasting and other
jobs from 1951 to 1970. He now lives in Melbourne and
works as a freelance writer. Like James K. Baxter (q.v.)
and Mike (Charles) Doyle (q.v.) he reacted against the
'island story' thesis of New Zealand literature put
forward by Allen Curnow (q.v.), declaring himself more
influenced by 'Auden [q.v.], Yeats [q.v.], Pound, men
whose vision appeared unlimited by the back fence'.
From the conscious nationalism of poets such as R.A.K.

Mason (q.v.) or A.R.D. Fairburn (q.v.) he turned to the personally felt and experienced, aside from any 'New Zealand' quality it might have. His incisive and unsettling analysis of New Zealand urban society led to his being dubbed 'the poet of subtopia'. His poetry blends social concern with a strong sense of the poet's role and in this his work resembles that of Baxter, with whom he edited *Numbers* (1954–60) together with Mike Doyle. His first collection, *Stanza and Scene* (1945), struck this vatic note and *The Sun Among the Ruins* (1951), subtitled 'Myths of the Living and the Dead', maintained a similar approach. Later collections include *The Dark Glass* (1955) and, in collaboration with Baxter, Doyle and Kendrick Smithyman (q.v.), *The Night Shift* (1957), 'Poems on Aspects of Love' ('suddenly, in middle-age, I have found my feet as a poet in the mysteries of love'). A selected poems volume, *Bread and a Pension* (1964), was followed by his first Australian-published book, *Land Like a Lizard: New Guinea Poems* (1970). *Fires and Patterns* appeared in 1976.   [PQ]

JOHNSON, PAMELA HANSFORD (1912–81). Novelist, born in London and educated at Clapham County Secondary School. After working for some years in a bank, she turned full-time writer. Her volume of autobiographical reflections, *Important to Me* (1974), includes memories of her early love affair with Dylan Thomas (q.v.) whom she might have married but for his bohemianism. Her marriage to Gordon Neil Stewart (1936), of which there were two children, ended in divorce, and in 1950 she married the novelist C.P. Snow (q.v.). Her first novel, *This Bed Thy Centre* (1935), whose title was supplied by Dylan Thomas, created something of a stir because its heroine, Elsie Cotton, a gauche young girl, sexually uninstructed in the bad old pre-permissive days, is at once hungry for consummation and loaded with inhibitions. 'I had thought of the novel simply as an attempt to tell the truth about a group of people in a London suburb, whose lives were arbitrarily linked', the author later claimed (Preface to 1961 reprint). But were Clapham schoolgirls ever quite so emotionally retarded as those we encounter? Such queries about the quality of her authorial insight are provoked by Johnson's continuing preoccupation with mundane realism unvisited by profundity or intensity, the major expression of which is the trilogy beginning with *Too Dear for my Possessing* (1940), and continued in *An Avenue of Stone* (1941) and *A Summer to Decide* (1949). But the sheer literary competence involved in the management of interlocking lives and various social contexts from the prewar to the postwar days must be granted, and the author has a limpid, unadorned directness of style that matches the documentary sobriety of her view. In *An Impossible Marriage* (1954) and *The Last Resort* (1956) she returns to the Clapham Common area of the first novel twenty years later, and the narrator-heroine, herself a novelist, is probably the most autobiographical of her portraits. Johnson's output was both prolific and unpredictable. In the three novels, *The Unspeakable Skipton* (1959), *Night and Silence Who is Here?* (1962) and *Cork Street, next to the Hatters* (1965), she assays a comic vein. Daniel Skipton, a study in artistic paranoia, is based on the life of

Frederick Rolfe ('Baron Corvo'). *On Iniquity* (1968) reflects on the Moors Murder trial which she attended.
[HB]

JOHNSTON, DENIS (1901–). Dramatist, born in Dublin, Ireland, and educated at Dublin, Edinburgh, Cambridge and Harvard University, Massachusetts, USA. He was called to the Bar in 1925. He has been theatrical producer in Dublin (Abbey and Gate Theatres) and for the BBC, and has held professorial posts in Massachusetts, California, New York and Washington. Wartime experiences as BBC correspondent in the Middle East and Europe are dashingly chronicled in *Nine Rivers from Jordan* (1953). His play *The Old Lady Says 'No'* (1929), a non-naturalistic, episodic piece whose title seems to reflect Lady Gregory's (q.v.) rejection of it when offered to the Abbey, was first performed at the Dublin Gate Theatre Studio in 1929 with Micheal Macliammoir as Robert Emmet, Irish revolutionary martyr. Emmet (or actor dressed up as such) floats timelessly through Dublin circles, rich and poor, with varying degrees of irrelevance to their interests. Use of quotations from well-known romantic poetry and heroic oration sharpens the irony. Johnston's determination to make his fellow countrymen rethink their sentimentalization of revolution is also evident in *The Moon in the Yellow River* (Abbey Theatre, 1931) in which republicans blow up a Free State hydroelectric power plant. In *The Scythe and the Sunset* (prod 1958) Johnston overtly challenges O'Casey's (q.v.) reading of the 1916 Easter Rising and the pacifist message he derives from it in *The Plough and the Stars*. For Johnston the British made a colossal psychological blunder in treating too seriously a rebellion that would otherwise have quickly caved in. The rising met the amateur soldiers' need (sharpened by the real war of 1914–18) for a gesture of aggressive self-assertion in the face of the contempt and ridicule of their countrymen. Johnston's output also includes *The Dreaming Dust* (prod 1940), a freely constructed play about Swift which opens in St Patrick's Cathedral, Dublin, with masquers representing the Seven Deadly Sins. Johnston's prefaces in his *Collected Plays* (two volumes, 1960) clamour wittily for that public attention to his work which many critics agree they merit. *The Brazen Horn* (1968) is autobiographical. The novelist Jennifer Johnston (q.v.) is Denis Johnston's daughter by his first wife, Shelagh Richards, whom he married in 1928.   [HB]

JOHNSTON, JENNIFER (1930–). Novelist, daughter of the playwright, Denis Johnston (q.v.). She leaped into full-blown maturity as a writer with her first novel, *The Captains and the Kings* (1972), and rapidly established herself as a leading Irish novelist with *The Gates* (1973) and *How Many Miles to Babylon?* (1974). Her presentation of the comedy and tragedy of human communication and failure of communication across the barriers separating class from class and nation from nation is deeply moving. There is painstaking portrayal of the Anglo-Irish landed gentry in their awkward relationship to retainers and peasants both in the years of simmering nationalism and imperial decline and in the postwar years. The author sees family problems extended through the generations. Major MacMahon of *The Gates* declines into alcoholic decay while his orphaned niece finds companionship only with a local peasant boy. *How Many Miles to Babylon?* is something of a tour de force. A young Irish heir, Alexander Moore, and a local peasant boy, Jerry, join up in the First World War as officer and private. Their friendship is sustained in defiance of military regulations and in spite of the social and political divides between them. The red tape of discipline, even more than the mud and the blood, bears down tragically upon a pair by nature and by race unfitted to subordinate feeling and impulse to the inhumanity of the military machine. In *The Christmas Tree* (1981) the heroine, Constance Keating, returns home from London to Dublin under sentence of death from leukaemia at the age of 45. She faces her few remaining weeks coolly, regarding death as 'an attractive alternative to life', which she has never found very satisfactory. Recollections of the past add a powerfully controlled intensity to the study of physical decay.   [HB]

JONES, DAVID (Michael) (1895–1974). Poet and artist, born in Brockley, Kent. His father was a printer from a Welsh-speaking family in Holywell, Flintshire; his mother was the daughter of a Thames-side mast-and-block maker. The mixed Welsh and Cockney ancestry became a matter of personal pride and, as such, a determining influence on Jones's work as a writer. Jones has been compared with Blake for his dual distinction as artist and poet. 'I cannot recall a time when drawing was not a preoccupation', he said; but writing and literature came later. He did not read until he was 8 but paid his sister a penny an hour to read to him and, refusing to go to the local grammar school, he attended the Camberwell School of Art from 1909 to 1914 instead. In 1915 he enlisted in the Royal Welch Fusiliers and served on the Western Front from December 1915 until he was wounded and sent home in March 1918. Long afterwards he met Siegfried Sassoon (q.v.) and exchanged memories of Mametz Wood. 'His Battalion relieved ours after my day out bombing the Prussian Guard', Sassoon discovered. The permanent effect of the war on Jones's work was significant, and crucial too was his conversion to Roman Catholicism. 'It was I think sometime in 1917 in the neighbourhood of Ypres that I first found myself wondering about the Catholic tradition. Four years later, in 1921, I found myself unable to do other than subscribe to that tradition.' (Broadcast talk, October 1954.)

In 1919 Jones went to the Westminster School of Art and in 1921 began his long friendship with Eric Gill. He was with Gill's community at Ditchling from 1922 to 1924, and joined Gill again at Capel-y-ffin near Llanthony in 1927, and at other homes in 1928. Jones left two portraits of Gill's second daughter, Petra, to whom he was for a time engaged; but he never married. His career as engraver and water-colourist was well begun when, fascinated with the relationship between artistic form and content, he turned aside to experiment in another medium. He was staying with his parents in Sussex in 1927 and down with the flu when he did the first bits of writing that turned eventually into *In Parenthesis**, a poem (largely prose in form) based on his experience of the war. It was only, however, because of encouragement from Harman Grisewood that he persisted with the work,

which was completed in 1932, although not published until 1937. A breakdown intervened and neurasthenia was to dog Jones intermittently for the rest of his life.

In Parenthesis deals with those early months of warfare which Jones came to see as having an amateurishness that left room for individualism – a phase ended by the wholesale slaughter of the 'relentless mechanical affair' that began with the Battle of the Somme. He was able therefore to set his picture of Welshmen and Londoners at war in the context of heroic Celtic legend and the Romano-British past. T.S. Eliot (q.v.) read the typescript and recognized it at once as 'a work of genius'. He noted the affinity of Jones's work with that of Joyce (q.v.), Pound and himself, and he prophesied the eventual growth of critical commentaries to elucidate it. Jones's next great work, *The Anathemata**, was published in 1952. It represents a development from *In Parenthesis* comparable in kind to the development between Joyce's *Ulysses* and *Finnegans Wake*, for whereas there is basic chronological narrative sequence in *In Parenthesis*, however festooned with overtones, *The Anathemata* has no such recognizable consecutiveness. Nevertheless W.H. Auden (q.v.) called it 'very probably the finest long poem written in English in this century'. If its apparent formlessness makes it at first sight forbidding, there is an inner unity woven of thematic recurrence. Though frankly fragmentary, the material is gathered 'by a kind of quasi-free association', personal only in that 'you use the things that are yours to use because they happen to be lying about the place or site or lying within the orbit of your "tradition"', objective in that it binds microcosm with macrocosm in epic portrayal of our historical and cultural past. The Catholic system of symbol and sacrament, extended incarnationally, makes a universal offering of life of which the mass provides central *signa*. The poem is written in a vigorous, packed style, influenced by Hopkins and Joyce. Vocabulary and imagery are astonishingly multifarious.

Jones's later years produced pieces of what appeared to be a further work in progress, *The Fatigue* (1965) and *The Tribune's Visitation* (1969). Like the former, the latter 'is concerned with troops of the Roman garrison in Palestine in the earlier decades of the first century AD (Introduction). Overtones draw the formula *Idem in me* from the Roman oath of military allegiance (the 'sacramentum') into a Christian context in the tribune's declaration: 'See! I break this barrack bread, I drink with you, this issue cup, I salute with you, these mutilated signa, I with you have cried with all of us the ratifying formula: *Idem in me*!' It is interesting that the piece shows a movement back to simpler narrative coherence. But the subsequent publication of further pieces, which to some extent overlap with each other, *The Sleeping Lord and other Fragments* (1974), *The Kensington Mass* (1975) and *The Roman Quarry and other sequences* (1981), has prompted the suggestion that all Jones's literary output after *In Parenthesis* consisted of one long unfinished epic work. (The subtitle of *The Anathemata* is 'fragments of an attempted writing'.)

See also David Jones, *Epoch and Artist: Selected Writings*, ed. Harman Grisewood (1959), *The Dying Gaul and Other Writings by David Jones*, ed. Harman Grisewood (1978), *Dai Greatcoat, A Self-Portrait of David*

Jones in his Letters, ed. René Hague (1980), and William Blissett, *The Long Conversation, A Memoir of David Jones* (1981).

In Parenthesis is based on Jones's experience as a private in the Royal Welch Fusiliers between December 1915 and July 1916. Jones's technique is to mix narrative and descriptive writing in the third person with dialogue that is direct and vivid but is not assigned to named speakers – though the context may allow specific characters to be distinguished. The poet can be identified with the central figure, Private John Ball, whose name also indicates his more general symbolic status. The seven sections of the work take us from pre-embarkation parade to France and the trenches, and there is a steady but inexorable progress to front-line action. In the climactic battle (part 7) Ball is wounded and many of his companions are killed.

The emphasis throughout is upon the impact of the war on all the senses and, through them, on the feelings. Jones's extraordinary skill lies in selectively accumulating concrete details of the outer scene – with all its horrors and strange beauties, its grotesque absurdities and racking discomforts – and in keeping the living voice of the participating soldier always at your ear. The work is thus perhaps the most powerfully evocative literary record of the First World War that we have. But in addition Jones gives epic dimension to the work by setting the deeds of the soldiers in the context of heroic legends from the past. In particular each section is prefaced by an epigraph from *Y Gododdin*, a sixth-century epic of a disastrous Welsh raid on the English at Catraeth (Catterick). Within the text echoes and overtones also introduce correspondences with events in the *Mabinogion*, Malory and Shakespeare's *Henry V*. The effect of the whole is to hold the Welsh and English traditions together under a powerful yoke.

The Anathemata has the subtitle 'fragments of an attempted writing' and the motto, 'This prophecy Merlin shall make for I live before his time', which together indicate the unstructured character of the presentation and the non-naturalistic quality of the content. In his preface Jones quotes the historian Nennius's introduction to his *Historia Brittonum*: 'I have made a heap of all that I could find'. Circular rather than progressive in design, the poem explores thematically what Jones calls his 'own "thing", which *res* is unavoidably part and parcel of the Western Christian *res*, as inherited by a person whose perceptions are totally conditioned and limited by and dependent upon his being indigenous to this island'. The accumulated residue of culture handed on to us from past phases when there were rich shared backgrounds, Jones defines as our 'deposits': from them he derives his themes; for from them he is himself derived. The word 'anathemata' means 'devoted things', things holy or unholy 'lifted up or in whatever manner made over to the gods'.

The poem is divided into eight sections. The starting-point of section 1 ('Rite and Fore-time') is the prayer of consecration in the mass, and overtones throughout the poem hold the mass in mind. Reflection moves to the beginnings of our race in prehistory, then in Roman and in Celtic times. In sections 2, 3 and 4 ('Middle-Sea and Lear-Sea', 'Angle-land' and 'Redriff') the focus is narrowed to

fasten on the incorporation of Britain into Roman civilization, the invasion of the Anglo-Saxons, and the specific home of Jones's maternal ancestry, Rotherhithe. From this narrow centre substance and vision surge out expansively again as though going through an egg-timer. 'The Lady of the Pool' (title of section 5) is the Virgin Mary, the patron of the pool of London, and also a daughter of the Thames awaiting annunciation. Related imagery of the Wood, the Tree, the Vessel, the Woman, the Church, gradually builds up a Joycean network of correspondences here and in section 6 ('Keel, Ram, Stauros'). The Nativity of Christ is a dominating theme in section 7, 'Mabinog's Liturgy', while the Crucifixion and the Last Supper provide the culminating imagery of the final section, 'Sherthursdaye and Venus Day', where the unity of intention is made evident in the drawing together of thematic motifs.

> He does what is done in many places
> what he does other
>   he does after the mode
> of what has always been done.
> What did he do other
>   recumbent at the garnished supper?
> What did he do yet other
>   riding the Axile Tree?

Most readers will require help in reading *The Anathemata*. It is provided by René Hague who wrote *A Commentary on the Anathemata of David Jones* (1977) with the poet's assistance. Reviewing this work in *The Times* (15.5.78), Harman Grisewood observed: 'The Anathemata is a comprehensive declaration of the link between the whole of humanity and the Redemptive Act, between art and sacrament, between Bethlehem and Calvary. It is a "poem for our time" because it exposes the very nature of our humanity, and, as only great poetry could, the course which may lead us to dehumanize ourselves'.   [HB]

JONES, GLYN (1905–). Poet, novelist and short-story writer, born in Merthyr Tydfil, Mid Glamorgan, Wales, educated there and at St Paul's College, Cheltenham. He worked as a schoolmaster in Glamorgan. In a broadcast in 1946 his friend Dylan Thomas (q.v.) described him as 'one of the few young Welshmen writing English poetry today who has a deep knowledge of *Welsh* poetry itself' (*Quite Early One Morning*, 1954). From the time of his first short stories (*The Blue Bed*, 1937) and his first published verse (*Poems*, 1939) Jones has been a regional writer deeply aware of the emotional and comic possibilities inherent in the rapturous lyricism and the ugly revulsion that the lighter and darker aspects of the Welsh rural and industrial scene can call out. His novels are rich in autobiographical material and they effect a unique blending of the rhapsodic and the grotesque. *The Valley, the City, the Village* (1956), a series of linked impressions, moves from childhood in the valley, to university days in the city, and to a post-finals holiday with college friends in the village of Llansant; and in the childhood section especially the prose throbs with human warmth and humour. *The Learning Lark* (1960) satirizes corruptions in the educational set-up in a Welsh valley. *The Island of Apples* (1965) is a remarkably vivid retelling of a myth in modern terms. It records the arrival of a strange, handsome young hero in a Welsh valley and his effect on his companions, and gives full play to Jones's verbal virtuosity. The theme allows of the extremes of realism and fantasy: the squalor, sordidness, dirt and vice in the poverty-stricken mining background are offset by rhapsodic boyish dream-pictures of romantic adventure and fulfilment. Jones's novels are above all galaxies of vivid human portraiture, detailed, eccentric, earthy, yet glowing with humour and vitality. *Selected Short Stories* (1971) brings stories from the earlier volumes together with some new ones. In *The Dream of Jake Hopkins* (1954) the title piece is a verse play for radio on the burdens of a schoolmaster, and it is eminently fitted for aural reception:

Here I stand, a middle-aged master,
My hair like tow and my face like plaster,
Awaiting my class – and awaiting disaster.

See also *Selected Poems* (1975).   [HB]

JONES, GWYN (1907–). Novelist and short-story writer, born in Gwent, Wales, educated at Tredegar Grammar School and University College, Cardiff. He had an academic career as English teacher and was Professor of English at University College, Cardiff, from 1965 to 1975. Among his historical novels *Richard Savage* (1935) studies the eighteenth-century poet of that name and *A Garland of Bays* (1938) studies the Elizabethan writer, Robert Greene. Nearer home, *Times Like These* (1936) pictures the 1926 General Strike in South Wales and *The Walk Home* (1963) portrays an illegitimate victim of nineteenth-century social barbarities. In the latter the style has an appropriate jauntiness and some Celtic exuberance, but the smell of the earth reaches the reader only through the library window. Jones first began publishing short stories with *The Buttercup Field* (1945) and *The Still Waters* (1948). His tales deal with homely Welsh characters and tend to be strong in narrative content. (See *Selected Stories*, 1974.) He is also an expert on folklore, Scandinavian as well as Welsh, and has translated Icelandic sagas into English. He has edited the *Oxford Book of Welsh Verse in English* (1977).   [HB]

JONES, T.H. (Thomas Henry) (1921–65). Poet, born in an isolated shepherd's cottage near Llanafan, Dyfed, Wales, where he spent his early childhood. His university course at Aberystwyth was interrupted by war service in the Royal Navy. After teaching English at the Portsmouth Naval Dockyard, he became a lecturer in English in the University of New South Wales in 1959. He published *The Enemy in the Heart* (1957), *Songs of a Mad Prince* (1960) and *The Beast at the Door* (1963). *The Colour of Cockcrowing* (1966) and *Collected Poems* (1976) followed posthumously. The mature work has an assured lyrical and metaphysical power. Key themes derive from the poet's physical exile from Wales and reflect his graver alienation from the cultural and religious pressures it imposed on his childhood. The displacement is universalized. The war and 'watching my betters die' increased the burden of guilt. Love is both an inescapable obsession and a threat to integrity. In 'Adam Wonders About Eve' Adam ponders whether, out of her fluency, Eve herself

may have taught the serpent to speak, or whether indeed she may perhaps have invented the whole story in order to submerge him in illusion and to control him as 'her lord, her clown'. The private dichotomy of imaged self and real self is added to the unresolved public paradoxes of lost home, nationality and belief. The tortures of increasing alcoholism give to some of the later poems the nightmarish pathos of Malcolm Lowry's (q.v.) (see 'Lines for the Death of an Alcoholic'). In a succinct and sympathetic critical study of 'Harri' Jones (*T.H. Jones*, 1976), Julian Croft has praised his 'combination of intricate aural decoration and a simple vocabulary'.   [HB]

JOSEPH, M.K. (Michael Kennedy) (1914–81). Poet and novelist, born in London. He went to New Zealand with his family in 1924. He was educated at the universities of Auckland and Oxford and after war service returned to teach at Auckland University, where he is now Professor of English. His first book of verse, *Imaginary Islands* (1950), was privately printed but his novel, *I'll Soldier No More* (1958), was published both in Auckland and London and is a classic imaginative documentation of the tension and inaction of life in the services. Subtle and perceptive in its analysis of the human effects of such an artificial existence, the work falters only in the over-neat contriving of the plot. *The Living Countries* (1959) was a further poetry collection which illustrated his charting of 'consciousness and self-consciousness, expressed in poems about New Zealand, about religion and about literature'. The novel *A Pound of Saffron* (1962) tested spiritual precepts dramatically against an academic background and *The Hole in the Zero* (1967) was a remarkable science-fiction-inspired exploration of human perspectives in a timeless context. Selected poems from the period 1945–72 were reprinted in *Inscriptions on a Paper Dart* (1974) which reaffirmed the quiet seriousness of his poetic work and, above all, his commitment to translating his own experience in terms which can reach others. The novel *A Soldier's Tale* (1976) was set in France in the Second World War. *Byron the Poet* (1964) is an outstanding critical study.   [PQ]

JOYCE, JAMES (1882–1941). Novelist, born in Rathgar, Dublin, Ireland, the second child of John Stanislaus Joyce and his wife Mary ('May') Jane (née Murray), but the first to survive. John Joyce had moved to Dublin from Cork, where he inherited property, and he was Collector of Rates for Dublin until the post was abolished in 1891, leaving him a pensioner at the age of 42. John was a gifted but recklessly extravagant man, a great talker and a great drinker. Four of his sons and six daughters survived infancy, and the gradual decay of his fortunes, for long mitigated by successive mortgages on the various Cork properties, became grave and painful in James's early teens. The Joyce household was always on the move about Dublin. Henceforward the change from house to house became a descent to squalor. James had been sent at the age of 6 to Clongowes Wood College, County Kildare, a school for the élite, where early enthusiasms for literature, music and Catholic piety became evident; but he was withdrawn when the financial blow of 1891 fell. After a brief spell at a Christian Brothers' school, he was offered a free place at Belvedere College, a Jesuit day school, through the kindness of Father John Conmee. Here he made excellent progress in his English studies as well as in French, Italian and Latin, and he won several scholarship prizes that enabled him to give the family an occasional taste of the lost luxuries of their more prosperous days. By the time Joyce left Belvedere in 1898, he had accumulated a considerable reservoir of literary material. The childhood view of Dublin streets and strands; the taste at school of repression, loneliness and homesickness; family life disordered by poverty, politics and thriftlessness; the living array of Dublin eccentrics racily magnified in John Joyce's boisterous banter: this much-to-be-used material was balanced by the stresses and ecstasies of an inner life that knew the extremes of adolescent piety and penitence, and the calls of sex, beauty and art.

Joyce entered University College, Dublin, in 1898 and took his BA degree in modern languages in 1902. Among student friends were J.F. Byrne (who was to figure in the novels as 'Cranly') and C.P. Curran, the author of *James Joyce Remembered* (1968). Joyce's brother Stanislaus was also close to him. (See Stanislaus Joyce, *My Brother's Keeper*, 1958.) In 1900 Joyce published his first article, 'Ibsen's New Drama', in *The Fortnightly Review*, and in 1901 issued 'The Day of the Rabblement', an Ibsenite attack on the Irish bias of the new national theatre. Rejection of Irish Catholicism and alienation from both nationalist and establishment opinion were already isolating him, but he managed to meet Russell (q.v.), Yeats (q.v.) and Lady Gregory (q.v.). Through them he was introduced to London editors, and the *Daily Express* gave him books to review. After going to Paris with the intention of studying medicine, he was recalled to Dublin in April 1903 by the impending death of his mother. 1904, the year to be celebrated in *Ulysses*, was packed and eventful. Joyce had poems in *Saturday Review* and elsewhere, and stories in *Irish Homestead*; he lived for a time in the Martello Tower at Sandycove with Oliver St John Gogarty (q.v.), taught at a school in Dalkey, won a bronze medal as a tenor soloist, started work on *Stephen Hero*, shared the platform with John MacCormack at a concert in the Antient Concert Rooms and met Nora Barnacle, a Galway girl who worked at Finn's Hotel. The two took their first evening walk together on 16 June, the day later chosen for the events of *Ulysses*. In October they threw in their lots together for life, going first to Paris and then to Switzerland, where Joyce began to earn his living by teaching English. His first poems, *Chamber Music*, a collection of short love lyrics, was published in London in 1907. His children, Georgio and Lucia, were born in Trieste in 1905 and 1907.

Joyce's life was thereafter that of an exile who nevertheless, as a writer, lived mentally in the city he had left behind, recalling the detail of its topography and its personalities with unremitting imaginative intensity. He visited Ireland in 1909 and again in 1912, but failed to get *Dubliners** published until 1915. This collection of fifteen felicitous short stories is the product of high artistic discipline and sensitivity. Events of childhood, youth and adulthood are dealt with successively. The nullifying effect of the Dublin social and mental environment is evident in human dreams, hopes and ambitions

pathetically unfulfilled. A rich vein of symbolism gives profundity to the tales. *A Portrait of the Artist as a Young Man** was issued serially in *The Egoist* in 1915 and in book form in 1916. This quasi-autobiographical novel reworked much material from *Stephen Hero*, a manuscript that has been posthumously published (1944). The *Portrait* is rooted in acutely felt personal recollection, and Joyce presents his hero's (Stephen Dedalus's) experience from within his own mind in idioms tuned to infant thought, childhood thought, adolescent thought and student thought successively; but authorial detachment adds a rich veneer of humour and irony.

The Joyces lived in Zurich during the First World War, were in Trieste shortly afterwards and eventually settled in Paris till the Second World War drove them out in 1940. They were in London in 1931, where Joyce and Nora legalized their marriage on 4 July. The long years of work devoted to writing *Ulysses** (1914–22) and *Finnegans Wake** (1923–39) had their burdens for Joyce in the form of uprootedness from home, a long struggle for publication and recognition, many operations for painfully defective eyesight, and, above all, the grief of Lucia's emerging schizophrenia. On the positive side Joyce was the recipient of public patronage through the influence of well-wishers like Yeats and of astonishingly generous private patronage from Harriett Weaver and others. The strength of his attachment to his wife and his children was always at the heart of his stability as an artist. His sense of humour and his Irish irony were crucial to him as man and as writer. The play *Exiles* (1918), coming between the *Portrait* and *Ulysses*, indicates, as its hot-house characters interchange their unnecessary torments, how right Joyce was to eschew Ibsenite naturalism.

When Sylvia Beach published *Ulysses* under the 'Shakespeare and Company' label in February 1922, she presented to the world an epic masterpiece. The modern Odysseus is a Dubliner, Leopold Bloom. For wanderings about the world of ancient myth we have wanderings about the city of Dublin; and all is compressed within one June day, the 16th, in 1904. The full development of the Joycean 'stream of consciousness' technique enables the hero's past life to be grasped in retrospect. The technique faithfully records the flow of thought and feeling, doing justice to persistent emotional currents and logical randomness alike. But devices of symbolism, labyrinthinism and intense connotative multiplicity are used to bind the multifarious material together in a unifying network of correspondences that universalize individual and national experience. (See Harry Blamires, *The Bloomsday Book, A Guide through Joyce's Ulysses*, 1966.) The achievement left Joyce anxious to push further his technique of connotative multiplicity and appease his hunger for the interlocking of the particular and the universal. *Finnegans Wake*, finally published in 1939, was the culmination of seventeen years devoted to thus developing the machinery of expression on a multilingual basis so as to contain the personal, the particular and the cosmic within an encyclopedic grasp. Joyce was worn out when this long-anticipated 'Work in Progress' was completed, and he died in Zurich in 1941. The standard biography is Richard Ellman's *James Joyce* (1959). See also James Joyce, *Letters*, volume 1, ed. S. Gilbert (1957), volumes 2 and 3, ed. R. Ellman (1966), and James Joyce, *Critical Writings*, ed. E. Mason and R. Ellman (1959). For help with *Finnegans Wake* see W. York Tindall, *A Reader's Guide to Finnegans Wake* (1969).

Dubliners is a collection of fifteen stories, several of whose characters reappear in *Ulysses*. They are accurate in naturalistic detail, shaped by patterned correspondences and sharpened by symbolic overtone. Joyce's overt directness and simplicity ('a style of scrupulous meanness' he called it) gives ironic impact to studies of events in which the paralysis and corruption of Dublin life frustrates vital impulse and negates idealism. The effect is not devastating because the pathos is touched with warm compassion and shot through with humour. 'Eveline' is typical. Eveline, who is bound to a laborious job and a hard father, lets the chance of escape overseas slip away through ingrained inability to act. Joyce's Ireland is suffocating: his message is at loggerheads with that of Irish Movement writers like Yeats. His skill lies in bringing his characters' experience to a point of crisis where simple acts or words are crammed with significance and illumination. The moment of sharpest focus is revelatory of the personal and national dilemma. Most celebrated, perhaps, are the more substantial stories, 'Grace' and 'The Dead'. 'Grace' is an ironic miniature epic of salvation. Protestant-born and Catholic backslider, Tom Kernan, starts his pilgrimage on the floor of an underground public lavatory, a little 'hell'. He finishes it sitting between his friends at the Jesuit church in Gardiner Street and listening to a moralistic sermon. 'The Dead' is a limpid yet densely symbolic masterpiece, presenting Gabriel Conroy, a writer who has uncomfortably come to terms with the world (as Joyce might have done), and his wife, Gretta, who can still weep for the death of a young man who loved her in Galway long years ago.

A Portrait of the Artist as a Young Man, a quasi-autobiographical novel, traces the infancy, childhood, adolescence and early manhood of Stephen Dedalus, the would-be Dublin artist. Joyce records his own experience, often with detailed accuracy. The reader gets a clear picture of home life in a decaying household with a feckless, irresponsible father and a suffering mother. Life at Clongowes school, at Belvedere and at University College, Dublin, is brought into sharp focus in selected events and conversations that mark crucial movements in personal attitude. For the emphasis is upon the development of the individual under the pressures of an environment and a culture too aridly repressive for the young artist's spiritual needs. Stephen's spiritual development and his sexual development are conjointly tested and strained in a Dublin society which confronts a boy with ready prostitutes on the streets and with hell-fire sermons in retreat. There is a phase of intense re-dedication to chastity and orthodoxy, but the climactic epiphany of a wading girl, skirts tucked up, gazing out to sea, is decisive, and Stephen accepts the implications of his artistic vocation. 'I will not serve that in which I no longer believe, whether it call itself my home, my fatherland, or my church.' But Stephen Dedalus (the names unite the first Christian martyr with the arch-artificer of classical legend), who reappears in *Ulysses*, is not a straight-forward self-portrait. He is at once hugged close in sympathy and distanced in irony. The blend of pathos and humour is important. 'I may have been too hard on that young man', Joyce averred.

Ulysses is an epic novel of which serialized excerpts had appeared in the *Little Review* and *The Egoist* prior to publication in Paris in 1922. Difficulties over censorship delayed publication in London (apart from small limited editions) until 1937. The framework of the book matches that of the *Odyssey*. Odysseus's years of wandering, his son Telemachus's search for him and the return to Penelope are paralleled in the story of Leopold Bloom, Dublin advertisement canvasser, Stephen Dedalus (would-be artist in search of spiritual fatherhood) and Molly, Bloom's much loved but sexually neglected wife. Dublin streets, shops, cafés, bars, library, churches, brothels and the like replace the world of ancient myth. All is compressd within a single day, 16 June 1904.

Leopold Bloom has been sexually separated from his wife for ten years since the birth and tragic death, eleven days later, of their longed-for son, Rudy. Leopold is a Jew and an outsider. His upgrading to epic status is not solely a matter of matching his lot with that of Odysseus. Joyce's imagery makes Bloom's difficulties, his longings and frustrations, as breadwinner and as husband, the focus of universal human tensions. His hunger for Molly is an aspect of man's hunger for his earth goddess, for his mother, for the warmth and security and fulfilment which earth can never permanently provide. It corresponds with man's idealistic turning to church and madonna, mystical Bride and divine Spouse. The book's imagery gives Molly a changing status, as Mother Country, Mother Church, or Mother of the Son of Man. Her infidelity with Blazes Boylan corresponds with Ireland's betrayal of her children, with Eve's betrayal of Adam and (via a symbolic reading of *Hamlet*) with the betrayal by the frail human flesh of the manhood it has mothered. The system of analogies enables Joyce to take a universal view of the human situation while never relaxing his grip on the particular: for *Ulysses* is alive throughout with the savour and salt of Dublin life, private and public, in 1904. Nevertheless the city becomes everyman's city, potential *Urbs Beata* or suburbanized and socialized 'New Bloomusalem'.

The work is divided into three books within which are eighteen episodes, twelve of them in the central book, and three in each of the other two books. Book 1 concentrates on Stephen Dedalus, book 2 on the wanderings of Bloom and book 3 on the coming together of Bloom and Stephen, first in shared companionship and finally in the mind of Molly. There is an implicit Dantean structure in that the great central book takes us spiralling down the circles of modern unreality (in newspaper office, library, bar and the like) to the depths of the twentieth-century Inferno in the brothels of Nighttown. The Joycean ethic is clear. In Molly's adultery we see the home betrayed from without and within (by Boylan's intrusion and by Bloom's fastidious neglect). Molly is Eve seduced by Satan, Ireland usurped by the British, the church betrayed from within, the flesh of humanity let down by the selfish masculine intellect. Ireland is betrayed by those who rend her dedicated prophetic leaders like Parnell, by those who sell her horses to the enemy, by those who sell her artistic soul (as establishment writers do) and by those who sell her young womanhood in the Dublin brothels.

The humour of the book matches its profundity: the stylistic virtuosity matches the magnitude of the conception. Each episode displays Joyce's literary skill in a distinct style or series of styles. Vast resources of parody and pastiche are brought into play to achieve multiplicity and universality. The Joycean dexterity with verbal and syllabic ambiguity effects a unique exploration of the connotative, associative and symbolic power of words.

Finnegans Wake occupied Joyce from 1923 to its publication in 1939. Fragments of it ('Work in Progress') began to be published as early as 1924, so the massive book was a focus of controversy long before its completion. In *Ulysses* Joyce had experimented with puns and with multiple compounds like 'menagerer' which derives a threefold connotation from 'manager', 'ménage' and 'menagerie'. In *Finnegans Wake* he developed this method of expression on a multi-lingual scale. His aim was to find verbal multiplicity adequate to contain concentric cycles of meaning. Basically one may say that *Finnegans Wake* is a tale of a Dublin publican and his family at Chapelizod; but there is no dramatic action. Children play in the evening outside the pub; they have supper and do their homework. H.C. Earwicker, the publican, serves his customers and gets drunk. The family and the related characters have multiple identities, local and universal, subjective and analogical, for the world of *Finnegans Wake* is the dream world in which we spend a good part of our lives, and where shifting identities, multiple significances and composite impressions, congruous or incongruous, are commonplace.

Joyce virtually manufactured his own language for *Finnegans Wake* and the exacting demand it makes upon the reader delayed intelligent appraisal of the work by all but the most fervid admirers. But the book is no longer regarded as an entertainment for cranks. The sheer rhythmic beauty of much-quoted descriptive passages has drawn attention to the quality of Joyce's prose, which is musical both in its direct aural claim upon the reader and in its interwoven figures and motifs. The lyricism, and the joyful humour that bounces from words and phrases even when they are but half-understood, gives a surface attractiveness that leads the reader to dig deeper.

So doing, he encounters an elaborate structure for which Joyce is indebted to the eighteenth-century philosopher of history, Giambattista Vico (*La Scienza Nuova*). Joyce utilized Vico's division of history into recurring cycles – the divine age, the heroic age, the human age and the *ricorso*, or return. 'I am trying to build many planes of narrative with a single aesthetic purpose', he said. And he was influenced, in his balancing of pairs and opposites, by the kind of philosophy of dualism that he found in William Blake and in Giordano Bruno, the sixteenth-century philosopher of Nola. Vico, Bruno and the magnificent arabesques of the *Book of Kells* help us to an understanding of an organization in which the fall of man, the story of Noah's Ark, the battle of Waterloo, the fall of Satan and of Humpty Dumpty as well, all have their place. Mythical and historical figures mingle and merge in a composite picture of human life. Humphrey Chimpden Earwicker (Here Comes Everybody and Haveth Children Everywhere) is all men and all mountains. Anna Livia Plurabelle is all women and all rivers. At the cosmic level we have the history of Dublin: at the private level the biography of the author. The formidableness of the style is inseparable from the vastness of the conception. 'His writing is not *about* something; *it is that something itself*', Samuel Beckett (q.v.) observed of Joyce's last book.   [HB]

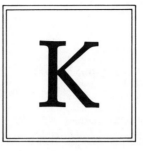

KAVAN, ANNA (1904–68). Novelist, born in France. Brought up partly in the USA, she lived also in the east, on the continent and in Australia and New Zealand, before settling in England. A heroin addict for the last thirty years of her life, she increasingly gave to her work the hallucinatory quality of the addict's perceptions and explored with tragic thoroughness the sense of detachment from the true self. After writing several run-of-the-mill novels in the 1920s and 1930s she began, in the experimental novel *The House of Sleep* (1947), retitled *Sleep Has His House* (1948), to work on her own experience of an unhappy childhood and consequent resort to an inner world. Her narrator counterpoints brief autobiographical recollections of daytime neglect and loneliness, humiliation and fear, with the phantasmagoric elaborations and intensifications of them that occur in the feverish dream-world of the night. Frustration and grief call out their compensatory opposites of exaltation and delight, and the verbal pyrotechnics tap a rich poetic vein. There are touches of surrealistic humour, like the description of the Major, symbol of respectable authority, who is equipped with a plug-in halo that lights up when switched on. There is comic cartoonery and delirious De Quinceyan rhetoric. There are anticipations of Beckett (q.v.) as well as reminders of Kafka and Joyce (q.v.).

A Scarcity of Love (1956) is a full-scale study of a wealthy woman whose uncanny self-centredness and self-admiration, and her resolve to fix men in adoring dependence upon her without the least surrender of her self, even her sexual self, assumes the integrity-consuming potency of witchery and devilry. The initial background, a castle in the Italian mountains, gives the Gothic atmosphere of Mrs Radcliffe's *Udolpho* to the early chapters and increases the intensity of the trance-like recognitions and disjunctions which Kavan defines so exactly.

The extent of Kavan's talents first became evident in her short stories, *Asylum Piece* (1940). A posthumous collection of short stories, *Julia and the Bazooka* (1970), has been edited and introduced by Rhys Davies (q.v.) who knew her personally. The title story is a frank account of a woman's dependence on the syringe (her 'bazooka') and other stories in the volume analyse the addict's experience of detachment from reality with pathos and acuteness. Other important novels are *Who Are You?* (1963) and *Ice* (1967). [HB]

KAVANAGH, PATRICK (1905–67). Poet, born in Inishkeen, County Monaghan, Ireland, son of a cobbler who also had a small farm. His childhood experience ('the usual barbaric life of the Irish country poor', he said), the conflict which developed between love of the land and ambition as a poet and the subsequent entry into the literary world – these things formed the substance of literary work in three media: the poetry itself, the fictional autobiography, *The Green Fool* (1938), and the autobiographical novel, *Tarry Flynn* (1948). As commentary upon, and corrective of, all three there is a brief *Self-*

Portrait (1964), first transmitted on Irish television. In this Kavanagh called *The Green Fool* a 'stage-Irish lie' written 'under the evil aegis of the so-called literary movement'; but the hardships and frustrations of peasant farming it records are real enough; local social, religious and political life is registered with vividness and humour, and the final drama of an escape to literary Dublin and London which proves to be no escape makes its point. But the book had to be withdrawn after a successful libel action by Oliver St John Gogarty (q.v.) on whom the aspiring young poet had called in Dublin. ('I mistook Gogarty's white-robed maid for his wife – or his mistress. I expected every poet to have a spare wife.') Of the earthier, unglamourized, often sardonic journey over similar autobiographical ground in *Tarry Flynn* Kavanagh continued to think well. It is 'not only the best but the only *authentic* account of life as it was lived in Ireland this century', he said (*Self-Portrait*). Indeed it is among the great studies of an artist growing up, highly perceptive in its record of family and friends, in its self-exploration and its humour; a rural counterpoise to Joyce's *Portrait of the Artist*.

Kavanagh's first book, *Ploughman and Other Poems*, was published in 1936 before he had forsaken his farm, but it was *The Great Hunger* (1942) that established him, and the self-projection in farmer Patrick Maguire won praise that Kavanagh later discounted ('it lacks the nobility and repose of poetry', op. cit.). By now he had come to Dublin ('the worst mistake in my life') to fall beneficiary to the literary cult of the peasant, to reject it along with the fake Ireland 'as invented and patented by Yeats [q.v.], Lady Gregory [q.v.] and Synge [q.v.]', and to become a frequenter of the bars that destroyed Brendan Behan (q.v.). Succeeding volumes of verse (*A Soul for Sale*, 1947; *Come Dance with Kitty Stobling*, 1960; and *Collected Poems*, 1964) contain highly individual short poems that are at once spare and intense, matter-of-fact in tone and naked of pretension; and they won Kavanagh the reputation of the greatest Irish poet since Yeats. The conscious dedication to everything that negates posture and showmanship ultimately made him turn on his own earlier work as being based on 'a myth that was a lie':

> Trees walking across the crests of hills and my
> rhyme
> Cavorting on mile-high stilts and the unnerved
> Crowds looking up with terror in their rational
> faces.
>
> ('Come Dance with Kitty Stobling')

He was wryly frank with his public and himself, disinfecting the poetic atmosphere with an idiom and a persona unhampered by literary or social protocols:

> There are people in the streets who steer by my
> star.
> There was nothing they could do but view me
> while I threw
> Back large whiskeys in the corner of a smoky bar
>
> ('The Same Again')

Reviewing Peter Kavanagh's *Sacred Keeper, A Biography of Patrick Kavanagh* (1980) in the *Times Literary Supplement* (13.6.80), James McNamara has pinpointed what ultimately put Kavanagh at odds with the world and with himself.

> Reading Kavanagh is to move as far as possible away from the nine-to-five view of life encountered among the 1950s Movement poets. He took the view that poetry was an ancient sacred flame, dangerous because it rose from the activity of the Holy Spirit, which jealously rendered the genuine poet fit for nothing else in life. [HB]

KENEALLY, THOMAS (1935–). Novelist, born in Sydney, New South Wales, Australia, and educated at St Patrick's College there. He prepared for the priesthood, an experience reflected in several of his works, but left two weeks before his ordination. He later studied law and worked as a teacher in Sydney in 1960–4; from 1968 until 1970 he lectured in drama at the University of New England, New South Wales. A prolific novelist, his books cover a wide range of topics and styles from *The Place at Whitton* (1964), which depicted witchcraft in a Catholic seminary, and the strange symbolic fable *A Dutiful Daughter* (1970) to more recent historical works such as *Gossip from the Forest* (1975) and *Season in Purgatory* (1976) which explore, respectively, the period of the 1918 Armistice and the partisan movement in the Mediterranean during the Second World War. *Bring Larks and Heroes* (1967) was a milestone in modern Australian fiction with its vivid, heavily patterned, historical re-creation of Sydney's convict period as a testing-ground for spiritual values. *Blood Red, Sister Rose* (1974) showed a similar interest, this time in the life of Joan of Arc. *Three Cheers for the Paraclete* (1968) and *The Survivor* (1969) both explored the conflicting demands of spiritual and worldly duties, the former in a seminary and the latter over an arena stretching from academe to Antarctica. *The Chant of Jimmie Blacksmith* (1972) was a powerful novel centring on the actual murder of a white family; in its skilful combination of strongly presented scenes, complex characterization and overall mythic significance it illustrated his writing at its best. *Confederates* (1979) once again demonstrated Keneally's ability to bring alive a historical situation in his fiction; this time his focus is the American Civil War. [PQ]

KENNEDY, MARGARET (1896–1967). Novelist, born in London and educated at Cheltenham Ladies College and at Somerville College, Oxford. At Cheltenham she won a prize for a narrative poem in a competition which was adjudicated by Yeats (q.v.). She married David Davies, former secretary to Asquith, in 1925. Her first novel, *The Ladies of Lyndon* (1923), was quickly overshadowed by *The Constant Nymph* (1924), which became one of the best-selling and most discussed books of its age. 'It's topping', wrote John Galsworthy (q.v.) to Edward Garnett; and indeed it is cunningly fashioned, and its presentation of spirited individualism in conflict with class-ridden conventionality sheds interesting light on the ethos of the period. Fourteen-year old Tessa is one of the motley brood ('Sanger's Circus'), legitimate and illegitimate, of the eccentric composer Albert Sanger. Brought up in bohemian freedom in a Swiss chalet, the children are left by his death to find their feet in an unsympathetic world. Tessa's unspoken, selfless devotion to the adult musician, Lewis Dodd, outlasts his incongruous marriage into high society, but heart disease kills her when the two of them are finally brought together. There were successful stage and screen versions of the book. Among later novels were the sequel, *The Fool of the Family* (1930), *Together and Apart* (1936), *The Feast* (1950) and *Troy Chimneys* (1953). Margaret Kennedy repeatedly shows imaginative power in depicting the sufferings of childhood and growing up. Of her plays the most notable was *Escape Me Never* (1934), which was also filmed. *The Ladies of Lyndon* and *Together and Apart* have both been reissued (1981). [HB]

KENNELLY, BRENDAN (1936–). Poet, born in Ballylongford, County Kerry, Ireland, educated at Tarbert, County Kerry, and at Trinity College, Dublin, where he is now Professor of Modern Literature. Since *Cast a Cold Eye* (1959) he has published numerous small volumes of poetry including *Dream of a Black Fox* (1968), *Islandman* (1977) and *The Visitor* (1978). 'I believe there is a poetry in everyday life and that the poet is one who tries to stay awake to that', he says, emphasizing the poet's 'continued struggle to discover and develop a proper language . . . a language of complete alertness, a vital and buoyant idiom'. 'Alert', 'vital' and 'buoyant' are appropriate adjectives for the idiom of a poet who has evoked both the rural and the urban scene with imaginative acuteness, pinning down what is heard and seen with rare verbal ingenuity.

> Braying on its mercy mission
> The white hysterical bully
> Blows all things out of its way . . .

That is the ambulance ('Ambulance') cutting its way savingly through 'the slack city' like a surgeon's knife through the human body. But, in the title poem of *Good Souls to Survive* (1967), for instance, Kennelly emerges also as a poet of calmly weighed – if more abstract – philosophic reflection on the human lot.

> If merit is measured at all,
> Vulnerability is the measure;
> The little desire protection
> With something approaching passion,
> Will not be afraid, cannot face error.

Kennelly edited the *Penguin Book of Irish Verse* (1970) and has written two novels, *The Crooked Cross* (1963) and *The Florentines* (1967). [HB]

KEYES, SIDNEY (1922–43). Poet, born in Kent, and brought up by a tempestuous grandfather who threw the furniture about. He went up to Oxford on a history scholarship in 1940, joined the army in 1942, was commissioned, served in North Africa, and was killed near Sidi Abdulla, having run into the enemy when sent out on a dawn patrol. From being a frail, introspective child, he became a reflective, impenetrable but not isolated young man, whose intense inner life was nourished on past English poetry. Of contemporaries he admired Eliot (q.v.), Charles Williams (q.v.), Graves (q.v.) and his friend John Heath-Stubbs (q.v.). Yeats (q.v.) too impressed him greatly. *The Iron Laurel* (1942) was his

first volume of poetry, and he was dead by the time the second, *The Cruel Solstice* (1944), came out and won the Hawthornden Prize. As a soldier-poet in the tradition of Owen (q.v.), Keyes dwells much on pain and death. In 'The Foreign Gate', written as he went into the army, the dead of past wars speak of their experience and the poet wrestles with the need to conquer the enemy, death.

> The great have come home and the troubled spirits
>   have spoken:
> But help or hope is none till the circle be broken
> Of wishing death and living time's compulsion,
> Of wishing love and living love's destruction.

'The Wilderness' owes much to Eliot in its rhythms and imagery. It extends the preoccupation of the soldier to a wider view of the need for personal surrender.

> All who save their life must find the desert –
> The lover, the poet, the girl who dreams of Christ.

Keyes's *Collected Poems* was published with an Introduction by Michael Meyer in 1945, and Meyer also edited *Minos of Crete: Plays and Stories* (1948). [HB]

KHAN, ISMITH (1925–). Novelist, born in Port-of-Spain, Trinidad, educated there and at Michigan State University and the New School for Social Research, New York. He has worked as journalist, librarian and university teacher.

He highlights uncommon facets of the multifarious Caribbean reality. In popular superstition the jumbie bird's song is death's summoner, and *The Jumbie Bird* (1961) dramatizes deracinated bewilderment among Muslim indentured immigrants (and their descendants) inveigled to Trinidadian sugar estates from India. Their pleasures but chiefly their disillusion are concentrated in the awakening consciousness of Jamini, grandson of the fiery old Kale Khan. After India's independence, shrivelled hopes of repatriation hasten Kale Khan's death, but Jamini and his father painfully find their true selves, having learned that, despite mutability, 'life have something special that go last forever'. *The Obeah Man* (1964) invests a practitioner of vestigial African religious practices with an artist's sensibility and dedication to his fellow West Indians' needs. Zampi's initial relationship with the woman Zolda is splendidly enacted through their powerful matching sexuality, but the novel buckles when Khan settles for what K. Ramchand calls 'a naive philosophy of self-control' (*The West Indian Novel and its Background*). [AR]

KINSELLA, THOMAS (1928–). Poet, born in Dublin, Ireland, son of an employee at Guinness's Brewery, educated by the Christian Brothers and at University College, Dublin. He worked for the Irish Department of Finance until 1965 and has since been Professor of English at Southern Illinois University and at Temple University, Philadelphia. He has published over twenty volumes of verse, beginning with *The Starlit Eye* (1952). *Selected Poems 1956–1968* (1973) contains samples from *Poems* (1956), *Another September* (1958), *Moralities* (1960), *Dowstream* (1962), *Wormwood* (1966) and *Nightwalker and Other Poems* (1968). 'It is my aim to elicit order from significant experience, with a view to acceptance on the basis of some kind of understanding. Major themes are love, death and the artistic act' (quoted J. Vinson, *Contemporary Poets*, 1975). Kinsella contemplates the poet's role and worries over an Ireland that seems to have exchanged 'a trenchcoat playground for a gombeen jungle' ('A Country Walk'). He refuses to talk down, and his intellectualism gives his introspection a sometimes forbidding density (see 'Baggot Street Deserta'), but when the cogitation is earthed in public history and stiffened by recognizable practical concern (see the passage on working in the Civil Service in 'Nightwalker', part I) the texture tends to be more lucid. 'In the Ringwood' is a captivating visionary ballad, 'Cover Her Face' a moving elegy, and 'Phoenix Park' a poem of searching scrutiny on departure from Eire. Yet in the pressurized self-exploration of later collections, such as *Notes from the Land of the Dead* (1972) and *A Technical Supplement* (1976), Kinsella cuts adrift from surface coherence and plunges into seemingly hypnotic deeps of haphazardly associative imagery. Of the former collection one tongue-in-cheek reviewer noted, 'Our man from the Land of the Dead is sending back no hard news'. See also *Fifteen Dead* (1980) and *Poems 1956–1973* (1980).

[HB]

KIPLING, RUDYARD (1865–1936). Poet and short-story writer, born in Bombay, India, where his father, a man of Yorkshire stock, taught at the School of Art. His mother's sister Georgina was wife of Sir Edward Burne-Jones, while her sister Louisa was mother of Stanley Baldwin. Rudyard's name is that of the Staffordshire lake where his parents first met. He was sent back to England to school in 1871, and six miserable years spent in the home of a Southsea hell-fire evangelical were brightened only by visits to the Burne-Joneses where 'Aunt Georgy' treated him lovingly and 'Uncle Topsy' (William Morris) was an entrancing visitor. Kipling was removed to the United Services College, Westward Ho, in 1878, where he began to read ravenously and where a Triple Alliance was formed with two other boys, to be featured later in the schoolboy stories, *Stalky & Co* (1899). In 1882 he returned to India to work as journalist, first with the Lahore *Civil and Military Gazette*, then with the Allahabad *Pioneer*. At once 'my English years fell away, nor ever, I think, came back in full strength' (*Something of Myself*, 1937). Pursuit of news coverage took him into multifarious corners of Indian life, he was much in army circles, he joined the Freemasons, and soon his early verses (*Departmental Ditties*, 1886) and early stories (*Plain Tales from the Hills*, 1888) were blazing his name in England and a wit was praying for those better days

> When the Rudyards cease from Kipling
> And the Haggards Ride no more.

The Kipling ethic began to be formulated – an emphasis on duty and the job to be done rather than on personal feelings, a sense of overriding law to which men must selflessly submit. The 'imperialist' tag was soon to damage him in the eyes of liberals, though his emphasis on the cost in personal discipline that ruling the lesser breeds extorts is a rigorous one, and he does not worship success: rather he sympathizes with the failures and the unknown victims of bungling powers-that-be.

Kipling came to London in 1889 to enjoy a meteoric rise in repute and income, but bad health sent him cruising to Italy, South Africa, Australia and India. Back in England again, he married Caroline Starr Balestier in 1892 and honeymooned in Canada and Japan before settling for four years at Vermont in New England. He had published his novel *The Light that Failed* in 1890 (the failing light is the eyesight of an artist who wants to complete a great work while there is yet time) and the stories *Life's Handicap* also in 1891. The Vermont years saw the publication of *Barrackroom Ballads* (1892), the short stories *Many Inventions* (1893) and the two *Jungle Books* (1894 and 1895), which introduce us to Mowgli, a boy brought up by a wolf-pack after being lost in a forest in infancy. Accepted by the animal world, he acquires their lore and learns that justice of the jungle that puts human justice to shame. Kipling did not hit it off with his New England neighbours and the family were back in England in 1896, though it was some time before they found their permanent home. This was Bateman's, at Burwash in Sussex, where they settled in 1902 and where Kipling indulged that passion for early motor cars (including the steam variety – see 'Steam Tactics' in *Traffics and Discoveries*, 1904) which Henry James (q.v.) was to make such sport of and Ford Madox Ford (q.v.) was to record so hilariously in *Return to Yesterday*. The Kiplings had two daughters, one of whom died of pneumonia in infancy, while their son John (born 1897) was killed in action in 1915.

Kipling's *Kim* (1901) is the story of an Irish orphan from the native quarter of Lahore who goes travelling with a Tibetan lama, runs into his father's old regiment and gets taken into Secret Service work. Kipling realized his incapacity to write a 'real novel'. *The Light that Failed*, he said, was 'only a *conte* – not a built book', while *Kim* was 'nakedly picaresque and plotless' (op. cit.). But his proficiency in the control of material as a short-story writer won lasting popularity for *Just So Stories for Little Children* (1902) which are whimsically phrased for reading aloud to a perhaps self-consciously childlike child audience. Kipling thought them his best work in prose, but the narrative is laced with parenthetical cajoleries, archly salted with the inconsequential 'logic' of infancy, coy abbreviations (' 'stute' for 'astute') and other devices patronizingly imitative of childhood inarticulacy. Nevertheless the cosy babyisms decrease as the book proceeds and there is no trace of the twee in the direct fable-style tale 'The Cat that Walked by Himself'. *Puck of Pook's Hill* (1906) and *Rewards and Fairies* (1910) are directed at older children and use the device of a meeting with Puck so that youngsters can be told tales of past ages in England. Poems of a pleasingly archaic comeliness are interposed between the stories. Kipling's stories for adults are very diverse, and show his great inventiveness and his skill in planting a tale to give it impact – framing it in the recollections of a participant or observer. Tales of India predominate at first, but Kipling's travels gave him material from many other parts of the world, and the 1914–18 war later supplied a heroic touchstone by which tested, proven or broken old soldiers could measure subsequent trials (see 'The Woman in His Life', *Limits and Renewals*, 1933). Kipling prided himself on his 'economy of implication' and pruned his stories ruthlessly in composition. The result is a cryptic reliance on obliquities, a mannered authorial stance – sometimes tight-lipped, sometimes obtrusively jocular – and a tiresome fondness for narration in dialect. Such devices make some of the later stories difficult to disentangle as well as jerky to read.

As a poet, Kipling remains a voice that cannot be drowned. The rhythms of swinging balladry and stately hymns undergird a vigorous rhetoric and the fluent 'catchiness' is the product of superb control. He has a flair for rolling out the right words. Poems like 'If', 'Gunga Din' and 'The Road to Mandalay' are among the best-known in the language. So too is Kipling's own favourite, 'Recessional', published in *The Times* after Queen Victoria's Jubilee Celebrations. Kipling refused the Laureateship in 1895 and the OM in 1916 and in 1924. He was buried in Westminster Abbey. The official biography, *Rudyard Kipling* (1978), which Lord Birkenhead completed in 1948, was suppressed throughout her lifetime by Kipling's daughter, Mrs Bambridge, who had commissioned it.   [HB]

KIRKUP, JAMES (1923–). Poet, born in South Shields, County Durham, the son of a joiner, and educated at South Shields and at Durham University. Kirkup has given us a lively picture of his infancy and upbringing in the two autobiographical books, *The Only Child* (1957) and *Sorrows, Passions and Alarms* (1959). They evidence a remarkably acute memory and an unnerving early sensitivity to external impressions. The privations of a Tyneside upbringing in the grim days of inter-war slump are courageously assimilated into a family life rich in sympathy, humour and love. Kirkup makes the reader feel privileged to meet his parents at second hand. Lack of resentment, and liberality of praise and gratitude make Kirkup a writer to whose magnanimity the reader warms. A pacifist, he worked on the land in the Second World War. He held the first Gregory Fellowship in Poetry at Leeds University in 1950 to 1952 and later held academic posts in Sweden and (as Professor of English Literature) in Spain, Malaya and (more extensively) Japan. Kirkup has been prolific in producing volumes of poetry, books about the east, translations from French and German, and a novel. His facility as a poet and his apparent readiness to versify on any topic at the drop of a hat have made him suspect to some critics. But facility is not pretentiousness, and Kirkup's total absence of arrogance, cynicism or small-mindedness is refreshing. Perhaps *The Submerged Village and Other Poems* (1947) first gave evidence of his quality, but it was the title poem in *A Correct Compassion and Other Poems* (1952) that compelled general attention. It is a careful first-hand description of a heart operation ('Mitral Stenosis Valvulotomy') observed in the General Infirmary at Leeds. Powerful dramatic reportage, it conveys a sharp reassessment of the character of compassion:

Cleanly, sir, you went to the core of the matter.
Using the purest kind of wit, a balance of belief
    and art,
You with a curious nervous elegance laid bare
The root of life, and put your finger on its beating
    heart.

The succeeding volume, *The Spring Journey and Other Poems* (1954), confirms Kirkup's distinctiveness, notably in the title poem about a day trip by car from Leeds to Whitby, and in the companion pieces, 'Summertime in Leeds' and 'A Visit to Brontëland'. If sometimes the reader feels that Kirkup's pleasures and interests have been taken up under pressure of producing a poem therefrom, the gift for objective delineation remains nevertheless versatile. *The Prodigal Son: Poems 1956–1959* (1959) contains work of comparable quality, and 'Tea in a Space-Ship' is quite funny. Later volumes include *White Shadows, Black Shadows: Poems of Peace and War* (1970) and *The Body-Servant: Poems of Exile* (1971). 'The Core of the Matter', from the former, returns to Kirkup's earlier preoccupation with heart surgery, neatly reflecting on press reports of a heart transplant in Capetown in which the donor was a pregnant black and the recipient a white ex-policeman. Kirkup's prolific output includes plays, translations, travel books and fiction.
                                                    [HB]

KLEIN, A.M. (1909–74). Poet, born in Montreal, Quebec, Canada, and educated at McGill University and the University of Montreal. He was called to the Bar in 1933 and practised until 1954. Early poems were published in 1929 and he appeared in the important anthology *New Provinces* (1936) edited by A.J.M. Smith (q.v.) and F.R. Scott (q.v.). His work explores the variety of Jewish culture with scholarship and wit, his first collection *Hath Not a Jew* (1940) coming at the close of a ten-year involvement with the zionist movement in Canada. It was a brilliant focusing of the riches of Jewish tradition within a contemporary context. In 1944 he published *Poems* and the bitterly satirical collection *The Hitleriad*. *The Rocking Chair* (1948) illuminated new perspectives in its involvement with French-Canadian culture, his familiarity with Jewish tradition and social or family bonds enabling him to respond perceptively to analogous French-Canadian patterns. *The Second Scroll* (1951) he termed a novel, but it employs a first-person narrator and includes some of his own work papers within its complex format. Its narrative thread traces actual and spiritual journeys of Uncle Melech Davidson through twentieth-century history, but for all its outward Jewishness it is fundamentally a secular work whose message is humanist in tone.   [PQ]

KOESTLER, ARTHUR (1905–83). Novelist and political thinker, born in Budapest, Hungary, and educated at the University of Vienna. As a journalist he rose to be Foreign Editor of *B.Z. am Mittag*, Berlin. He joined the Communist Party and worked for it until 1938. He could not remain in Hitler's Germany and was in Russia in 1933 and in Spain, reporting on the Civil War, in 1936. Captured by the nationalists and condemned to be executed, he was saved under a Red Cross prisoner-exchange agreement. His *Spanish Testament* (1938) tells the story. Koestler renounced communism, and disillusionment with revolution became a dominant theme of his writing. He was imprisoned in France in 1939, joined the Foreign Legion in 1940 and then escaped to England, first to serve in the Pioneer Corps and subsequently to work for the Ministry of Information. He became British by naturalization and began to write in English. Of his autobiographical volumes *Scum of the Earth* (1941) describes prison experience in France at the beginning of the war, *Arrow in the Blue* (1952) covers his early years up to joining the Communist Party and *The Invisible Writing* (1954) continues the story. Among his works of political and social analysis are *The Yogi and the Commissar* (1945) and *The Trail of the Dinosaur* (1955).

Koestler's novels bring acute philosophical and psychological insight to bear on the dilemma of political man and ethical man. *The Gladiators* (1939) (translated from German) deals with the revolt of the Roman slaves in 73–71 BC. *Darkness at Noon* (1940) (also translated from German) is a powerful portrayal of the career of Rubashov, a composite portrait of one of the Bolshevik old guard whose execution becomes politically expedient during the Stalinist purges of the 1930s. Rubashov is arrested and subjected to prolonged interrogation, first by a former friend and comrade-in-arms, Ivanov, and then by Gletkin, a coldly fanatical representative of the new generation of communists for whom the state is infallible. As Rubashov broods in his cell, his past is revealed to us as that of a revolutionary who has served and suffered for the cause, has eliminated others where necessary, but for whom queries now arise over the cost in individual suffering that the state demands. Yet, although he is deeply disillusioned, the brainwashing is effective. For Ivanov 'the principle that the end justifies the means is and remains the only rule of political ethics'. For Gletkin 'truth is what is useful to humanity' and Rubashov is persuaded that 'Honour is to be useful without vanity'. He signs a false confession so comprehensive that execution is inevitable.

Koestler's next novel *Arrival and Departure* (1943) is set in Neutralia (a fictionalized Portugal) in 1941. Petya Slavek, a disillusioned Balkan communist who has been tortured by a collaborationist government, faces the moral choice between escape to America and going to England to offer himself for dangerous work behind the enemy lines. A moving psychological study of a courageous yet guilt-laden hero is presented within a sweeping examination of the historic significance of the European conflict – an examination made possible by confrontations between nationals on neutral ground. *Thieves in the Night* (1946) deals with the Jews in Palestine. *The Age of Longing* (1951) is a pessimistic parable of the anti-utopian genre about the end of Europe. Koestler returned to fiction with *The Call Girls* (1972), an amusing and instructive satirical picture of an international conference held by a small group of top-grade boffins and eggheads who are nicknamed 'call girls' because they are always on tap for expense-free get-togethers, and make a career of it. Their interdisciplinary symposium is hilariously useless in getting to grips with imminent threats to continuing human survival. Koestler's marriage of scientific and political interests with literary imagination is a fruitful one. He matters as a novelist with real intellectual nourishment to offer. See also his *Bricks to Babel, Selected Writings with the Author's Comments* (1982).   [HB]

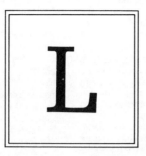

L

LA GUMA, ALEX (1925–). Political activist and novelist, born and educated in Cape Town, South Africa. A son of politically conscious parents, he joined the Communist party and was on its Cape Town Committee until the party was proscribed in 1950. For helping to organize the Freedom Charter (1955) he was among 156 South Africans accused in the infamous Treason Trial (1956) which ended with the charges dropped in 1961. After working as a clerk, book-keeper and factory-hand, he joined the radical paper *New Age* in 1960. As an executive member of the Coloured People's Congress he was detained for five months during the state of emergency after Sharpeville (1960) and was arrested again in 1961 for organizing a strike. In 1962, without trial, he was placed under twenty-four-hour house arrest for five years, prohibited from speaking publicly, publishing or being quoted. He spent two periods in solitary confinement in 1963 and 1966, as did his wife Blanche, also in 1966. They and their two children went into exile and settled in London from 1966 until 1978, when he moved to Havana as representative of the African National Congress.

In a 1977 interview, La Guma explains that after reading a brief newspaper report in the 1950s of a youth being shot by police, he decided to write a fictional account of how that death might have come about. The result was the first draft of the short novel *A Walk in the Night*. He had no thought of publication and it lay in a drawer until Ulli Beier, on behalf of Mbari in Nigeria, asked whether he had manuscripts for possible publication. Thus, its author banned from publishing in South Africa, *A Walk in the Night* (1962; London, 1967) came out in Nigeria. Mbari also published some of his short stories in *Black Orpheus* between 1960 and 1964. Set in the now demolished Cape Town coloured slum, District Six, *A Walk in the Night* is both an indictment of the sordid realities of poverty and racial segregation and a celebration of life that persists despite them. D. Rabkin writes that the 'characters who are condemned to walk the streets of District Six . . . are there not for their own "foul crimes", but as a consequence of the social and political system . . . Hell is not a state of mind, but a system of legislation'.

The prime object of all La Guma's fiction is to reveal through concrete particularities how that system of legislation with its bloated bureaucracy blights the lives of black South Africans and warps the humanity of black and white alike. To the white policemen in District Six all young males are *skollies* or thugs, and the main action shows how the pustule of anger in Michael Adonis over his dismissal for 'cheeking' a white foreman swells and eventually bursts in his mindless killing of a down-and-out old white actor, his escape when police mistake the layabout Willieboy for the murderer and his joining a gang of thugs. The streets, alleyways, overcrowded tenements, inadequate sewerage, the rot and stench of District Six, are brilliantly projected in terse, sinewy language, with sentence inversions and Afrikaans expressions in the dialogue authentically suggesting the rhythms and accents of 'Cape Coloured' Afrikaans. Toughness, violence, crime are shown to be inevitable in an environment more suited to cockroaches than people. La Guma's outlook is not wholly determinist, however; amidst the sordidness there is tenderness in the family life of the Lorenzos and in Joe's attachment to 'the mysterious life of sea things' by the shore and his belief that 'A man's got a right to look after another man'. The grim ending, with Willieboy dead in the police van, Raalt the white policeman feeling no compunction, Michael Adonis about to start a career of crime, is counterpointed with Joe wondering at the 'beauty of starfish and anemone' and Grace feeling the new knot of life within her.

La Guma's settings are circumscribed and localized, and he uses characterization not to explore individuality but to exemplify the human costs of South Africa's socio-economic system. Thus in *And a Threefold Cord* (Berlin, 1964) the setting is a shanty-town on the Cape Flats, the theme people's attempts to fashion rudimentary habitations out of 'flattened fuel cans . . . waterproof paper, cartons, old pieces of metal'. The will to prevail against such odds is expressed in the warm sense of community among the shanty-dwellers, while the inability of the isolated white character to form relationships where he wants to dramatizes the human sterility in many white South Africans.

In *The Stone Country* (Berlin, 1967; London, 1974) La Guma achieves an unusual merging of realism and symbolism. The setting, entirely within a prison, becomes an apposite image of all South Africa: white warders in absolute control work partly through privileged black trusties, while among the prisoners are intellectual 'politicals', petty criminals, murderers, all subject to the prevailing currents of naked force. Yet, even here, the apparently brutalized condemned murderer is capable of 'a flicker of light . . . like a spark of faulty electricity' towards the narrator who has befriended him.

In the *Fog of the Season's End* (1972), about the underground black resistance, is characteristically rich in details about life under apartheid. It is, however, La Guma's weakest novel, for he attempts to construct a highly heroical tale (in genuine tribute to the resistance) upon his accustomed framework of realism. His own unease is betrayed in an excessively adjectival style overloaded with far-fetched similes that distract. In *Time of the Butcherbird* (1979) he regains his poise with the theme of the South African government's policy of tidying up their ethnic map by forcibly removing tribal people from their ancestral lands and dumping them on waste land. The twin narratives of private revenge and of communal resistance to removal are placed in a fully realized rural locality and La Guma extends his range by dealing more extensively than before with white characters.

La Guma has also edited an anthology, *Apartheid* (New York, 1971; London, 1972), and written an account of his travels in Russia, *A Soviet Journey* (1978). He was awarded the Afro-Asian Writers' Lotus Prize (1969). [AR]

LAL, P. (1929–). Publisher, poetry publicist and poet, born in Kapurthala, India, and educated in Calcutta. He taught at St Xavier's College, Calcutta, from 1952 to 1967 and at the University of Calcutta from 1967, besides holding visiting professorships abroad.

Of prodigious literary energy, Lal has published many volumes of his own poetry since 1960, including *Collected Poems* (1977), and half a dozen critical books; he has edited many anthologies, notably *Modern Indian Poetry in English* (1969), and translated (or as he would have it 'transcreated') numerous works from Sanskrit and other Indian languages, such as *The Mahabharata* (1969–74). His verse is generally cultivated and taut, but disappointingly often lapses into triteness or image-mustering. S. Mokashi-Punekar observes that Lal's poetry reveals a sensitive response to natural beauties and to the twists of human nature; increasingly in recent years he has come under Indian classical literary influences and turned an angry satirical eye upon modern urban life.

As founder-manager of the publishing house Writers Workshop, Calcutta, and editor of its *Miscellany*, he has consistently encouraged young writers and contributed immeasurably to the continued writing of poetry in English in India. [AR]

LAMMING, GEORGE (1927–). Novelist, born and educated in Barbados, receiving encouragement at school from Frank Collymore, editor of the literary magazine *Bim*. After schoolmastering in Trinidad, he migrated to London, where he has since lived, when not holding visiting professorships or travelling abroad. He received the Maugham Award in 1957.

Lamming was in the vanguard of writers who left the West Indies to work and publish in London. His richly metaphoric imagination commands the English language in supple, suggestive and ingenious ways. *In the Castle of My Skin* (1953) was soon and deservedly recognized as a major West Indian work, but his later books are of unequal quality. Perhaps such early success was unfortunate for Lamming's development. At the centre of *In the Castle* is the growing up of four peasant boys on a small Caribbean island, but the theme of change and growth embraces the entire colonial society, as it develops from dependence upon a decaying, land-owning family, through labour unrest and social uncertainty, towards political awareness and independence. In poverty and parochialism, with Empire-day school parades punctuating revivalist meetings, the boys nevertheless enjoy a pristine freedom as they amuse themselves on the beach, unravel in confused argument the life around them, steal into the grounds of the big house at night and behold wonders: ' "You never been so close", Trumper whispered . . . "Never ever", said Boy Blue. " 'Tis like a next world, the music an' the drink an' all that, an' particular the way they hold on to one another." " 'Tis like a Christmas", Trumper said.' In biblical cadences the old people comment wisely and stoically upon the mutability overtaking them, while the boys and the community as a whole are shown clearly, often lyrically, undergoing inevitable, natural metamorphosis. A vanishing way of life is sympathetically recorded, without sentimentality, and what is replacing it greeted with nervous expectation.

Launching into optimistic emigration to England and finding only dashed expectations is the theme of *The Emigrants* (1954). Its characters have little of the insouciant resilience that Selvon (q.v.) gives his in *The Lonely Londoners*; instead there is the overwhelming sense that 'W'at it is we searchin' for, others got, an' they ain't any happier'. Although Lamming's linguistic exuberance produces splendid scenes in *The Emigrants*, there are weaknesses in design, such as the disproportionately long voyage, and many improbabilities in the plot.

Of Age and Innocence (1958), set on the fictional West Indian island, San Cristobal, during the agitation for independence, contrasts Ma Shephard's gritty but incomplete peasant wisdom and the plottings, violent deaths and counter-murders of politics, with the youthful ability of boys of different racial origins to form friendship and trust beyond race, thus auguring well for the island's future. Though some parts of *Season of Adventure* (1960) are irritatingly over-written, the theme of the heroine's hesitant finding of a genuinely West Indian identity is well integrated with her desire to know who her real father was, and with her half-fearful, but ultimately accepting, involvement in the 'souls' ritual and drum music that are a Caribbean inheritance from Africa via slavery.

In *Water with Berries* (1971) Lamming applies his eccentric reading of the Caliban–Prospero relationship as that of colonized and colonizer to a group of artists in London who try to integrate their metropolitan present with their colonial past. *Natives of My Person* (1972), about a seventeenth-century voyage of colonization to the Caribbean, is a complex mélange of themes: freedom, imperialism, government and mercantilism, the past in relation to the present, love and sexuality, the innermost and the verbally communicable. These are two very ambitious novels, full of wonderful pieces of artistry that attempt vastly comprehensive orderings of experience which too often sound solemn reverberations, indiscriminately, so that the patterns of meaning being striven after evade apprehension.

Lamming has also published a collection of essays, *The Pleasures of Exile* (1960), which reiterates his Caliban–Prospero interpretation variously, and has edited an anthology of modern black writing, *Cannon Shot and Glass Beads* (1974).   [AR]

LARKIN, PHILIP (1922–). Poet, born in Coventry, West Midlands, and educated at King Henry VIII Grammar School there. He read English at St John's College, Oxford, from 1940 to 1943. His first post was in the public library at Wellington, Shropshire. From there he moved into academic librarianship at University College, Leicester (1946), Queen's College, Belfast (1950), and Hull University (1955) where he still remains. *The Less Deceived* (1955) and his inclusion in Robert Conquest's (q.v.) anthology, *New Lines* (1955), established him as a poet. He was thus associated with the 'Movement' that turned its back on high-flown diction and gesture in favour of the language used in conversation, and that ironically played down any poetic claim to influence the public world. Succeeding volumes were *The Whitsun Weddings* (1964), *The Explosion* (1970) and *High Windows* (1974). Larkin asserts that it is the work of Thomas Hardy which represents the best body of poetry this century. Though he took Hardy as a model for not posturing as a poet but being himself, it is his strength that he cannot readily be categorized. His poems are rooted in day-to-day events lifted out of ephemerality by

the wry probings of a reflective sensibility. His words heighten the commonplace experience, concretely in respect of its impact on the senses, disquietingly in its half-realized implications for men and women unsure of their significance. In 'Ambulances' children in the road and women coming from the shops suddenly catch sight of

> A wild white face that overtops
> Red stretcher blankets momently

and sense the 'solving emptiness / That lies just under all we do'. In the celebrated 'Church Going' the unbeliever enters an empty church in habitual curiosity and lingers, teased by his own questions of the 'serious house on serious earth'. The title poem in *The Whitsun Weddings* describes a Whitsuntide train journey on which the poet gradually wakes up to the sequence of wedding parties encountered at stations en route, and here the response is wholly unironic and life-affirming. More characteristic is the bleak pessimism with which the poet considers his predecessor in a furnished room in 'Mr Bleaney'.

Some of Larkin's harsher mockeries in *High Windows* (see 'Posterity', 'This Be the Verse', 'Vers de Société') use colloquial coarseness so devastatingly that irony topples over into crude cartoonery ('the drivel of some bitch / Who's read nothing but *Which*'). Crucial lines sum up the attitude and feelings which caught a certain current mood of cynical disengagement and gained Larkin a vastly increased readership: 'Still going on, all of it, still going on' (of the seaside holiday scene in 'To the Sea'); 'There's something laughable about this' (of the way the moon sweeps through the clouds, 'high and preposterous and separate' in 'Sad Steps'); and 'I'm stuck with this old fart at least a year' (his future biographer's thought as he works on the poem in question, 'Posterity'). Larkin is a masterly craftsman in using received stanzaic forms with lucidity and naturalness. His novel *Jill* (1946) is autobiographically interesting in that its hero, John Kemp, a policeman's son from the north, finds wartime Oxford socially discomfiting and psychologically mortifying. Katherine Lind, of his second novel, *A Girl in Winter* (1947), is also displaced: she is a continental refugee in an English provincial town in wartime. In *All that Jazz: A Record Diary 1961–68* (1970) we meet Larkin the jazz feature writer of the *Daily Telegraph* from 1961 to 1971. Larkin has received signal academic recognition in honorary D Litts from Belfast, Leicester, Warwick, St Andrews and Sussex universities. He edited *The Oxford Book of Twentieth-Century English Verse* (1973), and it bears the stamp of his preference for poems that are 'well made and show decorum', as Auden (q.v.) has observed with approval. But critical enthusiasm which the cool scrupulousness of Larkin's craftsmanship early evoked has now been tempered by some unease at the suburban narrowness of his vision. See also Anthony Thwaite, ed., *Larkin at Sixty* (1982).   [HB]

LAVIN, MARY (1912–). Irish novelist and short-story writer, born in Massachusetts and a graduate of Dublin University. She has lived most of her life in Ireland and was President of the Irish Academy of Letters from 1971 to 1973. *The Stories of Mary Lavin*, two volumes (1964 and 1974), contains stories from several collections dating back to 1942. Tales of Irish life, they fasten on significant events in personal and family affairs – quarrels, estrangements, bereavements, incongruous marriages – mixing pathos with quiet humour in an entertaining and illuminating manner. The novel *The House in Clewe Street* (1945) traces the growth and maturation of Gabriel Galloway, grandson and heir of a well-to-do property-owner, Theodore Coniffe, and son of his youngest daughter, Lily. The Coniffes live in a small country town, Castlerampart. Gabriel loses both parents in childhood and is then brought up by two frustrated spinster aunts, the elder soured and authoritarian, the younger sweet but ineffective; he breaks out and runs away to Dublin with a servant girl. There is no background of political or public event in Mary Lavin's world, but she has deep understanding of psychological differences due to temperament, class, upbringing and environment. She sees the feminine world freshly from the outside as well as acutely from within, and her men are masculine. The development of Gabriel under the peculiar tyrannies of thwarted spinsterhood and of a preselected, 'privileged' social role is penetratingly defined. Mary Lavin has moral urgency in her larger design and yet she can pin down the minor dilemmas of domestic sociability and human intercourse with delicious irony. *Mary O'Grady* (1950) is another Irish family history. Frank O'Connor (q.v.) noted Lavin's imperviousness as a writer to Ireland's public troubles. 'Of the principal Irish writers of the period only Mary Lavin has come out of it unmarked. Her work seems to be in a class by itself. It is deeply personal, and there are a great many doors in it marked "Private"' (*The Backward Look*, 1967). [HB]

LAWRENCE D.H. (David Herbert) (1885–1930). Novelist and poet, born at Eastwood near Nottingham, Nottinghamshire, in an area where coal-mining impinged on farming and drab villages on the beauty of nearby Sherwood Forest. Such dichotomies stamped themselves on Lawrence's mind and work. There was the contrast between the warm, instinctive cameraderie of the underground workers in their dark world of toil and the womenfolk's daylight world of home-making and child-rearing. Lawrence's parentage epitomized the antithesis. His mother, Lydia, had been a school-teacher and had married beneath her in succumbing to a handsome and vital but almost illiterate miner. Daily familiarity with her husband's crudities repelled her. She went on cultivating her mind and brought up her five children in a warm little circle from which their father was excluded. He took refuge in drink and revenge in domestic wrath. Bert (D.H.L.) won a scholarship to Nottingham High School. When he left, he worked first as a clerk in a surgical appliance factory at Nottingham, then as a pupil-teacher in Eastwood ('three years' savage teaching of collier lads', he called it, and it provided the picture of Ursula's early teaching days in *The Rainbow*). His elder brother, Ernest, the apple of his mother's eye, who had risen to an office job in London, died of pneumonia. Lydia was plunged in apathetic despair until Bert himself went down with pneumonia and replaced his dead brother as the object of her devouring possessiveness. The pressure stultified Bert's long and at first idyllic relationship with Jessie Chambers, whose family lived at Haggs Farm nearby. After Mrs Lawrence's death from cancer in 1910

Lawrence admitted this to Jessie. 'I've *loved* her, like a lover. That's why I could never love you.' (See *D.H. Lawrence* by 'E.T.', Jessie Chambers, 1935.) The dilemma is frankly reproduced as the central theme of *Sons and Lovers*. Lawrence took a two-year teacher-training course at University College, Nottingham, and it was here that he met Louise Burrows to whom he was for a time engaged. (His letters to her have been published as *Lawrence in Love*, edited by J.T. Boulton, 1968.) A rather different relationship arose when Alice Dax, a radical, a suffragette and a married woman like Clara Dawes in *Sons and Lovers*, took him to her bedroom and 'gave' him 'sex' as an instant recipe for completing a troublesome poem.

Lawrence was teaching at Croydon when Jessie Chambers sent some of his poems to the *English Review* on her own initiative. The result was a meeting with Ford Madox Ford (q.v.) who then read the manuscript of Lawrence's novel, *The White Peacock*, and proclaimed him a genius. The novel was published in 1911. Written in the first person, it deals beautifully and lovingly with the countryside Lawrence knew, but promotes the characters he knew on to a somewhat unreal level of leisured affluence, and the style ascends to keep up with them. Lawrence's second novel, *The Trespasser* (1912), transposes into fiction the tragic love affair of Helen Corke, a teacher he met in London, whose lover, a married violinist, committed suicide. Lawrence was never healthy, and illness as well as inclination drove him to abandon school-teaching. Hoping to apply for a job at a German university, he sought the help of Professor Ernest Weekley, the philologist, whose teaching he had appreciated at Nottingham. Weekley (who later became widely known through his books, *The Romance of Words*, 1912, and *The Romance of Names*, 1916) generously invited him to lunch. The lunch cost him his happiness, for Lawrence and Weekley's German wife, Frieda von Richthofen, who was 32 and mother of three children, set each other alight at first meeting. The two eloped to the continent and thereafter, until tuberculosis killed Lawrence at the age of 44, they led a wandering life in Europe, Australia, New Mexico and elsewhere. The war years kept them in England where, as a result of Frieda's German nationality and Lawrence's outspokenness on the conflict, they fell under suspicion and were harassed by the police. A rasping fictionalized account of the harassment is incongruously inserted in *Kangaroo*. The couple were able to marry after a divorce in 1914. Frieda's isolation from her children was a source of strain, the marriage always had its tempestuous side and Frieda's marital infidelities neither began nor ended with Lawrence; nevertheless her vitality and full-bloodedness as a mate, and her downrightness in countering her husband's more eccentric personal and ideological claims, are stamped on his work.

*Sons and Lovers** (1913) is Lawrence's finest work, notable alike for its autobiographical richness, its psychological insight as a study of growing up, and its intense evocation of family life and local background. The references to warmth and joy ('Everybody was mad with happiness in the family') must be set against Lawrence's later rejection of Eastwood and what it stood for. ('I hate the damned place', he said on his last visit in 1926.) *The Rainbow* (1915) covers the lives of three generations of a

Nottinghamshire family, the Brangwens, in a repetitive cyclic pattern of mating, birth and death that matches the rhythmic continuity of farming life. Love is threaded through with the antagonisms, battles and rages consequent upon Lawrence's obsession with 'love that was keenly close to hatred'. The men in the mines are the property of the machine that employs them and home, for them, is 'a little side-show'. Ursula Brangwen, whose girlhood is traced with the thoroughness of Paul Morel's boyhood in Sons and Lovers, pits herself against the domination of the machine. At the end, after rapturous love and let-down, she is left with her hope in the rainbow, 'the world's new architecture' that symbolically replaces the archaic cathedral arch. For 'the older world is done for, toppling on us. . . . There must be a new world', Lawrence explained in a letter about the book. The theme ramifies in Women in Love* (1921) where the lives of Ursula and her sister Gudrun are followed further in what is probably Lawrence's most cohesive book.

Aaron's Rod (1922) shows Aaron, a miner, breaking out of servitude in marriage, but 'everybody hates Aaron's Rod – even Frieda', Lawrence conceded. In Kangaroo (1923) the marital ups and downs of Richard Lovat Somers, a writer, and his wife Harriet, project Lawrence's struggles with Frieda. (There is a chapter of sustained analysis, 'Harriet and Lovat at sea in marriage'.) Against a superlatively rich portrayal of Australian life and scenery, a would-be fascist dictator, Cooley (called 'Kangaroo'), heads a movement of ex-servicemen intent on a national take-over. Somers, needing the living fellowship with other men that Lawrence himself craved for, is drawn to Cooley but then rejects his philosophy as being too spiritualized. Somers cherishes 'the dark god at the lower threshold'. The Plumed Serpent (1926), set in Mexico, develops the theme of a cult rooted in sex and blood-consciousness, and one becomes aware of a seemingly demonic urge driving Lawrence towards the assertion of unexplored naturalistic allegiances to replace the civilizational values he hated. Lady Chatterley's Lover* (1928) became Lawrence's most notorious book. A sexual parable, it offsets the paralysis of the traditional order by renewal from the vigorous earth. 'The usual sloppy English', said James Joyce (q.v.) after sampling it, and indeed much of Lawrence's prose is cluttered with sentimental turgidities that smack of women's magazines.

Lawrence's output also included travel books (Sea and Sardinia, 1921), short stories (St Mawr, 1925) and polemical works like Psychoanalysis and the Unconscious (1921) and, more notably perhaps, Fantasia of the Unconscious (1922), in which he develops sex-based anti-intellectualist theories, opposing 'living experience' and 'sure intuition' to our prevailing 'science of the dead world'.

Lawrence's poetry was gathered together in Collected Poems (1928) and Last Poems (1932). Much of it is autobiographical in character. Look! We have come through (1917) registers the depths and heights of the first years with Frieda. 'They may have come through', Bertrand Russell is reputed to have observed, 'but I see no reason why I should look.' Some of the poetry is satirical ('How beastly the bourgeois is') but the best of it is poetry of observant response to natural life. Here, in recapturing the sensuous and emotional flavour of an encounter with

bird or beast or flower, Lawrence's verbal power to pin down the instant and the immediate comes into its own. Lawrence's readiness to disregard conventional metrical inhibitions invited accusations of carelessness, but they have been countered: 'He is always happiest when, trusting his intuitive response to the emotional demands of his theme, he sets his words dancing to an inner music, unconstrained by the rules of prosody' (John Press, A Map of Modern English Verse, 1969).

Frieda Lawrence wrote a book of personal memories, Not I, But the Wind (1935). Lawrence was an indefatigable letter-writer. Aldous Huxley edited his Selected Letters (1932). The Collected Letters in two volumes, edited by H.T. Moore (1967), is now being superseded by James T. Boulton's seven-volume collection, The Letters of D.H. Lawrence. See Volume I 1901–1913 (1978) and Volume II 1913–1916 (1982).

Sons and Lovers is an intensely autobiographical novel. In a finely realized account of mining life in the Midlands, the situation of the Morel family parallels that of the Lawrences. Mrs Morel's background was middle-class and the passion that caused her to marry her miner husband has not survived close encounter with the crudities of his calling and the animal insensitivity of his make-up. Her four children are brought up to hate their father and to enjoy an intimacy of heart and mind that excludes him. Mrs Morel fastens her special affection with consuming possessiveness upon her son William and, after his death, on the younger son Paul. Paul's psychological development is traced with insight and subtlety. Leaving school, he goes (like Lawrence) to work in a surgical appliance factory at Nottingham, but his interest in books and painting remains strong. Paul finds happiness outside his home at a nearby farm where Miriam Leivers lives with her brothers. The love between Paul and Miriam (the Jessie Chambers of Lawrence's own experience) is doomed because of the overpowering emotional bond imposed on Paul by his mother's love. The personality of Miriam, pitted against the hostile competitive demands of Mrs Morel – who dies of cancer – is movingly realized. In a second love affair, with Clara Dawes, a radical suffragette living apart from her husband (and modelled on Alice Dax), Paul again fails to achieve a fulfilling relationship. 'The shock of Sons and Lovers gave the death-blow to our friendship', Jessie Chambers wrote long afterwards (op.cit.). The book is seminal Lawrentian themes ('Only from the middle class one gets ideas, and from the common people – life itself, warmth', Paul avers) but the angle of judgement is one that Lawrence would later have corrected. 'I would write a different Sons and Lovers now: my mother was wrong, and I thought she was absolutely right.'

Women in Love continues the story of the Brangwen family begun in The Rainbow, but with a surer focus and portraiture, for Lawrence concentrates on the two sisters, Ursula and Gudrun, and constructs a work that is shapely in respect both of the balanced human studies and of the carefully spaced dramatic set-pieces. The setting is at first the small mining town of Beldover, but the action shifts to London and Austria. Gudrun, aged 25, an art student, 'beautiful, passive, soft-skinned, soft-limbed', is paired with Gerald Crich, wealthy heir to mine-ownership, a handsome, strong, masterful representative of industrial efficiency. Ostensibly he succeeds with women, but it is the shallow effectiveness of mechanical efficiency, and real love cannot be managed like a business. So the affair with Gudrun fails, Gerald's hollowness is laid open, and he goes out to a symbolic death in the cold Austrian snow. Ursula, aged 26, now a schoolteacher, whose hostility to machine-domination was made clear in *The Rainbow*, is here matched with Rupert Birkin, school inspector and spokesman for the passionate self that must assert its integrity against the cramping pressures of mechanized industrialism and the domination of intellect. There is much of Lawrence and Frieda in the working out of this tense, sometimes violent, but ultimately fulfilling relationship. In the picture of the gatherings at Breadalby, the Georgian mansion, and more especially in the study of Hermione Roddice, Lawrence draws on experience of Garsington and of Lady Ottoline Morrell; while for the London scenes at the Pompadour café he draws on the contemporary bohemian world to which his growing literary reputation had given him entrée.

Lady Chatterley's Lover was published in London in an expurgated edition in 1928 and privately, without expurgations, in Paris in 1929. The first full authorized editions were published in 1959 (New York) and 1960 (London). Three versions of the novel exist (see *The First Lady Chatterley* and *John Thomas and Lady Jane*). The setting is Wragby Hall, a family seat in the industrial Midlands. Sir Clifford Chatterley has returned from the war paralysed below the waist. His impotence is symbolic of the sterile upper-class establishment. Indeed, Sir Clifford is turned into a monstrous personification of the moribund mechanical 'Thing' Lawrence detested, and it might be argued that Lawrence's artistry becomes too mechanical in assaulting it. Mellors, the gamekeeper, earthy and lowly, but sensitive and self-educated, a representative of working-class virility, provides the sexual fulfilment that Chatterley's wife, Connie, desperately needs, and she becomes pregnant. Mellors plans to divorce his wife and, though Sir Clifford refuses to divorce Connie, the two lovers determine to go and settle down together. Lawrence's free use of 'four-letter' words in Mellors's love-talk, designed to intensify the simple genuineness of the relationship, fails to retrieve the terms for such a purpose. But the collision between what is vital and what is moribund has some force, and Lawrence's estimate of the book, like his aim, was earnest enough: 'To me it is beautiful and tender and frail as the naked self is'.

LAWRENCE, T.E. (Thomas Edward) (1888–1935). Writer of prose and man of action, an illegitimate son of an Anglo-Irish aristocrat and a Calvinist mother. The father raised a second family with her after leaving his first wife and changing his name. Lawrence was educated in Oxford at the High School and at Jesus College, where he gained first-class honours in modern history. He worked in archaeological excavation in the Middle East and, when the war came, joined the Arab Bureau in Cairo for intelligence work. In 1916 he went to the desert to engineer the guerrilla warfare of Arabs against the Turks. He adopted Arab costume, won the confidence of Arab chieftains and gave rein to his romantic temperament in active leadership, train-wrecking and

intrigue which readily assumed an aura of larger-than-life mystery and heroism. After the war he became the symbol of dashing, courageous achievement in a theatre of war that could be glamorized, as the Western Front could not. Lawrence wrote up his campaigns in *The Seven Pillars of Wisdom* (privately printed, 1926; issued publicly, 1935) of which an abridged version, *Revolt in the Desert*, appeared in 1927. The book is a ranging account of exciting action, evocative of atmosphere and locale and shot through with a high-pitched straining after epic dimension in human interchange and reflection:

> To be of the desert was, as they knew, a doom to wage unending battle with an enemy who was not of the world, nor life, nor anything, but hope itself; and failure seemed God's freedom to mankind.

The growth of the 'Lawrence of Arabia' legend between the wars was not hindered by Lawrence's over-advertised determination to seek obscurity. He tried to hide in the lowest ranks of the Air Force, taking the name first of 'Ross' then of 'T.E. Shaw'. It became popularly understood that he had made promises to the Arabs on the government's behalf that were later dishonoured and that he shrank thereafter from involvement in affairs at any level where he might be tainted with acquiescence. But the 'legend' has come under fire. Though it is plain that Lawrence's courage needed no supplementation from fiction, it is being accepted that he exploited his own enigmatic persona in contributing to a myth of youthful precocity and in supplying material for the exaggeration of his prowess, brilliance and importance. Richard Aldington (q.v.) (*Lawrence of Arabia*, 1955) sees him as a perpetual leg-puller, romancer and confounder of fact with fiction, whose irresistible propensity for self-dramatization and self-advertisement was fuelled by the basic insecurity of an illegitimate with a homosexual nature. G.B. Shaw (q.v.) described him as 'a pure undiluted actor'. Even Charlotte Shaw, in whom Lawrence found a motherly confidante, declared him 'an infernal liar'. Lawrence met his death when travelling too fast on his motor bike on a return drive from Bovington Camp, Dorset, to his cottage, Clouds Hill. He had just dispatched a telegram to Henry Williamson (q.v.) who, it appears, was toying with the idea of a meeting between Hitler and Lawrence as a potential English counterpart. Lawrence's *Letters* were edited by David Garnett (q.v.) in 1938.   [HB]

LAWSON, HENRY (1867–1927). Short-story writer, born on the goldfields in Grenfell, New South Wales, Australia, in 1867. A lonely child, Lawson's early years were unhappy and his introspective tendencies were exacerbated by irregular education and by partial deafness from the age of 9. He began work at about 13, and in 1883 his mother left with himself and his two younger brothers for Sydney. In 1887 the Sydney *Bulletin* (q.v.) published his 'Song of the Republic' and he subsequently established a reputation for stirring verses depicting the lot of the working man or heralding a glorious and independent Australia. In 1892 Lawson spent eighteen months working in the area around Bourke in western New South Wales and the experience crystallized for him not only the physical horrors of outback life but also the compensating qualities of stoicism and wry humour possessed by those whose everyday environment it was. This relatively brief period provided material for much of Lawson's best work, in which a deceptively simple style and structure allow him to explore characters and situations that are both 'typically Australian' and universally significant. A volume of verse, *In the Days When the World Was Wide* (1896), was followed later the same year by a collection of prose, *While the Billy Boils*. Also in 1896 Lawson married Bertha Bredt, and the couple spent time in Perth and a year in New Zealand, where he wrote much of *Joe Wilson and His Mates* (1901). For two years he then held down an office job in Sydney, but in 1899, with encouragement from the Governor of New South Wales, Lord Beauchamp, the family left for England. Lawson's drink problem of the past four years was now severe and Bertha soon returned to Sydney with the two children, followed by her husband. The marriage was in ruins, and the period until his death in 1927 was to be one of physical and artistic decline in spite of proffered help from friends. Much of Lawson's importance for his contemporaries lay in his verse, but today his stories are more highly regarded. Their dramatic yet subtle presentation of outback life broke with an earlier, more stylized, treatment of Australia and opened a realm which has ever since exercised a fascination for Australian writers, artists and critics. Widely praised in his day for its supposedly documentary picture of bush life, the craftsmanship of Lawson's 'fictional world' is now valued for its intense concentration upon, and reworking of, a limited range of experience which he renders capable of bearing complex human emotions.   [PQ]

LAYTON, IRVING (1912-). Poet, born in Neamtz, Romania. He arrived in Canada with his parents at the age of one. He took a degree in agricultural science at MacDonald College, Sainte Anne de Bellevue, Quebec, and after war service in 1942-3 took an MA in economics at McGill University, Montreal. A varied and distinguished career as teacher, poet and writer-in-residence followed, and since 1969 he has been Professor of English at York University, Toronto. Throughout his career Layton has worked within the academic establishment, but his poetic stance has always been calculatedly anticonformist and often deliberately shocking - at least by the standards of conservative Canadian society. He was an associate editor of the seminal American journal *Black Mountain Review* in the 1940s and was a central figure in the Canadian poetry revival of that period. Layton is a prolific writer who published fifteen volumes of verse between his earliest book, *Here and Now* (1945), and the *Collected Poems* of 1971 (which contained 385 titles). The publication of *In the Midst of My Fever* (1954) and *The Cold Green Element* (1955) marked a significant development in his work from the technically accomplished but sometimes strained and satiric outrageousness of early books such as *Now is the Place* (1948) and *The Black Huntsman* (1951) to a more mellow outlook which often holds romance and irony in tension. Layton has retained from his early verse a romantic conception of the poet as outsider, prophet and medium of the true voice of instinctive feeling - but the new stringency was reaffirmed in *Improved Binoculars: Selected Poems*

(1956) which had an introduction by William Carlos Williams. Layton's Foreword to *A Red Carpet for the Sun: Collected Poems* (1959) stated that the volume contained all the poems written between 1942 and 1958 that he wished to preserve and stressed that they belonged to a period of his life that was over - 'testing, confusion, ecstasy'. He now saw himself as 'an angry middle-aged man, going into courage and truth'. *Selected Poems* appeared in 1974, and more recent poetry includes *Lovers and Lesser Men* (1973) and *The Pole Vaulter* (1974). His published views on a wide range of topics (which at their most provocative give little indication of the fine poet Layton can be at his best) were collected in *Engagements: The Prose of Irving Layton* (1972). In the Foreword to the 1971 *Collected Poems* Layton wrote: 'My early childhood experiences in Montreal put a crease into my mind neither theology nor socialism has been able to straighten out. I see life as a Dionysian Cock-and-cunt affair with time off, though precious little of it, for meditation and good works'. In considering the question 'Am I a Canadian poet?' he declined to deal in 'abstractions and thick evasive words', claiming: 'My country is wherever there are concrete objects to touch, taste, feel and enjoy'. *The Uncollected Poems, 1936-1959* was published in 1976; *Taking Sides* (1977) gathered social and political writings from the period since 1935.
                    [PQ]

LEACOCK, STEPHEN (1869-1944). Canadian humorist, born in England. He was 6 when his parents emigrated, grew up on a farm near Lake Simcoe, Ontario, and was educated locally, at Upper Canada College and at the University of Toronto. He was a master at Upper Canada College from 1889 until 1898 when he began postgraduate studies at the University of Chicago, Illinois. In 1903 he was appointed lecturer in economics and political science at McGill University, Montreal, became head of the department in 1908 and remaind there until he retired in 1936. Leacock's first book, *Elements of Political Science* (1906), was a standard textbook for many years, but the appearance of *Literary Lapses* in 1910 immediately established his international reputation as humorist - the book was first published privately but was republished the same year in New York and London and subsequently went through some twenty editions in as many years. His colourful career as a humorist nevertheless ran parallel to that of the academic who published almost one hundred articles and more than two dozen books. Collections of his humorous pieces total over thirty, his work having first appeared in American and Canadian magazines as early as 1894. It combines satire, irony, parody and pure nonsense in varying proportions within the framework of the sketch or essay. In *Sunshine Sketches of a Little Town* (1912) and *Arcadian Adventures with the Idle Rich* (1914) Leacock sought to extend his talents in portraits of (respectively) Canadian small town and city life. He also wrote (less interestingly) on the theory of humour in *The Greatest Pages of American Humour* (1916), and in his admiring studies *Mark Twain* (1932) and *Charles Dickens* (1933). His fullest exploration of the topic is to be found in *Humour: Its Theory and Technique* (1935) and *Humour and Humanity: An Introduction to the Study of Humour*

(1937) though his artistic practice excels his academic theories. Leacock also wrote several books dealing with Canadian history, and his unfinished biography, *The Boy I left Behind Me* (1946), is a lively account of his family and career which touches upon many issues of the day. [PQ]

LEAVIS, F.R. (Frank Raymond) (1895–1978). Critic, born and educated in Cambridge, Cambridgeshire, where he taught English and held a fellowship at Downing College from 1936 to 1962. His wife, Queenie Leavis (author of *Fiction and the Reading Public*, 1932), was also a teacher and critic. Leavis became the master of a school of criticism through his work as a tutor and his predominant role in the founding and editing of the literary quarterly *Scrutiny* which, from 1932 to 1955, fought to uphold critical standards and adjust erroneous evaluations. Leavis believed that a serious interest in literature must be a serious interest in the quality of life, in social equity and cultural health. The study of English is a discipline directed at inheriting and sustaining a living creative literature embodying the cultural tradition that guarantees our human values. We are now involved in a crisis of civilization in that home, school and university corroborate the debasement of standards and erosion of significance presided over by highbrow and lowbrow media alike. Minorities, rigorous in judgement and disciplined in response, must work to restore the moral health and intellectual integrity that mass industrial civilization has destroyed. Leavis's astringency and bellicosity bred acrimonious controversy and he paid for his prophetic zeal by years of neglect at the hands of the academic establishment he censured. Influential books include *Mass Civilization and Minority Culture* (1930), *New Bearings in English Poetry* (1932), *The Great Tradition* (1948), *D.H. Lawrence, Novelist* (1955) and *The Living Principle* (1975). *Scrutiny* was reissued in twenty volumes in 1963. [HB]

LEDWIDGE, FRANCIS (1891–1917). Irish poet, born in Slane, County Meath, Ireland, into a peasant family. He got into print through the encouragement of Lord Dunsany, to whom he sent a copybook full of verse in 1912 and who wrote prefaces for his *Songs of the Field* (1915), *Songs of Peace* (1916) and the final and posthumous *Complete Poems* (1919). Ledwidge joined the 5th Royal Inniskilling Fusiliers in which Dunsany held commissioned rank and was killed on the Western Front. Ledwidge was essentially a nature poet. The Irish countryside remained his constant inspiration. Even later poems written from barracks or front line for the most part use the immediate environment only as background for nostalgic dreams of the home land. But though there are too many facile poeticisms in the earliest work, there is also evident from the start a clarity of observation and an imaginative responsiveness that, as Dunsany observed, defy patronization 'by the how interesting! school'.

> Above me smokes the little town
> With its white-washed walls and roofs of brown
> And its octagon spire toned smoothly down
>   As the holy minds within.
>   ('Behind the Closed Eye' from *Songs of the Field*)

That the experience of war and exile was beginning to extend Ledwidge's range and the practice of his craft to sharpen his technique is evident from finely conceived poems like 'Thomas MacDonagh', 'In the Shadows' and 'After Court-Martial'. [HB]

LEHMANN, JOHN (1907–). Poet, editor and publisher, born in Buckinghamshire, brother of Rosamond Lehmann. He was involved with Leonard and Virginia Woolf in running the Hogarth Press, founded and edited *New Writing* in the 1930s and *Penguin New Writing* in the 1940s, established his own publishing business in 1946 and edited the *London Magazine* from 1954 to 1961. His *Collected Poems 1930–1963* was published in 1963. Lehmann writes close-packed, thoughtful verse which has rhetorical comeliness if not passion or intensity. His autobiography, *In My Own Time: Memoirs of a Literary Life* (1969), was issued in three volumes, *The Whispering Gallery* (1955), *I Am My Brother* (1960) and *The Ample Proposition* (1966). It is an interesting mine of literary history. Lehmann has been prolific as critic and as editor. *A Nest of Tigers* (1968) is a study of Edith, Osbert and Sacheverell Sitwell (q.v.). Later books include *Virginia Woolf and Her World* (1975) and *Thrown to the Woolfs* (1978). [HB]

LEHMANN, ROSAMOND (1905–). Novelist, born in Buckinghamshire and educated privately and at Cambridge. She married the Hon. Wogen Philipps (later Lord Milford) in 1928, but the marriage was dissolved. *Dusty Answer* (1927) traces the development of a sensitive girl, Judith. *Invitation to the Waltz* (1932) and *The Weather in the Streets* (1936) respectively present Olivia at an ingenuous 18 and ten years later with a divorce behind her. (Both novels were reissued in 1981.) In respect of mores those books are too strenuously in period not to have dated. The author's most ambitious book, *The Echoing Grove* (1953), explores a love triangle in which Dinah Burkett shares her sister Madeleine's husband, Rickie Masters, against the background of the 1930s and the war years. Presentation by indirect recollection phased in a series of deftly counterpointed time-shifts is technically impressive. There is subtlety and depth of delineation in the studies of the two women and their reactions, but the men are improbable. In a suffocatingly feminine context they analyse themselves obsessively as emotional specimens. 'No wonder you're scared you may be women in disguise', says Georgie, Rickie's last mistress, and Rickie replies 'Perhaps we are'. Rosamond Lehmann's autobiographical work, *The Swan in the Evening; Fragments of an Inner Life* (1967), looks back to the death of her daughter Sally from polio, a loss which interrupted her productivity as a writer for many years. Her later novel, *A Sea-Grape Tree* (1976), is a romantic fantasy. [HB]

LEONARD, HUGH (pseudonym of John Keyes Byrne) (1926–). Dramatist, born in Dalkey, County Dublin, and educated at Presentation College, Dun Laoghaire. He worked in the Civil Service in Dublin before turning full-time writer in 1959, when he moved to England. The London theatre has never provided him with the successes his work deserved and he returned to Ireland in the 1970s. He began his career with *The Italian Road* (prod 1954) but first became known outside Ireland for his dramatic adaptation of Joyce's *Portrait of the Artist as a Young Man* and *Stephen Hero, Stephen D.* (1962). *The Poker Session* (1963) is a play of considerable verbal subtlety and structural ingenuity. It exploits the tension and uncertainty surrounding the return home from a lunatic asylum of a young man with various grudges to work off on family and friends. They are invited to meet him, and a fellow inmate comes along to assist in a probing post mortem in which dialogue teeters on either side of the boundary separating sanity from insanity. Questions press upon the audience: Is he still mad or pretending to be? Who drove him mad in the first place? The suspense is palpable, but the tangle of motivations and machinations (involving a murder) is too dense for the final dénouement to be theatrically effective. *The Patrick Pearse Motel* (prod 1971), intended as a satire on the new prosperity of the time, is a riot of implausibilities and zany logic.

Da (prod 1973) represents a much surer-footed workmanship and it was a runaway success in the USA. Charlie, a man in his early forties, returns to Ireland from England to bury his foster-father. As he goes through remaining effects in the old home, the past he broods on is re-created, acted out by Da, his mother and his younger self. The dialogue is witty, and there is a most sympathetic study of a warm-hearted father. *Time Was* (prod 1976) presupposes that in the near future human nostalgia for the past will have upset the time-system of our world, dislodging people from their proper decades. The recurrence of the past here involves the re-entry of the dead among the living on the same plane of action, and smacks of gimmickry. But the technique of *Da* is pressed further in *A Life* (prod 1979), a touching study of a Dublin civil servant who learns, on the eve of his retirement, that he has terminal cancer and seeks to repair a broken friendship. Desmond Drumm and his wife, Dorothy, visit Mary and her husband, Larry Kearns. Drumm, an educated, cautious and conscientious fellow, lost Mary long ago to Larry, a warm-hearted but feckless idler. All four characters are duplicated as stage flashbacks counterpoint episodes from forty years previously with the current scene. The double unravelling of the past enables Leonard to uncover emotional cross-currents that produce moments of powerful ironic impact. And deeper implications are raised by the contrast between the rather desiccated civil servant with a life of dogged routine behind him and the lovably generous wastrel who perhaps in more ways than one has beaten him at living.

[HB]

LESSING, DORIS (1919–). Novelist, born of British parents in Kermanshah, Iran, where her father was a bank manager. In 1924 he sought a new life by purchasing a farm in Southern Rhodesia and settling there. Doris left the farm for Salisbury, married a civil servant in 1939, had two children and was divorced in 1943. Her second marriage (to Godfried Lessing) also ended in divorce, and she came to England in 1949, bringing her first novel, *The Grass is Singing* (1950). A later non-fiction book, *In Pursuit of the English* (1960), gives an account of her departure from Africa and her confrontation with

the English, and it opens with vivid recollections of her eccentric father. *The Grass is Singing* traces the doomed life of the Turners, a white couple in Rhodesia who are unequal to the superior role the racial set-up requires of them.

Doris Lessing's major achievement is the sequence of five novels about Martha Quest, eventually called *Children of Violence*. It comprises *Martha Quest* (1952), *A Proper Marriage* (1954), *A Ripple from the Storm* (1958), *Landlocked* (1965) and *The Four-Gated City* (1969). It records Martha's African upbringing, her development as a sexual, social and political being, her encounter with postwar London, and finally it takes a prophetic leap into the future. Lessing has been highly praised for her portrayal of modern women. Martha's experience matches her own in many respects: indeed the personal tone and the heavy documentation often have the flavour of undoctored autobiography. Martha is a highly strung young woman, obsessively aware of herself physically and emotionally. The analysis of her continuing struggle to find her own 'completeness' has the detail of a professional casebook. Her forceful instinctive rejection of the patterned social and personal role which parental and environmental pressures would impose on her is defined in terms of the accepted progressive ideologies of the 1930s and 1940s. A current of emotional vehemence gives the work at times a quivering intensity; but it is not sustained. Indignation lacks focus and defined objective. Martha's spirit is at war, not just with hide-bound convention, but also with healthy norms of useful work and sobriety. The world Doris Lessing evokes has credibility and authenticity that extend over a panoramic range of interests and portrayals, yet experience is recorded in too raw a state: the quintet seems to grow by aggregation, and there is no recurringly felt rhythm of presentation, piece by piece or over the work as a whole, to give it dramatic shape.

A later novel, *The Golden Notebook* (1962), sets out to describe the intellectual and moral climate of the time through the study of Anna Wulf, a writer suffering a block over the question of the relationship between the writer's real and projected self. 'I keep four notebooks, a black notebook, which is to do with Anna Wulf the writer; a red notebook concerned with politics; a yellow notebook in which I make stories out of my experience; and a blue notebook which tries to be a diary.' The golden notebook is to unify what has thus been divided. *Briefing for a Descent into Hell* (1971), a study of mental breakdown, reflects the author's interest in Sufism. In *Shikasta* (1979) our radiation-fouled planet (Shikasta, 'the stricken') exists within the colonizing reach of the Canopus Empire and receives a needful visitation. It was called 'Rohanda', the fruitful, until the supply of the benign, air-like fluid SOWF (substance-of-we-feeling) was reduced, degeneration set in, and an enquiry was called for into our century of destruction. This tale was the first of a projected cosmic chronicle called *Canopus in Argos: Archives*. The second tale, *The Marriages Between Zones Three, Four, and Five* (1980), was followed by *The Sirian Experiments* (1981), *The Making of the Representative for Planet 8* (1982) and *The Sentimental Agents in the Volyen Empire* (1983).

Doris Lessing's output as a short-story writer was

garnered in 1978 in two volumes of Collected Stories, *To Room Nineteen* and *The Temptation of Jack Orkney*.   [HB]

LEVINE, NORMAN (1924–). Novelist and short-story writer, born in Ottawa, Ontario, Canada, where he grew up. After war service he went to McGill University, Montreal, Quebec, graduating in 1948. He has lived in England since 1949, with spells in Canada as a university writer-in-residence. His local human landscape of St Ives, Cornwall, often forms an important element in his work, and his writing is firmly rooted in his own personal, immediate situation. Although only in *Canada Made Me* (1958) does he deal directly with his feelings as an expatriate and a writer, these concerns shape much of his best work. The novel *From a Seaside Town* (1970) explores the role of a writer in relation to everyday life and its relevance to his own sense of identity. The fifteen stories in *I Don't Want To Know Anything Too Well* (1971) were collected from a variety of journals and exemplify the neutral, objective, yet first-person narrative position adopted with such effect in much of his work. Atmosphere and analysis are established tellingly through a spare, precise use of language and the artful distancing of any personal element. *Selected Stories* (1975) underlined the self-questioning character of his writing. Although he lived abroad his work is an important part of contemporary Canadian fiction for its exploration of a personal world which is made capable of reflecting larger issues. He returned to Canada in 1980.

[PQ]

LEWIS, ALUN (1915–44). Poet, born at Aberdare, Mid Glamorgan, Wales. He went from Cowbridge Grammar School in 1932 to study history, first at University College, Aberystwyth, for his BA, then at Manchester University for his MA. He began work as a schoolmaster in 1938 but volunteered for the Royal Engineers in 1940. He was sent out to India in 1942 and his regiment was in Burma, up against the Japanese, when Lewis was 'accidentally wounded by a pistol shot'. Lewis was not a happy warrior, but a bored, frustrated civilian in uniform. The celebrated 'All Day It Has Rained' evokes the drab tedium of life under canvas on a wet Sunday.

> I saw a fox
> And mentioned it in the note I scribbled home;
> And we talked of girls, and dropping bombs on
>   Rome,
> And thought of the quiet dead and the loud
>   celebrities.

This is one of the poems in *Raider's Dawn* (1942). Lewis published a book of short stories, *The Last Inspection*, in 1943, but his next volume of poems, *Ha! Ha! Among the Trumpets* (1945), was posthumous. Since then *In the Green Tree* (1948), containing letters and stories, and *Selected Poetry and Prose* (1966), edited by Ian Hamilton, have appeared. Lewis has been described as a natural prose writer in whose poetry one can point to a fluency too easy and a verbal discrimination too slack, but his voice is unmistakably that of a generation of reluctant soldiers and there is sharp descriptive exactness in poems of the Indian landscape like 'The Mahratta Ghats':

> The valleys crack and burn, the exhausted plains
> Sink their black teeth into the horny veins
> Straggling the hills' red thighs

Jeremy Hooker and Gweno Lewis (the poet's widow) have edited *Selected Poems of Alun Lewis* (1981), to which Hooker contributes a thoughtful 'Afterword'.   [HB]

LEWIS, C. S. (Clive Staples) (1898–1963). Novelist and man of letters, born in Belfast, Northern Ireland, the son of a solicitor. His mother died of cancer in 1908. In *Surprised by Joy* (1955), an autobiographical study of his early life, Lewis tells how he hated both his schools, Wynyard School, Hertfordshire ('Belsen'), and Malvern College ('Wyvern'), and was eventually entrusted to a private tutor. He won a scholarship to University College, Oxford, in 1917 but was soon in the army in France, then wounded and sent home. He took firsts in Greats and in English and was Fellow of Magdalen College, Oxford, from 1925 to 1954, when he transferred to Magdalene College, Cambridge, to be Professor of Medieval and Renaissance English. Lewis's conversion from atheism to Christianity in 1929 was the climax of personal search and intensely felt reasoning, and it determined the character of his literary career. The personal account of his conversion is contained in *Surprised by Joy*, the analytical record in *The Pilgrim's Regress* (1933), 'Allegorical Apology for Christianity, Reason and Romanticism', which traces the progress of its pilgrim John ('born in the land of Puritania') through the shires of contemporary intellectual apostasy and unbelief. Lewis had already published a narrative allegorical poem, *Dymer*, in rhyme royal (1926). Henceforward his work as a literary critic was highly distinguished (see *The Allegory of Love*, 1936; *A Preface to Paradise Lost*, 1942; *English Literature in the Sixteenth Century*, 1954; *Experiment in Criticism*, 1961) and continues to delight and nourish students of English literature as the fruits of one of the best-stocked minds of the age; but Lewis himself always set a higher value on creative writing which involves invention, and by this he would have wished to be judged. By this and by the numerous works of popular theology which proved him a skilful expositor, able to clarify and illuminate, without cheapening or diluting, the orthodox doctrine which gave body to his own religious thinking. *The Problem of Pain* (1940) and *The Screwtape Letters* (1942) – the latter a series of letters from a devil, Screwtape, to his nephew, Wormwood, giving advice about how to secure a human 'patient' from commitment to the divine 'Enemy' – were the first of a series of works of apologetic and moral theology which for two decades made Lewis the most influential Christian teacher of the day.

A religious impulse lay also at the heart of his imaginative work. The trilogy of science fiction is his main fiction for adults. *Out of the Silent Planet* (1938) takes the hero Ransom unwillingly to Mars, the victim of two wicked scientists, while *Perelandra* (1943) (later renamed *Voyage to Venus*) takes him to Venus, where the same scientists try to corrupt an innocent woman as Eve was corrupted on Earth by Satan. The spread of evil from a fallen planet to unfallen beings is at issue. There is more immediate human interest and subtler psychological content in the third volume, *That Hideous Strength* (1945), where the conflict is carried on at home in contemporary England. *Till We Have Faces* (1956) is a reinterpretation of the classical myth of Cupid and Psyche.

Probably Lewis's finest work as an imaginative writer is in the Chronicles of Narnia, seven stories for children, of which the first, *The Lion, the Witch and the Wardrobe* (1950) represents the divine power of redeeming love in the person of the awesome lion, Aslan. Lewis's device of taking four children (fewer in the later stories) to a land abounding in marvellous beings and multifarious adventures exactly matched his extraordinary inventiveness, his vast resources from the reading of legend and literature, and his instinctive power to endow events with mysterious overtones and mythic dimensions. The finely articulated symbolism, which shadows aspects of the human situation at large as the Christian sees it, is not the product of calculation but of a rare visionary grasp of all things in terms of divine purpose and cosmic conflict. Among the series are *The Voyage of the 'Dawn-Treader'* (1952), *The Silver Chair* (1953) and *The Last Battle* (1956).

Lewis married his friend and admirer, Joy Davidman, an American citizen resident in England, in 1956 in order to save her from deportation, but the marriage became a deeply affectionate one. She died of cancer in 1960 (see *A Grief Observed*, published in 1969 under the pseudonym, N.W. Clerk). [HB]

LEWIS, PERCY WYNDHAM (1884–1957). Artist, novelist and thinker, born at sea off the American coast of English parents and educated, eventually, at Rugby and the Slade School of Art. In 1914 he edited the quarterly periodical *Blast* and with Ezra Pound launched the term 'Vorticism' to advertise an artistic movement that grew out of Imagism – in which 'energy creates patterns'. The emblem of the electrified cone was used as a symbol of circulating energies, local and historic, drawn centripetally into the artist's creative vision. Lewis's output as a painter includes memorable portraits of T.S. Eliot (q.v.) and Edith Sitwell (q.v.). His prodigious intellectual vigour and his titanic dissatisfaction with the Zeitgeist emerge in almost everything he wrote. The early days of shock-tactics and ardent campaigning are vividly recaptured in the later autobiographical work, *Blasting and Bombardiering* (1937), which covers the years up to 1926. War experience, in which he advanced from bombardier to battery officer, is documented in a series of vital sketches: we meet at close quarters the three writers with whom Lewis is historically most firmly associated, Pound, Eliot and Joyce (q.v.), as well as Ford Madox Ford (q.v.), T.E. Lawrence (q.v.) and T.E. Hulme (q.v.): the record of an encounter with Joyce in Paris is hilariously comic reportage.

Lewis's immense output as a writer can be roughly divided into polemical or critical books and works of fiction. Among the former *Time and Western Man* (1927) is central. Like all his work, this philosophical study runs counter to fashionable currents of thought, for Lewis accepted the objectivity of value and the supremacy of intellect. He saw traditional respect for metaphysics and for inherited wisdom threatened not only by modern subjectivity but also by the current obsession with time and consequent preoccupation with movement and

change for their own sake. Lewis's reaction against subjectivism and internality made him critical of the 'stream of consciousness' technique employed by Joyce, while his respect for intellect put Lawrence's exploitation of the unconscious out of court. His works of literary criticism include *The Lion and the Fox* (1927), a study of 'the role of the hero in the plays of Shakespeare', *Men Without Art* (1934) and *The Writer and the Absolute* (1952). In the latter Orwell (q.v.), as well as Sartre and Camus, comes under fire for descending into the market place and seeking an absolute outside art itself.

Lewis projected himself in aggressive Kierkegaardian isolation as 'the Enemy': his assault upon his age thrust widely and cut deeply. The dull, 'oppressive respectability' and tedious predictability of standard twentieth-century revolutionaries was as much the target of his scorn as the philistinism of the masses. (See *The Art of Being Ruled*, 1926.) He was tireless in setting ideas in motion: Eliot described him as 'the greatest journalist of my time'. Lewis's detestation of the mediocre and the meretricious, allied to his temperamental antagonism and isolation, turned him into a satirist of devastating acuity. At the same time his literary credo gave him a classical attachment to form and externality that was in tune with his graphic talent but at loggerheads with much contemporary experimentation. 'You stand for Impressionism. It is finished', he told Ford Madox Ford. 'You and Conrad [q.v.] had the idea of concealing yourself when you wrote. I display myself all over the page.' (Ford's version, in *Return to Yesterday*, 1932.) The indignation of neglected genius sharpened his assault upon current philistinism. 'Contemporary man is allergic to the masterpiece', he wrote in *Rude Assignment* (1950), a further burst of autobiography, lamenting the 'isolation and stultification' of society's 'most intellectually energetic and imaginative individuals'.

For Lewis the artist's vision is a central, not an eccentric, one. He opens our eyes to life and prepares the ground for civilized intelligence to operate. His first novel, *Tarr* (1918), a virile assault upon bohemian life in Paris before the First World War, was greeted enthusiastically. Eliot's famous review of it spoke of Lewis's work as combining 'the thought of the modern and the energy of the cave-man', while Rebecca West (q.v.) drew comparison with Dostoevsky. The narrative technique, Lewis averred, 'was denuded of those rhetorical ornaments to which the English critic had become accustomed in a work of fiction' (*Blasting and Bombardiering*). In *The Apes of God* (1930) Lewis subjected the cultural scene of the day to fiercely ironic ridicule for the flabbiness and sentimentality of its bogus 'liberalism'. 'And it is also a book of *action*', Lewis insisted (*Men Without Art*), stressing that he set great store by its much criticized '*externality*, in a world that is literally inundated with sexual viscera and the "dark" gushings of *The Great Within*'. Lewis's blasting of Bloomsbury no doubt encouraged that neglect of him which his antagonistic independence provoked, and an apparent dalliance with fascism (see *Hitler*, 1931) was hurtfully magnified. But Lewis had produced his most astonishing imaginative work to date in 1928, when *Childermass* was published. This vision of 'migrant humanity' awaiting entry to Heaven formed the first volume of *The Human Age**, a planned tetralogy of which the fourth part, *The Trial of Man*, was never written, and whose second and third parts, *Monstre Gai* and *Malign Fiesta*, did not appear until 1955. The trilogy as it stands represents Lewis's most substantial achievement as a writer.

Lewis's other later works include the volume of stories, *Rotting Hill* (1951), and the novel, *Self-Condemned* (1954). There was also earlier a collection of verse, *One Way Song* (1933). Lewis was blind at the end of his life and wrote courageously on the approaching affliction of total darkness in *The Listener* in 1951: 'I shall then have to light a lamp of aggressive voltage in my mind to keep at bay the night'. See, E.W.F. Tomlin, ed., *Wyndham Lewis: An Anthology of His Prose* (1969), and C.J. Fox, ed., *Enemy Salvoes: Selected Literary Criticism by Wyndham Lewis* (1975). Alan Munton has edited the *Collected Poems and Plays* (1980).

The Human Age consists of the first three parts of an unfinished tetralogy. The setting of *Childermass* is 'outside Heaven', where two friends, Pullman and his former fag, Satters, meet in a region of hallucinatory character. The vast panoramic setting around the 'magnetic city' owes something to Milton and something to memories of the Western Front in the First World War. Over-congested descriptive writing delays arrival at the main substance of the book – a tribunal at which the dead are admitted into the city. Their examination is conducted by the Bailiff, a grotesque figure, ugly, hump-backed, big-nosed, who operates from a Punch and Judy theatre. He represents neither morality nor reason; indeed what he is and what his credentials are become questions at issue as a series of awkward people from among those he is examining challenge him. The challengers do not represent definable standpoints, argument is cluttered with digression and abuse, the Bailiff is uncontaminated by earthly logic and no clear intellectual dialectic is worked out. Nevertheless some of Lewis's pet theses – against time-ridden notions of progress, against radicalism and against contemporary devaluation of 'the great' and supremacy of mediocrity – are given an airing. The stylistic debt to Joyce is immense, flattering imitation married with satirical parody. In general the first part brings massive talent into play and fails disappointingly to discipline it.

In *Monstre Gai* Pullman and Satters get inside the city, but it is not Heaven. The Third City, in which civilization functions ostensibly as on earth, is ruled by the Padishah, an angelic being. The angelic regime is puritanically non-alcoholic and all women are confined to a special sector, the Yenery. The Bailiff is subverting the Padishah's authority with a fifth column whose affiliation is to Hell, and the Third City is under periodic attack from Hell that is terrifying. On to this conflict are superimposed tensions within the City caused by radical opposition to the Bailiff from such parties as the Hyperideans, the Catholics and the communists. Pullman, a well-known writer on earth, is an ex-Catholic whose worldliness in life has now led him naturally to sympathy with the Bailiff, a being of supreme bogusness and the 'Gay Monster' of the title. He is gradually seduced into the Bailiff's service (installed comfortably in the luxury of the Phanuel Hotel) to the extent that when the Padishah's

authority is finally reasserted he has to accept the Bailiff's offer of flight to Hell. This second book is compact, disciplined, subtle in its exploration of Pullman's gradual moral decay and stylistically all the better for its freedom from Joyceanisms.

In *Malign Fiesta* Pullman and Satters are brought to Matapolis, a city of Hell. Sammael, or Satanael (Satan), rules the place in puritanic style (there are no women) and contact with him is at first overwhelmingly sinister and unnerving. His hatred of God's creation, mankind (women especially), was the root of his alienation from God who, he says, has given him the job of moral scavenger. Thus Hell receives sinners and the Punishment Service subjects them to appalling torture in Punishment Cells and a House of Fire whose horrors bring Belsen and Dachau to the aid of Dante. Pullman manages to ingratiate himself with Sammael and is given a post at Haus Europa, an Adult University through whose work Sammael hopes to educate and humanize the angels. Pullman aids and abets him in planning the introduction of human women, the gradual amalgamation of angel status with human status, the inauguration of the Human Age (of the title) and the abandonment of the devilish functions. In his soberer moments Pullman sees wicked defiance of God in 'arranging the contamination of the angel nature. . . . To save his skin, he had been actively assisting at the annihilation of the Divine'. He is, however, deeply implicated with Sammael; prayers and repentance intrude only at moments of personal peril. At the end, in a heavenly angelic incursion, he is seized by White Angels and carried off. [HB]

LINDSAY, JACK (1900–). Novelist, born in Melbourne, Victoria, Australia, the eldest son of the writer and artist Norman Lindsay (q.v.). He was educated at the grammar school and university in Brisbane, graduating in classics in 1921. He was associated with the Sydney magazine *Vision* (1923–4), went to London in 1926 and later achieved considerable success with the Fanfrolico Press which published fine limited editions until its closure in 1930. A truly prolific writer, he is the author of over forty novels and over fifty critical books. He has edited another twenty books on topics as diverse as William Morris and J.M.W. Turner, of whom he published an important critical biography in 1966. His classical interests show not only in his critical studies but also in over twenty-five books of translation from the Greek and Latin. Devotion to poetry is matched by an ardent Marxism which strengthens rather than qualifies his humanist principles; his respect for 'the vital unity of the individual expression, the image' is well demonstrated in his recent volume of collected critical essays *Decay and Renewal* (1976). He has described his writing as 'derived wholly from poetry . . . as the highest point of human consciousness'. No brief account can do justice to the range of his work: *Betrayed* Spring (1953), together with the companion novels *A Local Habitation* (1957) and *All on the Never-Never* (1961), explore 'the British Way of Life'; *Rome for Sale, Caesar is Dead* (both 1934) and *Last Days with Cleopatra* (1935) brought together his classical and contemporary interests; *Life Rarely Tells* (1958) and *Fanfrolico and After* (1962) are autobiography. [PQ]

LINDSAY, MAURICE (1918–). Poet, born in Glasgow, Strathclyde, Scotland, educated at Glasgow Academy and at the Scottish National Academy of Music, Glasgow. After service in the Second World War he worked in Scottish journalism as music critic and drama critic, became a well-known BBC reporter and commentator on Scottish television and, in 1961, the first Programme Controller of Border Television at Carlisle. He is married and has four children. His first published poetry was *Perhaps Tomorrow* (1941). In 1957 George Bruce (q.v.) gathered poems from Lindsay's volumes to date in *The Exiled Heart* and wrote an introduction drawing attention to the quality of his early war poetry, his Scots poems about Scottish people and places, and his descriptive lyrics. Lindsay's own selection, made later, *Selected Poems 1942–1972* (1973), confirms him as a detached, quiet-voiced observer capable of vivid strokes:

> She rolled the Easter egg of her belly
> through the pinging-open door . . .
>
> ('Fruits')

There is pathos, irony and humour in the neat portraits ('Games Mistress', 'School Prize Giving' and 'Farm Widow'), an occasional more disturbed reflectiveness ('The Vacant Chair' and 'Country Funeral') and some moving personal poems ('An Elegy' and 'These Two Lovers'). Lindsay edited the *Poetry Scotland* series that began in 1943, *Modern Scottish Poetry 1920–45* (1946) and other volumes. His prose output includes *The Scottish Renaissance* (1949), *Robert Burns* (1954) and *History of Scottish Literature* (1976). He has also edited *Modern Scottish Poetry* (1976) and *Scottish Comic Verse* (1981).

[HB]

LINDSAY, NORMAN (1879–1969). Novelist and artist, born at Creswick, Victoria, Australia, which features as 'Redheap' in the witty novels *Redheap* (1930), *Saturdee* (1933) and *Halfway to Anywhere* (1947). From 1896 he lived a bohemian existence in Melbourne as an illustrator, but drawings for the *Decameron* brought him critical recognition and a job with the Sydney *Bulletin* (q.v.) in 1901. *A Curate in Bohemia* (1913), his first novel, reflects his reckless years in Melbourne. He was in Europe in 1909–10 and fell seriously ill with tuberculosis soon after his return; for the rest of his life he lived mostly at Springwood, in the Blue Mountains of New South Wales. The magazine *Vision* (1923–4), which was started by his eldest son, Jack (q.v.), and Kenneth Slessor (q.v.), was an important focus for the literary and artistic movement which Lindsay inspired. His main intellectual position found expression in *Creative Effort* (1920) and *Madam Life's Lovers* (1929) in addition to *Vision*. The drawings 'Pollice Verso' and 'Crucified Venus', first exhibited in 1904 and 1912 respectively, shocked established opinion by their frank sensuality; in both works sensual enjoyment is contrasted with the destructive forces of church and state. Lindsay described Rabelais and Nietzsche as 'the two supreme gods of my Olympus' – even *Redheap* was banned by the Australian authorities until 1958 – and remained a vital if lonely revolutionary in the arts during the between-wars epoch in Australia. He also wrote and illustrated the classic Australian children's book, *The Magic Pudding* (1918), in addition to later novels such as *The Cautious Amorist* (1934) and *Age of Consent* (1938). *My Mask* (1970) is autobiography.

[PQ]

LINKLATER, ERIC (1899–1974). Novelist, born at Dounby, Orkney, Scotland. His father was of Norse descent. Linklater was educated at Aberdeen Grammar School. Medical studies at Aberdeen University were interrupted by service in the First World War. Linklater was a private in the Black Watch and was wounded in the head. After the First World War he abandoned medicine for English. After two years in India as a journalist and a brief spell as a teacher at Aberdeen University, Linklater went to the USA as a Commonwealth Fellow to work towards the study *Ben Jonson and King James* (1931), but the best-selling comic novel *Juan in America* (1931) proved to be more than a minor by-product of the venture and Linklater gave himself thereafter to writing. He served again in the Second World War, first as a major in Orkney, then at the War Office. In 1933 he married Marjorie MacIntyre and they had four children. He wrote three autobiographical books, *The Man on My Back* (1941), *A Year of Space* (1953) and *Fanfare for a Tin Hat* (1970). Linklater's output contains some sixty titles, including over forty novels. The zest of the man bubbles over in words whenever his tireless pen touches paper. It is difficult to be fair to a writer who was so unfair to himself that he wrote far too much. Talented penmanship is always on tap. There are passages of conversational cut and thrust in *Poet's Pub* (1929) that have a scintillating satirical bite, and the genre is that of neo-Peacockian early Huxley. *Juan in America* (1931), a modern picaresque tour of the States, effervesces with riotous satirical studies of American gangsterism, academics, bootlegging, politics and a dozen other facets of life, all tapped for their joke content, often in the hectoring hyperbolic style of the comic columnist. But the flippant mock-heroics that flower in verbal cadenzas on every other page become wearisomely predictable and voluminous. A far maturer work, *Private Angelo* (1946), gives evidence of the artistic discipline that so much of Linklater's work lacks and it has generally been accounted his best novel. The portrayal of an unheroic Italian soldier's exploits in 1943 and 1944 when the American and British armies are pushing the Germans steadily up north through Italy, it is altogether subtler in its wit and in its ironies, more succinct in phrase and sharper in dialogue. And though the war is initially just a backcloth for escapades and high jinks, a more serious philosophic vein surfaces fitfully in reflections upon destruction, death and suffering. Yet it is essentially a comic book, heavily dependent on stock and sometimes embarrassingly insular notions of English, American and Italian national characteristics. A versatile and copious writer, rich in invention, Linklater relied on a mannered literary idiom, traditional in flavour, but in need of a revivification that he did not attempt and an economy that he rarely practised.

[HB]

LIVESAY, DOROTHY (1901-). Poet, born in Winnipeg, Manitoba, Canada. She graduated from the University of Toronto in 1931 before going on to study in Europe. She was a social worker, newspaper correspondent, documentary scriptwriter and teacher, and later worked in France and Zambia with UNESCO 1958-63. Since 1966 she has held posts at various Canadian universities. Her sustained output and originality over some fifty years make her an important and respected figure in Canadian writing. Early collections such as *Green Pitcher* (1928), her first, and *Signpost* (1931) contained lyrical poems and showed an Imagist influence, though the latter already suggested the socially and politically committed work of *Day and Night* (1944) and *Call My People Home* (1950). Thirty years' writing is represented in her *Selected Poems* (1956) and her experience in Zambia is reflected in *The Colour of God's Face* (1965). In this book, as in *The Unquiet Bed* (1967), her poetry 'reverted to personal statement'; the love poetry in this latter volume and in *Plainsongs* (1971) is available in *Collected Poems: The Two Seasons* (1972). In this book the range, variety and unwavering commitment to poetic innovation of her work is fully illustrated. Her belief in the human worth of poetry – it is 'speech and communication and should be said aloud' – has not always informed her feeling for the magic of words. *Right Hand Left Hand* (1977) is a work in complex format with a self-explanatory subtitle: 'A True Life of the Thirties: Paris, Toronto, Montreal, The West and Vancouver. Love, Politics, The Depression and Feminism'. [PQ]

LIVINGS, HENRY (1929-). Dramatist, born in Lancashire. He has worked as an actor with Theatre Workshop and other companies. As playwright he has focused on inadequate or deranged personalities at loggerheads with the established social system and its frameworks of operative authority. In *Big Soft Nellie* (prod 1961) slapstick with a television cabinet and antics by a half-mad mechanic turn an electrical shop into a hilarious madhouse. In *Eh?* (prod 1964, pubd 1965) a demented boilerman, located at the heart of a vast, mechanized factory, creates pandemonium and blows the place up. Humour tends to be submerged under absurdity. There is no touchstone of rationality by which inanity can be fathomed and irony salted. Of Livings's numerous plays perhaps *Kelly's Eye* (prod 1963, pubd 1964) comes nearest to achieving human substance in the figure of the fugitive murderer, Kelly. A man early attuned to violence by service in the First World War and with the Black and Tans in Ireland, Kelly is given to searching analysis of the human self that entrances a girl victim of establishment mores. *Pongo Plays* (1971) contains six short plays produced in 1969 and 1970: they are folksy comic sketches in which a Lancashire smart-Alec scores off the powers-that-be. They were followed by *Six More Pongo Plays* (1975). [HB]

LOGUE, CHRISTOPHER (1926-). Poet, born in Portsmouth, Hampshire, educated at Pryor Park College, Bath, and Portsmouth Grammar School. He spent some years in France and published his first volume of verse, *Wand and Quadrant* (1953), in Paris. His output includes some twenty titles of published verse. Logue became known as a protest-poet experimenting with wildly unconventional forms of expression, who brought poetry to the 'pop scene' and wrote poster-poems. Yet he is a many-sided personality and has a compelling voice:

> I want my poems to be in your mind
> so you can say them when you are in love
> so you can say them when the plane takes off
> and death comes near
> (Foreword to *New Numbers*, 1970)

His verse adaptations of passages from Homer's *Iliad* (*Patrocleia*, 1962; *Pax*, 1967, from books XVI and XIX respectively) are racy and virile renderings. The selection, *Ode to the Dodo* (1981), represents his verse to date, much of it clamantly instantaneous in its appeal. He has also written plays for stage and screen. [HB]

LONGLEY, MICHAEL (1939-). Poet, born in Belfast, Northern Ireland, educated at the Royal Belfast Academical Institute and at Trinity College, Dublin, and a schoolmaster until he became Assistant Director of the Arts Council for Northern Ireland in 1970. His first collection of poems, *No Continuing City* (1969), marked him as a poet who could combine colloquialism effectively with traditional metrics. *An Exploded View* (1973) showed an extension of human concern and of technical range. Longley's interest in the animal world is evident. 'Casualty' studies the corpse of a sheep whose disintegration ends in a scattering of ribs and wool 'as though hunger still worked there'. The volume also touches on the Troubles and includes the celebrated poem, 'Wounds', which connects the fatal long-term effects on his father of damage inflicted on the Somme ('I am dying for King and Country, slowly') with the current sectarian murder of soldiers and a bus conductor, who

> collapsed beside his carpet-slippers
> Without a murmur, shot through the head
> By a shivering boy who wandered in . . .

Other volumes include *After Fishing in the Sky* (1975) and *Man Lying on a Wall* (1976). *Selected Poems 1963-1980* (1981) confirms Longley as a poet with a winningly unaffected speaking voice and a refined technical accomplishment. [HB]

LOWRY, MALCOLM (1909-57). Novelist and poet, born near Liverpool, Merseyside, the son of a wealthy cotton broker, and educated at The Leys School, Cambridge. Before proceeding to the university he persuaded his father to get him a job as a deck-hand on a freighter, SS *Pyrrhus*. The family influence, and the family limousine which drove him to the docks to embark, did not endear him to his shipmates, and the novel, *Ultramarine* (1933), traces his sufferings on the voyage to the east as a misfit tormented by the desire to prove himself. A revised version of the book was published in 1935. A wound received on his first voyage was later to debar him from service in the Second World War. After taking his degree at Cambridge, Lowry spent periods of time in Spain, Paris, New York, Hollywood and Mexico. His first marriage, to Jan Gabrial, a former child actress, ended in divorce. In 1940 he married Margerie Bonner, an American writer, with whom he settled in British Columbia, occupying a shack among a community of squatters on Dollarton beach, Vancouver, from 1940 to 1954. Eventually the authorities evicted the squatters, burned the shacks and turned the land into a public park complete with picnic tables and car space. The Lowrys fled to Italy, then to England, where Lowry died in a cottage they had taken at Ripe, Sussex. The pressures of loneliness and isolation, and the initiation into heavy drinking, turned Lowry into a personality tortured by alcoholism and guilt.

> When the doomed are most eloquent in their
>   sinking
> It seems that then we are least strong to save.

So Lowry writes in 'The Doomed in their Sinking', one of the confessional poems in his posthumous *Selected Poems* (1962) which scarcely have parallel outside the tragic outcries of Cowper in such verses as 'The Castaway'.

The novel *Under the Volcano* (1947) does for drunkenness what De Quincey did for drug addiction. A work of searing self-revelation, it has a hysterical yet disciplined eloquence. It is set in Mexico in 1938. The characters' pasts are recaptured in flashbacks while immediate events are concentrated in one day on which the former British Consul in Quauhnahuac, Geoffrey Firmin, is surprised by the unexpected return of his divorced wife, Yvonne, who left him the year before. Firmin's half-brother, Hugh, is himself in love with Yvonne. The trio take a day trip by bus to a bullthrowing at Tomalin, and it proves fatal for both Geoffrey and Yvonne. Geoffrey is an alcoholic so damaged by drink and Yvonne's absence that he cannot grasp the love she now offers and they both desperately need. In presenting Firmin, Lowry uses Joycean techniques for fusing the outer with the inner world, and the sober with the drunken currents of the latter. The merging of lucid reasoning with increasingly lurid and demented fantasy is powerful in effect. The erosion of Geoffrey's will and the demonic horrors of delirium tremens make an unnerving impact by virtue of Lowry's volcanic prose. Hugh, a communist idealist, is guiltily aware of contemporary events (the Crossing of the Ebro) in the Civil War in Spain, and a window is opened on to the claustrophobic study of Firmin by a sense that

inebriety is more than a personal, clinical matter ('if our civilization were to sober up for a couple of days it'd die of remorse on the third'), and that the alcoholic's choice is symbolic of man's fall. 'Do you like this garden which is yours? We evict those who destroy it', runs the Spanish epigraph.

Lowry had planned a Dantesque group of novels to be called *The Voyage That Never Ends*, of which *Under the Volcano* was to be the *Inferno*. There is evidence that the short story, 'The Forest Path to the Spring', included in the collection *Hear us O Lord in Heaven Thy Dwelling Place* (1961), was meant as a sketch for a *Paradiso*. The stories are 'essentially monologues on travel, memory, art and life, marital love, and atonement', writes Daniel B. Dodson (*Malcolm Lowry*, 1970), but they lack drama and economy. Other posthumous publications are *Selected Letters* (1965) and two novels put together from material among his papers by his widow: *Dark as the Grave Wherein my Friend is Laid* (1968) and *October Ferry to Gabriola* (1971).   [HB]

LUCIE-SMITH, EDWARD (1933–). Poet, born in Jamaica, the only child of a colonial administrator. His first volume of poems, *A Tropical Childhood* (1961), includes a poem ('The Lesson') recalling how he heard the news of his father's death from his boarding-school headmaster at the age of 10. Later he came to King's School, Canterbury, and Merton College, Oxford. 'I did not want to be a professional poet, though I did want to be a professional writer', he has recorded in his autobiography, *The Burnt Child* (1975). In fact he was closely associated with Philip Hobsbaum (q.v.) in the founding of the 1950s movement known as the 'Group'. He has written over twenty books of verse, and is the editor of numerous influential collections including the Penguin *British Poetry Since 1945* (1970). Conscious artistry, applied to a wide range of subjects, gives his work a cultivated 'literary' flavour. *Towards Silence* (1968) includes 'Fragments of a *Tristan*' and a poem about the Crécy campaign in 1346 ('A Game of French and English'), while *The Well-Wishers* (1974) opens with a sequence spoken by a marooned Irish monk in the Dark Ages ('Hermit's Island'). Later works include the novel *Dark Pageant* (1977).   [HB]

M

MACAULAY, ROSE (Dame) (1881–1958). Novelist, born at Rugby, Warwickshire, where her father G.C. Macaulay was a master at the school. Macaulay senior's family was that of Lord Macaulay, the historian. His wife's family, the Conybeares, had for centuries been rich in scholars and divines. Emilie Rose was the second of seven children (five girls and two boys). Her mother, Grace Macaulay, suffered from a menacing tubercular infection of the throat and her husband decided in 1887 to abandon his career and transport the family to Italy, where the children enjoyed a sunny seaside upbringing at Varazze. The effect on Mrs Macaulay's health was so beneficial that the family moved back to England in 1894. They first settled in Oxford, where the author attended the High School and in 1900 began to read history at Somerville College. A failure of health or of nerve occurred at the time of her final examination in 1903 and she was awarded an Aegrotat. By this time the family had moved to Aberystwyth, where her father was Professor of English Language and Literature from 1901 until his move to a lectureship at Cambridge in 1906.

Rose Macaulay's first novel, *Abbots Verney* (1906), was well received and another six novels followed in the next eight years, including *The Secret River* (1909), *Views and Vagabonds* (1912) and *The Lee Shore* (1912). They set the lines of Macaulay's future development in displaying touches of ironic brilliance, serious concern with the damage done by narrow-mindedness, a Jamesian aware-

ness of the way varying levels of perceptiveness affect human relationships and a persisting interest in human failure and being at loggerheads with society. When she was well established as a writer she tried to suppress her pre-First World War novels. 'She did not want to be identified with books that she had come to regard as painfully naive' (Constance Babington Smith, *Rose Macaulay*, 1972). Rupert Brooke (q.v.) ('a family friend from our childhoods') has been seen as the model of the young hero poet in *The Secret River*. She met him in Grantchester and in London. It was through him and through Naomi Royde-Smith that she made contact with the capital's literary circles. From 1915 she had a post at the War Office, and here she fell in love with Gerald O'Donovan (q.v.), a married man, with whom, for some twenty years, she had a constant relationship that was at once the source of great happiness and, on account especially of her Anglican upbringing, of deep inner conflict.

Meanwhile her literary career flowered in *Potterism: A Tragi-Farcical Tract* (1920), a coruscating satirical assault on the mediocrity, cant, greed and sentimentality of the established well-to-do, who are epitomized by Mr Potter, a press lord, and his wife (pen-name Leila Yorke), a trashy novelist. The young Potter twins, like other young idealists – religious, political and scientific – pit themselves against the juggernaut of humbug and commercialism that is 'Potterism', and in their various ways fail or succumb. A 'murder' plot provides a hinge for the action.

Narrative is distributed between participants who view matters differently according to their own emotional interest in events. Yet the book has Rose Macaulay's prevailing weakness in being too many things at once. She can misfire through uncomfortable juxtaposition of what is humanly sad and tragic with flippant commentary by narrator or author. *Told By An Idiot* (1923) is a three-generation study in similar vein. Aubrey Garden leads his family a merry dance in his giddy pursuit of religious truth. Rose drew him 'rather sketchily' from Matthew Arnold's brother, Tom, who 'spent his life migrating from one church or no-church to another and back again' (*Letters to a Friend*, ed. C.B. Smith, 1961). *They Were Defeated* (1932) is a historical novel, fruit of a lifelong interest in the seventeenth century. An original impulse to write a biography of Robert Herrick was transformed as she brooded on the poet as a live person surrounded by friends. So the novel's action starts in Herrick's parish in Devonshire and the period covered is from October 1640 to May 1641. The book is packed with contemporary event and controversy, and varied scenes from the life of country and town. A vein of symbolism links personal act and public issue. Period authenticity is closely guarded.

A personal crisis occurred in 1939 when Rose, who was accustomed to take holidays with Gerald O'Donovan (discreetly, to avoid giving pain or causing scandal), crashed her car into another at the fell-top on the Penrith–Alston road and injured her lover. Though Gerald recovered from the stroke that followed the accident, he died of cancer in 1942. Meanwhile Rose's London flat had been destroyed in an air raid in 1941. She suffered a breakdown herself and it was many years before she wrote another novel. Not surprisingly, therefore, *The World My Wilderness* (1950) is a work of different timbre from its predecessors, notable for the compassion with which it portrays the lost young people of the immediate postwar years. A sense of moral disintegration is symbolically matched with the ruins left by the war. (Rose Macaulay's next book, *The Pleasure of Ruins*, 1953, is an ambitious and scholarly attempt 'to explore the various kinds of pleasure given to various people at various epochs by the spectacle of ruined buildings', Introduction.) How Rose herself found spiritual peace in reconciliation to sacramental practice as an Anglo-Catholic is revealed through the published correspondence with her friend and spiritual mentor, Father Hamilton Johnson (*Letters to a Friend*). Something of the moral and spiritual turmoil she endured can be gleaned from her last novel, *The Towers of Trebizond* (1956), where her personal dilemma intrudes, incongruously but eloquently, into a work otherwise garrulously ironic, bursting with travel anecdote and simmering with chuckles. The narrator, Laurie, comes to see her adultery as 'a meanness and a stealing, a taking away from some one what should be theirs, a great selfishness, and surrounded and guarded by lies lest it should be found out. And out of this meanness and this selfishness and this lying flow love and joy and peace, beyond anything that can be imagined'. See also Rose Macaulay, *Last Letters to a Friend*, ed. C.B. Smith (1962), and *Letters to a Sister*, ed. C.B. Smith (1964).
                                                                        [HB]

McAULEY, JAMES (1917–76). Poet, born at Lakemba, New South Wales, Australia, and educated at Fort Street High School, Sydney, and at the University of Sydney. Together with the poet Harold Stewart he wrote the 1944 'Ern Malley' poems, a literary hoax perpetrated on the Adelaide magazine *Angry Penguins*. From 1946 until 1960 McAuley lectured in government at the Australian School of Pacific Administration, and was often in New Guinea, a country which made a profound impression on him and which he wrote about perceptively in the Sydney journal *Quadrant* (19, Winter 1961), which he edited from 1956; 'I could see exemplified in the small field of New Guinea the great drama of the disintegration of traditional cultures, and the groping for the means of creating a new social order in the modern world'. The conception of order or 'ceremony' as a necessary basis for the deepest human, and therefore also artistic, values is fundamental for McAuley. It is in this sense that his work can rightly be seen as classical, Augustan, rather than Romantic, not in form but in its underlying conception of man and his world. He visited Europe and the United States for the first time in 1960, and in 1961 was appointed Reader in Poetry in the University of Tasmania, Hobart, and subsequently Professor of English. McAuley's first book of poems, *Under Aldebaran* (1946), displayed a wide variety of techniques and interests, though many of the works conveyed the unease of the period, notably the opening poem 'The Blue Horses'. This early collection, however, also included 'Envoi' and 'Terra Australis', poems whose blend of metaphysical conceit and meditative calm in charting the landscape of the mind has made them classic anthology pieces:

> Voyage within you, on the fabled ocean,
> And you will find that Southern Continent,
> Quiros' vision – his hidalgo heart
> And mythical Australia, where reside
> All things in their imagined counterpart.

A second collection of poetry, significantly titled *A Vision of Ceremony* (1956), amply confirmed McAuley's range and power; 'An Art of Poetry' presents issues of art and faith with consummate delicacy, while the three-poem series, 'The Hero and the Hydra' (to which McAuley added a fourth part in 1949), explores the paradoxes of man and his civilization, tending to a stoical conclusion. It was to be his last poetic statement in this realm before his conversion to Catholicism in 1952 provided the foundation for a more positive, life-enhancing attitude. The long poem 'A Letter to John Dryden' wittily takes note 'That things are not the same as when you wrote' and sets out McAuley's hopes and doubts as a poet seeking to communicate in 'this vacant sly / Neurotic modern world' where 'A formless relativism ends our days, / And good and evil are but culture-traits'. This collection also contained work which established McAuley as a fine love poet, while his lyric work was marked by a sureness of control which in no way precluded essential simplicity.

McAuley furthered his contribution to debate on the roots of contemporary civilization with a collection of essays on literature, art and culture, *The End of Modernity* (1959). Modern culture is seen as the manifestation of a civilization in decay, while the liberalist outlook, which McAuley regards as opposed to 'the natural pieties of the human mind', is typical of 'the anti-metaphysical modern mentality'. The underlying issue in these essays is what McAuley defines as 'the idea which is creeping like a deathly chill over the Western world that the normal mind is the uncommitted mind, without fixed principles or certainties'. It is important to realize that for McAuley tradition (and, in poetic terms, the use of traditional forms) is not restrictive but liberating; 'subtlety, complexity, and balance are all on the side of the traditional verse. It provides the best combination of freedom and order'. *Selected Poems* (1963) made available again some of McAuley's earlier work, and in the same year a study of Christopher Brennan (q.v.) was published. The concluding analysis of Brennan's short-comings as a poet reflects McAuley's classical conception of the artist's role: 'Brennan's work is ultimately solipsistic; it really contains only one living being, one powerful consciousness projecting its inner agonies into "myth" . . . instead of a unified world scheme Brennan had to make do with "a void dismantled universe" . . . lighted by wrecked drifting constellations and furnished only with miscellaneous symbolist bric-a-brac'.

In his Introduction to a 1963 selection in the 'Australian Poets' series McAuley wrote 'The subjects that seem, in looking back, to recur in my poetry are: love, human and divine; order and crisis in the soul and in the city of man; creative energy in life and art; the heroic virtues. Yet if I had to state in a phrase what was my constant concern, I should say it has been the search for, and the struggle to express, an intuition of the True Form of Man'. *Captain Quiros* (1964) broke new ground in this search; a narrative poem of epic dimensions, it centres upon the subjective world of the sixteenth-century Portuguese navigator and the metaphysical implications of his aims. The poem is ambitious both in scope and form; as a record of a lifetime's spiritual journey it also provides a complex framework of historical fact and myth through which McAuley can draw together themes whose interest for him are already apparent in his earlier work. The very scale of the attempt perhaps meant that there would inevitably be flaws, but it is nevertheless an impressive achievement. Significantly, in the Introduction to the 'Australian Poets' selection he wrote: 'The hardest problem confronting the poet in my time . . . is the struggle for an adequate symbolism'. A critical work, *The Personal Element in Australian Poetry* (1970), examined selected poets from the late nineteenth century through to his contemporaries, seeking to understand 'the relation between poetry and personal experience'. He concluded that when no accepted moral or rational structures remain 'the poet can fall back upon a record of his random sensitivities: the private world does not then complement the public one; it proclaims the ruin of the public world as well as its own disorder'. In *The Grammar of the Real, Selected Prose 1959-1974* (1975) he applied his tenets to a wide range of topics and the volume provides a good introduction to the man. *A Map of Australian Verse* (also 1975) is a valuable guide to the twentieth-century poets and includes not only texts but notes and selected criticism.

McAuley stands as a somewhat lone figure in Austra-lian poetry, articulating sincerely views which many would characterize as conservative – even reactionary. He himself knew this only too well and saw it as the inevitable reward of those who stand against the tide. Fashion, style and creed aside, his work commands attention by virtue of the quality he thought lacking in Christopher Brennan; 'the final thing necessary: that force of poetic genius which overcomes and subdues everything to its own sure purpose'. The collection of poetry *Music Late at Night* was published in the year of his death, 1976.   [PQ]

MacBETH, GEORGE (1932-). Poet, born in Strath-clyde, Scotland, educated at King Edward VII School, Sheffield, and New College, Oxford. He has worked in an editorial capacity for the BBC since 1958. A poet of astonishingly ready talent, he has been generally acclaimed for his giftedness, inventiveness and breadth of interest, but sometimes scolded for flamboyant and frivolous poetic self-indulgence. He already had some thirty published titles to his credit when *Collected Poems 1958-1970* (1971) drew on them, gathering the poems under four heads. It is the work in the first section, where 'the theme is public crisis, interleaved with family deaths', that most emphatically exemplifies MacBeth's capacity for bringing disciplined artistry to bear on matters of earnestness and moment such as war, torture, abortion, childhood memories and bereavement. The personal and the particular are probed in imagery that intensifies the immediate and extends its implications universally. Technically the metaphorical and metrical sleight of hand can be stunning. MacBeth's capacity for lively poetic entertainment is a rare gift. The experimentation in other sections of the volume (devoted to 'white goddess' poems, poems for children of any age, poems for performance and new poems) sometimes ends up in sheer foolery; at other times in intense yet fluent and readable poems such as the sustained narrative of an affair, 'Light in Winter'. MacBeth added several further volumes in the 1970s. *Poems of Love and Death* (1980) reveals him still a poet of Audenesque facility, seduced at times by his own virtuosity into theatrical sensationalism, but capable also of tensely intimate personal poems clean of spectacular effects. In *Poems from Oby* (1982) he speaks from the Norfolk countryside in a more consistently measured voice.   [HB]

MacCAIG, NORMAN (1910-). Poet, born in Edinburgh, Lothian, Scotland, and educated there at the Royal High School and the university. He married Isabel Munro in 1940 and has two children. He was a schoolmaster, then a headmaster, until he joined the teaching staff at the University of Stirling in 1970. Since *Far Cry: Poems* came out in 1943 he has published volumes of verse steadily. They include *Riding Lights* (1955), *The Sinai Sort* (1957), *A Common Grace* (1960), *A Round of Applause* (1962), *Measures* (1965), *Rings on a Tree* (1968), *Midnights* (1970), *The White Bird* (1973) and *The World's Room* (1974). MacCaig is a poet of extraordinary perceptiveness in describing Scottish scenery. He evokes the feel of it with a sensuous acuteness that wakens the reader's sensibilities ('The night tinkles like ice in glasses'). MacCaig is also a 'metaphysical' both in the sense that his imagery, like Donne's,

demands active intellectual and imaginative responsiveness –

> Light perches, preening, on the handle of a
> pram. . . .
> Far out in the West
> The wrecked sun founders though its colours fly.
> ('Nude in a Fountain')

– and in the sense that he speculates philosophically
about the relationship between appearance and reality,
between the observer and the object. Hugh MacDiarmid
(q.v.) called him 'the best Scottish poet writing in English
at the present time' (*The Company I've Kept*, 1966). [HB]

MacCARTHY, DESMOND (1878–1952). Journalist
and critic, educated at Eton and Cambridge. He became
an influential figure in the Bloomsbury Group, literary
editor of the *New Statesman* and later leading critic of the
Sunday Times. He collected articles and essays in a series
of volumes (*Portraits*, 1931; *Criticism*, 1932; *Experience*,
1935 etc). *Memories*, ed R. Kee (1953), a posthumous
collection of literary essays (many of them on contemporary writers), contains a portrait of MacCarthy by
Cyril Connolly (q.v.). MacCarthy was knighted in 1951.
  [HB]

McCRAE, HUGH (1876–1958). Poet, born in
Melbourne, Victoria, Australia, and educated at
Hawthorn Grammar School there. Articled to a
Melbourne architect for a time, he turned to verse and
drawings for the Melbourne *Punch*, the Sydney *Bulletin*
(q.v.) and the New York *Puck*. In 1914 he tried writing and
theatre work in the United States, without success.
Friendship with Norman Lindsay (q.v.) resulted in superb
editions of his work from the Fanfrolico Press in which his
own accomplished verse and Lindsay's illustrations
evoked an antiquity of fauns, satyrs and 'fat young
nymphs'. Although somewhat dated now, McCrae's
work, like that of Lindsay, is important for its often witty
acknowledgement of a European and classical heritage at
a time when Australian cultural life often tended towards
the national and chauvinistic. *Satyrs and Sunlight* (1909)
and *Colombine* (1920) are collector's examples of his
early poems, but his best work is available in the *Poems*
(1939) and the *The Best Poems of Hugh McCrae* (1961). *My
Father and My Father's Friends* (1935) contains interesting recollections – his father was a poet and a friend of
the Australian writers Clarke, Kendall and Gordon.
Georgiana's Journal (1934), which he edited, is the diary
of his grandmother. His own letters were edited for publication (1970) by R.D. Fitzgerald (q.v.). [PQ]

**MacDIARMID, HUGH (pseudonym of Christopher
Murray Grieve)** (1892–1978). Poet and leader of the
Scottish Renaissance, born in Langholm, Dumfriesshire,
Scotland, son of a postman, and educated at Langholm
Academy. As a child, he tells us in the autobiographical
book, *Lucky Poet* (1943), 'I boasted I would be world-
famous by the time I was thirty', and the truculence was
characteristic. MacDiarmid forsook teacher-training in
1911 and started in journalism, to which he returned
after war service in the RAMC. He married Margaret
Skinner in 1918 and there were two children of the

marriage. The family lived in Montrose during the 1920s.
MacDiarmid was active in Labour Party politics, and he
was involved in the founding of the Scottish National
Party in 1928. He had a brief spell in London in 1929,
when Compton Mackenzie (q.v.) induced him to work on a
radio magazine that failed (*Vox*), and a brief spell in Liverpool in 1930. Difficulties, personal, domestic and financial, came to a head at this time. MacDiarmid was
divorced in 1932. He married Valda Trevlyn in 1934 and
went to settle at Whalsay in the Shetlands. He suffered a
breakdown and the Shetland years were ones of hardship
and privation. In 1941 the war drove MacDiarmid to
Clydeside where he undertook heavy manual work in a
factory. He later transferred to the Merchant Service. He
was awarded a Civil List pension in 1950 and in 1951 he
moved to the little two-roomed cottage near Biggar,
Strathclyde, where he remained and which his fame
turned into a place of pilgrimage for admirers throughout
the world.

MacDiarmid joined the Communist Party in 1934, but
was expelled four years later partly, it would seem,
because of his involvement with Scottish nationalism and
partly for his enthusiastic advocacy of Douglas's Social
Credit scheme. It was typical of his instinct for con-
trariety that he should have rejoined the Communist
Party in 1957 when everyone else was leaving it in disgust
at the take-over of Hungary. Radicalism was in
MacDiarmid's bloodstream. So was nationalism, and his
Anglophobia sometimes verged on hysteria. His dream of
a Celtic Workers Republic uniting Cornwall, Scotland,
Ireland and Wales derived much of its passion from
detestation of 'the English Ascendancy, the hideous khaki
empire' ('Cornish Heroic Song') and 'the baneful drug of
over-Anglicization' (*Lucky Poet*) to which bourgeois
Scotland has succumbed. 'Modern Scotland is a disease
in which almost everything has turned into mud' (op. cit.).
But in *The Company I've Kept* (1966), another autobiographical volume, MacDiarmid draws attention to
David Daiches's positive judgement on his work for a
Scottish Renaissance. It is bound up with forgotten
questions of Scottish identity. 'Nationalism for him is only
superficially a political programme. At bottom, its object
is to provide a means of responding properly to experience.' For MacDiarmid's driving vision was that of 'the
fulfilled man in the fulfilled society'. Neither *The
Company I've Kept* nor *Lucky Poet* is forthcoming about
intimate personal matters. They are rather works of
polemical apology.

After somewhat unpromising early efforts in English
verse, MacDiarmid began to write lyrics in a synthetic
Scots whose vocabulary, though genuinely vernacular, is
derived from diverse periods and localities. He drew
much on Jamieson's *Dictionary of the Middle Scots
Tongue* and other treasuries of archaism, and the compound is therefore not the language of any spoken dialect,
but a literary fabrication by an artist determined to
eschew the worn-out verbal currencies of established
usage. The fruits of this pursuit of a style disencumbered
of familiar idiom and recognizable influence were
collected in *Sangschaw* (1925) and *Penny Wheep* (1926).
MacDiarmid was right in believing that a ransacked and
new-minted vernacular could comprehend a variety of
moods and attitudes with startling emotional clarity and

down-to-earth directness. The method reaches its culmination in MacDiarmid's most celebrated poem, *A Drunk Man looks at the Thistle* (1926). This is a long dramatic monologue, a phantasmagoric sequence of reflective lyrics in various stanzaic forms. MacDiarmid spoke in the Author's Note of the logic of drunkenness as though to discourage the search for coherence, but in fact the ranging speculation on Scotland, poetic creation and the realities, mundane or metaphysical, of the human lot, is packed with intellectual vigour and imaginative richness. Scotland's thistle is a versatile symbol, now Yggdrasil, now the phallus. The verbal dexterity and wit are astonishing; the vividness of mood is intense; the provocative persona is larger than life:

> Like staundin' water in a pocket o'
> Impervious clay I'pray I'll never be,
> Cut aff and self-sufficient, but let reenge
> Heichts o' the lift an benmaist deeps o' sea.
>
> ('A Vision of Myself')

To Circumjack Cencrastus (1930) is a less coherent sequence. Cencrastus is a mythical Scottish serpent. To 'circumjack' is to lie around (*circumjacere*). Indeed the remarkable concentration and passionate rigour of the *Drunk Man* were but fitfully attained in the succeeding output. Critics blamed the increasing political preoccupation evident in *First Hymn to Lenin and Other Poems* (1931); but MacDiarmid's spirit never faltered:

> And as for me in my fricative work
> I ken fu' weel
> Sic an integrity's what I maun ha'e
> Indivisible, real,
> Woven owre close for the point o' a pin
> Onywhere to win in.
>
> ('The Seamless Garment')

However, the dilution of the Scots idiom in *Scots Unbound* (1932) and *Stony Limits* (1934) heralded an eventual return to English. In the later poetry there was also a drift away from metrical formalities to prosaic rhythms. MacDiarmid was always a volcanic poet, but the verbal helter-skelter of 'Let us arise' (from *In Memoriam James Joyce*, 1955) is unrestrainedly indigestible by ear or mind, and the deafening stridencies of the 'Cornish Heroic Song' (from *A Kist of Whistles*, 1943) include such unpalatable lines as:

> So collapsed Cornwall's viridical qualities
> In Wesleyans and myxoedematous sectaries like
> these
> Felled by the abundant centrifugally-spreading
> hyphae

MacDiarmid initially and triumphantly harked back to Dunbar and to the Scottish tradition of wit and speculation, fleering satire and ironical parody. He admired Burns as a symbol of the Scottish character grappling with the need for native self-expression, but he lambasted the 'bourgeois Burns cult, a monstrous misappropriation of Burns, whitewashed and respectablized and made, like statistics, to prove anything and everything except the inadmissible things for which he essentially stood'. His own best work has the quality he most valued – it is thought deriving its essence rather than merely its shape

from words. His range of concern extended from the philosophical and the political to the domestic and the personal. Reviewing his *Complete Poems 1920–76 Vols 1 & 2* (1978), John Montague (q.v.) argued that the quality of the lyrics to be found in the 1930s volumes established MacDiarmid 'and not the modish Auden' as 'the major poet of the thirties' (*Guardian* 30.11.78). K. Buthlay edited a selection of MacDiarmid's prose in *The Uncanny Scot* (1968) and D. Glen edited some of his literary criticism in *Selected Essays* (1969).   [HB]

MacDONAGH, DONAGH (1912–68). Dramatist and poet, born and brought up in Dublin, Ireland, and a District Judge in the Irish courts. MacDonagh was the son of Thomas MacDonagh, himself a poet and lecturer in English at University College, Dublin, who was one of the leaders of the 1916 Easter Rising and was executed. Donagh MacDonagh's volume of poems, *The Hungry Grass* (1947), contains a moving tribute, 'Maud Gonne', and a deeply felt radio masque about the 1916 Rising, 'Easter Christening'. The verse comedy, *Happy as Larry*, is a tale of murder and wife-stealing cheerfully presented in the rhythms and idiom of rollicking balladry. ('I thought that it might be possible, by using the technique of the Marx Brothers and the circus, to lure the unsuspecting public into the theatre and then land dollops of verse in their laps.') It was first put on at the Mercury Theatre, London, in 1947. *Step-in-the-Hollow*, first produced at the Gaiety Theatre, Dublin, in 1957, is a racy Irish farce involving a randy septuagenarian judge who is unexpectedly visited by an official Inspector. The Inspector sits at his side on the bench on the very day an irate mother brings a case about invasion of her daughter's bedroom; and the judge himself is guilty. The tables are happily turned at the end.   [HB]

McGAHERN, JOHN (1934–). Novelist, born and educated in Dublin, Ireland. He has given a harrowing portrayal of provincial Irish life in the two novels *The Barracks* (1964) and *The Dark* (1965). The former records the decline and death of Elizabeth Reegan in her forties. The second wife of a policeman who is eaten up with violent resentment against his superior officer, she copes with her stepchildren and relives mentally her Irish girlhood and her nursing experience in the London blitz. *The Dark* traces a motherless boy's struggle through childhood and adolescence to the winning of a university scholarship in the teeth of his father's tyrannical brutality. McGahern eschews 'plot'. His books take inner emotional direction from the pattern of family affliction, the rhythm of growing and dying. A claustrophobic defeatism broods over these powerfully controlled studies in which even intensely dislikeable men touch nerves of sympathy and affection. In the third novel, *The Leavetaking* (1974), which takes a swipe at Ireland's attitude to divorce, McGahern is effective where he treads similar ground again, but unconvincing when he forsakes Ireland for London and sophistication. *Nightlines* (1970) showed McGahern's mastery as a short-story writer. *Getting Through* (1978) confirms a rare gift for creeping quietly into the lives of ordinary people in a variety of environments and undemonstratively dissolving what might be otherwise drab or prosaic in their confusions and failures in rich imaginative sympathy. The novel *The Pornographer* (1979) studies a pornographic writer who wants loveless sex and gets a girl pregnant. He learns something eventually from her love and through the death of his aunt from cancer; but the book lacks the emotional logic and psychological plausibility of the early Irish novels. [HB]

MACHEN, ARTHUR (1863–1947). Novelist, born at Caerleon-upon-Usk, Gwent, Wales, and educated at Hereford Cathedral School. His interests as a writer were in fantasy and horror, Celtic legend and myth, the supernatural and the occult. In 1900 he joined the hermetic Order of the Golden Dawn of which Yeats (q.v.) was also a member. He worked in publishing and journalism and with the Frank Benson Shakespeare Repertory Company. He was helped in early life by a legacy and in late life (from 1932) by a Civil List pension. His early fiction includes *The Great God Pan* (1894) and *The Hill of Dreams* (1907). Though much of Machen's work belongs in composition to the 1890s, it was in the 1920s that it was widely recognized. By then his famous short story of the First World War, 'The Bowmen', first published in the *Evening News*, had bred the popular legend of the Angels of Mons. In 'The Bowmen' a British soldier instinctively repeats the prayer for aid, 'Adsit Anglis Sanctus Georgius', and St George brings a company of unseen Agincourt bowmen who leave 10,000 Germans dead. The story was reprinted in Machen's *Tales of Horror and the Supernatural* (1949), a collection that shows his indebtedness to the Gothic tradition of Mrs Radcliffe and Horace Walpole as well as to Wilkie Collins and Conan Doyle (q.v.). The narrative writing is heavily laden with words as well as with atmosphere. The modern reader is likely to find the mystery and tension somewhat synthetically fabricated. *Children of the Pool* (1935) is a late collection of stories. *Far Off Things* (1922), *Things Near and Far* (1923) and *The London Adventure* (1924) are autobiographical. [HB]

MacINNES, COLIN (1914–76). Novelist, born in London but educated in Australia, the son of Angela Thirkell, a writer. He carved out a distinctive niche for himself in novels that racily portray the contemporary London of teenage cults, pop-music addiction, drinking, drugs, prostitution and delinquency. *City of Spades* (1957) recounts the experience of Johnny Fortune, a Nigerian who tries to make a go of it in London. *Absolute Beginners* (1959) centres on a contemporary teenage cult and is narrated by an 18-year-old dealer in pornographic photography. MacInnes's accuracy in depicting the world of drinking-clubs, ponces, hustlers and the like has its sociological interest, as has his careful differentiation of current cults and their related gear. He projects a vivid undercover life in the capital with conviction and energy. *Mr Love and Justice* (1960) is a book of the same genre, in which Frankie Love, a ponce, is allegorically balanced against Ted Justice, a policeman. Much of MacInnes's effectiveness derives from his invention of a diction that gives identity to the sub-world. Its vocabulary is rich in words for human types – conscript, oldie, serf, sperm, chicklet, tax-payer, spade, mug, non-mug, kiddo, yobbo, zombie, oafo and slob. As literature, however, the books

display in their crisp presentation and hotted-up diction the flavour of grown-up comics.

Of later novels *All Day Saturday* (1966) goes back to prewar Australia, while *Westward to Laughter* (1969) and *Three Years to Play* (1970) go back to the eighteenth century and to the Elizabethan Age respectively. *Out of the Garden* (1974) reverts to the earlier concern with the contemporary social scene. *Out of the Way: Later Essays* (1978) includes many pieces which MacInnes contributed to *New Society* under the heading, 'Out of the Way', as well as contributions to *Spectator* and *Encounter*. On the strength of them, he has been acclaimed an essayist in the tradition of Hazlitt and Orwell. [HB]

McKAY, CLAUDE (1890–1948). Poet and first Negro West Indian novelist, born in Jamaica. He emigrated to the United States after publication of his poems, *Songs of Jamaica* (1912). Unsustained college study between 1912 and 1914, during which he was profoundly influenced by Du Bois's *The Souls of Black Folk*, was followed by four years as a railway waiter. His rousing sonnet addressed to fellow Negroes, 'If we must die', appeared in *The Liberator* (1919). Two uncomfortable years in England ended with the publication of *Spring in New Hampshire* (1920), which, with *Harlem Shadows* (1922), reveals a poet of social protest who affirms Negro identity. Fêted in Moscow in 1922, he worked and travelled through France, Spain and Morocco from 1923 to 1934. The novels *Home to Harlem* (1928) and *Banjo* (1929) made him a central Harlem Renaissance figure and, as K. Ramchand notes, show his 'preoccupation with the place of the Negro in white civilization . . . a celebration of Negro qualities . . . and attacks upon the civilized white world'. Less explicitly polemical, *Banana Bottom* (1933) convincingly presents an educated West Indian woman finding her true self in the village community of her birth, 'dancing down the barrier between high breeding and common pleasures'. The autobiography *A Long Way from Home* appeared in 1938. [AR]

McKENNA, STEPHEN (1888–1967). Novelist, born in London, nephew of the financier and statesman, Reginald McKenna, who became Chancellor of the Exchequer in 1915. Stephen McKenna, educated at Westminster School and Oxford, describes himself in the autobiographical volume, *While I Remember* (1921) – a curiously impersonal book – as 'an Irish boy brought up in England and sent to a tory stronghold by a father who had reared him on the pure milk of late Victorian radicalism'. In fact McKenna became an interestingly detached and philosophical commentator on his age in his sociopolitical novels, of which *Sonia* (1917) proved the most successful, perhaps because of the nostalgia it breathes for the pre-1914 political and social scene. 'This book may then perhaps have something of historical value in portraying a group of men and women who were at the same time my personal friends and representative of those Governing Classes in politics, journalism, commerce and society.' The survey of the World at the Top is held together by a romantic narrative thread of a wayward, self-centred girl, Sonia Dainton, who is painfully disciplined into maturity and integrity through the love of an Irish rebel's son who is wounded and blinded in

France. Covering the years from late summer 1898 to August 1915, the book tracks the careers of the fated generation from public school to war service, military or civilian. Socially and politically aware, the novel ambles through 'the four years of carnival that ended with the war' and the opening of the war itself, achieving a sense of the big movements of history and shot through with percipient philosophical observations, often aphoristically pinpointed. Other novels include *The Reluctant Lover* (1912), *Sonia Married* (1919), *An Affair of Honour* (1925), *Last Confession* (1937) and *A Place in the Sun* (1962). McKenna also wrote the memoir, *Reginald McKenna 1863–1943* (1948). He worked in the War Trade Department in the First World War and again in the Ministry of Economic Warfare in the Second World War. He is not to be confused with Stephen MacKenna (1872–1934), the Fenian associated with the Irish literary revival and translator of Plotinus who as 'Martin Daly' published *Memories of the Dead* (1916). [HB]

MACKENZIE, COMPTON (Sir) (1883–1972). Novelist and miscellaneous writer, born at West Hartlepool, County Durham, when his actor-parents were on tour. He was educated at Oxford. His eventful career included a year as a full-time Anglican lay-reader bent on ordination, residence in Capri, reception into the Roman Catholic Church in 1914, service in the Royal Marines in the Dardanelles, wartime intelligence work in Athens, founding *The Gramophone* in 1923, ownership of the Shiant islands in the Outer Hebrides and advocacy of Scottish nationalism. D.H. Lawrence's (q.v.) malicious caricature of Mackenzie in 'The Man Who Loved Islands' was, according to Norman Douglas (q.v.), his reward for having befriended Lawrence on Capri. Mackenzie's first two novels, *The Passionate Elopement* (1911), a period romance, and *Carnival* (1912), a story of stage life, were immensely successful; his third, *Sinister Street* (1913), an attempt 'to present in detail the youth of somebody handicapped by a public school and university education', uses autobiographical material in studying the formation of a personality. Ford Madox Ford (q.v.) called it 'the history of a whole class . . . during a whole period' (quoted in D.J. Dooley, *Compton Mackenzie*, 1974). Henry James (q.v.) acclaimed the young novelist, but he was to go on to write a hundred books and, though the readiness of his humour and his narrative inventiveness guaranteed him continuing success as an entertainer, he paid the price of facile over-production in the general critical estimate of his contemporaries. Yet there has always been some unease about this estimate. Edmund Wilson noted how Mackenzie tried 'to plead in his books for the rights of the small nations and cultural minorities' and he ridiculed the comparatively disproportionate critical respect given to Somerset Maugham (q.v.), 'a writer with none of Mackenzie's distinction' (ibid.). D.J. Dooley himself asserts, 'He has been a kind of English Proust, evoking the moods of past time. He has written some of the funniest novels in the language'. Of Mackenzie's serious novels *The Altar Steps* (1922), *The Parson's Progress* (1923) and *The Heavenly Ladder* (1924) form a religious trilogy on the Anglo-Catholic movement, but his most ambitious work is the immense six-volume sequence, *The Four Winds of Love* (1937–1945), which presents a panoramic portrayal of Mackenzie's own times, moving from hero John Ogilvie's schooldays at the time of the Boer War in *The East Wind* (1937) to the deteriorating international situation of the 1930s in *The North Wind* (1944–5). Lighter works like *Whisky Galore* (1947), in which a cargo boat laden with whisky is conveniently grounded off a Hebridean island during a wartime whisky famine, exploit stock comic recipes with unflagging zest and resourcefulness. Mackenzie's monumental autobiography, *My Life and Times*, was issued in ten volumes (called 'Octaves') between 1963 and 1971. [HB]

MACKINTOSH, ELIZABETH (1897–1952). Born in Inverness, Scotland, and trained in Birmingham as a teacher of physical training. She achieved a remarkable success when John Gielgud played the title role in her historical play, *Richard of Bordeaux* (1933), a study of Richard II; three-quarters of the action takes place before the point at which Shakespeare's play begins. For this and for other plays, as well as for her biography, *Claverhouse* (1937), Mackintosh used the pseudonym 'Gordon Daviot'. As 'Josephine Tey' she wrote mystery novels, including *The Franchise Affair* (1948) and *The Daughter of Time* (1951). In the latter a hospitalized Scotland Yard man exercises his detective ingenuity on vindicating Richard III from his reputation for villainy. [HB]

MacLENNAN, HUGH (1907–). Novelist and essayist, born at Glace Bay, Cape Breton, Nova Scotia, Canada, the son of a Scottish Canadian doctor. He graduated from Dalhousie University in 1929, went to Oxford as a Rhodes Scholar and travelled widely in Europe before completing his classical studies with a doctorate at Princeton University, New Jersey. He worked for a time as a schoolteacher before joining the English Department at McGill University, Montreal, Quebec, in 1951. MacLennan's first novel, *Barometer Rising* (1941), illustrates his classic compositional method in its patterning of local history (the Halifax munitions explosion of December 1917, which he witnessed) within a context of personal fulfilment and national destiny which raise it towards the level of myth. MacLennan here contrives that the explosion can suggest a cataclysmic resolution not only in the characters' lives but in Canada's actual and spiritual history, but the requirements of naturalism and the demands of a symbolic approach are not always reconciled in later works. *Two Solitudes* (1945), which explores dimensions of the French–English conflict in Quebec, contains some fine writing (especially in the first part) but the final effect is that of an over-schematic approach. *The Precipice* (1948) traced the restrictive effects of puritanism upon Canadians and Americans and this theme was pursued with more success within the microcosm of a Cape Breton mining village in *Each Man's Son* (1951), arguably his best work. *The Watch that Ends the Night* (1959) adopted first-person narration which permitted extended reflection and analysis through the central character, George Stewart, a professor and political commentator. A new complexity of method makes this MacLennan's most ambitious work, but the wide-ranging commentary it contains is more suited to the kind of urbane essay found in *Cross Country* (1949), *Thirty* *and Three* (1954) and *Scotchman's Return* (1960) in which he shows himself to be an astute, witty and experienced commentator on life – including that of his own country. In *Seven Rivers of Canada* (1961) reflections on history and geography are blended with the demands of the travel book. *Return of the Sphinx* (1967) explored the issue of separatism in Quebec (first broached in *Two Solitudes*) partly through the character of Alan Ainslie, who was a boy in *Each Man's Son*. This is a tightly written novel, which, through its calculated links with his earlier works, evolves a complex response. In its sweeping delineation of issues touching upon the national consciousness the work is of great importance, though many would feel that the era for novels of such classic scope is now past. MacLennan's own vision demands a large canvas, but his particular character studies – especially of women – are often insufficiently subtle to bear the weight which the overall design requires.   [PQ]

MacNEICE, LOUIS (1907–63). Poet, born in Belfast, Northern Ireland, the son of a clergyman (later a bishop), educated at Marlborough and at Merton College, Oxford. He got a first in Greats and in 1930 became a lecturer in classics at Birmingham University. In 1936 he moved to Bedford College, London, as lecturer in Greek, and in the 1940s he became attached to the BBC, writing and producing 'features' and plays.

MacNeice has been popularly grouped with Auden (q.v.), Spender (q.v.) and Day Lewis (q.v.), 'poets of the thirties', but he never shared the political commitment of the other three. He was neither a Marxist nor one who aligned himself with the English proletariat. A scholar in equipment – but lacking the scholar's temperament – he early evolved a style that is at once prodigal in imagery, acute in its observation of familiar things and conversationally easy on the ear. The ease with which the reader latches on to MacNeice's mood and is carried on the current of his music distinguishes him from more taxing contemporaries. 'There is no code to crack in MacNeice', G.S. Fraser (q.v.) has written.

MacNeice published his first volume of poems, *Blind Fireworks*, in 1929, and it was followed by *Poems* (1935) and *The Earth Compels* (1938). From the start, in these volumes, there is a metaphorical vein that has vitality and immediacy and reflects alert observation:

That never-satisfied old maid, the sea
Rehangs her white lace curtains ceaselessly.
                    ('The lugubrious, salubrious seaside')

Dazzling images are thrown off with a casual air:

Down the road someone is practising scales,
The notes like little fishes vanish with a wink of
    tails.
                    ('Sunday morning')

And the ambiguous connotative throwback from fishes' tails to 'scales' is a characteristically lavish bonus. Technical virtuosity in the masterly control of rhythm, image, aphorism and double-rhyme is immense:

The sunlight on the garden
Hardens and grows cold,
We cannot cage the minute
Within its nets of gold . . .
                    ('The sunlight on the garden')

But it was the long poem, *Autumn Journal* (1939), which brought MacNeice's gifts into play. in a peculiarly apt and, as it turned out, historically important way. The *Journal* has 24 cantos and covers the period from August 1938 to New Year 1939. It is intimate, informal and spontaneous rather than gravely pondered. The poet thinks aloud; there is frank introspection, uneasy observation of the current scene and some grappling with the mystery of things. Canto IV gives us a touching portrait of MacNeice's first wife (the marriage had ended in divorce), canto VIII of early married happiness and canto XI of the broken relationship. In canto V the threat of impending war intrudes on London life ('The bloody frontier / Converges on our beds'), in canto X the start of a new term at Bedford College throws the memory back to early days at Marlborough and canto XVI takes us to Ireland. In canto XVIII disillusionment with the contemporary scene is acute and devastating. The country is 'a dwindling annexe to the factory / Squalid as an after-birth'. There are times when one suspects that MacNeice's aloof detachment is allowed to confer the right to castigate indiscriminately; but MacNeice himself is not unaware of this suspicion:

But most of us lack the right discontent, contented
    Merely to cavil.

The implicitly dismissive juxtapositions ('The Sleeping Beauty or the Holy Ghost' and 'The gentleman farmer, the village idiot, the Shropshire lad') make a telling impact before the reader has time to ask what the Irish irony is up to. Yet *Autumn Journal* remains perhaps the most powerfully evocative work of the decade in the way it plays on the nerve of nostalgia and registers the temper of the time – the moods of melancholy abandon, the trapped expectancy of doom.

It is doubtful whether MacNeice bettered this sombrely entrancing achievement. The long *Autumn Sequel* (1954) seeks to repeat the success fifteen years later and MacNeice struggles heroically with terza rima through twenty-six cantos, yet the whole has a forced, run-down feel. Even the echoing of other poets seems here not so much to intensify connotation as to dissolve the personal stamp. There are vivid vignettes of old friends and reminiscences of places. Imagery and aphorism leap to life at times; but at other times the reader is conscious of an aimless versified garrulity. The melancholy awareness of a lack of centre breaks through:

I sometimes think
That I am an actor too, that the Muse has
    defaulted
And left me an apparatus, rivet and link,
With nothing to link or rivet.

D.B. Moore (in *The Poetry of Louis MacNeice*, 1972) avers that 'MacNeice was afflicted with a guilty agnosticism because to be an agnostic was to be traitor to an upbringing that had taken place in an atmosphere of unquestioning belief'. What Moore calls his 'troubled lack of conviction' is one aspect of his uneasy remoteness. However real the world MacNeice re-creates for us, there hangs about it a rather sad air of disclosure denied at the deepest levels of personal encounter.

MacNeice's prose work, *Modern Poetry*, came out in 1938. Walter Allen has described *Modern Poetry* and *Autumn Journal* as 'expressions of one single impulse'. MacNeice himself describes the book as 'a plea for *impure* poetry, that is, for poetry conditioned by the poet's life and the world around him', and he goes on to insist that the poet is 'both critic and entertainer' and must steer a middle course between propaganda and escapism. In a chapter on 'The Personal Factor' he lists things that conditioned his own poetry – 'having been brought up in the North of Ireland; having a father who was a clergyman; the fact that my mother died when I was little; repression from the age of 6 to 9' and so on. The facts hinted at here have been posthumously laid bare in the publication (*The Strings are False*, 1965) of auto-biographical material that MacNeice left in the hands of his friend, E.R. Dodds. Not everything in the book endears one to the writer, for MacNeice can speak superciliously of near relations and domestic servants; but the sheer zest of the work is captivating and its wry ironies bring a complex personality before us.

MacNeice's output includes a translation of the *Agamemnon* (1936), a study, *The Poetry of W.B. Yeats* (1941), and plays and features for radio too numerous to be consistently inspired. It has sometimes been argued that his work shows little development of talent. But there is no falling-off in the latest volumes of verse, *Solstices* (1961) and *The Burning Perch* (1963). At the end there is notable tautness and discipline to match the uncanny brilliance of the 1930s that gave us the rollicking 'Bagpipe Music'. E.R. Dodds edited the *Collected Poems* (1966). [HB]

MAHON, DEREK (1941–). Poet, born in Belfast, Northern Ireland, educated at Belfast Institute and Trinity College, Dublin. After two years in America and Canada, he returned to Ireland in 1967 to teach for a year at Belfast High School, then to be lecturer at the Language Centre of Ireland in Dublin, and later (in 1977) at the New University of Ulster in Coleraine. His *Night-Crossing* (1968) is an engaging collection, wide-ranging in theme, eclectic in style, the work of a poet who seems capable of writing wittily and tuneably on whatever subject offers itself. 'Grandfather' and 'My Wicked Uncle' are entertaining portraits, 'In Belfast' and 'In Carrowdore' (at the grave of Louis MacNeice) more searchingly meditative, and 'An Unborn Child' a captivating monologue from inside the womb. In *Lives* (1972) presentation is more complex, the Irish problem raises its head and a more sombre note is struck. 'Ecclesiastes' is a brilliant ironic squib, 'Rage for Order' looks at destruction in a Belfast street under the light from a poet's attic, and 'Beyond Howth Head' is a cunningly constructed Audenesque verse-letter from Dublin to London. *The Snow Party* (1975) was succeeded by *Poems 1962–1978* (1979) in which Mahon collects and, in some cases, revises the contents of the three earlier volumes and adds some new poems. 'Of all the poets to have emerged from the North (of Ireland), Mahon seems to be the least locally attached', Blake Morrison has written, noting too Mahon's 'sympathy with a post-Movement tradition of the poem as anecdote-and-moral' (*Times Literary Supplement*, 15.2.80). At its most forceful Mahon's impact is immediate:

Wonders are many and none is more wonderful
    than man
Who has tamed the terrier, trimmed the hedge
And grasped the principle of the watering-can.'
                                    ('Glengormley')

Seamus Heaney (q.v.) has declared *The Hunt by Night* (1982) Mahon's 'most exuberant and authoritative single volume to date. . . . It is as if the very modernity of his intelligence has goaded a primitive stamina in his imagination.' There is scintillating technical brilliance (including a display of Joycean pastiche). There is also the sombre bafflement evident in the title poem on the painting of the same name by Uccello. Perhaps our own long 'hunt by night' is not after all a great adventure, 'but some elaborate / Spectacle put on for fun'. [HB]

MAIS, ROGER (1905–55). Painter and novelist, born in Jamaica. He grew up in the rural Blue Mountains area, and later in Kingston. On leaving school he worked as civil servant, journalist, gardener, salesman and photographer. His political consciousness ignited by the Kingston riots in 1938, he ardently supported the National Movement; from it, claimed Norman Manley, Mais drew 'direction and power and purpose'. He flung himself into political, social, intellectual and artistic polemics with 'his entire capital of affections' (John Hearne, q.v.). In 1944 Mais was imprisoned for writing a 'subversive' article. He went abroad in 1952, living in London, Paris and the South of France until returning to Jamaica shortly before his death.

With Mittelholzer (q.v.), Reid (q.v.), Selvon (q.v.) and Lamming (q.v.), Mais helped to create modern West Indian literature. His short-story volumes published in Jamaica, *Face and Other Stories* (1942) and *And Most of All Man* (1943), with his novels, *The Hills Were Joyful Together* (1953) and *Brother Man* (1954), established his initial reputation for social realism. It is true that, like *The Children of Sisyphus* by Patterson (q.v.), they delineate very concretely the squalor and futility of Kingston slum life, that the title of the first novel is a highly sardonic echoing of Psalm 98, that the rhythm of the natural seasons is counteracted by the jangling disorders of poverty and viciousness, that the couple with the most fulfilled relationship in *The Hills Were Joyful Together* meet violent deaths; nevertheless, this novel, which most patently achieves Mais's self-declared intention of revealing 'the dreadful condition of the working classes', contrasts despair with many gleams of tenderness and humanity. In *Roger Mais* (1978) Jean D'Costa insists that *Brother Man* complements *The Hills*, observing that in the latter: 'The forces of life exist, but in a posture of defeat. In *Brother Man* the pattern is altered: . . . its imagery is triumphant'. At the cost, however, of sentimentalizing Brother Man's Christ-like career. Although K. Ramchand (*The West Indian Novel and Its Background*) underplays the permanent value of the first two novels, he rightly stresses that in *Black Lightning* (1955) Mais's 'art and understanding are in greatest harmony'. The rapid cinematic technique of juxtaposed dramatic scenes is more economical, the forest setting allows more subtly enriching relationships between nature and mankind, the exploitation of dialogue as characters stumble towards understanding is pliant and deft, but, especially, the non-realist adaptation of the Samson motif of strength and weakness intermixed allows a comprehending tempering of suffering with fulfilment. [AR]

MALGONKAR, MANOHAR (1913-). Soldier, far-mer, novelist, born in Bombay, India. He received an anglicized upbringing close to a princely court and graduated BA (Hons), Bombay, in 1936. After profes-sional big-game hunting, he was a civil servant in 1937-42 and soldier in 1942-52, rising to lieutenant-colonel. Since 1959 he has farmed at Jagalbet. Author of two plays and five books of non-fiction, Malgonkar accurately characterizes his fiction as attempting stories 'full of meat, exciting, well-constructed, plausible, and with a lot of action'. Shyamala Narayan questions the plausibility of The Devil's Wind (1972), about the 1857 'Indian Mutiny', and regards Open Season (1979) as 'entertaining'. Shalimar (1978) is based upon Krishna Shah's film. His best novels reflect his own energetic experience: Distant Drum (1960), about an army officer's career; The Princes (1963), like Anand's (q.v.) similar novel, on Princely India's extinction; A Bend in the Ganges (1964), concerning the 1947 Partition upheavals (on the same theme, see Singh (q.v.) and Nahal (q.v.)). Combat of Shadows (1962), however, ventures into the psychology of British tea-planters before Indian indepen-dence. Malgonkar is politically conservative; momentous events furnish backgrounds to individual behaviour, not thematic motifs. Since 1974 he has published three volumes of short stories. The Men Who Killed Gandhi (1978) is a meticulously researched and professionally written account of the plot that led to the assassination of the Mahatma in 1947. [AR]

MALOUF, DAVID (1934-). Poet and novelist, born in Brisbane, Queensland, Australia. He has lived in Italy for several years. On his father's side Malouf's family is from the Lebanon and on his mother's from London; his own writing has reflected a personal odyssey in its timeless yet personal exploration of that inner world which reflects and refracts the outer. Educated at Brisbane Grammar School and at the University of Brisbane, he went on to teach at the latter for two years before teach-ing in England for nearly ten years from 1959. After returning to Australia he was appointed a senior lecturer at Sydney University and was active in both writing and publishing poetry. Bicycle and Other Poems (1969), Neighbours in a Thicket (1974) and Poems 1975-6 (1976) established him firmly as an important contemporary voice in Australia, and although he now lives as an expatriate he has little sympathy for heated debates on whether Australian writers should live in Australia. The convenience yet comparative isolation (and cheapness) of his present village home allow him to concentrate on his creative work; he considers himself an Australian writer who happens to live in Europe. His first work of fiction was Johnno (1974), a novel which drew deeply upon his own Queensland childhood, while An Imaginary Life (1978) took the form of a story told by the exiled Roman poet Ovid of his encounter with a wolf-boy and their ensuing relationship. A moving and disturbing fable which questioned the very bases of 'civilized' existence, it

was praised internationally and confirmed Malouf as a writer of varied talents and great promise. [PQ]

MANDER, JANE (1877-1949). Novelist, born near Auckland, New Zealand. 'I am an Aucklander by birth and a North Aucklander by environment' she wrote in 1935. Her father travelled the wild North Auckland area running timber milling enterprises and this area she came to know so well is reflected in her work as a spiritual testing place, not simply as local testing. The Story of a New Zealand River, written in 1914-16 and published in 1920, was a powerful depiction of the woman's lot in the stark North Auckland setting. The Passionate Pilgrim (1922) and The Strange Attraction (1923) were less successful novels exploring colonial tensions, but all three books attracted censure in New Zealand for their frank treatment of 'sex problems'. In 1923 she settled in London; Allen Adair, her finest work, was published in 1925 but aroused little interest in New Zealand. She now felt 'a hankering to get back to my original environment in writing' and returned to Auckland in 1932, but, weighed down by a daughter's duties to her aged father until his death in 1942, and by ill-health after that, she wrote no more fiction. Allen Adair is again set in 'that gum country of the north which is in my blood and bones' and, written by a then expatriate, stands as her final treatment of the pull between New Zealand and 'Home' and – within New Zealand – between urban life and the bush she knew and loved. [PQ]

MANNING, OLIVIA (1917-80). Novelist, born in Portsmouth, Hampshire, of a naval officer and an Irish mother, and privately educated. She spent much of her youth in Ireland. In 1939 she married Reginald Smith, a British Council lecturer in Bucharest. German invasions drove them first out of Romania to Athens, then out of Greece to Egypt. The experience culminating in the successive evacuation provided the material for the author's most outstanding work, her Balkan Trilogy: The Great Fortune (1960), The Spoilt City (1962) and Friends and Heroes (1965). Earlier novels (School for Love, 1951; A Different Face, 1953) had demonstrated penetration and precision: the trilogy is a fine documentary record of how the shallow and the frivolous, the hedonist and the idealist, behave as Nazi tyranny and brutality intrude upon English residents against the background of a crumbling culture, a corrupt regime and a wretchedly unequal social order. The gradual encroachment of disaster exercises a cohesive, fatalistic pressure against which the coolly exact detailing of gossipy futilities has both comic and ironic power. Threaded through the whole is a remarkably subtle study of personal adjust-ment between a wife, Harriet Pringle, and her husband Guy, whose infuriatingly indiscriminate generosity and public self-commitment (his 'easy, almost feckless willing-ness to adopt the world') preclude the loving domestic privacies she hungers for. This collision of temperaments at the personal level has ideological overtones: they fuse with public issues that are simultaneously in crisis, and a unity of purpose emerges to compensate for the often excessive documentation.

Olivia Manning set out deliberately to chronicle her age, believing that the novel form is 'perfectly adapted to the expression of our bewildered and self-conscious civilization'. She took up the story of the Pringles again in the Levant Trilogy, consisting of *The Danger Tree* (1977), *The Battle Lost and Won* (1978) and the posthumous *The Sum of Things* (1980). Set largely in Egypt, it follows in sequence upon the Balkan Trilogy. Guy and Harriet, their marriage crumbling, are involved in the idle social life of Cairo while the army bloodily confronts Rommel in the desert. In the last novel they are separated for most of the time, and the ultimate reconciliation is not all that consolatory. 'In an imperfect world, marriage was a matter of making do with what one had chosen.'   [HB]

MANSFIELD, KATHERINE (pseudonym of Katherine Mansfield Beauchamp) (1888–1923). Short-story writer, born at Wellington, New Zealand, the daughter of an established merchant and banker. After local schooling she was educated privately for three years at Queen's College, Harley Street, London, before returning to New Zealand in 1906. She loved London, 'to live there is a real existence', and after a quarrel with her father she was allowed to return in 1908. Granted an allowance, which continued all her life, she was supposed to study music but a reckless and self-demanding search for experience led to an impetuous marriage in the following year and to a pregnancy (not by her husband) which miscarried while she was in Germany, where she had been sent to convalesce by a well-meaning but unknowing mother. Her bitter feelings at this time are reflected in the stories first published serially in *The New Age* in London and collected the next year as *In a German Pension* (1911). The situation of 'Frau Fischer' reflects her own, but the later stories have a more moderate tone and also use a recollected Wellington family setting (with Andreas Binzer as her father) rather than her immediate European one. She had lived apart from her husband since the marriage and, in 1912, she met John Middleton Murry (q.v.), to whose magazine *Rhythm* she had recently contributed 'The Woman at the Store'. This was an untypical but striking story with a wild New Zealand setting which in many ways foreshadowed much subsequent New Zealand fiction.

Mansfield did not marry Murry until 1918, when her first husband divorced her, but their personal and literary partnership gave her something of the security she needed, and although some of her contributions to *Rhythm* (which collapsed in 1914) were witty parodies and articles (at which she excelled) she also developed the vein first revealed in such stories as 'A Birthday' from her first collection. Her writing now included stark New Zealand tales ('The Woman at the Store', 'Ole Underwood' and 'Millie'), her various satirical writings in assorted London journals and stories centring upon childhood innocence in conflict with parental authority, such as 'The Little Girl' and 'New Dresses'. 'An Indiscreet Journey' (1915), which reflected her own trips to Paris, was a technical advance but the dramatic change came in February 1915 with the arrival from New Zealand (to enlist) of her young brother Leslie, to whom she had always been close. Their shared family memories give a distinct atmospheric quality to 'The Wind Blows' and 'The Apple Tree'; for the first time she was able to draw deeply upon the New Zealand background which was to be the source of her finest work. When Leslie was killed in October she was heartbroken, but her resolve to write was strengthened: 'I've got things to do for both of us'. From December she was living at Bandol, in the South of France, and in January 1916 she recorded in her *Journal*: 'I want to write about my own country. . . . Not only because it is a "sacred debt" that I pay . . . because my brother and I were born there, but also because in my thoughts I range with him over all the remembered .places'. Her commitment to her writing now joined with her sense of being a New Zealander and her work gained a strong and certain intention: 'I want . . . to make our undiscovered country leap into the eyes of the old world'. By early March she had written 'The Aloe', which she revised in 1917 for publication as 'Prelude'; in this deceptively simply story of a New Zealand family moving house her gifts for shifting perspective, complex statement and evocative concrete detail are perfectly combined. In 1917 tuberculosis was suspected (the first haemorrhage came in February the following year) and she left again for Bandol where she wrote 'Je ne parle pas français', partly based on her brief stay in Paris with Murry in 1913. In August 1918 'Bliss' was published in the *English Review* – her first success with such a prestigious journal – and her best work to date was collected in *Bliss, and Other Stories* (1920), which was acclaimed by many critics though she herself thought it 'trivial . . . not good enough'. In *The Garden Party and Other Stories* (1922) awareness of her own approaching death is but a personal instance of that enveloping sense of mortality represented by the war (particularized for her in Leslie's death), and the stories bring to recollections of a sheltered New Zealand childhood the adult recognition of that mysterious 'diversity of life . . . Death included'. The book was well reviewed as a second collection from a promising young writer. Eleven months later (January 1923) she was dead. The posthumous collections *The Dove's Nest* (1923) and *Something Childish* (1924) show her talent still growing, though several of the stories are unfinished. Her *Journal* was first published by Murry in 1927 (with a 'definitive edition' in 1954), the two-volume *Letters* in 1928 and *The Scrapbook of Katherine Mansfield* in 1939. *Letters to John Middleton Murry* (1951) printed the full correspondence, but after Murry's death in 1957 the extent of his rearrangement of her personal papers was realized from the full material he then made available. *The Letters and Journals of Katherine Mansfield*, edited by C.K. Stead (1976), provides a useful selection; a complete edition of the papers is in preparation. Her personal writings form a valuable complement to the stories and confirm her status as one of the classic short-story writers of the twentieth century. Critical biographies have been published by A. Alpers (1953 and, more importantly, 1980). Mansfield's personal writings are a valuable complement to her published material and confirm her status as an outstanding writer; her full importance will probably only be clear when the definitive edition of her writings is published from material being researched by Margaret Scott in the Turnbull Library, Wellington.

[PQ]

MARKANDAYA, KAMALA (Mrs Taylor) (1924–). Novelist, born in South India. She studied at Madras University and became a journalist. In London, early in her writing career, she worked in a solicitor's office. Married, with one daughter, she lives in Britain.

As W. Walsh remarks, her novels 'are remarkable for their range of experience': peasant poverty, village life, city squalor, Indian princely privilege, art and patronage, nationalist politics, middle-class marriage, immigrant deracination. Her courage in attempting such a gamut of imaginative understanding is wholly admirable, but it has been at some cost of authenticity and linguistic appropriateness; for instance, in *Two Virgins* Indian villagers occasionally use contemporary British colloquial expressions.

The first novel, *Nectar in a Sieve* (1954), is a tale of grinding peasant labour reaping only elemental subsistence, sometimes starvation, but also of stoical, ennobling strength. The device of a peasant narrator is less successful than in *Kanthapura* by Raja Rao (q.v.); though it contributes immediacy, one is sceptical of Rukmani's range of thinking and language. On such grounds Indian critics regard Markandaya's novels less warmly than foreign commentators like Walsh and S.C. Harrex. Of *The Golden Honeycomb*, but with other novels also in mind, Shayamala Narayan writes: 'the locale lacks authenticity because it is given no precise geographical location' and 'the people have no particular language'. In *A Handful of Rice* (1966) the spirited hero confronts not the elements but urban man-made penury, and his moral integrity and herculean efforts prove unavailing.

Markandaya's strength is her use of characterization to unravel human consciousness and complex relationships, as with the tensions between a religious wife and her rationalist husband – presented with great insight – in *A Silence of Desire* (1960), though the pat resolution disappoints. *Two Virgins* (1974) delicately traces the unfolding consciousness of a village girl. Such explorations of selfhood combine penetratingly, though sometimes too schematically, with Anglo-Indian relations in *Some Inner Fury* (1955), where an Indian girl renounces her love for an Englishman during the quit-India campaign; in *Possession* (1963), with the artist-hero breaking from his English patroness to rediscover his Indian roots; and in *The Coffer Dams* (1969), which explores the conflicting attitudes of an English engineer and his wife to Indian life. With a more solidly realized setting than usual, *The Nowhere Man* (1973) describes an Indian immigrant's discomfiture as British racial prejudice mounts. Sadly, *The Golden Honeycomb* (1977) betrays some response to mere fashion in its pseudo-modernist style, structure and sexual titillation.

Pleasure City (1982) is a bravely ambitious attempt, through the relationship between an unusually resourceful young Indian villager and a sensitive British businessman, to deal with neo-colonialism and its imperial origins. Though with an admirably conceived design about the impingement of historical processes upon character and individuality, the novel would seem to require a matching linguistic inventiveness that the novelist hasn't quite delivered. [AR]

MARSH, EDWARD (Sir) (1872–1953). Civil servant who became Winston Churchill's private secretary in 1905. He devoted his wealth to the encouragement of poetry and edited the celebrated volumes of *Georgian Poetry* that were issued between 1912 and 1922. He had connections with many distinguished writers and artists and published an informative autobiography, *A Number of People* (1939). See Christopher Hassall's biography, *Edward Marsh* (1959). [HB]

MARTYN, EDWARD (1859–1924). Dramatist from County Galway, Ireland. He was closely involved with Yeats (q.v.) and George Moore (q.v.) in the foundation of the Irish National Theatre, which was launched in 1899 with productions of Yeats's *The Countess Cathleen* and Martyn's *The Heather Field*. The latter is an Ibsenesque study of an Irish landowner given to idealistic dreaming whose aspiration for land-reclamation outruns his means. His idée fixe, strengthened by opposition from his wife and friends, leads to financial disaster and his mind gives way. Martyn's play *Maeve* (prod 1900) has nationalistic overtones. Maeve O'Heynes, daughter of the Prince of Burren, is due to marry a wealthy Englishman to restore the family fortunes. Another mystical idealist, she is found dead on her wedding morning. Martyn also wrote *Grangecolman* (prod 1912) and *The Dream Physician* (prod 1914). He was a devout and obedient Roman Catholic, and an expert on church music and architecture. His oddly incongruous friendship with George Moore is chronicled in Moore's *Hail and Farewell* and lightly mocked in Yeats's *The Cat and the Moon* ('Did you ever know a holy man but had a wicked man for his comrade and his heart's darling?'). [HB]

MASEFIELD, JOHN (1878–1967). Poet, novelist and dramatist, a copious writer with about a hundred books to his credit. He was born 'in or near' Ledbury, Herefordshire. *Grace Before Ploughing* (1966) recaptures the joy and wonder of childhood in a region of orchards, hills, rivers and old buildings, not to mention mail-coaches and kind folk who still talked of the Civil War 'against Oliver'. When he eventually began to write, 'the scenes of my tales were those peculiar to my childhood' (*St Katherine of Ledbury*, 1951). His mother died when he was 6 and his father's mind gradually gave way until he was confined in 1890 and died in 1891. The aunt who assumed responsibility for the six orphaned children was totally unsympathetic to young John's bookish interests and aspirations. At the age of 13 he became a trainee on HMS *Conway* on the Mersey and, years later in the autobiographical volume, *New Chum* (1944), he remembered climbing up to the cross-trees and drinking in the outspread 'miracle' of the Mersey scene – cities of shipping, and mountains in the distance. Soon, with two years' sea-training behind him, Masefield was working as a pot-boy in a New York bar (see *A Tarpaulin Muster*, 1907). He then spent twenty-two months at a Yonkers carpet factory. Here, as he recorded in another autobiographical volume, *In the Mill* (1941), he was deeply moved by the industry and cameraderie of the mill-hands; but he was already exploring English literature, writing verse, and trying his hand at a novel. He worked his way back to England, determined to make a literary career.

There followed the Bloomsbury years described in the poem 'Biography' (from *Philip the King and Other Poems*, 1914). They were 'blank with hardship' but yet warmly remembered for the friendship known in Yeats's (q.v.) company ('that old room – above the noisy slum – / Where there was wine and fire and talk') and especially for the long night walks with J.M. Synge (q.v.) ('Now I miss / That lively mind and guttural laugh of his'). 'When he is gone I shall be gloomy enough', Yeats lamented of Masefield's eventual removal to the country.

The influence of Yeats is detectable in Masefield's first volume of verse, *Salt Water Ballads* (1902), which, together with its successor, *Ballads* (1903), contains many of the most popular anthologized poems such as 'Sea-Fever' and 'Cargoes'. Fluent rhythmic vitality complements a hard-won intimacy with the seas and seamen. We know from *In the Mill* that Masefield's experience on ship and in factory left him angry that 'deeds of work' were not publicly heeded like 'deeds of sport' ('I knew that there was some defect in our sense of value'). Real outrage gave authenticity to the poem, 'A Consecration', prefixed to *Salt Water Ballads*:

> Not of the princes and prelates with periwigged charioteers
> Riding triumphantly laurelled to lap the fat of the years, –
> Rather the scorned – the rejected – the men hemmed in with spears.

Masefield devoted himself to sing of the unknown men worn or damaged in toil or battle. 'Of these shall my songs be fashioned, my tales be told.' Thus many of the *Salt Water Ballads* versify the rough chatter and yarning of seamen in Kiplingesque lingo, though others – both here and in *Ballads* – have recourse to romantic story-book nauticality ('A Ballad of John Silver' and 'An Old Song Re-Sung') and to gentler Yeatsian nostalgia ('The West Wind' and 'A Wanderer's Song'). Masefield's work on the sea is alive with the lore of seamanship, technical and mythological, and it is imbued with unpatronizing respect for the skill and fortitude of very ordinary men.

The narrative poems represent Masefield's most distinctive achievement. They were written for a big audience and they won it. They are contemporary in substance and their appeal resides in sheer story, uncomplicated by psychological investigation or polemical undercurrent. *The Everlasting Mercy* (1911) created a sensation. 'Nine-tenths sheer filth' and 'wicked licentiousness' declared Lord Alfred Douglas. Written in octosyllabic couplets, it recounts in the first person the story of Saul Kane, poacher, drunkard and debauchee, who undergoes a violent evangelical conversion. He disputes poaching ground with Bill Myers and fights it out. He wins, but has a bad conscience because he has lied. After a drunken debauch at the pub he runs amok and is then moved to repentance by the rebuke of a Quaker, Miss Bourne. A storm of controversy arose when the poem appeared in the *English Review*. The religious fervour ('And in my heart the drink unpriced, / The burn-ing cataracts of Christ') cheek-by-jowl with pub scenes that contain their due quota of obscenities and blasphemies shocked some, while the intrusion of rough back-chat into 'poetry' offended others:

> 'You closhy put'
>   'You bloody liar'
> 'This is my field'
>   'This is my wire'
> 'I'm ruler here'
>   'You aint'
>   'I am'
> 'I'll fight you for it'
>   'Right, by damn.'

The succeeding narrative poem, *Dauber* (1913), deals with the kind of dilemma young Masefield himself must have faced in his dual role as determined seaman and would-be writer. Dauber goes to sea as lampman and painter, moved by ambition to be an artist who can paint sea and ships with inside understanding. His artistic dedication made him hated at home; now it makes him despised at sea. Bravery in a month of storm and struggle off Cape Horn proves him in his own eyes and establishes him with the crew, but in a later storm he falls from a yard-arm to his death. The poem is in rhyme-royal: busy scenes afloat, above deck and below, have vigour and reality. *The Daffodil Fields* (1913) has comparable life and fluency, but is overloaded with stereotyped sentiment. A triangular relationship between Mary Keir and two friends, Michael and Lion, turns to grief when Michael, the loved and betrothed one, goes off to Argentina and forgets her. One is reminded of Tennyson's *Enoch Arden*, for Mary marries Lion, but when Michael returns the rivals destroy each other. *Reynard the Fox* (1919), an exciting account of a fox-hunt in rollicking couplets, is generally regarded as Masefield's finest narrative poem. Masefield remarked that only at a fox-hunt, or perhaps a funeral, could one see 'the whole of the land's society brought together, focused for the observer, as the Canterbury pilgrims were for Chaucer' (*Recent Prose*, 1926). The Chaucerian stamp is there in a lively picture of the hunters, a powerful evocation of the countryside, and a breathless commentary on the pursuit.

'The novel exists because life is not exciting enough: the poem exists because life has excited the poet', Masefield averred. As a novelist himself, he displays narrative inventiveness even to the point of excess, but complex character-relationships are not among his interests and plausibility is at a discount. Nevertheless individuals come alive and, in *Sard Harker* (1924) for instance, the presentation of heroic personal fortitude sustained through countless testing adventures attains the moral status of a parable. A fitting charm in romantic adventure (*Jim Davis*, 1911) and in wonderful fantasy (*The Midnight Folk*, 1927) is finely gauged in stories for children, where as a prose story-teller Masefield fully comes into his own.

In his early years in London Masefield was involved with Yeats, Gordon Bottomley (q.v.) and others in attempting to establish poetic drama on the stage and in the 1920s he became the driving force behind amateur theatricals at Boar's Hill. His play, *The Tragedy of Nan* (1909), a rustic melodrama, first produced in 1908 under the direction of Granville Barker (q.v.), depicts a country girl brought up by a brutal aunt, and it has been suggested that her scathing outbursts against her aunt reflect something of Masefield's own feelings. Nan's desperation ends when she stabs the man she loves and throws herself into the river Severn. The three-act prose play, *The Tragedy of Pompey the Great* (1910), is static rather than dramatic and the dialogue is awkwardly unfluent. *Philip the King* (1914), a one-act study in rhyming verse of how the news of the Armada's loss was received in Spain, makes a poem of dignity, but scarcely a play. Later plays included *The Trial of Jesus* (1925) in prose, and *The Coming of Christ* (1928), a verse play, the first to be performed in Canterbury Cathedral on the initiative of Dr G.K.A. Bell, the Dean.

During the First World War Masefield had periods of service with the Red Cross in France and in the Dardanelles. His book *Gallipoli* (1916) presented the Dardanelles campaign in heroic epic terms and was an enormous success. It inspired the British Commander-in-Chief, Sir Douglas Haig, to invite him to go out and give the same treatment to the Battle of the Somme. But Masefield's visit to France in 1917 for this purpose was rendered null on his return by the failure of the War Office in London to put the necessary material at his disposal, and the venture petered out in two brief studies, *The Old Front Line* (1917) and *The Battle of the Somme* (1919). In later years Masefield added further autobiographical volumes, *So Long to Learn* (1952) and *Grace Before Ploughing* (1966). Masefield married Constance de la Cherois-Crommelin in 1903. He became Poet Laureate in 1930. 'I think the government has done well and that you will touch hearts nobody else could have touched', Yeats wrote in congratulation; 'those poems you read and sang to me in Woburn Buildings will be recognized for the classics that they are.' (C. Babington Smith, *John Masefield*, 1978.) Masefield was awarded the OM in 1935. [HB]

MASON, A.E.W. (Alfred Edward Woodley) (1865–1948). Novelist, born at Dulwich, London, educated there and at Oxford. He turned from acting to writing and had an enormous success with *The Four Feathers* (1902) and *The Broken Road* (1907). The former is an interesting period-piece. Harry Feversham, scion of a military family, is so afraid of disgracing its name by cowardice that he leaves the army when ordered to Egypt. The four white feathers presented to him by three comrades and his now lost fiancée are ultimately taken back and all ignominy redeemed by the courageous acts he undertakes in reparation. Highly accomplished in presentation, drenched in sentimental clichés, the book could no more fail than could *Land of Hope and Glory* or *The Lost Chord*. *At the Villa Rose* (1910), the first of a series of popular detective stories, introduces Hanaud, the French detective. [HB]

MASON, R.A.K. (Ronald Arthur Kells) (1905–71). Poet, born near Auckland, New Zealand, and educated at the university there. He travelled briefly to various Pacific countries but in effect lived his life in Auckland as teacher, public works employee and union official in addition to various other jobs. With James Bertram he edited the short-lived but influential left-wing magazine *Phoenix* (1932–3), whose contributions included Charles Brasch (q.v.), A.R.D. Fairburn (q.v.) and Allen Curnow (q.v.). He remained a committed Marxist all his life. An early love poem was printed in *Phoenix* and his first collection, *The Beggar*, appeared in 1924 when he was only 19. It was sombre in tone and led on to *No New Thing* (1934) – a very rare book – in which he himself described his poems as 'sponges steeped in vinegar / useless to the happy-eyed / but handy for the crucified'. It was only with this volume that his work became known in New Zealand; it was not only an important element in the New Zealand poetry scene of the mid 1930s but also represented him at his best. He was very active politically during the Depression, a period which stimulated writers such as John Mulgan (q.v.) and Frank Sargeson (q.v.). Curnow has written of New Zealand poetry that 'the thirties released – or tapped – a spring', but Mason himself wrote very little. *This Dark Will Lighten* (1941) contained the best work from his earlier collections but *Squire Speaks* (1938) and *China* (1943) did not add to his reputation. His best work is available in *Collected Poems* (1962), to which Curnow contributed a useful introduction. [PQ]

MATHERS, PETER (1931–). Novelist, born in London. He went to Australia as a child and has lived mostly in Melbourne, Victoria, since, though he was for a time in London and the United States in the 1960s. *Trap* (1966), set on the north coast of New South Wales – 'a fictitious state, like Faulkner's' – was widely acclaimed. It probed inherited Australian attitudes through the spare yet evocative depiction of the contemporary experiences of Jack Trap, part-aboriginal worker. Sure control over material and a taut prose style made the work not just a picaresque entertainment but a powerful and unsettling portrait of a nation and its people; 'To write, to put something down, is an act of subversion. . . . The aim of the novelist should be to subvert the society around him.' *The Wort Papers* (1972) again employed a complex but finely balanced fictional structure in its exploration of personal ambition and guilt through the present and past of Thomas Wort, a prosperous business executive. Through the autobiography of his artist-brother and the reminiscences of their father, the novel extends the family dimension towards an epic of national awareness and the role of individual lives in it. The strength of both works rests in their unobtrusive charting of broader issues through the perceptive depiction of day-to-day events. [PQ]

MAUGHAM, W. SOMERSET (1874–1965). Novelist, short-story writer and dramatist, born in Paris of English parents who had both died by the time he was 10. He was brought up at Whitstable, Kent (fictionalized as 'Blackstable'), by his uncle, the local vicar, educated at King's School, Canterbury ('Tercanbury'), and Heidelberg

University, and then studied medicine at St Thomas's Hospital, London, qualifying as a doctor in 1897. These years get full coverage in *Of Human Bondage* (1915), Maugham's frankly autobiographical novel in which 'the emotions are my own, but not all the incidents are related as they happened' (Foreword). The orphan, Philip Carey, suffers from a club foot as Maugham suffered from a stammer. His uncle William, a narrow-minded clergyman, represses him, while his aunt Louisa mothers him lovingly. The agonies of physical disfigurement, boarding-school miseries, loss of faith, sexual initiation, an attempt to turn artist in Paris, arduous years of training to be a doctor and a desperate struggle to bring ideal into some kind of relationship with reality in sexual love – these themes are pursued with devastating thoroughness and intensity. If the tormented hero is in some respects his own worst enemy, the soul's damage by physical disability is largely to blame. Maugham's sharp eye for hypocrisy and his gift for scathing commentary on life's let-downs gives some sort of homogeneity to an otherwise shapeless sequence of experiences. The publication of the book marked a turn in Maugham's career as a writer. He had first started as a novelist in 1897 with *Liza of Lambeth*, making use of his first-hand experience of the London slums and the miseries of childbirth there. But he forsook practice for travel, lived in bohemian Paris and slowly made his way as a writer. Success came to him first as a playwright, and by 1908 he had four plays running simultaneously in the West End. But at the age of 37, 'firmly established as the most popular dramatist of the day' (op. cit.), he suddenly began to refuse managers' contracts and settled down for two years' work on *Of Human Bondage*. Finding fulfilment in this medium, he followed it with *The Moon and Sixpence* (1919), a novel based on the life of Gauguin. ('It was written during the summer of 1918 while I was recovering on a hill-top in Surrey from the tuberculosis I had contracted earlier in the war', Preface.) Charles Strickland, a middle-aged stockbroker, suddenly forsakes wife and children and goes to Paris, then to Tahiti, hag-ridden by the compulsive inner urge to paint. The man who opts out of society, defying its conventional norms, was to be the theme of a later, more ambitious book, *The Razor's Edge* (1944), where an unsuccessful attempt is made to picture a human disinterestedness of saintly yet placidly unheroic dimensions in Larry's pursuit of self-perfection.

Maugham came back into the theatre with resounding success in the 1920s. *The Circle* (1921) and *Our Betters* (1923) reflect his professional adroitness in meeting the mood of the day. In the former a wife escapes from marriage and thus repeats her mother-in-law's romantic kick against respectability a generation later. In the latter the target is wealthy American women who buy themselves into the English aristocracy, fail to adjust and take refuge in promiscuity. The attempt at Wildean wit is void of brilliance and acuity: paradox degenerates into cynicism, humour into flippancy. Maugham settled permanently on the French Riviera in 1927, but extensive travel continued to enrich his work. In estimating his own gifts in the autobiographical book *The Summing Up* (1938) he rightly claims 'an acute power of observation'. This gift, allied to conscious pursuit of stylistic lucidity and reinforced by a talent for narrating in a persuasive speak-ing voice, made him an impressive writer of short stories. The volume, *Ashenden* (1928), was founded on his wartime experiences in the Intelligence Department. The complete short stories were collected in three volumes in 1951. *Cakes and Ale* (1930) has been acclaimed as Maugham's best novel. It is notorious for its reputed representation of Thomas Hardy (q.v.) as Edward Driffield and, more justifiably, of Hugh Walpole (q.v.) as Alroy Kear. The supercilious, urbane narrator casts a sophisticated, worldly eye on the tedious game of life in which most people exist to be scored off. But acidity is laid aside for the study of Rosie, whose hearty promiscuities have a cleansing guilelessness. (She is said to be based on Ethelwyn Sylvia Jones, daughter of the dramatist Henry Arthur Jones. See Ted Morgan, *Somerset Maugham*, 1979.) Maugham's clinical approach to the human scene has won him the image of sardonic cynic, and indeed his books abound in dislikeable people; love is often reduced to coition; women pant with lust; altruism and generosity are grudgingly allowed for. Extravagant claims have been made for Maugham when in fact his style is pedestrian, subsidiary material proliferates indigestibly and issues broached are too deep for the technical and imaginative resources available. [HB]

MEHROTRA, ARVIND KRISHNA (1947–). Poet, born in Lahore, India, and educated in Allahabad and Bombay. A university lecturer since 1968, he was in the United States from 1971 to 1973.

Mehrotra, who admits to the influence of *Manifesto of Surrealism* on his writing, is perhaps the most inventive and rapidly maturing of the younger Indian poets. *Bharatmata: A Prayer* (1966), a poem on 'Mother India', won considerable praise; it was followed by *Woodcuts on Paper* (London, 1967), *Pomes / Poemes / Poemas* (1971) and the more substantial *Nine Enclosures* (1976). His translations of poems from other languages have appeared in American and British journals. Co-editor of *damn you*, an arts magazine, in 1965–8, he founded a literary press, Ezra-Fakir, 1969; with the poets Adil Jussawala, Gieve Patel and Arun Kolatkar, he established Clearing House, 1976. Mehrotra's earlier knotty, avant-garde verse has led to a maturely associative use of imagery, by which limpid, subtly ironic observation of concrete realities and fragmentary childhood memories give forth sonar-like echoes of uncertainty or menace:

> Clouds cannot always be trusted
> This one broke into the house
> Went behind the cupboard, barked
> I left the city
> And like any hunting dog
> It picked up the scent.

[AR]

MEHTA, VED (1934–). Journalist and biographer, born in Lahore, India. Blind from the age of 3, he attended a special school in Bombay. His first book, *Face to Face* (1957), describes his childhood, the family migration into India at the Partition in 1947 and his youthful years in America after 1949. Mehta studied at Pomona College, California, and the Universities of Oxford and Harvard. Since 1960 he has worked on *The New Yorker*, in which the material for most of his books first appeared. *Walking the Indian Streets* (1960) is a cliquishly Oxonian account of a return visit to India in 1959. *Fly and the Fly-Bottle* (1963) and *The New Theologians* (1966) are based on *New Yorker* interviews with, respectively, historians and philosophers, and Christian thinkers. Other works of lively journalism are *Portrait of India* (1970), *John Is Easy to Please* (1971), *The New India* (1978).

Mehta's best writing is biographical, especially the unpretentious, engaging *Daddyji* (1972) and *Mamaji* (1979), which colourfully capture the Third World experience of a family's progression from peasantry to the professions. His single novel, *Delinquent Chacha* (1967), is comedy somewhat in the vein of Desani (q.v.); K.R.S. Iyengar (*Indian Writing in English*) calls it 'pure – almost transcendent – fun'.   [AR]

MERCER, DAVID (1928–80). Dramatist, born in Wakefield, West Yorkshire, and educated at Durham University. He was a laboratory technician and a school-teacher before turning full-time writer in 1962. He made his name with a group of three television plays, *The Generations* (1964), and continued to write for that medium. The TV comedy *A Suitable Case for Treatment* (prod 1966) contains a celebrated and characteristically witty exchange:

> *Morgan* Did you hear what the white rat said to the other white rat?
> *Analyst* What?
> *Morgan* I've got that psychologist so well trained that every time I ring the bell he brings me something to eat.

Mercer took an increasing interest in personalities at loggerheads with their social environment and human condition. This theme dominates the stage play *Flint* (Aldwych Theatre, 1970), the study of an Anglican clergy-man, Ossian Flint, who is unfrockably shocking in moral conduct and wittily unhypocritical about it. 'I rather admire the aberrated fellow', says his bishop. 'His appetites are grotesque, but at least they are matched by the power of his brain.' Mercer's linguistic versatility has Beckettian and Pinterian qualities. Brisk verbal acerbities festoon the dialogue with catchy epigram. The mutually comforting relationship between the 70-year-old parson and a delinquent girl is a source of both riotous fun and touching pathos. *After Haggerty* (Criterion Theatre, 1970) is another play alive with comedy and authentic human substance. Bernard Link, drama critic, moves into a flat previously occupied by one Haggerty, whose former mistress turns up with his illegitimate baby to take venge-ful possession of the place. The subsequent arrival of Bernard's father, a retired train-driver from Yorkshire, brings a clash of manners and mores rich in fun and meaningfulness. Mercer had ideas, energy of mind and rare verbal dexterity, but his later plays, such as *Duck Song* (prod 1974), did not make the forceful impact of his best work. Though there is sharp dialogue at the beginning of the TV play *Happy Bear* (1976), about an erratic dentist with a breast-fixation, the escalating course of the farce snaps authenticating links with human reality. *Cousin Vladimir* (1978), a stage play, has a potentially fruitful theme involving an English nuclear physicist who

has opted out of serving the establishment in favour of alcoholism and a Russian opposite number who has fled the Soviet Union, but Mercer's wit and humour falter and the study of disintegration and disillusionment comes across as sadly negative and pessimistic.   [HB]

MEW, CHARLOTTE (1869–1928). Poet, born in London, daughter of an architect who died young and left his wife to bring up their four children in poverty. Two of them became insane. Charlotte Mew was awarded a Civil List pension in 1923 on the recommendation of Hardy (q.v.), De la Mare (q.v.) and Masefield (q.v.). Hardy declared her 'the best woman poet of our day'. After many tribulations, she took her own life. Her first collec-tion of verse, *The Farmer's Bride* (1916), contained in its title poem a little masterpiece, the lament of a farmer who has taken a young wife only to find her frightened into sexual rejection of himself and all men. The controlled tension, the sheer naturalness of voice, and the pathos with which the half-hidden compassion and anguish of the farmer come through, mark the writer as a passionate recorder of grief and mystery and loss.

> She sleeps up in the attic there
>   Alone, poor maid. 'Tis but a stair
> Betwixt us. Oh! my God! the down,
>   The soft young down of her, the brown,
> The brown of her – her eyes, her hair, her hair!

Harold Monro (q.v.) wrote of this poem, 'The outline would have resolved itself in the mind of Mrs Browning into a poem of at least two thousand lines; Browning might have worked it up to six thousand. Charlotte Mew tells the whole touching story in forty-six lines.'

This is only one of a cluster of poems in Charlotte Mew's two published collections (*The Rambling Sailor* followed in 1929) which by their sincerity, economy and passion mark her as one of the most strangely neglected poets of the age.

Val Warner has edited Charlotte Mew's *Collected Poems and Prose* (1981). The prose consists of stories and articles which were published in journals before she devoted herself to poetry.   [HB]

MIDDLETON, STANLEY (1919–). Novelist, born and educated in Nottingham, Nottinghamshire, where he returned as a schoolmaster after war service. In a series of some eighteen novels, beginning with *A Short Answer* (1958), Middleton has used his knowledge of the Nottingham locality and its inhabitants – especially the professional middle class – to explore the complexity of human response and behaviour at points of life where problems and crises create situations of special tension or bewilderment. The action is not shaped into a contrived plot. It is usually confined to a few months, and flashbacks fill out life stories where necessary. A weak-ness is that interest tends to sag about halfway through when the impact of initial shocks has been assimilated. In *Distractions* (1975) Edward Fielding, head of a prosperous firm of building contractors, having looked after a mentally declining wife, Anna, for many years, finally forsakes her for a mistress, Hilda. As the book opens, Anna has just committed suicide. The subsequent period of trial and adjustment for Edward, Hilda and

Edward's son, Jeremy, is registered with tact and penetration. *Two Brothers* (1978) studies lifelong fraternal opposites, extravert and introvert, successful businessman and struggling schoolmaster-poet. The former married the girl whom the latter also loved, and in middle life the past boils up again. In *In a Strange Land* (1979) a brilliant young musician, temporarily marooned in a provincial city, is drawn into a series of emotional entanglements which produce their quota of crises, breakdowns, bereavements and other predicaments, haphazard and mostly unsensational, but amounting to a good deal in personal wear and tear. *Entry into Jerusalem* (1982) is about a provincial artist, John Worth, who scorns profitable compromise and then, ironically, leaps to fame with his painting 'Christ's Entry into Jerusalem', which portrays a skinhead Saviour on a motorbike.

Middleton is regarded as a master of the commonplace, the upsets that ruffle workaday life with all its minor frictions and uncertainties, and the cautious hesitancies they call out. He projects the inconclusive element in human relationships and the littering of life with loose ends. At its best his style has a ferial spareness and sturdiness appropriate to the undemonstrative outlook on the world. [HB]

MILLIN, SARAH GERTRUDE (née Liebson) (1889–1968). Novelist and confidante of Smuts and Chaim Weizmann, born in Lithuania. She grew up on the Vaal River diamond diggings near Barkly West, South Africa. Her husband, Philip Millin, became a Supreme Court judge. Her first published short story and novels like *The Dark River* (1920), *The Sons of Mrs Aab* (1931) and *King of the Bastards* (1950) present miscegenation as resulting inevitably in physical, moral and social degeneration. Her most popular novel on this theme, *God's Stepchildren* (1924), with an attitude diametrically opposed to that in *Turbott Wolfe* (1925) by William Plomer (q.v.), was applauded by the Nazis as a cautionary tale on the evils of racial impurity, though as a Jew Millin was anti-Nazi. D. Rabkin writes that white South Africans reacted to it 'as the plausible and articulate ejaculation of their racial nightmares'. However misguided her racial diagnosis, she conveys compassion for people in harsh circumstances and has a genuine tragic sense. Her own experience of life on the diggings enabled her to become the first thorough-going realist in South African fiction, and she was the most prolific writer of her time. In addition to seventeen novels, she published a volume of short stories, two autobiographical books, six wartime diaries (1944–8), three books on South Africa and two biographies, *Rhodes* (1931) and *General Smuts* (1936). [AR]

MILNE, A. A. (Alan Alexander) (1882–1956). Children's writer, dramatist and light entertainer, born in Kilburn, London, the third and youngest son of John Vine Milne who ran a preparatory school, Henley House, where H.G. Wells (q.v.) was for a time science master. Frank Swinnerton (q.v.) (*The Georgian Literary Scene*) speaks of 'a photograph which shows H.G. Wells as a wispy young assistant master, and Milne as a ringleted child of about eight years old'. Milne was educated later at Westminster School and Trinity College, Cambridge, where he edited *Granta* and got a third-class honours degree in mathematics. His decisive ambition was to write; he was soon doing freelance work and by 1906 he was assistant editor of *Punch*. He stayed with *Punch* until 1919, getting well known as a light essayist and fluent versifier. He then made a name as a successful playwright with a taste for whimsy, fun and pathos which naturally called out comparison with Sir James Barrie (q.v.). In the three-act comedy, *Wurzel-Flummery* (prod 1917), for instance, two proud men have fortunes left to them on condition that they change their names to Wurzel-Flummery. *Mr Pim Passes By* (prod 1919) was a comparable exercise in blowing light sketch material up to dramatic size. *Toad of Toad's Hall* (1929) is a dramatic adaptation of Kenneth Grahame's *The Wind in the Willows*. Milne published an autobiography, *It's Too Late Now*, in 1939.

Milne married Dorothy de Sélincourt in 1913, and their son, Christopher Robin, was born in 1920. The parental need to turn bedtime entertainer uncovered in Milne a remarkable talent as a children's writer. Two volumes of verses, *When We Were Very Young* (1924) and *Now We Are Six* (1927), gave little Christopher Robin archetypal status as the lovable, imaginative youngster whose doings and day-dreams, voiced with impeccable rhythmic charm, are all happily contained within a frame of comfortable domesticity. The two prose volumes, *Winnie-the-Pooh* (1926) and *The House at Pooh Corner* (1928), vivify the toy animals that are the companions of Christopher Robin's homely adventures. Appropriate human characteristics – lovable slow-wittedness (Pooh Bear), plaintive self-pity (Eeyore), pathetic ineffectiveness (tiny Piglet) and diminutive 'cheekiness' (Roo, pocket edition of Kanga) – are read into the toy animals according to their appearance. Stuffed limbs, suitably bedraggled, and stitched eyes, were vividly realized in E.H. Shepard's illustrations and the books made Milne one of the most successful children's writers of the century. A signal honour was conferred on the lovable bear when *Winnie-the-Pooh* was translated into Latin by Alexander Leonard in 1960 as *Winnie ille Pu*. Frederick C. Crews's jeu d'esprit, *The Pooh Perplex* (1963), subjects Pooh and Co. to satiric analysis from fashionable critical viewpoints, Marxist, Freudian and the like (Pooh is 'tragically fixated at the narcissistic stage of development'). [HB]

MITCHELL, ADRIAN (1932–). Poet, born in London, educated at Dauntsey's School, Wiltshire, and Christ Church, Oxford. He has been a journalist and has held academic posts. Known as a 'protest' poet for whom poetry contributes towards revolution, and linked sometimes with the American 'Beats', he has used his talent in support of radical and humanitarian causes. *Poems* (1964) was followed by *Out Loud* (1968), *Ride the Nightmare* (1971) and *The Apeman Cometh* (1975). Mitchell has also published three novels and has had plays staged and televised. An enthusiast for public poetry readings, Mitchell has produced easily assimilated, vigorous verses with a ready rhetorical verve:

I was run over by the truth one day.
Ever since the accident I've walked this way

So stick my legs in plaster
Tell me lies about Vietnam.

('To Whom It May Concern')

'Most people ignore most poetry because most poetry ignores most people', Mitchell avers. If he often pays the price of populism and can lapse into sloganizing and slush, his most disciplined verses benefit from the telling forthrightness. See his *For Beauty Douglas, Collected Poems 1953-79* (1982). [HB]

MITCHELL, W.O. (1914-). Novelist, born in Weyburn, Saskatchewan, Canada, and educated at the University of Manitoba, Winnipeg, and at the University of Alberta, Edmonton, from which he graduated in 1942. He has held various jobs and most recently has been a teacher; he was writer-in-residence at the University of Calgary, Alberta, 1968-71. His writing career resembles that of Sinclair Ross (q.v.) in that his first book, *Who Has Seen the Wind* (1947), is his best, depiction of the awakening of childhood towards adult tensions providing immediate emotions never equalled in the more contrived works which followed. The story of Brian O'Connal's developing awareness of time and complex reality allowed the focus to be held on him, whereas *The Kite* (1962), in which Keith Maclean recalls Brian O'Connal, is less successful because of the author's failure to control the more complicated structure. *The Vanishing Point* (1973), a revised version of 'The Alien' which was originally published in serial form during 1953-4, also suffered from lack of adequate structure. The strength of his best writing lies in the simple but subtle presentation of everyday life so as to illuminate universal truths through specific events. [PQ]

MITCHISON, NAOMI (1897-). Novelist, born in Edinburgh, Lothian, Scotland, daughter of Professor J.S. Haldane, a physiologist. She spent her childhood in country houses and castles, was educated at St Anne's College, Oxford, and at 18 married G.R. Mitchison, barrister and later Labour MP and Life Peer. In a long and fecund life (five children, nineteen grandchildren) Lady Mitchison has championed many good causes, engaging actively in farming, forestry and overseas relations. She was for twenty years a member of the Argyll County Council and is 'Mother' to the Bakgatla tribe of Botswana. The historical novel is her forte. *The Conquered* (1923), set in Caesar's Gaul, portrays Meromic, son of a Gallic chieftain, torn by conflicting loyalties in the last doomed rebellion against Roman domination. *Cloud Cuckoo Land* (1925) fastens on the fate of Alxenor, son of a ruling family in a small Aegean island state, caught up in the struggle between Athens and Sparta in the fifth century BC. Other novels of the ancient world are *The Corn King and the Spring Queen* (1931), set in the Crimea, and the more recent *Cleopatra's People* (1972). Besides novels and short stories, Lady Mitchison has written numerous children's books, serious historical, political and documentary works, and the autobiographical *Return to the Fairy Hill* (1966). *Mucking Around* (1981) is a record of her travels in five continents over fifty years. [HB]

MITFORD, NANCY (1904-73). Novelist and biographer, born in London, the eldest of the seven children (six of them girls) of Lord Redesdale, a tempestuous sportsman who used to retreat from them into his 'child-proof room' at their country house in the Cotswolds. The family did not escape notoriety: Diana married Oswald Mosley, the British fascist; Unity became Hitler's admirer; Jessica became a communist. Nancy married the Hon. Peter Rodd in 1933 but was divorced in 1958. Captivated by French culture and civilization, she settled in Paris and fell in love with a French colonel. Her last four years were a painful struggle against Hodgkin's Disease. Her early novels (*Highland Fling*, 1931; *Christmas Pudding*, 1932) were frolicsome farces portraying the frivolities of the 1920s in the manner of early Waugh. Her mature novels, *The Pursuit of Love* (1945) and *Love in a Cold Climate* (1949), are astonishingly successful in depicting the closely knit English aristocratic circles of the inter-war years at their social game and in the bosom of their families. Fanny Logan, the narrator in both books, soft-pedals the intimacies of her own story (as does Anthony Powell's (q.v.) narrator in his *A Dance to the Music of Time* novels) and focuses in the first on Uncle Matthew's nest of excitable, untamed young, more especially cousin Linda and her pursuit of love, and in the sequel on the rebellious sexual struggle of Polly against her parents, Lord and Lady Mountdore. Irascible Uncle Matthew, a hilariously fictionalized portrait of Lord Redesdale, is matched in insuppressible dynamism and oddity only by the female counterpart, Lady Mountdore, an outsized Lady Bracknell. In each book there is underlying serious concern for young minds neglected and feelings bruised amid all the indulged eccentricities of moneyed adults. The portrayal of imaginative, resourceful youngsters with their gleeful, conspiratorial camaraderie is brilliant. Nancy Mitford's humour scintillates, for she can parody the idiosyncractic attitudes and conversational cadences of the aristocracy with delicious irony and deadly authenticity. Two further novels followed in the same genre (*The Blessing*, 1951; *Don't Tell Alfred*, 1960), but the author devoted her later years to historical biography, notably in *Madame de Pompadour* (1954) and *The Sun King: Louis XIV at Versailles* (1966). 'She was a self-trained historian who illuminated periods of history which academic historians veiled under draperies of clichés', Rebecca West (q.v.) has written (*Sunday Telegraph*, 6.9.75). Nancy Mitford edited *Noblesse Oblige: An Enquiry into the Identifiable Characteristics of the English Aristocracy* (1956), a jeu d'esprit that gave currency to the light-hearted distinction between 'U' (upper-class) and 'non-U' as labels for habits of speech and behaviour. [HB]

MITTELHOLZER, EDGAR (1909-65). Novelist, born and educated in New Amsterdam, Guyana, of a family of Swiss origin settled there since the eighteenth century. His diffident father, an ill-paid clerk, left his children's upbringing to their puritanical, overbearing mother. At 11 Mittelholzer became an avid reader of Buffalo Bill and Nelson Lee stories, eventually encompassing Clive Bell's *Civilization*; reading, stamp-collecting and, from 1921, compulsive story-writing probably constituted escape into art from the smothering reality of home life, for, as his autobiography, *A Swarthy Boy* (1963), suggests, the pettily stern restrictions imposed by his mother early engendered a fierce desire for absolute personal freedom and the destruction of all social conventions that impinged upon it. In maturity this desire became a passion that often found inconsequential expression in his published fiction. After failing to obtain the Senior School Certificate in 1927, he determined to become a writer and was soon sending stories and, in 1929, a novel to London editors and publishers. As they came back rejected by one, he would promptly dispatch them to another, and start on new pieces in a process he regarded as a form of warfare under the motto 'Sieg oder Tod!'

But victory was long delayed. He wrote *Corentyne Thunder* in 1938, while working as a minor customs official in New Amsterdam, but not until 1941 did it become the first of his twenty-three published novels. The title suggests his attempted design – the integration of East Indian peasantry with the landscape and climate of the Corentyne coastal plain. But while always striving for, Mittelholzer seldom achieves, authentic design, whether philosophic, psychological, moral or artistic. Despite L. James's claim, *Corentyne Thunder* fails to harmonize the very successful realism through which the meagre lives of Ramgolall and his family are projected, with the precious romanticism, which in over-written passages describes climatic phenomena in terms of the characters' varying moods. Perhaps Mittelholzer's youthful study of the First World War harmed his literary career, for he tended to write with a frenzy not unlike that with which Western Front generals committed their troops to battle.

He is, however, one of the most important flawed novelists of the century. *Corentyne Thunder* heralded the extraordinary outburst of mid-century Caribbean literary achievement, including Mittelholzer's subsequent books, that has created a Caribbean consciousness transcending the scattered parochialisms of the area, precipitating the elements of a Caribbean identity, and, most importantly, decolonizing literature in the West Indies. Less sophisticated and profound than his compatriot Wilson Harris (q.v.), he nevertheless, like Harris, works the turbulence of Guyanese landscape and history into meaningful constitutents of the Caribbean imagination.

It was nine years before Mittelholzer could find a publisher for his second novel, *A Morning at the Office* (1950), perhaps the best crafted of his books, in which his skills submitted to the discipline of a strictly limited action that yet allowed for complex personal and social interactions. Set in a single office in Port of Spain, Trinidad (where Mittelholzer lived from 1941 to 1948), the action, which takes place in one morning, revolves around the anonymous declaration of a black office boy's love for the manager's coloured, middle-class secretary. While attention shifts to the backgrounds and aspirations of each of the fourteen characters, with the exact social nuance of every degree of skin pigmentation graphed, the central fission of racial, social, professional and personal relationships is brilliantly sustained, producing something of the emotional texture and artistic unity of classical drama in miniature.

Yet Mittelholzer's best-known work is on the grand scale, the Kaywana sequence: *Children of Kaywana*

(1952, including *Kaywana Heritage*, separately published from 1976), *The Harrowing of Hubertus* (1954, later retitled *Kaywana Stock*) and *Kaywana Blood* (1958). It is a saga, covering the years 1612–1953, of the descendants of two seventeenth-century Dutchmen (Vyfuis and van Groenwegel) and Kaywana, a half-Indian, half-English woman of indomitable spirit. Its popularity is explained by the vigorous, often melodramatic narrative, the exoticism of time and place, the titillation of frequent sexual episodes and, more legitimately, the energy of the writing and an impressive interplay of imagination with historical research. Each van Groenwegel generation is measured by its inheritance of Kaywana's virtues of courage and fire-like spirit, even if they take the perverted forms of burying an ailing slave alive or castrating a close friend for coupling with a favourite slave girl. Yet F.M. Birbalsingh is right in concluding that Mittelholzer is neither moralist nor pornographer. Like their creator, the van Groenwegels assert their own individualism as the sole means of survival in a world they see as utterly nonmoral. It would seem that the mean hypocrisies of Mittelholzer's boyhood New Amsterdam so disgusted him, even while he found fulfilment as an Anglican altar-server, that in his writing he could seldom reconcile a deep craving for order with an equally deep need for licentious freedom. In contrast to the Kaywana novels, in which this need constantly surfaces, *Shadows Move Among Them* (1952) and *The Mad MacMullochs* (1959) present attempts to create egalitarian, self-sufficient, sexually uninhibited communities, ostensibly free of restraints, yet both rigidly controlled by autocratic authority. The authorial disapproval of racial prejudice in *A Morning at the Office* is contradicted by the apparent sanctioning of the hero's anti-black sentiments in *Latticed Echoes* (1960). Yet the movingly naïve integrity and moral resilience of the heroine in *The Life and Death of Sylvia* (1953) proclaims simultaneously a burning faith in the power of the human spirit and its tragic ineffectuality in a corrupt world. All these disparate elements, along with half-baked theories of modern psychology, eugenics, transcendentalism, make Mittelholzer an uneasy and not yet satisfactorily explicated twentieth-century writer.

Mittelholzer settled in England in 1948. In 1965 he committed suicide by fire in a Sussex field, much like the hero of his last novel, *The Jilkington Drama* (1965). Was his misfortune as man and writer the inability to distinguish between life and art? [AR]

MONRO, HAROLD (1879–1932). Poet, educated at Radley, whence he appears to have been expelled for drinking, and at Caius College, Cambridge. After an unfortunate marriage and working as a land agent in Ireland, he settled down on private means to literary life in London. He edited first *The Poetry Review*, then *Poetry and Drama* and, above all, ran the Poetry Bookshop in Devonshire Street, where the first volume of Edward Marsh's (q.v.) *Georgian Poetry* was published in 1912 and where new poets appeared regularly at poetry readings. Monro's generosity was instrumental in encouraging many poets, and he did not restrict his interest to poets of the 'Georgian' school to which his own early work belonged. T.S. Eliot (q.v.) wrote an Introduction to Monro's posthumous *Collected Poems* (1933) of which there is now an up-to-date edition (1970) with a Preface by Ruth Tomalin and biographical information supplied by Alida Monro, the poet's second wife. Some early poems, like 'Great City', have notable impressionistic lucidity and the celebrated 'Milk for the Cat' is charming – though Monro grew to resent its inclusion in school anthologies. But Monro's most remarkable work is in one or two deeply felt late poems such as 'Living', 'The Sickroom' and 'Bitter Sanctuary' (for which Monro's alternative title was 'The Alcoholics'). The suffering of alcoholics in the face of delirium tremens is registered with painful authenticity.   [HB]

MONTAGUE, C.E. (Charles Edward) (1867–1928). Novelist and journalist, born in London of Irish stock, and educated at the City of London School and at Oxford. War service apart, he spent his life working for the *Manchester Guardian*. He married the daughter of its editor, C.P. Scott, and rose to be leader-writer. His first novel, *A Hind Let Loose* (1910), is a comic account of a journalist who writes leading articles for rival Liberal and Conservative newspapers, daily anathemizing himself reciprocally in print. When the First World War came, Montague dyed his hair (he was 47) and enlisted as a private (the only man whose hair turned black overnight through courage, it was said). In 1916 he became an officer in intelligence. His *Disenchantment* (1922), a book of war memoirs, traces the transmutation of spirit that training and front-line experience wrought in the at first eager recruits of 1914 and 1915. It portrays the incompetence of the men giving the orders, the muddle, the contrast between front line and GHQ, between military life and civilian life. There is heavy-fisted irony about the high command and a scathing record of the ordinary solider's progress through disillusionment, suspicion and distrust to postwar 'apathy, callousness and lassitude'. The same traumatic experience provided the impetus for *Fiery Particles* (1923), a book of short stories, and *Rough Justice* (1926), a novel. The Garth family of *Rough Justice* ('They're England, really, these Garths') live in a house which is itself bottled English history. Father (Thomas), son (Auberon) and adopted daughter (Molly) share a native integrity. Thomas, in public life, has the honesty and wisdom that prevent him from rising to political leadership. Auberon and Molly serve selflessly in the war to become 'unconscious symbols of all that had saved England'. By contrast Montague lays into the empty-headedness and self-seeking of the ruling classes, the corruption in the services, the irrelevance of public-school clap-trap, the profiteering and the jockeying for safety. It is done with zest and spirit. One is often conscious of reading the mannered prose of a leader-writer and Montague lacks that artistic selectivity which makes for narrative intensity and dramatic impact. Nevertheless the novel is a moving document of the period. Montague published *A Writer's Notes on His Trade* in 1930.   [HB]

MONTAGUE, JOHN (1929–). Irish poet, born in Brooklyn, New York. He came to an Ulster farm at the age of 4 for his childhood years. Educated at Armagh, University College, Dublin, Yale University, Connecticut and Iowa, he has lived in Ireland, America and France. He has

published about a dozen volumes of verse, including *Forms of Earth* (1958), *Poisoned Lands* (1961), *Tides* (1971), *The Rough Field* (1972) – an epic sequence made up of ten sections – *The Cave of Night* (1974) and *The Great Cloak* (1978). *Selected Poems* (1982), the poet's own selection from earlier collections, contains also some new poems. Montague's worried and passionate absorption with his Ulster inheritance, notably evident in *The Rough Field*, is never a limiting interest. His preoccupation with Ireland is that of a writer with a historical perspective and a world-view:

> To be always at the periphery of incident
> Gave my childhood its Irish dimension; drama of
>   unevent.

So he writes in 'Auschwitz, mon Amour', a poem about watching a film of Auschwitz. 'An Irish poet seems to me in a richly ambiguous position with the pressure of an incompletely discovered past behind him, and the whole modern world around', Montague wrote in introducing *The Faber Book of Irish Verse* (1974) which he edited. His own strength as a poet lies in acute observation of the contemporary combined with intellectual flexibility in relating it to the past. Penetrating and unparochial both on public matters (see 'What a View', *Tides*) and on personal and local matters (see 'The Cage', *The Rough Field*), he is a poet with an apophthegmatic sineviness, who eschews grand gesture and can pack lucid lines with a contained intensity. What Montague has learned technically from William Carlos Williams, Ezra Pound, W.H. Auden (q.v.) and others has been merged with a distinctively Irish poetic tonality.   [HB]

MOORE, BRIAN (1921–). Novelist and short-story writer, born in Belfast, Northern Ireland. He emigrated to Canada in 1948. He moved to the United States in 1959 and now lives in California. His position is necessarily that of an outsider, and this may partly explain his skill at creating lonely characters in the depiction of whose fates ironic detachment blends with compassion. His first two novels, *Judith Hearne* (1955) and *The Feast of Lupercal* (1957), were set in Northern Ireland and presented with moving accuracy and wry humour characters tormented by their own crumbling values in a world of faded pretensions. The tragi-comic tale *The Luck of Ginger Coffey* (1960) had Montreal as its setting, and featured an Irish immigrant whose dreams of social status and financial success in Canada are gradually shattered – a process which almost costs him both his self-respect and his wife. The hero of this novel has both left Ireland and married – the attractiveness yet seeming impossibility of these two actions features large in all Moore's Irish settings. The tone of the book is lighter, and its comic exploration of the problems and compensations offered by life in Canada makes it the best Canadian novel on the plight of the immigrant. *An Answer from Limbo* (1962) gave ample scope for his love of Irish colour, this time with a mother-figure who goes to New York to look after her son's children. The book conveys Moore's reaction not only to the hostile urban waste of New York but also to the destructive professionalism (as he saw it) of some writers there; by sacrificing concern for his wife and mother in order to further his art, the central character loses everything. *The*

Emperor of Ice Cream (1965) drew upon his experiences in wartime Belfast. *While I am Mary Dunne* (1968) re-examines that crumbling core of self-identity which had occupied him in *Judith Hearne*, this time against a setting which in real time covers twenty-four hours in New York, but which the recollections of Mary Dunne extends to twenty years in various parts of Canada. This novel illustrates not only Moore's skill in controlling time and structure but also his profound understanding of the human psyche. *The Revolution Script* (1971), a 'non-fiction novel', depicted the Canadian crisis of October 1970 and focused the issue of separatism for Quebec. *Fergus* (1970) and *Catholics* (1972) explored Irish and religious themes with mixed success, but *The Great Victorian Collection* (1975) showed at its best his ability to combine artistic inventiveness and wit with a subtle probing of human hopes and fears in a contemporary fable about an academic whose dream becomes reality (an idea already pursued in *Fergus*): 'Can it be said that he first envisaged the Collection in his dream? Or did he create it in its entirety?' Moore sees this as his first fully Canadian work (it contains no Irish or immigrant characters) although the setting is American. In the delicate intimacy with which it questions artistic success and the conditions for distinguishing reality from illusion this book confirms his position as an outstanding writer whose gift is to unite his own complex background in works of unusual integrity and power. In *The Doctor's Wife* (1976) Sheila Redden leaves both husband and son in Belfast for an affair with a young American student. *The Mangan Inheritance* was published in 1979.   [PQ]

MOORE, GEORGE (1852–1933). Novelist, dramatist and man of letters, born at Moore Hall in County Mayo, Ireland, and at school for a time in Birmingham. His father was an MP and the family moved to London in 1868. George wanted to become an artist, and studied painting with increasing determination after his father's death in 1870. In 1873 he went to Paris. There he eventually abandoned painting for writing, and he published poems, *Flowers of Passion*, in 1878, and *Luther*, a verse play, in 1879. The Paris years of café life and contacts with artists such as Manet and Degas were later written up in *Confessions of a Young Man* (1888), the first essay in a brand of autobiographical reminiscence that was to prove to be Moore's most effective genre. (The second work in this vein was *Memoirs of My Dead Life*, 1906.) It was Wilde's quip that Moore conducted his education in public, book by book. Moore was an artist, always ready to touch up his experience in print: he fictionalized himself, his acquaintances and his past; the tendency to self-caricature was as objective as his tendency to caricature others.

Financial difficulties on the family estate brought Moore home from Paris to Mayo in 1880 and back to London in 1881, where he began to write his naturalistic novels under the influence of Zola. *A Modern Lover* (1883) pictures Lewis Seymour, an artist in whose making three women have a hand, and for two of them it is a costly achievement. In *A Mummer's Wife* (1885) Kate Ede, a dressmaker and the wife of a draper, goes off with an actor in a touring company. A romantic creature, with little moral strength, she makes her way through

jealousy, drunkenness and poverty to a sordid death. *Esther Waters* (1894) crowned Moore's early work with a popular success. Esther Waters comes as a kitchenmaid to the Barfields at Woodview. Everyone there except Mrs Barfield, a devout fellow Plymouth Brother who befriends her, is obsessed with racing and gambling. Esther is seduced, leaves Woodview and is abandoned. Her subsequent hardships and suffering, unsparingly registered, are eventually mitigated by marriage to her child's father, but at his death she is left penniless. She returns at the end to Woodview and Mrs Barfield, twenty years older but unchanged in basic fortitude. Moore's next novel was *Evelyn Innes* (1898) in which his interest in music (he was an enthusiastic Wagnerian) is apparent. The heroine's father is modelled on Arnold Dolmetsch. Evelyn herself is a vital and intense woman, an opera singer who fails to find either in love or in music the fulfilment she needs and who decides to become a nun. The sequel, *Sister Theresa*, followed in 1901.

With *Evelyn Innes* and a stage play behind him (*The Strike at Arlingford*, 1893), Moore was a covetable literary figure when W.B. Yeats (q.v.) and Edward Martyn (q.v.) won his co-operation in the founding of the Irish Literary Theatre. This venture, together with his interest in the Gaelic League and his disgust with the current imperialistic spirit unleashed by the Boer War, led him to leave London for Dublin in 1899 and to settle there in 1901. Martyn's play, *The Heather Field*, and Yeats's *The Countess Cathleen* launched the theatre in Dublin in 1899. Martyn's next effort, the comedy *The Tale of a Town*, was so poor (in Yeats's, Lady Gregory's and Moore's eyes) that he handed it over to Moore who rewrote it as *The Bending of the Bough*. Moore and Martyn, according to Yeats, were 'cousins and inseparable friends, bound one to the other by mutual contempt'. Moore collaborated with Yeats in *Diarmuid and Grania* (prod 1901) but it was not a comfortable partnership. 'Because his mind was argumentative, abstract, diagrammatic, mine sensuous, concrete, rhythmical, we argued about words', Yeats averred. Differences with Yeats and disillusionment with Ireland led Moore back to London in 1911, where he lived until his death. The activities in Ireland, however, provided much of the best material in the culminating autobiographical work, *Hail and Farewell** (1911–14), in which Edward Martyn and AE (George Russell (q.v.)) are treated to comic yet not unappreciative dissection, while tongue-in-cheek accounts of Yeats's pomposities scintillate with caustic denigration. Yeats created in *Dramatis Personae* (1935) a frank picture of Moore as a gossipy raconteur who would destroy his own reputation as easily as anyone else's for the sake of conversational effect, and as a fellow who could be absurdly ignorant in mundane practical matters. 'He said to a friend: "How do you keep your pants from falling about your knees?" "O," said the friend, "I put my braces through the little tapes that are sewn there for the purpose." A few days later he thanked the friend with emotion.' However that may be, the reader of Moore's *Hail and Farewell* is carried through the three volumes (*Ave, Salve, Vale*) on an irresistible tide of good humour.

The Untilled Field (1903), a collection of short stories of life in priest-ridden Irish parishes, was another product of Moore's Irish phase. Indeed he claimed that his original intention was to burn the English versions as soon as they were translated into Irish, but the Irish translations failed to sell. Meanwhile Moore's approach to the novel had undergone a change. Symbolism and a richer, more resonant prose gave a new authority to *The Lake* (1905), the story of an Irish priest whose inner conflicts lead to his forsaking his parish and his country. (It was based on the case of Gerald O'Donovan, q.v.) Indeed the development of Moore's style (or 'styles' – for he had many) from the accurate recording of the first novels to the finely wrought graces and fluencies of the last is impressive; and the art of the story-teller matured correspondingly. *The Brook Kerith* (1916) deals with a Jesus who does not die on the cross but is saved by Joseph of Arimathea and lives as a shepherd until Paul discovers him. *Héloïse and Abelard* (1921) presents the lovers feelingly and authentically against a thought-out background of eleventh-century life that is packed with detail and rich in imagery. Finally *Conversations in Ebury Street* (1924) reproduces the mature Moore's talk with his friends: there are penetrating and provocative critical judgements on Hardy (q.v.) and George Eliot, on Conrad (q.v.) and Mrs Gaskell ('the most commonplace of all English writers'), and surprises like the tribute to Anne Brontë's *Agnes Grey* as 'the most perfect prose narrative in English literature'.

Hail and Farewell, a three-volume work of autobiographical reminiscence, was for Moore at once 'the cause of my being' and 'the turning-point in Ireland's destiny'. *Ave* moves from London to Dublin for the opening performance of the Irish Literary Theatre in 1899. Moore's swift sequence of imaginatively intensified recollections re-creates rehearsals and performances, a famous dinner at the Shelbourne Hotel, visits to Lady Gregory (q.v.) at Coole and to Frau Wagner at Bayreuth. A surge of controlled comic deflation washes around the figures of Edward Martyn and Yeats – portraits that are subtly and evocatively realized; and there is self-irony to match. *Salve* contains much about the Gaelic League, a captivating and affectionate portrait of AE and conversation with Moore's brother Maurice that brings back childhood and schooldays. Moore argues on the incompatibility of literature and Catholic dogma, concludes that Ireland must cease to be Catholic if she is to be culturally reborn, declares himself a Protestant and decides to return to England. In *Vale* flashbacks recall early days in London and Paris; and there are more sketches of Dublin personalities, AE, James Stephens (q.v.), Lady Gregory, John Eglinton and Douglas Hyde among them. At the last the love affair with 'Stella' – who followed him to Ireland – is terminated, and there is a visit to Moore Hall where the author's life-story began. Moore's reminiscences bubble up from moods and moments charged with associative significance, while themes and personalities move in and out of the pattern recurringly. In these respects Moore can be aligned with Proust. The detached humour, the irony and the impressionistic mode of composition align him with Joyce (q.v.). For the text is a moving panorama of smoothly controlled transitions between reflection and description, dialogue and recollection. Personal and public matters, gossip and fact and reverie, are cunningly woven together. The flavour of the most entertaining passages owes much to the accumulation of

nuances rich in devastatingly good-humoured denigration. The artistic credo is firmly pronounced: 'The artist should keep himself free from all creed, from all dogma, from all opinion. . . . He is almost unaware of your moral codes, he laughs at them when he thinks of them'.   [HB]

MOORHOUSE, FRANK (1939–). Short-story writer, born in New South Wales, Australia, and educated at Nowra High School and Wollongong Technical College. He worked in journalism for a time but his 'reformist zeal to change society by peaceful means' engaged him in the Workers' Educational Association and he now writes full-time. *Futility and Other Animals* (1969) was a frank, even sensational, series of 'interlinked stories' dealing with contemporary Australian society – 'a modern, urban tribe which does not fully recognize itself as a tribe'. He described the 'central dilemma' of the book as 'that of giving birth, of creating new life'. In its exploration of the urban counter-culture the work established him as a accomplished and controversial writer. *The Americans, Baby* (1972), 'a discontinuous narrative of stories and fragments', furthered his charting of urban subculture, but with greater depth and flexibility than the earlier book. In 1973 he edited the annual anthology *Coast to Coast*, and in the following year published *The Electrical Experience*, another discontinuous series of 'narratives' and 'fragments' which gave a shrewd and witty picture of the life and love of T. George McDowell in an Australian small town 'somewhere south of Nowra'. *Conference-Ville* (1976) was a witty charting of that country of the mind, while *Tales of Mystery and Romance* (1977) explored complex aspects of the environment, 'both internal (anxieties, pleasures and confusions) and external (the houses, streets, hotels and experiences)', with great perception. Apart from books he is actively involved with the alternative press in Australia and in writing film scripts, notably *Between Wars* (1974), directed by Mike Thornhill. Speaking of earlier days, Moorhouse says that as he developed 'away from the humanist tradition of the Australian story – sympathetic to the working class and kind to kangaroos' his stories were rejected from the literary magazines. While certainly never 'establishment', today his writing commands deserved attention.   [PQ]

MORAES, DOM (Dominic) (1938–). Poet, born in Bombay, India. Since graduating from Oxford in 1959, he has worked as television scriptwriter, documentary-film maker and magazine editor.

Outside India probably the best-known Indian poet writing in English, Moraes was the first non-British recipient of the Hawthornden Prize (1958) for his collection *A Beginning* (1957). It was followed by *Poems* (1960), *Fifteen Poems for William Shakespeare* (1964), *John Nobody* (1965), *Poems 1955–1965* (1966) and *Bedlam Etcetera* (1966). He writes chiefly about interior experience, often confrontation with mythic, even grotesque, creatures; many are figurings of his own anxieties. 'The Visitor' illustrates the nature of his attempts to reconcile private individuality with existence in general: 'Dark angel of the world, who moves behind / Dayfall, and whispers truth to innocence, / Hurting it to tears'. Despite his considerable metrical gifts and the honesty, wit and *gravitas* of this poem and others, like 'At Seven o'clock', 'Melancholy Prince' and especially 'Kanheri Caves', Moraes has not yet poetically, in S. Nagarajan's words, 'found any convincingly felt solution to his personal problems'. He has also written various works of non-fiction, most notably *My Son's Father: An Autobiography* (1968). Other publications include *East to West: A Collection of Essays* (1971) and *Mrs Gandhi* (1980) [AR]

MORGAN, EDWIN (1920–). Poet, born and educated in Glasgow, Strathclyde, Scotland. He has taught in the English Department at Glasgow University since 1950. He has published volumes of verse steadily since *Cathkin Braes* (1952): they include *The Second Life* (1968) and *From Glasgow to Saturn* (1973). Morgan is versatile in his gifts and interests. Aspects of day-to-day Glasgow life are neatly registered in poems such as 'King Billy' and 'Trio' and deep feeling is captured with unobtrusive imaginative ingenuity in 'One Cigarette', where the poet reflects on the burning cigarette left behind by his visitor. ('No smoke without you, my fire.') 'In the Snack-bar' is a touching account of helping an old blind man to the toilet from a snack-bar.

> Wherever he could go it would be dark
> and yet he must trust men.
> Without embarrassment or shame
> he must announce his most pitiful needs
> in a public place.

Morgan has also experimented with 'concrete poetry', achieving a catchy Joycean spiritedness with his dexterous blend of Scottishness and humour. He has published translations of *Beowulf* (1952), poems from Eugenio Montale (1959) and from the Hungarian poets, Sándor Weöres and Ferenc Juhász (1970). He has edited *Scottish Satirical Verse* (1980), noting Scotland's 'two deep self-inflicted wounds – Calvinism and the Union', and the self-critical vein stemming from this dividedness. The collection *Poems of Thirty Years* (1982) proves Morgan's rare inventiveness and prodigality as a poet who rejects modish cold-bloodedness and cynicism, and can celebrate love or the charm of daily experience with moving exuberance. [HB]

MORTIMER, JOHN (1923–). Dramatist, born in Hampstead, London, educated at Harrow and Oxford. Called to the Bar in 1948, he became a QC in 1966. His play *The Dock Brief* (radio and television production 1957; stage production 1958) is an imaginatively conceived confrontation in gaol between a murderer and his counsel, a struggling old barrister to whom the case matters more than it does to the resigned, hen-pecked working man who has got rid of his wife. This dichotomy between the artifice and human irrelevance of the legal game and the reality of living and doing is more fully explored in *The Judge* (prod 1967), in which a judge returns at the end of his career to conduct the assize in his native town where lives the woman whom he believes he wronged and by whom he obsessively demands to be judged himself. *A Voyage Round My Father* (prod 1970) has autobiographical significance as the study of a barrister who, like Mortimer's own father, has gone blind and forced himself to ignore the affliction to the

maximum. The play is clumsily episodic in construction. There is greater presentational polish in the sequence of four one-act sex comedies, *Come as You Are* (prod 1970), where ironies of marriage and the sex-game are flavoured with a liberal sprinkling of farce. Mortimer has written for screen, radio and television. His autobiographical book, *Clinging to the Wreckage* (1982), sheds light on the part he has played professionally in the legal defence of writers against charges of obscenity, as well as on his view of literature as the writer's 'defence and safety-valve' in sublimating anger and humiliation. [HB]

MORTIMER, PENELOPE (1918–). Novelist, born in Rhyl, Clwyd, Wales, the daughter of a clergyman. She has been twice married, the second time to the playwright John Mortimer (q.v.), and has six children. She has done a good deal of journalism, including the reviewing of fiction. Her novel *Johanna* (1947) was published under her first married name ('Dimont'), but she first made an impact with *A Villa in Summer* (1954). Her fictional terrain is almost exclusively sexual and domestic. In *Daddy's Gone A-Hunting* (1958) (in USA as *Cave of Ice*) Ruth Whiting, a suburban bundle of fears and guilts, finds a tenuous bond with her daughter only when the latter becomes pregnant and mother and daughter have to conspire over secret abortion, in league against a brute husband-father who seems to belong to a lower species. In *My Friend Says It's Bullet-Proof* (1967) Muriel Rowbridge is teetering neurotically on the edge of breakdown after a cancer operation has removed a breast. She learns to accept herself through a casual liaison, but not to accept the man who has obliged. Penelope Mortimer's women give themselves to inwardness, .capriciousness and 'privileged despair': the male world is alien. Later novels are *The Home* (1971) and *Long Distance* (1974).

[HB]

MOTTRAM, R.H. **(Ralph Hale)** (1883–1971). Novelist, born in Norwich, Norfolk. He followed his father into banking until he made his way as a writer. Something of the family tradition can be gathered from *Our Mr Dormer* (1927), the chronicle of a rising East Anglian family, beginning in 1813 and finally glancing forward to the 1920s. Mottram served in Flanders as an interpreter in the First World War and his friend John Galsworthy (q.v.) (whom Mottram celebrated in *For Some We Loved*, 1956) wrote a Preface for his war novel, *The Spanish Farm* (1924), written from the point of view of a civilian on the edge of the war. Madeleine Vanderlynden, daughter of a farmer, sticks it out in the farm 20 miles from the front, herself 'the implacable spirit of that borderland so often fought over' and forceful symbol of her country, ultimately 'pushing aside even her attractiveness to toil and bargain ruthlessly'. Mottram added two sequels, *Sixty-Four Ninety-Four* (1925) and *The Crime at Vanderlynden's* (1926), and interposed interludes to complete *The Spanish Farm Trilogy* (1927) on a scale to match the achievements of Galsworthy and Ford Madox Ford (q.v.). The two later volumes follow the war careers of English officers, Geoffrey Skene and Stephen Doughty Dormer respectively (the latter a scion of the house of *Our Mr Dormer*). The farm is used for billeting troops going up and down the line, and Skene has a brief affair with Madeleine. Mottram thus balances the resident peasant view of the war with the intruding serviceman's view, the French angle on the British with the British angle on the French. He gives a vivid and detailed picture of day-to-day military life and at the same time achieves a cosmic view of the passing years on the shifting Western Front and the changing communal mood and morale of succeeding waves of volunteers and conscripts. The second and third volumes are insufficiently distinct in character and purpose, but the chronicle as a whole, though defective in dramatic pattern, is an absorbing and acutely felt record of the war. Mottram's numerous later novels did not make a comparable impact. Among the latest, *To Hell, With Crabb Robinson* (1962) is a fantasy in which the author encounters his ancestral cousin, the early nineteenth-century writer Crabb Robinson, and conducts a dialogue with him, while *The Speaking Likeness* (1967) is the story of one of Mottram's predecessors as Mayor of Norwich. *The Window Seat* (1954) and *Another Window Seat* (1957) are collections of autobiographical pieces reflecting on (mostly public) events.　　　　　[HB]

MPHAHLELE, ES'KIA (formerly Ezekiel) (1919-). Critic, teacher, short-story writer and novelist, born in Pretoria, South Africa. He grew up in the tribal village of Maupaneng, Transvaal, and in the black 'location' of Marabastad, Pretoria. Educated at St Peter's School, Johannesburg, and Adams College, Natal, he graduated (BA 1949 and MA 1956) from the University of South Africa (external degrees) and took his PhD from Denver, Colorado (1968). Married in 1965, he and his wife Rebecca have five children. He worked as a messenger, as a clerk at an institution for the blind in 1941-5, as a schoolmaster from 1945 till dismissed 'for subversive activities', at various badly paid jobs in 1952-5, and for *Drum* magazine from 1955 until he left South Africa in 1957 to be a schoolmaster in Nigeria. He was in Paris in 1961-3 with the Association for Cultural Freedom; Nairobi in 1963-5 as Director of the Chemchemi Creative Centre; and Nairobi, Denver and Lusaka successively from 1965 to 1970 as university lecturer, until he was appointed a professor of English in Denver 1970. In 1978 he returned to South Africa and now works in the Institute for African Studies, University of the Witwatersrand, Johannesburg.

Mphahlele's first volume of short stories, *Man Must Live*, appeared in 1947, but his autobiography, *Down Second Avenue* (1959), won him international recognition as a writer. *The Living and the Dead*, short stories, was published in Nigeria in 1961. In 1962 his pioneering critical book, *The African Image*, appeared; it was to have an immense influence throughout Africa. He was a co-editor of *Black Orpheus* in 1960-4 and in 1964 edited *Modern African Stories* with Ellis Komey. In 1967 there was another collection of his short stories, *In Corner B*, and his edition of the Penguin anthology, *African Writing Today*. A substantial novel, *The Wanderers*, appeared in 1971, another, *Chirundu*, in 1979, a volume of critical essays, *Voices in the Whirlwind*, in 1972, and a selection of stories and poems, *The Unbroken Story*, in 1981. Over the years he has written frequently for international periodicals.

Down Second Avenue is the finest of a virtual genre of black South African autobiographies, including *Tell Freedom* (1954) by Peter Abrahams (q.v.) and Bloke Modisane's *Blame Me on History* (1963). That is not the main reason why it has become a classic and been translated into about a dozen languages. It is a vivid, candid, often angry account of the development of a highly intelligent, sensitive human personality in the face of appalling poverty and all the other disadvantages of growing up in South Africa's black ghettos under the virtually intolerable restrictions in every department of living imposed by the apartheid state. It tells of a childhood still close to surviving traditional African ways in an impoverished village, of an adolescence amid scenes of urban slum brutality, of a desperate struggle for literacy and education, achieved only through the sacrificial labours of mother, aunts and grandmother. Such experiences are shown to be common for all urban black children in South Africa, but made concrete in the particularity of the author's own life. By the very narration of facts which might even strike an outsider as wild fantasy, the book unselfconsciously testifies to the resilience of the human spirit. Mphahlele's unsubdued humanity and reverence for life give *Down Second Avenue* extraordinary warmth and vitality. It not only made him an eloquent interpreter of black experience in South Africa, but struck a chord in black people's hearts throughout Africa, the United States and the Caribbean, and won the admiration of others.

The African Image was the first serious, comprehensive, critically discriminating study of African writing and of the treatment of Africans in fiction by European and white South African authors. It went into the larger cultural questions of the black man's acquisition of 'European' education and the relationship between African identity, literature and society in modern African countries. J. Jahn's *Muntu* (1961), G. Moore's *Seven African Writers* (1962) (one of the seven is Mphahlele) and *The African Image* created the theoretical groundwork for the study of African literature which blossomed in African universities after two important literary conferences, in Dakar and Freetown, in 1963, in both of which Mphahlele was a vigorous participant. Of the three books Mphahlele's has been the most influential, as much for the width of its approach as for the pertinency of its execution. Because of his serious reservations about the continuing validity of the francophone writers' theory of négritude and his very pragmatic treatment of African nationalism and the idea of the African Personality, *The African Image* profoundly affected writers and critics in anglophone Africa. What above all distinguishes it is the imaginative extent of the politico-cultural territory it covers, in close association always with incisive critical evaluation of actual texts. The second edition (1974) is almost a new book; which brings *The African Image* up to date by reviewing the rich growth of African writing that had occurred since 1962 and by relating African literature more closely with Afro-American writing.

Another impressive volume of criticism, *Voices in the Whirlwind*, came out in 1972, essays which reflect his American experience in a number of articles on Afro-American literature.

The novel *The Wanderers* (1971) tends to confirm the

impression that Mphahlele's major contribution to literature is as a practising critic rather than as a writer of
fiction. The Wanderers follows the broad outlines of
Mphahlele's life, first as an opponent of apartheid within
South Africa, then as an exile; while the earlier part, set
in South Africa, recaptures some of the immediacy and
vivacity of Down Second Avenue, the structure and
fictional realization falter when the scene moves
elsewhere. About a politician in an African state who is
corrupted by power, Chirundu (1979) fails to resolve convincingly in fictional terms the connection between individual morality and political integrity.

Extensive as Mphahlele's political, cultural and literary view is, it grows out of his painful experience as a
black South African, and his commitment to the cause of
his long-suffering people is stamped upon everything he
has written. The exhilaration of his first few years as a
free man living outside his native land gave way to a disturbing sense of exile from everything, both good and ill,
that had impelled him to become a writer. Among exiled
opponents of apartheid his return to South Africa, with
apartheid still intact there, has been bitterly criticized,
but it cannot dim his achievement as the author of Down
Second Avenue and The African Image. [AR]

MTSHALI, OSWALD MBUYISENI (1940–). Poet,
born in Vryheid, Natal, South Africa, and educated there
and in Johannesburg, after which he worked as a
messenger. While in prison on mere suspicion, the incon-
sistency in a violent condemned prisoner's kindnesses to
him stimulated a desire to transpose experience into
poetry. His work started appearing in South African
periodicals; in 1971 he published Sounds of a Cowhide
Drum: Poems, which sold a record 16,000 copies in the
first year. Some of the acclaim was mere white liberal
patronization which overlooked his weaknesses: thinking
that is often undistinguished ('Love and Truth / are sugar-
coated words / offered to Sunday school children'),
similes that don't illumine but distract (the sun setting
compared to a coin working a parking meter in 'Sunset'),
rhythmic slackness where conversational effects are
intended. But within South Africa he broke the black
writers' silence that had lasted for a decade after
Sharpeville and heralded the new poetry represented in
the anthology Black Poets in South Africa (1974). Mtshali
records, often ironically, the deprived lives of blacks in
the segregated urban areas. He hits sarcastically at
colour-bar restrictions ('Pigeons in the Oppenheimer
Park'); or shows the humiliations ('Men in Chains') and
cruelties ('Ride upon the Death Chariot') imposed by
apartheid, with 'men shorn / of all human honour / like
sheep after shearing'; or dramatizes vividly ('An
Abandoned Bundle') the contempt for life that the system
induces among the ghetto-dwellers. But, as in the title
poem, he also proclaims the indomitable African spirit.
Another volume, Fireflames, appeared in 1981. [AR]

MUIR, EDWIN (1887–1959). Poet and critic, born in
Orkney, Scotland, one of six children of a tenant farmer
who was eventually compelled by ill-health and financial
difficulties to sell out. He moved to Glasgow when Edwin
was 14. The Orkney upbringing, with the intense loves

and fears of a sensitive, nervous childhood, provided
much of the stuff of later poetry, and the early days are
feelingly recaptured in Muir's Autobiography (1954), an
expanded version of The Story and the Fable (1940).
Glasgow depressed Muir, and the deaths of his father,
two brothers and his mother in rapid succession intensified his distress as he moved through various menial jobs
to a beer-bottling factory and thence to a factory at
Fairport for reducing bones to charcoal. Meantime he
embraced socialism and read avidly, drawing special
sustenance from Heine and Nietzsche. He met Willa
Anderson, a St Andrews graduate, in 1918 and married
her the following year. The couple moved to London, with
no evident prospects ('Sensible friends shook their
heads', Autobiography), but the marriage proved 'the
most fortunate event in my life'. Muir worked as a freelance journalist, writing articles and reviews for The
New Age, The Scotsman and The Athenaeum, while his
wife taught. At this time he underwent psychoanalysis,
for throughout his life he had extraordinary dreams, alive
with grotesque, fantastic and cataclysmic manifestations. Vivid waking trances of mythic intensity are also
recorded by Muir and seem to justify the psychoanalyst's
warning to him that his 'unconscious was far too near
the surface for my comfort and safety, and that I should
hurry to put something soundly substantial between me
and it'.

The Muirs spent several years abroad after the war,
living in Prague, Dresden, Hellerau, Italy and Austria.
Using their knowledge of German, they gradually turned
themselves 'into a sort of translation factory. . . . It began
as a resource and hardened into a necessity'. But, at the
age of 35, Muir had begun to write poetry and the years of
his childhood came alive for him again. 'Horses' restored
his father's plough-horses to life; the 'Ballad of Hector in
Hades' (about the pursuit round the walls of Troy) 'was
really a resuscitation of the afternoon when I ran away in
real terror from another boy as I returned from school.
The bare landscape of the little island became, without
my knowing it, a universal landscape over which
Abraham and Moses and Achilles and Ulysses and
Tristram and all sorts of pilgrims passed'. The statement
defines a poetic method Muir used repeatedly: the two
poems named were included in First Poems, accepted by
Virginia Woolf (q.v.) for the Hogarth Press and published
in 1925, the year the Muirs returned to Britain. During
the Second World War they lived at St Andrews and,
after the war, Muir held British Council posts in Prague
and Rome, then served as Warden of Newbattle Abbey
College near Edinburgh.

Muir's prose output includes The Structure of the
Novel (1928), John Knox – Portrait of a Calvinist (1929)
('too full of dislike of Knox', Muir said), Scottish Journey
(1935), which records impressions of a tour, Scott and
Scotland (1936), which considers the problem of the
Scottish writer in relation to the English tradition, Essays
on Literature and Society (1949) and three novels, one of
them, The Three Brothers (1931), set in sixteenth-century
Scotland. The Muirs together translated Kafka into
English, and Stephen Spender (q.v.) observed that 'Muir's
poetry has something of the obsessive search into ramifications of an object which is Kafka's true genius'. Cer-

tainly Muir's successive volumes of poems, *Variations on a Time Theme* (1934), *Journeys and Places* (1937), *The Narrow Place* (1943), *The Voyage* (1946) and *The Labyrinth* (1949), record a continuing meditative grappling with themes that arose naturally from the stark contrast between the vision awakened in the Orcadian childhood and the pressures of contemporary industrialism that Glasgow life first imposed upon him. (For this reason the *Autobiography* provides the most illuminating commentary on the poetry.) The contrasts between mortality and immortality, imprisonment and freedom, recur:

> My childhood all a myth
> Enacted in a distant isle;
> Time with his hourglass and his scythe
> Stood dreaming on the dial
> > ('The Myth', *The Voyage*)
> And now I'm locked inside
> The savage keep, the grim rectangular tower
> From which the fanatic neighbour-hater scowls
> > ('The Journey Back', *The Labyrinth*)

Muir's dreams, a source of vital imagery, load his poetry with natural and animal symbols, and mythic resonances echo the great archetypes of creation and fall, journey through waste and wilderness, imprisonment, the wanderer's return and rediscovering Eden. In *The Labyrinth* it· is Theseus who speaks, but the maze is universalized –

> the wild-wood waste of falsehood, roads
> That run and run and never reach an end,
> Embowered in error.

Thus Muir's imagination transfigures the mystery of his pilgrimage in parable. It was a pilgrimage that took him through a struggle against depression to the achievement of inner peace. The spiritual journey led from a hyper-emotional evangelical conversion as a boy, through a long phase of religious indifference, to a realization that 'quite without knowing it, I was a Christian' and finally to a deep understanding of the Incarnation, acquired in Rome. Muir belongs to no poetic group. He eschewed technical innovation, but one detects an occasional rhythmic or stylistic echo of Yeats (q.v.) and indeed of Eliot (q.v.). Muir's *Collected Poems: 1921-1958* was published in 1960 (revised 1963). His widow, Willa, wrote *Belonging: A Memoir* (1969), P.H. Butter edited his *Selected Letters* (1974) and Andrew Nobel has edited and introduced *Edwin Muir: Uncollected Scottish Criticism* (1982). One of Muir's three novels, *Poor Tom* (1932, reissued 1982), has autobiographical interest in relation to his early days in Glasgow.   [HB]

MULDOON, PAUL (1951–). Poet, born in County Armagh, Northern Ireland, and educated at St Patrick's College, Armagh, and at Queen's University, Belfast. His main collections of verse are *New Weather* (1973), *Mules* (1977) and *Why Brownlee Left* (1980). The first of these contained poems of remarkable technical authority for so young a poet, such as 'Elizabeth' and 'The Electrical Orchard'. Muldoon never wastes words, he is strangely indirect and remote, he seems to conduct a running com-

mentary on life without ever looking anyone in the face. Though he talks frankly to his neighbour, Elizabeth,

> My promised children are in your hands,
> Hostages by you in your father's old house
> > ('Elizabeth')

she is firmly shut inside, nowhere to be seen. This aloneness is sensed ironically as the narrator and his mistress speed together across country by car in 'Good Friday 1971, Riding Westward'. An inventive maker of images, a master of the natural inflexions of conversation, Muldoon is teasingly untransparent, for his characteristic poem, anecdotal or descriptive, leaves behind a legacy of unease. The title poem of *Why Brownlee Left* tells in fourteen lines how a farmer, who apparently had every reason for contentment, set out to plough one day and vanished. They found his pair of black horses,

> Shifting their weight from foot to
> Foot, and gazing into the future.

This potent blend of blankness and helpless compassion is a recurring note in Muldoon's work. The longer poem, 'Immram', an intoxicating verbal feast, is a narrative of search for the speaker's father in America, which takes him through seedy adventures in high spots and dark corners to a hotel penthouse where the boss of a drug-running empire (for which his father once worked) is holed up like a worn-out Howard Hughes. Muldoon seems to withhold from the reader only the ultimate key for which he himself is searching in shared bafflement.
                                                          [HB]

MULGAN, JOHN (1911–45). Novelist, born at Christchurch, New Zealand, and educated at Auckland and at Oxford universities. An informed concern for political and human issues which was first aroused by his experience of the 1932 Auckland unemployment riots is reflected in his writings from England for the New Zealand *Auckland Star* during 1936. He also edited the anthology *Poems of Freedom* (1938), to which W.H. Auden (q.v.) contributed a preface. An editorial note by Mulgan defended 'the liberalism of poetry in its oldest and widest sense' and, prophetically in the light of his own suicide seven years later, spoke of 'the essential nobility of the human race . . . which causes men to go forward and when they can no longer go forward, to die'. His sole work of fiction is *Man Alone* (1939) which marked a return to his New Zealand roots similar to that undergone by Katherine Mansfield (q.v.) and similarly personal and productive. The book traces the career in New Zealand, England and eventually in Civil War Spain of Johnson, a 'medium-sized . . . ordinary looking' immigrant of 1919. A perceptive and deceptively straightforward portrait of Johnson, his country and the period, the book stands as a classic study of the land and its poeple. The title invites comparison with, for example, the 'Arawata Bill' persona of Denis Glover (q.v.). The posthumous *Report on Experience* (1947) – 'only the draft and outline of a book I'd like to write' – was a profound and harrowing account of his experiences in Greece during the war, including his changing attitudes towards the country of his birth.
                                                          [PQ]

MUNRO, ALICE (1931–). Novelist and short-story writer, born in Wingham, Ontario, Canada. After high school she spent two years at the University of Western Ontario. She married in 1951 and moved to Vancouver, later to Victoria, in British Columbia. She has three daughters by this marriage. In 1972 she returned to Southwestern Ontario and now lives in Clinton with her second husband. Her first book was *Dance of the Happy Shades* (1968), a collection of stories in which her sure eye and ear for the revealing details of day-to-day living were already apparent. The novel *Lives of Girls and Women* (1971) exploited these talents in a moving, and at times amusing, depiction of the painfully enjoyable process of growing up. It is this world, located in the region of Canada that she knows so well and observed through the eyes of 'girls and women' whose experience often seems to echo her own, that Munro has established as hers; the book is a formidable achievement, rich in pathos and humour alike. The thirteen stories in *Something I've Been Meaning to Tell You* (1974) further strengthened her reputation as a writer, and in *Who Do You Think You Are?* (1978) Munro again demonstrated her humanity and her mastery of the craft of fiction in ten stories charting the career of Rose from school, through the traumas and delights of university, sex and married life, to her eventual hard-won independence as a mother who succeeds as actress and interviewer. Munro feels herself 'lucky to be a Canadian writer' and has a strong attachment to Southwestern Ontario: 'the part of the country I come from is absolutely Gothic. You can't get it all down. . . . I think that the kind of writing I do is almost anachronistic, because it's so rooted in one place'. On her achievements to date such doubts do her writing less than justice.   [PQ]

MUNRO, NEIL (1864–1930). Novelist, born in Inveraray, Argyllshire, Scotland. He worked as a journalist and was editor of the *Glasgow Evening News* from 1918 to 1927. He wrote romantic novels that glamorized Highland life, transposing the idioms and cadences of Gaelic into English for the dialogue of his clansmen. Historical novels in the tradition of Stevenson inlcuded *John Splendid* (1898), *Doom Castle* (1901) and *The New Road* (1914). John Buchan, who wrote a Preface to the posthumous collection, *The Poetry of Neil Munro* (1931), declared *The New Road* to be 'beyond question the best Scots historical novel since Sir Walter'. Set at the time of the pacification of the Highlands and the construction of General Wade's military road, it is a tale of murder and usurpation with an exciting hunt across the hills from Inveraray to Inverness. Munro also wrote humorous tales (*The Vital Spark*, 1906; *The Daft Days*, 1907). He sometimes used the pseudonym 'Hugh Foulis'.   [HB]

MURDOCH, IRIS (1919–). Novelist, born in Dublin, Ireland. She was educated at the Froebel Educational Institute, London, at Badminton School, Bristol, and at Somerville College, Oxford, where she read Greats from 1938 to 1942. She worked first in the Treasury in London, then with the United Nations Relief and Rehabilitation Administration in Europe, before returning to the academic world. After a year at Newnham College, Cambridge, she became a Fellow of St Anne's College,

Oxford, in 1948, and taught philosophy there until 1963. She married John Bayley, a fellow don (at New College), in 1956. Her first novel, *Under the Net* (1954), set the pattern of her books which are overloaded with incident, characters and theatrical high jinks. Murdoch is a philosopher who discounts the need for an overall view of the general end and meaning of existence. Correspondingly *Under the Net* reads like a patchwork of inadequately related set-pieces which suggest uncoordinated talent and purpose. Jake Donaghue, the hero, is a neurotic workshy literary hack; he is a stagey Irish individualist playing fast and loose with the world about him, putting his foot in it and getting it in the neck. Externalities are fluently observed. Farcical incident and psychological slapstick seem to be manufactured on the assembly-line of an efficient fun-factory. The recipe laid down for entertaining pantomine capers and side-splitting japes suggests that Murdoch is a farce-writer manqué. But there is no living human centre. The arid flippancy precludes acute seriousness and acute humour alike.

Claims have been made for *The Bell* (1958) on the grounds that the interplay between a number of disparate freaks and perverts, deluded idealists and neurotics, located in a monastic community, takes some symbolic quality from the apparent concern with spiritual ideals and with the installation of a new bell. But Murdoch's decisively secular artistic antennae do not register spiritual concerns or religious minds convincingly. *A Severed Head* (1961) confirms that, in terms of moral value, Murdoch's world is an anarchic one in which human beings prey on each other sexually in the quest for supposed liberation. Martin Lynch-Gibbon is another version of Jake in that he puts his foot in it as much by his innocence as by his guile; and to this extent ironical paradox makes parts of the book very funny. But Murdoch's farce is itself never sure-footed enough precisely because the fitful attempts to turn cartoon figures into human beings intrude incongruously upon her cheerful implausibilities. She moves uncomfortably between farce and half-cynical 'seriousness'. Other novels include *The Sandcastle* (1957), a domestic novel, *The Red and the Green* (1965), which is set in Dublin at the time of the 1916 Rising, and *Bruno's Dream* (1969), which focuses on the consciousness of an old man who is slowly dying.

The Black Prince (1973) was highly praised for its ingenuity. Something of a thriller, it is equipped with two Forewords, by a supposed editor and a supposed author, who are joined by four of the characters in supplying six Postscripts. This experimental exercise in multiple interpretation, it is claimed, 'hardens the core of apparent actuality at the same time as puncturing the authority of any narrator, including herself' (Ronald Hayman, *The Novel Today*, 1976).

Iris Murdoch's work divides critics sharply, as the reception of her later novels, such as *A Word Child* (1975) and *Nuns and Soldiers* (1980) continues to show. It has been observed that she has a professional philosophical interest in 'a central problem of literary aesthetics: how to reconcile the need for form in art with the need to respect contingent reality'. In this respect, as a practitioner, she provokes the extremes of praise and condemnation.   [HB]

MURPHY, RICHARD (1927-). Poet, born in County Galway, Ireland. He spent childhood years in Ceylon, and was then educated in England (Magdalen College, Oxford, 1945-8). He has held occasional academic posts at English and American universities, but lived more permanently in County Galway. *The Last Galway Hooker* (1961) records the history of the *Ave Maria* from its launching in 1922 to its purchase by the poet in 1959 to take tourists out fishing. The boat makes an apt image for registering time's changes and the slipping away of human lifetimes. 'The Cleggan Disaster' is a narrative poem about a night of storm off the west coast of Ireland in 1927 in which twenty-five fishermen were lost. Momentous public changes are implicitly brought home in two poems in which Murphy focuses on his own family and the lost ascendancy. *The Woman of the House* (1959) pays tribute to his grandmother, a lovable Irish patrician who lost her reason in old age. 'The God Who Eats Corn' is a portrait of his father, who retired from the British Colonial Service as Governor of the Bahamas to settle in Southern Rhodesia in 1950. These sustained poems (included in *Sailing to an Island*, 1963) are steadily pondered works of substance that claim attention unobtrusively. See also *Selected Poems* (1979). [HB]

MURRAY, LES (Leslie Allan) (1938-). Poet, born in Nabiac, New South Wales. He read modern languages at Sydney University, acquiring linguistic ability which he employed first as a translator at the Australian National University, 1963-7, and since then as a widely read and fiercely local poet. He lives on his 'forty acres' in New South Wales, and his life and work are richly located there, both articulating a delicate yet relaxed balance between an instinctively felt (and intimately understood) awareness of the land and its customs and what some (though not Murray) would see as the wider world of 'culture'.

Murray's first book, *The Ilex Tree* (1965), was written jointly with his poet-friend Geoffrey Lehmann, but *The Weatherboard Cathedral* (1969) illustrated his distinctive voice, though many of the poems reflected experiences during a visit to Europe. *Poems Against Economics* (1972) contained the fine 'meditation' (Murray's word) 'Walking to the Cattle Place', in which his ability to span time and place through the universality of country tasks produced one of the finest Australian long poems. As this poem shows, he is a great believer 'in integrations, in convergences'; he uses poems as 'a springboard for talking about matters of wider interest', and a recurring impulse in his writing is the belief that Australian culture is 'still in its Boeotian phase', and that any distinctiveness it possesses is 'still firmly anchored in the bush'. No narrow-minded nationalist, for Murray 'freedom is memory'. Yet his wide reading and interests attain their natural focus in the celebration ('I'll always be celebrating') of an inclusive civilization that has nothing to do with being metropolitan and everything to do with living as part of a natural community. 'I try to realize, through art, a certain spacious, dignified, and distinctive order which underlies our late colonial society and its imported idiocies'; Murray's term for this order is 'the vernacular republic', which was the title of a fine 1976 volume of selected poems. In pursuing this order he has achieved

the 'convergence' of Hesiod, whose work he greatly admires, and that of Australian Aboriginal writers from whose poetry and song he has learnt to respect 'a deeply familiar world in which art is not estranged, but is a vital source of health for all the members of a community'. Sympathetic to 'the public role poetry has had' in Australia, and capable of devastating humour, Murray is at 45 a massive figure whose ability to take on issues which demand boldness as well as poetic craft suggest that his stature will continue to grow. 'I am not European, nor is my English,' Murray once observed. The final line of his powerful poem 'The Returnees' expresses the fusion with characteristic laconic wit: 'We're country, and Western'. [PQ]

MURRY, JOHN MIDDLETON (1889-1959). Critic and thinker, born in London, educated at Christ's Hospital and at Oxford. His career as a journalist-critic included work for *The Westminster Gazette*, *The Nation*, *The Adelphi* and *The Athenaeum* (which he edited). He was closely associated with D.H. Lawrence (q.v.) and wrote *Son of Woman* (1931) about him. He married Katherine Mansfield (q.v.) in 1918 and, after her death in 1923, edited *The Letters of Katherine Mansfield* (1928), *The Scrapbook of Katherine Mansfield* (1939) and *Katherine Mansfield's Letters to John Middleton Murry* (1951). His critical works included *Keats and Shakespeare* (1925) and *William Blake* (1933). He joined the Peace Pledge Union in 1936 and edited *Peace News* during the Second World War. He ran an experimental community farm for a time. His aim was to bring Marxist thinking within a Christian orbit. See also his son Colin Middleton Murry's autobiographical volumes, *One Hand Clapping* (1975) and *Shadows on the Grass* (1977). [HB]

MYERS, L.H. (Leo Hamilton) (1881-1944). Novelist, born at Cambridge, Cambridgeshire. His father, F.W.H. Myers, was a man of letters and a founder member of the Society for Psychical Research. Eton made Leo a rebel against its social values. When F.W.H. Myers died in 1901, Leo and his mother went to America for a planned posthumous meeting with the deceased, but he failed to keep the appointment. Leo met Elsie Palmer, daughter of a Colorado general, and nine years his senior. He married her in 1908. They had two daughters. Leo was left wealthy enough to be independent. He was medically unfit for service in the 1914-18 war. He had begun work on his novel *The Orissers* in 1909 and when it was completed and published in 1922 it had a succès d'estime. The struggle between two families for the possession of a country estate is given the dimensions of a philosophical conflict between opposing ways of life. As Myers rebelled against the social values of the class to which he belonged – and whose privileges he enjoyed – so he rebelled against the social and moral values of the aesthetic circles to which his literary achievement gave him access. He kicked against the self-enclosed arrogance of the Bloomsbury Group and rejected their emphasis on 'states of mind' as having a validity independent of moral judgement. Thus, acutely conscious of the current disintegration of values and bitterly hostile to the corruptions of the social order, he ultimately turned to communism and projected his ideal on to Russia with a neurotic obsessive-ness. In April 1944 he committed suicide by taking an overdose of veronal.

Myers's great work is the tetralogy called *The Near and the Far*. The first three books, *The Near and the Far* (1929), *Prince Jali* (1931) and *Rajah Amar*, were published as a trilogy under the title *The Root and the Flower* in 1935 and the lengthy sequel, *The Pool of Vishu*, was added in 1940, when Myers gave the title *The Near and the Far* to the whole. The story is set in sixteenth-century India in the reign of Akbar, the Great Mogul; but Myers's India (he never went there), like the Abyssinia of Dr Johnson's *Rasselas*, is a convenient background for studying the individual human mind as it grapples with the demands of public life and the search for personal integrity. 'It *was* my object to create a world that I liked better than the existing one', Myers conceded in a letter to L.P. Hartley (q.v.) in 1929. The Emperior Akbar's two sons, Salim and Daniyal, are rivals to succeed him. Amar, Rajah of Vidyapur, father of Jali and a Buddhist, wishes to retire from the world, but is held back from achieving total detachment at the public level by the evil foreshadowed in the probable victory of Daniyal and at the private level by the devotion of his Christian wife, Sita. A vast ramification of political and personal intrigue, intertwined with varieties of philosophical speculation, allows Myers to pursue his bent for exploring the world of mind. His weakness is that abstractions and generalities outweigh concrete exemplification. The feel of real life is missing and the nerve of passion is not touched. An interesting feature is the satire of Bloomsbury in the homosexual Prince Daniyal's Pleasance of the Arts, a remote camp of pleasure houses where scandalmongering is the principal pastime ('everybody in the Camp was always ready to do a friend a bad turn') of a self-admiring, self-indulgent group of bogus aesthetes who live in obedience to the peremptory voice of fashion, depending for their fun 'upon a solid, shockable world of decorum and common-sense'. See G.H. Bantock, *L.H. Myers: A Critical Study* (1956).   [HB]

NAHAL, CHAMAN (1927–). University teacher, critic and novelist, born in India and educated there and in Britain. He teaches English in Delhi University, has been a Professor of English at Long Island University, New York, from 1968 to 1970 and has lectured in Malaysia and Japan. Nahal contributed a weekly literary column to the newspaper *Indian Express* from 1966 to 1973.

He has written books on D.H. Lawrence (q.v.), Hemingway and J. Krishnamurti, a volume of stories, *The Weird Dance* (1965), and novels. *My True Faces* (1973), about stresses in a marriage, Shyamala Narayan finds unconvincing for its 'heavily involved style'. *Into Another Dawn* (1977), set chiefly in the USA, affirms, through an Indian youth's love for a young American woman, that east can meet west. *The English Queens* (1979), a fantastical satire, attacks Indian élitism and its infatuation with the English language as the concomitant of contempt for native Indian culture. *The Crown and the Loincloth* (1981) is the first in a trilogy about Gandhi. Nahal's best novel, *Azadi* (1975), which won the Sahitya Akademi Award, is a warming account of Muslims, Hindus and Sikhs living peacefully in Sialkot before 1947, and of the Hindus' flight into India as refugees after the Partition. Despite their losses and great sufferings, their feeling of self-respect in independent India is successfully conveyed, though the love story of Hindu youth and Muslim girl is cliché-tinged.   [AR]

NAIPAUL, SHIVA (1945–). Novelist, born in Port of Spain, Trinidad, where he attended school before reading Chinese at Oxford. He lives in Britain but has travelled much in Africa, Asia, the Caribbean, Europe and the United States.

Three short stories appeared in *Penguin Modern Stories 4* before his first novel, *Fireflies* (1970), was published. Like other Caribbean writers of East Indian background, he records the steady wilting of Hindu culture and religion in the West Indies. In *Fireflies* this sharply observed attrition is partly offset by Mrs Lutchman's ultimately composed acceptance of loss, loneliness and dependence, but the depiction of Hindu cultural decadence is unrelieved by the heroical resistance to it that characterizes Biswas in *A House for Mr Biswas*, by his elder brother V.S. Naipaul (q.v.). In *The Chip-Chip Gatherers* (1973) the dominant note is the futility induced by an ethos that is moribund yet prevents participation in the broader flow of West Indian life. Both novels have won major literary awards. *North of South* (1978) is a sardonic account of travel in Africa, *Black and White* (1980) an angry report on American subcultures and Guyanese politics behind the People's Temple mass suicides of November 1978.   [AR]

NAIPAUL, V.S. (Vidiadhar Surajprasad) (1932–). Novelist, born in Chaguanas, Trinidad, son of Seepersad Naipaul, journalist and author of *Gurudeva and Other Indian Tales* (1943). After attending Queen's Royal

College, Port of Spain, Naipaul went to Oxford in 1950, graduated in English in 1953, and has since returned to the Caribbean only as a visitor. In 1955 he married Patricia Ann Hale. Editor of the BBC radio programme 'Caribbean Voices' in 1954–6, he reviewed regularly for the *New Statesman* between 1956 and 1960. Though living mainly in England, he has travelled frequently, in the West Indies, North and South America, India and Africa. One of the foremost twentieth-century novelists in English, he has received many literary awards, including the Rhys Memorial Prize (1958), the Maugham Award (1961), the Hawthornden Prize (1964), the Smith Literary Award (1968) and the Booker Prize (1971). He has enjoyed a higher reputation in Europe and North America than in the Caribbean, where his satirization of West Indian life and his non-fictional treatment of it in *The Middle Passage* (1962) have caused him to be regarded by many as an uncommitted, élitist writer, while two other works of non-fiction, *An Area of Darkness* (1965) and *India: A Wounded Civilization* (1978), have not endeared him to Indians. To regard him, however, as belonging to a metropolitan western mode of realism, as some critics would have it, is to mistake for the underlying attitude in his best work what is a sophisticated novelistic technique. While he habitually chooses to distance himself as a novelist from the material he is working with, his most acclaimed novel, *A House for Mr Biswas* (1961), is a work of immense implicit compassion for the heroically imaginative efforts of limited humanity in an inimical world. But it is true that the geniality of his early writings gradually gives way to an increasingly dark, more chilling view of man's lot.

This possibility was acknowledged by such discerning critics as K. Ramchand (*The West Indian Novel and Its Background*, 1970) and W. Walsh (*A Manifold Voice*, 1970). The latter's comment that Naipaul 'is engaged with the stresses and strains we recognize as crucial in our experience now' is an early perception of what was latent in Naipaul's specifically West Indian books culminating in *A House for Mr Biswas*, and cumulatively manifested in his subsequent fiction. The watershed in Naipaul's career was *An Area of Darkness*, ostensibly an account of his visit to India (from which his grandfather had migrated to Trinidad) but in reality his painful examination of what he had assumed was his own substratum of Indianness. In Walsh's words, it 'is a kind of metaphysical diary of the effort to shine a Western novelist's light into an interior area of darkness. It reconstructs, it doesn't simply record, this experience'. Each of Naipaul's books of non-fiction, but especially *An Area of Darkness* and the historical study of early Trinidad, *The Loss of El Dorado* (1969), seems to have prepared the way for the next phase in his development as a novelist; in each he has articulated more directly than a novelist can the gradual shifts in his perceptions of the world about him. More recent non-fictional books are *The Return of Eva Peron with The Killings in Trinidad* (1980) and *Among the Believers: An Islamic Journey* (1981).

Geniality characterizes Naipaul's first book (though third in date of publication), *Miguel Street* (1959), which treats the inhabitants of a small Trinidadian locality with a very sharp eye for gesture and facial expression and a sure ear for popular colloquial idiom. The mediating narrator is an expatriate adult drawing upon memories of the people and place of his childhood and adolescence. With good humour and an occasional touch of pathos, it commemorates a community with little opportunity for originality, few hopes, but great cockiness and vitality. *The Mystic Masseur* (1957) is a mock biography of Ganesh Ramsumair, masseur and mystic, who sees himself destined for greatness and achieves political prominence in Trinidad through a combination of good luck, crude exploitation of credulity and sharp, petty business acumen. Shaking himself loose from his already atrophied Hindu roots, and ending up as the colonial statesman G.R. Muir, MBE, he unwittingly illustrates how the very minds of colonial people become colonized. Behind Naipaul's satire of Ganesh and his environment lies a realization of the imperial pressures that have caused their client-identities; it is Naipaul's first treatment of deracination, which is to be found in various forms in all his later novels. Nevertheless, the satire contains much that is genial, as does that in *The Suffrage of Elvira* (1958), a spirited comedy about a legislative council election in rural Trinidad, which satirizes both the western democratic process and the peculiarly West Indian metempsychosis it undergoes, with racial-vote bargaining, fear of *obeah* or magic, and every kind of petty wheeler-dealing.

A House for Mr Biswas, a substantial novel of early maturity, is richer and more rewarding than *The History of Mr Polly* by H.G. Wells (q.v.), which, J. Carthew convincingly argues, served as a kind of model. It is a tragi-comic and deeply understanding study of the attempts of a mediocre little man in a desert-like cultural milieu, who feels himself destined for better things, to establish a distinctive personality and style of his own. The symbol of his quest is the individual ownership of a house, which he does attain, though, like everything else in his life, incompletely. By assuming the role of an official biographer of a notability, and consistently referring to the central character as *Mr* Biswas, Naipaul achieves a remarkable kind of detachment that enables him to present Biswas as simultaneously absurd and heroic. Biswas has not only to assert himself against a hostile social environment but also to clamber out of the status of a hanger-on in the household of his prosperous Indian in-laws, the Hanuman family. Through the detailed activities of a household of Indian origin in the second and third generations of settlement in Trinidad, Naipaul examines the clinging to a cultural heritage even while understanding of its customs and rituals steadily fades away – a deracinated people grasping after shadows. But Biswas's quest is also a vigorous rebellion against such an existence. It may be a satiric view of shrivelling Indian roots in the Caribbean, but it is also ultimately about large-scale deracination caused by imperial processes in the past, and while there is regret for what these West Indians have lost, there is also, in Biswas's limited achievement, a celebration of freedom from ways of life now irrelevant in the West Indies.

Mr Stone and the Knights Companion (1963) is Naipaul's only novel set wholly in England and with

English characters. L. White (*V.S. Naipaul: A Critical Introduction*, 1975) argues the skill with which Naipaul has exploited here his own sense of uncertainty about the English, even after twelve years among them. Mr Stone, nearing retirement and aware of the utter futility of his urban existence, devises the Knights Companion to bring sustenance into the lives of the lonely and aged, but the 'packaging' of his idea by his colleagues turns the generous concept into a mere public relations exercise for their firm. After a late springtime in which Stone believes that his gnarled life is growing into organic and ordered relationship with the city he inhabits, he realizes that 'all that was not flesh was of no importance to man', that there is only the nullity of 'man's own frailty and corruptibility'.

The *Mimic Men* (1967) examines personal nullity in relation to post-independence politics in the Third World. Of Hindu birth and élitist background, 'Ralph' Singh, educated in England, has a grander, more intellectual and more romantic vision than Biswas of his own distinctiveness in an orderless West Indian island. He pursues it politically, achieves power and finds that the vision translated into action spells only negation. After his overthrow, he becomes a recluse in a London hotel, and the novel takes the form of his intelligent and sensitive attempt to understand himself and his society through language. As M. Thorpe remarks (*V.S. Naipaul*, 1976), more sharply than Mr Stone, Singh comes to accept the reality of a corrupt world. *The Mimic Men* denies validity to existing notions of post-colonial independence, and offers a fresh, sweeping analysis as a possible new starting point.

After Naipaul's historical study, *The Loss of El Dorado*, A.J. Gurr (in a 1970 essay) and Thorpe wondered, understandably, whether his novel-writing was at an end, and the structure of *In a Free State* (1971) seemed to confirm their speculations. A Prologue and an Epilogue, presented as extracts from travellers' journals, enclose three separate fictions – about a Bombay Indian servant who obtains a very dubious freedom in Washington, about a West Indian immigrant destroyed mentally by his experience of England and about English expatriates in a 'free' African state during a political upheaval. The theme common to all five pieces is that freedom is illusory in whatever form it is commonly dreamed of in the twentieth century. *In a Free State* has been followed by two substantial novels with large political motifs. A hasty reading of *Guerrillas* (1975) could pronounce it a sordid story about twisted lives, but the theme is the relationship between individual searches for identity and for regenerative political action, with both search and action doomed by the sterile western capitalist ethos desolately mimicked in an acrid Caribbean setting. The three main characters, representative little victims, are a would-be Black Power leader, a white South African liberal and former political prisoner and a young Englishwoman whose political and orgasmic hopes of human possibility are forever being disappointed. Each makes guerrilla raids upon life. Their interaction leads to macabre catastrophe and emptiness – they have no roots, no place, no centre, no freedom, only the flickering potential to reach after them. *A Bend in the River* (1979) tragically acknowledges on a vaster scale than before the corruptibility of

the human heart and of the means it has devised to secure 'the good life' for many different kinds of modern community. Though set in an unnamed, but Zaïre-like central African state, which is realized fictionally on a scale comparable to Costaguana in *Nostromo* by Conrad (q.v.), this plenteous, sombre, apocalyptic novel is less about Africa, more about the west's perpetrations against the Third World and against itself, and the consequent wreckage in human distortions, apostasies, self-denials and brutalities. It may seem nihilistic, but it applies a stringently honest cant-test to most of the shibboleths of our century, diagnostically rather than autopsically. With a balancing honesty it conveys wonder at the human capacity to survive. As *Mr Biswas* consummated Naipaul's specifically West Indian novels, so *A Bend in the River* would seem to perfect the fiction that began with *The Mimic Men* but had its impetus from the experience contained in *An Area of Darkness*.   [AR]

NANDY, PRITISH (1947–). Editor and poet, born in Bhagalpur, India, and educated in Calcutta. Most determinedly modernist of the younger Indian poets, Nandy is also the most prolific. His first volume, *Of Gods and Olives* (1967), was followed within a dozen years by some sixteen collections of his poetry, including the verse drama *Rites for a Plebeian Statue* (1969); he also edited or translated more than a dozen selections from poets writing in Indian languages, and edited such anthologies as *Poems from Bangladesh* (1971) and *Indian Poetry in English Today* (1973).

Nandy has described his poetic aim: 'to achieve an entirely new breakthrough in form', involving 'the fusion of a modern language with [Indian] myths and symbols'. Thus the rhythmic effects forced upon the reader by unconventional spacing of words and phrases in *From the Outer Bank of the Brahmaputra* (1969); thus such swirling, tumbling language as in 'Eclogue 9':

> The Blue vein-map is
> the innocent depth
> standing before the farm
> like my mother's insides
> soft and afraid of the seed.

Thus the intense, conversational, poetic 'prose' of his more memorable poems, like 'Calcutta if You Must Exile Me', where sparse language strikes at raw realities. *The Selected Poems of Pritish Nandy* appeared in 1979.   [AR]

NARAYAN, R.K. (Rasipuram Krishnaswami) (1907–). Novelist, born in Madras, India, and brought up there by his maternal grandmother, with holidays in Chennapatna, Hassan and Mysore, where his father was successively a headmaster. He received his last two years of schooling under his father in Mysore. In 1930 he graduated from Maharaja's College of Mysore University and decided to become a writer. By 1933 some short stories had appeared in Madras publications and a lampoon of British novelists ('How to Write an Indian Novel') in *Punch*; he was also writing his first novel. After marriage he undertook regular hack-journalism, until, on the recommendation of Graham Greene (q.v.), Hamish Hamilton accepted his novel *Swami and Friends* (1935). By 1939 he had published two more novels, *The Bachelor* *of Arts* (1937) and *The Dark Room* (1938), had a contract with the Madras paper, *The Hindu*, for a weekly sketch or story and was working on film scripts. When his wife died of typhoid in June 1939, Narayan was inconsolable and thought he could never write again. He devoted himself to their daughter, with long periods of meditation leading to the consolation of psychic communion with his wife. His interest in psychic experience diminished when he found he had, in his own words, 'attained an understanding of life and death' (*My Days*, 1975). Gradually he resumed literary activity, editing the only four issues of a literary quarterly, *Indian Thought* (1942–3), and starting his fourth novel, *The English Teacher* (1945; *Grateful to Life and Death*, USA, 1953). He has since produced seven more novels, four collections of short stories, a prose translation (1972) of the Indian epic *The Ramayana* and a shortened prose translation of *The Mahabharata* (1979). Until his first visit abroad, on a Rockefeller Award (1956), Narayan lived in Mysore and its environs, surrounded by relations and numerous friends in all walks of life. *The Guide* won him the 1958 Sahitya Akademi Award and in 1967 Leeds University conferred an honorary doctorate on him.

All Narayan's novels are set in the fictional town of Malgudi, which W. Walsh (*R.K. Narayan*, 1971) declares 'is as familiar to his readers as their own suburbs'. *Swami and Friends* and *The Bachelor of Arts* are fresh, episodic novels of childhood and youthful self-exploration. *The Dark Room*, a solemn handling of Indian marriage, attempts the integrative theme of a wife's resentment, then stoical acceptance, of subordination to an autocratic husband. In contrast, *The English Teacher* celebrates a joyful marriage extended psychically after the wife's death; stylistically it is the most stilted and unaffective of Narayan's books, perhaps because he labours to treat with fictional objectivity the most profoundly formative experience of his own life. •

With *Mr Sampath* (1949; *The Printer of Malgudi*, USA, 1955) the Malgudi mode is truly established: the creation of a whole twentieth-century South Indian town, where a rich variety of people are occupied with mundane busynesses, yet influenced, often unconsciously, certainly ironically and tragi-comically, by the ancient conservative values of Hindu faith. Into such a world are released the disruptions of individualist aspirations that find expression in modernity, flamboyance, moral madness, lack of self-knowledge, but with a discernible movement towards understanding and humaneness. Amidst the surface stability of Malgudi, Sampath the small-time printer tries to become a big-time epic-film producer, engulfing financiers, actors, technicians with his cyclonic insubstantiality, turning Srinivas, editor of *The Banner*, which Sampath used to print, into a nominal scriptwriter. From it Srinivas nevertheless gains calmness, which could easily be mistaken for, but is not, acquiescence in nullity; he unfurls his modest *Banner* again, dedicated to improving the world, now and in Malgudi.

Similarly, behind the confused activities of the pavement money-lender, Margayya, at the very portals of the Co-operative Land Mortgage Bank in *The Financial Expert* (1952), is a pure, almost ennobling, devotion to the rituals of Lakshmi, Goddess of Wealth, which sours all his human relationships, does bring him riches through the publication of a pornographic book, but also acceptance of the goddess's disfavour when he loses everything. *Waiting for the Mahatma* (1955) displays Gandhi crystal-like as a manifestation of divinity and, set against this measure, the sadly mixed motives of his followers in the Quit India Campaign, such as the 'hero', Sriram, who becomes a *Satyagrahi* more out of love for Gandhi's protégé, Bharati, than out of understanding of the Mahatma's saintly teachings. In *The Man-eater of Malgudi* (1961) Vasu the taxidermist kills animals in order to 'preserve' them. He is abrasive, modern professionalism devouring everything in its path in Malgudi, but the novel quietly hints throughout that this over-sized, muscular, intelligent man is also endowed with the qualities of a *rakshasa* of Hindu mythology, an evil demon who, happily for humanity, is fated to destroy himself too. But the sharp, darkly comic contrast between Vasu and his main victim, the gentle Nataraj, illustrates, in M.K. Naik's words, that one 'can mismanage human relationships by practising both a militant egotism . . . and a timid altruism which submits tamely to evil'.

In his two most recent novels, Narayan refines further his manipulation of incongruities, first fully practised in *The Guide* (1958), so as to reach delicately behind absurdity or grossness for the desolating but humanizing wisdom of tragic experience. In *The Sweet-vendor* (1967; *The Vendor of Sweets*, USA, 1967), Jagan's belief that he is following ancient wisdom by conquering taste so as to conquer the self is belied by his indulgence of a son who flouts Jagan's orthodox principles on returning from America with the franchise for an electronic story-writing machine. Only when Mali disparages his father's sweet-making enterprise can Jagan view their relationship dispassionately. At 60 he chooses freedom in a life of meditation – but with a cheque-book among the few necessities in his shoulder-bag. In *The Painter of Signs* (1976) modernity erupts into Malgudi again as Daisy, a liberated woman working for the family-planning campaign. She captivates Raman into painting family-planning symbols, and into her bed. There is a fine ambivalence in Narayan's treatment of the desolated Raman when Daisy unexpectedly moves on elsewhere.

Narayan's fictive and imaginative powers are at their most impressive in *The Guide*, another of his deftly ambiguous titles, for Raju's life, lubricated by an easy loquacity, goes through the progression of railway newsagent, tourists' guide, impresario to a dancing-girl whom he foists on the public as a great dancer, financial mismanager of her earnings, and consequently gaolbird for two years. Then, having fortuitously sheltered in a disused temple, he gets mistaken for a holy man by the peasants and is venerated for his guidance of their lives. Ultimately, against his will, this confidence trickster, who has always delighted in pleasing others by whatever means, becomes a holy man in truth by undertaking a twelve-day fast to end a catastrophic drought: 'for the first time he was learning the thrill of full application . . . doing a thing in which he was not personally interested'. The enigmatic ending suggests that Raju dies on the eleventh day as the whole nation looks on.

Most critics have echoed Graham Greene's likening of Narayan's ironic art to Chekhov's. If the comparison provides a comfortable starting-point for western readers, it also denies Narayan's position within the ancient but living tradition of Indian story-telling. In lucid and deceptively simple English he superbly enriches that tradition, in technique no less than reference and outlook, and produces a very Indian interpretation of reality. [AR]

NEILSON, JOHN SHAW (1872–1942). Poet, born in Penola, South Australia. After some two years' formal education he began work on the land amid constantly failing family fortunes. Poor eyesight meant that after 1905 he could read and write only with great difficulty. His first collection, *Heart of Spring* (1910), was followed thirteen years later by *Ballad and Lyrical Poems* which in fact reprinted much of the earlier collection. *New Poems* (1927) extended his range and the *Collected Poems* of 1934 included twelve new poems. Neilson received a small literary pension in 1922 and a sinecure with the Melbourne County Roads Board in 1928 – his first regular income. His finely wrought lyrics, which combine response to natural beauty with a prevailing sadness, have won increasing respect in recent years. He draws, largely instinctively, upon romantic and symbolist techniques in a poetry which at its best possesses a striking visionary fragility, at worst sinks to sentimental cliché. *Unpublished Poems* (1947), a 1963 selection by Judith Wright (q.v.), and *The Poems of John Shaw Neilson* (1965, revised and enlarged 1973) have made available a comprehensive text of this lonely and highly individual writer who, apart from Christopher Brennan (q.v.), is the most interesting poet of the early twentieth century in Australia.   [PQ]

NESBIT, E. (Edith) (1858–1924). Children's writer, born in Kennington, London, the daughter of an agricultural chemist. Her father died in 1862 and thereafter Mrs Nesbit took her family to the continent where they roamed from place to place in the interests of her daughter Mary's health. They returned to England in 1870. Edith married Hubert Bland in 1880. A well-known Fabian and a political journalist, Bland proved a difficult husband, and Edith found herself bringing up two of his illegitimate children alongside her own. She was, however, a tough if impetuous and high-spirited personality. She first began to write for money in early married life when her husband was ill and his business partner absconded with the capital. She wrote stories, novels and verses, and the copious, if unremarkable, output no doubt supplied a discipline that stood her in good stead when she found her true métier as a children's writer with the first stories about the Bastable children. These appeared in the *Pall Mall Magazine* and the *Windsor Magazine* in 1898 and were then issued in book form as *The Story of the Treasure Seekers* in 1899. The Bastables – Oswald, Dora, Dickie, Alice, Noel and H.O., not to mention Albert-next-door – set their minds to work on the task of restoring the family fortunes from their 'poor but honest circs in a semi-detached house in the Lewisham Road'. Oswald is the narrator who mostly remembers to refer to himself in the third person, but whose detachment falls short of eschewing objective self-praise. It is a rich uncle who in fact transforms the family fortunes, and in *The Wouldbegoods* (1901) the children have acceded to affluence. *New Treasure Seekers* (1904) narrates further

Bastable exploits. The comic vein is rich and sturdy, never slyly adult. The Bastables themselves are scornful of cheap storybook clichés and sentimentality. A different family is involved in *The Railway Children* (1906) and their adventures include rescuing trains, babies and foreign refugees. More akin to the Bastables are the spirited family of *Five of us – And Madeline* (1925). Alongside stories rooted in the everyday world, Nesbit wrote several stories of magic and enchantment, notably *Five Children and It* (1902), *The Story of the Amulet* (1906) and *The Enchanted Castle* (1907), as well as the historical fantasies *The House of Arden* (1908) and *Hardy's Luck* (1909). See also Anthea Bell, *E. Nesbit* (1960).   [HB]

NEWBOLT, HENRY (Sir) (1862–1938). Poet, whose nautical and patriotic balladry gave him a great reputation in pre-1918 England. It is too much like diluted Kipling to be any longer fashionable. The melodramatic verses 'He Fell Among Thieves' (about an ex-public-school boy dying bravely in north-west India with the 'School Close' in mind) have been much anthologized. 'Vitai Lampada' ('There's a breathless hush in the Close tonight') has become a jocular symbol of public-school ethos. John Betjeman (q.v.) edited Newbolt's *Selected Poems* (1940).   [HB]

NEWBY, P.H. (Percy Howard) (1918–). Novelist, born at Crowborough, East Sussex, and educated at Hanley Grammar School, Worcester, and St Paul's College of Education, Cheltenham. A brief spell of schoolmastering was terminated by the war. Newby served in the RAMC, but in 1942 was seconded to Fouad Awal University in Cairo as Lecturer in English. He stayed in Cairo until 1946 when he turned full-time writer. He joined the BBC in 1949 and by 1958 had become Controller of the Third Programme. In *A Journey to the Interior* (1945), Newby's first novel, the hero, significantly named 'Winter', is sent abroad by his firm to recuperate after the death of his wife and her baby in childbirth. He comes to the sultanate of Rasuka whose atmosphere of corruption, despair and deceit recalls the territories of Conrad (q.v.) and Greene (q.v.). The legend of Rider, who disappeared mysteriously on a journey into the interior, becomes an obsession with Winter as a symbol to the dispirited widower of the kind of quest needed to wrest rebirth from desolation. *Agents and Witnesses* (1947) takes us to a fictional Mediterranean island which allows Newby to use his memories of Cairo, but *Mariner Dances* (1948) is set in England and *The Snow Pasture* (1949) mainly in Wales. In *A Step to Silence* (1952) and *The Retreat* (1953) Newby draws on his prewar experience of life in a teacher-training institution. Through the maturer novels (*The Picnic at Sakkara*, 1955; *Revolution and Roses*, 1957; and *A Guest and His Going*, 1959) Newby has established himself more surely with his public. They have the ingredients of farce alongside painful, discomfiting probes into human rationality and human relationships. *The Picnic at Sakkara* and *A Guest and His Going* explore Anglo-Egyptian relationships after the fashion of Forster's (q.v.) study of Anglo-Indian relationships in *A Passage to India*. Edgar Perry, lecturer in the Faculty of Arts at Gizeh, moves in some bewilderment among the extraordinary machinations of Muawiya Khaslat, devoted, admiring student who seeks to win his affection as an ardent disciple and becomes the Muslim Brotherhood's instrument to shoot him dead. Perry's ingenuous involvement with questions of student welfare draw him ironically into the labyrinth of political intrigue. Newby is a highly disciplined and economic writer and a master of the laconic. A teasing insight into human complexity and eccentricity is conveyed at a low emotional voltage. A low authorial profile allows of dryness and salt, but not intensity. His work does not catch fire. But plots are neatly and cunningly contrived and Newby can startle by the illuminating originality of phrase and image. Of later books *Something to Answer For* (1968) takes us back to Egypt at the time of the Suez crisis and *A Lot to Ask* (1973) presents a company director turned parliamentary candidate who has gone off his head. In *Kith* (1977) we are back up the Nile during the Second World War. *Feelings Have Changed* (1981), set in London and Egypt, sheds light on life at the BBC in the days of Louis MacNeice. [HB]

NGUGI WA THIONG'O (formerly James Ngugi) (1938-). Dramatist and novelist, born in Limuru, Kenya. He graduated in 1964 from Makerere University College, Kampala, Uganda, where he wrote his first two novels. His third novel appeared during a period of postgraduate study in Leeds. A lecturer at University College, Nairobi, from 1967, he resigned in protest when the Kenyan government closed the college in January 1969 after a student strike. Following a period abroad, he returned to Nairobi University as a lecturer, played a part in the decision to replace departments of English by departments of literature in East African universities, and later became Chairman of the Literature Department in Nairobi. Ngugi helped to found the Kamirithu Cultural and Community Centre, where *Ngaahika Ndeenda* (pubd Nairobi, 1980; English version, *I Will Marry When I Want*, 1982), a play in Gikuyu he co-authored with Ngugi wa Mirii, was successfully performed by the villagers in 1977, until unexpectedly banned by government order. Earlier that year another play, *The Trial of Dedan Kimathi*, by Ngugi and Micere Mugo, was published, as well as his fourth novel, *Petals of Blood*. On 31 December 1977 he was detained without charge under Kenya's Public Security Act. The University of Nairobi refused to reinstate him after his release in December 1978. *Detained* (1981) is his prison diary.

Ngugi's *Weep not, Child* (1964) was the first East African novel in English, and the first to deal with the Mau Mau guerrilla war of the 1950s from an African point of view. Much of the authenticity of observation and feeling derives from his adolescent experience during the 'Emergency', but *Weep not, Child* gains added importance by forming, with his subsequent novels, a cohesive view of Gikuyu history from pre-colonial times, through British colonialism, the Mau Mau rebellion and Independence, to the present of continuing poverty for the masses and affluence for the élitist minority. Though critical of missionary Christianity in Kenya, in the first two novels Ngugi applies the language of Christian inspiration to Gikuyu reactions to colonialism, but the description of social, economic and political conditions becomes markedly more secular and radical with each successive novel, and in *Petals of Blood* has a Fanonesque and Marxist enunciation.

The River Between (1965), though published after *Weep not, Child*, was written first. The story about rival villages unfolds during British penetration of Kikuyuland: first, missionaries preach the Christian Gospel, then their western-style schools undermine traditional culture, then government taxation hastens the dispossession of Gikuyu land. Waiyaki the hero, with a messianic vision of his role in Gikuyu history, fails because he believes that European education, without a comprehensive political programme, is an adequate instrument for countering European encroachment. His failure illustrates both African resolution and confusion during historical events like the female circumcision controversy of the 1920s and the Independent Schools Movement that it precipitated. Missionary incomprehension of African belief and custom allies Christianity with colonial power, while mission schools help to inspire African dissatisfaction with the condition of bondage.

The strength of *Weep not, Child* is its eloquent evocation of bewilderment and loss in another young hero, Njoroge, also imbued with messianic purpose, but frustrated by violent events during the Mau Mau war. By now the process of Gikuyu dispossession is well advanced, and Ngotho, Njoroge's father, is a mere paid labourer to the white settler, Howlands, on the lands that had been Ngotho's ancestral heritage. As in *The River Between*, Ngugi employs an unpretentious, taut, direct narrative style, but with a new, ironical, element — as in the chief antagonists' unconsciousness of how much experience, and suffering, they have in common. Nevertheless, there is authorial indulgence in Njoroge's soulfulness; he is unable, until the very end of the book, to resolve his blighted personal ambitions within the larger situation of his people's struggle.

With its orchestration of several characters' fates (rather than concentration on a single hero), with its disrupted time sequence intertwining present and past, and with its detached yet humane treatment of betrayal under great stress, *A Grain of Wheat* (1967) is a remarkable technical advance on Ngugi's first two novels. As E. Obumselu has argued, Ngugi's encounter with Conrad's *Under Western Eyes* had a catalytic effect upon his maturing as a novelist. This time the personal tragedy of Mugo (another character with messianic illusions) is satisfyingly integrated with political ideals and events; so also with the individual disillusion of other important characters. And behind the dramatization of weakness and betrayal is the suggestion that, at the very celebration of Independence, the ordinary Kenyan people who bore the brunt of the struggle for freedom are getting short measure from their political leaders. Like Conrad's Razumov, Mugo's conscience is 'washed clean' by a public confession of his betrayal of a Mau Mau leader during the war; and others learn to live with their past failures. While disturbing questions hang over the country's political dispensation, the novel ends with sober affirmation of human ability to gather up the threads of frayed lives.

Ten years elapsed before Ngugi's next novel. Meanwhile his play, *The Black Hermit*, was published in 1968; although first performed during Uganda's Independence celebrations (1962), it too hints at the African politicians' neglect of the masses. *This Time Tomorrow* (including two other plays, *The Rebels* and *The Wound in the Heart*) appeared in 1970. In *Homecoming: Essays on African and Caribbean Literature* (1972) and *Writers in Politics* (1981), Ngugi discusses literature in relation to the kinds of social reality, particularly the effects of colonialism upon the colonized, that he handles fictionally in his novels.

Petals of Blood (1977), Ngugi's most substantial and impressive work, is a culmination of earlier preoccupations. Again there is no single 'hero', but four major characters, each a misfit in Kenyan society seeking personal peace in the remote village of Ilmorog: Abdullah, former freedom fighter with the legendary Dedan Kimathi, unemployed after Independence, now keeping a scanty bar; Munira, unsuccessful son of a prosperous black Presbyterian landowner, now running the ramshackle village school; Wanja, 'good-time' city girl, now helping her grandmother to wrest a living of sorts from the parched land; Karega, expelled from school for questioning authority, reduced to selling odds and ends on Nairobi streets, now Munira's assistant. But the chief character is Ilmorog itself, its geographical location associated with legends of the heroic past but now a place of dust, destitution and disillusion. The villagers undertake an epic march to the capital to lay their troubles before the government; in the wake of the national publicity they attract, every kind of religious, political and commercial exploiter moves in to 'relieve' them. Ilmorog is 'developed' into New Ilmorog, the inhabitants deprived of their smallholdings through sharp practice by banks and other agencies of 'free enterprise', in which MPs and Ministers have a hand. Newcomers from the business world of the capital take over the town, though themselves merely 'Africanized' faces on the local boards of international companies. The rich detail with which Ngugi presents the predicament of peasants at the mercy of commercial and political cynicism gains power from the accomplished shifts in the narration, divided among the four major characters and an anonymous, representative inhabitant of Ilmorog. The novel is a massive indictment, often Marxist in language, of neo-colonialism in independent Africa, achieved on a concrete, fictional level by showing, uncompromisingly and movingly, how the already crippled lives of ordinary people are maimed and broken. Its logic spells a socialist solution with its roots in African communality.

The political logic just referred to leads to a linguistic and literary logic in Ngugi's next novel, *Devil on the Cross* (1982), for it is his own translation of his first novel in Gikuyu *Caitani Mutharabaini* (Nairobi, 1980), aimed, that is, in the first place at a popular indigenous African readership. The heroine Wariinga is a victim both of male sexism, indeed brutality, and of neo-colonialism, and the novel is her witnessing the enactment in real life of her recurrent nightmare of the crucifixion of the Devil with all his corruptions, but his being lifted down by black men who acquire 'a portion of his robes of cunning'. The discursive, explicit mode of oral tale and song is combined with satire and other literary modes, as much to anatomize the condition of the wretched of Africa as to urge them to communally corrective action.

Ngugi's writings demonstrate amply his faith in the social function of literature in Africa.   [AR]

NICHOLS, PETER (1927–). Dramatist, born in Bristol, Avon. He has worked as actor and schoolteacher. His play, *A Day in the Death of Joe Egg* (prod 1967), is something of a tour de force, exposing the stress on a husband and wife of handling a spastic daughter with damaged cerebral cortex, multiplegic, epileptic, in fact virtually a vegetable. They escape the hourly agony by freely opening the safety-valve of humour, though the 'fallacy of the sick joke' is that 'it kills the pain but leaves the situation just as it was'. A powerful play ('based on experience of our first child, who died when she was ten'), it is kept alive by Nichols's verbal agility. *The National Health* (prod 1969, pubd 1970), much less sure in its human impact, is a busily episodic presentation of hospital life in the raw – offset by a clever parenthetical send-up of the stereotyped fictional doctor–nurse romance. *Forget-Me-Not Lane* (1971), like its predecessors, employs music-hall techniques, this time in a study of family life, contrasting wartime Britain with contemporary Britain. *The Freeway* (1974) is gentle futuristic fun produced by the marooning of motorists in a massive traffic-jam. In *Chez Nous* (1974), a vital and ingenious comedy, a paediatrician's book on secondary education has been marketed by his publisher as trendy advocacy of teenage sex, and become a best-seller. The author and his family retire to their farmhouse in the Dordogne where non-theoretical permissiveness catches up with them uncomfortably if hilariously. *Privates on Parade* (1977) presents a service concert-party for the British army in Singapore in 1948. *Born in the Gardens* (1979) goes back to Nichols's home city of Bristol for a family gathering of middle-aged offspring around their newly widowed mother: the humour and the pathos have the authenticity of Nichols's first success. But *Passion Play* (1981), a sexual tangle, is awkwardly unreal, and *Poppy* (prod 1982) counterpoints earnest lecturettes on the Opium Wars against mock-up Victorian pantomime to entertaining rather than to sharply satirical effect.   [HB]

NICHOLSON, NORMAN (1914–). Poet and dramatist, born in Millom, Cumbria. He has lived there in the same terrace house ever since. He was educated at Millom Grammar School, but in 1930 tuberculosis was diagnosed and he was sent to a Hampshire sanatorium where he spent fifteen months in bed. Back in Millom in 1932, he had to husband his health and could neither proceed to a university nor do full-time work. Hence he made a career of writing, and his publications include topographical works (*Cumberland and Westmorland*, 1949, and *Portrait of the Lakes*, 1963) and biographical studies (*H.G. Wells*, 1950; *William Cowper*, 1951) as well as the critical study, *Man in Literature* (1943), editorial work like that for the Penguin *Anthology of Religious Verse* (1942) and two novels. Nicholson's stepmother had given him a Methodist upbringing, but he had been baptized into the Church of England, and it was to Anglicanism that he returned in the late 1930s after a period of alienation. George Every, of the Society of the Sacred Mission at Kelham, took an interest in his early poetry and brought about an introduction to T.S. Eliot (q.v.). Nicholson's

Christian faith interpenetrates his work as poet and playwright.

> Now that I have made my decision and felt God on
> my tongue
> It is time that I trained my tongue to speak of God.

Nicholson's rootedness in Millom has been equally crucial, but his reigionalism is not a narrowing factor. He rightly claims that his use of imagery from the immediate human and local environment enables him to see man in nature and man in society with concreteness and with clarity of focus. 'Cleator Moor', from the collection *Five Rivers* (1944), pictures the rich days of mining prosperity, then the slump, then the ironic wartime need to dig here again for the means of death. Simple quatrains are taut with energy. The surface is local and particular; the depths universal. In *Rockface* (1948) we find a similar tendency to universalize and moralize the local scene at length in 'Across the Estuary' and 'Silecroft Shore', and with fine economy and accuracy of detail in 'St Luke's Summer'. The soul, like the Cumberland park, has its 'brown October days'

> And yet while dead leaves clog the eyes
> Never-predicted poetry is sown.

The Pot Geranium (1954) brings the voices of local characters to enrich the universal themes ('They dug ten streets from that there hole' says the townsman in 'Millom Old Quarry') and in *A Local Habitation* (1972) this interest in people is further strengthened. Nicholson has learned to weave their colloquialisms into verse and find hidden meanings in their idioms. Moreover the wry ironic angle is now enriched with a warmer humour which does not lessen the profound gravities it overlays (see 'The Tune The Old Cow Died of'). In *Sea to the West* (1981) human interest is deepened by the contrast between the rapid personal changes in the local way of life and the slow movement of erosion and glaciation remoulding the natural background of water and rock. *Selected Poems 1940-1982* (1982) is characteristically modest in compass, but 'Nicholson's diction and images realize the texture and pieties of a whole way of life', as Seamus Heaney (q.v.) puts it.

Nicholson contributed *The Old Man of the Mountains* (1946) to the postwar revival of Christian verse drama. It plants the story of Elijah firmly in the Cumberland area and makes it real. The dialogue is wiry and disciplined; the action has vigour. The cast includes The Raven and The Beck who speak for God and nature respectively. *Prophesy to the Wind* (1950) projects a future post-industrial age into which one of our contemporaries is miraculously catapulted. *A Match for the Devil* (1955) goes back again to the Old Testament and presents Hosea, whose wife's adulteries epitomize Israel's infidelities to Yahweh. *Birth by Drowning* (1960) puts Elisha in a northern dale as a country GP.

Nicholson married Yvonne Gardner, a school-teacher, in 1956. In 1965 he was at long last pronounced free of all traces of tuberculosis. See his autobiography, *Wednesday Early Closing* (1975), a richly exact record of his Millom upbringing as a shopkeeper's son.   [HB]

NICOLSON, HAROLD (Sir) (1886–1968). Biographer and critic, born in Tehran, Iran, where his father was British minister, and educated at Wellington College and Balliol College, Oxford. He married the writer Victoria Sackville West in 1913. Nicolson had a successful career in the diplomatic service and was an MP from 1935 to 1945. His literary studies include *Tennyson* (1923), *Byron: the Last Journey* (1924) and *Benjamin Constant* (1949). Chosen as official biographer, he wrote *George V: His Life and Reign* (1952). Collections of essays include *Marginal Comment* (1939) and *The English Sense of Humour* (1947). *Some People* (1927, reissued 1983) was acclaimed on publication for its acumen both as autobiography and as social comment. It is a series of vignettes which weave the factual with the imaginary in portraying top people in the early decades of the century. His son Nigel Nicolson edited his *Diaries and Letters 1930-62* (three volumes, 1966-8). Since Nicolson's death these have been superseded by *Diaries and Letters 1930-64*, edited and condensed by Stanley Olson (1980).   [HB]

NICOLE, CHRISTOPHER (pseudonyms Andrew York, Peter Grange) (1930-). Novelist, born of European parentage in Georgetown, Guyana, and educated in Barbados and Guyana. After working for a bank from 1947 to 1956, he migrated to Guernsey. In 1951 he married Jean Barnett; there are four children.

With over thirty books published, Nicole is the most prolific writer from the Caribbean. The first eight novels, from *Off-White* (1959) to *White Boy* (1966), all set in the Caribbean, reveal his skill at well-turned, action-filled plots and vivid rendering of landscape and locality, his ability, as in *Shadows in the Jungle* (1961), to evoke the influence of landscape upon his characters' outlook, and his strong sense of Caribbean history, as in the 'Amyot' trilogy (1964–5). A tendency to sensationalism (e.g. *Ratoon*, 1962) foreshadows the thrillers and juvenile stories written under the York pseudonym, beginning with *The Eliminator* (1967). Since 1966 Nicole has written increasingly about situations in Europe. He describes his Peter Grange books as 'parodies of historical novels'. A. Boxill declares that Nicole's strengths are 'carefulness of craftsmanship' and 'economy of style'. He has published two histories, *West Indian Cricket* (1957) and *The West Indies* (1965).   [AR]

NORTJE, ARTHUR (1942-70). Poet, born in Oudtshoorn, South Africa, and educated in Port Elizabeth and at the apartheid University of the Western Cape. He went to Oxford (1965) and, after graduating there, chose self-imposed exile, with two years' teaching in Canada and a return to Oxford for graduate studies in 1970. He died in November 1970 of an (accidental?) overdose of drugs. During his lifetime individual poems appeared in periodicals; a substantial selection, *Dead Roots*, was published posthumously (1973). His earliest verse is much influenced by his former teacher Dennis Brutus (q.v.).

Dead Roots constitutes a cohesive unfolding of honest self-exploration (marred sometimes by self-pity over his coloured South African plight). It conveys the tragedy of exile, and of estrangement from normal human relationships, both personal and political. There is a clearly discernible, two-fold, connected development: a movement towards more flexible command of the resources of versification; and a steady drifting, analytically observed in the poetry, through self-indulgences and artificial stimulations that threaten to disintegrate the personality, towards the first hints of a resolution in poems written in Oxford during his last few months. He died a poet entering maturity.   [AR]

NOYES, ALFRED (1880–1958). Poet, born in Wolverhampton, who received gentle encouragement from Meredith and Yeats (q.v.) on the appearance of his first collection, *The Loom of Years* (1902), and from Swinburne on the publication of his more ambitious narrative poem, *Drake* (1906–8). Popular recognition was soon guaranteed by his talent for versification with a catchy rhythmic fluency and his resistance to fashionable impulses towards more demanding and sophisticated work. The easy memorability of poems like 'The Highwayman', 'Come down to Kew in lilac-time' and 'Sherwood in the twilight' won him a firm place for many years in school anthologies. Noyes became a Roman Catholic in 1927. In his autobiographical book, *Two Worlds for Memory* (1952), he tells how he spent ten years on his three-volume magnum opus, *The Torch-bearers* (1922, 1925, 1930), a study of great scientists. A visit to the Mount Wilson Observatory, California, and a suggestion by the astronomer George Ellery Hale that poetry might well concern itself with the 'fight for knowledge' bore fruit in these 10,000 lines of somewhat flaccid blank verse interspersed with lyrics. An anti-modernist, Noyes was proud to have once ordered Hugh Walpole (q.v.) (a self-invited guest) out of his house for recommending Joyce's (q.v.) *Ulysses* to his young daughter.   [HB]

O

OAKLEY, BARRY (1931–). Dramatist and novelist, born in Melbourne, Victoria, Australia, in 1931. After graduating in arts from Melbourne University he worked variously as teacher, advertising agent and with the Department of Trade and Industry before being able to write full-time. His short stories have been published widely in Australian journals. His first novel, *A Wild Ass of a Man* (1967), established his formidable ability as a witty but compassionate satirist of contemporary Australian life. *A Salute to the Great McCarthy* and *Let's Hear it for Prendergast* (both 1970) showed greater distancing of material and control of form. His caricatures of the opposite poles of Melbourne culture, Australian Rules football and academe, sometimes tended towards the dramatic set-piece in a way which hints at his talent for drama. Two plays, *The Feet of Daniel Mannix* and *Beware of Imitations*, were performed at the Melbourne alternative theatre, Pram Factory, in 1970 and 1972 respectively; *Bedfellows* (1975) confirmed his grasp of the dramatic form and gave full scope for that sense of life which informs his best comic writing. In general his humorous depiction of Australian life draws upon a deeply held belief in the writer's role in contemporary life; 'to be characteristically Australian in the worst sense is to allow ourselves to remain provincial and to be dominated by the worst of our parent cultures – British patriotism and insularity, American aggressiveness and materialism.' In his own writing he has tried to trap, and report on, the typical (but always surprising) 'homo suburbiensis, forever patrolling and mowing his front lawn'. A collection of his stories appeared in 1977 as *Walking Through Tigerland*.   [PQ]

O'BRIEN, EDNA (1932–). Irish novelist, born in Tuamgraney, County Clare, Ireland, educated at the National School, Scarriff, and the Convent of Mercy, Loughrea. After pharmaceutical training in Dublin, she worked for a short time as a pharmacist. She married the novelist and playwright Ernest Gebler in 1952, but the two have since been separated. She has two children. Her first novel, *The Country Girls* (1960), as a study of Irish childhood and upbringing, belongs to the same genre as Patrick Kavanagh's (q.v.) *Tarry Flynn* and provides a fit feminine counterpart. There are stock Irish ingredients – hard-working, long-suffering mother and thriftless, drunken father; descent from landownership to poverty; harshly puritanical convent education; bereavement, rebellion and escape – but they are vivified in the captivating portraits of Caithleen Brady and her better-off but much sillier companion, Baba (Bridget) Brennan. The details of village life are memorably recaptured, the dreams and strains of girlhood acutely realized. The naturalness of the book, its unforced directness of style and the piquant, pervasively feminine sensibility are refreshing; but whether the author has matched this achievement in her later work is doubtful. *Girl with Green Eyes* (1962) and *Girls in Their Married Bliss* (1964) tell us about the later lives of Caithleen and Baba. In *August is a*

Wicked Month (1965) the study of Ellen Sage, who has 'married above her mental means', has separated from her husband and shares the custody of their little boy, traces a firm moral pattern in which the attempt to find human comfort in free sexual companionships begins with deceptive pleasure ('In bed she opened wide. And christened him foxglove because it grew high and purple in a dark secretive glade') and escalates into sordidness. In *Casualties of Peace* (1967) Willa McCord, who has been damaged by frustrating sexual excitation at the hands of an impotent pervert, has to receive the full digital treatment by a Jamaican, Auro, to be released from lone self-torment into fulfilment. *Johnny, I Hardly Knew You* (1977) brings a welcome change of interest. It is a perceptive study of a middle-aged woman who has killed her lover and is in prison awaiting trial. The autobiographical *Mother Ireland* (1976) is a pleasing patchwork of personal reminiscence, of Irish lore, Irish portraiture and Irish nostalgia. *In Returning* (1982) is a collection of short stories, some of which first appeared in the *New Yorker*. O'Brien focuses again on the Ireland of her childhood, and her re-entry into the child's consciousness is often both penetrating and touching. [HB]

O'BRIEN, FLANN (pseudonym of Brian O'Nolan) (1911–66). Novelist. O'Nolan was born at Strabane, County Tyrone, Northern Ireland, the son of a Customs and Excise Officer and the third of a family that eventually numbered twelve. After a period in Tullamore, the family moved to Dublin in 1923, where Brian was educated at Synge Street School, Blackrock College and University College. Here he began to write in both English and Irish. 'He does not seem to have served his time as a writer but to have assumed magisterial status with a confidence which defied question', his brother Kevin has written in *Myles: Portraits of Brian O'Nolan*, ed. T. O'Keefe (1973). In the same book Niall Sheridan, companion of his university days (and represented as 'Brinsley' in *At Swim-Two-Birds*), has given a vivid account of the 'springtime' of a remarkable genius and the composition of *At Swim-Two-Birds*, a brilliantly experimental novel which was published by Longmans in 1939, then virtually forgotten until its re-publication in 1960. It is a work of surrealist character in which parodic techniques, often Joycean in scope and flavour, are exploited in a riotously comic counterpoint; for action is an interwoven fabric of 'plots' that belong to different levels of literary artifice and hilariously confuse the world of the narrator and that of his invented characters. Niall Sheridan's account of its genesis is pertinent. 'The plot, he [O'Nolan] explained, was simple: it would concern an author, Dermot Trellis, who was writing a book about certain characters who, in turn, were revenging themselves by writing about him.' But the scheme is complicated by the fact that the narrator of the whole has his own life too. Moreover, one of Trellis's characters, Finn MacCool, has his own epic tale to tell. The resultant send-up of the Fenian cycle is perhaps overdone for non-Irish readers; but in fact the published novel was cut down by a fifth from O'Nolan's manuscript at the judicious hands of Niall Sheridan., The hilarious phantasmagoria owes a good deal to Joyce (q.v.) (more especially to the 'Circe' episode in *Ulysses*), while ironic

conjuring tricks played with the novel form remind us that the book was almost contemporaneous with Beckett's *Murphy* (q.v.). Intermittent synopses as well as passages of comment and explanation occur. In one of them a novel is described as 'a self-evident sham to which the reader could regulate at will the degree of his credulity'. The right of characters to self-determination and a decent standard of living is defended. Trellis's fondness for sleep gives his characters their chance. 'Swim-Two-Birds' is the English translation of an Irish place-name that figures in Finn's tale of King Sweeny.

A year after the publication of *At Swim-Two-Birds* O'Nolan was writing to William Saroyan describing as 'finished' the next novel, *The Third Policeman*, which in fact achieved publication only posthumously in 1967. 'When you get to the end of the book you realize that my hero or main character (he's a heel and a killer) has been dead throughout the book and that all the queer ghastly things which have been happening to him are happening in a sort of hell which he earned for the killing.' O'Nolan makes the most of an after-life where macabre pantomime, unnerving symbolism and conversational exercises in ironic non-sequiturs that carry menacing overtones are fully in place. It is at once cunning fantasy and searching moral parable. *The Dalkey Archive*, published earlier (in 1964), though very different in subject and setting (around Dublin), unfortunately traverses the same ground again at some points, notably in developing comic 'business' with the man-plus-bicycle combination beloved of Beckett. An interesting feature is the reappearance in Ireland of James Joyce (his 'death' was faked), now repentant, seeking to become a Jesuit, but offered only a post in the household staff 'in charge of the maintenance and repair of the Fathers' underclothes in all the Dublin residential establishments'. It is sad that resentment against Joyce's growing fame possessed O'Nolan in his later days, for Joyce had praised *At Swim-Two-Birds*.

Under the pseudonym 'Myles na Gopaleen' O'Nolan wrote the highly popular column 'Cruiskeen Lawn' in the *Irish Times*, from which a selection has been published in *The Best of Myles* (1968). For his book in Irish, *An Béal Bocht* (1941), he used the same pseudonym. It was translated into English by P.C. Power as *The Poor Mouth* (1973). [HB]

O'BRIEN, KATE (1898–1974). Novelist, born at Limerick, Ireland, and educated at Laurel Hill Convent there and at University College, Dublin. She lived for many years in London and in Spain. She made her name with *Without My Cloak* (1931), a full-scale study of a wealthy small-town family, the Considines, Irish Forsytes, who proliferate during the years 1860 to 1877. The writing has distinction, the tapestry of Victorian life is unfolded at a leisurely pace in lilting prose, rhythmic and decorative. There is a moving study of the family beauty, Caroline: she fails to find sensual release in either her over-protective husband, Jim Lanigan, or her too sentimental would-be lover, Richard, who mistakenly 'lets desire wait on tenderness'. The predominant theme is the excessive paternal devotion of widowed Anthony Considine and its effect on his eldest son, Denis, a latterday Richard Feverel. Anthony's wife, Molly, has been killed by childbearing, the victim of marital love enjoyed in a pre-contraceptive society. In *The Last of Summer* (1943), a slighter book, Tom Kernahan is over-mothered by possessive, widowed Hannah, as Denis Considine was over-fathered. A brief family tangle in an Irish home on the eve of the outbreak of war in 1939 revitalizes an emotional dilemma of a generation back. A spiritual dimension is opened through Tom's sister, Jo, who has a religious vocation and sees emotional histories *sub specie aeternitatis*. *That Lady* (1946), set in Spain between 1576 and 1592, is 'not a historical novel' but 'an invention arising from reflection on the curious external story of Ana de Mendoza and Philip II of Spain' (Foreword). Other titles include *The Ante-room* (1934), *Mary Lavelle* (1936), *The Flower of May* (1953) and *Presentation Parlour* (1963).

[HB]

O'CASEY, SEAN (1880–1964). Irish dramatist, born into a Protestant family, and brought up in the Dublin slums by his mother, Susan. His father, a book-lover, died when Sean was 3: a little ladder he used in order to get at his bookshelves broke under him. Sean had little schooling but studied avidly. A Protestant rector (Rev. E.M. Griffin) encouraged him as a young man, but his revolutionary enthusiasms aligned him with the Gaelic League and the Irish Republican Brotherhood. Working as a labourer, increasingly influenced by Marx, he then joined the Transport Union; but eventually he moved away from the nationalistic factions. He wrote articles for journals such as *The Irish Worker* and in 1919 began offering plays to the Abbey Theatre. Lady Gregory (q.v.) accompanied rejections with encouragement ('not far from being a good play' and 'your strong point is characterization') and O'Casey persevered. *The Shadow of a Gunman* was accepted and performed at the Abbey in 1923. It is a two-act tragedy set in a Dublin tenement in May 1920. Donal Davoren, a poet, staying with Seumas Shields, is mistaken by the locals for a gunman on the run and plays up proudly. An IRA man has left a bag of Mills bombs in the house and, when the Black and Tans arrive, Minnie Powell takes the bag to her room, thinking she is helping a brave patriot – Davoren. The bombs are found. Minnie is seized, tries to get away and is shot. Not for the last time O'Casey shows Irish womanhood paying the price for masculine politicking and masculine vanity. He followed up this success with the magnificent three-act tragedy, *Juno and the Paycock**, produced at the Abbey in 1924, an altogether richer and more complex play, depicting events in a Dublin tenement during the Civil War of 1922. O'Casey was again working imaginatively on people he knew well, caught in the bitter conflicts he had lived through and speaking the idiom he loved and could touch with poetry. *The Plough and the Stars**, perhaps his finest play, followed in 1926. Dealing with the Easter Rising of 1916 and contrasting the vanity of fanatical revolutionaries with the suffering of their womenfolk, it caused riots at the Abbey. But O'Casey had now fashioned from Dublin's immediate past and still-living problems a group of plays astonishingly rich in high irony and searching tenderness, thick with shafts of humour and shafts of pain.

O'Casey came to England in 1926 and in 1927 married the young actress Eileen Reynolds who performed as Eileen Carey and who has written on Sean since his death (*Sean*, 1971). Thereafter he was physically an exile from Ireland where he had already become 'a voluntary and settled exile from every creed, from every party, and from every literary clique'. The O'Caseys eventually settled in Devon, bringing up their children there and often suffering financial hardship, for the productions of the 1930s did not match the successes of the 1920s. In more ways than one *The Silver Tassie* (1928) marked the turning-point. In Act I Harry Heegan, a strong young soldier, much liked by the girls, kicks the winning goal that gains his club a silver cup ('tassie'). In Act IV, at a party, crippled and pinned in a wheelchair, he watches his girl in the arms of another and hammers the cup till it is mangled as he is mangled himself. The intervening second act, set in France, gives an expressionist rendering of the First World War against a symbolic background of 'jagged and lacerated ruin' for which Augustus John provided the first set. Yeats (q.v.) turned the play down for the Abbey and O'Casey never forgot what he regarded as a bitter injustice. Shaw (q.v.) thought it 'a hell of a play' with 'no falling-off or loss of grip'. O'Casey pressed his expressionist experiments further in *Within the Gates* (1933) – the gates of a London park. Depersonalized figures ('The Dreamer', 'The Bishop', 'The Atheist', 'The Policewoman' etc.) play out in rhetoric an allegorical critique of contemporary England. After the heavily polemical representation of the fascist–worker conflict in *The Star Turns Red* (1940), O'Casey went back to Dublin in *Red Roses For Me* (1942), the most autobiographical of his plays. Ayamonn Breydon, the hero, is a self-portrait; Mrs Breydon is O'Casey's mother. A struggle between strikers and police (in which Ayamonn is killed) harks back to O'Casey's experience of the Great Lockout of 1913. A visionary transfiguration of drab Dublin and drab Dubliners occurs in Act III on a bridge over the Liffey.

Later plays, *Cock-a-Doodle-Dandy* (1949), *The Bishop's Bonfire* (1955) and *The Drums of Father Ned* (1960), continue the preoccupation with the condition of Ireland, but an Ireland no longer naturalistically registered. Symbol and allegory work out O'Casey's basic opposition between negation and affirmation in terms of Irish prejudice and the spirited fervour of youth. Myth and fantasy, farce and dance, all have their place. But perhaps what most surely matches up to O'Casey's dramatic triumphs of the 1920s is the six-volume autobiography: *I Knock at the Door* (1939), *Pictures in the Hallway* (1942), *Drums under the Window* (1945), *Inishfallen, Fare Thee Well* (1949), *Rose and Crown* (1952) and *Sunset and Evening Star* (1954). The record is presented in the third person and it overflows with vitality, with rollicking fun and with unsparing fidelity to the grotesque and the gruesome in the long struggle against poverty, pretentiousness and folly. After the great events of Irish history in books 3 and 4 (1906–16 and 1916–21) the last two volumes cover the period of settlement in England. For all his public provocativeness as a communist, O'Casey was a much-loved man who managed to get on famously with people like the Marchioness of Londonderry, Ramsay Macdonald, Harold Macmillan and Lady Astor: she called him 'an old Red', while Harold Macmillan coupled him with Ronald

Knox as two of 'the most saintly men' he had known. O'Casey was a prolific and often combative writer of public and private letters. David Krause is editing *The Letters of Sean O'Casey* in three volumes. See *Volume I: 1910–1941* (1975).

Juno and the Paycock, a three-act tragedy, is set in a Dublin tenement in 1922 when extreme republicans ('diehards') are fighting the supporters of the new Free State. 'Captain' Jack Boyle, work-shy and worthless, struts vainly about the Dublin bars 'like a paycock' with his crony, 'Joxer' Daly. Juno Boyle, his long-suffering wife, is steadfast, patient and practical, while her son John, who lost an arm in the Easter Rising, is unemployed and neurotic, and her daughter Mary is on strike. Mary's principles, like John's, are as costly to her mother as their father's indolence. Suddenly informed of a bequest from a cousin, 'Captain' Boyle goes on a spending spree and piles up debts. Mary is pregnant by a school-teacher who has conveniently gone abroad. The cousin's will turns out to have been legally ill phrased, and the expected fortune evaporates. Bailiffs cart the furniture away. John is executed for betraying a diehard who has been ambushed. Flamboyance and self-deception, bitterness and waste, are comically and tragically registered, while Juno's charity and fortitude shine out in contrast. Human realities of Ireland are present in powerful archetypes.

The Plough and the Stars, a four-act tragedy, crowned O'Casey's early group of plays with a masterpiece. It moves between a Dublin tenement, a public house and the street. Acts I and II take place in November 1915, Acts III and IV during the Easter Rising of 1916. The theme is the price paid, by suffering women especially, for fanatical revolution. Jack Clitheroe, a bricklayer, is made Commandant in the Irish Citizen Army, and his political fervour is shot through with vanity. His wife Nora tries to keep him at home, then to drag him from the scene of battle, and is brutally rebuffed. Clitheroe is killed, Nora's child is stillborn and she goes insane. Bessie Burgess, a wonderful, courageous and cantankerous old Protestant, is shot dead while trying to pull the demented Nora from a window. The play shows finer human feelings numbed and loving relationships shredded while men whose vanity has been inflated are hypnotized by savage patriotic rhetoric. The oratory in question incorporates passages verbatim from speeches by Padraic Pearse, the rebel leader, and there was a riot at the third performance at the Abbey Theatre; but Lady Gregory, who generously sponsored O'Casey, had no doubts. 'An overpowering play', she wrote. 'I felt at the end of it as if I should never care to look at another; all others would seem so shadowy to the mind after this.'   [HB]

O'CONNOR, FRANK (pseudonym of Michael O'Donovan) (1903–66). Irish writer who was born in Cork, Ireland, the son of an ex-bandsman in the British Army, and educated by the Christian Brothers. The contrast between the crude, drink-loving father and the fastidious, suffering mother turned him into 'the classic example of the Mother's Boy' (*An Only Child*) and he took his second Christian name and his mother's maiden name for his pseudonym. Interest in Irish nationalism grew in the traumatic aftermath of the British execution of the 1916 rebels. O'Connor went to a Dublin summer school run by the Gaelic League and gained a certificate as a teacher of Irish. He joined the Volunteers and fought with the anti-treaty forces in the Civil War. Imprisoned by Free State forces, he eventually lost his confidence in the republican hard line. Released in 1923, he met Lennox Robinson (q.v.) who encouraged him to train as a librarian. Thereafter he held library posts in Sligo, Wicklow, Cork and finally Dublin. He was among the young writers taken up by AE (George Russell (q.v.)), who published his stories in the *Irish Statesman*. Robinson introduced him to the Abbey Theatre circle. He became a director of the theatre in 1935, but in 1939 he responded to the advice of his publisher Harold Macmillan ('You've reached the stage where you must decide whether you're going to be a good writer or a good public servant. You can't be both') and resigned to turn full-time writer. He was in London during the Second World War, but his later years were spent between America and Ireland.

O'Connor's short stories were collected in two volumes, *Stories of Frank O'Connor* (1953) and *Collection Two* (1964). They show his rich versatility in this medium. In dialogue, feeling and presentation the stories are the work of a sensitive craftsman. 'O'Connor is doing for Ireland what Chekov did for Russia', Yeats (q.v.) claimed. The sheer power of the title story in the volume, *Guests of the Nation* (1931), is a case in point. It is about a Civil War execution of friendly English Tommies who are being kept as hostages by a republican battalion. *The Saint and Mary Kate* (1932), a novel, followed this first volume of short stories. O'Connor's story 'In the Train' was dramatized for the Abbey Theatre by Hugh Hunt in 1937. Hunt also collaborated with O'Connor in *The Invincibles* (1937), a play about the terrorists' assassination of the British Chief Secretary in Dublin in 1882. O'Connor excelled at verse translation from the Irish (*The Wild Bird's Nest*, 1932; *Lords and Commons*, 1938) and some fine specimens can be seen in his fascinating compendium, *A Book of Ireland* (1959). O'Connor's early days are portrayed in the autobiographical book, *An Only Child* (1961), and the period from the Truce to 1939 in its posthumous sequel, *My Father's Son* (1968). The former volume includes a moving portrait of Erskine Childers (q.v.) among reminiscences of the Civil War, and the latter vivid memories of AE, Lennox Robinson, Yeats, F.R. Higgins and other Dublin literary figures. *The Backward Look* (1967), O'Connor's survey of Irish literature, also concludes with some interesting sidelights on contemporary writers. *The Cornet-Player Who Betrayed Ireland* (1981) assembles twenty-one of O'Connor's previously uncollected stories. They evidence again his dexterity in delicately distancing himself from an exuberant presentation of Irish life. Sally Fitzgerald has edited *The Habit of Being* (1978), a collection of O'Connor's letters.   [HB]

O'DONOVAN, GERALD (1872–1942). Irish novelist, born in County Cork, Ireland. He became a parish priest in Galway, but left the priesthood, came to England, married, was for a time sub-warden of Toynbee Hall and eventually became wartime head of the Italian Section of the Department for Propaganda in Enemy Countries. Here he fell in love with one of his subordinates, the novelist Rose Macaulay (q.v.), with whom he was involved in a semi-clandestine relationship for the rest of his life. O'Donovan's first novel, *Father Ralph* (1913), became his best known. No doubt heavily autobiographical, it traces the career of an Irish boy pre-natally dedicated to the priesthood by his mother, sincerely pursuing that vocation, but gradually disillusioned by clerical corruption and hypocrisy until he is compelled to renounce his orders. The tone is sad rather than mockingly satirical. There are holy and selfless priests as well as time-servers. Ralph O'Brien's rebellion is against rigid dogmatism, ecclesiastical chicanery and clerical insensitivity to the suffering of the poor. The novel documents aspects of Irish life at the turn of the century with detailed fullness: peasant life, big house life, life in a seminary and at Maynooth. In imaginative terms it is diffuse and lacks intensity and the hero is too naïve for his inner conflict to be convincingly registered. Nevertheless the picture of small-town gerrymandering, by which political and social movements can be manipulated so as to suppress and damage those they are designed to liberate and benefit, has historical value.   [HB]

O'FAOLAIN, SEAN (1900–). Novelist and short-story writer, born in Cork, Ireland. The son of Denis Whelan, a constable in the Royal Irish Constabulary and loyal to the British Empire, he was born John Whelan. He began his studies at University College in 1918. Already he was a student of Gaelic and he served with the Irish Republican Army against the Free State forces in the Civil War of 1922. He went to Harvard on a Commonwealth Fund grant in 1926 and married Eileen Gould in Boston in 1928. He was a Lecturer in English at St Mary's College, Strawberry Hill, Middlesex, from 1929 to 1933. *Midsummer Night Madness* (1932), a volume of stories about the Troubles, with insights into IRA organization, bomb-making, guerrilla activities, the terror of the Black and Tans and the varying plights of the rich and the poor, was enthusiastically received, though O'Faolain has since reacted against the lush romanticism pervading the book. On the strength of it he returned to Ireland to write, and produced three novels of Irish life, *A Nest of Simple Folk* (1933), *Bird Alone* (1936) and *Come Back to Erin* (1940). The first, and best, of them tells the story of Leo O'Donnell, a farmer's son from Limerick, who turns Fenian and is killed in the 1916 Rising. The book portrays sixty years of Irish life with the vividness of transfigured family memories. Cornelius Crone, the hero-narrator of *Bird Alone*, is a lonely rebel against the political and religious establishments.

But it is in the later short stories that O'Faolain has most finely registered the conflicting undercurrents in Irish life. The cool simplicity of the human studies in *Teresa and Other Stories* (1947) is reminiscent of Joyce's *Dubliners*. A more satirical purpose is evident in *I Remember! I Remember!* (1961). Later collections include *The Heat of the Sun* (1966), *The Talking Trees* (1970) and *Selected Stories* (1978). O'Faolain is a short-story writer of great verve and acumen and of increasing technical flexibility. A lively capacity both to relish and to deflate flamboyant Irishness coexists with a finely exercised preference for 'secret, self-deceiving ambiguities' rather than the 'crisp certainties of the world at large'. The *Collected Stories* are now available in three volumes

(1980–2). Thus assembled, they reveal with what exhilaration and judiciousness he has exercised his virtuosity in this form. It is characteristic that the narrator of 'Persecution Mania' observes 'There are two types of Irishman I cannot stand. The first is always trying to behave the way he thinks the English behave. The second is always trying to behave the way he thinks the Irish behave.'

O'Faolain's hatred of censorship and the censorship mentality and his disillusionment with post-revolution, middle-class Ireland enlivened his editorship of *The Bell* from 1940 to 1946. He has written an autobiography, *Vive Moi* (1965), notable biographies of Daniel O'Connell (*King of the Beggars*, 1938), Hugh O'Neill (*The Great O'Neill*, 1942) and others, as well as travel books and critical works of which the most important is *The Vanishing Hero: Studies in Novelists of the Twenties* (1956).   [HB]

O'FLAHERTY, LIAM (1896–). Novelist, born on the Aran Islands off the coast of Galway, Ireland. He was educated at Rockwell College, Cashel, Blackrock College and (for one year) University College, Dublin. He had been destined for the priesthood, but he enlisted in the Irish Guards and served in France until he was wounded in 1917. After travelling abroad and earning his living as he could, he returned to Dublin in 1922, fought for the Republicans in the Civil War and in 1923 had to forsake Ireland for England, where he established himself as a writer. Most of his books were published in the 1920s and 1930s. Since that time he has lived chiefly in the USA. His first novel, *The Neighbour's Wife*, came out in 1923. When *The Black Soul* followed in 1924 AE (George Russell (q.v.)) declared, 'The Black Soul overwhelms one like a storm' (*Irish Statesman*). Three years later Yeats (q.v.) was writing to Olivia Shakespear of O'Flaherty's *The Informer* (1925) and *Mr Gilhooley* (1926), 'I think they are great novels and too full of abounding natural life to be terrible despite their subjects. They are full of the tragic farce we have invented.' They are also full of melodrama, lurid violence and sensationalism. Gypo Nolan in *The Informer* is a Dubliner of gigantic physique and small brain, a former policeman, dismissed for informing, who gets across Commandant Gallagher of the Revolutionary Organization and counter-informs so that his comrade in arms is trapped by the police and killed. The subsequent torment of Nolan, against the seedy Dublin background of doss-house, pub and brothel, and with all the paraphernalia of underground terrorism and secret midnight tribunal thrown in, is presented in extravagant yet stereotyped terms. Nolan lays about him like Desperate Dan. Gallagher is a Byronic study in sour, perverted fanaticism who utters volleys of 'almost inarticulate oaths' and rouses a 'tumultuous devouring passion' in Mary McPhillip by 'the deadly fascination of his face and of his voice'. There is too much shuddering, writhing, snarling and whining, convulsing of limbs, twitching of cheeks and grinding of teeth. Yet at the same time the book has an emotional dynamism, a rhetorical sweep and a vividness of presentation that explain why it was acclaimed as a masterpiece.

O'Flaherty continued to explore themes of violence, torment and disillusionment in subsequent novels. They include *The Assassin* (1928), *The Puritan* (1931) and

Skerrett (1932), a moving study of a struggling Aran schoolmaster. *Famine* (1937) has been praised for its more restrained, less melodramatic tone and its social authenticity. It gives a searing account of the Great Famine of 1845. Many of the short stories too are in O'Flaherty's less flamboyant, more naturalistic vein. Collections include *Spring Sowing* (1923), *The Tent* (1926), *Red Barbara* (1928) and *The Short Stories of Liam O'Flaherty* (1937). O'Flaherty had vivid memories of peasants and fishermen to draw upon. He is at his best in stories about animals, children and simple people, Frank O'Connor (q.v.) insisted (*The Backward Look*, 1967), arguing that he was a 'divided character' whose 'secondary personality blows up into outrageous, uproarious and sometimes absurd novels'. Later publications include the novel *Insurrection* (1950), *The Stories of Liam O'Flaherty* (1956) and the selection of stories *The Pedlar's Revenge* (1976). There was an early autobiography, *Shame the Devil* (1934).   [HB]

OKARA, GABRIEL I.G. (1921–). An Ijaw from the Niger Delta area of Nigeria, a poet who has also written a powerful novel, *The Voice* (1964). On leaving Government College, Umuahia, he trained as a book-binder and started writing plays and features for radio. A keen student of Ijaw oral literature, he gained wider literary training through extensive private reading. Known initially as a poet, he contributed to the first issue in 1957 of the pioneering African literary magazine *Black Orpheus*, and also to many other periodicals. During the 1960s he was an information officer in the Eastern Nigerian provincial administration and in the Civil War (1967–70) worked for the Biafran authorities. Since the war he has been in the Information Department at Port Harcourt. Poems by Okara have been included in many anthologies, and the long-awaited collection, *The Fisherman's Invocation*, was published in 1978. Okara's poetry is often elegiac in mood, melancholy sometimes, even nostalgic, especially for the innocent simplicity of childhood and its primal, instinctual life of the senses. But it is not sentimental: nostalgia not as an analgesic but as invocation to the sensuous vigour which opens man's inner quick to divine intimations. He regrets the loss of this open faculty and desires 'to unlearn all these muting things' – laughing 'with only my teeth', shaking hands 'without my heart' ('Once upon a Time'). Images of fire, the sun, the wind, waterflow, dance, song recur frequently, associated with hunger for spiritual release: 'the instinct's vital call / desire in a million cells / confined'. The imagery here is physiological but the poem continues: 'O God of the gods and me, / shall I not heed / this prayer-bell call' ('Spirit of the Wind'). Okara's poetry has a remarkably appropriate musical quality, achieved partly by skilful repetition and partly by a subtle use of participial phrases, often as in normal English usage but from time to time (especially when a 'dying fall' effect is intended) in a slightly un-English way which apparently derives from his native Ijaw. The technique produces very moving effects, as in 'The Snowflakes Sail Gently Down', in which an African in a northern winter laments deeds of dereliction being enacted in his homeland.

Such departures from Standard English make his novel, *The Voice*, one of the most memorable African novels of the 1960s, one which sets out to expand English in order to accommodate African thinking and feeling. Okara has said: 'I have endeavoured in my words to keep as close as possible to the vernacular expressions [of Ijaw]. . . . In order to capture the vivid images of African speech, I had to eschew the habit of expressing my thoughts first in English'. Not only does he employ literal translation of Ijaw words, expressions, proverbs, images but he also fits them sometimes into syntactical constructions quite deliberately intended to sound un-English. *The Voice* is a poetically conceived parable about the immediate post-Independence political situation in a fictional West African country and about the artist's commitment to his society. Okolo the hero (his name means 'voice') challenges the new political leaders by simply asking the ordinary people awkward questions about the quality of their lives. His integrity and his refusal to be bullied or bribed by the authorities lead to his death at their hands, but his words and actions have begun to undermine the position of the self-seeking rulers and there is some hope for the future. Okara's use of Ijaw-inspired syntax, idiom, even literary devices, gives his English a new edge, but also creates a gravity of tone that forces the reader into a slower pace than usual and thus involves him in precisely the same kind of questioning about personal and social values that Okolo seeks to stimulate among his people. Occasionally Okara overdoes his very unusual style but at its best it produces intensely poetic and convincing effects, as in this description of Okolo regaining consciousness painfully in a dark cell:

> When Okolo came to know himself, he was lying on a floor, on a cold, cold floor lying. He opened his eyes to see but nothing he saw, nothing he saw. For the darkness was evil darkness and the outside night was black black night. Okolo lay still in the darkness enclosed by darkness, and he his thoughts picked in his inside. Then his picked thoughts his eyes opened but his vision only met a rock-like darkness.

                    [AR]

OKIGBO, CHRISTOPHER (1932–67). Poet, son of a Roman Catholic school-teacher, born in Ojoto village, Eastern Nigeria. After attending a Catholic elementary school, he entered Umuahia Government College (1945). He graduated in classics from University College, Ibadan (1956). After working for two commercial companies, he was Private Secretary to the Nigerian Minister of Information, until he joined Fiditi Grammar School as Latin Master (1959). Assistant University Librarian at Nsukka in 1960–2, West African manager for Cambridge University Press in 1963–6, he joined the Igbo exodus to the Eastern Region after the Nigerian military coups and the massacres of Igbos in the north and west (1966). When the Civil War broke out in July 1967, he joined the Biafran forces, became a major and was killed in action between Enugu and Nsukka (August 1967). He and his wife Safinat were married in 1963 and had a daughter. He was a keen sportsman, generous and exuberant, a voracious reader and as deeply interested in music and the mythologies of different cultures as in literature. Two slim volumes of his poetry appeared during his lifetime.

Heavensgate (1962) and *Limits*. (1964); other poems were published in the journals *Transition* and *Black Orpheus*. Most of his poetry, however, appears in *Labyrinths*, which he prepared for publication, with revised versions of previously published poems and an introduction he wrote in 1965, though the book was published posthumously (1971).

Okigbo is the most eclectic of poets with echoes of phrase and rhythm from the classics, the Bible, the Catholic liturgy and many poets, including Hopkins, Pound and Eliot (q.v.). But even in his early work, where these echoes are most obvious, both as unconscious influence and as deliberate reference (as in *Heavensgate* and *Limits*), his own distinctive voice also finds utterance, chiefly in the patterning of each poem, but, increasingly, in the dependence of that patterning less on semantic than on 'musical' allusiveness, both in rhythmical effects and in the echoing of evanescent themes through the periodic, delicate repetition of phrases and images (as in 'Silences' and 'Distances'). 'Path of Thunder: Poems Prophesying War', the last group in *Labyrinths*, reveals a movement towards more social than personal themes yet retains a personal anguish, as the persona senses the preliminary rumbles of the thunderstorm that was to break over Nigeria; this movement involves a less cryptic, more conversational, use of language, though each poem remains an enactment of ritual. The eclecticism in Okigbo's poetry is put to a thoroughly individual, original end by a mind that glories in subtle correspondences among the diverse expressions of human aspirations in widely varied cultures; more accurately, a wide-ranging *cultural* eclecticism is used in a synthesizing act of imaginative creation to work out tentatively a mythological poetic that is at once very personal and much more than merely personal. A simple example of this cultural aspect of Okigbo's poetry is *'Lament of the Masks* – For W.B. Yeats: 1865–1939', written in 1964 or early 1965; it is composed in the manner of a Yoruba *oriki* or praisesong, and O.R. Dathorne observes that these lines are adapted and transformed utterly from an *oriki* in praise of a king of Ede:

> For like the dog's mouth you were never at rest,
> Who, fighting a battle in front,
> Mapped out, with dust-of-combat ahead of you,
> The next battle field at the rear –
>
> That generations unborn
> Might never taste the steel –
>
> Who converted a jungle into marble palaces
> Who watered a dry valley and weeded its banks –

Similarly, Okigbo's responsiveness to phenomena of the human mind and spirit could acknowledge no inherent contradiction between his Catholic upbringing and his reverence for the traditional Igbo religion, nor between religious worship and poetic creation. In an interview with M. Whitelaw (1965), he says:

> I am believed to be a reincarnation of my maternal grandfather, who used to be the priest of the shrine . . . where Idoto, the river goddess, is worshipped . . . that is, I should carry on his duties. . . . And in 1958, when I started taking poetry very seriously, it was as

though I had felt a sudden call to begin performing my full functions as the priest of Idoto.

Heavensgate opens with a supplication to Idoto by a penitent persona standing as a 'watchman for the watchword / at *Heavensgate*'. Of this five-part poem, Okigbo remarks ('Introduction', *Labyrinths*): '*Heavensgate* . . . originally conceived as an Easter sequence . . . later grew into a ceremony of innocence, something like a mass, an offering to Idoto; the celebrant . .'. is about to begin a journey. . . . The various sections of the poem . . . present this celebrant at various stations of his cross'. *Heavensgate* has no ordinarily 'logical' progression, but progression there is, analogous to that of musical composition, for the persona's awareness of his sensual nature contained within his spiritual quest seeks to break through the confinements of normalcy to reach definition of self and of the larger reality of which snatches of music and gleams of light are the metaphorical intimations.

In *Limits* the persona undergoes a similar experience, but now through the 'limits' imposed by a 'dream remembered', and he is now celebrant-as-poet, the first four poems mapping his growth in a quest which proves illusory, and the remaining eight concerned with the historical anguish of the community he has sprung from and his responsibility to it as poet-prophet.

The more incantatory effects of poetry are exploited in 'Silences'. Here Okigbo concentrates on the musical aspect of ritual and uses 'Crier' and 'Chorus' and talking drums instead of a single persona; the dramatized experience is again that of an intense striving to capture the elusive – of hearing strained to receive sound impulses from silence, for 'Silences are melodies / Heard in retrospect'. In 'Distances' there is a return to an individual voice lamenting its solitariness before a goddess, but personal anguish is counterpointed by awarenesses of the sufferings of others. In 'Path of Thunder' the persona and the poet merge as 'I, Okigbo, town-crier' proclaiming the times:

> The drowsy heads of the pods in barren farmlands
>   witness it
> The homesteads abandoned in this century's brush
>   fire witness it:
> The myriad eyes of deserted corn cobs in burning
>   barns witness it.

[AR]

OKOT P'BITEK (1931–82). Poet, born in Gulu, Uganda, educated there and at King's College, Budo. A schoolmaster before going to Britain in 1958, he obtained an education diploma at Bristol, a law degree at Aberystwyth and an Oxford B. Litt in 1964 on Acoli and Lang'o oral literature, an interest maintained for life. As a Makerere University College extramural lecturer he founded the annual Gulu Festival of Acoli Culture. He became Director of the Uganda Cultural Centre in 1966; after unexplained dismissal in 1968, he joined the University of Nairobi and organized cultural festivals throughout Kenya. A convinced advocate of communally performed cultural activities involving peasants, villagers and workers, he was scornful of academic study of the arts.

In 1953 Okot published an Acoli novel, *Lak Tar Miyo Wi Lobo*, about modern disruptions of traditional life in Acoliland, but his most important book was the long poem in English, *Song of Lawino* (1966), which defends native Acoli culture with verve, and robustly satirizes Africans whoring after western ways. In later poems, and in such writings as *African Religions in Western Scholarship* (1971) and *Africa's Cultural Revolution* (1973), he maintains that neo-colonialism is chiefly a form of cultural, not economic, hegemony, that the real struggle for Africans is between 'the fundamental assumptions of western civilization and the fundamental assumptions of African civilization' (*African Religions*).

Okot declared flatly that his English poetry owed nothing to western literature but had sprung from his knowledge of Acoli tradition. G.A. Heron (*The Poetry of Okot P'Bitek*, 1976) shows how Okot's 'songs' in English incorporate many techniques and conventions of Acoli oral poetry. *Song of Lawino* (a much modified translated version of a poem Okòt originally wrote in Acoli) is 'sung' by Lawino, partly individual, partly representative in characterization, to her kinsfolk about her westernized husband's contempt for her and her traditional ways. In vivid, lucid, rapidly moving verse full of images from rural life, it uses Lawino's 'naïve' outlook to describe Christian customs and western concepts satirically, e.g. segregation of the sexes in schools: 'And the young men / Sleep alone / Cold, like knives / Without handles'.

In *Song of Ocol* (1970) Lawino's husband replies. *Two Songs* (1971) contains 'Song of Prisoner' and 'Song of Malaya' (prostitute); both lament the continued plight of the African masses since independence. Okot's poetry has influenced the thinking of young people about African cultural identity, and in East Africa probably helped create the climate of thought that led to the transformation of English departments in Kenyan, Ugandan and Tanzanian universities into departments of literature.

The *Horn of My Love* (1974) consists of his translations of Acoli oral verse, and *Hare and Hornbill* (1978) of African folktales [AR]

ONDAATJE, MICHAEL (1943–). Poet, born in Colombo, Sri Lanka, and educated there and at Dulwich College, London, before going on to the University of Toronto. For four years he taught at the University of Western Ontario and in 1971 joined the English Department at Glendon College, York University, Toronto. The collection *Dainty Monsters* (1967) proved his eye and ear to be sharp for the wry or grotesque dimensions of everyday existence. It also illustrated a daunting proficiency in the handling of verse forms. In *The Man with Seven Toes* (1969) a growing interest in the surreal led to the omission of the personal lyrics to be found in the earlier volume. *The Left-Handed Poems: Collected Works of Billy the Kid* (1970) was an ambitious work which employed verse, prose and varied 'documentary' material to form a discontinuous narrative on this factual yet legendary character. The book provided ample scope for the probing, and re-creation, of that mysterious borderline between the everyday and the extraordinary

and was an important contribution to Canadian writing, not least in its imaginative grappling with an American folk-hero. *The Collected Works of Billy the Kid* was also produced on stage at Stratford, Ontario, in 1973. *Rat Jelly* (1973) extended Ondaatje's interest in the grotesque aspects of everyday existence while *Coming Through Slaughter* (1977) was a full-length prose work which re-created the life and times of Buddy Bolden, a jazz pioneer in New Orleans, in a varied format analogous to that of *The Left-Handed Poems*. Later publications include the poem *Elimination Dance* (1978) and the collection *There's a Trick with a Knife I'm Learning to Do* (1979). Ondaatje edited the short-story collection *Personal Fictions* (1977) and the Canadian selection *The Long Poem Anthology* (1979). [PQ]

ORTON, JOE (1933–67). Dramatist, born in Leicester, Leicestershire. He left school at 16, and two years later went to the Royal Academy of Dramatic Art. His first play, *Entertaining Mr Sloane* (prod 1964), was followed by *Loot* (prod 1966, pub 1967) and *Crimes of Passion* (*The Ruffian on the Stair* and *The Erpingham Camp*, prod 1967). *Loot* is a funereal farce whose slapstick with coffin and corpse tumbles from absurdity to absurdity but is redeemed from nullity by the distinctive wit ('HAL: We shared the same cradle. FAY: Was that economy or malpractice?'). Of Orton's television plays *Funeral Games* (prod 1968, pub 1970) is another corpse comedy and *The Good and Faithful Servant* (prod 1968, pub 1970) takes the mickey cleverly out of enforced jollities and cameraderies imposed by a works personnel and welfare services. *What the Butler Saw* (staged 1969) is a crazy farrago of undressing and pressing up: inspiration had plainly dried up. There is a school of thought, however, which finds Ortonesque anarchic farce, with its subversion of authority figures, language, and literary conventionalities, symptomatic of a significant 'post-modern sensibility'. See *The Complete Plays* (1976). [HB]

ORWELL, GEORGE (pseudonym of Eric Blair) (1903–50). Novelist, essayist and social polemicist, born in Bengal, India, the son of a customs official who early retired to England and sent him to the south-coast preparatory school pictured in the autobiographical title piece of *Such, Such Were the Joys* (1953). He was acutely conscious there of his relative poverty ('I had no money, I was weak, I was ugly, I was unpopular') and early evolved the notion that he was doomed to failure. ('In a world where the prime necessities were money, titled relatives, athleticism, tailor-made clothes, neatly-brushed hair, a charming smile, I was no good.') He won a scholarship to Eton and when he left there took a post in the Indian Imperial Police. He served in Burma from 1922 to 1927 and then came back to England. Rejection of the class values represented by his home and his schooling was now married to guilt at his involvement in imperial oppression ('I was not going back to be part of that evil despotism') and Orwell took the first of those extraordinary decisions which gave heroic integrity to his active career. He went to Paris to participate voluntarily in poverty and privation at its seediest. ('I wanted to submerge myself, to get right down among the oppressed, to be one of them and on their side against their tyrants', *The Road to Wigan Pier*.) The motives were no doubt complex. He was defying society's current money-values, expiating the guilt of police work, sharing working-class difficulties over employment and cancelling out his own family's ascent to a social status not worth having. And he was also getting excellent literary copy. After Paris he came back to England to gain experience of the native brand of destitution.

The first fruits of this self-identification with the world's oppressed was the autobiographical record, *Down and Out in Paris and London* (1933), in which we see him rescuing himself from starvation at the pawn-shop, tramping the streets of Paris looking for a job, washing dishes in hotel kitchens, and then coming to England to live as a tramp and sleep in doss-houses. The discomfiture provoked by devastating inequality is at times somewhat indiscriminately, even naïvely, rationalized by Orwell; but his knowledge of the poor gave him authority and he longed to make it more intimate ('At present I do not feel that I have seen more than the fringe of poverty'). However, in his next published book and first novel, *Burmese Days* (1934), he turned his fire on the evils of the imperialistic system he had seen at work seven years before as a policeman. ('In order to hate imperialism you have got to be part of it', *Wigan Pier*.) There is no sentimentalizing of the natives; rulers and subjects are alike involved in corruption and intrigue, but the gap between them indicates the failure of the system. The second novel, *A Clergyman's Daughter* (1935), is a somewhat mechanically fictionalized social document. Dorothy Hare, daughter of a clergyman who is little more than a caricature of selfish insensitivity, loses her memory under the strain of unrecognized overwork, unanswered desire for affection and fixed fear of sex. After plumbing the depths of poverty among tramps and hop-pickers, she eventually comes to rest as a teacher in a bad private school. (Orwell himself had worked in one.) At the end she returns home to take up again where she left off. Orwell emerges here as a socio-moralist in the tradition of William Godwin. The low point of Dorothy's fortunes comes when she can no longer afford to stay in Mary's, the prostitutes' doss-house, and has to spend her nights in the open. Orwell's dramatic presentation of the social outcasts in Trafalgar Square at night (it includes Mr Tallboys, an unfrocked clergyman eloquent in surrealistic blasphemies) is plainly modelled on the Nighttown episode in *Ulysses*.

There are occasional intrusions of Joycean pastiche into the next novel, *Keep the Aspidistra Flying* (1936), whose lonely hero, Gordon Comstock, is at war with his upbringing and defies the current money morality at a sacrificial cost to himself from which he is rescued only at the eleventh hour by the commonsense of the girl he loves. Orwell is brilliant at displaying the importance of money in the lives of those who lack enough. He knows at first hand that level of society where suffering, cold and hunger are daily routine, and that mentally more harassed level where financial calculations set their imprint on every personal interest and human contact. But he lacks sympathetic imaginative grasp of human personality and relationships. This is true of *Coming Up for Air* (1939), in some ways the best of his 'novels' and a lively autobiograpical record by a middle-aged insurance agent, George Bowling, who tries to come up for air by briefly forsaking the suburban treadmill and revisiting the village of his childhood. A historical running commentary on social conditions from the 1890s to the 1930s, delivered by the voice of a good-humouredly browned-off cynic, the book is packed with telling documentation – such as the account of the slow ruin of a one-man retail business run by George's father. But the characters – even George's wife – tend to enter the scene dragging their casebook social histories behind them. And Orwell's docketing of human beings by class definition, often entertaining in itself, is now so pervasive as to amount to an obsession.

Two books of a very different kind intervened between *Keep the Aspidistra Flying* and *Coming Up for Air*. Orwell accepted a commission to investigate conditions in the depressed areas for the Left Book Club and produced his severe revelations in *The Road to Wigan Pier* (1937). Immediately afterwards he went to Spain to report on the Civil War and impulsively joined a minority fighting group that was later treacherously denounced by the communists. He was wounded in the throat and returned to write *Homage to Catalonia* (1938), reporting what he had seen with such objectivity that neither Right nor Left found it palatable. It was during the Second World War that Orwell wrote his masterpiece, *Animal Farm** (1945), a scathing satirical attack on Stalinist communism, piquantly presented in the delightful idiom of an innocent animal fable for children. It was an immediate success. By this time Orwell was a well-known essayist, journalist and reviewer whose column 'As I Please' was a regular feature in *Tribune*. *The Collected Essays, Journalism and Letters* was edited in four volumes by S. Orwell and I. Angus (1968).

Orwell's never strong health failed him soon after the war. He went to the island of Jura in 1947 but was soon driven south by developing tuberculosis. *Nineteen Eighty-Four** (1949), his sour prophetic novel of submergence under totalitarianism, has a monochrome relentlessness. ('It wouldn't have been so gloomy if I hadn't been so ill.') Orwell was twice married; in 1936 to Eileen O'Shaughnessy, who died in 1945, and in 1949 to Sonia Brownell.

Animal Farm is a short satirical fable at the expense of dictatorship, more especially of the Stalinist regime that destroyed the Russian revolution. The animals at Manor Farm rebel against Farmer Jones, drive him out and rename their home 'Animal Farm'. Animalism is the new creed, with its idealistic Seven Commandments that can be summed up in the slogan, 'Four legs good, two legs bad'. The animals are betrayed by the pigs who, having the brains, corner the luxuries and keep the dumber beasts hard at work by deceptive propaganda. Comrade Napoleon ousts Snowball, his only rival, trains dogs as bodyguards, and establishes himself in comfortable supremacy, amending the revolution's commandments and slogans one by one to justify his indulgence. 'All animals are equal' is modified by adding 'but some animals are more equal than others'. Finally, when the pigs take to walking on their hind legs, the sheep are quick to stop bleating 'Four legs good, two legs bad' and substitute 'two legs *better*'. The allegory is full of shrewd and subtle shafts directed at the more cynical communist manipulations of people, events and facts, yet it is pervaded by good humour. The obvious affection for animals contributes to the book's freshness and mellowness.

Nineteen Eighty-Four is an anti-utopian novel in the mould of Huxley's *Brave New World*, and it foresees a triumph of totalitarianism so complete that individual thought is eradicated. The action is mainly in London, capital of Oceania, one of the world's three powers. Oceania is alternately at war with the other two, Eurasia and Eastasia, and is perpetually readjusting its propaganda accordingly. Dictator Big Brother rules Oceania and his portrait is plastered everywhere with the caption 'Big Brother is Watching You'. The small Inner Party keeps tabs on everyone by ubiquitous two-way telescreens from which members of the Outer Party can rarely escape observation. The masses (the 'proles') get by as best they can. At the mechanical and material level civilization is running down – but not in respect of the machinery of universal totalitarian surveillance and persecution. The Ministry of Peace keeps the current war going, the Ministry of Plenty rations things and the Ministry of Love, controlling the Thought Police, has perfected the most refined means of torturing dissidents. Winston Smith works in the Ministry of Truth, helping to subject history to continuous correction in accordance with the propaganda demands of the present. Restlessly out of key with the total denial of privacy and individuality, he deviates into the forbidden by having a love affair and keeping a diary: he is trapped and submitted to torture so ruthlessly engineered that his brain is ultimately washed clean of reason and meaning. 'He had won the victory over himself. He loved Big Brother.' A notable instrument of repression throughout is New-Speak, the approved language from which concepts dangerous to the prevailing non-thought are eliminated.
[HB]

OSBORNE, JOHN (1929–). Dramatist, born in London and educated at a 'rather cheap boarding school' which he left at the age of 16, first to work in journalism, then to enter the theatrical world with a touring company. Experience of provincial repertory stimulated him to write, and one of the early plays from this period, *Epitaph for George Dillon* (written in collaboration with Anthony Creighton), was later revised and put on in London. It was the English Stage Company that first produced Osborne's most celebrated play, *Look Back in Anger**, at the Royal Court Theatre in 1956. Historical factors in respect of changes in social mores and more specifically of changes in the theatrical climate contrived to give this play the status of a landmark and Osborne himself a symbolic importance. The play is a diagnostic projection of alienation in the figure of Jimmy Porter, a young man whose restless sense of estrangement from the postwar social framework – itself a disintegrating relic of a supposedly stabler and sunnier past – expresses itself in vengeful torture of his wife and neurotic self-laceration. The tirade is Jimmy's (and Osborne's) forte and the wayward energy of Osborne's dialogue made the hero whose emotion is dissipated in garrulity an apt vehicle for

him in representing what journalists rashly identified as the mood of a generation. The terms 'angry young man' and 'kitchen sink drama' became definitive clichés. But the habit of projecting irrational and compulsive garrulity does not encourage fastidiousness in the use of words or subtlety in the communication of meaning.

Osborne's next play, *The Entertainer*, in which Laurence Olivier played the lead, was performed by the same company at the Royal Court Theatre in 1957. It makes an interesting attempt to fuse the domestic and professional life of Archie Rice, faded variety actor, by interweaving home scenes and vaudeville turns. In questioning whether actors ever stop acting, and in showing home self and stage persona interlocked by fatal mutual contagion, it makes a point; but the incessant family backchat has the tedium of undoctored real-life converse among people who drink too much and think too little. This remains a weakness of much of Osborne's work: the drab repetitiveness of idiom has neither the ironic wit of Beckett (q.v.) nor the harmonic overtones of Pinter (q.v.). Osborne's sentimental attachment to the music hall, which Archie Rice's father, Billy, successfully dominated in its heyday, is on a par with the nostalgic backward look (in *Look Back in Anger* and elsewhere) to a 'secure' and 'stable' Edwardian world which never in fact existed. In this respect the lack of penetration or philosophic dimension makes it inappropriate to categorize Osborne's work as 'drama of ideas'.

Jimmy Porter's prototype is with us in the hero of *Epitaph for George Dillon* (prod 1957), a young, failing writer who accepts the hospitality of the suburban world he is trying to defy. Streaks of parasitical ingratiation and priggish contemptuousness foreshadow the unlovableness of Jimmy Porter. Osborne's attempt to get his own back on the men of the media in *The World of Paul Slickey* (1959), a musical, was not popular with its human targets. 'I dedicate this play to the liars and self-deceivers; to those who daily deal out treachery; to those who handle their professions as intruments of debasement' the dedication runs, but satirical thrust is dissipated in indiscriminate bad temper. In *Luther* (1961) Osborne turned to episodic historical chronicle under Brechtian influence, but it is a fragmented piece of work in which naïvely simplistic excursions into Freudian psychoanalysis serve little purpose other than to suggest that Luther's constipation helped to cause the Reformation. Osborne gives us a Luther whose shift from obedient monastic self-dedication to Protestant rebellion is neither set in an intelligible context of historic fact and change nor given the status of a spiritual pilgrimage with a driving logic of its own. There is neither external authenticity nor internal conviction.

Inadmissible Evidence (prod 1964) manages to harness Osborne's strength as a one-character-projectionist by presenting a leading character, Bill Maitland, who is on the stage throughout and does most of the talking. Maitland is a dishonest solicitor, inwardly on trial, estranged and isolated ultimately to the point of total breakdown. If the hero of *Luther* was Jimmy Porter draped in a monkish habit and afflicted with haemorrhoids, Pamela, the loquacious, failing actress of *Time Present* (1968), is Jimmy Porter after a semi-successful sex-change operation. There is superficial chatty trendiness about youthful naughtinesses with drugs and older naughtinesses in promiscuity which, like the liberated chaps' jokes about sanitary towels in *The Hotel in Amsterdam* (1968), perhaps help to identify the streak of immaturity that prevented Osborne from canalizing his verbal fluency either in morally anchored satire or in cheerfully amoral farce. *West of Suez* (1971) is a study of the middle-class daughters of a famous writer and their respective menfolk, who are emptily and meaninglessly at leisure on a Caribbean island. Dominant Frederica is at loggerheads with herself in the Porter tradition and baits her husband as Jimmy baits his wife; but the overall drift of the play confirms the presence in Osborne of a critical perspective and a satirical impulse that deserved to be disentangled from implicit relish of attitudes they discredit. Perhaps he is a Puritan moralist manqué. However that may be, the invention of the twentieth-century Comedy of Bad Manners and the itching hero who is everyman out of humour remains notable. *A Better Class of Person* (1981) is the first instalment of an autobiography.

Look Back in Anger. Jimmy Porter and his wife Alison share a flat in a Midlands town with Cliff Lewis, a like-able young man who finds himself the buffer between husband and wife. Jimmy, for all his university education, has elected to run a sweet-stall. He has struck another blow at convention by marrying the daughter of a respectable retired colonel and subjecting her to his way of life. He is alienated not only by the social and educational upheaval of his postwar generation but also by a deep seated personal fixation from the early death of his father which he watched as a child. Looking back on a dimly sensed one-time public and private 'security', he vents the anger of the uprooted and estranged in fluent vituperation, goading his wife as the representative of her class and tormenting himself in the process. Frustration and rebelliousness result in soap-box neurosis and virulent verbal diarrhoea. The action involves Alison's temporary departure from home (she is pregnant and the strain is telling) during which her friend Helena acts as substitute bed-mate. Osborne makes Alison and her father likeable characters, and the relationship between husband and wife has its tenderness sustained in intermittent reversion to an escapist childish fantasy in which they romp fondly together, playing squirrels and bears.   [HB]

OWEN, WILFRED (1893–1918). Poet, born in Oswestry, Shropshire, and educated at the Birkenhead Institute, Liverpool, and at University College, Reading. His mother, a devout Anglican, described him as a 'very thoughtful, imaginative child – not very robust', and he early found poetry fascinating. Keats became a decisive literary influence. A tutor at Bordeaux when the First World War broke out, he came home and enlisted in the Artists' Rifles in 1915, and in January 1917 he was sent out to the Somme front with the 2nd Battalion Manchester Regiment. He was soon recording the horrors in letters home – 'everything unnatural, broken, blasted; the distortion of the dead whose unburiable bodies sit outside the dug-outs all day, all night'. After shattering experiences in attack he was invalided home. In one of the letters sent from hospital in France he voiced disquiet of conscience

over the resort to arms by a supposedly Christian nation. Back home he was first at Netley Hospital, then at Craig-lockhart War Hospital, near Edinburgh, where Siegfried Sassoon (q.v.) was also a patient. 'One morning', Sassoon wrote, 'there was a gentle knock on the door of my room and a young officer entered. Short, dark-haired, and shyly hesitant' (*Siegfried's Journey*). The conversations of the two poets at Craiglockhart and their subsequent correspondence gave direction and inspiration to Owen. 'You have fixed my Life – however short', Owen wrote to Sassoon. Indeed Sassoon's positive criticisms seem to have helped Owen to correct a tendency to lush over-writing, and the older poet was generously appreciative as evidence of Owen's full gifts came to light. 'When contrasting the two of us', he wrote later, 'I find that – highly strung and emotional though he was – his whole personality was far more compact and coherent than mine.' (*Siegfried's Journey*.) Owen went back to France in August 1918, his nerves recovered. He was awarded the MC, but was killed a week before the Armistice while leading his men in an attempt to cross a canal.

Only four poems by Owen were published during his lifetime, one in the Craiglockhart magazine, *The Hydra*, in 1917 and three in *The Nation* in 1918. The great poems belong to the last twelve months or so in France and they were issued in 1920 with an introduction by Sassoon. Nevertheless Owen was sufficiently aware of the approval of important contemporaries to be writing confidently to his mother at the turn of the year (1917–18), 'I am held peer by the Georgians; I am a poet's poet. I am started.' He was right, for Edmund Blunden (q.v.) eventually described him as 'apart from Mr Sassoon, the greatest of the English war poets'. Owen put the soldier's suffering on paper with desolating verbal accuracy:

> Our brains ache, in the merciless iced east winds
>   that knive us . . .
> Wearied we keep awake because the night is
>   silent . . .
> Low, drooping flares confuse our memory of the
>   salient . . .
> Worried by silence, sentries whisper, curious,
>   nervous,
>   But nothing happens.
>
>   ('Exposure')

The use of half-rhyme (knive us/nervous, silent/salient) is peculiarly effective in dislocating the reader's responses with an upsetting sense of things strangely askew. 'Greater Love' ('Red lips are not so red / As the stained stones kissed by the English dead') probes disquietingly the contrast between sexual love and the searing physical surrender of the soldier in battle. 'Dulce et decorum est' is sickeningly vivid in portraying the squalor of death by gas as a commentary on the 'old lie' about the glory of dying for one's country. With the same steady ruthlessness Owen pictures the sordid case of a soldier who shoots himself ('The Dead-Beat') and the grotesquely hideous victims of shell-shock ('Mental Cases'), while 'Disabled' defines the fate of the former popular footballer and now returned legless hero from whom women avert their eyes. It clearly foreshadows O'Casey's *The Silver Tassie*. 'Anthem for Doomed Youth' ironically notes the funeral ceremonies that war provides for its dying: not bells, prayers or candles, but 'the monstrous anger of the guns' and the 'stuttering rifles' rapid rattle'. 'Strange Meeting', perhaps Owen's finest poem, pictures a soldier after death meeting with the enemy he has killed.

In the Preface he sketched for publication Owen wrote, 'Above all I am not concerned with Poetry. My subject is War, and the pity of War. The Poetry is in the pity.' Thus his compact verses spell out the suffering of the soldier and the brutality of the massacre with telling metaphors and uncanny rhythmic and assonantal effects that underline the unease. Yeats (q.v.) caused a fuss when he omitted Owen from *The Oxford Book of Modern Verse* (1936), but he defended his decision in a letter to Dorothy Wellesley ('He is all blood, dirt & sucked sugar stick'). See the *Collected Poems*, ed. C. Day Lewis (q.v.) (1963), and the *Letters*, ed. H. Owen and J. Bell (1967). See also H. Owen, *Journey from Obscurity: Wilfred Owen 1893-1918*, three volumes (1963-5). [HB]

PALMER, VANCE (1885–1959). Novelist and critic, born at Bundaberg, Queensland, Australia. After doing clerical and journalistic work locally he moved to London as a freelance writer but later worked as a tutor and book-keeper for Queensland landowners. He then returned to London and subsequently travelled in North and South America. He married in 1914; his wife, Nettie, wrote *Modern Australian Literature* (1924) and *Henry Handel Richardson* (1950). He was influential in literary, critical and dramatic circles from his novel *The Passage* (1930), a romantic story set in a Queensland fishing community, through to his important cultural study *The Legend of the Nineties* (1954), which sought to define the special importance of that period in Australian national life between the 1854 Eureka gold-diggers' rebellion and the Anzac Gallipoli landings of 1915. It held that 'the literary pioneers of the nineties' established 'a tradition of democratic writing' which distinguished Australian literature 'from most English writing where the style aimed at is a literary one and the point of view is fixed in a secure middle class'. This thesis touched a responsive chord and is still the subject of critical debate in Australia. Always a promoter of Australian literature, his own works employed a flat, documentary approach which succeeds best in the late trilogy *Golconda* (1948), *Seedtime* (1957) and *The Big Fellow* (1960), all set in Queensland.　　　　　　　　　　　　　　　　　[PQ]

PARTHASARATHY, R. (1934–). Poet, born at Tirupparaiturai, South India. A Bombay graduate, he obtained a linguistics diploma at Leeds University in 1964. After ten years' lecturing, he joined the Oxford University Press, and is an editor in its Madras office. From 1964, in journals and anthologies, a small number of meticulously wrought poems, with vivid, often startling visual imagery, gained him a considerable reputation and the *Poetry India* Ulka Prize (1966). Some vigorous articles on the validity of Indians writing poetry in English enhanced his reputation. *Rough Passage* (1977), his long-awaited first volume, was a disappointment to his admirers, because many of its thirty-seven poems (each forming 'part of a single poem') are second, or even third, revisions, and arguably not always improvements, of previously published versions. They are arranged in three sections: 'Exile' deals with alienation from both European and Indian city life; 'Trial' with unsatisfying erotic and poetic experience ('my throat reeks of the sweat / of words: their unmentionable / odour sustains me'); 'Homecoming' with an uneasy return to his Tamil heritage and a stoical contentment 'with the small change of uncertainties' – an acceptance of, in G.N. Devi's words, 'the tremendous "hollow" at the centre of his existence'.　　　　　　　　　　　　　　　　　[AR]

PATON, ALAN STEWART (1903–). Novelist, biographer, teacher, liberal politician, born and educated in Pietermaritzburg, Natal, South Africa. In 1928 he married Doris Francis (two children) and after her death Anne Hopkins (1969). After teaching for ten years, he was Principal of Diepkloof Reformatory, Johannesburg, from 1935 to 1948, where he gained much insight into black African experience of South Africa's racist laws. After his first novel, *Cry, the Beloved Country*, was published (1948), he devoted himself to writing and liberal politics, becoming founder and President of the Liberal Party in 1958, until its disbandment in 1968. His second novel, *Too Late the Phalarope*, had appeared in 1953, followed by *Debbie Go Home: Stories* (1961, as *Tales from a Troubled Land*, USA, 1965), *Knocking on the Door: Shorter Writings* (1975), various political and sociological studies (e.g. *Hope for South Africa*, 1958), two books of Christian meditation and two substantial political biographies: *Hofmeyr* (1964) and *Apartheid and the Archbishop: The Life and Times of Geoffrey Clayton* (1973). Paton has received numerous international awards, including the United States Freedom Award (1960), and honorary degrees.

The critical response to *Cry, the Beloved Country* has cooled since 1948, but the book remains historically important; both it and the film version helped release the first ripples of world-wide indignation against South Africa's racial system. Lyrical in conception, with carefully placed passages of poetic prose singing the natural glories and lamenting the human miseries of land and people, it is nevertheless a powerful indictment of arrogant and unjust government. The story of a simple rural African priest's personal sufferings through the effects of urban corruptions on members of his family is one of human endurance triumphing over bitter griefs, told with great compassion made eloquent by literal translations of Zulu idiom in the dialogue. Indeed, the novel is primarily aimed at opening white South African hearts to understanding and Christian charity, and thus, hopefully, at changing society. Politically, therefore, it can be judged naïve, with the author's undisguised antagonism to urban African political movements and the final symbol of a white man shaking hands with a black too flimsy to contain all the political realities that still prevent a just South African settlement. Yet these considerations cannot detract from Paton's highly intelligent analysis of white attitudes, or from the vivid realism with which the black slums near Johannesburg are described.

Too Late the Phalarope shows such a great advance in novel technique that Paton's decision to engage actively in public life rather than write more novels, though worthy of respect, cannot but be regretted. Set within an Afrikaner community, the theme is less the obvious race motif than the tragic inability of human beings in intimate relationships with one another to achieve and articulate understanding. It emerges chiefly in the confused relations between a father who keeps his emotions under iron control, and his son whose natural spontaneity is thereby driven underground (the title refers to the son's abortive attempt to mend the breach with the gift of a book on birds). Moreover, the son's love for his wife is blighted by her inability to respond to his sexuality. He cannot resolve the tension between his public personality (the very embodiment of manly Afrikaner virtues) and his sensuous emotional nature. Against his very nurture he finds unsatisfactory sexual solace with an African woman, is sentenced under the Immorality Act and brings his family to shame. The narrator is the hero's maiden aunt, who views his destruction compassionately though within the context of Afrikaner attitudes to inter-racial sex. Without condoning this mentality, Paton gives a profoundly sympathetic reading of the Afrikaner predicament. *Too Late the Phalarope* is about the twisting of human nature by an implacable self-destructive will-power and can indeed be read as a commentary upon what the collective Afrikaner consciousness has done to its own potentially generous humanity through unmalleable attitudes and policies.

In Paton's late seventies has come a new burst of creative energy. *Towards the Mountain* (1981) is the first, tautly written, wise and very honest instalment of his autobiography. *Ah, But Your Land Is Beautiful* (1981) is the first of a projected trilogy of novels. By means of a not entirely bonded mix of fiction, documentary and historical reporting, and personal authorial meditation, Paton tries to recapture the very feel of living in South Africa during the first decade of Afrikaner nationalism rampant and its policy of apartheid. Tha main characters, who do not always speak with the same vivacity and authenticity of accent as some of the minor figures, are white, black and Indian liberals, and the impression cannot be evaded that Paton is here placing on record his tribute to the political activities of the Liberal Party, which he led until its disbandment.   [AR]

PATTEN, BRIAN (1946–). Poet, born in Liverpool, Merseyside, and educated at Sefton Park Secondary School. He left school at 14 and worked briefly for a local newspaper. He had an early success with *Little Johnny's Confession* (1967), a collection of lyrical poems, best when read aloud, and straight from the adolescent world of pop, all-night parties, urban squalor and sleeping around. 'When in public poetry should take off its clothes and wave to the nearest person in sight; It should be seen in the company of thieves and lovers rather than of journalists and publishers', begins 'Prose Poem towards a Definition of Itself'. Patten found himself in demand for public poetry reading. In *Notes to the Hurrying Man, Winter '66 – Summer '68* (1969) a harsher critical note is heard. For instance in the brief 'Projectionist's Nightmare' a bird finds its way into the cinema and smashes itself by flying into the screen depicting 'a garden / a sunset and two people being nice to each other'. At the sight of real blood and intestines the audience screams, 'This is not what we came to see'. Later volumes include *The Irrelevant Song* (1971), *The Unreliable Nightingale* (1973) and *Grave Gossip* (1979).   [HB]

PATTERSON, ORLANDO (1940–). Sociologist and novelist, born in Jamaica, where he went to school and university in Kingston. He obtained a PhD at the London School of Economics in 1965, lectured there and in Jamaica and in 1971 became a Professor of Sociology at

Harvard. He wrote *The Sociology of Slavery* (1967), an important study of negro slave society in Jamaica.

Patterson received the Fiction Prize of the Dakar Festival of Negro Arts (1966). His first novel, *The Children of Sisyphus* (1964), vividly describes Kingston's garbage-dump slums and the self-defeat of its inhabitants (like the prostitute Dinah whose attempted break-away fails), with the Rastafarian cult as an opiate for despair. *An Absence of Ruins* (1967) develops this Camus-like, existential theme; the character Blackman says of himself, and by implication of his neo-colonial society: 'I must keep up the appearance of going in order to forget that I am not'. *Die the Long Day* (1972) realistically reconstructs a Jamaican slave estate and its brutalities, showing the masters as themselves enslaved by their system, but the story asserts the courage of body and mind that should make the slaves heroical, not shameful, to their twentieth-century descendants. [AR]

PAULIN, TOM (1949–). Poet, born in Leeds but brought up in Belfast, and educated there and at the universities of Hull and Oxford. His volumes of verse, *A State of Justice* (1977) and *The Strange Museum* (1980), placed him firmly among the Northern Ireland poets who came to prominence in the 1970s, such as Seamus Heaney (q.v.) and Paul Muldoon (q.v.). His poems (for instance, 'Before History' and 'Surveillances') often presuppose awareness of the current Irish troubles. Paulin's flatness and sobriety of utterance achieves a disturbing ironic force in the light of that awareness. The intensity of the reader's response derives, not from the text in itself alone, but from the discrepancy between its undemonstrative tone and the horrific reality:

And the sky is a dry purple, and men
Are talking politics in a back room.

('In the Lost Province')

[HB]

PEAKE, MERVYN (1911–68). Artist and novelist, born in China, the son of a medical missionary. He received his early education at Tientsin Grammar School. His parents brought him back to England when he was 11 (travelling via the trans-Siberian railway) and he was sent to Eltham College, Kent, and later to Royal Academy Schools. He first made his living by teaching at schools of art and by freelance work as pictorial artist. He married Maeve Gilmore, also an artist, in 1937. He had his first exhibition of drawings in 1938 and soon after began his career as a book illustrator. War service in the ranks strained him to the point of breakdown and he was invalided out of the army to work as war artist. Meanwhile he had started the celebrated *Gormenghast Trilogy**, working on the first novel, *Titus Groan*, while in the army. He published a children's story, *Captain Slaughterboard Drops Anchor*, in 1945 and a wry fantasy of polar exploration, *Letters from a Lost Uncle*, in 1948. Between these *Titus Groan* (1946) burst upon the literary world with the kind of succès d'estime that makes a man's name but does little for his pocket. The adjective 'Gothic' was soon being used in an inadequate attempt to define a vein of fantasy in which a grotesque world is created – vast in scale, intricate in detail, larger than life in characterization and essentially unfettered by canons of naturalistic plausibility. The intermingling of horror and comedy is skilful and often subtle. The setting is a castle so stupendous in size and labyrinthine in structure that the ruling lord's spinster twin sisters can perish of brutal incarceration by a kitchen boy turned rebel in a remote and forgotten chamber. The beings who inhabit the world of *Titus Groan* and its successor, *Gormenghast* (1950), have names like Steerpike, Fuchsia, Prunesquallor, Swelter, Sourdust and Barquentine. Figures of inspired caricature, whose faces are surveyed topographically like terrains, move in rhetorical grandeur against a background of prodigious panoramic scenery. Over all broods the stony spirit of the castle itself whose ceaseless ritual is a massive symbol of irresistible yet moribund tradition. In *Titus Alone* (1959), the last volume, Gormenghast is forsaken for a nightmare world of mingled modernity and absurdity, seductiveness and violence, to which the young heir, Titus, escapes and where his ineradicable attachment to the lost domain raises doubts about his sanity. A fourth volume was projected but never started. In his Introduction to *Drawings by Mervyn Peake* (1949) (a collection that includes heart-rending drawings made in Belsen shortly after the Allied armies moved in) Peake summed up the artistic aim that produced Gormenghast aptly: 'For it is one's ambition to create one's *own* world in a style germane to its substance, and to people it with its native forms and denizens that never were before, yet have their roots in one's experience'. Belsen was part of that experience.

Peake's other notable novel, *Mr Pye* (1953), was a product of his knowledge of Sark, where he lived for some years before marriage and again after the war for a time with his family (there were two sons and a daughter). It is a fable-like novel in which Mr Pye descends upon Sark full of evangelical zeal to convert the islanders to unselfishness and love in devoted friendship with the 'Great Pal' above. He achieves much, but doubts disturb him when he begins to grow wings. Driven to the only logical expedient, he tries to be wicked and with such success that the wings shrink and horns grow on his forehead instead. How he is delivered from the 'ding-dong battle between the warring forces of horn and feather' is divertingly told. The island whore, Tintagieu, 'five-foot-three-inches of sex', is a hilariously entertaining study.

The prolific creative energy Peake poured into pictorial and literary channels gives him a status comparable to that of Wyndham Lewis. The nervous cost – the drain on imaginative and emotional resources – can be gauged from the moving memoir written after his death by his widow, *A World Away* (1970), an intensely personal projection of a career that burnt itself out with tragic thoroughness. Peake's last preoccupations as a writer centred frustratingly on an unsuccessful attempt to turn playwright with *The Wit to Woo* (1957). A trembling of the hand was the first sign of a collapse which was diagnosed as 'premature senility' when he was only 46. 'I have played too much around the edge of madness', he wrote to his wife, and he withdrew mentally from all contact with humanity while he still had twelve years to live. See also Maeve Gilmore and Shelagh Johnson, eds, *Mervyn Peake: Writings and Drawings* (1974), and Maeve Gilmore, ed., *Peake's Progress* (1978).

The Gormenghast Trilogy of novels comprises *Titus Groan*, *Gormenghast* and *Titus Alone*. The setting of the first two is the castle of Gormenghast, an immense and fantastic structure whose inhabitants live a life dominated by ancient ritual. Gothic halls and turrets, corridors and underground passages, are mapped out in a fabric vast enough to allow for peril and conflict in virtually 'unexplored' recesses. Lord Sepulchrave, 76th Earl of Groan, a victim of chronic melancholia, is ultimately destined for insanity, in which he thinks himself an owl and is eaten by owls. The Countess lives amid a swarm of white cats and birds: there is a nest in her hair. Rottcodd, Keeper of the Hall of Bright Carvings, Swelter the cook and Sourdust the Master of Ritual are grotesque caricatures yet, like the warmer and subtler human studies (such as Dr Prunesquallor and the Countess's daughter, Fuchsia), they have substance and impact both momentous and disturbing. Titus, the young heir to a birthright of pre-formulated ceremonial, is soon 'restless for a world without Walls'. But rebellion of a more sinister kind infects the Gormenghast community with corrosive unease when the kitchen boy Steerpike, a cunning, ambitious radical, by subterfuge and villainy picks off enemies and rises to power. He arranges the burning of the Earl's library and is on the spot to act the brave rescuer in the nick of time. He deludes the Earl's dim-witted twin sisters, involves them in crime (they set fire to the library), blackmails them and murders them by incarceration. Disaster and horror have seeped through the life of Gormenghast on a sickening scale by the time Steerpike is unmasked. A climactic hunt for him coincides with a vast deluge that leaves the whole castle flooded up to its third storey. It is Titus who finally slays Steerpike, and then leaves Gormenghast, determined to escape the weight of its dead traditions. This is where the second book ends.

Titus Alone, the third book, is markedly different – economic in style and taut in structure – and the sequences are alive with a half-formulated satiric groundswell, for the world to which Titus escapes has nightmare resemblances to our own. A great, symbolic factory 'at the gate of hell' from whose windows hundreds of identical faces stare out blankly, hints at a tyranny more sinister than that of Gormenghast. An Under-River hide-out for refugees and outcasts is a sombre, desolate 'crepuscular region'. Surface consequentiality evaporates while persons and places loom before us with teasing illogical exactitude. The concluding attempt to send Titus mad tries him savagely, for a vast charade is prepared in the form of a crude mock-up of the lost Gormenghast that his deliriums have described in detail. [HB]

PETERS, LENRIE (1932–). Poet, born in Bathurst, Gambia, and at school there and in Freetown, Sierra Leone. He studied in Cambridge and London, graduating as MB, B Chir. in 1959. A Fellow of the Royal College of Surgeons, he has worked in British hospitals. In addition to a novel, *The Second Round* (1965), about the disintegration of a sophisticated African personality, Peters has published four verse collections: *Poems* (Ibadan, 1964), *Satellites* (1967, including most of the former), *Katchikali* (1971) and *Selected Poems* (1981). They contain many sensitively wrought poems showing a highly intelligent mind at work upon the physical and spiritual precariousness of modern life, and the circumscribed possibilities for fulfilment. Though individual poems seem almost cynical, despairing, disillusioned, his work as a whole achieves a sober equilibrium and muted hopefulness, 'for autumn is wonder and wonder is hope'. His cherishing of individuality is balanced by concern for the sufferings of others, in Africa and elsewhere; his intellectual naturalization in Europe by a controlled nostalgia for his African childhood. Images from the operating theatre enhance the delicate precision of his searching for composure amidst his intensely sensuous responses to experience, as he seeks to 'focus through words'. [AR]

PINTER, HAROLD (1930–). Dramatist, born at Hackney, East London. His father, Hyman Pinter, was a ladies' tailor, and the family were Jews of Hungarian or possibly Iberian extraction. Pinter's East End childhood gave him the idiom and imagery of decayed working-class environments so crucial to his work, but he experienced periods of evacuation to Cornwall during the Second World War. From Hackney Downs Grammer School, where the English master, Joseph Brearley, particularly inspired him ('He's a brilliant man', Pinter said), he went in 1948 to the Royal Academy of Dramatic Art, but stayed for only two terms. He objected to National Service, was not exempted, but persisted and was fined. He published two poems in *Poetry London No. 19* in 1950 and has continued to write poetry. (See *Poems*, selected by Alan Clodd, 1968.) Pinter sought work as an actor, trained further at the Central School of Speech and Drama, in 1951–2 toured Ireland with a Shakespearian company (see the brief autobiographical sketch, *Mac*, 1968), and in 1953 joined Donald Wolfit's season at the King's Theatre, Hammersmith. Here he first met the actress Vivien Merchant whom he married in 1956 (and from whom he was divorced in 1976). By this time he was touring the provinces in repertory and soon began to write plays.

The one-act play *The Room* was presented at the Hampstead Theatre Club in January 1960 and at the Royal Court Theatre two months later. Here, and in the companion one-acter *The Dumb Waiter*, the dialogue makes it evident that Pinter has mastered a new conversational tonality in which phrases and rhythms of day-to-day talk are reproduced with uncanny fidelity, yet so planted that their ordinariness, their reiteration and their inconsequentiality carry overtones of menace and mystery. The Pinter recipe is established from the start. Casts are small. Action is minimal. Plots scarcely exist except in so far as they can be constructed by guesswork on the part of an attentive audience – and even so they remain hypothetical: there is no confirmation. 'The desire for verification is understandable, but cannot always be satisfied', Pinter himself has said. People are not always honest, not always capable of accurate revelation. 'The more acute the experience the less articulate its expression.' What Pinter does achieve is the implicit universalization of his characters' situations on a scale that invites critics to talk in terms of mythic correspondences, ritual patterns and psychological archetypes. Thus, in *The Room*, the drab dialogue between Rose Hudd, her lorry-driver husband (who scarcely utters) and callers at their flat displays humanity desperately maintaining the routines of meagre 'security' against impending threats from the outside. The disturbing, the unexpected, the terror round the corner or under the floor is infinitely worse than 'living and partly living' – the repetitiveness of tedium accepted and embraced. In Pinter the intruder (like the blind black man in *The Room*) often embodies the threat most forcibly. And the danger of being supplanted, domestically or sexually, has its social and racial implications.

Pinter's first three-act play, *The Birthday Party**, exploits the theme of intrusion and menace, saucing it with acrid comedy. Two hearty guests descend upon a boarding house to persecute and ultimately remove a lone lodger. The audience can only guess what volume of terror and brutality underlies the iceberg tip of oppression teasingly floating through the drab establishment, but the potent verbal exchanges create a claustrophobic atmosphere resounding with sinister ambiguities. The first London performance in 1958 was received with almost total critical hostility. Harold Hobson alone recognized its quality in *The Sunday Times*. ('Mr Pinter, on the evidence of this work, possesses the most original, disturbing and arresting talent in theatrical London.') *The Caretaker** (1960) was more successful, in spite of its all-male cast of three and its obsession with a Beckettian level of human inadequacy and failure to communicate. Pinter's reputation was now established. In the one-acters, *The Collection* (prod 1961) and *The Lover* (prod 1963), both written originally for television and then transferred to the London stage, the focus shifts to middle-class life and to sexual fantasies which may offer, individually or in partnership, a seeming escape from boredom. Domestic and sexual usurpation are themes variedly treated in three plays written for television, *Night School* (prod 1960), *Tea Party* (1965) and *The Basement* (1967). *Tea Party*, the most substantial of the three, traces the gradual deterioration of Disson, boss of a sanitary ware firm. In marrying he acquires a wife who, with her brother, takes over his home, his firm, his secretary, himself, and he finishes up blind and deaf, struck down by a seizure. It is not of course clear what part conscious intention plays in the human takeover. The characteristic Pinteresque cloud of unknowing hangs over such questions. In *The Basement* a triangular struggle for place and partner is presented in vivid economic sequences. Here the focus is narrow and the contestants are two men to one woman. The later, fuller triangular struggle of *Old Times* (1971), a two-act play, involves two women to one man.

But before *Old Times* Pinter dealt with the intrusion theme in a two-acter, *The Homecoming* (1965), in which a son who has made good in America as a professor returns unexpectedly to his north London home. The reaction of father and brothers to Teddy's return is complicated by the fact that he brings with him the wife he secretly married on the eve of emigration and who falls back to her earlier habits. She is apparently ready to accept the status of a common household sexual property and a sexual money-earner too. Questions of plausibility cluster around her emergence as the archetypal all-purpose tart, but Pinter's practice as a whole is to forsake that kind of dramatic irony in which the audience's omniscience

collides with the characters' ignorance for the kind in which characters apparently know – or perhaps only suspect – what audiences can but dimly guess at.

James Joyce (q.v.) has been a significant influence on Pinter at the stylistic level (for instance in the comically incongruous verbal choreography) just as T.S. Eliot (q.v.) has been on Pinter's rhythmic liturgy of terse backchat. The influence of Joyce's *Ulysses* is evident in *Old Times* where the past is recaptured, with fantasy thrown in, and realized afresh alongside the present in controlled Joycean juxtaposition. Pinter's wise assimilation of Joyce and Eliot puts him in the mainstream of English literature.

Of later plays the production of *No Man's Land* in 1975 was notable for the brilliant double-act of Sir John Gielgud and Sir Ralph Richardson in an encounter between two ageing, contrasting former acquaintances, rich and poor respectively, with enough veiled rivalry between them to salt their confrontation with serio-comic discomfiture. *Betrayal* (1978) is an ingenious play, sharp in focus and characteristically teasing in impact. It has three characters and a waiter. Jerry has had a clandestine (as he thinks) affair with Emma, the wife of his best friend, Robert, for several years after their marriage in 1968, at which he was best man. Robert becomes aware of the betrayal in 1973 but says nothing and continues to treat Jerry as his friend. The affair is terminated in 1975. Jerry does not learn that Robert has been aware of the betrayal until two years later, in 1977. These are the bare bones of the action. The disturbing power of the play derives from Pinter's cunning presentation of key episodes in this story in reverse order, beginning in 1977, and moving back through events in 1975, 1974, 1973 and 1971 to 1968. This novel way of engaging the audience's curiosity adds to Pinter's remarkable technical equipment for disseminating compulsive unease. *The Hothouse*, first produced by the author himself at the Hampstead Theatre, London, in April 1980, is a play written back in 1958 which Pinter decided was worth presenting on stage after making a few cuts. It is set in a lunatic asylum where the senior staff, obsessed with their own career interests and locked in the world of their private passions, are finally slaughtered by the patients. The play plainly represents a stage in Pinter's development prior to the point when he learned to sustain economy of utterance and fine down the rhetoric of emotion and self-display to its telling minimum. The Beckettian influence, so fruitful in later Pinter, is here but half-assimilated.

Pinter has adapted several novels as film scripts, including L.P. Hartley's (q.v.) *The Go-Between* and John Fowles's *The French Lieutenant's Woman*. See also his *Poems and Prose 1949–1977* (1978).

The Birthday Party. The setting is a seedy boarding house in a seaside holiday resort. Stanley Webber has settled there. He seems to be a failed concert-party pianist, now idling and keeping indoors. Mothered by his landlady, Meg, he is at once childishly dependent, resentful and unbalanced. Two lodgers arrive and begin to take over, planning a birthday celebration for Stanley. Plainly he is their victim, and the back-slapping bonhomie of Goldberg, the dominant visitor, ironically offsets the clearly vengeful intentions of evident terrorists. Cross-questioning makes nothing clear except the gravity of the menace and the fact that Stanley is charged with betraying some organization. It is left to the audience to put two and two together. The second persecutor, an Irishman, Dermott McCann, calls for a Fenian toast at one point and there are enough scattered references to Ireland to conjure up thoughts of the IRA. The menacingly double-edged birthday celebrations reduce Stanley to a state of breakdown. There is more than a hint of torture off-stage. The visitors carry off a collapsed Stanley in a symbolic black car at the end.

The Caretaker. The setting is a junk-laden room in a derelict house in London. Aston, the tenant, brings in a tramp he has rescued from a brawl in a café. Aston seems to be a compulsive picker-up of oddities, and the tramp, Davies, takes his place among a clutter of inanimate objects. Davies can scarcely believe his good luck as he is offered hospitality by Aston and, later, the job of care-taker by Aston's brother, Mick, who owns the place and differs from the others by apparently having a business and earning a living. These three are the only characters and the action, such as it is, revolves around the doubt whether Davies, the intruder, may supplant Aston. The fascination, the mystery and the power of the play reside in the triangular interplay of three personalities on three levels of mental deprivation. Davies is merely dim. Aston has had a brain operation for lunacy and been left half-feelingless. His post-operative condition is a mental half-light in which facts are divorced from significance, procedures emptied of purpose, and responsiveness shaved down to a near-animal level of slowness and obtuseness. Mick exudes a highly articulate idiocy. He lives mentally and verbally in a world which sounds at times like other people's, but fantasy takes over and he is as abberational as those whose foothold is his for the giving. The fitfulness of contact between man and man is caught by Pinter in a display of isolating self-deceptions that are the product of thinking associatively rather than logically. Irrationalities are verbally parcelled up with a grim comic neatness. Man's claim on a place is the issue.
[HB]

PITTER, RUTH (1897–). Poet, born at Ilford, Essex, the daughter of teachers. After working as a War Office clerk during the First World War, she spent twelve years painting for the Walberswick Peasant Pottery Company, Suffolk, before going into partnership and building up her own Chelsea business in hand-painted fancy goods, known as Deane and Forester. The Second World War drove her back into a factory. Its strains also heightened a personal crisis which began to be resolved when she heard C.S. Lewis's radio broadcasts of Christian apologetic. She became a Christian. Her first volume, *First Poems*, had been published in 1920, *First and Second Poems* in 1930 and *A Mad Lady's Garland* in 1934. Other volumes followed until in 1968 she collected her work in *Poems 1926–1966* and wrote a substantial Preface. The output is that of a devoted craftswoman. Discipline 'leaves one so free', she says (*The Poet Speaks*, ed. Peter Orr, 1966). 'I want to have as an end-product something that will please and soothe', she adds, though not denying the need for 'some bitterness and some violence'. 'She combines an exquisite sensibility to the natural world with a power of intense spiritual vision', David Cecil has

said. The chiselled perfection of 'The Ermine' (from *The Ermine*, 1953) displays the integrity of her expression, the fineness of her texture. Here and elsewhere in this volume reflection is pinned delicately at stretch like a butterfly in a case. She has a beautifully cadenced rhythmic naturalness:

> How lonely seem the creatures then;
>   How lonely, even trees;
> But the conceiving minds of men
>   Are lonelier than these.
>
> ('The Tree at Dawn')

'The Other' is an exercise in mystical penetration that is unnervingly lovely in its music and its imagery. Ruth Pitter's mature range can be sampled in *Still By Choice* (1966) which contains a challenge to utter self-openness to God ('In the Open'), a humorous probe into moral attitude ('Charity and Its Object'), a finely woven response to new evidence from physicists that 'this order must pass' ('Who knows?') and a warm-heartedly unflinching portrait of human toil ('Yorkshire Wife's Saga') that has the profound honesty of R.S. Thomas. See also *End of Drought* (1975).   [HB]

PLAATJE, SOLOMON TSHEKISHO (1877–1932). Linguist, journalist, politician, novelist, of Barolong origin, born near Boshof, South Africa. Without formal secondary education he acquired extensive learning from private, spare-time study. Court interpreter in Mafeking during the siege of 1899–1900, he kept a manuscript diary, discovered by J.L. Comaroff and published as *The Boer War Diary of Sol T. Plaatje* (1973), a unique African view of the fighting. A newspaper editor for many years, as Secretary of the South African Native National Congress, founded in 1912, he energetically opposed the Natives' Land Act (1913), the foundation of all apartheid laws, and wrote indignantly on its earliest effects in *Native Life in South Africa* (1916): 'Awakening on Friday morning, June 20, 1913, the South African Native found himself . . . a pariah in the land of his birth'. This Act also motivated his idyllic treatment of Barolong religious, social and legal integrity and of the old African values in *Mhudi*, written about 1917 but published 1930 – the first South African novel in English by a black writer. T. Couzens has convincingly argued Plaatje's ironic and innovative use of the language for implicit contemporary political purposes, though the narrative is set in the 1830s.   [AR]

PLOMER, WILLIAM (1903–73). Poet and novelist, born of English parents in Northern Transvaal, South Africa. His early autobiographical book, *Double Lives* (1943), records the sharp contrasts of childhood, youth and schooling divided between England and Africa. It also records Plomer's meeting with Roy Campbell (q.v.) in 1926 and their brief collaboration on the anti-racialist journal *Voorslag* ('Whiplash'). After some years in Japan, Plomer settled in England and in 1937 became Literary Adviser to Jonathan Cape. Plomer had sent the manuscript of his first novel, *Turbott Wolfe*, to Leonard and Virginia Woolf (q.v.) whose Hogarth Press published it in 1926. Its presentation of the native African case caused anger in South Africa, and Plomer later spoke of it as 'a violent ejaculation, a protest' on the part of a 'solitary emotional youth' reacting 'convulsively to his surroundings' (*Double Lives*). In *Sado* (1931), published in America as *They Never Came Back* (1932), the setting is Japan, but *The Case Is Altered* (1932) is the product of Plomer's having taken lodgings in a Bayswater house where the attractive young landlady was butchered by her husband in what became a sensational case. *The Invaders* (1934) and *Museum Pieces* (1952) are also concerned with life in London. Plomer published several volumes of short stories and collected together a representative selection in *Four Countries* (1949) where he notes in his Preface his central concerns with inter-racial confrontation abroad and the 'comedy of class distinctions' at home in England. He regards his personal experience of transplantation as 'not uncharacteristic of this age of dislocation, disorientation and exile, this age of the Displaced Person'.

Plomer began to publish verse in 1927 with *Notes for Poems*, and the fruits of succeeding volumes were gathered in *Collected Poems* (1960), which was revised and brought up to date in 1973. He tells in the Preface (1973) how he emulated Pound's determination that poetry should 'move against poppycock', be harder, saner, 'austere, direct, free from emotional slither'. And indeed he made his biggest impact with jocular satirical ballads, narrative and anecdotal, whose crisp commentaries on social absurdities constitute a vivid record of inter-war decadence and aberration. In the best pieces the penetration is sharp, social nuances are deftly captured, there is precision in phrase and image, and – for all the slapstick and tomfoolery – the pressure of a positive moral stance comes through, and society's inner hollowness is probed sometimes with searing irony.

Plomer collaborated with Benjamin Britten in providing libretti for *Gloriana* (1953) and for other dramatic and choral works designed for church performance (*Curlew River*, 1964; *The Burning Fiery Furnace*, 1966; *The Prodigal Son*, 1968), which he nicknamed 'choperas'. When he died he was at work on revising and amalgamating the two autobiographical books, *Double Lives* and *At Home* (1958). The work has been posthumously published as *The Autobiography of William Plomer* (1975) with a postscript by his friend Simon Nowell-Smith. It has interesting sidelights on members of the Bloomsbury Group with whom he was acquainted and on his experience as a publisher's reader.   [HB]

PLUNKETT, JAMES (pseudonym of James Plunkett Kelly) (1920–). Novelist, born in Dublin and educated there by the Christian Brothers and at the College of Music. He was employed in the offices of the Gas Company, he became active in the Workers' Union of Ireland, and in 1955 he began to work in dramatic production for Radio Eireann, for whom he wrote several plays. His collection of short stories *The Trusting and the Maimed* (New York, 1955; London, 1959) won high praise from Frank O'Connor (q.v.) and established him as a writer versatile in his ability to vary tone and mood, and to enter penetratingly into the minds of the young or the old. Plunkett's diversity of range, his intimate understanding of the Irish scene, his skill in speaking through different 'voices', and his readiness to learn from his

predecessors, including Joyce (q.v.), bore fruit on a larger scale in his two historical novels of twentieth-century Dublin, *Strumpet City* (1969) and *Farewell Companions* (1977). The former covers the years 1907–14. 'Against the backcloth of social agitation', Plunkett explained, 'it is about the attitudes of the various strata of society – from Dublin Castle and people of property down to the destitute poor and the outcasts.' *Farewell Companions*, its sequel, covers the years up to the end of the Second World War. At the centre of the novel is Tim McDonagh, born in 1920, whose experience incorporates a good deal of autobiographical material. But Plunkett's cast is a large one. The background of public events, like the Easter Rising of 1916, the Anglo-Irish War, the Treaty, the Civil War and its legacy, impinges on the reader concretely in personal adventure and private tragedy lived through by a richly varied dramatis personae. Plunkett shows skill in keeping numerous strands before the reader and in weaving his episodic material together in a panoramic tapestry. The mosaic-like patterning within the five 'movements' of the work is not conducive to sustaining either intensity of focus or a highly charged emotional current, but there is throughout an ever-present human warmth both in humour and in suffering, and the total achievement is an impressive one. See also the non-fiction work *The Gems She Wore: A Book of Irish Places* (1972).   [HB]

PORTER, HAL (1917–). Novelist, short-story writer and poet, born in Melbourne, Victoria, Australia. He first worked as a teacher, taught children of the occupation forces in Japan in 1949–50 and later worked as a librarian in Victoria from 1954 to 1961 before becoming a professional writer. His first book was *Short Stories* (1942), and a further collection, *A Handful of Pennies* (1958), drew upon his experiences in Japan and established the sharp eye for the grotesque, the complex prose style and the autobiographical note which mark much of his best work. *The Actors* (1968) was an incisive study of the uneasy juxtaposition of tradition and new values in modern Japan (the illustrations for which also proved his talent as an artist). *The Tilted Cross* (1961), set in Hobart, was an inventive exploration of the tragic dimension within a Christian setting. His first volume of autobiography, *The Watcher on the Cast-Iron Balcony* (1963), was widely acclaimed, and the sequence continued in *The Paper Chase* (1966) and *The Extra* (1975). A prolific writer, Porter has also published plays and poems, the most recent poetry collection being *In An Australian Country Graveyard and Other Poems*, and stories, *Fredo Fuss Love Life* (both 1974). A collection, *The Portable Hal Porter*, appeared in 1978 and he wrote the story of his boyhood home in *Bairnsdale: Portrait of an Australian Country Town* (1977). He feels that most writers in Australia are regional writers – 'the place is so big . . . I'm a southern Victorian – cold winds, bare apple trees, all that'.   [PQ]

PORTER, PETER (1929–). Poet, born in Brisbane, Queensland, Australia, and educated at grammar schools there and in Toowoomba, Queensland. He left Australia at the age of 22 and has made his home in London. He worked for many years in journalism, bookselling and advertising and currently works as a freelance writer. His first book, *Once Bitten, Twice Bitten* (1961), was followed the next year by his inclusion, together with Kingsley Amis (q.v.) and Dom Moraes (q.v.), in *Penguin Modern Poets 2*. These volumes established his ability to handle a wide range of verse forms and his strong interest in European history and culture as a context for the dispassionate, often sardonic, probing of contemporary vanities. Music and painting are recurrent influences, especially in later works. *Poems Ancient and Modern* (1964), which illustrated this trait, was followed by *Words Without Music* (1968) which represents 'a kind of gathering crisis'. *A Porter Folio* (1969) was in similar vein and *The Last of England* (1970) reflected his ever-growing range of topics and perspectives, a variety extended in other ways by *After Martial* (1972), the fruit of his long-standing 'unconscious desire to create ... afresh' the Latin originals – 'he is amazingly modern'. *Preaching to the Converted* (1972) mirrored the 'coming to terms with the psychological pressure of death and how to cope with it', while *Jonah* (1973) was a poem sequence illustrated by the Australian artist Arthur Boyd. *Living in a Calm Country* (1975) confirmed his status as one of the most important poets writing in England; he remains closely in touch with the Australian poetry scene and his relationship with his country of birth has been the source of some fine poems.   [PQ]

POTTER, BEATRIX (1866–1943). Writer and illustrator of children's books, born in London to parents with money in Lancashire cotton. Strictly brought up and deprived of outside contacts, she found solace in sketching, especially on family holidays in Scotland and the Lake District. An unpublished book on fungi was followed by *The Tale of Peter Rabbit*, printed privately in 1900 and later in colour by F. Warne & Co (1902). The story was an expanded version of an illustrated letter sent to a child and, like several others among her tales, featured a household pet. Beatrix Potter became engaged to Norman Warne, her publisher, in 1905 but he died the same year from leukaemia. The little square books of animal stories, exquisitely illustrated with remarkable accuracy of detail, appeared in regular succession and include *The Tailor of Gloucester* (1903), *The Tale of Benjamin Bunny* (1904), *The Tale of Two Bad Mice* (1904), *The Tale of Mrs Tiggy-Winkle* (1905), *The Tale of Tom Kitten* (1907) etc. They are written in a highly individual yet wholly natural idiom, are devoid of sentimentality or patronization, and tinged with delicate irony. After her marriage in 1913 to Tom Heelis, a solicitor, Beatrix Potter settled down to sheep-farming in the Lake District. Her own first small Lakeland farm, Hilltop, Sawrey, was bequeathed to the National Trust and is now open to the public. Beatrix Potter's 200,000-word diary has been decoded and transcribed as *The Journals of Beatrix Potter 1881–97* by Leslie Linder (1966). See also the biography *The Tale of Beatrix Potter* (1946, revised 1968) by Margaret Lane.   [HB]

POWELL, ANTHONY (Dymoke) (1905–). Novelist, born in London. His father was an army colonel and Powell was educated at Eton and at Balliol College, Oxford. The clear impress of school and university experience can be found in *A Question of Upbringing* –

though the book is in no sense 'autobiographical'. Powell married Lady Violet Pakenham in 1934 and he has two sons. His life and literary output are both divided into two by the Second World War. Before the war he had a job in publishing (with Duckworth's), then as film scriptwriter, and he published half a dozen novels. During the war he was an officer in the Welch Regiment and then in the Intelligence Corps. After the war (in which he won distinctions and rose to the rank of major) he returned to writing as book reviewer and novelist. He had been working during wartime leaves on John Aubrey, the seventeenth-century antiquary, and he published the biography, *John Aubrey and His Friends*, in 1948. He also edited a volume of Aubrey's work, *Brief Lives and Other Selected Writings of John Aubrey* (1949). The interest in so kindred a spirit – arch-accumulator of gossip and anecdote – is notable.

The first of the prewar novels, *Afternoon Men* (1931), is a deft registration of the fashionable and arty 1920s. It has affinities with early Waugh (q.v.) and Huxley (q.v.) as an exposé of vapidity and boredom and in its focus upon social drifters, but Powell has neither the cutting moral edge of Waugh nor the dazzling intellectual fireworks of Huxley. His technique is a direct, even terse, recording of dialogue and setting, pervaded by the humour of quiet irony. The laconic style piquantly flavours the vacuities it presents. There is no 'plot'. People meet in pubs, flats, taxis, art galleries and the like. They go to parties, they drink and they gossip endlessly. Significantly enough, the one excitement of the book is a climactic non-event. The artist Pringle finds his girl in the arms of one of his guests, goes off to commit suicide in the sea, leaving behind him his clothes and a farewell note, only to return later, having changed his mind and got rescued by fishermen. The deadpan management of the episode is superb. Moreover Powell has subtlety in noting personal interplay at the social game and the sex game. Dialogue sometimes lays a crisp, cryptic surface over naturalistic redundancy and mistiness of meaning that seems to pre-echo Pinter. The sardonic authorial tone is slyly devastating in a wholly comic and non-condemnatory way. Of the other prewar novels *From a View to a Death* (1933), with its picture of village society disturbed by the intrusion of a vigorous young artist, shows movement towards solider presentation of human character, while in *Agents and Patients* (1936) antics degenerate into farce.

After the war Powell decided to write a single 'really long novel' running through many volumes. A motive was the quite justifiable one of artistic economy – that one would thus 'pick up in that way all you lose by ending a book and starting again with a lot of entirely new characters'. The work as a whole is called *A Dance to the Music of Time**. It is a sequence of twelve novels which cover the period of Powell's own life and form a choreographically structured panorama of upper-class and middle-class life against the background of public events. Especially notable volumes for sampling the work are *The Acceptance World* and *Casanova's Chinese Restaurant* along with the crucial first volume, *A Question of Upbringing*, which lays the foundation for the rest by presenting a nucleus of early friends of the narrator, Nicholas Jenkins, who matches the author in social background and career.

Powell has now completed a multi-volume series of

memoirs, *To Keep the Ball Rolling*, with I. *Infants of the Spring* (1976), II. *Messengers of the Day* (1978), III. *Faces in My Time* (1980) and IV. *The Strangers All are Gone* (1982). The first two volumes, covering the Eton and Oxford days and the early years in London, are notable for substantial portraits of contemporary writers, Green (q.v.), Orwell (q.v.), Waugh (q.v.), and the Sitwells (q.v.) among them. The third volume covers the eventful period from the author's marriage into the aristocratic Pakenham family in 1934 to the point of embarking on the *magnum opus*. The fourth volume covers the years since 1952 in a loosely knit patchwork of recollections of literary activities, journeys, personalities and musings.

A Dance to the Music of Time falls into four trilogies, the first consisting of *A Question of Upbringing* (1951), *A Buyer's Market* (1952) and *The Acceptance World* (1955). In *A Question of Upbringing*, the narrator of the whole series, Nicholas Jenkins, describes his schooldays and university days in the early 1920s, introducing, among a host of others, Charles Stringham, Peter Templer and Kenneth Widmerpool, whose courses through life are to run contemporaneously with his own. In *A Buyer's Market*, in which Nicholas falls frustratingly in love with the same girl as Widmerpool, we are in the late 1920s; but throughout the work as whole the narrator, in focusing upon a given period, draws correspondences – sometimes long ones – with previous or later phases of life. Thus Powell's intricate design involves multiple time-shifts that contribute towards the overall achievement of dimensional richness and anecdotal density. In *The Acceptance World*, against the background of hunger marches and means-test protests of the early 1930s, the interchanging of partners within marriage and without is part of the 'formal dance with which human life is concerned', while the rise of the pushy, vulgar Widmerpool and the decadence of Stringham and his class suggest 'a whole social upheaval, a positively cosmic change in life's system'.

Nicholas is 28 or 29 at the beginning of the second trilogy (*At Lady Molly's*, 1957; *Casanovas's Chinese Restaurant*, 1960; *The Kindly Ones*, 1962). His engagement (in *At Lady Molly's*) to Isobel Tolland takes him and the reader into close contact with an aristocratic family whose ten sons and daughters, with their love affairs and other relationships, come tumbling into a field of gossip already densely populated. The sexual jostling is now so thick, the interchange of partners so rapid, that the reader's head reels. It takes place against a lightly sketched public background – in *Casanova's Chinese Restaurant* of the Spanish Civil War and the Abdication crisis. The narrator's private life remains shadowy, his own engagement and marriage intentionally little dwelt upon ('It is hard to describe your wife').

Perhaps such unity of substance as the work as a whole possesses belongs chiefly to the first six volumes, for the third trilogy (*The Valley of Bones*, 1964; *The Soldier's Art*, 1966; *The Military Philosophers*, 1968), covering the Second World War, is in many respects separately conceived. In the first year of the war (*The Valley of Bones*) Nicholas has a commission in a Welsh regiment that is for a time stationed in Northern Ireland and later in southern England. By the end of the book he is ironically

made junior officer to Widmerpool ('I saw that I was now in Widmerpool's power') at the same moment that Paris falls into Hitler's hands, but in the succeeding volumes Nicholas is transferred to the Intelligence Corps. The war trilogy is linked to its predecessors by the renewal of old gossip while on leave, by odd meetings with faces from the past, and above all by sombre news of the deaths of figures dominant in the earlier volumes. Thus the dominion of death imposes its own pattern on the disrupted lives and its own moral on the futilities and sensualities it terminates. The first two volumes of the final trilogy introduce new characters and have at least a superficial separateness. *Books Do Furnish a Room* (1971) deals with the immediate postwar years and *Temporary Kings* (1973) moves on to 1955. *Hearing Secret Harmonies* (1975) concludes the sequence, bringing us up to the early 1970s.

Nicholas Jenkins is a detached yet compassionate observer, freed by a quiet integrity from the vanities and sensual excesses of the society he moves in. Perhaps he is too unassuming. His lack of interest in self – either analytical or dynamic – deprives the series of a continuing narrational thrust such as Proust's Marcel supplies. But there is thematic continuity in the basic contrast between Nick himself, the man of sensitivity and imagination, and his foil, Kenneth Widmerpool, the man of ambition. Widmerpool's clumsy insensitivities make him something of a butt at school, but by the fourth volume (*At Lady Molly's*) he is in the City and 'supposed to be rather good at making money'; he rises quickly to the rank of colonel in the war ('for the army is a world of the will', *The Valley of Bones*) and is a Labour Life Peer in the penultimate volume (*Temporary Kings*), narrowly escaping trouble in the aftermath of the Burgess–Maclean affair for suspicious contacts across the Iron Curtain.

The sequence as a whole, Powell tells us, 'is intended to illustrate and bring up to date considerations of the way in which the middle and upper classes live in England'. As a fictional social document on the years it covers (from Nick's pre-First World War childhood to the 1970s) its perspectives are revealing, if limited by the social territory focused upon and the emphasis selected. The image of the dance of time, based on a painting by Poussin (in which the Seasons dance hand in hand), provides a central symbol for the structure of the work, in which human beings move in and out in sequence, changing partners with dizzying rapidity. The design is developed by accumulation. The figures whose lives are intertwined with Nicholas's in the first book have their relations and connections, and the reader is introduced to an expanding number of them. The society is one in which men and women marry two, three and four times and in which there is no limit to extra-marital liaisons. On this basis Powell interknits a vast array of human beings in a network of promiscuous intra-marital and extra-marital permutations. In so far as this represents the breakdown of marriage morality and the advent of cynicism, we see the foundations of permissiveness laid by people in whose conversation even the personal tragedies of their friends can be flippantly capsulated in witty, dismissive jocularities. For the detailed notation of gossip abounds in conversational quips that falsely externalize by summing up changes in human relationships too neatly. To this extent there is a moral drift, fitfully underlined by the narrator in pointing to acts that represent landmarks 'in the general disintegration of society in its traditional form'.

Powell remains essentially a recorder of life from the outside, lavishly feeding the appetite for 'fact' and allowing the inner life to be presupposed. It is the public face and the conversational report that weigh: many characters have anecdotal rather than psychological solidity. Nevertheless the Proustian scale of the work is impressive.   [HB]

POWYS, JOHN COWPER (1872–1963). Novelist, the eldest son of Rev. C.F. Powys and brother of the writers T.F. Powys (q.v.) and Llewelyn Powys (q.v.). J.C. was born at Shirley Vicarage near Ashbourne, Derbyshire, and educated at Sherborne School and at Corpus Christi College, Cambridge. The Rev. C.F. Powys, father of a family of eleven, had moved from Derbyshire in 1879 to Dorchester and in 1885 he went on to become Vicar of Montacute, Somerset. Powys disappointed his parents' expectation that he would follow family tradition and take holy orders. He taught first in girls' schools and then established himself as a freelance lecturer on literature, becoming popular in the USA. His marriage in 1896 began inauspiciously with a male friend's company on the honeymoon and ended eventually in separation. Significantly, no doubt, Powys refers to his brother-in-law in the Autobiography as 'my son's uncle'. This Autobiography (1934) is a remarkably frank and buoyant piece of eccentric self-portraiture, copious and fertile like all his work. Powys published volumes of poetry in 1896 and 1899, collaborated with his brother, Llewelyn, in the autobiographical Confessions of Two Brothers, and published three novels between 1915 and 1925; there were also books in the field of criticism and philosophy; but his career as a major novelist began only in 1929, when he was already 57 years old, with the publication of Wolf Solent. The first of four Wessex novels, it is set in the countryside of Powys's schooldays and Sherborne is fictionalized as Ramsgard. Wolf, the son of a passive, amoral father and a spirited, demanding mother, has a characteristically Powysian need for two women: Gerda, a country girl associated with nature and the earth, and Christie, a more complex representative of the world of imagination and intellect.

> What might be called the purpose and essence and inmost being of this book is the necessity of opposites. Life and Death, Good and Evil, Matter and Spirit, Body and Soul, Reality and Appearance have to be joined together, have to be forced into one another, have to be proved dependent upon each other.

So Powys wrote later of this book with characteristically cumulative wordiness. In A Glastonbury Romance (1932), perhaps his most celebrated work, Powys set himself 'to convey a jumbled-up and squeezed-together epitome of life's various dimensions', and he wove a massively variegated web of pictorial scene and human interplay, with the Grail quest at the heart of the symbolism. Bulk gives the book a certain unwieldiness, for control of

narrative design is not Powys's strong point; but he works through distinct thematic patterns with a buoyancy of thrust and an intensity of moment-by-moment awareness that endow his work with a fitful, half-realized grandeur.

Powys has a breathless oratorical fluency which J.B. Priestley (q.v.) has attributed to his long platform experience. 'He is too rhapsodical for cold print' (Introduction to the Autobiography). And indeed Powys himself admitted in the Autobiography that what really paid him for lecturing was not the money but 'the actual sensation I got from it and the life-energy I imbibed from it. Such sucking up of crowd-magnetism I found to be one of the most marvellous of human restoratives'. Weymouth Sands (1934) is a story of the sea as the symbol of destiny over against which drifting human beings work out their lonely failures and losses. Maiden Castle (1936) takes us to Dorchester itself where Dud No-Man settles to write a historical novel. He saves a young circus-performer, Wizzie Ravelstone, from exploitation and takes her home (reminding the reader of Rogue Herries's rescue of Mirabell Starr in Hugh Walpole's (q.v.) Rogue Herries); but he is impeded in love by prior entanglement with his dead mother and his dead virgin wife, and by inability to consummate, and Wizzie leaves him. The discovery of his father – a half-mad Welshman, Enoch ('Uryen') Quirm, who is trying to revive the cult of the old gods of Maiden Castle and thinks himself a reincarnation of their power – represents one more failure by 'No-Man' to realize satisfying self-identity.

An aura of unreality pervades much of Powys's work. The reader seems to be required to jump between imaginative worlds as disparate as those of T.F. Powys and Charles Williams (q.v.), Thomas Hardy (q.v.) and Mervyn Peake (q.v.). Exploration of inner thought and day-dream at a level of acute twentieth-century awareness is pursued within a nineteenth-century novelistic framework. It is as though Virginia Woolf (q.v.) were trying to work to Arnold Bennett's (q.v.) technical rule-book. Counterpoint between outer dialogue and inner train of thought is powerful in contrast yet clumsy in presentation. The intermingling of surface concern and private indifference, of ideal and contrasting reality, is sharply ironical nevertheless. So is the exploration of defective communication between male and female. One of Powys's notable strengths is his gift for defining the sexual terrain we occupy, 'moving, as we all have to do, in the midst of a flickering cat's cradle of erotic currents'. But Powys himself, a lifelong visual enthusiast for female knees and ankles, was scarcely normal sexually. 'As often as he understood women – and when he did it was with startling insight – he disliked them', observes H.P. Collis in John Cowper Powys, Old Earth-man (1966).

Powys moved to Wales in 1934 and settled in a cottage at Blaenau Ffestiniog for the near thirty years of life that remained to him. His later works include the Welsh novels, Morwyn (1937) and Owen Glendower (1941), and the historical fantasy, The Brazen Head (1956). The posthumous novel, After My Fashion (1980), written soon after the First World War, reflects Powys's experience of America, and of New York especially. Collections of letters include I.C. Peate, ed., Letters 1937–1954 (1974), and M. Elwin, ed., Letters to his Brother Llewelyn 1902–1925 (1975).   [HB]

POWYS, LLEWELYN (1884–1939). Born in Dorset, the youngest of the three writer-brothers (see J.C. Powys (q.v.) and T.F. Powys (q.v.)). He collaborated with J.C. (the eldest) in *Confessions of Two Brothers* (1916) and then wrote sketches of African and English life, *Ebony and Ivory* (1923) and *Black Laughter* (1925), which display his natural gift for evocative descriptive writing. This power, rather than any fictional imaginativeness comparable to that of his brothers, is what distinguishes him, and his 'imaginary autobiography' *Love and Death* (1939) is more highly regarded than his novel *Apples be Ripe* (1930). Powys also wrote travel books and two books of reminiscences, *Skin for Skin* (1926) and *The Verdict of Bridlegoose* (1927).   [HB]

POWYS, T.F. (Theodore Francis) (1875–1953). Novelist and writer of short stories, born at Shirley in Derbyshire, the third of the eleven children of Rev. C.F. Powys, an Evangelical clergyman. His brothers include J.C. Powys (q.v.), also a novelist, and Llewelyn Powys (q.v.), writer of essays and travel books. The family moved to Dorchester in 1879, and thence to Montacute, Somerset, where the Rev. C.F. Powys held the living for thirty years. Theodore had no university education, but after schooling at Dorchester, Sherborne and Aldeburgh, he was launched by his father into farming in Suffolk. The venture was a failure ('I was far too often in the shade of a tree, reading, when I should have been among the furrows') and, after six years of it, he buried himself in rural Dorset where he lived in hermit-like seclusion, first at Studland, then from 1904 to 1940 at East Chaldon, and for the rest of his days at Mappowder. He married Violet Rosalie Dodd in 1905 and there were three children. Powys gave himself to writing and to meditative quietness. He was suspicious of mechanical work: it was man's invention to avoid contemplation. ('Man works in order to keep God at bay.') He scarcely stirred from his home and averred that he believed in monotony. He and his family were dependent for many years on a small allowance from his father, for though the years between 1902 and 1931 were productive of books, many of these were very slow to get into print. It follows that publication dates are not a sure guide to order of composition. The struggle with poverty began to be relieved only with the publication of *The Left Leg* (with *Hester Dominy* and *Abraham Mew*) in 1923. It is a short tale presenting a sharp contrast between Farmer Mew, a ruthless, grasping egoist, and Farmer James Gillet, pious and unworldly, whose daughter Mary is Mew's victim and the vehicle of retribution. In the extreme moral dualism, the savagery, the comedy and above all in the activity of Old Jar, travelling tinker and God himself, the Powys recipe is laid down. Among other earlier works were *Black Bryony* (1923), *Mark Only* (1924) and *Mr Tasker's Gods* (1924).

Powys's style is distinctive. His clipped, terse sentences build up short paragraphs by aggregation. Sturdiness and incisiveness are his qualities rather than graciousness of phrase or rhythm, and he seems to have emulated Bunyan. Dialect in the dialogue matches the narrative in angularity. For Powys's concern is with the simplest activities of rural life – of farmers, inn-keepers, labourers, tramps, tradesmen and the like. His field of interest was that of the poet George Crabbe, whose work

gave him especial pleasure. Exploited servants, feckless idlers and drunken rogues throng his pages. Hypocritical clergymen are mercilessly pilloried: but there are compassionate, self-sacrificing clergymen too; for Powys's world is inhabited by stark extremes. His books are twentieth-century moralities in which the seven deadly sins confront their opposites; avarice against generosity, cruelty against kindness and egotism against love. The vein of Swiftian savagery is strong. Mr Tasker (*Mr Tasker's Gods*) feeds a dead horse to his pigs (his 'gods') and gets rid of his unwanted father by maddening his wild dog with the father's old hat. The scent does its work. The dog gets its teeth into the old man's throat. The pigs, smelling blood, eat him up. It would be difficult to think of a more detestable character than Mr Tasker – or than those ghoulish, witch-like women who inhabit Powys's books (Mrs Vosper in *Mr Weston's Good Wine* and old Tabitha in 'The Spittoon and the Slate') and whose dominant passion is to purvey untried village virgins to the squirearchy and the well-to-do for instant debauching. On the other hand Powys's good characters are haloed personifications of gentleness, humility and unselfishness. Henry Turnbull (in *Mr Tasker*) is a revealing study of the sort of being Powys especially cherishes – a vicar's son who is unfitted for life in a working, self-seeking society by an ingenuous unworldliness that verges both on sanctity and on idiocy. Naïve simplifications of the beastliness of the vicious and the purity of the virtuous sometimes involve peculiar moral thrust and emotional engagement, but can also produce moralistic sentimentality and a failure of authenticity.

Powys's short stories have the same strengths and weaknesses, notably *Fables* (1929), a volume whose title was later changed to *No Painted Plumage* (1934). The hero of 'John Pardy and the Waves' is a favourite Powysian victim – a rejected, good-for-nothing brother who returns from abroad to sponge on his respectable relations; the values of people who get on in life are always under stern judgement in Powys. In 'The Corpse and the Flea' God speaks through a flea ('I will not leave you comfortless' and 'I will be with you always') to a revived corpse and reconciles it to death; and in 'Mr Pim and the Holy Crumb' God converses appropriately through an articulate crumb of consecrated Communion bread. In some cases ('The Clout and the Pan' and 'The Hassock and the Psalter') the moral insights offered scarcely justify the laboured artifices of dialogue between inanimate objects. Powys is generally reckoned to be at his best in *Mr Weston's Good Wine** (1927) in which God figures as a travelling wine-salesman who visits a Dorset village. In *Unclay* (1931) a village receives a momentous visitation of a different kind, this time by John Death. A much lighter story, *Kindness in a Corner* (1930), achieved some popularity.

Powys's symbolism gives pattern and dimension to his study of a world under judgement. If there is much bitterness in his work, there is also resignation and consolation. 'As regard his religion he is a Christian, and believes a good deal too much in God', he wrote of himself. But, like his books, what he said of himself leaves much unexplained. An unresolved tension remains. 'Mr Powys gives the impression that he knows a disreputable secret about life, but does not convince us that the real secret of life is disreputable', Edwin Muir observed. See also Powys's *Soliloquies of a Hermit* (1918).

Mr Weston's Good Wine takes its title from Jane Austen's *Emma* (chapter xv). Emma finds herself alone in a carriage with Mr Elton. 'She believed he had been drinking too much of Mr Weston's good wine, and felt sure he would want to be talking nonsense.' Folly Down, a village based on East Chaldon in Dorset, where Powys lived for twenty years, is visited one November evening by God in the person of Mr Weston, a travelling wine-salesman who is accompanied by his angelic assistant Michael. They come in a Ford delivery van, advertising Mr Weston's Good Wine. Mr Weston declares that his wine 'is as strong as death and as sweet as love'. There is 'no trouble incident to this fretful and changing life of man' that it cannot cure. Time is suspended during the course of the evening and judgement appropriately worked out on the wicked and the virtuous. Among the former is Mrs Vosper who ensnares young maidens so that a farmer's lusty sons can enjoy them under a symbolic village oak tree. Among the latter is Tamar, daughter of Rev. Nicholas Grobe, the unbelieving vicar. She has dreamed of surrendering herself to an angel – and does, in the person of Michael. Luke Bird is a saintly Powysian idealist who preaches to the beasts of the field. The rare blend of caricature appropriate to parable, of allegorical pattern and complex symbolism, with a Swiftian focus on the animality of rural man, is made palatable by a piercing emotional intensity and a crisp ironic humour.

[HB]

PRATT, E.J. (Edwin John) (1882–1964). Poet, born in Western Bay, Newfoundland, Canada, a small fishing community, son of a Methodist minister. He learned at first hand of the tragi-heroic relationship between man and the sea where 'Eternity / had fashioned out an edge for human grief' ('Ground Swell'). Pratt was ordained himself but entered the University of Toronto in 1907, graduating in philosophy in 1911. He went on to take his MA and a PhD in theology before joining the English Department at Victoria College, Toronto University, in 1920. The sea, in its both realistic and symbolic aspects, was always of great importance for Pratt, and his first book of poetry, *Rachel* (1917), described a mother awaiting news of her drowned son. *Newfoundland Verse* (1923) also dealt extensively with the sea's moods and rhythms as they interacted with those of man, though the volume contained (in Pratt's own words) 'theories and reflections of theories about life . . . bald, very bald generalizations'. Little of this early work appeared in *Collected Poems* (1944). Pratt's second collection, *The Witches Brew* (1925), was an irreverent and witty extravaganza on alcohol, seen by some as a satire on prohibition in Canada (abolished in Ontario in 1927). His virtuosity as a narrative poet was now clear, and this was displayed to the full in *Titans* (1926), an allegory on war and an epic poem on the struggle between a whale and its hunters. An interest in conflict on a vast scale, with its profound human implications, underlies most of Pratt's later work, most notably *The Titanic* (1935), in which the conjunction of man's pride and natural forces in the liner's sinking in 1912 gave Pratt a subject which evoked some of his finest

poetry. His vision of the tragedy is·complex, for although the iceberg is apparently victorious in this clash of primitive barbarism and sophisticated (yet superficial) technology, there are contrary tensions within the overall pattern. Though 'defeated', man triumphs through acts of heroism which stand undiminished against the seemingly unconquerable 'grey shape' of the iceberg. Pratt's admiration for acts of collective heroism determined his poetic involvement in the wartime years; the growing scourge of fascism is reflected in *The Fable of the Goats* (1937), and four of Pratt's other books deal with the Second World War: *Dunkirk* (1941), *Still Life and Other Verse* (1943), *They are Returning* (1945) and *Behind the Log* (1947). Pratt turned inland for themes of heroism in *Brébeuf and his Brethren* (1940) and *Towards the Last Spike* (1952) which dealt respectively with early Jesuit missions to the Indians and the building of the Canadian Pacific Railway. Never committed to any fashion or faction in his work, Pratt contributed a new dimension to modern Canadian poetry through his heroic vision of man and his ability to express this vision in narrative poetry of outstanding sensitivity and power. On his chosen ground he is without equal, and the publication in 1958 of *Collected Poems* (with an important introduction by Northrop Frye) enabled the scope and talent of his poetry to be readily appreciated by a new generation of poets and readers.

[PQ]

PRESCOTT, H.F.M. (Hilda Frances Margaret) (1896–1972). Novelist and historian, born in Cheshire, educated at Wallasey High School, Lady Margaret Hall, Oxford, and Manchester University. She was Vice-Principal of St Mary's College, University of Durham, from 1943 to 1948. Her purely historical works include *Spanish Tudor* (1940), a life of 'Bloody' Mary, and *Jerusalem Journey* (1954) with its sequel *Once to Sinai* (1957), on fifteenth-century pilgrimages to the Holy Land. The early novels, such as *The Unhurrying Chase* (1925) which is set in twelfth-century France, pale into insignificance beside the extensive two-volume work *The Man on a Donkey* (1952), which presents a record of Henry VIII's dissolution of the monasteries and the opposition it provoked in the north. The story is told in chronicle form and covers the years 1509 to 1537. Centring first on the small Priory at Marrick in Swaledale, its range expands to touch upon crucial events in London involving such figures as Cardinal Wolsey, Thomas Cromwell, Katherine of Aragon, Anne Boleyn and Jane Seymour, and to give a stage-by-stage account of the swelling northern resistance to Henry's tyrannies that came to a head in the ill-fated Pilgrimage of Grace led by Robert Aske. Aske was lured by false promises of pardon to dismiss his followers and to go to discuss grievances with Henry personally, and was treacherously hanged at York in 1537. The patient fullness of detail with which the life of the period is accurately re-created makes this a notable work.

[HB]

PRIESTLEY, J.B. (John Boynton) (1894–). Novelist, dramatist and essayist, born in Bradford, West Yorkshire, the son of a schoolmaster. He left school early, took a job in the office of a woollen mill, and started writing for local newspapers. He served for five years in the Duke of Wellington's and Devon Regiments (1914–19), rising to command of a front-line company, and then went to Trinity Hall, Cambridge, on an ex-officer's grant. He read history and English literature and Quiller-Couch (q.v.) suggested that he might stay on at Cambridge to teach, but he moved to London in 1922 'with a young wife, no regular job and a total capital of less than fifty pounds'. (He married Pat Tempest in 1921, Mary Wyndham Lewis in 1926 and, after divorce, the writer Jacquetta Hawkes in 1953.) His first novels, *Adam in Moonshine* and *Benighted*, were both published in 1927 and *Farthing Hall*, written in collaboration with Hugh Walpole (q.v.), followed in 1929, but it was the astonishing popular success of *The Good Companions** (1929) and *Angel Pavement* (1930) that rocketed Priestley to fame and wealth. He acquired a house on the Isle of Wight in 1934, but he has lived more recently at Alveston in Warwickshire.

Priestley's vast and variegated output includes twenty-six novels and over thirty plays, and a list of other miscellaneous prose works (including essays, autobiography, criticism, radio talks etc.) can run to fifty titles. The lack of an obvious masterpiece means that the question of Priestley's relative importance as a writer becomes a question about the value of quantity and diversity. Single works do not select themselves for emphasis by virtue of being landmarks in a personal artistic progress, still less in the development of the literary form in question. The habit of having a lot to say about anything and everything of current social interest, and of cultivating a vein of grumbling jocularity in saying it, has turned Priestley into a public figure in the mould of Shaw and Chesterton, but there is neither the wit of the one nor the dexterity of the other to give equivalent literary substantiality to the figure.

Among the novels Priestley himself pleads especially for his favourite, *Bright Day* (1946), a first-person record by a middle-aged film script writer, Gregory Dawson, whose recall of sunny prewar boyhood in Bruddersford (Bradford) and the succeeding break-up of a hopeful era contains a good deal of autobiographical material. Priestley presses too the claims of *Festival at Farbridge* (1951), a rumbustiously comic and topical picture of contemporary English provincial life timed for the 1951 Festival of Britain, and of *The Image Men* (1968), which he describes as 'a sharp satire, very topical, on our ideas of education, our mass media, advertising, business expertise etc.'. But many still regard *Angel Pavement* as his best novel. This study of London in the 1920s centres on a small firm in the City (Twigg and Dersingham of Angel Pavement) which is respectably going downhill till it becomes first the beneficiary, then the victim of an international shark, Mr Golspie. He descends upon it with a recipe for instant commercial prosperity, enriches himself, tricks his partner ruinously, then absconds. The effect, first of success, then of failure, on each of the firm's employees and their intimates is impressively registered against the background of postwar unsettlement and rising unemployment. There is a sharp awareness of the threat of poverty overhanging the meagre consolations of suburban working-class life. The book has an overall social and moral impetus to match its structural

tidiness, and Priestley's prodigality of reflection and of inventiveness in characterization serve him well. Even so, Priestley's fundamental lack of restraint damages his work here as elsewhere. The practice of telling the reader what is inside every newspaper, shop, tram, café or human head encountered en route palls. The minutiae of family life and the vapidities of personal conversation are reproduced with the fidelity associated with routine radio serials. Moreover, Priestley's assumption of the epic novelist's detachment practised by Fielding and Thackeray is not always ballasted by felt sympathy. Too often we hear the voice of one who is superior to the people he writes about, sometimes indeed the voice of someone who is trying to get his own back.

Priestley, it is said, now regards himself as primarily a dramatist, and in plays, of course, the god-like authorial commentator is silenced and only his characters speak. If the silencing of the authorial voice allows a fresher and more independent authenticity to characterization, it also deprives the plays of the humorous and ironic dimensions of the novels. *Eden End* (1934) is a somewhat melancholy play portraying a north-country doctor's family whose lost sheep, daughter Stella, returns home temporarily and with pathetic consequences. Three of Priestley's most talked-of plays reflect his interest in the problem of time. *Dangerous Corner* (1932), his first play, is an interesting experiment in representing the might-have-been alongside the has-been by tracing both from a common junction. Thus the opening of the first act is repeated in summary at the end of Act III, but the dangerous corner (a remark that led to devastating revelations in Acts I and II) is this time smoothly negotiated by the characters. The doctrine of Serial Time expounded by J.W. Dunne in *An Experiment with Time* left its mark on *Time and the Conways* (1937) in which the lives of the Conway family leap forward twenty years in Act II, to return in Act III to the 'present' of 1919. But it is rather the melancholy dominion of time than man's possible liberation from it that is confirmed by thus transposing the chronology and showing hopes dashed in the future before they are entertained in the present. The theory of Ouspensky (*New Model of the Universe*) and Circular Time supplements that of Dunne and Serial Time in *I Have Been Here Before* (1937), when a young headmaster finds the wife of a fellow guest in his arms while holidaying at a village inn in North Yorkshire. *Laburnham Grove* (1934), *When We are Married* (1938) and *An Inspector Calls* (1945) are other plays that achieved popularity. But perhaps Priestley is at his most natural when he is phrase-spinning *in propria persona* as an old-fashioned essayist. A collection of earlier pieces was edited by Eric Gillett in 1956 (*All About Ourselves and Other Essays*). The later, maturer Priestley consciously lays aside the native role of West Riding grumbler to capture life's brighter moments in the neatly fashioned essays, *Delight* (1949).

Priestley's admirers, resenting critical neglect of his work, argue that the talent is so prodigal, so versatile, that critics, who like to define and docket a limited artistic achievement, have been overwhelmed by abundance and have decided to look the other way. Priestley was awarded the OM in 1977. Among works of autobiographical rumination are *Midnight on the Desert* (1937), *Rain upon Gadshill* (1939), *Margin Released* (1962) and *Instead of the Trees* (1977).

The Good Companions is a large-scale novel, rambling and picaresque in interest but carefully structured around the decisions of three characters to break from their routine surroundings. Jess Oakroyd, a carpenter of Bruddersford, Yorkshire, nagged by his wife and sacked by his firm, takes to the road with his tool bag. Inigo Jollifant, a schoolmaster at a private school, is dismissed for not putting up quietly with the tyrannies of the headmaster's wife. Elizabeth Trant, liberated from a comfortable small-town rut by her father's death, buys a car and sets off on a tour. The three come together alongside a failing concert-party, the Dinky Doos. Elizabeth has money and altruism, Inigo has musical talent as well as an irrepressible sense of humour, and Jess is the born stagehand and odd-job man. A new company is formed, The Good Companions. Days of near-total failure and heartbreak are lived through before everybody finds succcess and happiness appropriate to his desires – Inigo as a song-writer, the Companions' comedienne Susie Deans as a London actress, Elizabeth in marriage, and Jess in escape to his loving married daughter in Canada. There is much humour in the book, some of it hearty and heavy-handed, the best of it lightly ironic. The indulgent, omniscient author keeps the reader's ear, chuckling, sentimentalizing, and pulling the curtain open and shut.

[HB]

PRINCE, F.T. (Frank Templeton) (1912–). Poet, born and brought up in Kimberley, South Africa. He came to Balliol College, Oxford, in 1931 and, after service in the Intelligence Corps in the Second World War, joined the English Department at Southampton University and was Professor of English there from 1957 to 1974. His poetic output has been small. *Doors of Stone; Poems 1938–1962* (1963) contains 'all I wish to preserve from two previous books, as well as a number of more recent poems' (Prefatory Note). In the celebrated war poem 'Soldiers Bathing' the poet strives towards the meaning of his men's recreation in the sea and finally sees them transfigured under a sunset streaked with redness like Christ's blood. The climactic image is Marlowe's. And in the fine sequence of love poems beginning with 'The Inn' sharp echoes of Eliot (q.v.), Shakespeare and especially Donne enrich a text that is charged with metaphysical wit yet also immediate and deeply felt: Prince blends the old and the new with something of Eliot's assurance. *Memoirs in Oxford* (1970) is an autobiographical poem. Using the five-lined stanza of Shelley's *Peter Bell the Third*, it traces personal and poetic development by retrospective glances at childhood and young manhood, and does so with limpid clarity and frankness. *Drypoints of the Hasidim* (1975) goes back to the eighteenth-century revival of Hasidism by Polish Jews to shed light on the Catholic Church today. Stephen Spender (q.v.) has spoken of the 'packed quietness, the result of intense meditation' that marks Prince's later poetry (*Sunday Telegraph*, 24.8.75). [HB]

PRITCHETT, V.S. (Victor Sawdon) (1900–). Novelist, short-story writer and critic, born in Ipswich, Suffolk, and educated at Alleyn's School, Dulwich, London. He abandoned business for journalism in 1923 and in 1926 took up an influential position as critic on the *New Statesman*. His own novels do not rise above the derivative in substance or presentation. *Nothing Like Leather* (1935) exploits Pritchett's knowledge of the leather trade in studying Burkle, a zealous money-maker. *Dead Man Leading* (1937) portrays an explorer, Harry Johnson, who is obsessed by his missionary father's disappearance in the Brazilian jungle and achieves the same fate. *Mr Beluncle* (1951), the portrait of a silly businessman with a gift for cheerfully blinding himself to facts, belongs to the genre of Wells's light fiction, but it fails to hang together. In the short stories Pritchett's economy, his fine paragraph-by-paragraph control, his subtle verbal craftsmanship, his sense of humour and his gift for pin-pointing significant idiosyncrasy, all come into their own without the air of contrivance found in the novels. The seminal essence of *Mr Beluncle*, for instance, is satisfyingly capsulated in 'The Saint'. Pritchett's special interest is in lower-middle-class characters outside the world of culture, infected with 'puritanism' and often eccentrically assertive. The collections of stories began with *The Spanish Virgin* (1930) and include *It May Never Happen* (1945), *Collected Stories* (1956), *When My Girl Comes Home* (1961), *Blind Love* (1969) and *The Camberwell Beauty* (1974). Critical works include *The Living Novel* (1946) and *The Working Novelist* (1965), and there two autobiographical books, *A Cab at the Door* (1968) and *Midnight Oil* (1971). The latter, in portraying Pritchett's father, a Christian Scientist, shows the theme of *Mr Beluncle* as his 'obsessive subject'.

Pritchett edited *The Oxford Book of Short Stories* (1981), and his introduction sheds light on his theory of the way the shaping of a well-crafted story can convey the sense that 'our now restless lives achieve shape at times and that our emotions have their architecture'. The publication of *Collected Stories* (1982) drew critical acclaim for Pritchett's achievement over fifty years in memorably defining changing nuances of social life through succeeding decades. [HB]

PYM, BARBARA (1913–80). Novelist, born in Oswestry, Shropshire, and educated at Huyton College, Liverpool, and St Hilda's College, Oxford. She worked for many years at the International African Institute and edited the journal *Africa*. A series of novels published in the 1950s gave her only a limited readership and after *No Fond Return of Love* (1961) her books went out of print until her work was cited coincidentally in the *Times Literary Supplement* in 1977 by both David Cecil and Philip Larkin among the most underestimated novels of the century. This roused a new interest in Barbara Pym's work. She completed two new novels, *The Sweet Dove Died* and *Quartet in Autumn* (1978), and two of the earlier ones were soon reprinted: *Excellent Women* (1952) and *A Glass of Blessings* (1958). These last two are quiet but subtly perceptive studies, the first of a good-natured, much-put-upon spinster, the second of a married woman with too little to think about and, though earnest and well-meaning at heart, too ready to have her head turned by flattery. The books are first-person narratives and the dialogue and comment, while superficially direct and ingenuous, often carry deliciously comic overtones. The irony has no acerbity, and the author has been compared to Jane Austen for the delicate polish of her artistry; but sometimes the slightly stylized conversations conjure up rather the image of an Ivy Compton-Burnett (q.v.) exorcized of her gloom and converted to Anglo-Catholic cheerfulness.

The Sweet Dove Died and Quartet in Autumn are no less percipient, but they lack the early ebullience. In the latter the portrayal of lonely, inadequate characters is effected with a somewhat chilly poignancy. Two men and two women in their early sixties work in the same office but otherwise go their solitary ways. As the two women retire and one goes downhill under terminal cancer, the sense of the absurdity of individual self-protectiveness adds some comedy to the pathos. The posthumous novel A Few Green Leaves (1980), however, is sunnier in tone – a comedy of village life as it is lived.

[HB]

QUILLER-COUCH, ARTHUR ('Q') (Sir) (1863–1944). Novelist and critic, born in Bodmin, Cornwall, and educated at Clifton College and Trinity College, Oxford, where he read classics. He made his name in the 1880s with historical romances after the fashion of R.L. Stevenson's – spirited adventures with some psychological interest. Q was a devoted Cornishman. Fowey, where he eventually made his home, figures as 'Troy' in *Troy Town* (1888) and other Cornish novels and stories. He has been accused of sentimentalizing the life of the Duchy in insipid Arcadian vein and certainly the cheerful stage Cornishry can seem trivial – as, for instance, in *Shining Ferry* (1905). A more effectively earnest vein runs through *Hetty Wesley* (1903), a study of John Wesley's sister. Quiller-Couch edited *The Oxford Book of English Verse* (1900) and in 1912 he became King Edward VII Professor of English Literature at Cambridge, where he gathered an enthusiastic following by lectures later published as *On the Art of Writing* (1916) and *On the Art of Reading* (1920). As a stylist he cultivated mannered graces that now firmly date him.

[HB]

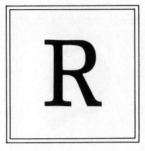

RAINE, CRAIG (1944–). Poet, born in County Durham and educated at Oxford. He has published *The Onion, Memory* (1978), *A Martian Sends a Postcard Home* (1979) and *A Free Translation* (1981). The title poem of the second volume, which observes our world through the eyes of a visitor from Mars –

> Rain is when the earth is television.
> It has the property of making colours darker.

– inspired the use of the word 'Martian' to describe a new drift in certain poets towards using extravagantly fanciful imagery as a means of revitalizing our view of the familiar world. See 'The Grocer':

> He shakes the air into a paper bag and,
> eggs pickpocketed inside, trapezes it.

[HB]

RAINE, KATHLEEN (1908–). Poet, born in Ilford, Essex, educated at Ilford County High School and Girton College, Cambridge, where she read natural science and later, in 1955, became a Fellow. Her spiritual home was in rural Northumberland where she lived for some years in childhood with an aunt. Her mother's people were Scottish and her first autobiographical volume, *Farewell Happy Fields* (1973), shows how the lost northern landscape and village formed her childhood paradise. ('In Northumberland I knew myself in my own place; and I never "adjusted" myself to any other'.) Her second autobiographical volume, *The Land Unknown* (1975), covers the period of her unsuccessful marriages to Hugh Sykes Davies, the Cambridge English don, and to Charles Madge, the poet, and of her temporary conversion to Roman Catholicism. *The Lion's Mouth* (1977) completes the autobiographical trilogy.

Kathleen Raine's first volume of verse, *Stone and Flower* (1943), was succeeded by *Living in Time* (1946), *The Pythoness* (1949) and *The Year One* (1952); and *Collected Poems* (1956) gathered together what she considered worth preserving. It shows her a poet of transparent sincerity in the tradition of those whom the perennial philosophy of Platonic idealism has in one way or another inspired – Blake, Shelley and Yeats among them (and she has written critical books on Blake, Coleridge, Yeats (q.v.) and David Jones (q.v.)). 'The ever-recurring forms of nature mirror eternal reality; the never-recurring productions of human history reflect only fallen man, and are therefore not suitable to become a symbolic vocabulary for the kind of poetry I have attempted to write.' (Introduction.) Edwin Muir (q.v.), reviewing her work, spoke of its 'natural beauty undecorated and undefaced by influence'. At her best she has a fine lyrical control of word and rhythm, and can achieve compelling memorability. Meditative in manner, intimate in tone, refined in feeling and delicately poised in presentation, her finest work illuminates disturbingly. *The Lost Country* (1971) is rich in technique and varied in substance. It derives its title from the moving poem, 'In Answer to a Letter':

> The only Paradise, Proust said,
> Is the lost country that has passed
> Out of time and into mind. . . .
> Plato, that we come from thence,
> Out of mind and into time,
> In a forgetful sleep descend,
> And by remembering return
> Where memory and hope are one

Of later collections *The Oval Portrait* (1977) contains a sketch of her mother in its title poem, and *The Oracle in the Heart* (1980) reveals again her scientific precision of natural observation alongside her mystical hunger for 'imageless / Plenitude of soul'. *Collected Poems 1935–1980* was published in 1981. [HB]

RAMANUJAN, A.K. (1929–). Poet and translator, born in Mysore, India. He studied at the universities of Mysore in 1946–50 and Indiana, Bloomington, USA, in 1959–63. He married Molly Daniels in 1962; they have two children. He taught in India from 1950 to 1958; since 1962 he has been in the Linguistics Department, University of Chicago. A poet in both English and Kannada, he has translated various volumes of poetry and prose from Tamil and Kannada into English.

The Striders (1966), *Relations* (1971) and *Selected Poems* (1976) contain English poems of exquisite workmanship that very delicately unravel the perplexities of an Indian of conventional Hindu upbringing who lives in the United States. They are among the finest poems on the twentieth-century experience of the exile's unease, all the more unusual for eschewing self-dramatization, affirming, instead, the fertile influence of an ambivalent existence, with the emotional and intellectual see-saw thus produced constantly surprising and wryly delighting.

The Striders (a British Poetry Book Society Recommendation) won praise for the delicacy and precision of the verse, the purity of its language and, in K. Ireland's words, 'a style which avoids ambiguity and strives after neat syntax, clarity, and easy rhythm'. This wholly merited emphasis on perfection of style and technique has often, however, both in India and abroad, carried a murmur that Ramanujan's poetry is a virtuoso performance of a very thin melody. S. Nagarajan undermines, indeed contradicts, his statement that Ramanujan could become 'perhaps the most considerable Indian poet in English', by claiming that he 'may not have much to say'. G. Devi argues convincingly that the title poem in The Striders, an image of a water-insect motionless upon 'the ripple skin / of a stream', is a symbol of fixity-within-flux, which constitutes the ambiguous theme of Ramanujan's poetry. Indeed, this interplay of contraries also occurs in Ramanujan's use of subtle, detailed memories of his Indian childhood and family (developed further in *Relations*) that steal upon him in his American academic life.

The phenomenon is illustrated in 'Snakes' (The Striders). A characteristically conversational opening, 'No, it does not happen / when I walk through the woods', puzzles the reader for twelve lines, until he discovers that it is among 'aisles of bookstacks' that the persona thinks of snakes. There follows a description of snakes in a dusty, rural setting, then vivid memory-flashes of his own terror of ritual cobras in his parents' home, so that even his sister's braids seemed snake-like, until walking home one night his heel 'slushes on a snake', purging his fear and making it psychologically safe to walk through woods. The irrational childhood phobia, as irrationally 'cured', surfaces unexpectedly in an American library, owing to the faintest colour and texture resemblances between book-spines and reptiles. There is brilliant clarity in the 'objects' described, but it is an ironically observed, ambivalent experience that simultaneously juxtaposes, links, contrasts, merges two cultures, past and present, childhood and maturity – the disparate contents of a mind. Devi believes that such concern with the poet's own mind marks an alienation from human relationships which Ramanujan jealously conserves as a means of self-discovery, but the fundamentally ironic attitude in poem after poem persuades the reader to regard Ramanujan's interior experience as an instance of the workings of the *human* mind, at once disturbing and full of wonder. [AR]

RANSOME, ARTHUR (1884–1967). Children's writer, son of a Professor of History at Leeds University who took his family for annual holidays on a farm at Nibthwaite near Coniston Water in the Lake District. Ransome went to Russia in 1913 seeking the material which produced *Old Peter's Russian Tales* (1916) and became Russian correspondent for the *Daily News*, then for the *Manchester Guardian*. But it was memories of early Lake District holidays (and also East Anglia holidays) that inspired and furnished his major work, the twelve books for and about children, beginning with *Swallows and Amazons* (1930) and forming a consecutive chronicle in which figure the Walker children (John, Susan, Titty and Roger) who holiday by the lake and have a little sailing dinghy, *Swallow*, and their friends the Blackett children (Nancy and Peggy), with their benevolent bachelor Uncle Jim ('Captain Flint' and Ransome's self-portrait), who reside in the area. The series of stories includes *Swallowdale* (1931), *Peter Duck* (1932), *Winter Holiday* (1933), *Pigeon Post* (1936), *Secret Water* (1939) and *Great Northern?* (1947). *Coot Club* (1934) and *The Big Six* (1940) take us to the Norfolk Broads and feature other children (the Callums). The posthumous publication of *The Autobiography of Arthur Ransome* (1976) shows how accurately related to Ransome's own experience are the details of the children's adventures. The air of reality, so appealing to children, is thus explained. Technical expertise in sailing, camping and other outdoor pursuits gives substance to the adventures. [HB]

RAO, RAJA (1908–). Novelist, born at Hassan, South India, into an ancient Brahmin family. His childhood was influenced by his grandfather's spiritual interests and by rural village life at Harihalli. His father, H.V. Krishnaswamy, taught at Nizam's College, Hyderabad, where Rao attended the Madarsa-e-Aliya, the only Hindu in a Muslim school. At the Muslim University of Aligarh, along with Ahmed Ali (q.v.), he was introduced to European culture by Eric Dickinson. After matriculating there, he returned to Hyderabad, graduating from Nizam's College in 1928. A scholarship took him to the University of Montpellier, then the Sorbonne; in France he married Camille Mouly (divorced 1949). In 1965 he married the American actress Katherine Jones. Back in India in the early 1930s, Rao visited the ashrams of holy men like Aurobindo, Gandhi and Taranath. While involved in Gandhi's 'Quit India' movement he edited the periodical *Tomorrow* with Ahmed Ali in 1943–4. His personal spiritual quest, which began in France, eventually found direction when he met Sri Atmananda Guru at Trivandrum in 1943. He was appointed a professor of philosophy in the University of Texas in 1965, and has since travelled regularly between the United States and India, thus maintaining touch with the traditional sources of his spiritual values.

'Spiritual' and 'metaphysical' are inescapable words in trying to describe Raja Rao's writings. His earliest fiction (short stories in his own language, Kannada, and in English) was written in the 1930s though not collected in a volume, *The Cow of the Barricades and Other Stories*, until 1947. Most of them show him beginning to experiment with means of adapting English to convey Indian thought and feeling, and dealing with the themes of village life and Hindu religious experience that form the stuff of his first novel, *Kanthapura* (1938).

In the Foreword to *Kanthapura*, Rao writes: 'One has to convey in a language that is not one's own the spirit that is one's own. . . . We cannot write like the English. We should not. We cannot write only as Indians. We have grown to look at the large world as part of us.' In the copious manner of the *Mahabharata* and *Ramayana*, with the episodic structure of the puranas, the stirring story of Kanthapura is told in a homely, conversational style, as if by a rural grandmother drawing upon her repertoire of traditional tales. The everyday lives of the fictional inhabitants of Kanthapura, beside the River Himavathy in South India, are created in rich, full, realistic detail, all closely integrated with worship of the goddess Kenchamma – with the ceremonies and festivals that make the 'god-world' seem 'true and near and brilliant'. The age-old rhythms of the natural year are daily made manifest in the village, so that, as C.D. Narasimhaiah observes, 'the sense of the past comes into meaningful union with the present' and 'the individual has no existence of his own apart from the community'. As Kenchamma gives every activity significance, Moorthy, the Brahmin follower of Gandhi, is able to arouse the community to non-violent resistance to the British: the independence struggle is thus subsumed into the millennia-old religious experience of India, even though locally the authorities triumph and 'neither man nor mosquito' is left in Kanthapura.

The relationship of 3000 years of Hindu myth to life in the twentieth century is central to Rao's second, and hitherto most important, novel, *The Serpent and the Rope* (1960); the love between the characters Rama and Savithri is a skilful modern re-interpretation of the legend of Satyavan and Savithri in the *Mahabharata*. But this story, and the novel itself, are also very much more. Other themes, all intertwined, include the relationship between India and the west (Rama and his French wife

Madeleine), between the earthly and the spiritual (Rama's love of women/Woman and desire for God), between the physical and metaphysical worlds (the 'waves' and 'water' of the superscription), between personal identity and godhead (exemplified in Rama's quest) and supremely, as the title indicates, between illusion and reality (the apparent world symbolized by the serpent, the illusory image superimposed upon the rope – Brahman or absolute reality). M.K. Naik describes it as a 'philosophical novel'. Ahmed Ali declares: 'The philosophy *is* the story'. Rama's marriage to Madeleine breaks down, but through his ideal, 'platonic' love of Savithri, which endures even her 'real' marriage to another, he begins to realize himself and his Indian heritage and goes on to seek out a guru who can 'vouchsafe the vision of Truth'. Above all, perhaps, the novel maps this spiritual quest of Rama's, and it is in trying to read the map that western readers usually find Rao much less accessible than other Indian novelists in English. Without some attempt at Vedantic philosophy (though the novel itself does help the ignorant but willing reader), it is all too easy to be stupefied by dialogue containing a sentence like 'When the I is, and where the Nothing is, what is the Nothing but the "I" '. For all the intimate knowledge Rao displays of France and England, of Christian (and Islamic, Buddhist and Hindu) doctrines, of movements in western thought and feeling, for all the appeal the book makes to the reader to surrender himself to the pull of its currents, it is debatable whether Rao addresses himself as much to western as to Indian readers. Narasimhaiah and Naik think it the most richly and genuinely *Indian* novel yet written in English. It undoubtedly makes strenuous demands on non-Indians, but to try to meet them proves an invigorating and expanding intellectual and emotional experience, part of which derives from the extraordinary fusion of western and Indian modes of story-telling. In his lucid book on Rao, Naik remarks that the Indian form to which the novel comes closest is 'the Purana – that unique blend of history, literature, philosophy and religion', and that Rao's use of English is 'a conscious attempt to forge an English prose style based on . . . features of Sanskrit rhythms'.

The Cat and Shakespeare (1965) is a revision of 'The Cat' published in the *Chelsea Review* (New York, 1959). It has been called 'symbolical', 'surrealist', 'a comic extravaganza and a realist tale'. Rao has again adapted traditional Indian story-telling and philosophy to modern experience. The bustling, loquacious central character, Govindan Nair, who 'has an explanation . . . for everything' and believes that 'We would all be kittens carried by the cat', acts as a mediator for divine grace and love. Against the background of 'corrupt' petty bureaucracy in India during the Second World War, he enables the narrator Ramakrishna Pai (who wonders at the beginning if God will ever bless him) to become the recipient of grace, symbolized by the cat, and ultimately to 'hear the music of marriage' despite earlier discords – much as the married partners in Shakespeare's romances do. Like the eleventh-century commentator Ramanuja, Rao emphasizes in this apparently shapeless story the philosophy of self-surrender through love, so that grace descends upon human beings, not through the suppression of the human will, but as its union with God's will. *The Serpent and the*

Rope ended with Rama's submission to a guru; *The Cat and Shakespeare* goes beyond, to the wonder of a oneness with the deity.

Comrade Kirillov, written in English but first published in French translation (1965), then considerably reworked, appeared in English in 1976. Largely a philosophic satire of communism, especially of the anti-nationalist role of Indian communists in 1939–45, but also of theosophy and of British liberal-leftish attitudes in the 1930s and 1940s, it asserts the unconscious Indianization of foreign creeds. Less enduring than Rao's other books, its acute but genial exposure of inherent contradictions in various political and philosophical stances nevertheless makes it a scintillating satiric performance.

The Serpent and the Rope won the Sahitya Akademi Award in 1964. [AR]

RATTIGAN, TERENCE (1911–77). Dramatist, born in London, educated at Harrow and Oxford, and a full-time playwright, apart from his war years in the RAF, from 1934. *French Without Tears* (prod 1936), an upper-class farce, ran for over 1000 performances and established Rattigan as a reliable entertainer. More serious plays include *The Winslow Boy* (1946), based on a famous Edwardian case of a naval cadet who was wrongly accused of theft and whose father almost ruined himself through determination to clear his name, and *The Browning Version* (prod 1948), a one-act study of a public-school master who is a failure. *Adventure Story* (prod 1949) essays the portrayal of Alexander the Great's career in chronicle form, disposing episodic presentation of his gradual descent into tyranny between a prologue and an epilogue that show him on his deathbed. *The Deep Blue Sea* (1952) is a psychological study in obsessional infatuation on the part of the wife of a good-natured judge for an easy-going and inadequate former test pilot. *Ross* (1960) is about Lawrence of Arabia. Rattigan's theatrical craftsmanship guaranteed a steady narrative interest. He defended himself against charges of shallowness and obviousness on the grounds that the box-office relies on 'Aunt Edna', the archetype of limited intelligence and cultural mediocrity. (Preface to volume 2 of the *Collected Plays*, published in four volumes, 1953–78.) [HB]

RAYMOND, ERNEST (1888–1974). Novelist, brought up along with 'Dot' in the strange household of Major-General George Blake ('Dum') and 'Aunt Emily'. He only very gradually discovered he was the son of Blake and Emily's sister, 'Aunt Ida', while Dot was the daughter of Blake and Emily. Raymond's first autobiographical volume, *The Story of My Days* (1968), records steps in the discovery, as well as schooldays at St Paul's, London, training at Chichester Theological College, service as a chaplain in the First World War, and its climax in the Gallipoli campaign that inspired his first novel, the runaway best-seller *Tell England* (1922). 'Tell the Spartans, stranger, that here we lie, obedient to their laws', wrote Simonides of those who fell at Thermopylae. 'Tell England, ye who pass this monument / We died for her, and here we rest content', is Raymond's epitaph on heroes who fell in the Dardanelles. The impact of the book derives from the way Raymond brings a long, conven-

tional, boys'-magazinish account of the schooldays of his heroes, with all its scrapes and rigours, hopes and dreams, to ironic consummation on the fatal peninsula of classical history and legend. Sophisticated critics tore the book to shreds, and Raymond later came to feel reservations about its 'naive romanticisms . . . too facile heroics and too uncritical patriotism', but it was the firm launching-pad for a literary career that produced over forty novels, the last, *Under Wedgery Down* (1974), completed just before his death. Raymond relinquished his Orders during a religious crisis after the war. The later autobiographical volumes are *Please You, Draw Near* (1969) and *Good Morning, Good People* (1970). [HB]

READ, HERBERT (Sir) (1893–1968). Poet and critic, born near Kirbymoorside, North Yorkshire, the son of a farmer. He was educated at Crossley's School, Halifax, and at Leeds University. He fought as an infantry officer in the First World War and was awarded the DSO and the MC. Afterwards he held a civil service post in the Treasury, then at the Victoria and Albert Museum, and he became Professor of Fine Art at Edinburgh University from 1931 to 1933. Thenceforward he worked in various publishing, editorial (the *Burlington Magazine*) and academic (Charles Eliot Norton Professor of Poetry at Harvard, 1953–4) capacities. Francis Berry (*Herbert Read*, 1961) shows how the contrast between idyllic childhood on a farm and years of trench warfare provides a clue to understanding the temper and direction of Read's creative and critical output. *Annals of Innocence and Experience* (1940) in its later edition (1946) reprints autobiographical recollections of his country childhood, *The Innocent Eye* (1933), in conjunction with *In Retreat* (1925) and *Ambush* (1930), two volumes about the war in which the combatant analyses the feelings of those involved. The polarities recur elsewhere. In Read's one novel, the allegory *The Green Child* (1935), a South American president, Olivero, feigns assassination and returns quietly to his old home in rural Yorkshire where he and the symbolic Green Child descend to the utopian underwater realm of Green Children. Over against this curious exercise in fantasy stands the celebrated poem *The End of a War* (1933), a crisp and concentrated exercise in metaphysical speculation inspired by a bloody incident on 10 November 1918. A wounded German officer lured a British battalion into a village supposedly abandoned by the retreating Germans, and thus into a machine-gun ambush. The three parts of the poem are 'Meditation of the Dying German Officer', 'Dialogue between the Body and the Soul of the Murdered Girl' (her naked mutilated corpse was found in a cottage) and 'Meditation of the Waking English Officer' (who survived to reflect on the armistice). Read's *Collected Poems* (1946) reveal him the master of sharp observation, succinct and direct in style. The title poem of the later volume, *Moon's Farm* (1955), is a moving dramatic dialogue on the poet's return to his home area in Yorkshire after fifty years. Read's prolific prose output in the critical, aesthetic and sociological fields marks him as one of the most stimulating minds of the age. *Collected Essays in Literary Criticism* came out in 1938 and *Selected Writing* in 1963. [HB]

READ, PIERS PAUL (1941–). Novelist, the son of Sir Herbert Read (q.v.), brought up in Yorkshire and educated at Ampleforth College and at Cambridge. He is a Roman Catholic, and his novels are notable for the working-out of ideas and the exploration of moral problems. In *The Junkers* (1968) a panoramic view of the Second World War, seen from the German side, is conveyed through the accumulating files and investigations of an English diplomat posted to Berlin in 1963. *Monk Dawson* (1969) is the study of a priest who moves from an exclusive community to work in the Archdiocese of Westminster, then, increasingly finding his faith irrelevant, gains release from his vows to plunge into London life. *The Professor's Daughter* (1971) effectively grasps developments of political and social and moral thinking that came to a head in the radical and violent student movement for 'liberation' in America in the 1960s. In *The Upstart* (1973), a much less convincing book, Read pictures a man so damaged by class snobberies in youth that he tries to ruin the local aristocrats who condescendingly befriended him – the son financially, the daughter sexually. *Polonaise* (1976) centres on a Polish count who has lost his faith and *A Married Man* (1979) on a middle-aged English barrister who rebels in 1973, becoming a Labour candidate for Parliament and taking a mistress. Read's strength is that of a conspectus-novelist, summing up phases of recent history and probing the moral issues involved in their social and personal crises. The novels have intellectual substance and are immensely readable. *The Villa Golitsyn* (1981) is a story of real or suspected espionage by Foreign Office staff. Complex in design, but melodramatic in substance, it purports to probe seriously the collision between private morality and public loyalty. *Alive* (1974), Read's factual account of the Andes plane crash of 1973 and the cannibalism of the survivors, was a big commercial success.   [HB]

REANEY, JAMES (1926–). Poet and playwright, born near Stratford, Ontario, Canada, and educated at the University of Toronto. After graduating in 1948 he lectured for seven years at the University of Manitoba, taking an MA and PhD at the University of Toronto. Since 1960 he has taught English at the University of Western Ontario. He founded and edited the magazine *Alphabet* (1960–71), a publication 'devoted to the iconography of the imagination' which reflected his own mythopoeic approach to literature. His first poetry collection, *The Red Heart* (1949), blended satire, extravagant wit and a sense of spiritual mystery with great technical virtuosity. The darker poems in the collection observed the human comedy against the eternal background of decay and death, finding the truer values in childhood than in the frightening yet superficial adult world. A second collection, *A Suit of Nettles* (1958), contained twelve pastoral eclogues in imitation of Spenser's *Shepheardes Calender* (1579) and extended his criticism of worldly values through the immediate reference of local satire. A prolific playwright, Reaney's blend of naturalism and fantasy is best represented in *The Killdeer* which was acclaimed on its first production at Vancouver (1960). It was published in *The Killdeer and Other Plays* (1962) and a revised version (produced at Vancouver 1970) in *Marks of Child-*

hood (1970). The publication of *Collected Poems* (1973) allowed a full appreciation of his range and distinctive talent. *The Dismissal, or Twisted Beards and Tangled Whiskers* (1978) was written to mark the 150th birthday of the University of Toronto.   [PQ]

REED, HENRY (1914–). Born in Birmingham, West Midlands. He wrote one of the most read poems of the 1939–45 war, 'The Naming of Parts', which brilliantly parodies the instruction of an NCO based on phrases in a military manual. Its initial echoing of Auden's 'Spain' and its sexual double-entendres add to the impact.

> To-day we have naming of parts. Yesterday,
> We had daily cleaning. And to-morrow morning,
> We shall have what to do after firing. But to-day,
> To-day we have naming of parts.

The poem is one of three in the same vein (II 'Judging Distances', III 'Unarmed Combat') called 'Lessons of the War' and included in *A Map of Verona* (1946) alongside a celebrated parody of T.S. Eliot (q.v.), 'Chard Whitlow'. Reed has also written plays and scripts for radio.   [HB]

REEVES, JAMES (1909–78). Poet, born in London, educated at Stowe School and Cambridge University. He was a schoolmaster, then a college of education lecturer, until 1952 when he turned to full-time writing and editing. A specialist in juvenile literature, he has been prolific in providing prose and verse material for children. As an editor, he has over forty titles to his credit, most of them directed at the educational market. His own poetry is the work of a quietly ruminative mind, dissatisfied with depersonalizing forces in the contemporary social environment, not often stirred to ferocity, but capable of wry deprecation at the tone of an income tax demand:

> Couched in the smoothest, most obsequious terms;
> But what it meant was: 'We can break you,
>   Reeves;
> You'd better pay up quick, you worm of worms!'
>   ('Indirect Speech')

Reeves writes of the worries and consolations of private emotional life with a studied, undemonstrative assurance and, when the inspiration flares to match the unobtrusive craftsmanship, he achieves moments of exemplary imaginative authority. *Collected Poems 1929–1974* (1974) includes 'all the poems I want to reprint'. The *Times* obituarist observed that 'his poems had all the virtues and none of the vices of Georgian poetry'.   [HB]

REID, VIC S. (Victor) (1913–). Novelist, born and educated in Jamaica, where he has worked in journalism and advertising, with extensive travel abroad.

One of the older post-1945 West Indian writers, Reid has a powerful but unequal talent. *New Day* (1949) created a wholly new sense of indigenous historical identity, when most West Indians believed they inhabited historyless and cultureless deserts. At Jamaican Independence in 1944, an aged narrator, speaking a convincing approximation to Jamaican dialect, describes the Morant Bay Rebellion of 1865, which he witnessed. Through him, Reid imposes a historical continuum from the catastrophe of 1865 to Independence, with Jamaicans, at one with landscape and natural growth, becoming a distinctive people. In *The Leopard* (1958), about Mau Mau in Kenya (see Ngugi, q.v.), Reid's manipulation of negritudinist theory and primitivist sexuality makes the fiction creak, but he redeems it with the honestly rendered relationship between an African father and half-white son – the latter 'symbolic of all cultures produced by a meeting of civilizations' (Louis James). The seventeenth-century Maroon hero of *The Jamaicans* (1976) embodies a prophetic vision of Jamaican national integrity relevant for Jamaicans today.

Reid has also published some books of children's fiction. [AR]

REITZ, DENEYS (1882–1944). Politician, soldier and writer, born at Bloemfontein, South Africa, third son of F.W. Reitz (President of the Orange Free State, 1889–96, and Secretary of State, Transvaal Republic, 1898–1902). Seventeen at the outbreak of hostilities, Deneys Reitz fought against the British throughout the Anglo-Boer War (1899–1902) and went into self-imposed exile in 1902 rather than submit. His wartime leader, General Smuts, eventually persuaded him to return and help work for Afrikaans–English unity in South Africa. In 1914–18 he fought under Smuts against the Germans in South-West Africa and Tanganyika and, after severe wounds in France as colonel commanding the 1st Royal Scots Fusiliers, led the battalion into Germany in 1918. He was a cabinet minister under Smuts in 1921–4 and in the Hertzog-Smuts administration of 1933–9, then in Smuts's wartime government in 1939–43 he was Deputy Prime Minister. In 1943 he became South African High Commissioner in London, at which post he died.

In 1929 Reitz published *Commando*, about his experiences in the Anglo-Boer War, which he had written in 1903 in exile in Madagascar. It is one of the finest accounts in English of personal experience in war, conveyed in a sparse, economical style that tells of extraordinary feats of daring, endurance and youthful zest as if they were commonplaces. In two and a half years he covered vast distances on horseback, scouting, skirmishing, fighting, galloping off to re-form, reduced to rags, wearing only an old grain bag in the bitter winter of 1901, suffering every kind of physical deprivation, but buoyed up by an unshakeable faith in the forlorn cause of the Boer republics. The second half of *Commando* deals with Reitz's part in the daring Smuts raid into the Cape Colony with a force of 300 men, constantly harried by superior British forces, frequently evading capture by incredible exploits in mountain and forest country, until they controlled hundreds of square miles of the North-Western Cape Colony. The simple, fast-moving narrative generates a moving sense of an epic struggle in which the vast landscape reduces human action to the barest levels of endurance and survival. It is an unpretentious, frank, ingenuous revelation of the hidden reserves of the human spirit in the face of what would normally be regarded as utterly overwhelming physical conditions. Above all, the immense variety of detail and incident is skilfully orchestrated so that the narration of elemental facts becomes a remarkable feat of the creative imagination.

Reitz wrote two other autobiographical books: *Trekking On* (1933) and *No Outspan* (1943). [AR]

RENAULT, MARY (pseudonym of Mary Challans) (1905–). Novelist, born in London, educated at Clifton High School, Bristol, and St Hugh's College, Oxford. She became a State Registered Nurse, served as such during the Second World War and afterwards went to live in South Africa. Her best-known 'straight' novel, *The Charioteer* (1953), a story of the Second World War, draws on her nursing experience. It focuses on homosexuals (including wounded ex-servicemen) with an intensity that is not alleviated by samples of schoolgirlish dialogue (' "Oh you," said Bunny coquettishly') and coy observation ('A leisured view of the room yielded so many awful little superfluities, so many whimsies and naughty-naughties'). But Mary Renault is primarily a historical novelist, specializing in the classical and ancient world. *The Last of the Wine* (1956) is set in Athens at the time of Socrates. *The King Must Die* (1958) and *The Bull from the Sea* (1962) are set in the mythic Minoan world and centre on Theseus, King of Athens. The first novel tells the story of his youth; the second takes up with his return from Crete after slaying the Minotaur and his accession to his father's throne. The books are not free of the staginess in tone and dialogue that snare historical novelists.

Fire from Heaven (1970) and *The Persian Boy* (1972) trace the career of Alexander the Great and are more fictional biographies than dramatically shaped novels. The former covers the first twenty years of Alexander's life; the latter covers his last seven years, and is narrated by his favourite boy, Bagoas, a Persian eunuch from the court of King Darius. Alexander's journeys, with the attendant battles, intrigues and conspiracies, have a ready-made interest which the author exploits with considerable skill, but the emotional core of the book is limitedly and cloyingly homosexual. *Funeral Games* (1981) turns the sequence into a trilogy by chronicling events in the decade after Alexander's death. [HB]

RHYS, JEAN (1894–1979). Novelist, born in Roseau, Dominica. After some schooling in England, she worked as chorus girl, mannequin and artist's model. The first of her three marriages led to ten post-1918 years of European bohemianism, chiefly Parisian. *The Left Bank* (1927), stories about artists in Paris, was published with encouragement from Ford Madox Ford (q.v.), on whom she apparently partly modelled the egotistical Heidler in her first novel, *Postures* (1928; as *Quartet*, New York, 1929, and subsequently). These two books and three further novels, *After Leaving Mr Mackenzie* (1930), *Voyage in the Dark* (1934) and *Good Morning, Midnight* (1939), form Rhys's first literary career, which, despite the modernity of her treatment of female sexuality, made little contemporary impact. She lived in Devon, forgotten until her finest novel, *Wide Sargasso Sea* (1966), won the Royal Society of Literature and W.H. Smith awards and the reissue of her earlier books. Two volumes of stories followed: *Tigers Are Better-looking* (1968) and her most designed and delicate collection of short fiction, *Sleep It Off, Lady* (1976).

Jean Rhys's dedicated craftsmanship, drawing much upon her own experience without being merely 'autobiographical', achieves extraordinarily clear-sighted understanding of uprooted, insecure, intense, life-seeking but defenceless personalities. Her heroines form a series of steadily developing studies of intelligent, independent-minded, rebellious, but directionless, vulnerable women. Exploiting their own sexuality, sometimes as if it were a cash crop (as in *After Leaving Mr Mackenzie* and *Good Morning, Midnight*), they are essentially passive victim-figures. They reject their genteel origins, but blindly, pursuing unattainable absolute personal freedom and recapture of past happinesses. To wonder whether actually working for a living might not have cured their lugubrious tendencies is equally a tribute to the novelist's art and a reservation about her moral vision. Nevertheless, in *Voyage in the Dark* and *Good Morning, Midnight* metaphor, imagery and the use of first-person narration give central characters and readers simultaneously a profounder understanding of how any form of exploitation, personal or social, diminishes humanity.

Entirely independent of *Jane Eyre* in its technique and artistry, *Wide Sargasso Sea* convincingly creates the story of Rochester's mad wife, using her and Rochester as sensitive, alternating narrators, who both become victims of a decadent Caribbean society and lush but menacing tropical ambience. Antoinette's deepening experiences of dependence, loneliness, cruelty, and the intensity of her responses, push her tragically into the insanity that mere gossip originally assigned to her. It is a wholly satisfying consummation of Jean Rhys's novelistic skills. [AR]

RICHARDS, FRANK (pseudonym of Charles Hamilton) (1875–1961). Writer of school stories. He had his first effort accepted by a periodical at the age of 17 (see *The Autobiography of Frank Richards*, 1952) and never looked back. Stories published in the *Gem* (1907–39) and the *Magnet* (1908–40) endeared him to generations of boys as the creator of Greyfriars School, Tom Merry, monocled Arthur Augustus D'Arcy and the greedy, irrepressible and eminently bashable fat boy, Billy Bunter. Richards has been credited with 80 million words and with never being slipshod. Facsimile reissues of his stories have continued to prove popular. [HB]

RICHARDSON, DOROTHY (1873–1957). Novelist, born in Abingdon, Oxfordshire. Inheriting the fruits of her grandfather's success as a grocer, her father turned gentleman and declined into bankruptcy, and her mother committed suicide. Dorothy, one of four sisters, left home and worked as a teacher in Hanover and London, then, from 1896, as secretary-assistant to a Harley Street dentist. She began to write and translate and to mix in progressive socialist and feminist circles. An affair with H.G. Wells (q.v.) ended in pregnancy and miscarriage in 1907. She married Alan Odle, an artist fifteen years her junior, in 1917. Though a victim of tuberculosis, he survived until 1948. Richardson devoted herself to a mammoth work, *Pilgrimage*, which ultimately consisted of thirteen novels: *Pointed Roofs* (1915), *Backwater* (1916), *Honeycomb* (1917), *The Tunnel* (1919), *Interim* (1919), *Deadlock* (1921), *Revolving Lights* (1923), *The Trap* (1925), *Oberland* (1927), *Dawn's Left Hand* (1931), *Clear Horizon* (1935), *The Dimple Hill* (1938). These twelve were collected as *Pilgrimage* in 1938. *March Moonlight* was completed at her death and and published posthumously in *Pilgrimage* (1967). In substance *Pilgrimage* is trans-

figured autobiography. Richardson uses the stream-of-consciousness technique in anticipation of Virginia Woolf and does so in a conscious attempt to produce a feminine counterbalance to masculine realism. Miriam Henderson, the heroine, has a career parallel to Richardson's and something of her creator's tendency to undermine the close relationships she enters. H.G. Wells is portrayed as Hypo Wilson. ('People are nothing to him but the foolish hope of an impossible unanimity at the service of his plan.') His affair with Miriam reaches its climax in the last two chapters of *Dawn's Left Hand*. *Pilgrimage* never achieved sales commensurate with its critical reputation. Richardson's impressionistic method is rich in detail and has a flickering vitality, but sustained intensity is sacrificed through a failure to select from personal experience only what can be interestingly shared with a reader. There is nothing to match the thematic and symbolic patterning that structures the work of Joyce (q.v.) and Woolf (q.v.). [HB]

RICHARDSON, HENRY HANDEL (pseudonym of Ethel Florence Richardson) (1870–1946). Novelist, born in Melbourne, Victoria, Australia, the daughter of a Protestant Dublin doctor who had come to the gold-rush town of Ballarat in 1852. He had practised for three years in England after qualifying in Edinburgh in 1849, but at Ballarat he worked for four years as a gold-digger, and later as a storekeeper, before taking up the medical profession again. Profits enabled him to take his family to Europe in 1874 but while abroad his investments collapsed and his career as a doctor in Australia from 1877 was one of failure, progressive incapacity and madness. He was placed in a Melbourne private asylum in 1878 and died early the following year. These events provide the basis for his daughter's finest novel, *The Fortunes of Richard Mahony*. This work was first published in three parts: *Australia Felix* (1917), *The Way Home* (1925) and *Ultima Thule* (1929); a revised omnibus edition was published in 1930. Her first book, *The Getting of Wisdom* (1910), reflected her education at the Melbourne Presbyterian Ladies College after her father's death. Her musical talent was such that her mother took her to Leipzig at the age of 17 to study the piano at the Conservatoire. She passed three happy years there, came to recognize that she had not the temperament for a concert pianist, but determined to satisfy her other love, of writing. In Leipzig she had met J.G. Robertson, a young literary scholar, and they married in 1895. *Maurice Guest* (1908) was begun two years later and captures her growing awareness and individuality during the Leipzig period. She and her husband lived in Strasbourg until his appointment as Professor of German at London University in 1903. After that she lived in England, first in London and, after her husband's death in 1933, in Surrey; she made a brief trip to Australia in 1912 to obtain material for *Richard Mahony*. She read widely in European literature and her books are better understood in this context than in relation to the work of Australian writers of the time. She lived a retiring life and her work was little known in England or Australia until the appearance of *Richard Mahony*, in which her talents found full scope – although both her early novels displayed a skill in depicting personal relationships. Mahony's spiritual restlessness is traced through a declining career and the inadequacy of his aspirations revealed in a moving sequence of events which establishes his increasing isolation from his family and from humanity at large. An attempt to escape to England from what he sees as the grossness and provincialism of Australia only results in his feeling equally alienated from the close-knit circles of English society. Cultural tensions between England and Australia, and the difficulty of establishing a satisfying imaginative relationship with a new land, are themes which have occupied many Australian writers and artists. In *Richard Mahony* these issues are both immediately relevant and also assume profound spiritual dimensions as obsessions of Mahony's disordered mind. The final section of the book represents the supreme achievement of Richardson's work in its economical yet powerfully moving depiction of Mahony's growing isolation and lapse into insanity. A full study of her life and work is available in *Ulysses Bound* (1973) by Dorothy Green.   [PQ]

RICHLER, MORDECAI (1931–). Novelist and short-story writer, born in Montreal, Quebec, Canada, and educated at Sir George Williams University there. He left to spend two years in England and returned to Canada briefly in 1952 where he joined the staff of the Canadian Broadcasting Commission for a time. He married in 1959 and has five children. Richler was awarded a Guggenheim Fellowship in 1961 and was writer-in-residence at his old university in 1968–9 and at Carleton University, Ottawa, in 1972. Since 1953 he has lived in Europe (mainly in London) writing for film and television (including adaptations of his own works) in addition to his novels and short stories. Richler's most successful works are those which draw deeply upon the remembered poverty of his own childhood in the old Jewish ghetto of Montreal's St Urbain's Street. This impulse informs *The Apprenticeship of Duddy Kravitz* (1959) and *Son of a Smaller Hero* (1965). In these books he explores the conflicting pressures on a young Jew growing up in modern society in a prose whose range and wit mirrors the tragic-comic complexity of its subject. In a series of books set in Europe, Richler exposed the ruthlessness and hypocrisy of modern commercial and political values through characters and situations which veer between social realism and satire. *The Acrobats* (1954) centres upon a young idealistic Canadian outsider in Spain who dies at the hands of a psychopathic ex-Nazi. In *A Choice of Enemies* (1957) a Canadian expatriate is again the central character, this time in a cult-world of London left-wingers and film producers which Richler clearly knows all too well. *Cocksure* (1968) also draws, not altogether successfully, upon this setting. *St Urbain's Horseman* (1971) is again set in London, but through the childhood and family memories of Jake Hersh, a Canadian-Jewish film producer, opens perspectives on to areas of world guilt. It contains black humour and social satire in the outrageous story of how Hersh has to 'pay the price of the colonial come to the capital'. It is his most fully realized work. The *Incomparable Atuk* (1963) was a heavy satire set in Toronto which allowed for fantasy and farce in its depiction of the corrupting effects of modern materialistic culture on an innocent Eskimo. Although truly inter-

national in reputation, Richler still regards himself very much as a Canadian writer, not simply because his central characters are themselves Canadian – either uneasily 'at home' in Canada or plainly expatriate: 'All my attitudes are Canadian. I'm a Canadian; there's nothing to be done about it'. His artistic achievement, like that of A.M. Klein (q.v.) in a different vein, has been to define his own very particular experience in such a way that it not only mirrors the sentiments of other Canadians but conveys the universal dimension of that Canadian experience to readers everywhere. Richler's journalistic collections, *Hunting Tigers under Glass* (1968) and *Notes on an Endangered Species* (1974), are valuable for an approach to his work; *Shovelling Trouble* (1972) collected entertaining essays and reviews.   [PQ]

RICKWORD, EDGELL (1898–1982). Poet, born in Essex, educated at Colchester and Oxford. He served in France in the First World War and produced a handful of powerful, compressed poems about life in the trenches whose emotional austerity makes a chilling impact (see 'The Soldier Addresses His Body' and 'Trench Poets'). The influence of Donne and the metaphysicals puts the early Rickword in line with T.S. Eliot (q.v.) (see 'Sir Orang Haut-ton at Vespers'). The postwar social and political scene became the target for harsh satire, and Rickword added Swiftian octosyllabics ('The Handmaid of Religion') and Popish decasyllabics ('The Encounter') to his armoury. 'To the Wife of a Non-Interventionist Statesman' (published in 1938), a communist's outraged protest against western connivance at Franco's butcheries, is precisely prophetic of the price soon to be paid:

> already Hull and Cardiff blaze,
> and Paul's grey dome rocks to the blast
> of air-torpedoes screaming past.

Rickword added little to his poetry after 1930. See *Collected Poems* (1947) and *Collected Poems and Translations* (1974).   [HB]

RIDLER, ANNE (1912–). Poet, born in Rugby. She married Vivian Ridler in 1938 and has four children. *The Nine Bright Shiners* (1943), *The Golden Bird and Other Poems* (1951), *A Matter of Life and Death* (1959) and *Some Time After and Other Poems* (1972) are the work of a poet with a finely cultivated lyrical gift for recording and celebrating events of domestic life with frankness and clarity of feeling that is never clamant yet always fervent. Themes include wartime separation from her husband, married love, birth, motherhood, the growing up of children, visits, anniversaries and the like. The verse play *The Shadow Factory* (prod 1945) played its part in the revival of Christian drama that grew out of Eliot's *Murder in the Cathedral*. It is a nativity play with a difference in that its setting is a contemporary factory where welfare and culture for the workers subserve productive efficiency. ('New factory is but old Priestley writ large.') *The Trial of Thomas Cranmer* (1956) was written for the 400th anniversary of Cranmer's martyrdom and handles the theme of redemptive suffering with a convincing straightforwardness of presentation. More recent plays are *Who Is My Neighbour?* (prod 1961) and *The Jesse Tree* (1972), a masque on 'the glory of the world and the mystery of evil' that uses the Jesse Window in Dorchester Abbey (scene of the first performance in 1970) as the starting-point. [HB]

RIVE, RICHARD (1931–). Fiction writer and critic, born in Cape Town, South Africa, where he graduated in 1949. While a schoolmaster in the 1950s, his brisk, authentic stories of slum life under apartheid appeared in local journals; *African Songs* (Berlin, 1963) is a collection of them. A novel, *Emergency* (London, 1964; New York, 1970), deals with political disturbances after the Sharpeville massacre in 1960. Rive edited *Quartet* (1964), containing four stories one each by himself, La Guma (q.v.), James Matthews and Alf Wannenburgh, and the much reprinted anthology, *Modern African Prose* (1964). His Oxford DPhil thesis (1974) was on Olive Schreiner (q.v.); he has published many critical articles. Though widely travelled in Africa, Europe and America, he is the only black protest writer of his generation not to seek exile. Rive's best stories are terse and laconic, relying chiefly on skilful transpositions of 'Cape Coloured', mainly Afrikaans, speech into English dialogue; they range from the semi-documentary treatment of daily black humiliations, as in 'Willie-boy' and 'Drive In', to impassioned hope in 'African Song', and a fanciful but morally implacable presentation of Christ's second coming, as a black man in South Africa, in 'The Return'. *Writing Black* (1981) is an autobiographical volume. [AR]

ROBERTS, MICHAEL (1902–48). Poet, and Principal of the College of St Mark and St John, Chelsea, London, in his last three years. He had published *Poems* (1936) and *Orion Marches* (1939) and had edited *The Faber Book of Modern Verse* (1936). Janet Adam Smith, Roberts's widow, has described the genesis of this influential anthology. On T.S. Eliot's (q.v.) initiative its purpose was 'not to be a comprehensive anthology of the "best poems" of the age but rather . . . to define the modern movement in a way that was not just chronological but a question of sensibility and technique' (*Times Literary Supplement*, 16.6.76). The result was a volume that almost totally excluded the Georgians, ignored Edward Thomas (q.v.) and vastly over-represented 'poets of the Thirties' such as Stephen Spender (q.v.) and Cecil Day Lewis (q.v.). Roberts's own *Collected Poems* (1958), which has a memoir by his widow, reveals a poet of disciplined artistry who wrote when he had something to say. Frederick Grubb has edited Roberts's *Selected Poems and Prose* (1980). [HB]

ROBINSON, LENNOX (1886–1958). Irish dramatist, born in County Cork, Ireland, and educated at Bandon Grammar School. He moved to Dublin in 1908 when his play *The Clancy Name* was produced at the Abbey Theatre. *The Cross Roads* (1909) and *Harvest* (1910) followed; Robinson became manager of the theatre and continued to supply lively comedies of Irish life. In his play *The Lost Leader* (1918) Parnell turns up as a porter in a West of Ireland hotel, not dead after all, but suffering from amnesia. Robinson was competent enough in laying hands on current devices and motifs to produce stageable antics of domestic upheaval (see *Crabbed Youth and Age*, 1922) and he was capable of an amusing character study such as the amiably scatter-brained Mrs Brennan in the

three-act comedy, *The Round Table* (1921), but his ventures into Ibsenesque analysis are gratingly ill-digested (see *The White Blackbird*, 1925). Probably his best play, *The Big House* (1926), chronicles the late stages in the melancholy decline of a once-prosperous Anglo-Irish Ascendancy family in County Cork. We see a home stricken successively by the First World War in 1918, by guerrilla activity and the Black and Tans in 1921, and by republican reprisals in the Civil War in 1923. Robinson became a director of the Abbey Theatre in 1923 and was largely responsible for determining its policy in the years immediately following the death of Lady Gregory (q.v.) in 1932, when his fondness for knockabout comedies met with opposition from Frank O'Connor (q.v.) and others. Robinson's *Collected Plays* came out in 1928. Later works are *W.B. Yeats, A Study* (1939) and *Curtain Up* (1942). He edited *The Irish Theatre* (1939). [HB]

RODGERS, W.R. (William Robert) (1909–69). Poet, born in Belfast, Northern Ireland, and educated at Queen's University, Belfast. He was for twelve years a Presbyterian minister in County Armagh till in 1946 he became a BBC producer, working on Irish topics. His first volume, *Awake! and Other Poems* (1941), is marked by rhythmic vigour and by metaphorical over-abundance that suit well with certain moods of exuberance, but too often (e.g. in 'Summer Holidays' and 'End of a World') the proliferation of imagery, clever as it is , bludgeons the reader into mental dizziness. Feeling is apt to get shouted down by the hectoring declamation intended to voice it. The texture is generally less dense in the succeeding volume, *Europa and the Bull and Other Poems* (1952). The title poem, a bounding recapitulation of the myth, is a riot of image and movement. The 'Easter Sequence', a series of commentaries on the events of Holy Week, written first for broadcasting, is looser in its flow and less tangled with excess metaphor. [HB]

ROLFE, FREDERICK WILLIAM (1860–1913). Novelist. He claimed the title 'Baron Corvo' and used the form 'Fr Rolfe' authorially. He was born in Cheapside, London, into a family that manufactured pianos. He left school at 15 but managed to earn a living as a schoolmaster until, at 25, a convert to Catholicism, he offered himself for the priesthood and eventually gained a place at Scots College, Rome. His expulsion from the college caused lifelong embitterment. He tried to make his way as a painter before committing himself to writing, but in no sense did he ever thereafter earn a stable living, and the story of his frustrations and privations – as failed priest and unprofitable writer – is a sad one. He was not without friends and potential collaborators, and publishers' commissions occasionally came to his rescue, but an incurable quarrelsomeness and a mania for self-justification so possessed him that friendship and patronage were rewarded with acrimony and vituperation. Persecution mania and a chronic paranoiac vindictiveness drove him to resentful ingratitude even against men on whom he had sponged for day-to-day subsistence. We have an extraordinary picture of Rolfe in his last years. After ten years of literary struggle at home, he went off to Venice in 1908 and thereafter refused to come back. Unpaid hotel bills mounted up; there were floods of letters levering money from abused friends who supported him; he indulged his homosexual proclivities to a degree of marked depravity; at times he was penniless; and he died of a sudden heart attack.

The unattractive biographical portrait is important, for it contains the stuff of his significant literary work. *Stories Toto Told Me* (1898) – folk-lore legends of saints – appeared first in *The Yellow Book* and, with many new fables added, reappeared in *In His Own Image* (1901). In *Chronicles of the House of Borgia* (1901) Rolfe thought himself back into the past with zest, vividness and infectious verbal flamboyance. *Don Tarquinio* (1905), 'A Kataleptic Phantasmatic Romance', is the history of one day in the life of a man of fashion in the era of the Borgias. Of the three books which most powerfully and shamelessly fictionalize the persona and career of Rolfe himself, *Nicholas Crabbe*, or 'The One and the Many', first published posthumously (1958), covers the years of literary struggle in London, pillorying publishers and literary acquaintances, and *The Desire and Pursuit of the Whole*, also published posthumously (1934), covers the final Venice years. It libels English residents against the background of Nicholas Crabbe's wish-fulfilling love for a wholly submissive and dependent boyish girl ('the form of a noble boy, in all but sex') called Gilda. Nicholas Crabbe, writer, gives place to his alter ego, Arthur George Rose, in Rolfe's most celebrated novel, *Hadrian the Seventh* (1904). In this most glorious of all day-dreams of getting one's own back, Rose, twenty years after rejection as a candidate for priesthood, is summoned by ecclesiastical authority to accept reparation for the acknowledged injustice. He is priested and then, after an electoral impasse at the conclave in Rome, made Pope. As Supreme Pontiff (Hadrian VII), Rose makes sweeping innovations, rides roughshod over sticklers for the status quo, sorts out the nations, walks about Rome doing good, rolls his own cigarettes and indulges in idiosyncratic dispensation of patronage. Rolfe has great fun with the vocabulary of hierarchy and ceremony, liturgy and protocol. But the book falters imaginatively through excessive personal self-justification and eventually topples into hysterical anti-socialism. Successive collections of Rolfe's *Letters* to various correspondents have been edited by Cecil Woolf (1959, 1960, 1962, 1963 and 1974) and Miriam K. Benkovitz (1977). [HB]

ROSENBERG, ISAAC (1890–1918). Poet and artist, born in Bristol of an immigrant Jewish family from Russia. His father, Barnard Rosenberg, was 'a poor Jewish pedlar and a scholar of his traditional culture' (Jean Liddiard, *Isaac Rosenberg*, 1975). The family moved to London in 1897 and Isaac was brought up in the East End. He was apprenticed to an engraver from 1904 to 1910, was supported at the Slade School of Art by a wealthy Jewess, went to South Africa in 1914, returned to England in 1915 and, though his father was a Tolstoyan pacifist, volunteered out of desperate need to supply some income for his impoverished family. His health and physique were poor, he did not make a good soldier, and his service in the Bantam Regiment was a long agony ('the army is the most detestable invention on earth', he told Lascelles

Abercrombie (q.v.)) not mitigated by the fact that he was 'forbidden to send poems home, as the censor can't be bothered with going through such rubbish' (letter to Edward Marsh (q.v.)). He was killed near Arras on April Fool's Day 1918, having remained a private. He published *Night and Day* (1912), *Youth* (1915) and *Moses* (1916), an incomplete verse play, all at his own expense. After his death Gordon Bottomley (q.v.) edited his poems and Laurence Binyon (q.v.) contributed a memoir (1922). Collected editions appeared in 1937 and 1949 with forewords by Siegfried Sassoon (q.v.). Rosenberg began to write under the influence of Rossetti, but 'the vague and nebulous disappeared from both his art forms' (op. cit.); his language lost romantic mistiness; he learned the value of exactness and clarity. Rosenberg consciously determined to saturate himself with the strange and extraordinary experience of war so that it could refine itself into poetry. He never felt or voiced the heroic or patriotic spirit like Rupert Brooke (q.v.): conversely he never expressed nostalgic regret for a broken culture or lost pastoral peace; for he had no lost peacetime Arcadia to mourn. War brought an intensification of hardships and sufferings which poverty, a reserved temperament and frail physique had already introduced him to. His 'August 1914', 'Returning we hear the larks' ('my best poem'), 'Dead Man's Dump' and 'Break of Day in the Trenches' are among the most painfully aware war poems we have.

> A man's brain splattered on
> A stretcher-bearer's face;
> His shook shoulders slipped their load,
> But when they bent to look again
> The drowning soul was sunk too deep
> For human tenderness.
>
> ('Dead Man's Dump')

Incisive yet complex, compassionate yet acutely penetrating and detached, Rosenberg's best poems are organic pieces in which poetic logic has its own way, neither overlaid by expected sentiment nor pressed into ready-made rhythmic pattern. See *The Collected Works of Isaac Rosenberg: Poetry, Prose, Letters, Paintings, and Drawings*, edited by Ian Parsons (1979). [HB]

ROSS, SINCLAIR (1908–). Novelist, born in Shellbrook, Saskatchewan, Canada. He worked for the Royal Bank of Canada in Winnipeg and later in Montreal. He retired in 1968 and now lives in Spain. His position in Canadian literature is secured by his first novel, *As for Me and My House* (1941), which drew deeply upon his own boyhood memories in raising a picture of prairie life towards the level of myth. The dramatic yet understated conflict between man and landscape provided a perfectly tuned setting for the delicate analysis of tension and frustration which leads to a complex and satisfyingly ambiguous conclusion. The novel has become a classic of Canadian literature, but the later works, *The Well* (1958) and *Whir of Gold* (1970), failed to equal the intensity yet immediacy of the early book. *The Lamp at Noon* (1968) collected some fine short stories, the title story again using a prairie setting in a sober charting of human tenacity. Ross's best recent work is *Sawbones Memorial* (1974). [PQ]

RUSSELL, GEORGE WILLIAM (pen-name AE) (1867–1935). Poet, born at Lurgan, County Armagh, Northern Ireland, of Protestant stock. He studied art in Dublin, then met Yeats (q.v.) in 1866 and became interested in theosophy, Irish mythology and poetry. *Homeward, Songs by the Way* (1894) was his first volume of poems. Others followed, including *Collected Poems* (1926) and *Selected Poems* (1935). Russell's poetic development matched Yeats's in character if not in quality or inspiration: the well-known octosyllabics, 'On behalf of Some Irishmen not followers of Tradition', are neat and eloquent:

> We would no Irish sign efface
> But yet our lips would gladlier hail
> The firstborn of the Coming Race
> Than the last splendour of the Gael.

Russell edited *The Homestead* and *Irish Statesman* and occupied a dominant role in Dublin as literary legislator, much loved by his protégés and generous in the discovery and encouragement of new talent. 'This was the man who was father to three generations of Irish poets', Frank O'Connor (q.v.) says of him (*My Father's Son*). Russell is portrayed with subtle appreciation in George Moore's (q.v.) *Salve*, with comic solemnity in the 'Scylla and Charybdis' episode of Joyce's *Ulysses* (q.v.). He was unsympathetic to the hard-line republican case, felt that De Valera had gravely damaged Ireland and finally, in disillusionment, gave up his Dublin house and moved to London. He died in Bournemouth.   [HB]

S

SACKVILLE-WEST, VICTORIA (1892–1962). Novelist and poet, born and brought up at Knole, near Sevenoaks, Kent, the palatial ancestral home which the Sackvilles had owned since the sixteenth century and which was to exercise a lifelong spell on her imagination. 'Vita' married Harold Nicolson (q.v.) in 1913. She accompanied her husband on his diplomatic postings to Constantinople and Tehran, she bore two sons and the marriage was ultimately an unshakeable one, but Vita's turbulent relationship with Violet Trefusis caused serious tension between 1918 and 1921 (see Nigel Nicolson, *Portrait of a Marriage*, 1973). Her most celebrated work in verse was *The Land* (1926), a pastoral poem that moves through the seasons, celebrating the life of the Kent countryside in the manner of Virgil's *Georgics*. *Collected Poems* came out in 1933. Vita made her début as a novelist with *Heritage* (1919), but it was *The Edwardians* (1930) and *All Passion Spent* (1931) that brought big-scale literary success. *The Edwardians* is an invaluable first-hand picture of life in a ducal residence such as Knole in the years following 1905 when the younger generation first sensed the possible impermanence of the feudal tradition that history had imposed on them. The social and moral codes of the Edwardians are neatly analysed ('Appearances must be respected, though morals might be neglected'; 'Thou shalt not be found out'; 'Only the vulgar divorce'). *All Passion Spent* is a study of an octogenarian widow, Lady Slane, whose life of dutiful devotion to her husband has precluded the fulfilment of her own early artistic ambitions. Vita's own private and family problems are reflected within these books. Her non-fiction output includes *Knole and the Sackvilles* (1923), an account of the ancestral home, *Passage to Teheran* (1926) and the biography *Aphra Behn* (1927). Virginia Woolf's (q.v.) affection for Vita is expressed in the imaginative portrayal of her in *Orlando*.

[HB]

SAHGAL, NYANTARA (née Pandit) (1927–). Journalist and novelist, born in Allahabad, India. She graduated in history from Wellesley College, Massachusetts in 1947. A daughter of Nehru's sister, her upbringing was permeated with Gandhi's ideals; she describes it in *Prison and Chocolate Cake* (1954). The tensions arising from her 1949 marriage into an affluent business family remote from Gandhian principles are perceptible in another autobiographical book, *From Fear Set Free* (1962). She began serious journalism in 1965; divorce came in 1967.

Her well-written novels constitute an intellectual repository of the dedicated, humane Gandhian values that overthrew imperialism, and she examines, in Jasbir Jain's words, 'the men and women behind political ideas and actions' (*Nyantara Sahgal*, 1978). In *A Time to Be Happy* (1958) and *This Time of Morning* (1965) politics fail to cohere satisfactorily with the major characters' troublous love stories, but *Storm in Chandigarh* (1969) successfully dramatizes the effacement of the old idealistic politicians in Punjab by new men of opportunism. *The Day in Shadow* (1971) searchingly anatomizes the new Indian leadership who proclaim 'time to bury Gandhi'. *A Situation in New Delhi* (1977), her most cogent fictional expression of Gandhian political morality, examines various concepts of revolution.   [AR]

ST OMER, GARTH (1940?-). Novelist, born in Castries, St Lucia, who graduated in French from the University of the West Indies, Jamaica. For some years he lived in turn in France, Ghana and Britain.

St Omer's is the starkest, bleakest West Indian vision of the moral paralysis that neo-colonialism induces in sensitive minds. As Jacqueline Kaye observes, he is influenced by the French existentialists, and his characters perform various masquerades to hide their utter futility. Except in 'Syrop', a novella published in *Introduction 2* (Faber, 1964), his major figures rebelliously refuse to take the places in neo-colonial society for which they have been educated, but can find no meaningful alternative. *A Room on the Hill* (1968), *Nor Any Country* (1969), *J—, Black Bam and the Masqueraders* (1972), and the two novellas in *Shades of Grey* (1968) are closely related in situation, characterization and tone; only Breville in *Nor Any Country* performs an act of reconciliation with other individuals in what G. Moore regards as an attempt to redeem his past. This flicker is dowsed by the prevailing mood of the next novel: 'We not only make cakes of mud. We eat them as well.'   [AR]

SAINTSBURY, GEORGE (1845–1933). Literary historian and critic, born in Southampton, Hampshire, educated at King's College School, London, and Merton College, Oxford. He was schoolmaster, then journalist and eventually Professor of Rhetoric and English Literature at Edinburgh University. He read omnivorously and wrote copiously about what he read. Publicatons include *A Short History of English Literature* (1898), *A History of Criticism* (three volumes, 1900–4) and *The Peace of the Augustans* (1916). Saintsbury has been described as 'the first and in many ways the greatest of the long line of academic critics who, in the last 60 years or so, have turned the study of English Literature into a humanistic discipline for undergraduates which may, in the long run, replace Latin and Greek' (G.S. Fraser, *The Modern Writer and His World*, 1964).   [HB]

SAKI (pseudonym of Hector Hugh Munro) (1870–1916). Short-story writer, born in Burma, son of a police officer and brought up by maiden aunts in Devonshire. He started a career in the Burma Police which failure of health quickly terminated. He then turned to journalism and writing. As a correspondent he visited the Balkans, Warsaw, St Petersburg and Paris, then settled in Surrey. Hugh Walpole (q.v.) tells how 'he was to be met with at country houses and London parties, apparently rather cynical, rather idle, and taking life so gently that he might hardly be said to be taking it at all' (quoted in *The Bodley Head Saki*, 1963, ed. J.W. Lambert). *Reginald* (1904) gathered together fifteen sketches that had appeared in the *Westminster Gazette*: they record the conversation of a frivolous, cynical, urbane young man. *Reginald in Russia* (1910) expands sketches into something more like

'stories', continuing to make game of society life. *The Chronicles of Clovis* (1911) and *Beasts and Super-Beasts* (1914) bring Saki's short-story technique to maturity. Here and in the book-length story, *The Unbearable Bassington* (1912), Saki deals satirically with the vagaries and hypocrisies of high living, at his best achieving a witty epigrammatic bite in the mode of Wilde. ('To be clever in the afternoon argues that one is dining nowhere in the evening.') The mannered polysyllabic narrative style is much of its period, but the dialogue of society women, especially when scoring bitchily off one another, is often hilarious, and the gift of amusing paradox a rare one. ('The art of public life consists to a great extent of knowing exactly where to stop and going a bit further.') *When William Came* (1914) pictures an England under German occupation. Saki enlisted as a private at the age of 44 and was killed on the Western Front. The wartime sketches, *The Square Egg*, were published posthumously (1924). There is enough direct and oblique evidence of mysogyny and of interest in cruelty and bloodthirstiness to make Saki's life and works a happy hunting-ground for psychoanalytical critics. ('I'm God! I'm going to destroy the world', he shouted as a boy as he chased his sister round the nursery with a burning hearth-brush.)

A.J. Langguth includes 'Six Short Stories Never Before Collected' in his *Saki: A Life of Hector Hugh Munro* (1982).   [HB]

SALKEY, ANDREW (1928-). Novelist, born in Colon, Panama. He attended Jamaican schools and London University, graduating in 1955. From 1952 he worked variously for BBC radio, which broadcast his plays and poems. He won the Deutscher Kinderbuchpreis (1967) for such outstanding children's novels as *Hurricane* (1964), *Earthquake* (1965) and *Drought* (1966). He has edited many anthologies.

Salkey's zestful but sceptical novels emphasize the bleak West Indian experience of poverty at home and ghetto-culture in London. *A Quality of Violence* (1959), like Lamming's (q.v.) *Season of Adventure* and Sylvia Wynter's *The Hills of Hebron* (1962), vividly describes pocomania spirit possession, including mutual flagellation to the death, though Salkey's central theme is human irrationality. In *Escape to an Autumn Pavement* (1960), more ambitious style and structure almost disguise the aridity of a West Indian's initiation into London life and sex. *The Late Emancipation of Jerry Stover* (1968) reveals individualist freedom as unavailing in the continuing colonialism of Jamaican politics. Abused by English society, the Jamaican hero of *The Adventures of Catullus Kelly* (1969) goes insane, while *Come Home, Michael Heartland* (1976), though sympathetic to 'the knife thrust of Black consciousness' in Brixton, questions its outcome. Salkey has also published poetry, e.g. *In the Hills Where Her Dreams Live* (1979) and *Away* (1980).   [AR]

SANSOM, WILLIAM (1912–76). Novelist and short-story writer, educated at Uppingham, Leicestershire. He worked in a bank, then in advertising, till he joined the National Fire Service on the outbreak of the Second World War. His first stories drew on experience of the London blitz (see *Fireman Flower*, 1944): twenty years later *The Stories of William Sansom* (1963) selected thirty-three tales from the various collections to date, and Elizabeth Bowen (q.v.) introduced them enthusiastically ('To a point, all Sansom stories are scenic stories. . . . The substance of a Sansom story is sensation. . . . A Sansom story is a *tour de force*'). Sansom was less successful as a novelist. *The Body* (1949) has been highly praised for its descriptions of parts of London. It is a study of a simple-minded middle-aged husband whose escalating tendency to self-immolation fabricates tormenting jealousy on the basis of a brash neighbour's interest in his wife. Among later novels are *A Bed of Roses* (1954), *The Loving Eye* (1956) and *The Cautious Heart* (1958). *The Last Hours of Sandra Lee* (1961) reworks Sansom's most characteristic vein, blanketing the heroine's desperation with a jaded ironic nonchalance. Sandra Lee, innocent office girl of 21, is reluctant to plunge into the permanent security of affectionate marriage until she has acquired 'some kind of past with which to face the future' ('You're a good girl who wants to be bad', her friend tells her). [HB]

SARGESON, FRANK (1903–82). Short-story writer and novelist, born in Hamilton, New Zealand, and educated at the University of New Zealand, Canterbury. His early works arose out of his experience of the 1930s Depression, which 'put a sort of community into life' in spite of the hardships. They are deceptively simple monologues which, by the artful employment of a naïve narrator, achieve a poignant tension between surface story and perceived meaning: 'this new way of writing consisted in writing sentences which suggested more than they said'. This indirect, understated and ironic method found a realistic basis in the spare colloquialisms of local speech: 'I was as much excited by the thought of the advance I had made towards bringing an appropriate New Zealand language to light as I was by the substance of the story'. *Conversations with My Uncle* (1936) collected these early short stories and was followed by *A Man and his Wife* (1940). After *That Summer and Other stories* (1946) technique and subject matter became more varied, the shift in focus outgrowing the stock-character of the laconic rural underdog established by the earlier stories and reflecting an increasingly complex postwar society in New Zealand. *I For One* (1952) represented a decided break with his earlier pattern of writings which, although they were quickly recognized as classics, were criticized by some as both constricting his talents as a writer and presenting a one-sided picture of New Zealand life. This novel, set in 1950, follows the frustrations of a schoolmistress by presenting her diary entries for the three months following the death of her father; it was a convincing demonstration of his new-found breadth as a writer. *Memoirs of a Peon* (1965) was 'a picaresque novel' which took the form of reminiscences by a former lady-killer. The blend of human comedy, ironic charting of New Zealand social manners in the 1920s and complex satire (directed as much at the pedantically facetious narrator as at the milieu he describes) produced a highly original book which further enhanced his stature as a writer: 'I realized that if I could assume the mask of a more literate person it opened up a great deal more'. *I Saw in My Dream* (1949) expanded an earlier story of 1945 ('When the Wind Blows') in

exploring the contradictions between a puritan upbringing and the dominant yet superficial values of an acquisitive society. The book fails largely because of greater complexity in the (later) second section which squares oddly with characters already sketched. The theme has direct New Zealand relevance, as the poet James K. Baxter (q.v.) has observed, and was pursued further in *The Hangover* (1967), a more tightly constructed work and the first novel with an urban setting. *Joy of the Worm* (1969), a tragi-comic novel which depicted the effects of parental domination, also dealt with emergence from the protective, religious peace of childhood into the problems of adulthood, while the title story of *Man of England Now* (1972) presented New Zealand society over the previous fifty years through the eyes of a young English migrant. An old people's home was the setting for *Sunset Village* (1976). The memoir trilogy, *Once is Enough* (1972), *More than Enough* (1975) and *Never Enough* (1978), provides a good introduction to his life and work. Arguably the outstanding New Zealand prose writer of his time, in his early work Sargeson established a worldwide reputation which did much to enable other New Zealand writers to regard the novel as a possible form; his own later work built on this foundation but extended the range and form of comment so that his published works now constitute a major study of the society of which he was a lively part all his life. [PQ]

SASSOON, SIEGFRIED (Captain Siegfried Loraine Sassoon, CBE, MC) (1886–1967). Poet and prose writer, born in the Kentish Weald and brought up there by his mother who had separated from her husband. She was a Thornycroft, daughter of Thomas Thornycroft, sculptor, sister of Sir John, the naval architect, and of Sir Hamo, sculptor. The Sassoons were Jews with social and financial status. ('Ever since I could remember, I had been remotely aware of a lot of rich Sassoon relations. I had great-uncles galore, whom I have never met and they all knew the Prince of Wales' – *The Old Century*.) Siegfried was educated privately at home, then at Marlborough and at Cambridge, which he left without a degree, for he was too interested in poetry and sport to work at law. The war poetry which catapulted him into fame must not, for all its importance, be overvalued in relation to the extraordinary prose output which provides an essential commentary upon it. He wrote two autobiographical trilogies. The first is a semi-fictionalized record in which Sassoon figures as George Sherston: *Memoirs of a Fox-Hunting Man* (1928), *Memoirs of an Infantry Officer* (1930) and *Sherston's Progress* (1936). The three were issued together as *The Complete Memoirs of George Sherston** in 1937. But the presentation of a soldier-huntsman could scarcely do full justice to the inner life of a soldier-poet and Sassoon wrote a second and factual series of memoirs: *The Old Century and Seven More Years* (1938), *The Weald of Youth* (1942) and *Siegfried's Journey, 1916–1920* (1945). Less even in accomplishment perhaps as a whole than the Sherston trilogy, and inevitably affected adversely at times by the necessity to go over the same ground twice, the volumes are packed with rich evocations of persons and events and also constitute 'an outline of my mental history'. *The Old Century* recaptures childhood with a prose artistry that blends the re-minted voice of spontaneous childhood simplicity in counterpoint with the idiom of adult reflection. Sassoon's humour (as well as his searing gravities) resides in just such stylistic dualities.

The Weald of Youth records the entry into poethood. Sassoon issued privately printed collections before the war but came to see that his 'pseudo-archaic preciosities' bypassed the real physical world. He made a preliminary breakthrough with The Daffodil Murderer (1913), which began as a parody of Masefield's The Everlasting Mercy and turned into a not unflattering pastiche. So far 'one half of me was hunting-field and the other was gentleman writer'. The war wrought the change. From experience as a second lieutenant in the trenches on the Somme (where he won the MC) he came home on sick leave in 1916. It is at this point that Siegfried's Journey begins the astonishing story that reached its climax after Sassoon came back to England a second time with a shoulder wound from the Battle of Arras in 1917. The gap between the real war and the home picture of it tormented him. The torment fused with a newly discovered 'talent for satirical epigram' to produce war poems which exploded the established myths of heroic militarism. The work of this, the crucial phase of Sassoon's poetic output, is represented by The Old Huntsman and Other Poems (1917), Counter-Attack and Other Poems (1918), The War Poems (1919) and Picture Show (1919). But Sassoon's revulsion against the war was not just a literary matter. He issued a protest against the prolongation of the war which was calculated to result in court martial and imprisonment. But the authorities sent him to Craiglockhart War Hospital, where he met Wilfred Owen (q.v.) and where he was restored. On his third posting to the front he was wounded again after a rash foray across No-Man's-Land. Siegfried's Journey goes on to record his postwar involvement with the Labour Party: he became Literary Editor of the Daily Herald. It is also crowded with informative reminiscences of the many literary figures his talents first, then his celebrity, introduced him to. They include Hardy (q.v.), Gosse (q.v.), Robert Ross, Bennett (q.v.), De la Mare (q.v.) and Osbert Sitwell (q.v.).

Sassoon's war poems shocked by ironically juxtaposing the raw realities of the trenches with the easy slogans of conventional patriotism and morale-boosting uplift. In 'They' a bishop explains that when the boys come back 'they will not be the same', having fought in a just cause. Legless, blind, broken and syphilitic boys admit that indeed they have changed – 'And the Bishop said, "The ways of God are strange"'. The conciseness is telling. Sassoon needs only eight lines in the famous 'Blighters' to present the packed home theatre shrilling a jingoistic music-hall chorus ('We're sure the Kaiser loves our dear old Tanks') and to demolish the falsity of it with the image of a real tank lurching down the stalls to the tune. It would put an end to the jokes and the intolerable mockery of the riddled corpses on the battlefields.

'The Hero' briefly pictures a soldier's mother receiving news of her son's death at the front in grief and pride. 'The colonel writes so nicely', she says. But the officer who has brought the missive knows the truth. Jack was a 'cold-footed, useless swine' who panicked. Sassoon's capacity for thus crisply buffeting the reader's sensibilities is allied to a telling verbal resourcefulness in spread-

ing out before him the sickening environment of battle – rotten corpses, legs and trunks in the sucking mud, sodden buttocks, clotted heads, and the smoke, the fire and the shrieks (see 'Counter-Attack'). The harshness of the exposure and the satirical bitterness of tone touch at times an almost hysterical pitch and, after this revelation of what the war did to a ruminative young 'booby-trapped Idealist', the later poetry was bound to be an anti-climax. But Sassoon was conscious of the need to find a new style and cites his own 'Early Chronology' as providing a fresh pattern 'in which I assumed a laconic, legato tone of voice and endeavoured to be mellow, sophisticated, and mildly sardonic'. His latest work was influenced by his reception into the Roman Catholic Church in 1957. See the Collected Poems (1961). See also D. Felicitas Corrigan, Siegfried Sassoon: Poet's Pilgrimage (1973) and Rupert Hart-Davis, ed., Siegfried Sassoon's Diaries 1920–1922 (1981).

The Complete Memoirs of George Sherston is a trilogy of fictional autobiography in which Sassoon represents himself as George Sherston. The first volume, Memoirs of a Fox-Hunting Man (1928), re-creates the rural 1890s of the well-to-do. Sherston, the narrator, made wiser by time, looks back on the boy and the young man he was with nostalgia for the idyllic days of hunting and cricket, but with many a side-glance at youth's thoughtlessness and waywardness. Yet a tolerant good-humour pervades the retrospective moral strictures. ('As I remember and write, I grin, but not unkindly, at my distant and callow self.') George is a sensitive, imaginative young person in love with the countryside, and he learns hunting the hard way. Though he reads a lot (before the hunt becomes a passion) and likes symphony concerts, Sassoon has made him a hero much less cultivated than himself ('only me with a lot left out', he says in The Weald of Youth and 'a simplified version of my outdoor self', he adds in Siegfried's Journey). The book is rich in lovable (as well as some unlovable) portraits who evoke delight in the kindly values of the lost regime they represent at its best. The stylistic texture of the book is remarkable; country scenes are saturated with an atmosphere of tranquillity; the narrative and descriptive flexibility is such that it can cope with subtly abrupt shifts of viewpoint that are productive of humour, irony or ominous pre-echo of what is to come. Towards the end the war intrudes and takes Sherston into the Yeomanry with a deceptive lack of fuss ('For me so far the War had been a mounted infantry picnic in perfect weather'), then to a commission in the Royal Flintshire Fusiliers. We leave him at the front 'staring across at the enemy I'd never seen'.

Memoirs of an Infantry Officer (1930) is a moving personal record of the war and 'its effect on a somewhat solitary-minded young man'. We accompany Sherston through the Somme offensive of 1916 and the Battle of Arras in 1917. He is at home on leave, first sick, then wounded: he wins the MC. The outer scenes are presented with startling clarity while the inner workings of Sherston's restless mind maintain a counterpoint that weaves agony with humour, bitterness with idealism. The subtle complexities of moral and psychological motivation are laid bare in candid exposure of the many men who make up one man. Alongside dare-devilry in his fighting exploits there is wholesale disillusionment with institutionalized war. On leave in 1917 he meets Thornton

Tyrell (Bertrand Russell) and makes the famous formal protest against the continuation of the war. Seeking a court martial as heroically as he sought danger in battle, he is diverted to Slateford Hospital for shell-shocked officers. *Sherston's Progress* (1936) traces the hero's restoration and his voluntary return to the front. A brief but highly entertaining sequence takes us to Ireland, and Sassoon is at his funniest here. But the multiplicity of selves portrayed is what gives the work its depth. Robert Graves (q.v.) (portrayed in the book as 'David Cromlech') has said that Sassoon's 'unconquerable idealism changed direction with his environment', and in Sherston's last weeks at the front he is feeling 'strong and confident in the security of a sort of St Martin's summer of Happy-Warriorism' and yet also defining himself as 'a company commander with a suppressed anti-war complex'. The quality of reflection is sustained throughout the trilogy. The war has a hated yet irresistible grip on those it embraces: it is an alien, monstrous aberration, defiling nature and mankind. Yet Sherston is the better for it. [HB]

SATCHELL, WILLIAM (1860–1942). Novelist, born in England, educated partly in Germany. He had ventured into print with verse and prose at the age of 23 before going to New Zealand in 1886. His fortunes as a pioneer and storekeeper did not prosper but in 1895 he made money as a stockbroker. Throughout his life he published journalistic writings but his importance rests on two works, *The Land of the Lost* (1902) and *The Greenstone Door* (1914). *The Toll of the Bush* (1905) and *The Elixir of Life* (1907) suffer excessively from the over-complicated plots and sterotyped characters which also mar the other works. *The Land of the Lost* establishes the desolate North Island setting as an arena for metaphysical as well as physical stress in writing that recalls Thomas Hardy (q.v.) and foreshadows that of Jane Mander (q.v.). The novel shows a real imaginative appreciation, unrealized though it is ultimately, of ways in which a specific New Zealand setting could be used for a truly universal drama. *The Greenstone Door* is set in the period 1830–60 in the form of recollections of childhood by the hero, Cendric Tregarthen, who is brought up by a Maori chief after his father is killed. Later events which shatter his boyhood idyll include the troubled period after the Treaty of Waitangi (1840) and the siege of Orakau Pa (1864). Something of a historical classic, it nevertheless lacks the imaginative dimensions of the earlier novel. [PQ]

SAYERS, DOROTHY L. (Leigh) (1893–1957). Novelist and dramatist, the daughter of a clergyman, brought up in Norfolk and educated at Somerville College, Oxford, where she took first-class honours in French. After working successively at school-teaching, in publishing and in advertising, she established herself as a detective novelist in a series of books beginning with *Whose Body?* (1923). The series includes *Lord Peter Views the Body* (1928), *Have His Carcase* (1932), *The Nine Tailors* (1934) and *Busman's Honeymoon* (1938). Its success depends largely on the charm and brilliance of the amateur detective, Lord Peter Wimsey, a handsome cultured aristocrat, unashamed of upper-class mannerisms and highbrow erudition. A faithful manservant, Bunter, and a down-to-earth Scotland Yard man, Parker, are useful foils. Sayers

took seriously her craft of detective fiction ('the art of framing lies – but mark! of framing lies in the *right way*', she said). She wrote for an intelligent public, spicing her dialogue with wit and sophistication. Corpses and clues become the concern of characters who have plenty of other things to talk about as well. Sayers re-created a varied series of backgrounds from her own experience – an advertising agency in *Murder Must Advertise* (1933), the artists' community in Kirkcudbright in *Five Red Herrings* (1931) and Oxford in *Gaudy Night* (1935).

Busman's Honeymoon was made into a successful play, and the author turned her attention to religious drama. She wrote *The Zeal of Thy House* for the Canterbury Festival in 1937, taking the story of William of Sens, architect and re-builder of the cathedral. The play explores the theme of divine and human creativity and is not without dramatic power. *The Emperor Constantine* (1951) is theatrically ineffective, but Sayers scored a great success with her prose play cycle on the life of Christ, written for radio, *The Man Born to be King* (prod 1941). A sequence of twelve episodes, covering events from the Nativity to the Resurrection, it is at once direct in impact, biblically authentic in substance and attuned to the modern mind. Sayer's last work was her translation of Dante's *Divine Comedy*.

As a young woman, Dorothy Sayers had her eccentricities, and later she became very secretive about her private life. Since her death it has become known that she bore an illegitimate son in 1924 and that her marriage in 1926 to Oswald Arthur Fleming gave her no equal companionship but a lot of drink bills to pay. See James Brabazon, *Dorothy L. Sayers: The Life of a Courageous Woman* (1981). [HB]

SCANNELL, VERNON (1922–). Poet and novelist, born in Spilsby, Lincolnshire, and educated at Queen's Park School, Aylesbury, Buckinghamshire. From 1941 to 1945 he served with the Gordon Highlanders in the Middle East and in Normandy, where he was wounded. Scannell has been an amateur and professional boxer and an English teacher: he won the Heinemann Award for Literature for *The Masses of Love* (verse) in 1960 and he turned freelance writer in 1962. Of his novels *The Fight* (1953) and *The Big Time* (1965) reflect the boxing experience and *The Face of the Enemy* (1961) pictures ex-servicemen failing to adapt to postwar life. Scannell has also written a book on *Edward Thomas* (1962) and an autobiography, *The Tiger and the Rose* (1971). But he is primarily a poet, and the volumes of verse include *A Sense of Danger* (1962), *Walking Wounded* (1965), *Company of Women* (1971) and *The Loving Game* (1976). A craftsman in accepted stanza forms (with a hint of Auden), he is a poet for whom a visit by an insurance agent, a radio interview with a celebrity, or a 9-year-old boy's destruction of a cat with Daddy's stick sparks off a sharply observed summary of the world we know. Scannell has told us that an actual incident in Normandy lay dormant within him for eighteen years till it produced the celebrated title poem of *Walking Wounded*, a powerful recapturing of a morning procession of damaged men from the front. A wry preoccupation with life's more ironic let-downs is evident. The walking wounded lack the 'noble wounds' of the 'heroic corpses' and will be fit to fight again. The faded middle-aged lovers of 'Taken in Adultery' are too zestless, tired and melancholy to exude the glamour of sin. Scannell's *Not Without Glory* (1976) is a critical study of poets of the Second World War. *New and Collected Poems 1950–1980* (1980) shows Scannell continuing steadily to respond to and reflect on the life around him with anecdotal substance and technical directness that stand in refreshingly lucid contrast to current impressionistic trends. [HB]

SCHREINER, OLIVE (1855–1920). Champion of women's rights and many unpopular causes, moralist, novelist, born at Wittebergen Mission Station, Cape Colony, South Africa. What little formal education she received from her German father and English mother was later supplemented by wide reading, including Spencer's *First Principles* and Emerson's *Essays*, both of which greatly influenced her thinking. From youth she was unconventional in behaviour, unorthodox in ideas. Chronic asthma was a possible cause of moodiness that often strained her relationships with others, though her ardent faith in humane principles lay behind her estrangement from political figures like Rhodes. South African politicians, including Smuts, courted her views on politics after 1890, but seldom heeded them. While a governess on farms near Cradock in the Karoo (1874–81), she completed at least one novel and worked on two or three others. She went to England in 1881 and had a novel accepted by Chapman and Hall on Meredith's advice. Published as *The Story of An African Farm* (1883), it went into three editions that year. She was lionized by literary London, the first 'colonial' writer to achieve metropolitan acclaim. She formed a close friendship with the young Havelock Ellis, encouraging his early work on the psychology of sex, which was related to her own passionate interest in the disabilities women suffered in Victorian society; she became an influential spokesman in Britain (1883–9) for the political aspirations of women and the working class.

Returning to South Africa in 1889, she settled for almost three years in the Karoo hamlet of Matjesfontein. It was a period of better health and some tranquillity which saw the publication of *Dreams* (1891), an intensification of her interest in Southern African politics, and her composition of most of the posthumously published *Thoughts on South Africa* (1923). In 1892 she returned to the Cradock district, and in 1893 visited England again and published *Dream Life and Real Life*, mostly allegories. In 1894 she married a Cradock farmer, S.C. Cronwright, who changed his surname to Cronwright-Schreiner. A shared opposition to Rhodes's political aims and methods contributed to their early married happiness, soon overshadowed when an only child died at birth (1895). Later her continuing ill-health and the volatile political situation meant they were often separated, though they visited Europe together in 1896–7. Olive Schreiner's burning sense of political justice found expression in a short novel, *Trooper Peter Halket of Mashonaland* (1897) (a courageously uncompromising attack on Rhodes's materialism and his Chartered Company's inhuman treatment of the blacks in what became Rhodesia), and in *A South African's View of the Situation* (1898) (a pamphlet pleading with the British not to make war on the two Boer republics). These publications contracted her own personal life by alienating many of her former English admirers. When the 1899–1902 war broke out, she publicly championed what she saw as the heroic Boer struggle against a rapacious British imperialism and came under military observation in the Cape village of Hanover.

With characteristic political foresight she realized shortly after the Boer defeat of 1902 that they were a resilient people who would recover from humiliation, and her sympathies turned more consciously to the plight of black South Africans. In 1906 she wrote: 'No one needs me here now except the Natives'. She tried to reconstruct parts of her large work on women and sex (destroyed in manuscript in the war); they appeared as *Woman and Labour* (1911), an influential argument for women to share fully in 'men's' work and for their enfranchisement. One of her finest pieces of political and social analysis appeared in *The Transvaal Leader* (1908; separately 1909): *Closer Union: A Letter on the South African Union and the Principles of Government*. U. Edmands rightly regards it as Olive Schreiner's 'most eloquent plea for justice and equality of opportunity for all members of society'.

In 1913 she went to Europe, vainly hoping for a cure for her asthma, but 1914 found her stranded in England, where her German name, her abhorrence of war and her defence of conscientious objectors in an article (1916) made her increasingly unpopular. Lonely, depressed, her health rapidly declining, she aged so much that when her husband finally joined her in London in 1920 he failed to recognize her. She knew she was dying and sailed for South Africa, while he remained in London. She died alone in a Cape Town hotel. Cronwright then busied himself on behalf of her literary reputation and published *The Life of Olive Schreiner* and edited *The Letters of Olive Schreiner* (both 1924). He had had *Thoughts on South Africa* published (1923) and brought out two novels she had begun in the 1870s and frequently reworked during her life: *From Man to Man* (1926) and *Undine* (1929).

Despite the four novels, Olive Schreiner did not think of herself as a novelist – a thinker and writer, yes; one who believed that in a colonial situation, at least, it was a writer's pre-eminent task to apply the strictest civilized standards to the realities of everyday life, and not to flinch from drawing the logical moral conclusions. Hence, for all the repetitiveness, the weak construction, the sometimes blatant moralizing, her fiction, especially *An African Farm*, can still move a modern reader by its sheer moral authority, even on issues, like women's rights, where much dust of battle has now settled. The device of Christ appearing to Peter Halket may be cumbersome fictionally, but it enables her devastatingly to apply professed Christian principles to the sordid practices of colonialism with a moral power similar to that of Conrad (q.v.) in *Heart of Darkness*. Her methods belong rather to the tradition of inspired preaching; hence her predilection for dreams, visions and allegories, which appear even in her fiction, and for logical and suasive argument, as in *Closer Union*, with its rich postulation of a justly ordered and truly united South Africa. Her creed is thoroughly humanist, devoid of the consolations of religion, yet numinous in its whole-hearted pursuit of truth.

[AR]

SCOTT, ALEXANDER (1920–). Poet, born in Aberdeen, Scotland, educated at Aberdeen Academy and Aberdeen University. After war service, in which he gained the Military Cross, he held university posts, first at Edinburgh for a year, then at Glasgow from 1948, where he became Head of the Department of Scottish Literature in 1971. Scott has written a number of plays for stage and radio, lively, boisterous and rich in comic inventiveness; but he is primarily a poet. The Latest in Elegies (1949) was followed by Selected Poems (1950) and Mouth Music (1954), but it was Cantrips (1968) which first won really wide acclaim for him as a spirited, sinewy writer, with a vigorous-delight in rhyme and rhythm and irresistible gusto as a comic and satiric commentator on his age. Later collections include Selected Poems 1943–1974 (1975). Scott matches up to the standard Sassenach conception of the Scots Maker, a heady, hectoring, rumbustious poetic persona, rich in exaggeration yet plain-spoken and down-to-earth, and capable of hard seriousness as well as of riotous fun. There is tenderness, too, in his love poetry. [HB]

SCOTT, F.R. (Francis Reginald) (1899–). Poet, born in Quebec City, Canada, and educated at Bishop's College, Lennoxville, Quebec, then at Oxford as a Rhodes Scholar. He pursued a varied and distinguished career as both an academic and a practising lawyer, his literary activities being but part of a wider involvement in national affairs. During his time at McGill University, Montreal (after his return from Oxford in 1927), he met A.J.M. Smith (q.v.) who interested him in poetry. Together with Smith, A.M. Klein (q.v.) and others he became a prominent supporter of a modernist and cosmopolitan poetic, partly through his editorship with Smith of the McGill Fortnightly Review (1925–6). In 1936 they edited the important poetry anthology New Provinces, and in 1957 The Blasted Pine, 'An Anthology of Satire, Invective and Disrespectful Verse', which was a more lighthearted illustration of Scott's aversion to convention and conservatism. He was associated with Preview and the Northern Review during the period 1942–7. His first book, Overture (1945), revealed a talent for biting and immediate social and satirical verse alongside a varied range of lyrical poems dealing with love and the natural world. Events and Signals (1954) showed a moderation of his satirical stance, but The Eye of the Needle (1957), subtitled 'Satires, Sorties, Sundries', was a selection from such works. Selected Poems was published in 1966, and The Dance is One (1973) included travel poems and translations from the French. Scott remains an important figure in Canadian literature, for his sustained criticism of reactionary opinion as much as for his poetic example. Essays on the Constitution (1977) collected a series of essays and papers published between 1928 and 1971. [PQ]

SCOTT, PAUL (1920–78). Novelist, born in Palmer's Green, North London, son of a commercial artist. He served in the army from 1940 to 1946 and was sent to India as an officer cadet in 1943. There he became an air supply specialist and travelled as such over the length and breadth of the country, meeting an immense variety of British and Indian soldiers and civilians. After the war he worked in publishing and in a literary agency until he was able to turn full-time writer in 1960, settling down in Hampstead Garden Suburb. He married Nancy Avery in 1941 and had two daughters. His first novel, Johnnie Sahib, came out in 1952. The Alien Sky (1953) and The Mark of the Warrior (1958) both make use of the Indian background. The Chinese Love Pavilion (1960) takes us to the Malayan jungle. A planter and guerrilla leader, Saxby, has disappeared, and Tom Brent, a major in the intelligence, narrates the search for him. The Birds of Paradise (1962) is the autobiographical narrative of William Conway, son of a political agent in one of the princely states of India – his childhood, his marriage, his career and his terrible experience in a Japanese prisoner-of-war camp.

Scott's key achievement is his monumental quartet of novels which attempts a comprehensive dissection of the closing years of British rule in India: The Jewel in the Crown (1966), The Day of the Scorpion (1968), The Towers of Silence (1972) and A Division of the Spoils (1975). The Raj Quartet (1977) is an intricately constructed record of a momentous phase – the sudden dropping of the curtain on 200 years of British domination, with all its complex social consequences and human undercurrents. The Jewel in the Crown centres on events in August 1942 after British military setbacks in Malaya and Burma, when Japanese invasion and the 'Quit India' campaign create a new insecurity for the ruling British. A well-meaning English girl, Daphne Manners, niece of a former provincial Governor, is in British eyes over-friendly with a young Indian, Hari Kumar, who has had an English public-school education as Harry Coomer. When Daphne is raped by unknown assailants in the Bibighar Gardens, Mayapore, and rash arrests are made (including that of Kumar), riots follow and Daphne's compromising relationship with Kumar complicates and intensifies the clash of attitudes. The reader picks up narrative essentials piecemeal and sometimes peripherally from the spoken or written records of various participants and observers, all seemingly garrulous, but none of them fully informed or free of prejudice. Daphne's personal story is reserved for the end. Though the subject of this first novel inevitably recalls Forster's (q.v.) A Passage to India in tracing an intensification of mutual racial and social misunderstanding consequent upon an assault, Scott's four-volume study ripples out forwards and backwards from this challenging moment to embrace an immense historical phase in its coverage, effectively transcending Forster's work if not in subtlety of analysis, at least in panoramic fullness of documentation. Relationships between ruling British and ruled natives are explored multi-dimensionally through Scott's continuing awareness of all the facets of the life of each. The pressures of historical fact and of personal need, of political impetus and private passion, are finely balanced and Scott gets under the skin of native and British with the same uncanny penetration. The Day of the Scorpion, in its analysis of the public role demanded of a ruling class and the need for costly and dishonest private adaptation to the collective inheritance of domination, excellently reveals how 'here the British came to an end of themselves as they were'. 'It's time we were gone', the sensitive, sympathetic Sarah Layton observes. After completing the Raj Quartet Scott portrayed a retired ex-army couple lingering on in the new India in *Staying On* (1977), a book with a good deal of comedy which nevertheless, according to Philip Larkin (q.v.), manages to carry 'the emotional impact of a lifetime, even of a civilization' (*The Times*, 24.11.77).   [HB]

SCOTT, TOM (1918-). Poet, born in Glasgow, Strathclyde, Scotland. He started life as an apprentice in the building trade but, after war service and subsequent experience of various jobs including those of postman and dishwasher, he went to Newbattle Abbey at the suggestion of its Warden, Edwin Muir (q.v.), and thence to Edinburgh University. He has been acclaimed as the most gifted of the poets to have written in Scots, following in the wake of Hugh MacDiarmid (q.v.). His early book of translations, *Seven Poems o Maister Francis Villon* (1953), was succeeded by *The Ship and Ither Poems* (1963) of which the title poem is a long allegorical study of civilizational collapse based on the sinking of the *Titanic* and the catastrophe of the First World War. *At the Shrine o the Unkent Warrior* (1968) is a sustained denunciation of war throughout the ages. Scott has told how T.S. Eliot (q.v.) led him back to Villon and MacDiarmid led him back to Dunbar. The conjunction of modernist influence with the medieval tradition has been fruitful for him. His work has passion, acuity and sturdiness. Scott was joint editor (with John MacQueen) of the *Oxford Book of Scottish Verse* (1966) and editor of the *Penguin Book of Scottish Verse* (1970). Among later volumes are *Musins and Murgeonins* (1975) and *The Tree* (1977)   [HB]

SCOVELL, E.J. (Edith Joy) (1907-). Poet, born in Sheffield, South Yorkshire, educated at Casterton School, Westmorland, and Somerville College, Oxford. She married Charles Sutherland Elton in 1937. Her small output comprised only two books of verse published in the 1940s and the collected volume *The River Steamer* (1956), until she wrote *The Space Between* (1982). She writes with unaffected delicacy and with an unobtrusive precision of observation, using traditional forms easily and gracefully. Philip Hobsbaum (q.v.) has praised her 'almost mystical sense of the presence of life' and perhaps her most notable poems – those about children – have a searching, unsentimental tenderness in conveying this sense.   [HB]

SCUPHAM, PETER (1933-). Poet, born in Liverpool, Merseyside, a Cambridge graduate and an English teacher. He is frankly absorbed with the complexities and the finesse of poetry as a word-game and his work is disinfected equally of self-indulgent subjectivism and of grand gesture. But he is no mere miniaturist of the observed and captured immediate, for his inspiration is rooted in an acute awareness of history and of human mortality. *Prehistories* (1975) earned critical praise for its scrupulous craftsmanship and its packed text. *The Hinterland* (1977) contains memorable meditations on an environment secretly alive with a peopled past (like 'Dissolution' or 'The Green Gate'). Its title piece is a sequence of fourteen sonnets, each linked to its successor

by a common concluding and opening line, with a fifteenth sonnet neatly formed from these same now heavily weighted pentameters. It examines the inescapable overshadowing pressure of the First World War, and to a lesser extent the Second World War, on the subsequent years of our century.

> August, September, hang their weights upon
> The rim of summer, when great wars begin.

Summer Palaces (1980) is distinguished by exactness of observation, spareness of style and attentive directness of focus.   [HB]

SELVON, SAMUEL (1923-). Novelist, born in Trinidad of Indian origin and educated at Naparima College. He served with the Trinidad RNVR, 1940-5. In 1947 he married Draupadi Persaud and in 1963 Althea Nesta Daroux, and has three children. While working as a journalist with the *Trinidad Guardian* in 1946-50, he wrote verse and short stories that were well received in Trinidad. In 1950 he moved to London and became a civil servant with the Indian High Commission, until in 1954 he decided to earn his living by writing. Since 1952 he has published one volume of short stories and nine novels, and written radio plays. Selvon has twice held Guggenheim Fellowships (1954, 1968), scholarships from the Society of Authors (1958) and the Trinidad government (1962), a British Arts Council grant (1967-8) and been a writer-in-residence at British and American universities. In 1969 he was awarded the Trinidadian Humming Bird Medal.

Selvon's first novel, *A Brighter Sun* (1952), is a vigorous yet tender account of the personal maturing of a young Trinidadian Indian couple, Tiger and Urmilla, flung together at 16 into a traditional arranged marriage, given the bare necessities for existence, and left to make of their lives what they can. From a wholly peasant background, Tiger grows into manhood and acquires literacy, their marriage becomes mutually sustaining, and they undergo the process of creolization, a process accelerated by the Second World War, by which racial and cultural barriers in their semi-urban surroundings are eroded. As the title suggests, deracination promises a more fulfilling future, and the words spoken by old Sookdeo in a dream that precedes his death sum up part of the novel's tendency: 'Don't mind you is creole and I is coolie! Everybody must live together as friend!'

Selvon's major contribution to West Indian writing has been his successful pioneering of the use of West Indian dialect for more than merely quaint or comic purposes, and it is the source of much of the vitality and authenticity in his work. In *A Brighter Sun* the narration itself is mostly in Standard English, but in the course of the story it shifts increasingly to dialect, both when it modulates obviously, but also sometimes by no means unambiguously, into *oratio obliqua*. He uses the device conservatively, modifying Trinidadian dialect considerably to make it widely intelligible. Nevertheless, he brings the accents of popular speech so fully into West Indian fiction that it can be used to express the full range of emotions that a novelist needs to deploy. In his later books, he extends and refines the technique, producing sophisticated effects to control the reader's responses to story and character. For this reason, Lamming (q.v.), in *The Pleasures of Exile*, praises Selvon as 'the greatest . . . folk poet the British Caribbean has yet produced'. Another aspect of Selvon's originality is his being thoroughly conversant with the lives and speech of Trinidadians from non-Indian backgrounds. Unlike V.S. Naipaul (q.v.), he uses them for major supporting roles in his fiction: besides the central Indian couple, Tiger and Urmilla, other important characters are Negro, Chinese and Portuguese, while some vivid minor figures are American and English.

In *Turn Again, Tiger* (1958) Selvon continues the story of the couple's creolization and break with their Indian and sugar-cane-dominated youth, the psychological effects of which they learn both to overcome and yet to acknowledge as part of themselves. In praising the 'pointed finish' and 'rounded artistry' of Selvon's short stories in *Ways of Sunlight* (1958), I. Van-Sertima writes of 'the episodic fragmentation' of the novels, but in her introduction to the 1979 reissue of *Turn Again, Tiger*, S. Pouchet Paquet ably demonstrates the structural cohesion of the novel. Selvon deals with similar themes in his other novels set in Trinidad, *An Island Is a World* (1955), *I Hear Thunder* (1963), *The Plains of Caroni* (1969) and *Those Who Eat the Cascadura* (1972), but it is doubtful whether he achieves the same delicate blending of comedy and pathos as in the 'Tiger' novels. *The Plains of Caroni* takes further the evolution of peasantry into proletariat by dealing with the violent protests of sugar-cane workers against mechanization and by making the educated and articulate hero conscious of the need to break with the past and establish a new, modern society, but K. Ramchand rightly regrets that the 'frustrated lovers are unsubtly and melodramatically presented'. The setting-up and then ironic undermining of racial stereotypes as a basis for characterization, so successful elsewhere in Selvon's fiction, fails in *Those Who Eat the Cascadura*, especially in the love affair between the Indian girl and the visiting Englishman.

Between 1950 and 1962 many thousands of West Indians emigrated to seek jobs and better pay in England by supplying labour for the meaner forms of employment that British workers were able to vacate during the years of affluence. Another of Selvon's notable achievements has been his interpretation of the West Indian immigrant experience in England, in the spirited buoyancy of *The Lonely Londoners* (1956) and *The Housing Lark* (1965). Without incongruity he moves from farce, through gradations of satire and comedy and gentle humour, to true pathos. He develops his literary adaptation of Trinidadian dialect so that it becomes an inclusive instrument of West Indianness, and now, with the narration wholly in dialect, England, especially London, is seen in an entirely new literary perspective. It is a new growth of Selvon's sensitivity to human behaviour in a situation of social change, and to the psychic hurts that accompany it. Structure seems loose and shifts of mood arbitrary – from nostalgia for the tropics, through the frustrations of the struggle for jobs and housing, through seeming insouciance and the temporary effervescence of alcohol and sex, to the varied desperate searchings for community and belongingness. But it forms a mosaic of cultural patterns that are both outside British life and beginning to enrich it. However comic the mode, serious undercur-

rents are always present, as in this passage from *The Lonely Londoners*:

> the English people starting to make rab about how too much West Indians coming to the country: this was a time, when any corner you turn, is ten to one you bound to bounce up a spade. In fact, the boys all over London . . . and big discussion going on in Parliament about the situation, though the old Brit'n too diplomatic to clamp down on the boys.

British 'diplomacy' proved temporary and *Moses Ascending* (1975) records later, grimmer immigrant experience. Moses is a West Indian who has materially 'made good' in a minor way by aping the shoddy methods of English landlords, and even acquiring a white servant. The book is full of ironic reversals, like the West Indian night-worker who comes to feel that London's shops and offices have been abandoned to his ownership after dark. The tone is often acerbic and the satire, whether of 'liberal' whites or amateurish Black Power groups, penetrating and pungent.

Selvon now lives in Canada.   [AR]

SEROTE, MONGANE WALLY (1944–). Poet, born in Sophiatown, South Africa, and educated in Lesotho and Johannesburg's apartheid townships. In 1969 he was imprisoned, without charge, for nine months. In the mid-1970s he attended Columbia University, New York.

His first two volumes, *Yakhal'inkomo* (1972) and *Tsetlo* (1974), established him as the most inventive and imaginative of the black-townships poets. Like Mtshali (q.v.), he laments the dehumanization suffered by South Africa's urban blacks, and voices their deep anger, for instance in 'Black Bells', which ends in shouted 'nonsense' syllables powerfully articulating inarticulate rage. He writes a flexible, lyrical, free verse and the seemingly detached persona in the poems is affected by the very observations on ghetto life being recorded. Serote's intuitive craftsmanship is supported by a solid sense of historical process, for instance in 'The Growing', where he comes to understand how one people's aspirations have choked those of another people, or in the unravelling into consciousness, in 'Ofay-watcher Looks Back', of the confidence trick history has played on black South Africans. Some of his poems exult in the new confidence that distinguishes Serote's Black Consciousness generation from their fathers.

In *No Baby Must Weep* (1975), a long poem, the speaking voice chants the young urban black experience of choking in arid dust and dreaming of life-restoring waters. The mood is bitter and despairing, but the rapid, jazz-like verse and assertive language convey faith for the future. There have followed *Behold Mama, Flowers* (1978) and his first novel *To Every Birth Its Blood* (1981).   [AR]

SHADBOLT, MAURICE (1932–). Novelist and short-story writer, born in Auckland, New Zealand, and educated at the university there. He worked as a journalist and with the New Zealand National Film Unit in the 1950s. In 1957 he turned to freelance writing and journalism and lived in Europe until 1960. *The New Zealanders* (1959), 'A Sequence of Stories', revealed his close involvement with contemporary New Zealand society in its physical and spiritual dimensions – 'a bruised Eden, my country' – although the stories covered both New Zealand settings and the Europe from which he had recently returned. A further collection, *Summer Fires and Winter Country*, was published in 1963. His first novel, *Among the Cinders* (1965), was less demanding than the stories but its picaresque quality and the New Zealand bushlands setting gave it popular success there. *The Presence of Music* (1967) marked another change of form, the three novellas exploring 'the situation of the artist, not in some limbo, but in a particular time and place'. The demands of the New Zealand context, and the often isolated quality of an existence where nature is the only comfort, featured in the ambitious novel *This Summer's Dolphin* (1969) and, through the eyes of an immigrant writer, in *An Ear of the Dragon* (1971). *Strangers and Journeys* (1972) undertook a massive chronicling of New Zealand society over two generations and is an impressive if flawed work. *Danger Zone* (1975) set personal fulfilment in the context of the French nuclear tests in the Pacific and reflects his own involvement in sailing into the testing area. His work has considerable range and variety but in general illustrates his own contention that 'at its best the short story is the purest and most penetrating of literary forms'. *Figures in Light: Selected Stories* (1979) gathered previously published writing.　　　　　　　　　　　　　　　[PQ]

SHAFFER, PETER (1926–). Dramatist, born in Liverpool, Merseyside, the twin brother of Anthony Shaffer who has also written plays. Both were educated at St Paul's School, London, and at Cambridge. Peter's play *Five Finger Exercise* (1958) is a tense drama of middle-class life in a weekend cottage where a young German tutor brings hot-house relationships between father, wife, son and daughter to boiling point. *The Royal Hunt of the Sun* (1964), a play about the conquest of Peru, sets out 'to realize on stage a kind of "total" theatre involving not only words but rites, mimes, masks and magics' (Author's Notes). There is a grandiose attempt to project the massiveness of the adventure and the collision of civilizations, but voguish anti-institutionalism and be-yourself anarchism are foisted somewhat incongruously on to the costumed past, and Pizarro talks too much like a 1960s playwright peddling pop-radicalism and disillusionment. *Black Comedy* (1965) is a slapstick romp supposedly in darkness. *Equus* (1973) tackles the case of a stable boy who has blinded six horses with a metal spike. A psychiatrist takes him on and restores him to a normality he no longer believes in himself. In *Amadeus* (1981) Shaffer goes back to the dying Mozart's accusation that his rival, Antonio Salieri, had poisoned him.　　　　　　　[HB]

SHAPCOTT, THOMAS (1935–). Poet, born in Ipswich, Queensland, Australia, where he was a public accountant. His first collection *Time on Fire* (1961) won immediate recognition for a lyrical note which derived from an intensely observed actual context but whose expression had a challenging linguistic dexterity. Many of the poems between this collection and *The Mankind Thing* (1964) link the tenuous pattern of reality to the certainty of the family circle, but already apparent was an

interest in music, painting and French literature as inspirational sources. These interests also related to a feeling for historical characters and scenes which emerged as a major preoccupation in *A Taste of Salt Water* (1967) and *Inwards Towards the Sun* (1969). In 1968, together with Rodney Hall (q.v.), he contributed an important introduction to the anthology *New Impulses in Australian Poetry*, which sought 'to clarify the accomplishment of Australian poetry in breaking fresh ground . . . since 1960'. *Australian Poetry Now* (1970) was a further anthology, while *Contemporary American and Australian Poetry* (1976) sought to illustrate comparative developments with mixed success. *Shabbytown Calendar* (1975) was a poem sequence in diary form reflecting the life-rhythm of a small Queensland town. *Selected Poems* was published in 1978.　　　　　　　　　　[PQ]

SHAW, GEORGE BERNARD (1856–1950). Dramatist and polemicist, born in Dublin, Ireland, of an amiable feckless drinker and his more indomitable wife, a singer. The family was officially Protestant (but in fact religiously indifferent). Shaw claimed that his schools did little for him, but he early began to read, and he lived in a home where operatic and choral music was constantly rehearsed. Opera and theatre captivated him. After working as a land-agent's clerk, Shaw moved to London (1876) where his mother had already gone to earn a living by teaching singing. There was a small family inheritance and Shaw had his share of its meagre benefits as he studied in the British Museum and struggled to make a career as a writer, producing five novels including *Cashel Byron's Profession* (the profession is boxing). He embraced vegetarianism, socialism and teetotalism. He became acquainted with William Archer who helped him into journalism. As 'Corno di Bassetto' he was music critic for the *Star*, and in 1895 he began a three-year stint as dramatic critic for the *Saturday Review*, a post in which he was succeeded by Max Beerbohm (q.v.). Meantime Shaw had got to know William Morris and through him Florence Farr, the actress, with whom he had a love affair and who played Blanche (a heroine modelled on herself) in his first play, *Widowers' Houses* (prod 1892). The practice of living on the rents of slum property is the controversial heart of the play. It was published in 1898 as one of the 'unpleasant' plays in *Plays Pleasant and Unpleasant*, and was partnered there by *The Philanderer* and by *Mrs Warren's Profession*, whose target is the practice of living on the indirect profits of prostitution. Shaw thus began dramatic writing as an unashamed propagandist against corruption in the fabric of contemporary society.

In the 'pleasant' plays message is, in varying degrees, tempered with greater humour and more purely human interest. *Arms and the Man* (prod 1894) takes us to Bulgaria during the war with Serbia of 1885. Bluntschli, a fugitive Serbian officer, breaks into the room of Raina Petkoff, a romantic young lady whose lover, Sergius, has led a Bulgarian cavalry charge. Bluntschli is in fact a Swiss mercenary totally disillusioned with war and its supposed heroisms. Events press home the contrast between human idealism and realism in relation to war and love, and the comedy scintillates. *You Never Can Tell* (prod 1900) plays no less dazzlingly with the theme of women's emancipation and the difficulty of insulating the young New Woman against masculine ingenuity and masterfulness. Richly displaying the early Shaw's inspired humour and assured theatrical craftsmanship, it became a great box-office draw and Shaw began to feel dissatisfied with it. ('I was ashamed of its tricks and laughs and popularities.') The most serious of the 'pleasant' plays is *Candida*. Candida Morell mothers the sensitive young poet, Marchbanks, whom her husband, a clergyman, has befriended. Marchbanks falls in love with Candida and claims her from Morell, a genial, energetic, robust extravert. At the crisis Candida has to choose between her husband, offering his strength, honesty, ability and authority, and Marchbanks, offering only his weakness, his desolation and his heart's need. 'I give myself to the weaker of the two', says Candida, and the young poet realizes immediately that he has lost her.

Shaw followed an arduous career of public speaking in the socialist cause during the 1880s and 1890s. He joined the Fabian Society in 1884 and his connection with the Webbs brought about his meeting in 1896 with Charlotte Payne-Townshend, an Irish heiress, whom he married in 1898. The union, if not at the start, very shortly became one from which sexual activity was excluded. Shaw's copious and devoted correspondence with Ellen Terry and his tempestuously unconsummated affair with Mrs Patrick Campbell give further evidence of a curious relationship to women. Beatrice Webb averred that he did not understand them, that his sensuality had 'all drifted into sexual vanity' (Janet Dunbar, *Mrs G.B.S.*, 1963).

Candida was successfully staged at the Royal Court Theatre by Harley Granville-Barker (q.v.) in 1904, and thus the partnership between Barker and J.E. Vedrenne began. It marked a theatrical revival, for Shaw's plays were highly popular. Whatever their deficiencies, in the eyes of some critics, in the way of shapely tailoring and traditional plotting, they established drama as a vehicle for airing current social problems and pressing radical solutions. It can be argued that in Shaw convincingness of characterization is jeopardized by the insatiable relish for paradox and perversity, that the rhythm of action is submerged under argumentative dialogue and human interest sacrificed to polemical thrust: nevertheless the Shavian versatility of range, fluency and wit, and the sure eye for theatrically telling topsy-turvydoms make the impact of his best work irresistible. In *The Devil's Disciple* (prod 1897) the scene is set in a New Hampshire town during the American War of Independence. Men are being hanged by the British to discourage rebels. It is the dashing young foe of local piety and respectability (the self-confessed 'Devil's disciple') who turns hero in sacrificing himself to save the local minister; and the minister then turns man of action to save his saviour. *Caesar and Cleopatra* (first English performance 1907) sets the Shakespearian record straight by presenting Julius as a virtuous superman and the Queen of Egypt as a spoilt, ignorant child. *John Bull's Other Island* was written in 1904 at the request of Yeats (q.v.) 'as a patriotic contribution to the repertory of the Irish Literary Theatre'. In fact it proved too ambitious for the resources of the new Abbey Theatre and also 'uncongenial to the whole spirit of the neo-Gaelic movement' (Shaw's Preface), but was a huge success at the Court Theatre. Moving from con-

temporary London to an Irish village, it is a brilliantly entertaining improvisation on the serio-comic collision between Irish and English character and mentality. In *Major Barbara* (prod 1905) Shaw returns to the conflict 'between real life and the romantic imagination' (Preface), this time arguing that the Salvation Army can do less for man than the power of money, for poverty is 'the vilest sin of man and society'. *The Doctor's Dilemma** (prod 1906), *Getting Married* (prod 1908) and *Androcles and the Lion* (prod 1912) were further 'thoughtful' comedies in the phase which reached its climactic success in *Pygmalion** (prod 1914).

A more urgent note was struck in *Heartbreak House*, written between 1913 and 1916, and representing 'cultured, leisured Europe' at the time of its drift towards the abyss of war. The witty comedy of wayward love-relationships allegorizes the parlous condition of English society, adrift and navigationless. Then the serious Shaw took over with a vengeance and created *Back to Methuselah**, a massive epic drama of creative evolution requiring two or three nights for performance and propagating that religion of the 'Life Force' which Shaw had already proclaimed (but more lavishly decorated with comedy – and therefore more palatable) in *Man and Superman**. But the words 'his greatest play' tend nevertheless to be used of his chronicle, *Saint Joan** (prod 1924). Of later plays, *The Apple Cart* (prod 1929) takes us forward to the court of King Magnus of England at the end of the twentieth century, and *In Good King Charles's Golden Days* (prod 1939) takes us back to Isaac Newton's house and the Queen's boudoir in the reign of Charles II.

Among the devices Shaw developed for projecting the public persona of clowning showman and prophetic sage were the lengthy Prefaces he added to his plays on publication. In these he let fly at social abuses and probed such queries as 'What is an Irishman?' and 'Is Shaw better than Shakespeare?' 'It's the yoking together of the quick & dead', said T.E. Lawrence (q.v.) of the marriage between play and preface, but the garrulous outbursts complement a considerable independent prose output, including *The Quintessence of Ibsenism* (1891), *The Perfect Wagnerite* (1898) and *The Intelligent Woman's Guide to Socialism* (1928). See also *Ellen Terry and Shaw, A Correspondence* (1931), *Correspondence Between Shaw and Mrs Patrick Campbell*, ed. A. Dent (1952), and *Letters to Granville Barker*, ed. C. Purdom (1957). Dan H. Laurence has edited Shaw's complete music criticism in three volumes, *Shaw's Music* (1981).

The Doctor's Dilemma, a five-act play, is labelled a 'tragedy', but much of it is comic. A conversation at St Mary's Hospital between the Shaws and Sir Almoth Wright was interrupted by an enquiry whether the doctor could add another to the tuberculosis patients undergoing his new special treatment. The doctor asked, 'Is he worth it?' and the idea for the play was born, enabling Shaw to bait the medical profession with witty satirical studies of their class. Sir Colenso Ridgeon has a new cure for tuberculosis but can handle only ten patients at once and already has nine when Jennifer Dubedat appeals to him to treat her husband, an artist. Louis Dubedat is brilliant as a painter but morally unscrupulous, and Ridgeon cannot take him on without excluding a poor but worthy GP, Blenkinsop. This is the dilemma. Dubedat rules himself out by blackguardism: the comically confident Sir Ralph Bloomfield Bonnington takes him on, and he dies, reciting his creed, 'I believe in Michaelangelo, Velasquez, and Rembrandt; in the might of design, the mystery of colour, the redemption of all things by beauty everlasting'. In Act V, at a posthumous exhibition of Dubedat's paintings, Ridgeon tells Jennifer that he is in love with her; but she has already remarried. 'Then I have committed a purely disinterested murder!' Ridgeon observes.

Pygmalion, a five-act comedy, was first produced in London in 1914 with Mrs Patrick Campbell as Eliza and Beerbohm Tree as Higgins. It was to become Shaw's most successful play commercially and eventually to suffer transmogrification into the musical, *My Fair Lady*. The legend of Pygmalion tells how the artist created a beautiful statue, fell in love with it, and successfully begged the goddess Aphrodite to give it life. Shaw updates the artist into a contemporary professor of phonetics, Henry Higgins, who guarantees that he can so transform the speech of an ill-spoken cockney flower-girl, Eliza Doolittle, as to pass her off as a duchess in a few months. The experiment is made, Higgins paying Eliza's father, a dustman, five pounds. When Eliza is first produced at Higgins's mother's 'At Home' she has faultless pronunciation but is less sure on vocabulary and utters the famous 'Not bloody likely!' Later she makes her successful appearance in society as a duchess. Higgins's professional achievement satisfies him, but Eliza now refuses to be simply the object of an experiment. She is a sensitive woman with a problem of social adjustment – and with an emotional awakening that Higgins's intellectual bachelordom cannot cope with. In this respect the play concludes ambiguously.

Man and Superman, a four-act play called 'A Comedy and a Philosophy', was first performed, incompletely, in 1905, and completely ten years later. In structure it is a standard comedy into which a lengthy dream-scene is interpolated. This episode, Don Juan in Hell, forms most of Act III which itself amounts to 40 per cent of the total text. John Tanner, a wealthy revolutionary with a Shavian capacity to shock the conventional over social and moral matters, finds himself joint guardian of Ann Whitefield after her father's death. Tanner correctly recognizes that woman is the huntress and man the hunted in the sex game but is slower than his cockney chauffeur, 'Enry Straker, to observe that he has himself been marked out by Ann. Waking up to it, he flees by car to Spain, is captured by brigands in the Sierra Nevada, caught up there by the pursuing Ann, and conquered. The famous dream, a sustained debate, takes place during captivity. In it the chief brigand is the Devil, Tanner is Don Juan, Ramsden (Tanner's fellow guardian) Don Gonzalo and Ann, Donna Anna. The philosophy of the Life Force is expounded by Don Juan in the dream before, as John Tanner, he becomes the victim of it, overtaken by woman's eternal pursuit of man. The play as a whole is tediously over-wordy, though Shavian epigrams glitter here and there ('An Englishman thinks he is moral when he is only uncomfortable' and 'What is virtue but the Trade Unionism of the married?').

Back to Methuselah, an epic drama in five acts, called by Shaw a 'Metabiological Pentateuch', written between 1918 and 1921, was first produced in 1922 (New York) and 1924 (London). It demands the best part of a day if it is to be performed at a sitting. It is a fantastic presentation of the doctrine of Creative Evolution, pressing man's need to determine consciously his own development and recognizing that this involves transcending the seventy-year life-span which inhibits human potential. Part I ('In the Beginning') is set in the Garden of Eden where Eve learns from the Serpent the way of human renewal by birth and foresees ever new wonders for her race. Part II ('The Gospel of the Brothers Barnabas') shows contemporary postwar thinkers, the Barnabases, expounding the theory that man may will to live 300 years, to politicians who caricature Lloyd George and Asquith. Part III ('The Thing Happens') takes us on to AD 2170 when it emerges that two disciples of the Barnabases have in fact broken through the barrier and are over 250 years old. Part IV ('Tragedy of an Elderly Gentleman') takes us to Ireland in AD 3000. One of the now obsolescent race of short-livers, very much in the shape of the author himself, is visiting a region where the established race of long-livers find him incomprehensible, and he dies. Part V ('As Far as Thought can Reach') is set in AD 31920 when men and women are born full-grown from eggs and can die only as the result of an accident. At the end Adam and Eve, Cain and the Serpent appear again and Lilith speaks of the continuing progress of her seed towards the mastery of life.

The impracticable demands of the play obviously deter would-be performers; so does the theoretical character of its central interest, the lack of overall structure and of human conflict. For all the vigour of Shaw's thinking the text is often verbose, repetitive and undistinguished. Shaw wrote the play to be the supreme expression of his 'religion'. It was necessary, he said, because in *Man and Superman* his dramatic parable in Creative Evolution had been 'too brilliantly and lavishly' decorated through the over-abundance of his 'invention and comedic talent'. In a postscript to the play after twenty-five years (1944) he sustained his claim for it as a masterpiece. 'Back to Methuselah is a world classic or it is nothing.' It is not a world classic.

Saint Joan, a chronicle play about Joan of Arc in six scenes and an epilogue, was first produced in London in 1924 with Sibyl Thorndike as Joan, a part she made her own. The peasant maid is called by her 'voices' to go to Orleans, become a soldier and raise the English siege. She manages to impress the Dauphin and is given her chance. After victory at Orleans, the Dauphin is crowned, but Joan is eventually captured and handed over to the English. She is brought to trial before the Inquisition, signs a confession under intense moral pressure and threat of execution, but tears it up when she hears that life imprisonment is to be her sentence and is taken off to the stake. The trial is the high point of the play. The exposition of the church's case against Joan is logically set out in terms of the spiritual and moral threat represented by individualistic rebellion against institutional authority. The readiness to destroy bodies in order to save souls is voiced without melodramatic caricature. An epilogue shows the Dauphin dreaming about Joan twenty-five years later and her future canonization is foreseen. It was indeed the canonization of Joan in 1920 that led to Shaw's work on what is his finest serious play. Its success transformed his public image. 'Henceforth, whatever he said or did was treated with respect, tinged with awe.' (Hesketh Pearson, *Bernard Shaw*.) [HB]

SHERRIFF, R.C. (Robert Cedric) (1896–1975). Dramatist and novelist, born at Kingston upon Thames, Surrey, and educated at Kingston Grammar School. Work for the Sun Insurance company was interrupted by the war, in which he served on the Western Front with the rank of captain. He wrote several plays for amateur performance and then *Journey's End* was put on at the Savoy Theatre in 1929 and was a stupendous success. It is a straightforward portrayal of trench life set in a front-line dug-out near St Quentin in March 1918 when a German attack is awaited. The emotional situation is fraught with tension when a young subaltern, Raleigh, joins the company. He is fresh from school, where the present company commander, Captain Stanhope, was and is the idol of hero-worshipping youngsters: moreover Stanhope is in love with Raleigh's sister. But after three shattering years at the front the idol is a half-broken man, heavily reliant on drink. Raleigh's dilemma is terminated by German gunfire. Sherriff failed to repeat his success in subsequent plays, *Badger's Green* (1930) and *Windfall* (prod 1933), but achieved a best-seller with the novel *The Fortnight in September* (1931) and thereafter prospered as film-script writer. His autobiography is *No Leading Lady* (1968). [HB]

SKELTON, ROBIN (1925–). Poet, born in Yorkshire and educated at a grammar school near York, at Cambridge University and at Leeds University, from which he graduated in 1950. After war service he taught at Manchester University for over ten years before emigrating to Canada where he has proved a stimulating presence on the literary scene. He is currently Chairman of the Department of Creative Writing at the University of Victoria, British Columbia. In 1967 he became joint editor of the *Malahat Review* and in 1972 editor. A prolific poet, critic and editor – and distinguished in all three fields – his verse draws upon the spectrum of classical and European culture just as his critical studies have ranged from John Ruskin and Irish writers to general works on poetry and the poet, such as *The Practice of Poetry* (1971) and *The Poet's Calling* (1975). Early collections, such as *Third Day Lucky* (1958), suggest a similarity to the 'Movement' poetry of the English 1950s in their flat and understated manner, but more recent work has been outstanding not only for its range and variety but also for a distinctive, and often outspoken, voice. *Selected Poems 1947–1967* (1968) provides a useful cross-section of his poetry. More recent works include *Private Speech: Messages 1962–1970: Poems* (1971) and *Fools Wisdom* (1975). [PQ]

SILKIN, JON (1930–). Poet, born in London and educated at Dulwich College. After national service and a period of factory work, he became Gregory Poetry Fellow at Leeds University and took a degree there. Since then he has held lectureships in the USA and Australia. He

helped to found the quarterly magazine *Stand* in Newcastle upon Tyne in 1968. His early collection of verse, *The Peaceable Kingdom* (London, 1954; New York, 1969), included a much-anthologized poem 'Death of a Son' (at the age of one in a mental hospital) of moving frankness and directness. This directness, if not the accompanying lucidity, have been maintained in later collections. Silkin's determination to probe meditatively teasing issues of human life, of growth and death, with immediacy and with imaginative concreteness has bred a metaphorical trenchancy that can sometimes seem too strident; but the firm reflective voice always sounds authoritative. *The Re-Ordering of Stones* (1961) was followed by *Nature With Man* (1965), a collection containing a series of flower poems in which floral life and growth is characterized so as to suggest correspondences with human life. The poems, Silkin tells us, 'concentrate closely on the flowers, and it is towards their centrality they tend to draw *human* life as, in *The Peaceable Kingdom*, I was trying to draw human life in the direction of certain animals, and a powerful consortium of all animals'. Among later collections are *Amana Grass* (1971), which bears marks of his residence in the USA, and *The Principle of Water* (1974), which includes a sustained dramatic sequence, 'The People', with a central theme harking back to the birth and death of a handicapped baby recorded in 'Death of a Son'. There is some critical dissatisfaction with the syntactical liberties that Silkin's Imagistic method seems to entail, as the reception of *The Psalms and their Spoils* (1980) showed. [HB]

SILLITOE, ALAN (1928–). Novelist, born in Nottingham, Nottinghamshire. He left school at 14, served in the RAF from 1946 to 1949, and in 1959 married the American poet Ruth Fainlight, with whom he and Ted Hughes (q.v.) collaborated in *Poems* (1971). Sillitoe's novel *Saturday Night and Sunday Morning* (1958) portrays Arthur Seaton, mechanic in a Nottingham bicycle factory, who finds release from drudgery in weekend drinking, and adultery with two married sisters. His brother Fred, like the reader, is sometimes 'forced to admit that Arthur was not a very nice bloke'. After *The General* (1960) and *Key to the Door* (1961), Sillitoe essayed in *The Death of William Posters* (1965) a full-scale study of an intelligent working man's walk-out from domestic and industrial servitude in Nottingham, 'where he had been born bred and spiritually nullified'. Frank Dawley's career is a sexed-up version of the twentieth-century escape pattern laid down by Wells's (q.v.) Mr Polly. Frank's banal sub-Lawrentian clichés somehow set fire to respectable female hearts as the peripatetic rebel seeks to throw off his working-class sense of persecution symbolized in ubiquitous proclamations that 'Bill Posters will be Prosecuted'. We leave him gun-running in Algeria at the end, but his story continues in *A Tree on Fire* (1967). The title story in the book of short stories *The Loneliness of the Long-distance Runner* (1959) is an impressive study of a Borstal boy's psychological dilemma when entered in a big race by his governor, and shows Sillitoe at his most subtle. Among later novels *The Flame of Life* (1974) pictures an experimental English kibbutz which fails.

Contrasts between order and anarchy, complexity and simplicity are standard themes in Sillitoe, who has detected a duality in himself deriving from differences in his maternal and paternal background. Later collections of short stories include *Down to the Bone* (1976) and *The Second Chance* (1980). [HB]

SIMPSON, N.F. (Norman Frederick) (1919–). London-born dramatist, labelled an exponent of the Theatre of the Absurd when two short plays, *A Resounding Tinkle* and *The Hole*, were produced at the Royal Court Theatre in 1958. The delivery of an elephant to a semi-detached house in the former, and diverse spectacles witnessed by diverse eyes down a hole in the road in the latter, spark off lunatic verbal sequences sub-Beckettian in flavour. In the full-length *One Way Pendulum* (prod 1959, pubd 1960) the antics of a mad household include the attempt to train Speak-Your-Weight weighing machines to sing Handel in chorus. Simpson's maniac logic is unanchored to a bed of significance, associative or imaginative. It is comic-column nonsense that, unlike Beckett's (q.v.), rarely seems to animate authentic metaphor. But in *The Cresta Run* (prod 1965, pubd 1966) a plausible vein of satire emerges through the *reductio ad absurdum* of the irreducible absurdities of secret service espionage. Simpson's nonsense novel, *Harry Bleachbaker* (1976), is advertised as a book which 'once having been put down, clamours as perhaps no other book ever written has clamoured, to be left lying where it is'. [HB]

SINGH, KHUSHWANT (1915–). Journalist, novelist, historian, born in Hadali, in pre-partition India, and educated in Delhi, Lahore and London. A lawyer in 1938–47, an Indian government journalist in 1947–58 and editor of *The Illustrated Weekly of India* from 1969, he has written books on Punjabi and Sikh history and culture, notably his two-volume *History of the Sikhs* (1963, 1966), edited others and translated Punjabi works into English, such as Amrita Pritam's *The Skeleton* (1964). *A Bride for the Sahib and Other Stories* (1967) is one of four collections of his English stories: they are sceptical, sardonic treatments of human irrationality. Of his novels in English, *Train to Pakistan* (New York, 1955, as *Mano Majra*, 1956; London, 1956) is more accomplished and less disillusioned than *I Shall Not Hear the Nightingale* (1959). With cinematic clarity, the former dramatizes communal tensions in Mano Majra, a fictional village on the new Pakistan–India border in 1947. The selflessness of a Sikh dacoit sacrificing his life in saving a trainload of Muslim refugees from slaughter is set, parable-like, against the complacency of officials, the moral hollow-ness of an intellectual activist and the acquiescence of Sikh villagers when zealots plan to massacre the Sikhs' former Muslim neighbours. R. Singh has edited collections of his non-fictional writings: *Khushwant Singh's India without Humbug* (1977), *Around the World with Khushwant Singh* (1978), *Good People, Bad People* (1978). [AR]

SISSON, C.H. (Charles Hubert) (1914–). Poet, born in Bristol, Avon, and educated at the university there. He served in the British Intelligence in India during the Second World War and has since made his career in the Civil Service and his recreation in poetry. A series of volumes of poems and translations culminated in *In the Trojan Ditch: Collected Poems and Selected Translations* (1974), to which he soon afterwards added *The Poem of Nature* (1976), a version of Lucretius's *De Rerum Naturae*, and *Anchises* (1976), a collection of further original poems. Sisson's Foreword to *In The Trojan Ditch* (which includes translations from Heine, Catullus, Ovid and Horace) defines the nature of the poet's problem revealingly ('I was forced into verse . . . through having something not altogether easy to say. . . . There is no question . . . of filling note-books with what one knows already') and goes on to express sympathy for Dryden who, after a lifetime of poetic experiment, finally took most pride in translation. 'He was glad, I imagine, to be able to release the energies of poetry without passing for having said anything of his own.'

Sisson's rejection of fashionable assumptions ('The writing of poetry is, in a sense, the opposite of writing what one wants to write') and his attachment to the Church of England give him the status of a rebel against current mores. The quality of his original verse can be gauged from 'A Letter to John Donne'. Recalling Donne's incumbency of Sevenoaks and an occasion when he visited Knole, it is one of a group of poems (see also 'The Crucifix') in which Sisson achieves immediacy of impact and urgency of reasoning reminiscent of Donne himself. By contrast 'The Queen of Lydia' is a deftly ironic piece. King Candaules, boastful of his wife's beauty, arranges for his general, Gyges, to spy at night on her undressing. Next day the queen gives Gyges the choice of killing the king and marrying her or of being killed by her husband.

> And the Queen's motive? She believed
> (The Lydians are barbarians)
> To be seen naked was a shame
> Which only death could expiate
> Or marriage, as in Gyges' case.
> So you see how barbarians are.

One can understand John Mole's observation on Sisson's later collection, *Exactions* (1980): 'His achievement is to have developed a style which directs attention to its own finest passages and lodges them in the memory'.

Sisson's translation of Dante's *Divine Comedy* (1980) in unrhymed colloquial free verse has been praised for its readability. His critical study, *English Poetry 1900–1950: An Assessment* (1971), is a useful survey. [HB]

SITWELL, EDITH (Dame) (1887–1964). Poet and prose writer, born at Scarborough, North Yorkshire, the eldest child of Sir George Sitwell, Bt. On the maternal side the grandparents were Lord and Lady Londesborough. The child lacked love and sympathy from her mother and father, for she was not beautiful and could be exasperatingly frank and wilful. The unflattering portraits of her parents in the autobiography *Taken Care Of* (1965), granted that they are exercises in caricature from a sick bed, bear record to crudely damaged childish sensitivities. The girl grew up with an eccentric father and a mother whose fashionable tastes she could not share, and she withdrew into an inner world, her loneliness mitigated at first only by family servants and later by her governess, Helen Rootham. Her brothers, Osbert (q.v.) and Sacheverell (q.v.), when they were not away at school, shared the mingled blessing and inconvenience of upbringing in the ancestral seat, Renishaw Hall in Derbyshire, and all three turned thence to literature like sophisticated, upper-class Brontës. At the beginning of the First World War Edith went to earn her living in London and she was soon publishing her own poems (*The Mother*, 1915) and editing the poems of others in a serialized anthology, *Wheels* (1916–21), in which the young Aldous Huxley figured. It was not a conformist publication for she realized that the flat verbal and rhythmic predictability of contemporary verse made vital innovation a matter of necessity. She herself was both influenced by the French symbolists and stimulated by the study of earlier English poetry, study which was later to bear fruit in *A Poet's Notebook* (1944). This contains interesting notes on Chaucer, Dunbar, Skelton, Jonson and Herrick as well as Pope, Smart, Blake, Wordsworth and Hopkins. The keen interest she had from the first in rhythm and texture is reflected in her early enthusiasm for Swinburne and for Pope (whose 'Rape of the Lock' she knew by heart in girlhood).

Façade (1922) and *Bucolic Comedies* (1923) represent the first phase of her work, in which technical virtuosity in the manipulation of clamorous rhythmic effects and in the interplay of aural devices like rhyme and assonance is matched by startling experimentation in metaphorical transposition ('The light is braying like an ass'). When the *Façade* poems were provided with a musical accompaniment by William Walton, and were publicly declaimed through a megaphone against an orchestration of comparable vigour and novelty, something of a cultural sensation occurred and it was not easy thereafter for the poet to live down the one-sided image that her light-hearted excursion into nonsense verse had created. But in *The Sleeping Beauty* (1924) the satiric mood was abandoned for one of romantic nostalgia. It is a work of transfigured autobiography whose setting is the rich garden of Renishaw, and it opens with a haunting sureness of touch:

> When we come to that dark house,
> Never sound of wave shall rouse
> The bird that sings within the blood
> Of those who sleep in that deep wood.

The use of family memories to fashion a fairy-tale world whose scenes and characters can be identified by the initiated (the celebrated 'Colonel Fantock' is another case in point) perhaps makes accusations of privatism understandable, but the woven fabric of music and imagery is compellingly rich in itself.

The publication of *Gold Coast Customs* (1929) marked an astonishing development. The imaginative and rhythmic intensity of this work gives it a macabre and harrowing power as a picture 'of a world where all the natural rhythms of the spirit, of the soil, of the seasons, have broken down', to quote the poet herself. It has been called her 'Waste Land', for it juxtaposes the celebration of barbaric Ashantee rites, involving orgy and slaughter after the death of a rich man, with Lady Bamburgher's smart parties and 'the cries of the slums' at home. Sustained underlying drum beats add ominous insistency to stark Websterian imagery. Yet there was a gap of ten years – during which the need for money drove Edith

Sitwell to write prose works – before the culminating phase of poetic output began with the onset of the Second World War. In the celebrated poem, 'Still Falls the Rain', written out of experience of air raids in 1940, the rain of fire is equated with the rain of redeeming blood from the suffering Christ:

> Still falls the Rain –
> Dark as the world of man, black as our loss –
> Blind as the nineteen hundred and forty nails
> Upon the Cross.

The poet became a Roman Catholic and began to speak to the age of cataclysmic disaster and change in a new, more universal idiom, eschewing the esoteric and the private. A vivid, wide-ranging symbolism – biblical, literary and natural – was now at her disposal in a series of odes, majestic in cadence and stately in movement. 'Invocation', 'An Old Woman' and 'Eurydice' are visionary proclamations of faith. The 'Three Poems of the Atomic Bomb' powerfully declare the defilement of earth and the lust for gold, but yet again find hope through Christ's coming 'in the terrible rain'.

There were those who, like Siegfried Sassoon (q.v.), regretted that the 'gifted fantastical writer' should have 'assumed the robes of a prophetess and oracle' more fitting an Eliot (q.v.) or a Yeats (q.v.), but Edith Sitwell's popular reputation flowered in her last years as she became a Dame of the British Empire and accumulated honorary D Litts. She was known as a personality, grandly eccentric in dress, aristocratic in bearing and impatient – sometimes waspishly so – of nonsense and criticism. She was generously helpful to young writers and gladly gave her backing to Dylan Thomas (q.v.) for instance. Among her prose works *Alexander Pope* (1930) stands out as one fervent and sensitive technician's tribute to another. It rehabilitated Pope the man as well as Pope the poet. *I Live Under a Black Sun* (1937) curiously transfers the story of Swift, Stella and Vanessa into the twentieth century for fictional treatment. Dame Edith's royal biographies include *Victoria of England* (1936) and *Fanfare for Elizabeth* (1946). Volumes of *Collected Poems* were published in 1930 and 1957. J. Lehmann and D. Parker have edited the *Selected Letters* (1970). Victoria Glendinning has written a fine biography, *Edith Sitwell, Unicorn among Lions* (1981).   [HB]

SITWELL, OSBERT (Sir) (1892–1969). Poet, novelist and man of letters. He was the eldest son of Sir George Sitwell, Bt, and succeeded to the baronetcy in 1943. The magnificent family home, Renishaw Hall in Derbyshire, and the house at Scarborough provided the early background for the three literary Sitwells, Edith (q.v.), Osbert and Sacheverell (q.v.), whose upper-class Edwardian upbringing did not prevent them from becoming a terrible trio, self-consciously crusading for culture and conducting 'a series of skirmishes and hand-to-hand battles against the Philistine' as 'advocates of compulsory Freedom . . . the suppression of Public Opinion . . . and the rationing of brains' (Osbert in *Who's Who*). After being educated 'during the holidays from Eton', Osbert served in the Brigade of Guards from 1912 to 1919 and celebrated the news of his postwar demobilization in the South of France by launching his uniform in a hamper out to sea. His considerable poetic output is that of a witty observer, fluent and graceful in versification. In *Poems About People* (1965) he gathered together the earlier volumes, *England Reclaimed* (1927), *Wrack at Tidesend* (1952) and *On the Continent* (1958), verse portraits respectively of country people, inhabitants of watering places and English residents abroad. The studies have amusing clarity of outline and fitful satiric bite, but they lack epigrammatic memorability.

As a novelist Sitwell achieved a notable success with *Before the Bombardment* (1926), a satirical picture of prewar Scarborough ('Newborough'), where the wealthy widows and spinster daughters of Victorian magnates spin out their comfortable days in residential hotels, and the thudding sea – from which the town is finally to be shelled by German cruisers – roars ominously in the background. Arnold Bennett (q.v.) understandably complained that 'the man *describes* characters instead of showing them'. *Miracle on Sinai* (1933), a more Peacockian exercise, takes us to a luxury hotel for satire on cartoonified eccentrics (including D.H. Lawrence (q.v.) as 'T.L. Enfelon') who picnic on Mount Sinai and witness a miraculous revelation (new tablets of the law). Sitwell also wrote short stories (see *Collected Stories*, 1953) and polemical pieces such as *A Letter to My Son* (1944) which made unfashionable complaints about the indiscriminate human and cultural price of war. But it is generally claimed that his major achievement is the massive autobiography in five volumes, *Left Hand! Right Hand!* (1944), *The Scarlet Tree* (1946), *Great Morning* (1948), *Laughter in the Next Room* (1949) and *Noble Essences* (1950), to which *Tales My Father Taught Me* was added as a pendant in 1962. 'I *want* my memories to be old-fashioned and extravagant . . . I *want* this to be gothic . . . full of others . . . crowded with people of every sort', he wrote in his Introduction. The volumes can fascinate with their personal reminiscence and their evocation of a historic phase that began with 'the sunset hour of one of the great periodic calms of history', and an impressive outsized portrait of the Sitwells' eccentric father bestrides the pages. Yet the work as a whole is too unselective, too insubstantially eloquent, for greatness. *Left Hand! Right Hand!* was chosen as title for the whole 'because, according to the palmists, the lines of the left hand are incised inalterably at birth, while those of the right hand are modified by our actions and environment and the life we lead.' [HB]

SITWELL, SACHEVERELL (Sir) (1897–). Poet and prose writer, the younger brother of Edith (q.v.) and Osbert Sitwell (q.v.). He was born at Scarborough, North Yorkshire, educated at Eton and at Balliol College, Oxford, served in the Guards during the First World War, married Georgia Doble in 1925 and has two sons. He succeeded to the baronetcy on Osbert's death in 1969, and now lives at Weston Hall, Northamptonshire – the county of which he served as High Sheriff in 1948–9. His vast prose output (fifty to sixty titles) includes a good deal of critical work based on lifelong experience of works of art all over the world. Commentator on architecture, the decorative arts and music too, he has also produced travel books (*The Netherlands*, 1948; *Spain*, 1950;

Portugal & Madeira, 1954; *Denmark*, 1956; *Malta*, 1958, and others), having made himself sufficiently known abroad to be a freeman of Lima and to have a restaurant named 'Le Sitwell' after him in Noto, Sicily. Of the prose works in Sitwell's evocative poetic vein the 'Autobiographical Fantasia', *All Summer in a Day* (1926), and the rhapsodic pot-pourri, *Splendours and Miseries* (1943), have each been called 'masterpieces' (the latter manages to pack the Victorian suspect murderess Madeleine Smith, the atrocities of the Nazis, and the London blitz among the miseries; picnics and Pisan frescoes among the splendours). *Southern Baroque Art* (1924) 'created a revolution in English taste', Lord Clark avers. *British Architecture and Craftsmen* (1945), a survey of taste, design and style from 1600 to 1830, has also been influential. But probably Sitwell would wish to be judged first as a poet. In *Journey to the Ends of Time* (1959) he speaks with delight of the renewal of the youthful poetic impulse in later years. 'To be once more a poet, and not driven to write prose.' He has indeed an 'enormous facility for mellifluous verse-making', and it can be argued that generally 'the intellectual muscles are too relaxed to produce that concentration of thought, wit and imaginative vision that is the especial province of poetry' (John Lehmann, *A Nest of Tigers*, 1968). Moreover the subjects of the more ambitious poems, like the sequence *Canons of Giant Art: Twenty Torsos in Heroic Landscapes* (1933), distance them from the impact of direct personal experience. 'Agamemnon's Tomb' ('among the greatest of modern poems', Osbert averred in his Preface to Sacheverell's representative *Selected Poems*, 1936) is a grandiose assemblage of reflections on death and its horrors, but too arduously fashioned for current taste. More immediately palatable is the delightful vignette of the Edwardian heyday that one finds in so modest a poem as 'Week Ends' (from the first volume, *The People's Palace*, 1918), where the dialogue between the grand lady, her guest and her gardener makes its point tellingly and entertainingly:

> 'Well then, you see,
> I want the treetops trimmed,
> And then at tennis
> One can watch the steamers
> Through Lord Dodo's chimneys.'
>   'Exactly.'
>   'Yes! M'um.'

A frequent critical comment on the vast output in both verse and prose (over seventy titles) is that it 'awaits revaluation and rediscovery' (G.S. Fraser). See also the autobiography, *For Want of a Golden City* (1973). [HB]

SLESSOR, KENNETH (1901–71). Poet, born at Orange, New South Wales, Australia, and educated at Mowbray House School, Chatswood, and the Church of England Grammar School, Sydney. At the age of 19 a job on the Sydney *Sun* began a long career with the press. He was joint editor with Norman Lindsay (q.v.) of the four issues of the witty and polemical journal *Vision* (1923–4), and in 1923 he edited the collection *Poetry in Australia* with Lindsay's eldest son, Jack (q.v.). After working for two years on the Melbourne *Punch* and *Herald*, in 1927 he joined the staff of *Smith's Weekly* in Sydney and later became editor. During the war he was Official War Correspondent with the Australian Army and from 1956 to 1961 edited the literary magazine *Southerly* (1939–). He was an editor of the *Penguin Book of Australian Verse* (1958). Slessor's earliest poems appeared in *Vision*, and in their romantic tone and imagery were in studied contrast to the then predominant bush-ballad tradition. *Thief of the Moon* (1924) had been privately printed in Sydney, and the next collection, *Earth Visitors* (1926), was a limited edition from the Lindsay Fanfrolico Press in London which displayed a dazzling mastery of language and technique hardly matched by seriousness of subject. The visual influence of Norman Lindsay's art is apparent in the richly sensuous imagery and careful patterning. The title poem was dedicated to Lindsay, and reflects the poet's youthful enthusiasm for the literary and artistic movement that he headed. Such poems are marred by escapist images and evocations of a lost Eden of erotic beauty; 'The Night Ride', by contrast, shows Slessor focusing his visual sensibility and verbal dexterity upon an apparently everyday experience to produce a poem of striking originality and suggestiveness. The poems in *Cuckooz Contrey* (1932) showed further advance, and in 'Captain Dobbin' and 'Five Visions of Captain Cook' Slessor succeeded in expressing a variety of experience within a finely worked dramatic structure. 'Five Visions' in particular is a richly evocative and whimsical charting of Australia's literal and spiritual history: 'So Cook made choice, so Cook sailed westabout, / So men write poems in Australia'. The work's tracing of youth's decline into death reflects that sardonic disenchantment which characterizes so much of Slessor's poetry. Yet the movement of the poem also celebrates the complexity of life's voyages and visions, and leads to a satisfyingly balanced conclusion. In the title elegy of *Five Bells* (1939) his poetic art attains its highest point, personal feelings for his drowned friend being expressed in images which both capture the immediate scene of Sydney harbour and set up profound reverberations. The sensuous variety of remembered experience and the desolation wreaked by time, themes which recur so often in his work, are here wrought into a poem of satisfying complexity and control. *One Hundred Poems* (1944) was a collection of the poems he wished to preserve, and the later book *Poems* (1957) contains only three unimportant additions. *Bread and Wine* (1970) collected journalism of peace and war, together with articles from *Southerly*. Slessor's achievement is within a limited compass (his self-imposed silence after *One Hundred Poems* suggests recognition of this) but its quality assures it an important place within modern Australian literature. [PQ]

SMITH, A.J.M. (1902–80). Poet, born in Montreal, Quebec, Canada, and educated at McGill University, Montreal, where he edited the *McGill Daily Literary Supplement* and later founded the *McGill Fortnightly Review* which introduced the new poets of the 'Montreal Group' who were instrumental in promoting modern poetry in Canada. Smith took his doctorate at Edinburgh in 1931 and returned to the United States where he

worked as a teacher until joining the English Department at Michigan State University, East Lansing, in 1936; he became professor in 1960. He was a major directing influence as an editor, remaining a poet of severely restrained output but high theoretical and practical ability. Two small volumes, *News of the Phoenix and Other Poems* (1943) and *A Sort of Ecstasy* (1954), were followed by *Collected Poems* (1962) and *Poems: New and Collected* (1967). Smith's doctoral research had been on seventeenth-century metaphysical poetry in English and in his own writings he turned away from any overt involvement in 'Canadian poetry' while maintaining a deep commitment to Canadian writing. This interest is reflected in his editorship of over fifteen anthologies, among these *The Book of Canadian Poetry* (1943, 1948, 1957), to which he contributed an important introduction, and *The Oxford Book of Canadian Verse* (1960, 1965). More recently he edited *Masks of Fiction: Canadian Critics on Canadian Prose* (1961) and a companion volume on verse the following year. In 1973 a revised edition was issued of *Exploring Poetry*, originally published (with M.L. Rosenthal) in 1955. *The Book of Canadian Prose* (two volumes, 1965 and 1973) and *Modern Canadian Verse* (1967) were followed by his own important contribution to an area he had done so much to make known with the publication of *Towards a View of Canadian Letters: Selected Essays 1928–72* (1973). [PQ]

SMITH, IAIN CRICHTON (1928–). Poet and novelist, born on the Isle of Lewis in the Outer Hebrides, Scotland. He was brought up in a Gaelic-speaking community, but he read English at Aberdeen University and became English master at Oban High School in 1955. He has published short stories in both Gaelic and English. His volumes of English verse include *The Long River* (1955), *Deer on the High Hills* (1960) (a single poem), *The Law and the Grace* (1965), *The Bourgeois Land* (1969) and *Notebooks of Robinson Crusoe* (1974). Smith uses his Scottish background to great effect, sketching it deftly and portraying its inhabitants and their dilemmas with a somewhat melancholy sensitivity to human loneliness and vulnerability, but without sentimentalizing the pathos. An easy conversational style is crisply adjusted to richly varied human portraiture with undertones from a groundswell of passion, suffering, frustration or even sheer courage. Robin Fulton has edited Smith's *Selected Poems 1955–1980* (1982). Among Smith's novels, *Consider the Lilies* (1968) tells of an old Highland woman at the time of the Sutherland Clearances, *The Last Summer* (1969) of a 16-year-old Highland boy, and *Goodbye Mr Dixon* (1974) of Tom Spence who is writing a novel about a novelist and, through seeking copy, discovers a girl who draws him from his fictional world into a real world. *An End to Autumn* (1979) studies conflict consequent upon the well-meaning introduction of mother-in-law into the marital home. Smith's collections of short stories include *Survival Without Errors* (1970), *The Hermit and Other Stories* (1977) and *Murdo and Other Stories* (1981). In the last his somewhat idiosyncratic taste for the grotesque and the bizarre gives a winning piquancy to tales of humdrum daily life. [HB]

SMITH, PAULINE JANET (1882–1959). Novelist and short-story writer, born in Oudtshoorn, South Africa, in the Little Karoo region of the Cape Province. Her father, Herbert Urmson Smith, an English physician who settled there in 1879, was an energetic man of wide cultural interests, whose death at the age of 43 in 1898 permanently clouded her life. When Pauline Smith was 13, she and her younger sister were sent to school in Britain, where she spent the rest of her life, except for some lengthy visits to South Africa between 1905 and 1938 and travel in Europe. In 1909 Arnold Bennett (q.v.) saw some of her early attempts at writing; his faith in her ability and his hectoring encouragement enabled her to overcome the debilitating effects of chronic ill-health and personal diffidence. She was devoted to him as a father-figure friend, but was not his studio pupil. In August 1923 Middleton Murry (q.v.) printed her story 'The Pain' in *The Adelphi* and others followed over the next few years. Eight of these stark, tragic tales of Afrikaner (Boer) peasantry were published as *The Little Karoo* in 1925. Her novel, *The Beadle*, appeared in 1926. *The Little Karoo* was enlarged in 1930 with the addition of 'The Father' and 'Desolation'. *A.B.* came out in 1933, two years after Bennett's death – a slim but very sensitive and discriminating tribute to Bennett, which describes his generosity to her yet honestly acknowledges that they belonged to vastly different literary and moral worlds. Her last published work, *Platkops Children* (1935), was a collection of children's stories written in her youth. These four volumes and some stories in South African newspapers constitute her published work, but on *The Little Karoo* and *The Beadle* rests her firm reputation as possibly South Africa's purest writer of fiction in English. Indeed, *The Little Karoo* is among the finest collections of short stories published in Britain in the 1920s.

Her writing is austere and highly economical, apparently very simple, but of the finest and most delicate workmanship. That she wrote slowly and little was due as much to her uncompromising craftsman's respect for the medium as to ill-health. In adapting English sentences to the rhythms and sometimes the constructions of colloquial Afrikaans, she found a means well suited to analysing the most secret inner lives of elemental, dour peasant people, both when their flesh gave way under the strains of their demanding Calvinist faith and when their lives were congruent with it. Through her concrete presentation of the outward signs of their joys and sorrows, she created, out of an isolated regional setting, richly compassionate images of human courage, endurance, love and misery. A writer with an English-South African background, she nevertheless penetrates an obscure corner of the Afrikaner cultural situation. Shortly before her death at Broadstone, Dorset, she was presented with an illuminated address signed by twenty-five South African writers, praising her for having 'transcended the barriers of race and language'.

[AR]

SMITH, STEVIE (Florence Margaret) (1902–71). Poet, born in Hull, Humberside, educated in London, where she worked in publishing. She produced volumes of poetry at intervals from 1937 (*A Good Time Was Had By All*). *Selected Poems* (1962) and *Collected Poems* (1975) are decorated with her own odd drawings whose effect is to underline the flippant aspect of verse which inhabits a grey area between ingenuous, ballad-like directness and comic doggerel. It is an area where jeux d'esprit can teeter on the edge of profundity. Smith's own mental ambivalence is evident in her obsessional running battle with Christianity, which somehow never wholly lets her go. Her most innocent poems ('The Singing Cat') can captivate; her most serious poems (the title poem of *Not Waving But Drowning*, 1957) can disturb. Often she winds up the machinery of anecdotal nonsense verse, then lets it run down into casual inconclusiveness or throwaway banality behind whose obviousness a sting seems surely to lurk. She can versify comment on topicalities (see 'Valuable' or 'Why are the Clergy . . .?') with journalistic spontaneity and immediacy. She can make a stunningly obvious pun tingle with new resonance:

> Private Means is dead
> God rest his soul, officers and fellow-rankers said.
> ('Private Means is Dead')

The pervasive sense that poetry is not worth too much ardour or toil is made explicit in 'My Muse' ('When I am happy I live and despise writing') and has its obverse implications for life itself. She seems to make of blankness a destination, yet her way of crossing and re-crossing the frontiers between naïveté and sophistication, between glee and melancholy, pathos and malice, exercises the kind of fascination that could easily create a cult. She wrote three novels, *Novel on Yellow Paper* (1936), *Over the Frontier* (1938) and *The Holiday* (1949). Like her poems, they project an unhappiness with which her distrust of seriousness cannot cope. Jack Barbera and William McBrien have edited *Me Again* (1981), her 'Uncollected Writings'. [HB]

SMITH, SYDNEY GOODSIR (1915–75). Poet, born in New Zealand, educated at Malvern College and at the universities of Oxford and Edinburgh. Settling in Edinburgh, he chose to write in Scots and soon became, after Hugh MacDiarmid, the major poetic voice of the Scottish Renaissance. A steady output of verse began with *Skail Wind* (1941), which includes in 'Epistle to John Guthrie' a defence against the charge of writing a language no one speaks:

> And so, dear John, ye jist maun dree
> My Scots; for English, man,'s near deid,
> See the weeshy-washy London bree
> An tell me then whaes bluid is reid!

Under the Eildon Tree (1948), a sequence of twenty-four elegies on great lovers of history and myth, is regarded as his finest achievement. Personal, subjective material is subsumed into meditations on the fate of figures like Orpheus and Eurydice, Dido and Aeneas. The patriotic play *The Wallace* (1960) was produced at the Edinburgh Festival in 1960. *Collected Poems* came out in 1975. Smith's language is at once vigorously alive with contemporary raciness and steeped in the poetic tradition reaching back to the Middle Scots makars. *Carotid Cornucopius* (1947), a novel, is a word-drunk fantasy in Scots, Joycean in character. [HB]

SMITHYMAN, KENDRICK (1922–). Poet, born in Te Kopuru, Auckland, New Zealand, and educated at Auckland University College. After war service – 'all my war was on paper' – he was a primary school teacher until 1963 when he became a senior tutor in the Auckland University English Department. His early collections, *Seven Sonnets* (1946) and *The Blind Mountain* (1950), were followed by *The Gay Trapeze* (1955), all of them demonstrating his careful craftsmanship and his wryly dispassionate translation of personal experience. *The Night Shift* (1957) – 'poems on aspects of love' – was a joint volume with James K. Baxter (q.v.), Mike (Charles) Doyle (q.v.) and Louis Johnson (q.v.). A rich poetic and cultural awareness and a sharply individual wit combine in his best work to give a striking interpretation of the local, felt experience in terms which demand a wider, considered understanding. This genuine complexity of approach was confirmed not only by the poetry collection *Inheritance* (1962), but also by his major study of New Zealand poetry, *A Way of Saying* (1965). This book explored the relevance to the New Zealand literary situation of the 'provincial' and 'regional' distinction first made by the American critic Allen Tate: 'Nationalism, provincialism and regionalism are far from being merely New Zealand concerns. The thoughts of writers overseas who have wrestled with these matters should not be ignored by us if we would get our own thinking clear.' The book focuses upon New Zealand poetry itself, but by seeking to answer questions of wider import (which also recur in the poetry) it faces directly that relation between life and literature which features so strongly in Smithyman's own work. An increased assurance of tone and a constantly adventurous technical range characterize *Flying to Palmerson* (1968), and the later collections, *Earthquake Weather* (1972), *The Seal in the Dolphin Pool* (1974) and *Dwarf with a Billiard Cue* (1978), confirmed his status as one of the most rewarding poets writing in New Zealand. His own introduction to the selection in the 1956 anthology by Charles Doyle was typically self-effacing in its complexity: 'Often enough I wrote a poem because I proposed to myself some technical problem for which the equivocal solution was a piece of writing. Such things were not inevitably poems.' [PQ]

SNOW, C.P. (Charles Percy) (1905–80). Novelist, born in Leicester, Leicestershire, where his father worked in a boot and shoe firm. He was educated at Alderman Newton's Grammar School and at Leicester University College where he gained a first-class BSc in chemistry in 1927 and an MSc in physics in 1928. He then went to Christ's College, Cambridge, as a research student, gained a fellowship and later a tutorship. But already his ambition was to break through from science to literature. 'I knew my own ultimate vocation from the time I was about eighteen', he has said. A piece of research that went wrong in 1933 provided both the impetus to change direction and the subject of his third novel, *The Search* (1934). In 1935 he conceived the idea of the series of novels that became his life work as a writer, and he wrote the first, *Strangers and Brothers* (1940), before putting the project aside for the duration of the Second World War. He was involved in the organization of scientists for the war and became a civil servant. As Director of Per-

sonnel in the Ministry of Labour, and later as a Civil Service Commissioner concerned with scientific appointments, he was, until 1960 (when he retired from the Civil Service), at the centre of decision-making that straddled the government service and the academic world. Snow married the novelist Pamela Hansford Johnson (q.v.) in 1950. Between 1947 and 1964 eight volumes were added to the cyclic scheme of related novels, but Snow was lured back into the world of public affairs in 1964 when he became Parliamentary Secretary to the new Ministry of Technology in Harold Wilson's first Labour administration. He was subsequently made a Life Peer as Baron Snow of Leicester. He resigned his office in 1966 and the sequence of novels was then completed by the publication of *The Sleep of Reason* (1968) and *Last Things* (1970). Snow now renamed the first novel of the series *George Passant* and adopted the title *Strangers and Brothers** for the cycle as a whole.

Snow's ascent from a lower-middle-class home in the provinces to the Whitehall 'corridors of power', his transit through Cambridge Senior Common Rooms en route, his contacts with the scientific, social and political establishments, together equipped him uniquely as a recorder of his time, and what he calls 'insights into society' can be detected in his ingenious eleven-volume conspectus of the masculine world of politicking – politicking in neatly graded milieux from provincial educational institution to Cabinet. Snow's 1959 Rede lecture at Cambridge, *Two Cultures and the Scientific Revolution*, is concerned with the split between traditional culture, literary in character, and the specialized scientific world, and with the dangers inherent in continuing fragmentation. He saw himself as a bridge-maker across the divide.

Strangers and Brothers is a series of eleven linked novels covering the years 1914 to 1968 from the point of view of Lewis Eliot, Snow's alter ego, whose career in essential respects matches his own. Three of the books (the third, sixth and last) concentrate on Lewis's private life and provide an autobiographical framework for the rest. The other eight books focus more objectively on persons and events of which Lewis is an off-side spectator. *George Passant* (originally published as *Strangers and Brothers*, 1940) tells the story of Passant, a solicitor's assistant in Lewis's unnamed home town (Leicester). A brilliant but inadequately disciplined man, he teaches in the local college in the evenings and gathers about him a group of youngsters inspired and infected by his progressive permissiveness. *The Light and the Dark* (1947) tells the story of a brilliant but mentally unstable Cambridge research scholar, Roy Calvert, to his death on a bombing mission over Germany in 1943. *Time of Hope* (1949) deals with Eliot's early days, the gradual fulfilment of his ambition to rise and practise at the Bar, and his unfortunate marriage to the deeply unresponsive Sheila Knight. *The Masters* (1951) fastens on Lewis's Cambridge college for a probing analysis of intrigue and the power game in electing a new master. *The New Men* (1954), covering the years 1939 to 1954, explores the moral attitude of scientists at an atomic research establishment and the problem posed by the dropping of a bomb on Hiroshima. Lewis's younger brother, a nuclear researcher, is a key figure in the exposure of a communist

in the nest. *Homecomings* (1956) initiates a second revolution of the cycle by tracing Lewis's autobiography from
1938 and the death of his first wife to 1951 when, happily
married to Margaret and father of a son, he has risen to
the heights of Whitehall. *The Conscience of the Rich*
(1958) concerns a wealthy Jewish family first encountered by Lewis in 1927 when a fellow law student,
Charles Marsh, took him home. *The Affair* (1960) goes
back to the Cambridge college for another crisis in the
Senior Common Room sixteen years after *The Masters* (it
is now 1953 to 1954). *Corridors of Power* (1964), sometimes cited as Snow's most controlled, homogeneous and
structured work, takes us to the top with an account of
political manoeuvring over the Cabinet's nuclear deter-
rent policy. *The Sleep of Reason* (1968) fastens on the
years 1963 to 1964, first to bring Lewis's personal story
up to date, then to take him back to his home town for the
trial of two young lesbians who have murdered a little
boy. One of them is Passant's niece. The relationship
between Passant's career as a prophet of freedom for the
instincts and the horrific murder which is the fruit of permissiveness thirty years later makes for an element of
moral patterning, but it is not an issue deeply embedded
in the total current of thought. *Last Things* (1970) sees the
next generation trying their hand at idealistic radicalism,
and attempts some sort of philosophic conclusiveness in
Lewis's response to near-death after an eye-operation.

Snow's hero-narrator is so much more virtuous than
most of the people he deals with that he embarrasses the
reader, not least when he has recourse to modest dis-
claimers that do not ring true. He is recurrently in receipt
of testimonials from all around to the value of his friendship, his patience and his merits. Recorded by the recipient, such tributes endow him with priggishness. Snow
has argued that the 'inner design' of the work resides in
'the resonance between what Lewis Eliot sees and what
he feels', and there is some attempt at thematic continuity in relation to possessive love, love of power, and
renunciation of power, but as succeeding volumes focus
on different overlapping individual careers, the overall
pattern inevitably brings to mind the image of a filing-
cabinet with an efficient built-in cross-reference system.
At his best – in *Corridors of Power* – Snow portrays the
excitements of public life with some discernment; but
sometimes the cryptic style rings hollowly: emotional
exchanges are minuted like committee meetings, and
attempts to fabricate tension out of reiterated generalities fall flat. [HB]

SOMERVILLE, E.O. (Edith Oenone) (1858–1949) and
ROSS, MARTIN (1862–1914). Novelists, who wrote in
collaboration and were remarkable in achieving a joint
style. Edith Somerville, though born in Corfu, came of an
Irish family of Castle Townshend, County Cork, and eventually became mistress of the family home there. Her
cousin Violet Florence Martin came from Ross House,
near Oughterhead in County Galway, whence she took
her pseudonym 'Martin Ross'. Somerville was passionately devoted to her cousin ('Deep in her was a profound
distaste for the opposite sex', Maurice Collis, *Somerville
and Ross*, 1968) and continued to attribute her work to the
partnership after Violet Martin's death from a brain
tumour. In spiritualist seances she held what she

regarded as conversations with her former collaborator
which enabled her to continue to write. The list of
published books contains nearly thirty titles, including
works of travel (*Through Connemara in a Governess Cart*,
1892; *In the Vine Country*, 1893), reminiscence (*Irish
Memories*, 1917; *Wheel-Tracks*, 1923), articles and
essays (*Some Irish Yesterdays*, 1906; *Stray-aways*, 1920).
The novel, *The Real Charlotte* (1894), studies two women,
tragic victims respectively of inescapable personal ugliness and personal charm, but it was the succession of
stories of Irish life, *Some Experiences of an Irish R.M.*
(1899), which made the authors famous overnight. Major
Sinclair Yeates, the R.M. (Resident Magistrate), settles at
Shreelane and is joined by a strong-minded bride. Round
him revolves a series of stories – many of them horse and
hunting stories – that are rich in down-to-earth comedy.
The humour relies largely on rural personalities and
dialogue and on hilarious Irish ingenuity in stage-
managing scrapes, practical jokes and mischances. The
astonishing verve and spontaneity were maintained in the
subsequent collections, *Further Experiences of an Irish
R.M.* (1908) and *In Mr Knox's Country* (1915). The best of
the books published after Violet Martin's death is the
novel *The Big House at Inver* (1925), an ambitiously
spacious account of 'one of those minor dynasties that, in
Ireland, have risen, and ruled, and rioted, and have at
last crashed in ruins'. In fact it concentrates on a formidable illegitimate female descendant's determination, on
behalf of her legitimate brother, that 'the King shall have
his own again'. Somerville writes with a multitude of
literary graces – verbal embellishments, ironic asides,
parenthetic felicities – and manages her wilful
characters with fond parental good-humour. Edith
Somerville was a cousin of Bernard Shaw's wife and
Violet Martin was a cousin of Lady Gregory (q.v.). [HB]

SORLEY, CHARLES HAMILTON (1895–1915).
Poet, born in Aberdeen, Scotland, educated at Marlborough College. He spent some months in Germany just
before the First World War, then joined up, was commissioned, and killed in action. *Marlborough and Other
Poems* (1916) included a celebrated sonnet rejecting the
shallow postures of jingoism:

> When you see millions of the mouthless dead
> Across your dreams in pale battalions go,
> Say not soft things as other men have said

In such poems Sorley anticipated the complex reaction to
the war which the later, wholesale slaughter was to
provoke from Sassoon (q.v.), Rosenberg (q.v.) and Owen
(q.v.). *The Letters of Sorley* (1919), edited by W.R. Sorley,
reinforce the impression of a talented and powerful
thinker prematurely cut off. [HB]

SOUTAR, WILLIAM (1898–1943). Poet, born in
Perth, Perthshire, Scotland. He served in the navy from
1916 to 1918 and contracted a spinal disease which eventually incapacitated him. He took a degree in English at
Edinburgh University in 1923, but he was totally bed-
ridden for the last thirteen years of his life. From his bed
he published several volumes of poetry, and Hugh
MacDiarmid edited his *Collected Poems* (1948) after his
death. Selections were also published from his journal,

under the title *Diaries of a Dying Man* (1954). Soutar's work contains powerful short poems in English, like the anti-bloodsport outburst, 'The Guns', and a haunting cry about the cost of killing in battle, 'The Unknown'. But his finest work is in Scots. He revitalizes the ballad form with an uncanny fidelity to its essential character and idiom. There is finely compressed emotional energy in simple songs of love and loss, like 'The Tryst' and 'O! shairly ye hae seen my love'; while 'Birthday' is a rich, wild gothic tale of night-riders who encounter a unicorn in the Grampians:

Nae man brac'd back the bridle
Yet ilka fit stüde still
As thru the flichterin' floichan-drift
A beast cam doun the hill.

It steppit like a stallion,
Wha's heid hauds up a horn,
And weel the men o' Scotland kent
It was the unicorn.

[HB]

SOYINKA, WOLE (1934–). Dramatist, actor, producer, poet, novelist, teacher, born in Abeokuta, Western Nigeria, and educated in Ibadan and at the University of Leeds in 1956–8. After working with the Royal Court Theatre, London, he founded 'The 1960 Masks' in Nigeria and later the Orisun Theatre. His play *A Dance of the Forests* was produced for the Nigerian Independence celebrations in 1960. In 1967 he was charged with substituting a radio tape of his own for one due to be broadcast by the Western Nigerian Prime Minister, but was acquitted. Later in 1967, after the Nigerian Civil War broke out, he was detained and held in Kaduna Prison for over two years, mostly in solitary confinement. He has taught in the universities of Ife and Lagos, and in 1969 became head of the School of Drama, University of Ibadan. He lived in Ghana in 1972–5, where he edited the journal *Transition*. Since then he has been at Ife, though intermittently a visiting lecturer in Britain and the United States. In 1966 he was a joint winner of the John Whiting Drama Prize; in 1969 he was awarded the Jock Campbell Prize and in 1973 an honorary doctorate of the University of Leeds. He was a co-editor from 1960–64 of the important journal *Black Orpheus* and edited an anthology, *Poems of Black Africa* (1975). He is not only the most versatile and prolific but also the most politically involved of anglophone African writers.

His first published work consisted of some short stories in magazines (1954–7). In 1959 the Royal Court Theatre produced his still unpublished play, *The Invention*. Three Plays (containing *The Swamp Dwellers*, *The Trials of Brother Jero*, *The Strong Breed*) appeared in Nigeria in 1963. In the same year *A Dance of the Forests* and *The Lion and the Jewel* were separately published in London. While the Jero play and *The Lion and the Jewel* are sparkling comedies that satirize both traditional rural and modern urban ways (in the latter, the schoolmaster's aspirations include dining off 'breakable plates'), the tragic dimensions of *The Swamp Dwellers* and *The Strong Breed* involve darker questionings both of ancient communal beliefs and of modern individualistic attitudes to

them. *A Dance of the Forests* remains Soyinka's most complex and theatrically ambitious play. It is steeped in the beliefs of his Yoruba background, and its characters include the Yoruba gods, or Forest Dwellers, who respond equivocally to a village's request for two representative ancestors to be sent back from the dead in order to join in a great Gathering of the Tribes. For these two visitors from the time of the legendary Yoruba king, Mata Kharibu, bring no glory but are shown to have behaved even as selfishly and sordidly, centuries before, as the living characters in the play. The point is made by means of a flashback to Mata Kharibu's court and underlined dramatically by the same actors playing corresponding roles in both past and present. In the final 'trial' of the living and the dead, the chief deity, Forest Head, underlines the sombre drift of the play: 'My secret is my eternal burden – to pierce the encrustations of soul-deadening habit, . . . hoping that when I have tortured awareness from [human] souls, perhaps, only perhaps, in new beginnings', and his voice trails away. Soyinka uses Yoruba songs translated into English and adapts old rituals and dances to produce particular dramatic effects on the modern stage, yet the play carries a caustic commentary upon violence and corruption in the very society whose new-born nationhood it was commissioned to celebrate.

This ironical strain in *A Dance of the Forests* develops into the full political satire of *Kongi's Harvest* (1967), about a modern demagogic ruler who tries to assume the symbolic legitimacy of the traditional, quasi-religious *oba* or chief. Neither side gains a clear-cut victory, but the blatant lust for power of the new style of African leader is satirized in superbly comic scenes.

Meanwhile in 1965 *The Road*, despite its satirical undercurrents, had carried further Soyinka's interest in Yoruba beliefs about interaction between the living and the dead (a theme he was to explore fully in the essays in *Myth, Literature and the African World*, 1976). The characters in *The Road* are drawn from the lower reaches of Nigerian urban society, associated with motor vehicles and the new sacrifices that the god Ogun demands in the form of victims of road crashes. The central character is the ironically named Professor who seeks The Word that will explain death. His voracious and futile collecting of every kind of printed word and his understanding that a man wearing a ritual mask partakes of the life of the spirit personated thereby suggest that Soyinka is sounding out the contradictions within a society moving from intuitive communication with the spirit world to literacy and rationalism. Again Soyinka employs ingenious dramatic devices to convey his theme – the liberal use of untranslated Yoruba songs and traditional dances at moments of particular intensity.

If his novel, *The Interpreters* (1965), does have a fully realized, coherent theme (it is highly regarded by critics like E.D. Jones and G. Moore), it would seem to be the difficulty that the intellectual Nigerian élite have in resolving the conflicting pulls of communality and highly developed individualism. In different ways the four intellectuals who are the main characters believe they should be interpreters to their society of 'modern' ways, but, with one enigmatic exception, are themselves confused. Despite its clever satire of many absurdities in modern Nigeria, despite its immense energy and linguistic gusto, *The Inter-*

preters is an untidy novel in which exuberances like Sagoe's 'philosophy' of voidancy grow out of proportion to the purposes they seem intended to serve.

The long title poem of *Idanre and Other Poems* (1968) explores the dual nature of the Yoruba god Ogun in an attempt to resolve the paradox of renewal out of destruction ('growth is greener where / Rich blood has spilt'). While it partly seeks to habilitate the old gods in the twentieth century, it is very much a convoluted personal poem about knowledge and belief. Verbal complexity in 'Idanre' often enacts the poet's profound sensibility but sometimes it only glitters on the surface in this volume, resulting in acrobatics of word and image that produce portentousness where wry wisdom is aimed at (e.g. 'To My First White Hairs', 'Easter'). 'Massacre October 1966 Written in Tegel' is, however, a closely textured, shocked, personal confrontation with a national atrocity that seeks in 'brotherhood of ill' with Nazi Germany to 'stay the season of a mind'.

One effect of Soyinka's imprisonment in 1967-9 was the incubation of three plays, a translation of Euripides's *The Bacchae*, a novel, a volume of poetry and the vitriolic account of that prison experience, all published between 1971 and 1975. Another was a greater attention to literary form; Soyinka's words still tumble in a stream of energetic creativity but there is now less mere ebullience, a greater directing power, as the sweep of his imagination translates the acrid details of actual experience into patterns of passionately affirmatory vision. The prison book, *The Man Died* (1973), should be read along with the play *Madmen and Specialists* (1971), the novel *Season of Anomy* (1973) and especially the poetry of *A Shuttle in the Crypt* (1972). Many of these poems were composed in gaol as part of the rigorous self-discipline, so vividly described in *The Man Died*, that Soyinka imposed upon himself to conserve his sanity. *Season of Anomy* is a finely structured, disturbing novel, in which Soyinka unflinchingly measures the obscene reality of what Nigerian did to Nigerian, African to African, in 1966-70. Yet, despite the detailed scenes of massacre, despite the descent into an underworld of inhumanity by the characters Ofeyi (Orpheus) and Iriyise (Eurydice), the book is affirmatory in a particularly Yoruba way. The near-utopian communal settlement of Aiyéró is both crypto-Christian and traditionally Yoruba in its ideals and practices and is presented as an image of hope for African society. Its ideals embody the dual nature of Ogun's activities, the god who plunges into self-destruction in order to re-create and re-energize. In political terms, the Soyinka of *A Dance of the Forests* (who makes Forest Head himself shudder at the violence of the human beings he has created) has become a revolutionary in *Season of Anomy*: the character known as the Dentist is a political assassin, but his name indicates exactly Soyinka's concept of the legitimate use of violence – as a beneficent surgical operation upon the body politic. Set against the life-sustaining values of Aiyéró, and for the time being triumphant over them, are the capitalist Cartel and its military machine. But the last sentence of the novel ('In the forests, life began to stir') shows the beginning of a new cycle confirmed by the titles of the five sections into which the book is divided: 'Seminal', 'Buds', 'Tentacles', 'Harvest', 'Spores'.

Dr Bero in *Madmen and Specialists* is the antithesis of the Dentist: a medical practitioner who becomes a 'specialist' medical executioner of those deemed unreliable by the military regime. The roles of his sister and the Earth Mothers show that he has abandoned his life-saving functions in favour of destruction, for gain and out of power lust. Bero's 'mad' father had served human flesh in an officers' mess as a logical demonstration of all that war implies, and the play exposes the ugly dehumanization that occurs in war. One of the group of maimed characters who are the flotsam of armed conflict satirically parodies an African political speech – Soyinka's estimate of the Nigerian Civil War: 'Excuse me, please, but we are entitled to match you history for history to the nearest half-million souls'. Presumably 'you' refers to the Europe of 1914-18 and 1939-45.

In *Death and the King's Horseman* (1975), Soyinka returns to the Yoruba belief that 'present life contains within it manifestations of the ancestral, the living and the unborn' (*Myth, Literature and the African World*). The play demonstrates that an individual's deliberate, ritual willing of his own death is, in fact, an affirmation of communal life and continuance.

Ogun Abibimañ (1976), inspired by the Soweto Children's Uprising in South Africa that year, is an extended poem that invokes the Yoruba god Ogun and the Zulu hero-king Shaka to serve as a clarion call to all black people, everywhere, to help in the liberation of their fellows in South Africa. *Opera Wanyosi* (prod 1977, pubd 1981), a very lively and inventive adaptation of Brecht's *Threepenny Opera* and Gay's *The Beggar's Opera*, satirizes greed and chicanery in Nigerian society, and political corruption and power-lust throughout Africa. *Aké: The Years of Childhood* (1981) is an extraordinarily engaging account of innocence and growing experience in a Christian compound in the midst of Yoruba culture and belief.

Soyinka has the gifts of verbal inventiveness, a passionate sense of justice and humanity, and an original, transcending imagination. The acute deprivations he endured in solitary confinement seem to have steeled his mind and acted catalytically in his development as a craftsman of letters. [AR]

SPARK, MURIEL (1918–). Novelist, born in Edinburgh, Lothian, Scotland, of a Jewish father, Bernard Camberg, and a Presbyterian mother, Sarah Uezzell. She was educated at James Gillespie's School for Girls, Edinburgh. 'Edinburgh is the place that I, a constitutional exile, am essentially exiled from', she has said (quoted in K. Malkoff, *Muriel Spark*, 1968), and from the age of 18 until 1944 she lived in South Africa, where she married S.O. Spark in 1938. She had one son, but the marriage was dissolved and in 1944 she came back to England to work in the Political Intelligence Department of the Foreign Office. She was editor of *Poetry Review* from 1947 to 1949; she published a volume of poetry, *The Fanfarlo and Other Verse*, in 1952; and she worked for some years in the literary field, publishing *Child of Light* (1951), a book about Mary Shelley, *John Masefield* (1953), and (in collaboration with Derek Stanford) *Emily Brontë, Her Life and Work* (1953). She also edited *The Brontë Letters* (1954), *My Best Mary: The Letters of Mary Shelley* (1953) and *Letters of John Henry Newman* (1957), the last two again in collaboration with Derek Stanford.

Muriel Spark wrote the winning entry for a short-story competition in the *Observer* at Christmas, 1951, but it was only after prompting from Macmillan, the publishers, that she began to think of the novel as her medium and wrote *The Comforters* (1957). By this time she had moved through Anglo-Catholicism to become, in 1954, a Roman Catholic. She has since been labelled a 'Catholic writer', sometimes by critics who use the label pejoratively. The fact that her view of life presents a radical challenge to current humanistic and hedonistic presuppositions in the critical world cannot be regarded as putting her off-centre in relation to larger canons of artistic integrity. It is necessary to say this because there have been attempts to write off Spark's as a minor talent and a flawed artistry as against writers whose basic dogma is a trendy, if irresponsible, commitment to moral and social decomposition. Muriel Spark's is an astonishingly rare and subtle genius. That it relies on economies of form and of imaginative focus is a strength, not a weakness. Like Jane Austen she does not try to camouflage her identity as a woman, and her presentation of the male is all the shrewder and livelier for the unmistakable femininity of the authorial voice. Her second novel, *Robinson* (1958), is the record of January Marlow and how, along with two other survivors of a plane crash (Jimmie Waterford and Tom Wells), she spent nearly three months on an island inhabited only by Robinson and his servant boy, Miguel. January's experience puts aspects of the human situation under a microscope. Macrocosmic overtones give open-ended mythic status to the man-shaped island (January would now be tempted to declare it 'a time and landscape of the mind', did she not have relics of the place about her) and to the mysterious Robinson whom January thinks of 'as a kind of legendary figure'. Moreover the pattern of human relationships in the intensified 'laboratory' conditions of exile from normality recapitulates and concentrates for January moral problems she has left behind; for Jimmie matches one of her brothers-in-law and Tom Wells the other. The temporary disappearance – and apparent murder – of Robinson, who is benefactor, healer, host and provider, yet also authoritative inhibiter and intrusive regulator of behaviour and attitude, makes possible a perceptive exploration of the consequent effect of the 'freedom' he thus designedly contrives for the survivors. Spark's opening up of extra-naturalistic dimensions gives her work a poetic validity and a universality of status that will outlast her own age, while her resistance to identifiable allegorizations safeguards her against propagandist didacticism.

In successive novels Muriel Spark has fastened on experiences which correspondingly sharpen responsiveness to the inescapable human lot. In *Memento Mori* (1959) the main characters are aged, and they are subjected to periodic telephone calls from a mysterious voice, delivering the terse message, 'Remember you must die'. The power of the book rests on the contrast between the simple reality of the message and the dominant concerns of the transient lives it upsets. Worldly obsession with wills and bequests on the part of the near-senile well-to-do and their would-be inheritors accelerates ironically in inverse relation to decreasing life-expectancy. In *The Ballad of Peckham Rye* (1960) Dougal Douglas, a Scots graduate, takes a job with a south-bank textile firm who want an 'Arts man to bring vision into the lives of the workers' and incidentally to solve the absentee problem. Douglas double-crosses them by accepting and holding a similar post with their rivals and by stirring up restlessness among the workers. For all his insidious use of blackmail and his diabolical deformities (he is a hunchback and has incipient horns), he is no crude Morality devil and his whirlwind career in waking people up is by no means wholly evil in intent or effect. Action, however, seems to belong to the world of fantasy, whereas in *The Prime of Miss Jean Brodie** (1962) the author brings acute analytical powers to bear on the career of a Scots spinster schoolmistress, and in particular her psychological and moral influence upon a group of pupils carefully differentiated in temperament and malleability, but all subjected to her highly pressurized educative technique. In *The Girls of Slender Means* (1963) a fire at a girls' hostel in London in 1945 is the catalytic event that brings the lives of the girls and one of their boyfriends under judgement, by suddenly shifting the angle of vision. Tragedy lays human selfishness open *sub specie aeternitatis*.

Muriel Spark is a witty, economic writer whose dialogue is crisp and telling. Time-shifts, pre-echoes of future events and changes in mode of narrative presentation are deftly manipulated and the story-line is rarely single-track. If echoes of graceful past masters of aphorism have been caught in her earlier work (Beerbohm (q.v.) has been cited), the flavour of Beckett (q.v.) can be detected in *The Driver's Seat* (1970), where cumulative illogicalities and insane obsession with detail mark the last hours of an unloved woman who provokes a freshly released sex-maniac to kill her. After completing her longer, denser novel, *The Mandelbaum Gate* (1965), whose setting is divided Jerusalem, the author vowed never again to write a long book, but *The Takeover* (1976) is a substantial work. Its setting is the lake of Nemi of Frazer's *The Golden Bough*. At a time of contemporary crisis a revival of the ancient cult of Diana coincides with the breakdown of the proprietorial safeguards sustaining our decadent plutocracy. We are entering 'the Dark Ages II'. *Territorial Rights* (1979), a further exploration of evil, is also set in Italy. A story of robbery, violence and espionage, it tackles the subject of public betrayal as *The Prime of Miss Jean Brodie* tackled that of private betrayal. *Loitering with Intent* (1981) is a fictional autobiography of a writer whose experience as a novelist in some respects parallels Muriel Spark's own. The narrator's reflections on her work have thus a special interest for the reader.

The Prime of Miss Jean Brodie is a study of Jean Brodie, a teacher at Marcia Blaine School for Girls, Edinburgh, in the 1930s. She challenges authority by a supposedly progressive educational method in which the arts have precedence over the sciences and individuality over the team spirit. Her way of preserving the culture of the élite is to cultivate a group of pupils ('the Brodie set') and mould them in her image to be 'la crème de la crème'. The process involves opening up to them her own love life – in the past with a soldier killed in the war, in the present with the married art master, whom she nobly renounces, and with the music master, who temporarily answers the consequent physical need while the art master retains her devotion. The girls are finely characterized; the flavour of their thinking, from the age of 10 to the age of 18, is subtly captured in appropriate idiom at each stage. It is to Rosa Stanley that Miss Brodie looks for vicarious sexual fulfilment with the art master; but her fellow pupil, Sandy Stranger, actually takes her place and Sandy is the one who 'betrays' Miss Brodie to the headmistress, making it possible for the authorities to dismiss her. 'It's only possible to betray where loyalty is due', Sandy claims at the end when she has become a nun, Sister Helena of the Transfiguration. A higher ethic has supervened. [HB]

SPENCER, BERNARD (1909–63). Poet, born in Madras, India, and educated at Marlborough College and Corpus Christi College, Oxford. He was for a time classics master at Westminster School and from 1942 worked for the British Council, serving abroad for the most part. He contributed poems to Grigson's New Verse in the 1930s and, after the war, to the London Magazine. He published three volumes of verse: Aegean Islands (1946), The Twist in the Plotting (1960) and With Luck Lasting (1963). Collected Poems (1965), published posthumously, has now been superseded by Collected Poems (1981), edited by Roger Bowen.

Grigson described Spencer as 'a sprite, of rather low pressure', and the characteristic of his small but distinctive output is a quiet fastidiousness which precludes any incivility or excess. There is never a hint of the flamboyant or the coarse-grained. 'I think I like ordinary people because I am listening', he said. But he seems to have listened and watched until the pressures within built up to bursts of revealing creativity. His imagery could be memorably meticulous:

A dog's pitched
Barking flakes and flakes away at the sky.
('Night-time: Starting to Write')

Spencer had a remarkable gift for fastening on the workaday minutiae of life and seeing them transfigured. In 'Part of Plenty', as he looks up from his book to watch his wife laying the table,

there is an importance of beauty
Which can't be accounted for by there and then,
And attacks me

Again, in 'Train to Work', he studies a puzzled-looking commuter on the Underground and senses the burden of his days so powerfully that he finds 'poetry roaring from him like a furnace'. Over against the prevailing scrupulous undemonstrativeness, words like 'attacks', 'roaring' and 'furnace' acquire compelling force. Spencer is one of those minor poets whose work, as Anthony Thwaite (q.v.) puts it, carries 'the flavour of a distinct and irreplaceable personality' Times Literary Supplement, 1.1.82). [HB]

SPENDER, STEPHEN(1909–). Poet and critic who has also written fiction and drama, born in London, the son of Harold Spender, the Liberal journalist and biographer of Asquith and Lloyd George. Spender was educated at University College School and at University College, Oxford. At Oxford he became acquainted with W.H. Auden (q.v.) who, two years his senior, held court in grand intellectual assurance ('Calling on Auden was a serious business. One made an appointment', World Within World). Spender spent two years in Germany in the 1930s (for a time in close touch with Isherwood (q.v.)): he became a communist, joined the party and went to Spain during the Civil War to help the Republican cause. Forward from Liberalism (1937) voices his political convictions at this stage ('Liberals must reconcile Communist social justice with their liberal regard for social freedom . . . must accept the methods that it might be necessary to use in order to defeat Fascism'), but later experience reversed the movement back to liberalism. Though it has since become fashionable to portray literary flirtations with communism in the 1930s as conveniently trendy, cosy, abstract and even adolescent, it is clear that Spender was both disturbed by social inequalities and drawn by idealistic Marxist utopianism.

Spender's first volume of poetry, Poems (1933), made a great impression and very soon Spender was being linked by the critics with Auden, Day Lewis (q.v.) and MacNeice (q.v.). These poets were seen as a young group responding to the events of an economically and politically afflicted decade with a new verbal vitality and a frank social awareness. In point of fact Spender's best work is personal in stamp, deriving as much from a Forsterian hang-up on the privacies of personal relationship as from matters of public moment. (Spender thinks Forster 'the best English novelist of this century'.) It has been argued that the 1933 volume contains what really matters in Spender's considerable output and that he might have done better not to have gone further (C.H. Sisson, English Poetry 1900–1950). It has also been argued that 'his later poems are . . . often his profounder work' (G.S. Fraser in The Penguin Companion to Literature). The succeeding volumes include The Still Centre (1939), Poems of Dedication (1946), The Edge of Being (1949) and Collected Poems (1955) in which Spender revises somewhat, but carefully explains his aim of improving without 'cheating', that is without forgetting the obligation to remain true to the 'felt experiences' from which the poems arose. Spender is a poet whose most frequently anthologized poems do full justice to his talent. 'The Pylons' contrasts the old 'secret' of the hills – stone cottages, crumbling roads, hidden villages – with the stark intruders:

Pylons, those pillars
Bare like nude, giant girls that have no secret

and it is done with sharpness and economy; while in 'I think continually of those who were truly great' there is flowing rhetoric to proclaim what is precious in the Spenderian personal ethic – 'never to forget / The essential delight of the blood'

Never to deny its pleasure in the morning simple
light

Nor its grave evening demand for love.

The same rhetorical vigour serves a different purpose in 'After they have tired' where 'comrades' are exhorted, 'after the failure of banks / The failure of cathedrals and the declared insanity of our rulers' not to lack 'the Spring-like resources of the tiger', and the imagery flashes into life:

We have come at last to a country
Where light equal, like the shine from snow,
    strikes all faces.

Such power is perhaps but fitfully displayed over Spender's later poetry. He remains capable of capsulating a familiar mood neatly, but it is not hard to find infelicity of rhythm and prosody, a lack of memorability in substance and form, and a degeneration of rhetoric into diffuseness. Sometimes one fears that the postures are 'romantic' stereotypes, that a youthful textbook rebelliousness has been prolonged into middle age.

Spender's autobiography, World Within World (1951), provides an apt commentary on his poetry – poetry in which sometimes the frequency of the first personal pronoun suggests a man too interested in himself. That World Within World is full of lively, gossipy impressions of contemporaries (such as Auden, Isherwood, Eliot (q.v.), Virginia Woolf (q.v.) and the Bloomsbury Group) cannot be denied: but they are surface impressions for the most part. Reflection is more interesting for the state of mind revealed than for illumination shared. ('Critics like Virginia Woolf, who reproached our generation for writing too directly out of a sense of public duty, failed to see that public events had swamped our personal lives and usurped our personal experience.')

Spender's verse play, Trial of a Judge (1938), 'a tragic statement in five acts', is a study of the collapse of 'liberal' justice under pressure from the fascist right. The communist left is naïvely glamorized, but then the age is the age of Hitler. The jargon of political polemics is mixed up with strained, sometimes ill-digested, imagery and does not make for a palatable brew. Spender has been active as a critic. He joined with Cyril Connolly (q.v.) in editing Horizon which aimed to keep literary sensitivities afloat during the war, and he was co-editor of Encounter from 1953 to 1965. He published The Destructive Element in 1936, analysing 'the deep consciousness of destructive forces threatening our civilization, which was to be found in the work of Henry James, James Joyce, T.S. Eliot' and others. The Making of a Poem (1955) is a collection of essays, 'the notes of a writer on writing'. The Struggle of the Modern (1963) discusses books, 'commenting on the characteristics which relate to the problems of inventing a specifically modern kind of art', and playing with such 'opposites' as 'recognizers' and 'non-recognizers' of the modern situation (such as Wilfred Owen (q.v.) on the one hand and De la Mare (q.v.) on the other). In 1970 Spender was made Professor of English Literature at University College, London. See also Lee Bartlett, ed., Letters to Christopher (1981), Spender's letters to Christopher Isherwood written between 1929 and 1939, and two journals belonging to 1932 and 1939 respectively.   [HB]

SPRING, HOWARD (1889–1965). Novelist, born in Cardiff, South Glamorgan, Wales, son of a gardener. He was a journalist until his third novel, O Absalom! (1938) – later retitled My Son, My Son – proved a best-seller. A story of two Manchester men, English and Irish respectively, who are close friends and whose matching ambitions for their sons are frustrated when the one kills the other, it covers the period from the 1890s to the Irish Civil War. Packed with incidents and characters, most of them fictional stereotypes, it lacks thematic concentration and substitutes sentimentality for emotional intensity. Among later novels were Fame is the Spur (1940) and The Houses in Between (1951). There are also three autobiographical books: Heaven Lies About Us (1939), In the Meantime (1942) and And Another Thing (1946).   [HB]

SQUIRE, J.C. (Sir John Collings) (1884–1958). Poet, born in Plymouth, Devon, educated at Blundell's School in Devon and Cambridge University. He became the first literary editor of The New Statesman in 1913, contributing under the pseudonym 'Solomon Eagle'. Later he was editor of the London Mercury (1914–34) in which he generously championed the cause of the Georgian poets and thereby gained for them the name 'the Squirearchy'. As Eliot (q.v.) and the poets of the 1930s displaced this conservative group, Squire became, not unjustly, the symbol of an obsolete movement. He had, however, shown himself a skilled and witty parodist (see Collected Parodies, 1921), and his assimilative sensibility gives a derivative character to much of his serious verse, which began with Three Hills (1913). Collected Poems (1959), introduced by John Betjeman (q.v.), contains a handful of notable poems, among them the favourite, 'The Stockyard', dedicated to Robert Frost, a movingly unfussy account of a visit to the Chicago Abattoir ('You have come to see the filthiest thing in the world') with its sickening assembly-line slaughter. Squire's output included literary criticism, short stories and an autobiography, The Honeysuckle and the Bee (1937). He was knighted in 1933.   [HB]

STALLWORTHY, JON (1935–). Poet, born in London, educated at Rugby School and Magdalen College, Oxford. From 1959 to 1977 he worked for Oxford University Press. He began publishing poetry with The Earthly Paradise (1958) and The Astronomy of Love (1961), but he has confessed that his early poems often 'reflected too faithfully for their own good their maker's lack of involvement in the world around him. They are the poems of an observer rather than a participator' (James Gibson, ed., Let the Poet Choose, 1976). The collection Root and Branch (1969), however, included 'The Almond Tree', a poem 'written from the inside', recounting the shock of learning in the hospital corridor that his new-born son was a mongol. Stallworthy draws attention to the importance of the image of the tree in his work and recommends a companion piece from the same volume, 'Elm End', in which the human end of a dynasty coincides with the felling of an avenue of centuries-old elms on the family estate. In his poetry generally the substance is often weighty, its unfolding narratively alive. 'A Letter from Berlin' is a telling record of skilful, but unsuccessful, experimental hysterectomies in prewar Berlin. To hindsight the surgical failures now seem to have foreshadowed the more efficient blood-lettings of Buchenwald. Stallworthy's subsequent collections, which include *Hand in Hand* (1974), *The Apple-Barrel, Selected Poems 1956-1963* (1974) and *A Familiar Tree* (1978), have strengthened his reputation as a quiet and meticulous craftsman who allows neither artifice to smother compassion nor detachment to iron out agony, and whose use of words is rarely self-indulgent. He edited the *Penguin Book of Love Poetry* (1974) (USA, *A Book of Love Poetry*).   [HB]

STEAD, CHRISTINA (1902–82). Novelist, born in Rochdale, New South Wales, Australia. She moved to Sydney in 1917 and was educated at Sydney High School. Trained as a teacher, she resigned from the Education Department in 1924 and sailed for England in 1928 where she wrote *Seven Poor Men of Sydney* (1934). She worked in Paris in 1929–35, and this is reflected in *House of All Nations* (1938). She later travelled in Europe and visited the United States, where she lived from 1937 until after the war. In 1974 she returned to Australia from England. *The Man Who Loved Children* (1940) and *For Love Alone* (1944) are arguably the finest Australian works of this period, confirming the sense of atmosphere and skill in acute analysis of family relationships shown in her first novel. Set in the United States and in Sydney (later in England) respectively, both books explore with sensitive yet ruthless perception the destructive aspects of love turned to selfishness. *Letty Fox: Her Luck* (1946) drew on her American experience in following the search of the heroine for fulfilment during the troubled 1930s. *The Dark Places of the Heart* (1966), first published in New York and published the following year in London as *Cotter's England*, is set in England of the 1950s. *The Puzzleheaded Girl* (1967) was four novellas, while *The Little Hotel* (1973) focused European material in revealing the hopes and fears of the various guests. 1976 saw the publication of *Miss Herbert (The Suburban Wife)*.   [PQ]

STEPHENS, JAMES (1880?–1950). Irish poet and novelist. He once gave 2 February 1882 as his birthday (it also happens to be Joyce's). St John Gogarty (q.v.) thought him the son of a Dublin vanman, Francis Stephens, and born 9 February 1880. Possibly Stephens was illegitimate. The known facts appear to be that at the age of 6 he was arrested for begging on the Dublin streets and committed to Meath Protestant Industrial School for Boys, Dublin, which he left in 1896. He drifted from one job to another and was a clerk in a solicitor's office when AE (George Russell (q.v.)) discovered him through poetry published in *Sinn Fein*. His first book of poems, *Insurrections*, was published in 1909. Meanwhile Stephens had formed a liaison with his landlady, Millicent Josephine ('Cynthia') Kavanagh (née Gardiner), whose husband left her. Their son, James Naoise, was born in 1909. Of Cynthia's two daughters by her husband, Iris remained with her mother. The son James was to die tragically by stepping on a live rail at a London station in 1937.

Stephens's reputation as a boy from the slums who had known hunger, slept rough, tramped the roads and even fought with swans for a piece of bread gave its aura to a man of great spiritedness, vigour and humour who stood scarcely four feet six high, had large eyes in a droll face and recited prose and poetry with irresistible rhythmic fervour. (His most recent reputation was that of an entrancing broadcaster for the BBC.) His first novel, *The Charwoman's Daughter* (1912), is the story of Mary Makebelieve who lives 'with her mother in a small room at the very top of a big dingy house in a Dublin street'. Among those she knows by sight from her daily walks are figures we can recognize as AE, Yeats (q.v.), Synge (q.v.) and George Moore (q.v.). The girl's sexual awakening is registered with feeling and subtlety. Stephens's outer simplicity of presentation is powerful in its effect. He underlines the threadbare poverty of tenement life, not by direct emphasis, but by fully exploring the day-dreams of better things in which Mrs Makebelieve finds solace. The Makebelieve household seems to show Ireland in miniature. Stephens thought the novel his best book, but it was *The Crock of Gold* (1912) whose success made his name and induced him to turn freelance writer. It is a book of extraordinary charm in the rich Irish vein which allows the mingling of myth and folklore, the god Pan and the leprechauns, with policemen who arrest murderers and the inmates of their cells who have tasted grinding privation. The book is at once fairy tale and parable, fantasy and philosophy and nonsense. At the centre is a Philosopher who needs to learn that 'thought, as we know it, is a disease and no more'. The theme is the search for happiness, and the book abounds in gnomic apophthegm and burlesque aphorism, in wise saws and pseudo-epigrams. *Deirdre*, the celebrated romance, was published in 1923.

Stephens gathered his successive volumes of poems into *Collected Poems* in 1926. 'The duty of the lyrical poet is not to express or explain, it is to intensify life', he proclaimed in the Preface. His work has consistent craftsmanship and clarity, and ranges from the high romantic strain, like 'Deirdre' –

Do not let any woman read this verse.
It is for men, and after them their sons,
And their sons' sons.

– to realistic studies of slum squalor like 'A Street' ('Two narrow files of houses scowl, / Blackened with grime'), from outbursts of delight like 'Mary Hynes' to devastating ironic squibs like 'Blue Blood'. 'Mary Hynes' is one of the poems he fashioned by paraphrase of Blind Raftery, the early nineteenth-century Irish poet.

Apart from a period in Dublin, as Registrar of the National Gallery between 1915 and 1924, Stephens moved mostly between London and America. He knew Joyce (q.v.), who thought him the right man to complete *Finnegans Wake*, should death cut him off. He was awarded a British Civil List pension in 1942 and a grant from the Royal Bounty enabling him to go to Dublin to receive an honorary D Litt in 1947.

Augustine Martin has selected and introduced a number of his short stories in *Desire and Other Stories* (1981).   [HB]

STEWART, DOUGLAS (1913–). Poet, born in Eltham, New Zealand, and educated at Victoria University College. He worked as a journalist in New Zealand before leaving for Sydney in 1934 in the hope of joining the staff of *The Bulletin* (q.v.). The job did not materialize and, after freelancing for a few months in Sydney and Melbourne, Stewart returned to New Zealand. He later worked his passage to England, and finally joined *The Bulletin* in 1938. Stewart is usually thought of as a contributor to Australian literature, though it is worth noting that he has often been attracted by themes which embrace the whole Pacific and not just Australia. His first collection of poems, *Green Lions* (1936), was followed by *White Cry* (1939). This early lyric poetry is extended in two wartime volumes, *Elegy for an Airman* (1940) and *Sonnets to the Unknown Soldier* (1941). In his introduction to a 1963 selection of his poems published in the 'Australian Poets' series he explains that the 'Elegy' was written for a boyhood friend killed while serving with the RAF: 'We had met in London not long before his death. I wrote it after I had come to live in Australia and, looking back nostalgically to New Zealand, remembered how beautiful the country really was.'

Ned Kelly (1943) was a poetic drama based on the last stand of the famous Australian bushranger. Stewart links his interest in the Kelly story with the genesis of an earlier poetic drama for radio, *The Fire on the Snow* (1944), which had been first broadcast by the Australian Broadcasting Commission in June 1941: 'I was still most deeply interested – as I am today – in what I called "the heroic image": voyagers, explorers, men of daring: pursuing the line of thought that Robert D. Fitzgerald [q.v.] was afterwards to express so clearly in "Heemskerck Shoals" '. This account of the play's fascination for him is important for an understanding not only of Stewart's own work, but also that of other contemporary writers and artists: 'three interests – the "discovery" of Australia, the study of the "heroic image", the romance of the bushrangers – blended together in my mind, and the play was the result'. *The Fire on the Snow* was based on the fate of the 1910 Antarctic Expedition, and in a Foreword to a new edition (1954) Stewart confesses that he wrote it 'under blind compulsion . . . because Scott's story had always fascinated me'. The play attracted a good deal of attention at the time ('more . . . than, alas, I have ever known since') and in 1944 Stewart published another radio play, *The Golden Lover*, a delicate and fanciful comedy based on a Maori legend, and also a volume of short stories, *A Girl with Red Hair* (1944). *The Dosser in Springtime* (1946) was Stewart's first collection of Australian poetry, and demonstrated an interest, and expertise, in the ballad form which was to mark much of his later work. A volume of criticism, *The Flesh and the Spirit* (1948), brought together much of his work for the *Bulletin's* Red Page (which he had written since 1941). His next poetry collection, *Sun Orchids* (1952), included the important narrative poem 'Terra Australis' about an imaginary meeting in mid-Pacific between the seventeenth-century Portuguese navigator Captain Quiros and William Lane, the radical idealist who left Australia to found a utopian New Australia in Paraguay in 1893. *The Birdsville Track* (1955) was a commissioned sequence of poems, some of

which formed the 'commentary' to the 1954 prize-winning documentary film *Back of Beyond* by John Heyer on the outback mail run from Mallee to Birdsville in South Australia. Stewart contributed an important introduction to his selection of *Modern Australian Verse* (1964) in which he made clear his belief that enjoyment rather than any standards of 'Australianness', theme or style, was the basis for his choice of verse: 'when you are in the business of writing or criticizing poetry, surrounded and bombarded by controversy, you do tend to forget that this is an art meant to provoke not argument but pleasure'. In *The Flesh and the Spirit* Stewart had seen major poetry as an 'art which accepts and presents a heroic image of the life of man', whereas the art and literature of our own age tends to reject life or retreat into subjectivism. His interest in narrative, dramatic and lyrical poetry, together with his belief in 'the isolation and clarification of the image', lead him to distrust work which is too abstract or didactic. At its best his work succeeds in presenting the 'heroic image' but does not always avoid the danger of stressing heroism while failing to discriminate in literary and moral values. In 1967 *Selected Poems 1936–1967* appeared, and a *Selected Poems* the following year. *The Broad Stream* (1975) was criticism.　　　　[PQ]

STEWART, J.I.M. (John Innes Mackintosh (1906–). Novelist, who published 'serious' novels under his own name and crime novels under the pseudonym 'Michael Innes'. He was born in Edinburgh, Lothian, Scotland, educated at Edinburgh Academy and Oriel College, Oxford, and has held university posts in English literature at Leeds, Adelaide, Belfast and finally (from 1949) Christ Church, Oxford. The detective fiction (there are over thirty titles) is noted for ingenious stories about professional (often academic) and well-to-do characters. It is written for an intelligent public with a smattering of culture, and the favourite detective, Inspector Appleby, has himself a genteel background. The straight novels presuppose a readership with some intellectual pretensions, sophisticated enough to be interested in the technical and trade patter of artists and writers and the psychological demands their calling makes – *Mark Lambert's Supper* (1954), *The Guardians* (1957), *A Use of Riches* (1957), *The Man Who Won the Pools* (1961) and *The Last Tresilians* (1963) are examples. Henry James's (q.v.) influence is evident in the presentation of characters and the unravelling of their meditations as well as often in narrative substance. The quest for the supposedly dead artist, John Arnander, in *A Use of Riches*, smacks at first of *The Aspern Papers*. The emotional dilemma of Jill Craine/Arnander who finds herself with two husbands is inadequately realized, yet cerebralism runs riot in detailed technical criticism of imaginary works of art. Stewart's casual urbanity sustains a genteel remoteness from dust and sweat. There is subtlety without intensity. Emotions are defined, not felt. In *Mungo's Dream* (1973), the story of an Oxford friendship, what appeals is the percipient humour in the portrayal of aristocrats and the literary witticisms embedded in quotation-bespattered dialogue. A five-novel sequence of high life at Oxford began with *The Gaudy* (1974) and reached its term with *Full Term* (1978).

The pentalogy is now called *A Staircase on Surrey*. Stewart contributed volume XII to the *Oxford History of English Literature: Eight Modern Writers* (1963). [HB]

STOPPARD, TOM (1937–). Dramatist, born in Czechoslovakia. The war drove the family first to Singapore, then to India, and in 1946 they came to England where Stoppard's education continued in Nottinghamshire and Yorkshire (Pocklington School). He worked as a journalist from 1954 to 1963. His first play, *A Walk on the Water*, was televised in 1963, but it was *Rosencrantz and Guildenstern Are Dead* (prod Edinburgh, 1966; London, 1967) that earned him widespread recognition. Stoppard's express aim was 'to exploit a situation which seemed to me to have enormous dramatic and comic potential – of the two guys who in Shakespeare's context don't really know what they are doing' (quoted in C.W.E. Bigsby, *Tom Stoppard*, 1976). The dislodged, bewildered pair, unsure of identity and objective, indulge a Beckettian mix of routine small talk and the chop-logic of philosophical questioning. The contrast between twentieth-century conversation and Shakespearian blank verse, the skating between 'real' and 'theatrical' worlds at various levels, and the clash of nonsense against tightly jointed rationality make the recipe for high farce with a core of pathos at man's condition. If the Beckettian shadow is too intrusive here, Stoppard later grows out of mere derivative dependence. *Jumpers* (1972) juxtaposes Professor George Moore's preparation of a lecture on the existence of God, the problem of value and, in particular, the objectivity of good and evil, with murder committed at a party in his home, and the whole is both riotously comic and philosophically cohesive. *Travesties* (prod 1974) focuses on Zurich in 1918 where Lenin is working towards the Russian revolution and James Joyce towards the completion of *Ulysses*. The historical basis of the play lay in Joyce's arrangement for a production of *The Importance of Being Earnest* by a company of English players and in particular his choice of Henry Carr from the British Consulate for the part of Algernon. The juxtaposition of artist and revolutionary has rich implicit significances that Stoppard allows to speak for themselves. The Wildean pastiche is brilliant. The parody of *Ulysses* (a sustained catechetical dialogue burlesques the style of the 'Ithaca' episode) is hilarious. Stoppard breaks new ground by thus feeding on the literary tradition and has perhaps opened a new way forward for English drama.

Stoppard is a *writer* to his finger-tips. His rare command of language and his theatrical versatility make his continuing productivity an exciting feature of the current literary scene. *Night and Day* (1978) is set in an imaginary African country whose dictator-president faces a rebellion. British reporters come to cover events. From their diverse attitudes and motives Stoppard constructs a thoughtful and sometimes witty debate that involves penetrating judgement on Fleet Street journalism. *On the Razzle* (1981) is Stoppard's adaptation of *Einen Jux will er sich machen* by the nineteenth-century Viennese playwright, Johann Nestroy. The theme is the old tale of country mice who escape to the town for a day of illicit freedom. The day-off involves a grocer, his daughter and his employees, who each have their different motives for going on the spree. Stoppard frankly exploits stock situational devices to make the entertainment a riotously comic romp, and his dialogue scintillates with elaborate double-entendres, puns and music-hall backchat. If *On the Razzle* exudes traditional theatrical expertise, *The Real Thing* (1982) breaks new ground in presenting successive episodes from the real-life story of a writer (Henry), his wife, his mistress (actresses by profession) and her husband (an actor) alongside episodes from the plays Henry has written in which the other three perform. The plays reflect the living experience of writer and performers, and Stoppard is able to probe subtleties of personality and relationship all the more piquantly by moving between direct and indirect projection, between mental, actual, and theatrical levels of experience. [HB]

STOREY, DAVID (1933–). Novelist and dramatist, born in Wakefield, West Yorkshire, the son of a miner. He financed his studies at the Slade School of Art in London by playing as a professional for Leeds Rugby League and commuting. Arthur Machin, the hero of his first novel, *This Sporting Life* (1960), is also a footballer, and his obdurate love for the middle-aged widow, Mrs Hammond, his landlady, represents the assertion of the physical against emotional impregnability, while in the second novel, *Flight into Camden* (1961), the heroine Margaret Thorpe's wilful love for the married artist, Howarth, represents the assertion of spiritual independence against the powerful pressures of the family's moral cohesiveness. A great strength is the realistic force with which northern temperament is delineated and working-class dialogue composed. The philosophical schematization of *Radcliffe* (1963) has a Lawrentian directness. The clash between the vital, earthy working class and the faded, once-cultured upper class is embodied in a homosexual relationship whose pressurized tensions result finally in somewhat melodramatic violence. If the analysis of neurosis in this dark book all but drifts into the pornography of despair, *A Temporary Life* (1972) restores the balance somewhat. An art teacher moves between the asylum where his insane wife is confined and the outside world of art education which is perhaps only officially saner. In *Pasmore* (1972), a tense and sombre book, Colin Pasmore, a university lecturer, capriciously undermines the happiness of his wife and children, and eventually his own mental balance, by an adulterous liaison that is less convincing to the reader than the embittered reaction of his miner-father back home. 'A man that leaves his wife and kiddies. Why, an animal wouldn't do that.' The lengthy, and apparently autobiographical, novel of a boy's upbringing in a miner's home, *Saville* (1976), suffers from laborious over-documentation. But *A Prodigal Child* (1982) is one more powerful study of displacement from a northern working-class background, this time on the part of Bryan Morley, a boy of 'prodigal talent', who is taken up by a wealthy couple and becomes a sculptor, but who makes the 'prodigal's' return to his native environment. Storey has justly been compared with Arnold Bennett for the sheer accuracy and fullness with which he portrays people's working lives.

Storey's first play, *The Restoration of Arnold Middleton* (1967), is a vital and entertaining piece. Arnold is an excitable schoolmaster who carries the classroom tricks of the trade (mock-pedantry, noisy bonhomie, playful histrionics) into his home life, partly to ease the tensions caused by the presence of his mother-in-law. The act escalates into real madness, relieved only by the departure of the mother-in-law at the end. In Celebration (1969), a family drama, brings the three sons of a Yorkshire miner back home for their parents' wedding anniversary, and explores the complex conflicts between working-class oldsters and supposedly educated but ill-adjusted middle-class sons. Home (1970), set in an asylum, reverts to the preoccupation with insanity. Action is minimal, and The Changing Room (prod 1971, pubd 1972) is an animated tableau from the world of rugby football. Neither Life Class (prod 1974, pubd 1975), with its crude slapstick, nor Mother's Day (prod 1976, pubd 1977), which makes representation of modern urbanism's alleged sexual rapacity a pretext for tedious vulgarity, has advanced Storey's reputation as a dramatist. He appears to take his work as a novelist more seriously. [HB]

STOW, RANDOLPH (1935–). Novelist and poet, born in Geraldton, West Australia, and educated at the University of Western Australia. Although childhood images of the coastline and desert inland of the area inform much of his writing, the local is always realized as a microcosm of the universal; a strong sense of place, both immediate and national, blends with a deep interest in indigenous cultures and a questioning of the tenets of 'white' Australia. The early novels, The Bystander (1957) and A Haunted Land (1956), together with Act One: Poems (1957) were enthusiastically acclaimed and, perhaps inevitably, this led to a certain falling off in critical reaction and a degree of withdrawal by the author. To the Islands (1958, rev. 1981) was compared to Voss by Patrick White (q.v.), published the previous year, in its employment of the Australian landscape as a spiritual testing-place, although Stow's work was more personal and in some ways the stronger for it. The two books were recognized as heralding a new departure in the Australian novel but although Stow's book arguably benefited from the themes first broached by White, in retrospect the powerful story of the failed missionary Heriot, and his journey to the islands of the dead, can best be seen as one realization of concerns which recur throughout his work. A fine verse collection, Outrider; Poems 1956–1962 (1962), was illustrated by the Australian artist Sidney Nolan and demonstrates the extent to which Stow was working well beyond the confines of a notional 'Australian' literature. The range and genuine complexity of his work place him among the most important Australian writers, though one consequence of this openness, and of his move from Australia to England, has been a severing of ties with his homeland, and an exploration of increasingly personal worlds in his writing. His first novel for five years, Tourmaline (1963), was set in an Australian ghost town but employed it, together with character and chronology, in a manner which required a complex spiritual and literary response; compare his twelve-poem series 'From the Testament of Tourmaline, Variations on Themes of the Tao Teh Ching' published in Poetry Australia for 12 October 1966, a version of which was reprinted in A Counterfeit Silence three years later.

Stow has travelled widely, spending several years as a patrol officer in the Trobriand Islands, over a year as a writer-in-residence at the University of Leeds, and a year in the United States as a Harkness Fellow, during which he wrote The Merry-go-round in the Sea (1965). Partly autobiographical, this novel had a new simplicity of approach and sensitively explored dimensions of personal and national awareness through the experience of a young boy growing up in Western Australia before and during the Second World War; 'The world the boy had believed in did not, after all, exist. The world and the clan and Australia had been a myth of his mind, and he had been all the time an individual.' Not the least valuable element of the book is its moving yet restrained account of the impact on the Australian consciousness (seen through the boy, his relations and his boyhood idol Rick, who goes as a prisoner to Changi concentration camp) of defeat, and possible invasion, at the hands of the Japanese. The painful transition from childhood to adolescence and the shattering of a nation's confidence in itself are linked in a study which lifts personal experience to mythic proportions without contrivance. The incommunicable richness of the individual experience, and the consequent strangeness of the poet's role, was stressed in the character, and title, of his next book, A Counterfeit Silence (1969), a demanding poetry collection. In a characteristically brief afterword to an anthology selection of his work Stow wrote in 1971: 'I really have nothing to say about poetry in general (except that mine tries to counterfeit the communication of those who communicate by silence). And these poems are mostly private letters.' For many years he has lived quietly in an English village near the area from which his ancestors first emigrated to Australia. In 1967 he published Midnite, The Story of a Wild Colonial Boy, an outstanding work for children which blended family anecdote, historical awareness and humour to great effect. Recently he has extended his interest in music, writing the libretti for two pieces in conjunction with the composer Peter Maxwell Davies: Eight Songs for a Mad King (1969) and the 'rant', Miss Donnithorne's Maggot (1974). In Visitants (1979) and Girl Green as Elder Flower (1980) his talent for fiction showed itself to great advantage in widely differing forms, reaffirming his status as an important contemporary writer. [PQ]

STRACHEY, LYTTON (1880–1932). Biographer and critic, born in London, one of the thirteen children (eleven survived) of General Sir Richard Strachey, who had an impressively effective administrative career in India. He was educated at Abbotsholme School, Derbyshire (briefly), at Leamington College, Liverpool University College, and Trinity College, Cambridge, where he read history. At Leamington he 'experienced his first homosexual crushes' so emotionally stirring that they lasted for him as symbols of 'the ideal companionship which he was always seeking to recapture in later life' (Michael Holroyd, Lytton Strachey by Himself, 1971). At Cambridge he came across G. Lowes Dickinson, Bertrand Russell and G.E. Moore, but he failed to get the fellowship at Trinity that he coveted, and returned to London in 1905 to take up a literary career as essayist and reviewer. Strachey's appearance was odd. Tallish, but extremely thin, he had a droopy, sagging posture and a large brown beard. Homosexual infatuations were a continuing obsession: romantic agonies of devotion to his cousin, Duncan Grant, were committed to his diary in feverish rhetoric; and when he suddenly proposed to Virginia Woolf (q.v.) in 1909, he was wisely rejected. The exchange of letters between Strachey and Virginia Woolf, extending over twenty years of friendship, was edited by Leonard Woolf and James Strachey (*Virginia Woolf and Lytton Strachey, Letters*, 1956). Strachey became a central figure in the literary and artistic circle known as the Bloomsbury Group. It included E.M. Forster (q.v.), Clive Bell and Desmond MacCarthy as well as Leonard and Virginia Woolf. The coterie shared a common revulsion against the cramping inhibitions of the middle-class Victorian mind. Strachey, who was numbered among Lady Ottoline Morrell's friends, unsuccessfully declared himself a conscientious objector in 1916, although his physique put military service out of the question for him.

Strachey had published *Landmarks in French Literature* in 1912, but it was *Eminent Victorians* (1918) that made his name. The book comprises sketches of Cardinal Manning, Florence Nightingale, Dr Arnold and General Gordon. Strachey's method is to deflate the standard heroic figures of the Victorian age by witty ironies handed out in the temperate tones of an urbane commentator. Evidence accumulates of the petty, vain and unworthy characteristics of the cherished idols and contemporary opinion was duly shocked. Yet in the succeeding volume, *Queen Victoria* (1921), the Queen comes off less ignobly from her confrontation with the cynical biographer than might have been expected. For all the fun about the familiar pomposities of the Victoria-and-Albert protocols and domesticities, a current of sentiment is stirred in her portrayer by the sheer durability of Victoria's enigmatic integrity. Strachey's imaginative presentation of the figures he delineates is like the work of a skilled novelist, though his recourse – often for ironic effect – to ready-made novelistic tricks of style vulgarizes the tone. Virginia Woolf, to whom the work is dedicated, wrote to him in high praise, but she also had this to say: 'My only criticism . . . is that occasionally I think one is a little too conscious of being entertained'. Strachey's other works include *Elizabeth and Essex* (1928) and *Books and Characters* (1922). The latter contains a much-cited essay, 'Shakespeare's Final Period'.

The success of *Queen Victoria* enabled Strachey to buy Ham Spray House, near Marlborough, Wiltshire, where he lived from 1924. His strange ménage in later days involved the artist Dora Carrington, who was in love with Strachey, and her husband Ralph Partridge, with whom Strachey was for a time in love. Soon after Strachey's death Carrington committed suicide. She put on Strachey's dressing-gown and shot herself. [HB]

STRONG, L.A.G. (Leonard Alfred George) (1896–1958). Novelist, short-story writer and poet, born in Plymouth, Devon. His father was half-Irish and his mother wholly Irish. Strong was educated in Brighton College and at Oxford and earned his living as a schoolmaster until he turned full-time writer in 1930. The novels include *Dewar Rides* (1929), *The Jealous Ghost* (1930), *The Brothers* (1932), *The Bay* (1941) and *The Hill of Howth* (1953), and the collections of stories include *Doyle's Rock* (1925), *The English Captain* (1929), *Travellers* (1945) and *Darling Tom* (1952). A perceptive and sympathetic observer of life, especially of rural life in Ireland and in the West Country, Strong was also a gifted poet (see *Dublin Days*, 1921; *Selected Poems*, 1931), restrained and polished in technique, who wrote some lively verses by working instinctively within the compass of his gifts. His autobiographical volume, *Green Memory* (1961), contains interesting personal reminiscences of numerous literary acquaintances, including Yeats (q.v.) and Ralph Hodgson (q.v.). [HB]

SUTHERLAND, EFUA THEODORA (1924–). Theatre director and playwright, born and educated in Cape Coast, Ghana. She undertook further teacher-training at Homerton College, Cambridge, and studied linguistics at SOAS, University of London. On returning home about 1950, she researched into the rich Ghanaian folk culture that her urban, Christian upbringing had shut her off from. She has held appointments in the University of Ghana.

Between 1958 and 1961 Sutherland founded Experimental Theatre and Drama Studio in Accra and helped establish the cultural journal *Okyeame*, which printed her plays, *Foriwa* (1964; separately, Accra, 1967) and *Edufa* (1966; separately, London, 1967), the latter about the polarities of egoism and devotion in marriage, and of modern business and traditional faith. She has written many plays for her theatre groups; some have been published in Ghana and in periodicals elsewhere. She has also written an authoritative study, *Anansegoro* (Accra, 1975), of the Akan trickster tales about Ananse and their development into an Akan specialist drama. In *The Marriage of Anansewa* (London, 1975) she has skilfully adapted one of these comic, wryly philosophical Ananse stories as an English play, incorporating singing, ritual, fluid staging, audience participation and other conventions of popular Akan theatre. [AR]

SWINNERTON, FRANK (1884–1982). Novelist and critic, born in London. He started work as an office boy, rose to reading and editorial work in publishing and became a well-known critic on various journals. He has written about forty entertaining novels, unpretentiously geared to middle-brow taste. *Nocturne* (1917) first made his name. 'I must say you young writers . . . spread your butter thin and make it go a long way. There are pages and pages of "Nocturne" that would not last me half a line', Bernard Shaw (q.v.) wrote to him and Swinnerton records the judgement frankly in his *An Autobiography* (1937), one of a group of books of literary reminiscences which also includes *Background with Chorus* (1957) and *Figures in the Foreground* (1963). *Harvest Comedy* (1938) has been praised as his best novel. More important for the student of literature is *The Georgian Literary Scene* (1934), a personal literary panorama containing neat studies of the many famous novelists and poets whom Swinnerton encountered in his publishing days. It is a mine of shrewd judgements and gossipy portraiture. [HB]

SYMONS, ARTHUR (1865-1945). Poet and critic, born in Milford Haven, South Wales, of Cornish stock. His father was a Methodist minister and was soon transferred to Guernsey where 'Victor Hugo once stopped the nurse to smile at me' (*Spiritual Adventures*, 1905). Symons struggled hard to establish himself as poet and critic. *Days and Nights* (1889), his first published verse, won praise from Pater and Meredith, and he became a member of the Rhymers' Club. Yeats (q.v.), a fellow member, encouraged him and later praised him in *Autobiographies* ('Arthur Symons, more than any man I have ever known, could slip as it were into the mind of another, and my thoughts gained in richness and in clearness from his sympathy'). Symons's *Poems* (two volumes, 1902) selects from previous collections. Later volumes were *Lesbia* (1920), *Love's Cruelty* (1923) and *Jezebel Mort* (1931). Delicate in technique but inclined to be misty and melancholy in substance, Symons's poetry never fulfilled its early promise. But his output as a critic was massive and influential. Tragedy overtook him in 1908 when he was confined in an asylum with what was diagnosed as 'General Paralysis of the Insane' and given at most two years to live. In fact the diagnosis and the prediction were incorrect. Symons's was a case of manic-depressive psychosis and he made a slow recovery. He gave an account of his illness in *Confessions* – 'an extraordinary recital, a fantastic exploration into the unknown continents of the human mind' (Roger Llombréaud, *Arthur Symons: A Critical Biography*, 1963). [HB]

SYNGE, J.M. (John Millington) (1871-1909). Irish playwright, born near Dublin, Ireland, into a Protestant landowning family with strong religious convictions, having clergy and several bishops in the ancestry. Synge's father died in 1872 and John, the youngest of four brothers, was brought up by a widowed mother with a strongly evangelical turn of mind, who early frightened him with talk of hell. In his teens he reacted by renouncing Christianity. He studied music at the Royal Academy of Music, learned the violin, and in 1892 took his degree at Trinity College, Dublin. His unbelief proved the decisive obstacle in his first love affair with a girl whose father was a Plymouth Brother. In 1893 he went to Germany as a music student, then moved to Paris where he read much literature, interested himself in Irish studies and attended meetings of the Irish League. Yeats (q.v.) met him in Paris in 1896 and urged him to go to the Aran Islands to get the islanders' way of life into his blood in preparation for playing his part in the Irish literary renaissance. In a series of prolonged visits to Aran, Synge collected stories and imbibed the spirit of the peasants, whose charm and humour, independence and skill in hardship and danger he learned to love. Synge formed a prose idiom for dramatic dialogue at once rich and rhythmic. Its suppleness made it apt for those extremes of the tragic and the farcical, the ironic and the lyric, which his sensitivity compassed. His early prose work, *The Aran Islands*, did not get into print until 1907, and *In Wicklow, West Kerry and Connemara* was published only after his death. Material found its way into the plays from these firsthand records which do justice to both the humour and the grief of the people he got to know. The plays are permeated with Synge's strangely compelling sense of place.

The Irish Literary Theatre was founded in 1899, and in 1902 the Irish National Theatre Society was formed to continue its work on a more permanent basis. The society moved into the Abbey Theatre in 1904 and Synge was one of the first directors. His first play for the company, *In the Shadow of the Glen*, had been performed in the Antient Concert Rooms in October 1903, and *Riders to the Sea* in 1904. His first play to be performed at the Abbey Theatre was *The Well of the Saints* – in February 1905. *In the Shadow of the Glen* is a one-acter in which Dan Burke shams death and thereby puts his frustrated young wife, Nora, to the test. A tramp arrives at the cottage and is left with the 'corpse' while Nora goes to communicate her news. By the time she returns with her chosen young man, Michael Dara, the 'corpse' has let the tramp into the secret. The upshot of Nora's failure in the fidelity test is that she is turned out by her husband and goes off with the tramp, while Michael remains to drink Daniel's health. The frank, implicit sexuality of the play and Synge's sympathetic representation of the rebellious wife provoked opposition and prompted the charge that Synge was not serving nationalist aspirations by his denigratory portrayal of Irish life. *Riders to the Sea*, on the other hand, is a stark tragedy in one act, the scene a cottage on an island in the west of Ireland. Old Maurya has lost her husband and five of her six sons at sea. She and her two daughters are still waiting for the body of Michael, the most recent victim, to be washed ashore. The remaining son, Bartle, cannot be dissuaded from setting out in a storm for Connemara and he is drowned before ever he gets afloat. Maurya has epic grandeur as the symbol of suffering womanhood. The cumulative encroachment of doom gives the work the oppressive fatalism of Greek tragedy. *The Well of the Saints* is altogether less gloomy. Martin and Mary Doul, two old blind beggars, have a touching cheerfulness in disability, heightened by the illusion (implanted by the villagers who chaff them) that they are handsome. When the saint (a wandering friar) heals them with holy water the shock of each other's ugliness turns them to bitterness and strife. The effect of the cure wears off, blindness returns, and when the chance of a second (and permanent) cure is offered by the friar, they resist, Martin dashing the holy water to the ground. They are happier in their blindness.

Synge seems to have been a quiet, gentle, self-absorbed man who neither spoke in praise of others' work nor made claims for his own, yet his inner confidence was immense. Yeats told George Moore (q.v.), 'Synge has always the better of you, for you have brief ghastly moments during which you admit the existence of other writers; Synge never has'. Synge's work for the Irish theatre was rooted in Irish life but was not motivated by political aim. Nevertheless the production of *The Playboy of the Western World** at the Abbey Theatre in 1907 caused opposition to Synge to explode in riots. Plot and language were alike judged offensive. There was uproar at the first performance. People 'booed, hooted, blew tin trumpets' (Lady Gregory) and police had to be called in. *Freeman's Journal* condemned the play as an 'unmitigated, protracted libel upon Irish peasant men and, worse still, upon Irish girlhood'. The spectacle of Irish villagers hero-worshipping a supposed murderer and the frankness of their utterance proved too much and the play was judged defamatory to the nation. Yeats and Lady Gregory (q.v.) staunchly and loyally defended it and refused to abandon the production. The storm of controversy was still raging when the company toured the United States with the play in their repertoire in 1911. It remains Synge's masterpiece and one of the greatest comedies of the century. Synge's last play, *Deirdre of the Sorrows**, was left unfinished at his death but put into shape by Yeats and Lady Gregory. This tragedy of love occupied Synge as his own early death (from a tumour) approached and the part of Deirdre was lovingly designed for Molly Allgood to whom he was engaged. She would visit him to act it for him as he wrote it, a little at a time, between bouts of despondency. Ann Saddlemyer edited the *Plays* in two volumes (1968) as well as *Letters to Molly: Synge to Maire O'Neill* (1971) and *Some Letters to Lady Gregory and Yeats* (1971). Alan Price constructed Synge's *Autobiography* (1965) from manuscripts.

The Playboy of the Western World is a three-act comedy whose action takes place near a village on the coast of Mayo. Christy Mahon is on the run, for he thinks he has killed his father, when he comes one night into the village public house and meets Pegeen Mike, the innkeeper's daughter. She worms his story out of him and it does not shock: it provokes admiration and adulation from Pegeen and later from the local girls, so much so that Christy plays up and dramatizes himself into a hero. He agrees to stay: there is rivalry for him as a future husband between Pegeen and Widow Quinn. Christy has in fact been a spineless good-for-nothing, and when old Mahon turns up with a bandaged head to lay bare the facts of the case, the heroic image is shattered. But the irony is that the boost has been the making of Christy – who is now capable of carrying off all the trophies at the local games – and father is finally proud of his regenerate son: the two go off reconciled. The readiness of Irish girls to lionize a parricide, together with the use of 'bad language', was the cause of the furore. Synge himself wrote: 'Any one who has lived in real intimacy with the Irish peasantry will know that the wildest sayings and ideas in this play are tame indeed, compared with the fancies he may hear in any little hillside cabin in Geesale, or Carraroe, or Dingle Bay'.

Deirdre of the Sorrows, a three-act tragedy, was performed at the Abbey Theatre, Dublin, in 1910. The story is from the saga of Cuchulain and it had already been used in poetic drama by Yeats. Deirdre is a beautiful girl doomed by prophecy to bring disaster on those who love her, and the ageing King Conchubor brings her up in seclusion and isolation in the hope of defeating the curse and making her his wife. Deirdre meets Naisi, nephew to the king, and falls in love with him. Helped by Naisi's two brothers, the lovers escape to Scotland. After seven years Conchubor offers them pardon and invites them to return to Ireland. They do so, and walk into a treacherous trap. Naisi and his brothers are killed by Conchubor's men; but Deirdre frustrates the king's aims by suicide. Synge's version gives an archetypal poignancy to the situation of the two lovers by its emphasis on the threat that time holds over a couple who have been happy in each other for seven years. Deirdre is inwardly suspicious of Conchubor's invitation to them to return; but she is equally afraid that to prolong safety in exile with Naisi is to run the risk of love fading as the years pass.   [HB]

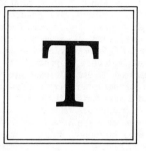

TAYLOR, ELIZABETH(1912–75). Novelist and short-story writer, born in Reading, Berkshire. She worked for a time as a governess, married J.W.K. Taylor in 1936 and had two children. Her first novel, *At Mrs Lippincote's* (1945), is a wartime story of an RAF officer's wife condemned to follow his posting and set up home in a furnished house. Succeeding titles include *Palladian* (1946), *A Wreath of Roses* (1949) and *The Sleeping Beauty* (1953). The author tends to focus on affluent families living in commuterland. *In a Summer Season* (1961) presents Kate Heron's life with her second husband, Dermot. He is the antithesis of her first husband, Alan, who has died, in lacking any purpose, in sharing none of her cultural interests, and in being ten years her junior. To enhance the tricky situation there are two children of Kate's first marriage and a fond widower next door who belongs to that past of Kate's which Dermot never shared. Taylor follows the diverse threads of each individual's emotional life with extraordinary percipience and astuteness, and weaves them together into pattern with an unfailing sense of balance. *The Wedding Group* (1968) has a deliciously subtle account of a cranky simple-life community dominated by a religious artist, Harry Bretton, whose Christs tend to look like himself. One of his grandchildren, the girl Cressy, falls 'in love with the present time' and escapes to marry a man who is himself the victim of his deserted mother's possessiveness. There is a tactful artistic perfection in the working out of a pattern in which vital individuals impinge on each other's deep isolated-ness. There are no clichés in Elizabeth Taylor's work. She has humour and compassion as well as sharpness. Her technique eschews all wastage or superfluity. Brief flashes of living dialogue and reflection succeed each other rapidly, and deft sketches suggestively fill in the wider background, giving social dimension and solidity to the whole. Her range may be limited but her characters come vividly alive in a world where meals, weather, drains, gardens, cars and commuting are matters of daily concern. It is understandable that she has been compared with Jane Austen. Her short stories are contained in *Hester Lilly* (1954), *The Blush* (1958) and *The Devastating Boys* (1972).   [HB]

THOMAS, D.M. (Donald Michael) (1935–). Poet and novelist, born in Redruth, Cornwall, educated at the grammar school there, then at University High School, Melbourne, and at New College, Oxford. He became Senior Lecturer in English at Hereford College of Education in 1963. Early volumes of verse included *Two Voices* (1968) and *Logan Stone* (1971). He became known as a writer of verse monologues and narratives reflecting his interest in science fiction. But it was his novels, beginning with *The Flute-Player* (1979), that widened his reputation, and *The White Hotel* (1981) quickly became a best-seller.

Thomas, himself a translator of Russian poets, sets *The Flute-Player* in a vaguely conceived Soviet-style country where the population suffer oppression and privation at the hands of ill-defined authorities. Struggling against the ever-present threat of mysterious disappearance, torture and imprisonment, characters representative of the free human spirit – poetry, sculpture, drama, painting etc. – revolve in arabesque around Elena, a persisting symbol of vitality, beauty, and love unquenchable. The relationships are drenched in a sexuality cloyingly crude and repetitive. The White Hotel explores the case history of Lisa Erdman, an imaginary patient of Freud's, whose childhood experiences have left a damaging legacy, conscious and unconscious. While suffering from severe sexual hysteria she commits her often pornographic fantasies to paper for Freud's analysis and the reader's delectation. The Freudian psychoanalytical framework licences the registration of sexual excess, and the historical framework of the holocaust requires the registration of obscene violence. The mixture sent reviewers reaching for superlatives that sober criticism can scarcely corroborate.   [HB]

THOMAS, DYLAN (Marlais) (1914–53). Poet, born and brought up in Swansea, West Glamorgan, Wales, where his father, D.J. Thomas, taught English at the grammar school. The names D.J. gave his son claimed a bardic vocation for the boy. 'Dylan' was found in the *Mabinogion* and 'Marlais' derived from Gwilym Marles Thomas, D.J.'s uncle, a popular preacher-bard of radical views and the family's great man. Dylan did not learn Welsh: his father did not like it. Neither did he like Christianity, though his atheism permitted him one day, looking out of the window, to exclaim, 'It's raining again, blast Him!' However, Dylan's mother took him to chapel. The lasting bond between father and son was enriched by Dylan's achievement of the literary life D.J. had vainly desired for himself and had then predestined for the boy. He handed on too his habit of supplying oracular wit night by night in the local pub. Ultimately D.J.'s death inspired one of Dylan's most moving poems, the villanelle 'Do not go gentle into that good night'. At Swansea Grammar School Dylan's passion for poetry seems to have been the sole evidence of academic interest or talent, and he left to work as a reporter for the *South Wales Evening Post*. By 1933 he was freelancing and, for the rest of his life, he earned his living precariously by his pen. (Commissions for film scripts eased the financial strain in the war years.) Before he left Swansea for London important friendships were established, notably with Dan Jones, the composer, Glyn Jones (q.v.), the writer, and Vernon Watkins (q.v.), the poet. Thomas's *Letters to Vernon Watkins* (1957) together with those he wrote to Henry Treece and to Pamela Hansford Johnson (q.v.), with whom he was for a time in love, shed interesting light on his poetic development.

Constantine Fitzgibbon (*The Life of Dylan Thomas*, 1965) notes that three-quarters of the poet's work in verse 'dates in style, in concept and often in composition' from the early Swansea period, for Thomas went on using his early notebooks for many years, transforming early material by maturer craftsmanship. His first book, *Eighteen Poems*, was published in 1934. Speaking of its most quoted poem, 'The force that through the green fuse drives the flower', G.S. Fraser (q.v.) sees Thomas 'massively identifying the body of man with the body of the world' (*Dylan Thomas*, 1957). Symbolism of sexual frustration abounds in this first volume and indeed Thomas accepted the orgastic character of poetic utterance. 'Man should be two-tooled, and a poet's middle leg is his pencil', he wrote in a letter to Charles Fisher. But in *Modern Poetry* (1938) Louis MacNeice (q.v.) cited 'Light breaks where no sun shines' in *Eighteen Poems* as 'the almost automatic collocation of a number of emotional (primarily sexual) symbols, thrown up as a drunk man throws up phrases', and Thomas encountered some critical resistance from Richard Church of Dent's over the contents of his second volume, *Twenty-five Poems* (1936). He was accused of surrealism, defended himself, but conceded, 'I think I do know what some of the main faults of my writing are: Immature violence, rhythmic monotony, frequent muddle-headedness, and a very much overweighted imagery that leads too often to incoherence'. Nevertheless 'And death shall have no dominion', with its rhetorical swing, helped to win popular interest in *Twenty-five Poems*. The volume contains an interesting piece of poetic self-examination, vis-à-vis the poses required of the eloquent poet, in 'I have longed to move away', as well as the densely contorted sonnet sequence, 'Altarwise by Owl-light'.

Thomas married Caitlin Macnamara in 1936 and, for all the stresses consequent upon his way of life, the love between the two remained central to his existence. They lived much in cottages in Wales, notably at New Quay and Laugharne, but Thomas's intermittent spells in London ('my capital punishment') involved him in bohemian excesses that soon made a legend of his wild drinking and his sexuality. Thomas, who once called himself 'the Rimbaud of Cwndonkin Drive', seems to have played out his hag-ridden dipsomaniac self-immolation with self-parodic yet tragic thoroughness. 'At the core a typical Welsh puritan and non-conformist gone wrong', Augustus John averred. The human costliness of his 'act' is clear from Caitlin Thomas's books published since his death, *Leftover Life to Kill* (1957) and *Not Quite Posthumous Letter to My Daughter* (1963). The climactic consequences are laid bare in J.M. Brinnin's *Dylan Thomas in America* (1955), for the need for money drove Thomas the actor-reader to make the United States his stage (there were gruelling lecture trips in 1950 and 1952) and the second of two visits in 1953 killed him.

The poetry that guarantees Thomas's reputation derives chiefly from *Deaths and Entrances* (1946). Thomas, who had turned his back on the fashionable poetic postures and idioms of the socially conscious thirties, here reaches his peak in deliberate celebration of basic personal realities ranging from the transfigured recapture of boyhood holidays at his aunt's farm in 'Fern Hill' to the fine elegiac outcry in 'A Refusal to mourn the death, by fire, of a child in London'. This poem and 'Ceremony after a fire raid' stand among war poems where Thomas would have most wished them to stand – beside Wilfred Owen's (q.v.) – and the refinements of construction and of metaphorical sequence justify the poet's own claim: 'I am a painstaking, conscientious, involved and devious craftsman in words'. Yet Thomas's variability must be accepted. Within the same volume, *Deaths and Entrances*, the title poem fails by congestion and incoherence, while 'The Conversation of Prayer' is a triumph of artistry. There is high artistry too in *In Country Sleep* (1952). The name poem (intended to be the first piece of a bigger work, *In Country Heaven*) is a father's blessing on his little daughter as she goes to bed after fireside fairy tales. Thomas's essential poetic dedication did not of itself deteriorate. In a note prefaced to *Collected Poems* (1952) he wrote, 'These poems, with all their crudities, doubts, and confusions, are written for the love of Man and in praise of God, and I'd be a damn' fool if they weren't'.

Thomas's prose work is unfailingly rich in imaginative and verbal vitality. The *Portrait of the Artist as a Young Dog* (1940) is a collection of stories, some of them shaped with *Dubliners* as model. (Joyce (q.v.) was 'his most admired prose writer', Vernon Watkins tells us.) Autobiographical material adds rich colour to our picture of the poet's early days – childhood and young manhood, journalism and pub-crawling. Among the broadcast talks published in *Quite Early One Morning* (1954) 'Reminiscences of Childhood' and 'Return Journey' (to Swansea in search of the young Dylan) fill out our understanding of the man with a freshness and intimacy not predominant in the poetry. The popular radio play, *Under Milk Wood**, recording a day in the life of a Welsh seaside village, was finished shortly before his death and broadcast posthumously in January 1954. See Dylan Thomas, *The Poems*, ed. Daniel Jones (1971). See also Constantine Fitzgibbon, ed., *Selected Letters* (1966), and J.P. Harries, ed., *Selected Writings* (1970).

Under Milk Wood has neither dramatic structure nor active encounters between characters. Instead, its personae, dwellers in a Welsh seaside village called 'Llareggub' (a name that should also be read backwards), are overheard in vocal self-revelation during the course of a single day. The technique of mental projection, with its cheerful blend of sentiment, humour and bawdy, owes something to the 'Circe' episode in Joyce's *Ulysses*. The work makes few concessions to naturalism and the cast is little more than a collection of animated cartoons with stagey 'Welsh' names like Mrs Ogmore-Pritchard, Organ Morgan, Dai Bread and Rev. Eli Jenkins. Willy Nilly, the postman, brings advance news of the contents of such missives as he delivers. Polly Garter is tumbled by all the farm boys. Mae Rose Cottage lies in clover drawing circles in lipstick round her nipples. Rev. Eli Jenkins prays understandingly and understandably:

> We are not wholly bad or good
> Who live our lives under Milk Wood,
> And Thou, I know, wilt be the first
> To see our best side, not our worst.

The idea from which the work sprang was that of a mad village visited by an inspector, certified as collectively insane and sealed off so as not to infect the rest of the world. In conclusion it was to turn out to be the only sane and happy place surviving in a mad world. In fact the work became a series of impressions, rooted no doubt in knowledge of village life in Laugharne and New Quay, but hilariously fantastic in flavour and too static to allow of developmental interest. [HB]

THOMAS, EDWARD (1878–1917). Poet and prose writer, born in London of Welsh stock. His father, Philip Henry Thomas, came from Tredegar. Member of a large family of tin-plate workers and miners, he had established himself in the Civil Service with a clerkship at the Board of Trade: the achievement nourished a paternal concern for his son's security that was to be sadly at loggerheads with the precarious literary career to which Edward eventually committed himself. Edward was educated at various schools, the last of which was St Paul's, where he overlapped with Chesterton (q.v.) and E.C. Bentley. In 1894 Thomas first met the writer and critic James Ashcroft Noble, who helped and encouraged him in his early efforts as a writer and whose daughter Helen brought him companionship that soon deepened into love – despite maternal opposition on both sides. There was a gap between leaving St Paul's in 1895 and going to Oxford in 1897. Walking, reading and writing were Thomas's occupations, and personal enthusiasm took him to Wiltshire to explore the Jefferies country. (The observant delight in nature and in rural life that gave Jefferies's prose work its charm was highly congenial to Thomas, and he was later to write a deeply sympathetic critical study, *Richard Jefferies*, 1909.) In 1897 Thomas's first book, *The Woodland Life*, was published with a dedication to Helen's now deceased father. Helen herself held posts as governess. She became pregnant and the couple married in 1899 before Thomas's university course was completed. He took his finals in 1900 and then set out with Helen on a life of parenthood (there were three children) and authorship in which Edward's financial difficulties and Celtic melancholy were together sometimes too overwhelming to be kept at bay by arduous literary exertion. The years of study – by no means all penurious or shadowed by depression – were spent in various cottages, first in Kent, then in Hampshire. The vicissitudes were finely and movingly recorded by Helen Thomas, after her husband's death, in *As It Was* (1926), which traces events from the first meeting with Edward in her father's study to the birth of their son, and its sequel, *World Without End* (1931), which takes the story up to Edward's last departure for the front line in France. It is a record of family life intensely cherished against the pressures of back-breaking toil to fulfil publishers' commissions (books on the countryside, books on English writers, edited anthologies etc.) and to supply reviews, essays and articles. Titles include *Rose Acre Papers* (1904), *Beautiful Wales* (1905), *The Heart of England* (1906), *Feminine Influence on the Poets* (1910), *The Isle of Wight* (1911), *George Borrow* (1912), *The Icknield Way* (1913), *Keats* (1916), *A Literary Pilgrim in England* (1917).

There is much in Thomas's immense prose output that bears the marks of composition under pressure, and the gracious prose is often sentimental and over-written, but Thomas's fierce integrity matured in technical self-judgement over the years of prose writing. One can see the poet in the making, not only in the highly perceptive detection of the subtly worthy and the subtly worthless in his critical treatment of other writers' work, but also in the rarely exact descriptive writing at which his artistry operated with increasing self-discipline. He showed himself a poet in his prose: Gordon Bottomley (q.v.), W.H. Hudson (q.v.) and De la Mare (q.v.) were among those who made the point to him. It finally sank in when the friendship of Robert Frost came to enrich his last years with a congenial and stimulating poetic fellowship. Ralph Hodgson (q.v.) introduced Thomas to Frost in 1914. Frost urged Thomas to take his own prose cadences and turn them directly into verse.

When the poetic flow came, in the last three years of his life, it proved to represent a breakthrough from Georgian mellifluousness and decorativeness into a plainness of phrase and rhythm that have the ring of unique honesty. There is no place for sentimentality nor for literary word-tasting. Thomas had criticized other writers for verbal connoisseurship, labelling it 'philately'. He himself eschewed conscious graces and found a directness of utterance that choked all pretence and pretentiousness:

> How weak and little is the light,
> All the universe of sight,
> Love and delight,
> Before the might,
> If you love it not, of night.
>
> ('Out in the Dark')

Thomas hammers syntax into stanzaic shape like a stonemason, and the effect on the reader is of an intimate entry into his brooding. Thomas read this poem to his wife on his last leave at home. 'He reads me some of the poems he has written that I have not heard – the last one of all called "Out in the Dark". And I venture to question one line, and he says, "Oh, no, it's right, Helen, I'm sure it's right" ' (World Without End). The 'rightness' is indisputable.

Thomas's blank verse is an apt vehicle for the less tense purpose of bringing memorable incidents, places or personalities to life. 'Lob', 'Up in the Wind' and 'Wind and Mist' might be cited. In the last named there is a Wordsworthian encounter with a stranger who admires the view of what is in fact the poet's former house – and the scene of much personal unsettlement. Dialogue is woven neatly into decasyllabics as it also is in the remarkable poem, 'As the Team's Head-Brass', in which the poet sits on a fallen elm while a ploughman makes his circuits, exchanging a few words with the poet at each turn round. Brief question and answer about the war, threaded through the steady record of unchanging farm-work, make an impact all the heavier for the low-key wryness that is Thomas's vein.

> 'Have you been out?' 'No.' 'And don't want to
> perhaps?'
> 'If I could only come back again, I should,
> I could spare an arm. I shouldn't want to lose
> A leg. If I should lose my head, why, so,
> I should want nothing more . . .'

Of the compact lyrics that show Thomas's uncanny gift for opening out complex moods with sureness and sincerity one may mention 'The Owl', 'When First' and 'Adlestrop', each rooted in precise incident, and 'And You, Helen' and 'No One Such as You', two poems addressed to his wife. That Thomas is a powerful war poet emerges indirectly in what are ostensibly 'country' poems, like 'As the Team's Head-Brass', and directly in such searchingly frank outcries as 'No Case of Petty Right

and Wrong' and 'No One Cares Less Than I'. In 'Lights Out' quietly he faces the prospect of death with a prophetic courage that transfigures his deep melancholy and frustration:

> I have come to the borders of sleep,
> The unfathomable deep
> Forest where all must lose
> Their way, however straight,
> Or winding, soon or late;
> They cannot choose.

Thomas had joined up in July 1915. By November he was a lance corporal in the Artists' Rifles and by April 1916 a corporal. In August 1916 he became a cadet in the Royal Artillery and was commissioned second lieutenant in November. In spite of his age, he volunteered for service in France, and he was killed in the bombardment that opened the Battle of Arras on Easter Monday 1917. See Collected Poems, ed. R. George Thomas (1978), and Selected Poems, ed. R.S. Thomas (1965).

Thomas's widow, Helen, lived on into her eighties. His daughter, Myfanwy, has selected material from her mother's letters and writings and brought her own memories to bear on them in Time and Again (1978). Edna Longley has gathered and introduced selected prose by Thomas in A Language Not To Be Betrayed (1981). See also Myfanwy Thomas's memoirs One of These Fine Days (1982).   [HB]

THOMAS, R.S. (Ronald Stuart) (1913–). Poet, born in Cardiff, South Glamorgan, Wales, and educated at the University College of North Wales, Bangor, where he read classics and took his degree in 1935. He went for theological training to St Michael's College, Llandaff, and was ordained priest in 1937. He held curacies at Chirk and at Hamner and in 1942 became Rector of Manafon, a remote and not notably attractive village in Montgomeryshire some ten miles south west of Welshpool. After twelve years there he became in 1954 Vicar of St Michael's Eglwysfach, a hill village in Cardiganshire on the road between Machynlleth and Aberystwyth. In 1967 he moved into Carnarvonshire to the tip of the Lleyn Peninsula to be Vicar of St Hywyn, Aberdaron with St Mary, Bodfern. In 1973 he became Vicar of St Aelrhiw, Rhiw with Llanfaerlrhys.

Thomas's first publications were issued from small Welsh presses, The Stones of the Field (1946) from the Druid Press, Carmarthen, and An Acre of Land (1952) and The Minster (1953) from the Montgomeryshire Printing Company, Newtown. A commendation by Alan Pryce Jones on the BBC Critics' programme in 1952 caused these editions to be sold out and in 1955 Thomas gathered together what he considered to be the best work in them, added some Later Poems, and published the whole as Song at the Year's Turning. An Introduction to the volume by John Betjeman (q.v.) paid generous tribute to the newly discovered poet. A retiring personality, he had not sought an introduction, but the publishers wanted a 'name' to help sell the book. 'The "name" ', Betjeman wrote, 'which has the honour to introduce this fine poet to a wide public will be forgotten long before that of R.S. Thomas.' Betjeman recognized that here was a priest-poet, personally zealous to win souls for the Christian faith, looking 'at man and nature in the light of eternity'. Casting about for comparisons, critics have compared Thomas to Crabbe for the way he comes to grips with the harsh realities of rural life – the dirt, the cruelty, the near-bestiality – and to Edward Thomas for his 'slow medita-tive manner' (Edward Lucie-Smith (q.v.)) and his dis-ciplined verbal sparseness. All agree that he has nothing in common with his counterpart in name and fame, Dylan Thomas (q.v.). Yet perhaps comparison might also be made with George Herbert. However different in temperament the two may be – for Thomas has none of Herbert's sunniness, rarely tastes the peace of tension resolved, and is much less direct and explicit than Herbert in reference to priestly duties – nevertheless the two careers of hidden devotion to human ministry with the marriage of literary to personal discipline seem to match across the centuries. Thomas's succeeding vol-umes include *Poetry for Supper* (1958), *Tares* (1961), *The Bread of Truth* (1963), *Pietà* (1966), *Not That He Brought Flowers* (1968), *H'm* (1972), *Laboratories of the Spirit* (1975) and *Frequencies* (1978). His dominant interests recur in them with no slackening of perception or crafts-manship. *Between Here and Now* (1982), however, includes a very distinctive group of poems on Impression-ist paintings in the Louvre.

English-speaking by unbringing, Thomas taught himself Welsh, and the Wales he represents is a country-side decaying inwardly by the invasion of a threatening 'Elsan culture' and the 'thousands of mouths . . . emptying their waste speech / About us' ('Looking at Sheep', *The Bread of Truth*). 'At fifty he was still trying to deceive / Himself' that his country 'was still Wales'. But the land has 'no more right to its name / Than a corpse'. It lies like a bone 'thrown aside and of no use' ('A Country', *The Bread of Truth*). Thomas is too big a man and a poet to see the local dilemma in isolation. There is no banner-waving and there are no concessions to sentimentality or to any inherited attitudes in his presentation of the Welsh peasant. Among the human studies in which the harshly repellent aspects of daily toil and stench, dirt and death, are faced, the recurring poems about Iago Prytherch, the hill-farmer, reveal an appreciation of a prototype of human endurance, 'quietly repairing the rents of history' and, in 'Servant' (*Pietà*), he is even imaged in terms that give him his own cultural status. The poet turns from his own questionings and doubts –

> To where you read in the slow book
> Of the farm, turning the field's pages
> So patiently, never tired
> Of the land's story; not just believing,
> But proving in your bone and your blood
> Its accuracy.

Thomas's concern with the dual power of nature to brutalize and to heal is rooted in his Christian sense of paradox and his awareness of the openness of human nature to the bestial and the spiritual. If the men of the moors have not yet 'shaken the moss' from their savage skulls or 'prayed the peat from their eyes' ('A Priest to his People'), nevertheless, in 'Valediction' ('You failed me, farmer'), the farmer is rebuked for lacking the grace and beauty that belong to his background:

> Your uncouthness has
> No kinship with the earth, where all is forgiven,
> All is requited in the seasonal round
> Of sun and rain, healing the year's scars.

Alan Brownjohn (q.v.), the poet, has pinpointed the corresponding stylistic paradox of Thomas's 'harshly refined' manner and his 'piercing plainness' of statement.

The poems in which Thomas speaks more revealingly of his calling and the personal tensions the priestly life imposes are shorn of posture and pretence, and reflect ruthless self-exposure in varying moods of bewilderment – 'Someone must have thought of putting me here. . . . What do I find to my taste?' ('Who?') – of spiritual testing ('In Church') and of hope glimpsed ('The Belfry'). The terse, spare, yet unsparing precision and economy of the man is essentially and inextricably both a literary and a spiritual fact. Its unique impact understandably provokes comments such as that of Kingsley Amis (q.v.): 'His example reduces most modern verse to footling whimsy'. For the tensions and ambivalences inherent in the cultured and compassionate priest's encounter with what attracts and what disgusts in those he would serve are explored with force and penetration that universalize the parochial.   [HB]

THOMPSON, FLORA (née Timms) (1873–1947). Prose writer, daughter of a stonemason, brought up in the Northamptonshire hamlet, Juniper Hill. Leaving school at 14, she worked in the village post office at Fringford, 8 miles away, and later at Grayshott, Surrey, where she served Conan Doyle (q.v.) and Bernard Shaw (q.v.) with stamps. After her marriage she and her husband ran the post office at Liphook, where she turned out 'small sugared love stories' and started the Peverel literary society. Flora Thompson was 'a born observer' and her three autobiographical volumes, *Lark Rise* (1939), *Over to Candleford* (1941) and *Candleford Green* (1943), later issued in one volume as *Lark Rise to Candleford* (1945) (Candleford is Buckingham), record the day-to-day life of the 1870s and 1880s with fascinating detail and memor-ability. The agricultural labourer has 10 shillings a week but manages to contrive 'a rough plenty' from his pig, his vegetables, his beehives and his gleanings from harvest and hedgerow. With water still carried in buckets on a shoulder yoke and cooking done over the fire, the villagers bemoan the extravagant upkeep of a turnpike road now made redundant by the railways. We are shown Aunt Dorcas in her village post office-cum-smithy with the new 'telegraph instrument' under a velvet cover and Irish har-vesters admitted unofficially after hours to send postal orders to starving wives at home. It is a world where fried mice are served up to prevent bed-wetting and a black slug is bound upon a wart to charm it away; but it is seen by eyes aware of the bigger social and historical perspec-tives. A fourth volume of reminiscences, *Still Glides the Stream*, was added in 1948. Margaret Lane has made a selection from Flora Thompson's earlier work and introduced it by a useful biographical essay in *A Country Calendar and Other Writings* (1978). [HB]

THWAITE, ANTHONY (1930–). Poet, born in Cheshire, educated in Yorkshire to the age of 10, then for four years in the USA, finally at Kingswood School, Bath, and Christ Church, Oxford. He has held university posts in Tokyo (1955–7) and Benghazi (1965–7), worked as BBC radio producer, as literary editor of the *New Statesman* and as co-editor of *Encounter*. *Home Truths* (1953) shows an early-established control of technical niceties, the tone is unapologetic and the movement of thought agile. *The Owl in the Tree* (1963) contains in 'Mr Cooper' a powerful poem on the riddle of death suddenly encountered while visiting the urinal of a Manchester pub. *The Stones of Emptiness* (1967) shows the historical sense awakened by Thwaite's sojourn in Libya, and *Inscriptions* (1973) brings to fulfilment Thwaite's rare power to touch the nerves of our mortality in briefly etched encounters with the reality of the present or the ruins of the past. Each poem is here distinct, all of a piece, resonant with meaning, supply and expertly fashioned. *New Confessions* (1974), the fruit of Thwaite's long fascination with St Augustine of Hippo, is 'an inner commentary on Augustine, partly in verse, partly in prose, which would be written in the margin, as it were, of Augustine's writings, but which would also be a personal book of meditation and transmutation' (Prefatory Note). *A Portion for Foxes* (1977) is an appetizingly diversified collection of short poems inspired by objects, places, people ('For Louis MacNeice' pays tribute to the poet under whom Thwaite worked at the BBC) and personal memories or worries. The last group (see 'Called For', 'Jack' and 'Marriages') show Thwaite's reflectiveness at its most accessible. *Victorian Voices* (1980) is a fine collection of Browningesque dramatic monologues by nineteenth-century characters who failed to reach genuine eminence, the painter Alma-Tadema, the potter Edward Bingham and the literary hack John Churton Collins among them. Perhaps the most rewardingly skilful of these perceptive and richly evocative studies is 'A Message from Her', Mary Ellen Meredith's account of the break-up of her marriage, appropriately matching and countering her husband's 'Modern Love'. Thwaite is a knowledgeable and stimulating critic of recent and contemporary English poetry. See his *Twentieth-Century English Poetry: An Introduction* (1977). [HB]

TOLKIEN, J.R.R. (John Ronald Revel) (1892–1973). Writer of fantasy, born in Bloemfontein, South Africa. He came to England in 1896. He was later to speak of the 'long-seeming' childhood years 'between learning to read and going to school' as neither golden nor happy, but 'sad and troublous' ('On Fairy Stories'). He was educated at King Edward VI School, Birmingham, and at Exeter College, Oxford, where he took his BA degree in 1915. He served with the Lancashire Fusiliers from 1915 to 1918, and was at the front on the Somme as signalling officer in 1916 until 'trench fever' brought him home. 'One has indeed personally to come under the shadow of war to feel fully its oppression', he wrote later. 'By 1918 all but one of my close friends were dead.' Tolkien was early

fascinated by the study of language and attained academic distinction as a philologist. He worked on the *Oxford English Dictionary* from 1918 to 1920 and then spent five years at Leeds University as Reader and as Professor of English Language successively. He returned to Oxford as Rawlinson and Bosworth Professor of Anglo-Saxon in 1925 and held a fellowship at Pembroke College until he moved to Merton in 1945 to be Merton Professor of English Language and Literature, a chair he held until 1959.

'A real taste for fairy-stories was awakened by philology on the threshold of manhood', Tolkien wrote ('On Fairy Stories'). As father of four children (he married Edith Mary Bratt in 1915 and had three sons and a daughter), he understood what children like but he insisted that 'if fairy-story as a kind is worth reading at all it is worthy to be written for and read by adults'. His story *The Hobbit; or There and Back Again* (1937) tells how Bilbo Baggins, a hobbit, is involved with a group of dwarfs in an adventurous expedition that takes him from his cosy home at Hobbiton in the Shire to the Lonely Mountain and battle with the dragon Smaug. The dragon holds the treasure-hoard and the kingdom that rightly belong to the dwarf Thorin Oakenshield. The journey takes the company to Rivendell where they stay with Elrond and the elves at the Last Homely House of the West, then over the perilous Misty Mountains and through the terrifying gloom of Mirkwood. There are trolls, goblins and wargs to oppose them and eagles as well as elves to help. Above all there is the wizard Gandalf. His mysterious comings and goings are resonant with echoes of a cosmic struggle between good and evil within which the current venture is microcosmically set. Moreover the adventures are enriched by hints of a mighty history in the background. Thus we are prepared for the vast expansion of the moral and imaginative dimensions represented in Tolkien's subsequent work, *The Lord of the Rings**, an epic in which appear several of the same characters (and many many more) and the same terrain (with much much more of it). In *The Hobbit* Bilbo comes into possession of an evil magic ring which is the key to absolute power, and possession of which is the central issue of the succeeding epic. The easygoing unambitiousness of the hobbits prevents their being readily corrupted by the ring. Hobbits are little creatures between two and four feet high. Their feet have tough leathery soles and are hairy – the only 'animal' characteristic in a species whose name seems to combine *homo* and *rabbit* in a portmanteau word. Loving peace and quiet in a pre-industrial countryside, and revelling in food, drink, tale-telling and tobacco, they symbolize the simple, unpretentious, homely 'goodness' that tyranny hates and technology erodes. In being comparatively innocent, simple in their tastes, and courageous beyond their magnitude when dealing with full-size and outsize foes, the four hobbits of the epic parallel the four children of C.S. Lewis's Narnia stories.

The Fellowship of the Ring, the first volume of *The Lord of the Rings*, was published in 1954; *The Two Towers* and *The Return of the King* followed in 1955 and 1956. As Tolkien worked on the earlier part of the epic during the late 1930s and the 1940s he would read succeeding chapters aloud to the little group of writers and scholars that gathered round C.S. Lewis (q.v.), calling themselves

'The Inklings'. Common to several of the group (which included Charles Williams (q.v.)) was an interest in fantasy and a related religious position (Roman Catholic in Tolkien's case) that gave theological status to the sub- and super-natural and down-graded fashionable literary canons of naturalistic plausibility and servitude to fact. (Tolkien thought the critical standards of drama – which is by nature anthropocentric – baleful in their influence on narrative literature.) Thus Tolkien defended the fairy story as offering Fantasy, Recovery, Escape, and Consolation – freedom from fact, renewal of vision, and that happy ending of which the gospel story of redemption is perhaps the ultimate archetype. Nevertheless he disliked straight allegory that imposes an interpretation, preferring 'history, true or feigned, with its varied applicability to the thought and experience of readers'. (His revealing little parable, 'Leaf by Niggle', suggests that what Tolkien called 'applicability' many would call 'allegory'.) The enormous success of *The Lord of the Rings* turned Tolkien into a student cult on the campuses of the USA and made him one of the most celebrated literary figures of the 1960s.

Other works include *Farmer Giles of Ham* (1949), a light-hearted, mock-heroic 'medieval' tale of a very ordinary farmer who accidentally achieves heroism by shooting a giant and then takes on an idiosyncratic dragon, Chrysophylax. *Smith of Wootton Major* (1967), in which Smith, a visitor to Faery, finally chooses to return to his home, has been read as Tolkien's farewell to his art like Shakespeare's *The Tempest*. The children's story *Mr Bliss* (1982) has been published posthumously. *The Silmarillion* (1977), also published posthumously, is the history of the First Age of the World antecedent to the chronicles of Hobbitry. Tolkien conceded that it was 'primarily linguistic in inspiration'. His son Christopher put it together from his father's papers. *J.R.R. Tolkien, A Biography* (1977) by Humphrey Carpenter is illuminating. Tolkien's *Tree and Leaf* (1961) contains the essay 'On Fairy Stories', quoted above, and 'Leaf by Niggle'. Humphrey Carpenter, assisted by Christopher Tolkien, has edited *Letters of J.R.R. Tolkien: a Selection* (1981).

The Lord of the Rings is an epic trilogy in prose comprising *The Fellowship of the Ring*, *The Two Towers* and *The Return of the King*. This vast fantasy is presented as history – the history of Middle-earth in the Great Year of its Third Age. It purports to be derived from ancient annals – source manuscripts located at places within the story and source memoirs attributed to characters within the story. An array of appendices and indices at the end of the last volume covers 127 pages. It includes fragments of 'legends, histories and lore' relative to the story as edited and representing a massive network of pseudo-history that is summed up in genealogical trees and chronological tables. The main language of the ancient scripts from which the material has supposedly been transcribed is fully described and other tongues used by races of beings in the book are touched upon. In all, story and explanatory material together constitute a monumental achievement by a scholar richly versed in the philology, mythology and literature of the older European languages.

The story begins sixty years after the events described in *The Hobbit*. Bilbo Baggins retires from Bag End to the home of the elves at Rivendell, bequeathing to Frodo, his chosen heir, the magic ring of absolute power that corrupts all who desire to possess it. Sauron, the dark lord of the evil and desolate land of Mordor, wants it in order to complete his conquest of Middle-earth and to enslave all its inhabitants. It becomes Frodo's burdensome quest, freely undertaken, to convey the ring to the one place where it can be put beyond the grasp of the Enemy. He must cast it into the Cracks of Mount Doom in the land of Mordor. Three other hobbits set out with Frodo: Sam, Merry and Pippin. As perils accumulate the four are divided into two couples and later into four individuals, and Tolkien is thus able to keep a hobbit-presence within each main strand of his complex narrative. For the quest to destroy the ring is only one move in the campaign to resist Sauron's overt and subversive aggressions against the neighbouring territory of Gondor and further realms – even to the far Shire where hobbits live in supposed security. In the early chapters Sauron's Nine Ring-wraiths, faceless Black Riders, are already abroad in the Shire. Meanwhile the wizard Saruman's treachery has made of Isengard, near the Gap of Rohan, an outpost of Mordorism and a place to match his mind, 'a mind of metal and wheels' that cares nothing for growing things. The climax of the open struggle comes at the siege of Minas Tirith, capital of Gondor, where Aragorn should rightly rule. (Sauron's orcs killed his father.) Resistance to Sauron is master-minded by Gandalf, the wizard. He is aided by the Ents, treelike tree-shepherds, who destroy Isengard, and by the forces of men and elves who, with Aragorn, finally converge on the beleaguered fortress of Minas Tirith. After struggling through forest and tunnel, over desert and mountain, to the Mount of Doom, Frodo and Sam lose the ring at the last moment to Gollum, the haunting incarnation of unscrupulous self-centredness. Dancing with delight at his triumph, he slips into the Crack of Doom and takes the ring with him.

Tolkien's imaginative scheme has a powerful inner logic, for his inventiveness is disciplined in a patterning consistent with a Christian reading of the character and operation of good and evil. (Trolls, for instance, are mock-Ents, while orcs are mock-elves.) The style is self-consciously 'epic' and reverberates with the cadences of Anglo-Saxon verse. At its best it has poetic energy equal to its function. Inevitably invention sometimes slides into empty repetitiveness and style slackens correspondingly.

[HB]

TOMLINSON, CHARLES (1927–). Poet, born at Stoke-on-Trent, Staffordshire. He read English at Queen's College, Cambridge. He worked as a school-teacher and private secretary before reading for a London MA and (in 1956) joining the teaching staff at the University of Bristol, where he later became reader in English poetry. He has also held professorships in the USA. He married Brenda Raybould in 1948 and has two daughters. His published volumes include *Relations and Contraries* (1951), *The Necklace* (1955), *Seeing is Believing* (1960), *A Peopled Landscape* (1963), *American Scenes and Other Poems* (1966), *The Way of a World* (1969), *Written on Water* (1972), *The Way In* (1974) and *The Flood* (1981). From the first Tomlinson managed to submit himself to the world he observed without intruding a restless or defiant persona. He indulges no poetic self-projection, either excited and flamboyant or cool and clever. He found in the French symbolists and in American poets like Marianne Moore and Wallace Stevens 'something which released me from the dilemma of either Dylan Thomas or William Empson' (*The Poet Speaks*, ed. P. Orr, 1966). Tomlinson's gift is to pin down the particular with spare precision and with intellectual accuracy that is neither dry nor pretentious. A note of self-withdrawal gives a rare objective intensity to his work.

> Do not call to her there,
> but let her go
> bearing our question
> in her climb: what does she
> confer on the hill, the hill on her?
> ('The Hill')

He can be bitingly comic in such human studies as those of 'Mr Brodsky', the American would-be Scot, 'Chief Standing Water', the reservation hotelier, or Ludmilla Quatsch of 'Beethoven Attends the C Minor Seminar'. The free metres adopted disinfect the verse of the known emotional currencies vested in metronomic musicality. The effect is of a consistent freshness and 'rightness' of touch. In *The Way In* Tomlinson returns to his early Midlands surroundings and other urban areas to track the story of post-Victorian decay and post-1945 demolition in graphic vignettes with nostalgic overtones.

> It took time to convince me that I cared
> For more than beauty: I write to rescue
> What is no longer there – absurd
> A place should be more fragile than a book.
> ('Dates: Penchull New Road')

The sustained discipline – some would say 'austerity' – of Tomlinson's work is the mark of poetic integrity. See his *Selected Poems 1951-1974* (1978) and the *Oxford Book of Verse in English Translation* (1980) which he chose and edited. Tomlinson, who also draws and paints, has produced pictures to illuminate his poems and an Arts Council Exhibition of his graphics, *The Graphic Work and Poetry of Charles Tomlinson*, toured the country in 1980. *Some Americans, A Personal Record* (1981) recalls visits he made to five American poets who influenced him: William Carlos Williams, Marianne Moore, Ezra Pound, Louis Zukofsky and George Oppen.　　　　[HB]

TONKS, ROSEMARY. Novelist and poet, born in London. She lived for a time in West Africa and Pakistan, and has told how she was later living alone in Paris in near poverty and recovering from poliomyelitis when working on her first novel in the early 1960s (*The Times*, 12.5.76). Her poetry (*Notes on Cafés and Bedrooms*, 1963; *Iliad of Broken Sentences*, 1967) reflects the bittiness of modern urban life in dramatic jottings, often feverishly vivid. Her novels (*Opium Fogs*, 1963; *Emir*, 1963; *The Bloater*, 1968, etc.) focus on the feminine mind. *The Bloater* tracks the sex-play of a temperamental, scatter-brained, inconsequentially womanly woman whose sophisticatedly

unsophisticated ploys finally claim their victim. She seemingly speaks for her creator when she says: 'Taste in the arts and the theatre should never be confused with "good taste", which is static and middle-class'.　　　　[HB]

TOYNBEE, PHILIP (1916–81). Novelist and poet, born in Oxford, Oxfordshire, the son of the historian Arnold Toynbee, and of Rosalind, daughter of the classical scholar, Gilbert Murray. He was educated at Rugby School, from where he was expelled, and at Christ Church, Oxford, where he joined the Communist Party for a time. After war service in intelligence and in the Ministry of Economic Warfare, Toynbee worked on the editorial staff of *The Observer* and became widely known as an influential book-reviewer. His first novel was *The Savage Days* (1937), but it was with *Tea with Mrs Goodman*, published in the USA as *Prothalamium* (1947), that he began to experiment in narrative technique, entering in succession the minds of a group of people at a tea-party to construct a collage of inner visions poetic rather than dramatic in effect. *The Garden to the Sea* (1953, London; 1954, New York) focuses comparably on the diverse 'selves' of a single character.

Toynbee's major work was the four-volume verse novel known as the 'Pantaloon' series, an opus in seven sections ('The First Day of the Valediction of Pantaloon, The Second Day of the Valediction . . .'). *Pantaloon* (1961) contains the first four 'Days', while the fifth, sixth and seventh 'Days' followed respectively in *Two Brothers* (1964), *A Learned City* (1966) and *Views from a Lake* (1968). The work is an attempt at tragi-comic epic of the 1914–46 period, and its hero, Dick Abberville, looks back on this period from a future point at the end of the twentieth century. His great age, his sometimes acute but sometimes fallible memory, and his liability to confusion provide some justification for the innovatory method of presentation in which narrative sequence is eschewed and memories flow in disconnected succession. The whole Toynbee called 'a mosaic of insights, a constellation of enlightening moments'. He sought to avoid any progression false to real remembering and to do justice to the way in which the new moment is always laden with the weight of the past. The verse is fluent and flexible, individual sections often have memorable imaginative vitality as a series of static visions, but the discrete, oblique method creates unnecessary obstacles to ready responsiveness in the reader.　　　　[HB]

TRAVERS, BEN (1886-1981). Dramatist, born in London and educated at Charterhouse School. He served in the Royal Naval Air Service in the First World War, then began to write as a novelist. When he adapted his novel *A Cuckoo in the Nest* (1922) for the stage in 1925 it proved to be the first of a series of extremely popular farces. *Rookery Nook* (prod 1926), another adaptation of a novel, *Thark* (prod 1927), *A Cup of Kindness* (prod 1929), *Turkey Time* (prod 1931) and many others followed. These 'Aldwych farces' are cunningly structured comedies of mistakes and gaucheries culminating often in bedroom scrapes. Men are caught with their trousers down and women in their underclothes and recourse is had to desperate expedients in the cause of salvaging respectability. Teetering by deception on a tenuous tight-rope of plausibility over an abyss of confirmed impropriety proves a sure recipe for hilarity and suspense. As late as 1975 Travers staged a lively and indeed thoughtful farce, *The Bed Before Yesterday*, which could hold its own with contemporary productions. See also Travers's autobiography, *Vale of Laughter* (1957). [HB]

TRESSELL, ROBERT (pseudonym of Robert Noonan) (c. 1870–1911). Novelist, probably born in Dublin, Ireland. He lived in South Africa just before the turn of the century and in Hastings, Sussex, from 1902, working as a painter and sign-writer. He died of tuberculosis. His novel, *The Ragged Trousered Philanthropists* (1914), posthumously published by his daughter, was a drastically cut-down version of the full work later edited by Frederick C. Ball (1955). A group of workmen in Mugsborough (Hastings) are immune to the socialist propaganda of the protagonist, their fellow employee Owen. The irony lies in this immunity, for their lives are a laborious struggle for survival in conditions of miserable privation. In Owen's eyes they are philanthropists, altruistically toiling to enrich the capitalist class and demanding no share in the fruits of their labours. But they accept exploitation as part of the nature of things: the material comforts they earn for others are 'not for the likes of us'. The work is a valuable documentary of working-class life and attitudes in the Edwardian age. [HB]

TREVOR, WILLIAM (William Trevor Cox) (1928–). Novelist and short-story writer, born in County Cork, Ireland, and educated at St Columba's College and Trinity College, Dublin. He has been a schoolmaster and a sculptor, and has settled in England. His second novel, *The Old Boys* (1964), marked him as a writer of distinction who has learned – but not slavishly – from Beckett (q.v.) and Ivy Compton-Burnett (q.v.), developing his own brand of terse, cryptic dialogue, stylized yet alive, in order to portray human misfits, sometimes evil, sometimes harmless, but usually funny. A story of committee intrigues in an old boys' association and of the annual reunion allows Trevor to bring his laconic objectivity to bear on the seediness and drabness of old men fixated on the codes that have mutilated them. *The Boarding House* (1965) gathers together another group in an establishment where quirkiness and crankiness in thought and speech and act are counterpointed in curt, ironic sentences, smouldering with inner humour. Trevor's inventiveness with potty fads and rogueries of mildly or screwily inadequate personalities is unfailingly entertaining. Though tenderness and compassion do not intrude largely on the sardonic portraiture, Trevor's dry humour is itself infectiously warming. *Mrs Eckdorf in O'Neill's Hotel* (1970) portrays a down-at-heels Dublin hotel, now guestless and used as a brothel, whose loss of its former glory lures a woman photographer in search of her next coffee-table documentary. The tracing of simultaneous threads in Dublin life harks back to the 'Wandering Rocks' episode in Joyce's (q.v.) *Ulysses*. Trevor applies the same technique in *Elizabeth Alone* (1973) to a group of women fortuitously gathered together in a hospital ward for hysterectomy operations, but there is evidence here of

technique taking over where inspiration flags. *The Children of Dynmouth* (1976) concerns a teenage delinquent at large in a Dorset seaside resort. In *Other People's Worlds* (1980) Julia Ferndale, an officer's widow and a Roman Catholic, marries a television actor fifteen years her junior. He is a liar and a sham, complete with abandoned wife, neglected parents, forsaken mistress and illegitimate child. His life-style and his contacts open up contemporary hells.

Trevor is an accomplished writer of short stories. *Angels at the Ritz* (1975) was proclaimed the best collection since Joyce's *Dubliners* by Graham Greene (q.v.). Perhaps Trevor's concern with the frustrations and anti-climaxes of personal life and the tendency of emotional strategies to peter out or go off at half-cock called out the comparison. The story 'Mrs Silly' is an acutely sensitive study of a boy's dilemma at a boarding school when his affectionate but socially clumsy mother visits him. The title story of *Lovers of their Time* (1978) tells amusingly how a married travel agency clerk and a shop assistant make free use of a bathroom at a large hotel in the absence of more suitable premises for their love-making. *Beyond the Pale* (1981) is a series of stories which fracture the frame of seeming normality by juxtaposing external decorum with hidden vice. The veil is lifted from a world of prim social proprieties to uncover depths of savagery and squalor. The title story, for instance, concerns an idyllic Antrim country house, the favourite haunt of English holidaymakers (two seemingly innocuous couples), where a sudden tragedy uncovers a connection with IRA violence costly in misery for Irish and English alike. The discovery exacts its price too in bringing to light what kind of people the holiday couples themselves really are.

A trilogy for television, *Matilda's England* (prod 1979), covering events in the life of a farming family from the 1930s to the 1950s, was greeted with critical acclaim. [HB]

TUOHY, FRANK (1925–). Novelist and short-story writer, born in Uckfield, Sussex, educated at Stowe School and at Cambridge. He has held university teaching posts in English literature in Finland, Brazil, Poland, Tobago and the USA. His first novel, *The Animal Game* (1957), was set in Sao Paulo, Brazil, and the second, *The Warm Nights of January* (1960), in Rio de Janeiro. Tuohy exercises rare evocative power in conveying the feel of distinctive locales, exotic or drab, without wasting a word, and he has aphoristic neatness in pinpointing subtly observed aspects of human sensitivity or human attitudinizing. He fastens on problems of human isolation and alienation acutely evident where foreign colonies, themselves diverse in nationality, impinge upon native cultures likewise mixed and heterogeneous. The English oil executive in Sao Paulo in *The Animal Game* becomes painfully aware of the 'moral vacuum' sucking at people cut adrift from the accustomed social adjustments and pressures imposed in Europe on feelings and attitudes. He narrowly escapes fatal entanglement with a woman of corrupt sensuality. In *The Warm Nights of January* the focus is upon a Frenchwoman, an artist, who finds herself inescapably bound in passion to a Negro fifteen years her junior who is frank ('Everyone here knows French women are whores'), uninhibited, struttingly dominant in confident masculinity and yet battens on her shamelessly for a life of cheap pleasure at her expense. Tuohy here analyses numerous subtle failures of contact and understanding in a seething melting-pot of racial and cultural cross-currents. In *The Ice-Saints* (1964) the setting is Poland. *The Admiral and the Nuns* (1962) and *Fingers in the Door* (1970) are collections of short stories.

[HB]

TUTUOLA, AMOS (1920–). Story-teller, born in Abeokuta in the Yoruba area of Nigeria. He attended school intermittently between 1934 and 1939, when his father died. Drought frustrated his efforts to farm his father's land, so in 1940 he went to Lagos and learned to be a blacksmith. He served in the RAF as a blacksmith in 1942–6. In 1947 he married and he and his wife Victoria have two children. He was employed as a messenger by the Department of Labour in Lagos in 1946–52 and, after publication of his first book, as a storeman by the Nigerian Broadcasting Corporation in Ibadan. As a child he had enjoyed listening to old people telling stories from the abundant Yoruba oral tradition and at school he told stories to his fellows. He has said that as a result of reading a synopsis in a Nigerian magazine of the Yoruba writer D.O. Fagunwa's *Ogboju Ode Ninu Igbo Irunmale* (translated later by Soyinka, q.v., as *The Forest of a Thousand Daemons*), he responded to an advertisement in the same magazine, wrote *The Palm-Wine Drinkard* in a few days, and sent it to the United Society for Christian Literature, which conveyed it to Faber's in London.

And so, with the publication in 1952 of, to give its full title, *The Palm-Wine Drinkard and His Dead Palm-Wine Tapster in the Dead's Town*, West African literature in English can be said to have started. In the introduction to Tutuola's second book, *My Life in the Bush of Ghosts* (1954), G. Parrinder considers Tutuola as inaugurating a new type of 'Afro-English literature' of imaginatively reshaped traditional African tales written in a kind of English startlingly unorthodox in vocabulary, grammar and syntax yet fully intelligible to an English reader. Parrinder's prophecy has been fulfilled in part by the rapid and substantial West African literature in English subsequently produced by such writers as Achebe (q.v.), Okara (q.v.), Okigbo (q.v.) and Soyinka (q.v.), who in very different ways also draw upon traditional African material, but none has followed Tutuola, except chronologically. His writing remains unique.

Although his books are often called novels, the term is a misnomer, and hence the description of him, above, as 'story-teller'. Partly inspired by, at first partly imitating, Fagunwa's books, Tutuola draws upon the rich repertoire of Yoruba folk-tales, usually linking them in an individual book within a journey or quest framework. In *The Palm-Wine Drinkard* the narrator and his friends are prodigal drinkers of palm-wine, until the narrator's palm-wine tapster's sudden death cuts off their supply. The drinkard sets off into the forests to seek out his tapster in the country of the dead. In a series of fantastic episodes, the drinkard encounters every possible kind of African deity and spirit and endures many incredible adventures until he finds his tapster, who is, however, not allowed to leave the Dead's Town. Instead, he gives the drinkard a magical

egg. When the hero returns home, he appears to have gained greatly in wisdom and is able to advise his people how to offer the sacrifice that symbolizes the submission of Earth to the superior power of Heaven, thus bringing rain to end a long drought. Until this more permanent solution, the drinkard's magical egg has supplied his village with food. Starting as a selfish consumer, he has thus developed into a communal provider. This brief summary may exaggerate the narrative coherence of the book, for its structure is essentially episodic. In a London University thesis, A.A. James claims that twenty-nine of the thirty episodes are based on Yoruba folk-tales, including the incident of the 'complete gentleman', a conflation of three variant tales. The quality of both Tutuola's imagination and his idiosyncratic English is illustrated in this passage:

> I could not blame the lady for following the Skull as a complete gentleman to his house at all. Because if I were a lady, no doubt I would follow him to wherever he would go, and still as I was a man I would jealous him more than that, because if this gentleman went to the battle field, surely, enemy would not kill him or capture him and if bombers saw him in a town which was to be bombed, they would not throw bombs on his presence, and if they did throw it, the bomb itself would not explode until this gentleman would leave that town, because of his beauty.

The Palm-Wine Drinkard created a stir outside Africa and among its enthusiastic reviewers was Dylan Thomas (q.v.). Its strange English was regarded as an exciting, highly inventive adaption of the language to convey the exotic features of an African imagination. Much of this early enthusiasm was misplaced or patronizing, and some very extravagant symbolical meanings have been read into his books by western critics, though G. Moore (*Seven African Writers*, 1962), while recognizing that all 'his heroes or heroines follow out one variant or another of the cycle of the heroic monomyth, Departure-Initiation-Return, as analysed by Joseph Campbell in *The Hero with a Thousand Faces*', keeps his feet on firm ground by declaring that Tutuola's books are 'like a fascinating cul-de-sac ... full of wonders, but ... nonetheless a dead end'. At first Nigerians were horrified, believing that Tutuola's 'semi-literate' English was giving the world a damaging impression of the English of educated West Africans. The truth is that Tutuola is not a sophisticated writer and uses the best English he is capable of – that of someone whose formal schooling stopped at Standard VI. But he is in the vital tradition of the African village teller of tales, who not only retells what he has heard from an older generation but has the imaginative creativity to mould the material afresh as he relates it. Among his own additions to the Yoruba spirit-world is the Television-handed Ghostess in *My Life in the Bush of Ghosts*; it is a book with a stronger unifying thread than *The Palm-Wine Drinkard*, for the quest motif is dramatized through the narrator's twenty-four-year, purgatorial experience of many kinds of evil treatment, involving physical pain, terror and despair, so that he learns the meaning of 'good' and 'bad'.

Simbi and the Satyr of the Dark Jungle (1955) shows more conscious characterization than its predecessors and conveys a folk-tale moral of a disobedient daughter who matures through suffering she has brought upon herself. By the time Tutuola wrote *The Brave African Huntress* (1958) he had read Edith Hamilton's *Mythology* and the denizens of his African bush, now consistently called 'the jungle', include, unconvincingly, nymphs, goblins and gnomes. Further non-African influences appear in *Feather Woman of the Jungle* (1962), designed as a ten nights' entertainment with an old chief telling his people of his youthful exploits and hardships. *Ajaiyi and His Inherited Poverty* (1967) is another story of many episodes, some two-thirds of them based on Yoruba folk-tales. Though in general much like its predecessors, *The Witch-Herbalist of the Remote Town* (1981) shows a more conscious attempt at narrative shaping, though a publisher's note points to changes made 'in preparing Amos Tutuola's manuscript for publication'.

In an interview with O. Leslie, Tutuola declared that he wanted to keep the past, not to allow Yoruba culture to die under the pressure of European culture, but that he wrote in English because he also wanted people outside Africa to know the Yoruba past. He is no mere translator but an oral artist who, paradoxically, writes, and even more paradoxically does so in what English he can muster, thus opening up very directly a whole world of African imagination to English readers. [AR]

TUWHARE, HONE (1922–). Poet, born in Kaitoke, near Wellington, New Zealand, and educated at schools in Auckland and at technical colleges there and at Otahuhu, near Wellington. After army service in 1945–7 he worked as a boilermaker and was also active in union affairs and in left-wing politics. His first collection, *No Ordinary Sun* (1964), found a wide readership in New Zealand and established him as an important new poet, largely through its perceptive exploration of the personal tensions between his Maori inheritance and the predominantly pakeha (white man's) New Zealand of today. Familiar problems of the technological age (the title poem refers to the atom bomb) are given new and powerful expression in a local situation, often through reference to landscape or to traditional Maori and western myth. In a Foreword to the book his friend R.A.K. Mason (q.v.) welcomed him as the first 'member of the Maori race qualifying as a poet in English and in the idiom of his own generation, but still drawing his main strength from his own people'. Mason relates the value of his work to 'the clear vision of one who knows life by . . . hard work with his hands' (Tuwhare was a 'boiler-maker on an out-back construction job' at the time) and many poems are indeed specific in time and place, while allowing full scope for his sense of colourful vitality. *Sap-Wood and Milk* (1972), a limited edition with graphics by the Maori artist Ralph Hotere, showed a move from the earlier, somewhat rhetorical, poetry towards an increasing use of the conversational and colloquial. This search for an appropriate poetic voice continued (with more success) in *Something Nothing* (1974), where it reflected the personal / cultural dilemmas explored in the volume. A poem to the late Ron (R.A.K.) Mason takes up the question of inheritance and tradition that Mason himself had broached in his Foreword to *No Ordinary Sun*: 'You've joined your literary / ancestors, whilst I have problems still in / finding mine'. A fine poem on the death of James K. Baxter (q.v.) exemplifies his ability to blend bold phrases of the kind Baxter himself loved ('Joy for the brother sun chesting over / the brim of the land') with a spare colloquialism which nevertheless captures the poignancy of the situation ('a tired old mate in a tent / laid out in a box / with no money in the pocket'). He is one of the most promising, as well as one of the most important, New Zealand poets. A collection of poems and short stories, *Making a Fist of It*, appeared in 1978. [PQ]

UPWARD, EDWARD (1903–). Novelist, born in Romford, Essex, educated at Repton School and Corpus Christi College, Cambridge. He taught for thirty years in a London grammar school and then retired to the Isle of Wight. He was for sixteen years a member of the Communist Party, which he left in 1948 because of opportunist 'revisionism' in the official British party line. Upward was early associated with the Auden–Spender group: he joined with Christopher Isherwood (q.v.) in fabricating a fantasy world called Mortmere, and his short story, *The Railway Accident* (1969), written in 1928, an allegory of the real world breaking in on the world of middle-class unreality, represents his rejection of Mortmere. *Journey to the Border* (1938), a semi-fantastic story with a Kafkaesque flavour, records the Marxist pilgrimage and conversion of an unnamed 'tutor', at loggerheads with the false, archaic world of the middle class, scornful of his own adaptation to its mores, but given over to 'passive fantasies which left his real situation unchanged' until the will to act impels him to get in touch with the workers' movement. Upward published nothing for twenty years, then forsook fantasy for mundane realism in *In The Thirties* (1962). It presents Alan Sebrill, a middle-class poet who joins the Communist Party. *The Rotten Elements* (1969), its sequel and the second part of a trilogy, finds Alan and his wife dissenting from the official party line for its deviation from correct Marxism-Leninism under the postwar Labour government. The emotional agonies and intellectual worries of the characters presuppose in the party a quasi-religious authority and compulsiveness. In the Author's Note to the first volume Upward promised a third novel which would 'aim to vindicate poetry as having its own kind of truth, which the poet must not subordinate to political truth' and *No Home But the Struggle* has carried the story into the 1950s and early 1960s, the days of CND, the whole trilogy having been published as *The Spiral Ascent* (1977). The total undertaking suffers from unrelieved heaviness and solemnity.

[HB]

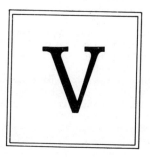

V

VAN DER POST, LAURENS (1906–). Journalist, farmer, soldier and writer, born near Philippolis, South Africa. He attended school in Bloemfontein and worked aboard Durban whalers as a youth. While a journalist in Durban in 1925-6, he co-operated with Roy Campbell (q.v.) and William Plomer (q.v.) on the seminal periodical *Voorslag*. With Plomer he visited Japan in 1926. He moved to London and married Marjorie Wendt in 1928; divorced in 1949, he then married Ingaret Giffard. In 1930 van der Post was in Cape Town as a journalist, but returned to England in 1934 to farm in Gloucestershire. In 1939 he enlisted and served as a British commando in Ethiopia, North Africa, Syria, Sumatra and Java, where he was captured and narrowly escaped death while a prisoner of war (1942-5). He was military attaché in Djakarta in 1945-7 and received the CBE. Editor of the *Natal Daily News* in 1948, he next led explorations for the British government in Nyasaland in 1949 and the Kalahari in 1950-2. Since then he has divided his time between England and South Africa, and written six novels and some of the finest twentieth-century books of travel and exploration.

Van der Post's mythopoeic imagination, which has made him immensely critical of modern western rationality, was formed in childhood on the family farm in South Africa where he first heard Bushman and other African legends from a variety of tribal backgrounds. With senses delicately tuned by tracking and hunting, his mind opened to the intuitive and the instinctive, to the secret bonds between people, animals, plant-life and landscape. This faculty was nurtured by wartime action behind enemy lines, by expeditions into remote parts of Africa, by reading William Blake and D.H. Lawrence (q.v.) and by friendship with Carl Jung. He has come closer than other white writers to the life of traditional, pre-colonial Africa, and found in it symbolic meanings akin to those evolved by francophone négritude writers. By responding with sensitive receptivity to different cultures in Africa and Asia, van der Post has exiled himself from his native Afrikanerdom, while remaining a native of Africa rather than Europe.

His literary career began with a prewar novel, *In a Province* (1934), though he had earlier had some poems and essays published in Afrikaans. More than a decade before Paton (q.v.), *In a Province*, inspired by Plomer's *Turbott Wolfe*, is the first novel by a South African that analyses and seriously questions white South African treatment of blacks. Praising it in *The African Image*, Mphahlele (q.v.) regards it as van der Post's best novel. Unlike his later fiction, it is conceived in a wholly realist mode, despite the authorial apostrophe at the end. Trenchant in his depiction of white racism, van der Post does not, however, allow the hero to join his Marxist friend's political activities, but makes him draw back in the belief that Marxism dehumanizes by denying individuality and personal responsibility – an attitude that persists into the later fiction. The grandiloquent, over-written *Flamingo Feather* (1955) is a melodramatic,

Buchanesque tale of adventure hinging upon the frustration of a Marxist plot in Africa. *A Far-Off Place* (1974) discredits Marxist involvement in African liberation movements, though with greater understanding of why men seek social and economic justice through revolution.

The Face Beside the Fire (1953) is a heavily psychological novel about an artist's spiritual exile, as he moves between a Europe and an Africa ponderously endowed with symbolic meanings intended to explicate the contradictions within his personality. *The Seed and the Sower* (1963) consists of three stories (including 'A Bar of Shadow', separately published, 1956) thematically related to two characters' experiences in Japanese prisoner-of-war camps, as, years later in England, they come to terms with their bruised identities and attain humane comprehension of their captors' codes of honour and duty which had so often been expressed in ritualized brutalities. *The Hunter and the Whale* (1967), *A Story like the Wind* (1972) and its sequel *A Far-Off Place* less portentously combine realism with symbolism; tales of physical action, perilous journeying and extreme endurance, they embody psychological quests for individual wholeness that bring the characters vividly to life, while mystically suggesting that re-creation of the human spirit can save modern man from annihilation. These strange, temperamental, seemingly rambling novels, so unlike the densely textured novels of Wilson Harris (q.v.), nevertheless reveal a fertile associative imagination which, like Harris's, is acutely aware of the dangers of cultural, racial, national solipsism, and presses the novel into the service of seeking anew ancient, forgotten ways of perception that will counteract man's over-reliance upon rationality and its perversions.

Just as Harris has gathered together what survives of Arawak myth and legend, so in his two most important books, *The Lost World of the Kalahari* (1958) and *The Heart of the Hunter* (1961), van der Post describes his expedition to the few surviving groups of Bushmen, and pieces together the fragments of their myths and legends, carefully unravelling imagery and symbolism, relating them to rock-painting, dancing and history, and taking from them compass readings for mankind's safer journeying in today's world. It is arguable that van der Post's novelistic skills are better managed in non-fiction than novels. Parts Three and Four of *Venture to the Interior* (1952), about his exploration of Mount Mlanje and the Nyika Plateau (Nyasaland), compellingly dramatize men pitted against nature and needing to overcome imbalances within themselves in order to maintain physical equilibrium. The detailed, concrete rendering even persuades one of the mystique the author attributes to the prehistoric cedars of Mlanje. In *The Night of the New Moon* (1970), about his prisoner-of-war experiences, the vivid telling produces a drama between absolute power and the only puny weapon against it, a psychological grasp of the captors' minds. Both books achieve a narrating artistry superior to that in the fiction associated with them, *Flamingo Feather* and *The Seed and the Sower* respectively. *A Mantis Carol* (1975) reports on the charismatic life of a circus-perfoming Bushman, Hans Taaibosch, in the United States; though the author learned of him only at second hand, Taaibosch's gentleness and moral courage have all the substantiality of skilful characterization. The other non-fictional writings are: *The Dark Eye of Africa* (essays, 1955), *Journey into Russia* (as *A View of All the Russias* in USA, 1964), *A Portrait of Japan* (1968), *Jung and the Story of Our Time* (1976).

Despite many inequalities of execution (e.g. the disproportionately discursive Parts One and Two of *Venture to the Interior*, and much melodrama in the novels), fiction and non-fiction alike are powerful, at their best superbly written, ventures into the human unconscious. [AR]

WADDELL, HELEN (1889–1965). Novelist, translator and medieval historian, born in Tokyo, Japan. Her father was a scholarly Presbyterian missionary from County Down, Ireland ('the Vicar of Wakefield turned Chinese scholar', Helen called him). Her mother died when Helen, the youngest of ten children, was two. Her father remarried, brought the children home to Ulster and died himself when Helen was 11. She was educated with her elder sister Meg at the Victoria High School for Girls, Belfast ('This one I will educate for nothing', the percipient headmistress exclaimed of Helen), and at Queen's College, Belfast. Her first book, *Lyrics from the Chinese*, was published in 1915 but it was not until 1920 that, freed from heavy domestic obligation by the death of her stepmother, she went to Somerville College, Oxford, for further study. From here she moved first to London, then (with the aid of the Susette-Taylor Travelling Fellowship) to Paris. *The Wandering Scholars* (1927) and the translated verse which followed it, *Mediaeval Latin Lyrics* (1929), are the work of a scholar whose imagination gives colour and vitality to everything it touches. The graceful lyricism of Helen Waddell's verse and prose is matched by a deeply felt entry into the heart of the past and a tender sympathy with its poets and thinkers. These qualities give her work a haunting, nostalgic magnetism and her ambition to be a creative writer bore full fruit in the novel, *Peter Abelard* (1933).

The wish to write on Abelard (born 1079) had been at the back of Helen Waddell's mind for twenty years. She was captivated by the figure of the great medieval theologian and teacher who fell in love with his young pupil, Héloïse, niece of Fulbert, a Canon of Notre Dame. The two became lovers and Fulbert, who was at first outraged, nevertheless was prepared to accept that they should marry in secret in order to preserve Abelard's reputation. Héloïse unselfishly refused to ruin Abelard's career by marrying him. She preferred to be his mistress. Fulbert plotted Abelard's castration, ruining prospects for priesthood or marriage alike. Héloïse faithfully took the veil at Argenteuil and became Abbess. Many years later moving letters were exchanged between the former lovers. So deep was Helen Waddell's eventual involvement with the story that in 1924, while ill in Paris, she had a dream in which she was identified with Héloïse and the decision to make the book a novel was formed. It proved an enormous success and has since been translated into nine European languages. The power of the book lies in the scholarship brought into play. Helen Waddell faithfully reproduces the intellectual climate of the age, doing justice to the philosophical and theological controversies that Abelard was involved in, and binding them so tightly with his personal dilemma that the whole acquires the status and dimensions of an archetypal study in Christian self-surrender – moral, intellectual and spiritual.

Waddell's intention was to write 'the second part of the story as Héloïse saw it', but the distractions of other claims – social, literary and personal – and then the difficulties of English life in wartime, denied her the conditions for its composition. Her play, *The Abbé Prévost*, was performed in 1933 and *The Desert Fathers*, a selection of fragments translated from the *Vitae Patrum*, was published in 1936. Literary recognition and academic honours crowded upon her but, after the war, her spirits flagged and she began to suffer intermittently from loss of memory. She spent her last years in total oblivion. 'She did not suffer, she was not unhappy. She smiled gently to herself and knew no one' (Monica Blackett, *The Mark of the Maker, a Portrait of Helen Waddell*, 1973). [HB]

WAIN, JOHN (1925–). Poet and novelist, born at Stoke-on-Trent, Staffordshire. He was educated at the High School, Newcastle-under-Lyme, and at St John's College, Oxford. A damaged eye kept him out of the forces and he became a wartime undergraduate among the small body of medical rejects and injured servicemen. As a pupil of C.S. Lewis (q.v.) he felt the force of the then vigorous Oxford Christian Literary movement associated with Lewis and Tolkien (q.v.), and Wain, himself a child of dedicated pacifist Anglican parents, has interesting things to say about these various formative influences (and how he eventually rejected them) in his autobiographical volume, *Sprightly Running* (1962). Wain was awarded a three-year research fellowship at St John's College in 1946 and in 1947 became also a lecturer in English at Reading University. In 1955 he took the difficult decision to forsake teaching for freelance writing. The genuine element of personal dedication and self-sacrifice involved in fleeing the securities of salary and pension, while at the same time setting his face against all vulgar recipes for cheap literary popularity, has sometimes assumed an abrasive dominance in his public thinking.

Wain's first novel, *Hurry on Down* (1953), follows the career of a young man unfitted for life at any social level by the combination of a working-class Midlands upbringing and a university education. 'I never rebelled against ordinary life: it just never admitted me, that's all', Charles Lumley finally claims after a series of false starts including window-cleaning, hospital-portering, car-delivery and drug-running. The picaresque presentation is often lively and amusing, and the study of the social misfit has fitful authenticity, but at times comic detachment seems to falter and one detects an injured authorial ego on the rampage. Wain has complained about the easy journalistic simplification that linked him, after *Hurry on Down*, with John Osborne and others as an Angry Young Man, but he is a writer with so many moral and social dislikes and disapprovals that the glib categorization is certainly understandable, and perhaps not wholly unjust. *Strike the Father Dead* (1962) is a later study in social rebellion, this time by the 17-year-old son of a redbrick university professor. *The Smaller Sky* (1967), a work of admirable economy and discipline, presents Arthur Geary, a scientist who can find release from tension only by living permanently on Paddington Station. *A Winter in the Hills* (1970), a more ambitious and cumbersome effort, takes us to a North Wales village where rabid Celtic nationalism and a heroic attempt to defend a one-man business (running a bus) against take-over are themes that allow crude values of mass-civilization to be contrasted with simple local and personal ideals. But the prose is sometimes undistinguished, goodies and baddies identify themselves at sight by their faces, and clichés like the heroine's caddish first husband with whom marriage has been a living death are embarrassing. In *The Pardoner's Tale* (1978) a disillusioned writer's dilemmas and aspirations are mirrored in those of his central character in a novel-within-the-novel, but again the book suffers from verbal flabbiness.

Wain has published several volumes of literary criticism and his biographical work, *Samuel Johnson* (1974), is a portrait of the writer he early identified as 'my favourite author, my moral hero' with whom as a young man he could identify in 'stoical resistance against hopeless odds' (*Sprightly Running*). But he regards his poems as 'the best things I have done' (op. cit.). *Mixed Feelings* appeared in 1951 and *A Word Carved on a Sill* in 1956. The latter fully established Wain as involved in the so-called 'Movement' which sought to replace the rhetoric of the romantic 1940s with disciplined, formalized verses (terza rima and villanelle are favourites) that have an aphoristic compactness, are charged with wit, and by quiet directness and polish underplay whatever moral gravity they may carry. Some readers find Wain's cleverness cold, his mannered graces archaic, but there is vitality and bite in his work at its best. *Weep Before God* (1961) brings the epigrammatic gift to maturity.

> A false coin dropped on a stone farmhouse floor
> Is heard as false: but every coiner knows
> This cannot happen on the boardroom carpet.

So he writes in 'A Boisterous Poem About Poetry', a verse credo of one who finds the poet's language the great antiseptic and antibiotic for minds rotted by slogans. The question remains whether he can himself escape the paradox that his own bundle of 'radical' postures is now sufficiently standardized to be vulnerable to an assault on slogans. 'A Song about Major Eatherley', a poem dealing with the subsequent fate of an American pilot who carried an atomic bomb to Nagasaki, is a case in point.

Wain's later attempt at wider-ranging work in a variety of verse forms, *Wildtrack* (1965), is disconcerting in its surface discreteness. *Feng* (1975), a long poem on a version of the *Hamlet* story, focuses on Feng, the 'Claudius' of the piece, a 'sick and hallucinated person who seizes power and then has to live with it'. *Poems for the Zodiac* (1980) is a collection of twelve poems accompanying twelve drawings by Brenda Stones. *Poems 1949–1979* (1981) is highly selective. Wain was Professor of Poetry at Oxford from 1973 to 1978. [HB]

WALCOTT, DEREK (1930–). Dramatist and poet, born in Castries, St Lucia, where he went to school before studying at the University of the West Indies, Kingston, Jamaica, and graduating in 1953. After working as a teacher and journalist in Jamaica, he has been, since 1959, founding director of the Trinidad Theatre Workshop and made various visits abroad.

Unlike most West Indian writers of his generation, Walcott did not migrate to Europe or the United States to establish himself as a man of letters, but dedicated himself to the task of working, from within, towards the creation of a genuine West Indian culture. This was not to be predominantly black, Indian or European, even though it meant fashioning a literary West Indian dialect from various patois, as well as using the English language associated with a metropolitan culture whose local adherents despised the home-grown as vulgar, 'every endeavour / as that of the baboon' ('At Last'). A taxing, almost disillusioning labour, it probably contributed to the steadily developing preference in his poetry for grey tints and salty moods. His earliest volumes of verse, *Twenty-Five Poems* (1948), *Epitaph for the Young* (1949) and *Poems* (1953?), were published in Trinidad, Barbados and Jamaica respectively. *In a Green Night: Poems 1948–1960* (1962) was the first of the collections published in London and New York which have established Walcott as the West Indian poet with the widest range of modulation and as one of the most gifted present-day poets writing in English, a reputation often recognized internationally, for instance by the Jock Campbell Award (1974) and the Welsh Arts Council International Writer's Prize (1980).

So far Walcott's poetic career would seem to fall into two main phases: the first tentative, rather 'literary', full of both ardour and uncertainty, a poetry of innocence, consisting of *In a Green Night*, *Selected Poems* (1964), *The Castaway* (1965), *The Gulf* (1969) and culminating in the splendid autobiographical poem *Another Life* (1973); the second, blossoming out of the integrative, summative experience of composing *Another Life*, and consisting of *Sea Grapes* (1976), *The Star-Apple Kingdom* (1980) and *The Fortunate Traveller* (1982), mature, often sombre or elegiac, a poetry of experience beyond disillusion offering great promise of further growth in craftsmanship. *Selected Poetry* (1981), edited by the younger poet Wayne Brown, is a sensitive choice from all these volumes, except the last. With its freer, more exploratory metrics, its more rigorous control of language, its drive towards greater simplicity of expression, *Another Life* undoubtedly takes Walcott into poetic maturity. K. Ramchand describes it as 'a record of a struggle to accept loss without having to doubt the value of what has been lost, and to cherish what has been gained'. Nevertheless, the evolution from early to mature work has been gradual and organic, anguished too, a steady refining away of verbal and rhythmic echoes from English poets of the earlier twentieth century, as Walcott has tuned idiom and versification into fit instruments for his ironic, antithetical, highly individual imagination.

The nature of the daunting task the young poet set himself (to create an authentic West Indian poetic in an undeniably metropolitan language) corresponded with his ability to imagine stark contrasts in some sort of balance, to confront both the European and the African in his family origins, to rage against Elizabethan sea-dog precursors of colonialism as 'Ancestral murderers *and poets*' (my italics), but to acknowledge 'That Albion too, was once / A colony like ours' and that, thus, 'All in compassion ends / So differently from what the heart arranged' ('Ruins of a Great House', *Green Night*). The word 'compassion' provides no facile resolution, but a complex ambivalence of attitude generated in the poem's entirety. Even the early 'A City's Death by Fire' (*Green Night*), about the disaster that engulfed Castries in 1948, exemplifies this faculty by holding against the shock of 'his wooden world' blazing the idea of 'Blessing the death

and the baptism by fire'. Despite the often surface simplicity of the words, much of Walcott's poetry is, in very unsimple ways, about the violent cultural and racial crucible of West Indian history; his most personal poems of self-definition include that history in his awareness of his own racial and small-island origins. Even far-distant political issues intrude into his being; so, in a poem on the Mau Mau rebellion in Kenya, his pity for both black and white victims of violence becomes a deeply personal problem: 'how choose / Between this Africa and the English tongue I love? / Betray them both, or give back what they give? / How can I face such slaughter and be cool?' ('A Far Cry from Africa', *Green Night*.)

The relationship between what he feels as his fragmented personality and the topography, history and everyday life of the West Indies finds fullest expression in *The Castaway* and *The Gulf*, the titles themselves hinting at the nature of his vision. His concurrent sense of artistic isolation from the common people and of great love for them, and his compassion for the sufferings of Arawak, Carib, African and Indian (even for the tropical exile of European masters), merge into a comprehensive celebration of the landscapes and seascapes that physically create the island limbos, parochialisms and rivalries, 'Our hammock swung between Americas' ('Elegy', *Gulf*), yet facing Africa and Europe. The many delicate passages of pictorial description that measure his own and his peoples' states of existence also, usually without sentimentality, certainly without mere glamour, sensitize the Caribbean landscape for occupation by the creative imagination. It is neither literary programme, nor personal 'ambition as a searing meteor', but a necessity forced upon Walcott's sensibility by a 'sun-stoned' climate, by 'The unheard, omnivorous / jaws of this rain forest' that have produced 'too much nothing here' ('Air', *Gulf*). In 'Crusoe's Journal' (*Castaway*) he sees his work as a Man Friday occupation, though shaping 'where nothing was / the language of a race'.

The sensibility is religious, in the least dogmatic sense, yet the mind is also astringently sceptical, another cause of his feeling exiled even within the Caribbean, as in 'Crusoe's Island' (*Castaway*) he longingly observes unsophisticated peasants responding to a church bell: 'And nothing I can learn / From art or loneliness / Can bless them as the bell's / Transfiguring tongue can bless'. The religious temper is found in numerous poems that with increasing artistic detachment meditate upon selfhood, love, time, death and private and public experience of all kinds; for instance, the title poem of *Sea Grapes*, composed around a classical Greek and Caribbean parallelism of theme and imagery, ends 'The classics can console. But not enough', while in 'The Cloud' and 'Adam's Song' he uses the Adam–Eve–Eden story to comprehend his modern perceptions and intuitions. Middle-aged perspectives come edging into *Sea Grapes* through his sceptical tones, which in poems like 'Party Night at the Hilton' and 'Dread Song' reserve for the political apostasy of Third World leaders more scorn and anger than he has spent upon imperialists. The title poem of *The Star-Apple Kingdom* is Walcott's fullest and most powerful single poem on the intimate connection between Caribbean (in this case Jamaican) history, geography and present political climate. The opening poem, 'The

Schooner *Flight'*, uses individual personae as representative, almost allegorical figures, thus establishing more clearly than before the close links between his poetry and his plays.

Ramchand declares 'that Walcott the poet is inseparable from Walcott the dramatist, and that a profound dialogue and a balance exist between the presences and problems explored in the social worlds created in his plays, and the dark internalizations of his poems'. *Henri Christophe* (prod and pubd 1950), *Henri Dernier* (pubd 1951), *Ione* (prod 1957, pubd 1954), *Drums and Colours* (prod 1958, pubd 1961) were published in the West Indies, the rest abroad: *The Dream on Monkey Mountain*, with *Ti-Jean and His Brothers*, *Malcochon* and *The Sea at Dauphin* (New York, 1971; London, 1972); *The Joker of Seville*, with *O Babylon* (New York, 1978; London, 1979); *Remembrance*, with *Pantomime* (1980). In his plays Walcott has evolved a drama based on such indigenous West Indian folk activities as singing, story-telling and dancing. They thus have an emphasis on bodily expression, which, however, reacts with richly metaphoric dialogue, frequently in verse, that draws discriminately upon colloquial West Indian speech, including phrases from the Creole French of St Lucia. 'What the Twilight Says', Walcott's 'Overture' to the *Monkey Mountain* volume, is an important and eloquent essay on the creative imagination in the West Indies, and the most illuminating introduction to his practice as a dramatist.   [AR]

WALEY, ARTHUR (1889–1966). Oriental historian and translator, born in Tunbridge Wells, Kent. He changed his surname from Schloss to his mother's maiden name in 1914. Educated at Rugby and Cambridge, he became Assistant Keeper in the British Museum Department of Prints and Drawings, and lectured in oriental studies at London University. He published many translations from Chinese and Japanese. They include *170 Chinese Poems* (1918), *More Translations* (1920), *The Nō Plays of Japan* (1921), *The Tale of Genji* (1925–32, six volumes) and *Chinese Poems* (1946). *The Tale of Genji* (*Genji-monogatari*), regarded as the greatest work in Japanese literature, is a lengthy eleventh-century novel of amorous adventure by Murasaki Shikibu. Waley also wrote books on Chinese art, history and philosophy. His scholarship is supported by rare feeling and insight as well as by sustained verbal felicity in translating, and he is an illuminating interpreter of the east.   [HB]

WALLACE, EDGAR (1875–1932). Popular novelist, born at Greenwich, London, the illegitimate son of an actress, Polly Richards. He joined the army at 18 and served in South Africa, where a poem to Rudyard Kipling he wrote for the *Cape Times* won him a meal with the great man – and the neglected advice, 'For God's sake, don't take to literature as a profession'. Wallace became *Daily Mail* correspondent, made a name as a journalist, then as the author of the mystery novel *The Four Just Men* (1905), the West African stories, *Sanders of the River* (1911) and *Bones* (1915), a flood of sensational thrillers, and such gripping plays as *The Ringer* (1926) and *On the Spot* (1930). He earned massive sums, yet ran himself heavily into debt by gambling and other extravagances. He sustained himself through days and nights of continuous work by drinking endless cups of sugared tea, and died of diabetes. (See Margaret Lane, *Edgar Wallace*, 1938.)   [HB]

WALLACE-CRABBE, CHRIS (1934–). Poet, born in Melbourne, Victoria, Australia, and educated at Melbourne Grammar School and at Melbourne University, where he now teaches English. His first book of poetry, *The Music of Division* (1959), showed his deep interest in politics and history at a universal level, as well as in their specific and complex reflection in present-day Melbourne. *In Light and Darkness* (1963) was followed by contributions to the anthology *Eight by Eight* and the editing of *Six Voices* (both 1963), the latter his selection from 'the six leading Australian poets today'. In 1967 he published *The Rebel General*, a further collection of his own work. The long poem 'Blood is the Water', in *Where the Wind Came* (1971), confronted the brutal human realities resulting from politics, and marked a new note in what had previously been largely restrained and consciously wrought academic poetry. *Selected Poems* (1973) was followed by two important books of cultural and critical essays, *The Australian Nationalists* (1971) and *Melbourne or the Bush* (1974), the latter a valuable personal introduction to the poet and his world as well as a perceptive analysis of Australian culture from the viewpoint of the practising author. In 1980 he published a book of poems entitled *The Emotions are Not Skilled Workers* and edited the collection of twentieth-century Australian verse, *The Golden Apples of the Sun*.   [PQ]

WALPOLE, HUGH (Sir) (1884–1941). Novelist, born at Parnell, Auckland, New Zealand, where his father, Somerset Walpole, future Bishop of Edinburgh, was incumbent. Hugh was sent home to boarding schools in England in 1893, but his father was appointed Principal of Bede College, Durham (a church training college), in 1898 and Hugh then became a day boy at Durham School. The superior attitude of the close to the community at Bede provoked a backlash twenty-five years later in Walpole's novel *The Cathedral* (1922). 'I think the Durham snobbery has been boiling in me for years', Hugh wrote to his mother while working on the book. He was at Emmanuel College, Cambridge, from 1903 to 1906 and got a third-class degree in history. Brief experience as a preparatory-school master at Epsom College, Surrey, provided the impulse for what is sometimes regarded as Walpole's most disciplined and perceptive book, *Mr Perrin and Mr Traill* (1911). Set in a Cornish boarding school, Moffat's, it shows inbred tension, staleness and frustration among masters whose early hopes have been eroded by time. Middle-aged Mr Perrin is one such. Young Mr Traill comes as his assistant and succeeds where he fails, becoming popular with the boys and getting engaged to the girl Perrin has secretly loved. Amid claustrophobic intensities of hostility and bitterness, Perrin's obsessions degenerate into mental disintegration. He tries to kill Traill, then sacrifices his own life in the attempt to save him. There is effective use of irony and some technical originality in presentation, but Henry James (q.v.) put his finger on the book's weakness: 'I don't quite recognize here the *centre of your subject*, that . . .

fixed point from which one's ground must be surveyed'.

In 1909 Walpole had set himself up as a writer in London and embarked on his lifelong career of getting to know the right people by approaches which his own generosity and good-nature seem to have made irresistible. The list of writers with whom he corresponded eventually included Henry James, Conrad (q.v.), Virginia Woolf (q.v.) and Arnold Bennett (q.v.). The latter twitted him amiably from above ('You know nothing' about style) while J.B. Priestley (q.v.) worshipped conveniently from below. Conversely Somerset Maugham (q.v.) pilloried him as the time-serving, snobbish novelist, Alroy Kear, in Cakes and Ale. During the war Walpole was in Russia, serving with a Russian medical unit in the Carpathians and later in a British propaganda bureau in Petrograd. Russian experience bore fruit in The Dark Forest (1916), which includes on-the-spot registration of the Carpathian campaign of 1915, and The Secret City (1919), a tale of Petrograd in the March revolution of 1917. Back in England Walpole served in the Ministry of Information until 1919 when he became his own master for life. Thereafter increasing literary success enabled him to enjoy a London home, a country house overlooking Derwent Water and triumphant tours of America. Jeremy (1919), a book about boyhood, had two sequels, Jeremy and Hamlet (1924) and Jeremy at Crale (1927). Jeremy introduces us to Polchester in Glebeshire, a cathedral city supposedly in the south west, but Durham as well as Truro and Polperro contributed to its topography. Polchester provides the setting for The Cathedral (1922) in which Trollope-style intrigue among ecclesiastics is embedded in heavy moralistic cartoonery. Archdeacon Brandon, a study in arrogance and selfishness which masquerades as devotion to the church, is unknowingly eroding the happiness of his wife and family. Yet the sledgehammer strokes with which he is ground into the dust have a too melodramatic obviousness. Characterization is unsubtle and fails to carry conviction. The occasional, incongruous intrusion of a narrating 'I' underlines James's point about the lack of a focusing-point in Walpole's work. Nevertheless Walpole has skill and fluency in story-telling and in the management of a diverse dramatis personae, and he exudes an air of professionalism. These qualities were pressed into service for a magnum opus about the Lake District, The Herries Chronicle. The first (and best) volume of the tetralogy, Rogue Herries (1930), traces the life of the Herries family in the eighteenth century, more especially of Francis Herries who settles in a wild farm in Borrowdale. A faintly Byronic figure, the family rogue, redeemed by devotion to his son and to his second wife, the girl Mirabell, he is the centre-piece in a gallery of standard romantic postures personified. Every ingredient in the romantic novel cookbook is aggregated and flavoured with historical name-dropping in a sequence of picture-postcard scenes. What impresses most is Walpole's extraordinary assimilative instinct evident in the range of his derivativeness – from Scott, the Brontës, Hardy and Galsworthy. Yet the sentimentality has a touchingly honest obviousness. Succeeding volumes, Judith Paris (1931), The Fortress (1932) and Vanessa (1933), bring the saga up to the twentieth century. But they do not gather vitality en route, and the mind boggles at Walpole's long-term plans for four further volumes covering the Elizabethan age, the Civil-War, James II and William III and Queen Anne periods. Death intervened. Walpole suffered from diabetes, was strangely careless about the prescribed diet and weakened his heart by erratic use of the insulin needle. He was knighted in 1937.

[HB]

WARNER, REX (1905–). Novelist, born in Birmingham, West Midlands, educated at St George's School, Harpenden, Hertfordshire, and at Wadham College, Oxford. He worked first as a schoolmaster, served in the Home Guard during the Second World War and became Professor of English at the University of Connecticut in 1963. Warner is a classical scholar whose output includes works of translation from Euripides, Aeschylus, Xenophon, Thucydides, Plutarch and Caesar. His early novels are exercises in allegory; his later fiction is historical biography. In The Young Caesar (1958) Julius Caesar tells his own story up to the close of his first consulate; Imperial Caesar (1960) is the sequel. Pericles the Athenian (1963) is a fictional biography and The Converts (1967) a novel of early Christianity. It is the earlier novels, however, that constitute Warner's main achievement as an imaginative writer. The Wild Goose Chase (1937) uses a symbolic method closely akin to Kafka's. 'Wild Goose, I made you a symbol of our Saviour' begins the poem inserted as epigraph. Three brothers set off by bicycle in pursuit of the Wild Goose. All cross the frontier into a land bound by totalitarian tyranny, whose deity is a stuffed wild goose. Bureaucracy and technology impose a deadly grip that keeps the urban masses and the peasantry in miserable servitude. The youngest brother, George, heads a peasant revolution in the name of comradeship, honesty, hard work and a Lawrentian preference for flesh and blood over intellect. For all its power to fascinate, passage by passage, the book as a whole is clumsily diffuse, its edges blunted by superfluity. But The Aerodrome (1941, reissued 1982) is a much finer piece of work and the nearest English equivalent to Kafka's The Castle. A stereotyped English village, dominated by rector and squire whose family lives are entangled in infidelity and corruption, stands for the shabby and decayed but untyrannical and traditional English way of life. The Air Force that first neighbours and then supplants it stands for ruthless, dehumanized efficiency. The hero, Roy, apparent son of the rectory, is recruited into the service of the Air Vice Marshal to negate 'the stupidity, the ugliness and the servility of historical tradition', 'to escape the bondage of time', and to obtain total mastery over self and environment. Warner manages to combine Orwellian clarity of political message with Kafkaesque sense of mystery and depth. The symbolism is not exhausted by political exposition but has disturbing moral and philosophical dimensions. Imaginative reach and allegorical inventiveness give the work an importance that prevailing naturalistic critical fashion has so far failed to reckon with. It is the most telling of three novels – they include also The Professor (1938) – which register the political stresses of the 1930s as urgently as did contemporary poets.   [HB]

WARNER, SYLVIA TOWNSEND (1893–1978). Novelist, short-story writer and poet, born in Harrow, Middlesex, the daughter of a schoolmaster, and privately educated. A musicologist, she was one of the editors of the standard *Tudor Church Music*. A left-winger politically, she went to Spain during the Civil War. Her poetry (*The Espalier*, 1925; *Time Importuned*, 1928; *Opus 7*, 1931) does not have the distinction of her prose. The first novel, *Lolly Willowes* (1926), subtitled *The Loving Huntsman*, tells of the 'conversion' of a well-to-do spinster aunt from being an inhibited piece of family furniture by the discovery that she is 'a witch by vocation'. In the Devil's service a woman can have 'a life of one's own, not an existence doled out to you by others'. The style is like Jane Austen's: mannered phrases and neatly turned sentences deftly sum up people and attitudes with the authorial accents of indulgent ironic amusement. The overturning of a settled fabric of life through the incursion of the fantastic or the supernatural is Warner's forte. Timothy Fortune, bank clerk, then missionary, in *Mr Fortune's Maggot* (1927), suffers a 'conversion' comparable to Laura Willowes's. In *Summer Will Show* (1936) Sophia Willoughby, the lady of Blandamer House, Dorset, has something of the frustrated spiritedness of George Eliot's Dorothea Brooke and Meredith's Diana Warwick ('It was boring to be a woman, nothing that one did had any meat in it'), and the quality of Sylvia Warner's thought and style make such comparisons natural. Sophia breaks out of her nineteenth-century social framework to become the comrade-in-arms of her husband's Parisian mistress in the 1848 Revolution. A woman 'brought up in a world policed by oughts', she discovers the 'intoxication of being mentally at ease'. *The Corner That Held Them* (1948), a book altogether quieter and drier in tone, chronicles the history of an English Benedictine convent in the fourteenth century. Though a work of fascinatingly detailed imaginative reconstruction, it lacks the dramatic impetus of the earlier novels. Warner was a writer of great subtlety and versatility. In addition to the eight novels, she wrote some dozen volumes of short stories (including *Elinor Barley*, 1930; *The Cat's Cradle Book*, 1940; *Winter in the Air*, 1955; and *The Innocent and the Guilty*, 1971) and a biography of T.H. White (q.v.). A collection of pieces originally written for *The New Yorker* and posthumously published as *Scenes of Childhood* (1981) sheds light fascinatingly on the upper-middle-class social background of her youth. At the time of her death she was preparing her *Collected Poems* (1982), now edited by Claire Harman. [HB]

WATERHOUSE, KEITH (1929–). Novelist, born in Hunslet, Leeds, West Yorkshire, the son of a greengrocer. He left Osmondthorpe County School, Leeds, at the age of 15 and gradually found his way into journalism, first in Yorkshire, then in Fleet Street. He travelled widely as a feature writer and has run a regular column in the *Daily Mirror*. Waterhouse made his name as a comic novelist with *There is a Happy Land* (1957) and *Billy Liar* (1959). The latter studies Billy Fisher, incorrigible addict of compulsive day-dreaming, of wishful self-aggrandizement in fantasy. Perpetually improvising his own fictional world and allowing it to intrude into actuality, Billy entangles himself in a network of impromptu opportunist fibbing.

Billy's home town, Stradhoughton, is a challengingly depressing environment inhabited by stage Yorkshiremen muttering their dry, ironic obliquities. Waterhouse pays the penalty of the comic writer who tries too hard. Satire· of indefatigable joke-men is apt to be too heavy-handedly jokey. Nevertheless his exploration of the conflict between dream and reality has perceptiveness. It recurs in *The Bucket Shop* (1968) in the study of William's vain attempt to latch on to the life of the trendies by running an antique shop; but the humour becomes forced, for too much is asked of the comic formulas. We meet Billy Liar in middle age, but by no means cured of his escapist fantasies, in *Billy Liar on the Moon* (1975). There is a selection of journalistic articles in *Mondays, Thursdays* (1976). Clement Gryce, the hero of *Office Life* (1978), gets a job at the central offices of a massive conglomerate, British Albion, and joins a conspiracy of employees trying to find out what they are employed in doing. [HB]

WATKINS, VERNON (1906–67). Poet, born in Maesteg, Mid-Glamorgan, Wales, educated at Swansea Grammar School, Repton School and Cambridge. Then, apart from wartime service in the RAF, he worked in Lloyds Bank, Swansea, until 1965. He was Visiting Professor at the University of Washington when he suddenly died. His first volume, *Ballad of Mari Lwyd* (1941), has for its title poem a dramatic treatment of the Welsh custom of carrying a wooden Grey Mare ('Mari Lwyd') from house to house on New Year's Eve and claiming refreshment by challenge to a rhyming contest. Later volumes include *The Lady with the Unicorn* (1948), *The Death Bell* (1954), *Cypress and Acacia* (1959), *Selected Poems 1930–1960* (1967) and *Fidelities* (1968). Watkins's lifelong friendship with Dylan Thomas (q.v.) is recorded in Watkins's *Dylan Thomas: Letters to Vernon Watkins* (1957), where Watkins observes that 'natural observation in poetry meant nothing to us without metaphysical truth'. Thus Watkins's dedication to poetry was that of a religious devotee who had caught a visionary glimpse of reality that transformed his estimate of the significance of time.

> History is a pageant, and all men belong to it.
> We die into each other: remember how many
> Confided their love, not in vain, to the same earth.
> 　　　　　　　　　　　　　　　　　　　　　('Triads')

Watkins saw in the Welsh landscape symbols of the eternal reality of which our time-ridden world offers but shadowy images. A prophetic sense of vocation as an interpreter of the truth gave him integrity of purpose ('For me neglect and world-wide fame were one', *Fidelities*) and it has led admirers to draw comparisons with Blake and Vaughan as well as with Yeats (q.v.). [HB]

WATSON, WILLIAM (Sir) (1858–1935). Poet, born in Burley-in-Wharfedale, West Yorkshire, on the edge of Ilkley Moor. *Wordsworth's Grave and Other Poems* (1890) won widespread approval. A writer of great accomplishment, Watson seemed all set to assume the mantle of Tennyson. His 'Lachrymae Musarum', published on Tennyson's death, is stately, deftly orchestrated rhetoric. That Watson did not succeed to the vacant laureateship (for which his anti-imperialist opposition to the Boer War was blamed) proved a lifelong disappointment. His aim was to sustain the rhythms, tone and attitudes of the past great – Milton, Wordsworth and Tennyson; but the carefully moulded, dignified verses too often lacked inspiration and the resistance to innovation proved arid. [HB]

WAUGH, EVELYN (Arthur St John) (1903–66). Novelist, born in Hampstead, London. His father, Arthur Waugh, was a literary journalist, distinctly conservative in taste, who wrote an autobiography, *One Man's Road*. His elder brother, Alec, at the age of 17 wrote a notorious novel attacking public schools, *Loom of Youth* (1917): the book made it impossible for Evelyn to follow Alec at Sherborne, and he was sent to Lancing instead. A church public school, Anglo-Catholic in persuasion, it was considered especially appropriate for a boy already deeply religious in temperament, though in fact Waugh lost his faith there, as he described in *A Little Learning: The First Volume of an Autobiography* (1964), a revealing record of his childhood, his father and his education. Waugh won a history scholarship to Hertford College, Oxford, where he fell for 'the prevalent illusion that a man of parts could idle for eight terms and at the end sit up with black coffee and master the required subjects in a few weeks'. He did not work, developed a 'mutual dislike' for his tutor, drank, got into debt, acquired a reputation for dandyism and for artistic trendiness, and finally 'wasted' time on study in his valuable last term – a matter of later regret since he only got a third anyway. Among the friends made at Oxford were several writers, including Harold Acton, Anthony Powell (q.v.), Henry Yorke (Green (q.v.)), Alfred Duggan (q.v.) and Cyril Connolly (q.v.): Harold Acton's *Memoirs* record the undergraduate life of the time which Waugh himself was to recapture in *Brideshead Revisited*. After Oxford he was briefly a student at Heatherley's Art School, then a schoolmaster at two private schools, the first of which, in Flintshire, though he found it 'depressingly well-conducted', provided in its second master the living model of the incredible Grimes of *Decline and Fall*. Waugh then turned his interest to cabinet making, so that it was as a student carpenter that he sought the hand of the Hon. Evelyn Gardner, daughter of Lord Burghclere, whom he married on the strength of his first book, *Rossetti: His Life and Works* (1928). It was published by Duckworth, but they found his novel, *Decline and Fall**, too shocking and Waugh took it therefore to Chapman and Hall, the firm of which his father was managing director. They issued it with a few expurgatory alterations in 1928. It is a riotously funny book, illustrated by the author's own line-drawings, and containing a lively pack of sharply delineated comic figures amongst whom the picaresque hero proceeds through a heady sequence of careering misadventures. But it was the second novel, *Vile Bodies* (1930), that made the sensation and the money. It chronicles the life of the young smart set in the 1920s. A decisive generation gap divides the bright young things from the old brigade. The party is the symbol of the new permissiveness. 'Oh, Nina, what a lot of parties', says Adam Fenwick-Symes, the novelist hero. 'Masked parties, Savage parties, Victorian parties, Greek parties, Wild West parties . . . all that succession and repetition of massed humanity. . . . Those vile bodies'. Adam's quest

for money to enable him to marry Nina is pursued in a world where money is acquired in casual, trivial and arbitrary ways. Waugh has become a novelist whose surrealistic sense of humour transmutes the stuff of biting social satire into comedy. There are characters common to *Decline and Fall* and *Vile Bodies* and indeed to *Black Mischief* (1932), a third comic novel, but *A Handful of Dust* (1934) anticipates a later, more serious, vein. Its idealistic hero, Tony Last, suffers a series of losses – his wife by infidelity, his son by a fatal accident, and then the ancestral home he loves. His physical and mental world having collapsed about him, he is fantastically involved in a quest to discover a lost city in South America, and his agony reaches a climax of incongruity in the faraway jungle. ('I will show you fear in a handful of dust' is a quotation from T.S. Eliot's *The Waste Land*.)

Waugh's first marriage ended in separation in 1929. In 1930 he became a Roman Catholic. After his first marriage was annulled by the church in 1936 he married Laura Herbert, granddaughter of the Earl of Carnarvon. He had published a biography of the Jesuit martyr *Edmund Campion* in 1935 and was to write a biography of Ronald Knox many years later (1959). He became an unapologetic, blusteringly aggressive Catholic flag-waver somewhat in the Chestertonian tradition. The conversion to Catholicism and the renewal of European war in 1939 determined the character of his later novels. *Put Out More Flags* (1942) turned his magnifying lens on the survivors of the hectic 1920s of his earlier books as they adapted themselves to the Phoney War 'before the Churchillian renaissance'. *Brideshead Revisited** (1945) was intended to show 'the operation of divine grace on a group of diverse but closely connected characters'. It works powerfully with the theme of divorce as a key point of collision between Catholic and secular morality. Waugh's alleged surrender in this book 'to the glamour of beauty, food, rank, love, church, society', not to mention 'fine writing' (Rose Macaulay, *Evelyn Waugh*, 1948) made it more popular with the public than with fastidious critics. Indeed the tendentious moral drift and the earnestness of tone apparent under its hilarities provoked regrets at the evident demise of the essentially comic satirist of the early novels.

Waugh's war service with the Royal Marines and his participation in a British Military Mission to Yugoslavia in 1944 provided material for his trilogy, *Sword of Honour: Men At Arms* (1952), *Officers and Gentlemen* (1955) and *Unconditional Surrender* (1961), in which he sought to do for the Second World War what Ford Madox Ford (q.v.) had done for the first in *Parade's End*. He presents an impressively monitored documentary of army life in which the pervasive humour is more genial and the authorial companionship more relaxed than heretofore. The interest is heavily masculine: the central theme is Guy Crouchback's epic pilgrimage through a war which begins as a love affair with the army, for he is a Catholic aristocrat of romantic impulse and deep integrity, and which proves ultimately to be a progress into the modern age and to a 'surrender' that has many facets. Waugh's other late novel, *The Ordeal of Gilbert Pinfold* (1957), had special interest for its frank and startling autobiographical content. Gilbert Pinfold is a successful writer to whom middle age (assisted by excessive use of drugs and drink) brings a nervous breakdown. He hears hallucinatory voices which plot against him. The escalating fantasies, involving organized surveillance, conspiratorial persecution and incrimination, are laughably grotesque yet they reflect in exaggerated form the victim's own image of himself. That image, presented in neat summary at the beginning of the novel, is a finely objectified self-projection by the author. Donat Gallagher has edited Waugh's journalism in *A Little Order* (1977), Michael Davie has edited his *Diaries* (1976) and Mark Amory has edited his *Letters* (1980). See also Christopher Sykes, *Eyelyn Waugh, A Biography* (1975).

Decline and Fall. Paul Pennyfeather, a 'blank-page' hero to whom things happen, sometimes fortunately but more often disastrously, has his career determined in both respects by his contacts with the English upper class. Sent down from Oxford for indecent behaviour after being forcibly debagged by drunken aristocratic louts, he is then employed at a hilariously bogus boarding school in Wales from whence he is whisked away to high life as the intended husband of a pupil's widowed parent, Margot Beste-Chetwynde. But the source of her wealth is the white-slave traffic, as Paul discovers when he is arrested on his wedding day and gaoled for his ingenuous part in assisting the transit of young ladies to 'cabaret' jobs in South America. Margot marries the Minister of Transportation instead and consequently wires are pulled and Paul is marvellously rescued from prison by a fake operation and 'death' which enable him to be smuggled abroad. There is pointed satire in the presentation of a corrupt, self-protective upper class that can rig the machinery of society to ensure that it is always other people who pay for its follies and vices both in fact and in reputation. But page by page, in the riotously comic antics on the human scene (at the school especially), satirical drive is often swamped under inspired tomfoolery. The cartoonery has a grotesque, Dickensian flavour: the dialogue has crisp ironic vitality.

Brideshead Revisited. Captain Charles Ryder (in peacetime a celebrated architectural painter) finds his regiment in the Second World War posted to Brideshead, seat of the Marquis of Marchmain with whose family his life has been inextricably involved since the Marquis's younger son, Sebastian Flyte, became his loved friend at Oxford twenty years earlier. The Flytes are Roman Catholics and Waugh shows the grip of their faith and their institutional practice surviving personal sinfulness and wilful apostasy. Charles Ryder, loved and cherished as he is by the family and valued for his personal integrity and unselfishness, is an agnostic, a spiritual outsider bewildered by the persisting intrusion of the church into their lives. The tragic climax of the book arises from the fact that Ryder and Julia, Sebastian's sister, fully discover their love for each other only years after the two have made incongruous and unhappy marriages. They become lovers; divorces are arranged and everything seems set for a happy ending in conventional twentieth-century secular terms when, after the old Marquis's deathbed reconciliation to the church, Julia's long-smouldering sense of Catholic obligation bursts into flame and she breaks with Ryder. The religious theme itself is forcefully articulated. The weakness of the book lies in the tendency to equate the aristocractic tradition, good living, good taste, and everything under threat from the mediocrity of modernity, with the Roman Catholic Church.   [HB]

WEBB, FRANCIS (1925–74). Poet, born in Adelaide, Australia, and educated at Christian Brothers' Schools in Sydney. After the war he was at Sydney University for a year and also spent time in Canada and England before returning to Australia to live. The linked fifteen-poem sequence, *A Drum for Ben Boyd* (1948), which had first been published in *The Bulletin* (q.v.) two years earlier, presented versions of the 'truth' about a mid-nineteenth-century Australian merchant venturer and in conception resembled 'voyager poems' by poets such as Kenneth Slessor (q.v.) and James McAuley (q.v.). Yet Boyd was no typical hero; the difficulty and complexity of a search, whether for truth or some more intangible, spiritual goal, is a recurrent theme in Webb's poetry. In the title poem of his second collection, *Leichhardt in Theatre* (1952), he turned to the eccentric explorer who also partly inspired *Voss* (1957) by Patrick White (q.v.). Over-ambitious in its range from tragedy to melodrama, the sequence nevertheless remains impressive, and in probing the explorer's inner doubts the poet maps issues to which he returned often in later works, notably in 'Eyre all Alone' from the 1961 collection, *Socrates and Other Poems*. Several other poems in *Leichhardt in Theatre* show him at his best, while *Socrates* contains 'A Death at Winson Green', an outstandingly moving example of his later work in which the physical setting perfectly embodies the spiritual issues. In his best work, as in this poem, the ordering through verse of his own personal suffering leads to perception of the underlying mysterious pattern of life itself.   [PQ]

WEBB, MARY (née Meredith) (1881–1927). Novelist, born at Leighton, Shropshire, and brought up in what she calls its 'magical atmosphere'. She married a teacher in 1912 but the two turned to market-gardening and Mary to writing novels. There was a long struggle against poverty; the books did not sell; the publisher was importuned for advances and loans (and once had his face slapped when he refused), but shortly after her death Stanley Baldwin, the Prime Minister, publicly eulogized her fifth novel, *Precious Bane* (1924), and it became a long-standing best-seller. In his farm amongst the isolated Ellesmere pools and ploughlands Gideon Sarn, hell-bent on making money, binds his sister Prue to himself in a life of unrelenting toil. Prue has an untreated hare-lip (Mary Webb's own affliction) but finds her soul mate nevertheless. The period is the early nineteenth century. A vein of gnarled rural archaism, appropriate to rough-hewn peasantry, enriches the style. The success of *Precious Bane* released a spate of 'primitive' rural fiction that was to be parodied by Stella Gibbons (q.v.) in *Cold Comfort Farm*.   [HB]

WELCH, DENTON (1915–48). Novelist, born in Shanghai, China, and educated at Repton School, from which he ran away at the age of 16. After a visit to his father in China he became an art student in London, but in 1935 he was knocked off his bicycle by a car and the damage to his spine slowly and painfully killed him. *Maiden Voyage* (1943), an autiobiographical novel covering school days, escape and the visit to China, is artlessly direct and unshaped: it carries an air of innocence and immaturity but registers the experience of the senses with remarkable acuteness. *In Youth is Pleasure* (1945) has been reissued (1982) with an introduction by John Lehmann (q.v.). It is a tenuous but characteristically limpid study of a schoolboy who spends a summer vacation at a country hotel. The adolescent's view of the world has a disturbing intensity. Death prevented the completion of *A Voice through a Cloud* (1950) which records a victim's response to his personal calamity. Jocelyn Brooke (q.v.) edited Welch's *Journals* (1952). [HB]

WELDON, FAY (1935-). Novelist, born in Alvechurch, Worcestershire, and a graduate of St Andrews University, married with three children. Her novels include *Female Friends* (1975), *Little Sisters* (1978), *Praxis* (1979) and *Puffball* (1980). They concentrate on the lives of postemancipation women who seem to have exchanged the toils of disciplined monogamy and externally imposed masculine domination for those of fecklessly damaging permissiveness and wilfully embraced subservience. Nature is at the back of it all. The disposition of good, unselfish women to allow themselves to be trampled on is only one side of the coin whose other face is motherhood. The sense of femininity rampant and combative coexists with that of femininity richly at peace in being fitfully cherished, indulged and impregnated. Promiscuity, careerism and disaffection seem to go hand in hand, yet no 'moral' is drawn. For the narrative technique encourages an existential focus upon the present for its own sake. Jerky, aggressive, often in the present tense and electrically alive with shocks, apophthegms and compulsive outbursts of feminine self-revelation or witty bitchiness, it interleaves dialogue, reflection, involuntary exclamation and detached, ironic commentary in a richly textured fabric. In presentation Fay Weldon tends to span the decades, assembling her story piece by piece in apparent chronological haphazardness. In *The President's Child* (1982) the expendability of women's interests is at issue, but handled with characteristic sportiveness. 'Feminism and high-class entertainment converge once more', Patricia Craig observes (*Times Literary Supplement*, 24.8.82). [HB]

WELLS, H.G. (Herbert George) (1866-1946). Novelist and sociological controversialist, born in the High Street, Bromley, Kent, the son of a feckless, failing shopkeeper who eked out a living by playing cricket. His mother Sarah, a woman of Northern Irish ancestry, had left domestic service to marry, and when Wells was 14 she escaped the now desperate financial struggle at home and went back to Up Park, near Midhurst, as housekeeper. Visits to his mother there gave Wells a view of the lives of the gentry. Sarah Wells had managed to send him to a dame school and to Bromley Academy before apprenticing him to a draper at Windsor. He did not give satisfaction and was dismissed. After various subsequent false starts and a second abortive apprenticeship to a draper, at Southsea, he became a pupil teacher at Midhurst, studied hard in the evenings and in 1884 won a scholarship to the Normal School of Science at South Kensington. There the lectures of T.H. Huxley made a

deep impression on him ('the greatest man I was ever likely to meet') and he was excited to have reached 'the fountain head of knowledge'; but the diversity of his interests, a bout of tuberculosis, and his temperamental restlessness militated against examination success and he did not graduate until 1890. Meantime he had started teaching and held a series of posts, since his schoolmastering was chequered by intermittent illness. In 1895 he was firmly launched on a literary career by the publication of *The Time Machine*, *The Wonderful Visit* and *The Stolen Bacillus* (short stories). By 1896 he was making over £1000 a year; thereafter his annual income touched £50,000 at its peak and his output of books eventually totalled over a hundred. Scientific study and social radicalism gave substance to his imaginative work and his personal experience was exhaustively drawn upon: much of Wells's fiction is transfigured autobiography. His remarkable sex life played its part. Wells fell in love with his cousin Isabel and married her in 1891. 'After six "engagement" years of monogamic sincerity and essential faithfulness, I embarked, as soon as I was married upon an enterprising promiscuity', he wrote in his lively *Experiment in Autobiography* (1934). The girl involved, Ethel Kingsmill, was the first of a long series of women on whom Wells's voracious sexual appetite and his romantic idealism fastened for appeasement and fulfilment. His elopement with Catherine Robbins, who became Mrs Wells in 1895 (he called her 'Jane'), provided him until her death with a devoted and loyal anchorage at home, but the adventures continued. The affair with young Amber Reeves, by whom he had a child, shocked members of the Fabian circle that had brought the two together, and the scandal intensified the provocative notoriety of Wells's outspoken novel *Ann Veronica** (1909) in which the heroine offers herself to her biology tutor as his mistress. Rebecca West (q.v.) was 19 when she reviewed his permissive novel *Marriage* (1912) and made his acquaintance. Two years later their son Anthony West was born.

Wellsian science fiction began with *The Time Machine* (1895), a book of seminal importance. Wells forsook the serious scientific canons accepted by Jules Verne for the realm of fantasy. 'I make use of physics. He invents!' Verne said. The Time Traveller travels forward in time in a machine he has invented and has hair-raising adventures in the Thames Valley as it will be in AD 802,701. The earth is a garden, nature has been subjugated, disease wiped out. But man has become differentiated into two species, beings of the Upper World, Eloi, and subterranean man, the Morlocks. These are the old haves and have-nots, aristocracy and mechanical servants, and they have degenerated into mere beautiful futility on the one hand and cannibalism on the other. In the abolition of danger and trouble, the answering human qualities of vigour and versatility have been lost too. *The Wonderful Visit* (1895), *The Invisible Man* (1897), *The War of the Worlds* (1898), *The War in the Air* (1908) and, much later, *The Shape of Things to Come* (1933) are exercises in similar genre. They gathered prestige from Wells's knack of prophesying developments that later events realized or made more plausible. But technological advance and the increasing sophistication of science fiction have now blunted the edge of Wellsian fantasy.

There remains a small body of early novels that keep

their freshness and a handful of short stories, fanciful and inventive in substance (see *The Country of the Blind*, 1911). The novels are social comedies and they evoke the feel of their age with vivacity and candour. 'Whatever Wells writes is not only alive but kicking', Henry James (q.v.) observed. The bubbling brightness can stale, the bouncing jocularity can pall, but the authenticity of *Love and Mr Lewisham* (1900), for instance, is exciting on historic and personal grounds. The book traces Lewisham's arduous struggle to rise by education, and wryly elaborates a conflict between ambition and love in which the latter is happily victorious. The emotional pattern is coherent and central: social theorizing is as yet an enrichment, not an obsession. *Kipps** (1905) is neatly homogeneous, though wider in its human range and social dimensions. *Tono-Bungay* (1909) ('I warn you this book is going to be something of an agglomeration') is a hotchpotch, but a versatile and invigorating one. 'Tono-Bungay' is an all-purpose patent medicine, 'slightly inferior rubbish', that makes a fortune by effective sales promotion – 'a monstrous payment for courageous fiction, a gratuity in return for the one reality of human life – illusion'. Like *Kipps* and *Love and Mr Lewisham*, the book is shot through with autobiography. So too is *The History of Mr Polly** (1910), a high-spirited study of a lower-middle-class failure who leaps out of the rut of respectability to find self-fulfilment. *Mr Britling Sees it Through* (1916) proclaims its purpose. 'This story is essentially the history of the opening and of the realization of the Great War as it happened to one small group of people in Essex, and more particularly as it happened to one human brain.' The British and the Britling quality are equated as the changing mood on the home-front is explored.

Wells's many literary acquaintances included Shaw (q.v.) and Conrad (q.v.), Henry James (q.v.) and Gissing, and above all Arnold Bennett (q.v.) whom he called 'the best friend I ever had'. He was in many respects a wayward personality, turbulent in spirit and perhaps rootless at heart. 'He always seemed to be coming from somewhere rather than going anywhere', G.K. Chesterton (q.v.) said (*Autobiography*). He came to believe in the novel as a medium of argument and persuasion in the cause of social development. This was not a recipe for artistic achievement, and hasty over-productiveness damaged him as a thinker, but among the notable novels of social analysis are *The New Machiavelli* (1911), which contains caricatures of contemporaries such as Sidney and Beatrice Webb, and *The World of William Clissold* (1926), a three-volume exercise in setting the world to rights.

Kipps. Artie Kipps is brought up by his uncle and aunt and becomes an apprentice draper, undergoing the experience of Wells's own boyhood. His early love for Ann Pornick, the girl next door, is forgotten, and he falls in love with the evening-class instructress, Helen Walsingham, a member of the educated class to which he aspires. Out of the blue comes an inheritance of £24,000 from his grandfather (Kipps is illegitimate and his father dead). The incongruities, human and social, produced by sudden accession to wealth are explored with humour and satire. The attempt to turn Kipps into a 'gentleman' fails, he rediscovers Ann, and he runs out of his engagement to Helen Walsingham just in time to save his happi-

ness, but not his fortune, which has been left in charge of Helen's brother, a solicitor. He has embezzled it and absconded. Fortunately a competence remains and a share which Kipps generously bought in a play turns lucky. The irrelevance of wealth to happiness is a theme. The absurdly arbitrary nature of its distribution is another. But the light authorial touch and the ingenuous likeableness of hero and heroine give the book its charm.

Ann Veronica is a protest novel against the domestic and economic servitude of women. Ann Veronica Stanley, a 21-year-old biology student, repressed in the 'wrappered life' of her middle-class suburban home by her widowed father (a solicitor) and her aunt, rebels and leaves home to fend for herself in London. Involvement with the Fabians, then with a suffragette demonstration, culminates in a prison sentence. Goaded into spirited rejection of current mores, she offers herself to the man she really loves, her biology tutor, who is separated from his wife, and escapes with him to happiness. Though Wells too often makes his point at the expense of unconvincing caricatures of conventional respectability, Ann Veronica herself is a finely realized study who learns the hard way that neither her own nature nor the notions of the idealistic feminists are quite what they seemed.

The History of Mr Polly. The theme is that of the downtrodden, lower-middle-class victim of routine and privation who has never quite lost his romantic dreams and impulsively throws off the shackles in middle life. Alfred Polly is suffering from physical and imaginative indigestion, body and mind having been badly nourished. Fifteen years a failing shopkeeper (like Wells's father), at loggerheads with Miriam, his wife, and face to face with bankruptcy, he plans to commit suicide and burn his shop so that his widow can collect the insurance. The fire succeeds, not the suicide, and Polly becomes a hero in rescuing a neighbour. He clears out nevertheless and finds fulfilment as odd-job man at a country pub where the landlady has to be protected from a criminally psychopathic nephew called 'Uncle Jim'. By coincidence Miriam believes that her husband is drowned, and she starts a tea-shop on the strength of the life-insurance benefit. The book makes a serious point about the social absurdity and waste implicit in 'that vast mass of useless, uncomfortable, under-educated, under-trained, and altogether pitiable people we contemplate when we use that inaccurate and misleading term, the Lower Middle Class'. Its strength lies in unfailing liveliness and good humour rather than in any notable psychological validity.

[HB]

WENDT, ALBERT (1939–). Novelist, short-story writer and poet, born in Western Samoa, an area of which he tries to present in his writings 'an honest view . . . as far as I can'. After elementary school in Samoa, Wendt gained a government scholarship to New Zealand and eventually returned to Apia in 1975 with an MA in history from Victoria University, Wellington. Since 1974 he has been at the University of the South Pacific in Suva, but feels that he 'can't live away from Samoa for too long'. *Sons for the Return Home* (1973) was the first novel by a Western Samoan and has (on his own analogy) a Camus-like sense of man's indomitable spirit in the hero: 'his life is a series of new beginnings. . . . He refuses to be turned into a tame Pacific Islander'. The stories in *Flying Fox in a Freedom Tree* (1974) are 'modern fables' set mostly in 1950s Samoa ('pre-Independence, that is') and a strong sense of place was also evident in the poems of *Inside Us the Dead* (1976), a collection at times painful in its charting of disillusion and distaste but always innovative and arresting. Wendt says he has 'learned a lot about the writing of prose from writing poetry' and certainly *Pouhuili* (1977) had remarkable tautness in its exploration of the uncharted borderland between reason and madness, existential constriction and freedom. *Leaves of the Banyan Tree* (1978) was a longer work in both bulk and time span which incorporated *Flying Fox in a Freedom Tree* as its central section. The book traces the life and culture of a small community over three generations; 'the whole concept is Faulknerian'. The political and cultural complexity of his terrain is important for Wendt, and he writes with a historical awareness rooted in the here and now: 'I am of two worlds, but I do belong to the South Pacific'. [PQ]

WESKER, ARNOLD (1932–). Dramatist, born in the East End of London into a Jewish working-class family. His father was a Russian tailor and his mother a Hungarian. Wesker's numerous early jobs included furniture-making, plumbing, farm-labouring, building and kitchen work. His play *Chicken Soup with Barley* (prod 1958), the first of a trilogy, presents a Jewish communist household in the East End. The first act takes place in October 1936 on the day of a provocative march by Mosley's fascists through East London which left-wing workers resisted and which terminated in violence. Atmosphere and technique are reminiscent of O'Casey's *Juno and the Paycock* (q.v.). In acts 2 and 3 the decades pass and by the end of the play the 1956 Hungarian rising has been squashed. Harry Kahn, the stereotyped inert, easygoing, unheroic father, has become paralysed; Sarah his wife, the magnificent, indomitable matriarch, sustains her belief in the cause, while her son Ronnie begins to feel that 'political institutions, society – they don't really affect people that much' and daughter Ada opts for the simple life in rural Norfolk. *Roots* (1959) then takes us to Norfolk to a family into which Ronnie Kahn is about to be married; but Beatie Bryant, his girl-friend of three years' standing, cannot shake off her innate, inherited peasant nullity when it comes to ideas, culture and intellect, and Ronnie backs out at the last moment. *I'm Talking About Jerusalem* (1960), the last of the three plays, traces the failure of Ada and her husband Dave in their attempt to live by making tasteful furniture in a Norfolk cottage devoid of mod cons and so to build Jerusalem in England's green and pleasant land. Wesker has thus entangled with his capitalist–socialist antithesis dichotomies between the city and the country, mechanization and craftsmanship, media-infected illiteracy and traditional culture. In fact Wesker tried to do something about the relationship between the artist and socialist society by establishing Centre 42, which was designed to revive popular arts with trade union co-operation, but which failed to get the kind of trade union involvement he had visualized. *Chips With Everything* (1962) is a bait-the-establishment set-

piece showing an anti-authoritarian RAF recruit corrupted into conformity. *Their Very Own and Golden City* (prod 1965) presents another failure to build the New Jerusalem by tracing the working-out of an architect's socialist ideal of building six Golden Cities co-operatively owned. *The Friends* (1970), an exercise in group neurosis, is the work of a Wesker who seems disillusioned with rationality as well as with the unresolved dilemma: 'You can't come to the people and claim that the things you like are superior to the things they like, because that will place you in a class that you're asking *them* to overthrow'. See *The Plays*, two volumes (1976–7). [HB]

WEST, REBECCA (Dame) (1892–1983). Novelist and critical thinker, born in County Kerry, Ireland, as Cicily Isabel Fairfield. She married Henry Maxwell Andrews in 1930. She adopted her pseudonym from the heroine of Ibsen's *Rosmersholm*. She was educated at George Watson's Ladies College, Edinburgh, came to London after leaving school and made her mark as a journalist advocating female suffrage and other advanced causes. Her meeting at the age of 19 with H.G. Wells (q.v.) led to the birth of the writer Anthony West in 1914 and to a long entanglement which she terminated by ultimatum in 1923. 'He could leave Jane and marry her; go on living with her with a guarantee of £3000 a year; or say goodbye. She knew that the last was the only possible choice.' (N. and J. Mackenzie, *The Time Traveller, The Life of H.G. Wells*, 1973.)

Rebecca West's first novel, *The Return of a Soldier* (1918), a war novel with a feminist emphasis, deals with amnesia due to shell-shock, which throws the victim, a married man, mentally back to his former sweetheart of fifteen years before. *The Judge* (1922) centres first on Ellen Melville, an Edinburgh girl mentally caught up in advanced suffragist and socialist causes. A little volcano of suppressed instinct, frustrated idealism and dammed-up individuality, she falls in love with the somewhat unconvincing neo-Byronic Richard Yaverland. The second half of the novel relates the life of Richard's mother, wronged village girl, seduced by the squire, raped by his butler, and now possessively and reciprocally fixated on Richard, the squire's son. 'He cannot love Ellen because he loves me too much', she confesses, before removing herself by suicide. 'Every mother is a judge who sentences the children for the sins of the fathers.' Social awareness and philosophic dimension are evident, but, for all its intensities and its thoughtfulness, the book is sprawlingly diffuse and descends to melodrama.

Rebecca West's non-fiction output includes the study *St Augustine* (1933), *The Meaning of Treason* (1949) – on issues raised by the trial of William Joyce ('Lord Haw Haw') who broadcast German propaganda to Britain during the Second World War – and *The Court and the Castle, A Study of the Interrelations of Political and Religious Ideas in Imaginative Literature* (1958), which argues against romantic notions of human perfectibility by natural ability and accepts the cruelty and irrationality of man's situation in purely human terms. *The Fountain Overflows* (1957) is probably Rebecca West's best novel. An unmistakable and powerful autobiographical vein runs through the picture of the Aubrey family. The girlhood of Rose Aubrey and her sisters is registered with great sensitivity and humour and, individually, the studies of the two parents are shrewd and penetrating. Piers, the brilliant father, selfishly hopeless with money and compulsively unhelpable, is fascinatingly portrayed from the child's angle. Individual facets of the novel – psychological, sociological, philosophical – give it remarkable richness and depth, and the observation is Dickensian in range and acuity. Rebecca West's weakness as a novelist is the lack of focus: she does so many different things in the same book (and does them well) that one cannot delimit her fictional genre. Her 85th birthday was marked by the publication of *Rebecca West: A Celebration Selected from her Writings* with an Introduction by Samuel Hynes (1977). A subsequent resurgence of interest in her work is evidenced by the reissuing of *The Judge* and *The Return of the Soldier* in 1982, the filming of the latter and the publication of the *The Young Rebecca: Writings of Rebecca West 1911–1917* (1982), a collection of her articles, essays and miscellaneous pieces, edited by Jane Marcus.   [HB]

WHITE, PATRICK (1912–). Novelist, born in London during one of his parents' visits to Europe. Born into a well-established Australian family, he was next in England as a 13-year-old pupil to be 'ironed out' (his own phrase) at Cheltenham College. Two years spent working on his father's lands followed before White returned to England again, this time to read modern languages at Cambridge University. He was already writing novels and when he came down from Cambridge in 1936 drama was also a strong interest; two plays had been staged in Sydney. Until the outbreak of the Second World War he lived in London. The painter Roy de Maistre was a close friend – 'he taught me to write by teaching me to look at paintings and get beneath the surface' – and White's first published novel, *Happy Valley* (1939), was dedicated to de Maistre. His second book, *The Living and the Dead* (1941), vividly portrayed elements of the London scene that he knew so well, but the war years were to be spent in the intelligence section of the Royal Air Force, mainly in the Middle East, Palestine and Egypt. The final stages of the war took him to Greece, 'where perfection presents itself on every hand', and it was here that he met Manoly Lascaris, with whom he has lived since his return to Australia in 1946. Family tradition and personal experience gave him a rich awareness of European life which he exploited brilliantly in *The Aunt's Story* (1948), begun in England. He had also travelled extensively in the United States before returning to Australia, and this spiritual odyssey of a spinster, from childhood in Australia through travels through 'the aching wilderness of Europe' to the 'pathetic presumption of the white room' in an American mental institution, reflects the spiritual unease of both the writer and the times. The early novels were well received in London and his decision to return 'home, to the stimulus of time remembered' was taken to avoid the danger, as he saw it, of 'ceasing to be an artist and turning into that most sterile of beings, a London intellectual'. Initially he worked a smallholding at Castle Hill, an area which was then on the rural outskirts of Sydney, but out of his fresh encounter with Australian society grew another novel, *The Tree of Man* (1955); 'it was the

exaltation of the average that made me panic most'. The book took the clichés of Australian 'dun-coloured realism' – a pioneer's struggle against drought, bush fire and flood – and raised them to the level of myth in its charting of the intense spiritual life of Stan Parker, an apparently 'average' farmer. In *Voss* (1957) he re-created both the times and inner history of Ludwig Leichardt, a nineteenth-century German explorer who disappeared while trying to lead an expedition across Australia. The novel attempted (in White's own words) to convey 'the textures of music, the sensuousness of paint' and was a work of striking historical scope yet with profound relevance to contemporary Australia – 'A pity that you huddle', said the German, 'your country is of great subtlety'. Although a sharp depiction of local rural landscape has remained an intrinsic feature of his work, *Riders in the Chariot* (1961) marked a turning to the city as focus at a time when White himself moved from Castle Hill, which had been engulfed by suburban sprawl, to Centennial Park within the city of Sydney proper. The concluding sections of both *The Tree of Man* and *Riders in the Chariot* reflect this change. The tragic complexity of recent European history also continued to inform his writing, although the main focus is always Australian, and it is this rich awareness which helps to give his books a universality which complements his vivid satiric sense. A fine collection of short stories, *The Burnt Ones* (1964), illustrated this within the strict demands of a form which served to purge his style of its occasional excesses. Another collection, *Four Plays*, was published the following year and marked the end of his experiments with drama – 'your novel might last, but your performance won't'. *The Solid Mandala* (1966) focused on 'the poor unfortunates' in a suburban setting, while in *The Vivisector* (1970), dedicated to the contemporary Australian painter Sidney Nolan, the artist-figure almost always present in his work occupies centre stage. In this book the call of Europe, the beauty yet vulgarity of Australia as Hurtle Duffield sees it, and the all-demanding yet therefore potentially destructive needs of the artist are wrought in White's compassionate, but often humorous, presentation into a rich and varied work. *The Eye of the Storm* (1973) takes a bed-ridden but once beautiful lady as its central figure, extending a concern with old age, its horrors and compensations, which was already apparent in *The Vivisector*, where the artist's final vision comes only after the 'stroke' of God. A collection of six 'shorter novels and stories', *The Cockatoos*, appeared in 1974 while the novel *A Fringe of Leaves* (1976) marked a return to an Australian historical setting in a further exploration of the values and limitations of 'civilization' through physical and spiritual suffering. White returned successfully to drama with the 1977 production of *Big Toys*, while Europe was the setting for the highly wrought, though not always successful, novel, *The Twyborn Affair* (1979).

In 1973 White was awarded the Nobel Prize for Literature, an event which confirmed his importance within contemporary writing in English but also points to his special significance for Australian literature. No other single Australian writer has produced such a volume of varied and demanding works which, while they are all concerned with the fate of the individual in an alien and largely hostile environment, spiritual as well as geographical, nevertheless also embrace an infinitely documented spectrum of Australian society. If, at the highest level, his concern has been to explore the unknown depths of the human psyche and to stretch the limits of the novel form in so doing, at the immediate level his writings have amply proved the inexhaustibility of the local setting. *Flaws in the Glass: A Self-Portrait* was published in 1981. [PQ]

WHITE, T.H. (Terence Hanbury) (1906–64). Novelist, born in Bombay, India, the son of a District Superintendent who was born in Ireland. Father and mother were at loggerheads: the father took to drink; the mother was a jealous, demanding woman. 'She managed to bitch up my loving women', White wrote later in his diary, and it may well be that the study of the jealous, selfish and possessive Morgause in *The Queen of Air and Darkness* bears the burden of his feeling for her. However, from 1911 the boy had six years of more settled English upbringing with his maternal grandparents. He was at Cheltenham College from 1920 to 1924, hating the crude dragooning but finding a sympathetic master (C.F. Scott) to encourage him in writing in the sixth form. He went up to Queen's College, Cambridge, in 1925 and read English. Illness overtook him and, when tuberculosis was diagnosed, he interrupted his Cambridge studies and spent several months in Italy; but he got a first-class degree in 1929. He had already published a volume of poems, *Loved Helen* (1929), and was soon at work on another book, *Three Lives* (one of them was that of Joanna Southcott, the eighteenth-century religious fanatic), but it did not achieve publication. He taught in a preparatory school, wrote fiction and began to pursue expensive upper-class sports, starting with hunting. From 1932 to 1936 he was head of the English Department at Stowe and was soon shooting and fishing as well as captivating his pupils by stimulating teaching and indeed by his publishers' careless revelation of the secret of the pseudonym ('James Aston') under which he had written the novel *They Winter Abroad* (1932). *Farewell Victoria* (1934), in its study of the sufferings of a patient, uncomplaining stable groom, reveals 'his old-fashioned esteem for goodness and faithfulness' (Sylvia Townsend Warner, *T.H. White*, 1967). A Surtees-type novel, *Earth Stopped* (1934), had a sequel, *Gone to Ground* (1935), but White's first real success was *England Have My Bones* (1936), a book pervaded by his passion for outdoor sports. He left Stowe for solitary life in a Buckingham cottage in 1936.

Thereafter White's mode of life was an extraordinary one. Though he intermittently roamed about, staying in hotels, he spent long periods living alone but in the company of dogs to which he became so passionately attached that the death of his setter, Brownie, had the effect on him of a close personal bereavement. Among his animal pets were hawks. He experimented in training them in the proper tradition of falconry, and his first such experience was recorded in *The Goshawk* (1952). White's magnum opus, the Arthurian tetralogy *The Once and Future King*★ (1958), began with *The Sword in the Stone* (1938), whose success at home and in the USA transformed White's financial position. In 1939 he went to Ireland, intending a brief visit, but settled down in a farmhouse in County Meath, and the war was over when he returned to England to isolate himself in a cottage on the fell top in Swaledale. From there, in 1946, he moved to the Channel Islands and settled in Alderney for the rest of his days. Of *The Sword in the Stone* White at first said, 'It seems impossible to determine whether it is for grown-ups or children', but the succeeding volumes seem to presuppose an adult readership. A fifth book in the series, *The Book of Merlyn* (1977), remained unpublished during White's lifetime as not matching up to the others in quality. The quartet was transmuted into an American musical, *Camelot*, in 1960, much to White's enrichment. His other works include *Mistress Masham's Repose* (1947), in which descendants of Lilliputians brought home by Gulliver play a part; *The Elephant and the Kangaroo* (1948), in which an angel descends down the chimney into an Irish home to warn of a new flood; *The Book of Beasts* (1954), a translation of the Roxburgh Bestiary ('a genuine, though unimportant little bit of useless scholarship on which I have now spent in a scatter-brained way twelve years of love'); and *The Master* (1957) ('my Treasure Island story').

White was a curiously unpredictable personality, intensely aware of his moments of joy and of his recurring periods of unhappiness. He was given to sudden rages and sought refuge from his deep underlying unease in fitful bouts of heavy drinking. 'A good man with bad patches of him', Siegfried Sassoon (q.v.) averred. 'Some exuberant demon takes control of him and plays havoc with his spiritual stability.' He died on board ship after a highly successful lecture tour in America.

The Once and Future King is a tetralogy of novels in which White recasts material from the Arthurian cycle. The parts are *The Sword in the Stone* (1938), *The Queen of Air and Darkness* (first called *The Witch in the Wood*, 1940), *The Ill-Made Knight* (1941) and *The Candle in the Wind* (1958). When issuing the books together in 1958 White revised the earlier volumes. The setting is 'medieval', richly informative and detailed in respect of the appurtenances and occupations of fine life (there is much fascinating detail about jousting, tilting, hawking and the like), imaginary in respect of characters and historical context (Robin Hood and Maid Marian appear among the cast) and idealized in respect of action and ethos. *The Sword in the Stone* tells of young Arthur's upbringing at the side of Kay in the castle of Kay's father, Sir Ector. Arthur's identity is unknown. He is nicknamed 'The Wart', but he has Merlyn for tutor and his eccentric but effective education includes personal transformations that enable him to have first-hand experience of life with fish, birds and beasts. Merlyn, a wizard whose pots cheerfully wash themselves up, is moving backwards through time and therefore remembers the days of top hats and possesses the 14th edition of the *Encyclopaedia Britannica*. His past is other people's future. Arthur becomes king at the end, having alone proved capable of taking the sword from the stone. *The Queen of Air and Darkness* centres on the 'Orkney clan' from whom destruction ultimately overtakes the king. Morgause is at once mother of Agravaine by Lot, her husband, and mother of Mordred by Arthur (whom she seduces and who is unaware that she is his half-sister). Agravaine and Mordred embody the retribution which is to destroy the king's great work. Conversely the second book also shows the king's work launched in the establishment of the Round Table. Arthur's plan is to 'harness Might so that it works for Right' by means of an order of chivalry. There is a light and lively flavour about the first book and a good deal of cheerfully pantomimic horseplay in the second book (see the Questing Beast especially), but the tone gradually changes and *The Ill-Made Knight* is an intensely moving reconstruction of the love between Lancelot and Guenever. A few of Lancelot's quests are recounted, for 'they were not made to win him reputation. They were an attempt to escape from Guenever'. Lancelot's personal dilemma is analysed with sharpness and subtlety. White meanwhile traces the moral change at Camelot as the use of might to serve right degenerates into a chivalric competitiveness that is a game in itself, carried on for its own sake. ('It has turned into sportsmanship ... Games-Mania', Arthur complains.) Then, in the next stage, when the country of Grammarye has been civilized and 'the ends have been achieved', 'there is nothing for them to use their might on' and the knights begin to go 'to rot'. Hence the re-invigorating spiritual quest initiated by Arthur, the quest for the Holy Grail, which is achieved but in which the best knights go to their deaths. *The Candle in the Wind* traces the final disintegration. Mordred and Agravaine compel the king to take public note of the queen's adultery. Lancelot is banished to France. Arthur faces the last battle with Mordred as the book ends.

White chooses his themes from Malory carefully (more or less ignoring Tristram and Iseult, for instance) and presses them into relationship within a moral design. He makes Arthur's kingdom at its best a Merry England of one's dreams, over against which there are 'mythological families such as Plantagenets' and 'legendary kings like John'. 'I am trying to write of an imaginary world which was imagined in the 15th century', White said. 'I allow anachronisms up to the 15th century.' But White's view sweeps the real centuries from time to time and, while Arthur is the embodiment of Englishry, Mordred is not only 'the invincible Gael' but also more particularly a rebel of the same breed as the IRA. Moreover White often turns with scathing irony to contrast twentieth-century permissiveness with the medieval ethic of idealized chastity and monogamy. 'In those days people loved each other for their lives, without the conveniences of the divorce court and the psychiatrist.'   [HB]

WHITING, JOHN (1917–63). Dramatist, born in Salisbury, Wiltshire, educated at Taunton, Devon. He trained at RADA, became a repertory actor, served in the Royal Artillery from 1939 to 1944 and managed thereafter to achieve a series of commercial failures in the theatre with plays whose evident quality puts him among the handful of significant postwar playwrights. His last work, *The Devils* (prod 1961), about a case of demonic possession among seventeenth-century nuns, and based on Aldous Huxley's (q.v.) *The Devils of Loudon*, provided a brief taste of success before Whiting died of cancer at the age of 45. *Saint's Day* (prod 1951) won the Festival of Britain play competition. The sombre theme (that it is 'the purpose of any memory – of any experience – to give foundation to the state of death') is explored with some profundity but with fatal lack of clarity in dramatic terms. *Marching Song* (prod 1954) makes more conces-

sions to dramatic explicitness, but the personae remain inadequately identifiable. The play studies the clash between private reality and public face. A disgraced general in a defeated European country chooses sacrificial suicide after involvement in a moral pilgrimage whose criteria (unlike those of Eliot's Becket, for instance) seem to be manufactured to meet the changing moment. *The Gates of Summer* (prod 1956) opposes romantic fiction to reality in focusing on a disillusioned philanderer who is on the point of sacrificing himself in a revolutionary cause. The tone of the whole is ambiguous: the graver paradoxes of man's condition tend to be assimilated into the frivolous topsy-turvydoms of comedy. Whiting remains important because he is deeply in tune with great twentieth-century writers. He learned from Shaw (q.v.), Eliot (q.v.) and Fry (q.v.), and his idiom, like Beckett's (q.v.), sometimes harks back to Wyndham Lewis (q.v.). Ronald Hayman has edited *The Collected Plays of John Whiting* (1969) in two volumes with notes.   [HB]

WIEBE, RUDY (1934–). Novelist, born in northern Saskatchewan, Canada. After early education at the Alberta Mennonite High School, Coaldale, he spent time at the universities of Alberta, Tübingen, Manitoba and Iowa. He now teaches at the University of Alberta. His first novel, *Peace Shall Destroy Many* (1962), traced the fortunes of a small group of Mennonites who had left the hardships of Russia for the farmlands of Saskatchewan, charting in particular the conflict of conscience in one man, during the Second World War period, whose pacifism contradicts his patriotism. *First and Vital Candle* (1966) explored the religious doubts of a white trader against the background of native sufferings and beliefs, concerns which inform the bulk of Wiebe's fiction: 'The stories we tell of our past are by no means merely words: they are meaning and life to us as *people*, as a *particular* people; the stories are there, and if we do not know of them we are, simply, like animals, memory ignorant, and the less are we people.' In *The Blue Mountains of China* (1970) Wiebe again turned to the Mennonites as immediate focus in a work spanning the forty years from 1920 through the lives of individuals. The larger meaning of the book, however, lay in Wiebe's vision of faith, struggle and the sanctity of personal life, elements which reached fine expression in *The Temptations of Big Bear* (1973). An ambitious blend of historical records and fiction techniques, this book is a deeply personal reading of an Indian leader's experiences during the prairie unrest of the 1870s and 1880s. A similar complex format was also used, not so successfully, in *The Scorched Wood People* (1977), which re-created Louis Riel's struggle for a homeland for the Canadian halfbreed (Métis) people. Wiebe is a fiercely committed regionalist and has contributed to the theatre, broadcasting and to many anthologies, including *Alberta: A Celebration* (1979). In 1974 he published *Where Is the Voice Coming From?*, a collection of short stories. 'What I suppose I'm doing', he says, 'is trying to unbury the story that I see is there.'   [PQ]

WIJENAIKE, PUNYAKANTE (1932–). Writer of fiction, born and educated in Sri Lanka. She is married and has three daughters. Her themes, even in the few stories humorously treated, reflect the transitoriness of human experience and often a tragic sense of the individual's isolation. Of her first book, *The Third Woman and Other Stories* (Colombo, 1963), Y. Gooneratne writes: 'there is none of her chosen themes that she does not handle with competence, sometimes with real distinction'. Despite its final, though awkwardly executed, affirmation of family love within a hostile community, her novel, *The Waiting Earth* (Colombo, 1966), with its skilful simulation of colloquial village speech, is a tragedy of a simple couple's inability to express the tenderness they feel for each other. A. Niven praises especially the artistry with which Wijenaike exposes the inner workings of her characters' minds and her unobtrusive use of descriptions of nature to convey their emotions. In the novella *Giraya* (Colombo, 1971) she experiments boldly, though not entirely successfully, with the diary form to explore the sterile lives of a decaying aristocratic family unable to keep pace with a changing world. She has also published stories for children. *The Rebel* (1979) is a collection of short stories.

[AR]

WILDING, MICHAEL (1942–). Short-story writer and novelist, born in Worcester, England, and educated at Oxford University. He was lecturer in English at Sydney University from 1963 to 1966 and returned to Australia in 1969. His first work of fiction was *Aspects of the Dying Process* (1972) which collected nine short stories with Australian settings. *The West Midland Underground* (1975) was a larger and more varied collection which confirmed his position as an important new writer exploring aspects of contemporary society in Australia. His work can be compared with that of Frank Moorhouse (q.v.), with whom he has been an editor of *Tabloid Story* since 1972. *Living Together* (1974), his first novel, was a witty and perceptive account of contemporary urban life, while his second novel, *The Short Story Embassy* (1975), was published by the company he had co-founded the year before. A demanding fable exploring a microcosm 'embassy' within which personal and artistic problems are acted out, it broke new ground in contemporary Australian fiction. *Scenic Drive* (1976) was a further collection of short stories which probed existential fears and fantasies with a fine blend of frankness and humour. [PQ]

WILLIAMS, CHARLES (1886–1945). Poet, novelist and dramatist, born in Holloway, London. When Charles was 8 his father's failing eyesight (he was a clerk) drove the family to St Albans, where they opened an artists' supply shop. Charles was educated at St Albans Abbey School and St Albans Grammar School. He went to University College, London, on a scholarship in 1901, but the family could not afford to keep him there and he left to take a job in publishing. In 1908 he joined the London office of Oxford University Press, in whose service he remained for the rest of his life. Weak eyesight kept him out of the army in the First World War. He married Florence Conway in 1917 and settled in Hampstead. Florence was not always comfortable with his way of publicly chanting poetry aloud wherever he might be; so he called her Michal (Saul's daughter who mocked David for dancing before the Lord) and the name stuck. Williams was indeed a fervent, unselfconscious enthusiast whose flow of talk and incantation enchanted his admirers. An interest in the occult led him to be con-

nected for a time with the Order of the Golden Dawn, but his dominating sense of the human being as supernaturally involved in a cosmic conflict between the powers of light and darkness was rooted in theological orthodoxy (Anglican), and the supernatural mythology which he employed in his novels is not just fictional machinery but credible Christian symbolism. So it is misleading to label his novels 'crypto-Gothic'. His imaginative world is nearer to Milton's than to Anne Radcliffe's. Williams's novels (*War in Heaven*, 1930; *Many Dimensions*, 1931; *The Place of the Lion*, 1931; *The Greater Trumps*, 1932; *Descent into Hell*, 1937; *All Hallows' Eve*, 1945) open up the daily lives of twentieth-century characters to a full range of spiritual influences from without – whether divine or diabolical in origin. The central moral issue is that of self-giving: for the ego that seeks mastery is possessed and destroyed by the demonic. Williams's key thinking is incarnational, and relies on a theology of Romantic Love also developed in his critical study of Dante, *The Figure of Beatrice* (1943), and in *He Came Down from Heaven* (1938). The lover's idealization of the loved one is a vision of her in a glory that appertains to all created things and beings properly accepted. In Williams's doctrine of the Affirmative Way sees Woman, Nature, Art, and City (the harmonious community) as Images, each in their respective modes, corresponding to that of the New Jerusalem in specifically religious experience. Williams knew T.S. Eliot (q.v.), who thought he approximated 'more nearly than any man I have ever known familiarly, to the saint' (see below), and his verse play, *Thomas Cranmer of Canterbury* (1936), was performed at the Canterbury Festival the year after Eliot's *Murder in the Cathedral*. But Williams's verse plays, including *The House of the Octopus* (1945) and *Seed of Adam* (1948), show a talent that is poetic and metaphysical rather than dramatic. His friend John Heath-Stubbs (q.v.) (*Charles Williams*, 1955) regards Williams as essentially a poet and indeed a major one. The claim rests chiefly on the two sequences of poems on the Matter of Britain, *Taliessin Through Logres* (1938) and *The Region of the Summer Stars* (1944). There is a commentary on these works by Williams's friend C.S. Lewis (q.v.) in *Arthurian Torso* (1948), a volume which also contains a posthumous fragment by the poet on *The Figure of Arthur*. 'Logres is Britain regarded as a province of the Empire with its centre at Byzantium. . . . The argument of the series is the expectation of the return of Our Lord by means of the Grail and of the establishment of the kingdom of Logres (or Britain) to this end' (Williams's Preface to *The Region of the Summer Stars*). Taliessin is the king's poet. The style is compact, taut, often terse, yet at the same time rich in ritual and rhetoric. The lyrics are disparate narrative sketches and monologues. The 'Byzantine' blend of mathematical lucidity and colourful heraldic imagery gives the work a disturbing static intensity.

Williams was evacuated to Oxford with Oxford University Press in 1939 and became a member of the literary circle associated with C.S. Lewis. Lewis, J.R.R. Tolkien (q.v.) and Dorothy Sayers (q.v.) were among those who contributed to *Essays presented to Charles Williams* (1947), a posthumous tribute. See also Williams's *Selected Writings* (1961), edited by Anne Ridler (q.v.), and her Introduction, quoted above, to *The Image of the City* (1958), a collection of Williams's essays. [HB]

WILLIAMS, EMLYN (1905–). Dramatist and actor, born in Mostyn, Clwyd, Wales, and educated at Oxford. He had his first big success with *Night Must Fall* (1935), a murder play theatrically clever in its manipulation of the audience's curiosity and suspense. A play he then wrote for John Gielgud, *He Was Born Gay* (1937), 'a romance' about pretenders to the French crown set in 1815 at the time of Waterloo, was not a success. *The Corn is Green* (1938), Williams's best-known play, is an autobiographical tribute to the school-teacher, Miss S.G. Cooke, who had spotted his talent and helped him to get to the university. (See also his book *George: An Early Autobiography*, 1962.) The sentimentality of the play dates it. The same may be said of *The Light of Heart* (1940), a study of a great actor ruined by drink. After the war Williams made a new career by reviving Dickens's practice of giving one-man dramatic readings. See also his *Collected Plays* (1961) and *Emlyn: An Early Autobiography 1927–1935* (1973). [HB]

WILLIAMSON, DAVID (1942–). Dramatist, born in Melbourne, Victoria, Australia. He graduated from Monash University in mechanical engineering. He wrote revues at university, but his first full-length play was *The Coming of Stork*, first performed in 1970 but not published until 1974. This work was later filmed in Australia and was staged (with revisions) in Sydney in 1973. *The Removalists* (1972) and *Don's Party* (1973) established him as Australia's leading playwright and were followed by *Jugglers Three* and *What If You Died Tomorrow* (performed 1972 and 1974 respectively and published 1974 with *Stork*). He has described his plays as being 'social documentaries to some extent'; they all create a powerful – often violent – sense of contemporary Australian life. He stresses that 'content is more important than style' in his concern to present 'real people in an ongoing situation'. His plays are an important dimension of the kind of contemporary writing in Australia which sees life in terms of what Williamson calls a 'wealth of types, sub-cultures and lifestyles'. At its best his work explores those subcultures with a blend of directness and poise which enables the local setting and style to carry a universal significance which is never stated but which gives the situation its vitality and form. The differing worlds of academe and Australian Rules football were explored in *The Department* (1974) and *The Club* (1977). *Travelling North* (1979) centred on old age and 'the very real difficulties of facing one's death'. [PQ]

WILLIAMSON, HENRY (1895–1977). Novelist and naturalist, born in Dorset. His experience in the infantry on the Western Front in the First World War marked him indelibly. Personal involvement in spontaneous front-line fraternization with the Germans at Christmas 1914 left him with a sense of the absurdity of the war and the falsity of the enmity. He became an ardent disciple of Richard Jefferies. 'People who don't see the earth and sea and stars plainly are spiritually corrupt – and spiritual

corruption begets physical corruption. That is the real cause of the Great War.' His main heroes, the cousins Willie and Phillip Maddison, are both prophetic idealists, tortured martyrs, bundles of resentments, prickliness, neurosis and also self-criticism. They find mystical release only with nature and fail largely with human beings. They conduct running battles with conventional Christianity, militarism, patriotism, moralism and respectability. They live much alone and write. Willie figures in the series *The Flax of Dream* (*The Beautiful Years*, 1921; *Dandelion Days*, 1922; *The Dream of Fair Women*, 1924; *The Pathway*, 1928) to which Willie's own 'masterpiece', *The Star-born* (1933), forms a pendant. Phillip dominates the even more ambitious saga, *A Chronicle of Ancient Sunlight*, a sequence of fifteen novels reaching from *The Dark Lantern* (1951), a Victorian tale of the courtship and marriage of Phillip's parents, to *The Gale of the World* (1969), in which Phillip, now 51, with two wars, a deceased first wife and a broken second marriage behind him, gets down to work on his magnum opus in a hut on Exmoor. The work closes with scenes of the disastrous Lynmouth flood of 1952. Five of the intervening novels deal with the First World War: *How Dear Is Life* (1954) with the First Battle of Ypres, *A Fox Under My Cloak* (1955) with 1915 at the time of Loos, *The Golden Virgin* (1957) with the year of the Somme, *Love and the Loveless* (1958) with 1917 and Passchendaele, and *A Test To Destruction* (1960) with the 5th Army in France in 1918.

Williamson's great strength is as a percipient observer and recorder of natural life, and his great successes were the two patiently researched animal tales, *Tarka the Otter* (1927) and *Salar the Salmon* (1935). In the novels of human experience action is often swamped under the weight of natural detail. Unbalanced political outbursts also disfigure the novels. Williamson's flirtation with fascism and praise of Hitler damaged him with the public and he was interned briefly at the beginning of the Second World War. Polemical passages in *The Gale of the World* quote Sir Oswald Mosley rhapsodically. Williamson was neither a happy nor a likeable man. (See Daniel Farson, *Henry, An Appreciation of Henry Williamson*, 1982.) His powers were considerable, but he over-wrote grossly, he could lapse into slush, and there is much repetition between book and book and within books individually. Volumes of autobiography include *The Story of a Norfolk Farm* (1941) and *A Clear Water Stream* (1958). [HB]

WILSON, A.N. (Andrew Norman) (1950–). Novelist, born in Stone, Staffordshire, and educated at Rugby and New College, Oxford. In his neatly plotted first novel, *The Sweets of Pimlico* (1977), a young London school-teacher, a woman, encounters an ageing but strangely fascinating German in Kensington Gardens. Questions about the mysterious nature of his past, his character, his connections and the future disposition of his immense wealth enmesh her emotionally and psychologically. She is taken over. In *Kindly Light* (1979) a Roman Catholic convert and priest, a feckless young man to whom things just happen, learns thereby to discard the 'juvenile notion that life consisted of a series of choices'. His story, and the manner in which satire topples over into farce, are both reminiscent of Waugh's (q.v.) *Decline and Fall*. The book contains some sharp and amusing studies of trendy clergy and liberated nuns.

Wilson's most praised novel has been *The Healing Art* (1980). It makes ingenious use of a hospital mix-up between X-ray reports on two women who are having their first check-up after mastectomies. The ageing suburban housewife is wrongly pronounced clear; the 39-year-old English don, Pamela Cooper, bravely tries to reconcile herself to a misdirected death-sentence. The setting is Oxford. Pamela, a medievalist and an Anglo-Catholic, is persuaded by her parish priest to take a trip to the shrine at Walsingham in search of healing. An apparent 'miracle' inevitably ensues. The contemporary scene is registered with a wickedly keen relish, and yet compassion seeps through. Wilson's style is polished, his tone cool and his humour captivatingly unassertive.   [HB]

WILSON, ANGUS (1913–). Novelist, born in Bexhill, East Sussex. His father was of Scots descent and his mother South African. Angus was the youngest of six sons and separated by thirteen years from the brother nearest in age. The father was 'a generous, attractive, witty, even lovable man entirely ruined by total self-indulgence', Wilson has said (*The Wild Garden*, 1963). A raffish, boastful fellow, he lived without working and on a diminishing income, leading the family from hotel to boarding house as gambling and borrowing permitted. The world of Wilson's family and of the small hotels 'was essentially the world of the comedy (and the pathos) of manners' (op. cit.). Here Wilson, a keen observer with a gift for verbal mimicry, found human evidence of drift, failure, pretence and dissipation, from which later he peopled his fiction. Wilson became a pupil at a preparatory school where one of his brothers was the headmaster and he went as a day boy to Westminster School in 1927. His hard-pressed mother died when he was 15. Her colonial upbringing, amid plentiful servants, had ill fitted her for the life her husband's irresponsibility condemned her to. Wilson's family background and his isolation by age seem to provide a classic preparation for the creation of fiction, but it was many years before a deep personal need drove him to tap the reservoir of human material as a writer. After taking a degree in medieval and modern history at Merton College, Oxford, in 1936 (a legacy from his mother had provided the means), he was appointed to the British Museum's Department of Printed Books. He was to return to the museum after the war and to remain there till 1955. He went as a lecturer in English to the University of East Anglia in 1963 and was appointed professor in 1966. But wartime service with the Foreign Office, from 1942 to 1946, had sent him to a country billet where eventually tension and loneliness culminated in a nervous breakdown. He began to write as therapy, and indeed the high praise rightly given to Wilson for his courageous confrontation as a writer with the effects of mental illness sometimes tends to blur critical estimate of his literary achievement.

In the two early volumes of short stories, *The Wrong Set* (1949) and *Such Darling Dodos* (1950), Wilson was much concerned with the degree to which middle-class people understand themselves, as evidenced by their response to events that break intrusively upon their routine existence. 'Self-realization was to become the theme of all my novels', Wilson has said (op. cit.). In *Hemlock and After* (1952) Bernard Sands, successful novelist, meets practical failure in the very moment of apparently realizing his idealistic scheme to make Vardon Hall a government-subsidized haven for young writers; at the same time he finds personal failure as a trusting homosexual in the sudden detection of his own susceptibility to sadistic excitation. Gentle, all-tolerant humanism proves inadequate to the human reality. Wilson rejects Christianity yet makes this judgement, wittily capturing the emptiness of middle-class chatter and posturing, and the evasion of mutual contact it involves. But for all his subtle recording of conversational nuance, satirical impact is weakened by a registration of homosexual whimsy and sensibility too involved and titillatory for detachment. In *Anglo-Saxon Attitudes* (1956) Gerald Middleton, a retired professor of medieval history, finds his inner poise eroded by evidence of lifelong failure as man and scholar, failure in a career of easy evasion by which, in home and university, he has left vacuums for insensitive people to exploit damagingly. Finally Gerald acts, both as man and as scholar, facing the reality of his failed marriage and ferreting out the facts of an archaeological fraud about which he has long been suspicious. Wilson attempts a Dickensian breadth of social portraiture but the book lacks narrative intensity and dramatic thrust, suspense is absurdly attenuated, and structure is lost in sprawl. Wilson claims that, of the central figures in his first three novels, he consciously identified himself only with Meg Eliot, heroine of *The Middle Age of Mrs Eliot* (1959), whose success in friendship, good works, cultural interests and social life is challenged by the sudden death of the husband to whom she has been deeply, if also dependently and even devouringly, devoted. The event that gives direction to the book occurs after ninety pages of waiting for what the dust-jacket has promised, and Meg's self-discovery is as slow and frustrating for the reader as it is for herself. An unlikely pacifist brother, running a nursery with a collection of cranks, packs out the volume. Imaginative energy flags and falters. Wilson's thoroughness in recording his characters' submergence in self-analysis and their obsession with how they appear to others drives him doggedly through many a verbal morass of unalleviated flatness. In *The Old Men at the Zoo* (1961) the rival claims of administration and of devotion to wild life are brought into conflict in a story of a London zoo and a 'future' war in the 1970s. The dichotomy between contemplation and social activity is, for Wilson, the humanist's secularized form of the grace-and-good-works paradox. *No Laughing Matter* (1967) chronicles some fifty years of family life from 1912. Wilson tries his hand at some Joycean techniques and verbally at least there is vitality and ingenuity. Later novels are *As If by Magic* (1973) and *Setting the World on Fire* (1980), the latter an elaborately contrived exercise structured on the antithesis between the baroque and the classical, inspiration and order.   [HB]

WILSON, COLIN (1931-). Prose writer, born in Leicester, Leicestershire. He broke into prominence with an ambitious philosophical study of alienation, *The Outsider* (1956), whose success initiated a succession of polemical works, several of them exploiting the novel form (e.g. *Ritual in the Dark*, 1960; *The God of the Labyrinth*, 1970). Themes of violence, sex and crime are treated within a framework of metaphysical exploration into modern man's condition. [HB]

WINGFIELD, SHEILA (1906-). Poet, born in Hampshire and educated at Roedean. She married the heir to an Irish viscountcy in Co. Wicklow and became Lady Powerscourt. She was determined to be a poet from her childhood, but the claims of public and private life kept her out of literary circles and limited her productiveness. *Poems* (1938) drew praise from Yeats (q.v.) and De la Mare (q.v.), and was succeeded by *Beat Drum, Beat Heart* (1946) which Herbert Read (q.v.) declared 'the most sustained meditation on war that has been written in our time'. Its four sections, 'Men in War', 'Men at Peace', 'Women in Love' and 'Women at Peace', compare men in war with women in love and men at peace with women out of love in what the poet herself has called 'psychological–philosophical' fashion, yet totally devoid of philosophical or abstract vocabulary. The fabric is finely compounded of images raked from whole cultures and peoples and histories. The lines are alive with memorable metaphors that sum up known experience in accessible terms, and the changing moods and meditations are voiced with rhythmic and tonal flexibility.

Her *Storms, Selected Poems 1938–1977* (1977), which has a preface by G.S. Fraser (q.v.), includes the whole of this major poem and selects from all her volumes (*A Cloud Across the Sun*, 1949; *A Kite's Dinner*, 1954) up to and including *Admissions* (1977). 'Each word / Each event, shows me its own,/ Natural tact', Sheila Wingfield has written, and an immense reverence for words shines through her fastidiously turned reflections on places and people, birds and relics.

'A Melancholy Love' evokes Dublin nostalgically with a handful of deftly planted images. 'One's Due' mines a rare vein of self-analysis. The poet ponders the eternal doom of wife-beaters, liars, and child-torturers, of people eaten up with envy or pride, before quietly analysing her own less spectacular but no less valid claims on a place in the pit. A final powerful stanza pictures Lazarus, newly called back to life and swaying unsteadily on his feet. Just so the poet must 'try out my tongue again'. Wingfield's work carries an air of effortless application by a long-practised hand.

Delicacy of finish, directness of tone and sometimes an engaging obliqueness of reference give her laden, economic verses a rare richness which G.S. Fraser has compared with that of Landor's latest work. [HB]

WODEHOUSE, P.G. (Sir) (1881–1975). Novelist, whose initials stand for 'Pelham Grenville' and whose familiar nickname was 'Plum', born at Guildford, Surrey. His father was a judge in Hong Kong and, with his parents out east, Wodehouse was educated at preparatory schools and at Dulwich College, while being in the care of various aunts in the vacations – 'passed from aunt to aunt', he says in his autobiographical book *Over Seventy*

(1957). Aunts were to become notable symbols of age and authority in Wodehouse's fictional world, and a convenient device for avoiding souring the relationship between parent and child in the necessary literary process of pitching rebellious youth against sober seniority. The real aunts had connections in society that gave young Wodehouse inside knowledge of what life is like in the homes of the aristocracy – and not only in the rooms above stairs. 'My mind today is fragrant with memories of kindly footmen and vivacious parlour maids' (op. cit.). Disappointed of a place at Dartmouth and a future naval career by defective eyesight, Wodehouse was destined by his parents for a career in banking and became a clerk in the London branch of the Hong Kong and Shanghai Bank, but in 1902 he cut a page out of a new ledger (in which he had unwisely been writing a 'piece' on the Formal Royal Opening of the book) and the 'Bank decided (and a very sensible decision too) that the only way to keep solvent was to de-Wodehouse itself' (op. cit.). He now struggled to establish himself as a freelance writer and eventually got a permanent weekly column in *The Globe*. His early successes were school stories, many written in serial form. *The Pothunters* (1902), his first published novel, was originally written for the *Public School Magazine*. He wrote also for *Captain* and *Chums*.

Wodehouse had a holiday in the USA in 1904 and returned there in 1909 to begin a connection that gave him a second home and a second career. For the accumulating sixty-odd novels were not the only source of the income that enabled him, by the 1930s, to keep a butler, footman, chauffeur, cook, housemaid, parlourmaid and scullery maid to help run his Mayfair home for self, wife and stepdaughter. (He married Ethel Rowley Wayman, a widow, in 1914.) He contributed as author of script, and sometimes of lyrics, to the manufacture of eighteen musical comedies. Events in the lucrative partnership in show business with Guy Bolton are brightly recorded in *Bring On The Girls* (1954), written jointly by the two of them.

But of course it is the prodigious output of comic novels and linked short stories on which his literary reputation rests. Among them, outstandingly, the books featuring Jeeves and Bertie Wooster and the books dealing with life at Blandings Castle form a corpus whose characters are household names in both Britain and America, for they inhabit a vast saga-like realm of make-believe which lends itself to the kind of serio-comic documentation that Sherlock Holmes fans learnedly disseminate, bypassing the author in their involvement with his world. *My Man Jeeves* (1919), *The Inimitable Jeeves* (1923) and *Carry On, Jeeves* (1925) launched the Jeeves series and succeeding titles lead right on to *Stiff Upper Lip* in 1963 and *Much Obliged, Jeeves* in 1971. The Blandings series includes *Something Fresh* (1915), *Leave it to Psmith* (1923) and *Summer Lightning* (1929) and ends with *A Pelican at Blandings* (1969). Jeeves the butler, rock of stability and wisdom, is the deft sorter-out of problems for his bungling master, Bertie Wooster. Wooster, in narrating, assumes the mantle of lovable fathead, tempting bait for designing females and wayward victim of Aunt Agatha's brutal attempts to bring him to heel. A Robin Hood streak drives him to rush impetuously to the aid of fellow sufferers from society's restrictive sanities, such as Bingo Little. The combined possibilities in such partnerships for putting your foot in it and finishing up in the hottest seat are such that Jeeves's skill in privately arranging for social cataclysms to overtake persecuting bounders and offended rigorists is tested to the full. The aristocratic life as lived at Blandings Castle by Lord Emsworth and his ménage is an idealized Edwardian day-dream, whose material details may in some respects be outdated as the years pass, but whose fairy-tale status remains secure. This is escapist literature. And by an unfaltering felicity of control, Wodehouse manages to clinch social absurdities by the fistful without allowing humour to slide into satire.

· Wodehouse perfected a style of unique comic intensity. It was especially fitted to its main function of representing the speech, thought and acts of characters like Wooster and Psmith, whose mercurial vitality of spirit, whether through their being mentally one step behind or one step in front of their fellows, digests incongruities like fresh air. Snippets of well-known poetry, slang, drawing-room smarm, echoes of literary Victorianese and bits of technical jargon are mixed up to an inimitable recipe, and metaphor abounds. People 'pour', 'trickle' or 'filter' into a room. They 'biff' about and 'shimmer off'. Wooster 'lubricates the good old interior' when he has a drink. The craftsmanship is highly disciplined, and the care and effort which Wodehouse expended on his work can be gauged from the 'Self-Portrait in Letters' arranged by Wodehouse's lifelong friend and correspondent, W. Townend, under the title Performing Flea (1953). 'In a Jeeves story every line has to have some entertainment value', Wodehouse writes. He demonstrates the assiduous stages of composition which even a 'popular story' must pass through. He maps out a plot, splits it up into scenes, thinks of the characters as actors in a play, writes a 30,000-word scenario and then is ready to begin. Wodehouse's workmanship was appreciated. Belloc (q.v.) once called him the best of living English writers. Oxford gave him an honorary D Litt in 1939. Leavis (q.v.) mocked the solemn award, but Oxford was right.

The saddest thing in the Wodehouse story is that, being resident at Le Touquet in 1940, he fell into the hands of the Germans and, after internment, was persuaded to give some broadcasts in English. They were innocuous, but their lightly ironic postures left room for misrepresentation which broadcasters and journalists at home, who ought to have known better, exploited. Postwar scrutiny completely cleared Wodehouse, but not before years had passed in which calumny made return to England unwise, even unsafe. He stayed in the USA and became an American citizen in 1955. It was in 1961 that the BBC broadcast an 'Act of Homage and Reparation' by Evelyn Waugh (q.v.) and in 1975, the year of his death, that he was created a knight in the New Year Honours List. See also Over Seventy: An Autobiography with Digressions (1957) and J.H. Heineman and D.R. Benson, eds, P.G. Wodehouse: A Centenary Celebration (1981).

[HB]

WOOLF, VIRGINIA (1882–1941). Novelist, born in London. Her father was Sir Leslie Stephen, the Victorian critic and rationalist agnostic who edited the Dictionary of National Biography. Virginia inherited her father's agnosticism but not the confident cheerfulness that accompanied it. She married Leonard Woolf, the political thinker, in 1912, and her sister Vanessa married the art critic, Clive Bell. Together the two couples were at the centre of the Bloomsbury Group, a coterie of artists and intellectuals which included Lytton Strachey (q.v.) and E.M. Forster (q.v.). The group was not a movement with a programme, but they were conscious of their superiority to the ordinary run of humanity and they shared a common revulsion against the cramping inhibitions of the middle-class Victorian mind. The value they set on freely indulged personal relationships had its positive and negative aspects artistically in their work and practically in their lives. In reading Virginia Woolf's novels one is aware of the sad havoc wrought by time and change, separation and sickness on the most promising of such relationships. Virginia Woolf suffered acutely from depression and mental unbalance. Indeed the founding of the Hogarth Press by the Woolfs in 1917 had a therapeutic motive. The personal unease combined with the melancholy built into Virginia Woolf's philosophical position to plant a sadness at the core of her novels. In March 1941, when the Woolfs were living in Sussex, the German air raids aggravated worries about her own mental condition and she took her own life by drowning.

The first volume of the Letters of Virginia Woolf 1888–1912, edited by Nigel Nicolson and published in 1975, reveals the writer's surprising capacity for practical triviality and insensitivity and sheds a curious light on her sexual nature. Lesbian leanings are evident and the relationship to her future husband was oddly based. 'As I told you brutally the other day, I feel no physical attraction in you.' The enigmatic aspects of Virginia Woolf's personality are perhaps not irrelevant to the persisting critical disagreement about her artistic status. Yet her dissatisfaction with the standard fictional techniques of narrational plotting and character projection, which for her constituted an artistic servitude to the crude external sequence of events, was immensely salutary for the English novel and her response innovatory in a way that gives her affinities with Joyce (q.v.) – in spite of the fact that she found Ulysses unsatisfactory. ('It fails because of the comparative poverty of the writer's mind', she said.) In 'Modern Fiction' (included in The Common Reader, 1925) she assaulted the current bastions of literary fashion by declaring Wells (q.v.), Bennett (q.v.) and Galsworthy (q.v.) artistic 'materialists . . . concerned not with the spirit but with the body' who 'spend immense skill and immense industry making the trivial and the transitory appear the true and the enduring'. For her part Virginia Woolf dispenses with the standard techniques of presentation – description, narrative and dialogue arranged in sequential chunks. She floats the reader on a 'stream of consciousness' where he can savour the fluidity of her characters' inner life and the sharp richness of their moment-by-moment response to sensation and experience.

Virginia Woolf's first novels, The Voyage Out (1915) and Night and Day (1919), both studies of young girls, were straightforward in technique, but experimentation began in Jacob's Room (1922), where clear narrative outline is dissolved, and reached fulfilment in Mrs Dalloway (1925) in which sequential chronological patterning is burst wide open. The book fastens on a single summer's day in the life of Clarissa Dalloway, a woman of 51 whose external concern is simply to prepare for and run a party she is giving in the evening. The event brings into new focus in her inner life all that has brought her to the emotional present as wife of a successful MP and might-have-been wife of a failed but intensely alive old friend, Peter Walsh, newly returned from India. Thus the substance of the book is contained in the reflections and flashbacks that reconstruct Mrs Dalloway's past. Throughout the book the progress of the well-to-do towards their evening of expensive pleasure is counterpointed by the lot of Septimus Warren Ward and his wife Lucrezia. Septimus, a victim of delayed shell-shock, careers through escalating insanity to gruesome suicide. News of the tragedy is brought to the party because one of the guests, an eminent Harley Street psychiatrist, is delayed by his involvement in the case. The intrusion of death is powerfully articulated and the interwoven themes, in contrast and cohesiveness, have clarity and tidiness. To the Lighthouse* (1927) develops the technique of Mrs Dalloway, extending to its furthest reach at the time the author's gift for exploring human awareness at that level of inner moment-by-moment sensitivity where the truth of imagination locates the basic stuff of human life. By now Woolf has achieved rare poetic skill in bringing out the transforming power of trivial incidents on the inner life, and ironic ingenuity in tracking the entanglement of the subjective element in supposedly objective act and word.

Orlando (1928), the next novel, is technically a tour de force. Time's tyranny is destroyed in a fantasy which extends the life of Orlando over four centuries. Orlando is at first a young Elizabethan nobleman, but he changes sex to become Lady Orlando in the reign of Queen Anne and is hopping out of a car to shop at Marshall and Snelgrove for bath salts before we take leave of her, having sampled the delights of succeeding centuries. The book can be understood only in the light of its private purpose of celebrating Vita (Victoria) Sackville-West (q.v.) with whom Virginia Woolf had a close friendship. 'The effect of Vita on Virginia is all contained in Orlando, the longest and most charming love letter in literature, in which she explores Vita, weaves her in and out of the centuries, tosses her from one sex to the other, plays with her, dresses her in furs, lace and emeralds, teases her, flirts with her, drops a veil of mist around her, and ends up by photographing her in the mud at Long Barn, with dogs, awaiting Virginia's arrival next day' (Nigel Nicolson, Portrait of a Marriage, 1973). Vita was bisexual. Violet Trefusis, with whom she earlier had a passionate love affair that threatened both their marriages, is introduced into Orlando as Sasha, a Russian princess.

The Waves* (1931) brings Virginia Woolf's artistic experimentation to its logical conclusion. The externals of action and dialogue are totally submerged and the reader is taken into the minds of a group of growing characters mutually familiar. The personality of each is reflected in the minds of the others so that a kaleidoscopic pattern emerges, corresponding in its glittering fluidity to the movement of the sea. There is no distinctive development in The Years (1937), but in Virginia Woolf's last novel, Between the Acts (1941), which was published posthumously, she pushes her symbolic technique further by fixing the tentatively poised relationships of a group of

characters against the background of a village pageant. The amateur theatricals indulge a refreshing, if artistically ambiguous, vein of comic burlesque.

Virginia Woolf's critical essays, including those that formed the two volumes called The Common Reader (1925 and 1932) and those published in the posthumous volumes, The Death of the Moth (1942) and The Moment and Other Essays (1947), have been edited in four volumes of Collected Essays (1966-7) by her husband, Leonard Woolf. A Room of One's Own (1929), an essay based on papers originally read at the women's colleges at Cambridge, is a lively feminist protest. 'A woman must have money and a room of her own if she is to write fiction.' Virginia Woolf filled thirty books of diaries between 1915 and her death, and the material is now being edited by Anne Olivier Bell. See The Diary of Virginia Woolf, vols 1-4 (1977-82), covering the years 1915-35. See also The Flight of the Mind: The Letters of Virginia Woolf, vols 1-4 (1975-8), edited by Nigel Nicolson and Joanne Trautmann.

To the Lighthouse. The Ramsay family and their hangers-on are at their holiday home in the Isle of Skye before the First World War. A projected visit to the lighthouse 'tomorrow' is seen as the evening falls to be increasingly unlikely. It is a matter of ecstasy or agony to the youngest of the eight children, James. Mr Ramsay, a study based on Virginia Woolf's father, Leslie Stephen, and a philosopher, brusque and eccentric, accurately forecasts the calling-off of the expedition. Mrs Ramsay, a woman of deep sensitivity and unselfishness, prefers to let James down more gently. This difference sums up the antithetic balance of a husband-wife relationship that itself epitomizes the universal marital dichotomy. Well over half the book is given over to the events of the single evening. A central transitional passage called 'Time Passes' briefly sums up the passage of ten momentous years during which the house is left desolate, Mrs Ramsay dies, son Andrew is killed in battle in France and daughter Prue dies in childbirth. The lighthouse becomes a moving symbol of the shifting light and darkness of the human lot. In part three, 'The Lighthouse', it is Mr Ramsay's two youngest children, James and Cam, now 16 and 17, who at last make the trip to the lighthouse, the two of them now bound in common secret alienation from their insensitive father. These are the survivors of time's devastation.

The Waves is based on the lives of six characters, Bernard, Neville, Louis, Susan, Rhoda and Jinny, who are brought up together in childhood but whose ways diverge thereafter. All is contained in the minds of the characters, and their stylized dialogue (mature and metaphor-ridden from infancy) is not spoken conversation but inner reflection tangential to such outward communication as takes place between them. The current of emotion and sensation, threading its way through the parallel careers, is counterpointed by the progress of sun and tide from dawn to sunset, 'the majestic march of the day across the sky' and the movement of the waves beneath. The group of friends drift apart but gather in young adulthood at a London restaurant to say goodbye to their common friend, Percival, who is leaving for India and who is later killed. He has loved Susan, who in turn has loved Bernard; but both have married outside the group, Susan to a farmer.

A later reunion at Hampton Court occurs when the group are middle-aged. Virginia Woolf's preoccupation with the inner life enables her to hold the moment, outwardly undramatic, when 'something is made' through common personal feeling. 'Time tapers to a point. . . . These are the true events.' And they sort ill with the conventional artifices of fiction. 'They want a plot, do they?. . . It is not enough for them, this ordinary scene?' Neville muses, while Bernard the writer ('We are all phrases in Bernard's story', Neville reflects), summing life up, observes, 'Of story, of design, I do not see a trace then.'
[HB]

WRIGHT, DAVID (1920–). Poet, born in Johannesburg, South Africa, educated there and at Northampton School for the Deaf and Oriel College, Oxford. He had to overcome the disability of total deafness (see *Deafness: A Personal Account*, 1969) in order to establish himself as journalist and editor. He married Phillipa Reid in 1951 and now lives in Cumbria. His poetry to date (beginning with *Poems*, 1949) was gathered in *To the Gods the Shades, Collected Poems* (1977). It is never pretentiously complex but has the compactness and ease of highly disciplined conversation. Much of it breathes an unrufflable equanimity, is cheerfully aloof from manufactured angst, and bypasses metaphysical unease by concentrating on 'the fine point of existence, the instant's span'. But there is quietly voiced grief and perturbation too, notably in poems on South Africa and on memories of wartime London in *Metrical Observations* (1980). Wright collaborated with John Heath-Stubbs (q.v.) in editing *The Faber Book of Twentieth-Century Verse* (1953, revised 1975) and has also edited, *inter alia*, the Penguin *Mid-Century English Poetry 1940–60* (1965). He has also written three books on Portugal.
[HB]

WRIGHT, JUDITH (1915–). Poet, born on the family property near Armidale, New South Wales, Australia, where she spent much of her childhood. Her education began with the Correspondence School, but at 13 she boarded at the New England Girls School, Armidale. She read English at Sydney University, and also gained a wide acquaintance with European literature, philosophy and history. After graduating in 1936 she spent a year in England and Europe before working at secretarial jobs in Sydney. From 1941 to 1943 she lived with her father on the family property, 'Wallamumbi', in New South Wales, and then went to Brisbane as a clerk. In 1947 she joined the university permanent staff as a statistician, and during this period met Jack McKinney, a philosopher, whom she was to marry. His interests in many ways complemented her own, and they worked together until his death in 1966.

Her father's family had been in Australia for almost a century; his mother's grandfather had founded the property and vineyard 'Dalwood' in the Hunter Valley, New South Wales, in 1828. The strong tradition of family links with Australia, reinforced by her own country childhood experiences, forms a central aspect of her poetry. She had always wanted to be a writer, and had been actively writing poetry, when time and money allowed, since her Sydney typist days. Her first book of poems, *The Moving Image* (1946), established her at once in Australia

as an important new poetic talent. The volume's epigraph from Plato, 'Time is a moving image of eternity', pointed to a preoccupation which was explored in poems which took the world she knew and loved as fabric but strove for a timeless significance. The title poem juxtaposes the treasured memories of childhood, 'the green world of a child', with the experienced disillusionment of the war years – 'Dust blows from the airfield; dust in the mouth'. A deeply human concern for man's situation, 'caught in the endless circle of time and star', also informs two other poems from this early collection which are still among her finest, 'Bullocky' and 'South of my Days'. In both these works she explored her inheritance of a family pastoral tradition which she recognized as representative of a period in her nation's history.

During her time at 'Wallamumbi' she had read her grandfather's twenty-five-volume diary, and in 1947 she received a grant from the Commonwealth Literary Fund to work on a family history. This was a productive period also for poems and short stories, though the family history failed to find a publisher and so did not appear until 1959, as *The Generations of Men*. It remains one of the best introductions to her work. A second book of poems, *Woman to Man* (1949), challenged, and offended, many critics by its frank, sensitive exploration of feminine emotion, although some poems continued the vein of landscape poetry established in the first collection. On the basis of her established reputation she was invited to edit the new *Oxford Book of Australian Verse* (1956). The success of this volume led to Oxford also publishing *The Generations of Men* and a work for children from the same period, *Kings of the Dingoes* (1958). A third collection of poems, *The Gateway* (1953), revealed the constant tuning of her poetry to carry more varied and complex meanings. *The Two Fires* (1955) encompassed not only her continuing intellectual quest, but also human events as disparate as the birth of her daughter Meredith in 1956, the tragic muddle of the Korean war and the shadow of the atomic bomb. The volume's epigraph from Heraclitus suggests the balancing of the fire of destruction by the creative kindling of human life and love. Yet in spite of this suggested balance, the fine concluding poem, 'The Harp and the King', expressed a dilemma that so much of her poetry strives to reconcile – the necessity, and impossibility, of man's work transcending time if life is to have meaning. The harp replies to the king's anxious questions by singing praises of mutability, but this is no solace to the aged king; 'Make me believe in my mortality, / since that is all I have, the old king said'. The progression of the poem asserts the possibility of release from time's bondage, but the overall effect is that 'Time strips the soul and leaves it comfortless'. 'Gum-trees Stripping' employs the symbol of the tree, always important in her work, in a precise, lyrical image of the poet's art. *Birds* (1962) reflected an increasing concern with conservation, while *Five Senses* (1963), a selected poems volume with an additional section ('The Forest'), was followed by a 1963 selection in the 'Australian Poets' series with a practical and perceptive Introduction by herself.

Recognizing the fact that today poetry 'like medicine, is not often taken for its pleasant taste; it is prescribed', Wright argued that even so its vital gift can be received: 'Poetry ought not to be thought of as a discipline, but as a kind of praise'. The historical or human dimensions which inform the poetry also characterize her criticism, which has opened up important new lines of approach. Studies of the Australian poets Shaw Neilson (q.v.) and Charles Harpur (both 1963) were followed by *Preoccupations in Australian Poetry* (1965), a major critical work which not only included illuminating studies of particular writers but also put forward challenging interpretations of the intimate relationship between national geography and cultural self-awareness. A further poetry volume, *The Other Half* (1966), and a collection of short stories, *The Nature of Love* (1966), were followed by *Collected Poems* (1971), which included previously unpublished poems in the section 'Shadow'. *Because I was Invited* (1975) brought together writings on a wide range of topics. She has often disappointed and annoyed critics by the extent to which each new book has broken new ground, and she herself feels that poetry does not merely describe man and his world but should be the ordering principle of it: 'modern man is something like a survival of poetry, which once shaped and interpreted his world through language and the creative imagination. When poetry withers in us, the greater part of experience and reality wither too'. Her celebration of poetic truth has produced poetry which blends lyric grace and intellectual rigour. Her work has moved away from the natural beauty of the early books, and at times later work has relied too readily upon a strained use of symbolism instead of writing from felt experience. At its best her work, including her criticism, is marked by a range of compassion and understanding which assures her of a central place in modern Australian literature. Of her recent books *Fourth Quarter* (1977) is poetry while *The Coral Battleground* (1977) charts the threat to the Barrier Reef from man's encroachment. They spring from the same commitment to life.   [PQ]

WYNDHAM, JOHN (pseudonym of John Benyon Harris) (1903–69). Novelist, brought up in Birmingham, West Midlands, educated at Bedales School. He worked variously in farming, law, commercial art and advertising, then, after war service in the army, won acclaim in the science fiction field with *The Day of the Triffids* (1946). Most of the human population are deprived of sight through visual contact with a rare meteoric phenomenon. Simultaneously the vegetable world acquires mobility through the multiplication of a strain of monstrous sentient plants called triffids. Wyndham's fictional recipe is a productive one. The precariousness of our civilization is made evident as handfuls of survivors struggle to adapt to cataclysms that destroy the familiar framework of material life and mental assumption ('how *easily* we have lost a world that seemed so safe and certain'). In *The Kraken Wakes* (1953) the threat comes from a hostile consciousness in the deepest regions of the sea: it sends 'sea-tanks' to depopulate sea-coasts, destroys shipping with lightning blows and finally extends the sea's domain by melting arctic ice. Wyndham continued to explore momentous shifts in the balance of nature consequent upon what are at first marginal alterations in man's relative capacity: *The Chrysalids* (1955), *The Midwich Cuckoos* (1957), *The Trouble with Lichen* (1960).   [HB]

YEATS, W.B. (William Butler) (1865–1939). Poet and dramatist, born in Dublin, Ireland, of Protestant stock. His father, John B. Yeats, was an artist. Family connections with Sligo gave young Yeats an early knowledge and lasting love of that area, but the family moved to London in 1868, to return again to Ireland in 1880. Thus Yeats was at the Godolphin School, Hammersmith, from 1874 to 1880, then, in Dublin, attended Erasmus High School and, later, the Metropolitan School of Art, where he began his lifelong friendship with George Russell (AE) (q.v.), the future poet and visionary. The Yeats family were back in England by 1887 and movement between England and Ireland was to remain a feature of much of Yeats's adult life. Early works included two poems in the *Dublin University Review* in 1885, an article the following year on Samuel Ferguson, the Irish poet and Gaelic scholar whose lays helped to make Celtic legend and mythology known, and *Mosada* (1886), a Moorish tale in dramatic verse. *The Wanderings of Oisin and Other Poems* was published by private subsidy in 1889. St Patrick receives back in Ireland the unrepentant heathen Oisin (Ossian), bent, bald and blind after three centuries of 'dalliance with a demon thing'. The rhymed dialogue, rich and varied in image and rhythm, won praise from William Morris. Three major interests determined Yeats's experience at this time – the Rhymers' Club; Maud Gonne and the Irish nationalist movement that claimed her devotion; and theosophical and hermetic studies which gave direction to Yeats's already awakened interest in oriental religion and occultism. The last two of these interests remained matters of passionate concern for the rest of Yeats's life. The Rhymers' Club met at the 'Cheshire Cheese'. Lionel Johnson, Ernest Dowson and Arthur Symons (q.v.) formed with others a group of poets noted for decadence and dissipation, and subsequently called by Yeats the 'Tragic Generation'. The influence of MacGregor Mathers led Yeats, who was fascinated by ancient symbol and ritual, to join the Order of the Golden Dawn, a cabbalistic order. He believed that he found in magic and hermetic studies an intellectual centre for his life and his work as a poet.

In 1889 Yeats first met Maud Gonne, and was captivated by her beauty and her masterful energy. Her father's death had left her with an independent income and she dedicated herself to the cause of revolutionary Irish nationalism. Yeats first proposed to her in 1891 and was rejected; but the friendship lasted and the frustrated devotion bore fruit for long afterwards in Yeats's poems and plays. Maud Gonne's revolutionary extremism was such that Yeats's deeply humane and idealistic spirit could neither approve her methods nor supply her with literary propaganda to her taste. Later, in 1908, in 'No Second Troy', he wrote:

> Why should I blame her that she filled my days
> With misery, or that she would of late
> Have taught to ignorant men most violent
>   ways. . . ?

But Yeats's own aspirations for Ireland were real and

fervent enough, and The Countess Cathleen*, a verse play published in 1892, projects and transfigures Maud Gonne into a lady who 'martyrs' herself for the starving Irish peasantry by the sale of her soul. Yeats was already formulating that 'theory and practice of a dramatic art where symbol replaces character, events are allegories and words keep more than half their secrets to themselves' (Joseph Hone, W.B. Yeats, 1942). The Land of Heart's Desire, another verse play, was produced in London in 1894. A newly-wed, Mary Bruin, calls, 'Fairies, come take me out of this dull world'. A Faery Child intrudes and, after a struggle with the parish priest, claims Mary and she dies.

Yeats's poetic output of the 1890s is often richly decorative in style, haunting in rhythm, dreamy in tone. The melancholy is pervasive. 'The Lake Isle of Innisfree', 'When you are old' and 'The White Birds' belong to the miscellaneous verse and prose collection, The Celtic Twilight (1893). 'The Rose', 'The Song of Wandering Aengus', 'He wishes his beloved were dead' and 'He wishes for the cloths of Heaven' belong to the later and more disciplined volume, The Wind Among the Reeds (1899). Up to this point the use of Irish legend is notable; the rather stagey Yeatsian self-projection oddly foreshadows the ruthless and ironic self-disclosure of the future; but the swooning music gives no hint of the more exacting and strenuous utterance to come. There is no doubt that, had Yeats died early, The Wind Among the Reeds would have represented the culminating fruit of a distinctive and spell-binding lyricism, Pre-Raphaelite in its origin. Moreover Yeats had published Irish tales of the supernatural in prose in The Celtic Twilight (1893), The Secret Rose (1897) and Stories of Red Hanrahan (1897).

Meanwhile, together with Lady Gregory (q.v.) and Edward Martyn (q.v.), Yeats had thrown himself into the work of establishing the Irish Literary Theatre, and had involved George Moore (q.v.) in the theatrical and other activities that were to draw him from London to Ireland and provide the substance and inspiration of his Hail and Farewell. In 1899 the company produced The Countess Cathleen and in 1902 Cathleen-ni-Houlihan*, the most popular of Yeats's dramas, in which a mysterious wandering woman, a symbol of Ireland (Maud Gonne, on the stage), lures a young man to revolutionary sacrifice on the very eve of his wedding, and of which Yeats was to ask years later:

Did that play of mine send out
Certain men the English shot?

('The Man and the Echo')

The financial support of Miss A.E. Horniman, an Englishwoman, enabled the theatrical group, now the 'Irish National Theatre', to establish themselves at the Abbey Theatre, Dublin, where Yeats's On Baile's Strand* was produced on the opening night in 1904 along with Lady Gregory's Spreading the News. By now Yeats had sustained the shock of Maud Gonne's marriage to the nationalist, John MacBride, an incongruous union which dismayed many and soon resulted in separation. However, Lady Gregory's home at Coole Park became for long a place of refuge and restoration for the poet. For years he spent his summers there, indebted to Lady Gregory for material and moral sustenance. 'I doubt if I should have done much with my life but for her firmness and care', he wrote (see Autobiographies, 1956). The Abbey Theatre for long continued to claim Yeats's attention in both a managing and a literary capacity. His Deirdre* was performed there in 1906.

In The Green Helmet and Other Poems, published in 1910, the year in which he accepted a Civil List pension, Yeats voiced his pain at Maud Gonne's view of him:

My darling cannot understand
What I have done, or what would do
In this blind bitter land.

('Words')

But a new note of more muscular decisiveness is heard in Responsibilities (1914) where in the preliminary address to his ancestors ('Pardon, old fathers') Yeats forcefully achieves his aim – to make his work 'convincing with a speech so natural that the hearer would feel the presence of a man thinking and feeling' (Letter to his father, 1913). The Easter Rising took Yeats by surprise. It is said that Ireland did not want it; but the British reaction in executing leading rebels transformed the national mood permanently and Yeats's poem summed up the transformation in haunting lines:

All changed, changed utterly:
A terrible beauty is born.

('Easter 1916')

John MacBride was among those executed. Yeats approached Maud Gonne again about marriage and met with a negative response. He proposed to her daughter, Iseult, and was again rejected. Shortly afterwards, in 1917, he married George Hyde-Lees, an Englishwoman much younger than himself whom he had met six years before. They lived first in Oxford, then in Dublin. A daughter was born in 1919, and a son followed. 1919 also saw the publication of The Wild Swans at Coole which includes 'In Memory of Major Robert Gregory' and 'An Irish Airman Foresees His Death' (Lady Gregory's son was killed in action with the Royal Flying Corps in 1917); and Yeats acquired the castle tower and cottage near Gort, County Galway, for many years his summer home and called by him 'Thoor Ballylee'. In the 1920s and 1930s, increasingly honoured throughout the world, Yeats was elected to the Irish Senate, received the Nobel Prize for Literature (1923), was given an honorary D Litt at Oxford (1931) and edited, if somewhat idiosyncratically, The Oxford Book of Modern Verse (1936).

Meanwhile the most astonishing poetic career of our age reached its climax in a series of volumes that represent Yeats's full immersion in a poetry utterly and naturally expressive of the man, his passions and the interests, private and public, that claimed them – Michael Robartes and the Dancer (1921), The Tower (1928), The Winding Stair (1933), A Full Moon in March (1935) and Last Poems and Two Plays (1939). Looking back on his earlier work and the 'masterful images' that possessed him, he is ruthlessly honest with himself:

Now that my ladder's gone,
I must lie down where all the ladders start,
In the foul rag-and-bone shop of the heart.

('The Circus Animals' Desertion')

The metaphor is characteristic of the imaginative intensity, the concentration and complexity, which give his late work its dynamic thrust. When he died in France in 1939, T.S. Eliot (q.v.) spoke of him as 'the greatest poet of our time' and 'one of the few whose history is the history of our time, who are a part of the consciousness of their age, which cannot be understood without them'. Yeats's body was brought to Ireland after the war and re-buried at Drumcliff in 1948: a stone at the grave-head is inscribed with the words he wrote for the purpose:

Cast a cold eye
On life, on death.
Horseman, pass by.

See Yeats's *Collected Poems* (1952), *Collected Plays* (1952), *Autobiographies* (1953), *Letters*, ed. Allan Wade (1954), *Essays and Introductions* (1961) and *Memoirs* (including the *Journal*) (1972). See also *Interviews and Recollections*, ed. E.H. Mikhail (1977).

The Countess Cathleen is a blank-verse play in five scenes 'laid in Ireland in old times'. Famine is ravaging the country. Two demons, disguised as merchants, lure Shemus Rua and his son, Teigne, to sell their souls for money. The demons aim to gain the costly soul of Countess Cathleen, who is already laying out her riches to buy food for the peasantry. They deceive her with reports that her plans to bring in cattle and meal have miscarried, then steal her remaining treasure, and finally, as other peasants are succumbing to the merchants, she sells her own soul in return for those of the peasants and for the needed resources. The play was dedicated to Maud Gonne, and her legendary self-sacrificial efforts for evicted Donegal peasants were in Yeats's mind. More-over, the role of the poet Aleel, who loves the Countess and tries to save her from self-immolation, reflects Yeats's anxiety to draw Maud Gonne from violent political extremism. The play, in its second version, was performed, along with Martyn's *The Heather Field*, in the Antient Concert Rooms at the launching of the Irish Literary Theatre in 1899. Rumours of theological heterodoxy, stimulated by F. Hugh O'Donnell's pamphlet, *Souls for Gold*, aroused controversy, yet Yeats's con-clusion is anything but Faustian. An Angel declares that the dead Countess is 'passing to the floor of peace' for 'The Light of Lights / Looks always on the motive, not the deed, / The Shadow of Shadows on the deed alone'. Later Yeats (in *Dramatis Personae*, 1935) recognized that the theme really demanded a Countess who, having signed away her soul, would be transformed and would immediately 'mock at all she had held holy', horrifying the peasants. He came to regard the drama as no more 'than a piece of tapestry'.

Cathleen-ni-Houlihan is a one-act play in prose, the scene being the 'interior of a cottage close to Killala in 1798'. Peter Gillane, his wife Bridget and young son Patrick are excitedly anticipating the wedding next day of the elder son Michael, who brings in the dowry of £100. It is a happy family occasion into which intrudes a strange old woman who is doomed to wander because there are too many strangers in her house who have taken her land, 'her four beautiful green fields'. A symbol of Ireland, she tells of those who have died for love of her. She refuses food, drink and money. 'If any one would give

me help, he must give me himself, he must give me all.' Her prophecies of coming sacrifice are followed up by news of the arrival of the French fleet at Killala. Michael tears himself away from his home and his bride-to-be. This patriotic play, with its implicit call to forsake home and ambition and die for Ireland, was highly popular with the nationalists. Maud Gonne herself acted the part of Cathleen at the first performance in St Teresa's Hall, Dublin, in 1902, when it was presented along with AE's *Deirdre*. Immediately afterwards came the formation of the Irish National Theatre, with Yeats as President. *Cathleen-ni-Houlihan* was the 'first play where dialect was not used with an exclusively comic intention', Yeats said (*Dramatis Personae*), admitting too that it was written with the help of Lady Gregory.

Deirdre, a one-act play in blank verse, is more confined in scope than Synge's (q.v.) subsequent play, *Deirdre of the Sorrows*, which derives peculiar pathos from the pre-sentation of the story with its full time-scale. Yeats's play concentrates on the last events. At King Conchubar's guest-house in a wood Fergus receives back Naoise and Deirdre, now supposedly pardoned by the king. (Years ago Naoise took away Deirdre, Conchubar's destined bride.) Fergus believes in Conchubar's honour, Naoise in the king's pledged word, while Deirdre is uneasy. The treacherous king, who wants both vengeance on Naoise and Deirdre at last for bride, has Naoise murdered; but Deirdre begs to be allowed to tend her husband's corpse and seizes the opportunity to stab herself. The tragedy has intensity and acts impressively. '*Deirdre* and *On Baile's Strand*', Yeats wrote (op. cit.), 'are more profound than the sentimental *Land of Heart's Desire*, than the tapestry-like *Countess Cathleen*.'

On Baile's Strand. The High King Conchubar visits Cuchulain, King of Muirthemne, and exacts an oath of obedience. A Young Man comes from Aoife's country to challenge Cuchulain to combat. He is, in fact, the son of Cuchulain and Aoife, the fierce woman-fighter with 'stone-pale cheek and red-brown hair' whom Cuchulain mastered long ago. Cuchulain has no knowledge of his birth, but the strange inner memories his appearance recalls make him refuse to challenge until driven by Conchubar and others to the belief that he has been bewitched. In combat he kills the young man, then learns his identity, goes mad and rushes into the sea to fight the waves. Where events have immediate high seriousness the dialogue is in blank verse, but a Fool and a Blind Man who, Chorus-like, keep the audience informed about back-ground facts, speak in prose. The practice of using material from the heroic Celtic legends and tales suited Yeats's purpose for making the Irish aware of their cultural heritage and Yeats returned to Cuchulain in 'The Death of Cuchulain' (*Last Poems and Two Plays*, 1939).
                                                                    [HB]

YOUNG, ANDREW (1885–1973). Poet and naturalist, born in Elgin, Scotland. Shortly after his birth the family moved to Edinburgh where he was educated, eventually taking his MA at Edinburgh University in 1908. He entered the Presbyterian ministry in 1912, first serving at Berwick-on-Tweed. He married in 1914, worked in France with the YMCA during the First World War, and after it moved to England to take charge of a church at

Hove. It was not until 1938 that he joined the Church of England. He was ordained in 1939, became Vicar of Stonegate, Sussex, in 1941 and Canon of Chichester Cathedral in 1948. He published a small collection of poems as early as 1911 (*Songs of Night*) and other such volumes followed in small editions from London booksellers. After getting to know Viola and Francis Meynell he had *Winter Harvest* (1933) published by the Nonesuch Press. This was followed by *The White Blackbird* (1935) and *Collected Poems* (1950), both published by Jonathan Cape. Fourteen years later came another *Collected Poems* (1950). Meanwhile Young had published a prose work about wild flowers, *A Prospect of Flowers* (1945), and indeed, with one notable exception, Young's verse output up to 1950 was that of a nature poet pre-eminently. The exception was *Nicodemus*, a 'mystery' play on the Crucifixion and the Resurrection, written largely in blank verse. It was published in 1937 and was broadcast that year with music by Imogen Holst.

Young's nature poems are those of an unerringly accurate observer who never wastes a word. They are often sharply, even startlingly, metaphysical, yet never strained in style. There is a neat coalescence of conversational tone with imaginative concentration. The complete absence of posture, sentimentality or pretentiousness gives the reader an unshakeable trust in the poet: yet it is a trust that stops short of familiarity. Young emerges as a strong, deeply tranquil but not intimately knowable person. Perhaps this is because of his objectivity. He makes you look at what he is looking at, not at himself. Detail is unforgettably captured:

> It was the time of year
> Pale lambs leap with thick leggings on
> Over small hills that are not there.
>
> ('A Prehistoric Camp')

Paradox is used judiciously: 'This wind brings all dead things to life', 'A Windy Day' begins, and 'Winter Morning' ends –

> Here where the grass is dank
> The sun weeps on this brightening bank.

In the prevailing poetic unobtrusiveness deeper implications are always unforced, and sometimes might pass unnoticed. Yet Young is sensitive to the awesome mystery and wonder of the earth he knows so intimately. In 'The Chalk-Cliff', face to face with 'the blazing height of chalk', he stands 'like a soul strayed / In Paradise / Hiding my blinded eyes'; while in 'In Teesdale' he puts off his visit to the great waterfall till morning daylight, turning at night rather to the warmth of the lighted farm:

> To-night I fear the fabulous horses
> Whose white tails flash down the steep water-
>   courses.

Robert Frost and Edward Thomas (q.v.) have both been cited as influences.

There came a change in Young's output in 1952 when he published *Into Hades*, a poem which prefigures the poet's death and the subsequent experience on the edge of another life yet still within reach of this one. He hovers about his old haunts, playing the ghost, while his own burial is in progress, yet sees his new body 'though not yet adopted', glimpses the New Earth (for 'Sun, moon and stars lay in that tomb with Christ'), and, when beatific silence swells into an explosive heavenquake, he is stunned, 'assaulted by the sight'. Thus visionary insight allied to stylistic concreteness makes for a powerful presentation of the virtually unpresentable – separation of soul from body and sudden deliverance from temporal and spatial limitation. The old powers of observation operate to new purpose in a new dimension. When it seems that space is upturned:

> It brought to mind
> How waterdrops fall *up* to a lake's surface
> Reflecting drips from an oar.

To this substantial work, in 1958, was added the sequel (even longer) *A Traveller in Time*, the two poems being joined under the title *Out of the World and Back*. The second poem follows the pilgrim soul on a journey outside time which involves visits to medieval tiltyard and abbey, to the mysteries at Eleusis and the Old Testament world of Hoseas. Glimpses of men 'living in their own time though long since dead' culminate in brief, vivid recapturings of Jesus and the Virgin Mary at Nazareth and Jerusalem; and Christ is known finally as the Light of whom all other lights in history were begotten and partook. At the end the poet sits side by side on a stone with Richard Rolle, the medieval mystic, sharing his seat as he shares his vision. In publishing this last big work Young confessed that he was not altogether sorry when the spring of short nature poems ran dry for, intense as was his interest in nature, 'it was not as deep as the underlying interest that prompted me to change my style and write *Into Hades*'.

Young's first book on wild flowers, *A Prospect of Flowers*, was followed in 1950 by *A Retrospect of Flowers*. These two are the work of a man of letters with literary quotations and apt anecdotes at his finger tips, and at the same time the work of a lover of flowers and plants with vast botanical knowledge based on a lifetime's pursuit of them. In *A Prospect of Britain* (1956) Young writes affectionately of places as well as of flowers – on inns and barns, woods and moors, cathedrals and railway stations. Leonard Clark arranged *The Collected Poems of Andrew Young* (1960) and edited *Andrew Young: Prospect of a Poet* (1957).   [HB]